musicHound r&b

The Essential Album Guide

Gary Graff, Josh Freedom du Lac and Jim McFarlin

Forewords by Huey Lewis and Kurtis Blow

DETROIT • NEW YORK • TORONTO • LONDON

musicHound™ R & B
The
Essential
Album
Guide

Published by Visible Ink Press®
a division of Gale Research
835 Penobscot Building
Detroit, MI 48226-4094

Visible Ink Press, MusicHound, and A Cunning Canine Production are trademarks of Gale Research.

Most Visible Ink Press books are available at special quantity discounts when purchased in bulk by corporations, organizations, or groups. Customized printings, special imprints, messages, and excerpts can be produced to meet your needs. For more information, contact Special Markets Manager, Gale Research, 835 Penobscot Bldg., Detroit, MI 48226. Or call 1-800-776-6265.

Cover photo of Aretha Franklin © Jack Vartoogian

Library of Congress Cataloging-in-Publication Data

MusicHound R & B : the essential album guide / edited by Gary Graff,
   Josh Freedom Du Lac, and Jim McFarlin.
         p.   cm.
      Includes bibliographical references (p.   ), list of World Wide
Web pages (p.   ), and indexes.
      ISBN 1-57859-026-4
      1. Rhythm and blues music—Discography. 2. Sound recordings-
-Reviews.   I. Graff, Gary.   II. Du Lac, Josh Freedom, 1970-   .
ML156.4.B6M87 1998
781.643'0266—dc21   97-37692
                                                              CIP
                                                              MN

ISBN 1-57859-026-4
Printed in the United States of America
All rights reserved

10 9 8 7 6 5 4 3 2

musicHound introduction

Rhythm & blues represents perhaps the greatest synthesis to come out of the great American musical melting pot. It's music for the dance floor, the bedroom, and the church. It's raw and righteous. It can be contemplative, rowdy, and raunchy—all at the same time. And that's just Ray Charles we're talking about.

R&B is a distinctly American music rooted in the tribal thunder that came over on the slave ships from Africa. Here it mixed with the hymns that these new captive residents were force fed on Sunday mornings. It's the blues—the country kind from the Mississippi Delta and the city variety from Detroit, Chicago, and other centers of black immigration—blending with the gospel styles that evolved in the post-Civil War Baptist churches.

But it's also sophisticated, equally touched by the growth of jazz and lush, pre-rock pop music during the first half of the twentieth century. As Charles himself once said, "It wasn't something I thought about; it was just something I did. I went to church. I heard a lot of blues . . . and jazz. When I made my music, that was all part of it."

R&B has always been a malleable form, whether it was Bessie Smith and Billie Holiday picking up the torchy ways of their times, or George Clinton and Sly Stone figuring out how to add electric guitars and rock 'n' roll attitude (not to mention the influence of certain pharmaceuticals) to their songs. Disco begat modern electronic music, while hip-hop has opened new avenues of aural alchemy—not to mention combustible oratory.

The element unifying all these approaches is a passion that's unique to R&B. It's the heat heard in Holiday's yearning, the desire in Otis Redding's pleading, the exclamation in Wilson Pickett's testifying, the edge in 2Pac's anger. There's a reason why they once called it soul music, after all. But that powerful expression extends far beyond the African American experience where R&B first found voice to speak of a greater, more universal truth. Ask a roomful of rock stars how many of them would like to be James Brown, and a lot of hands will be raised. Everyone, it seems, has soul—at least a little bit. And they always want more.

The mission of *MusicHound R&B* is to present this breadth and depth in order to convince you to do one thing—go out and get the music. We aim wide; we want you to listen to Billie and Brother Ray, to Aretha and Otis and Diana and Michael and Janet and Maxwell, to the Tempts and the Tops and to Stevie, in his little and big incarnations. We also want you to hear the Rolling Stones and Rod Stewart and Beck, and to pick up a little hip-hop (or a lot) while you're at it.

Ultimately, every artist or act in this book exhibits that R&B passion. The voice. The beat. The groove. More than displays of craft and muscianship—though there's plenty of that—R&B performances tend to cleanse the soul, creating a catharsis and uplift. Like any genre, R&B has its share of piffle; you can only shake your booty so many different ways, after all. But the best of it is transcendent, wanting to take you higher.

As Huey Lewis mentioned in his foreword, R&B can be a challenging form for record consumers. Only pop music seems to have the sales figures to convince record companies to keep catalogs stocked up. Hundreds of classic R&B titles have fallen out of print, and hip-hop—which is primarily a singles medium, anyway—is particularly ephemeral, with albums deleted from the catalog within weeks of their release.

The situation is improving, however, thanks to passionate, history-minded folks at Rhino, PolyGram's Chronicles, EMI Capitol Music Properties, The Right Stuff, Hip-O, and other labels that realize there's an appetite for the music. Scores of compilations are keeping individual songs alive, but various labels seem to be developing a desire to preserve the albums and let the world recognize that many of these artists had more to offer than whatever made the charts at the time.

We also feel that we've tapped into R&B at an exciting time, when hip-hop's appeal to inner city and suburban youths has opened a portal to the entire genre, when new fans are looking back to find out exactly what the inspirations had to offer beyond the samples. The music is there; it's just a question of having a good guide.

And that guide should be *MusicHound R&B*. This isn't exactly an encyclopedia, but it is a compendium of information that will give you a sense of where these performers came from and what their sound means in the wide pantheon of R&B. Our writers approached their entries with a sense of zeal, generally hoping to convince you that their artists are to be listened to in earnest, and recommending where to start. But the Hound is not tame; we'll call a turkey a turkey, or a fire hydrant a fire hydrant. And you know what a good Hound does to one of those. . . .

So enjoy your trip through the wide world of R&B. Find that act—or acts—that you're vaguely familiar with and take a chance on further investigation.Whether you find a whole new world or just a new piece of landscape, we'll be looking for you out in the land of a thousand dances.

So how do you use *MusicHound R&B*? Here's what you'll find in the entries, and what we intend to accomplish with each point:

• An introductory paragraph, which will give you not only biographical information but also a sense of the artist's or group's sound and its stature in the R&B—and overall music—pantheon.

• **what to buy:** The album or albums that we feel are essential purchases for consuming this act. It may be a greatest hits set, or it may be a particular album that captures the essence of the artist in question. In any event, this is where you should start—and don't think it wasn't hard to make these choices when eyeballing the catalogs of Stevie Wonder, James Brown, Sarah Vaughan, and some of the other R&B titans. Note that for acts with a limited catalog, **what's available** may take the place of **what to buy** and the other sections.

• **what to buy next:** In other words, once you're hooked, these will be the most rewarding next purchases.

• **what to avoid:** Seems clear enough. This is Hound poop.

• **the rest:** Everything else that's available for this act, rated with the Hound's trusty bone scale (see below for more on this). Note that for some artists with sizeable catalogs, we've condensed this section down to **best of the rest.**

• **worth searching for:** An out-of-print gem. A bootleg. A guest appearance on another artist's album or a film soundtrack. Something that may require some looking but will reward you for the effort.

• ◀◀ : The crucial influences on this act's music.

• ▶▶ : The acts that have been influenced by this artist or group. Used only where applicable; it's a little early for Erykah Badu or Maxwell to have influenced anybody.

We should also remind you that *MusicHound R&B* is a *buyers' guide.* Therefore, for the most part we only discuss CDs that are currently in-print and available in the United States.

Now, you ask, what's with those bones? (Down, boy! Sheesh. . . .) It's not hard to figure out—🦴🦴🦴🦴🦴 is nirvana (not Nirvana), a **woof!** is dog food. Keep in mind that the bone ratings don't pertain just to the act's own catalog, but to its worth in the whole music realm. Therefore a lesser act's **what to buy** choice might rate no more than 🦴🦴🦴; some even rate 🦴🦴, a not-so-subtle sign that you might want to think twice about that act.

As with any opinions, all of what you're about to read is subjective and personal. MusicHound has a bit of junkyard dog in it, too; it likes to start fights. We hope it does, too. Ultimately, we think the Hound will point you in the right direction and, if you buy the 🦴🦴🦴🦴🦴 and 🦴🦴🦴🦴 choices, you'll have an album collection to howl about. But if you've got a bone to pick, the Hound wants to hear about it—and promises not to bite (but maybe bark a little bit). If you think we're wagging our tails in the wrong direction or lifting our leg at something that doesn't deserve it, let us know. If you think an act has been capriciously excluded—or charitably included—tell us. Your comments and suggestions will serve the greater *MusicHound* audience and future projects, so don't be shy.

musicHound **c r e d i t s**

Editors

Gary Graff is an award-winning music journalist and supervising editor of the *MusicHound* album guide series. A native of Pittsburgh, Pennsylvania, his work is published regularly by Reuters, *Replay, Guitar World, ICE,* the *San Francisco Chronicle,* the *Cleveland Plain Dealer,* Michigan's *Oakland Press,* SW Radio Networks, *Country Song Roundup,* Mr. Showbiz/Wall of Sound, Jam TV, Electric Village, and other publications. His weekly "Rock 'n' Roll Insider" report airs on Detroit rock station WRIF-FM (101.1), and he also appears on public TV station WTVS' *Backstage Pass* program. He is a board member of the North American Music Critics Association and co-producer of the annual Detroit Music Awards. He lives in the Detroit suburbs with his wife, daughter, and two stepsons.

Josh Freedom du Lac was born in the Haight-Ashbury in 1970, which explains his middle name—but not necessarily his affinity for R&B and hip-hop. Whens, whys, and hows aside, he distinctly remembers listening frequently to KSOL, which played a little too much Gap Band. He also recalls being mesmerized by Run-D.M.C., Kurtis Blow, Whodini, and Newcleus, among others, at his first-ever concert in 1984. A year later, he appeared in his middle school yearbook wearing a nylon Nike athletic suit and Pumas with fat laces. Within a decade, he found himself writing about music professionally as the pop critic for *The Sacramento Bee,* where he is about to become a grizzled, five-year veteran. He is also a regular contributor to Wall of Sound and has done some other freelance work that's simply too insignificant to mention. A graduate of Whittier College, where he majored in something (business administration) that has nothing to do with music criticism, he currently lives in Sacramento, California, with his girlfriend, their fat cat, and a bonsai tree that gets plenty of sun.

Jim McFarlin is a nationally respected, award-winning critic and columnist on music, pop culture, and the media. Named "Best Critic" in the inaugural Michigan Rock Awards, his work has appeared in *People, Life, Hit Parader, Entertainment Weekly, USA TODAY, Electronic Media, USA Weekend, The Detroit News, The Detroit Sunday Journal,* the NAACP's *Crisis,* and, internationally, in *The Rock Yearbook* (St. Martin's Press U.K.). Featured as a pop culture expert on *Entertainment Tonight* and other national TV programs, McFarlin is a contributing editor for the new interactive online entertainment service FantastiCON, and has worked alternately as a TV and radio talk show host, voiceover talent, public speaker, and stand-up comedian.

Managing Editor

Dean Dauphinais is an editor at Visible Ink Press and a contributor to *MusicHound Rock.* The co-author of two books, *Astounding Averages!* and *Car Crazy,* he lives in suburban Motown with his wife, Kathy, and two sons, Sam and Josh. He plans on being buried with his Prince, Marvin Gaye, and Frank Sinatra CDs.

Associate Managing Editor

Judy Galens is a senior editor at Visible Ink Press and the managing editor of the 1998 titles *MusicHound Jazz* and *MusicHound Folk.* She has edited books on inventing, sports, and food festivals, but her heart belongs to the Hound. She resides in the Detroit suburbs with her hip-hop-loving husband, two cats, and a hound of her own.

Copy Editor

Brigham Narins is a freelance editor, writer, and slowly advancing doctoral candidate who lives in suburban Detroit. A long-time guitar enthusiast (a Fender man), he is known around the house as the Notorious B.R.I.G.

Publisher

Martin Connors

MusicHound Staff

Michelle Banks, Christa Brelin, Jim Craddock, Beth Fhaner, Jeff Hermann, Brad Morgan, Leslie Norback, Terri Schell, Carol Schwartz, Devra Sladics, Christine Tomassini

Art Director

Tracey Rowens

Photographers Extraordinaire

Ken Settle is a Detroit-area photographer who has specialized in music photography for over 16 years. His photos have been published worldwide in magazines such as *Rolling Stone, People, Guitar Player, Playboy, Audio,* Japan's *Player,* France's *Guitarist,* and Australia's *Who Weekly.* His work also appears in *MusicHound Country* and *MusicHound Blues.*

Jack and Linda Vartoogian grew up in late 1950s Detroit and heard, but did not get to see, the best performers in R&B and blues. To compensate, they have devoted themselves to photographing musicians (and dancers) from across the country and around the world. While their New York City home virtually guarantees that, eventually, most acts come to them, they continue to seek opportunities to discover new talent and new venues—the farther from home the better. Their images appear regularly in *The New York Times, Time, Newsweek, Living Blues,* and *Jazz Times,* among many others, as well as in innumerable books, including their own *Afropop!* (Chartwell Books, 1995) and *The Living World of Dance* (Smithmark, 1997), and *MusicHound Blues* and *MusicHound Jazz.*

Graphic Services

Randy Bassett, Pam Reed, Barbara Yarrow

Permissions

Maria Franklin

Production

Mary Beth Trimper, Dorothy Maki, Evi Seoud, Shanna Heilveil

Data Entry

Kathy Dauphinais

Technology Wizard

Jeffrey Muhr

Typesetting Virtuoso

Marco Di Vita of the Graphix Group

Marketing & Promotion

Marilou Carlin, Kim Intindola, Betsy Rovegno, Susan Stefani

MusicHound Development

Julia Furtaw

Contributors

Steve Braun is a Chicago-based national correspondent for *The Los Angeles Times.* He covered the second Woodstock and the Rock and Roll Hall of Fame concert and has written about Jerry Lee Lewis's brushes with the law.

Mike Brown is a DJ, a rave organizer, and a system administrator for Hyperreal, an Internet web site that provides a home for alternative culture and expression.

Ken Burke is a singer/songwriter whose column "The Continuing Saga of Dr. Iguana" has inspired a loyal (albeit deeply disturbed) following in small press publications since 1985.

Salvatore Caputo is a freelance writer living in Phoenix with his wife and three kids. He was the pop music critic for the *Arizona Republic* from 1990 to 1997.

Norene Cashen writes for *Alternative Press,* Detroit's *Metro Times,* and *Etch.*

Roger Catlin is the rock critic for the *Hartford* (Connecticut) *Courant.*

Jeff "DJ Zen" Chang is a writer, a record company hack, and, most shockingly, a father living in the Bay Area on little more than rice and water. He has written for more magazines than you've ever heard of.

Brian Coleman is a freelance writer and DJ from Boston who feels that Sun Ra, Lee "Scratch" Perry, Rahsaan Roland Kirk, and Kool Keith should have made beautiful music together, not apart.

MC Connors grew up in Detroit listening to CKLW and its 80,000 watts, and later discovered that he had the sounds of Motown ingrained on his brain, a not unpleasant sensation.

Dan Cooper is the former associate editor at the Country Music Foundation in Nashville, Tennessee.

Logan Creed is a freelance writer based in Florida. His work has appeared in too many music publications to list.

Dean Dauphinais is managing editor of Visible Ink Press' *MusicHound* series.

Eric Deggans is the television and pop culture critic for the *St. Petersburg Times* newspaper in Florida, where he's inspired by three children, a wife, and two cats. In that order.

Daniel Durchholz is editor of *Replay* magazine and a contributing editor at *Request* and Requestline. He lives in St. Louis, Missouri.

Andy Ernst is a longtime record collector and pop-R&B devotee, and a journalism major at Western Michigan University in Kalamazoo, Michigan.

David Feld is a contributing writer for *Blues Access* magazine and plays guitar and bass in the Diminished Capacity Revue. By day, he is a deputy public defender in Alameda County, California.

Christina Fuoco is a resident of Berkley, Michigan, and a music journalist for *The Observer & Eccentric* newspapers based in Livonia, Michigan.

Lawrence Gabriel is a Detroit-based writer, poet, and musician who is also editor of Detroit's *Metro Times.*

David Galens is the editor of Gale Research's *Drama for Students* print series and *Contemporary Authors* on CD, and a regular contributor to Gale's *Contemporary Theatre, Film, and Television* and *Contemporary Authors* print series. He is also a member of the Detroit-based band the Civilians.

Simon Glickman is the lead singer and lyricist for the L.A. band Spanish Kitchen. He has written for *Contemporary Musicians, Uncommon Heroes, Entertainment Today, Rockrgrl,* and other publications, and served as co-editor of *Native North American Biography.*

Gary Pig Gold is a contributor to *MusicHound Rock* and *MusicHound Country* and leads a Hoboken, New Jersey-based band called the Ghost Rockets, whose "maximum rhythm 'n' bluegrass" rendition of "Love Rollercoaster" already has the Ohio Players on the phone to their lawyer.

Mike Greenfield plays guitar, writes songs, and works in advertising and public relations in Youngstown, Ohio.

Stacey "Hot Mixx" Hale is an 18-year veteran Master Mixer/DJ with numerous awards to her credit. She is president of the Detroit Regional Music Conference, an annual event she founded in 1993.

Jill Hamilton is a Los Angeles-based freelance writer whose stories have appeared in the *Ann Arbor* (Michigan) *News, Rolling Stone,* and other publications.

Steve Holtje is a freelance writer and editor in New York whose work has appeared in *Creem, New Power Generation,* the *New Review,* and other publications. A contributor to *MusicHound Rock* and *MusicHound Country,* he is co-editor of *MusicHound Jazz.*

Barbara Ingalls is a graphic designer and union troublemaker and works at *The Detroit Sunday Journal.*

Todd S. Inoue writes about music for *Metro Newspaper* in San Jose, California. His work has also appeared in *Pulse!,* the *Village Voice, Giant Robot, Option 8,* and *P.O.V.*

Michael Isabella is a radio account manager in Detroit. His love of music was nurtured in his native Cleveland—where all his friends looked just like Drew Carey.

Jazzbo is Joseph Monish Patel, a San Francisco-based music journalist and writer who contributes to several print and Internet publications, including *Rap Pages, The Source, URB, Raygun,* and Mr. Showbiz.

Jim Kamp is an editor/writer with 10 years of reference publishing experience and an acute interest in the history of popular music, including country, rock, R&B, and jazz.

Steve Knopper is a Chicago-based freelance writer who has contributed to *Rolling Stone, George, Newsday,* the *Chicago Tribune, Request, Billboard, Yahoo! Internet Life,* the Knight-Ridder Newspapers wire service, and SW Radio Networks. The former music critic for Boulder, Colorado's *Daily Camera,* he's editor of *MusicHound Lounge: The Essential Album Guide to Martini Music and Easy Listening,* to be published by Visible Ink Press in 1998.

Michael Kosser is a Nashville-based freelance author and songwriter who has had 10 books published—six nonfiction books on popular music and four historical novels about Native Americans—and has heard his songs recorded by numerous pop and country artists.

Greg Kot is the rock critic for the *Chicago Tribune* and has contributed articles to numerous publications, including *Rolling Stone, Request, Replay,* and *Guitar World.*

Bryan Lassner is a student at the University of Michigan and, in his spare time, enjoys playing and composing on the piano and keyboard.

Matt Lee is the former leader of the Detroit-based R&B/rock band the Suspects. He now works as music buyer for a record store in Royal Oak, Michigan, and heads his own company specializing in public relations and music promotion.

Tali Madden is a contributing writer to *Blues Access* magazine and a freelance music journalist. A former NPR-affiliate jazz and blues broadcaster/programmer, he is currently based in Portland, Oregon.

Brian Mansfield is the co-editor of *MusicHound Country.* A resident of Nashville, Tennessee, he has written for *USA TODAY, Request,* and other publications, and is the Nashville correspondent for CountryNow.com. He is co-editor of *MusicHound Folk,* to be published by Visible Ink Press in 1998.

Lynne Margolis is a music critic and feature writer at the *Tribune-Review* in Pittsburgh, Pennsylvania, who believes pop music falls into two categories: BB and AB, as in Before the Beatles and After the Beatles.

Patrick McCarty has written about rock 'n' roll for the past 20 years for various publications, including Richmond, Virginia's *Times-Dispatch* and *News Leader, Style Weekly,* and *MusicHound Rock.* He's a classically trained musician, producer, and songwriter, but we don't hold that against him.

Andre McGarrity is a 1995 screenwriting graduate from New York's prestigious School of Visual Arts, where he won the school's coveted Dusty Award for best screenplay. He currently works as creative editor for impact! interactive! inc., a Southfield, Michigan-based New Media company specializing in providing content for the Internet.

Jonathan "Corky" Meadows plays keyboards for the Detroit-based R&B group One Way. He is also the minister of music at his church and an aspiring film score writer.

David Menconi is the music critic at the *Raleigh* (North Carolina) *News & Observer* and has written for *Spin, Billboard, Request, MusicHound Rock,* and *MusicHound Country.*

David Okamoto is the music editor for the *Dallas Morning News* and a contributing editor to *ICE* magazine. His work has also appeared in *Jazziz, Rolling Stone,* and *CD Review.*

"Lisa Lisa" Orlando is a top-rated disc jockey by night, spinning urban and dance-oriented music for Detroit's WDRQ-FM. By day, as Lisa J. Orlando, she is a practicing attorney specializing in entertainment law and a certified aerobics instructor.

Allan Orski has written for *Rolling Stone* Online, *Replay,* Requestline, *Black Book,* and SW Radio Networks, as well as for *MusicHound Rock* and *MusicHound Country.* He lives in a loft under the Manhattan bridge, where he alienates his peers by singing along with Sam Cooke records.

Tamara Palmer is the associate editor of *URB* magazine. Her work has appeared in various publications, including *Rolling Stone, Wired, Option,* and *Raygun.*

Alan Paul is senior editor of *Guitar World* magazine, executive editor of *Guitar World* Online, and a contributor to *People* magazine, *MusicHound Rock, MusicHound Country,* and *MusicHound Blues.*

Franklin Paul is a New York–based journalist and R&B music critic for Reuters. He was awarded the 1997 Music Journalism Award for excellence in online interviews.

Bob Paxman is a Nashville-based entertainment journalist whose works have appeared in *Country Weekly, Billboard, TV Host,* and numerous other publications.

Damon Percy is an associate editor for Gale Research's *Dictionary of Literary Biography* online series and a freelance writer. His work has appeared in the *Detroit Free Press, VIBE,* and the hip-hop magazine *Beat Down.*

Doug Pippin is an advertising copywriter in New York and a drummer who ran the band music practice facility Jamland.

Bill Pollak is a technical writer, editor, and manager of a technical communication group at a research institute in Pittsburgh, Pennsylvania. By night, he is an R&B singer and recording artist known professionally as Billy Price. He has released six independent recordings, the latest of which—*The Soul Collection* ♪♪♪♪ (Green Dolphin, 1997, prod. Billy Price, H.B. Bennett)—features a cameo appearance by Otis Clay.

Barry M. Prickett is a Sacramento-based musician and freelance writer who has never met an opinion he didn't like to give.

Doug Pullen is the music and media writer for the *Flint* (Michigan) *Journal* and Booth Newspapers. He is a contributor to *MusicHound Rock*, *MusicHound Country*, and *MusicHound Blues*.

Bob Remstein is a keyboardist and composer who was music editor for *Los Angeles View* before he began writing for publications in cyberspace, where he now resides.

Sherese L. Robinson is a graduate of the School of Visual Arts in New York City and a professional screenwriter (and personal acquaintance of Irene Cara). She is presently pursuing her master's degree in film from Columbia University.

Leland Rucker has been writing about popular music since 1975 and is the managing editor of *Blues Access* magazine. He is the co-author of *The Toy Book* (Knopf, 1992) and editor of *MusicHound Blues*.

Christopher Scapelliti is an associate editor of *Guitar* magazine and a contributor to *MusicHound Rock* and *MusicHound Country*.

Joel Selvin has covered pop music for the *San Francisco Chronicle* since 1970 and has contributed to *MusicHound Rock* and *MusicHound Country*. His seventh book, *Sly and the Family Stone: On the Record*, will be published in the spring of 1998.

Greg Siegel is the managing editor of *ICE* magazine and has written for *Detour*, *Virtually Alternative*, *Modern Drummer*, *Raygun*, *Audio*, *Los Angeles Magazine*, and *Request*.

Dana G. Smart is the manager of A&R at Universal Music Special Markets and the former manager of catalog development at Motown Records. He lives with his family in Long Beach, California, where he still buys his records, whenever possible, on vinyl.

Tim A. Smith is a nationally known gospel music journalist and Detroit-based radio personality.

Spence D. is a Bay Area journalist who first began writing about hip-hop culture in 1990 for the underground rap 'zine *The Bomb*. The Writer Also Known As Spence Dookey regularly contributes to *The Source*, *URB*, *Raygun*, *Option*, *Gavin*, *Bikini*, and *Slap*, and even writes about film for Roughcut.com.

Corey Takahashi is a freelance journalist based (for now) in banana-slug-infested Santa Cruz, California. His work has appeared in *The* (Portland) *Oregonian*, *SF Weekly*, *A.Magazine*, and *Asian Week*.

Tom Terrell is a freelance music journalist based in New York who claims to know everything about pop music since 1955 — and remembers it all despite a longtime backstage association with George Clinton and Funkadelic.

Chris Tower is a freelance writer and college radio broadcaster who lives in Richland, Michigan, with his ghost cat, Bumba-Head. His work has appeared in *CyberHound's Web Guide*, *The Kalamazoo* (Michigan) *Gazette*, and a variety of national and international magazines.

Aidin Vaziri is the breakdancing world champion and night manager of KFC #617.

Oliver "O-Dub" Wang is a contributing editor at *URB*. His work has also appeared in the *San Francisco Bay Guardian*, *Vinyl Exchange*, *A.Magazine*, *Asian Week*, and *Yolk*.

Todd Wicks is a Detroit freelance writer whose work has appeared in the fanzines *Jam Rag* and *Renegade*, the *Detroit Jewish News*, and the suburban Detroit *Observer & Eccentric* newspapers.

David Yonke writes about popular music for *The Toledo* (Ohio) *Blade*.

MusicHound R&B was a blast; not that the other *MusicHound* books were any less enjoyable, but there was something about this particular volume that made it even more joyful. Maybe it's because, four books into the series, we're getting better at it.

Or maybe it was the company.

With three editors, *MusicHound R&B* was like, well, a three-ring circus. But a good one—Barnum & Bailey variety, if you know what I mean. After doing *MusicHound Rock* as a one-man show, I went from lonely to looney, with the three of us peppering each other with ideas, questions, and challenges—a wee-hours music critic skull session that went on for six months.

So my cheers and thanks firstly to Jim McFarlin and Josh Freedom du Lac, who made this project an absolute riot. Jim, my onetime Detroit newspaper rival and now *compadre,* kept things lively with his quick one-liners and some of the most memorable expressions of editing angst I've ever heard. Josh brought his West Coast cool and a gift of translating certain realms of hip-hop to us older dudes. They brought expertise and great enthusiasm to the book, and I'm grateful for both.

Dean Dauphinais at Visible Ink remains the mother of all project managers, a steady hand who took a lot from us and deflected an equal amount so that we wouldn't have to deal with it. I'm sure there were times Dean was ready to tear his hair out, but since he shaved it all off when the Red Wings won the Stanley Cup, that wasn't an option. The rest of the Visible Ink gang—Martin Connors, Terri Schell, Kim Intindola, Judy Galens, and Marilou Carlin, who all left their hair intact—were as encouraging and supportive as always. We continue to be appreciative of Brian McCafferty's efforts at PolyGram Special Markets.

Everyone who was thanked in *MusicHound Rock* and *MusicHound Country* gets the nod again, and I'd like to offer particular thanks and welcome to our new contributors in *MusicHound R&B*; welcome to da *real* dog pound. Five bones also to my good pals and colleagues Dan Durchholz, Jim Lynch, and Kent Woodman, who kept me sane and working, as well as to my friend and attorney Stephen Scapelliti, who's become so much a part of the pound that he has his own stash of bones. Thanks also to Chris Richards of Repeat the Beat for helping us compile our list of entries, to David Dorn and the other folks at Rhino Records for helping with research, and to Bill Schulte at PolyGram Distribution's Detroit branch. And much respect to my assorted editors and employers for their indulgence as we worked on this project: John Loscalzo and Barry Jeckyll at SW Radio Networks; Steve Gorman at Reuters; Marylynn Hewitt at the *Oakland Press*; Erik Flanigan at Wall of Sound; Brad Tolinski and Tom Beajour at *Guitar World*; Isaac Josephson and Scott Hess at Jam TV; Shelton Ivany at *Country Song Roundup*; Joel Selvin at the *San Francisco Chronicle*; Allan Walton and Scott Mervis at the *Pittsburgh Post-Gazette*; and Phil Jacobs and Gail Zimmerman at the *Detroit Jewish News.*

I'm honored by Huey Lewis's willingness to write one of the forewords for the book and by the great job he did. And I appreciate the support and input from Huey and the other members of the News, as big a bunch of R&B fanatics as you're likely to encounter in the rock world.

To my brothers and sisters in the Metropolitan Detroit Council of Newspaper Unions—well, here we are again. I thought, hoped, and prayed that by this time our struggle would be over, but it continues. The courage and stamina you've all shown during the past two-and-a-half years is awe-inspiring, and we can only hope it will be rewarded in due time. A special note to Emily Everett, who works her heart out to keep our precious *Detroit Sunday Journal* alive; you're a hero.

To my family—my parents Ruthe and Milt, my brother Harvey and his wife Vicki, my stepsons Ben and Josh, my daughter Hannah, and my beloved wife Judy—well, here's another one. Your patience, support, and love helps make these books happen in ways you might not understand or imagine, and, as always, the last word in these acknowledgments always goes to you.

Gary Graff

When I agreed to work on this book (and it was hardly a tough choice), my girlfriend reacted by saying, simply: "Cool." Several months later, though, there was a computer sitting on our dining room table; CDs, magazines, and reference books were scattered all over our living room; and our one-way conversations went mostly like this: "Do you have to work on that damn book again tonight?" Even though the computer is still sitting on the dining room table (but not for long—really), the conversations have become interesting again and now flow two ways. To which I say, simply: Laura, I love you. Thank you for your patience. Of course, being a music junkie herself, she also helped out in other ways, assisting me with my research and answering several questions that had stumped me. For that I am ever thankful.

Also deserving much thanks are my mother, Diana Jow du Lac, and my father, Jean-Antony du Lac, who provided encouragement when I needed it most and, in the case of my father, even offered proofreading help when I needed it least. (When nobody has turned in any copy yet, Dad, there's nothing to proofread. But thanks anyway!) My brother, Chris, deserves a nod, too, for turning me on to the Jonzun Crew, the Jungle Brothers, and Stetsasonic before I'd heard them anywhere else.

My editors at *The Sacramento Bee* (Gregory Favre, Rick Rodriguez, Scott Lebar, Bruce Dancis, and Jeannie Wong) were especially kind, allowing me to suffer through the deadline crunch in relative peace—and then immediately sending me away to the South to find the ghost of Elvis and forget about *this* Hound dog for a while. Those same editors were also nice enough to take a risk and give me a job as a pop music critic in the first place.

Special thanks to Jeannie Wong and Marcos "Jerky" Breton, whose friendship and personal and professional advice have been invaluable. All of my other colleagues at *The Bee* deserve thanks, too, but especially Jose Luis Villegas and Tom Negrete, who also offered some helpful words that made a difference.

It was an honor and a delight working with all of the writers whose names appear in this book under the hip-hop entries, even if they thought otherwise as I ranted and raved via e-mail about how much I hated deadlines (especially missed ones) and left strange voice mail messages about missing entries that weren't actually missing. Special thanks to Jazzbo for laughing in the face of a ridiculous workload and picking up so many entries while, somehow, finding time to talk baseball, too. And extra-large ups, too, to Jeff Chang—the invisible co-editor—for all of the invaluable suggestions, names, phone numbers, and deep (and not-so-deep) thoughts. *You* are Tiger Woods. You are not, however, Kurtis Blow. There's only one of them, and I'd like to thank him for rocking the house at the first concert I ever went to and, especially, for being gracious enough to write a foreword for this book. You rule the *MusicHound* world.

Ever-helpful others who deserve four pats on the back—and a free copy of this book: My best friend, Kevin Wong, who stole my Black Moon album but gave me his copy of "In Control" and a strange remix of "The Message" to make up for it; Mixxula, who has more opinions than the Supreme Court; "One-Can" Dan Charnas, who should stop fronting and start writing that book he keeps talking about; Cheo Hodari Coker, Tracii McGregor, Billy Jam, and Kris Ex, who were all here in spirit; Roberta Magrini and Kym Norsworthy, the most helpful hip-hop publicists in the business; Bill Adler, the most helpful ex-publicist in the business; Zack Layton at the Virgin Megastore and Rob Fauble at The Beat, who let me spend lots of time looking at albums and computer kiosks in their stores; Brad Kava, who always tells me something interesting; Mixmaster Mike, who listened to KPOO almost as much as I did; and anybody else who deserves to be thanked and otherwise acknowledged for *something*.

Finally, a sincere "thank-you" goes out to *MusicHound* managing editor Dean Dauphinais and my lead co-editor, Gary Graff, for giving me a shot—and for not shooting me when I was late. It was a fun, challenging ride. And also, one final nod to my other co-editor, Jim McFarlin, who was a major source of inspiration at the finish line. Misery always loves company!

Josh Freedom du Lac

The longer I live, the more I'm convinced that life is one never-ending succession of ironies. When Gary Graff shocked me with an out-of-the-blue invitation to be co-editor on this project, I had just made a solemn vow to myself to "do a book" in 1997, and was busily drafting proposals on various subjects in hopes of attracting a publisher. Irony number one.

None of those proposals remotely resembled a book about contemporary music, much less a comprehensive reference work like this one. However, even though I hadn't written about pop music in anger since I covered the beat for a Detroit newspaper in the 1980s, Graff—whom I had been conditioned to view as my sworn enemy and hated rival when he covered the same beat for a competing paper—reassured me that I not only had the talent for the task, but also possessed a body of knowledge that would be essential for the editor of an R&B guide: specifically, a vivid recollection of—and affection for—long-extinct soul groups from the disco era, acts few other people will admit to remembering. Age holds some odd advantages at times.

I signed on to the *MusicHound* experience with my eyes wide open, fully expecting it to be a massive, totally involving challenge. I was wrong. As difficult as I thought it would be, it proved twice that hard, and I stand in awe and utter disbelief that Gary could have compiled and edited the rock edition of this *MusicHound* series entirely by his lonesome. His experience, wisdom, common sense, understanding, and comforting mantra—"I think we're in good shape"— meant more to this neophyte book editor than he will ever know. Gary, I take back all those things I thought and mumbled about you over the years. I'd like to think that this gracious, thorough professional—the man with whom I couldn't co-host a Detroit radio program many years ago because we couldn't stand sitting together in close studio quarters too long, who is now my editor for the weekly *Detroit Sunday Journal* published by locked-out Detroit newspaper workers—is not only my partner in publishing, but also my newest friend. Irony number two.

I found another invaluable source of support in my other co-editor, Josh Freedom du Lac, a man I have never seen (three ironies, and counting) but whose wealth of insights about modern-day rap and R&B music, and shared frustrations and incremental victories as a fellow first-time editor, helped me put numerous issues into perspective through countless e-mail conversations and long-distance calls. Our *MusicHound* managing editor, Dean Dauphinais, was an absolute rock of guidance and advice, one of the most tolerant and considerate men to whom

I've ever had to give excuses. How he put up with me sometimes, I'll never know. I'm sure he may be wondering as well.

I cannot tell you how astonished and disappointed I was by the number of talented, knowledgeable music people I contacted who initially embraced this writing concept with great enthusiasm only to quickly dump their assignments or vanish altogether. (I will spare you the embarrassment of listing you by name here; you know who you are.) That made me truly appreciate the correspondents who not only followed through but also performed above and beyond the call. Topping this list were Andre McGarrity, who endured more demands and verbal rantings from me than I would have in his position; Tim Smith, who kept accepting additional gospel music responsibilities with grace and good cheer; Chris Tower, a godsend who took on many of the gigantic artist discographies (that make lesser writers quiver) with refreshing zeal and aplomb; and Lisa Orlando, who dashed off several important entries at zero hour and made me wish I'd contacted her months earlier.

Sincerest thanks, too, to Beth Larsen, who spent many long hours searching the Internet on my behalf when she should have been working (hope your boss buys the book but never reads this section); Heather Chamberlain, my summer assistant, for allowing me to focus on this job by making my other jobs easier, and who will hopefully remember me when she becomes the next Martha Graham; Julie St. Anne, for turning me on to the Music City writing Mafia; and Deborah Smith Pollard, Larry Kaplan, and Tony Hoye for direction and goodwill.

Jazz Now magazine publisher and editor-in-chief Haybert K. Houston, Daniel R. Clemson of the Mills Brothers Society, and music journalist Scott Yanow provided timely assistance, as did Internet websites too numerous to mention.

I dedicate my portion of *MusicHound R&B* to my guiding light and role model, my late mother, Caribell; my 93-year-old father, Hildry, who probably won't understand a word of this but will be able to boast about his son the published author nonetheless; and to my heart and soul, my wife, Elaine, the funniest, most even-tempered and loving woman I've ever known, who (almost) never got mad over not seeing me crawl out of my office for days at a time. Thank you for keeping the music playing, darling.

Jim McFarlin

musicHound r&b

A

A+

Born Andre Levins.

Part of a new generation of rappers who were reared solely on hip-hop, A+ launched his recording career at the tender age of 14. Though the raspy-voiced teen didn't generate much noise in the crowded hip-hop field with his debut, his big-name supporters—including Q-Tip, AZ, Mobb Deep, the Lost Boyz, and Heavy D.—insist he'll only get better with age.

what's available: *The Latch-Key Child* ♪ (Universal, 1996, prod. Q-Tip, Kedar, others) is the young rapper's only album and is redeeming only for its collaborations. "Me and My Microphone," for instance, is given a boost by smooth-voiced poet Q-Tip, and A+ is joined by AZ for the aptly titled "A+Z"—arguably the album's best song.

influences:
◄◄ Nas, Method Man, Mobb Deep, Chi-Ali, Kris Kross

Jazzbo

Aaliyah

Born Aaliyah Haughton, January 16, 1979, in Brooklyn, NY.

Success was in the cards for Aaliyah since she began performing at age nine. Her warm-up gigs included a stint on television's *Star Search* and a jam session in Las Vegas with Gladys Knight, the ex-wife of her uncle, Barry Hankerson. As a 15-year-old, Aaliyah (Arabic for "the highest, the ex-

alted one, the best") certainly lived up to the title of her debut album, *Age Ain't Nothing but a Number*; she held a 3.8 grade point average at Detroit's High School for the Performing Arts and was clearly on her way to being the Person Most Likely to Become a Recording Artist. And a successful one at that, as her first album sold more than 1 million copies. Aaliyah also experienced some tabloid exposure, thanks to (unfounded) rumors that she married her mentor, R. Kelly.

what's available: *Age Ain't Nothing But a Number* ♪♪♪ (Atlantic/Jive, 1994, prod. R. Kelly) blends the hip-hop sassiness of Mary J. Blige and the soul of Motown. This established Aaliyah as a New Jill to watch, thanks to hits such as the poignant ballad "At Your Best (You Are Love)" and the anthemic "Throw Your Hands Up." *One in a Million* ♪♪♪ (Blackground Enterprises/Atlantic, 1996, prod. Jomo Hankerson, Michael Haughton, Craig Kallman) is a collage of sensual songs that show off her new-found musical and personal confidence; the video for the title track shows off her body (in a skin-tight silver lame crop top and pants) as well as her never-ending vocal range. Aaliyah salutes Janet Jackson with her relentlessly addictive dance-party take on Marvin Gaye's "Got to Give It Up," which features a duet with Slick Rick, while Naughty by Nature's Treach duets with her on the smooth "A Girl Like You."

influences:
◄◄ TLC
►► Lil' Kim (sans profanity)

Christina Fuoco

Gregory Abbott

Born April 2, in New York, NY.

Gregory Abbott's background is an unusual one for a pop star. He started playing music during the 1970s to help pay his tuition while working on a master's degree at Berkeley and Stanford universities. Even though he was academically interested in psychology, Abbott was no stranger to music. He learned piano at an early age, and was singing with the St. Patrick's Cathedral Choir in New York when he was only eight. Abbott taught English at Berkeley for a while before he decided to give music his full attention. He debuted with the libidinous *Shake You Down*, on which he performed vocals, keyboards, and drums. The album went gold and stayed on the charts for 22 weeks. The title track followed, hitting #1 on the *Billboard* pop, adult contemporary, black, and dance charts. "Shake You Down" also received BMI's Pop Song of The Year award for the most performed song of 1988. Abbott's second record, the out-of-print *I'll Prove It To You*, didn't enjoy the success of his debut. But by then he was a celebrity and sex symbol, modeling for layouts in *Playboy* and voted one of the 10 sexiest male artists in *Playgirl*. He also had a role on the popular soap opera *All My Children*. After a long break from recording, he released *One World* in 1995, attempting to connect with his Caribbean roots. The record includes covers of Bob Marley songs and original material. Abbott's second record for Musik International was scheduled for release in 1997.

what to buy: *Shake You Down* ♫♫♫ (Columbia, 1986, prod. Gregory Abbott) really captures Gregory Abbott at his best.

the rest:
One World ♫♫♫ (Musik International Records, 1995)

influences:
◀◀ Bob Marley, Bill Withers, Johnny Nash
▶▶ Johnny Gill, Al B. Sure, Ralph Tresvant, Rome

Norene Cashen

Paula Abdul

Born June 19, 1963, in Los Angeles, CA.

Following a lead set by the ultimate pop/R&B vixen, Madonna, Paula Abdul was among the lucky few dance artists of the mid-1980s to score major pop success despite a startling lack of singing talent. A choreographer for the Los Angeles Lakers cheerleaders by age 17, Abdul turned her high-profile gig into work choreographing videos—first for the Jacksons and then Janet Jackson's dance-heavy breakthrough videos—becoming a star herself when the clips exploded on MTV. After doing similar work for ZZ Top and *The Tracey Ullman Show,* among others, Abdul soon signed a record deal, releasing a critically-drubbed but commercially successful dance-pop debut album. Critics primarily objected to Abdul's singing—a thin, nasal wail that needed lots of processing to sound listenable. Her own stylized, MTV-friendly videos won the day, however, showing that, perhaps for the first time, you could be a successful R&B diva with little or no singing ability. A second record also did well, but trouble loomed when a backup singer on Abdul's first record claimed to have sung lead vocals on all the tunes. Given Abdul's lack of vocal talent, it was a serious charge, resolved by a Los Angeles court decision in Abdul's favor. But by the time the suit was concluded, younger, hip-hop-influenced dance divas were ruling the charts, and Abdul's 1995 album came and went without much notice. Now on her second marriage, Abdul has resorted to acting in made-for-TV movies to stay in the public eye.

what to buy: Her debut, *Forever Your Girl* ♫♫ (Virgin, 1988, prod. Keith Cohen, L.A. Reid, Babyface, Oliver Leiber, Dave Cochrane, Jesse Johnson, Elliot Wolff, Glen Ballard, Curtis Williams), perfectly distills the 1980s-era, studio-centered ethic that has hobbled modern R&B. It's basically a record steered by a boatload of producers and even more studio musicians, crafting a sonic artifact to go with an incredibly videogenic star. The songs are almost an afterthought, but funk-tinged fare such as "Opposites Attract" and "Straight Up" are worth hearing more than once—even if it's only at your next aerobics workout.

what to avoid: *Shut Up and Dance (The Dance Mixes)* **woof!** (Virgin, 1990, prod. Elliot Wolff, Keith Cohen, The Bomb Squad, Curtis Williams, Oliver Leiber, Frankie Foncett, Shep Pettibone, L.A. Reid, Babyface) provides vapid and uninspiring remixes of songs that weren't that great to begin with—really just an excuse to put another Abdul video into heavy rotation.

the rest:
Spellbound ♫♫ (Virgin, 1991)
Head Over Heels ♫♫♫ (Virgin, 1995)

worth searching for: The collection of videos from her debut disc, also titled *Straight Up* (Virgin, 1990), if only to see the real reason why she got a record deal—videogenic dance moves and well-packaged video showcases.

influences:
◀◀ Janet Jackson, Madonna, Donna Summer
▶▶ Mariah Carey, Gillette

Eric Deggans

Paula Abdul (© Ken Settle)

Above the Law

Formed 1988, in Pomona, CA.

Cold 187um (born Gregory Hutchison), vocals; KM.G the Illustrator (born Kevin Gulley), vocals; Total K-oss (born Anthony Stewart), vocals.

Brazen with its approach, though formulaic in content, ATL stands as one of the most overlooked fixtures of the southern California legacy known as gangsta rap. If longevity is any gauge, the group—which started under Eazy-E as members of his Ruthless Posse—easily outranks the hit-and-fold wonders of today. Nearly a decade into the game, ATL's funk beats, garnished with hustler braggadocio, maintain a certain authenticity in light of topical cliches such as cars, money, and quick women. Thank the double-barrel delivery of raspy-voiced KM.G, plus 187um's faculty for hilarious and plentiful sound bites. While money-making and violence are the fodder feeding most of ATL's rhymes, the lyricists' tongue-in-cheek style makes clear that what they rap about isn't necessarily what they condone. Add to their music flashes of political and social commentary,

and you have a group that's entertainingly confused. Ultimately, the best way to enjoy ATL is not to expect much consciousness-raising, but rather to relish the elaborate production of a group that plays its own instruments, sings its own hooks, and consistently makes rap for the street rather than the radio.

what to buy: *Time Will Reveal* 𝒹𝒹𝒹𝒹 (Tommy Boy, 1996, prod. Above the Law) is an intoxicating pimpography that includes lyrical flash, musical funk, and occasional self-reflection. The highlight of this and other ATL albums is found in the production, which, at its best, harmonizes gangsta funk with street-level R&B. "Evil That Men Do" is an operatic epic on sin, while "Gorillapimpin" offers one example of that evil: "Wherever we go/A nigga play a ho." Car culture and high-profiling is immortalized on "100 Spokes," and "Apocalypse Now" ties together all the strengths of ATL, establishing the group's unique place in modern rap.

the rest:
Livin' Like Hustlers 𝒹𝒹𝒹 (Ruthless/Epic, 1990)

Vocally Pimpin' EP ℐℐℐ (Ruthless/Epic, 1991)
Black Mafia Life ℐℐℐ (Ruthless, 1992)
Uncle Sam's Curse ℐℐℐ (Ruthless, 1994)

influences:

◀◀ N.W.A., Too $hort, Ice-T

▶▶ Dr. Dre, Dove Shack, Westside Connection

Corey Takahashi

Colonel Abrams

Born Colonel Abrams IV, in Detroit, MI.

In that great rhythm-and-blues tradition of virile, powerful male singers with military names (Major Lance, General Johnson, Gary "U.S." Bonds), Colonel Abrams exploded out of the U.S. dance/house music experience somewhere between the crash that crippled Teddy Pendergrass and the high-torque emergence of Keith Sweat. Steeped in the Motown music heritage until moving to New York at age 10, Abrams organized a child singing group and began entering Apollo Theater amateur contests almost immediately upon his arrival. As the New York underground music scene erupted around him, Abrams hooked up with a local DJ who needed a singer to accompany the instrumental mixes he was playing in clubs and on radio. The rabid audience response to one such collaboration, "Runnin'," landed Abrams a deal on the independent Streetwise label, which folded after releasing his second single. Undaunted, he cut an 8-track recording of a feverish, calypso-style dance number called "Trapped"—written while he was stuck on a New York expressway—which became the most-requested song in clubs and record stores. Picked up by MCA, "Trapped" went on to sell an astonishing 1.3 million copies in Europe alone and raced to #1 on the U.S. dance charts in 1985. Abrams went on to release a string of lesser hits, including "The Truth," "I'm Not Gonna Let (You Get the Best of Me)," and "How Soon We Forget," and recorded tracks produced by Cameo leader Larry Blackmon. In the 1990s, the Colonel has shifted his theater of operations to Britain, where he is revered as a legendary figure in the acid jazz and house music movements.

what's available: Virtually none of Abrams's sizzling 1980s work is commercially available today. His last U.S. release, *Make a Difference* ℐℐℐ (Music USA, 1996, prod. various), really doesn't—sizzle, that is. It's useful as a representative sample of the singer's raw, propulsive style, but it lacks the sexual urgency of earlier work like "Trapped" and "I'm Not Gonna Let."

worth searching for: If you can lay your hands on any of the Colonel's mid-1980s promo singles for MCA—like "Nameless," "Speculation," or "How Soon We Forget"—or his British import LP *Voice of the Underground* (Smack, 1995)—with the tune "So Proud"—or the out-of-print U.S. release *About Romance* (Scotti Brothers, 1992)—with its acid jazz mix of "In the Groove"—you'll be in line for a field promotion. This is all compelling, convincing Abrams funk. And, of course, keep stalking the vinyl cut-out bins for his earliest MCA LPs, *Colonel Abrams* and *You And Me Equals Us*.

influences:

◀◀ Luther Vandross, Al Jarreau, Patti LaBelle, David Ruffin, Dennis Edwards, Levi Stubbs, Teddy Pendergrass

▶▶ Keith Sweat, Jodeci, Sandy B, Tyrone Summer, The Tony Rich Project

Jim McFarlin

Johnny Ace

Born John Marshall Alexander Jr., June 9, 1929. Died December 25, 1954.

During his lifetime, Johnny Ace was just a popular R&B balladeer. After his death, he became a tragic, romantic icon for teenagers who found added resonance in his posthumously released hit "Pledging My Love." Before he officially became "Rock 'n' Roll's First Fatality," John Alexander worked in Adolph Duncan's popular Memphis band and played piano on recordings with B.B. King's Beale Street Boys. After King and Bobby "Blue" Bland left, Alexander renamed the group The Beale Streeters and took over the lead vocal spot. When Alexander signed with Duke Records in 1952, he changed his stage name to Johnny Ace so as not to embarrass his father, a Memphis preacher. Ace's first release, "My Song," sounds poorly recorded and off-pitch today, but the vocal was warm and vibrant, and the record was a #1 R&B hit for nine weeks. (Johnny Otis and his orchestra were eventually brought in to supplement Ace's recording sessions.) In 1953, "Cross My Heart" was a Top 5 single, and its echo-laden follow-up, "The Clock," stayed in the #1 spot for five weeks. Ace's winning streak with cozy, vibe-accented ballads continued into 1954 with "Saving My Love For You," "Please Forgive Me," and "Never Let Me Go," prompting disc jockeys to vote him the year's Most Programmed Artist in a *Cashbox Magazine* poll. Ace dealt with the pressure of stardom one time by sticking the barrel of an empty .32 revolver in his mouth, pulling the trigger and, after the weapon sounded an empty click, laughing at the horrified expressions of those around him. On Christmas Eve in 1954, backstage at a Houston concert, Ace pulled the same stunt with a loaded pistol and died. He was only 25 years old. The wave of publicity surrounding the death of Johnny Ace resulted in "Pledging My Love" not only hitting #1 on the R&B charts for 10 weeks, but peaking at #17 on the pop charts as well. A second posthumous single, "Anymore," was Ace's final Top 10 R&B hit and was all Duke Records had left to issue. Johnny Ace tribute songs became an R&B vogue for awhile, and Duke Records tried to cash in by hiring Ace's younger brother, St. Clair Alexander, to record under the name Buddy Ace. "Pledging My Love" remains a staple of oldies radio and '50s rock 'n' roll compilations, where Ace's is the one pleadingly heartfelt voice in a sea of frivolity.

what's available: Currently, there are two versions of the *Johnny Ace Memorial Album*: *Johnny Ace Memorial Album* 🎵🎵🎵🎵 (MCA, 1973) has 12 tracks; its evil twin, *Johnny Ace Memorial Album* 🎵🎵🎵 (MCA Special Products, 1987), is a budget version containing only eight tracks. The 12-song version is an exact reproduction of the LP Duke released in 1955. Ace's work seems ripe for a major repackaging; he recorded 10 singles for Duke, usually coupling a ballad with a rocking jump blues number. Of the 12 songs available, most are ballads, with "Please Forgive Me" being conspicuously absent, and there are no useful session or liner notes.

influences:

◀◀ Bobby "Blue" Bland, B.B. King

▶▶ Chuck Willis

Ken Burke

Ace of Base

Formed 1990, in Gothenborg, Sweden.

Jenny Cecilia Berggren, vocals; Malin Sofia Datarina "Linn" Berggren, vocals; Jonas Petter "Joker" Berggren, keyboards; Ulf Gunnar "Buddha" Ekberg, keyboards.

It's appropriate that you can file Ace of Base's albums right after ABBA's in your collection. Like the Swedish Europop pioneer that preceded it, Ace of Base consists of two men and two women playing insidiously catchy tunes that are guilty pleasures, pure and simple. Don't come to Ace of Base looking for deep lyrical insights or philosophical musings when all you really need are a pair of dancing shoes and a taste for pop escapism at its finest. If you do take the time to dig beneath the exuberant grooves, though, you'll find an occasional melan-

choly streak running through the Ace's lyrics. Has this Scandinavian quartet not gotten enough sun, or is it simply that pop music demands a certain amount of drama from Top 40 fodder? Trust me: When the synth-bass lines start pumping on songs like "All That She Wants" and "Don't Turn Around," it will scarcely matter.

what to buy: The group's debut, *The Sign* 🎵🎵🎵 (Arista, 1993, prod. Joker/Buddha) offers a trio of massive international hits—"All That She Wants," "Don't Turn Around," and the title track—all of which sound remarkably alike: a curious mix of toy reggae, Eurodisco, and new wave synth-pop bouncing along at 95 or so beats per minute. The European version of the album is available in a slightly different configuration under the title *Happy Nation*.

the rest:

The Bridge 🎵🎵🎵 (Arista, 1995, prod. Joker/Buddha)

influences:

◀◀ ABBA, C+C Music Factory

Daniel Durchholz

Barbara Acklin

Born Barbara Allen, February 28, 1943, in Chicago, IL.

Barbara Acklin is one of the vital elements of the late 1960s/early 1970s Chicago soul sound. She made her first foray into music when her cousin Monk Higgins cut a couple of sides on her for his Secret Agent label, a record that went nowhere. Acklin's big break would come after joining Brunswick Records in 1966 as a secretary/receptionist and songwriter. After an impromptu audition for label superstar Jackie Wilson—Acklin co-wrote Wilson's hit "Whispers (Gettin' Louder)"—she was soon in the studio. Many of her early releases were duets with labelmate Gene Chandler. It was the release of "Love Makes a Woman" during the summer of 1968 that would confirm her status as a powerful solo vocalist. While "Love Makes a Woman" was her best chart performer, she wrapped up the decade with equally catchy midtempo groovers such as the funky "Just Ain't No Love," "After You," and "Am I the Same Girl"—though chart prospects of this one were unfortunatetly hampered by the release of The Young-Holt Unlimited's instrumental version, "Soulful Strut," a few months prior. "Same Girl" nevertheless caught the ear of Swing Out Sister, who issued an excellent, faithful cover version on their *Get In Touch with Yourself* album in 1992. By the turn of the decade, Acklin and her writing partner, Chi-Lites' frontman

Eugene Record—whom she eventually married—began funking up Acklin's sound while continuing to issue records with that sweet, smooth, soulful Chicago groove, all with the hopes of recapturing the chart success of "Love Makes a Woman." That type of reward, though, would only come after her defection from Brunswick to Capitol in 1974.

what's available: The best of Acklin's Brunswick work is collected on *Greatest Hits* &&&& (Brunswick, 1995, prod. various). All of the hits are here, including the two with Gene Chandler ("Show Me the Way to Go," "From the Teacher to the Preacher"), and the album is fleshed out with some excellent B-sides and album tracks. The staff of the recently reincarnated Brunswick Records wisely—thankfully!—drew the bulk of the bonus material from her soul output, leaving the marginal pop material that was *de rigeur* for 1960s-era R&B in the can. The album's only flaw is the omission of Acklin's three charting records for Capitol. But the writing, musicianship, and production of Brunswick Records at its late 1960s/early 1970s zenith is so strong—as it's represented here—that you barely notice they're missing.

influences:

◀◀ Curtis Mayfield, Mary Wells, Jo Armstead

▶▶ Patrice Rushen, Phoebe Snow, Swing Out Sister

Dana G. Smart

Johnny Adams

Born January 5, 1932, in New Orleans, LA.

Johnny Adams's warm vocals and extraordinary range have earned him the title of "the Tan Canary" in New Orleans. He is equally comfortable singing blues, jazz, R&B, and country in a rich, strong tenor that soars from round, low notes to a soulful falsetto, from a whisper to a scream. Among New Orleans singers, only Aaron Neville comes close to approaching the elegance and grace which Adams brings to each song. One can still hear in his voice his beginnings as a gospel singer with groups such as the Soul Revivers and Bessie Griffin and her Soul Consolators. In 1959, he started recording rhythm & blues for Ric Records and scored a big local hit with "I Won't Cry." Legend has it that Berry Gordy loved Adams's voice and wanted him for Motown, but a threatened lawsuit by Ric president Joe Rufffino ended that possibility. Adams continued recording for regional labels and charted with the country-flavored "Release Me" and "Reconsider Me" on SSS International Records in the late 1960s. For

many years, Adams teamed up with guitarist Walter "Wolfman" Washington every weekend at Dorothy's Medallion Lounge, a club that featured 300-pound go-go dancers performing with snakes. In 1984, Adams began an association with Rounder Records and producer Scott Billington which resulted in a series of excellent recordings and well-deserved national renown.

what to buy: *Johnny Adams Sings Doc Pomus: The Real Me* &&&&& (Rounder, 1991, prod. Scott Billington, Mac Rebennack) is a glorious tribute to the literate and complex songs of the great Doc Pomus. Rebennack gets high marks for co-producing, playing keyboards, and co-writing seven of the 11 tunes, and Red Tyler adds exquisite arrangements to songs like the clever and poignant "Imitation of Love" and the jazzy ballad "Blinded by Love." Adams finds his way to the heart of lyrics like this from "My Baby's Quit Me": "The dust is three inches thick/Ain't a clock in the house sayin' tick." *I Won't Cry: From the Vaults of Ric & Ron Records* &&&& (Rounder, 1991, prod. Jeff Hannusch) is a collection of Adams's earliest recordings from 1959–62. The youthful singer displays almost overwhelming power and emotion on these dates, which also feature the young Mac Rebennack. The title tune, Adams's first recording, is a doo-wop number with huge vocals penned by "Tutti Frutti" composer Dorothy Labostrie, a neighbor of Adams who brought him to Ruffino after hearing him sing "Precious Lord" in the bathtub. *Good Morning Heartache* &&&& (Rounder, 1993, prod. Scott Billington) is a dream match-up: Legendary arranger Wardell Quezergue meets the Tan Canary on a set of jazz standards. This is late-night, brandy-sniffing, romance-enhancing music, as Adams wraps his chords around gorgeous songs like "You Don't Know What Love Is" and "Come Rain or Come Shine." *One Foot in the Blues* &&&& (Rounder, 1996, prod. Scott Billington) is another inspired grouping, matching Adams with Dr. Lonnie Smith's Hammond B-3 organ for a satisfying set of soulful blues.

what to buy next: Adams's other tribute album, *Walking on a Tightrope: The Songs of Percy Mayfield* &&&& (Rounder, 1989, prod. Scott Billington), features the songs of "the poet laureate of the blues." A contract writer for Ray Charles for many years, as well as a distinctive vocalist in his own right, Mayfield composed hundreds of songs. Backed by various jazz and blues musicians (including Walter "Wolfman" Washington and Duke Robillard on guitars), Adams brings elegance and emotion to the slow blues of the title cut and swing tunes like "Look the Whole World Over." The highlight is a brilliant reading of "Danger Zone," one of the greatest songs ever written.

the rest:
From the Heart 🎵🎵🎵🎵 (Rounder, 1984)
After Dark 🎵🎵🎵🎵 (Rounder, 1986)
Room with a View of the Blues 🎵🎵🎵🎵 (Rounder, 1987)
The Verdict 🎵🎵🎵🎵 (Rounder, 1995)

worth searching for: Adams shows up as a guest vocalist on a diverse group of recordings. Look for him on Maria Muldaur's *Fanning the Flames* (Telarc, 1996, prod. Maria Muldaur, John Snyder, Elaine Martone) and *Lost in the Stars: The Music of Kurt Weill* (A&M, 1985, prod. Hal Willner, John Telfer).

influences:

◀◀ Percy Mayfield, Johnny Hartman, Bobby Bland

David Feld

Oleta Adams

Born May 4, 1962, in Seattle, WA.

Reared in the soul-shouting confines of a gospel-fed church in Seattle, Adams recorded a couple of jazzy albums during the 1980s with a trio in Kansas City, Kansas, and was well on her way to membership in the Holiday Inn lounge singer hall of fame when fate walked into a gig. Actually, Adams was something of a minor legend in Kansas City for her elaborate lounge shows, one of which captivated Tears For Fears frontmen Roland Orzabal and Curt Smith during a chance visit in 1986. They eventually plucked Adams from her lounge work to help fire up the slow-going recording sessions for their 1989 *Seeds of Love* album and brought her along for the tour, where she turned heads with her soulful, emotive vocals and piano playing. Orzabal and Tears producer David Bascombe returned the favor by producing her first album, recorded for Orzabal's own label. Her cover of a Brenda Russell tune, "Get Here," topped the charts thanks to its timely selection as a theme for the Persian Gulf War. It seemed the start of a great career, but her lounge-singing roots led her to stock two subsequent albums with ill-fitting cover tunes and a listless jazz/R&B sound that doomed them to the cut-out bin.

what to buy: Hands down, Adams's debut *Circle of One* 🎵🎵🎵🎵 (Phonogram/Mercury, 1990, prod. David Bascombe, Roland Orzabal) is easily her most accomplished. The Tears production team artfully straddles a tenuous line between clear, focused renditions of jazzy R&B covers such as the Quincy Jones tune "Everything Must Change" and Orzabal's uncannily well-arranged Fairlight keyboard sequencing on danceable pop tunes such as "Rhythm of Life"—originally intended for "Seeds of Love"—and the title track. And, while the Gulf War circum-

> *I used to work in bars. You work through anything--the blender, the waitresses, groups from conventions coming through, even people falling over you drunk. You know those things called 'The Yard'? When you sing in a place that has some of those and you get a bunch of guys together and they decide to compete, they're going 'Go! Go! Go! Go! Go!' and you're in the middle of 'Send in the Clowns' and you really learn how to get over it.*
>
> **Oleta Adams**

stances helped make "Get Here" a pop hit, it's Adams's powerful, passionate vocals that turned it into an instant classic.

what to buy next: There's a clarity of purpose and a perfect mix of music, voice, and message on her gospel album, *Come Walk with Me* 🎵🎵🎵🎵 (Harmony/Relativity, 1997, prod. Michael J. Powell), that makes Adams's secular work seem almost forced. It's easy to tell, especially on "What Price" and "This Love Won't Wait," from whence her inspiration flows.

what to avoid: Reeling from a sophomore record that tanked, Adams tried to reach out to the R&B community with her third record, *Moving On* **woof!** (Mercury, 1995, prod. Vassal Benford, Michael J. Powell, Alan Rich, Judd Friedman), an album filled with listless R&B that couldn't be more calculated if it was made by Casio. Ironically, her effort came at a time when the R&B charts were dominated by young, hip-hop inspired divas, consigning her effort to a commercial pit even her army of producers—veterans of projects by Whitney Houston, Mariah Carey, and Anita Baker—couldn't avoid.

the rest:
Evolution 🎵🎵🎵 (Phonogram/Mercury, 1993)
Come Walk with Me 🎵🎵🎵🎵 (Harmony/Relativity, 1997)

worth searching for: Adams's vibrant piano work and able vocals dueting with Orzabal on the percolating "Woman in Chains" and "Badman's Song" on the Tears For Fears album *The Seeds of Love* 🎵🎵🎵🎵 (Mercury, 1989, prod. David Bascombe and Tears For Fears) provide more than a few spine tingling moments.

influences:

◀◀ Nina Simone, Aretha Franklin, Anita Baker

▶▶ Sabelle, Deborah Cox

Eric Deggans and Franklin Paul

Afro Rican

Whoomp, here it is. Before Tag Team or the 69 Boyz or many of the other '90s sex-crazed bass heads had their three-and-a-half uptempo, butt-shaking minutes in the Sunbelt spotlight, there was Afro Rican. The multi-ethnic group's remarkably infectious 128 bpm single, "Give It All You Got (Doggie Style)," became a mix-show and club hit, memorable for its snatch of Foxy's "Get Off" and its instructions to "break it down/let's do it doggie style."

what's available: *Give It All You Got 95* 🎵🎵 (Hip Rock, 1995, prod. Afro Rican) resurrects the otherwise out-of-print title hit and contains the song "Rollercoaster," but is not otherwise notable. Amusing titles, though ("Make that Booty Jump," "Gotta Get My Freak On," "68 and IOU 1").

influences:

◀◀ 2 Live Crew, Egyptian Lover, Kraftwerk, Afrika Bambaataa

▶▶ 95 South, 12 Gauge, Tag Team, 69 Boyz, A-Town Players, Ghost Town DJs, Quad City DJ's

Todd Inoue

Ahmad

Born Ahmad A. Lewis, in Los Angeles, CA.

Long before hip-hop reached the age of 18 (in recorded commercial form, anyway), it had already lost its innocence. So, too, had Ahmad well before he'd become old enough to vote. "Back in the days, when I was young/I'm not a kid anymore/But some days I sit and wish I was a kid again," the South Central rapper with the affected British accent and half-decent singing voice crooned sweetly in his endearing breakthrough hit, "Back in the Day." Recorded when Ahmad was 18, the song looks in the rearview mirror and cringes at the rapidly fading view of a simpler, easier, carefree time—circa 1985—when all the pre-teen rapper had to worry about was homework and girls, who were sporting biker shorts en masse, thanks to J.J. Fad. Of course, listening to the rest of the funky, largely upbeat *Ahmad* you almost begin to wonder if the young artist really has many more worries now, as he invests much of his time pursuing women ("The Palladium"), bonding with his friends ("Homeboys First"), and exhorting you to dance and/or party ("Touch the Ceiling," "We Want the Funk," "Can I Party?"). But he eventually does get serious, examining peer pressure on "You Gotta Be . . ." and giving a big recorded kiss to his mother on "Ordinary People" to make for a promising, well-balanced debut that lyrically recalls the great hip-hop storyteller Slick Rick. Oddly, though, the album has yet to see a follow-up.

what's available: The centerpiece of *Ahmad* 🎵🎵🎵🎵 (Giant, 1994, prod. Ahmad, others) is clearly "Back in the Day," which appears in original form plus two remixes. The first remix, which uses a large sample from Teddy Pendergrass's "Love T.K.O." to great effect, is actually the version of the wistful song that introduced Ahmad to the masses and went gold, perhaps changing his view about the present. Although Ahmad promises that he's "not gonna sing another sad song," he does just that with the well-conceived "You Gotta Be . . .," taking on the roles of both an impressionable inner-city kid who doesn't want to be in a gang and a gangster who applies just enough pressure to get him to join. "Is it a lie that I must be a roughneck and wear a frown just to be down? . . . Forget about respect/I refuse to be the next guy fitted for a casket," he says, before slipping into his second role and instructing: "Either with it or get blasted." Ahmad eventually gets with it and is given a .22 and sent into a store, where he summarily gets shot before winding up in jail. "Niggaroes, come together because divided we fall," he says, slipping into morality-play mode before bringing people together himself with one of his uplifting party jams, "We Want the Funk."

worth searching for: Ahmad and fellow wordsmiths Saafir and Ras Kass teamed up for the memorable posse cut "Come Widdit" off the *Streetfighter* soundtrack (VRS, 1994), although Ahmad really finished third in the competitive three-way rap race.

influences:

◀◀ Slick Rick, Pharcyde, Volume 10, Young M.C., Domino

▶▶ Skee-Lo

Josh Freedom du Lac

Akinyele

Born Akinyele Adams.

As with Nas, Akinyele introduced himself to the hip-hop world with a 45-second stint on the Main Source's classic posse cut, "Live at the Barbeque." On the legendary track, Akinyele debuted what would become his trademark—delivering the last words of a couplet a couple octaves lower than his normal voice. Though he had people "oooohing" and "aaaaahing" at first, Akinyele quickly wore out his hackneyed rhyming style by using it whenever he recorded.

what's available: Never accuse Akinyele of not being direct. His only album to date, *Vagina Diner* 🎵🎵 (Interscope, 1993, prod. Large Professor), offers less-than-subtle insight into the rapper's primary interests. Thanks to the Large Professor's tightly constructed beats, "Outta State" and "Checkmate" are the album's most redeeming songs. A third, "I Luh Huh," might be worth listening to if it weren't for its blatant offensiveness, with Akinyele reviewing various ways he can make his girlfriend's pregnancy go away.

influences:

◀◀ Main Source, Juice Crew, Chubb Rock

Jazzbo

Gerald Albright

Born 1957, in Los Angeles, CA.

To his fans, saxman Gerald Albright must seem like a mystery wrapped in an enigma. Dubbed "Wonderfunk" by his musical peers, Albright is arguably the most in-demand R&B session player of the 1990s; it's almost easier to list the best-selling soul, jazz, and gospel LPs he *hasn't* performed on over the past decade than the recordings his silvery-smooth harmonies have graced. He is the saxman of choice for such top-drawer artists as Quincy Jones and Take 6, works with acts as diverse as Third World and the Boys Choir of Harlem, and owns credits on some of the most prominent rhythm-and-blues LPs of recent years (Whitney Houston's *I'm Your Baby Tonight*, Patrice Rushen's *Straight from the Heart*, and BeBe and CeCe Winans's *Heaven* among them). But while Albright is clearly a superior instrumentalist (having originally studied piano before switching to tenor sax, and experimenting with electric bass in college), and has been signed to Atlantic Jazz as a solo act since 1988, the quality of his own albums has generally been spotty and unconvincing at best. It's as if he's content to collect his triple-scale paycheck playing behind others rather than let his solo talents soar to the fore, as have so many of his sax contemporaries. Among Albright's live appearances was a national tour called "Just the Sax," accompanied by Everette Harp, Bobby Watson, and Art Porter. Maybe he's just more comfortable in groups.

what to buy: Even though only half of the 10 cuts were actually recorded there, *Live at Birdland West* 🎵🎵🎵🎵 (Atlantic Jazz, 1991, prod. Gerald Albright) is a stunning exception to Albright's usual elementary pop-funk formulas. Shifting easily between alto and tenor horns and joined by tenor star Kirk Whalum, Albright ennobles his most unapologetic jazz outing with haunting versions of "Georgia on My Mind" and "Limehouse Blues," while welcoming guest star Eddie Harris for a joyous track called "Bubblehead McDaddy." This is the album where Albright dropped his guard and let his pure talent blaze through.

what to buy next: Although Albright's work is solid, *Smooth* 🎵🎵🎵 (Atlantic, 1994, prod. various) may be his most accessible LP (particularly for the jazz-impaired) due to its glittering array of guest stars. His RSVP list includes singers Howard Hewett ("This Is for the Lover in You") and Will Downing ("Just 2 B with You"), guitarist Lee Ritenour ("G & Lee"), and the incomparable bassist Stanley Clarke (on the atmospheric "Sedona"). When you've played behind as many stars as Albright has, you can call in some pretty impressive markers.

the rest:
Just Between Us 🎵🎵🎵 (Atlantic Jazz, 1987)
Bermuda Nights 🎵🎵🎵 (Atlantic Jazz, 1988)
Dream Come True 🎵🎵🎵 (Atlantic Jazz, 1990)
Giving Myself to You 🎵🎵🎵🎵 (Atlantic Jazz, 1995)

influences:

◀◀ Earl Bostic, King Curtis, Tom Scott, Clarence Clemons, Patrice Rushen, Najee, Grover Washington Jr.

▶▶ Kirk Whalum, David McMurray, Kenny G, Dave Koz, Everette Harp, Boney James

Jim McFarlin

Arthur Alexander

Born May 10, 1940, in Florence, AL. Died June 9, 1993, in Nashville, TN.

Alexander wrote songs that helped define early 1960s popular music, yet he never achieved wide or sustained notoriety outside the music industry. With a smooth and plaintive vocal style, Alexander wedded country with soul to create music that was unique, outstanding, and enduring. His first hit, 1962's "You Better Move On," was recorded in Muscle Shoals, Alabama, and helped to establish that locale as a hotbed of soul and R&B talent. Alexander's music was also an early influence on John Lennon and Paul McCartney, who covered his biggest hit, "Anna (Go To Him)," on the Beatles' 1963 debut album; two years later, the Rolling Stones used Alexander's "You Better Move On" on *December's Children*. Bob Dylan ("Sally Sue Brown"), Elvis Presley ("Burning Love"), and Otis Redding ("Johnny Heartbreak") were among the other pop luminaries who recorded Alexander's works. But his own career languished, due mainly to substance abuse and a record industry that insisted on pegging him as a country artist. Disillusioned, he retired from recording and moved to Cleveland, Ohio, where he drove a bus for a social services agency. Marshall Crenshaw kept Alexander's music alive by covering "Soldier of Love (Lay Down Your Arms)" on his 1982 debut album, and in 1991, Alexander was coaxed into performing at a songwriters workshop at The Bottom Line in New York. That sparked him to record a new album and resume his career; tragically, though, he suffered a fatal heart attack on the eve of a concert tour to celebrate his return. Alexander was never really a household name, but he'll always be remembered as one of the great early influences on rock & roll.

what to buy: *The Ultimate Arthur Alexander* ♫♫♫♫ (Razor & Tie, 1993, prod. various) is an outstanding compilation that houses Alexander's original versions of the songs that were covered by so many influential artists of the 1960s. These are mostly mid-tempo ballads featuring great melodies and lyrics that are hauntingly personal and direct, with a recurring theme of relationships gone wrong.

what to buy next: *Lonely Just Like Me* ♫♫♫♫ (Elektra Nonesuch, 1993, prod. Ben Vaughn, Thomas Cain) was recorded shortly before Alexander's death and offers some great new originals in the style of his best work, along with some updated versions of his older songs. This was an unexpected treasure for fans who had assumed Alexander would never record again. *Adios Amigo: A Tribute to Arthur Alexander* ♫♫♫♫ (Razor & Tie, 1994, prod. various) is a memorable tribute from a wide range of

artists paying their respects in song. Elvis Costello's burning version of "Sally Sue Brown" is worth the price of admission alone.

what to avoid: While it has some great moments, *Rainbow Road: Arthur Alexander, The Warner Brothers Recordings* ♫♫ (Warner Bros., 1994, prod. Tommy Cogbill) is inconsistent and for major fans and completists only.

the rest:
Soldier of Love ♫♫♫ (Ace, 1987)

worth searching for: *A Shot of Rhythm and Soul* ♫♫♫♫ (Ace, 1982), a well-annotated vinyl-only collection that contains all the big hits and some great songs such as "Sally Sue Brown," which are not represented on *The Ultimate Arthur Alexander*.

influences:

◀◀ Eddy Arnold, Hank Williams, Elmore James, Jimmy Reed, B.B. King, Junior Parker, the Drifters, the Clovers, Billy Ward and the Dominoes

▶▶ The Beatles, Marshall Crenshaw, Elvis Costello, the Rolling Stones, Otis Redding, Ike & Tina Turner, Humble Pie, Ry Cooder, the Bee Gees, Rod Stewart

Michael Isabella

Tha Alkaholiks

Formed 1992, in Los Angeles, CA.

J-Ro (born James Robinson), vocals; Tash (born Rico Smith), vocals; E-Swift (born Eric Brooks), DJ.

Nobody can ever accuse the 'Liks of not being able to have a good time. The trio's love of parties and beer led rhyme-crony King Tee to give them their fittingly irreverent moniker, and the group has incorporated that theme into nearly everything it does. J-Ro, Tash, and E-Swift made it their mission to spread good times through beats and rhymes, and in doing so they helped launch the rebirth of the post-gangsta Los Angeles hip-hop scene.

what's available: If nothing else, Tha Alkaholiks are consistent. The group's debut, *21 & Over* ♫♫♫♫ (Loud/RCA, 1993, prod. E-Swift, Loot Pack), features a potent mix that has become the group's infallible formula: Upbeat, arm-waving grooves and sharply delivered lyrics. The well-conceived "Mary Jane"—which takes a cue from Rick James, metaphorically relating the pursuit of marijuana to that of a woman—is the wittiest of all the songs that have exposed hip-hop's love affair with blunts. And the screaming horns and driving rhymes of the album's first single, "Make Room," nearly caused the floor to cave in at a 1993 music conference when Tha Alkaholiks performed the song live. On *Coast II Coast* ♫♫♫ (Loud/RCA, 1995, prod. E-Swift, Diamond D), the group's mandate for making universal party music is re-inforced. Tash's rhyming, which developed immensely between albums, highlights cuts such as "Let It Out," which is a Diamond D production that uses an intoxicating, spy-fi guitar loop sam-pled from the Bruce Lee classic, *Enter the Dragon.*

worth searching for: Tha Alkaholiks were introduced on "I Got It Bad Y'all," a funky, liquor-induced posse cut from mentor King Tee's *The Triflin' Album* (Capitol, 1993).

influences:

◀◀ King Tee, WC and the MAAD Circle

▶▶ Xzibit, The Loot Pack

Jazzbo

All-4-One

Formed 1993, in Los Angeles, CA.

Tony Borowiak, vocals; Alfred Nevarez, vocals; Jamie Jones, vocals; Delious Kennedy, vocals.

All-4-One's formation seemed predestined. Tenor Tony Borowiak and bass singer Alfred Nevarez grew up in Lancaster, California (notorious as the town where Frank Zappa and Cap-tain Beefheart were raised), and threw their lot together in a harmony group. During a talent contest, they competed with another group that featured tenor Jamie Jones. Both groups soon broke up, and the three vocalists, who had admired each others' singing at the contest, got together. Jones had lined up some radio jingle work, and they soon found their voices blended well. Jones met up with producer Gary St. Clair while singing in a church choir. St. Clair was impressed by Jones's voice. He told the trio that producer Tim O'Brien of Blitzz Records—no doubt inspired by Boyz II Men's huge success with harmony-oriented material—wanted someone who could sing "So Much in Love," the 1963 doo-wop hit by The Tymes. So the trio went in search of a fourth voice. Following the previous pattern, they found tenor Delious Kennedy by accident when Borowiak and Jones were messing around trying to win some money at a karaoke contest.

what to buy: *All-4-One* ♫♫♫ (Blitzz/Atlantic, 1994, prod. Gary St. Clair, Tim O'Brien, David Foster, DJ Gill) is *the* album by All-4-One, until maybe a greatest hits album comes along. The group excels at doo-wop harmony, although the sound is so pristine that it recalls the Beach Boys as much as the Clovers—which, in a sense, is unsurprising for a group from Southern California.

Vocal quality aside, the album's main deficiency is a lack of memorable songs. The group tries gamely but doesn't seem to have the heart for the derivative hip-hop doo-wop of numbers such as "(She's Got) Skillz" and "The Bomb." The megahit "I Swear" is one of those faceless but catchy pop tunes that dom-inated the middle-of-the-road charts during the late 1980s and early 1990s. It was a major country hit for John Michael Mont-gomery, too, but All-4-One cut the superior version.

what to buy next: *And the Music Speaks* ♫♫♫ (Blitzz-Atlantic, 1995, prod. Gary St. Clair, Tim O'Brien) features the group's other big hit, "I Can Love You Like That," and a great album-closing a cappella number, "We Dedicate," that takes some of the starch out of the sound. However, the memorable-moments quotient is low.

the rest:

All-4-One Christmas ♫♫♫ (Blitzz-Atlantic, 1995)

My Brother's Keeper N/A (Atlantic, 1997)

worth searching for: "Someday," the group's contribution to the *Hunchback of Notre Dame Soundtrack* ♫♫♫ (Hollywood, 1996, prod. Walter Afanasieff).

influences:

◀◀ The Flamingos, the Dells, Harold Melvin & the Blue Notes

Salvatore Caputo

Almighty RSO

Formed in Boston, MA.

Ray Dogg, vocals; Tony Rhome, vocals; E-Devious, vocals; Deff Jeff, DJ.

Is it really true that any publicity is good publicity? The Almighty RSO might forever be remembered for something en-tirely other than its music, thanks to a highly publicized 1994 letter written by the co-editor of *The Source*, James Bernard, that charged the hip-hop journal's publisher, David Mays, with a conflict of interest. The letter alleged that Mays was the man-ager of the Almighty RSO and claimed that he had sneaked an article about the then-unknown group into the magazine—without alerting Bernard and the rest of the editorial staff. Mays, for his part, denied having any proprietary interest in the group. But still.

what to buy: The thing is, the Almighty Real Solid Organization or Rock Shit On (or whatever "RSO" stands for) isn't bad. While stylistically uneven and far from groundbreaking, the group's full-length debut *Doomsday: Forever RSO* ♫♫♫ (Rap-a-Lot/Noo Trybe, 1996, prod. Havoc, Kay Gee, others) is still a mostly interesting examination of ghetto life in which the narrators (and guests from Mobb Deep to Eightball & MJG) exhort fellow youngbloods to "Keep Alive" and insist that there's "Gotta Be a Better Way" while also rapping about "Killin 'Em" and "Illicit Activity." And on "You Could Be My Boo," the group teams up with the ghetto-fabulous singer Faith Evans for a sort of low rent "I'll Be There for You/You're All I Need to Get By."

the rest:
Revenge Uv Da Badd Boyz 𝄞𝄞𝄞 (RCA EP, 1994)

influences:
◀◀ Lost Boyz, Naughty by Nature, Mobb Deep

Josh Freedom du Lac

Gerald Alston
Born November 8, 1942, in North Carolina.

Like so many R&B singers, Gerald Alston is a product of the church; his father was a preacher and his uncle, Johnny Fields, was part of the famed gospel group the Blind Boys. Alston went secular in 1971 when he began a 17-year stint with the Manhattans that included hits such as "Kiss and Say Goodbye," "It's You," and "Shining Star." But despite a fine, expressive voice and some minor hits in the U.K., his solo career never took off. There were too many singers like him—Luther Vandross and Freddie Jackson—with more promotional juice behind them for Alston to ever get over in a big way.

what's available: *First Class Only* 𝄞𝄞 (Scotti Bros., 1994)—also released as *Kiss and Say Goodbye*— is a tepid affair, especially in this age of New Jack sensibilities.

worth searching for: The out-of-print *Open Invitation* 𝄞𝄞𝄞 (Motown, 1990) is Alston's best effort, showing potential that merits more success than he had.

influences:
◀◀ The Blind Boys, the Soul Stirrers, Sam Cooke, Marvin Gaye
▶▶ El DeBarge, Freddie Jackson, Babyface

Gary Graff

Anotha Level
Formed 1991, in Los Angeles, CA.

The critical success of groups like the Pharcyde, Freestyle Fellowship, and Tha Alkaholiks rejuvenated the L.A. hip-hop scene, and this teenage quintet's record deal was a product of the industry's newfound interest in Southland rap. While the five MCs' voices never belied their ages (they came together while attending L.A.'s Westchester High School), the group also couldn't hide its Pharcyde influence, immediately turning off those listeners who felt that Anotha Level didn't have the charisma—or creativity—to match.

what's available: The group got off on the right foot with "What's That 'Cha Say," a light, jazzy single that became a consummate California spring song. But the ensuing debut, *On Anotha Level* 𝄞 (Priority, 1994, prod. Laylaw, D-Maq) was filled with too many Pharcyde allusions, making it difficult to appreciate the young group's sincerity.

influences:
◀◀ Pharcyde

Jazzbo

Apache
Born Anthony Teaks in Jersey City, NJ.

Differentiation is the key to standing out in a crowded field, and that's exactly what Apache tried to do, taking his name from his partial Native-American background. Judging by his short-lived career, though, it simply wasn't enough. Ironically, although Apache is considered a ruffneck, he's also known for his undying devotion to female MC Nikki D.

what's available: *Apache* 𝄞𝄞 (Tommy Boy, 1993, prod. A Tribe Called Quest, Large Professor, Diamond D, Apache, others) did little to captivate listeners, save for one track: "Gangsta Bitch," a uniquely charming—if ogre-like—love song that became a mini-anthem in the summer of '93.

worth searching for: Although Apache nemesis Queen Latifah might disagree, finding the "Gangsta Bitch" single is a better investment than buying *Apache*.

influences:
◀◀ Naughty by Nature, Flavor Unit

Jazzbo

Joan Armatrading
Born December 9, 1950, in Basseterre, St. Kitts, West Indies.

Armatrading's loyal cult following has kept her touring and recording for more than 25 years. Her revealing, emotionally

Joan Armatrading (© Ken Settle)

charged lyrics and excellent though underrated guitar playing reveal a solid, consistent talent. Raised in England, Armatrading's first public notice came in 1970 when she appeared in *Hair* and began a folk collaboration with songwriter Pam Nestor. After one duo album, Armatrading went solo with a sound that blended jazz, Caribbean, and rock influences into a folk format; she was also among the first to bring synthesizers into an essentially acoustic setting. Her later work featuring electric guitars is less satisfying, but her steady songwriting skills have maintained the integrity of the music. The coordination and interplay between her vocals and her guitar playing lends distinction to much of her work.

what to buy: *Joan Armatrading* ✍✍✍✍ (A&M, 1976, prod. Glyn Johns) is full of pining lyrics and sparse arrangements that color and enhance her pleasing, husky voice. The anthemic gospel ending to "Love and Affection" tops off one of the most joyous and revealing looks at the effects of love. Some of her electric stuff does hit, and *The Key* ✍✍✍✍ (A&M, 1983, prod. Steve Lillywhite, Val Garay) is one of Armatrading's least introspective forays. There's a taste of the old Joan on "Drop the Pilot," "(I Love It When You) Call Me Names," and the title song, but she also casts an eye on the social ravages of drugs and violence. *Greatest Hits* ✍✍✍✍✍ (A&M, 1996, prod. various) is exactly what it says.

what to buy next: Much of what fans like most about Armatrading is on *Back to the Night* ✍✍✍✍ (A&M, 1975, prod. Pete Gage), a spare, folkish work with great songs such as "Dry Land," "Cool Blue Stole My Heart," and "Body to Dust."

what to avoid: Armatrading's ability to produce a hook or memorable line largely evaded her songs on *Hearts and Flowers* ✍✍ (A&M, 1990, prod. Joan Armatrading), although the title tune is a keeper.

the rest:
Whatever's for Us ✍✍✍ (A&M, 1972)
Show Some Emotion ✍✍✍ (A&M, 1977)
To the Limit ✍✍✍✍ (A&M, 1978)
Me, Myself and I ✍✍✍✍ (A&M, 1980)
Walk Under Ladders ✍✍✍ (A&M, 1981)
Track Record ✍✍✍✍ (A&M, 1983)
Sleight of Hand ✍✍✍✍✍ (A&M, 1986)
Classics, Vol. 21 ✍✍✍✍ (A&M, 1986)
The Shouting Stage ✍✍✍ (A&M, 1988)
Square the Circle ✍✍✍ (A&M, 1992)
What's Inside ✍✍✍✍ (A&M, 1995)

worth searching for: The hard-to-find *Secret Secrets* ✍✍✍✍ (A&M, 1985, prod. Mike Howlett) contains some of Armatrad-

ing's most densely produced music, including horns, but the change does her good. There's a pervasive joy here so that even a bluesy lyric such as "Friends Not Lovers" gets delivered with a bouncy, infectious beat.

influences:

◀◀ Odetta, Joni Mitchell

▶▶ Tracy Chapman, Dionne Farris

Lawrence Gabriel

Louis Armstrong

Born August 4, 1901, in New Orleans, LA. Died July 6, 1971, in New York, NY.

Armstrong stands out as one of the giants of 20th-century music. A trumpeter, vocalist, and entertainer par excellence, Armstrong put the stamp on all jazz singing and improvisation that would come after him; his stylings also made their mark in the R&B, pop, and rock communities, where his hit "What a Wonderful World"—which took on a new life after its inclusion in the film *Good Morning Vietnam*—has become a popular cover choice. Born and raised in New Orleans as the jazz age was taking off, Armstrong was the first improviser to blend disparate riffs and accents into extended solos that hung together as unified musical statements. This was obvious during his early days with the King Oliver and Clarence Williams groups, but his recordings with his own bands—Hot Five and Hot Seven—are some of the most important works of any music. These were just studio bands, but their musical treatments took New Orleans jazz out of the collective improvisation mode into that of the featured solo improviser. Pieces such as "Potato Head Blues," "Hotter Than That," and "Cornet Chop Suey" set standards for improvisation and composition. "Heebie Jeebies" put him on the map as a vocalist and popularized scat singing; Armstrong's gruff voice could wring emotion out of jazz, blues, ballad, or pop song. Armstrong put it all together with an unequaled technical mastery that so overshadowed his contemporaries that he was held as a model for all to follow.

what to buy: Armstrong's early recordings are historic, and many of them are included on the four-CD set *Portrait of the Artist as a Young Man, 1923–1934* ✍✍✍✍✍ (Columbia/Legacy, 1994, comp. Nedra Olds-Neal). This is an essential Armstrong collection with recordings from his Oliver and Williams days in addition to seminal collaborations with Bessie Smith ("St. Louis Blues"), Lonnie Johnson, Jimmie Rogers (yes, the country-western guy), and others. The Hot Five/Seven stuff is here, along with some of his early big band work. *The Complete Studio*

Recordings of Louis Armstrong and the All Stars ♫♫♫♫ (Mosaic, 1993, comp. Michael Cuscuna) completes the picture with a six-CD set of Armstrong recordings spanning 1950–58. This is a great collection showing the band in top form with the likes of Earl Hines, Jack Teagarden, Trummy Young, Barney Bigard, Lucky Thompson, and Gene Krupa on board. Many of the standards ("Muskrat Ramble," "Struttin' with Some Barbecue," "Body and Soul," "Lazy River") are here, captured fresh without the burden of an audience to entertain. "Baby, Your Slip Is Showing" provides a taste of how Armstrong could still capture the old feeling. Both sets include excellent booklet essays and photos.

what to buy next: *Hot Fives and Hot Sevens—Vol. 2* ♫♫♫♫ (CBS, 1926/Columbia, 1988, prod. various) shows Armstrong's first flush of maturity and defining of the art of jazz.

what to avoid: *What a Wonderful World* **woof!** (Decca, 1970, prod. Bob Thiele) contains little of what made Armstrong great, pandering to the rock generation with electric bass and guitar on covers that include "Give Peace a Chance" and "Everybody's Talking."

the rest:
Louis Armstrong and Earl Hines ♫♫♫♫ (CBS, 1927/Columbia Jazz Masterpieces, 1989)
The Essential Louis Armstrong ♫♫♫♫ (Vanguard, 1987)
Stardust ♫♫♫♫ (CBS, 1988)
Laughin' Louie ♫♫♫ (RCA, 1989)
The Sullivan Years ♫♫ (TVT, 1990)
Mack the Knife ♫♫♫♫ (Pablo, 1990)
Rhythm Saved the World ♫♫♫♫ (Decca, 1991)
In Concert with Europe 1 ♫♫♫♫ (RTE, 1992)
Blueberry Hill ♫♫♫ (Milan, 1992)
The California Concerts ♫♫ (MCA, 1992)
Sings the Blues ♫♫♫♫ (BMG, 1993)
Young Louis Armstrong—(1930–1933) ♫♫♫ (BMG, 1993)
Louis Armstrong and His Friends (Pasadena Civic Auditorium, 1951) ♫♫♫ (GNP, 1993)
Happy Birthday Louis ♫♫♫ (Omega, 1994)
Swing that Music ♫♫♫ (Drive, 1994)
Pocketful of Dreams, Vol. III ♫♫♫♫ (Decca, 1995)
Satchmo at Symphony Hall ♫♫♫♫ (MCA, 1996)
Disney Songs the Satchmo Way ♫♫♫♫ (Disneyland, 1968/Walt Disney Records, 1996)

worth searching for: *Ella Fitzgerald and Louis Armstrong* (Verve, 1957, prod. Norman Granz) offers a double treat with two of the world's greatest classic jazz singers swinging together. A great cast of Oscar Peterson, Herb Ellis, Ray Brown, and Buddy Rich back them up.

influences:

◀◀ Joe "King" Oliver, Buddy Bolden, Kid Rena

▶▶ Bix Beiderbecke, Dizzy Gillespie, Wynton Marsalis, Victoria Williams, Buster Poindexter, Chicago, Blood, Sweat & Tears

Lawrence Gabriel

Vanessa Bell Armstrong

Born October 2, 1953, in Detroit, MI.

Vanessa Bell Armstrong (too often confused with the fine black actress Vanessa Bell Calloway) has been inspiring, uplifting, and delivering the Good News to gospel audiences everywhere since her early teens, traveling the concert circuit with the likes of the late Rev. James Cleveland, Dr. Mattie Moss Clark and the Clark Sisters, the Mighty Clouds of Joy, and the Winans. In 1984, Armstrong began her recording career by signing with Benson's Onyx label. The late Min. Thomas Whitfield produced her first album, *Peace Be Still*, which went to the top of the gospel charts. Three years later, she received Grammy and Dove Award nominations for her album *Following Jesus* and, on another note, beat out Aretha Franklin and Patti LaBelle for the high-profile assignment of singing the theme song "Shine On Me," for the NBC sitcom *Amen*. After several label changes and battles over royalties, Armstrong signed in 1987 with her current label, Verity Records, and began to take more control over her career. Her recent recordings have featured guest appearances from the likes of jazz guitarist-vocalist Jonathan Butler and the celebrated "Prince of Gospel," John P. Kee, whom Armstrong hand-picked to produce her 1995 LP *The Secret Is Out*.

what to buy: *Vanessa Bell Armstrong* ♫♫♫♫ (Verity, 1987, prod. various) showcases Armstrong's decidedly urban slant to gospel music. Tried-and-true gospel fans literally despised this album, accusing Armstrong of "backsliding" and "selling out," but for true lovers of good music, this is a valued addition to any CD stack. It includes her "controversial" crossover hit, "You Bring Out the Best In Me."

what to buy next: Continuing on her journey through the wilds of R&B/urban music, *Wonderful One* ♫♫♫ (Verity, 1989, prod. various) does its best to get Armstrong out to the mainstream through her duet with Jonathan Butler on the ballad "True Love Never Fails" (also heard on Butler's LP *More Than Friends*). Although some of the songs are shallow lyrically, just to hear Armstrong's soaring voice here is worth the price of admission.

the rest:
Peace Be Still ♫♫♫♫ (Benson/Onyx, 1984)

Following Jesus ♫♫♫♫ (Jive, 1987)
The Truth about Christmas ♫♫♫ (Jive, 1990)
Something on the Inside ♫♫♫ (Verity, 1993)
The Secret Is Out ♫♫♫♫ (Verity, 1995)
VIP (Victory In Praise) Music and Arts Seminar Mass Choir ♫♫♫ (Verity, 1996)

worth searching for: The Onyx/Benson material captures Armstrong at her gospel best. If you should happen to stumble upon *Greatest Hits* ♫♫♫♫ (Muscle Shoals Sound Gospel, 1991), don't hesitate: Pick it up, say "Thank you, Lord," and head straight for the cash register.

influences:

◀◀ Dr. Mattie Moss Clark, Rev. James Cleveland, Aretha Franklin, Patti LaBelle, Luther Vandross

▶▶ Vickie Winans, Charlene Bell

                                              Tim A. Smith

Arrested Development /Speech /Dionne Farris

Formed 1988, in Atlanta, GA. Disbanded 1996.

Speech (born Todd Thomas), vocals; Headliner (born Tim Barnwell), DJ; Rasa Don (born Donald Jones), vocals, drums; Aerle Taree, vocals, dancer, stylist (1988–94); Montsho Eshe, dancer, choreographer; Baba Oje, spiritual adviser; Dionne Farris, vocals (1992-94); Ajile, vocals, dancer (1994–96); Kwesi, DJ, vocals (1994–96); Nadirah, vocals (1994–96).

Billed as the "positive" rap band that would counter all the "negative" gangstas and braggarts, Arrested Development borrowed liberally from Sly & the Family Stone and built on De La Soul to make one of the best albums in 1992 pop. Led by the upbeat young rapper Speech, the band eschewed violence, hatred, and misogyny and played up African-American self-esteem and even Christianity. Drawing a connecting line through the history of 20th-Century black music, AD built its songs out of blues samples and '70s funk riffs. Spike Lee was so impressed with the band's sense of history that he gave AD the leadoff track ("Revolution") to his jazz- and R&B-dominated *Malcolm X* soundtrack. Unfortunately, the band had little staying power, breaking up after its tedious sophomore album. Dionne Farris, a part-time singer in the band, surprisingly outshone Speech when her solo album was better received and became a bigger hit than his.

what to buy: Packed with sunny chants and Dionne Farris's strong singing, the hit single, "Tennessee," was just one of the many highlights on the band's terrific debut, *3 Months, 5 Months & 2 Days in the Life of . . .* ♫♫♫♫♫ (Chrysalis/EMI, 1992, prod. Speech). Among the others: The decidedly anti-gangsta "People Everyday," which slyly reworks "Everyday People."

what to buy next: Farris's solid solo debut, *Wild Seed—Wild Flower* ♫♫♫♫ (Columbia, 1995, prod. Dionne Farris, others), led off with the year's funkiest hit, "I Know."

what to avoid: *Unplugged* ♫♫ (Chrysalis, 1993, prod. Alvin Speights, Speech) doles out inferior alternate versions of the debut's fresh songs.

the rest:
Zingalamaduni ♫♫ (Chrysalis, 1994)

worth searching for: The *Malcolm X Soundtrack* ♫♫♫♫♫ (Reprise/Warner Bros., 1992, prod. Spike Lee, Quincy Jones) brilliantly lines up AD's "Revolution" (also released on an extended EP), with classics by bluesmen Joe Turner and Junior Walker; jazz legends Billie Holiday, John Coltrane, and Duke Ellington; and R&B stars Ray Charles, Louis Jordan, and Aretha Franklin.

solo outings:
Speech:
Speech ♫♫♫ (Chrysalis, 1996)

influences:

◀◀ Public Enemy, De La Soul, Sly & the Family Stone, Gang Starr, Jungle Brothers, Dream Warriors, Last Poets, Boogie Down Productions

▶▶ Fugees, Digable Planets, Basehead, Spearhead

                                              Steve Knopper

Steve Arrington

See: Slave

The Art of Noise

Formed 1983 in London, England. Disbanded 1990.

Anne Dudley, keyboards, string arrangements; J.J. Jeczalik, Fairlight, keyboards; Gary Langan, engineer (1983–86).

Hailed by hip-hop and techno musicians for its pioneering use

Speech of Arrested Development (© Ken Settle)

of samplers as song construction tools rather than random noise boxes, The Art of Noise was formed in 1983 as a side project of studio wizards Jeczalik, Langan, and Dudley, who had been brought together by Trevor Horn for the production of Yes's *90125* album and Frankie Goes to Hollywood's *Welcome to the Pleasuredome* sessions. The group's first experiments, captured on *Into Battle* and *Who's Afraid?*, were catchy, arty instrumentals assembled almost entirely from pre-recorded sound snippets via Horn's newly-purchased Fairlight sampling keyboard—one of the first such devices ever made. After scoring dance club and chart success with "Beat Box" and its drastically remixed counterpart, "Close (to the Edit)," the Art of Noise split from the ZTT camp in 1985 over creative differences. Its subsequent releases through China Records, although generally well-received, included dodgy novelty collaborations (a dance track featuring manufactured media personality Max Headroom, a cover of Prince's "Kiss" featuring Tom Jones, and the Grammy award-winning "Peter Gunn" remake with twang legend Duane Eddy), syrupy orchestral arrangements, and an uninteresting trough of remixes, compilations, and repeated reissues of the same material. An amicable parting in 1990 allowed Dudley and Jeczalik to pursue solo projects; Dudley continued her orchestral work for film soundtracks, while Jeczalik collaborated with Ten Years After's Alvin Lee before entering the techno scene in 1995–96 with The Art of Silence.

what to buy: An electronic music classic, the concept album *Who's Afraid Of? (The Art of Noise!)* 𝄢𝄢𝄢𝄢 (ZTT/Island, 1984, prod. Trevor Horn, Paul Morley, Art of Noise) has itself been sampled by scores of musicians in tribute. *In Visible Silence* 𝄢𝄢𝄢𝄢 (China/Chrysalis/Off Beat, 1986, prod. Art of Noise) is more accessible and equally competent, although it is markedly different from—in fact, almost a parody of—the band's ZTT-era sound. Although bombastic at times, *In No Sense? Nonsense!* 𝄢𝄢𝄢𝄢 (China/Chrysalis, 1987, prod. Anne Dudley, J.J. Jeczalik) is an engaging, stereophonic tour de force, seamlessly gliding from string interludes to boys choirs to dance tracks and beyond; worlds away from "Beat Box," it is the cream of the post-ZTT Art of Noise.

what to buy next: Dismissed as "pretentious" by some critics, *Below The Waste* 𝄢𝄢𝄢 (China/Polydor, 1989, prod. Anne Dudley, J.J. Jeczalik) is the least experimental of the band's output but makes a good follow up to *In No Sense? Nonsense!*. The African-influenced tracks—"Dan Dare," "Chain Gang," and "Yebo!"—are well worth the price.

what to avoid: All the post-ZTT cash-in compilations—*The Best of the Art of Noise* 𝄢𝄢 (China/Polydor, 1988/1997, prod. Art of

Noise), *The Ambient Collection* 𝄢𝄢 (China/Polydor, 1990/1997, prod. Art of Noise), *The FON Mixes* 𝄢𝄢 (China, 1991/1997, prod. Art of Noise), and *The Drum and Bass Collection* 𝄢 (China, 1997, prod. Art of Noise).

the rest:
Into Battle with the Art of Noise 𝄢𝄢𝄢𝄢 (ZTT/Island, 1983)
Re-Works of Art of Noise 𝄢 (China/Chrysalis, 1986)
The Best of the Art of Noise 𝄢𝄢 (China, 1992)

worth searching for: The import-only compilation *Daft* 𝄢𝄢𝄢𝄢 (ZTT/Warner, 1986, prod. Art of Noise), which contains all of *Who's Afraid . . .* plus remixes of "Moments In Love" and a long version of "Snapshot."

solo outings:
Anne Dudley:
(With Jaz Coleman) *Songs from the Victorious City* 𝄢𝄢𝄢𝄢 (China/Polydor/TVT, 1991)
(With Jaz Coleman) *Alice In Wonderland: Symphonic Variations* 𝄢𝄢𝄢 (Sound Stage, 1994)
(With Jaz Coleman) *Ancient and Modern* 𝄢𝄢𝄢 (The Echo Label, 1995)

J.J. Jeczalik:
The Art of Sampling 𝄢𝄢𝄢 (AMG, 1994)
(With Art of Silence) *artofsilence.co.uk* 𝄢𝄢𝄢𝄢 (Permanent, 1996)

influences:
◄◄ Kraftwerk, Tangerine Dream, Mike Oldfield, John Cage, environmental noise recordings

►► Future Sound of London, The Orb, 808 State, William Orbit, Yello, Shinjuku Thief, Global Communication, Severed Heads

Mike Brown

Artifacts

Formed in Newark, NJ.

Tame One, vocals; El Da Sensai, vocals.

Two graffiti artists from New Jerusalem (Newark, New Jersey, to the rest of us), Tame One and El Da Sensai earned more than just constant play on the hip-hop airwaves with their homage to graffiti bombing, "Wrong Side of Da Tracks." They also earned respect from their hip-hop peers for acknowledging a rarely celebrated facet of hip-hop culture.

what's available: *Between a Rock and a Hard Place* 𝄢𝄢𝄢 (Big Beat/Atlantic, 1994, prod. T. Ray, Redman, Artifacts, others) is more like a collection of tight, consistent singles than a cohesive, wholly conceptual entity. The hefty drums and familiar horns of "Wrong Side of Da Tracks" received the most attention, but

Nickolas Ashford (l) and Valerie Simpson (© Ken Settle)

"Come On Wit Da Get Down" and "Dynamite Soul" are certainly worth checking out. There aren't too many surprises with the Artifacts. They stick with the same formula on *That's Them* 🎵🎵🎵 (Big Beat/Atlantic, 1997, prod. Lord Finesse, Da Beatminerz, others). "Art of Facts" has a laid back vibe that suits the group well, but the album becomes tedious with its 16 tracks, including "Return to Da Wrongside," a sequel to the group's first graffiti-loving hit.

influences:

◀◀ Lord Finesse, Diamond D

Jazzbo

Ashford & Simpson

Formed 1964.

Nickolas Ashford (born May 4, 1943, in Fairfield, SC); Valerie Simpson (born August 26, 1948, in New York, NY).

If your collection includes albums by Marvin Gaye and Tammi Tyrell, Diana Ross or the Shirelles, chances are you know the work of the husband and wife writing/performing/producing duo Valerie Simpson and Nickolas Ashford, who have written such modern classics as "Ain't No Mountain High Enough," "Your Precious Love," "You're All I Need To Get By?," "Ain't Nothing Like the Real Thing" (for Gaye and Terrell), and their own "Solid." They met and began their careers as gospel singers at White Rock Baptist Church in Harlem. They started writing gospel songs together, then collaborated in 1966 on "Let's Go Get Stoned" for Ray Charles. Their subsequent career has produced 22 gold and platinum records and more than 50 ASCAP songwriting trophies, including the prestigious Founders Award. They record and tour as a duo, and are in-demand producers for artists such as Gladys Knight, Teddy Pendergrass, and Quincy Jones. They also host a daily radio show on New York's KISS-FM and continue to write hits, most recently "I'm Every Woman" for the motion picture *The Bodyguard* starring Whitney Houston.

what to buy: *Capitol Gold—The Best of Ashford & Simpson* 🎵🎵🎵 (Capitol, 1993, prod. Ashford & Simpson), a comprehensive overview of the main portion of their performing career. It includes "Solid" and "I'll Be There For You" among their better songs. *Is It Still Good To You?* &&&& (Warner Bros., 1978/Ol' Skool, 1996, prod. Ashford & Simpson) has some dated disco-style arrangements, but their love song formula remains intact.

what to buy next: *Been Found* &&&& (Ichiban, 1996, prod. Ashford & Simpson) is an intriguing collaboration with poet Maya Angelou, whose spoken word passages mesh nicely with the duo's melodies. *Count Your Blessings: The Gospel According to Ashford & Simpson* &&&& (EMI, 1996, prod. Ashford & Simpson) makes a case that their spiritual music is as good—and perhaps better—than their secular fare.

what to avoid: *A Musical Affair* && (Warner Bros., 1978/Ol' Skool, 1996, prod. Ashford & Simpson) is a tired effort. There's still some great singing, but look harder for better recordings.

the rest:
So So Satisfied &&& (Warner Bros., 1977/Ol' Skool, 1996)
Send It && (Warner Bros., 1977/Ol' Skool, 1996)
Stay Free &&& (Warner Bros., 1979/Ol' Skool, 1996)

worth searching for: *Solid* &&&& (Capitol, 1984, prod. Ashford & Simpson) is out of print but lives up to its title as one of the duo's most consistent albums. You should also make a point to score versions of their songs recorded by Marvin Gaye and Tammi Terrell; *Tammi Terrell's Greatest Hits* (Motown, 1970), contains every soulful, heartbreaking song the two recorded before Terrell's untimely death from a brain tumor.

solo outings:
Valerie Simpson:
The Best of Valerie Simpson &&& (Motown, 1991)

influences:

◀◀ Ray Charles, Smokey Robinson, Burt Bacharach and Hal David, Lieber & Stoller, Carole King & Gerry Goffin, Smokey Robinson, Holland-Dozier-Holland

▶▶ Marvin Gaye, Tammi Terrell, Lionel Richie, Barbara Ingalls

Gary Graff

Rick Astley

Born February 6, 1966, in Newton-le-Willows, England.

Discovered by the production team of Stock, Aitken, and Waterman, Rick Astley sent many teenage girls' hearts aflutter with his soulful voice and patented dance songs, but it never got deeper than that. His first album was a hit, but as Astley's fans got older—and his crack production team got weaker—he began a long, slow fadeaway.

what to buy: *Whenever You Need Somebody* &&& (RCA, 1987, prod. Phil Harding, Ian Curnow, Daize Washbourn) made Astley a certified teeny-bop star with the hits "Never Gonna Give You Up," "Together Forever," "It Would Take a Strong, Strong Man," and the oft-covered "When I Fall in Love."

the rest:
Hold Me In Your Arms && (RCA, 1988)
Free &&& (RCA, 1991)
Body and Soul && (RCA, 1993)

influences:

◀◀ Sam Cooke, Marvin Gaye, Daryl Hall, Paul Young, Boy George/Culture Club

▶▶ Jamaroqui, Lisa Stansfield

Christina Fuoco

Atlantic Starr

Formed 1976, in White Plains, NY.

David Lewis, guitar, vocals; Jonathan Lewis, trombone; Wayne Lewis, keyboards; Sharon Bryant, vocals (1976–84); Clifford Archer, guitar (1976–85); Porter Carroll, drums (1976–85); Koran Daniels, saxophone (1976–85); Joseph Phillips, drums (1976–94); William Sudderth, trombone (1976–85); Barbara Weathers, vocals (1985–90); Rachel Oliver, vocals (1991–94); Aisha Tanner, vocals (1994–96).

Atlantic Starr started out as a funk band, but over the course of 10 albums it eventually set a standard for sweet, 1980s adult contemporary ballads. The often-overlooked group, led creatively by the Lewis brothers, made a name for itself early in R&B circles by crafting a number of sensitive ballads and smooth mid-tempo tunes. They made "soft" classics such as "Am I Dreaming" and "Send for Me," with live instruments at a time when techno-pop and rap were all the rage. The band's membership changed drastically—and perhaps for the better—before the release of its appropriately named (and out of print) 1985 work *As the Band Turns*. Four members were set free, and lead singer Sharon Bryant went solo. With new lead singer Barbara Weathers on board, the group scored several chart-topping pop hits, including "Secret Lovers" and "Always." After Weathers left to record a solo album in 1990, the band tried a number of other lead vocal combinations, but could only manage one other hit song, 1992's "Masterpiece."

what to buy: *Secret Lovers—The Best of Atlantic Starr* &&&&& (A&M, 1986, prod. various) is a mighty collection of ballads and soul favorites that allows one to appreciate both the great songwriting of the Lewis Brothers and the precious subtleties of both of the band's female lead singers.

what to buy next: *All In the Name of Love* 🎵🎵🎵 (Warner Bros., 1987, prod. David Lewis, Wayne Lewis) has several great songs, though it suffers from a mild case of overproduction.

the rest:
Love Crazy 🎵🎵🎵 Warner Bros, 1992)

solo outings:
Sharon Bryant:
Here I Am 🎵🎵 (PolyGram, 1989)

Barbara Weathers:
Barbara Weathers 🎵🎵 (Reprise, 1990)

influences:
◀◀ Earth, Wind & Fire, Rene & Angela, the Commodores
▶▶ Starpoint, Midnight Star

Franklin Paul

Audio Two /Milk

Disbanded 1992.

Gizmo, vocals; Milk (born Kirk Robinson), vocals.

Audio Two's Gizmo and Milk became hip-hop immortals by recording one of the genre's true classics, "Top Billin'." The first hip-hop group to perform at famed Carnegie Hall, Audio Two also garned attention outside rap circles by collaborating with everybody from Mary J. Blige to Sinead O'Connor (along with hip-hop artists Positive K and Milk's sister, MC Lyte).

what to buy: *What More Can I Say?* 🎵🎵🎵 (Atlantic/First Priority Music, 1988, prod. Audio Two) features "Top Billin'" and the funny "Hickies Around My Neck." But the rest of the songs are mostly just variations on the same ("Top Billin'") theme.

the rest:
I Don't Care 🎵🎵 (Atlantic/First Priority Music, 1990)

solo outings:
Milk:
Never Dated 🎵🎵 (American Recordings, 1994, prod. Milk)

influences:
◀◀ Run-D.M.C.
▶▶ Positive K, MC Lyte, Stetsasonic

Jazzbo

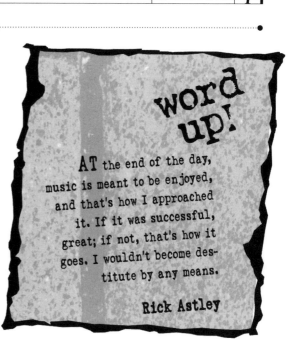

word up!

AT the end of the day, music is meant to be enjoyed, and that's how I approached it. If it was successful, great; if not, that's how it goes. I wouldn't become destitute by any means.

Rick Astley

Patti Austin

Born August 10, 1948, in New York, NY.

Patti Austin has one of the purest, most familiar voices in all of pop music. A favorite of urban and contemporary jazz audiences, Austin has paradoxically enjoyed even more success as the Unknown Voice in countless advertising jingles. A protege of both Dinah Washington and Sammy Davis Jr., Austin has been a pro since the age of five. In 1969, United Artists released her debut single "Family Tree," which was a hit in the Northeastern corridor. For Austin, however, "Family Tree" was aural Fool's Gold, as her career didn't quite take off. Instead she plunged into the profitable yet anonymous world of demo, jingles, and backup sessions, avenues which are still her bread and butter gigs to this day. In 1976, Austin released her solo debut, *End of a Rainbow*, on CTI Records to the favor of the burgeoning progressive urban audience. The next year's followup, *Havana Candy*, made her a kind of overgrown cult fave. During this period, Austin sang on albums by Quincy Jones (*Sounds & Stuff*), George Benson (*Give Me the Night*), and Paul Simon (*One Trick Pony*), which gained her a much wider following then her own recordings. Austin's career took a quantum leap in 1981 when "Razzamatazz," her tune from Jones's *The Dude*, went gold. Signed to Jones's Qwest label the following year, Austin enjoyed her only platinum success with the James

Ingram duet "Baby Come To Me"; *Every Home Should Have One*, the LP that featured the song, was also very successful. She recorded three more records for Qwest, but she never again reached those previous heights. Austin moved to GRP in 1990, and although she's still a radio favorite, her glory days with the general public seem, at the moment, to be over.

what to buy: *Every Home Should Have One* 𝄞𝄞𝄞𝄞 (Qwest, 1981, prod. Rod Temperton, Quincy Jones) is the crown jewel of Austin's career, a pop confection equal to Michael Jackson's epochal *Off the Wall* LP. *Live at the Bottom Line* 𝄞𝄞𝄞 (CTI, 1979, prod. Creed Taylor) is loose (epitomized by her wry country-western take on Randy Newman's "Rider in the Rain") and endearing, capturing Austin in a rare concert setting.

what to buy next: *The Ultimate Collection* 𝄞𝄞𝄞 (GRP, 1995, prod. various) is a good display of Austin in her most current incarnation.

the rest:
The Real Me 𝄞𝄞𝄞 (Qwest, 1988)
Love Is Gonna Getcha 𝄞𝄞𝄞 (GRP, 1990)
That Secret Place 𝄞𝄞𝄞 (GRP, 1994)
The Best of Patti Austin 𝄞𝄞𝄞 (Epic, 1994)

worth searching for: Austin has guested on plenty of albums, including the soundtrack to *The Blues Brothers* 𝄞𝄞𝄞 (Atlantic, 1980/1995). She also appears in the movie.

influences:
◀◀ Dinah Washington, Dakota Staton, Barbara Lewis
▶▶ Phyllis Hyman, Luther Vandross, Siedah Garrett, Dianne Reeves

Tom Terrell and Gary Graff

Automator
Born Dan Nakamura.

Although he's a veteran of the Bay Area hip-hop scene, Automator only recently became known worldwide for orchestrating the rebirth of famed Ultramagnetic MC Kool Keith as Dr. Octagon. The classically trained musician not only produced Dr. Octagon, as well as Kool Keith's other solo ventures, but his home-based Glue Factory has been the recording studio of choice for cutting-edge artists from DJ Shadow and Blackalicious to the underground turntablist, Q-Bert.

what's available: Automator's first release in over seven years, *A Better Tomorrow* 𝄞𝄞𝄞 (Ubiquity, 1996, prod. Automator) is an EP of melodious, moody beats that survey a range of musical styles. DJ Shadow and Q-Bert's work in The Glue Factory seems to have rubbed off on such drum-heavy songs as the title track and "The Truth."

worth searching for: In 1989, Automator released the vinyl-only "Music to be Murdered By," an allusion, perhaps, to the Jeff Alexander- and Alfred Hitchcock-penned song of the same name.

influences:
◀◀ Mantronix, Prince Paul, Dust Brothers

Jazzbo

Average White Band
Formed 1972, in London, England. Disbanded 1980. Re-formed 1989.

Alan Gorrie, bass, vocals; Onnie McIntyre, guitar, vocals; Roger Ball, keyboards, saxes; Malcolm Duncan, tenor saxophone (1972–80); Robbie McIntosh, drums (1972–74, died 1974); Hamish Stuart, guitar, vocals (1972–80); Steve Ferrone, drums (1974–80); Alex Ligertwood, vocals (1989–90); Eliot Lewis, vocals, keyboards, bass, and guitar (1990–present), Pete Abbott, drums (1994–present).

Whenever a new AWB cut hit R&B radio during the 1970s, the response was often the same: These guys are Scottish? Indeed, Average White Band held the title (shared perhaps with Tower of Power) as the funkiest white boys in black music. Formed by a mix of members from several Scottish soul tribute groups, AWB (the name was supposedly bestowed by Bonnie Bramlett of Delaney & Bonnie)—working with producer Arif Mardin—concocted a funky mix of James Brown-style funk and old-school R&B that captivated the then-emerging disco movement. A 1973 debut record failed to catch fire, but the band soon struck gold with Atlantic in 1974. Unfortunately, success took its toll, as drummer Robbie McIntosh died at a Hollywood party, snorting a fatal mix of heroin and morphine (Alan Gorrie reportedly inhaled the same mixture but was kept awake by Cher and survived). Friend and Bloodstone member Steve Ferrone replaced McIntosh, helping the band sharpen its focus on authentic funk sounds. But as disco killed off funk, AWB's material became more and more watered down—until fans of its original funk flavor stopped buying records. Disbanded in 1980, AWB was revived by Gorrie, Ball, and McIntyre in 1989 (with former Santana vocalist Alex Ligertwood as lead singer), though the relative failure of its comeback album doomed the band to the nostalgia circuit. Back with a 1997 album, the group continues to mine a blue-eyed, retro funk feel.

what to buy: Fans of 1970s funk *must* own the group's first two Atlantic releases, *Average White Band* 𝄞𝄞𝄞𝄞 (Atlantic, 1974, prod. Arif Mardin) and *Cut the Cake* ♪♪♪♪♪ (Atlantic, 1975, prod. Arif Mardin). These records helped set the tone for the era, ranging from horn-fueled workouts like the instrumental "Pick Up the Pieces" to silky slow jams such as "Schoolboy Crush," "If I Ever Lose This Heaven," and "Person to Person." Unlike many Europeans trying to do funk, AWB sounded as authentic as any other act on R&B radio—a feat as impressive as it was surprising.

what to buy next: Greatest hits packages, when done well, are the best way to get the essence of an act's career without the clinkers. And few collections do this job better than *Pickin' Up the Pieces: The Best of the Average White Band, 1974–80* ♪♪♪♪ (Rhino, 1992, prod. Arif Mardin, Jerry Greenberg, Gene Paul, David Foster, Average White Band). Here, fans can check out the group's biggest successes and album cuts on one generous 18-track excursion.

what to avoid: The band's reunion, *Aftershock* **woof!** (Track Record, 1989, prod. John Robie) plumbs new depths of disappointment. Featuring just three original members and a formulaic sound, this record reminded everyone why the band broke up in the first place.

the rest:
Show Your Hand ♪♪♪ (MCA, 1973/Foundation, 1997)
Put It Where You Want It ♪♪♪ (MCA, 1975)
Soul Searching ♪♪♪ (Atlantic, 1976)
Person to Person ♪♪♪♪ (Atlantic, 1977)
Warmer Communications ♪♪ (Atlantic, 1978)
Feel No Fret ♪♪ (RCA, 1979)
Average White Band, Vol. 8 ♪♪♪ (Atlantic, 1980)
Shine ♪♪ (Arista, 1980)
Cupids In Fashion ♪♪ (RCA, 1982)
Best of the Average White Band ♪♪♪ (RCA, 1984)
Soul Tattoo ♪♪♪ (Foundation Records, 1997)

worth searching for: Members of AWB have lent their talents as session musicians to works by several artists, including Chaka Khan, Paul McCartney, Eric Clapton, Duran Duran, and Tom Petty—often making better contributions there than on their own records. Particularly notable is *Benny and Us* ♪♪♪♪ (Atlantic, 1977, prod. Arif Mardin, Jerry Greenberg), a collaboration with R&B great Ben E. King.

influences:

◀◀ James Brown, Tower of Power, Brian Auger, Ben E. King, Wilson Pickett

▶▶ Prince, KC & the Sunshine Band, Little Steven & the Disciples of Soul, the Commitments

Eric Deggans

Roy Ayers
Born September 19, 1940, in Los Angeles, CA.

The legend of Roy Ayers begins when he was five years old and was presented with a pair of mallets by vibraphonist Lionel Hampton. Maybe that had something to do with his choice to switch from piano to vibes when he was in high school. In his early twenties, an accomplished Ayers played with Teddy Edwards, Chico Hamilton, Wayne Henderson, and Gerald Wilson's big band on the Los Angeles jazz scene. During the mid-1960s he signed with Atlantic. Ayers played with the renowned jazz flutist Herbie Mann from 1966–70, a major influence who opened many doors for him; Mann, in fact, produced Ayers's first three records on the label. In 1970 the newly formed Roy Ayers Ubiquity (drummer Billy Cobham, guitarist George Benson, trombonist Wayne Henderson, and vocalist Dee Dee Bridgewater) signed with Polydor and released several critically acclaimed jazz records. In 1976, Ayers bravely stepped away from the warm embrace of jazz circles by experimenting with the sounds of R&B on *Mystic Voyage* and *Everybody Loves Sunshine*. His undaunted innovations paid off when both records charted, and his fans seemed to follow him through a series of ever-changing styles. After 1977's *Vibrations*, Ayers entered a mellow period that yielded softer, smoother grooves. In 1980 he toured Africa with Fela Anikulapo Kuti and made *Africa, Center of the World* (Polydor, 1981). As much as he has been inspired by his collaborations and tours with artists from around the world, Ayers has been an inspiration to many. On April 6, 1986, the city of Los Angeles celebrated an official "Roy Ayers Day."

what to buy: The two discs of *Evolution: The Polydor Anthology* ♪♪♪♪ (Polydor, 1995. prod. various) is a thorough overview featuring guest artists such as Sonny Fortune, Billy Cobham, Ron Carter, and Gloria Jones. The tracks were originally produced by Roy Ayers, Myrnaleah Wiliams, and Jerry Schoenbaum.

the rest:
Roy Ayers Live at the Montreaux Jazz Festival ♪♪♪♪ (Verve, 1972)
Naste' ♪♪♪♪ (RCA, 1995)
Best of Roy Ayers ♪♪♪♪ (Polydor, 1997)

worth searching for: *Mystic Voyage* ♪♪♪♪ (Polydor, 1976, prod. Roy Ayers), his first full-fledged foray into the R&B world, which benefitted from his tasty fusion sensibility.

influences:

◀◀ Lionel Hampton, Herbie Mann, Leroy Vinnegar, Fela Anikulapo Kuti

▶▶ A Tribe Called Quest, Guru (of Gang Starr), Brand Nubian, Galliano, Groove Collective

Norene Cashen

AZ

Born Anthony Cruz, in Brooklyn, NY.

An able MC whose style resembles that of his compadre Nas, AZ is but another member of The Firm to represent the tri-realism of sex, money, and murder in his decidedly New York rhymes. Particularly central to his mindset is money—and how he will amass it. Not surprisingly, this is what sets him apart from the more sagacious Nas, who better handles a variety of issues beyond material hunger. AZ shines, no doubt, but his relentless devotion to capitalism eventually grows tiresome, tarnishing his lyrical skills like an old nickel.

what to buy: *Doe or Die* 𝄞𝄞𝄞 (EMI, 1995, prod. Pete Rock, AZ, others) is the debut from this thug-mafioso whose rhymes reflect an urgency to maximize life and profit in the turbulent '90s. His best song, "Sugar Hill," presents these themes in a slickly produced, laid-back track that finds its inspiration in the old school. A touch of poignancy is provided on "Your World Don't Stop," which humanizes the condition and struggle of locked-up homies.

the rest:
Pieces of a Man N/A (Noo Trybe/Virgin, 1997)

worth searching for: Prior to dropping *Doe or Die*, AZ caught the hip-hop world's ear with a complicated and lightning-quick verse on "Life's a Bitch" from the Nas album *Illmatic* 𝄞𝄞𝄞𝄞 (Columbia, 1994, prod. various). A sample: "Visualizing the realism of life and actuality/Fuck who's the baddest, a person's status depends on salary."

influences:
◀◀ Nas, Raekwon

▶▶ Cormega

Corey Takahashi

B

Babyface
/L.A. Reid and Babyface

Born Kenneth Edmonds, April 10, 1959, in Cincinnati, OH. Antonio "L.A." Reid born June 7, 1957, in Cincinnati, OH.

Michael Jackson, the King of Pop? Forget about it. Since the late 1980s, Babyface wears the crown. The triple threat songwriter-producer-performer has had a hand in more than 100 Top 10 pop and R&B hits, and in sales of 26 million-selling singles and 72 million-selling albums. Too bad most of those hits sound like they were taken off a greeting card; only recently has Babyface's work begun to resonate with personal passion. It all began during the early 1980s, in his hometown of Cincinnati, where Edmonds—dubbed "Babyface" by noted stand-up comic and whirlwind bassist Bootsy Collins—met drummer L.A. Reid in the funk band the Deele. By the group's third and most successful album, the gold *Eyes of a Stranger* (1987), the duo was co-producing the band and solidifying a creative partnership that would help define the New Jack Swing era. Reid and Edmonds moved to Atlanta in 1989, and their LaFace label helped turn the city into an R&B mecca. Among their triumphs were Boyz II Men's massive single "End of the Road" and Whitney Houston's multiplatinum soundtrack for "The Bodyguard"; the duo collected Grammys for both efforts, but soon after began working separately. Yet the Babyface juggernaut only got stronger, with increasingly high-profile clients such as Madonna (the 1995 #1 "Take a Bow") and Eric Clapton (the Grammy-winning 1996 single "Change the World"). As a performer, a distinct Babyface persona began to emerge on four increasingly successful solo albums. "Whatever happened to chivalry?" is the question posed on one of his early songs, and he proffered a silky yet vulnerable portrait of a lady's man that made the most of his pleasant but thin voice.

what to buy: Edmonds's lyrics often settle for cliches instead of specifics, and his arrangements can sound coldly synthesized, but *The Day* 𝄞𝄞𝄞 (Epic, 1996, prod. Babyface) makes some tentative strides toward a more personal tone, particularly on the title track, written about the birth of his son Brandon; the boyhood reminiscence "Simple Days"; and the spouse-abuse indictment "How Come How Long."

what to buy next: *For the Cool in You* 𝄞𝄞𝄞 (Epic, 1993, prod. Babyface) is smooth as usual, but the marvelously understated ballad "When Can I See You" is framed by Babyface's acoustic guitar—the first time in years that a major R&B hit had been built around the sound of an acoustic instrument. *A Closer Look* ♫♫♫ (Solar/Epic, 1991, prod. L.A. Reid, Babyface) provides an overview of the early solo work, notably the jazzy torcher "Whip Appeal."

what to avoid: Babyface's debut on the first Deele record, *Street Beat* ♫♫ (Solar, 1983, prod. Reggie Calloway), finds the singer-guitarist contributing to a competent funk outing by a bunch of Prince/Time wannabes.

the rest:
(With The Deele) *Material Thangz* ♫♫♫ (Solar, 1985)
(With The Deele) *Eyes of a Stranger* ♫♫♫ (Solar, 1987)
Lovers ♫♫♫ (Solar/Epic, 1987)
Tender Lover ♫♫♫ (Solar/Epic, 1989)
Unplugged N/A (Epic, 1997)

worth searching for: The soundtrack for the film *Phenomenon* ♫♫♫♫ (Reprise, 1996, prod. various) features "Change the World," Babyface's coolly understated (and immensely successful) collaboration with Clapton.

influences:

◀◀ Prince, Time, Luther Vandross, Dionne Warwick

▶▶ Boyz II Men, Whitney Houston, Toni Braxton, Bobby Brown, TLC

Greg Kot

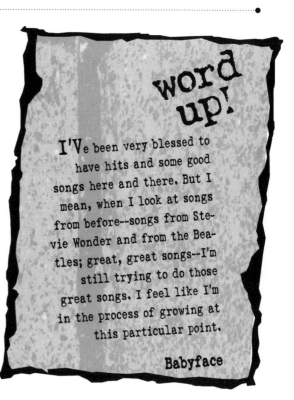

word up!

I'Ve been very blessed to have hits and some good songs here and there. But I mean, when I look at songs from before--songs from Stevie Wonder and from the Beatles; great, great songs--I'm still trying to do those great songs. I feel like I'm in the process of growing at this particular point.

Babyface

Backstreet Boys

Formed mid-1990s, in Orlando, FL.

Brian Littrell, vocals; A.J. McLean, vocals; Nick Carter, vocals; Kevin Richardson, vocals; Howie Dorough, vocals.

If at first you don't succeed. . . . Well, Backstreet Boys *did* succeed, just not in its home country at first. The quintet, which grew up in the shadow of Walt Disney World, brought out its eponymous debut album of frilly, R&B-laced pop in 1995. U.S. audiences, caught up in modern rock, yawned, but the rest of the world lapped up nearly 5.5 million copies. So the Boys tried again at home in 1997, and early responses indicated a more favorable reception for the first single, "Quit Playing Games (With My Heart)." If America is ready for another teenybop sensation (samplers included with makeup kits?), this could well be it.

what's available: Though they could be the male counterpart to the Spice Girls—this is pretty sugary stuff—*Backstreet Boys* ♫♫♫ (Jive, 1997, prod. various) at least shows some good taste and melodic sensibility. Producers include Full Force and P.M.

Dawn, while the songs demonstrate that the five singers are not groove impaired. Definitely one to keep an eye on.

influences:

◀◀ Bobby Brown, New Kids on the Block, All-4-One

Gary Graff

Erykah Badu

Born Erica Wright, February 26, 1971, in Dallas, TX.

Few divas have arrived on the scene as full-formed as Erykah Badu. Dressed like a proud African queen and with a voice that recalls Billie Holiday, the singer espouses "Baduizm," a self-made philosophy of Afrocentrism and spirituality. Her name, she says, is a sound you make while scat singing, and it means "manifest truth" in Arabic. Whatever. Ultimately, it's Badu's honeyed vocals, sensual grooves, and seemingly bottomless well of self-confidence that wins the day. Classy and sassy, the singer is part of the current crop of young R&B artists (D'Angelo, Maxwell, Me'Shell Ndegeocello) that is reviving the form by looking to elders such as Stevie Wonder, Marvin Gaye, and Chaka Khan for both their smooth grooves and their hard-won wisdom. Already it seems certain Badu & Co. will take the music to the next level.

what's available: On her debut, *Baduizm* ✍✍✍ (Kedar Entertainment/Universal, 1997, prod. various), the accompaniment is minimal, the vibe is retro, but the lyrics are conscious and the beats prove Badu knows from hip-hop production. "On & On," the song that drove *Baduizm* to the upper reaches of the charts, is a spare anthem about perseverance in the face of hard times; the shimmering "Next Lifetime" chronicles the formation of a love triangle; and "Drama" deals with a host of social ills. Badu is not without a sense of humor, though; the freeform skit "Afro," throws out some wicked lines as Badu delivers a bluesy a cappella vocal. Finally, there's a nice cover of the Atlantic Starr chestnut "4 Leaf Clover." All in all, it's amazing how together this debut album is. It'll be interesting to see where Badu takes it from here. Her second album, *Live* N/A (Kedar/Universal, 1997), was scheduled for late 1997 release.

influences:
◀◀ Billie Holiday, Stevie Wonder, Chaka Khan

Daniel Durchholz

Bahamadia
Born Antonia Reed, in Philadelphia, PA.

Like Jeru the Damaja and Group Home before her, Bahamadia's career was launched with the release of an *Ill Kids* compilation of undiscovered talent put together by Guru. The DJ-turned-MC and mother of two embraces experimentation, and, indicative of her chameleon logo, traverses from one lyrical style to the next with both ferocity and finesse.

what's available: Bahamadia's debut, *Kollage* ✍✍✍✍ (EMI, 1996, prod. Da Beatminerz, DJ Premier, others) is one of the most underappreciated hip-hop albums of the '90s. The spontaneous patchwork of words and phrases on "Word Play" and "Innovation" is textbook lyricism. "Da Jawn" is a reworking of the Funky Four + 1's classic, "The Joint," with music supplied by fellow Philly residents, the Roots.

worth searching for: Bahamadia has established a strong camaraderie with the Roots, guesting on two of their songs: "Proceed III," a luxurious remix of the group's breakthrough single, "Proceed" (DGC, 1995); and "Push Up Yo Lighta," from *illadelph halflife* (DGC, 1996).

influences:
◀◀ MC Lyte, Sha-Rock, Salt-N-Pepa, Gang Starr, Digable Planets
▶▶ Nonchalant

Jazzbo

Philip Bailey
Born May 8, 1951, in Denver, CO.

Philip Bailey achieved fame as the strikingly high falsetto vocalist in Earth, Wind & Fire, a group that—arguably—rose in the charts on the strength of his singing on such hits as "Reasons." The year before the group broke up in 1984, Bailey released his first solo album and struck gold on his sophomore release with a catchy duet with Genesis singer/drummer Phil Collins ("Easy Lover") that went all the way to #2 on *Billboard*'s pop singles chart at the end of 1984. He never again matched that success as a solo artist and has sung with the re-formed Earth, Wind & Fire. Additionally, he recorded several albums of Christian music, one of which won a Grammy. The only interesting feature of these albums for non-believers is his singing.

what to buy: *Chinese Wall* ✍✍✍ (Columbia, 1984, prod. Phil Collins) has "Easy Lover," but the best tracks are the haunting "Children of the Ghetto" and "Walking on the Chinese Wall."

what to buy next: The production on Bailey's first solo album, *Continuation* ✍✍✍ (Columbia, 1983, prod. George Duke) sounds very much of its time, but the songwriting (especially "I Know") is good, and Bailey's singing is spectacular.

what to avoid: *Philip Bailey* ✍ (Zoo, 1994, prod. various) finds an array of producers (including PM Dawn and Chuckii Booker) attempting to bring Bailey into the 1990s, and, in the process, steamrolling over his strengths.

the rest:
Inside Out ✍✍ (Columbia, 1986)

worth searching for: Bailey found religion in 1975 and has made a number of slickly modern gospel records, of which *The Wonders of His Love* ✍✍✍ (Myrrh/A&M, 1984, prod. Philip Bailey) was one of the better-distributed. Writing collaborators include George Duke and Skip Scarborough (who also play on a number of tracks), while EWF vets Don Myrick and Andrew Woolfolk lend their sax talents to a song each; this ensures a high degree of musical continuity from Bailey's secular work—in fact, these tracks don't particularly sound like gospel, though perhaps only believers will appreciate the extremely religious lyrics. On some other tracks, the organ swirls and backing chorus are laid on thick, and Bailey drops into his lower voice, sounding more like standard modern gospel.

influences:

◀◀ Maurice Williams, Marvin Gaye, Al Green

▶▶ Sylvester, Paul Young

Steve Holtje

Anita Baker

Born December 20, 1957, in Toledo, OH.

Abandoned by her teen-age birth mother at age two, Anita Baker quickly found singing offered a release from the tension and tough times she experienced as a network of family and friends raised her in inner city Detroit. Singing in church led to singing in local bands, including the renowned 10-piece outfit Chapter 8, which scored a record deal while touring in Los Angeles and had a minor hit with the tune "Ready for Your Love" in 1980. When Chapter 8 folded, Baker got a job as a secretary in a legal firm, recording her first solo record for the Beverly Glen label in 1983. Slowly, the record—filled with Baker's sumptuous vocals but hampered by uninspired songwriting—caught the ears of adult fans just getting hip to the Quiet Storm format of romantic, jazzy soul. But the singer, in a pattern that would be repeated many times in her career, was kept from recording a follow-up for years while fighting to get out of her Beverly Glen contract. Three years later, she assembled her breakthrough record, *Rapture*, for Elektra Records, with former Chapter 8 bandmate Michael J. Powell producing. Powered by her fearless vocals and lithe, energetic delivery, the record went on to sell more than 10 million copies, establishing Baker as the female flipside of Luther Vandross's vocal-centered, pop-drenched R&B love songs. Though subsequent records seemed to mine the same musical vein—marrying the singer's expansive vocals to sinewy jazz funk arrangements—fans bought the albums. Before long, Baker's personal troubles mounted, including three miscarriages, a reported feud with Vandross while on tour, and a non-stop work schedule that brought a brief breakdown in 1991. Returning to the limelight with an album in 1994, Baker sold a million copies within the first week of release. But she grew dissatisfied with both her record label, management, and attorneys, filing lawsuits against them all in mid-1996. By the end of the year, Elektra had agreed to allow the six-time Grammy winner to transfer to another record company owned by WEA Entertainment Group, Atlantic Records.

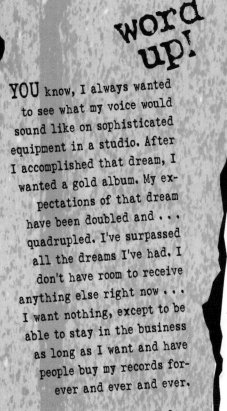

word up!

YOU know, I always wanted to see what my voice would sound like on sophisticated equipment in a studio. After I accomplished that dream, I wanted a gold album. My expectations of that dream have been doubled and . . . quadrupled. I've surpassed all the dreams I've had. I don't have room to receive anything else right now . . . I want nothing, except to be able to stay in the business as long as I want and have people buy my records forever and ever and ever.

Anita Baker

what to buy: If music were sports, then Baker's *Rapture* 𝄐𝄐𝄐𝄐 (Elektra, 1986, prod. Michael Powell, Marti Sharron, Gary Skardina) would be a home run. Until this point, Baker's sultry, soaring vocals and romantic, jazzy approach were inspired concepts in search of quality songs to hang on. And *Rapture* offers some of the best tunes in the singer's career, from smash hits such as the breezy "Same Ole Love" and triumphant "Sweet Love" to signature simmering numbers like "Been So Long" and "Mystery." Add crack session players such as the Yellowjackets' Jimmy Haslip and former Stevie Wonder sideman Ricky Lawson and you have the makings of a true R&B classic.

what to buy next: It's true, nobody really needs to hear another cover of "The Look of Love," but that's the only misstep on *Rhythm of Love* ♪♪♪ (Elektra, 1994, prod. Anita Baker, Tommy LiPuma, Arif Mardin, Barry J. Eastmond, Gerard Smerek, George Duke), a triumphant comeback record that melds emotive covers of tunes such as "Body and Soul" and "My Funny Valentine" with soulful original stuff like "Wrong Man" and the hit "I Apologize." Easily her most consistent record since the mid-1980s.

what to avoid: Blessed with a soaring voice, focused style, and lots of charm, Baker has one vulnerability—none of it works without good songs. So it's not surprising that her worst album, *Compositions* **woof!** (Elektra, 1990, prod. Michael Powell), would be the one with the worst tunes overall. The singer's formula is so strong it drowns these halfhearted songs in a similar barrage of slinky bass lines, ambitious vocal lines, and funk-tinged grooves. Only for the biggest of fans.

the rest:
Giving You the Best That I Got ♪♪♪ (Elektra, 1988)

worth searching for: The "soundtrack" to the hit NBC-TV show *Mad About You* called *The Final Frontier* ♪♪♪ (Atlantic, 1997, prod. various) features Baker lending her trademark vocals to the show's theme song, also called "Final Frontier" and co-written by series star Paul Reiser.

influences:

◀◀ Roberta Flack, Brenda Russell, Chaka Khan

▶▶ Oleta Adams, Regina Belle, Rachelle Ferrell

Eric Deggans

LaVern Baker

Born Delores Williams, November 11, 1929, in Chicago, IL. Died March 10, 1997, in New York, NY.

LaVern Baker's sassy, gospel-drenched vocals made her novelty hits exhilarating to teenagers of the 1950s and helped pave the way for 1960s soul music. Baker got her professional start in Chicago nightclubs under the name Little Miss Sharecropper, where she would dress in raggedy clothes and amuse spectators by outshouting the great Joe Williams. Billed variously as Little Miss Sharecropper, Bea Baker, and LaVern and Maurice King & His Wolverines, she recorded unsuccessfully with National, RCA, and Columbia/Okeh before joining the Todd

Rhodes Orchestra and settling on the name LaVern Baker for her lone outing on King Records. She signed with Atlantic in 1953, and her first chart offerings for them ("Soul On Fire," "Tomorrow Night") were soulful ballads. "Tweedlee Dee," a Latin-tempoed novelty with nursery rhyme lyrics, was Baker's breakthrough hit. Teens loved it—when they could hear it, that is. It was common practice at the time for white singers to cover black R&B hits, and pop singer Georgia Gibbs's version of "Tweedlee Dee" (recorded with the same musicians and arrangements) garnered far more airplay and greater sales. (Gibbs also covered Baker's "Tra-La-la.") Baker unsuccessfully mounted a lawsuit over the theft of her sound. Eventually, disc jockeys such as Alan Freed boycotted competing white versions of R&B hits, and Baker's career took off in earnest. The torchy "Play It Fair" and "I Can't Love You Enough" were solid hits on the R&B charts, but during 1956 another teen-oriented shouter, "Jim Dandy" (the flipside of "Tra-La-la"), was a crossover smash. A sequel record, "Jim Dandy Got Married," did not fare as well. Baker appeared in two of Alan Freed's teen flicks *Rock, Rock, Rock* (1956) and *Mister Rock 'n' Roll* (1957); in the latter she lip-synched "Humpty Dumpty Heart," a trite ditty sung to the tune of "A Froggy Went-A-Courtin'." It was her last nursery rhyme-type success, as 1958 saw the release of Baker's biggest hit and best ballad, "I Cried a Tear," which featured King Curtis on sax.

At a career crossroads, Baker wanted her music to take a more adult direction; however, though her 1958 LP *LaVern Baker Sings Bessie Smith* was critically well-received, sales were disappointing. Baker returned to alternating teen novelties with heartache ballads, but her chart clout had diminished; 1960's "Bumble Bee" was a small hit, though a stylistic anachronism. Baker's career was briefly revived when producers Jerry Lieber and Mike Stoller had her cut a rough and ready version of Chuck Willis's "C.C. Rider" ("See See Rider") and the raving gospel classic "Saved." Vocally, Baker was at her peak, but no more hits were forthcoming. In 1964, she left Atlantic. She cut an unsuccessful LP at Brunswick, as well as a rousing duet with Jackie Wilson. In 1969, after a troop entertainment tour of Vietnam resulted in bronchial pneumonia, Baker moved to the Philippines for her health. During the next 20 years, she operated a serviceman's club in Subic Bay, where she periodically sang. In 1990, she returned to America to replace her friend and former lablemate, Ruth Brown, in the critically acclaimed Broadway revue "Black & Blue." That year, Baker was voted into the Rock 'n' Roll Hall of Fame and received a career achievement award from the Rhythm & Blues Foundation. Baker also resumed recording,

Anita Baker (© Ken Settle)

doing an LP for the DRG label, a live LP for Rhino Records, duets with Ben E. King and a memorable, sexy blues cut on the *Dick Tracy* soundtrack. Diabetes eventually forced the amputation of her legs, but she sang until her death from a wheelchair, with all the gusto and verve at her command.

what to buy: *Soul On Fire—The Best of LaVern Baker* 𝒜𝒜𝒜𝒜𝒱 (Rhino/Atlantic, 1991, prod. Ahmet Ertegun, Jerry Wexler; reissue produced by Yves Beuavis) contains 20 of her best-known recordings ("Tweedlee Dee," "Jim Dandy") but is skewed more towards her adult titles such as "Saved," "I Cried a Tear," and "Tomorrow Night."

what to buy next: *LaVern Baker Sings Bessie Smith* 𝒜𝒜𝒜𝒜 (WEA/Atlantic, 1958, prod. Nesuhi Ertegun) is an excellent tribute/compilation of Smith's songs ("Gimme a Pigfoot" is a real stand-out), and Baker does not compromise her own sound one iota.

what to avoid: *Woke Up This Mornin'* 𝒜𝒜 (DRG, 1992, prod. Hugh Fordin) contains some unlikely covers (James Taylor's "You've Got a Friend," the Bee Gees' "To Love Somebody") mixed with updated blues standards. Not bad really, but not the best place to start.

the rest:
Live in Hollywood 1991 𝒜𝒜𝒜 (Rhino, 1991, prod. Mark Linnet, Andy Paley)

worth searching for: *Blues Side of Rock 'n' Roll* 𝒜𝒜𝒜𝒜𝒱 (Star Club, 1993, prod. Ahmet Ertegun, Jerry Wexler) is a top-notch, 26-song import boasting several of Baker's lesser teen-oriented hits ("Bumble Bee," "Tra-La-La," "Humpty Dumpty") as well as much of the material on the Rhino disc. *Dick Tracy Soundtrack* 𝒜𝒜𝒜𝒱 (Sire Records, 1990, prod. Andy Paley) has one track by Baker, the wonderfully lewd "Slow Rollin' Mama." *The Sullivan Years—The Rhythm & Blues Revue* 𝒜𝒜𝒱 (TVT, 1993, prod. Steve Gottlieb) is hampered by dull sound, but Baker is terrific on her live version of "Tweedlee Dee."

influences:
◀◀ Bessie Smith, Esther Phillips
▶▶ Aretha Franklin

Ken Burke

Long John Baldry

Born January 12, 1941, in East Maddon, England.

A bonafide giant of a man, both in height (6-foot-7) *and* in stature, Long John Baldry's background in folk, blues, and jazz, and his uncanny blending of all three, paralleled the very birth of the entire British rock scene, and history rightfully records the man as a key player in its subsequent development. Upon first hearing Sonny Terry's "Silver Fox Chase" as a child, Baldry's fate was set, and after discovering the work of Big Bill Broonzy several years later, and acquiring his first guitar as a result, he became, along with Alexis Korner, the accompanist-of-choice for visiting U.S. bluesmen. Consequently, the late 1950s found Baldry touring the U.K. alongside Champion Jack Dupree, Memphis Slim, and Roosevelt Sykes, and both Eric Clapton and Spencer Davis cite their attendance at such shows as inspiring them to pick up *their* first six-strings. Baldry also toured his homeland several times with Ramblin' Jack Elliot, laying the seeds of the British folk renaissance in the process. Alexis and Baldry eventually joined forces in 1962 to form Britain's first electric blues band, Alexis Korner's Blues Incorporated, through whose ranks passed many of the country's giants-to-be, including Mick Jagger, Charlie Watts, Paul Jones, and Jack Bruce. Their *R&B from The Marquee* 𝒜𝒜𝒜𝒜 album (MFSL, 1996, prod. Jack Good) captures Baldry at his earliest—and raunchiest. As the result of a coin toss following a German tour, LJB left Blues Incorporated to join Cyril Davies' All-Stars in January of 1963, and exactly one year later, following Davies's death, formed from its remnants Long John Baldry & The Hoochie Coochie Men, which featured a young Rod Stewart (whom Baldry had discovered waiting for a train). This volatile arrangement, with the addition of Brian Auger and Julie Driscoll in 1965, transformed into Steampacket, Britain's first blues/rock "supergroup," but the ever-restless Baldry soon quit to form Bluesology, which spent the mid-1960s touring Europe with a young Reginald Dwight on keyboards, duly renamed by Baldry as Elton John. During 1967 and 1968, Baldry enjoyed his only breakthrough pop hits with a series of lush beat-ballads, including the British chart-topper "Let the Heartaches Begin," but his much-belated introduction to America didn't come until 1971, when he corralled old pals Stewart and John to produce a side apiece of the *It Ain't Easy* album; its biographical "Don't Try to Lay No Boogie Woogie on the King of Rock and Roll" became an FM staple, leading Baldry to belatedly undertake his first North American tours. The mid-1970s were spent hop-scotching back and forth across the Atlantic, touring, hosting a syndicated History of British Rock radio series, working with an Icelandic band called The Studdmen, and even recording two "white suit" albums for Casablanca at the height of the disco craze (records which, Baldry believes today, were "melted down for Donna Summer singles"). He soon after sought refuge in the comparative calm of Canada, becoming a citizen there in 1980. He resides to this day in Vancouver, where he not only continues to record and perform but also enjoys a lucrative side-career as a commercial voice-over artist (including Captain Robotnik in the "Sonic the Hedgehog" cartoon series). He was also a member, alongside Mose Allison and Rob Wasserman, of the Willie Dixon Dream Band and was on the Board of Directors of Dixon's Chicago-based Blues Heaven organization. Baldry still tours Europe regularly, where his fanbase—particularly in Germany—has remained strong for more than 30 years. With typically self-effacing style, Baldry sums up his most colorful life and career thusly: "Legend? Of course, dear boy. So when does the next set start?"

what to buy: Tough, vital, smoky, but with the man's inimitable air of class, *On Stage Tonight: Baldry's Out!* &&&&&&& (Stony Plain, 1993, prod. Holger Petersen) captures Long John and a crack back-up combo blasting it out on the stage of Hamburg's Fabrik Club to a suitably ribald crowd. This is everything R&B, and a live album of it, should be.

what to buy next: Both *Let the Heartaches Begin/Wait for Me* &&& (Beat Goes On, 1995, prod. Tony Macauley) and *A Thrill's a Thrill: The Canadian Years* &&&& (EMI Music Canada, 1995, prod. various) provide fine retrospectives of Baldry's late 1960s and early 1980s work, respectively.

the rest:
It Still Ain't Easy &&&& (Stony Plain, 1991)
Right to Sing the Blues &&&& (Stony Plain, 1996)

worth searching for: Another BGO import, *Long John's Blues/Looking at Long John* &&&& (Beat Goes On, 1995, prod. various) combines the man's sizzling 1964 and 1966 Pye albums on a single disc. File alongside *John Mayall's Bluesbreakers* as prime examples of the British blues revival at its best.

influences:
◀◀ Big Bill Broonzy, Leadbelly, Willie Dixon, Lonnie Johnson, Muddy Waters

▶▶ Eric Clapton, Mick Jagger, Rod Stewart, Elton John, Frankie Miller

Gary Pig Gold

Hank Ballard

Born November 18, 1936, in Detroit, MI.

Radio may have banned his biggest 1950s hits, and Chubby Checker cashed the big paycheck for his "The Twist," but Hank Ballard towered on the R&B landscape of the day. His 1954 record "Work with Me Annie" proved too hot for the timid

times, but the song inspired many sanitized rewrites and answer records. Censorship didn't slow down Ballard, who followed the record that blared out of jukeboxes across the country with "Annie Had a Baby" and the even more incendiary "Sexy Ways." While Hank Ballard & the Midnighters served as a fixture on the rhythm and blues charts through the 1950s, the group didn't hit home on the pop Top 10 until 1960 with "Finger Popping Time" and "Let's Go, Let's Go, Let's Go." Ballard joined doo-woppers the Royals in time to cut the group's first R&B chart entry, "Get It," in 1953 and set the stage for the historic recordings they made together. The group finally disbanded in 1965, and Ballard went on to tour and record with James Brown before reviving the Midnighters during the 1980s and recreating his classic 1950s stage show.

By bucking the sexual mores of the times, he may have been denied his just due on the charts, but Hank Ballard's records serve to demonstrate an important point—R&B never got any better than this, only different.

what to buy: *Sexy Ways: The Best of Hank Ballard and the Midnighters* &&&& (Rhino, 1993 prod. various) is the only Midnighters collection necessary. The 20 tracks cover all the highlights of his original King sessions.

what to buy next: An English import, *Live at the Palais* &&& (Charly, 1987, prod. John White), captures Ballard's current stage show, merrily mixing his classic R&B with more contemporary soul.

the rest:
Their Greatest Jukebox Hits &&&& (King, 1956)
Spotlight on Hank Ballard &&& (King, 1960)
Hank Ballard and the Midnighters &&& (King, 1961)
What You Get When the Gettin' Gets Good &&&& (Charly UK, 1986)

worth searching for: The 1954 10-inch album *Their Greatest Jukebox Hits* is one of the prime collector's items of 1950s R&B, invariably bringing more than $1,000 for a copy in reasonable condition.

influences:
◀◀ Gene Autry, Jimmy Rushing, Five Royales

▶▶ James Brown, Swamp Dogg, John Fogerty

Joel Selvin

Afrika Bambaataa

Born Kevin Donovan, April 10, 1960, in the Bronx, NY.

Jamaican expatriate DJ Kool Herc may be commonly credited

with creating hip-hop music, but Afrika Bambaataa brought hip-hop culture to the world. As a DJ and leader of the Universal Zulu Nation, Bambaataa brought together DJs, rappers, break-dancers, and graffiti artists into a singular, worldwide hip-hop movement that disregarded such obstacles as race and sex. Bambaataa's classic singles "Planet Rock" and "Looking for the Perfect Beat" not only broke down the barriers and revolutionized music, but they ushered in a new paradigm for universal youth culture as well. Born and raised in the Bronx, where hip-hop itself was born, Bambaataa named himself after a 19th-Century Zulu chief whose name meant "affectionate leader." In 1976, he formed the Universal Zulu Nation, an organization of hip-hop's cultural sentinels dedicated to peace and survival in the modern world. Ironically, the group grew out of a not-so-peaceful gang called the Black Spades that Bambaataa had once been a member of. Because hip-hop didn't yet exist, pioneering DJs Bambaataa, Herc, and Grandmaster Flash had to create it using the musical elements around them; using two copies of the same record, they would isolate the funkiest part of a song—the percussion break—to prolong the crowd's enthusiasm. Often called the "Master of Records" because nobody's collection could rival his, Bambaataa's m.o. was to create a sweaty, rhythmic orgy using everything from rare Latin rock to European disco and even the Monkees. In creating his own music, Bambaataa was influenced as much by the Sex Pistols and Kraftwerk as he was George Clinton and James Brown (perhaps explaining why he was so popular with the punk rock kids in his early club-spinning days). Time Zone—Bambaataa's floating collection of rappers, singers, and DJs—even collaborated with then-former Sex Pistol Johnny Lydon in 1984 on the aptly Orwellian New Wave hit, "World Destruction." Still, although Bam's electro-funk creations eventually inspired hip-hop offspring like house and techno, that freewheeling spirit often gets lost in today's insular view of what hip-hop is and isn't. These days, while Bambaataa still rocks parties and the occasional rave and makes frequent appearances on radio stations, he's nowhere near the top of hip-hop's Fortune 500. But as one of the most influential DJs ever, he owns a major place in hip-hop history and reaps perhaps the biggest reward of all: Respect.

what to buy: Recently, Bambaataa's long-time label reissued *Planet Rock: The Album* 🎵🎵🎵🎵 (Tommy Boy, 1986, prod. Afrika Bambaataa, Arthur Baker, others), an after-the-fact anthology that contains the classic singles "Planet Rock" and "Looking for the Perfect Beat," as well as three previously unreleased songs from Melle Mel, Trouble Funk, and Soul Sonic Force. But you don't necessarily have to look back to appreciate Bam-

baataa's music. Although it's been almost 20 years since he released his first single, "Zulu Nation Throwdown," on Winley Records, he still continues to make music that would drive any B-boy wild. The latest, from his group Time Zone, is the 22-track *Warlocks and Witches, Computer Chips, Microchips and You* 🎵🎵🎵 (Profile, 1996, prod. Afrika Bambaataa), a kinetic, non-stop jam. "Throw Your Fuckin' Hands Up" is the club favorite, but one of the best tracks is "Zulu War Chant," which, as the title suggests, features chants repeated over beats. Can anyone trace the lineage of black music better than Bam?

what to buy next: Another recent Tommy Boy reissue is the EP *Unity* 🎵🎵🎵 (Tommy Boy, 1984, prod. Afrika Bambaataa, Arthur Baker, James Brown), which was recorded with the legendary Godfather of Soul, James Brown. A number of seminal singles have been re-released, too, on CDs and vinyl, including "Planet Rock," "Looking for the Perfect Beat," and "Renegades of Funk." All are worth picking up. Released under the moniker Afrika Bambaataa and Family, *1990-2000: The Decade of Darkness* 🎵🎵🎵 (EMI, 1991, prod. Afrika Bambaataa) covers the myriad musical styles that Bambaataa continues to embrace: "Just Get Up & Dance" became a big house hit, "Say It Loud" continues Bam's running ode to James Brown, and "Freedom" and "Electro Funk Express" are reminiscent of the DJ's earlier days.

the rest:
(As Shango) *Shango Funk Theology* 🎵🎵🎵 (Celluoid, 1984)
Beware (The Funk Is Everywhere) 🎵🎵🎵 (Tommy Boy, 1986)
The Light 🎵🎵🎵 (EMI, 1988)
Don't Stop Planet Rock 🎵🎵🎵 EP (Tommy Boy, 1992)
Time Zone (Planet Rock, 1993)

worth searching for: Bambaataa continues to release a bevy of house, techno, and hip-hop singles for the European labels DFC and ZYX, and a few sides have been released by his own stateside independent labels, Planet Rock Music and Perfect Beat Records. In 1987 a bootleg record was released by Blatant Records featuring "Zulu Nation Throwdown" and "Death Mix," a legendary recording that is actually a copy of one of Bam's Zulu party DJ sets. Other incredible (and incredibly hard-to-find) singles include the Jazzy 5-featuring "Jazzy Sensation" (Tommy Boy, 1981), "Bambaataa's Theme" (Tommy Boy, 1986), and "Return to Planet Rock" (York's, 1989), which features the Jungle Brothers and Soul Sonic Force. All of these singles are worth the hunt.

influences:
◄◄ Kraftwerk, James Brown, Parliament/Funkadelic, Gary Neuman

▶▶ All of hip-hop, electronica

Jazzbo

Ant Banks

The dual threat producer-rapper is hardly a new thing in hip-hop. Erick Sermon and Parrish Smith, for instance, began making lots of dollars—not to mention some pretty vital self-produced records—as EPMD nearly a decade ago. But what about producers who can't rap, yet try anyway? And, no, we don't mean Sean "Puff Daddy" Combs. Instead, it's East Oakland's Ant Banks we're talking about. As a producer, Banks has been money: All slippery keyboards and deep, shuddering basslines, his trademark East Bay Area funk sound has graced hit records by Spice 1 and Too $hort, as well as recordings by the likes of Mac Mall, Goldy, and Off Da Hook. But as a rapper, well, Banks is much poorer. On his 1994 album, *The Big Badass*, for instance, he's completely upstaged by his guest contributors, including Spice 1, Too $hort and, especially, Boots of the Coup. Of course, by the time Banks finally decided to slip back into the production booth and go the producer compilation route on 1997's *Big Thangs*, his sound had become somewhat stale. So, too, had the lyrical concerns of his guests, which included usual suspects $hort, Spice 1, MC Breed, plus E-40, Ice Cube, and 2Pac.

what's available: Although *Big Thangs* 𝄢𝄢 (Priority, 1997, prod. Ant Banks) hit in Northern California, it's really a way-too-familiar-sounding dud, with Banks and a who's who cast of West Coast rap gangstas and playas covering well-worn sonic and thematic territory (bitches, ballin', and bangin', of course). The album is, however, notable for at least one track: "4 Tha Hustlas," which features $hort, Breed, and, in one of his several posthumous cameos, 2Pac. It doesn't hurt that "Hustlas" closes with guitarist Shorty B's mournful, fuzzy Eddie Hazelisms, which add a shot of texture and musical emotion to an album that's way too short on both. Of the albums that prominently feature Banks as a vocalist, *The Big Badass* 𝄢𝄢 (Jive, 1994, prod. Ant Banks) is the most recommendable, mostly for the guest list (Boots, $hort, Spice 1, Goldy, saxman J. Spencer, etc.). Also available are *Sittin' On Something Phat* 𝄢𝄢 (Jive, 1993) and *Do Or Die* 𝄢𝄢 (Jive, 1995).

influences:

◀◀ Too $hort, Spice 1, Parliament-Funkadelic, Sir Mix-A-Lot

▶▶ Off Da Hook, Mac Mall, Mike Mosely

Josh Freedom du Lac

The Bar-Kays

Formed 1966, in Memphis, TN.

Jimmy King, guitar; Ronnie Caldwell, organ; Carl Cunningham, drums; Phalon Jones, sax; Ben Cauley, trumpet; James Alexander, bass.

Although one of Memphis's many black high school bands, the Bar-Kays were just not like the other guys. The Bar-Kays—a band on fire—became, within a year of its formation, the demo band at Stax Records. The fortunes and fates were simultaneously sealed when they scored a national hit with 1967's summer anthem "Soul Finger" and became Otis Redding's tour band. Tragically, the entire band save Cauley and Alexander perished along with Redding in a plane crash near the end of the year. Bravely, the survivors re-formed the band and released the comeback, "Gotta Groove," in 1969. While not a bad record, the magic of "Soul Finger" was gone. Two years later the Bar-Kays returned with their acid-funk manifesto *Black Rock*. Now attired in Funkadelic-inspired space gear, their philosophy was clear: funky country freak was the new deal. In 1976, the band signed with Mercury, commencing a 10-year run that yielded 10 albums and a successful mid-level concert career. Since the beginning of the decade the Bar-Kays have been without a major label deal; though they continue to tour.

what to buy: *Best of the Bar-Kays* 𝄢𝄢𝄢𝄢 (Mercury Chronicles, 1993, prod. various) is a well-paced, well-thought out compilation of the band's most productive period. Check out "Freak Show" (preferably on the dance floor).

what to buy next: *Black Rock/Gotta Groove* 𝄢𝄢𝄢 (Stax, 1995, prod. various) is the ideal two-volume chronicle—one finds a band on the ropes, the other is a portrait of hard-won fearlessness and humor. *Money Talks* 𝄢𝄢𝄢 (Stax, 1978, prod. Allen Jones, Phil Kaffel) is a short collection of lean, no-nonsense stanky funk that is primarily perpetrated by the testifying fever of "Holy Ghost" and "Holy Ghost (Reborn)." *Soul Finger* 𝄢𝄢𝄢 (Rhino, 1994, prod. various), a classic case of a dream deferred, is a great party album full of BBQ rib grease and breaded chicken wings. This band would have gone places.

what to avoid: *48 Hours* 𝄢𝄢 (Basix, 1994, prod. Larry Dodson, James Alexander) offers only the skeletal remains of a once-promising outfit.

the rest:
Best of the Bar-Kays 𝄢𝄢𝄢 (Stax, 1991/1992)
Too Hot to Stop 𝄢𝄢𝄢 (Rebound, 1996)
Best of the Bar-Kays, Vol. 2 𝄢𝄢𝄢 (Mercury Chronicles, 1996)
Do You See What I See? 𝄢𝄢𝄢 (Stax, 1996)

worth searching for: The Bar-Kays' performances as a Stax session band. Among the best is Isaac Hayes's *Black Moses* 𝄢𝄢𝄢 (Stax, 1980/1990, prod. Isaac Hayes).

influences:

◀◀ Booker T. & the MG's, James Brown, Jimi Hendrix

▶▶ Meters, Funkadelic, Gap Band

Tom Terrell and Gary Graff

Dave Bartholomew

Born December 24, 1940, in Edgard, LA.

One of the true unsung heroes of R&B and rock 'n' roll, bandleader Dave Bartholomew laid one of the music's cornerstones with the records he made with Fats Domino starting in 1949. But, as the New Orleans-based artist and repertoire director for Imperial Records, the trumpeter and songwriter conducted a series of rich, vibrant recordings with dozens of lesser-known artists throughout the 1950s that never traveled far beyond jukeboxes in the deep South. While the Domino million-sellers were Bartholomew's only taste of nationwide success as a producer, he made equally satisfying records, steeped in the traditional sounds of New Orleans, with the same studio musicians backing himself, Smiley Lewis, Tommy Ridgely, the Spiders, Earl King, as well as visiting R&B dignitaries such as Big Joe Turner, Roy Brown, T-Bone Walker, and Charles Brown. His solo records have been covered by an eclectic and select few artists such as the Fabulous Thunderbirds—who did a marvelous job with Bartholomew's "The Monkey"—Elvis Costello, and Buster Poindexter. He went into semi-retirement during the early 1960s, although he continued to play music around New Orleans and occasionally joined Fats Domino's band on tour. But his work as one of the prime designers of the New Orleans R&B sound echoes throughout the rock world to this day.

what to buy: A double-disc set, *The Spirit of New Orleans: The Genius of Dave Bartholomew* 𝄢𝄢𝄢𝄢 (EMI, 1992, prod. Dave Bartholomew), blends his solo recordings with his productions of other artists, a detailed panoramic look at his landmark work.

what to buy next: Bartholomew's work hovers over the four-disc boxed set, *Crescent City Soul: The Sound of New Orleans 1947–1974* 𝄢𝄢𝄢 (EMI, 1996, prod. various) like one of those floats in Macy's Thanksgiving Day parade. The set samples not only his work with artists such as Fats Domino, Smiley Lewis, and many lesser-knowns, but also key Bartholomew productions such as "Lawdy Miss Clawdy" by Lloyd Price. Unfortunately, the

set duplicates many of the selections from *The Spirit of New Orleans* and ranges far beyond only Bartholomew's work.

worth searching for: His early solo recordings for the DeLuxe and King labels were collected on a British CD, *In the Alley* 𝄢𝄢𝄢 (Charly, 1991, prod. various).

influences:

◀◀ Louis Armstrong, Fats Pinchon, Louis Jordan

▶▶ Allen Toussaint, Paul McCartney, Dirty Dozen Brass Band

Joel Selvin

Rob Base & D.J. E-Z Rock

Formed 1982, in Harlem, NY.

Rob Base (born Robert Ginyard), vocals; E-Z Rock (born Rodney Bryce), DJ.

Did a single party or DJ set go by in 1988 that *didn't* include "It Takes Two"? The uptempo, bottom-heavy million-selling smash was the song of the moment in the second half of '88, and it was probably responsible for the obliteration of about half the woofer cones produced that year. Robert Ginyard and Rodney "Skip" Bryce began their artistic partnership in the early '80s, forming a group (in the fifth grade, no less) called Sureshot Seven. Seven eventually became two, and "It Takes Two" begat an album of the same name. Don't call Rob Base & E-Z Rock one-hit wonders, though: Proving that two was their magic number, they also had success with a second single, "Joy and Pain," although the group's joy eventually turned to pain when Frankie Beverly sued for copyright infringement over the uncredited use of lyrics from a Maze song of the same name.

what to buy: *It Takes Two* 𝄢𝄢𝄢 (Profile, 1988, prod. various) is a durable piece of hip-hop nostalgia. The undeniably funky title track might just be the sound of the hip-hop nation collectively taking a deep breath before diving back into the increasingly deep music of the day (Public Enemy, N.W.A., et al.).

the rest:

Break of Dawn 𝄢 (Funky Base, 1994)

worth searching for: Former hip-hop journalist and current record executive Dan Charnas recorded a hilarious faux-commercial for an L.A. radio station in 1997 that "announced" the return of Base and E-Z Rock by turning various parts of "It Takes Two" into songs of their own. The line "stay away from me/if you're contagious," for instance, becomes a "serious" song about disease, while "don't smoke buddah/can't stand zest" meets Flava Flav to become an anti-drug message. Bobby Jimmy and the Critters would be proud.

solo outings:
Rob Base:
The Incredible Base ♫♫ (Profile, 1989)

influences:
◄◄ Spoonie Gee, Run-D.M.C., Boogie Down Productions
►► Coolie, L.V., Puff Daddy

Todd Inoue and Josh Freedom du Lac

Basehead
Formed 1990, in Washington, DC.

Michael Ivey, vocals, guitar, bass, keyboards, drum programs; Brian Hendrix, drums; Paul "DJ Unique" Howard, turntables (1990–92); Bill Conway, bass (1992–present); Marco Delmar, guitar (1990–93); Bob DeWald, bass (1990–93); Bruce "Cool Aid" Gardner, drums (1990–93); Clarence "Citizen Cope" Greenwood, turntables (1992–present); Keith Lofton, guitar, (1992–present).

Basehead, the brainchild of the multi-talented Michael Ivey, impressed critics and a small cult of fans during the early 1990s with its moody, psychedelic blend of hip-hop and rock. Ivey's cynical and self-deprecating manner and somnambulistic vocals worked in striking contrast to his frequently trenchant lyrics, and Basehead's sleepy grooves, redolent of pot smoke and dorm-room angst, have an insinuating power.

what to buy: Basehead's debut, *Play with Toys* ♫♫♫ (Imago, 1992, prod. Michael Ivey), is a compelling mix of phat grooves, lean Hendrix and Zep-inspired guitar lines, edgy sarcasm, and hilarious sketches.

the rest:
Not in Kansas Anymore ♫♫♫ (Imago, 1993)
Faith ♫♫♫ (Imago, 1996)

solo outings:
Michael Ivey:
B.Y.O.B. ♫♫♫ (13/Rykodisc, 1994)

influences:
◄◄ Jimi Hendrix, Led Zeppelin, De La Soul, Stetsasonic, Arrested Development
►► Spearhead

Simon Glickman

Fontella Bass
Born July 3, 1949, in St. Louis, MO.

Born into a gospel singing family, Bass turned her back on that music to play piano in a series of blues bands during the early '60s. She stumbled into singing after filling in one night for a drunk Little Milton and later became a featured vocalist in the Oliver Sain Revue. Bass brought a brassy gospel voice to her blues and R&B singing; her biggest hit came in 1965, when "Rescue Me" hit the top of the R&B charts and garnered a Grammy nomination. Her marriage to avant garde trumpeter Lester Bowie led to life in Paris from 1968–71 and a largely unrecognized body of jazz work—although the powerful "Theme De Yoyo" on the Art Ensemble of Chicago's *Les Stances a Sophie* album shows her in top form. After divorcing Bowie, Bass was off the scene during most of the 1970s and 1980s raising her family, and when she returned, she slipped back into gospel.

what to buy: Her 1960s work is compiled on *Rescued—The Best of Fontella Bass* ♫♫♫♫ (MCA, 1992, prod. various), a good accounting of gospel-influenced 1960s soul with "Don't Mess with a Good Thing" and "Joy of Love."

what to buy next: Her recent gospel work still touches the jazz world. *No Ways Tired* ♫♫♫♫ (Nonesuch, 1995, prod. Wayne Horvitz) features jazzmen Bowie, David Sanborn, and Hamiett Blueitt. *Everlasting Arms* ♫♫♫♫ (Silver Spring, 1991, prod. Fontella Bass, Leroy Jodie Pierson) is an unusually naked performance of Bass singing traditional gospel songs accompanied only by herself on piano.

worth searching for: Bass injects some soul into a couple of songs on the World Saxophone Quartet's 1994 release *Breath of Life* (Nonesuch, 1994).

influences:
◄◄ Bessie Smith, Dinah Washington, Clara Ward
►► Tina Turner, Chaka Khan, Mariah Carey

Lawrence Gabriel

Shirley Bassey
Born Shirley Veronica Bassey, January 8, 1937, in Cardiff, Wales.

Known to some as the James Bond soundtrack star, Shirley Bassey's career shows that she is indeed much more. Long before she applied her flamboyant vocal treatment to 007 anthems in *Goldfinger* (1964) and *Diamonds Are Forever* (1972), making the songs worldwide hits, Bassey was a blossoming cabaret star. She was signed to Phillips in 1957 and recorded a cover version of Harry Belafonte's "Banana Boat Song" that hit #1 on the charts that year. Her songs "Kiss Me Honey Kiss Me" and "As I Love You" both entered the Top 10 in 1959. Bassey emerged full-force as a vocal stylist and dazzling live performer after signing to Columbia during the early 1960s, the peak of her career. Enchanting interpretations of "Climb Ev'ry Mountain" (1961) from *The Sound of Music* and "What Kind of Fool Am I?" (1963) from *Stop the World I Want to Get Off* showed Bassey's flair for show tunes. Her successful recording of "Goldfinger," her only major hit in America, led to a contract deal with United Artists in 1967. She also sang the theme song for the less triumphant 1979 James Bond film *Moonraker*. While she may not have directly influenced many singers in her genre, Bassey's glitzy show-stoppers inspired the most unlikely of artists—including Detroit rocker Mitch Ryder, whose only solo hit was a cover of Bassey's "What Now My Love" (Dyna Voice, 1967), and English rockers Status Quo, who covered her "I Who Have Nothing" (Pye, 1966). Bassey lives in Switzerland but travels to the U.S. occasionally to record and perform.

what to buy: *Goldsinger: The Best of Shirley Bassey* ♫♫♫ (EMI, 1995, prod. various) offers a little of everything from her film and show tune interpretations to her innovative approaches to pop.

the rest:
Sassy Bassey ♫♫♫ (Pair, 1991)
Shirley Bassey Sings the Songs of Andrew Lloyd Weber ♫♫♫♥ (EMI, 1995)

worth searching for: Bassey made a guest-appearance on the Swiss synth-pop duo Yello's album *One Second* ♫♫♫♫ (Mercury, 1987). *The Best of James Bond* ♫♫♫♥ (EMI, 1992) features Bassey's Bond contributions, plus some outtakes, in the illuminating context of the rest of the film franchise's musical *oeuvre*.

influences:

◀◀ Josephine Baker, Harry Belafonte, Lena Horne, Dinah Washington, Nina Simone

▶▶ Phyllis Hyman, Anita Baker, Vanessa Williams

Norene Cashen

Beastie Boys
/DJ Hurricane
/Money Mark

Formed 1981, in New York City, NY.

Mike D (born Michael Diamond), vocals, drums; MCA (born Adam Yauch), vocals, bass; John Berry, guitar (1981–82); Kate Schellenbach, drums (1981–82); King Ad-Rock (born Adam Horovitz), vocals, guitar (1982–present).

Many have read racial implications into the Beasties' massive, mid-'80s multi-platinum crossover success: For a time, the group held the distinction of having the best-selling rap album ever, which critics decided had more to do with old-fashioned American racism than well-deserved popularity. The truth will always remain somewhere in between. While a similar backlash would have destroyed a lesser white rapper or group, the Beastie Boys have continued to make albums that have extended both their musical reach and fan base—if not, as some might persuasively contend, transformed the face of both hip-hop and alternative rock. Over time, the Beasties have headed towards a common ground across genres, a vision that seems iconoclastic in the fragmented '90s.

what to buy: What hip-hop, metal, or alternative rock fan doesn't possess a copy of *Licensed to Ill* ♫♫♫♫ (Columbia, 1986, prod. Rick Rubin, the Beastie Boys)? Along with Run-D.M.C.'s *Raising Hell*, *Ill* turned hip-hop into big business and set it on its march towards the mainstream. In retrospect, it seems like a juvenile record—one which even the Beasties seem somewhat embarrassed about. But the album, which bridged the gap between frat keggers and 'hood house parties for a few seasons in the mid-'80s, stands up remarkably well to the test of time—especially Rubin's stripped-down rhythms, Ad-Rock's nasally vignettes, and MCA and Mike D's memorable punch-lines. Hindsight reveals another interesting twist: While most white suburban kids may have zeroed in on the Beasties' endless toying with pop culture icons (White Castle, Ted Knight, the famous Mr. Ed!), the crew's own fascination with Schoolly D and its willingness to adopt that style (see "The New Style") anticipates the phenomenal success of gangsta rap by a half decade. Bummed about royalty disputes and burnt on the New York scene, the Beasties fled for L.A.—and a new label—shortly afterward. There, they moved into a mansion, hooked up the like-minded Dust Brothers (who were mining Van Halen and obscure '70s metal-funkers Ballinjack for Top 10 hits with Tone Loc and Young M.C.) and engineer Mario Caldato and, finally, set about transforming themselves into free-minded freestylers. *Paul's Boutique* ♫♫♫♥ (Capitol, 1989, prod. Beastie Boys, Dust Brothers) was the result. A 180-degree turn, the record sounds like boutique clutter, crammed with samples of everybody from the Band to The Incredible Bongo Band and lyrical allusions to Bob Dylan, *A Clockwork Orange,* and Kurtis Blow. It's a beautifully incongruous mess. Sonically, the record stands as a high point of hip-hop's pre-sample clearance era.

Adam "MCA" Yauch of the Beastie Boys **(© Ken Settle)**

Anticipating the mood, the Beasties bridge hip-hop history and the next school, with nods to the coming old-school revival, DJ culture, and breakbeat digging.

what to buy next: By *Check Your Head* 🎵🎵🎵 (Capitol/Grand Royal, 1992, prod. Beastie Boys), the rest of the world had begun to catch up with the Beasties, so they moved to a mixture of live instruments and sampled sound in creating not just hip-hop, but dub psychedelia ("Something's Got to Give"), punk ("Time for Livin'," a Sly and the Family Stone cover), and—with the help of "Money Mark" Ramos Nishita—'70s organ/guitar funk grooves ("In 3's," "Groove Holmes"). Forget singles (except maybe "So Whatcha Want")—the Beasties are now an album band. *Ill Communication* 🎵🎵🎵 (Capitol/Grand Royal, 1994, prod. Beastie Boys) completes the transformation from '80s brats to '90s bohemians. Environmental and Buddhist concerns, plus Yauch's Tibetan activism, emerge as the main themes, as Yauch rhymes: "Been learnin from the elders/Now it's time to speak."

the rest:
Some Old Bullshit 🎵🎵🎵 (Capitol/Grand Royal, 1995)
Root Down 🎵🎵🎵 (Capitol, 1995)
The In Sound from Way Out 🎵🎵🎵 (Capitol/Grand Royal, 1996)

solo outings:
DJ Hurricane:
The Hurra 🎵🎵🎵 (Capitol/Grand Royal, 1995)

Money Mark:
Money Mark's Keyboard Repair 🎵🎵🎵 (Mo Wax/ffrr, 1995)

influences:
◀◀ T-La Rock, Schoolly D, Bad Brains, Biz Markie, Led Zeppelin
▶▶ Cypress Hill, Pharcyde, Red Hot Chili Peppers, Sublime, Bloodhound Gang

Jeff "DJ Zen" Chang

Beatnuts
Formed mid-1980s, in New York, NY.

Psycho Les (born Les Fernandez), vocals; JuJu (born J. Tineo), vocals; Kool Ass Fashion/Al Tariq (born Bertony Smalls), vocals (mid-1980s–96).

The Latino trio initially made its reputation as producers of considerable versatility, working the samplers and boards for a slew of underground artists including Chi-Ali, Monie Love, Powerule, Fat Joe, the Jungle Brothers, and Kurious. Sort of the rat bastard sons of the Native Tongues Movement, they didn't

aspire to get the party started right, instead going straight for the buzzing euphoria and the falling-down ugliness of the *end* of the party. As a chorus to one of their irrepressible grooves went: "I wanna fuck, drink, and smoke some shit!"

what to buy: There is no denying that these are among the best producers hip-hop has produced, sharing with Large Professor, in particular, a sixth sense about the funkiest loops from rare jazz LPs and funk 45s. Lyrically, well, they don't leave much to the imagination. *The Beatnuts* 🎵🎵🎵 (Relativity, 1994, prod. Beatnuts) presents the group in the best light, with "Are You Ready," "Yeah You Get Props," and "Fried Chicken" simply jumping off the platter.

what to buy next: The follow-up, *Stone Crazy* 🎵🎵🎵 (Relativity, 1997, prod. Beatnuts) has the group carrying on sans Fash, but with a half dozen or so new guests. It's no great leap forward lyrically, but the production keeps getting better—peep the eerie organs, quirky snips, and oddball loops on "Bless the M.I.C.," "Off the Books," and "Niggaz Know." In some sections, the group's debut EP, *Intoxicated Demons* 🎵🎵🎵 (Relativity, 1993, prod. Beatnuts) is a two-copy-mandatory DJ favorite (see "On the 1+2"). But aside from the instantly memorable "No Equal," most of the lyrics are strictly low-brow: lots of hoo-hah about guns, blunts, and oral sex.

the rest:
Stone Crazy 🎵🎵🎵 (Relativity, 1997)

worth searching for: Behind the boards, the group reworked Johnny Guitar Watson to make for Mad Skillz' best track ever, "The Nod Factor" (Big Beat, 1995).

solo outings:
Kool Ass Fash/Al Tariq:
God Connections 🎵🎵🎵 (Correct, 1996)

influences:
◀◀ A Tribe Called Quest, De La Soul, Jungle Brothers
▶▶ Diggin' In the Crates Crew

Jeff "DJ Zen" Chang

Beck
Born Beck Hansen, July 8, 1970, in Los Angeles, CA.

Best known for the rock/folk/hip-hop marriage on his brilliant single, "Loser," the ultra-prolific Beck changes musical genres

Beck (© Ken Settle)

almost as often as he does record labels. The son of hip, counter-culture parents, Beck first gained recognition as an eccentric folkie songwriter/performer in Los Angeles. Finding his niche mixing creaky acoustic guitar with oddball, stream-of-consciousness lyrics, Beck recorded several hard-to-find singles and independently-released albums until the intentionally goofy "Loser"—with Beck rapping badly over a hip-hop beat—set off a bidding war between labels. Any sense of a one-hit wonder was dashed with the release of his 1996 album _Odelay_, a blending of nearly every imaginable non-classical musical genre into a stew that was breathtaking in its scope but completely accessible at the same time. His inclusion on bills for Lollapalooza _and_ the HORDE only underscored the broad range of his artistic vision.

what to buy: _Odelay_ 🎵🎵🎵🎵 (DGC, 1996, prod. Dust Brothers) is a tremendous melding of styles, eclectic and melodic at the same time. The approach, with its woozy rhythms and furious beats, is by its nature subversive, but that didn't stop "Where It's At" or "Devil's Haircut" from becoming some of the best singles of 1996–97.

what to buy next: _Mellow Gold_ 🎵🎵🎵 (DGC, 1994, prod. various) offers a style-hopping cornucopia of sounds that establishes him as more than a one-hit wonder.

what to avoid: _One Foot in the Grave_ 🎵🎵 (K Records, 1994, prod. Beck) is a post _Mellow Gold_ project that sounds muted and indulgent after its predecessor's engaging eclecticism.

the rest:
Steropathetic Soul Manure 🎵🎵🎵 (Flipside, 1994)

worth searching for: Worth getting is the original "Loser" CD single (DGC, 1994, prod. various); it includes the title track plus four unreleased selections, including the fan favorites "Alcohol" and "Soul Suckin' Jerk."

influences:
⏪ Robert Johnson, Public Enemy, Miles Davis, Chet Baker, Bob Dylan, Pavement, Guided By Voices

Todd Wicks and Gary Graff

The Bee Gees

Formed 1958, in Brisbane, Australia.

Barry Gibb, vocals, guitar; Robin Gibb, vocals (1958–69, 1970–present); Maurice Gibb, vocals, bass, keyboards, guitar, percussion.

Before John Travolta strode down the sidewalk eating pizza to the disco sway of "Stayin' Alive," the Bee Gees were regarded as a pop vocal group of estimable talent that could take a good song and make it sound great. The trio had a few of those early on—"New York Mining Disaster 1941," "To Love Somebody," "Run to Me"—but it wasn't until the group recorded a few songs for the _Saturday Night Fever_ soundtrack that they became a phenomenon, making hits not just for itself but also for singer Yvonne Elliman and their late younger brother Andy Gibb. The brothers Gibb are, first and foremost, pop craftsman with an intuitive knack for harmonies and decent melodic sensibilities. Were it not for the film—and the subsequent co-starring role in the disastrous _Sgt. Pepper's Lonely Hearts Club Band_—the Bee Gees likely would have remained modest also-rans in the pop pantheon, neither celebrated nor scorned. As a result, however, they have a lot of money—and an artistic albatross that they haven't been able to shake since 1977. There was a sense of new embrace, though, from pop's hip elite when the trio was inducted into the Rock and Roll Hall of Fame in early 1997.

what to buy: _Main Course_ 🎵🎵🎵 (RSO, 1975/Polydor, 1994, prod. Arif Mardin) is a transitional album, pop with R&B touches that would turn into a full-fledged disco movement for _Saturday Night Fever_. On _Main Course_, however, it's a welcome switch from the bland pop path the Bee Gees were on before, yielding tuneful hits such as "Jive Talkin'" and "Nights on Broadway." _Bee Gees Gold_ 🎵🎵🎵 (Polydor, 1976, prod. various) is a solid gathering of pre-_Fever_ favorites.

what to buy next: Worth considering—but carefully—is the box set _Tales from the Brothers Gibb_ 🎵🎵🎵 (Polydor, 1990, prod. various). Its four discs cover everything you would want, but also plenty you wouldn't.

what to avoid: _Spirits Having Flown_ 🎵 (RSO, 1979/Polydor, 1994, prod. the Bee Gees, Karl Richardson, Albhy Galuten) the slick, calculated, and vapid follow-up to the _Fever_ success.

the rest:
Bee Gees 1st 🎵🎵🎵 (Atco, 1967/Rebound, 1994)
Odessa 🎵🎵 (Atco, 1969/Polydor, 1988)
Best of the Bee Gees, Vol. 1 🎵🎵🎵 (Atco/Polydor, 1969)
To Whom It May Concern 🎵🎵 (Atco, 1972/Polydor, 1992)
Best of the Bee Gees, Vol. 2 🎵🎵🎵 (Atco/Polydor, 1973)
Mr. Natural 🎵🎵 (RSO, 1974/Polydor, 1992)
Children of the World 🎵🎵🎵 (RSO, 1976/Polydor, 1994)
Here at Last . . . Live 🎵🎵🎵 (RSO, 1977/Polydor, 1990)
Size Isn't Everything 🎵🎵 (Polydor, 1993)
Still Waters 🎵🎵🎵 (Polydor, 1997)

worth searching for: The _veddy_ late 1960s _Cucumber Castle_ 🎵🎵 (Atco, 1970, prod. Robert Stigwood, the Bee Gees), recorded by Barry and Maurice during Robin's brief hiatus from the band, has hysterical Medieval cover art that company will get a kick out of.

influences:

◄◄ The Four Freshmen, the Kingston Trio, the Beatles, the Beach Boys

▶▶ Yvonne Elliman, Andy Gibb, Air Supply, Bread, Mr. Mister

Gary Graff

Bell Biv DeVoe
See: New Edition

Archie Bell & the Drells
Formed mid-1960s, in Houston, TX. Disbanded 1979.

Archie Bell (born September 1, 1944, in Henderson, TX); Huey "Billy" Butler (mid-1960s–69); Joe Cross (mid-1960s–69); James Wise; Charles Gibbs (1968–69); Willie Pernell (1969–73); Lee Bell (1969–79); Lucious Larkins (1973–79).

Once a synonym for soulful suavity, Archie Bell had a string of smooth, dance-oriented hits during the late 1960s and 1970s. Bell, a native of Texas, formed his Drells during high school but recorded his first big hit during a three-week leave from the military. "Tighten Up" topped both the R&B and pop charts during 1968, but Bell wasn't around to enjoy it; he was stationed in Germany at the time, and, in his absence, a number of groups billed themselves as *faux* Drells. Upon leaving the Army and re-establishing his rightful claim, Bell and his Drells worked with Philadelphia soul producers Bunny Sigler, Kenny Gamble, and Leon Huff for the better part of a decade. Bell also recorded as a solo performer during the early 1980s.

what to buy: *Tightening It Up: The Best of Archie Bell & the Drells* ♫♫♫ (Rhino, 1994, prod. various) collects 20 singles from the group's recordings for Ovide, Atlantic, TSOP, and Philadelphia International labels. Nearly all of these songs—"(There's Gonna Be a) Showdown," "Do the Choo Choo," and "Let's Groove" among the most popular—were made for the dance floor, but even when the Bell was singing a song called "I Can't Stop Dancing," he seemed to never break a sweat.

the rest:
Strategy ♫♫ (Philadelphia International, 1979/The Right Stuff, 1993)

influences:

◄◄ Curtis Mayfield, the Impressions, Major Lance

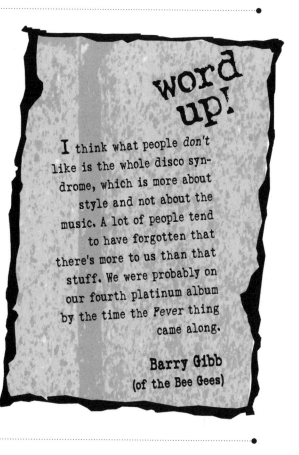

▶▶ Charles Wright & the Watts 103rd Street Rhythm Band, Harold Melvin & the Blue Notes

Brian Mansfield

William Bell
Born William Yarbrough, July 16, 1937, in Memphis, TN.

As both a songwriter and a vocalist, William Bell helped shape the Memphis soul sound of the 1960s and 1970s. Bell wrote or co-wrote many of the enduring classics of the Stax/Volt legacy: "Born Under a Bad Sign," "Private Number," and "I Got a Sure Thing," to name a few. The elegant, understated grace of his vocal delivery exhibited a songwriter's faith in the song. Much more a balladeer than a hard soul singer like labelmates Otis Redding, Sam Moore (of Sam & Dave), or Ollie Nightingale (of Ollie & the Nightingales), Bell endured the 15-year odyssey of Stax/Volt and left behind an impressive body of work that is as

$\frac{4}{2}$ *regina belle*

fresh and moving today as it was 30 years ago. Bell's initial recording for Stax, "You Don't Miss Your Water" (1961), was the first country-soul ballad from Memphis to gain national attention, establishing a paradigm that would be followed by Bell and many others for years to come. The best of his Stax ballads—"Share What You Got (Keep What You Need)" (1966), "Everybody Loves a Winner" (1967), "I Forgot to Be Your Lover" (1968), and "Lovin' on Borrowed Time" (1973)—belong on the short list of the masterpieces of Memphis soul. In 1975, after the demise of Stax, Bell moved to Mercury and had the biggest hit of his career with "Tryin' to Love Two" (1977).

what to buy: *Soul of a Bell* ✍✍✍✍ (Stax, 1967/ WEA/Atlantic, 1991, prod. various) was originally released in 1967 and contains all of Bell's early singles for Stax, plus outstanding covers of perennials such as "Do Right Woman, Do Right Man" and "I've Been Loving You Too Long." *Do Right Man* ✍✍✍✍ (Charly, 1984, prod. various) overlaps somewhat with *Soul of a Bell* but also includes "A Tribute to a King," a deeply moving remembrance of Otis Redding written by Bell and Booker T. Jones days after Redding's death.

what to buy next: *Best of William Bell* ✍✍✍ (Fantasy/Stax, 1988, prod. various) is a greatest hits collection from the period immediately after Stax's distribution arrangement with Atlantic Records ended in 1968. *Wow/Bound to Happen* ✍✍✍ (Stax, 1971 / Stax, 1969 / Fantasy/Stax, 1997, prod. various) collects two fine Bell LPs from 1971 and 1969, respectively. In a departure from standard operating procedures, *Wow* was recorded in Muscle Shoals, Alabama. Bell recorded a number of fine duets with Carla Thomas, Mavis Staples, and, most successfully, Judy Clay ("Private Number" and "My Baby Specializes," both from 1968). These are collected on *Duets* ✍✍✍ (Stax, 1968 / Fantasy/Stax, 1992, prod. various). *A Little Something Extra* ✍✍✍ (Fantasy/Stax, 1992, prod. various) contains outtakes and unreleased items from the Stax vaults, many of which are good enough to make you wonder what else might be in there.

what to avoid: Bell's releases on Wilbe, his own label, unfortunately consist of inferior modernized versions of his songs, re-recorded on the cheap with drum machines and electronic instruments. Skip *Bedtime Stories* **woof!** (Ichiban, 1992, prod. William Bell), *Vol. 1—Greatest Hits* **woof!** (Ichiban/Wilbe, 1994, prod. William Bell), *Vol. 2—Greatest Hits* **woof!** (Ichiban/Wilbe, 1995, prod. William Bell), and *On a Roll* **woof!** (Wilbe, 1995, Prod. William Bell).

the rest:
Phases of Reality ✍✍✍ (Stax, 1973)
Relating ✍✍✍ (Stax, 1974)

It's Time You Took Another Listen ✍✍✍ (Mercury, 1977)
Comin' Back for More ✍✍✍ (Razor & Tie, 1977)

worth searching for: Ace Records of Great Britain leases Stax product from Fantasy in the U.S., and the Ace catalog includes material that is unavailable in the U.S. *Stax Revue—Live at the 5/4 Ballroom* ✍✍✍✍ (Ace/Fantasy, 1995) offers rare live recording of Bell, Booker T. & the MG's, Rufus Thomas, and others from the mid-1960s.

influences:

◀◀ Sam Cooke, Jerry Butler, Curtis Mayfield

▶▶ Otis Redding, James Carr, O.V. Wright, Clarence Carter

Bill Pollak

Regina Belle

Born July 17, 1963, in Englewood, NJ.

Regina Belle was more than ready for stardom when New York City radio jock Vaughn Harper discovered her during the early 1980s while she performed in Greenwich Village clubs. By then she'd already studied voice at the Manhattan School of Music, played violin and sung with the Rutgers University jazz ensemble, and could play tuba, steel drums, and trombone. Harper hooked her up with soul group the Manhattans, who took her on tour and helped broker her record deal. Her first hit songs—"So Many Tears" and "Show Me the Way" from *All By Myself*—were well-received and made her a comer in a then-crowded field of adult female vocalists. *Stay with Me* put her out in front of the pack on the strength of her dynamic vocal prowess and the album's diversity. Successive album's weren't as tight, but Belle hit it big with "A Whole New World (Aladdin's Theme)" (from the Disney smash *Aladdin*), her Grammy-Winning 1993 duet with Peabo Bryson. A popular and tireless concert performer, she ended her relationship with Columbia Records in 1996 and signed with MCA.

what to buy: *Stay with Me* ✍✍✍ (CBS/Columbia, 1989, prod. Narada Michael Walden, Nick Martinelli) showcases Belle's hearty-yet-tender alto voice melting over mostly mid-tempo songs of yearning ("Make It Like It Was") and emotion ("Baby Come to Me"). Sadly, it's not until *Reachin' Back* ✍✍✍ (Columbia, 1995, prod. various) that she again finds material well suited for her voice. That's mostly because the album is a collection of 1970s cover tunes from the vaults of Philly International Records (e.g., Teddy Pendergrass's "Love T.K.O" and the Delfonics' "Didn't I (Blow Your Mind This Time)."

what to buy next: Although dense with mood and jazz flavor, *Passion* ✍✍✍ (Columbia, 1993, prod. Narada Michael Walden) isn't nearly as exciting as its title implies. But it does contain two exceptional songs, "A Whole New World (Aladdin's Theme)" and "If I Could."

what to avoid: *All By Myself* 🎵🎵 (Sony/Columbia, 1987, prod. various) suffers from a lack of direction, with too many up-tempo wannabe dance tunes. It does, however, contain her breakthrough first single, "So Many Tears."

worth searching for: The tune "Men Are from Mars, Women Are from Venus," from the CD of the same name (Angel, 1997). This a companion to the popular book and it features Belle in a pleasant duet with crooner Jeffrey Osborne.

influences:

⏮ Nancy Wilson, Patti Austin, Phyllis Hyman

⏭ Rachelle Ferrelle, Toni Braxton

Franklin Paul

Jesse Belvin

Born December 15, 1933, in San Antonio, TX. Died February 6, 1960, in Fairhope, AK.

Jesse Belvin's cozy, expressive vocal style brought the influence of Nat King Cole and Billy Eckstine to '50s R&B. A talented song-writer and vocalist, he seemed destined for a career as a major crossover artist before his death in an auto accident. Belvin got his professional start at age 16, singing with Big Jay McNeely's vocal group 3 Dots & a Dash and recording give-away records for L.A.'s Dolphin Records store. (One of their locally made discs was handed out free with the purchase of a major label disc. Try something like that today.) Belvin and Marvin Phillips eventually left McNeely to sign with Specialty Records. Billed as Jesse & Marvin, they had a Top 10 R&B hit with "Dream Girl" in 1953, but the act was broken up when Belvin was drafted into the Army. (Phillips formed a new duo with Joe Josea, billed as Marvin & Johnny, who hit with "Cherry Pie" in 1954.) While in the army, Belvin met future-Penguin Curtis Williams and, with Gaynel Hodge, wrote the doo-wop anthem "Earth Angel." Upon dis-charge, Belvin signed with Modern Records and began to record as a group called the Cliques: Belvin was the only actual Clique, however—he overdubbed all four parts of the group's vocals. Surprisingly, one of these experimental recordings, "Girl of My Dreams," was a fair-sized regional hit. Belvin also recorded with the Satellites, the Sheiks, and the Californians. Belvin could sing hopped-up blues, jazz, and a little gospel, but soft, sensu-ous ballads were what brought him national fame. In 1956, Belvin wrote and recorded the romantic classic "Goodnight My Love," a major R&B hit and, like "Goodnight Sweetheart, Good-

night" by the Spaniels, a favorite sign-off tune of late night disc jockeys everywhere. After a short string of less successful records, Belvin left Modern for RCA in 1958. RCA encouraged Belvin to record more standards with lusher musical arrange-ments, but he never stopped writing. "Funny" was a small hit in 1959, but the lovingly rendered "Guess Who," which Belvin co-wrote, was his breakthrough record on the pop charts, peaking at #13. (Years later, Dean Martin cut a version almost as sweet, but not quite.) With the era of rowdy R&B over, Belvin seemed poised to accomplish great things as a pop singer. He was only 26 when he died.

what to buy: *Golden Classics* 🎵🎵🎵🎵 (Collectables, 1997, prod. various) is a 26-track compilation containing Belvin's RCA hits "Guess Who" and "Funny," plus "Goodnight My Love" and the Cliques' "Girl of My Dreams." Most of his best adult-contempo-rary offerings such as "Secret Love" are here, too.

what to buy next: *Goodnight My Love* 🎵🎵🎵🎵 (Flair, 1993, prod. various) features 25 tracks from the Modern Records era, in-cluding the title track, the Cliques' "Girl of My Dream," the Space Riders' "My Satellite," and four previously unreleased alternate takes. *Goodnight My Love* 🎵🎵🎵🎵 (Ace Records, 1997, prod. various) is an almost identical and equally fine offering. *For Sentimental Reasons* 🎵🎵🎵🎵 (Alpha Records, 1987, prod. var-ious) contains 21 recordings for Modern and Specialty. "Good-night My Love" is here. So is the Jesse & Marvin hit and some Nat King Cole-influenced pop mixed in with earlier R&B tracks. Rare, but in some catalogs.

the rest:

My Last Goodbye 🎵🎵🎵 (RCA, 1990)
Mr. Easy 🎵🎵🎵🎵 (RCA, 1996)

worth searching for: *The Blues Balladeer* 🎵🎵🎵🎵 (Specialty, 1990, prod. Art Rupe, Bumps Blackwell) is a nice blend of Belvin's early in-store demos for the Dolphin label, his sides as part of the duo Jesse & Marvin and his first solo attempts. For serious fans mostly, but worth it.

influences:

⏮ Nat King Cole, Billy Eckstine, Big Jay McNeely

⏭ Marvin Phillips, Brook Benton, Sam Cooke

Ken Burke

Eric Benet

Born October 5, 1969, in Milwaukee, WI.

Soul singer Eric Benet is one of the true finds of 1996–97. After releasing a miserably promoted self-titled album with his band

$\frac{4}{4}$ *george benson*

George Benson (© Jack Vartoogian)

Benet (EMI, 1992, out of print), his potential shines on his debut solo album *True to Myself.* Following in the footsteps of Motown artists and even Luther Vandross and Seal, Benet's knack is for passionate, romantic R&B ballads, but he's just as successful at showing off his funk side.

what to buy: *True to Myself* ♫♫♫ (Warner Bros., 1996, executive prod. Alison Ball-Gabriel; prod. Eric Benet, George Nash Jr., Demonte Posey, Roger Troutman, Christian Warren) is the soul-wrenching story of his recovery from the death of Tami Marie Stauff, his girlfriend and mother of his daughter, India. The wah-wah, synth-fuzz bass flavor of the title track leads his tribute to those who helped him—India, his family, and God. "Let's Stay Together" was featured in the Martin Lawrence comedy *A Thin Line between Love and Hate,* while "Just Friends" and "Spiritual Thang" show Benet can notch the tempo up when he wants.

influences:

◀◀ Al Green, Marvin Gaye, Luther Vandross, Seal

Christina Fuoco

George Benson
Born March 22, 1943, in Pittsburgh, PA.

The stellar career of George Benson can be traced along two distinct and equally successful planes: as a singularly phenomenal jazz guitarist and a silky-smooth pop-soul singer. Like Nat "King" Cole before him, Benson has achieved enormous crossover acclaim in both instrumental and vocal recording circles. Cutting his guitar chops as a teenager on Blue Note and Prestige sessions with organ legends "Brother" Jack McDuff and Jimmy Smith, "Bad Benson" emerged as the heir apparent to his mentor Wes Montgomery, universally regarded as the greatest of jazz guitarists. Benson was signed to Columbia in the mid-1960s by legendary record producer John Hammond, the man who also discovered electric guitar trailblazer Charlie Christian. Benson's three records for Columbia, with Hammond producing, showcase an amazingly articulate player who's finding his own style while simultaneously paying grateful homage to Montgomery. Later, Benson told interviewers that in order to ink his deal with Columbia, singing was mandatory; if that was the case, it wasn't evident on these releases. It was also during this period that Benson became the first guitar player ever to record with Columbia labelmate Miles Davis. He earned the admiration of megaproducer Creed Taylor, who signed him first to the Verve label (where he cut the jazz-funk epiphany "Giblet Gravy") and then to A&M. The latter move saw the guitarist gain more control over every aspect of his sound, most evident on the LP *The Other Side of Abbey Road*, Benson's interpretation of the entire Beatles classic. When Taylor formed his own CTI label in 1971, it was only natural for Benson to join his amazing stable of artists: CTI's talent pool was a fertile climate in which performers could cross-pollinate and flourish. Here, as both soloist and accompanist, Benson was able to collaborate with such creative equals as trumpeter Freddie Hubbard and saxman Stanley Turrentine. The Taylor-produced sessions, often featuring arrangements by Don Sebesky, were more lush and fully orchestrated than Benson's previous projects with Hammond. Benson recorded nine albums for CTI, creating an impressive body of mostly-instrumental music which cemented his reputation as one of the great jazz improvisors of all time.

In 1975, Benson was wooed and won by producer Tommy LiPuma and Warner Bros. in a deal that reportedly included the largest signing bonus ever given to a jazz artist. The results lived up to the hype: Benson and LiPuma crafted a work which became the biggest-selling jazz LP in history. *Breezin'*, punctuated by pop-oriented material and emphasizing George's trademark scat singing, set the tone for an extraordinarily successful string of pop hits. Still shifting his skills at will while bonding jazz and mainstream musical stylings, Benson continues to captivate fans with a versatility only a handful of entertainers can match.

what to buy: Benson's breakthrough CTI recording, *White Rabbit* 𝄢𝄢𝄢𝄢 (CTI/CBS, 1987, prod. Creed Taylor) displays the artist solidly in his creative element. The title track, a trademark piece of the Jefferson Airplane, receives a stunningly different treatment from the original, yet the standout cut here is the 10-minute-plus, Latin-flavored "El Mar." The disc also features one of the first recorded performances from a young jazz guitarist named Earl Klugh. The live recording *George Benson in Concert: Carnegie Hall* 𝄢𝄢𝄢 (CBS, 1976, prod. Creed Taylor) includes after-the-fact overdubs by bassist Will Lee and drummer Steve Gadd; nevertheless, the total effect is breathtaking. Hubert Laws was there onstage to add his signature flute to the mix, and Ronnie Foster's keyboards soar above all the fusion, as they did on many Benson projects of this era. An excellent

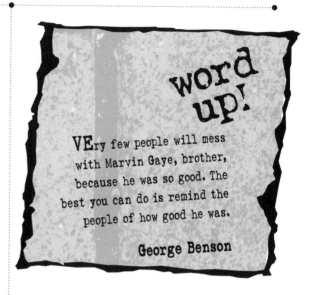

word up!

VEry few people will mess with Marvin Gaye, brother, because he was so good. The best you can do is remind the people of how good he was.

George Benson

overview of Benson's instrumental work can be found on *George Benson Verve Jazz Masters #21* 𝄢𝄢𝄢𝄢 (Verve, 1994, compilation prod. Michael Lang). The title tune from A&M's *The Shape of Things to Come* and selections from *The Other Side of Abbey Road* elevate this disc; also noteworthy is a fantastic guest appearance by Benson's former boss, Jimmy Smith, on a track entitled "The Boss." "I Remember Wes," a tribute to George's most profound guitar influence, is also included here, available for the first time on any release other than a CTI sampler.

what to buy next: *Breezin'* 𝄢𝄢𝄢 (Warner Bros., 1976, prod. Tommy LiPuma) is as big a hit album as any artist could hope to achieve. The title track, penned by soulman Bobby Womack, is one of the only instrumentals Womack has ever composed. Leon Russell's "This Masquerade" stands as the centerpiece of this LP, with Ronnie Foster and Phil Upchurch (keyboards and bass, respectively) providing seamless support. The "Dream Team" of Benson and production immortal Quincy Jones live up to all expectations on *Give Me the Night* 𝄢𝄢𝄢 (Warner Bros., 1980, prod. Quincy Jones); not only did the title song become a smash single, but the disc also gave a nod to days gone by with the exquisite cut "Moody's Mood." *Weekend in L.A.* 𝄢𝄢𝄢 (Warner Bros., 1977, prod. Tommy LiPuma) followed *Breezin'* with almost equal impact. Commercial hits were scored with its treatment of the Leiber/Stoller classic "On Broadway," as well as with the movie soundtrack theme "The Greatest Love of All."

The Best of George Benson ♫♫♫♫ (CBS, 1989, prod. Creed Taylor) and I Like Jazz: The Essence of George Benson ♫♫♫♫ (Legacy, 1993, compilation prod. John Snyder) present the cream of Benson's CTI and Columbia works, with never-before-released material on the CBS disc. Big Boss Band ♫♫♫ (Warner Bros., 1990, prod. George Benson) affirms that the guitarist will never turn his back on his jazz roots. Recorded with the Count Basie Orchestra, the project makes good on a promise Benson made to the renowned bandleader to someday join forces with his big band on an album.

what to avoid: 20/20 ♫♫ (Warner Bros., 1984, prod. Russ Titleman) doesn't remotely approach the standard of what came before or after. Bland, formulaic three- and four-minute pop tunes fall embarrassingly flat, and even guest artists such as Patti Austin, Roberta Flack, and James Taylor can't salvage the overall product.

the rest:
The New Boss Guitar of George Benson with the Brother Jack McDuff
    Quartet ♫♫♫♫ (OJC, 1964)
(With the George Benson Quartet) The Most Exciting New Guitarist on
    the Jazz Scene Today—It's Uptown with the George Benson Quar-
    tet ♫♫♫♫ (Legacy, 1966)
(With the George Benson Quartet) The George Benson Cookbook ♫♫♫♫
    (Legacy, 1966)
Body Talk ♫♫♫ (CTI/CBS, 1973)
Beyond the Blue Horizon ♫♫♫ (Legacy, 1973)
Bad Benson ♫♫♫♫ (CTI, 1974)
Good King Bad ♫♫♫ (CTI/CBS, 1975)
George Benson and Joe Farrell ♫♫♫ (CTI/CBS, 1976)
In Flight ♫♫♫♫ (Warner Bros., 1976)
Livin' Inside Your Love ♫♫♫♫ (Warner Bros., 1979)
The George Benson Collection ♫♫♫♫ (Warner Bros., 1981)
The Best ♫♫ (Rebound, 1981)
In Your Eyes ♫♫♫ (Warner Bros., 1983)
While the City Sleeps ♫♫♫ (Warner Bros., 1986)
Silver Collection ♫♫♫♫ (Verve, 1987)
Compact Jazz ♫♫♫ (Verve, 1987)
Love Remembers ♫♫ (Warner Bros., 1993)
Witchcraft ♫♫ (Jazz Hour, 1995)
The Best of George Benson ♫♫♫♫ (Warner Bros., 1995)
That's Right ♫♫♫ (GRP, 1996)
Revue Collection ♫♫♫♫ (One Way, 1996)
This Is Jazz #9 ♫♫♫♫ (Legacy, 1996)
Talkin' Verve ♫♫♫♫ (PGD/Verve, 1997)

worth searching for: The energy between Benson and good friend Earl Klugh captured on Collaboration ♫♫♫ (Warner Bros., 1987, prod. Tommy LiPuma) is truly inspirational. These are exceptional instrumentals. The Other Side of Abbey Road ♫♫♫♫

(A&M, 1995), now available only as a Japanese import, is also a brilliant example of musical interpretation.

influences:
◀◀ Wes Montgomery, Charlie Christian, Grant Green
▶▶ Earl Klugh, Stanley Jordan, Mark Whitfield

Matt Lee

Brook Benton
Born Benjamin Franklin Peay, September 19, 1931, in Camden, SC.
Died April 9, 1988, in New York City, NY.

With his satin-smooth baritone and easygoing delivery, Benton became one of the few black crooners of the 1950s to successfully cross over into the pop-rock realm. Benton cut his teeth first on the gospel circuit and later with writer/producer Clyde Otis, singing and co-writing demos for hundreds of other musicians (including Nat King Cole and Clyde McPhatter). By the late 1950s, Benton was signed by Otis to Mercury, where he put his deep, rich voice to work on lushly orchestrated R&B songs. The arrangements were the perfect showcase for Benton's intimate vocal style, and he scored an impressive 21 gold records in five years. In a move typical of record labels of this period, Mercury teamed Benton with a popular female singer—his labelmate Dinah Washington—whose easygoing voice meshed delightfully with Benton's. Together they scored a number of hits on the R&B charts—"Baby (You've Got What It Takes)," "A Rockin' Good Way"—until Washington's untimely death in 1963. Benton's encore was the 1970 hit "A Rainy Night in Georgia," an emotionally powerful deep-blues ballad that is the finest recording of his career. Although he never charted again, he remained a popular tour attraction into the early 1980s.

what to buy: Anthology ♫♫♫ (Rhino, 1986, prod. various) is a fine 24-track retrospective of Benton's long and varied career, but it loses points for excluding Benton's mid-1960s stint at RCA, where he made a number of excellent recordings of pop standards. But it does serve up the early hits—"It's Just a Matter of Time," "Kiddio," "Fools Rush In"—the duets with Washington—"Baby (You've Got What It Takes)," "A Rockin' Good Way")—and his later classic recordings for Atlantic's Cotillion label, including the hit "Rainy Night in Georgia."

what to buy next: This Is Brook Benton ♫♫♫ (BMG/RCA, 1989, prod. various) fills the gaps in Rhino's Anthology. This 20-track compilation of his 1965-66 recordings for RCA features Benton backed by a full orchestra on a wide number of pop standards

Chuck Berry (© Jack Vartoogian)

of the day, including "Call Me Irresponsible," "A Nightingale Sang In Berkeley Square," and Nat King Cole's signature tune, "Unforgettable." A pleasant reminder that Benton could croon as well as he could swing.

what to avoid: It is, in all likelihood, impossible to put out a bad album of Benton hits. So while *Greatest Hits* ⅃⅃ (WEA/Atlantic/Curb, 1991, prod. various) isn't necessarily poor, it is a lackluster sampling of Benton's catalog. Any of the other compilations listed here would be a stronger choice.

the rest:
Best of Brook Benton ⅃⅃⅃⅃ (PolyGram, 1987)
All His Best ⅃⅃⅃ (Charly Budget, 1992)
Greatest Songs ⅃⅃⅃ (WEA/Atlantic/Curb,1995)

worth searching for: *40 Greatest Hits* ⅃⅃⅃⅃ (Mercury, 1989, prod. Clyde Otis) is the best retrospective of Benton's Mercury years ever assembled. Although the album is out of print, sharp shoppers can usually locate unpurchased or used copies.

influences:
◄◄ Arthur Prysock, Frank Sinatra, Nat King Cole
►► Etta James, Ray Charles, Clyde McPhatter, Joe South

Christopher Scapelliti

Chuck Berry

Born Charles Edward Anderson Berry, October 18, 1926, in St. Louis, MO.

Next to Elvis Presley, Chuck Berry is rock 'n' roll's most influential performer—yet in terms of innovation, he stands second to no one. Berry's ringing guitar gave the nascent genre its most identifiable sound, and his wide-ranging, poetic lyrics gave it a vision. A black man with a taste for country music as well as the blues, Berry's souped-up anthems to teendom were irresistible, and because of his well-enunciated, theoretically "raceless" vocals, they were acceptable for airplay on radio stations that refused to broadcast R&B. But how the mighty have fallen. Beyond these staggering accomplishments, Berry's contributions to rock 'n' roll include sexual deviancy—he was jailed for transporting a teenaged prostitute across state lines during the early 1960s, and fined for videotaping the bathroom activities at his Wentzville, Missouri, restaurant during the early 1990s—and tax evasion, for which he was sent to prison during the late 1970s. Embittered, perhaps justifiably so, at the treatment he has received in exchange for his music, Berry for years has toured in a mercenary fashion, insisting on payment in cash, not rehearsing the pickup bands that back him, and phoning in his performances. He was the father of rock 'n' roll, and somehow turned into its deadbeat dad.

what to buy: Featuring 71 cuts on three discs, *The Chess Box* 🎵🎵🎵🎵🎵 (Chess/MCA/1988, prod. Leonard and Phil Chess) is an essential purchase for any serious fan of contemporary music. It covers all his essential hits—some of which topped the R&B charts, while others went pop—and delves into other areas, such as his blues playing, and includes some of the instrumental jams that the Chess brothers recorded surreptitiously in the studio and used to flesh out Berry's albums. Those on a tighter budget are directed to *The Great Twenty-Eight* 🎵🎵🎵🎵 (Chess, 1982, prod. Leonard and Phil Chess), which gets right down to the business of Berry's best, with no frills, though some essential material is missing. Still it's solid from start to finish.

what to buy next: Berry wasn't really an album-oriented artist, so deciding which of his individual albums to own largely depends on the hits contained therein. Of his many original classic albums, the two that remain in print are *Chuck Berry Is On Top* 🎵🎵🎵🎵 (Chess, 1959, prod. Leonard Chess) which includes "Johnny B. Goode," "Maybelline," "Roll Over Beethoven," "Carol," and "Little Queenie," which pretty much qualifies it as one of the best and most important albums ever. *New Juke Box Hits* 🎵🎵🎵 (Chess, 1961, prod. Leonard and Phil Chess) contains "Thirteen Question Method," one of Berry's slyest pieces of writing ever. For those who own the basics, *Rock 'n' Roll Rarities* 🎵🎵🎵🎵 (Chess, 1986, prod. Leonard and Phil Chess) offers a host of previously unreleased versions of Berry's hits as well as a number of stereo remixes.

what to avoid: Berry left Chess during the mid-1960s to record for Mercury, and most of the undistinguished work he turned in there is justifiably out of print. Still available, though, are *Golden Hits* **woof!** (Mercury, 1967, prod. Chuck Berry) which features not the definitive Chess versions but rerecordings of them, and *Live at the Fillmore Auditorium* 🎵🎵 (Mercury, 1967, prod. Abe Kesh) a less-than-impressive concert recording. *The London Chuck Berry Sessions* 🎵🎵 (Chess, 1972, prod. Esmond

Edwards) yielded one of Berry's biggest hits, the novelty song "My Ding-a-Ling," but the album is a marginal effort nonetheless. Finally, Berry's work has been repackaged many times on many labels. Unless you know enough to know what you're looking at, don't buy it.

the rest:
Hail! Hail! Rock 'n' Roll 🎵🎵🎵🎵 (MCA, 1987)
His Best, Volume 1 🎵🎵🎵🎵🎵 (MCA/Chess, 1997)
His Best, Volume 2 🎵🎵🎵🎵 (MCA/Chess, 1997)

worth searching for: Nearly all of Berry's original Chess albums are worth a listen. In the wake of the box set, they were reissued a few years back on MCA, but are out of print once again. Still, there may be a few lingering in used-CD bins. The latter two volumes in the Rarities' series, *More Rock 'n' Roll Rarities* 🎵🎵🎵🎵 (Chess, 1986, prod. Leonard and Phil Chess) and *Missing Berries: Rarities, Vol. 3* 🎵🎵🎵🎵 (MCA/Chess, 1990, prod. Leonard and Phil Chess) are also out of print, and die hard fans will dig 'em both.

influences:
◄◄ Muddy Waters, Louis Jordan, T-Bone Walker, Hank Williams
►► The Beatles, the Rolling Stones, the Beach Boys, Bob Dylan, and the whole of the first and second generation of rock 'n' rollers

Daniel Durchholz

Richard Berry

Born April 11, 1935, in Extension, LA. Died January 23, 1997, in Los Angeles, CA.

Richard Berry died a happy man. For most of his life he was a forgotten doo-wopper, practitioner of a musical genre that dated as fast as unrefrigerated milk. But a song he scribbled on a napkin between sets in an L.A. nightclub in 1957 became the quintessential, mindless rock 'n' roll song, a Latin-tinged blues number by the name of "Louie Louie." For years after Berry's own version sank without a trace and even after the Seattle-based Kingsmen drove FBI agents goofy trying to decipher their garbled cover, Berry received little recognition and no residuals. It took radio, "Louie Louie" marathons, and the support of lawyers, music critics, and thousands of lovers of garage rock to win Berry the royalties and honor he deserved. Stricken with polio not long after his family moved to Los Angeles during his childhood, Berry was on crutches until he was six. By high school, he was playing the ukulele and had met a pack of future doo-wop stars, among them crooner Jesse Belvin and future Coaster Cornell Gunter. The high school friends soon joined in a rotating roster of R&B groups—the Flairs, the Dreamers, the

Pharoahs—and recorded for Dolphin, Modern, and Flip. Berry was a natural songwriter, able to spin double entendres in "Jelly Roll" and satirize the mañana mentality in "Next Time." But it was his menacing, sex-dripping voice that became his stock-in-trade. Leiber and Stoller used him, uncredited, as the lead singer on the Robin's classic "Riot in Cellblock #9," and he was the nasty Henry voice in "The Wallflower," Etta James's answer song to Hank Ballard's "Work with Me, Annie." Session work kept him in clover for awhile, but by the late 50s, Berry's star was fading. He kept churning out records, among them "Louie Louie." The song is a take-off on Chuck Berry's "Havana Moon" and the calypso craze, but it was so overlooked that Flip Records released it as the B-side to a fluffy version of "You Are My Sunshine." Berry had already relinquished his rights when scuffling bands in Seattle found old copies of the song in the early 1960s. Soon, every Seattle band had "Louie Louie" in its repertoire; the Kingsmen and Paul Revere and the Raiders were the first to record it. It was the Kingsmen's noise-congested version, shouted up at a high-hung microphone, that sent dozens of FBI agents hunting around the country—and eventually interviewing a bewildered Berry—in a vain attempt to identify obscene lyrics. The song did nothing for Richard Berry until the 1980s, when new versions began to litter the landscape like forest toadstools—ranging from truly pornographic live Iggy Pop performances to kazoo band marches. Berry won back some royalties, and when the song rights were sold again in 1992, he won a substantial settlement. In recent years, he had begun to perform again, mostly in the L.A. area—a promising development cut short by his death from a heart attack.

what to buy: *Get Out of the Car* 𝄢𝄢𝄢𝄢 (Flair, 1994, prod. Joe Bihari) is funky, uptempo L.A. doo-wop and dreamy ballads, almost all written by Berry. Includes "Jelly Roll" and "The Big Break"—the sequel to "Riot in Cellblock #9"—but no "Louie Louie."

what to avoid: *Best of Louie Louie Vol. 1* 𝄢𝄢 (Rhino, 1988, prod. various) is only for "Louie" fanatics. Berry's version is here, and so is the Kingsmen's, but can you really stand a second listen to the Sandpipers or the Rice University Marching Owl Band?

worth searching for: *The Best of Flip Records, Vols. 1–3* 𝄢𝄢𝄢𝄢 (Titanic, 1997, prod. Max Freitag) documents Berry's Pharoah recordings, mixed in among tough doo-wop by Arthur Lee Maye (who went on to a career as a Baltimore Orioles slugger) and some cloying girl group ditties. "Louie Louie" is on *Vol. 3*, and on *Vol. 1* is "Have Love Will Travel," covered by the Sonics in the 1960s and 20 years later in a riotous version by Bruce Springsteen on his Tunnel of Love tour. Sound is spectacular, but these are Italian imports, so you'll have to dig.

influences:

◀◀ Jesse Belvin, Big Jay McNeely, Chuck Berry, Harry Belafonte

▶▶ The Kingsmen, the Kinks, Paul Revere & the Raiders, the Sonics, the Beach Boys, Iggy Pop, Toots and the Maytals, Bruce Springsteen, Dave Barry

Steve Braun

Big Chief

Formed 1989, in Ann Arbor, MI.

Barry Henssler, vocals; Mark Dancey, guitar; Matt O'Brien, bass; Phil Durr, guitar; Mike Danner, drums.

Paying tribute to its geographical roots, Big Chief took the hard edge of Ann Arbor legends the Stooges and the MC5 and combined it with the Motor City funk sounds of George Clinton's Parliament-Funkadelic projects. The result was an aggressive, powerful mix—as much hardcore funk as funky hardcore. Big Chief tempered its big sounds with liberal doses of humor (the members also worked on the popular underground humor/culture mag *Motorbooty*). The album *Platinum Jive*, for example, was a mock greatest hits collection with booklet pictures of the members' purported solo outings—such as Henssler's *The Sexual Intellectual*. But due to low record sales, Big Chief was dropped by Capitol Records in 1995, and the group is on hiatus while some of its members work with singer Thornetta Davis.

what to buy: *Mack Avenue Skullgame* 𝄢𝄢𝄢𝄢 (Sub Pop, 1993, prod. Big Chief, Al Sutton) is the funky "original soundtrack" to the non-existent movie of the same name. Judging by the music, the movie would have been a gritty, violent 1970s flick with plenty of females, flares and 'fros.

what to buy next: *Face* 𝄢𝄢𝄢 (Sub Pop, 1992, prod. Al Sutton, Big Chief) came out on a Seattle label in the prime days of grunge, but Big Chief rises above the fray with more of an in-your-face, heavy metal/soul melange.

what to avoid: Big Chief choked on its major label debut. The lightheartedness of the concept of *Platinum Jive* 𝄢𝄢 (Capitol, 1994, prod. Phil Nicolo, Big Chief) didn't translate to the generally heavy-handed music.

the rest:
Drive It Off 𝄢𝄢𝄢 (Get Hip, 1991)

worth searching for: Big Chief was a big supporter of vinyl and put out several limited edition singles, most of them on colored vinyl. The most coveted of these is the band's first, the "Brake Torque" b/w "Superstupid" (Big Kiss, 1989, prod. Big Chief) 7-inch on mauve and green vinyl.

influences:

◀◀ Parliament-Funkadelic, James Brown, MC5, the Stooges

Jill Hamilton

Big Daddy Kane

Born Antonio M. Hardy, September 10, 1968, in Brooklyn, NY.

Just about everything you need to know about Big Daddy Kane is summed up in the album art of his 1988 debut, *Long Live the Kane*. On the cover, the hip-hop Lothario is wearing a gold-trimmed toga and a suave but serious expression as three at-tractive and attentive women surround him, happily, dutifully of-fering their services. This represents Kane's Big Daddy Don Juan side—the one that helped him become hip-hop's first bona fide sex symbol. Inside, the same Greco-Roman scene is repeated, only now, Kane is wearing a sly grin, suggesting that he's also got a sense of humor. (Which he does, as confirmed by the "Pickin' Boogers" song he wrote for Biz Markie before kicking off his own career and, especially, by his own collaboration with Rudy Ray Moore two albums later.) And then there's the picture of a wholly confident Kane showing off his hi-top fade, thick gold ropes, massive gold rings, impressively huge gold-crown pendant, and green, yellow, red, and black African symbol. This picture reminds us that the Five Percenter Kane is assured, Afro-centric, street-savvy, and skilled—a state-of-the-art rapper who is just as capable of rhyming about his own verbal prowess (the classic "Raw") or serving up a "Word to the Mother (Land)" as he is of coming off like the smooth-operating Barry White of rap. Soon, though, Kane would become most interested in exploring his Casanova side, performing a duet with White, ditching the toga in favor of silk pajamas, posing nude in *Playgirl* and Madonna's *Sex* book, hanging out with porn stars, and other-wise becoming obsessed with his status as the sexy prince of darkness. It was no surprise, then, that the rap world quickly began to lose interest in Kane's steadily declining records, opt-ing instead to swap rumors about his sex life and related health.

what to buy: After working as a writer for the Juice Crew and DJing for the Crew's Roxanne Shante, Big Daddy Kane busted out on his own in 1987 with the roughneck anthem "Raw" and its hyperspeed vocals. That classic uptempo declaration of skills appeared a year later in remix form on the full-length debut *Long Live the Kane* 𝄢𝄢𝄢𝄢 (Cold Chillin', 1988, prod. Mar-ley Marl), an album on which Kane's hard but smooth delivery is a perfect match for producer Marley Marl's dense beats and samples. Lyrically, the effective remake "I'll Take You There" promises a fantastic voyage to a better, safer place, but Kane is

even more fantastic on the funked-up "Ain't No Half-Steppin'," spelling out in no uncertain terms who he is and why we should care: "I'm the B-I-G-D-A/Double-D-Y-K-A-N-E/Dramatic, Asiatic, not like many/I'm different, so don't compare me to another/ They can't hang, word to your mother."

what to buy next: The layered-funk production on the followup, *It's a Big Daddy Thing* 𝄢𝄢𝄢𝄢 (Cold Chillin', 1989, prod. Big Daddy Kane, Teddy Riley, Marley Marl, Easy Mo Bee, Mister Cee, Prince Paul) is top notch, with the Teddy Riley-produced "I Get the Job Done" the New Jacked highlight. But lyrically, Kane is already suffering a bit, with "Children R The Future" a well-meaning but ineffective message song and "Pimpin' Ain't Easy" simply a bad sign of things to come.

what to avoid: The weak, played-out *Daddy's Home* 𝄢𝄢 (MCA, 1994).

the rest:
Taste of Chocolate 𝄢𝄢𝄢 (Cold Chillin', 1990)
Prince of Darkness 𝄢𝄢 (Cold Chillin', 1991)
Looks Like a Job for Big Daddy Kane 𝄢𝄢 (Cold Chillin', 1993)

influences:

◀◀ Barry White, Marley Marl, Grandmaster Caz, Kurtis Blow

▶▶ Biz Markie, Three Times Dope, Def Jef, Naughty by Nature, Roxanne Shante

Josh Freedom du Lac

Big L

Born L. Coleman, in Harlem, NY.

Like Nas, O.C., and Redman, Big L initially made a name for himself by dropping fat cameo rhymes on other people's records. Representing Harlem, Big L came to prominence as a peripheral member of the Diggin' in the Crates Crew, popping up on the remix of Lord Finesse's "Yes You May" and, later, on Showbiz and A.G.'s "Represent."

what's available: With tight-knit production provided by the Diggin' in the Crates Crew, the beats on *Lifestylez Ov Da Poor & Dangerous* 𝄢𝄢𝄢 (Columbia, 1995, prod. Lord Finesse, Buckwild, Showbiz, others) are strictly East Coast, filled with tight drums and minimalistic samples. Big L's verbal delivery is sharp and snappy, but his high tenor can become a little grating at times. The album is loaded with several posse tracks, including the choice Buck Wild-produced cuts "8 Iz Enuff" (featuring eight of Big L's partners in rhyme) and "Da Graveyard" (featuring the entire Diggin' in the Crates Crew).

worth searching for: Prior to the release of *Lifestylez*, Columbia issued a DJ-only 12-inch promo of "Devil's Son."

influences:

⏪ Diamond D, Fat Joe, Kid Capri, Lord Finesse, Showbiz and A.G., Nas

Spence D.

Bigfood

See: Defunkt

Biz Markie

Born Marcel Hall, April 8, 1964, in New York City, NY.

The lispy beat-boxing giant Biz Markie burst onto the scene with a whale of a track, backing up the young Roxanne Shante in real time with his orchestra of mouth noises on 1986's "The Def Fresh Crew." He has since become the man of a thousand cameos, the patron saint of beat-collecting rap producers—the accidental martyr who changed the future of sampling. He'll likely go down as the most likable b-boy ever to spit on a mic. Originally a member of Marley Marl's Queensbridge-based Juice Crew All Stars, Biz avoided the pitched Bronx versus Queens battle between his homey M.C. Shan and KRS-1 on his way to making a number of classic tracks. When everyone went hardcore, Biz Markie kept it real *successful* by rhyming about picking his nose, going shopping at Albee Square Mall and dating ugly women. He soon bought a second house in New Jersey just to store his records. This prolific collection soon got him in deep water, though, as Gilbert O'Sullivan came calling over Biz's uncleared 1991 use of his composition "Alone Again (Naturally)" on *I Need A Haircut*. The huge settlement shook the foundations of the nascent hip-hop industry to their core. In fear of a legal reckoning, rap releases since "I Need A Haircut" have lost their scratchy old 45 funk flavor, replacing it largely with clean studio "extrapolations" or basic two-chord drones. Meanwhile, Biz continues to dig through his collection for tracks he releases on his independent 12-inch releases and keeps busy with a steady demand for cameo appearances.

what to buy: *Going Off* 𝄢𝄢𝄢𝄢 (Cold Chillin', 1988, prod. Marley Marl) is an unsung classic of the '80s—a record with much down-to-earth humor and some breakthrough beats. First the music: Marley Marl's shift from drum machines to samplers results in a sound as influential as the Bomb Squad's. By 1990, Marl's sound had transformed American R&B, British soul, and, of course, hip-hop itself. Biz Markie's beat boxing is showcased

on his first single, "Make the Music with Your Mouth Biz." But more importantly, he emerges as a hilarious, earthy storyteller, recounting adolescence on "Picking Boogers" and letting neighborhood turncoats know they've caught "The Vapors." "Nobody Beats the Biz" demonstrates the rapper's skills with some of hip-hop's most quotable lines ("Reagan is the prez but I voted for Shirley Chisholm!") and becomes a blueprint for all battle rhymes to follow.

what to buy next: *The Biz Never Sleeps* 𝄢𝄢𝄢 (Cold Chillin', 1989, prod. Biz Markie) loses some in the way of directness, as Biz takes over the production and indulges his weird side. Over the years, he's relied increasingly on re-creations and parodies of old funk and AM radio hits—the path that simultaneously lead him to create the sublime "Just a Friend" on this record and to face O'Sullivan in court. At the same time, his studious use of incredibly funky and obscure samples inspired two generations of producers, including Large Professor and DJ Shadow. All of Biz's records have moments of dusty brilliance, such as "Check It Out" or "I Told You," off *I Need A Haircut* 𝄢𝄢𝄢 (Cold Chillin', 1991, prod. Biz Markie). But, then, you have to endure karaoke session fodder like "Let Me Turn You On" off *All Samples Cleared* 𝄢𝄢𝄢 (Cold Chillin', 1993, prod. Biz Markie, Large Professor, others). Generally, though, it's not possible to lose with The Biz.

the rest:

Biz's Baddest Beats 𝄢𝄢𝄢 (Cold Chillin', 1996)

worth searching for: Biz's performance on Roxanne Shante's "The Def Fresh Crew"/"Biz Beats" (Pop Art, 1986, prod. Marley Marl) is essential. Of his numerous cameos, anything he's done with De La Soul is bound to rock your body.

influences:

⏪ Marley Marl, Big Daddy Kane, Roxanne Shante

⏩ De La Soul, Large Professor, Main Source, DJ Shadow, Jurassic 5, Del Tha Funkee Homosapien, A Tribe Called Quest, Doug E. Fresh, Kid Capri, Kwest Tha Madd Lad, Snoop Doggy Dogg

Jeff "DJ Zen" Chang

Black Moon
/Boot Camp Clik

Formed in Brooklyn, NY. Disbanded 1996.

Buckshot (born Kenyatta Blake), vocals; 5ft. Excellerator, vocals; Evil Dee (born Eward Pewgarde), DJ.

The trio garnered acclaim by creating the kind of dark, edgy soundscapes that ultimately influenced the '90s East Coast sound of artists from Mobb Deep to Notorious B.I.G. While Evil Dee and his Beatminerz production team were earning notoriety for their work with old soul breaks, Buckshot was being hailed as the next Rakim. But the group dissolved amidst legal issues in 1996, with Buckshot Shorty eventually re-emerging with the all-star Boot Camp Clik.

what to buy: When Da Beatminerz remixed the Black Moon single "I Got Cha Opin," using a strings-and-horns Barry White sample, it became an instant hit. But following one of the most inexplicable marketing trends in hip-hop, fans buying the group's debut album, *Enta Da Stage* ♫♫♫ (Wreck/Nervous, 1993, prod. Da Beatminerz), found not that hit version, but, rather, the original. Nonetheless, the album is a vivid marker of hip-hop's evolution, with "How Many MCs" and "Who Got the Props" achieving near-classic status.

what to avoid: After the group dissolved amidst legal issues, Nervous Records scrambled to capitalize on the Black Moon name, releasing the haphazard collection of remixes, freestyles, and B-sides *Diggin' In Dah Vaults* ♫♫ (Wreck/Nervous, 1996, prod. Da Beatminerz). While the album does include the "I Got Cha Opin" remix, it's hardly worth its full album price.

the rest:
Boot Camp Clik:
For the People ♫♫♫ (Duck Down/Priority, 1997)

worth searching for: The "I Got Cha Opin" remix single is essential Black Moon.

influences:
◀◀ Eric B. & Rakim, Gang Starr, EPMD, Showbiz and A.G.

▶▶ Smif-N-Wessun/Da Cocoa Brovaz, Heltah Skeltah, O.G.C., Mobb Deep, Blahzay Blahzay, Cella Dwellas

see also: *Heltah Skeltah, O.G.C.*

Jazzbo and Spence D.

Black Sheep
Formed 1983, in North Carolina.

Dres (born Andres Titus), vocals; Mista Lawnge (born William McLean), vocals.

With a sharp-witted, sardonic tongue and an against-the-grain attitude, Black Sheep was, indeed, the black sheep of the Native Tongues family that included De La Soul, A Tribe Called Quest, Jungle Brothers, and Queen Latifah. More than happy to dish out the comic diatribes, Dres and Mista Lawnge also subtly provided hip-hop with a conscience when it needed one most.

what to buy: *A Wolf In Sheep's Clothing* ♫♫♫♫ (Mercury, 1991, prod. Andres Titus, William McClean) combines playfully jazzy beats with an uncompromising, intelligent wit that's hardly been matched in hip-hop since. Dres's exaggerated gangsta introduction on "U Mean I'm Not" still stands as one of the most convincing parodies the music has ever seen, while "Flavor of the Month," "Similak Child," and "In the Meantime" have lyrics that could double as a stand-up routine. As the hit single "The Choice Is Yours" proves, Dres also has the lyrical ability to match the humor.

what to buy next: Part autobiographical and part observational, *Non-Fiction* ♫♫ (Mercury, 1994, prod. Showbiz and A.G., Andres Titus, William McClean, others) is an attempt to reveal a more serious side of the group. Although it doesn't quite match the high standards set by its predecessor, *Non-Fiction* does include some skilled writing and production work on such songs as "BBS" and "Gotta Get Up." Still, it remains worthwhile only for the true fan.

worth searching for: Talentless rapper M.C. Hammer had the gall to diss Black Sheep in song, saying: "Black Sheep, you're wack." So the group responded with "Ha," a three-and-a-half-minute B-side to "Without a Doubt" that lambastes all things Hammer.

influences:
◀◀ De La Soul, Jungle Brothers, Showbiz and A.G., Nice and Smooth

▶▶ Chi-Ali

Jazzbo

The Blackbyrds
Formed 1973, in Washington, DC. Disbanded early 1980s.

Donald Byrd, trumpet; Allan Barnes, reeds; Stephen Johnson, reeds; Barney Perry, guitar; Orville Saunders, guitar; Kevin Toney, keyboards; Wesley Johnson, keyboards; Joseph Hall, bass; Perk Jacobs, percussion; Keith Killgo, drums.

Detroit native Donald Byrd rose fast in the mid-1950s New York jazz scene. A young lion, his horn contemporaries were Lee Morgan, Freddie Hubbard, and Booker Little. By the early 1960s, Byrd was a Blue Note artist with top-selling albums. In 1968, a burned-out Byrd retreated into academia, directing Howard University's newly-formed Jazz Institute. Recognizing all the untapped student talent, Byrd decided to audition prospects from his classes for a long-term music industry workshop. Three years later, the workshop had dwindled down to six students, and the musician/educator now had his Blackbyrds. In 1974, Byrd secured the fledglings a contract with the pop Fantasy label. Shortly after, the Blackbyrds released their self-titled debut. The record fit right into the burgeoning black progressive scene (Roy Ayers, Earth, Wind & Fire, Gil Scot-Heron) of the times with a mix of both the funky ("Walking In Rhythm") and the jazzy ("April Showers"). The Blackbyrds' second release, *Flying Start*, established their jazzy party formula and it gave them an unlikely U.K. hit in "Rock Creek Park," a song that directly influenced future acts such as Incognito, Sade, and Olympic Runners. The Blackbyrds would continue for six years, touring nationally and in the U.K., and releasing four more albums and one soundtrack for *Cornbread, Earl & Me.*

what to buy: *Blackbyrds* ♪♪♪♪ (Fantasy, 1974/1996, prod. Donald Byrd) is the only Blackbyrds album still in print. It's also their best. A fine balancing act of jazz and pop-funk, Blackbyrds is a thinking man's party record.

what to buy next: *Greatest Hits* ♪♪♪ (Fantasy, 1995, prod. various) gets points for "Rock Creek Park," "Do It Fluid," and "Soft and Easy," but loses some for not including "April Showers" and "Funky Junkie." A proper anthology is in order.

influences:

◀◀ Roy Ayers, Miles Davis, Sly & the Family Stone

▶▶ Pieces of a Dream, Incognito, Groove Collective

Tom Terrell

J. Blackfoot

Born John Colbert Jr., November 20, 1946, in Greenville, MS.

If Otis Redding were alive today, he'd sound a lot like J. Blackfoot. One of the most incendiary performers in R&B today, Blackfoot draws from the same soul-stirring gospel roots as his idol, Redding, and performs with the same charismatic, fiery passion of a Southern Baptist preacher. Unfortunately, not many people know about this dynamic soul singer. Blackfoot is known among middle-aged and older blacks who make up the bulk of the traditional R&B audience today—an audience that is underserved by black radio but flocks to concerts by artists such as him, Latimore, Clarence Carter, and better-known brethren such as Bobby "Blue" Bland and Bobby Womack. Blackfoot's career has been steady, if obscure, marked by sporadic recording, constant touring, and a growing international audience that includes fans in Japan and Italy, where he is featured at an annual festival in Redding's honor. Though he's had some radio success, and better known artists have covered his songs, including rock singer Bryan Ferry, who recorded Black-

foot's hit "Taxi" for an album of covers bearing the same name. Ferry wasn't the first music notable to catch Blackfoot fever. David Porter and Isaac Hayes signed him to legendary Memphis soul label Stax on the strength of an impromptu audition he gave singing to songs on a jukebox. They built a group around him, Soul Children, which cut several moderately successful albums before the label went bankrupt. Blackfoot ventured out on his own after the group broke up with a solo debut, "City Slicker," and his first solo hit, "Taxi," which led to best new artist honors at the 1984 Soul Train Awards. With a husky tenor, an emphatic vocal style, and probing, confessional songs about love and lust, Blackfoot has carved out a niche in black music as one of its most passionate, seductive singers. Most of his albums are now out of print, but he's shopping for a label after three releases on the Platinum Blue imprint and as of this writing is working on an answer song to Patty Scott's novelty hit "Bill," called "Jill."

what to buy: Blackfoot always sings like he means it, and never is that passion more telling or convincing than on *Love-A-Holic* ♪♪♪ (Platinum Blue, 1991, prod. Homer Banks, Lester Snells), a balanced mix of his gospel, funk, blues, and soul roots that features his beautiful hit ballad "Just One Lifetime," a duet with Ann Hines.

what to buy next: *Room Service* ♪♪♪ (Platinum Blue, 1993, prod. Homer Banks, Lester Snells) is just about as good as *Love-A-Holic*, with a title song that proved a worthy successor to the more devotional "Just One Lifetime."

the rest:
Reality ♪♪♪ (Platinum Blue, 1995)

worth searching for: Only Blackfoot's Platinum Blue releases are still in print, but his work for the Memphis indie Sound Town was equally impressive, if somewhat less focused. Best among them is *City Slicker* ♪♪♪ (Sound Town, 1984, prod. Homer Banks, Chuck Brooks), which is available on import. Even though his Soul Children releases on Stax are long out of print, Blackfoot's management says that Fantasy has purchased the masters and may release the *Chronicles* (Stax, 1981, prod. various) album, a hits collection that's a pretty good overview of that overlooked soul group's talent. Keep your fingers crossed.

influences:

◀◀ Otis Redding, Wilson Pickett

▶▶ Al Green, Latimore

Doug Pullen

BLACKstreet

Formed 1993, in Virginia Beach, VA.

Teddy Riley, keyboards, vocals, voice box; Chauncey "Black" Hannibal, lead vocals; Levi Little, vocals (1993–95); David Hollister, vocals (1993–95); Mark Middleton, tenor (1995–present); Eric Williams, baritone (1995–present).

At first, fans of New Jack Swing were clamoring for a reunion of Guy, the groundbreaking hip-hop trio formed by superstar producer/composer/mastermind Teddy "Street" Riley, which split acrimoniously in 1991. Then two years later, Riley turned his attentions from building on his stack of 30-plus platinum albums working with artists ranging from Michael Jackson to the Winans and created his own new group, a quartet dubbed BLACKstreet. Now fans can't remember why they were so upset. Underscoring the title of their breakthrough 1996 LP, BLACKstreet took the New Jack hybrid of hip-hop and R&B that Riley is credited with inventing to *Another Level*, blending the vocals of three exceptional solo singers with Riley's and emphasizing a return to classic soul structures he calls "Heavy R&B." The distinctions between Riley's first group and his current outfit weren't as apparent upon the release of BLACKstreet's self-titled debut album in 1994. The new ensemble was definitely more powerful and Riley's production was typically superior, but the music itself was virtually a carbon copy of Guy's previous recordings. New Jack Swing hadn't evolved much between the end of Guy and the beginning of BLACKstreet, which proved a mixed blessing: BLACKstreet's virtually identical sound worked to gain the group immediate fans hungry for new Guy material, but did little to create an energy or identity uniquely their own. Then in 1995, singers Levi Little and David Hollister left suddenly to pursue solo careers, leaving Riley and writing partner Chauncey Hannibal as the only BLACKstreet originals until Mark Middleton and Eric Williams were tabbed as replacements. Surprisingly, the new vocal blood made the group even more formidable on *Another Level*, thanks in part to the distinctive, hypnotic groove of their #1 crossover smash "No Diggity" (street slang for "No doubt"), the single that mercifully knocked the Macarena off the top of the charts and features West Coast rapper *extraordinaire* Dr. Dre. The impact of "No Diggity" and the companion single "If You Need a Fix" (guest-starring Guns N' Roses guitarist Slash, Ol' Dirty Bastard from the rap group Wu-Tang Clan, and the ska band Fishbone) established BLACKstreet as a Teddy Riley production that can shine brilliantly on its own merits, and one of the preeminent singing ensembles in pop music today.

what to buy: *Another Level* ♫♫♫♫ (Interscope, 1996, prod. Teddy Riley) is far and away the most mature, cohesive work Riley has ever produced. Unlike Guy, which frequently sounded like a producer (Riley), a lead singer (Aaron Hall), and a supporting voice (Damion Hall) working in overlapping spheres, the revamped BLACKstreet trades on tight, inseparable Philly-style harmonies and a breathtaking diversity of layered, Jeep-friendly sounds. The music ranges from the hip-hop heaven of "No Diggity"—a song Riley penned without negativity, so that his daughter could listen to it—to Hannibal's obvious contributions on the slow jam "Don't Leave Me Girl," to the gospel-laden "The Lord Is Real (Time Will Reveal)," to a soul reworking of the Beatles "Can't Buy Me Love."

what to buy next: *BLACKstreet* ♫♫♫ (Interscope, 1994, prod. Teddy Riley) is a very good album, but it lacks the fullness, maturity, and exhilaration of *Another Level*. In this case, the first should definitely be last.

influences:

◄◄ Guy, the Temptations, the Delfonics, the O'Jays, Michael Jackson, Today

►► Jodeci, Dru Hill, 112

Andre McGarrity

Blahzay Blahzay

Formed in Brooklyn, NY.

Out Loud, vocals; P.F. Cuttin', DJ.

The Brooklyn hip-hop duo's m.o. is Classic Crooklyn: Hardcore, no-nonsense lyrics matched with big, deceptively simple beats. Indeed, Out Loud is all ruff-n-rugged vocals, while DJ P.F. Cuttin' favors piano loops, gritty basslines, shards of tweaked-out blues guitar, and turntable antics.

what's available: Propelled by a catchy hook that includes scratched snippets of A Tribe Called Quest's Q-Tip, "Danger" was a huge underground hit and gave the group a prominent—if not permanent—place on the hip-hop map. *Blah Blah Blah* ♫♫♫♫ (Fader/Mercury, 1996, prod. P.F. Cuttin', Out Loud) includes that breakthrough track, plus "Danger Part 2," which features new lyrics, a fat new beat, and a guest rhyme by Smoothe Da Hustler. Elsewhere, the verbal ruckus of "Don't Let This Rap Shit Fool You" is shrouded in eerie, mystical organ lines, and "Long Winded" undulates with weird scratchbatics.

influences:

◄◄ Black Moon, Gang Starr, Jeru the Damaja, Smoothe Da Hustler

Spence D.

Bobby "Blue" Bland (© **Jack Vartoogian**)

Bobby "Blue" Bland

Born January 27, 1930, in Rosemark, TN.

Bobby "Blue" Bland's lack of impact on white audiences during his 1960's heyday speaks more to the fickle caucasian view of bluesmen than it does his actual stature in the genre. The R&B charts and black clubs have known since the 1950s that although Bland is neither handsome, a guitar player, or even distinctly urban, his style of meaty crooning and mid-tempo sexiness put him in company with Ray Charles and Sam Cooke. His big-band brand of Texas blues allows him to inject even middling material with nearly unparalleled sweeps of emotion and delicate phrasing. Bland's sophisticated, subtle, lady-killer vocals reflect his Southern gospel beginnings as well as jazz and soul. This versatility marked his 20-year stint at Duke records, where his silky ballads influenced artists as far-reaching as Little Milton and the Band. Indeed, many lesser singers have burnt out their throats attempting Bland's "squall," a climactic strangled outburst punctuating his more dramatic moments.

Ironically, Bland started to make more of a dent in white markets with the release of his mid-1970s albums (*California Album, Dreamer*), which were clear erosions of his Duke glories. Years of ceaseless touring, health problems, and time itself have damaged and restricted his instrument, as the hit and miss quality of his recent albums indicate.

what to buy: For a single album, the early classic *Two Steps from the Blues* ♫♫♫♫ (MCA, 1961/1989, prod. Joe Scott) is a model of Bland's sizzling ballads and strikingly mature delivery. *I Pity the Fool/The Duke Recordings Vol. 1* ♫♫♫♫ (MCA, 1992, comp. Andy McKaie) captures the singer struggling to find a hit while forming the Texas blues sound that would carry him for the next two decades. The title track and "Cry, Cry, Cry" are but two gems that indicate his ease with uncluttered, divergent styles. Certainly his zenith, *Turn On Your Love Light* ♫♫♫♫ (MCA, 1994, comp. Andy McKaie) is a tour-de-force of Bland's mid-period mastery; from the aching "Share Your Love with Me" to the supercharged title track and the pop-jumpiness of

"Blue Moon," his command is undeniable, his approach intermittently gritty and smooth.

what to buy next: There's a slight dip in quality evident in *That Did It! The Duke Recordings Vol. 3* 𝄢𝄢𝄢 (MCA, 1994, comp. Andy McKaie), which documents his final years at Duke. Overall, his least-known period is more restrained and the songs lack the impact of his seminal work; but there are plenty of rewarding moments to be unearthed here.

what to avoid: The injustice inherent in a singer of Bland's stature singing Rod Stewart's "Tonight's the Night" makes *Sad Street* 𝄢 (Malaco, 1995, prod. W. Stephenson, T. Couch) that much more difficult to swallow. Never mind that his voice is a ravaged hulk by this point.

the rest:
Best of Bobby "Blue" Bland 𝄢𝄢𝄢𝄢 (MCA, 1972)
His California Album 𝄢𝄢𝄢 (MCA, 1973/1991)
Dreamer 𝄢𝄢𝄢 (MCA, 1974/1991)
(With B.B. King) *Together For the First Time . . . Live* 𝄢𝄢𝄢𝄢 (MCA, 1974)
(With B.B. King) *Together Again . . . Live* 𝄢𝄢𝄢𝄢 (MCA, 1976/1980)
Here We Go Again 𝄢𝄢 (MCA, 1982)
Members Only 𝄢𝄢 (Malaco, 1985)
After All 𝄢𝄢 (Malaco, 1986)
Blues You Can Use 𝄢𝄢 (Malaco, 1987)
First Class Blues 𝄢 (Malaco, 1987)
Midnight Run 𝄢𝄢𝄢 (Malaco, 1989)
Portrait of the Blues 𝄢𝄢 (Malaco, 1991)
Years of Tears 𝄢𝄢 (Malaco, 1993)
(With B.B. King) *I Like to Live the Love* 𝄢𝄢𝄢 (MCA, 1994)
You've Got Me Loving You 𝄢𝄢 (MCA, 1995)
How Blue Can You Get?: Classic Live Performances 1964–1994 𝄢𝄢𝄢 (MCA, 1996)

worth searching for: Any vinyl copies of anything from his Duke heyday should be seized with a firm grip, whether it's *Call On Me* 𝄢𝄢𝄢𝄢 (MCA, 1963), *Ain't Nothing You Can Do* 𝄢𝄢𝄢𝄢 (Duke, 1964), or *Here's the Man* 𝄢𝄢𝄢𝄢 (Duke, 1962). They're all stellar and should be treated as such.

influences:
◄◄ Ray Charles, Sam Cooke, Johnny Ace, B.B. King
►► The Band, Little Milton, Mighty Sam McClain

Allan Orski

Mary J. Blige
Born Mary Jane Blige, January 11, 1971, in New York, NY.

Mary J. Blige was crowned "The Queen of Hip-hop Soul" after her crossover success with the much-heralded debut *What's the 411?* Influenced by R&B stalwarts such as Al Green, the O'-Jays, and Donny Hathaway, Blige was 16 when she cut a demo tape version of Anita Baker's "Caught Up in the Rapture." It made its way into MCA Records' A&R department, which quickly signed her to a deal. Their excitement was justified when Blige's *What's the 411?* sold more than three million copies and scored a #1 hit with "Real Love." Blige hasn't changed her approach since; she's still blending hip-hop with classic R&B elements, though her follow-up albums haven't proven as cohesive or successful as *What's the 411?*

what to buy: The multi-platinum debut, *What's the 411?* 𝄢𝄢𝄢 (Uptown, 1992, Dave "Jam" Hall, Devante Swing, Mark Morales, Sean "Puffy" Combs, Tony D, others), strikes a delicate balance between hip-hop and soul, especially on the hits "Reminisce" and "Real Love."

the rest:
My Life 𝄢𝄢𝄢 (Uptown, 1994)
Share My World 𝄢𝄢𝄢 (MCA, 1997)

influences:
◄◄ The O'Jays, Al Green, Donny Hathaway, Roberta Flack, Ann Peebles, Salt-N-Pepa
►► Janet Jackson, Robin S., Missy Misdemeanor Elliot

Christina Fuoco

Blood of Abraham
Benyad (born Benjamin Mor), vocals; Mazik (born D. Saevitz), vocals.

As children of Israel, Benyad and Mazik are modern-day descendants of Abraham. They're justly proud of their heritage, with Jewish themes and references spread judiciously through their music and lyrics. But there are other influences and references, too: Dr. Suess, Joseph Campbell, and Nietzsche's *Genealogy of Morals,* not to mention mentor Eazy-E.

what's available: You know there's something different going on when an album's liner notes explain the Five Stages of Wisdom. (In seeking wisdom, the first stage is silence, the second is listening, the third remembrance, the fourth practicing, the fifth teaching.) But while *Future Profits* 𝄢𝄢𝄢 (Ruthless/Relativity, 1993, prod. Bret "Epic" Mazur, others) places a heavy-handed emphasis on knowledge and self-respect, you can't ignore the music, what with its cholesterol-heavy beats, catchy loops, and subtly progressive shifts. "This Great Land Devours" is a loping, flute-infused jam that samples Musical Youth and Melvin Van Peebles. "Stick to Your Own Kind" is awash in weird, psychedelic horns and guitar. "That Ol' Dupree Shit" is a gritty, dusted hip-hop blues. Perhaps the most radical song, though, is "Niggaz and Jewz (Some Say Kikes)," in which Benyad and Mazik wreck some racial epithets with the help of Eazy-E and Willonex, providing a tentative answer to the question about the relationship between Jews and Blacks in hip-hop.

influences:

◀◀ 3rd Bass, Goats, KMD

Spence D.

Bloodstone
Formed 1962 as the Sinceres, in Kansas City, MO.

Harry Williams, vocals, percussion; Charles Love, vocals, guitar; Charles McCormick, vocals, bass (1962–82, mid-1990s–present); Roger Durham, vocals, percussion (died 1973); Willis Draffen Jr., vocals, guitar, piano; Melvin Webb, drums (died 1973); Kenneth Smith, vocals (1962–mid-1980s); Eddie Summers, vocals, drums (1973–mid-1980s).

With only one hit—1973's "Natural High"—that made significant impact on the pop charts, Bloodstone has never enjoyed the props it deserves as a versatile, multi-faceted unit that managed to make current-sounding music through the soul-drenched 1960s, the funky early 1970s, and the disco era. Bloodstone's members wrote most of the material, too, though it worked with a variety of producers at the myriad labels it recorded for. Formed from two different groups in Kansas City, the Sinceres gigged around the city—from barbeque joints to hot clubs—until a 1968 trip to Los Angeles secured them their first recording contract and a permanent move to the West Coast. Before talking off for London, the group's manager suggested a name change to something more current and valid, so the Sinceres became Bloodstone. An opening spot for Al Green in London earned the group a new major label deal, and Bloodstone hit pay dirt with the *Natural High* album. The band earned a good live reputation—Williams would come out dressed in a blond wig and a skirt to sing Martha & the Vandellas' "Heat Wave"—but somehow it got lost amidst the 1970s other powerhouse R&B bands. After suffering the deaths of Webb (from diabetes) and Durhan (from internal injuries suffered in a fall from a horse in England), Bloodstone soldiered into the early 1980s—recording for labels such as London, Motown, and T-Neck—but slowly faded away. The group became more active during the early 1990s, however, though its latest release, *The Ultimate Collection*, is an unnecessary batch of re-recorded hits.

what to buy: *The Very Best of Bloodstone* ♪♪♪♪ (Rhino, 1997, prod. various) is a strong compilation with all the key songs, though it could stand a few more selections from *Natural High*.

what to buy next: *Natural High* ♪♪♪ (London, 1973/Rhino, 1996, prod. Mike Vernon, others) is Bloodstone's best individual album, a broad-reaching effort that includes funk, pop, psychedelic touches, a nod to old-time rock 'n' roll on a medley of "Bo Diddley" and "Diddley Daddy," and even a cover of "Little Green Apples." The reissue includes several bonus tracks.

what to avoid: *The Ultimate Collection* ♪♪ (I.T.P., 1996, prod. Charles Crews, Bloodstone). A comeback based on re-recordings of previous hits doesn't bode well for the group's future.

the rest:

Unreal ♪♪♪ (London, 1973/Rhino, 1996)

worth searching for: On *Lullaby of Broadway* ♪♪♪ (Decca U.K., 1976/T-Neck, 1985, prod. Mike Vernon), Bloodstone takes on show tunes with both respect and spirited irreverence—a balance few R&B acts have been able to achieve in taking on the standards.

influences:

◀◀ The Temptations, the Spinners, Rare Earth, Al Green

▶▶ B.T. Express, Lakeside, the Deele

Gary Graff

Kurtis Blow
Born Kurtis Walker, August 9, 1969, in New York, NY.

Blow is certainly not one of the most talented or distinctive rappers the music world has ever seen. But he still owns an important place in hip-hop history, namely as one of the genre's most accomplished and influential pathfinders. A part of the early wave of late-'70s/early-'80s Coke La Rock-inspired MCs, the Harlem artist had a number of hip-hop firsts: first artist to land a major-label deal (with Mercury Records, whose stable he never left after his 1979 signing); first rapper to earn gold certification for a 12-inch single ("The Breaks" in 1980); and the first bona fide rap superstar. Blow was also one of the genre's most directly influential lyricists; among those his simple but resonant style touched were LL Cool J, Kool Moe Dee, and Joseph Simmons, who called himself "Son of Kurtis Blow" before changing his moniker to Run. Blow's time in the spotlight didn't last long, though. He was gradually surpassed both commercially and stylistically by his hip-hop disciples, and his recording career came to a halt in 1988 after his stale-sounding eighth album, *Back By Popular Demand*, was released to little demand. Blow hasn't disappeared totally, though, working as a DJ on a Los Angeles radio station, promoting occasional old-school rap concerts, serving as the de facto narrator in the rapumentary, *Rhyme and Reason*, and, in the fall of 1997, compiling the three-volume *History of Rap* series for Rhino Records. In 1996, Blow also saw his music resurrected, thanks to Nas's hit cover of "If I Ruled the World." Imagine that.

what's available: All eight of Blow's studio albums are out of print. Then again, as with most early rappers, Blow was a singles-oriented artist whose full-length records were typically uneven collections highlighted by a couple of hits (but otherwise bogged down with forgettable filler). As such, the only Blow album you'll ever need to hear is *The Best of Kurtis Blow* ♪♪♪♪ (Mercury, 1994, prod. Kurtis Blow, others). All of Blow's seminal singles and B-sides are represented, from "Basketball" and "Christmas Rappin'" to "Hard Times" (hip-hop's first piece of social commentary). Also here is "If I Ruled the World," an optimistic and uplifting song that features the punchiest vocal performance of Blow's career. Perhaps to remind you that filler was such a major part of early hip-hop, the 14-track collection does contain a single gratuitous entry: The late-career, defiantly rap-free falsetto ballad "Daydream," which deservedly was never a hit.

influences:

◀◀ Coke La-Rock, Melle Mel, DJ Hollywood, Pete DJ Jones, Lovebug Starski

▶▶ LL Cool J, Run-D.M.C., Kool Moe Dee, Big Daddy Kane

Josh Freedom du Lac

The Blues Brothers

Formed 1977, in New York, NY.

Jake Blues (a.k.a. John Belushi), vocals (died 1982); Elwood Blues (a.k.a. Dan Aykroyd), harmonica, vocals.

During *Saturday Night Live*'s heyday, pals and blues enthusiasts Belushi and Aykroyd came up with a revue-style act to perform on the show. Backed by authentic soul veterans (including Booker T. & the MG's alums Steve Cropper and Donald "Duck" Dunn), the two adopted dark-suited, sunglassed personas and performed enthusiastic (if not always accomplished) renditions of R&B classics. The Blues Brothers became a popular recurring segment on SNL and even toured behind its million-selling albums; in 1980, director John Landis turned the concept into a hit film. Belushi's death from a drug overdose in 1982 ce-

mented the Blues Brothers as cult legends. Aykroyd used his Elwood persona to promote his House of Blues nightclub chain and plans to re-launch the Blues Brothers on film and record with actors James Belushi (John's brother) and John Goodman.

what to buy: *The Definitive Collection* ♪♪♪♪ (Atlantic, 1992, prod. various) contains all the favorites, including their popular versions of Sam and Dave's "Soul Man," the Spencer Davis Group's "Gimme Some Lovin'" and the quirkier numbers sung by Aykroyd.

the rest:

Briefcase Full of Blues ♪♪♪ (Atlantic, 1978)
Made in America ♪♪♪♪ (Atlantic, 1980)
The Blues Brothers ♪♪♪♪ soundtrack (Atlantic, 1980)
The Best of the Blues Brothers ♪♪♪♪ (Atlantic, 1980)

influences:

◀◀ Ray Charles, James Brown, Sonny Boy Williamson, the Blues Project, Stax-Volt

▶▶ Blues Traveler, Treat Her Right

Todd Wicks

The Bobbettes

Formed 1956, in Harlem, NY.

Reather Dixon, lead vocals; Emma Pought, second lead; Jama Pought, soprano; Laura Webb, tenor; Helen Gathers, alto.

In the early 1960s girl groups became a big deal, but in the mid-1950s they were as scarce as female pro hoop teams. One night in 1956, five girls between the ages of 11 and 13 showed up to compete on Amateur Night at the Apollo Theater under the name The Harlem Queens. A talent manager named James Dailey got wind of them, but thought Harlem Queens a bit too racy for a group of children, so they were renamed The Bobbettes and went on to make their mark in music history as the first R&B girl group to claim a legitimate hit on the rock 'n' roll charts. After landing a deal with Atlantic Records, their first release, in June, 1957, was "Mr. Lee," a catchy riff about a teacher who some of the girls knew but didn't particularly like. By July, "Mr. Lee" was a Top 10 pop hit and made it to #1 on the R&B charts. The Bobbettes never came close to a song of that magnitude again, though the sequel "I Shot Mr. Lee" made it to the middle of the pop lists three years later. They backed Johnny Thunder on his 1963 single "Loop De Loop," and later that year recorded "Love That Bomb" for the Peter Sellers movie *Dr. Strangelove*. In all, they released 28 singles for 10 different labels over a period of 17 years and remained active performers into the 1970s, but precious little of their work remains available today.

what's available: You can hear "Mr. Lee" on the superior compilation *The Doo Wop Box II: 101 More Vocal Group Gems from the Golden Age of Rock 'n' Roll* 🐾🐾🐾🐾 (Rhino, 1996, prod. various).

influences:

◀◀ LaVern Baker

▶▶ The Chantels, the Shangri-las, the Marvelettes, the Supremes, Martha Reeves and the Vandellas, the Pointer Sisters

Michael Kosser

Angela Bofill

Born 1954, in New York, NY.

Though sometimes classified as a jazz singer, Angela Bofill's recorded output all lies firmly within the realm of slick pop, though at both the beginning of her professional career (with Dizzy Gillespie, Cannonball Adderley, and others) and then after it had waned she performed in genuine jazz contexts. The Hispanic multi-instrumental prodigy grew up in the Bronx and performed on the Latin music scene, most notably with the salsa band led by Ricardo Morrero known simply as the Group. Flutist Dave Valentin of that band introduced her to the owners of GRP, who launched her career with an album that made the jazz charts. After her second album for GRP, she disputed her royalties and subsequently her contract was moved to Arista, which promoted her solely as an R&B artist and similarly focused the production on her albums. Though she never broke through to the mainstream, she had a number of R&B hits, and her mid-1980s albums charted consistently. She had the greatest success with Narada Michael Walden, who, like Bofill, steered jazz chops in a commercial direction. By the latter part of the decade, however, her sound was no longer current, and later efforts to update it came off awkwardly. Finally on her Shanachie album she returned to her old style, at least sounding comfortable again.

what to buy: *Best of Angela Bofill (1978–1985)* 🐾🐾🐾 (Arista, 1986, prod. various), in trying to represent her entire GRP/Arista career, ends up with too much of her mediocre work, but it's all that's available at the moment from that period, and it does have some of the good Narada Michael Walden material.

what to buy next: *Love in Slow Motion* 🐾🐾🐾 (Shanachie Cachet, 1996, prod. Rex Rideout, Angie B.) is Bofill's most recent album and marks a return to her old virtues, if in somewhat muted form, with a mellow jazziness that has come back in style at some radio formats if not on the singles charts.

what to avoid: *Intuition* 🐾 (Capitol, 1988, prod. Norman Connors, others) flitted desperately from cliche to cliche, both lyrically and sonically, as Bofill's producers weighed her down with inferior songs except for the old Gino Vanelli hit "I Just Wanna Stop"—dire straits indeed when this is the high point.

the rest:

Angie 🐾🐾 (GRP/Arista, 1978)
Angel of the Night 🐾🐾 (GRP/Arista, 1979)
Something About You 🐾🐾🐾 (Arista, 1981)
Let Me Be the One 🐾🐾🐾 (Arista, 1984)
Tell Me Tomorrow 🐾🐾🐾 (Arista, 1985)
Love Is in Your Eyes 🐾🐾 (Capitol, 1991)
I Wanna Love Somebody 🐾🐾 (Jive, 1993)

worth searching for: Of Bofill's out-of-print material, a pair of 1983 albums stand out as worthy of reissue. *Too Tough* 🐾🐾🐾🐾 (Arista, 1983, prod. Narada Michael Walden, Angela Bofill) flaunts her four-octave vocal range on a mix of pretty ballads and slightly uptempo tracks mildly inflected with dance production effects on Walden's half of the album (originally Side 1 of the LP). Bofill wrote or co-wrote all the tunes on her side, which is gentler and falters on the sappy closing track "Rainbow Inside My Heart," complete with kiddie chorus. *Teaser* 🐾🐾🐾🐾 (Arista, 1983, prod. Narada Michael Walden, Denny Diante) is energetic enough that the dated production doesn't dampen the fun. It helps that Walden and various songwriting collaborators (including Bofill) came up with plenty of massive hooks for Bofill to belt out.

influences:

◀◀ Dionne Warwick, Minnie Riperton

▶▶ Whitney Houston, Mariah Carey

Steve Holtje

Gary U.S. Bonds

Born Gary Anderson, June 6, 1939, in Jacksonville, FL.

Regardless of what Bruce Springsteen may think, it just may be that Gary U.S. Bonds is little more than a cipher, a singer with a gritty and soulful, but ultimately unexceptional voice, who happened to be in the right place at the right time—twice. Bonds's first 15 minutes of fame came thanks to producer Frank Guida, who put Anderson in front of a mic, multitracked his voice and added a party ambience to songs such as "New Orleans," "Quarter to Three," and "School Is Out." His fame slipped away almost as fast as it came, and Bonds hit the oldies circuit, where Springsteen—who frequently performed "Quarter to Three" in concert—found him, got him a record deal, and co-produced a pair of albums for him. Except for brief appearances on albums by Springsteen cohort Steven Van Zandt, Bonds slipped into relative obscurity once again.

what to buy: *The Best of Gary U.S. Bonds* ♫♫♫ (Rhino, 1990, prod. various) collects the hits from Bonds's early days. If you and your friends are mindful of rock 'n' roll's past, you couldn't ask for a better party tape. Confusing as it may be, another album called *The Best of Gary U.S. Bonds* ♫♫♫ (EMI, 1996, prod. Bruce Springsteen, Miami Steve Van Zandt) completes the story, collecting the cream from his latter-day period, including "Rendezvous," "This Little Girl," and "Out of Work," and padding it out with live versions of "Quarter to Three" and "New Orleans."

the rest:
Dedication ♫♫♫ (EMI America, 1981)
On the Line ♫♫♫ (EMI America, 1982)

influences:
◀◀ Fats Domino, Little Richard

▶▶ Bruce Springsteen, Southside Johnny, Peter Wolf

Daniel Durchholz

Bone Thugs-N-Harmony
Formed in Cleveland, OH.

Layzie Bone (born Steven Howse), vocals; Krayzie Bone (born Anthony Henderson), vocals; Flesh-and-Bone (born Stanley V. Howse), vocals; Wish Bone (born Byron McCane), vocals; Bizzie Bone (born Charles Scruggs), vocals.

Although Bone Thugs-N-Harmony have distinguished themselves with their penchant for the supernatural and strange, their lives were characterized by very real ghetto struggle. Their break came when they decided on a whim to leave Cleveland for Los Angeles—a trip that led the group to future mentor Eazy-E, who eventually turned Bone into mega-platinum stars. Before making their leap of faith to L.A., the tight-knit rappers (Layzie and Flesh are brothers, Wish is a cousin, and Bizzie and Krayzie are friends) had never strayed from East 99th and St. Clair Streets in Cleveland in a transient teenhood riddled with bouts of drug-selling and homelessness.

what to buy: The group's first single, "Thuggish Ruggish Bone," on Eazy-E's Ruthless Records became a surprise breakout hit on The Box pay-video outlet and helped bring the EP, *Creepin On Ah Come Up* ♫♫♫ (Ruthless, 1994, prod. Eazy-E, Yella, DJ Uneek, Rhythm D), a triple-platinum payday. The record is standard street fare (slow, Dre-influenced beats and gospel-style singing, with lyrics that range from revenge murders to Ouija boards), characterized only by unique, rapid-fire, singsongish rhyme flows. Certainly, the Freestyle Fellowship stylized this type of rhyming better, but there's no doubt that Bone rode it to the most commercial success. And within months, imitators had sprung up across the country. *E. 1999 Eternal* ♫♫♫♫ (Ruthless, 1995, prod. DJ Uneek) opens the music up considerably, allowing Bizzie Bone and Krayzie Bone, in particular, to shine. The singles are excellent: "Crossroads" is yet another "dead homies" track, but it's deeply felt and well-performed; and "1st of Tha Month," with its humorous and light angle, might have been the song that led morally bankrupt conservatives to champion welfare reform. Elsewhere, titles like "Die Die Die" tell the whole story.

what to avoid: *Faces of Death* **woof!** (Stoney Burke, 1993, prod. Bone) was the group's first independent release, and it shows none of the promise Eazy-E was later able to hear in their auditions.

the rest:
(As Flesh-N-Bone) *T.H.U.G.S.—Trues Humbly Gatherin' Souls* ♫♫♫ (Def Jam, 1996)
Mo Thugs: Family Scriptures ♫♫♫ (Relativity, 1996)
The Art of War (Ruthless, 1997) N/A

influences:
◀◀ Geto Boys, Freestyle Fellowship, Tung Twista, Eazy-E

▶▶ Crucial Conflict

Jeff "DJ Zen" Chang

Boogie Down Productions /KRS-One
Formed 1986, in South Bronx, NY.

KRS-One (born Lawrence Kris Parker), vocals; Scott La Rock (born Scott Sterling; died August 25, 1987, Bronx, NY), DJ.

Though its nebulous performing roster has changed numerous times over the last 11 years, BDP has always found its creative focal point in the person of KRS-One. As a homeless teenager on the streets of New York, Lawrence Kris Parker spent his time studying philosophy and religion and honing his rapping skills. It was at a homeless shelter where Parker met social worker Scott Sterling, who also happened to be the DJ Scott La Rock. Calling himself KRS-One (or, Knowledge Reigns Supreme Over Nearly Everyone), Parker formed Boogie Down Productions in 1986 with La Rock. With the help of the Ultramagnetic MC's Ced Gee, the two delivered their now-classic debut, *Criminal Minded*, the following year and were immediately hailed as the new leaders of the rap world. *Criminal Minded* was one of the first true hardcore East Coast albums and the first to combine reggae dancehall rhythms with bare-boned New York rap sounds. (It was also one of the first great diss records, thrashing M.C. Shan and Marley Marl with the one-two punch "South Bronx" and "The Bridge Is Over" simply because the Queens-based rapper and DJ had dared to assert that their burough—and not the birthplace, the Bronx—was hip-hop central. Bad mistake.) Though the modern-day connotations of the "hardcore" tag are less than flattering, *Criminal Minded* was infused with affirmative messages (relatively speaking), historical information, and pleas for positive change. However, in the summer of 1987, La Rock was killed, and his death hit KRS-One hard. The murder undoubtedly inspired the rapper's obsession with blending strident hip-hop and educational data; in later years, KRS even coined the phrase "Edutainment." La Rock's death, too, played a hand in KRS-One's dedication to the Stop the Violence Movement, which culminated in "Self-Destruction," hip-hop's more locally focused answer to "We Are the World." Today, KRS-One is still widely respected in the hip-hop world—and (to a lesser degree) in non-rap circles—as a source of scholarly wisdom. That image is so firmly entrenched that the artist with the oratory gift has engaged in debates with internationally recognized philosophers, earned an honorary college degree and even provided social commentary on TV talk shows.

what to buy: The definitive BDP/KRS-One album remains *Criminal Minded* ♪♪♪♪♪ (B Boy, 1987, prod. KRS-One, Scott La Rock, Ced Gee). Filled with such strident songs as "The P Is Free" (does drug commentary get any better than "The girlies are free/'Cause the crack costs money"?) and the title track, the album is a heady stew of funk, reggae, hip-hop, and South Bronx attitude. There's even an AC/DC riff ("Dope Beat"), as well as a lyrical disclaimer ("We're not promoting violence/ We're just having some fun") that seems to set up the next album, *By All Means Necessary* ♪♪♪♪ (Jive/RCA, 1988, prod. KRS-One). This recording ranks second primarily because it was released after *Criminal Minded*. But it still

may be the best pure example of hip-hop "edutainment" ever produced, with KRS-One and Co. dropping serious knowledge and beats from the first track ("My Philosophy") through the 10th ("Necessary"). Hip-hop with a conscience; what a concept.

what to buy next: A decade after the release of *Criminal Minded,* KRS-One hasn't lost a step. While hundreds of other hip-hop artists have watched time, trends, and, ultimately, dreams of career longevity pass them by, the solo *I Got Next* ♪♪♪♪ (Jive, 1997, prod. KRS-One, Showbiz, DJ Muggs, others) is decidedly contemporary, boasting all the latest in production styles—and anti-materialism messages. "I don't wear Versace/I wear DJs out quickly at the party," hip-hop's Jesse Jackson says, serving up lyrics that might sound trendy rolling off the tongue of a less-credible MC, what with rap's anti-Big Willie revolution in full swing. Coming from KRS-One, though, it's hard to argue. KRS is also a gifted live performer. Bursting with energy, yet compellingly intimate, *Live, Hardcore & Worldwide* ♪♪♪♪ (Jive/RCA, 1991, prod. Dwayne Sumal) is the only live hip-hop album that matters. It's also a semi-best-of collection, featuring many of the better songs from the first half of KRS-One's productive career.

what to avoid: *Sex and Violence* ♪ (Jive/RCA, 1992, prod. BDP) is a forgettable release which proves that knowledge isn't always power.

the rest:

Ghetto Music: The Blueprint of Hip-Hop ♪♪♪♪ (Jive/RCA, 1989)
(Stop the Violence Movement) *Self Destruction* ♪♪♪♪ EP (Jive/ RCA, 1989)
(Ms. Melodie) *Diva* ♪♪ (Jive/RCA, 1989)
Edutainment ♪♪♪ (Jive/RCA, 1990)
(Harmony) *Let There Be Harmony* ♪♪♪♪ (Virgin, 1990)
(D-Nice) *Call Me D-Nice* ♪♪♪ (Jive/RCA, 1990)
(H.E.A.L.) *Civilization vs. Technology* ♪♪♪ (Elektra, 1991)
The Return of the Boom Bap ♪♪♪♪ (Jive/RCA, 1994)
KRS-One vs. M.C. Shan: The Battle for Rap Supremacy ♪♪♪♪ (Cold Chillin', 1996)
(Heather B.) *Takin' Mine* ♪♪♪ (EMI, 1996)

influences:

◀◀ Grandmaster Flash & the Furious Five, Treacherous Three, Run-D.M.C., Schoolly D, Ice-T

▶▶ Public Enemy, N.W.A., Rage Against the Machine, Arrested Development, Digable Planets, Schoolly D, Ice-T, X-Clan, Channel Live, Mad Lion

Andre McGarrity and Josh Freedom du Lac

Boogiemonsters

Formed 1990, at Virginia State University.

Mondo, vocals; Vex, vocals; Myntric, vocals (1990–95); Yodared, vocals (1990–95).

The Boogiemonsters came together in 1990 while the four MCs were attending Virginia State University, but it wasn't until a scholastic sabbatical and a move to New York four years later that the underappreciated group introduced itself to the hip-hop world.

what to buy: *Riders of the Storm: The Underwater Album* ♫♫♫ (Pendulum/EMI, 1994, prod. Boogiemonsters, others) is a deft mixture of liquescent grooves and smooth, mysterious lyrical flows. The underground hit, "Recognized Thresholds of Negative Stress," burbles with ethereal shifts and loping basslines, and the group's metaphysical philosophy is further documented on "Altered States of Consciousness." But it's the dark, ominous mood of "Mark of the Beast" and the thoroughly haunting "Old Man Jacob's Well" that pack the greatest impact. The latter is an apocalyptic, graphically mesmerizing tale of an elderly child molester/serial killer that's told from the vantage point of both Old Man Jacob and his next young victim over misty basslines and serpentine guitar. Brilliant.

what to buy next: At first listen, *God Sound* ♫♫♫ (EMI, 1997, prod. Boogiemonsters, others) isn't nearly as compelling as the debut. But the album grows on you, thanks to subtly hypnotic production and quality rhymes. Now a duo, the Boogiemonsters are gravitating toward the religious side of life, with song titles such as "The Beginning of the End," "Behold a Pale Horse," and "Sodom & Gomorrarah" reflecting this newfound slant. The group also redefines "MC" as "Mental Calisthenics" on the song of the same name and brings Bahamadia in for an exercise in cameo lyricism on "Say Word."

influences:

◀◀ De La Soul, Digable Planets, Gravediggaz, OutKast, Pharcyde, Roots, A Tribe Called Quest

▶▶ Bahamadia

Spence D.

Booker T. & the MG's

Formed 1961, in Memphis, TN.

Booker T. Jones, organ; Steve Cropper, guitar; Al Jackson Jr., drums; Lewis Steinberg, bass (1961–63); Donald "Duck" Dunn (1963–present); Willie Hall, drums (1975–77); James Gadson, drums (1994); Steve Potts, drums (1994).

This racially integrated quartet mapped out the instrumental blueprint of 1960s Southern soul not only on deceptively simple ensemble instrumental sides, but as the house band at Stax/Volt recording studios. The four original musicians appear to interact instinctually, stitching together tight, intricate musical lines with evident ease. The band's 1962 Top 10 hit "Green Onions" put the small regional soul label on the nationwide map, setting the stage for a soul music uprising that echoes ever more resonantly through the years. At the core of this signature sound was the collaborative backbone of Booker T. and the MG's, whose members often ended up as part-writers of the many classics they created in the studio with giants like Otis Redding ("Dock of the Bay") or Albert King ("Born Under a Bad Sign"). On their own, the band members sculpted a trademark sound—a churning, throbbing tidy knot of sound topped by Jones's mellifluous organ and tacked together by Al Jackson Jr.'s left foot—a style they became comfortable and conversant enough with to stretch out considerably on later albums. In the wake of Stax's dissolution in the early '70s, the band also disintegrated. Jones moved to the West Coast and produced hit Willie Nelson albums. Cropper and Dunn joined the Blues Brothers. Al Jackson Jr., who carried on the tradition playing on Al Green recordings, was murdered in his home in 1975. The other three members began performing together again in 1990, and have appeared most notably as the house band at the Bob Dylan tribute at Madison Square Garden in 1992, backing Neil Young on a 1994 summer tour, and at the 1995 Rock 'n' Roll Hall of Fame concert in Cleveland. But none of the MG's many latter-era accomplishments match the towering contributions of the Memphis recordings.

what to buy: The band's fourth album, *Hip Hug-Her* ♫♫♫♫ (Stax, 1967/Rhino, 1992 prod. Jim Stewart), brims with confidence and seamless instrumentals—from succulent originals like the haunting title track, the rousing "Double or Nothing," or the cool "Slim Jenkins' Joint," to radically transformed covers like "Groovin'" and "Sunny."

what to buy next: The jazzy *Melting Pot* ♫♫♫ (Stax, 1983, prod. Booker T. & the MG's) and the tour-de-force instrumental rendering of the Beatles *Abbey Road* titled *McLemore Avenue* ♫♫♫ (Stax, 1971, prod. Booker T. & the MG's), named after the street where the Stax studios were located in Memphis, capture the mature, confident band stretching its sound into new, rich realms.

what to avoid: The reincarnation's major label outing, *The Way It Should Be* ♫♪ (Columbia, 1994, prod. Booker T. Jones), suffers from over-directing by the Columbia A&R department and a palpable lack of spirit.

the rest:
Green Onions ♫♫♫ (Atlantic, 1962)
Soul Dressing ♫♫♫ (Atlantic, 1965)
And Now ♫♫♫ (Atlantic, 1966)
In the Christmas Spirit ♫♫♫ (Atlantic, 1966)
The Mar-Keys and Booker T. & the MG's: Back to Back ♫♫♫ (Atlantic, 1967)
Doin' Our Thing ♫♫♫ (Atlantic, 1968)
Soul Limbo ♫♫♫ (Stax, 1968/1991)
Booker T. Set ♫♫♫ (Stax, 1969/1987)
The Best of Booker T. & the MG's ♫♫♫ (Atlantic, 1984)
The Best of Booker T. & the MG's ♫♫♫♪ (Stax, 1986)

worth searching for: While the two volumes of the 1967 European tour by the Stax/Volt entourage, *The Stax/Volt Revue: Volume One—Live In London* ♫♫♫♫ (Atlantic, 1967, Prod. Jim Stewart) and *The Stax/Volt Revue: Volume 2—Live In Paris* ♫♫♫ (Atlantic, 1967, Prod. Jim Stewart) capture Booker T. & the MG's serving as the protean house band for the Memphis soul caravan, *The Complete Stax/Volt Singles 1959–1968* ♫♫♫♫ (Atlantic, 1991, prod. various) is really nothing more than a nine-disc tribute to the greatest soul accompanists of all-time.

influences:
◀◀ The Mar-Keys, Cannonball Adderley

▶▶ Creedence Clearwater Revival, Elvis Costello & the Attractions

see also: *The Mar-Keys, the Blues Brothers*

Joel Selvin

Chuckii Booker
Born 1966, in Los Angeles, CA.

A crack multi-instrumentalist, Chuckii Booker showed skill as both a guitarist and drummer by age 14. He was soon signed to a production deal by Barry White, an arrangement that ended when White refused to release an album Booker had recorded. Gigging with bands in the L.A. area, Booker quickly developed a reputation as a producer and session player, working with acts such as Troop, Kool & the Gang, and Lalah Hathaway. By 1989 he was signed to Atlantic, turning in a record mostly featuring his own playing, with some able assistance by his piano-playing mother on one track. He served as musical director for

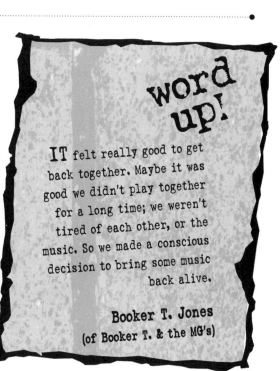

word up!

IT felt really good to get back together. Maybe it was good we didn't play together for a long time; we weren't tired of each other, or the music. So we made a conscious decision to bring some music back alive.

Booker T. Jones
(of Booker T. & the MG's)

Janet Jackson's "Rhythm Nation" tour before releasing his second record, another solo tour de force that found a little more success on the R&B charts—but not enough to keep him from working sessions with everyone from Go West to David Cassidy.

what to buy: Booker's sophomore effort, *Niice 'n' Wiild* ♫♫♫♫ (Atlantic, 1992, prod. Chuckii Booker) features all of the stuff that made his debut so impressive—lots of funky grooves, soaring vocals and inspired instrumental turns. He also has some impressive songs, including the #1 R&B hit "Games" (co-written with Gerald Levert) and the textured, atmospheric groove "Love Is Medicine."

the rest:
Chuckii ♫♫♫♪ (Atlantic, 1989)

worth searching for: Booker has played on albums for everyone from En Vogue to Philip Bailey and his godfather, Barry White, but one of his coolest appearances comes on pop band Go West's *Indian Summer* ♫♫♫ (EMI, 1993, prod. Peter Wolf), spicing up the track "I Want You Back" with an incendiary keyboard solo and some spot-on bass synth work.

influences:

◀◀ Prince, James Brown, Marvin Gaye

▶▶ Dallas Austin, Teddy Riley

Eric Deggans

James Booker

Born December 17, 1939, in New Orleans, LA. Died November 8, 1983, in New Orleans.

James Booker stood in for Huey "Piano" Smith on tour and Fats Domino in the studio, and the Clash covered his theme song, "Junco Partner," on *Sandinista!* There are many authorities who gladly testify to his amazing abilities, from Dr. John to Harry Connick Jr. In a city noted for great piano players, Booker was the greatest—if judged on sheer technique, not on hits or personal stability. Born into a musical family, Booker had an amazing musical memory and excelled at classical piano (giving recitals at age six) but was seduced by boogie woogie. By the age of 11 he was playing regularly on a local radio station, and at 14 he cut his first single, "Doing the Hambone/Thinkin' About My Baby," for Imperial Records, produced by Rock & Roll Hall of Famer Dave Bartholomew—who gave Booker session work based on his ability to copy anybody's style instantly. But though he had a hit with his 1960 record "Gonzo," made singles for a variety of labels during the 1950s and 1960s (often under aliases), and was a sideman on records by everyone from Joe Tex, Bobby Bland, and Lloyd Price, to Maria Muldaur, the Doobie Brothers, and Ringo Starr, Booker didn't record an album of his own until 1976, partly because he spent the middle of the 1960s in prison. He went through periods of drug abuse; though New Orleans guitarist Earl King backs up Booker's rationalization that he wasn't an addict because his metabolism allowed him to quit with no ill effects. After his prison stint (for drugs), Booker did a little session work and then more or less retired. He reappeared in 1975 for a European package tour which garnered him recording offers. He played regularly in New Orleans thereafter, until his death.

what to buy: Every Booker album is great and precious and full of awe-inspiring keyboard feats, but *New Orleans Piano Wizard: Live!* ♫♫♫♫ (Rounder, 1981, prod. Bernard Henrion) wins top recommendation for the crucial repertoire it includes: "Come Rain or Come Shine," "Please Send Me Someone to Love," and especially his diametrically opposed favorites "On the Sunny Side of the Street" and the heartfelt "Black Night." His vocals have a narrow stylistic range but are utterly appropriate. *Spiders on the Keys* ♫♫♫♫ (Rounder, 1993, prod. Scott Billington, John Parsons) draws on hours and hours of recordings at the Maple Leaf Bar to present a fascinating picture of Booker as strictly a pianist. His left hand is so strong that he makes even the Beatles' "Eleanor Rigby" totally *fonky.*

what to buy next: *Junco Partner* ♫♫♫♫ (Hannibal, 1976, prod. Joe Boyd, John Wood) was Booker's first album and one of only two studio albums. It's crucial not only for "Black Minute Waltz" (showing his classical side) and a great "Junco Partner" but also for George Winston's liner notes, analyzing the pianistic and compositional particulars of each performance. The other studio effort is *Classified* ♫♫♫♫ (Rounder, 1982, prod. Scott Billington, John Parsons), the only album available in the U.S. on which Booker recorded with a band (including saxophonist Alvin "Red" Tyler, long Booker's bandleader); the album's highlight is his tune "Classified," which Dr. John covered. For the feeling of an all-stops-out club date, *Resurrection of the Bayou Maharajah* ♫♫♫♫ (Rounder, 1993, prod. Scott Billington, John Parsons) can't be beat. The rowdy, rollicking set (at 76+ minutes the most generous in his catalog) of Maple Leaf Bar performances has lots of vocal tunes (everything from "St. James Infirmary" to "Bony Maronie") and a total lack of inhibition or playing it safe.

worth searching for: Any of Booker's original vinyl singles, which carry collector's values—and fetch collector's prices, for sure.

influences:

◀◀ Huey "Piano" Smith, Tuts Washington, Professor Longhair, Jelly Roll Morton, Frederic Chopin, Louis Moreau Gottschalk, Meade Lux Lewis

▶▶ Little Richard, Dr. John, Allen Toussaint, Henry Butler, George Winston

Steve Holtje

Boo-Yaa T.R.I.B.E.

Formed early 1980s, in Los Angeles, CA.

Godfather Rock "Te" (born Ted Devoux), band leader, vocals; Ganxsta Ridd, lead rapper; Monsta "O, " bass, vocals; Kobra, beats, vocals; others.

Treated largely as a novelty act by the record industry during its career, the Samoan Boo-Yaa T.R.I.B.E. stands as a testament to the West Coast's diversity and hip-hop's multi-cultural promise. For years, the musicians had played American gospel songs in their church on weekends, sneaking in funk numbers by Rare Earth or Slave whenever their father, the head minister, wasn't around. When hip-hop moved west in the early '80s, the six Devoux brothers made an early impact on the young Los Angeles rap scene, first as hardcore gangbangers (whose nickname fast became slang for the murderous snap of a gun), then as poplockers and breakdancers—and finally as one of the West Coast's first rap bands. By 1986, the Boo-Yaa T.R.I.B.E. was touring internationally and opening for James Brown, on the way to Lollapalooza and other festival stages. Critics never failed to stereotypically comment on the brothers' imposing physicality—without saying a word about their musicianship, let alone the gripping story of Islander immigrants adjusting to the hard inner-city streets. And so it would go.

what to buy: *New Funky Nation* 𝄞𝄞𝄞 (Island, 1990, prod. Joe "The Butcher" Nicolo, the Dust Brothers, Tony G., Boo-Yaa T.R.I.B.E.) presents an energetic musical mix of samples, live instrumentation, sing-along harmonies, and chants, and the lyrics are correspondingly upbeat in comparison to the more bloody street tales of the group's L.A. homies Ice-T and Ice Cube. The album is a fair representation of the Boo-Yaa's concert sound, if not of the members' street life.

what to buy next: As the years passed, two of the Devoux brothers were shot up in separate drivebys, and only one survived. The group itself became a casualty of corporate mergers and executive gutlessness. In 1992, after Los Angeles cops brutally shot the group's friends Pouvi and Italia Tualaulelei in their backs, the Boo-Yaa T.R.I.B.E. turned in its most harrowing tracks ever, including "Shoot Em Down" (which documented the case) and "MODC (Millions of Dead Cops)." Their timing could not have been worse: Time Warner had just sacked Ice-T for his "Cop Killer" track, and many record labels began to screen rap records for potentially inflammatory lyrics. When corporate executives at Disney, which owned the group's new label, Hollywood, heard the tracks, they stopped the album from being released. Years later, some of the tracks recorded during this period were released overseas on *Doomsday* (Bullet Proof, 1994). None of this music, though, has seen the wide domestic distribution it rightfully deserves. Boo-Yaa has since returned to releasing records on its own independently distributed label. *Occupation Hazardous* 𝄞𝄞 (Samoan Mafia/First Kut Music, 1995, prod. Monsta "O") is a much darker set of stories, although the music does not sustain the same level of tension and engagement.

worth searching for: *Rumours of a Dead Man* 𝄞𝄞𝄞 (Hollywood BASIC, 1993, prod. Boo-Yaa T.R.I.B.E.) is a three-song single that shows a growing maturity, as the group comments on the irrationality of gang violence.

influences:

◀◀ Ice-T, N.W.A.

Jeff "DJ Zen" Chang

Bo$$

Born Lichelle Laws, 1973, in Southfield, MI.

Manufacturing her steel-hard mettle on the outskirts of the Motor City, Bo$$ roared onto the rap scene in 1993 with her debut album, *Born Gangstaz*. Despite her upbringing as a middle-class Catholic schoolgirl, the rapper managed to convince the hip-hop establishment that she was every inch the streetwise sistah straight out of the 'hood. That image was undoubtedly fostered by her recording formula (smoothly pitting a penetrating, Detroit-brewed lyrical flow against slick, first-class West Coast production) as well as her intense hardcore posturing and a gutsy frankness that hit listeners right between the ears.

what's available: Instead of inventing a completely fictitious bad-girl persona, Bo$$ proclaims her personal reality by acknowledging her prep-school past and suburban roots on *Born Gangstaz* 𝄞𝄞𝄞 (Def Jam/CHAOS/Columbia, 1993, prod. Erick Sermon, Jam Master Jay, DJ Quik, others), a solid effort that finds her spitting out gangsta rhymes with venom and electricity on such songs as "Deeper" and "Recipe for a Hoe." She makes it clear that she's only in it for the money, and where she comes from really doesn't matter. Honesty never sounded so unrefreshing. Of course, Bo$$ may have gotten the fast $$ she desired, but she didn't remain in charge for long, quickly disappearing from the rap scene.

influences:

◀◀ MC Lyte, Queen Latifah, N.W.A., Too $hort, Yo Yo

▶▶ Lady of Rage, Da Brat, Lil' Kim, Foxy Brown, Conscious Daughters

Andre McGarrity

Earl Bostic

Born April 25, 1913, in Tulsa, OK. Died October 25, 1965, in Rochester, NY.

Saxophonist Earl Bostic started in jazz, and his minimalist approach and subtle phrasing were at odds with the "busier" playing styles of other swing-era musicians. But it was well-suited for R&B, to which Bostic turned during the 1950s as a band leader and performer. He did most of his key recording for King Records, including the 1951 smash "Flamingo" and other well-known songs such as "Temptation" and "You Go to My Head." A heart attack slowed him during the early 1960s, and the jazz influence crept back into his music, though he never lost the honking R&B edge that helped establish his reputation.

what to buy: *The Best of Earl Bostic* 𝄞𝄞𝄞𝄞 (Deluxe, 1956/King, 1989, prod. various) and *All His Hits* 𝄞𝄞𝄞𝄞 (King, 1996, prod. various) are pretty much what the titles describe and are both good introductions to this under-celebrated talent.

what to buy next: *Dance Music from the Bostic Workshop* 𝄞𝄞𝄞𝄞 (King, 1988) focuses on the funkier selections in Bostic's catalog.

the rest:
For You 𝄞𝄞𝄞 (King, 1956)
Let's Dance with Earl Bostic 𝄞𝄞𝄞𝄞 (King, 1957)
Alto Magic in Hi-Fi 𝄞𝄞𝄞𝄞 (King, 1958)
Blow a Fuse 𝄞𝄞 (Charly)

worth searching for: The out-of-print *25 Years of Rhythm and Blues Hits* 𝄞𝄞𝄞𝄞𝄞 (King, 1960) is the best compilation of Bostic material, if you can find it.

influences:
◀◀ Lionel Hampton, Charlie Creath, Edgar Hayes
▶▶ John Coltrane, Stanley Turrentine, King Curtis

Gary Graff

Jean-Paul Bourelly

Born November 23, 1960, in Chicago, IL.

Jazz fans know the guitarist Jean-Paul Bourelly for his work on Miles Davis, McCoy Tyner/Elvin Jones, Muhal Richard Abrams, and Cassandra Wilson albums (he co-produced Wilson's *Dance to the Drums Again*), while R&B/hip-hop fans have heard him on records by Jody Watley, D.J. Jazzy Jeff & Fresh Prince, Bel Biv Devoe, and Charles & Eddie. Unbelievably, he's only been able to put out albums on German and Japanese labels (Enemy at least has a New York office). He has combined the influences of a number of greats to invent his own distinctive, uniquely rich guitar sound. Mixing jazz/blues/rock playing and his gruffly soulful vocals with funk and hip-hop rhythms, often with his group Blue Wave (sometimes Bluwave) Bandits, he builds dense, complex music he calls

"New Breed Funk Jazz." Bassists Melvin Gibbs (Rollins Band), Darryl Jones (Rolling Stones), and Me'shell NdegeOcello all passed through his groups prior to their more famous gigs, and "Kundalini" Mark Batson of the hip-hop group Get Set VOP plays Sly Stonesque keyboards and sometimes raps for Bourelly's Blue Wave Bandits.

what to buy: The seven live tracks (plus a previously unreleased studio effort) on *Fade to Cacophony* 𝄞𝄞𝄞𝄞 (Evidence, 1996, prod. Jean-Paul Bourelly, Kazunori Sugiyama) provide a cross-section of his first three albums with added concert vigor, and this U.S. release may be the easiest to find. *Saints & Sinners* 𝄞𝄞𝄞𝄞 (DIW, 1993, prod. Jean-Paul Bourelly, co-prod. Kazunori Sugiyama) distills the core of his stylistic fusion on "Got to Be Able to Know" and "Rumble in the Jungle," while "Muddy Waters (Blues for Muddy)" is a slow, simmering update of the blues. Many tracks, especially "Skin I'm In," show his matter-of-fact socio-political/racial consciousness without being preachy.

what to buy next: *Trippin'* 𝄞𝄞𝄞𝄞 (Enemy, 1991, prod. Jean-Paul Bourelly) features some of Bourelly's best guitar playing, focusing on his integration of lead and rhythm, and some of his tighter material. The lush, intensely lovely instrumental rave-up "Love Crime" is especially memorable.

what to avoid: *Tribute to Jimi* 𝄞𝄞𝄞 (DIW, 1994) covers the music of Hendrix better than many such tributes as far as authenticity goes (both vocally and instrumentally), but its very closeness to Hendrix's style forces inevitable comparisons that Bourelly's doomed to lose, though he does add his own stamp to the music.

the rest:
(With Ayibobo) *Freestyle* 𝄞𝄞𝄞 (DIW, 1993)
Blackadelic-Blu 𝄞𝄞𝄞 (DIW, 1994)

worth searching for: Bourelly's debut as a leader, *Jungle Cowboy* 𝄞𝄞𝄞𝄞 (JMT, 1987, prod. Stefan Winter, Jean-Paul Bourelly), is his best album and definitely the easiest way in for the uninitiated, so it's unfortunate that JMT's U.S. distributor, Verve, doesn't make it available. Its deep funk/blues hybrid with jazzy overtones predates Bourelly's incorporation of hip-hop beats, with late jazz sax great Julius Hemphill guesting. Bourelly plays extensively on jazz violinist Sonya Robinson's out-of-print *Sonya* 𝄞𝄞𝄞𝄞 (Columbia, 1987, prod. Jean-Paul Bourelly) and wrote most of the material. It lets Bourelly stretch out more than usual (even playing keyboards), in more of a jazz vein than his own records; this mostly instrumental album contains some of his prettiest writing.

influences:

⏮ Muddy Waters, Jimi Hendrix, Wes Montgomery, Jimmy Page, John McLaughlin, Sly & the Family Stone, Frank Zappa, Miles Davis

⏭ Dave Fiuczynski

see also: *Defunkt*

Steve Holtje

David Bowie

Born David Robert Jones, January 8, 1947, in London, England.

David Bowie was an indispensable voice of the 1970s, pursuing a rare compositional and emotional balance as he adopted a variety of guises and experimented with different styles of music. While most of his early records laid the blueprint for modern alternative rock music, some of Bowie's most successful forays were into R&B environs, reaching his peak in the field with the soul-tinged *Young Americans* album. The rhythmic undercurrents stayed with Bowie throughout most of his work that followed. During the 1980s, Bowie homogenized this sound for a series of straightforward pop records that scored him plenty of hits despite less than satisfying artistic results. His most recent work signals an artist who is desperately flailing to stay hep. During the past few years Bowie has moved from avant noise with Tin Machine to moody industrial with *Outside* to drum 'n' bass with *Earthling*.

what to buy: On *Young Americans* 🎵🎵🎵🎵 (RCA, 1975, prod. Tony Visconti), Bowie delves into soul grooves with dazzling results. It includes such sensuous groovers as the title track and "Fame." *Hunky Dory* 🎵🎵🎵🎵 (RCA, 1971, prod. Ken Scott) is a similarly moving affair, featuring meditative melodies and lush string arrangements for "Changes," "Oh, You Pretty Things," and "Life On Mars?" *The Rise and Fall of Ziggy Stardust and the Spiders from Mars* 🎵🎵🎵🎵🎵 (RCA, 1972, prod. David Bowie, Ken Scott) remains Bowie's crowning achievement, containing his finest fusion of concept and songs ("Moonage Daydream," "Suffragette City," and "Starman"). Driven by exquisite melodies, stellar playing, and the songwriter's singular vision it is one of the finest albums of the 1970s. Its follow-up, *Aladdin Sane* 🎵🎵🎵🎵 (RCA, 1973, prod. David Bowie, Ken Scott), pushes the boundaries of pop music by prominently incorporating jazzy pianos in the rock 'n' roll mix. Written during Bowie's "Ziggy Stardust" tour, the album focuses on the singer's peculiar view of life in America, as captured in songs like "Drive-In Saturday" and "Panic In Detroit."

what to buy next: To get a taste of Bowie's experimental side, *Station To Station* 🎵🎵🎵🎵 (RCA, 1976, prod. David Bowie, Harry Maslin), is a vital starting point. It marks Bowie's first real attempts at deconstructionism—which, in turn, led to the Bowie/Brian Eno collaborative trilogy of *Low*, *Heroes*, and *Lodger*. It includes ace pop tunes like "Golden Years" and "Wild is the Wind." Bowie also released several greatest hits packages throughout his career, which serve as excellent primers to the dynamic span of his work. *The Singles 1969–1993* 🎵🎵🎵🎵 (Ryko, 1993, comp. Jeff Rougvie) is the best, a double-album set that touches on every crucial move forward. As for the Bowie/Eno collaborations, *Heroes* 🎵🎵🎵🎵 (RCA, 1977, prod. David Bowie, Tony Visconti) is the highlight, incorporating some of Bowie's finest melodies into the atmospheric soundscapes. The title track is stellar, as are "Beauty and the Beast" and "Joe the Lion." Bowie's debut, *Space Oddity* (originally released as *Man of Words, Man of Music* 🎵🎵🎵🎵) (RCA, 1969, prod. Tony Visconti, Gus Dudgeon), still stands as a masterpiece. Psychedelic, innocent, and suggestive, it captures just the right balance of wide-eyed wondering and young man coming of age, particularly on such stirring songs as "Letter To Hermione" and "An Occasional Dream."

what to avoid: Most of David Bowie's latter recordings are criminally bland. The biggest culprit of this lot was the insipid *Never Let Me Down* **woof!** (EMI, 1987, prod. David Bowie, David Richards), known best for its listless single "Day In Day Out." Equally vulgar was the "Glass Spider" tour that promoted it.

the rest:

The Man Who Sold the World 🎵🎵🎵🎵 (RCA, 1970)
Pin Ups 🎵🎵🎵 (RCA, 1973)
Diamond Dogs 🎵🎵🎵🎵 (RCA, 1974)
David Live 🎵🎵🎵 (RCA, 1974)
Low 🎵🎵🎵🎵 (RCA, 1977)
Stage 🎵🎵🎵 (RCA, 1977)
Lodger 🎵🎵🎵 (RCA, 1979)
Scary Monsters 🎵🎵🎵 (RCA, 1980)
Ziggy Stardust: The Motion Picture 🎵🎵🎵 (RCA, 1983)
Let's Dance 🎵 (EMI, 1983)
Tonight **woof!** (EMI, 1984)
Sound + Vision 🎵🎵🎵🎵 (Rykodisc, 1989)
(With Tin Machine) *Tin Machine* **woof!** (EMI, 1989)
(With Tin Machine) *Tin Machine II* **woof!** (Victory, 1991)
(With Tin Machine) *Tin Machine Live: Oy Vey, Baby* **woof!** (Victory, 1992)
Black Tie White Noise **woof!** (Savage, 1993)
The Buddha of Suburbia **woof!** (Virgin, 1993)
Santa Monica '72 🎵🎵🎵 (Griffin, 1995)
Outside **woof!** (Virgin, 1995)

Earthling 🎜🎜🎜 (Virgin, 1997)

The Deram Anthology 1966–1968 🎜🎜🎜 (Deram/Polydor, 1997)

worth searching for: The deluxe edition of *Ziggy Stardust . . .* 🎜🎜🎜🎜 (Rykodisc, 1990, prod. David Bowie, Ken Scott) gives this album a royal treatment with superior sound quality, bonus tracks, and a lavish booklet to enhance an already marvelous listening experience.

influences:

◀◀ Pink Floyd, the Yardbirds, the Who, the Kinks, Easybeats

▶▶ Duran Duran, Suede, the Smiths, Smashing Pumpkins, Nirvana

Aidin Vaziri

The Box Tops

Formed 1967, in Memphis, TN.

Alex Chilton, vocals, guitar; Tom Boggs, drums; Rick Allen, bass; Gary Talley, guitar; Bill Cunningham, organ. Also, studio players: Reggie Young, guitar; Bobby Wood, piano; Bobby Emmons, organ; Tommy Cogbill, bass; Gene Chrisman, drums.

The Box Tops existed more as a tool for the production-songwriting team of Chips Moman and Dan Penn than it did as an actual band. Tool or not, though, it is the Box Tops who are now often credited as among the first white groups to assimilate Southern R&B into what's now commonly referred to as "blue-eyed soul." After the breakaway success of its first single, "The Letter" in 1967, the group (excepting Chilton) was replaced by studio musicians. The gruff and gravelly singer was a first-class belter with a flair for high drama and a budding sense of emotional unrest, despite his young age (16). The combination of Penn and Moman's heavy production and Chilton's own voice struggling to find a place in it lent the seemingly lightweight material more than a hint of urgency. Although a handful of singles rushed onto the charts, Chilton finally balked for good in 1970. The high sweet voice Chilton has sung with since then (with Big Star and his unruly solo work) leaves little doubt as to how much the Box Tops was really an extension of Penn after all.

what to buy: By far the best compilation on the market, *The Best of the Box Tops* 🎜🎜🎜🎜 (Arista, 1996, comp. Bob Irwin) has better sound and liner notes and makes the others seem skimpy by comparison. For his part, Chilton runs flat-out, infusing what at first glance seem like toss-offs ("The Letter," "Cry Like a Baby," and "Soul Deep") with a gripping delivery that elevates the singles into airy classics.

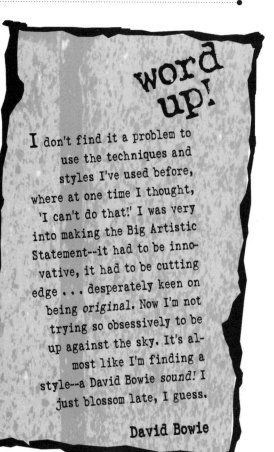

word up!

I don't find it a problem to use the techniques and styles I've used before, where at one time I thought, 'I can't do that!' I was very into making the Big Artistic Statement--it had to be innovative, it had to be cutting edge . . . desperately keen on being original. Now I'm not trying so obsessively to be up against the sky. It's almost like I'm finding a style--a David Bowie sound! I just blossom late, I guess.

David Bowie

the rest:

The Ultimate Box Tops 🎜🎜 (Warner Special Products, 1987)

influences:

◀◀ Otis Redding, the Beatles, Wilson Pickett, Percy Sledge

▶▶ Daryl Hall and John Oates, Big Star, Dan Penn, Neil Diamond

Allan Orski

Boyz II Men

Formed 1988, in Philadelphia, PA.

Wanya Morris, vocal; Michael McCary, vocals; Shawn Stockman, vocals; Nathan Morris, vocals.

After joining forces at Philadelphia's High School of Creative and Performing Arts, this quartet was discovered by New Edition's Michael Bivins, who helped them create a hook-laden fusion of East Coast swing, R&B, and pop. It was a hit from the start; the debut, *Cooleyhighharmony*, sold more than nine million copies. Following a record-setting hit "End of the Road" (from the *Boomerang* soundtrack), the Boyz showed that success was no fluke, jettisoning Bivins and releasing the monster-selling (though artistically lackluster) *II*, which sold more than 13 million copies and out-dueled Whitney Houston for the longest consecutive run at #1 on the *Billboard* charts with "I'll Make Love to You." Mixing traditions from 1950s doo-wop and 1960s Motown vocal groups and blending them with contemporary sounds, the Boyz seem to have hit on a formula that will make them timeless enough to continue on their commercial role well into the next century.

what to buy: On *Cooleyhighharmoney* 🎵🎵🎵 (Motown, 1993, prod. Dallas Austin, the Characters, Troy Taylor, Charles Farrar), the fun, carnivalesque feeling of "Motownphilly," the brooding sensuality of "Uhh Ahh," and the ballad "It's So Hard to Say Goodbye to Yesterday" are convincing tributes to the singing groups of the 1950s–1970s.

the rest:
Christmas Interpretations 🎵🎵 (Motown, 1993)
II 🎵🎵 (Motown, 1994)
Remix Collection 🎵🎵 (Motown, 1995)
Evolution 🎵🎵🎵 (Motown, 1997)

worth searching for: The soundtrack to the movie *Boomerang* 🎵🎵🎵 (LaFace, 1993, prod. various) contains "End of the Road" which broke Elvis Presley's record for the most weeks spent at #1 on the charts.

influences:
⏪ The Penguins, the Drifters, the Temptations, the Four Tops, Harold Melvin & the Blue Notes, the Dramatics, New Edition

Christina Fuoco

The Brand New Heavies

Formed 1986, in London, England.

Simon Bartholomew, guitars; Jan Kincaid, drums; Andrew Levy, bass; N'Dea Davenport, vocals (1989–96); Seidah Garrett, vocals (1996–present).

When a band relies on fashion runways and multi-screened video monitors in trendy mall clothing stores as the primary outlets for its music, it is obviously walking on dangerous ground. The Brand New Heavies have had an intimate under-

standing of this equation, and they have done a wonderful job of adapting at every turn. They were there with their electric grooves and love beads at the beginning of the decade when the British club scene started blowing up with bands such as Soul II Soul and Happy Mondays. When wine bar culture became the hip new scene, they donned the goatees and flares, and aligned themselves with outfits like James Taylor Quartet and Jamiroquai, turning out a wiry blend of jazz, soul, salsa, and house influences. In Britain, the Brand New Heavies gained recognition with a batch of club singles. In America, their success was instant and stellar; snatched up by hip Los Angeles indie Delicious Vinyl, their fresh sound and vision lent itself to a classic, self-titled debut album.

what to buy: Calling upon the cathartic talents of vocalist N'Dea Davenport—Donna Summer reborn in a plastic dress—and tightening up its sound, this formerly fey acid jazz band unleashed a string of hits that included "Never Stop," "Dream Come True," and "Stay This Way" on its stellar debut album *The Brand New Heavies* 🎵🎵🎵🎵 (Delicious Vinyl, 1991, prod. the Brand New Heavies). The London-based band bravely carries the torch of disco and funk into the 1990s.

what to buy next: The Brand New Heavies got in on hip-hop's early 1990s renaissance by pairing their electric sound with a collective of exalted rap stars, including Gang Starr, the Pharcyde, and Black Sheep, on *Heavy Rhyme Experience: Vol. 1* 🎵🎵🎵 (Delicious Vinyl, 1992, prod. the Brand New Heavies), the first successful building block for the too trendy jazz-hop genre. *Brother Sister* 🎵🎵🎵 (Delicious Vinyl, 1994, prod. the Brand New Heavies), meanwhile, marks an exuberant return to the Brand New Heavies' funk roots. With Davenport again handling the vocal duties, the album is full of spontaneity, lift, and live, impeccable mechanism, spanning moody airs like "People Giving Love" to bluesy stompers such as "Fake" to soul-to-the-bone earth shakers like "Mind Trips."

what to avoid: *Shelter* **woof!** (Red Ant, 1997, prod. the Brand New Heavies) lacks the livewire energy of the Brand New Heavies' earlier albums. Seidah Garrett, who was previously known for dueting with Michael Jackson on "I Just Can't Stop Loving You," lacks both the sexual charisma and frisky intensity of her predecessor. As a result, the songs on this effort suffer from tepid mid-tempo grooves and lackluster vocal dynamics, seeing the band move away from cutting-edge funk styles and toward the dreaded adult-contemporary market.

worth searching for: *Original Flava* 🎵🎵🎵 (Acid Jazz, 1994, comp. the Brand New Heavies) is a compilation of some of the band's earlier instrumental work. It features their only single from a misfired Chrysalis deal ("Got to Give") and some of the prototype material from their earlier incarnation as the K-Collective ("Rest of Me" and "Reality").

influences:

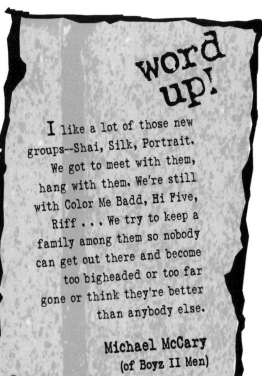 The JBs, Roy Ayers, Donna Summer, Average White Band, Sly & the Family Stone

▶▶ Jamiroquai, James Taylor Quartet, Incognito, Maxwell

Aidin Vaziri

Brand Nubian

Formed 1990, in New Rochelle, NY.

Grand Puba Maxwell (born Maxwell Dixon), vocals (1990–91); Derrick X/Sadat X (born Derek Murphy), vocals; Lord Jamar (born Lorenzo DeChalus), vocals; DJ Alamo, DJ (1990–91); Sincere Allah (born Terence Perry), DJ (1991–93).

Brand Nubian took the hip-hop community by storm when it emerged in 1990, deftly mixing Five Percent Nation diatribe with playful sex rhymes and bouncy production to create a unique blend of music that stimulated both the mind and the booty. While Derrick X and Lord Jamar were both equally competent on the mic, it was Puba who earned all the attention for his sing-song turns on *One for All*, a classic album that industry observers swear would have sold in the high hundreds of thousands—if only everybody in New York hadn't bought a bootlegged copy instead of an official release. Puba subsequently left the group (with Alamo in tow) to pursue a solo career, and pundits predicted the demise of Brand Nubian was imminent. They were wrong, though, as Derrick X (now Sadat X), Lord Jamar, and long-time friend, Sincere, successfully regrouped. All for one, indeed.

what to buy: On *One for All* 🎵🎵🎵🎵 (Elektra, 1990, prod. Grand Puba Maxwell, Brand Nubian), the dichotomy of Puba's sly sexual innuendo and Derek X's high-pitched nasal timbre and militant outbursts—coupled with impeccable production—makes for a bona fide rap classic. "Feel So Good" bobs and weaves with joyful exuberance, while the pointed political nature of "Concerto In X Minor" lays the groundwork for Derrick X's impending conversion to Sadat X. But the cornerstone of the album is easily the infectious "Slow Down," which transforms the popular Edie Brickell song "What I Am" into an anti-drug and (un)safe-sex hip-hop anthem.

what to buy next: Many figured that Brand Nubian would falter without the guidance and vocal flair of former frontman Puba. If

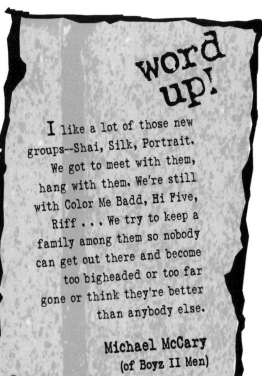

word up!

I like a lot of those new groups--Shai, Silk, Portrait. We got to meet with them, hang with them. We're still with Color Me Badd, Hi Five, Riff . . . We try to keep a family among them so nobody can get out there and become too bigheaded or too far gone or think they're better than anybody else.

**Michael McCary
(of Boyz II Men)**

anything, though, his departure makes for a leaner, meaner Brand Nubian, as *In God We Trust* 🎵🎵🎵 (Elektra, 1992, prod. Brand Nubian, Diamond D, others) sees the group shifting to a more hardcore approach, both musically and in delivery. With Sadat X, Lord Jamar, and Sincere accentuating their Muslim philosophies and beliefs, the album begins with "Allah U Akbar," a song that uses a Muslim chant as its musical foundation. Hardcore militancy also finds a home on the album in "Pass the Gat" and the seminal East Coast block rocker, "Punks Jump Up to Get Beat Down." Politically incorrect by some standards, the album is an uncompromising blast of New York hardcore. The Sadat X solo album *Wild Cowboys* 🎵🎵🎵 (Loud, 1996, prod. Diamond D, Buckwild, Pete Rock, others) combines rugged cowboy imagery with equally rugged rhymes. Sadat presides over a wild bunch of MCs, and, together, they dish out a solid set of 15 songs that roll and rumble over a pastiche of dark jazz and grit-soaked blues-funk samples, with the occasional Ennio Morricone floating in for dramatic, spaghetti-western effect. X marks the spot on the key track, "Open Bar," an all-too-brief reunion with Puba that's a minor hip-hop milestone. *Everything Is Everything* ♫♫♫ (1994, Elektra, prod. Lord Jamar, Buckwild, others) contains the group's familiar, trademark blend (militant, 5% Nation verbage, and ruffneck, East Coast attitude). But the trio now has a whole new musical perspective, bringing live instrumentation into the mix on five of the album's 16 tracks. The music is also marked by an ever-so-slight undercurrent of dank West Coast G-funk. And the few samples the group does use are diverse, to say the least—from the dark jazz trappings of Chico Hamilton to the blue-eyed soul of Simply Red. Grand Puba's solo debut, *Reel to Reel* ♫♫♫ (Elektra, 1992, prod. Grand Puba Maxwell, Kid Capri, others) sparkles in spots, but ultimately is disappointing, thanks largely to the dull grooves and lackluster samples, which restrict the rapper's fast-and-furious flow. *2000* ♫♫♫ (Elektra, 1995, prod. various) is even more disappointing, what with its soul-lite ambiance.

worth searching for: Prior to forming Brand Nubian, Puba was in Masters of Ceremony. The group's only album, *Dynamite* ♫♫♫♫ (Island, 1989, prod. various) is an underground classic.

influences:

◀◀ De La Soul, Public Enemy, Poor Righteous Teachers, A Tribe Called Quest

▶▶ Diamond D, Souls of Mischief, X-Clan, Dred Scott

Spence D.

Brandy
Born Brandy Norwood, February 11, 1979, in Macomb, MS.

As a multiplatinum-selling recording artist and the star of a hit TV show, teen sensation Brandy shows more poise than most people her age can muster even in the high school cafeteria. Mississippi-born and California-reared, Brandy's dream of a show-business career started as early as age four. Inspired by Whitney Houston, she sang with youth groups, in talent shows, and, at age 11, serenaded Arsenio Hall at a charity event with Houston's "The Greatest Love of All." Apparently, acting comes as naturally as singing to the talented teen, and she shone as the younger sister in the ABC show *Thea* before landing her own program, *Moesha*. On the recording tip, she was signed to Atlantic at age 14, and her self-titled debut rocketed up the charts, bolstered by a handful of singles that showcased her sweet

voice and still-maturing sensibility. Brandy is among the best and brightest of a new generation of multitalented performers.

what's available: The best thing about *Brandy* ♫♫♫ (Atlantic, 1994, prod. Keith Crouch, Somthin' for the People, Kipper Jones, Damon Thomas, Arvel McClinton, Kenneth Crouch) is that it's music made by a teenager *for* teenagers, and it's actually *about* teenage concerns, not the adult themes usually dealt with by young singers who want to be down so badly that they scarcely understand the material they've been handed. Brandy wants to be down too—so badly there's actually a song called "I Want to Be Down," but it's about finding a boyfriend, nothing more. "Best Friend" is a song for her younger brother, Willie Norwood Jr., a.k.a. Ray J, an actor and singer in his own right. And the three-part "Dedication" offers shout-outs to those who've been inspirations to her life and career. The rest—notably "Baby" and "Sunny Day"—are about relationships both real and hoped for, but they're neither sanitized nor quaint. Along the way, the beats are bumpalicious, and Brandy's vocals are surprisingly mature but full of precociousness and bubbly charm. *Brandy* is the product of a singer who's willing to listen to her elders but has plenty to say on her own as well.

influences:

◀◀ Whitney Houston, Mary J. Blige

▶▶ Ray J

Daniel Durchholz

Brass Construction /Skyy
Brass Construction formed as Dynamic Soul, 1968, in Brooklyn, NY. Disbanded 1984. Skyy formed early 1980s, in Brooklyn, NY.

Brass Construction: Randy Muller, vocals, keyboards, flute; Joseph Arthur Wong, guitar; Wade Williamston, bass; Wayne Parris, trumpet; Morris Price, trumpet; Mickey Grudge, saxophone; Jesse Ward, saxophone; Larry Payton, drums; Sandy Billups, percussion. Skyy: Randy Muller, vocals, keyboards, flute; Denise Dunning, vocals; Delores Dunning Milligan, vocals; Bonny Dunning, vocals; Solomon Roberts Jr., vocals, guitar, drums; Anibal "Butch" Sierra, guitar; Gerald Lebon, bass; Larry Greenberg, keyboards; Tommy McConnell, drums.

Brass Construction leader Randy Muller was born in British Guyana and lived there until he was 11, so it's not surprising that the group's music reflects the celebratory, Carnival vibe of the Caribbean, with strong, flowing grooves, chorale chants, and long, horn-drenched arrangements. A musical prodigy, Muller put the group together with school and neighborhood friends, many of whom were also Caribbean immigrants. The band was something of a side project while Muller studied at Hunter College in Manhattan, where he met budding music biz impressario Jeff Lane. But when the Muller-arranged "Do It ('Til You're Satisfied)" hit big for B.T. Express in 1974, he was able to parlay the success into a deal for Brass Construction. The nine-piece aggregation had little crossover success but was one of the premier funk bands of the 1970s and early 1980s, bringing sophistication *and* tremendous grooves to the dance floor via songs such as "Dancin'," "Get Up to Get Down," "Walkin' the Line," and "Partyline." Sadly, Brass Construction succumbed to record company pressure to make a more straightforward disco sound, which resulted in lower record sales and the eventual end of the band. Muller went to work with the group Skyy, whose chorale vocal approach—this time with the three Dunning sisters—recalled Brass Construction even if it didn't make as extensive use of brass.

what to buy: *Get Up to Get Down: Brass Construction's Funky Feeling* 𝄞𝄞𝄞𝄞 (EMI, 1997, prod. Randy Muller, Jeff Lane) could leave you gaping—if it didn't have you dancing non-stop around the room. This well-chosen 13-song retrospective shows that Brass Construction was one of the great uncelebrated funk bands, and it'll send you looking for more of its albums—which are, sadly, out of print.

the rest:
Brass Construction:
Golden Classics 𝄞𝄞𝄞 (Collectables, 1991)

Skyy:
Greatest Hits 𝄞𝄞𝄞 (The Right Stuff, 1996)

worth searching for: *Brass Construction* 𝄞𝄞𝄞𝄞 (United Artists, 1976, prod. Jeff Lane) and *Brass Construction II* 𝄞𝄞𝄞𝄞 (United Artists, 1976, prod. Jeff Lane) represent the kind of prodigious start that must have had rival groups shaking at the time.

influences:
◀◀ James Brown, Parliament, Ohio Players, B.T. Express
▶▶ Skyy, Brick, Prince, the Time

Gary Graff

Toni Braxton

Born Toni Michelle Braxton, in Severn, MD.

She's the flyest of the fly, but don't mistake Toni Braxton for just another pretty face. Under the tutelage of producers Antonio "L.A." Reid and Kenneth "Babyface" Edmonds, Braxton

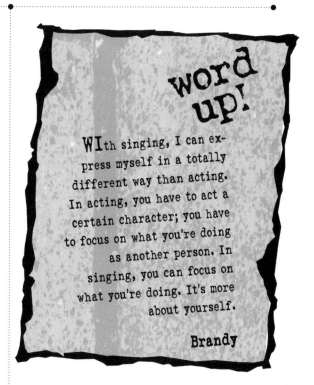

word up!

WIth singing, I can express myself in a totally different way than acting. In acting, you have to act a certain character; you have to focus on what you're doing as another person. In singing, you can focus on what you're doing. It's more about yourself.

Brandy

faced down a tide of nasty New Jacks and Jills and helped preserve R&B as a bastion of soulful, emotional balladry. And though she's but one among many through which the multitalented 'Face speaks, Braxton has been able to interject plenty of her own personality into the mix. On her debut she was the shy ingenue (a preacher's kid, after all), and sang mostly dejected love songs such as the smash hits "Breathe Again," "Another Sad Love Song," "Seven Whole Days," and "Love Shoulda Brought You Home." Four years and 11 million records sold later, the shy preacher's daughter was bustin' out, both of her clothes at various awards shows and in magazines (demolishing her laid-back image). After only a pair of albums, Braxton is already at the top of her game, and it'll likely be a long time before she has any reason to look down.

what to buy: Far from the chaste anthems of her debut, *Secrets* 𝄞𝄞𝄞𝄞 (LaFace, 1996, prod. Antonio "L.A." Reid, Kenneth "Babyface" Edmonds, Toni Braxton) presents Braxton as a self-assured and sexually liberated woman. "You're Makin' Me High," an erotic paean to desire and, um, self-gratification, busts

Braxton out of her rhythmic torpor, bobbing along atop a simmering beat. Equally plain-spoken is the song "Find Me a Man." "Un-Break My Heart" and the lovely "How Could an Angel Break My Heart" find Braxton back in top ballad form. On *Secrets*, Braxton proves she can have it both ways, fine and funky.

the rest:
Toni Braxton ⅃⅃⅃⅃ (LaFace, 1992)

worth searching for: The soundtrack for the film *Boomerang* ⅃⅃⅃⅊ (LaFace, 1992, prod. various) was a preview of what was to come with "Love Shoulda Brought You Home" and a duet with Babyface on "Give U My Heart."

influences:
◀◀ Luther Vandross, Chaka Khan, Stevie Wonder, Whitney Houston

Daniel Durchholz

The Braxtons
Formed late 1980s, in Severn, MD.

Toni Braxton, vocals (left 1992); Tamar Braxton, vocals; Towanda Braxton, vocals; Trina Braxton, vocals; Traci Braxton, vocals (left 1995).

Raised in a religious household—their father was an Apostolic minister—Toni Braxton paved the way for her younger sisters to have the freedom to listen to, and sing, secular music. It was a family act for some time, winning talent contests and even signing a recording deal in 1990. But after one single, Toni was scooped up by uber-producers Kenneth "Babyface" Edmonds and Antonio "L.A." Reid for their burgeoning LaFace label. The other sisters soldiered on, trimmed to a trio when Traci left in 1995. Toni continues to be supportive, and the Braxtons finally emerged with their major label debut in 1996.

what's available: *So Many Ways* ⅃⅃ (Atlantic, 1996, prod. Bryant Reid) is an average effort, marked by lush three-part harmonies and covers of Klymaxx's "I'd Still Say Yes" and Diana Ross's "The Boss"—none of which could push the album beyond the sea of mediocre R&B albums that surrounded it.

influences:
◀◀ The Supremes, Martha & the Vandellas, the Pips, TLC, SWV

Christina Fuoco

Toni Braxton (© Ken Settle)

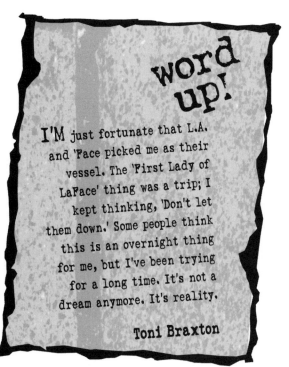

word up!

I'M just fortunate that L.A. and 'Face picked me as their vessel. The 'First Lady of LaFace' thing was a trip; I kept thinking, 'Don't let them down.' Some people think this is an overnight thing for me, but I've been trying for a long time. It's not a dream anymore. It's reality.

Toni Braxton

Brick
Formed early 1970s, in Atlanta, GA.

Jimmy Brown, vocals, saxophone, flute; Regi Hargis Hickman, vocals, guitar, bass; Ray Ransom, vocals, bass, keyboards, percussion; Eddie Irons, vocals, keyboards, drums.

Brick was one of the most ambitious bands to come out of the mid-1970s disco boom, flaunting jazz influences that gave real instrumental heft to its steamy jams—which were fat back before anyone started spelling it with a *ph*. The one-two punch of the group's first two albums, *Good High* in 1976 and *Brick* two years later yielded a batch of hits, including "Music Matic," "Dazz," and "(We Don't Wanna Sit Down) We Wanna Git Down." But as instrumentally facile as the group was, it was ultimately undermined by the lack of an equally accomplished singer; Brick was a faceless ensemble in a genre that thrives on personality, a handicap from which it never recovered.

what's available: It's individual albums are out of print, but *The Best of Brick* ⅃⅃⅃⅃ (Epic Legacy, 1995, prod. various) is a representative sample of the group's work that includes "Dazz," "Music Matic," and the other important jams.

worth searching for: Either the debut, *Good High* 𝄞𝄞𝄞 (Bang, 1976) or *Brick* 𝄞𝄞𝄞 (Bang, 1978) are as enjoyable as the hits set and go even deeper into the group's jazz roots.

influences:

◀◀ The Meters, Ohio Players, James Brown/the JB's, Parliament-Funkadelic, Charles Wright, Sly & the Family Stone

▶▶ The Commodores, Tony! Toni! Tone!

Gary Graff

The Brothers Johnson

Formed 1975, in Los Angeles, CA. Disbanded early 1980s.

George "Lightnin' Licks" Johnson (born May 17, 1953 in Los Angeles), guitar, vocals; Louis "Thunder Thumbs" Johnson (born April 13, 1955 in Los Angeles), bass and vocals.

These precociously talented brothers were playing professionally in their hometown before they were out of high school. Both started playing in Billy Preston's band while still teens, Louis following George; they spent two years with Preston and had their first taste of chart success with his 1974 hit "Struttin'." In 1975 they left Preston to concentrate on making their own demos and hooked up with famed producer Quincy Jones, who used them in his touring band and in the studio, where Louis in particular was in demand by acts such as Grover Washington Jr., Herbie Hancock, Bill Withers, Bob James, George Duke, and others. The brothers' first four albums under their own name were produced by Jones and exhibit examples of his trademark imagination (for instance, the carousel-like intro to "Strawberry Letter 23" and some still-striking synthesizer sounds) as well as his habitual polish, predilection for top-rank sessionmen (such as guitarist Lee Ritenour, keyboardist Dave Grusin, and drummer Harvey Mason), and mellow leanings. Louis's funky, popping basslines, George's fluid guitar facility and awe-inspiring Afro, and their comfortable tenor voices (often in close harmony) distinguished them as well, and they achieved considerable R&B singles chart success: three #1 songs in five years, all of which crossed over to become Top 10 pop hits. They also won the Best Instrumental Grammy in 1977 for "Q," their tribute to their producer. In 1981 they self-produced *Winners*, which became their first sub-million-selling LP, and that marked the beginning of their career decline. By the end of the 1980s they had split, with Louis moving to Japan, though they reunited in 1994 for a tour. Every group should be

so lucky when it comes to reissues: their four best albums are precisely the ones currently available on CD.

what to buy: The debut album *Look Out for #1* 𝄞𝄞𝄞𝄞 (A&M, 1976, prod. Quincy Jones) has not only the brothers' biggest crossover hit, "I'll Be Good to You," but also "Get the Funk Out Ma Face," the only time they managed to score two Top 40 hits on one LP. *Right on Time* 𝄞𝄞𝄞𝄞 (A&M, 1977, prod. Quincy Jones) is consistently as good as its big hit, Shuggie Otis's "Strawberry Letter 23," indelibly associated with the summer of 1977.

what to buy next: *Blam* 𝄞𝄞𝄞𝄞 (A&M, 1978, prod. Quincy Jones) wasn't quite the chart success of its predecessors, but the Ashford & Simpson-penned "Ride-O-Rocket" is among the brothers' best. *Light Up the Night* 𝄞𝄞𝄞𝄞 (A&M, 1980, prod. Quincy Jones) features the group's last crossover hit, the ultra-funky "Stomp!" (which most listeners assumed was called "In the Neighborhood"). Since it was also the last Jones-produced album, it's the last one you'll need to own.

what to avoid: *Greatest Hits* 𝄞𝄞𝄞𝄞 (A&M, 1996, prod. Quincy Jones, others) is fairly well-chosen, but 11 of its 15 tracks come (rightly so) from the first four albums, and there are some worthy album tracks that miss the cut. Since this is full-price and the above albums are mid-priced, the choice is clear: lovers of pop-funk will need the originals, while those who stubbornly want only hits will get this tuneful but chronologically jumbled and musically incomplete package, and will then suffer from massive duplication after they're captivated by the Johnson sound and discover that they too need the original albums.

the rest:

Winners 𝄞𝄞𝄞 (A&M, 1981)
Blast! The Latest and the Greatest 𝄞𝄞𝄞 (A&M, 1983)
Out of Control 𝄞𝄞 (A&M, 1984)
Kick It to the Curb 𝄞𝄞𝄞 (A&M, 1988)

worth searching for: Both the playing and songwriting of George and Louis are prominently featured on Quincy Jones's *Mellow Madness* 𝄞𝄞𝄞 (A&M, 1975, prod. Quincy Jones).

solo outings:

Louis Johnson:
Passage 𝄞𝄞 (A&M, 1981)

influences:

◀◀ Sly & the Family Stone, Earth, Wind & Fire, Ohio Players, Kool & the Gang

▶▶ Michael Jackson, Brand New Heavies, Incognito

Steve Holtje

The Brothers Johnson: George (l) and Louis (© Jack Vartoogian)

Bobby Brown

See: New Edition

Charles Brown

Born 1920, in Texas City, TX.

Ever wonder how pop piano music changed just after World War II from slick Gershwin tunes to hot, fast R&B? Blame Charles Brown. The blues pianist's first band, Johnny Moore's Three Blazers, modeled themselves after the slick hitmaker Nat "King" Cole's Trio. The band's primary talent, of course, was Brown—he penned the smooth 1945 hit "Driftin' Blues" and became a minor blues celebrity. Then Ray Charles, paying close attention to Brown's style and songwriting, copied the Three Blazers for his early bands. In "Driftin' Blues," like Brown's later classics "Merry Christmas, Baby" (covered most famously by Bruce Springsteen) and "Trouble Blues," you can hear both the cocktail-party-ready feeling of Cole's pop and the rocking-house-party feeling of Charles's R&B. Around 1956—when

Elvis Presley, not so coincidentally, was pushing rock 'n' roll onto the radio—Brown's stardom started to dry up. He continued to record and tour throughout the 1960s and 1970s, making a decent living, but he retired in the early 1980s. Then Bonnie Raitt, using her newfound star power to share fame with her blues influences, brought Brown on tour and recorded several duets. Since then, the revitalized singer-pianist has become prolific and multidimensional—his straightforward 1992 piano blues comeback album *Someone to Love* is almost as excellent as his confident 1996 jazz release, *Honey Dripper.*

what to buy: *Driftin' Blues: The Best of Charles Brown* ♪♪♪♪ (EMI, 1992, prod. Adam Block) does a great job of collecting the early Three Blazers hits (including, of course, the title track) and Brown's later work, such as "Merry Christmas, Baby." His 1992 collaboration with Raitt, *Someone to Love* ♪♪♪ (Bullseye/Rounder, 1992, prod. Ron Levy) is the sound of an old musician tickled to have such high-profile fans. Much more confident is *Honey Dripper* ♪♪♪♪ (Verve, 1996, prod. John Snyder), which stacks the goofy New Orleans novelty hit "Gee" against beautiful romantic ballads like "When Did You Leave Heaven" and "There Is No Greater Love."

what to buy next: Brown's pre-Raitt-tour comeback, *All My Life* ♫♫♫ (Bullseye/Rounder, 1990, prod. Ron Levy), is a solid piano blues album, but he hadn't yet hit his second recording career's stride. His post-Raitt material—*Just a Lucky So and So* ♫♫♫ (Bullseye/Rounder, 1994, prod. Ron Levy) and *These Blues* ♫♫♫ (Verve, 1994, prod. John Snyder)—is much more versatile and showcases Brown stretching out vocally.

what to avoid: Brown's best years were the 1940s and 1990s, and his singles between them—documented on *Southern Blues 1957–1963* ♫♫♫ (Paula, 1994, prod. Willie Dixon)—are uneven at best.

the rest:
Blues n' Brown ♫♫♫ (Jewel, 1971)
One More for the Road ♫♫♫ (Blueside, 1986/Alligator, 1989)
Driftin' Blues ♫♫♫ (Mainstream, 1989)
Cool Christmas Blues ♫♫♫ (Bullseye/Rounder, 1994)
Blues and Other Love Songs ♫♫♫ (Muse, 1994)

influences:
◀◀ Nat "King" Cole, T-Bone Walker, Art Tatum, Scott Joplin
▶▶ Ray Charles, Bonnie Raitt, Otis Spann, Floyd Dixon

Steve Knopper

Chuck Brown
& the Soul Searchers
Formed by guitarist Chuck Brown, 1968 in Washington, DC.

Washington, D.C. has always been a musicians' town. From the 1920s until the riot of 1968, the town was a hothouse of great musicians (Duke Ellington, Shirley Horn, Roberta Flack) and clubs. In the aftermath, the night scene shifted to rented ballrooms, juke joints, community and Veterans halls. R&B cover bands and mobile DJs (street jocks) often teamed up to satisfy the newer, younger non-club/concert audience. Into all of this came Chuck Brown & the Soul Searchers. Galvanized by Brown's bacon fat guitar and raw honey-fied tenor, the Soul Searchers quickly became the best in town. Brown changed the game rules forever when he invented Go Go music one hot summer's night in 1970. Knee deep into a groove and not wanting to pause between songs, he told the drummers to keep on funkin'. As the rhythms boiled, the crowd began to clap, chant, and bang on things. As the heat built, Brown's guitar chanked in and the horns, bass, and the Fender Rhodes fell in step. Too

soon, the music stopped. The band began to play some old hit, but the crowd wouldn't have it—they wanted the groove. That was the birth of the Go Go. From that point on, Soul Searchers live sets were non-stop and straight-up. To keep up, the other bands on the scene reconfigured to variations on Brown's lineup (vocalist/MC, congas, percussion, horns, drums, bass, guitar, and keyboard) and emulated his non-stop performances. During the early 1970s, Chuck Brown & the Soul Searchers became the first Go Go band to go national, releasing two albums (*We the People*, *Blow Your Whistle*) on the nationally-distributed Sussex label. In 1979, Brown and his crew made it all the way to "Soul Train" with "Bustin' Loose," the first national Go Go smash. Brown is the universal Godfather of Go Go to this day, respected and requested by a global audience that is trans-generational, cross-cultural, and pan-racial. There would be no Trouble Funk or DJ Kool without him.

what to buy: *Any Other Way To Go?* ♫♫♫♫ (Verve, 1987) is the only nationally-distributed Soul Searchers record. It's a killer live set recorded in front of the home folk. It's especially notable for Mayor Marion Barry's anti-drug rap on "D.C. (Go Go Drug Free)."

what to buy next: *The Other Side* ♫♫♫ (Liaison, 1992, prod. Chris Biondo), a sublime collection of choice blues, R&B, pop, and jazz standards, is a return to his Billy Eckstine/Sarah Vaughan roots. Joining him in vocal duets and solos is the incredible Eva Cassidy (sadly, she passed away in late 1996).

the rest:
Bustin' Loose ♫♫♫ (Valley Vue, 1979/1992)
This Is a Journey . . . Into Time ♫♫♫ (New Venture 4, 1993)

worth searching for: Jackson is on hand for two guest duets on Maxine Brown's *Greatest Hits* ♫♫♫ (Curb, 1996, prod. various), including a version of Sam and Dave's "Hold On, I'm Coming."

influences:
◀◀ T-Bone Walker, James Brown, Arthur Prysock
▶▶ All Go Go bands, DJ Kool, M'Shell Ndgeocello

Tom Terrell and Gary Graff

Foxy Brown
Born Inga Marchand, September 6, 1979, in NY.

Style, sexuality, and substance collide in the form of this veritable hip-hop heroiness. When not boasting about her appetite for designer labels, she's asserting a fluid femininity, jumping at a blink from seductive to hard-core. Largely in the vein of her clique

The Firm (Nas, AZ, and Cormega), Foxy Brown gives voice to a thuggish gotta-get-mine ethic, but kicks a calmer flow on R&B tracks that accentuate her self-styled femme fatale persona.

what's available: Foxy Brown (not to be confused with the reggae star of the same name) maintains unshakable poise on her debut, *Ill Na Na* 🎵🎵🎵 (DefJam, 1996, prod. Havoc, TrackMasters, others). Although she can rock a hard rhyme ("Foxy's Bells," which brings to mind LL Cool J's), the R&B elements in "No One's" and "Get Me Home" are more becoming to her style. The latter track is a perfect example of what makes Brown unique, melding her Tomboy delivery with the butter smoothness of BLACKstreet in what could be read as a challenge to traditional gender roles (i.e. female rapper, male crooners). "I'll Be" works to the same effect lyrically: "Na Na/Y'all can't touch her/My sex drive all night/Like a trucker."

worth searching for: Before dropping her debut, Brown gueststarred on a host of remixes and singles, joining everybody from LL Cool J to Toni Braxton. The best of these, however, featured Brown in a duet with rapper Jay-Z on 1996's "Ain't No Nigga."

influences:

◀◀ Nas, AZ, MC Lyte, Lil' Kim

Corey Takahashi

James Brown

Born May 3, 1933, in Barnwell, SC.

In terms of soul music, nobody can top the contributions or the pervasive influence of James Brown. He is a living link between the R&B swing bands of Louis Jordan and today's rap minimalists. The great soul singers of the middle and late 1960s—and more than a few rockers—took lessons from his early records and that animalistic scream he called a voice. Brown literally invented funk, still the dominant influence on black music—especially disco and rap. Like no one save Ray Charles, Brown faced off the spiritual passion and cadences of black gospel preachers with the supercharged sexual beat and rhythms of R&B. "Please, Please, Please," "Try Me," and "Think" introduced Brown's considerable skills to a generation of budding soul stars that would explode in the mid-60s. His stage show, from the corny-yet-effective cape routines to the rigorously rehearsed, ultra-professional, dapper Famous Flames revue, set a sweaty standard for any other such wannabes. Nobody worked harder than the self-dubbed Hardest Working Man in Show Business (a.k.a. Mr. Dynamite or the Godfather of Soul). Beginning in 1965, he began treating the recording studio with

the same precision and exuberance of an Apollo midnight performance, and his incredibly high standards for band membership paid off with "Papa's Got a Brand New Bag" (1965) and "It's a Man's, Man's, Man's World" (1966), music as revolutionary and innovative as any from the better-known and higher-praised Beatles, Rolling Stones, or Bob Dylan. As the 1960s wore on, Brown's lyrics became more strident and focused on the civil rights movement. As the lyrics eschewed sex and romance to stress black individualism over sex and romance ("Say It Loud, I'm Black and I'm Proud"), the music turned in on itself in ever more primal ways. Brown's band became an incubator of soul, home to innovative, talented musicians—such luminaries as Maceo Parker, Bobby Byrd, Fred Wesley, and Bootsy Collins—as stubborn, professional, moody, and self-determined as their boss. Solos and verse-chorus patterns were dumped in favor of extended, repetitive grooves pushed to fever pitch by Brown's call-and-response vocal chants ("Take me to the bridge!" "Give the drummer some!"). Before long, every instrument was playing some sort of percussion role—an approach that evolved into the dance music that became known as funk, then disco, and the even more fragmented hip-hop styles. Brown has achieved enormous wealth and success, but he's also been dogged by drug addictions and personal problems, which landed him in prison during the late 1980s. But there's no denying Brown's importance, the proof of which lays in 40 years of solid, ground-breaking grooves.

what to buy: Brown's recorded output is as fragmented as the funk he created; fortunately, he was more a singles artist, and whether you're at all interested in his importance or just want to shake your booty, nothing can possibly top *Star Time* 🎵🎵🎵🎵 (Polydor, 1991, prod. various), a comprehensive, chronological, and funkifying solid four discs of his very best and most important works, with many of the singles expanded back to their original lengths and liner notes that detail his accomplishments. If you're a bit more cautious, you shouldn't be without *Solid Gold 30 Golden Hits* 🎵🎵🎵🎵 (Polydor, 1986, prod. various) which boasts about half of those incredibly visionary, exhausting, and shake-your-booty singles. *Live at the Apollo* 🎵🎵🎵🎵 (King, 1963/Polydor, 1990 prod. James Brown) captures the midnight show of August 24, 1962, that put Brown on the national map, an electrifying documentation of pure show-time from the best live act of its time.

what to buy next: When Sid Nathan of King Records wouldn't release an instrumental called "(Do The) Mash Potatoes," Brown put it out on another label under a pseudonym (Nat Kendrick & the Swans), and, not surprisingly, it was a hit. His

James Brown (© Jack Vartoogian)

limitless proficiency on instrumental tracks matches (or at least augments) the creativity of the vocal hits, and many of his bands' finest performances are featured on *Soul Pride: The Instrumentals 1960–1969* 𝄞𝄞𝄞𝄞 (Polydor, 1993, prod. James Brown). The insights are tremendous; Brown, for instance, stands out as an intuitive organ player whose fluid style is perfectly suited to the music. *Roots of a Revolution* 𝄞𝄞𝄞 (Polydor, 1983, prod. Tim Rogers) is a producer's choice of recordings from 1956–1964, showing how Brown and his Famous Flames went from imitative to innovative in the years leading up to "Papa's Got a Brand New Bag." His blues side gets a rare spotlight on *Messing with the Blues* 𝄞𝄞𝄞𝄞 (Polydor, 1990, prod. Joe Scott), which illuminates his individualistic approach toward cover material and proves that he is as impressive a stylist as Ray Charles.

what to avoid: *Black Caesar* and *Slaughter's Big Rip-Off* 𝄞 (both Polydor, 1973, prod. James Brown), two blaxploitation film soundtracks that prove Brown was mortal after all.

best of the rest:
Please Please Please 𝄞𝄞𝄞 (King, 1959/PolyGram Chronicles, 1996)
Think 𝄞𝄞𝄞 (King, 1960/PolyGram Chronicles, 1996)
Papa's Got a Brand New Bag 𝄞𝄞𝄞 (King/PolyGram Special Products, 1965)
Sex Machine 𝄞𝄞𝄞 (King, 1970/PolyGram Chronicles, 1996)
Hell 𝄞𝄞𝄞 (Polydor, 1975)
Live at the Apollo, Vol. 2 𝄞𝄞𝄞𝄞𝄞 (Rhino, 1985)
20 All-Time Greatest Hits 𝄞𝄞𝄞 (Polydor, 1991)
Love Power Peace: Live at the Olympia, Paris, 1971 𝄞𝄞𝄞 (Polydor, 1992)
Funk Power 1970: A Brand New Thang 𝄞𝄞𝄞 (Polydor Chronicles, 1996)
Make It Funky: The Big Payback 𝄞𝄞𝄞 (Polydor Chronicles, 1996)

worth searching for: If you're interested in Brown's early recordings, the out-of-print collection *The Federal Years—Parts One and Two* 𝄞𝄞𝄞 (Solid Smoke, 1984) offers nascent versions of Brown's early vision and the growing pangs of the Famous Flames. Also, his collaboration with hip-hop pioneer Afrika Bambaataa, *Unity* 𝄞𝄞𝄞 (Tommy Boy, 1984, prod. Tom Silverman, Afrika Bambaataa), just in case you were wondering about Brown's connection to rap.

influences:

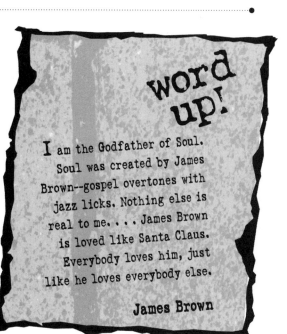 Hank Ballard & the Midnighters, Ray Charles, Louis Jordan, Bo Diddley, Wynonie Harris, Roy Brown, the Dominoes, Five Royales

Michael Jackson, Otis Redding, Sly & the Family Stone, Jim Hendrix, Mick Jagger, Parliament-Funkadelic, George Clinton, Bootsy Collins, Peter Wolf (J. Geils Band), Isaac Hayes, Chic, Afrika Bambaataa, Prince, Eric B. and Rakim, Hammer, Rod Stewart

Leland Rucker

Maxine Brown

Born April 27, 1932, in Kingstree, SC.

There's always been a nagging sense among R&B fans that Maxine Brown never had the career her wonderful voice should have given her, and it's hard to figure out why. Most likely it was a combination of label mistreatment, her own bad decisions, and some unfortuitous timing—like signing to Wand Records at the same as Dionne Warwick and being, at best, second fiddle. Brown was raised as a church singer, and during the late 1950s she moved to New York, where she sang with a couple of gospel groups. She signed with Nomar records and scored two quick hits in 1961—"All in My Mind" and "Funny"—before moving on to ABC and then Wand. With producer Luther Dixon, Brown did her best work at Wand, including the Gerry Goffin-Carole King song "Oh No Not My Baby" and duets with labelmate Chuck Jackson on "Something You Got," "Hold On, We're Comin'," and "Daddy's Home." Brown left Wand in 1971, moving on to Epic, Avco, and Commonwealth United, and she gradually—and sadly—faded from the scene.

what to buy: *Greatest Hits* 🎵🎵🎵 (Tomato, 1995, prod. various) is a generous 23-song set that has her key Wand tracks, including the duets with Jackson.

the rest:
Oh No Not My Baby: The Best of Maxine Brown 🎵🎵🎵 (Kent, 1990/1994)
Golden Classics 🎵🎵🎵 (Collectables, 1991)
Greatest Hits 🎵🎵🎵 (Curb, 1996)

influences:

Irma Thomas, Sam Cooke, Dinah Washington

Diana Ross, Martha Reeves, Ann Peebles, Dee Clark, Womack & Womack

Gary Graff

Roy Brown

Born September 10, 1925, in New Orleans, LA. Died May 25, 1981, in San Fernando, CA.

Roy Brown's wild jump blues and boogie records of the late 1940s and early 1950s were a spirited prelude to the joyous cacophony known as rock 'n' roll. His gospel-drenched squeals and shouts predated Little Richard's style, and by extension, the soul sounds of the 1960s. Brown's first recordings for Gold Star Records reflected his early love for the smoother sounds of Bing Crosby and Billy Eckstine, but once he signed on with Deluxe Records in 1947 he gave full vent to his wilder, more salacious influences. A talented songwriter as well as musician, Brown wrote the classic "Good Rocking Tonight" and offered it to his friend and idol Wynonie Harris, who didn't record his higher charting version until after Brown's rendition began to get airplay. Between 1947 and 1952, Brown scored an impressive string of hits with wailing blues and jump tunes such as "Hard Luck Blues," "Boogie at Midnight," "Miss Fanny Brown," "Rockin' at Midnight," "Cadillac Baby," "Good Rockin' Man," and "Long about Midnight." Brown's Deluxe contract was bought out by King Records in 1952, and although he continued to make remarkable music, his sales declined dramatically. Brown attempted to get across to the new teenage market by cutting sides with Bill Doggett's band under the name Tommy Brown, but the ploy failed. In 1957, Brown moved to Imperial Records, where producer Dave Bartholomew had him record closer to Fats Domino's style than his own. Brown's version of "Let the Four Winds Blow" was a Top 40 pop hit, but a limp cover version of Buddy Knox's "Party Doll" (his final chart appearance) stalled Brown's new momentum. During the 1960s, Brown continued to pump the blues and boogie for the Home of the Blues, Dra, Gert, Summit, Mercury, Gusto, and Bluesway labels without much commercial success. Between club dates and festival bookings, Brown supplemented his income by selling encyclopedias. His last sides were cut for his own record labels Friendship and Faith, which featured some occasionally great music, but sold poorly. Brown died of a heart attack in 1981, but the music he made way back when still rocks on.

what to buy: *Good Rocking Tonight: The Best of Roy Brown* 𝒥𝒥𝒥𝒥 (Rhino, 1994, comp. James Austin) is an 18-track compilation featuring his biggest hits and most influential sides for Deluxe, King, and Imperial. An essential disc for those who want to hear one of the true founding fathers or rock 'n' roll music. *Greatest Hits* 𝒥𝒥𝒥𝒥 (King Blues, 1997, prod. Henry Glover) is a nice budget disc featuring eight influential numbers such as "Good Rockin' Tonight," "Hard Luck Blues," and "Rockin' at Midnight." A good starter set, but the Rhino compilation has more.

what to buy next: *The Complete Imperial Recordings of Roy Brown* 𝒥𝒥𝒥𝒱 (Capitol Blues Collection, 1995, prod. Dave Bartholomew, comp. Pete Welding) is a 20-track collection featuring Brown's last chart records, "Let the Four Winds Blow" and "Party Doll." There are also cool tracks such as "Hip Shakin' Mama," "Slow Down Little Eva," and "We're Goin' Rockin' Tonight," as well as seven previously unreleased cuts. *Mighty Mighty Man* 𝒥𝒥𝒥𝒥 (Ace, 1993, prod. Henry Glover) contains 23 tracks from Brown's 1953–59 period at King and features some real gassers such as "Ain't Rockin' No More," "Gal from Kokomo," and "Shake 'Em Up."

what to avoid: *Good Rockin' Tonight* 𝒥𝒥 (Pilz, 1993) is a nine-song disc with undocumented live and studio tracks from later in Brown's career. Brown never gave a bad performance in his life, but the sound quality here is poor. For completists only.

the rest:
Battle of the Blues 𝒥𝒥𝒥𝒱 (King, 1986)
The Battle of the Blues, Vol. 2 𝒥𝒥𝒥𝒱 (King, 1989)
Battle of the Blues 𝒥𝒥𝒥𝒱 (King, 1989)

worth searching for: *Blues Deluxe* 𝒥𝒥𝒥𝒥 (Charly, 1993, prod. various) has 24 tracks from Brown's big years at Deluxe and King, with some additional material from his mid-1970s stay at Gusto Records. *Laughing But Crying* 𝒥𝒥𝒥𝒱 (Mr. R&B, 1994, prod. various) is a 16-track compilation of some of Brown's lesser known recordings and a few hits. Worthwhile.

influences:
◀◀ Louis Jordan, Wynonie Harris, Bing Crosby
▶▶ Bobby Bland, Little Richard

Ken Burke

Ruth Brown

Born Ruth Alston Weston, January 30, 1928, in Portsmouth, VA.

Modern audiences probably know Ruth Brown best as Motormouth Mabel in the 1988 film *Hairspray,* as the Tony Award-winning actress from the Broadway revue *Black & Blue,* or the host of NPR's "Blues Stage." Brown's more resonant legacy is her string of hits for Atlantic Records during the 1950s, which not only helped establish that label but also R&B's crossover appeal in the early rock era. Brown's first hits ("So Long," "Teardrops from My Eyes," "I'll Wait for You") were torchy jazz *a la* Billie Holiday and Dinah Washington, but as the age of rock 'n' roll dawned, she developed her own rough and ready style. Tunes such as "(Mama) He Treats Your Daughter Mean," "Wild Wild Young Men," "Mambo Baby," and "As Long as I'm Moving" were squealing, rocking paeans to youthful expectations, sexuality, and groove. Brown mixed her bawdy rockin' with sensual, romantic songs such as "Oh What a Dream" (written for her by Chuck Willis), "Love Has Joined Us Together" (with Clyde McPhatter), and "It's Love Baby." Her biggest hits were 1957's "Lucky Lips," a mainstream pop record that seems beneath her today, and the 1958 teen romper "This Little Girl's Gone Rockin'" (written by Bobby Darin), which eventually inspired a popular video on the Disney Channel. By the end of the 1950s, hits for Brown were not coming as easily, and she was lost in the shuffle on Atlantic's crowded roster of stars. Signing with Phillips/Mercury, Brown recorded two solid LPs and had a minor hit single with her version of Faye Adams's "Shake a Hand" in 1962. Brown's career tailspinned badly after that. Though she cut well-regarded LPs for the DCC and Capitol Jazz labels, sales were slow and live gigs were not plentiful. To keep her family fed and clothed, Brown joined the Head Start program and trained to be a beautician while working as a maid, nurse's aide, cashier, and babysitter. During the mid-1970s, comedian Redd Foxx helped revive Brown's career by bringing her to Los Angeles and casting her in bit parts on his hit sitcom *Sanford & Son.* Brown also had recurring roles on the ill-fated sitcoms *Hello Larry* and *Checking In,* but her experiences in live theater would ultimately prove more rewarding. Roles in *Amen Corner* and *StaggerLee* won her critical praise and led to her Tony Award-winning role in 1989's *Black & Blue.* Brown signed with Fantasy Records in 1988 and has recorded four well-regarded discs featuring fresh interpretations of jazz and blues standards as well as occasional rip-it-up R&B. Other successes just as important followed. Her decade-old legal battle with Atlantic over unpaid royalties was finally resolved in her favor, and her old label helped set up the Rhythm & Blues Foundation as part of the settlement. Brown was elected to the Rock 'n' Roll Hall of Fame in 1991. These days, Ruth Brown still records and plays live dates whenever time and health permits (often with protégé Bonnie Raitt), and 1996 saw the release of her autobiography *Miss Rhythm.*

what to buy: *Rockin' In Rhythm—The Best of Ruth Brown* ♫♫♫♫ (Rhino, 1996, prod. Ahmet Ertegun, Jerry Wexler, Herb Abramson, Jerry Leiber, Mike Stoller; reissue prod. James Austin, Peter Grendysa) contains 23 tracks featuring her biggest hits as well as previously unreleased live versions of "(Mama) He Treats Your Daughter Mean" and "Oh What a Dream" from 1959.

what to buy next: *Miss Rhythm: Greatest Hits And More* ♫♫♫♫♫ (Atlantic, 1989, executive prod. Ahmet Ertegun; reissue prod. Bob Porter) is a 40-song, two-CD set which not only includes all her Atlantic hits but also several pleasing LP tracks and four fine previously unreleased songs.

what to avoid: *Fine Brown Frame* ♫♫ (EMI/Capitol, 1993, prod. Sonny Lester; reissue prod. Michael Cuscuna) which is not so much a bad LP as it is a disappointing one. Brown is in fine voice, but the Thad Jones/Mel Lewis Orchestra distracts from her performance with its brassy, jazz effrontery. For completists only.

the rest:
Black Is Brown and Brown Is Beautiful ♫♫♫ (DCC Records, 1981)
The Soul Survives ♫♫♫ (DCC, 1982)
Takin Care of Business ♫♫♫ (Mr. R&B/Stockholm, 1984)
Have a Good Time ♫♫♫ (Fantasy, 1988)
Gospel Time ♫♫♫ (Lection Records, 1989)
Blues on Broadway ♫♫♫♫ (Fantasy, 1989)
Black and Blue ♫♫♫♫ (original cast recording) (DRG, 1989)
Help a Good Girl Go Bad ♫♫♫ (DCC Records, 1990)
Fine and Mellow ♫♫♫ (Fantasy 1991)
Sweet Baby of Mine ♫♫♫ (Route 66, 1992)
The Songs of My Life ♫♫♫ (Fantasy, 1993)

Live in London ♫♫♫♫ (Jazz House Records, 1995)
R+B = Ruth Brown N/A (Bullseye Blues, 1997)

worth searching for: *Late Date with Ruth Brown* ♫♫♫♫ (Atlantic, 1956, prod. Ahmet Ertegun, Jerry Wexler) is an import reissue of Brown's best early LP, with romantic standards gorgeously framed by arranger/conductor Richard Wess.

influences:
◄◄ Billie Holiday, Dinah Washington
►► Irma Thomas, Little Richard, Koko Taylor, Bonnie Raitt

Ken Burke

Shirley Brown
Born January 6, 1947, in West Memphis, AK.

The specter of Aretha Franklin looms over many female vocalists who recorded during the 1960s and 1970s. Thanks to her range, power, and accuracy in the high register, Shirley Brown is one vocalist who doesn't suffer from the comparison. Brown is to Aretha Franklin as Esther Phillips is to Dinah Washington: derivative, but worthy of attention in her own right. Brown is best known for having the last big hit on the Stax/Volt labels of Memphis, "Woman to Woman." Record sales of "Woman to Woman" delayed the inevitable padlocking of the doors. The record sold as it did for good reason; Brown's sassy spoken intro to a woman whose phone number appears one day in her old man's pockets (presumably Barbara Mason, whose "Shackin' Up" offered justification for man-stealing) represents one of the most entertaining explorations of this most enduring of soul music themes. It was the hottest thing on soul radio in 1975, touching off a flurry of quickly released rejoinders (e.g., "Man to Woman," Lonnie Youngblood; "From His Woman to You," Barbara Mason). Orphaned by the Stax/Volt bankruptcy, Brown enjoyed varied success during the next 10 years recording for Arista (where she was one of Clive Davis's first signings), 20th Century, Sound Town, and Black Diamond before hooking on with Malaco Records of Jackson, Mississippi. At Malaco, with the support of many of her fellow survivors from the golden age of Southern soul, Brown has fashioned a contemporary soul/blues sound based on the eternal verities— great songs, great sound, supportive musicianship, and transcendent singing.

what to buy: The follow-up to "Woman to Woman," "It Ain't No Fun," was an even more impressive display of Brown's astonishing vocal chops than its predecessor. Both songs are contained on *Woman to Woman* 🎵🎵🎵 (Stax, 1974/ Fantasy/Stax, 1994, prod. Jim Stewart, Al Jackson Jr.)—an essential release.

what to buy next: Among Brown's fine Malaco discs, *Diva of Soul* 🎵🎵🎵 (Malaco, 1995, prod. Shirley Brown, Bobby Manuel) has the strongest material and most uncluttered sound and production, and includes yet another variant on the woman-to-woman theme, "You Ain't Woman Enough to Take My Man." One caveat: Brown suffers from a common tendency among contemporary female vocalists to display all of her chops on every song she sings. She is truly a diva, but sometimes you wish she would show a bit of restraint. Approach this disc with caution, and keep something by Ann Peebles handy to cleanse the aural palate.

the rest:
Fire & Ice 🎵🎵🎵 (Malaco, 1978)
For the Real Feeling 🎵🎵 (United Artists/Stax U.K., 1979)
Timeless 🎵🎵🎵 (Malaco, 1990)
Joy and Pain 🎵🎵🎵🎵 (Malaco, 1993)

worth searching for: Two of Brown's earliest recordings for Nashville's A-Bet label appear on the outstanding AVI collections *Heart of Southern Soul: From Nashville to Memphis and Muscle Shoals* 🎵🎵🎵🎵 (Excello/AVI, 1995, prod. various) and *Uptown Down South* 🎵🎵🎵 (Excello/AVI, 1995, prod. various). Brown's 10 years in the wilderness between the Stax and Malaco years remain undocumented on CD. Those LPs are certainly worth searching for, particularly *Shirley Brown* 🎵🎵🎵 (Arista, 1977, prod. D.J. Rogers), *Intimate Storm* 🎵🎵🎵 (Sound Town, 1984), and *If This Is Goodbye* 🎵🎵🎵 (Black Diamond, 1986, prod. Shirley Brown, Winston Stewart, Jim Stewart). Finally, Brown contributes "I'm Gonna Stop You from Giving Me the Blues" to *Z.Zelebration: A Tribute to the Late Great Z.Z. Hill* 🎵🎵🎵🎵🎵 (Malaco, 1994, prod. Tommy Couch Jr., Wolf Stephenson), a wonderful compilation of songs associated with Malaco's flagship artist Z.Z. Hill, performed by other artists on the Malaco roster.

influences:
◀◀ Aretha Franklin, Clara Ward, Marion Williams, Shirley Caesar
▶▶ Whitney Houston, Mariah Carey

Bill Pollak

Peabo Bryson
Born Robert Peabo Bryson, April 13, 1951, in Greenville, SC.

Peabo Bryson emerged during the 1970s as one of the most promising and talented soul singers of his generation. Although the end of the decade threatened to eliminate sweet soul music by presenting most black artists singing funk, rock,

and disco, Bryson carried on the tradition of the beautiful balladeer. Before embarking on a solo career, he sang with Al Freeman & the Upsetters in 1965, Moses Dillard & the Tex Town Display from 1968–73, and Michael Zager's Moon Band until his debut album *Reaching for the Sky* was released in 1978 and established him as a comer in the industry. In addition to numerous solo hits over the last two decades, he has been equally successful recording award-winning duets with such artists as Regina Belle, Natalie Cole, Celine Dion ("A Whole New World" from Walt Disney's *Aladdin*), and Roberta Flack. Most recently, he was on tour in *The Wiz,* playing the Great OZ himself.

what to buy: *Reaching for the Sky* 🎵🎵🎵🎵 (Capitol, 1978, prod. Richard Evans, Peabo Bryson) is a superb debut display of silky soul crooning that features "I'm So Into You" and "Feel the Fire." *Crosswinds* 🎵🎵🎵 (Capitol, 1978) continued Bryson's momentum as a force to be reckoned with. His voice was at an expressive peak on this collection. *I'm So Into You: The Passion of Peabo Bryson* 🎵🎵🎵 (EMI, 1997, prod. various) is a good introduction to the man and his music, featuring the best of his solo hits as well as the choice duets with Cole and Flack.

what to buy next: *Straight from the Heart* 🎵🎵🎵🎵 (Elektra, 1984) offers a good mix of ballads, midtempo, and dance tunes. Bryson was at his vocal peak, and this collection produced his pop smash, "If Ever You're In My Arms Again." *Can You Stop the Rain* 🎵🎵🎵 (Columbia, 1991, prod. various) was the disc that put Bryson back in the big leagues and presents him sounding better than ever.

what to avoid: *Paradise* 🎵 (Capitol, 1980) tried to capitalize on Bryson's sentimental side. *Quiet Storm* 🎵 (Elektra, 1986) is another collection of ballads and mid-tempo songs that seemed devoid of sincerity and drive.

the rest:
We're the Best of Friends 🎵🎵🎵🎵 (Capitol, 1979)
Turn the Hands of Time 🎵🎵🎵 (Capitol, 1981)
I Am Love 🎵🎵🎵 (Capitol, 1981)
Born to Love 🎵🎵🎵🎵 (Capitol, 1983)
The Peabo Bryson Collection 🎵🎵🎵🎵 (Capitol, 1984)
Take No Prisoners 🎵🎵🎵 (Elektra, 1985)
All My Love 🎵🎵🎵 (Capitol, 1989)
Tonight I Celebrate My Love 🎵🎵🎵🎵 (CEMA, 1992)
Through the Fire 🎵🎵🎵🎵 (Columbia, 1994)
Peace on Earth N/A (Angel, 1997)

worth searching for: *Live and More* 🎵🎵🎵🎵 (Atlantic, 1980), a live double CD on which Bryson sings with Roberta Flack, is outstanding; an added attraction here are the background vocals by Luther Vandross.

Peabo Bryson (© Jack Vartoogian)

influences:

◀◀ Marvin Gaye, Sam Cooke, Smokey Robinson, Bill Withers, Al Green

▶▶ Luther Vandross, Freddie Jackson, Johnny Gill, James Ingram, Howard Hewett, Kenny Lattimore, Eric Benet

Damon Percy

B.T. Express

B.T. Express formed as the King Davis House Rockers, 1972, in Brooklyn, NY. Disbanded 1981.

Barbara Joyce Lomas, vocals; Bill Risbrook, vocals, saxophone; Wesley Hall, guitar, vocals; Michael Jones (a.k.a. Kashif), keyboards (1976–79); Rick Thompson, guitar; Dennis Rowe, percussion; Carlos Ward, reeds; Leslie Ming, drums; Jamal Rasool, bass, vocals; Louis Risbrook, bass, organ, vocals.

One of the three main groups—the others being Brass Construction and Skyy—that were mentored by producer Randy Muller and manager Jeff Lane, B.T. (a.k.a. Brooklyn Trucking) Express specialized in funky grooves that were fat before we started spelling the word with a ph. The group started with a band; its debut album, *Do It ('Til You're Satisfied)*, named after Bill Risbrook's title tune, launched two Top 10 pop hits—the title track and "Express." The album hit the Top 5 and earned a gold album award. The group never equaled that success again, however, and once Michael Jones left to record under the name Kashif, B.T. Express rather quickly came to a stop.

what to buy: With only compilations left in print, *The Best of B.T. Express* ♫♫♫♫ (Rhino, 1997, prod. various) is the best of the bunch. It has all the key hits—"Do It ('Til You're Satisfied)," "Express," "Give It What You Got/Peace Pipe"—in solid, remastered sound.

the rest:
Golden Classics ♫♫♫♫ (Collectables, 1991)
Do It!! Non Stop B.T. Express ♫♫♫♫ (Pair, 1993)

worth searching for: *Do It ('Til You're Satisfied)* ♫♫♫ (Roadshow, 1974, prod. Randy Muller) remains one of the quintessential 1970s funk albums.

influences:

◀◀ Sly & the Family Stone, James Brown, Watts 103rd Street Rhythm Band, Parliament, the Staple Singers

▶▶ Lakeside, Shalamar, Brick, Brass Construction

see also: *Kashif*

Gary Graff

Buckshot Lefonque

Branford Marsalis, saxophone; DJ Premier, DJ; DJ Apollo, DJ.

During the height of hip-hop/jazz fusion hype, it was common to see DJs and MCs incorporating jazz music into their sound. Rarely, though, did you see the opposite. Branford Marsalis—who, unlike his brother, Wynton, is renowned for his open-mindedness—not only attempted such a collaboration, he did so with great success. Of course, working with one of hip-hop's most talented producers, DJ Premier, didn't hurt.

what to buy: *Buckshot LeFonque* ♫♫♫♫ (Columbia, 1994, prod. Branford Marsalis, DJ Premier, others) is a groundbreaking volume of work. The melding of Premier's drumbeat construction and Marsalis's easy-going, soulful saxophone set the standard for all hip-hop fusion experiments. "Breakfast at Denny's" and "Some Cow Fonque" highlight the union of Premier's crisp, concise scratches and Marsalis's jazz intelligence. The importance of this project resonates in its contributors: Heralded young lion Roy Hargrove (trumpet), poet Maya Angelou (*I Know Why the Caged Bird Sings*), Death Row rapper Lady of Rage ("Blackwidow"), and even guitarist Albert Collins and bass whiz Victor Wooten.

what to buy next: *Music Evolution* ♫♫♫ (Columbia, 1997, prod. Branford Marsalis, others) is just as progressive, but not nearly as innovative—perhaps because of Premier's absence. In Premier's place is the wildly creative DJ Apollo, a member of San Francisco's Rock Steady DJs who actually was the touring DJ for the first project.

influences:

◀◀ Gang Starr, Brand New Heavies, Miles Davis

▶▶ DJ Quest, Greg Osby

Jazzbo

The B.U.M.S.

Formed in Oakland, CA.

E-Vocalist (born Evol Alexander), vocals; D-Wyze (born D'Angelo Smith), vocals.

The B.U.M.S. (or, Brothas Unda Madness) are part of a movement that's striving to redefine the parameters of Oakland's rap scene. To this end, they've eschewed the traditional Oakland mack/playa/pimp/bitch-and-funk blueprint (as created by Too $hort), favoring instead verbal gymnastics and loose musical grooves that are shaded jazzy-blue.

what's available: On *Lyfe and Tyme* ♫♫♫ (Priority, 1995, prod. King Tech, Joe Quixx, Baka Boyz, others), the B.U.M.S. deliver limber lyrics over a wide-reaching array of sounds, from the infectious bump of "Wreck Your Ears (Can Do)" to the swing-styled horns, bass, and vibes of "West Coast Smack." The album concludes with "Who Gives You the Right," a politically charged spoken word bit composed and delivered in the griot spirit of the Last Poets and Gil-Scott Heron.

influences:

◀◀ Souls of Mischief, the Coup, Saafir

Spence D.

Solomon Burke

Born 1936, in Philadelphia, PA.

Upon this rock they built the church. Solomon Burke, one of the crucial transitional figures in classic 1960s Southern soul, has seldom been recognized or celebrated for the key role he played in shaping the music's firmament. His hits on Atlantic Records were largely products a fruitful creative association with song-writer-producer Bert Berns, who launched his own estimable career with Burke's 1961 version of his "Cry to Me." Berns wrapped Burke's gospel fervor—the former "Wonder Boy Preacher"—in crisp, churchy sounds, inflected with Afro-Cuban accents that drove Burke to the edge of heartbreak in the songs. Together they mapped out a unique sound that bridged the gap between the mannered 1950s studio-conceived R&B of Leiber and Stoller to the rich, earthy Southern soul of Stax/Volt and Muscle Shoals. Burke's figure loomed large in those Southern states during his heyday, when he was known as "King of Soul" on the chitlin' circuit. During the four years he worked with Berns, Burke put out extraordinary record after extraordinary record, some of the definitive R&B recordings of their time. He also later made other fine records, including his biggest hit, "Got to Get You Off My Mind," but nothing equaled the drama and raw passion, the almost Gothic soul of his records with the brilliant producer. During the 1970s he virtually disappeared from the scene, tending to his large family, businesses, and his church in Los Angeles. But in recent years, Burke returned with several worthy albums for small independent labels that have helped get him some time back in the spotlight and have resuscitated a nearly forgotten but glorious career.

what to buy: The current double-disc retrospective of his Atlantic years, *Home In Your Heart* ♫♫♫♫ (Rhino, 1992, prod. various), covers the full expanse, although its deleted predecessor, a single-disc, 20-song collection, *The Best of Solomon Burke* ♫♫♫♫♫ (Atlantic, 1989, prod. various) might be more precisely to the point.

what to buy next: The whole sweaty, breathless majesty of his live performances gives Burke's music persuasive new dimensions, evidenced satisfactorily on *Live at the House of Blues* ♫♫♫ (Black Top, 1994, prod. Hammond Scott, Selassie Burke).

what to avoid: After leaving Atlantic, Burke made a modestly successful cover of "Proud Mary" for Bell records, but his subsequent work on MGM clearly shows a compromised artist lost in a sea of changing musical fashions.

the rest:
Soul Alive! ♫♫♫ (Rounder, 1985)
A Change Is Gonna Come ♫♫♫ (Rounder, 1986)
Home Land ♫♫ (Bizarre/Straight, 1991)
Soul of the Blues ♫♫♫ (Black Top, 1993)
The Definition of Soul ♫♫♫ (Pointblank, 1997)

worth searching for: His first album, *Rock 'N Soul* ♫♫♫♫♫ (Atlantic, 1961), a pricey collector's item these days, is one of the unrecognized landmarks of the golden age of soul.

influences:
◀◀ Robert Blair and the Fantastic Violinaires, Rev. Julius Cheeks

▶▶ Otis Redding, Joe Tex, Bruce Springsteen

Joel Selvin

Jerry Butler
Born December 8, 1939, in Sunflower, MS.

The Ice Man, Jerry Butler, is doo-wop's living link to soul music. Butler's early style was formed by singing with the Northern Jubilee Gospel Singers in Chicago. After meeting Curtis Mayfield at the Traveling Souls Spiritualistic Church, the two began singing in doo-wop groups such as the Quails and the Alphatones before joining the Roosters, an early version of the Impressions. Recording for the Vee-Jay subsidiary Falcon Records

in 1958, Jerry Butler & the Impressions recorded "For Your Precious Love," a romantic doo-wop ballad, which became a smash hit on both the pop and R&B charts. Butler's billing as soloist caused much dissension within the group, but after their two follow-up records failed to chart, billing became a moot point: Vee-Jay kept Butler and dropped the Impressions. (They would resurface during the 1960s with Mayfield as lead singer.) Butler's first solo records met with limited success, but when Mayfield rejoined him in the studio, their collaborations resulted in big hits such as "He Will Break Your Heart," "Find Another Girl," and "I'm A-Telling You." Butler broadened his appeal further with his hit interpretation of Henry Mancini's "Moon River," which beat the *Breakfast At Tiffany's* soundtrack version onto the charts by two weeks. The Burt Bacharach/Hal David penned "Make It Easy On Yourself" was a dual-market smash as well. Butler's cool mixing of gospel soul with supper club MOR kept him on the charts at a time when British acts had chased most American artists off pop playlists. Indeed, at the peak of Beatlemania, his duet with Betty ("The Shoop Shoop Song") Everett, "Let It Be Me," was a Top 5 pop hit. Despite Butler's continued success, Vee-Jay Records went bankrupt in 1966, and he signed with Mercury Records. Working with Philadelphia writer/producers Kenny Gamble and Leon Huff, Butler recorded a string of major crossover soul hits such as "Never Give You Up," "Hey Western Union Man," "Are You Happy," "Moody Woman," "Don't Let Love Hang You Up," "I Could Write A Book," and "Only the Strong Survive." These records helped establish Gamble & Huff's Philadelphia Sound, and they soon left to form their own label. Butler countered their loss by establishing the Songwriter's Workshop in Chicago, which nurtured the professional careers of Chuck Jackson, Brenda Lee Eager, and others. His 1972 duet with Eager, "Ain't Understanding Mellow," was a certified million-seller, and "One Night Affair" was a fair-sized dual market hit. But Butler's hit power ebbed considerably after that. (Butler and Eager also appeared in the 1973 documentary *Save the Children*). A 1975 deal with Motown resulted in five strong LPs, including a duet disc with Thelma Houston, but aside from 1977's "I Wanna Do It to You," few singles made much noise on the charts. In 1979, Butler signed with Gamble & Huff's Philadelphia International label, but despite a critically acclaimed LP, the reteaming produced no new hits. Since then, music has become something of a lucrative part-time job for Butler. In 1980, he began serving the first of four terms as Cook County Commissioner in Illinois. Butler was inducted into the Rock 'n' Roll Hall of Fame in 1991 and into the Rhythm & Blues Foundation in 1994. He still records sporadically for his own labels, has been featured in a CLIO Award-winning McDonald's commercial with Aretha Franklin, and plays live gigs whenever he has the time.

what to buy: *Best of Jerry Butler* 𝄞𝄞𝄞𝄞 (Rhino, 1987, comp. Bill Inglot) contains Butler's biggest hits with Vee-Jay and Mercury, as a solo artist, with Betty Everett, and with the Impressions. A great starting point.

what to buy next: *Iceman—Mercury Years Anthology* 𝄞𝄞𝄞𝄞 (PolyGram, 1992, prod. Kenny Gamble, Leon Huff) is a comprehensive two-disc, 44-track helping of Butler's work during his years as a major solo hit maker with Mercury. *The Ice Man—Jerry Butler* 𝄞𝄞𝄞𝄞 (Vee-Jay, 1992, prod. Calvin Carter) has 25 tracks of Butler's best from his Vee-Jay years, with and without the Impressions.

what to avoid: *Greatest Hits* 𝄞𝄞 (Pilz, 1993, prod. various) is a budget disc with some unusual source material but terribly muddy sound.

the rest:
Love's on the Menu 𝄞𝄞 (Motown, 1990)
Suite for the Single Girl 𝄞𝄞 (Motown, 1990)
Time & Faith 𝄞𝄞 (Ichiban, 1992)
Simply Beautiful 𝄞𝄞𝄞 (Valley Vue/Navarre, 1994)
Best Love 𝄞𝄞𝄞 (Capitol Special Products, 1994)

worth searching for: *Jerry Butler's Golden Hits Live* 𝄞𝄞𝄞𝄞 (Mercury, 1968) features live versions of material from his Vee-Jay years and showcases the cool stage presence and smooth, evocative style that caused a Philly DJ to admiringly dub him the Ice Man.

influences:
◀◀ Joe Williams, Curtis Mayfield
▶▶ Chuck Jackson, Donny Hathaway

Ken Burke

C+C Music Factory

Formed 1990, in New York, NY. Disbanded 1995.

David Cole; Robert Clivilles.

Even though the first record featuring the name C+C Music Factory didn't drop until 1990, the two Cs—producers David Cole

and Robert Clivilles—actually began their partnership years before, when Cole played live keyboards as Clivilles spun records at New York's Better Days nightclub. A growing force in underground dance since their 1987 club hit "Do It Properly" scored, the pair developed a reputation as ace remix artists, working for Natalie Cole and Luther Vandross, among others. They struck gold with the first C+C record, assembled with a former assistant engineer named Freedom Williams as the featured rapper and singer Zelma Davis. After the album was well on its way toward its more than 6.5 million sales tally, news broke that the muscular soul voice powering the initial hit "Gonna Make You Sweat" was actually Weathergirls singer Martha Wash—presumably excluded from the videogenic group because of her weight (she had once paired with another singer in a group called Two Tons O' Fun). Though the group tried to release another record, its calculated nature—combined with infighting that saw Williams attempt a quickly-aborted solo career—kept fans away. Despite Cole's death in 1995 from spinal meningitis, Clivilles attempted another C+C record with yet another cast of talent the next year—a record that quickly proved the Music Factory's 15 minutes had long since run out.

what to buy: Striking an inspired balance between the worlds of rap, R&B, dance, and pop, C+C's debut record, *Gonna Make You Sweat* 𝄞𝄞𝄞𝄞 (Columbia, 1990, prod. Robert Clivilles, David Cole), married an army of studio musicians, singers, and rappers to some impressive material. In particular, the title track and the freewheeling groove thang, "Things That Make You Go Hmmm," meld percolating dance pop with hip-shaking funk grooves.

what to avoid: The sophomore record, *Anything Goes* **woof!** (Columbia, 1994, prod. Robert Clivilles, David Cole), works outdated grooves with a cast of new talent that brings little to this mostly-uninspired material.

the rest:
C+C Music Factory 𝄞𝄞𝄞 (Columbia, 1996)

solo outings:
Clivilles and Cole:
Greatest Remixes Vol. 1 𝄞𝄞𝄞 (Columbia, 1992)

Freedom Williams:
Freedom 𝄞𝄞 (Columbia, 1993)

influences:
◀◀ Janet Jackson, Hammer, Taylor Dayne, Frankie Knuckles, Expose
▶▶ Spice Girls, Black Box, Backstreet Boys

Eric Deggans

The Cadets

Formed 1954, in Los Angeles, CA.

Aaron Collins, lead vocals, second tenor; Will "Dub" Jones, lead vocals, bass; Willie Davis, first tenor; Lloyd McCraw, baritone, manager; Ted Taylor, first tenor.

Owners of one of the first pure R&B hits to make the then-colossal leap onto the pop charts, the Cadets came together in L.A. in 1954 and within a year were doing double duty: they were recording for the Modern Records label as both as the Cadets (singing uptempo songs) and the Jacks (doing ballads and jump tunes). Their first single, a 1955 cover version of Nappy Brown's classic-to-be "Don't Be Angry," actually outperformed Brown's original on Savoy in many regions of the country. But the quintet's most famous record, "Stranded in the Jungle" by Ernestine Smith and James Johnson, was released the following year and emerged as a crossover triumph, hitting #15 on the pop charts while peaking at #4 on the R&B rankings. The song has been covered numerous times, most notably by David Johansen and the glam-rock 1980s band New York Dolls on their LP *Rock 'n' Roll*, artists wishing to offer a paean to the 1950s. The original Cadets version has been featured on several early-rock compilations over the years, including *Only Rock 'n' Roll 1955–1959 #1 Radio Hits* 𝄢𝄢𝄢𝄢 (JCI Associated Labels, 1996), the British import *Rhythm & Blues House Party* 𝄢𝄢𝄢 (Ace), and *Oldies But Goodies, Volume 1* 𝄢𝄢𝄢 (Original Sound Entertainment).

influences:

◀◀ The Feathers, the Jayhawks

▶▶ The Flairs, the Coasters, Elvis Presley, Teen Queens, the Nylons, David Johansen

Michael Kosser

The Cadillacs

Formed 1953, as the Carnations, in New York, NY. Renamed the Cadillacs in 1954. Disbanded in 1957. Re-formed in 1959. Also recorded as Jessie Powell & the Caddies, Speedo & the Original Cadillacs, Bobby Ray & the Cadillacs, and Ray Brewster & the Cadillacs.

Members have included vocalists Earl "Speedo" Carroll, Bobby Phillips, Cub Gaining, LaVerne Drake, James "Poppa" Clark, Johnny "Gus" Willingham, Earl Wade, Charles "Buddy" Brooks, James "J.R." Bailey, Bobby Spencer, Bill Lindsey, Champ Rollow, Caddy Spencer, Roland Martinez (Speedo & the Original Cadillacs), Kirk Davis (Speedo & the Original Cadillacs), Ronnie Bright (Speedo & the Original Cadillacs), Milton Love (Speedo & the Original Cadillacs), Reggie Barnes (Speedo & the Original Cadillacs), Curtis Williams (Speedo & the Original Cadillacs), Ray Brewster (Speedo & the Original Cadillacs), Irving Lee Gail (Speedo & the Original Cadillacs), Bobby Baylor (Ray Brewster & the Cadillacs), Fred Barksdale (Ray Brewster & the Cadillacs), Leroy Binns, Steven Brown, Johnny Brown, Gary K. Lewis.

Though they had less across-the-board success than many other vocal groups of the time, the Cadillacs left a lasting impact. Early hits such as "Gloria" and the boastful "Speedoo" set vocal standards for other groups to match, and following in the Cadillacs' footsteps was hard. They were one of the first groups to emphasize choreography, even hiring Charles Atkinson (Cholly Atkins), who would go on to map out moves for Motown acts such as the Miracles and the Supremes. The Cadillacs underwent numerous personnel changes, even before the oldies revival of the 1970s: in 1957, the group split, recording as the Original Cadillacs and Jessie Powell & the Caddies before reforming in 1959. The group recorded under at least seven different names during the 1950s and 1960s and continued to perform well into the 1990s.

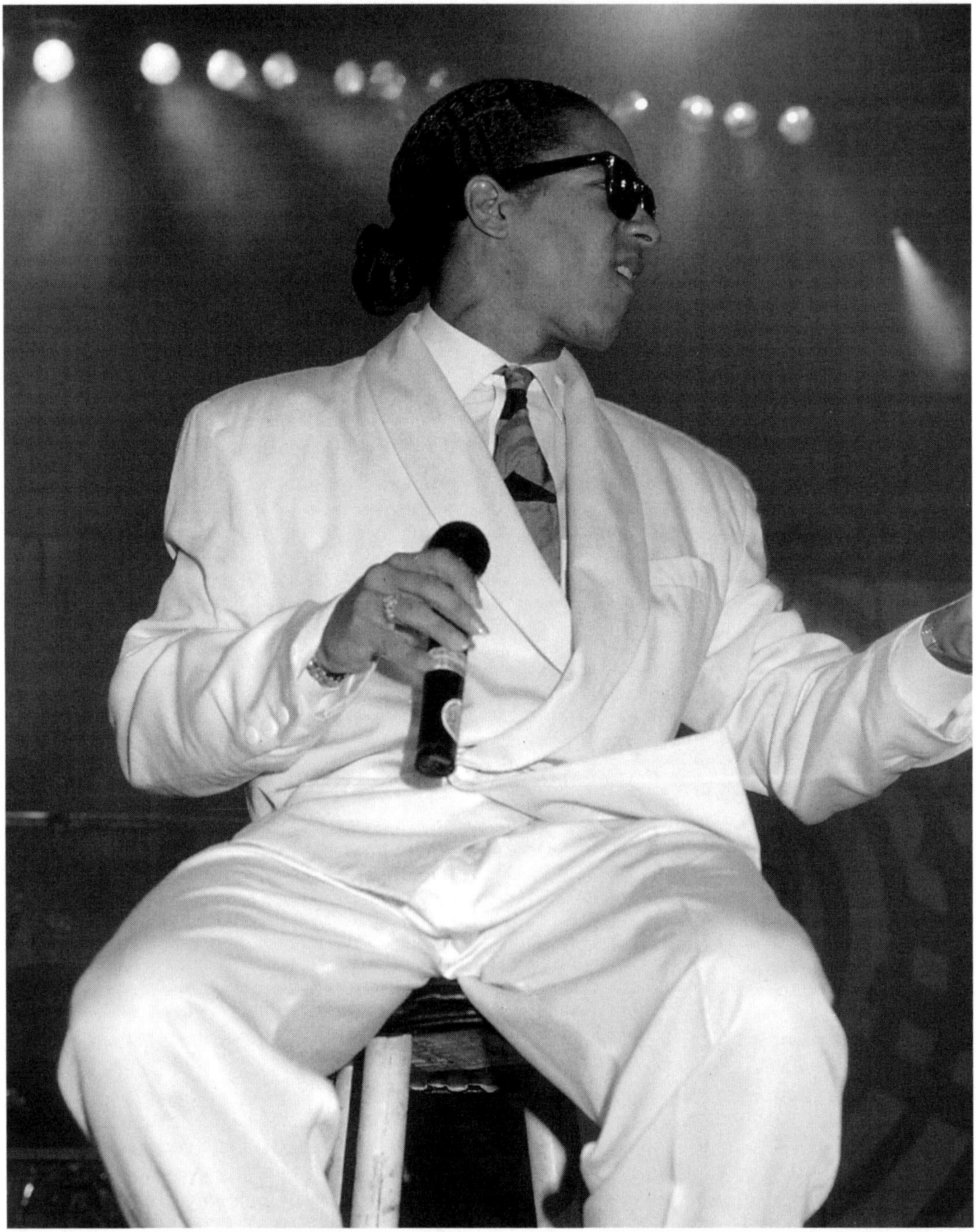

what to buy: At 18 cuts, *The Best of the Cadillacs* ♫♫♫♪ (Rhino, 1990) is the only Cadillacs disc most people will want—and it's by far the easiest to find. The compilation rightly focuses on the lineups for which Earl Carroll sang lead. The ballads ("Gloria," "Zoom") are just as fine as the better-know uptempo novelties ("Speedoo," "Peek-A-Boo"), though during the later recordings the Cadillacs had begun to cop the style of the Coasters (which Carroll joined in 1959).

the rest:
(With the Orioles) *The Cadillacs Meet the Orioles* ♫♫♫ (Collectables)

worth searching for: Two European imports, *Peek-A-Boo* ♫♫♫ (Remember, 1992) and *Please Mr. Johnson* ♫♫♫ (Dr. Horse), have similar content to the much more readily available Rhino compilation, though each has a few tracks that don't appear on the others. Anybody that interested in tracking down Cadillacs obscurities should spring for *For Collectors Only* ♫♫♫ (Collectables, 1992) instead—it's got two discs' worth of the hits and more.

influences:
◀◀ The Five Crowns, the Five Royales

▶▶ The Capris, the Frankie Lymon & the Teenagers, the Temptations, the Skyliners, the Marcels, the Moonglows

see also: *The Coasters*

Brian Mansfield

Shirley Caesar
Born October 13, 1938, in Durham, NC.

Shirley Caesar was singing gospel at the age of 12 to help support her widowed mother. In 1958 she joined the Caravans with gospel singers Albertina Walker, Bessie Griffin, Dolores Washington, Inez Andrews, Cassietta George, and Reverend James Cleveland on piano. Caesar's fiery zeal for Christian ministry inspired her to develop her own preaching style. She left the Caravans behind in 1966 (the reason they disbanded) and turned to Evangelism, preaching and singing in churches and venues around the country with her Shirley Caesar Singers. Shirley Caesar Outreach Ministries was founded during the 1980s to offer assistance and counseling to the poor in her hometown of Durham, North Carolina. In 1990, Caesar opened her own Pentecostal church. Most of Caesar's numerous albums are

Freedom Williams, featured rapper with C+C Music Factory (© Ken Settle)

recorded live, capturing the power of gospel music at its most gloriously witnessed moments.

what to buy: *He Will Come: Live* ♫♫♫♫ (Word, 1995, prod. Bubba Smith, Shirley Caesar) won a Grammy Award in 1996 for Best Traditional Soul Gospel Album. Most of the album was recorded live at Greater Bibleway Miracle Temple in Memphis and features Caesar's heaven-shaking version of the traditional "Revive Us Again."

what to buy next: *A Miracle In Harlem* ♫♫♫♫ (Word, 1997), which was recorded live with Hezekiah Walker at the Love Fellowship Church in Harlem, New York, is also excellent.

best of the rest:
Jesus I Love Calling Your Name ♫♫♫ (Word, 1983)
Sailin' ♫♫♫♫ (Word, 1984)
Christmasing ♫♫♫♪ (Word, 1986)
I Remember Mama (Word, 1989)
Live In Chicago with Reverend Milton Brunson ♫♫♫♫ (Word, 1989)
Her Very Best ♫♫♫♫ (Word, 1991)
He's Working It All Out for You ♫♫♫♪ (Word, 1991)
Stand Still ♫♫♫ (Word, 1993)
The Best of Shirley Caesar with the Caravans ♫♫♫♫ (Malaco, 1995)
Just a Word ♫♫♫♪ (Word, 1996)
Faded Rose ♫♫♫♪ (Hob Records, 1996)

worth searching for: *Till I Meet the Lord* ♫♫♫♫ (Savoy) features the Caravans with Caesar, taken from the group's two albums released by the Vee-Jay label during the 1960s.

influences:
◀◀ C.A. Tindley, Thomas A. Dorsey, Mahalia Jackson

▶▶ O'landa Draper & the Associates, the Winans, Aretha Franklin

Norene Cashen

Calloway
See: Midnight Star

Cab Calloway
Born Cabell Calloway, 1907, in Rochester, NY. Died November 19, 1997, in Hockessin, DE.

Cab Calloway had a long and distiguished career in jazz, pop, and R&B, but he's best known for the song "Minnie the Moocher" and its call-and-response "Hi-De-Hi-De-Hi-De-Ho" refrain—a staple at sporting events and frat parties. In 1930, Calloway headlined at Harlem's Cotton Club with Cab Calloway and His Orchestra, always wearing his trademark white tie and tails. It was from there that "Minnie the Moocher" was first broadcast. Calloway went to Hollywood in 1932, where he appeared in films such as *Stormy Weather* with Lena Horne and *The Singing Kid* with Al Jolson. He continued to tour, and during his peak years (the 1940s) he employed Cozy Cole and Dizzy Gillespie, who was fired from the band for allegedly throwing a spitball at Calloway during a gig in Connecticut. Calloway's big band lasted until 1948. During the early 1950s, he toured Europe and America with a company of George Gershwin's opera *Porgy and Bess*. In 1968, Calloway also starred in the New York and touring casts of an all-black version of *Hello, Dolly*, which co-starred Pearl Bailey. For the remainder of his career, Calloway worked mainly as a solo act, although he would occasionally perform with a big band, and he gained a new generation of fans for "Minnie the Moocher" with a hot version—performed in his trademark white outfit—in 1980's *The Blues Brothers* film. He also donned the outfit for Janet Jackson's 1989 video "Alright."

what to buy: *Are You Hep to the Jive?* ✵✵✵✵ (Legacy, 1994, comp. Bob Irwin) is a generous 22-track compilation of Calloway's hits and favorites from 1939–47. It's the best place to start.

what to buy next: *Cab Calloway featuring Chu Berry* ✵✵✵✵ (Legacy, 1993, comp. Michael Brooks) spotlights the Calloway big band with one of its finest soloists, saxophonist Leon "Chu" Berry. *Kings of the Cotton Club* ✵✵✵ (Laserlight, 1989) is a good historical piece that mixes selections from Calloway and Scatman Crothers.

what to avoid: *Mr. Hi-de-ho* ✵✵ (MCA Jazz, 1982), a thin compilation that pales next to *Are You Hep to the Jive?*

the rest:
Best of the Big Bands ✵✵✵✵ (Legacy, 1990)
Cruisin' with Cab ✵✵✵ (Topaz Jazz, 1995)

worth searching for: *Cab Calloway* ✵✵✵✵ (Classics Recordings, 1931) contains the original "Minnie the Moocher" as well as songs of other artists of the era, including the Vipers Drag, St. Louis Blues, and Mood Indigo. *Kicking the Gong Around* ✵✵✵✵ (ASV/Living Era, 1992) showcases the naughtier side of Calloway, chock full of songs of sex and substance abuse—much in the spirit of his live performances. The import *On Film (1934–1950)* ✵✵✵✵ (Flyright, 1995, prod. various) is a good collection of his celluloid performances.

influences:
◀◀ Duke Ellington, Al Jolson

▶▶ Louis Jordan, Spike Jones, Screamin' Jay Hawkins, Kid Creole & the Coconuts

Barbara Ingalls and Gary Graff

Cameo
Formed 1976, in New York, NY.

Larry Blackmon, drums, vocals, bass, keyboards; Tomi Jenkins, vocals, percussion; Nathan Leftenant, trumpet, vocals; Gregory Johnson, keyboards (1976–83); Charlie Singleton, guitar, vocals (1981–86, 1992–present); Arnett Leftenant, saxophone (1976–82); Eric Duram, guitar (1976–81); Gary Dow, bass (1976–81); Wayne Cooper, vocals (1976–81); Anthony Lockett, guitar (1981–82); Jeryl Bright, trombone (1981–82); Thomas Campbell, keyboards (1981–82); Stephen Moore, vocals (1981–82); Aaron Mills, bass (1981–82, 1992–present); Kevin Kendrick, drums, keyboards (1992–present).

Fired up by watching veteran performers such as James Brown and Otis Redding at New York's legendary Apollo Theater as a child, the Julliard School-trained Larry Blackmon developed the idea for Cameo while playing with a succession of New York funk bands. Cameo evolved from the 13-piece New York City Players, a hard-core funk band dedicated to opposing the disco craze sweeping Manhattan and the country. Signed to Chocolate City Records in 1976, Cameo was always controlled by Blackmon, who acted as producer on their first record date and every one to follow. Their early albums were mostly Parliament and Ohio Players-influenced funk, going mostly unnoticed until 1979's hit single "I Just Want to Be" assaulted the charts. By 1982, Blackmon knew the era of the big funk band was over, paring down Cameo's then-nine pieces to just five—himself, Leftenant, Jenkins, Singleton, and Johnson—moving the group to Atlanta and starting his Atlanta Artists label years before L.A. Reid and Babyface would turn the city into an R&B mecca. Touches of New Wave and rock became a greater part of Cameo's sound through the 1980s, culminating with their masterwork, 1986's "Word Up." At this point, Cameo was just Blackmon, Leftenant, and Jenkins, featuring a sinewy, processed sound spiced by session players such as sax master Michael Brecker. But as hip-hop took up more space in R&B, Cameo's bizarre visual image seemed more and more out of step. A succession of uninspired albums didn't help, dooming that 1990s-era Cameo to working the soul nostalgia concert circuit.

what to buy: No Cameo album is more consistent than its most successful work, *Word Up* ✵✵✵✵ (Atlanta Artists/PolyGram, 1986, prod. Larry Blackmon). Featuring only seven songs, the record crackles with whipshot drum sounds, lean grooves, and Blackmon's distinctive vocal yowls. The title track is already a dance floor classic, while the hard grooving "She's Mine" features a solo by Brecker that's nothing short of miraculous.

what to buy next: The flash of inspiration that brought *Word Up* continues on *Machismo* ♫♫♫ (Atlanta Artists/PolyGram, 1988, prod. Larry Blackmon), a record containing one of the most potent commentaries on race around, the percolating "Skin I'm In." Elsewhere, "Soul Tightened" harkens back to their early horn band roots and "Pretty Girls" continues the driving funk groove that "She's Mine" started. With its splashes of New Wave synths and hard rocking guitar, *She's Strange* ♫♫♫ (Atlanta Artists/PolyGram, 1984, prod. Larry Blackmon) is the first turn toward what would become *Word Up*. The title track is likely the band's second most-distinctive tune—with a signature galloping bass drum part—while "Talking Out the Side of Your Neck" lets Singleton rock out and "Hangin' Downtown" shows what may be the band's best ballad ever.

what to avoid: Thanks to the band's lack of songwriting consistency, there's no shortage of bad Cameo records out there (for example, everything before 1980's *Cameosis*). But for pure, wrongheaded mediocrity, *Emotional Violence* **woof!** (Reprise, 1992, prod. Larry Blackmon) sets a tough standard to beat. Chock full of bad songs fleshed out with arrangements that are weird for weirdness's sake, this record served as a fitting eulogy for a band long past its prime.

the rest:
Cardiac Arrest ♫♫ (Chocolate City, 1977)
Ugly Ego ♫♫ (Casablanca, 1978)
We All Know Who We Are ♫♫ (Casablanca, 1978)
Secret Omen ♫♫ (Casablanca, 1979)
Cameosis ♫♫♫ (Atlanta Artists/ PolyGram, 1980)
Feel Me ♫♫♫ (Casablanca, 1980)
Knights of the Sound Table ♫♫♫ (Casablanca, 1981)
Alligator Woman ♫♫♫ (Casablanca, 1982)
Style ♫♫♫ (Atlanta Artists/PolyGram, 1983)
Single Life ♫♫♫ (Atlanta Artists/PolyGram, 1985)
Real Men . . . Wear Black (Atlanta Artists/PolyGram, 1990)
The Best of Cameo ♫♫♫ (Mercury, 1993)
In the Face of Funk ♫♫ (Raging Bull, 1994)
Nasty ♫♫♫ (Intersound, 1996)

worth searching for: Guitarist Charlie Singleton's rollicking solo single with a band called Modern Man, dubbed, "Nothing Ventured, Nothing Gained" (Arista, 1987). Powered by an irresistible hook and Singleton's own instrumental prowess on keyboards, guitar, and drum programming, this wacky, propulsive tune made you wish he'd struck out on his own sooner.

influences:
◀◀ James Brown, Ohio Players, Parliament/Funkedelic
▶▶ Prince, Ready for the World, Toni! Tony! Tone!

Eric Deggans

Camp Lo
Formed in the Bronx, NY.

Sonny Cheeba, vocals; Geechi Suede, vocals.

Imagine crossing the 110 and catching a glimpse of Foxy Brown and Truck Turner standing on the street corner, snappin' their fingers and slangin' freestyle rhymes. That's the image invoked by Bronx bombers Geechi Suede and Sonny Cheeba. Forgoing the dark, menacing grooves and critical beatdown lyrics that have dominated mid-'90s New York City rap, the duo goes back in time to the days of throw-your-hands-in-the-air party jams and slick, creamy grooves. Part of Camp Lo's appeal is that, much like the blaxploitation-era pimps, players, hustlers, and private I's to whom they pay tribute, the two artists have created their own jargon, flipping a unique brand of slang amidst a dense mixture of fat grooves.

what's available: On its debut, *Uptown Saturday Night* ♫♫♫ (Profile, 1997, prod. Trugoy the Dove, others), Camp Lo looks backwards: "Park Joint" is a tribute to the old Bronx block parties, and "Nicky Barnes (a.k.a. It's Alright)" is all *Shaft* shuffle, thanks to the crackling blaxploitation beats that run underneath the duo's smooth tag-team verbal volleys. Elsewhere, both "Sparkle" and "Rockin' It (a.k.a. Spanish Harlem)" are steeped in cool Latin jazz, while the catchy "B-Side to Hollywood" (featuring De La Soul's Trugoy) is propelled by tweaked horns that could have been lifted from a Warner Bros. cartoon. Sparking, too, is the group's ultracool breakout hit, "Luchini (a.k.a. This Is It)."

influences:
◀◀ Digable Planets, De La Soul, Isaac Hayes

Spence D.

Tevin Campbell
Born November 12, 1978, in Waxahachie, TX.

Somewhat of a Renaissance man (boy), church choirboy Tevin Campbell actually began his professional career on television, starring in *Wally and the Valentines*. Quincy Jones introduced him to the world as a singer on his *Back on the Block* album, on which Campbell sang the title track and the #1 single "Tomorrow (Better You, Better Me)." Prince joined the fray by inviting Campbell to sing the future sing-along dance hit "Round and Round" on the soundtrack album to *Graffiti Bridge*. So it was with substantial credentials that Campbell began his own recording career, mixing his own releases with appearances on all-star collections such as *Handel's Messiah: A Soulful Celebration*, *A Very Special Christmas*, the soundtrack album to *A Thin Line Between Love and Hate*, *Songs from West Side Story*, and the *Rhythm of the Games* Olympics album.

what to buy: *T.E.V.I.N.* ♪♪♪ (Qwest, 1991, prod. Arthur Baker, Narada Michael Walden, Al B. Sure!, Kyle West, Prince, Quincy Jones) is a winner of an album, kicking off with a medley of "Round and Round," "Interlude," and "Over the Rainbow and On to the Sun." "Perfect World" and "Look What We'd Have (If You Were Mine)" show the range of the then-15 year old's vocal ability. After taking time to participate in *Handel's Messiah: A Soulful Celebration*, Campbell recorded *I'm Ready* ♪♪♪ (Qwest, 1993, prod. Daryl Simmons, Prince, Narada Michael Walden, Babyface). "Can We Talk," the catchy #1 single written by Babyface and Daryl Simmons, was nominated for Best R&B Song and Best R&B Vocal Performance in the 36th annual Grammy Awards.

the rest:
Back to the World ♪♪♪ (Qwest, 1996)

influences:
◀◀ Jackson 5, New Edition, Prince, Babyface
▶▶ Brandy

Christina Fuoco

Candyman

Born June 25, 1968, in Los Angeles, CA.

If former Tone-Loc sidekick Candyman was, indeed, a piece of candy, what type of candy might he be? Certainly not a jawbreaker, since the flavor-of-the-month rapper's stint in the spotlight didn't last long. A good guess might be candy corn, given that the pop rapper tended to come off as a gimmicky and, yes, corny MC who was destined to wind up on a K-Tel collection someday. And that he did, appearing on the label's *Rap's Most Wanted* collection with his crossover hit, "Knockin' Boots."

what to buy: The Candyman can (and will) be remembered for one PG-rated song: "Knockin' Boots," his hit ode to hittin' skins

that's included on the uneven debut, *Ain't No Shame In My Game* ♪♪♪ (Epic, 1990, prod. various).

the rest:
Playtime Is Over ♪♪ (Epic, 1991)
I Thought U Knew ♪♪ (I.R.S., 1993)

influences:
◀◀ Tone-Loc, Sir Mix-a-Lot, D.J. Jazzy Jeff & the Fresh Prince, Three Times Dope
▶▶ Paperboy

Josh Freedom du Lac

Capone-N-Noreaga

Formed in Queens, NY.

Capone, vocals; Noreaga, vocals.

Rappers Capone and Noreaga are among the newest wave of Queens-bred urban bards to make a dent on the worldwide hip-hop scene. And as contemporaries and associates of both Mobb Deep and Nas, their ties are legit and strong to that heritage, most of which still flows from the monumentally inventive pool of talent hailing from the infamous Queensbridge Projects, as well as the increasingly prolific LeFrak City section of the New York borough. Taking direct stylistic and thematic cues from their aforementioned Queensbridge counterparts, Capone-N-Noreaga also added a new lexicon to the street vocabulary of New York and rap in general, popularizing the renaming of their urban environment: Queensbridge is Kuwait, LeFrak is Iraq, Brooklyn is Baghdad, and so on. On their impressive 1997 debut *The War Report*, their real-life crime tales are given extra emphasis by their rugged but smooth flows, which glorify the thug and gangsta life without remorse or excuse. Although the duo is new to the scene, the continuing popularity of Queens-style rap should ensure that their blend of true skills with compelling storytelling capabilities will keep Capone-N-Noreaga relevant for years to come.

what's available: The opening salvo from this duo, *The War Report* ♪♪♪♪ (Penalty/Tommy Boy, 1997, prod. Khadafi, Marley Marl, EZ Elpee, others), isn't really as much a disparate album as it is a continuation of the revived Queensbridge saga that was kicked off by Nas's *Illmatic* and *It Was Written*, as well as by Mobb Deep's *The Infamous*. Featuring interesting production

Candyman (© Ken Settle)

work by EZ Elpee, Khadafi (formerly known as both Tragedy and the Intelligent Hoodlum) and the Godfather of the Queensbridge sound, Marley Marl, among others, songs such as "LA, LA," "Illegal Life," "Parole Violators," and "Bloody Money" are great examples of the duo's gritty street perspective and showcase the rappers' ability to tell stories in a stark and captivating manner. And the "Capone Phone" segments—recorded while the rapper was in the big lock-up (the two actually met doing hard time)—make it clear that the tales Capone-N-Noreaga tell come from first-hand perspectives of the mean streets.

influences:

◀◀ Kool G Rap, Nas, Mobb Deep, Rakim

Brian Coleman

Irene Cara

Born March, 18, 1958, in the Bronx, NY.

A multifaceted singer, musician, songwriter, dancer, and actor, Irene Cara is a star who burned twice as bright but dimmed far too soon, paying a heavy price for *Fame*. The child of performing parents, Cara was working professionally by the age of five and made her Broadway debut (in the Shirley Jones-Jack Cassidy musical *Maggie Flynn*) at nine. In 1972, her mother-manager landed Cara a role on the educational TV series *The Electric Company,* where she appeared for a year as a member of the show's rock-group-with-a-message, Short Circus. One of the few pop singers of the past 30 years who was an established, accomplished actor before making her musical breakthrough, Cara was an original cast member of the off-Broadway Fats Waller salute *Ain't Misbehavin',* and starred in such movies as *Sparkle* and *City Heat* and the TV docudramas *The Guyana Tragedy: The Story of Jim Jones* and *Roots: The Next Generation.* But she may always be best remembered for her performance in and exhilarating rendition of the title song to the 1980 motion picture *Fame,* a musical soap opera about the high hopes and hard realities of students at New York's High School of Performing Arts. The song "Fame" won the Academy Award for Best Original Song of 1980, Cara earned a Grammy (and plaudits as "Top New Female Vocalist" in *CashBox*), and the soundtrack album sold well over 1 million copies. In 1984 she repeated the formula, earning a Golden Globe Award and two more Grammys for her version of "Flashdance . . . What a Feeling," theme song to the movie *Flashdance.* Cara has been embroiled in a lengthy legal dispute with Geffen Records in recent years, which has caused her to become disillusioned with the music business. Though she still appears periodically on

television, her powerful, exuberant voice has been sorely missed among the crop of contemporary female vocalists.

what to buy: It's a testament to the brilliance and enduring popularity of *Fame* ℐℐℐℐ (PolyGram, 1980, prod. Michael Gore) that the CD version of the movie soundtrack remains widely available almost two decades after the film's release. While it's a full cast production, you can hear Cara's voice all over the place, most notably in "Out Here on My Own" and her breathtaking "I Sing the Body Electric."

the rest:
Flashdance ℐℐ (PolyGram, 1983)

worth searching for: Cara's first solo LP, *Anyone Can See* ℐℐℐ (Epic, 1982), and any video copy of *The Electric Company* circa 1972 (in which a precocious young Cara belts out "E on the End" like she was singing "The Star Spangled Banner"), have two things in common: they're both nearly impossible to find, and they're both remarkable collectors' items.

influences:

◀◀ Carmen Miranda, Lena Horne, Donna Summer, Gloria Gaynor, Barbra Streisand

▶▶ Madonna, Laura Branigan, Celine Dion, Paula Abdul, Taylor Dayne, Tiffany

Sherese L. Robinson

Mariah Carey

Born March 27, 1970, in Long Island, NY.

A product of a black Venezuelan father and Irish-American mother, Carey seemed born to be a pop star—wielding a soulfully astonishing seven-octave voice while offering a supermodel-ready look that barely hints at her ethnic origins. Working as a backup singer for various R&B sessions around Manhattan during her late teens—while supporting herself as the self-described "world's worst waitress"—the singer honed her songwriting talents with keyboardist Ben Margulies. On one such gig, backing R&B one hit wonder Brenda K. Starr at a party, Carey got her big break; Starr presented a demo tape of hers to Columbia Records chief Tommy Mottola, who was so taken with the material while driving home, he headed back to the party to meet Carey. Before long, with Mottola guiding her career—Mottola, who was eventually named president of Sony Music, married Carey in 1993 (they split in 1997)—the singer released a single, "Visions of Love," that went to #1 on the pop charts in 1990. Carey would eventually earn five consecutive #1 pop singles over her first two albums (a record for a new artist), along with two Grammy Awards. From that point, Carey—most often compared to fellow hitmaking diva

Whitney Houston—could do no wrong, offering an appealing pop sound leavened with touches of soul. An EP version of her *MTV Unplugged* performance soared to the top of the charts in 1992, along with her third record a year later. Though her first-ever concert tour in 1993 met with mixed reviews, a #1 duet with Boyz II Men in 1995 proved she still retained her golden touch. So far, she's sold 70 million albums worldwide, though she's recently been slighted in Grammy competition. And it remains to see how her split with Mottola will affect her career.

what to buy: For anyone looking at Carey's catalog, "what to buy" depends on what the collector wants. Fans of her treacly pop sound—a generically accessible approach that nearly suffocates her amazing vocal abilities—will want her debut disc, *Mariah Carey* ♬♬♬ (Columbia, 1990, prod. Mariah Carey, Walter Afanasieff, Rhett Lawrence, Narada Michael Walden, Ben Margulies, Ric Wake). Featuring the hit singles "Vision of Love" and "Love Takes Time," it's the most vibrant of her studio discs.

what to buy next: For those who yearn to hear Carey break free of her commercial prison, the closest you'll get is her *MTV Unplugged* ♬♬♬ (Columbia EP, 1992, prod. Mariah Carey, Walter Afanasieff). Though the 26-plus people appearing on this disc seem to belie the Unplugged ethic, Carey's vibrant live performance is nearly worth the heresy. As schmaltzy as it might seem, her take on the Jackson 5's "I'll Be There" really does impress—at least on the first hundred listens.

what to avoid: For fans of truly expressive soul music, everything in Carey's catalog goes down like a sawdust sandwich. But her *Merry Christmas* ♬♬ (Columbia, 1994, prod. Walter Afanasieff), mixing standards like "Silent Night" with original hits such as "All I Want For Christmas Is You," is enough to make any true soul fan reach for a few stiff shots of egg nog.

the rest:
Emotions ♬♬♬ (Columbia, 1991)
Music Box ♬♬♬ (Columbia, 1993)
Daydream ♬♬♬ (Columbia, 1995)
Butterfly ♬♬ (Columbia, 1997)

worth searching for: It's a bit gruesome, but it's worth seeing a videotape of 1995's Grammy awards telecast—if only for the horror on Carey's face as she is consistently edged out (and eventually shut out, despite four nominations) by Alanis Morissette and Annie Lennox.

influences:
◀◀ Whitney Houston, Minnie Riperton, Irene Cara

▶▶ Toni Braxton, Celine Dion

Eric Deggans

Jean Carne

Born Sarah Jean Perkins, in Columbus, GA.

Jean Carne has long bubbled under the R&B mainstream, a powerful singer who's never quite exploded into stardom. But it's not for lack of trying. Raised in New Orleans, Carne met her future husband, pianist Doug Carn, at Morris Brown College in Atlanta. They moved to Los Angeles and recorded three albums of well-known jazz instrumentals, to which Carne added lyrics—an ambitious move that nobody seemed interested in at the time. Carne began a solo career in 1974, singing with Earth, Wind & Fire, Mtume, and Duke Ellington. She also hooked up with Norman Connors, singing on his *Skewfoot* and *Saturday Night Special* albums before he introduced her to Kenny Gamble and Leon Huff, who signed her to Philadelphia International. She was there until 1982, moving on to Motown, where she recorded the *Trust Me* album with Connors. Despite the lack of success, Carne (she added the "e" to her surname during the early 1980s) has continued to record, including guest vocals for Roy Ayers, Rick James, and others. But mostly she works the club circuit, with particular success in Britain and Europe.

what's available: *Happy to Be with You* ♬♬♬ (Philadelphia International, 1979/The Right Stuff, 1994, prod. Dexter Wansel) is representative of her work on Philadelphia International, with relatively strong material, save an ill-advised cover of "You Light Up My Life."

worth searching for: Much of Carne's guest and session work is out of print, too, though she contributes some tasty vocals on Grover Washington Jr.'s *Strawberry Moon* (Columbia, 1987/ 1990).

influences:
◀◀ Sarah Vaughan, Dinah Washington, Ella Fitzgerald, Ann Peebles

▶▶ Anita Baker, Sade, Seal

Gary Graff

Clarence Carter

Born January 14, 1936, in Montgomery, AL.

For a blind guy, Clarence Carter sure did a lot of cheatin' and homewreckin'. Bad for the monogamists but good for us, as his leacherous ways produced a bona fide classic, "Slip Away." A back door proposition with Carter woefully copping to the tawdriness of it all as he slides his foot in the door, the song is a close second to "Dark End of the Street" as the greatest stolen-love R&B song ever. The rest of his body of work follows the tracks that "Slip Away" laid down, with no less lascivious results, as his trademark "heh-heh-heh" growl can still make the dudes pull their girlfriends a little closer.

what to buy: *Snatching It Back: The Best of Clarence Carter* 𝄞𝄞𝄞𝄞 (Rhino, 1992, prod. Rick Hall) is a solid 21-track compilation that contains "Slip Away" and "Patches" as well as other important tracks, such as his absurdly profound reworking of "Dark End of the Street." Preaching over the song's subtle groove, Carter fuses the sexual and the spiritual into a dizzying stir of desire.

what to buy next: *DR. C.C.* 𝄞𝄞𝄞 (Ichiban, 1987, prod. Clarence Carter) is highlighted by the gloriously lewd "Strokin'." In a handshake deal with Ichiban, Carter still releases albums sporadically.

what to avoid: *The Dr.'s Greatest Prescriptions* 𝄞𝄞𝄞 (Ichiban, 1992, prod. Clarence Carter) isn't a bad compilation, but the Rhino package renders it obsolete.

the rest:
Touch of Blues 𝄞𝄞𝄞𝄞 (Ichiban, 1988)
Hooked on Love 𝄞𝄞𝄞 (Ichiban, 1988)
Messin' with My Mind 𝄞𝄞𝄞 (Ichiban, 1988)
Between a Rock and a Hard Place 𝄞𝄞𝄞 (Ichiban, 1990)
Have You Met Clarence Carter? 𝄞𝄞𝄞 (Ichiban, 1992)
Legendary 𝄞𝄞𝄞 (MCA Special Products, 1995)

worth searching for: *Sixty Minutes with Clarence Carter* 𝄞𝄞𝄞𝄞 (Fame, 1973, prod. Rick Hall), Carter's out-of-print final session with the Muscle Shoals gang, brought some new and more modern elements into his mix.

influences:
◄◄ Lightnin' Hopkins, Otis Redding, Solomon Burke
►► Rick James, Aerosmith, Keith Sweat, R. Kelly

Allan Orski

Jimmy Castor
/The Jimmy Castor Bunch

Formed mid-1960s, in New York. Disbanded 1979.

Jimmy Castor (born June 22, 1943, in New York, NY), saxophones, percussion; Leonard "Lenny" Fridie Jr., percussion; Douglas Gibson, bass; Harry Jensen, guitar; Robert Manigault, drums; Gerry Thomas, keyboards, trumpet; Ken Mills, piano; Hillard Gibson, guitar; Paul Martinez, bass; Reginald Barnes, drums; Martin Charles, congas; Richard Landrum, congas; Ellwood Henderson Jr., drums; Jeffrey

Grimes, guitar; Paul Forney, bass; Ray Brown, keyboards; Leburn Maddox, guitar; Nate Wingfield, guitar; William King, bongos.

Nicknamed "the Everything Man," at least in part for the breadth of his musical style, Jimmy Castor has had a career spanning roles as part-time doo-wop singer and seminal hip-hop influence. During the 1950s, Castor attended the same public school as Frankie Lymon and even sang as an occasional Teenager when Lymon went solo. (Frankie Lymon and the Teenagers also covered Castor's first record, "I Promise to Remember.") Later, as a session musician, he played saxophone on Dave "Baby" Cortez's 1962 hit "Rinky Dink." Castor had his first hit as a bandleader in 1967 with "Hey, Leroy, Your Mama's Callin' You," which reached the Top 40 of both the pop and R&B charts. By 1972, he was billing his band as the Jimmy Castor Bunch, and the group had a string of R&B hits—mostly novelties and instrumentals—throughout the 1970s. Many of his tunes incorporated at least one recurring character, either Leroy from that first hit, or Bertha Butt, originally introduced in the 1972 crossover smash "Troglodyte (Cave Man)." After recording into the early 1980s (his last significant hit was 1988's "Love Makes a Woman" with Joyce Sims), Castor joined a touring oldies version of the Teenagers.

what to buy: *The Everything Man: The Best of the Jimmy Castor Bunch* 𝄞𝄞𝄞 (Rhino, 1995, prod. Jimmy Castor, others) includes "Hey, Leroy, Your Mama's Callin' You" and "Southern Fried Frijoles" from his Smash years, as well as the doo-wop "I Promise" from Jimmy Castor & the Juniors in 1956. But mostly this showcases Castor's funk in all its salacious glory with dance favorites like "Bertha Butt Boogie," "King Kong," and "Bom Bom."

the rest:
Hey Leroy Your Mama's Callin' You 𝄞𝄞𝄞 (Collectables, 1995)

influences:
◄◄ Frankie Lymon & the Teenagers, King Curtis
►► The Gapp Band, Ohio Players, Zapp, Defunkt

Brian Mansfield

The Catalinas

Formed 1958, in Myrtle Beach, SC.

Bob Meyer, lead vocals; Tommy Plyer, vocals; Jack Stallings; Johnny Edwards; Sidney Smith, Rob Thome; O.C. Gravitte; Johnny Barker, keyboards; Ronnie Gittens, trumpet; Danny Pierce, saxophone, vocals; Gary Barker.

Few people outside of the Carolinas have heard of the Catalinas, but the group's practically a household name with the clubgoing populace of the Myrtle Beach area. A white R&B band that made its first records in the early 1960s, the Catalinas have made their base in the Carolina region since then. "Summertime's Calling Me" was a huge hit in the region in 1975, and is largely credited with sparking a dance revival for "The Shag." The group has had approximately 60 members in the four decades of its existence.

what's available: Largely a group of covers, *Summertime's Calling Me: The Catalinas Anthology* ♫♫♫ (Ripete, 1994, prod. various) chronicles the Catalinas' 29-year recording history with music from seven different labels and four previously unreleased tracks. Starting with "Hey Little Girl," a Gladiolas' cover that appeared on Excello in 1961, and carrying through to a new version of Chuck Willis's "Hang Up My Rock and Roll Shoes" recorded in 1990, it's an enjoyable look at white soul styles. The title track and the Four Seasons-inspired "You Haven't the Right" have rightly become cult classics.

influences:
◀◀ The Embers, Maurice Williams & the Zodiacs, the Penguins
▶▶ The Tymes, the Entertainers

Brian Mansfield

Cella Dwellas

Formed in Brooklyn, NY.

Ug, vocals; Phantasm, vocals.

The Cella Dwellas rose from the Flatbush underbrush to drop liquid linguistics on Masta Ace's "4 Da Mind" in 1995. Ug and Phantasm wasted little time parlaying the cameo into a recording deal, and within a year, they dropped a debut of their own.

what's available: On *Realms 'N Reality* ♫♫♫ (Loud, 1996, prod. Cella Dwellas, others), Ug and Phantasm unleash their mystical freestyles and rugged lyrical workouts over a variety of East Coast-centric tracks that combine taut drum breaks with a weird, minimalistic dark-jazz ambience featuring processed guitars, ethereal xylophones, and wispy keyboard fills. Fulfilling a promise to deliver "proper tracks, style, and metaphoric creativity," the duo shines on such cuts as the brooding "Advance to Boardwalk," which compares the game of the streets to a Parker Bros. creation. The cool metaphors and twisted Park Place wordplay make the track an engaging listen.

worth searching for: Masta Ace Incorporated's "4 Da Mind," off *Sittin' on Chrome* (Delicious Vinyl, 1995), is a laid-back classic.

influences:
◀◀ Masta Ace, Mobb Deep, Busta Rhymes, Black Moon

Spence D.

Celly Cel

Born M. McCarver, in Vallejo, CA.

Celly Cel grew up around the corner from E-40 and is part of the Vallejo rap kingpin's extended Sick Wid' It posse. Lyrically and musically, he's decidedly West Coast.

what's available: Given Celly Cel's Sick Wid' It ties, it's not surprising that *Killa Kali* ♫♫♫ (Sick Wid' It, 1995/Jive, 1996, prod. Studio Tone, Mike Mosely, others) features the down-n-dirty mob style for which E-40 and the Click have become famous. On the dizzying knockout punch, "4 Tha Skrilla," Celly is even joined by E-40 and the Click's B-Legit. The rapper, who implores you to "Remember Where U Came From" and, elsewhere, duets with gangsta-rap guru Spice 1, also slows the pace down on the R&B-flavored "It's Goin' Down," which twists up an old Keith Sweat beat ("How Deep Is Your Love").

influences:
◀◀ E-40 and the Click, C-Bo, Dangerous Dame, Dru Down, Too $hort, Spice 1, Rappin' 4-Tay

Spence D.

Chairmen of the Board

Formed 1969, in Detroit, MI. Disbanded 1971. Re-formed 1972. Disbanded 1976.

Original lineup: General Norman Johnson, vocals; Danny Woods, vocals; Harrison Kennedy, vocals; Eddie Curtis, vocals.

After leaving the Showmen, which had recorded the rock 'n' roll anthem "It Will Stand" for Minit Records in 1961, General Norman Johnson recruited Harrison Kennedy from Stone Soul Children and Eddie Curtis—who had sung with Lee Andrews & the Hearts and Huey Smith & the Clowns—to form the Chairmen of the Board. The group had a number of hits during their seven-year career, most notably 1970's "Give Me Just a Little More Time" and "Pay the Piper," both produced by the Holland-Dozier-Holland team that had produced many classic Motown singles. The trio disbanded in 1976, but Norman and Woods recorded together under the Chairmen's name in 1981. Johnson also wrote songs for other artists, including Clarence Carter's "Patches" and the Honey Cone's "Want Ads." Johnson's music has been championed by rock singer Paul Weller of the Jam and

Style Council; he made occasional performances and recordings during the '80s.

worth searching for: Chairmen of the Board albums aren't easy to find these days, but *Greatest Hits* ♫♫♫ (HDH/Fantasy, 1990, prod. Holland-Dozier-Holland) captures the best of the group's 17 charting singles, including "Give Me Just a Little More Time" and "Pay the Piper." The group's first album, *Give Me Just a Little More Time* ♫♫♫ (Invictus, 1970, prod. Holland-Dozier-Holland) is also worth a listen. "Carolina Girls," a 1980 solo recording by Johnson, is available on the four-disc *Beach Music Anthology* ♫♫♫♫ (Ripete, 1992, prod. various), along with the Showmen's "It Will Stand" and "39-21-46."

influences:

◀◀ Lee Andrews & the Hearts, Stone Soul Children, Motown

▶▶ Clarence Carter, the Honey Cone, Style Council, Dexy's Midnight Runners

see also: *The Showmen*

Brian Mansfield

The Chambers Brothers

Formed 1954, in Los Angeles, CA.

George Chambers, bass; Willie Chambers, guitar; Lester Chambers, harmonica; Joe Chambers, guitar; Brian Keenan, drums.

With their roots in gospel, the Mississippi-bred Chambers Brothers would seem unlikely funk-psychedelic crossover pioneers, but they provided a reference point for other crossover groups beginning to hit their stride at the same time, including Parliament/Funkadelic and Sly & the Family Stone. The acoustic gospel band made its first amplified appearance at the 1965 Newport Folk Festival to great acclaim. After white drummer Brian Keenan joined, the band hit the rock club circuit, where a typical set would include any number of lengthy jams that would have made another young Southern brother act, the Allmans, proud. In 1968, the Chambers had a hit single with "The Time Has Come Today," an edited version of the powerful 12-minute pyschedelic epic on their Columbia debut—the first of six releases to chart. The band pulled together equal parts of Otis Redding, Wilson Pickett, and Haight-Ashbury, always with a nod back to their beginning at the Mount Calvary Baptist Church near Carthage in Lee County, Mississippi.

what to buy: A terrific sampling of the band is available on *The Chambers Brothers' Greatest Hits* ♫♫♫♫ (Columbia, 1971, prod. David Rubinson, the Chambers Brothers, Tim O'Brien), with the complete version of "Time Has Come Today" plus the blistering "I Can't Turn You Loose" and the more traditional gospel crooning of "People Get Ready."

the rest:

People Get Ready ♫♫♫ (Vault, 1965)
Chambers Brothers Now ♫♫♫ (Vault, 1966)
Shout! ♫♫♫ (Vault, 1968)
Time Has Come ♫♫♫♫ (Columbia, 1969/1989)
Love, Peace and Hapiness ♫♫♫ (Columbia, 1969)
Feelin' the Blues ♫♫♫ (Vault, 1970)
Chambers Brothers Live at Fillmore East ♫♫♫♫ (Columbia, 1970)
Unbonded ♫♫♫ (Avco, 1974)
Right Move ♫♫♫ (Avco, 1975)
Love, Peace and Happiness ♫♫♫ (GNP/Crescendo, 1994)
Time Has Come: The Best of the Chambers Brothers ♫♫♫♫ (Columbia, 1996)

influences:

◀◀ Wilson Pickett, Otis Redding, James Brown, the Animals

▶▶ George Clinton, Sly & the Family Stone, Run-D.M.C., War

MC Connors

Gene Chandler

Born Eugene Dixon, July 6, 1937, in Chicago, IL.

Gene Chandler's association with his first and biggest hit, the perennial oldies-station favorite "Duke of Earl," tends to overshadow a long and fruitful career as a consistently effective Chicago pop/soul stylist. Chandler's instantly recognizable, anguished tenor, polished by his years in doo-wop with the Dukays, proved to be a perfect vehicle for the urbane love songs of Chicago's greatest pop/soul composer, Curtis Mayfield. Chandler, Mayfield, and producer Carl Davis collaborated on a string of hits for the Constellation label during the mid-1960s, beginning with "Rainbow," Chandler's most overtly soulful offering, and continuing with "Man's Temptation," "Just Be True," "What Now," "You Can't Hurt Me No More," and "Nothing Can Stop Me," among others. Later Davis/Chandler collaborations on the Brunswick and Checker labels also produced outstanding R&B hits, many written or co-written by Chandler. In 1970, Chandler's self-produced LP for Mercury yielded another oldies-station perennial, "Groovy Situation," lighter and more pop-oriented than his 1960s material, but nonetheless irresistible. Again collaborating with Carl Davis at Davis's new label, Chi-Sound, Chandler scored two more dance-oriented hit records—"Get Down" (1978, completed by Davis and released

Gene Chandler (© Jack Vartoogian)

while Chandler was in prison serving time for a drug-related conviction) and "Does She Have a Friend?" (1980).

what to buy: *Nothing Can Stop Me: Gene Chandler's Greatest Hits* ♫♫♫ (Varese Sarabande, 1994, prod. various) is the most complete and well documented of many available collections of Chandler's recordings. It spans Chandler's entire career and includes "Duke of Earl," "Does She Have a Friend," and most of the big hits in between.

what to buy next: *Live at the Regal,* (originally released as *Gene Chandler Live on Stage in '65)* ♫♫♫♫ (Constellation, 1965/ Charly, 1986/Collectables, 1986, prod. Bill Sheppard) is a reissue of a 1965 performance at this Chicago theater, on the heels of James Brown's groundbreaking *Live at the Apollo* LP. This disc captures one of the greatest live performances ever committed to audio tape, "Rainbow '65," which was released as a 45 from the LP and gave Chandler his second hit with this Curtis Mayfield song. "Rainbow '65" shows a side of Chandler's

talents that his pop/soul records only hinted at. The interplay between Chandler and his admiring (mostly female) audience, as he builds ever so slowly to the song's cathartic climax, is positively scandalous. *Greatest Hits* ♫♫♫ (Collectables, 1994, prod. various) contains some of Chandler's early hits for Vee-Jay and Constellation.

the rest:
Just Be True ♫♫♫♫ (Constellation, 1964)
Greatest Hits by Gene Chandler ♫♫♫♫ (Constellation, 1964)
Gene Chandler ♫♫♫♫ (Checker, 1967)
The Girl Don't Care ♫♫♫♫ (Brunswick, 1967)
There Was a Time ♫♫♫♫ (Brunswick, 1968)
Two Sides of Gene Chandler ♫♫♫♫ (Brunswick, 1969)
Duke of Earl ♫♫♫ (Collectables, 1976)
When You're #1 ♫♫ (20th Century/Chi-Sound, 1979)
Get Down ♫♫ (20th Century/Chi-Sound, 1979)
Gene Chandler ♫♫ (20th Century/Chi-Sound, 1980)
`80 ♫♫ (20th Century/Chi-Sound, 1980)
Nothing Can Stop Me ♫♫♫♫ (Charly, 1980)

Here's to Love 🎵🎵 (20th Century/Chi-Sound, 1981)
Duke of Soul 🎵🎵🎵 (Chess, 1984)
60s Soul Brother 🎵🎵🎵 (Kent, 1986)
Duke of Earl 🎵🎵🎵 (Vee-Jay, 1993)
Gene Chandler 🎵🎵🎵🎵 (Vee-Jay, 1994)
Rainbow `80 🎵🎵🎵 (Collectable, 1994)
Soul Master 🎵🎵🎵 (MCA Special Products, 1995)
Tell It Like It Is 🎵🎵 (Black Tiger, 1995)
(With the Dukays) *The Duke* 🎵🎵🎵 (Vee-Jay, 1995)
Soul of Gene Chandler 🎵🎵🎵 (Brunswick, 1996)

worth searching for: Much of Chandler's work remains available only in vinyl. *The Gene Chandler Situation* 🎵🎵🎵 (Mercury, 1970, prod. Gene Chandler) is an excellent pop record produced by Chandler that includes "Groovy Situation." Also on Mercury from 1971 is *Gene & Jerry: One on One* 🎵🎵🎵 (Mercury, 1971, prod. Jerry Butler), a fine collaboration between Chandler and Jerry Butler.

influences:

◀◀ Curtis Mayfield, Jerry Butler, Billy Stewart, Pookie Hudson

▶▶ The Chi-lites

Bill Pollak

Change

Formed late 1970s, in Italy. Disbanded mid-1980s.

Paolo Granolio, guitar; David Romani, bass. Other members included: Luther Vandross, Timmy Allen, Jeff Bova, Rick Brennan, Michael Campbell, Vince Henry, Toby Johnson, James Robinson, Deborah "Crab" Cooper, Rick Gallwey.

More recording entity than band, Change was formed by Italian producer Jacques Fred Petrus, who recruited European and American musicians—notably stalwarts Pablo Granolio and David Romani. Change's greatest distinction was the presence of singer Luther Vandross on its first two albums, just before he began pursuing his solo career in earnest. Singer Deborah "Crab" Cooper went on to work with C+C Music Factory during the 1990s. Change was also one of the first bands produced by former Time members James "Jimmy Jam" Harris and Terry Lewis (on 1984's "Change of Heart"). A lack of crossover success eventually caused the band to fade away, and Petrus was fatally shot in 1987.

what's available: The only Change album available is also its best. *Glow of Love* 🎵🎵🎵🎵 (Warner Bros., 1980, prod. Jacques Fred Petrus) is an exceptional effort, mixing Vandross's old school crooning with the jazzy, Teflon slickness of late

1970s/early 1980s R&B. "A Lover's Holiday" and "Searching" are seminal tracks of the time.

worth searching for: *Change of Heart* 🎵🎵🎵 (Atlantic, 1984, prod. James "Jimmy Jam" Harris, Terry Lewis) isn't quite as good as *Glow of Love*, but it's an early look at the Harris and Lewis production style that would later revolutionize pop music with Janet Jackson and others.

influences:

◀◀ Steely Dan, Earth, Wind & Fire, Mtume, Stuff

▶▶ Luther Vandross, C+C Music Factory, Tony! Toni! Tone!

see also: *Luther Vandross*

Gary Graff

Channel Live

Formed in New Jersey.

Hakim, vocals; Tuffy, vocals.

Both former schoolteachers, Hakim and Tuffy received their break courtesy of the Teacha' himself, KRS-One. The two had attended several of KRS-One's lectures around New York and frequently ended up in deep conversation with him. When the veteran artist discovered they were also rappers, he listened to their tape and helped them get a record deal.

what's available: Though "Mad Izm" (produced by and featuring KRS-One) was an irrepressible hit in the summer of '94, Channel Live can't sustain the momentum over the course of its full-length debut, *Station Identification* 🎵🎵 (Capitol, 1994, prod. KRS-One, Channel Live). Still notable, however, are "Reprogram" and "Down with the Devil."

influences:

◀◀ KRS-One

Jazzbo

The Channels

Formed early 1950s, in New York, NY.

Earl Michael Lewis, lead vocals; Larry Hampden, first tenor; Billy Morris, second tenor; Edward Doulphin, baritone; Clifton Wright, bass.

The truth is, some of the greatest R&B records of all time never became national hits at the time of their release, either because the tiny labels which released them didn't have sufficient resources to promote or distribute them, or because the music was only beginning to establish itself in the collective consciousness of young America—particularly young white America. One classic example of such a song was "The Closer You Are," recorded in June, 1956 by the Channels for the brand-new Whirling Disc label. Featuring glorious, soaring harmonies throughout all the verses, and stirring falsetto counterpoints and bass vocal acrobatics that would be copied by other singers for years to come, "The Closer You Are" was a recording totally distinct from anything that came before it.

what's available: For whatever reasons, the song didn't become a national hit, but it has survived on compilation LPs such as the outstanding boxed set *The Doo Wop Box: 101 Vocal Group Gems from the Golden Age of Rock 'n' Roll* 𝄞𝄞𝄞𝄞 (Rhino, 1994, prod. Bob Hyde, Walter DeVenne) and in the repertoires of doo-wop groups ever since it first hit the airwaves. As for the Channels, they never recorded their breakthrough hit, but survived in various configurations for many years. Such is the power of one great, transcendent record.

influences:

◀◀ The Platters, the Flamingos

▶▶ The Crests, Dion and the Belmonts, the Drifters, Phil Spector, the Righteous Brothers, Billy Vera, Huey Lewis and the News

Michael Kosser

The Chantels

Formed late 1940s, in the Bronx, NY. Disbanded 1970. Re-formed 1973.

Arlene Smith, lead vocals (late 1940s–59, 1973–present); Lois Harris, first tenor (late 1940s–59); Sonia Goring, second tenor (late 1940s–70); Jackie Landry, second alto (late 1940s–70); Rene Minus, alto/bass (late 1940s–70); Richard Barrett, lead (1959–60); Annette Smith (1960–70); Barbara Murray (1973–present); Pauline Moore (1973–present).

The first successful, and arguably the best, R&B girl group of the 1950s and 1960s, the Chantels featured classically trained lead singer Arlene Smith, whose voice could match the emotional impact of solo acts such as Ruth Brown and LaVern Baker, though Smith's voice was much sweeter. The Chantels formed at St. Anthony of Padua School in the Bronx, New York, and by the time they hooked up with writer/producer Richard Barrett, the five singers were natural together. The group had a number of successes, most notably with 1957's "Maybe," before Smith left the group for a solo career in 1960. Barrett, who previously had sung in a doo-wop group called the Valentines, added a new singer, Annette Smith, and for a while fronted the band himself. Arlene Smith became a teacher in the Bronx and formed a revival version of the Chantels in 1973.

what to buy: Most people know only "Maybe" if they know any of the Chantels recordings at all, but the 18 cuts on *The Best of the Chantels* 𝄞𝄞𝄞𝄞 (Rhino, 1990, prod. Richard Barrett) show that the group, especially when fronted by Arlene Smith (as they are on 14 of the songs) was incapable of making a bad record. Smith's voice exudes passion and vulnerability, while the backing singers sound nothing short of angelic.

what to buy next: The 40 tracks on *For Collectors Only* 𝄞𝄞𝄞 (Collectables, 1992, prod. Richard Barrett) only reinforces the impression of the Rhino collection. It's probably a little more than most people would need, but it's a fine collection nonetheless.

the rest:
Chantels 𝄞𝄞𝄞 (Collectables, 1991)

worth searching for: *We Are the Chantels* 𝄞𝄞𝄞 (End, 1958), the group's first album (they'd had some EPs previously), was also one of the first rock-era albums released by a female group.

influences:

◀◀ Frankie Lymon, Dinah Washington, Ruth Brown

▶▶ The Crystals, the Marvelettes, the Shirelles, the Supremes, the Ronettes

Brian Mansfield

Ray Charles

Born Ray Charles Robinson, September 23, 1930, in Albany, GA.

Not for nothing is he known as the Genius. In a career almost unparalleled in American popular music, Ray Charles has done more than almost any other artist to obliterate the lines that once existed between R&B, gospel, country, pop, jazz, and rock. Beginning as an imitator of the urbane vocal stylings of Nat "King" Cole and the uptown blues of Charles Brown, Charles eventually forged his own style, combining gospel music and harmonies and the country music of his youth with decidedly earthier lyrics reflecting love, lust, heartbreak, and hard times. Though Charles's increase in popularity occured simultanously with the rise of rock 'n' roll, he correctly commented in his autobiography that his work has little to do with the nascent genre—it contained too much despair to compete on the charts with the uptempo ravings of Little Richard, Jerry Lee Lewis, and Elvis Presley. Yet Charles remains a seminal influence on rock, and he was rightfully inducted into the Rock 'n' Roll Hall of Fame in 1986. In R&B, Charles is revered both for his voice, which reveals a seemingly depthless capacity for heartache, and for his deftly intuitive ideas, which find him

Ray Charles (© Jack Vartoogian)

mining influences as varied as Count Basie and Hank Williams, and turning the result into works of staggering originality. A man of Herculean determination, few opponents from the world of music—or from life in general, for that matter—have faced him down. Not all of his decisions have been right ones, but he stands behind them all. And why not? He is one of the most recognizable figures in all of music, thanks to such timeless hits as "I Got a Woman," "What'd I Say," "The Night Time Is the Right Time," "Hit the Road Jack," "Georgia On My Mind," "Unchain My Heart," "You Don't Know Me," "Busted," and countless others, to say nothing of his famous "Uh-huh" Diet Pepsi commercials. There is no one else like him.

what to buy: Charles's illustrious career has been documented with several excellent box sets, but *Genius & Soul: The 50th Anniversary Collection* ✍✍✍✍ (Rhino, 1997, prod. various) stands above them all, if only for pulling together for the first time material from all facets of Charles career and from all of the labels he's recorded for. At five discs, it's a hefty investment in time and money, but it's an absolute treasure. Starting with an early single from his Seattle days, the set moves through his "genius" phase at Atlantic, to the even more unbridled innovation of his ABC days—recording soulful country & western classics and covering the Beatles—to the quiet classics (such as his recent reading of Leon Russell's "A Song for You") that he records to this day. *Genius & Soul* is one of the best box sets ever assembled. For those unwilling or unable to treat themselves, start with both *Anthology* ✍✍✍✍ (Rhino, 1988, prod. Sid Feller, Joe Adams) and *The Best of Ray Charles: The Atlantic Years* ✍✍✍✍ (Rhino, 1994, prod. Jerry Wexler, Zenas Sears, Neshui Ertegun, Ahmet Ertegun). The 20-track *Anthology* contains the ABC material, including "Georgia On My Mind," "Let's Go Get Stoned," "Eleanor Rigby," "Hit the Road Jack," and "Unchain My Heart." *The Atlantic Years*, which also contains 20 tracks, features "I Got a Woman," "What'd I Say," "The Night Time Is the Right Time," and "Drown in My Own Tears." Both are the best single-disc representations of those periods of Charles's music currently available.

what to buy next: They're advertised as country & western, but there are few recordings as soulful as Charles's takes on Eddy Arnold's "You Don't Know Me," Hank Williams's "You Win Again," and Frankie Laine's "That Lucky Old Sun." On *Modern Sounds in Country and Western Music* ♪♪♪♪ (ABC, 1963, prod. Sid Feller, Joe Adams) those songs and others stand as monuments to Charles's innovation and sheer audacity. During the heightened racial tensions of the early 1960s, what other black man could have pulled this off? *Live* ♪♪♪♪ (Atlantic, 1987/Rhino 1990, prod. Nesuhi Ertegun, Zenas Sears) combines a pair of essential late 1950s live recordings, *Ray Charles at Newport* and *Ray Charles in Person*. The set reveals Charles's intensity and charisma as a concert performer and includes explosive versions of "The Right Time," "What'd I Say," and "Drown in My Own Tears."

what to avoid: Some of Charles's albums are ill-conceived or carried out, but none are truly wretched. The things to beware of, however, are the numerous cheap repackagings of his hits. If it's not on Atlantic, ABC, Rhino, or DCC, proceed with caution.

the rest:
The Great Ray Charles/The Genius After Hours ♪♪♪ (Atlantic, 1958 and 1961/Rhino, 1987)
(With Milt Hinton) *Soul Brothers/Soul Meeting* ♪♪♪ (Atlantic, 1958 and 1962/Rhino, 1989)
The Genius of Ray Charles ♪♪♪♪ (Atlantic, 1959/Rhino, 1990)
The Genius Hits the Road ♪♪♪ (ABC, 1960/Rhino, 1997)
The Best of Ray Charles ♪♪♪♪ (Atlantic, 1970/Rhino, 1988)
Would You Believe? ♪♪ (Warner Bros., 1990)
The Birth of Soul: The Complete Atlantic Rhythm & Blues Recordings, 1952–1959 ♪♪♪♪♪ (Rhino, 1991)
My World ♪♪♪ (Warner Bros., 1993)
Ain't That Fine ♪♪♪ (Drive Archive, 1994)
Blues + Jazz ♪♪♪♪ (Rhino, 1994)
The Early Years ♪♪♪ (Tomato, 1994)
Strong Love Affair ♪♪♪ (Qwest, 1996)
Berlin, 1962 ♪♪♪♪ (Pablo, 1996)

worth searching for: At press time, Rhino Records was in the midst of an extensive program of reissuing Charles's ABC sides. One worth waiting for is *A Message from the People* ♪♪♪♪ (ABC, 1972), which includes "Abraham, Martin, and John," "There'll Be No Peace without All Men As One," and Charles's brilliant renderings of "Look What They Done to My Song, Ma" and "America the Beautiful." It's a protest album of sorts, from a man whose politics before this album, and since, have seldom been on display.

influences:

◀◀ Nat "King" Cole, Charles Brown, Count Basie, the Grand Ole Opry, Louis Jordan, Claude Jeter

▶▶ Van Morrison, Joe Cocker, Billy Joel

Daniel Durchholz

The Charms

Formed 1953, in Cincinnati, OH.

Otis Williams, lead singer; Richard Parker, bass; Rolland Bradley, tenor; Donald Peak, tenor; Joseph Penn, baritone.

One of the great things about R&B in the 1950s was that the record companies were spread all over the map, as opposed to today when the entire music industry is largely concentrated in three American cities. In those days, besides New York, Los Angeles and Nashville, there were important recordings being made in places like Houston, Memphis, Philadelphia, Detroit, Boston, Chicago, Seattle and Washington, D.C. And then there was Sid Nathan's King Records empire, based in Cincinnati, Ohio. From that city and that conglomerate came the Charms, a teen vocal group featuring a 16-year-old lead singer named Otis Williams (not the same Otis Williams who later starred with the Temptations). The Charms started recording for Nathan's subsidiary label, Deluxe, in 1953 and a year later released their cover version of the song "Hearts of Stone"—a cover only because the Jewels came out with their rendition of the tune exactly one week before them. The Charms were in turn covered by the Fontaine Sisters two weeks later, and it was the Fontaines who turned "Hearts of Stone" into a #1 smash on the pop charts. (The Charms's single was none too shabby, however, peaking at #15.) They put out several more cover tunes before coming out with their first true original, "Two Hearts," a powerhouse uptempo recording built around an electrifying lead vocal by Williams. But the Charms didn't lead a charmed life: "Two Hearts" was covered by Pat Boone and became Boone's first hit pop record, reaching #16 and leaving them underappreciated on the R&B charts. Both Boone and the Fontaine Sisters recorded for Randy Wood's Dot Records in Gallatin, Tennessee, and Wood had a remarkable ear for selecting songs to cover. The Charms had other notable hits, including "Ivory Tower" (#12 pop), but that one was covered by Gale Storm and Cathy Carr, both of whom scored even greater success with the tune. The original hits stopped coming, but the Charms continued to record for King's organization through the early 1960s.

what's available: In keeping with the Charms's legacy of rotten luck, however, the only known doo-wop reissue of "Two Hearts" is by the Jewels, included in the essential boxed set

The Doo Wop Box: 101 Vocal Group Gems from the Golden Age of Rock 'n' Roll 𝄢𝄢𝄢𝄢 (Rhino, 1994, prod. Bob Hyde, Walter DeVenne).

influences:

◀◀ The Orioles, the Ravens, Clyde McPhatter and the Drifters

▶▶ The Jewels, Pat Boone, Frankie Lymon and the Teenagers, the Temptations, Smokey Robinson and the Miracles, the Jackson 5

Michael Kosser

The Charts
Formed early 1950s, in Harlem, NY.

Joe Grier, lead vocals; Leroy Binns, first tenor; Steven Brown, second tenor; Glenmore Jackson, baritone; Ross Buford, bass.

Like many R&B groups of the 1950s, the Charts started out on the streets of Harlem, a bunch of young gang members who apparently graduated from crooks to crooners. Yet they stole one defining moment in pop music history. One of their members, Joe Grier, wrote a song called "Deserie," their rendition of which was good enough to get them onto the bill at the historic Apollo Theater for Amateur Night; unpolished enough to get them booed off the stage; and interesting enough to attract the attention of a rival group singer named Les Cooper. Cooper became their manager and landed the act a label deal. The Charts made the charts: "Deserie" was recorded in 1957, never went higher than #88 in the *Billboard* pop rankings—yet nonetheless became a doo-wop standard.

what's available: When you hear the song, as on the Rhino Records compilation *The Doo Wop Box: 101 Vocal Group Gems from the Golden Age of Rock 'n' Roll* 𝄢𝄢𝄢𝄢 (Rhino, 1994, prod. Bob Hyde, Walter DeVenne) you will understand. Raw and ragged, it was—and is—magnificent.

Michael Kosser

Chubby Checker
Born Ernest Evans, October 3, 1941, in Andrews, SC.

Chubby Checker is a fair to middling singer who happened to get extremely lucky when his version of Hank Ballard's "The Twist" hit the #1 (in both 1960 and in 1962) and spawned an unparrelled dance craze whose presence can still be felt in films such as "Pulp Fiction" and at any wedding or Bar Mitzvah reception. Unfortunately, Checker had little to say after "The Twist" (besides suggesting "Let's Twist Again"). Not that it mat-

tered, as it's been a consistent meal ticket. He even managed to squeeze more life out of it again in 1988 by way of a duet with rappers the Fat Boys.

what to buy: *Chubby Checker's Dance Party* 𝄢𝄢 (K-Tel, prod. various) is the most extensive compilation, with the innocent insistence of "The Twist" and its follow-up "Let's Twist Again." There are some other songs, too, if anyone's interested.

the rest:
All Time Greats 𝄢𝄢 (Special Music)
Mr. Twister 𝄢𝄢 (Charly, 1992)

influences:

◀◀ Fats Domino, Big Joe Turner

▶▶ Fat Boys, Allen Touissant, Billy Joel

Allan Orski

Cherrelle
Born Cheryl Norton, 1958, in Los Angeles, CA.

Cheryl Norton, a Detroit bank teller, got her big break—and became Cherrelle—during the late 1970s, when soul singer and guitarist Michael Henderson was taken by her singing on her Detroit day job. After four years of touring with Henderson, she landed at Tabu Records, where the house producers— Prince protégé's Jimmy "Jam" Harris and Terry Lewis—crafted a sound around the petite singer's powerful voice. The musical marriage paid off; their first hit, "I Didn't Mean To Turn You On," was followed by bigger successes—with more adult themes—such as "Saturday Love," her duet with Alexander O'Neal. Cherrelle's 1985 album *High Priority* spawned three hit R&B singles, and its follow-up, *Affair*, contained her biggest hit, "Everything I Miss at Home." But she never nabbed a crossover audience, even as her cousin, Pebbles, did, if only briefly. Cherrelle, one of the 1980s' most consistent R&B hitmakers, and a popular performer in the U.K., was not so fortunate during the 1990s, particularly after she and the production team parted ways.

what to buy: *The Best of Cherrelle* 𝄢𝄢𝄢 (Tabu/Motown, 1995, prod. various) is the obvious choice, both because Cherrelle was primarily a singles artist and because it may be near impossible to find prints of her first two albums.

what to buy next: *Affair* 𝄢𝄢𝄢 (Tabu, 1988, prod. James "Jimmy Jam" Harris III, Terry Lewis), is really two albums: a syrupy but genuinely sensitive work, which includes self-produced tunes like "My Friend" and "Lucky," and the polished, radio-friendly final work produced by Jam and Lewis.

what to avoid: *The Woman In Me* 🎵🎵 (Tabu/A&M, 1991, prod. various), her last original album, was supposed to be the work that showcased her voice and crossed her over to the pop market. But without Jam and Lewis at the helm, the work under-whelmed new listeners and alienated those accustomed to her sound.

worth searching for: *Fragile* 🎵🎵 (Tabu, 1984, prod. James "Jimmy Jam" Harris, III, Terry Lewis) and *High Priority* 🎵🎵 (Tabu, 1985, prod. James "Jimmy Jam" Harris, III, Terry Lewis), both out of print, are each entertaining, and interesting looks at early Jam and Lewis.

influences:
◄◄ Stephanie Mills, Evelyn "Champagne" King
►► Janet Jackson, Alexander O'Neal, S.O.S. Band

Franklin Paul

Neneh Cherry

Born Neneh Mariann Karlsson, March 10, 1964, in Stockholm, Sweden.

"You never seen a girl like this before/Because she's so sassy and completely secure," rapper Guru comments on the lead track of Neneh Cherry's sophomore album, perhaps as accurate and concise a summation of the singer/rapper's appeal as is possible. The daughter of Swedish artist Moki Cherry and West African percussionist Amadu Jah, Cherry is also the stepdaughter of avant-garde jazz trumpeter Don Cherry, and all of their work seems to have made an impact on her innovative, rhythmic, and jazz-inflected hip-hop/pop. Cherry performed with the ska band the Nails and the punk act the Slits before recording several albums as a percussionist with the irreverent jazz-fusion outfit Rip Rig + Panic, which in turn evolved into Float Up C.P. (both the latter two acts' albums are out of print). Cherry has enjoyed some popularity, but compared to the success of many lesser talents, she remains a tragically overlooked artist. Her mix of sung/spoken vocals presaged so-called "alternative" rap, and her sampledelic grooves paved the way for trip hop. She is a queen without a kingdom.

what to buy: Cherry's debut, *Raw Like Sushi* 🎵🎵🎵 (Virgin, 1989, exec. prod. Cameron "Booga Bear" McVey), leads off with the irrepressible and street-smart "Buffalo Stance," a single that blazed several hip-hop trials by incorporating jazz riffs, a sung chorus, and a strong, self-assured female perspective. The rest

of the album doesn't quite rise to that standard, but it has many fine moments, including the conscious "Inna City Momma" and "The Next Generation" as well as the breezy follow-up single "Kisses on the Wind" and the unabashedly sensualist "Outre Risque Locomotive."

the rest:
Homebrew 🎵🎵🎵 (Virgin, 1992)

worth searching for: For unknown reasons, Cherry's third album, *Man* 🎵🎵🎵 (Circa/Virgin, 1996) has never been released in the U.S. It contains her version of Marvin Gaye's "Trouble Man" and "7 Seconds," a duet with Yousou N'Dour.

influences:
◄◄ Don Cherry, Sex Pistols, Madonna
►► Fugees, Tricky, Bjork

Daniel Durchholz

Chi-Ali

An adopted member of the heralded Native Tongues posse who some incorrectly assumed was the mysterious kid "Jeff" from De La Soul's many B-sides, Chi-Ali was the protege of Black Sheep's Dres. Though he certainly had skills, the numerous references to his young age proved limiting. So, too, did that thing called puberty.

what's available: *The Fabulous Chi-Ali* 🎵🎵 (Relativity, 1992, prod. Beatnuts, Black Sheep) may be one of those albums only the die-hard Native Tongues fan should have: the posse cut "Let the Horns Blow" features one of Dres' better verses, and there's also a guest appearance from Phife of A Tribe Called Quest.

influences:
◄◄ Black Sheep, De La Soul, the Beatnuts
►► Kris Kross

Jazzbo

Chic

Founded 1977, in New York City, NY. Disbanded 1984. Re-formed 1992.

Nile Rodgers, guitar; Bernard Edwards, bass; Tony Thompson, drums; Alfa Anderson, vocals; Norma Jean Wright, vocals (1977); Luci Martin, vocals (1978–79); Luther Vandross, cameo vocals (1978–79).

From their first mega-hit single "Dance, Dance, Dance" in 1977 until the end of the disco era, Chic dominated the airwaves and the dance floors. Chic created some of the best bass-lines and grooves in the history of the industry; not just a 1970s throwaway/one-hit-wonder, Chic has been sampled by everyone from Queen to the Sugarhill Gang. Combined with Nile Rodgers' ear for a good riff and a healthy injection of Vandross's vocals, Chic can still hold it's own to any modern pop band. Sadly, Edwards' death from pneumonia in 1996 brought an end to one of the great trend-setting runs in R&B and pop history.

what to buy: *Dance, Dance, Dance: The Best of Chic* ✔✔✔✔ (Atlantic, 1991, prod. Nile Rodgers, Bernard Edwards, Kenny Lehman) has all the major hits from one of the best pop groups ever. Take some great guitar work, a good groove, crisp production, with a little funk and you've got a hypnotic rhythm laid under some of the best dance songs around. *Best of Chic, Vol. 2* ✔✔✔✔ (Rhino, 1992, prod. Nile Rodgers, Bernard Edwards, Kenny Lehman, Bob Edwards) follows up on the first *Best of* with a series of deeper album cuts. They weren't all big hits, but these tracks are no less worthy of praise, they remain beat-heavy enough for any dance floor, yet are still musically innovative and sufficiently varied to be enjoyed in any setting.

what to buy next: *Everybody Dance* ✔✔✔✔ (Rhino, 1995, prod. Nile Rodgers, Bernard Edwards, Kenny Lehman) is a budget-priced compilation of most of the hit songs plus a few seemingly random tracks to fill out the album; a good starting point to hear some of Chic's best hits without spending a lot of money. *C'est Chic* ✔✔✔✔ (Atlantic, 1978, prod. Nile Rodgers, Bernard Edwards) catches Chic at the height of the era. With both Alfa Anderson and Norma Jean Wright still on vocal duties, and Vandross' sublime backing help, Chic spawned their best LP and two hugely popular songs, "Dance, Dance, Dance (Yowsah, Yowsah, Yowsah)" and "Le Freak." Taking cues from the retro movement Chic re-formed after eight years to record *Chic-Ism* ✔✔✔✔ (Warner, 1992, prod. Nile Rodgers, Bernard Edwards). Years of producing acts like David Bowie and Madonna have left Rodgers with a keen sense of what goes into a good pop song, and while there's nothing revolutionary on here all the tracks are well crafted. If this had been released during the 1970s, it would have been a smash, but as it is the album provides a pleasant nostalgic feeling. If you want to hear some new disco songs, this is a good place to get them.

what to avoid: *Chic* ✔✔ (Atlantic, 1977, prod. Bernard Edwards, Nile Rodgers, Kenny Lehman, Bob Edwards) is not exactly bad, but beyond "Dance, Dance, Dance," it's not exactly good, either. With "Dance. . . ." on so many other, better, albums there should be no reason to take a second look at this one.

the rest:
Risque ✔✔✔✔ (Atlantic, 1979)
Real People ✔✔✔ (Atlantic, 1980)
Take It Off ✔✔✔ (Atlantic, 1981)

worth searching for: A few albums were released on vinyl but never made the conversion over to CD. These LPs are all currently out of print, but if you happen to see one in the bargain bin, you should pick it up: *Chic Chic* ✔✔✔ (Atlantic, 1981, prod. Bernard Edwards, Nile Rodgers); *Tongue In Chic* ✔✔✔ (Atlantic, 1982, prod. Bernard Edwards, Nile Rodgers); and *Believer* ✔✔✔ (Atlantic, 1984, prod. Bernard Edwards, Nile Rodgers)

influences:

◀◀ Parliament/Funkadelic, James Brown, Sylvester

▶▶ Mick Jagger, Madonna, David Bowie, Queen, Sugarhill Gang, Peter Gabriel, Bryan Ferry, Duran Duran, Al Jarreau, Philip Bailey, Sister Sledge, Diana Ross, Robert Palmer, Blondie

Bryan Lassner

The Chiffons

Formed 1960, in the Bronx, NY. Disbanded 1995.

Patricia Bennett; Barbara Lee; Judy Craig (1960–69); Sylvia Peterson (1962–95).

With infectious chants of "doo-lang, doo-lang" and a sugary sweet demeanor, the Chiffons epitomized all the most innocent qualities of the Girl Group sound, yet strong material and never less than assured performances helped them create several absolute classics which remain to this day among the best of their genre. Bennett, Lee, and Craig had already met and begun singing together in high school when a local writer named Ronnie Mack hired them in 1960 to record demo tapes of his songs. Impressed with their abilities, he cut a version of the Shirelles' "Tonight's the Night" with the trio and sold it to the small Big Deal label shortly thereafter, resulting in a minor national hit. The following year, Mack began working with the Tokens, hot off their chart-topper "The Lion Sleeps Tonight"; together they helped record Mack's song "He's So Fine" with the Chiffons, which hit #1 in March of 1963. The follow-up, "One Fine Day," was originally written for the Tokens by Gerry Goffin and Carole King: their demo recording, featuring Little Eva of "The Locomotion" fame on lead vocals and King's own distinctive piano accompaniment, was given to the Chiffons instead, who recorded their vocals over Eva's and sent it to #5 by July. That same year, two other Chiffons/Tokens collaborations were released under the pseudonym the Four Pennies, but the next

Chiffons release—their third of 1963 (and the third to use the word "fine" in its title)—stalled at a disappointing #40. Then the British Invasion banished practically every girl group not on Motown from the charts, and despite a slot opening for the Rolling Stones on their first-ever American tour, the Chiffons failed to place another record in the Top 10 until "Sweet Talkin' Guy" in 1966. It was their last U.S. best-seller, yet even after the departure of lead vocalist Craig in 1969, the group continued touring and occasionally recording (including a 1976 release of George Harrison's "My Sweet Lord," a song which Harrison had just been found guilty of "subconsciously plagiarizing" from "He's So Fine"). The Chiffons, in one form or another, persevered well into the 1990s, until Lee's death from a heart attack at the age of 48.

what's available: The sorrowfully skimpy *Chiffons' Greatest Hits* 🎵🎵🎵 (The Right Stuff, 1996, prod. various) is the easiest to find, and although it contains all of their most popular recordings, at a mere 10 tracks it's really too brief to offer the group the overview it deserves.

worth searching for: Two British imports, *The Fabulous Chiffons* 🎵🎵🎵 (Ace, 1992, prod. various) and *Greatest Recordings* 🎵🎵🎵🎵 (Ace, 1994, prod. various) are fairly readily available, and the latter contains many B-sides and album tracks which show there was much more than mere "doo-lang"-ing going on within the ranks. *One Fine Day* 🎵🎵🎵 (Laurie, 1963/Remember Records, 1996), a reissue of the Chiffons' third album, provides a picture-perfect glance at pre-Beatle Pop and R&B in its original form.

influences:

◀◀ The Chantels, the Shirelles, Phil Spector

▶▶ The Angels, the Go-Go's, George Harrison

Gary Pig Gold

The Chi-Lites

Formed 1960, in Chicago, IL.

Eugene Record (1960–75, 1980–88); Marshall Thompson; Robert Lester; Creadel Jones (1960–83, present); Clarence Johnson (1960); Stan Anderson (1973–80); David Scott (1975–80); Danny Johnson (1975–77); Vandy Hampton (1977–80); Anthony Watson (1990).

Led by Eugne Record's falsetto, the soft-soul of the Chi-Lites was but a gentle breeze compared to the usual gale force musical winds emanating from Chicago. Although the group made the charts with some socially charged message songs, its forte was mushy, candlelit ballads. Starting with "Give It Away" in 1969,

the group's yearning mellowness (a precursor to 1970s disco) earned them a string of hits, including "Oh Girl" and "Have You Seen Her," the latter enjoying a second life thanks to a late 1980s cover version by then-hot M.C. Hammer. Response cooled considerably during the late 1970s, and Record, who acted as both producer and songwriter, went solo with his high-pitched, loverman pipes. The group sputtered with line-up shifts until he re-formed the original members in 1980 for some light chart action. Subsequent member changes have been innumerable and far outnumber any remaining sparks of creativity.

what to buy: However close Record's production gets to syrup filled banality (and it veers right up to the edge at points), *Greatest Hits* 🎵🎵🎵 (Rhino, 1992, comp. Dave Booth and Gary Stewart) is a strong collection of the group's lightly sweeping ballads—"Have You Seen Her," "Oh Girl"—with social punch "(For God's Sake) Give More Power to the People"—mixed in now and then to spice up the swooning. Roll out the shag carpet and crack open the Asti Spumante.

what to buy next: *Greatest Hits, Vol. 2* 🎵🎵🎵 (Rhino, 1996, comp. Dave Booth) doesn't boast anything as memorable as "Have You Seen Her" but retains its mood lighting with some funky swaying, the pop beauty of "That's How Long" and the Spinners-like "Here I Am."

what to avoid: Unless keyboards and programmed drums are your idea of soul music, give *Just Say You Love Me* 🎵🎵 (Ichiban, 1990) a wide berth.

the rest:
Best of the Chi-Lites 🎵🎵🎵 (Kent, 1994)
Inner City Blues 🎵🎵 (Brunswick, 1996)

solo outings:
Eugene Record:
Welcome to My Fantasy 🎵🎵 (Warner Bros., 1979)

influences:

◀◀ The Spinners, Tavares

▶▶ Babyface, the Bee Gees

Allan Orski

Chill Rob G

Born Robert Frazier.

Chill Rob G first appeared in 1988 as a rapper from Mark the 45 King's Flavor Unit Family, a crew that included Queen Latifah, Apache, Double J, and Lakim Shabazz, among others. His stentorian, declamatory voice put him on par with the pre-eminent post-Run-D.M.C. rhymers, while his verbose, dense content anticipated the next generation of rappers like Organized Konfusion and Nas.

what's available: Beyond a few difficult-to-find early singles on Wild Pitch and an absolutely forgettable 1996 indie 12-inch, the only Chill Rob G release you'll find is his full-length *Ride the Rhythm* 🎵🎵🎵 (Wild Pitch, 1989/1990, prod. DJ Mark the 45 King). The record collects singles such as "Let Me Show You," "Wild Pitch," and the two best tracks Rob and the 45 King have ever made, "Court Is Now In Session" and "Let the Words Flow." The rhymes are equal parts social commentary and breathless rhyming, while Mark converts Graham Central Station's funk classic "The Jam" and the Police's post-punk-pop "Voices Inside My Head" into canonical B-boy loops on his SP1200. Later versions of the LP also include Rob's biggest hit, "The Power," which ironically was only made possible by a sample clearance lawsuit. The Eurodance group Snap! had placed Rob's a cappella from "Let the Words Flow" over a propulsive midtempo track on a gigantic 1989 import hit, but Wild Pitch prevented the American release of the record until a copycat version could be manufactured. In 1990, a Wild Pitch recording featuring Rob's original vocals over a secondhand track was released at the same time as Snap!'s musical version, which contained a vastly inferior rap. Both Snap! and Chill Rob G then faded slowly out of the limelight.

worth searching for: The Snap! version of "The Power" (Arista, 1990) may have been far more successful than the one credited to Power Jam Featuring Chill Rob G, but it was hardly superior. Better yet was the original Snap! import featuring Rob's vocals.

influences:

◀◀ Mark the 45 King, Latee, Public Enemy

▶▶ Lakim Shabazz, Organized Konfusion, Nas, Lord Finesse

Jeff "DJ Zen" Chang

Chino XL

Born Derrick Barbosa, in East Orange, NJ.

Oh, snaps. That's the reaction people might have upon hearing the lyrics of Chino XL, partially because it's hard to believe he says the things he does, but also because he follows the black tradition of playing the dozens, dishing out caps, insults, and, yes, snaps with reckless abandon. It's no idle boast when the quick-tongued and quicker-*witted* MC calls himself the king of the ill punch lines; his barbs and boasts can make your stomach turn with their tastelessness just as easily as they can

make your sides split from laughter. Who else in the rap world would call himself "ill as Liberace"? Who else would say that "your career was George Burns/I couldn't believe you wasn't dead yet"? And who else could boast that Quincy Jones refused to grant them sample clearance for saying "Strong like Miles Davis's heroin dependency/Fuckin' up lives like teenage pregnancy"? Then again, who would dare to?

what's available: On *Here To Save You All* 🎵🎵🎵 (American, 1996, prod. Kutmasta Kurt, D.J. Homicide, Dan Charnas, others), the former member of Art of Origin fights with his wits instead of his fists. Of course, his words can be just as devastating as a right uppercut to the chin, as he takes on—and takes out—everybody from Marion Berry to O.J. Simpson while poking metaphorical fun at anybody whose name happens to spring to mind. Nothing appears to be sacred as Chino is just as likely to mention Eazy-E's HIV-positive blood samples or before and after pictures of AIDS-stricken Arthur Ashe as he is Adina Howard or even 2Pac, who was none too pleased at the album's reference to the soap he may or may not have dropped while in jail. Not everything on this rugged album is a joke, though. Chino also takes pause to consider the relationship between guns and inferiority complexes and, on the minor hit "Kreep," wallows in self-pity—although not nearly as much as the alternarock group Radiohead did on the original "Creep."

worth searching for: Collectors should note that a sampler tape handed out well before the release of *Here To Save You All* includes a lyrical reference to Monie Love and chlamydia that wound up being censored on the album at the behest of record company lawyers.

influences:

◀◀ Naughty by Nature, Ultramagnetic MC's, Freestyle Fellowship

▶▶ Ras Kass, Mad Skillz

Josh Freedom du Lac

The Chords

Formed 1951, in New York, NY.

Carl Feaster, lead vocals; Claude Feaster, baritone vocals; Jimmy Keys, first tenor; Floyd "Buddy" McRae, second tenor; Ricky Edwards, bass.

Without meaning to sound too pretentious, it must be said that some songs are historical events. In 1954, America stood on the fault line of a cultural quake being triggered by the coming of rock 'n' roll—which was, to oversimplify, the selling of black

R&B music to white teenagers. Of the handful of pioneer songs that kicked off this phenomenon, perhaps the mightiest of them all was a sweet piece of aural candy by the Chords called "Sh-boom." Melding a broad variety of musical influences ranging from gospel and blues to jazz and pop, the five Chords came together in 1951; by 1954, they were discovered singing in a New York subway station by a talent agent whose associate got them a deal on Cat Records, an Atlantic imprint. "Sh-boom," their first release, came out in the spring of '54, was quickly discovered by California, and by July made its debut on both the pop and R&B charts. But it was then covered by a Canadian group called the Crew Cuts on Mercury Records, at a time when American pop radio programmers still thought there was something inappropriate about playing black music on their stations. The Crew Cuts went on to score the bigger hit with "Sh-boom," but before coming down too hard on the white artists of the time who did cover songs, keep in mind that cover records brought new sounds to millions of young ears which otherwise might never have heard them. It was only a matter of time before those rabid rock 'n' roll listeners would seek out and then demand the real thing. And once they did, the cover-song controversy vanished without a trace. And so did the Chords, after a 1954 lawsuit forced them to change their name to the Chord-Cats. But they left us with "Sh-Boom," a seminal song in the advancement of rhythm and blues as a universally accepted musical form. The tune was covered again in later years by the '50s nostalgia group Sha Na Na; even today, the Crew Cuts version tends to predominate in most oldies compilations.

what's available: To hear the true Chords, try the collections *Only Rock 'n' Roll, 1955–1965* 𝄞𝄞𝄞 (JCI Associated, 1995), *The Doo Wop Box: 101 Vocal Group Gems from the Golden Age of Rock 'n' Roll* 𝄞𝄞𝄞𝄞 (Rhino, 1994), or, strangely, the *Original TV Soundtrack: Happy Days Jukebox* 𝄞𝄞 (Nick at Nite, 1996).

influences:
◀◀ The Coasters, the Cadillacs
▶▶ The Crew Cuts, Sha Na Na

Michael Kosser

Lou Christie
Born Lugee Alfredo Giovanni Sacco, February 19, 1943, in Glen Willard, PA.

In the spirit of the great falsettos Del Shannon and Frankie Valli, 1960s heartthrob Christie wailed his way to stardom with a string of distinctive hit songs. From his early start as Roulette

Records' first breakthrough artist in 1962, Christie cut a figure as a tough-but-sensitive crooner, infusing his repertoire of "boy meets girl" tunes with just a blush of sexual urgency via his distinctive falsetto. By the late 1960s, he was part of the stable at bubblegum label Buddah Records, where he enjoyed one last hit ("I'm Gonna Make You Mine") before becoming a fixture in traveling revues.

what's available: *Enlightenment: The Best of Lou Christie* 𝄞𝄞𝄞 (Rhino, 1991, prod. various) dutifully collects his best songs— "The Gypsy Cried," "Two Faces Have I," "Rhapsody in the Rain," and his ambitious million-seller "Lightnin' Strikes."

influences:
◀◀ Del Shannon, Frankie Valli & the Four Seasons, Frankie Lymon
▶▶ The Delfonics, the Chi-Lites, Michael Jackson, Todd Rundgren, Mariah Carey

Christopher Scapelliti

Chubb Rock
Born Richard Simpson, May 28, 1968, in Jamaica.

Chubb Rock claimed that he jumped up on the scene with a dream that wasn't drafted to be pornographic, but the 1988 debut of the hefty Jamaican-born, Brooklyn-bred cousin of Howie Tee, *Chubb Rock Featuring Hitman Howie Tee*, seemed to suggest otherwise, showing him as a horny teenager with a narrow worldview. Chubb, however, quickly grew up, imploring fans to "Treat 'em Right" and generally rolling out rhymes that could be pointed and playful—all at once.

what to buy: Chubb's sophomore album, *And the Winner Is . . .* 𝄞𝄞𝄞𝄞 (Select, 1989, prod. Howie Tee), is his best, featuring deft production work and some insightful social commentaries that are leavened by Chubb's humorous streak. Chubb's deep, engaging voice gives him an air of authority, making his insights all the more credible.

what to buy next: Chubb's latest, *The Mind* 𝄞𝄞𝄞 (Select, 1997, prod. KRS-One, Easy Mo Bee, others), is more serious in tone, as the overweight ex-lover fights for his right to speak his mind, offering discourses on everything from the East-West feud to his own religious beliefs.

the rest:
Chubb Rock Featuring Hitman Howie Tee 𝄞𝄞 (Select, 1988)
The One 𝄞𝄞𝄞 (Select, 1991)
I Gotta Get Mine, Yo! 𝄞𝄞 (Select, 1992)

influences:

◀◀ Boogie Down Productions, Public Enemy, 3rd Bass

▶▶ Akinyele

Josh Freedom du Lac

Chunky A

Born Arsenio Hall, February 12, 1956, in Cleveland, OH.

A longtime amateur musician—he composed the theme for his long-running syndicated talk show himself—actor/talk show host Arsenio Hall got the idea to create a rap alter ego while his show was at its height. The character was a belligerent, overweight pain by the name of Chunky A. He seemed to be little more than an excuse for bad fat jokes and jabs at hip-hop culture—until Hall somehow got a record deal under this persona.

what to avoid: The record that resulted from the deal, *Large and In Charge* **woof!** (MCA, 1989, prod. various) was so bad that Vesta Williams's producer Attila Giles dreamed up a pseudonym for the album credit. Still, R&B sax master Gerald Albright and Williams did later admit to helping out, making a passable album best-known for its shameless rip-off of Cameo's "Word Up," the empty dance jam "Owww!" Ironically, it also describes the reaction of anyone forced to hear more than a few minutes of this vanity project.

influences:

◀◀ Bobby Jimmy and the Critters, Cameo, Fat Boys, CB4

Eric Deggans

Dee Clark

Born Delecta Clark, November 7, 1938, in Blytheville, AK. Died December 7, 1990.

Dee Clark was R&B's finest vocal chameleon. He could rock to the Bo Diddley beat, croon like Clyde McPhatter, scream like Little Richard, and utilize gospel tension and release techniques like Jackie Wilson. Clark was 14 years old when he made his first recording for Okeh Records as a member of the Hambone Kids in Chicago. From there he moved on to the Goldentones, which eventually became the Kool Gents, who were signed to the Vee-Jay Records' subsidiary Falcon (later Abner) Records in 1956. When recordings by the Kool Gents didn't sell, they reshuffled their line-up and became the Delegates, who had a novelty hit with "The Convention" (a tribute to the early rock movement, where Clark briefly imitates Frankie Lymon) that same year. After follow-up releases by the Delegates failed to chart, producer Calvin Carter convinced Clark to go solo.

Novelty tunes such as "Kangaroo Hop" and "24 Boyfriends" were regional hits, but Clark still wasn't finished tinkering with his style. When Little Richard temporarily retired at the peak of his fame, Richard's roadband the Upsetters recruited Clark to take his place. In retrospect, Clark's imitation of Little Richard on "Oh Little Girl" (and the unreleased "Emma Jean") tops later, similar attempts by Otis Redding and Paul McCartney for accuracy and gusto, but the disc flopped. Finally in late 1958, Clark established a hit groove with the Clyde McPhatterish "Nobody Else But You." He repeated that success the following year with "Just Keep It Up," which featured a happy flute sound and catchy bass voice on the chorus. A bigger hit by far was "Hey Little Girl," which had a Bo Diddley beat and Jackie Wilson-influenced vocal. Clark followed up with smaller chart records such as "How About That" and a cover version of the Eldorados' "At My Front Door" (better than Pat Boone's version, not as good as Johnny Carroll's). Once the Abner label was fully absorbed into Vee-Jay, Clark began to assert his own style. "You're Looking Good" and "Your Friends" were minor hits, but they featured an earthier, less imitative vocal from Clark. 1961's "Raindrops" was Dee Clark's masterpiece and greatest hit. Clark's vocal alternates observational detachment with gospel intensity and pain, and Calvin Carter's use of thunder claps and strings was innovative and imaginative. "Raindrops" should have heralded the start of a string of big records for Clark, but before he could take his new sound further, he left Vee-Jay in 1962. "Crossfire Time" was a medium-sized hit for the Constellation label the following year, but few releases afterwards did as well. Clark continued to write fine material (he composed "Nobody Else But You" and "Raindrops"), and his new hard tenor soared as never before. But he missed Calvin Carter's ear in the studio, and his career lost momentum. Clark played out his life recording for small labels and working oldies concerts. During the late 1980s, Clark participated in fundraisers to establish a rock 'n' roll retirement home and was still capable of astounding audiences with his dazzling array of vocal styles.

what to buy: *Raindrops* 𝄇𝄇𝄇𝄇 (Vee-Jay, 1993, prod. Calvin Carter) features 25 tracks, including his big hits "Just Keep It Up," "Nobody Else But You," "Hey Little Girl," the title tune, and early cuts with the Delegates, the Kool Gents, the Dells, and Jerry Butler, along with some cover songs that showcase Clark's uncanny ability to imitate some of the other big stars of his era.

what to buy next: *Raindrops* 𝄇𝄇𝄇 (Charly, 1994, prod. Calvin Carter) is an English import which also features the big hits but includes several tracks not on the U.S. version. Covers tunes such as "Old Man River" and showcases his Clyde McPhatter and Jackie Wilson influences. *Ultimate Collection* 🎵🎵🎵 (Marginal Records, 1996, prod. Calvin Carter) is an import from Holland. This one has 31 tracks of Clark's Vee-Jay material, which is just about everything he did for that label.

what to avoid: *Golden Classics* 🎵🎵 (Collectables, 1996, prod. various) features two re-recordings of his big hits and several later, non-Vee-Jay tracks. Clark's vocals are good and this collection is cheap, but better compilations are out there if you look.

the rest:
Keep It Up 🎵🎵🎵🎵 (Charly, 1980).
The Dee Clark Show 🎵🎵 (New Rose, 1993)
Hey Little Girl 🎵🎵🎵🎵 (Charly, 1995)

worth searching for: *How About That* 🎵🎵🎵🎵 (Abner, 1960, prod. Calvin Carter) and *You're Looking Good* 🎵🎵🎵🎵 (Vee-Jay, 1960, prod. Calvin Carter) are high quality Japanese vinyl reproductions of Clark's original Abner/Vee-Jay LPs put out by Line Records.

influences:
◀◀ Clyde McPhatter, Sam Cooke, Jackie Wilson
▶▶ Jerry Butler, Curtis Mayfield, Gene Pitney

Ken Burke

Dr. Mattie Moss Clark

Born 1925, in AL. Died September 22, 1994, in Southfield, MI.

Pianist, organist, arranger, singer, choir director, teacher, and recording artist, Dr. Mattie Moss Clark influenced virtually every facet of gospel music and played a major role in shaping the future direction of the genre. Indeed, her talented family alone supplied gospel with three of its most important acts: Clark herself; her brother and his family, Bill Moss and the Celestials; and her talented daughters, the Clark Sisters. Moving to Detroit in 1958, Clark achieved numerous milestones during a long and distinguished career, including the introduction of three-part harmony to gospel arrangements, the first gospel choir recording (1958), three gold albums, and composing over 700 songs, including the classics, "Climbing Up the Mountain" and "Salvation Is Free." This meticulous taskmaster accepted nothing less than the best, and gave the same in return.

what to buy: Although most of her music is not available on CD, true fans of Clark should enjoy *Dr. Mattie Moss Clark presents the COGIC National Mass Choir—Live In Atlanta* 🎵🎵🎵 (Sparrow, 1994, prod. Dr. Mattie Moss Clark, Eddie Howard, Dorinda Clark-Cole) and *Dr. Mattie Moss Clark presents the Michigan State Mass Choir Watch Ye Therefore* 🎵🎵🎵 (Crystal

Rose/Sparrow, 1994, prod. Eddie Howard, Dorinda Clark-Cole), both soul-satisfying works and solidly representative of this legendary figure. These discs were recorded while Clark was in failing health, but were seen through to the finish by her daughter, Dorinda, and keyboardist Eddie Howard.

the rest:
Dr. Mattie Moss Clark Presents a Reunion of the Southwest Michigan State Choir—Live at Bailey Cathedral COGIC, Detroit 🎵🎵 (Sparrow, 1994)

influences:
◀◀ Thomas A. Dorsey, Sister Rosetta Tharpe, Rev. C.L. Franklin, Mother Willie Mae Ford Smith, Clara Ward
▶▶ The Clark Sisters, Twinkie Clark, Clara Ward, Beverly Glenn, Aretha Franklin, Rance Allen, Vanessa Bell Armstrong, the Hawkins Family, Donald Vail, James Moore, the Winans

Tim A. Smith

The Clark Sisters

Formed 1973, in Detroit, MI.

Elbertina "Twinkie" Clark Terrell, vocals (1973–91); Karen Clark Sheard, vocals; Dorinda Clark Cole, vocals; Jacky Clark, vocals; Denise Clark, vocals (1973–88).

When the subject turns to girl groups in gospel music, the first name usually mentioned is the Clark Sisters. From a historical perspective, the Sisters—originally consisting of Twinkie, Denise, Jacky, Dorinda, and Karen, daughters of the late gospel giant Dr. Mattie Moss Clark—followed the lead of the Edwin Hawkins Singers and the crossover smash "Oh Happy Day" by taking their own inspirational single to mainstream audiences with the rocking "You Brought the Sunshine." The recording, which has become the group's signature song, not only became a favorite of their many gospel fans, but was also a huge dance-mix club hit. Singing together since Karen, the youngest, was three years old, the Sisters traveled extensively as children, performing on cross-country tours with their mother's choirs as well as sharing dates with another gospel singer who was climbing her way up the ladder, Shirley Caesar. Twinkie, the driving force behind shaping the Sisters' vibrant contemporary sound, left the act in 1991 to pursue a solo career; Denise left years earlier.

what to buy: BeBe Winans attempted to smooth out the Clark Sisters' gritty, hard-hitting gospel sound on *Miracle* 🎵🎵🎵🎵 (Sparrow, 1994, prod. BeBe Winans), removing their traditional vocal riffs, runs, and scats in favor of a clean, sleekly-produced sound, particularly evident on their rendition of "Amazing

Grace." Ironically, their longtime fans have had difficulty adjusting to the group's "new" direction, but this LP proves that the Clarks didn't need to perform all their vocal gymnastics to get their point across: They can just flat-out sing.

what to buy next: *Bringing It Back Home, Live* ♪♪♪ (Rejoice/Word, 1991) is hard to find but worth the search, recorded before Twinkie left the group and revealing the quintet in electrifying full voice and fully intact.

the rest:
Twinkie Clark Terrell Presents the Florida A&M University Gospel Choir (w/The Clark Sisters) ♪♪♡ (Chordant, 1996)

worth searching for: Hear Dr. Mattie Moss Clark together with her daughters on the exceptional release *Is My Living In Vain* ♪♪♪♪ (Sony Music Special Products, 1991).

solo outings:
Twinkie Clark:
The Masterpiece ♪♪♪♡ (Tribute, 1996)

influences:
◀◀ Dr. Mattie Moss Clark, Shirley Caesar

▶▶ Witness, Special Gift, Whitney Houston

Tim A. Smith

Otis Clay

Born 1942, in Waxhaw, MS.

Otis Clay's intense and enduring dedication to his craft has earned him the status as the 1990s torch-bearer for hard soul music, the last of the great soul men. Clay's style is rooted in the tradition of hard-shouting gospel quartet leads such as Julius Cheeks of the Sensational Nightingales (Clay was a member of the post-Cheeks Nightingales in his younger days). His secular recording career began in his hometown of Chicago for George Leaner's One-derful label, where he recorded under the guidance of mentors such as Harold Burrage and Cash McCall. Although crude by comparison to his later work, his One-derful recordings have an intensity and exuberance that few soul men have ever approached, most notably his relentless vocal performance of McCall's "That's How It Is." After One-derful, Clay recorded in Muscle Shoals, Alabama, for the Atlantic subsidiary Cotillion. His last Cotillion 45, the double-sided hit "Is It Over/I'm Qualified," was produced by Willie Mitchell in Memphis and led to the creative high point of Clay's career, his recordings for Hi Records. Clay recorded two LPs and a number of 45s for Hi with Mitchell and his Memphis production machine: the Hi Rhythm Section, the most precise and accom-

plished of the great Southern soul rhythm sections of the 1960s and 1970s; brother James Mitchell's brilliant horn and string arrangements; and the incomparable country/soul vocal trio of Rhodes, Chalmers, and Rhodes. Clay's biggest hit recording for Hi, "Trying to Live My Life without You," (later covered by both the J. Geils Band and Bob Seger) was only one of many equally strong performances. In particular, the ballads he recorded with Mitchell—"I Can't Take It," "I Die a Little Each Day," "Precious Precious," "The Woman Don't Live Here No More"—stand among the deepest, most intense performances in the genre. After a brief stint at TK Records in Florida, Clay recorded two brilliant live LPs in Japan that solidified his reputation as a tireless and electrifying live performer and touring artist, a reputation that he continues to earn to this day.

what to buy: *Hi Records Years: The Best of Otis Clay* ♪♪♪♪♡ (EMI/Right Stuff, 1996, prod. various) is the most thorough and well-documented available collection of Clay's recordings with Willie Mitchell in Memphis. Other excellent compilations are *That's How It Is* ♪♪♪♪ (Hi, 1991, prod. Willie Mitchell) and *The 45s* ♪♪♪♪ (Hi, 1995, prod. Willie Mitchell).

what to buy next: *Soul Man Live in Japan* ♪♪♪♡ (Bullseye Blues/Rooster Blues, 1984, prod. Otis Clay), the second of Clay's Japanese live recordings, features the Hi Rhythm Section and a strong collection of songs. Clay had suffered from a serious automobile accident a few months before the recording and is not quite in top vocal form. *I'll Treat You Right* ♪♪♪♡ (Bullseye Blues, 1992, prod. Ron Levy) is Clay's most recent studio recording. Although the production lacks the sparkling veneer of Clay's best work, this is a worthy collection of strong material, well executed and passionately sung. *On My Way Home: The Otis Clay Gospel Collection* ♪♪♪♡ (Bullseye Blues, 1993, prod. Ron Levy) includes a duet with the great Clarence Fountain of the Five Blind Boys of Alabama. Clay contributes an excellent vocal performance of O.V. Wright's "A Nickle and a Nail" on Roy Buchanan's *When a Guitar Plays the Blues* ♪♪♪ (Alligator, 1985, prod. Dick Shurman).

the rest:
Trying to Live My Life Without You ♪♪♪♪♡ (Hi, 1972)
I Can't Take It ♪♪♪♪♡ (Hi, 1977)
The Only Way Is Up ♪♪♪ (Waylo, 1985)
Watch Me Now ♪♪ (Waylo/Blues R&B, 1989)
His Precious Love ♪♪♪ (Paula, 1990)
When the Gates Swing Open ♪♪ (Echo, 1990)
Gospel Truth ♪♪♪ (Blind Pig, 1993)
(With Willie Clayton) *You Are My Life* ♪♪ (MMS, 1995)
(With Willie Clayton) *Chicago Soul Greats* ♪♪♪♪ (Hi, 1995)

worth searching for: Although difficult to find in the U.S., *Live in Japan* ✍✍✍✍ (JVC Japan, 1981, prod. Otis Clay) was the first and stronger of Clay's Japanese live recordings. Clay is in top form, backed by his tight, incendiary backup band Chicago Fyre. *Got to Find a Way* ✍✍✍ (P-Vine Japan, 1979, prod. various) is a collection of Clay's 19 recordings for One-derful. *A Memphis Soul Night Live in Europe* ✍✍✍ (Waylo, 1990, prod. Willie Mitchell) captures a live performance featuring Clay, Ann Peebles, Lynn White, and David Hudson, backed by Willie Mitchell and the Hi Rhythm Section. For a taste of Clay's earliest gospel work, see *Ring Them Golden Bells: The Best of the Gospel Songbirds* ✍✍✍ (AVI/Nashboro, 1995, prod. Robert Y. Kim, Opal Louis Nations). Clay is featured as lead vocalist on two songs, and he shares lead vocals with Maurice Dollison (later known as Cash McCall) on two others. Also featured is Chicago soul singer James Phelps. Clay performs a duet on "That's How It Is" with Billy Price on Price's *The Soul Collection* (Green Dolphin, 1997, prod. Billy Price, H.B. Bennett) ✍✍✍ and contributes some background vocals.

influences:

◀◀ Rev. Julius Cheeks (Sensational Nightingales), Joe Ligon (Mighty Clouds of Joy), Clarence Fountain (Five Blind Boys of Alabama), Harold Burrage, Cash McCall, James Carr, O.V. Wright

▶▶ Robert Cray, J. Geils Band, Bob Seger, Tyrone Davis

Bill Pollak

The Cleftones

Formed 1955, in Queens, NY.

Herb Cox, lead; Charlie James, first tenor; Berman Patterson, second tenor (1955–58, 1970–present); William "Buzzy" McClain, baritone (1955–58); Warren Corbin; Gene Pearson (1958–63); Patricia Spann (1958–present); Tony Gaines (1974–present); Nick Saunders.

Though the Cleftones were vocally one of the most solid groups of the doo-wop era, their sound is hard to pin down. One reason is because of their talent: though the group specialized in uptempo numbers such as "Little Girl of Mine" and "Heart and Soul," they also could pull off a passable ballad and the group's other singers would occasionally share leads with frontman Herb Cox. For awhile they also had a female singer, Patricia Spann, who added a different dimension to the group's sound. The Cleftones formed during a high-school election campaign and have stayed together in some form through four decades

(though they did not record from 1964–70). They have been regular performers on the oldies circuit well into the 1990s.

what to buy: *The Best of the Cleftones* ✍✍✍ (Rhino, 1990) contains the Cleftones best-known work for Gee and Roulette from 1955–62, including the group's biggest crossover single, a rocked-up treatment of "Heart and Soul" that hit the charts about three months after the Marcels did the same thing with "Blue Moon." These recordings usually feature honking sax work by Jimmy Wright, the leader of the Rama/Gee house band.

the rest:

For Collectors Only ✍✍✍ (Collectables, 1992)

influences:

◀◀ The Moonglows, the Penguins

▶▶ The Excellents

Brian Mansfield

Clever Jeff

Born Jeff Jones.

Jazzier than D.J. Jeff and fresher than the Prince of Bel Air, Jeff Jones is one of the better examples of what happens when a hip-hop artist just can't shake his jazz jones. The son of a female jazz singer, Jeff grew up playing drums and keyboards and formed a funk band in high school. In 1993, he hooked up with producer Dave G, signed a deal with Qwest and released an underrated debut, *Jazz Hop Soul*. The hip-hop world wasn't hip to the album, though, and Jeff was released by Qwest. The Bay Area-based artist recently resurfaced on the progressive San Francisco hip-hop/dance label, OM, to release his second album, *God Quality*.

what's available: Hip-bop hooray for *Jazz Hop Soul* ✍✍✍ (Qwest/Warner, 1994, prod. Dave G), a swinging, verve-filled album that isn't far removed in sound or spirit from Guru's Jazzmatazz. With a guest list that includes singer Mike Marshall (ex-Timex Social Club/Club Nouveau) and heralded young saxophonist Dave Ellis (ex-Charlie Hunter Trio), *God Quality* ✍✍✍ (OM, 1997, prod. various) has many of the same qualities that made *Jazz Hop Soul* such a winner. Of particular note is "The Ghetto Anthem," which makes a socially conscious effort to keep it real *positive*.

influences:

◀◀ Jazzmatazz, Dream Warriors

Josh Freedom du Lac

Jimmy Cliff (© Jack Vartoogian)

Jimmy Cliff

Born April 1, 1948, St. James, Jamaica.

Jimmy Cliff shot into international stardom in 1971 with his lead role in the movie *The Harder They Come* as well as his contributions to its allstar soundtrack, which still stands as Reggae 101. However, he had been recording since the early 1960s, making some of reggae's first sounds heard outside of Jamaica. Working with famed producer Leslie Kong, Cliff had a handful of hits on the island, leading to more far-reaching success with "Wonderful World, Beautiful People" in 1969. After the success of *The Harder They Come,* Cliff was ostracized by the Jamaican community, perhaps jealous at his newfound stardom, or merely insulted by his conversion from Rastafarianism to Islam. The sad truth is that for all the liberating forces at play during Cliff's moment in the sun, he's never been able to translate it into a consistent music or attain that level of success again. Instead, he's opted for a light MOR pop-soul approach that culminated in a two-album collaboration, *The Power and the Glory*

and *Cliff Hanger,* with Kool and the Gang during the first half of the 1980s. Besides nabbing a Grammy for *Cliff Hanger* (so keyboard-laden it could be the *Footloose* soundtrack), Cliff appeared in *Club Paradise* with Robin Williams and added seven songs to its soundtrack in 1986, although neither generated a wider audience for the singer.

what to buy: Perhaps the best quick indoctrination into 1970s reggae, *The Harder They Come* ♫♫♫♫ (Island, 1972, prod. various) is Cliff's crowning glory. A taut and yearning soundtrack filled with top-notch performances from all artists involved. Cliff's efforts on the title track, "Sitting in Limbo," "You Can Get It If You Really Want," and, most of all, "Many Rivers to Cross" remain timeless and moving as all classics do.

what to buy next: One of his more consistent studio albums, *Wonderful World, Beautiful People* ♫♫♫ (A&M, 1970, prod. Larry Fallon, Leslie Kong) paved the way to superstardom with its title track, the protest of "Vietnam" (which drew high praise from Bob Dylan) and the foreboding "Time Will Tell."

what to avoid: Cliff's records of late have a disturbing light-ness, and although *Hanging Fire* ♪♪ (Columbia, 1988, prod. Khalis Bayyan, I.B.M.C., Jimmy Cliff) is really not much better or worse than the bulk of his more recent releases, there's a sink-ing feeling that he may break into "Let's Hear It for the Boy" at any moment. Mediocrity from Cliff may not be so unsettling had he not once reached greatness.

the rest:

In Concert: The Best of Jimmy Cliff ♪♪♪ (Reprise, 1976)
Special ♪♪ (Columbia, 1982)
The Power and the Glory ♪♪♪ (Columbia, 1983)
Reggae Greats ♪♪♪ (Mango, 1985)
Cliff Hanger ♪♪ (Columbia, 1985)
Images ♪♪♥ (Cliff, 1991)
Struggling Man ♪♪♥ (Mango, 1993)
Live 1993 ♪♪♥ (Lagoon Reggae)
Samba Reggae ♪♪ (Lagoon Reggae, 1995)

worth searching for: Although it's a hit and miss soundtrack, *Marked for Death* ♪♪♥ (Delicious Vinyl, 1990) contains some stirring Cliff numbers. An ominous "John Crow" is stronger than anything he's done during the past 10 years.

influences:

◀◀ Toots and the Maytals, Desmond Dekker, Bob Marley

▶▶ UB40, Third World, General Public, Pinchers

Allan Orski

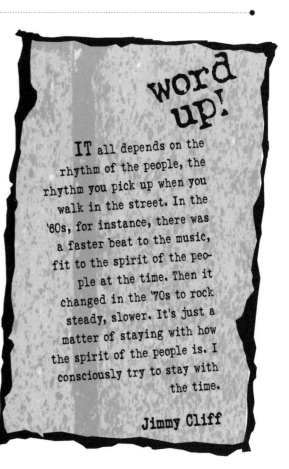

word up!

IT all depends on the rhythm of the people, the rhythm you pick up when you walk in the street. In the '80s, for instance, there was a faster beat to the music, fit to the spirit of the peo-ple at the time. Then it changed in the '70s to rock steady, slower. It's just a matter of staying with how the spirit of the people is. I consciously try to stay with the time.

Jimmy Cliff

George Clinton /Parliament-Funkadelic

Born July 22, 1940, in Kannapolis, NC.

MusicHound, meet the Atomic Dog. It's not like there weren't other funk bands around, but P-Funk distilled it to its purest elements and gave it metaphysical properties. For all the funk bands in the world, no other group has mastered the intricacy of layering rhythms, grooves, and vocals into a sophisticated whole the way Clinton and his P-Funk mob has done. And no other group has influenced black pop music as strongly over the last 20 years. After migrating to Detroit from New Jersey and flunking out at Motown during the mid-1960s, George Clinton and his Parliament pals (at that time a vocal group formed during the mid-1950s in Plainfield, New Jersey) de-cided to loosen up their music and take on a wild street image—in the process they revolutionized popular music and added multiple new agendas to black music. Clinton's rock-tinged raw music and irreverent black consciousness were like breaths of fresh air to the slick and suited veneer of most R&B acts. While P-Funk's antics spawned a growing under-ground buzz and occasional pop airplay, it wasn't until 1975's *The Clones of Dr. Funkenstein* that its heavy bass, chanted lyrics, wriggling guitars, and phat horn lines went over the top. From 1975–80, the P-Funk mob churned out hit after hit with the added spinoff groups, Bootsy's Rubber Band and the Brides of Funkenstein. In 1976, the group—a collective that ri-vals James Brown's assorted bands, with celebrated tenures by bassist Bootsy Collins, keyboardists Bernie Worrell and Walter "Junie" Morrison, guitarist Eddie Hazel, saxophonist Maceo Parker, and percussionist Larry Fratangelo—released five albums under four names for three different labels. Com-mon belief is that Clinton used the name Parliament for his more R&B, dance club-oriented records and Funkadelic for his

George Clinton (© Ken Settle)

rock side. That may be, but "Funkadelic" appeared when Clinton temporarily lost legal rights to the Parliament name. And when he lost legal rights to both names in the 1980s, he started recording under his own name. Regardless of the title, it's basically the same band; even after the group splintered in 1981, Clinton's records have featured many of the same musicians. Legal hassles dogged Clinton and other funkateers through much of the 1980s—though theirs was a peaceable induction into the Rock and Roll Hall of Fame in 1997—and the hits disappeared after 1982's "Atomic Dog"—though Clinton produced hit records for Thomas Dolby, the Red Hot Chili Peppers, and others. It was "Atomic Dog" that brought Clinton back in the 1980s as rapper after rapper sampled the track. Other P-Funk grooves followed and the funk presence brought Clinton back as an elder statesman. Not content to be just nostalgia, 1993's *Hey, Man . . . Smell My Finger* showed he could still throw down, while "If Anybody Gets Funk Up (It's Gonna Be You)" from *T.A.P.O.A.F.O.M.* signaled a full-scale return to form.

what to buy: Almost anything from the 1970s is a good choice, but Parliament's *Mothership Connection* ♪♪♪♪ (Casablanca, 1975, prod. George Clinton) lays out the P-Funk philosophy in a capsule with relentless grooves and happy horns. "Give Up the Funk (Tear the Roof Off the Sucker)" is the big hit, but the title tune is like losing yourself in a bumping cartoon. Funkadelic gets on the good foot, too, with *One Nation Under a Groove* ♪♪♪♪ (Warner Bros., 1987/Priority, 1993, prod. George Clinton). If you didn't like this record, you weren't dancing when you heard it.

what to buy next: For the early years, *Funkadelic's Greatest Hits* ♪♪♪♪ (Westbound, 1975, prod. George Clinton) covers things pretty well with "Can You Get To That," "I'll Bet You," and "I Got a Thing. . . ." The only essential early hit missing is the Parliament's "I Wanna Testify." The 10-minute title track of Funkadelic's *Maggot Brain* ♪♪♪♪ (Westbound, 1971, prod. George Clinton) proves that Jimi Hendrix wasn't the only black freaky rock guitarist.

what to avoid: Things looked bad for Funkadelic with *The Electric Spanking of War Babies* ✍ (Warner Bros., 1980, prod. George Clinton), which is burdened by no substantial jams and by Sly Stone's pathetic bleating on "Funk Gets Stronger."

the rest:
George Clinton:
Computer Games ✍✍✍ (Capitol, 1982)
U Shouldn't-Nuf Bit Fish ✍✍✍✍ (Capitol, 1983)
Some of My Best Jokes Are Friends ✍✍✍ (Capitol, 1985)
R&B Skeletons from the Closet ✍✍ (Capitol, 1986)
The Best of George Clinton ✍✍✍ (Capitol, 1986)
The Cinderella Theory ✍✍✍ (Paisley Park, 1989)
P. Funk All-Stars Live ✍✍✍ (Westbound, 1990)
George Clinton Family Series, Vol. 1–5 ✍✍✍ (AEM, 1992/1994)
George Clinton's Sample Some of Disc, Sample Some of D.A.T. Series, Vol. 1–6 ✍✍✍ (AEM, 1992/1994)
Hey, Man . . . Smell My Finger ✍✍✍ (Paisley Park, 1993)
Live Greatest Hits, 1972–1993 ✍✍✍✍ (AEM, 1993)
T.A.P.O.A.F.O.M. (The Awesome Power of a Fully Operational Mothership) ✍✍✍✍ (Sony 550, 1996)
Greatest Funkin' Hits ✍✍✍✍ (Capitol/EMI, 1996)
Lie and Kickin' N/A (Intersound, 1997)

Parliament:
Up for the Down Stroke ✍✍✍✍ (Casablanca, 1974)
Chocolate City ✍✍✍✍ (Casablanca, 1975)
Clones of Dr. Funkenstein ✍✍✍✍✍ (Casablanca, 1976)
Funkentelechy vs. the Placebo Syndrome ✍✍✍✍ (PolyGram, 1977)
P-Funk Earth Tour ✍✍✍✍✍ (Warner Bros., 1977)
Motor Booty Affair ✍✍✍ (Casablanca, 1978)
Gloryhallastupid ✍✍✍✍ (Casablanca, 1979)
Tear the Roof Off 1974–1980 ✍✍✍✍ (Casablanca/Chronicles, 1993)
The Best of Parlet featuring Parliament ✍✍✍✍ (Casablanca/Chronicles, 1994)
The Best of Parliament: Give Up the Funk ✍✍✍✍ (Casablanca/Chronicles, 1995)

Funkadelic:
Free Your Mind and Your Ass Will Follow ✍✍✍ (Westbound, 1970)
Funkadelic ✍✍✍✍ (Westbound, 1971)
America Eats Its Young ✍✍✍✍ (Westbound, 1972)
Cosmic Slop ✍✍✍✍ (Westbound, 1973)
Standing on the Verge of Gettin' It On ✍✍✍ (Westbound, 1974)
Let's Take It to the Stage ✍✍ (Westbound, 1975)
Hardcore Jollies ✍✍✍ (Warner Bros., 1976)
Uncle Jam Wants You ✍✍✍✍ (Warner Bros., 1979)
Music for Your Mother ✍✍✍✍✍ (Westbound, 1992)

worth searching for: *Music for Your Mother* ✍✍✍✍ (Ace/Westbound, 1992, prod. various), an import collection of Funkadelic singles, offers an interesting and valid perspective on what is, nevertheless, a definitely album-oriented band.

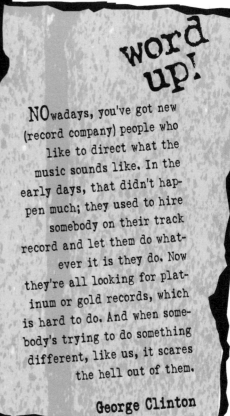

word up!

NOwadays, you've got new (record company) people who like to direct what the music sounds like. In the early days, that didn't happen much; they used to hire somebody on their track record and let them do whatever it is they do. Now they're all looking for platinum or gold records, which is hard to do. And when somebody's trying to do something different, like us, it scares the hell out of them.

George Clinton

influences:
◀◀ James Brown, Screamin' Jay Hawkins, Ike Turner, Sun Ra
▶▶ Dr. Dre, Prince, Groove Collective, Eric B & Rakim, Digital Underground, Red Hot Chili Peppers

see also: *Bootsy Collins, Maceo Parker*

Lawrence Gabriel

The Clovers

Formed 1946, in Washington, DC. Disbanded mid-1960s.

John "Buddy" Bailey, lead vocals; Harold Winley, bass vocals; Matthew McQuater, tenor vocals; Harold Lucas, baritone vocals; Bill Harris, guitar.

Following in the smooth, black pop-harmony tradition of such groups as the Ink Spots and the Mills Brothers, the Clovers was the first group to apply quartet harmonies to the rough and bawdy R&B style. Signed to Atlantic in 1950, the group's breakthrough came in 1951 with the #1 R&B hit "Don't You Know I Love You." The record—with its swinging beat, prominent bass harmony, and soulful lead vocals—became the template for subsequent R&B vocal hits by the Drifters, the Coasters, and the Midnighters. The Clovers changed lead singers a couple of times during the 1950s (notably with Charlie White and Billy Mitchell), but Atlantic's core creative team, including songwriter-arranger Jesse Stone and producer Ahmet Ertegun (who wrote "Don't You Know I Love You") kept the group's output consistent. The Clovers had scored 13 consecutive Top 10 R&B hits from 1951–54. The group's 1956 single "Love, Love, Love" crossed over to the pop charts. After leaving Atlantic for United Artists, the group scored once more on the pop charts with "Love Potion No. 9." The often-covered group's hits proved more profitable to a number of white singers, including Bobby Vinton ("Blue Velvet"), Bobby Vee ("Devil or Angel"), and the Searchers ("Love Potion No. 9"). The group broke up during the mid-1960s, though a number of suspect versions of the Clovers showed up on the oldies circuit during the 1970s.

what's available: *Down in the Alley: The Best of the Clovers* 𝄞𝄞𝄞𝄞 (Atlantic, 1991, prod. Ahmet Ertegun) is the only readily available collection of Clovers' tunes, so it's nice that it also happens to be a very good one. It features all of the 13 consecutive Top 10 R&B hits the group racked up in 1951–54, including "Ting-a-Ling," "Hey, Miss Fannie," and "Fool, Fool, Fool."

worth searching for: *Love Potion No. 9: The Best of the Clovers* 𝄞𝄞𝄞𝄞 (EMI America, 1991, prod. various) completes the picture, giving us a load of the group's time with United Artists, which produced the oft-covered title tune, the group's last big hit. Too bad the collection is out of print. Also worth seeking out is the single of "Love, Love, Love," a major Clovers hit that, oddly, is not included on *Down in the Alley*.

influences:
◀◀ Mills Brothers, Ink Spots

▶▶ The Coasters, the Penguins, Frankie Lymon & the Teenagers, the Jackson 5, New Edition

Salvatore Caputo

Club Nouveau

Formed 1986, in Sacramento, CA. Disbanded 1990.

Jay King, vocals; Valerie Watson, vocals; Alex Hill, keyboards.

If you blinked, you missed this band, which started during the mid-1980s as a spinoff from the Timex Social Club, a group that had its own out-of-nowhere hit with "Rumors" in 1986. One of the first producer-driven non-bands of the mid-'80s R&B-pop era, Club Nouveau featured three Timex members—King, Watson, and Hill, joined by the production team of Thomas McElroy and Denzil Foster. Unfortunately, McElroy and Foster left soon after the trio's 1986 debut album to mastermind R&B divas En Vogue's success, taking their New Jack pop smarts with them and precipitating Club Nouveau's demise.

what to buy: *Life, Love and Pain* 𝄞𝄞𝄞𝄞 (Warner Bros., 1986, prod. Jay King, Thomas McElroy, Denzil Foster) was an unqualified success, fueled by a monster hit cover of Bill Withers' "Lean on Me."

the rest:
Everything Is Black 𝄞𝄞 (Rip-it, 1989/1995)

influences:
◀◀ The Time, Rick James, Timex Social Club

Eric Deggans

The Coasters

Formed 1955, in Los Angeles, CA. Disbanded 1976.

Carl Gardner, tenor vocals; Billy Guy, baritone vocals (1955–65); Bobby Nunn, bass vocals (1955); Leon Hughes, tenor vocals (1955); Will "Dub" Jones, bass vocals (1956–65); Cornell/Cornelius Gunter, tenor vocals (1956–60); Earl "Speedo" Carroll, tenor vocals (1961–76); Ronnie Bright, tenor vocals (1965–76); Jimmy Norman, baritone (1965–76).

At the end of the white-bread 1950s, America's mainstream chose the comical Coasters as their most beloved black entertainers. Under the watchful eye of writer-producers Jerry Leiber and Mike Stoller, the Coasters issued a number of playful singles, which kept the group at the top of the charts well into the early 1960s. Although the contribution of Leiber and Stoller can't be overstated, the group's sound was just as earmarked by Nunn's low bottoms and Gardner's wolf-in-sheep's-clothing tenor.

what to buy: *50 Coastin' Classics: Anthology* 𝄞𝄞𝄞𝄞 (Rhino, 1992, prod. various), by far the best Coasters compilation on the market, is nearly overwhelming; going back to the pre-Coasters group, the Robins, the album has a wealth of obscurities and ample liner notes, with comments by Leiber and Stoller.

what to buy next: *The Very Best of the Coasters* 𝄞𝄞𝄞𝄞 (Rhino, 1993, prod. various) offers a compact version of *50 Coastin' Clas-*

sics that focuses on such chart-toppers as "Yakety-Yak," "Charlie Brown," and "Poison Ivy," as well as "What About Us," a track that argues that the band had more to offer than just yuks.

influences:

◀◀ The Drifters, Elvis Presley, Ernie K. Doe

▶▶ The Jimmy Castor Bunch, Weird Al Yankovic

Allan Orski

Joe Cocker

Born John Robert Cocker, May 20, 1944, in Sheffield, England.

With is gruff voice and passion-fueled delivery, Cocker is one of rock's great stylists—which can be as much a curse as a blessing. Because he seldom writes his own material, Cocker is usually at its mercy, and dependent on the producers who help him choose it and craft his sound. With sympathetic cohorts—Denny Cordell and Leon Russell at the start of his career, for instance—Cocker's brilliance, schooled in the classic blues and R&B of Ray Charles and Big Joe Turner, shines through; it takes *cajones* and rare talent to not only cover but to also re-invent prior hits such as the Beatles' "With a Little Help from My Friends" and Traffic's "Feelin' Alright." But Cocker has also laid his estimable pipes on some real schmaltz, even though sometimes it's brought him tremendous success ("Up Where We Belong" from the film *An Officer and a Gentleman*). In his fifties now, Cocker still has the voice—and his distinctive spastic air guitar performing style—that he began with in 1969. But each new venture is a crap-shoot, and we can only hope that he again finds the right combination of songs and collaborators to fulfill his potential.

what to buy: With a signature tune, "Delta Lady," as well as another hot Beatles cover ("She Came in Through the Bathroom Window"), *Joe Cocker!* 𝄫𝄫𝄫𝄫 (A&M, 1969, prod. Denny Cordell, Leon Russell) built on Cocker's triumphant Woodstock appearance and marked the arrival of a tremendous new talent. Though the band Russell assembled for the live *Mad Dogs and Englishmen* 𝄫𝄫𝄫𝄫 (A&M, 1970, prod. Denny Cordell, Leon Russell) at times seems loose and intrusive, Cocker really shows his mettle by never letting it overwhelm him. *Classics Volume 4* 𝄫𝄫𝄫𝄫𝄫 (A&M, 1987, prod. various) offers the best of his early period.

what to buy next: *The Best of Joe Cocker* 𝄫𝄫𝄫𝄫 (Capitol, 1993, prod. various) captures the best of his spotty later work, though every collection should have his rendition of "Unchain My Heart" and "You Can Leave Your Hat On." At four CDs, *The Long Voyage Home: The Silver Anniversary Collection* 𝄫𝄫𝄫

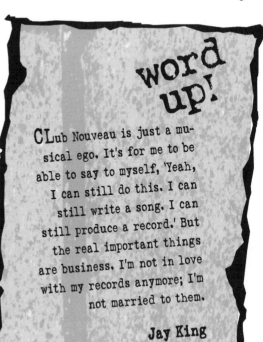

word up!

CLub Nouveau is just a musical ego. It's for me to be able to say to myself, 'Yeah, I can still do this. I can still write a song. I can still produce a record.' But the real important things are business. I'm not in love with my records anymore; I'm not married to them.

Jay King (of Club Nouveau)

(A&M, 1995, prod. various) is flabby in spots, but there are more than enough electrifying moments to compensate.

what to avoid: Tepid originals and vapid cover choices dog a couple of Cocker's latest albums, notably *Night Calls* 𝄫 (Capitol, 1992, prod. various) and *Have a Little Faith* **woof!** (Sony 550, 1994, prod. Chris Lord-Alge, Roger Davies).

the rest:

With a Little Help from My Friends 𝄫𝄫𝄫 (A&M, 1969)
Joe Cocker 𝄫𝄫𝄫 (A&M, 1972)
I Can Stand a Little Rain 𝄫𝄫𝄫 (A&M, 1974)
Jamaica Say You Will 𝄫𝄫𝄫 (A&M, 1975)
Sting Ray 𝄫𝄫 (A&M, 1976)
Live in L.A. 𝄫𝄫𝄫 (A&M, 1976)
Greatest Hits 𝄫𝄫𝄫𝄫 (A&M, 1977)
Luxury You Can Afford 𝄫𝄫 (A&M, 1978)
Sheffield Steel 𝄫𝄫𝄫 (Island, 1982)
Civilized Man 𝄫𝄫𝄫 (Capitol, 1984)
Cocker 𝄫𝄫𝄫 (Capitol, 1986)

Unchain My Heart 🎵🎵🎵 (Capitol, 1987)
One Night of Sin 🎵🎵 (Capitol, 1989)
Joe Cocker Live 🎵🎵🎵 (Capitol, 1990)
Organic 🎵🎵 (550 Music, 1996)

worth searching for: *Woodstock Twenty Fifth Anniversary Collection* 🎵🎵🎵🎵 (Atlantic, 1994) features portions of the performance that launched Cocker's career in the U.S.

influences:

⏪ Ray Charles, Big Joe Turner, James Brown, the Beatles, B.B. King

⏩ Kim Wilson (the Fabulous Thunderbirds), Roger Daltrey (the Who), Robert Palmer, Bryan Adams

Gary Graff

Nat King Cole

Born Nathaniel Adams Coles, March 17, 1917, in Montgomery, AL. Died February 15, 1965, in Santa Monica, CA.

He was known as the "King," and during his incredible, too-brief reign he actually ruled over two domains. Nathaniel Adams Cole was one of the finest jazz swing pianists in history, drawing deeply from the inspiration of Earl "Fatha" Hines. And he became one of the single most successful pop ballad singers of the 20th century, with a voice so warm, rich, and unmistakable that it seems nearly impossible to believe he spent the early years of his career trying to make it as a piano player! After his family moved to Chicago from the Deep South, Cole began taking keyboard lessons while playing the organ and singing in church. He made his professional debut in 1936 on *Eddie Cole's Solid Swingers*, a record fronted by his brother, Eddie, with brothers Fred and Isaac accompanying. He left the group to conduct the band for *Shuffle Along*, a touring music revue; when the show closed in Los Angeles, he settled there. Struggling to find his place in the music world, Cole finally managed to organize the King Cole Trio with guitarist Oscar Moore and bassist Wesley Prince and began performing on radio. The combo became popular when they recorded Cole's "Sweet Lorraine" in 1940, and other musicians (notably Art Tatum and Oscar Peterson) formed their own trios, inspired by his sound. Johnny Miller replaced Prince and the trio rose to prominence during that decade, recording exciting jazz music, mostly for Capitol, and performing in the movies *Here Comes Elmer* and *Pistol Packin' Mama* and the first-ever Jazz at the Philharmonic concert. Along the way, Cole grew more confident in his vocal ability and became increasingly more popular as a singer. When a string of now-classic recordings, including "The Christ-

mas Song," "I Love You for Sentimental Reasons," and "Nature Boy" culminated in a #1 hit with "Mona Lisa" in 1950, Cole became a pop singer fulltime. Though he continued to dabble in jazz, playing keyboards on the 1956 release *After Midnight*, Cole's vocals catapulted him to such superstardom that many of his newer fans weren't aware he could play piano. He landed his own NBC-TV series from 1956–57, an almost unheard-of accomplishment for a black man of the era. Despite being accompanied by the Nelson Riddle Orchestra and hosting many of the biggest stars of the day (Tony Bennett, Sammy Davis Jr., Peggy Lee), the show ultimately died due to lack of sponsorship and the refusal of some stations to carry it. Cole continued to be a major attraction, appearing in many movies (including *Cat Ballou* and *The Nat King Cole Story*) and becoming a musical holiday tradition at Christmas. One of the regal trademarks of the "King" was a lit cigarette in a cigarette holder, but when he died of lung cancer at the age of 47, the world mourned the loss of one of the most beloved voices of all time.

what to buy: Why it took the success of Natalie Cole's *Unforgettable* tribute to her father to prompt the release of a hit singles collection for Cole is inconceivable, but *The Greatest Hits* 🎵🎵🎵🎵 (Capitol/EMI, 1994, prod. various) is such a package. Covering the King's work from 1944 through 1963 in 62 minutes and 22 tracks, the collection skips some of his famous Christmas songs but does focus on his best pop productions such as "Mona Lisa" and "Sentimental Reasons." The cuts are arranged by style and quality rather than chronology, which gives an imperfect sense of history but a better sense of the music. *Jazz Encounters* 🎵🎵🎵🎵 (Blue Note, 1992, prod. Michael Cuscuna) combines the great work of jazz masters like Coleman Hawkins, Benny Carter, and Dizzy Gillespie with Cole's piano and vocal stylings. Here you'll find Cole's non-trio performances and some of his best collaborations with Woody Herman and Johnny Mercer.

what to buy next: If you're looking for big box sets, start with *Nat King Cole* 🎵🎵🎵🎵 (Capitol/EMI, 1992, prod. Lee Gillette), which boasts 4 discs and a 60-page booklet covering 20 years in 100 different tracks. As a side dish, you'll find the previously unreleased novelty "Mr. Cole Won't Rock & Roll" as well as Leonard Feather liner notes, complete track annotations, rare photographs, and some of the King's most inspiring jazz sets. Starting with records like *Lush Life* 🎵🎵🎵🎵 (EMI/Capitol, 1993) with the Pete Rugolo Orchestra, Cole was phasing out of trio work and trying to establish a vocal career over his keyboard fare. There's still jazz here, but lots of great vocals on tunes that are memorable and representative of Cole's best musical work.

what to avoid: Some musicians just could do no wrong—you didn't think they called him "King" simply because his last name was Cole, did you? His only albums worth avoiding are ones with weak or offbeat selections, such as *Greatest Country Hits* ♫♫ (Curb, 1990).

the rest:
Big Band Cole ♫♫♫♫ (EMI/Capitol, 1950)
The Billy May Sessions ♫♫♫♫ (EMI/Capitol, 1951)
Nat King Cole Live ♫♫♫ (A Touch of Magic)
Early American ♫♫ (A Touch of Magic)
(With the Nat King Cole Trio) *Hit That Jive, Jack: The Earliest Recordings (1940–41)* ♫♫♫♫ (Decca/MCA Jazz, 1990)
The Very Thought of You ♫♫♫♫♫ (Capitol/EMI, 1991)
The Jazz Collector Edition ♫♫♫♫ (Laserlight, 1991)
(With the Nat King Cole Trio) *The Trio Recordings* ♫♫♫ (Laserlight, 1991)
(With the Nat King Cole Trio) *The Complete Capitol Recordings of the Nat King Cole Trio* ♫♫♫♫♫ (Capitol/EMI, 1991)
(With the Nat King Cole Trio) *The Trio Recordings, Vol.2* ♫♫♫♫ (Laserlight, 1991)
(With the Nat King Cole Trio) *The Trio Recordings, Vol. 3* ♫♫♫ (Laserlight, 1991)
(With the Nat King Cole Trio) *The Trio Recordings, Vol. 4* ♫♫♫ (Laserlight, 1991)
The Unforgettable Nat King Cole ♫♫♫♫♫ (Capitol/EMI, 1992)
(With the Nat King Cole Trio) *The Best of the Nat King Cole Trio: Instrumental Classics* ♫♫♫♫ (Capitol/EMI, 1992)
The Piano Style of Nat "King" Cole ♫♫♫♫ (Capitol/EMI, 1993)
(With the Nat King Cole Trio) *Early Years of Nat King Cole Trio* ♫♫♫ (Sound Hills, 1993)
(With the Nat King Cole Trio) *Nat King Cole & the King Cole Trio: Straighten Up & Fly Right (Radio Broadcasts 1942–1948)* ♫♫♫ (VJC, 1993)
(With the Nat King Cole Trio) *The Nat King Cole Trio: World War II Transcriptions* ♫♫♫♫ (Music & Arts Programs of America, 1994)
Spotlight on Nat King Cole ♫♫♫ (Capitol/EMI, 1995)
The Jazzman ♫♫♫♫ (Topaz Jazz, 1995)
To Whom It May Concern ♫♫♫ (Capitol/EMI, 1995)
Swinging Easy Down Memory Lane ♫♫♫ (Skylark Jazz, 1995)
The Complete After Midnight Sessions ♫♫♫♫♫ (Capitol/EMI, 1996)
Sweet Lorraine (1938–1941 Transcriptions) ♫♫♫♫ (Jazz Classics, 1996)
The Vocal Classics ♫♫♫♫ (Capitol/EMI, 1996)
The Nat King Cole TV Show ♫♫♫ (Sandy Hook, 1996)
The McGregor Years (1941–1945) ♫♫♫♫ (Music & Arts Programs of America, 1996)
Love Is the Thing (Gold Disc) ♫♫♫♫♫ (DCC, 1997)

worth searching for: For a fascinating insight into the performing medium and the painstaking polishing of brilliance, Cole's *Anatomy of a Jam Session* ♫♫♫♫ (Black Lion, 1945) with drummer Buddy Rich is especially choice. Cole attacks the keys only, no vocals, and his dynamic jams with Charlie Shavers,

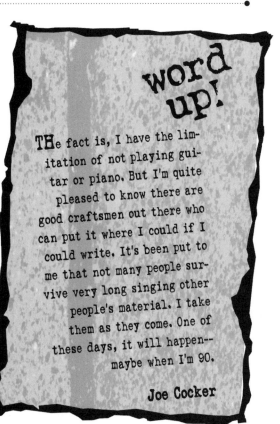

word up!

THe fact is, I have the limitation of not playing guitar or piano. But I'm quite pleased to know there are good craftsmen out there who can put it where I could if I could write. It's been put to me that not many people survive very long singing other people's material. I take them as they come. One of these days, it will happen—maybe when I'm 90.

Joe Cocker

Herbie Hayner, John Simmons, and Rich are superb. The solos that emanate from the 12 songs, five as a quintet, make this a very memorable disc and worth hunting down. Famous for his rendering of "The Christmas Song" and "Frosty the Snowman," Cole became the unofficial herald angel of Christmas. If you take the time to hunt down the reissues of *The Christmas Song* ♫♫♫♫ (Capitol, 1990, prod. Lee Gillette) and *Cole, Christmas and Kids* ♫♫♫♫ (Capitol, 1990, prod. Ron Furmack), you won't be sorry.

influences:

◀◀ Billy Kyle, Louis Armstrong, Louis Jordan, Duke Ellington, Teddy Wilson, Earl "Fatha" Hines

▶▶ Johnny Mathis, Frank Sinatra, Johnny Hartman, Oscar Peterson, Al Jarreau, Bing Crosby, Mel Torme, Billy Eckstine

Chris Tower

Natalie Cole

Born February 6, 1950, in Los Angeles, CA.

The second of Nat "King" Cole's five children, Natalie almost destroyed her career and her life under the weight of her father's enormous image, then rebounded to phenomenal heights because of it. Growing up in the Hancock Park section of Hollywood, Natalie thrived in the musical and entertainment environment and worshipped her father, making her singing debut with him at the age of 11. Tragically, the great "King" of pop vocalists died of lung cancer four years later. Natalie attended the University of Massachusetts at Amherst, earned a degree in child psychology, and began singing in local clubs with a group called Black Magic. However, the 1970s were difficult for Cole: arrested for possession of heroin in 1973, she struggled with alcohol and drug abuse through the 1980s. Despite those woes, her voice quickly earned commercial success and critical praise. During an appearance in Chicago, Cole was approached by record producers Marvin Yancy (whom she would later marry) and Chuck Jackson about making an album. That debut LP, *Inseparable*, produced two major hits, went gold, and won her two Grammy Awards. She was hailed as the next Aretha Franklin because of her powerfully soulful style. In the 1980s, she divorced Yancy and married Andre Fischer of the R&B group Rufus, but her continued drug and alcohol abuse plunged Cole into a career freefall from which she did not emerge until 1987. But in the 1990s, Natalie Cole rocketed to superstardom, sweeping the Grammy Awards and securing a platinum album with 1991's *Unforgettable*. The LP was her own tribute to her father after years of squirming beneath his massive shadow, and was inspired by the song she contributed to a Johnny Mathis tribute album in 1983. The title cut was a duet between Cole and the late Nat—his voice added through feats of engineering wizardry—and was named Song of the Year. In recent years, Cole has branched out into acting (appearing on the TV show *I'll Fly Away*, among others) and continues to release superior albums in a contemporary jazz-pop vein.

what to buy: Five million album buyers cannot be wrong, and *Unforgettable* ✶✶✶✶ (WEA/Elektra, 1991, prod. Andre Fischer, Tommy LiPuma, David Foster) shows that an album packaged to be a commercial gimmick can also be, in this case, what the title suggests. Showcasing Cole as a principal diva in the pop music world through its variety of Nat "King" Cole classics, the LP rises not only on the strength of its sentimentality but on its genuine beauty. Some sincerely argue that *Unforgettable* is one of the best albums ever recorded.

what to buy next: After *Unforgettable*, continue the exploration of Natalie's own musical repertoire with *The Natalie Cole Collection* ✶✶✶✶ (Capitol/EMI, 1988, prod. Chuck Jackson). A collection of Cole's 1975–1981 recordings on Capitol, almost all of which are out of print (including her excellent debut LP, *Inseparable*), the disc displays her stylings as a soul artist heavily influenced by Aretha Franklin. Songs like "Inseparable" and "This Will Be" highlight some of Cole's strongest vocal work. While *Take A Look* ✶✶✶✶ (WEA/Elektra, 1993, prod. Andre Fischer, Tommy LiPuma) was not as big a commercial success as *Unforgettable*, it was an equal critical achievement, with 18 gleaming jazz-seasoned tracks earning her a Grammy for Best Jazz Vocalist.

what to avoid: Cole parted ways with Capitol after recording *Don't Look Back* ✶✶ (One Way Records, 1980, prod. various); arguably, she left one album too late. Unquestionably her weakest work, with vocals lacking any trace of intensity or passion, this LP might have better been titled *Don't Look Here*.

the rest:
Natalie ✶✶✶✶ (One Way, 1976)
Thankful ✶✶✶ (One Way, 1977)
Natalie . . . Live ✶✶✶✶ (One Way, 1978)
I Love You So ✶✶ (One Way, 1979)
We're the Best of Friends w/Peabo Bryson ✶✶✶✶ (One Way, 1979)
Happy Love ✶✶ (One Way, 1981)
Dangerous ✶✶✶✶ (Modern, 1985)
Everlasting ✶✶✶✶ (WEA/Elektra, 1987)
Good to be Back ✶✶✶✶ (WEA/Elektra, 1989)
Unforgettable With Love-Special Edition w/video ✶✶✶✶ (WEA/Elektra, 1991)
Holly & Ivy ✶✶✶ (WEA/Elektra, 1994)
Stardust ✶✶✶ (WEA/Elektra, 1996)
This Will Be: Natalie Cole's Everlasting Love ✶✶✶✶ (EMI America, 1997)

worth searching for: Most critics agree that Cole's debut, *Inseparable* ✶✶✶✶ (Capitol, 1975), is a bravura, breakthrough performance. Though no longer in print, the album revealed that Cole is an amazing talent, a budding superstar in the same league as her father. It's worth the time investment to start beating down the used record bins. On the other end of the spectrum, Natalie pits her latter-day vocal prowess against the spectacular power of world-class tenors Jose Carreras and Placido Domingo on the holiday LP *A Celebration of Christmas* ✶✶✶✶ (Erato, 1996) and more than holds her own.

influences:
◀◀ Nat King Cole, Aretha Franklin, Diana Ross, Sarah Vaughan, Ella Fitzgerald, Billie Holiday, Roberta Flack, Patti LaBelle, Carmen McRae

Bootsy Collins (© Jack Vartoogian)

▶▶ Anita Baker, Whitney Houston, Mariah Carey, Taylor Dayne, Toni Braxton

Chris Tower

Bootsy Collins

Born William Collins, October 26, 1951, in Cincinnati, OH.

First known as a session musician in Cincinnati, Bootsy Collins came to the national spotlight when James Brown recruited him for his backing band in 1969. After fueling Brown's band for two years, the bassist left to join George Clinton's Parliament-Funkadelic menagerie. Within a few years, the colorful bassist—taken to wearing glitzy, sequined clothes with stars all over and playing a bass shaped like a huge star—became one of P-Funk's most popular ingredients, leading to a solo deal with his Bootsy's Rubber Band in 1976. Featuring fellow P-Funkers such as Bernie Worrell and past Brown sidemen Fred Wesley and Maceo Parker, the Rubber

Band presented a boatload of cartoon-like space-based tunes grounded in seriously psychedelic funk grooves. After six solo records filled with the same science-fiction funk, Bootsy turned to session work with artists such as Malcolm McLaren and Dee-Lite. But the funk returned again during the late 1980s, with Collins presenting a series of records even trippier than before, courtesy of his collaborations with avant-garde producer Bill Laswell.

what to buy: Collins's solo debut, *Stretching Out in Bootsy's Rubber Band* ♫♫♫♫ (Warner Bros., 1976, prod. George Clinton, Bootsy Collins), is one of the bassist's most consistent records, showcasing both his nimble, effects-filled bass work and out-of-this-world sense of humor. You have to fast-forward 12 years to get to his next-best effort, the aptly titled *What's Bootsy Doin'?* ♫♫♫♫ (Columbia, 1988, prod. Bootsy Collins, Bill Laswell). Recorded after a six-year layoff, it features some of the bassist's tightest, most powerful funk grooves, including the expansive workout "Party on Plastic."

what to buy next: As a convenient way to get the real funk without time-consuming detours, Collins's greatest-hits record *Back in the Day: The Best of Bootsy* 𝄞𝄞𝄞𝄞 (Warner Bros., 1994, prod. various) offers plenty of bang for the buck, collecting near-legendary singles such as "Bootzilla," "The Pinocchio Theory," and "Hollywood Squares" in the same package.

what to avoid: As an artist, consistent focus has never been one of Collins's strong points. Still, the all-over-the-place *Ultra Wave* 𝄞 (Warner Bros., 1980/1996, prod. Bootsy Collins, George Clinton) sets new lows for lack of direction and less-than-distinctive material. Collins's live album, *Keepin' Dah Funk Alive 4 1995* **woof!** (Rykodisc, 1995, prod. At'c Inoue) presents a mediocre band trying its best to re-create the bassist's legendary grooves.

the rest:

Ahh . . . the Name Is Bootsy Baby 𝄞𝄞𝄞𝄞 (Warner Bros., 1977/1996)
Bootsy? Player of the Year 𝄞𝄞𝄞𝄞 (Warner Bros., 1978)
This Boot Is Made for Fonk-N 𝄞𝄞𝄞 (Warner Bros., 1979)
The One Giveth, the Count Taketh Away 𝄞𝄞𝄞 (Warner Bros., 1982)
Jungles Bass 𝄞𝄞𝄞 (4th and Broadway, 1990)
Blasters of the Universe 𝄞𝄞 (Rykodisc, 1994)
Zillatron, Lord of the Harvest 𝄞𝄞𝄞 (Rykodisc, 1994)

worth searching for: *Funk Power 1970: A Brand New Day* 𝄞𝄞𝄞𝄞 (Polydor/Chronicles, 1996) chronicles Collins's term as a JB, showing the roots of the "space bass" style that would drive P-Funk and the Rubber Band in later years.

influences:

◀◀ James Brown, George Clinton, Larry Graham

▶▶ T.M. Stevens, Rick James, Flea (Red Hot Chili Peppers)

Eric Deggans

Color Me Badd

Formed in Oklahoma City, OK.

Bryan Abrams, vocals; Mark Calderon, vocals; Sam Watters, vocals; Kevin Thornton, vocals.

Much in the same vein as Boyz II Men, these Oklahoma City high school classmates resurrected the sound of vocal groups from the 1950s–1970s, with a slick pop sheen that characterized Top 40 hits of the late 1980s and early 1990s. The group was a hit out of the box; it's debut, *C.M.B.*, sold more than three million copies. That was also its zenith, and subsequent releases faltered, including a fan-alienating religious turn on the 1993 release *Time and Chance.*

what to buy: Teenage girls went crazy for *C.M.B.* 𝄞𝄞𝄞 (Giant, 1991, exec. prod. Cassandra Mills, Dr. Freeze, Howie Tee, Royal Bayyan, Hamza Lee, Nick Mundy), which features Color Me Badd's spirited bubblegum dance numbers and catchy pop songs, including "All 4 Love," "I Wanna Sex You Up," and "I Adore Mi Amor."

what to avoid: *Time and Chance* 𝄞 (Giant, 1993, prod. DJ Pooh, C.M.B., Hamza Lee, Howie Tee, Mark Murray, Jimmy Jam, Terry Lewis, David Foster), despite guest appearances by master musicians Bernie Worrell and Maceo Parker, as well as rapper Doug E. Fresh, couldn't be saved.

the rest:

Young, Gifted and Badd 𝄞𝄞 (Giant, 1992)
Now and Forever **woof!** (Giant, 1996)

influences:

◀◀ The Jackson 5, the Osmond Brothers, New Kids on the Block, New Edition

▶▶ Hanson

Christina Fuoco

Commissioned

Formed mid-1970s, in Detroit, MI.

Karl Reid, vocals; Marvin Sapp, vocals; Mitchell Jones, keyboards, drum programming; Fred Hammond, bass, keyboards, drum programming; Maxx Frank, keyboards/piano; Eddie Howard, synth bass; Mike Williams, drums, cymbals, drum programming.

The cutting-edge Commodores of gospel music, made-in-Motown ensemble Commissioned has influenced the sound of young mainstream R&B acts for more than a dozen years with their silky, distinctively refreshing vocal stylings while garnering a fan base that crosses the entire musical spectrum. Two of the group's original members, childhood friends Karl Reid and Mitchell Jones, laid the foundation for the group while attending Detroit's Mumford High School, where their classmates included BeBe and CeCe Winans. Commissioned kicked off its career as recording artists in 1985, signing with Light Records, and moved to Benson Records four years later. Unafraid to challenge the traditional boundaries for gospel performers, the group invited hard-rap pioneers Run-D.M.C. to guest on its Grammy-nominated album *Matters of the Heart*, and lent their singing talents to jazz guitarist Earl Klugh's 1994 instrumental LP, *Move*. Personnel changes have altered the size and the look of Commissioned through the years, but the focus of the group remains balanced between rich vocal harmonies and soul-stirring contemporary ministry.

what to buy: The group's *Irreplaceable Love* 🎵🎵🎵🎵 (Benson, 1996, exec. prod. Nathan DiGesare, Sherman M. Brown) is Commissioned at its best. The smooth, patented Commissioned soul flavor is there, updated with a zesty pop/AC twist. The LP includes a collaboration with Boyz II Men members Shawn Stockman and Wanya Morris, who wrote and produced the tracks "Irreplaceable Love" and "They Must Know," respectively.

what to buy next: For those who may be interested in hearing the development of Commissioned from their beginning stages, *Commissioned Complete* 🎵🎵🎵 (CGI, 1993, prod. Fred Hammond, Michael Brooks) provides a perfect background. This double disc contains the group's first two albums, *I'm Going On* and *Go Tell Somebody*, from the mid-1980s. This is classic stuff.

the rest:
Will You Be Ready? 🎵🎵🎵 (CGI, 1988)
Number 7 🎵🎵🎵🎵 (A&M, 1991)
Ordinary Just Won't Do 🎵🎵🎵 (CGI, 1993)
On the Winning Side 🎵🎵 (CGI, 1993)
A Collection 🎵🎵🎵🎵 (CGI, 1993)
Matters of the Heart 🎵🎵🎵 (Benson, 1994)
The Light Years 🎵🎵 (CGI, 1995)
State of Mind 🎵🎵🎵 (Verity, 1996)

influences:
◀◀ Harmonizing Four, Motown, Commodores, the Winans
▶▶ Boyz II Men, Jodeci, Shai

Tim A. Smith

The Commodores
/Lionel Richie

Formed 1968, in Tuskegee, AL.

Lionel Richie Jr. (born 1950 in Tuskegee, AL), vocals, piano, saxophone (1968–82); Walter "Clyde" Orange, drums, vocals; Milan Williams, keyboards, trombone, guitar (1968–89); Ronald LaPread, bass, trumpet (1968–86); William King Jr., brass, vocals; Thomas McClary, guitar (1968–83); James Dean "J.D." Nicholas, vocals, keyboards (1984–present).

You can mark the evolution of the Commodores' sound by the height of frontman Richie's afro. He piled it high in the early days, when the Commodores were a high-stepping funk outfit following the rock 'n' R&B path paved by Sly & the Family Stone

word up!

I found out the crowd wants to hear the song exactly like it is. I decided to take out the second verse of 'Three Times a Lady'; it's not important, they've heard it before. I got more people stopping me after the show saying, 'Why didn't you play the second verse? That's my favorite part.' I tried to leave out 'Brick House' . . . but they want to hear every friggin' song I ever did in life. That's a compliment, though. I'm not at all complaining when people fall in love with the songs and want to hear them.

Lionel Richie

and James Brown, testifying with crotch-thrusters such as "Machine Gun" and "Slippery When Wet" that tested the limits of the family crowds at concerts by the Jackson 5, whom the Commodores opened for between 1971–73. Towards the end of the 1970s, however, Richie took over and the group took a softer, more conservative trail, specializing in soft—but undeniably melodic—ballads such as "Sail On," "Still," and "Three Times a Lady." In true Motown fashion, it was only a matter of time until Richie spun off into a solo career, which he did with remarkable success during the 1980s before fading away in the 1990s. The

Commodores live on, though the group has never again been the chart denizen it was during the late 1970s. Can a reunion be too far off?

what to buy: *The Commodores Anthology* 𝄞𝄞𝄞 (Motown, 1995, prod. various) has it all; the early funk hits, the latter day love songs, the handful of post-Richie triumphs ("Nightshift," "Reach High"). A solid overview of one of the 1970s top acts. *The Ultimate Collection* 𝄞𝄞𝄞 (Motown, 1997, prod. various) is a solid single-disc gathering of the hits.

what to buy next: *Caught in the Act* 𝄞𝄞𝄞 (Motown, 1975, prod. James Anthony Carmichael, the Commodores) is vintage, fiery Commodores, before the mush took over. Richie became an obnoxiously ubiquitous presence during the 1980s, but his second solo album, *Can't Slow Down* 𝄞𝄞𝄞 (Motown, 1983, prod. Lionel Richie, James Anthony Carmichael) is a well-crafted, melodic affair loaded with hits such as "All Night Long (All Night)," "Hello," and "Stuck on You."

what to avoid: *Commodore Hits Vol. 1* and *Vol. 2* **woof!** (both Sound Barrier, 1992, prod. the Commodores) find the remaining Commodores trio clearly out of ideas, so they re-recorded the group's 1970s and early 1980s hits. Pathetic.

the rest:
The Commodores:
Hot on the Tracks 𝄞𝄞𝄞 (Motown, 1976)
Commodores 𝄞𝄞𝄞 (Motown, 1977)
All the Great Hits 𝄞𝄞𝄞𝄞 (Motown, 1982)
All the Great Love Songs 𝄞𝄞𝄞 (Motown, 1984)
Nightshift 𝄞𝄞𝄞𝄞 (Motown, 1985)
Greatest Hits 𝄞𝄞𝄞𝄞 (Motown, 1991)
Commodores Christmas 𝄞𝄞 (Sound Barrier, 1992)
No Tricks 𝄞𝄞 (Sound Barrier, 1993)

Lionel Richie:
Lionel Richie 𝄞𝄞 (Motown, 1982)
Dancing on the Ceiling 𝄞𝄞 (Motown, 1986)
Back to Front 𝄞𝄞𝄞 (Motown, 1992)
Louder Than Words 𝄞 (Mercury, 1996)

worth searching for: The out-of-print *Midnight Magic* 𝄞𝄞𝄞 (Motown, 1979, prod. James Anthony Carmichael, the Commodores) is a worth-hearing transitional album that finds the Commodores beginning the shift into highly commercial ballad mode.

influences:
◀◀ Sly & the Family Stone, James Brown, the Temptations, Blood, Sweat & Tears

▶▶ Prince, Steve Arrington, Frankie Beverly & Maze

Gary Graff

Common
/Common Sense
Born Rashied "Peteweestroe" Lynn, in Chicago, IL.

Chicago was a city doomed for hip-hop obscurity when Common Sense first rocked a Midwest mic. But by the time "Soul by the Pound" entered the remix rotation, the nasal-voiced wit of the Windy City was earning nods—and even odes—from the most scrutinizing of hip-hop purists. On both his albums (and, elsewhere, on a notable cameo on De La Soul's "The Bizness"), Common represents that which is pure and sensible in hip-hop: lyrics that require rewinding; jazzy beats that complement rather than carry his lyrics; and enough heart to underscore a lifelong kinship with the oral tradition.

what to buy: *Resurrection* 𝄞𝄞𝄞𝄞 (Relativity, 1994, prod. various) finds Common growing into his potential as one of hip-hop's most prolific poets. Here, he drops rhymes that reminisce and reflect on the influence Chitown and early hip-hop had in creating the voice we hear today. It is a resurrection, indeed, for an artist who had marred his debut with immature and misogynistic overtones. This follow-up, however, is a thought-out and thought-provoking work, with highlights including, "Thisisme," the metaphorically sly "I Used to Love H.E.R.," and the all-too-modest "Sum Shit I Wrote." A dexterous rapper, Common showcases his diversity of diction on "Communism" (an archive of words beginning with "com"), and his affinity for simile on "Watermelon": "I stand out like a nigga on a hockey team/I got goals/I can/Like a pop machine." If the rapper sounds as if he's slightly more creative and astute than your average MC, it's because he is. More humble, too. On "Pop's Rap" he lets a real old-schooler—his father—drop knowledge for a generation that derives much of its morals from the opportunistic and irresponsible.

the rest:
(As Common Sense) *Can I Borrow a Dollar?* 𝄞𝄞𝄞 (Relativity, 1992)
One Day It'll All Make Sense 𝄞𝄞𝄞𝄞 (Relativity, 1997)

influences:
◀◀ Das EFX, Rakim, De La Soul, Pete Rock & C.L. Smooth

▶▶ Nas, No ID

Corey Takahashi

Con Funk Shun
Formed 1968 as Project Soul, in Vallejo, CA. Disbanded 1986.

Michael Cooper, vocals, guitar; Louis McCall, drums; Cedric Martin, bass, keyboards; Danny Thomas, keyboards; Melvin Carter, key-

boards, vocals; Karl "Deacon" Fuller, saxophone; Zebulon Paulle Harrell, percussion, saxophone; Felton Pilate II, trombone, guitar, synthesizer, vocals.

Because it had almost no success on the *Billboard* pop charts—just two short-lived Top 40 hits, "Ffun" and "Too Tight"—Con Funk Shun does not enjoy the same crossover reputation as peers such as Cameo, Earth, Wind & Fire, and Kool & the Gang. Rather, CFS was an urban success story, bridging West Coast smoothness with Memphis soul grit for one of the most versatile of the 1970s funk band approaches. After having some success with Project Soul, Cooper and McCall moved to Memphis in 1972, where they met their future bandmates. After doing session work at Stax Records and touring as the Soul Children's backing band, the septet struck out on its own. Two singles for Stax lured Mercury Records, which signed CFS for what would be a long and fruitful association that also included producer Skip Scarborough. "Ffun" topped the R&B charts in 1977, and CFS would later slide into the R&B Top 5 with "Shake and Dance With Me" (1978), "Chase Me" (1979), and "Baby I'm Hooked (Right Into Your Love)" (1983), the latter produced by Eumir Deodato. After a collaboration with future New Kids on the Block mastermind Maurice Starr, Con Funk Shun burned out and faded away, disbanding in 1986.

what to buy: With the band's individual titles out of print, *The Best of Con Funk Shun* ♫♫♫♫ (Mercury Funk Essentials, 1993, prod. various) provides an excellent overview, with all the hits and some of the key album tracks. It makes a case that CFS didn't receive its propers while it was around.

the rest:
Best of Con Funk Shun, Vol. 2 ♫♫♫ (Mercury Funk Essentials, 1996)
Live for Ya ♫♫♫ (Intersound, 1996)

worth searching for: *Secrets* ♫♫♫♫ (Mercury, 1977, prod. Skip Scarborough) established CFS with "Ffun" and other well-crafted R&B tunes.

influences:

◄◄ James Brown, Earth, Wind & Fire, Kool & the Gang, Parliament

►► Zapp, Slave, L.T.D.

Gary Graff

Arthur Conley

Born April 1, 1946, in Atlanta, GA.

Otherwise a relatively minor star, Arthur Conley did assure his place in the Southern soul pantheon with "Sweet Soul Music";

a true 1960s horn-pumping, soul anthem, it's a literal roll call of homage to the decade's best soul men, name checking Sam Cooke (who is actually responsible for the song's melody) and Otis Redding, who co-wrote the song. Conley's career seemed to lose focus after Redding's death, despite a few minor singles such as "Funky Street" and a cover of the Beatles' "Ob-la di, Ob-la da." Conley eventually moved to Europe.

what's available: *Sweet Soul Music: The Best of Arthur Conley* ♫♫♫♫ (Ichiban, 1995, prod. David Nathan, Harry Young) is an excellent overview, containing many worthwhile lesser-known songs and a detailed history of the artist.

influences:

◄◄ Otis Redding, Sam Cooke, Sam and Dave

►► John Mellencamp

Allan Orski

Norman Connors

Born March 1, 1948, in Philadelphia, PA.

As a drummer, Norman Connors has performed with such jazz immortals as John Coltrane, Pharoah Sanders, and Archie Shepp. As a record producer, he owns credits with artists like Jean Carn, Michael Henderson, and singer-guitarist Norman Brown. As an impresario, he played a major role in guiding the early careers of protegees like Angela Bofill, and he recorded a vocal duet with the late Phyllis Hyman that many R&B fans hail as a contemporary classic. But no matter what Connors has done in the past, or may do in the future, he may forever be best remembered for a singular slice of aural perfection he sang all by himself in 1976—"You Are My Starship," a soaring, stratospheric love petition that landed as the black music response to the ethereal, grandiose "arena rock" of the period. Ironically, Connors piloted his "Starship" so superbly that it continues to overshadow virtually all his other impressive accomplishments. A drummer since the age of five, he broke in his musical chops as a teen doing session work for Coltrane, Shepp, and "Brother" Jack McDuff. Moving from Philly to New York, he cut several albums with Sanders before being wooed by two record labels as a solo artist. Connors has said that Atlantic Records "wanted to put me in that soul/jazz bag," but the Buddah subsidiary Cobblestone promised him the freedom to do whatever he wished. Those wishes transformed into a series of well-received albums, leading his own Starship Orchestra, collaborations as a songwriter as well as a producer, and the rare ability to be commercially viable and creatively ambitious at the same time. "Starship" is heavenly, but Norman Connors's legacy should be as a man with the knack for knowing how to bring out the best in others' talents as well as his own. In recent years, he has been recording for the Motown subsidiary MoJazz.

what to buy: Compilation experts the Right Stuff Records gained access to the Buddah vaults in 1997, and *The Best of Norman Connors & Friends* 🐾🐾🐾🐾 (The Right Stuff, 1997, prod. various) is one of the more glorious results. A "Best of" collection in the purest sense of the term, the CD's 10 cuts celebrate a range and depth of creative passion that extends far beyond "You Are My Starship," the opening track. Connors's other commercial hits, "Valentine Love" and "Once I've Been There," are on hand, as is his heartstopping duet remake of the Stylistics' "Betcha By Golly, Wow" with Phyllis Hyman.

what to buy next: To hear what Connors has been up to lately, check out *Easy Living* 🐾🐾🐾 (MoJazz, 1997, prod. Norman Connors, Jheryl Lockhart, Donald Tavie), an album of sturdy, sophisticated pop-jazz creations showcasing Connors on drums and percussion as well as vocals; he's aided and abetted here by saxman Gerald Albright and guitarist Doc Powell.

what to avoid: With the new Connors' compilation on the Right Stuff, there's little reason to recommend *The Best of Norman Connors* 🐾🐾 (Sequel, 1994, prod. various) which features "Starship," "Valentine Love," and a small selection of questionable choices.

the rest:
Saturday Night Special/You Are My Starship 🐾🐾🐾✓ (Sequel, 1996)
Remember Who You Are 🐾🐾🐾✓ (MoJazz, 1993)
Romantic Journey 🐾🐾🐾 (The Right Stuff, 1994)
You Are My Starship 🐾🐾🐾🐾 (Buddah, 1996)

worth searching for: Connors should enjoy a stellar reputation as a producer, but his studio skills haven't received the acclaim that some of his more-publicized contemporaries enjoy. The 1990s quality of his behind-the-glass work is evident in the LP by guitarist Norman Brown, *Just Between Us* 🐾🐾✓ (MoJazz, 1992).

influences:
◀◀ John Coltrane, Duke Ellington, Quincy Jones, Herbie Hancock, Stanley Clarke

▶▶ Barry White, the Artist Formerly Known as Prince, Brothers Johnson, Dee Dee Bridgewater, Michael Henderson, Luther Vandross, Phyllis Hyman, Jean Carne

Jim McFarlin

Conscious Daughters
Formed late 1980s, in Oakland, CA.

CMG, vocals; Special One, vocals.

Under the wing of mentor and label chief Paris, the not-necessarily *socially* conscious group became one of the few female acts to earn membership (and acceptance) in the boys club known as hardcore rap. The Daughters have even been called rap riot grrrrls, but that's wrong: Although their lyrical concerns occasionally do focus on gender ("What's a Girl to Do," "Widow"), they generally avoid the sort of in-your-face feminism the grrrls are known for, mostly coming off like two of the guys—or, maybe, two of the guys' harmless little sisters. They call that self-empowerment?

what to buy: With Paris burning up the G-funk from behind the boards, *Ear to the Street* 🐾🐾🐾 (Scarface/Priority, 1993, prod. Paris, others) is a fine cruising record, with the breakout single, "Something to Ride to (Fonky Expedition)," and the Lonnie Liston Smith-sampling "We Roll Deep" providing much funk for the trunk.

the rest:
Gamers 🐾🐾 (Priority, 1996)

influences:
◀◀ Bo$$, H.W.A., B.W.P.

▶▶ Suga T, Passion, Marvalless, Da Brat

Josh Freedom du Lac

The Contours
Formed 1958, in Detroit, MI.

Joe Billingslea, vocals; Huey Davis, vocals; Billy Gordon, vocals; Billy Hoggs, vocals; Hubert Johnson, vocals; Sylvester Potts, vocals.

Jackie Wilson is the one who persuaded a reluctant Berry Gordy Jr. to sign this rough-hewn soul group to his fledgling Motown label in 1961, even though it seemed an odd fit with the smooth, pop-oriented soul music that was the label's stock in trade. Wilson was the cousin of Hubert Johnson, who was the last Contour to join. Gordy was no more impressed after their first single "Whole Lotta Woman," flopped, but at Wilson's insistence, Gordy gave them one more chance. It came in the form of the Gordy-penned "Do You Love Me (Now That I Can Dance)?," an over-the-top dance number originally intended for the Temptations. It is the Contours' signature song, and their most copied, with versions by, among others, the British invasion group the

Dave Clark Five, who also had a hit with it in the early 1960s. Though none of the group's subsequent releases was able to generate the kind of heated excitement that song did, the vocal quintet did get a short-lived rep in the 1960s for urgent dance floor anthems like "Shake Sherry," "Can You Jerk Like Me," and "First I Look at the Purse," later covered by rock's J. Geils Band. Future Temptations singer Dennis Edwards and Joe Stubbs, brother of Four Tops singer Levi Stubbs, joined the group, which broke up in 1968 (Billingslea went on to become a Detroit police officer). It reformed during the mid-1980s and become a truly viable concern in 1987, after the box-office smash *Dirty Dancing*, which pushed the song to #11 on the *Billboard* charts. The Contours reunited in 1987 and appeared on the Dirty Dancing Live tour and album, and it continues to appear at concerts and private functions around the world.

what's available: The Contours' debut, *Do You Love Me (Now That I Can Dance)* 🎵🎵🎵 (Motown, 1962/1988, prod. various) is a gem that includes the title song, "Can You Jerk Like Me," and "First I Look at the Purse." Gordy and Smokey Robinson headed up a cast of producers that defined Motown's machine-like recording stucture.

influences:
◀◀ The Platters, the Drifters, Jackie Wilson

▶▶ J. Geils Band, the Village People, the Jackson 5, New Edition

Doug Pullen

Sam Cooke

Born January 22, 1931, in Clarksdale, MS. Died December 11, 1964.

Producer Jerry Wexler always thought Sam Cooke had the greatest voice of his generation. Considering Wexler made all those great records with Ray Charles and Aretha Franklin, among others, that says something. Cooke's life story is practically a parable for the story of soul music itself—from the innocence of shouting gospel to a sordid death outside a hooker's seedy hotel room. He became one of the first major black artists to establish his creative self-determination with a major label. He laid the cornerstones of the music called soul. As the lead vocalist (and sex symbol) of a top sanctified gospel group, the Soul Stirrers, Cooke had to hold his first pop sessions in secret, releasing the results under a pseudonym to relative indifference. But his next single, "You Send Me," went #1 in 1957, and Cooke never looked back. He not only expertly explored a vast cross-section of music on his own recordings—blues, supper club pop, epic ballads, Top

40 jive—but he wrote and produced brilliantly for other artists. His extraordinary impact cannot be over estimated. The pure sound in his throbbing, sensual voice intoxicated so many other vocalists—as well as listeners—that his style continues to echo throughout the pop scene long after his death. But his many and momentous accomplishments still live, well preserved in a number of different collections of his work.

what to buy: *The Man and His Music* 🎵🎵🎵🎵 (RCA Victor, 1986, prod. various) documents his commercial successes, from the early Soul Stirrers records to the towering final ballad, "A Change Is Gonna Come," over the chronological course of 28 selections. But no picture of Sam Cooke can be complete without *One Night Stand: Live at the Harlem Square Club 1963* 🎵🎵🎵🎵 (RCA Victor, 1985, prod. Hugo & Luigi). Here is sweaty, smokey, persuasive evidence of his mesmerizing powers over an audience from the scene of the crime.

what to buy next: His expressions covered so many different areas, and there are at least three albums immediately worth investigating. *Night Beat* 🎵🎵🎵🎵 (RCA, 1963/Abkco, 1995, prod. Al Schmitt), his 1963 small combo late night blues album, was one of soul's lost masterpieces until its digital release. *Sam Cooke with the Soul Stirrers* 🎵🎵🎵🎵 (Specialty, 1991, prod. various) contains some of the most sublime gospel vocals ever put to record. *Sam Cooke's SÁR Story* 🎵🎵🎵🎵 (Abkco, 1994, prod. Sam Cooke), a two-disc box that commemorates his skills as a writer and producer on one disc of rare gospel and another disc of obscure pop songs that originally appeared on his own record label.

the rest:
The Best of Sam Cooke 🎵🎵🎵🎵 (RCA Victor. 1963)
At the Copa 🎵🎵🎵 (Abkco, 1987)
The Rhythm and the Blues 🎵🎵🎵 (RCA Victor, 1995)

worth searching for: A number of rewarding selections that did not find their way onto CD remain resting in the original vinyl version of his album *Shake* 🎵🎵🎵 (RCA Victor, 1965), a collector's item that draws large bounties in record stores these days.

influences:
◀◀ R.H. Harris, Kylo Turner, Charles Brown

▶▶ Otis Redding, Rod Stewart, Steve Perry, Maxwell, D'Angelo, Tony Rich

Joel Selvin

The Cookies

Formed late 1950s, in Brooklyn, NY.

Ethel "Earl-Jean" McCrea, lead vocals; Dorothy Jones, vocals; Margaret Ross, vocals.

Though they had one exquisite hit single—1962's "Don't Say Nothin' Bad (About My Baby)"—and a few other lesser successes, the Cookies are more famous for whom they backed—Little Eva, Mel Torme, Ben E. King, Neil Sedaka—and for who covered their songs. After winning an amateur-night contest at the Apollo Theater, the three members of the Cookies began singing backup on records coming out of New York's Brill Building. When Little Eva, a babysitter that Cookies lead singer Earl-Jean McCrea introduced to songwriter Carole King, hit the top of the charts in 1962 with "The Loco-Motion," the Cookies followed with their first solo recordings. Three of their singles—"Chains," "Don't Say Nothin' Bad (About My Baby)," and "Girls Grow Up Faster Than Boys"—reached the pop Top 40, and Earl-Jean had a final hit of her own in 1964 with "I'm Into Something Good."

what's available: *Complete Cookies* 🎵🎵🎵 (Sequel, 1994, prod. Gerry Goffin, Russ Titleman) collects the recordings the trio made for Colpix Records between 1962–64. It's standard girl-group stuff—charming, but with less depth than the Shirelles and less punch than Phil Spector's records with the Ronettes, et al. In addition to "Don't Say Nothin' Bad (About My Baby)," the one song tough enough to raise these women out of anononymity, the album contains original versions of songs later made famous by the Beatles ("Chains"), the Drifters ("On Broadway," with very different lyrics), and Herman's Hermits ("I'm Into Something Good").

influences:

◀◀ The Chiffons, the Shirelles, the Crystals

▶▶ The Exciters, the Beatles, Herman's Hermits

see also: *Little Eva*

Brian Mansfield

Coolio

Born Artis Ivey.

With his trademark braids standing straight up off his head, Coolio comes off as funny as he is funky, a clown prince of hip-hop for the '90s. But don't mistake the former member of WC and the MAAD Circle for a fool: A reformed crackhead who has stood on both sides of the street, Coolio knows how to keep it real. Yet it's his penchant for fantasy—the good-time, non-stop vision of a Parliament/Funkadelic-style party out of bounds, not the nightmarish gangsta vision of Snoop Doggy Dogg and Dr. Dre, among others—that made him a voice to be reckoned with and a force on the charts.

what to buy: A virtual concept album about the simultaneous allure and repellence of ghetto life, *Gangsta's Paradise* 🎵🎵🎵🎵 (Tommy Boy, 1995, prod. Brian "the Wino" Dobbs, Poison Ivey, Coolio, Spoon, others) loses none of its credibility for Coolio's proselytizing on such cautionary tales as "Too Hot" (a safe-sex anthem), "Kinda High, Kinda Drunk" (an account of overindulgence) and "For My Sistas" (a rare appreciation—for rap, anyway—of the fairer sex). More freewheeling are the head-bobbing jams "Sumpin' New," "Cruisin'," and "A Thing Goin' On," the latter two of which reinvigorate classics by Smokey Robinson and Billy Paul, respectively. Best of all, though, is the triple-platinum, Grammy-winning title track, a harrowing mini-opera about life on the streets set against *Psycho*-style strings and vocalist L.V.'s plaintive choruses. Hard enough for the streets, but as uplifting as a Stevie Wonder album, *Gangsta's Paradise* is one of the best mainstream rap joints in recent memory.

the rest:

It Takes a Thief 🎵🎵🎵🎵 (Tommy Boy, 1994)
My Soul 🎵🎵🎵♪ (Tommy Boy, 1997)

influences:

◀◀ WC and the MAAD Circle, 7A3, Rob Base & DJ EZ-Rock, D.J. Jazzy Jeff & the Fresh Prince

▶▶ 40 Thevz, Ras Kass

Daniel Durchholz

The Counts

Formed 1971, in Detroit, MI.

If you're a fiend of the funk, the Counts is one of those undiscovered gems that you can't believe you've never heard. The group made some rumblings on the R&B and pop charts early in its career as the Fabulous Counts, with a couple of singles produced by Ollie McLaughlin—best known for his work with the Capitols, of "Cool Jerk" and "We Got A Thing That's In the Groove" fame. The biggest of the Fabulous Counts' early singles is the edgy, guitar-and-organ jam "Get Down People." By 1971, the group dropped the Fabulous and issued its first LP, *What's Up Front That—Counts*. Mostly instrumental, the album is a deep funk classic, a percolating syncopated assault. The highlight of the album is the title track, an extended jam with a super tough rhythm, steamy jazz/funk organ and guitar solos and an avant garde horn line.

what's available: *It's What's In the Groove* ♫♫♫♫ (Southbound, 1996) is the ultimate Counts collection and contains 20 tracks from 1973–75. *In Yo' Face Vol. 1 and 2: The Roots of Funk* ♫♫♫♫ (Rhino, 1994, prod. various) is good for freshmen still dunking their toes in the funk and includes the essential "Get Down People."

worth searching for: The British CD reissue of *What's Up Front That—Counts* ♫♫♫♫ (Westbound, 1971/Westbound/Ace U.K., 1994) features two previously unreleased tracks: "Motor City," a throw-away, and "What's It All About," which is an accomplishment—an uncomplicated, lush ballad with swirling strings that rivals any late Detroit-era Motown release. It's not easily found, but the title track and "What's It All About" alone make it worth the search. If you're looking for something more esoteric, check out the various artist collection *Funky Jams Vol. 5* ♫♫♫ (Hubbub U.K., 1996). It opens with "Get Down People" and just keeps it in the groove from there with super-rare but stone funk jams. Also worth investigating are the *Gettin' It Off—Westbound Funk* ♫♫♫♫ (Westbound/Ace U.K., 1993, prod. various) and *The Westbound Sound of Detroit* ♫♫♫♫ (Westbound/Ace U.K., 1994, prod. various) collections. *Gettin' It Off* features "What's Up Front That Counts" along with other rare and unreleased gems by the Ohio Players, Melvin Sparks, and Caesar Frazier, among others from the Westbound vaults. *The Westbound Sound* includes "What's It All About" as well as tracks from Unique Blend, the Detroit Emeralds, the Fantastic Four, and the Magictones. It's an excellent collection that shows that Detroit remained fertile soil for vocal group soul after the departure of the Sound of Young America.

influences:

◄◄ James Brown, Wilson Pickett, the Parliaments

►► The Ohio Players, the Young Disciples

Dana G. Smart

The Coup

Formed 1991, in Oakland, CA.

Boots, vocals; E-Roc, vocals; Pam the Funkstress, DJ.

Unrepentantly Black Marxist, unabashedly activist, and undeniably funky, the aptly-named Coup put out its first self-financed independent EP on Polemic Records in 1991. Part of a group of self-styled revolutionaries who called themselves the Mau Mau Rhythm Collective, the Coup went two steps beyond fellow rhyme motivators Chuck D. and Paris by holding their own

reading groups, organizing street youths, and regularly staging anti-police and anti-racist demonstrations at Oakland City Hall. Even before they reached a national stage, then, they could legitimately claim to be feared in the halls of power.

what's available: Both Coup albums on Wild Pitch deliver awareness wrapped in that greasy old East Bay funk. *Kill My Landlord* ♫♫♫ (Wild Pitch, 1993, prod. Boots) introduces Boots's clever and slippery rhyme skills. On "Not Yet Free" he manages to skewer the entire system of schooling without losing his funk or his sense of humor. E-Roc's more traditional East Bay flow, patterned much after E-40, provides a strong counterbalance. *Genocide & Juice* ♫♫♫♫ (Wild Pitch, 1994, prod. Boots) is even better. Boots stretches out for a '90s parable on the excellent "Fat Cats, Bigga Fish," while the crew's collaborations with notoriously violent Oakland rapper Spice 1, plus the ever-charming E-40, prove that they really do know how to get their message to the people without compromising their street integrity. The activists call it praxis.

worth searching for: *The Coup: The EP* ♫♫♫♫ (Polemic, 1991, prod. Boots) demonstrates the very praxis the group would become known for.

influences:

◄◄ Public Enemy, Boogie Down Productions, X-Clan, Paris, Disposable Heroes of Hiphoprisy, E-40

►► Mystik Journeymen, B.U.M.S.

Jeff "DJ Zen" Chang

Don Covay

Born March 24, 1938, in Orangeburg, SC.

Equally adept at, and hugely influential as, both a singer *and* a songwriter, Don Covay's 40-plus-year career in so many facets of the business is a testament not only to the man's great talent, but to his undeniable love of the music and of the people who make it. The son of a Baptist minister and a member from an early age of his family's gospel quartet, the Cherry-Keys, Covay's teen years were spent parking cars at Washington, D.C.'s renowned Howard Theatre, which quickly and indelibly exposed him to the more secular sounds of Clyde McPhatter and the Dominoes. Soon afterwards, as a member of the Rainbows (wherein the young Billy Stewart and Marvin Gaye also apprenticed), Covay enjoyed a minor local hit with "Mary Lee" in 1955, and followed this with a brief stint in the Moonglows. Two years later, opening a show for Little Richard, Covay so impressed the headliner that he was quickly asked to join his legendary back-up band the Upsetters and, under the name Pretty Boy, was duly signed to Atlantic Records. He found more success in subsequent years as a songwriter, however, penning hits for both Chubby Checker ("Pony Time") and Gladys Knight ("Letter Full of Tears"), while his own releases on a variety of labels made little impact. Finally, in 1964, he hit with his own recording of "Mercy Mercy" (which immediately made its way into the Rolling Stones's repertoire), followed by "See Saw" a year later. Now re-signed with Atlantic and working as both an artist and producer alongside the likes of Wilson Pickett, Joe Tex, Ben E. King, Solomon Burke, Otis Redding, and Arthur Conley, Covay won widespread acclaim and success in 1968 when Aretha Franklin scored huge hits with covers of "See Saw" and the Grammy-nominated "Chain of Fools." Covay then spent the 1970s working in a variety of capacities for both Mercury and Philadelphia International, and he toured with old pals Pickett and Burke as the Soul Clan during the early 1980s. But Covay was forced to slow his activities somewhat in recent years due to health problems. Nevertheless, his songs and style not only remain an important part of R&B's golden age, they continue to inspire writers and singers of all genres.

what to buy: One can't go wrong with *Mercy Mercy: The Definitive Don Covay* ♫♫♫♫ (Razor & Tie, 1994, comp. Billy Vera), which collects all of the key tracks, from Pretty Boy's first record, "Bip Bop Bip" onward.

what to buy next: *Checkin' In with Don Covay* ♫♫♫ (Mercury, 1992, prod. Don Covay) is a fine overview of the man's 1970s work, wherein he displays a vocal style more mature but with a passion and fire undimmed since his Howard Theatre days.

worth searching for: Tribute albums are usually anything but. One shining exception is *Back to the Streets: Celebrating the Music of Don Covay* ♫♫♫♫ (Shanachie, 1993, prod. Jon Tiven, Joe Ferry) on which dozens of fans and friends, from Jimmy Witherspoon to Iggy Pop, pay respectful yet entertaining homage to the man and his music in this thoroughly wonderful album.

influences:
◄◄ Soul Stirrers, Dells, Little Richard
►► Mick Jagger, Peter Wolf, Bad Acoustics

Gary Pig Gold

Craig G

Craig G cut his teeth as part of Marley Marl's acclaimed Juice Crew and appeared on the 1989 classic "The Symphony" with fellow Juice all-stars Big Daddy Kane, Masta Ace, Kool G Rap, and Roxanne Shante. While he proved himself to be one of the rap's most dexterous wordsmiths between 1989 and 1991, the rapper remained criminally underrated. After a brief disappearance, Craig resurfaced with a bang in 1994, taking out the rapper Supernatural in a now-legendary New Music Seminar freestyle battle.

what's available: Because hip-hop is a singles-based medium, very few albums have ever lived up to their allotted length. *Now That's More Like It* ♫♫♫ (Atlantic, 1991, prod. Marley Marl) is no exception, though songs like "Word Association," "Ummm," and "What You're Used To" certainly shine. *The Kingpin* ♫♫♫ (Atlantic, 1989, prod. Marley Marl) is recommended only if you need to hear more beyond *Now That's More Like It*. The title track stands out amongst the uptempo hip-hop and house tunes. Sadly, the album doesn't include "Take the Bait," the B-side to "Shootin' the Gift" single that's easily one of Craig G's best recordings.

influences:
◄◄ Ultramagnetic MC's, Kool G Rap, Big Daddy Kane, Biz Markie, Marley Marl
►► Masta Ace, D-Nice

Jazzbo

Craig Mack
Born Craig James Mack, on Long Island, NY.

Debuting nationally at the same time as former labelmate Notorious B.I.G., Craig Mack couldn't have been a more timely jester in the court of hardcore rap. Bumbling, yet endearing, the former EPMD roadie's lyrics document a range of inane thoughts, though he also delves into serious praises of God while rallying against art-inspired violence. Mack's beats, meanwhile, ring of high-tech, space-aged funk, a juxtaposition against his back-to-basic goofball forays on the mic. It's both refreshing and fun to listen to the against-the-grain breakthrough "Flava In Ya Ear," on which Mack sets a new standard for off-the-wall style: "And just like a piece of Sizzelean, you'll fit inside my stomach with the eggs and grits between." Hip-hop could use more humor.

what to buy: *Project: Funk Da World* ♫♫♫ (Bad Boy, 1994, prod. Easy Mo Bee, Craig Mack, others) debuts Mack's humorous disposition, reminding one of a new-school Biz Markie. Throughout the album, Mack scraps posturing in favor of feel-good party rhymes ("Get Down"), extensive boasting ("Funk Wit Da Style"), and nods to the divine ("When God Comes").

the rest:
Operation: Get Down 🎵🎵 (Street Life, 1997)

influences:
◄◄ Biz Markie, Redman, Das EFX, Busta Rhymes

Corey Takahashi

Hank Crawford

Born Bennie Ross Crawford Jr., December 21, 1934, in Memphis, TN.

Only from the musical melting pot that was Memphis during the 1940s could a seminal musician like Crawford emerge. A resourceful instrumentalist whose gutbucket alto sax obliterated the lines between classic jazz and R&B, Crawford was firmly entrenched by the late 1950s in Ray Charles's groundbreaking small band, a group that drew many new lines of its own and set the standard for almost every combo that would follow. As part of an all-star horn section which also included David "Fathead" Newman on tenor sax and trumpet virtuoso Marcus Belgrave, Crawford developed the ability to imbue a melody with phrasings as expressive as any of Brother Ray's featured vocalists. While directing Brother Ray's newly-expanded big band, he established himself as a solo artist with a string of Atlantic LPs before his relationship with Charles dissolved in 1963; by 1970, Crawford had moved to CTI Records, under the watchful eye of producer Creed Taylor. In recent years, Crawford has teamed with keyboardist Jimmy McGriff on the Milestone label, forming one of the great organ/sax duos of all time.

what to buy: The two-disc set *Heart and Soul: The Hank Crawford Anthology* 🎵🎵🎵🎵 (Rhino, 1994, comp. Joel Dorn) presents a wonderful overview of the artist in many different settings, with an astounding array of collaborators. B.B. King, Etta James, McGriff, and, of course, Ray Charles are all represented, with Crawford providing exquisite accompaniment in every situation.

what to buy next: Crawford has a knack of finding interesting guest musicians to join him, and *Tight* 🎵🎵🎵 (Milestone, 1997, prod. Bob Porter) is no exception. Drummer Idris Muhummad is featured on beautiful readings of the Nat King Cole classic "Mona Lisa" and the George Benson favorite "Breezin'." The mellow guitar of Jimmy Ponder takes center stage for much of Crawford's *Portrait* 🎵🎵🎵🎵 (Milestone, 1993, prod. Bob Porter), with old friend David "Fathead" Newman along for the ride. He teams with McGriff for *On the Blue Side* 🎵🎵🎵 (Milestone, 1989,

prod. Bob Porter), with "Hank's Groove" and "Jimmy's Groove" the standouts on a two-track digital recording.

what to avoid: The sum never quite equals the impressive parts on *Night Beat* 🎵🎵 (Fantasy, 1989, prod. Bob Porter). Despite the contributions of Bernard "Pretty" Purdie and Dr. John, this effort never cooks at the temperature this band should be capable of generating.

influences:
◄◄ James Moody, Duke Ellington, Count Basie
►► David Sanborn, Kenny G, Dave Koz, Clarence Clemons

Matt Lee

Randy Crawford

Born Veronica Crawford, February 18, 1952, in Macon, GA.

Soul crooner Randy Crawford seemed like a major force during the late 1970s when she sang the title tune of the Crusaders' 1979 *Street Life* album, their biggest hit, and released several of her own discs to good reviews. But her popularity has been greater in the United Kingdom than in her native land; her biggest successes here have been as a featured singer rather than the star. After "Street Life," her greatest chart outing here was in 1984, when she duetted with Rick Springfield on "Taxi Dancing," from the *Hard to Hold* soundtrack. Crawford, who graduated from church singing to club singing while still a teen, performed early on in a band that included William "Bootsy" Collins. She then moved on to a jazz band and later performed with George Benson, which brought her to the attention of Cannonball Adderley. These days, she's in the Whatever Happened To . . . ? category of nearly risen—or too quickly fallen—stars.

what to buy: *Raw Silk* 🎵🎵🎵 (Warner Bros., 1979, prod. Stephan Goldman), a fine album, is notable particularly for her gospel-influenced vocals on the finale, "Blue Mood"—a true testimony to her abilities.

what to buy next: With most of the Crusaders involved as producers and players, it's no surprise that *Randy Crawford* 🎵🎵🎵 (Warner Bros., 1980, prod. Wilton Felder, Stix Hooper, Joe Sample) delivers tasty, though syrupy, soul, as exemplified by the U.K. hit "One Day I'll Fly Away." But it also attempts to capitalize on disco with ill-conceived treatments such as "Blue Flame," which could have been a great funk tune if it weren't overproduced with synthesizers and other needless embellishments.

what to avoid: Bland is the word for *Secret Combination* ♫♫ (Warner, 1981, prod. Tommy LiPuma), a lifeless blend of MOR/smooth jazz/Lite FM Muzak covers that's an unfortunate example of talent gone to waste, considering the promise of Crawford's more soulful earlier work.

the rest:

Everything Must Change ♫♫♫ (Warner Bros., 1976)
Miss Randy Crawford ♫♫♫ (Warner Bros., 1978)
Now We May Begin ♫♫♫ (Warner Bros., 1980)
Windsong ♫♫♫ (Warner Bros., 1982)
Nightline ♫♫♫ (Warner Bros., 1983)
Greatest Hits ♫♫♫♫ (Telstar, 1984)
Abstract Emotions ♫♫♫ (Warner Bros., 1986)
Love Songs ♫♫ (Telstar, 1987)
Rich and Poor ♫♫♫♫ (Warner Bros., 1989)
Through the Eyes of Love ♫♫♫ (Warner Bros., 1992)
Don't Say It's Over ♫♫♫ (Warner Bros., 1993)
Naked and True ♫♫♫ (Blue Moon, 1995)
Best of Randy Crawford ♫♫♫♫ (Warner Bros., 1996)

worth searching for: Crawford's vocal on the title track of the Crusaders' *Street Life* ♫♫ (MCA, 1979) is her defining moment and the best thing on the album.

influences:

◀◀ Aretha Franklin, Dinah Washington

▶▶ Siedah Garrett, Toni Braxton, Anita Baker

Lynne Margolis

Robert Cray

Born August 1, 1953, Columbus, GA.

From the minute Robert Cray arrived on the national scene, with 1983's *Bad Influence*, he was marked as the great black hope of the blues, its best chance to come up from the underground and into suburban living rooms. He was, after all, a handsome young man with a soulful, pleasing voice and in possession of both a stinging, true blues guitar attack and an ear for a nifty pop hook. Indeed, Cray became the blues's first modern pop star three years later, with *Strong Persuader*, his Mercury debut. Since then, his music became ever more R&B-based and, unfortunately, largely less interesting. While his guitar playing and singing have only improved over the years, he has sadly lost some of the sense of fun and buoyancy which made his early

Robert Cray (© Jack Vartoogian)

> word up!
>
> I like my association with the blues, but it seems kind of strange that people overlook the R&B things. On all the other records we've done, we've always included R&B and blues. It's hard to classify what our music is; there's touches of so many things in it. I'd like to be in every section, to be honest.
>
> **Robert Cray**

music so special. On his recent albums Cray has settled into a monochrome groove that is mostly just boring. His success with classic covers on early albums—and on 1996's *Tribute to Stevie Ray Vaughan*—suggests that one way he may enliven his work in the future is to occasionally turn to the past for material.

what to buy: *Bad Influence* ♫♫♫♫ (Hightone, 1983, prod. Bruce Bromberg, Dennis Walker) is illuminated by that special spark that separates great music from good. Some of the performances are more than a little sloppy, but the album swings with a robust energy while spotlighting Cray's songwriting, sense of humor ("So Many Women, So Little Time"), and ability to seamlessly incorporate soul, rock, and pop touches into his blues. *Strong Persuader* ♫♫♫♫ (Mercury, 1986, prod. Bruce Bromberg) contains most of the same traits as well as better production values and a more pristine sound. Cray proved his true blue mettle with *Showdown!* ♫♫♫♫ (Alligator, 1985, prod. Bruce Iglauer, Dick Shurman), his sparkling collaboration with Albert Collins and Johnny Copeland.

what to buy next: On *Some Rainy Morning* 𝄞𝄞𝄞𝄞 (Mercury, 1995, Robert Cray) Cray rebounds nicely after several mediocre albums, ditching the horns and producing a taut album.

what to avoid: Cray followed up the success of *Strong Persuader* by trying to force out pop songs on the tepid-at-best *Don't Be Afraid of the Dark* 𝄞𝄞 (Mercury, 1988).

the rest:

False Accusations 𝄞𝄞𝄞 (Hightone, 1985)
Who's Been Talkin' 𝄞𝄞𝄞 (1980, Atlantic, 1986)
Midnight Stroll 𝄞𝄞𝄞𝄞 (Mercury, 1990)
I Was Warned 𝄞𝄞𝄞 (Mercury, 1992)
Shame + A Sin 𝄞𝄞𝄞 (Mercury, 1993)
Sweet Potato Pie 𝄞𝄞𝄞 (Mercury, 1997)

influences:

◀◀ Albert Collins, Eric Clapton, Magic Sam, O.V. Wright, Johnny "Guitar" Watson, Howlin' Wolf, Larry Davis, Buddy Guy

▶▶ Joe Louis Walker, Sherman Robertson, Eric Clapton, Clarence Spady

Alan Paul

Andrae Crouch

Born July 1, 1942, in Los Angeles, CA.

While soul and funk were expanding their boundaries from the late 1960s into the early 1980s, Andrae Crouch was busy revolutionizing the sound of gospel music through the use of strings and synthesizers. Breaking down long-established barriers between black and white gospel while bridging the gulf dividing contemporary and secular music, the bearded maestro injected R&B, funk, rock soul, and Latin themes into his compositions with state-of-the-moment recording techniques, forming a group called Andrae Crouch and the Disciples and landing his first hit LP, *Take the Message Everywhere*, in 1969. Developing a worldwide reputation for electrifying live concerts, Crouch's stature as a musical legend was enhanced by a breakthrough appearance on Johnny Carson's *Tonight Show* in 1972, and becoming the first gospel act ever to perform on *Saturday Night Live*. With nine Grammy Awards and an Academy Award nomination on his resume, Crouch has seen such mainstream stars as Stevie Wonder, Billy Preston, Earth, Wind & Fire's Philip Bailey, and Leon Russell grace his albums, while collaborating on the works of artists ranging from Elvis Presley and Michael Jackson to Madonna. Despite his phenomenal musical success, Crouch's career was severely marred by his 1982 arrest for cocaine possession, occurring shortly after he disbanded the Disciples upon the departure of lead vocalist Danniebelle Hall. He was eventually cleared of all charges, but then took a 10-year hiatus from recording, during which time he assumed the pastorate of his father's ministry, L.A.'s Christ Memorial Church of God in Christ, and composed the theme song for the TV sitcom *Amen*. He returned with a burst of creative energy in 1994, releasing the comeback LP *Mercy* and arranging music for *The Lion King* and *A Time to Kill* film soundtracks. Crouch has reclaimed his rightful position as one of popular music's most innovative minds. His twin sister, Sandra, is also a top gospel artist.

what to buy: Crouch's self-imposed absence had no effect on his genius. *Mercy* 𝄞𝄞𝄞𝄞𝄞 (Qwest, 1994, prod. Andrae Crouch, Scott V. Smith) demonstrates brilliantly just how far ahead he was—and is—of the entire gospel music industry. Combining the silken vocals of El De Barge, among others, the piano mastery of Joe Sample, and Crouch's uncanny use of diverse sound effects and musical imagery, his "revival" album is a refreshing, triumphant break from contemporary gospel's norm.

what to buy next: For those completely unfamiliar with Crouch's remarkable musical legacy, *Tribute: The Songs of Andrae Crouch* 𝄞𝄞𝄞 (Warner Alliance, 1996, prod. various) reviews his career through the sincerest form of flattery: his trademark works performed by the brightest stars of modern gospel. The heartfelt appreciation of his music soars on the Brooklyn Tabernacle Choir's rendition of "Soon and Very Soon," Take 6's electrifying treatment of "This Is Another Day," and a 70-voice, all-star choir including Patti Austin and BeBe Winans booming out "My Tribute (To God Be the Glory)."

the rest:

Live At Carnegie Hall 𝄞𝄞𝄞 (CGI, 1993)
Best of Andrae Crouch 𝄞𝄞𝄞𝄞 (CGI, 1993)
Autograph 𝄞𝄞 (CGI, 1993)
More of the Best 𝄞𝄞𝄞 (CGI, 1993)
Volume 1: The Classics 𝄞𝄞𝄞𝄞 (CGI, 1993)
Volume 2: We Sing Praises 𝄞𝄞𝄞𝄞 (CGI, 1993)
Take Me Back 𝄞𝄞𝄞𝄞 (CGI, 1995)
The Light Years 𝄞𝄞𝄞𝄞 (Light, 1995)
This Is Another Day 𝄞𝄞𝄞𝄞 (CGI, 1995)
Live In London 𝄞𝄞𝄞 (CGI, 1995)
Volume 3: Contemporary Man 𝄞𝄞𝄞 (CGI, 1995)
He's Everywhere 𝄞𝄞 (Hob, 1996)
Pray 𝄞𝄞𝄞𝄞 (Qwest, 1997)

worth searching for: The 1979–84 reissues *I'll Be Thinking of You* 𝄞𝄞𝄞𝄞 (CGI, 1993), *Don't Give Up* 𝄞𝄞𝄞𝄞𝄞 (Warner Alliance, 1996), and *No Time to Lose* 𝄞𝄞𝄞𝄞 (Warner Alliance, 1996) are three of Crouch's all-time best recordings and worth their weights in gold. None was previously available on CD until now.

influences:

◀◀ Min. Thomas Whitfield, Sandra Crouch, Doris Akers

▶▶ The Winans, BeBe and CeCe Winans, Take 6, First Call, Michael W. Smith, Twyla Paris

Tim A. Smith

The Crows

Formed 1951, in Harlem, NY.

Daniel "Sonny" Norton, lead; Harold Major, tenor; William "Bill" Davis, baritone; Jerry Wittick, tenor; Gerald Hamilton, bass.

If you don't think that "Sh-boom" was the first true rock 'n' roll hit, you probably believe the honor should go to "Gee," recorded and released by the Crows in the middle of 1953. Another group straight off the streets of Harlem, they won the Wednesday Amateur Night contest at the Apollo Theater and subsequently found themselves an agent named Cliff Martinez. He got them a shot on Jubilee Records, but their only release for that label didn't do much. They moved over to George Goldner's Rama Records, and their second release was "Gee," a pioneering doo-wop recording that featured a simple "Doot, do-do-doot, do-do-doot, do-do-do-do-do" harmony riff repeated throughout the verses, and a marvelous jazz guitar solo in the middle. The record had a long period of exposure and sales with a breakout in L.A. that propelled it to #14 on the *Billboard* pop charts in mid-1954 (and #6 on the R&B charts). This was several months before rock 'n' roll pioneer Alan Freed moved his radio show from Cleveland to New York; thus, in effect, the Crows had a hit rock 'n' roll record before the term "rock 'n' roll" was in general use. Still, it was out there, and the kids heard it. So when Freed began playing the Crows' original version of "Gee" and other recordings by black R&B groups, they said, "Oh, so *that's* where all those great records are coming from!" The Crows may never have had another hit, but they didn't have to in order to ensure their place in the history of rhythm and blues.

what's available: The compilation CD *The Best of Doo-Wop Uptempo* 𝄢𝄢𝄢 (Rhino, 1989, prod. various) contains "Gee" and several other seminal R&B classics.

Michael Kosser

Crucial Conflict

Formed 1994, in Chicago, IL.

Wildstyle, vocals; Kilo, vocals; Coldhard, vocals; Never, vocals.

Perhaps because of the city's status as the birthplace of house,

Chicago made virtually no impact on the national hip-hop scene in the '80s, but that began to change in the '90s with the emergence of Common Sense, Do or Die, and West Side quartet Crucial Conflict.

what's available: The group's debut, *The Final Tic* 𝄢𝄢𝄢 (Pallas/Universal, 1996, prod. Wildstyle) is built on an unpromising gimmick, dubbed "RODEO" (Rhymes of Dirty English Organization), which applies Old West imagery and sound effects to the inner-city frontier. But the polyrhythmic drive of the arrangements is undeniable, with layers of Latin percussion, industrial grind, cracking whips, and hi-hats that sizzle like rattlesnakes. The raps complement the grooves by leapfrogging one another in giddy games of call and response, and the brash hooks of the hit "Hay" and "Ride the Rodeo" suggest the emergence of a Midwestern hip-hop sound (see Bone Thugs-N-Harmony) primed to challenge the stylistic stranglehold of the East and West Coasts.

influences:

◀◀ Bone Thugs-N-Harmony, Freestyle Fellowship

Greg Kot

The Crusaders

Formed 1956, in Houston, TX.

Joe Sample, keyboards; Nesbert "Stix" Hooper, drums; Wilton Felder, sax and bass; Wayne Henderson, trombone (1956–72).

After playing together as junior high-school bandmates in their hometown of Houston, the Crusaders—or the Jazz Crusaders, to their most devoted fans—grew up to practically define the jazz/soul genre for more than three decades. By the late 1950s, the schoolboys, calling themselves the Nite Hawks, left Texas to relocate on the West Coast, playing mostly dance gigs at popular clubs in L.A. and Las Vegas. An all-day recording session in 1960 for the Pacific Jazz label yielded a minor hit, and the Jazz Crusaders were born. After establishing themselves as crossover kings through a slew of successful instrumental LPs that appealed to funk and jazz devotees alike, they shortened their name in 1972 to become simply the Crusaders. Following the departure of original member Hubert Laws (who went on to forge an illustrious jazz career of his own), the band's signature sound became centered on the seamless sax and trombone voices of Wilton Felder and Wayne Henderson, a front line combination which often sounded as if it were a singular instrument. With the funky electric piano of Joe Sample and rock-solid rhythms of Stix Hooper rounding out the sound, the Crusaders' initial successes were scored with cover versions of contemporary pop and soul hits, a formula which would consistently serve them well. Felder's searing saxophone became the band's secret weapon, providing him with plenty of outside session work on horn as well as electric bass. After nine years of recording for the Pacific Jazz label, the Crusaders subsequently hooked up with producer Stewart Levine, who was to become their most significant collaborator. Their partnership lasted several years, giving birth to the group's most creative works. The early records with Levine were released on the Chisa label and distributed by Motown; eventually, Chisa was absorbed by ABC's Blue Thumb label, where the band enjoyed its greatest commercial triumphs. Henderson left the group briefly in 1980, only to return; Sample departed to pursue a solo career, while Hooper left to work as a producer and manager. Undeterred by the loss of key members, the Crusaders continue their musical march as world-renowned performers known for their distinctive groove and polished musicianship to the present day.

what to buy: *The Crusaders: Way Back Home* ♪♪♪♪♪ (GRP-Blue Thumb, 1996, comp. Stewart Levine) is an astonishing compilation touching on all phases of the band's impressive history. The four-disc set includes early interpretations of such Lennon-McCartney classics as "Eleanor Rigby" and "Golden Slumbers." Also covered are tunes by Sly Stone and Carole King, along with funk-based originals recorded live as well as in the studio. The band's revolving bass and guitar spots have seen many fine players come and go, but none seemed to fill the roles as smoothly as guitarist Larry Carlton (widely regarded as "the Fifth Crusader") and Max Bennett on bass. *Scratch* ♪♪♪♪ (MCA, 1974, prod. Stewart Levine), recorded live at the Roxy in L.A., captures this lineup at its peak. The five tracks make for an enjoyable listen, highlighted by their extraordinary reworkings of Carole King's "So Far Away" and the Crusaders' own theme song, "Way Back Home."

what to buy next: *Old Sox, New Shoes* ♪♪♪♪ (MoJazz, 1971, prod. Stewart Levine) is the first recording with Levine at the controls, and the start of a great run for band and producer. Carlton's weeping guitar enhances *Southern Comfort* ♪♪♪♪ (Blue Thumb, 1974, prod. Stewart Levine). With the catchy groove of "Double Bubble" setting the pace, this album also includes the Crusaders' first true radio-friendly pop tune, "Keep That Same Old Feeling." So good were the vibes at the Hermosa Beach, California, club called the Lighthouse that the fellas recorded three albums there over four years. *Lighthouse 68* ♪♪♪ (Pacific Jazz, 1968, prod. Richard Bock) is the best of the three, featuring the band's first attempt at "Eleanor Rigby" with jazz bassist great Buster Williams holding down the bottom. *Happy Again* ♪♪♪ (Sin-Drome, 1995, prod. Wayne Henderson) finds the current squad in fine form, with old friends Carlton, Hubert Laws, and Roy Ayers back in the fold. Bobby Lyle provides excellent keyboard support, more than filling Sample's ample shoes. Bobby Caldwell ("What You Won't Do For Love") does a nice vocal turn on the Johnny Mercer chestnut "Fools Rush In," as well as on his own "Jamaica."

the rest:
Unsung Heroes ♪♪♪ (Blue Thumb, 1973)
Free As the Wind ♪♪♪ (Blue Thumb, 1977)
Street Life ♪♪♪ (MCA, 1979)

influences:

◀◀ Dizzy Gillespie, Art Blakey, Modern Jazz Quartet, Clifton Chenier

▶▶ King Curtis, David Sanborn, the Blackbyrds

Matt Lee

The Crystals

Formed 1961, in Brooklyn, NY. Disbanded 1967. Re-formed 1971.

Dee Dee Kennibrew, vocals (1961–67, 1971–present); Barbara Alston, vocals (1961–67); Dolores "La La" Brooks, vocals (1961–67); Mary Thomas, vocals (1961–63); Patricia Wright, vocals (1961–64); Frances Collins, vocals (1964–67); Marilyn Byers, vocals (1986–present); Gretchen Gale, vocals (1986–present).

A crucial yet oft-overlooked element in producer Phil Spector's Wall of Sound, the Crystals were the first—and most malleable—act he signed when he launched his own record company, and in many ways the group laid the groundwork upon which he, and many other artists and producers to follow, bridged the gap between R&B and the pop Top 10. Kennibrew, Alston, Brooks, Thomas, and Wright, who were all friends in high school, first came together musically to help songwriter Leroy Bates cut demo recordings of his material for Hill and Range Music (in fact, they named themselves after Leroy's daughter Crystal). Shortly after forming, they auditioned for Spector's new Philles label, and with one of Bates's tunes, "There's No Other (Like My Baby)," gave the company its first hit in 1962. The surprisingly (yet subliminally) topical "Uptown," written by Barry Mann and Cynthia Weil, provided the group with its second Top 20 entry only four months later, but a controversy surrounding the lyrics of "He Hit Me (It Felt Like A Kiss)" kept this third release from cracking the Hot 100. Rather than battle on behalf of this record, Spector decided to release instead a brand new Gene Pitney composition, "He's a Rebel," which he overheard while visiting friends at Liberty Records. Rushing to scoop Liberty's release of this song (planned for Vikki Carr), Spector tore across country to Los Angeles to surreptitiously record his own version utilizing the vocals of that city's hot new session trio, the Blossoms (Darlene Love, Fanita James, Gracia Nitzsche). Released in the fall of 1962 under the name the Crystals—though not one member of the group was involved in its recording—"Rebel" soared to #1 in November and became a Top 20 hit in England as well. The *real* Crystals, with Brooks now handling the majority of the lead vocals, scored twice more the following year with "Then He Kissed Me" and the classic "Da Doo Ron Ron." But by 1964 they were already tiring of Spector's increasingly tyrannical methods, not to mention the possible disgrace involved in promoting and touring behind records they did not actually record. Following a final pair of unsuccessful releases on Philles, they bought out their contract and signed with United Artists in 1965, where they cut several records in a Motown vein before being dropped the following year, after which they unceremoniously disbanded. However, unable to resist the lure of the oldies revival of the late 1960s, they re-formed five years later and continue touring to this day, though recently with Kennibrew as the sole original member.

what's available: The Wall of Sound was built with 45 RPM singles, and *The Best of the Crystals* ✍✍✍ (Abkco, 1992, prod. Phil Spector) contains no less than seven indisputable evergreens of the genre, along with enough intriguing B-sides and even inexplicable flops ("All Grown Up") to constitute no less than a virtual 19-track '60s Girl Group Primer.

influences:

◀◀ The Chantels, the Shirelles, Rosie & the Originals

▶▶ The Shangri-Las, Brian Wilson, the Motels, Sit 'n' Spin

see also: *Darlene Love, Phil Spector*

Gary Pig Gold

Culture Club /Boy George

Formed 1981, in London, England. Disbanded 1987.

Boy George (born George O'Dowd, June 14, 1961), vocals; Roy Hay, guitar, keyboards; Mikey Craig, bass; Jon Moss, drums.

Culture Club frontman Boy George brought pure ear candy with

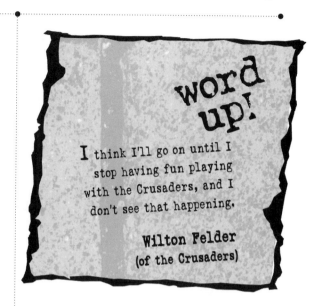

word up!

I think I'll go on until I stop having fun playing with the Crusaders, and I don't see that happening.

Wilton Felder (of the Crusaders)

a healthy dose of adrogyny to the top of the U.S. charts. Part of a long line of adrogynous rock singers, Boy George took it to the extreme, primping himself with makeup, braided hair, and tunics. The fad wore off after the group's first two albums—which launched a string of R&B-laden hit singles and earned the group a Grammy Award for Best New Artist in 1983. Personal dissensions and drug addictions eventually brought the group to an end. After a dry spell, Boy George's career was temporarily revived when his cover of Dave Berry's 1964 British hit "The Crying Game" was featured in the 1992 movie of the same name.

what to buy: Pop music doesn't get much better than *Colour By Numbers* ✍✍✍ (Virgin, 1983, prod. Steve Levine) and its danceable singles "Karma Chameleon," "Church of the Poison Mind," and "Miss Me Blind."

what to buy next: Culture Club's debut, *Kissing to be Clever* ✍✍✍ (Virgin, 1982, prod. Steve Levine) disarmed the masses with George's appearance and the plucky hits "Do You Really Want to Hurt Me?," "Time (Clock of the Heart)," and "I'll Tumble 4 Ya."

what to avoid: On the aptly titled *From Luxury to Heartache* ✍✍ (Virgin, 1986, prod. Arif Mardin, Lew Hahn) you can smell the end of the band coming.

the rest:
Waking Up with the House on Fire ✍✍♥ (Virgin 1984)

This Time: The First Four Years 🎵🎵🎵 (Virgin 1987)
At Worst . . . The Best of Boy George and Culture Club 🎵🎵🎵🎵 (SBK, 1993)

solo outings:
Boy George:
Sold 🎵🎵🎵 (Virgin, 1987)
High Hat 🎵🎵🎵 (Virgin, 1989)
The Martyr Mantras (Virgin, 1991)
Cheapness and Beauty 🎵🎵🎵 (Virgin, 1995)

influences:
◀◀ Queen, David Bowie, Bow Wow Wow, the Village People
▶▶ Right Said Fred, Pulp, Rupaul, Madonna

Christina Fuoco

Clifford Curry

Clifford Curry has been a popular Southeastern R&B mainstay whose recording career has usually involved Nashville, Tennessee. He started his career with such Southern vocal groups as the Echoes/the Five Pennies and the Bingos/the Hollyhocks. Later, he played in a middle Tennessee soul band that backed national singers as they came through town, and he recorded for Nashville's Excello label as Sweet Clifford. He hooked up with Nashville producer Buzz Cason for one regional hit, "She Shot a Hole in My Soul," and numerous other records. Most recently covered by Huey Lewis & the News, "She Shot a Hole in My Soul" became a favorite of the Carolina beach-music scene, and Curry continues to perform regularly there and throughout the Southeast. He was inducted into the Beach Music Hall of Fame.

what's available: *The Provider* 🎵🎵 (Appaloosa, 1994, prod. Fred James) is a thoroughly unremarkable album, self-penned music made with Nashville blues musicians. *She Shot a Hole in My Soul* 🎵🎵 (Collectables, 1995, prod. Buzz Cason, Mac Gayden), which collects the light pop-soul records made between 1967–73, is a distinct improvement, but even the title track doesn't have much more than a classic title and a nice horn riff going for it. Mac Gayden, who later wrote Carl Carlton's hit "Everlasting Love," plays guitar on much of this music.

influences:
◀◀ Joe Turner, the Drifters
▶▶ The Foundations, Carl Carlton

Brian Mansfield

word up!

IN Culture Club, I always made a point of making my songs ambiguous in that I never said 'he' or 'she.' I suppose as time goes by, I use the word 'he' more. The feelings still apply to everyone. Love is universal . . . people need to understand that there's no difference in the loving experience, no matter who it's between.

**Boy George
(of Culture Club)**

Frankie Cutlass

Although hardly a new concept, hip-hop producer compilations have been sprouting up left and right during the second half of the 1990s, with everybody from DJ Muggs to Ant Banks joining the fray. The Latino knob-twister Frankie Cutlass, too, assembled a group of rappers to add rhymes to his *Politics & Bullshit* beats but managed to separate himself from the pack simply by bringing the Juice Crew All-Stars back together for "Cypher: Part III."

what's available: Cutlass's guest list includes such New York heavyweights as Fat Joe, Kool G Rap, Sadat X, Busta Rhymes, the Coco Brovaz, Method Man, Keith Murray, Mobb Deep, and the Lost Boyz; but it's the Juice Crew's Roxanne Shante, Biz Markie, Craig G., and Big Daddy Kane who steal the show on

Politics & Bullshit ♫♫♫ (Violator/Relativity, 1997, prod. Frankie Cutlass). This album takes hip-hop fanatics on a magic carpet ride back to the genre's golden days with the "Symphony"-sampling "Cypher: Part III."

influences:

◀◀ Treacherous Three, Juice Crew All-Stars, Fat Joe, Sham & the Professor

Josh Freedom du Lac

Cypress Hill

Formed 1988, in Los Angeles, CA.

B-Real, vocals; Sen Dog, vocals; DJ Muggs, DJ.

Muggerud was an East Coast transplant to the hard streets of L.A.'s Southgate area who fell in with a number of rappers before finally hooking up with ex-local gang members Freese and Reyes. Although he'd previously produced an excellent crew called 7A3, it was with B-Real and Sen Dog that Muggs would find his greatest success. B-Real's nasal voice recalled King Ad-Rock, but he had the sort of street creed the Beastie Boys would never even dream of, carrying a slug in his body from a previous shooting. Sen Dog's own street life led him in and out of trouble before he completed the circle by becoming the group's hype man.

what to buy: When it was first released, *Cypress Hill* ♫♫♫♫♫ (Ruffhouse/Columbia, 1991, prod. DJ Muggs) felt to some West Coast true believers like another irrefutable answer to the Boogie Down Productions album *Criminal Minded*—the first, of course, being N.W.A.'s *Straight Outta Compton*. The record eventually went double-platinum because of East Coast support and, especially, because of the use of the chilly "How I Could Just Kill a Man" in the climax of Ernest Dickerson's film *Juice*; also important was the crossover legitimacy that the group's Lollapalooza stint brought. Still, everything about this record spoke West Coast: its murky, dusted samples; its hazy, ultraviolent, seedy midnight-on-Santa Monica Boulevard imagescape; its Spanglish accent; its earthy obsession with pot. Muggs is at his peak, deploying samples (both familiar and soon to be) in odd structures that complement B-Real's blunt-distorted storytelling and Sen Dog's punctuation marks. "Pigs," "Stoned Is the Way of the Walk," "How I Could Just Kill A Man," and "Hand On the Pump" redefine L.A. noir for the hip-hop generation, shot through with cop brutality, lowrider oldies, concentrated THC, and snarling driveby menace. That they again made marijuana (especially smoked in blunt form) the drug of choice for a generation was beside the point.

what to buy next: *Cypress Hill* represents a zone that Cypress never reenters. *Black Sunday* ♫♫♫ (Ruffhouse/Columbia, 1993, prod. DJ Muggs, T. Ray) is, the band admitted, a transitional record done hastily, and it rehashes the marijuana and guns motifs without covering any new ground. *Cypress Hill III—Temples of Boom* ♫♫♫ (Ruffhouse/Columbia, 1995, prod. DJ Muggs, the RZA) completes the group's move away from the layers of dusty funk samples of the first record and toward the warmer, more minimal feel of the Wu-Tang Clan, whose RZA guests on "Killa Hill Niggas." With Muggs now working with clean angular and atonal vibraphones, pianos, and strings to back up B-Real's psychedelia, it's easy to long for the wild abandon of the first record. While Cypress sat in a holding pattern, the label released *Unreleased & Revamped* ♫♫ (Ruffhouse/Columbia, 1996, prod. Muggs, Q-Tip, Prince Paul, Diamond D, Fugees, T-Ray), Cuban-born Senen left to work on other projects (including the Latino group Delinquent Habits), and Muggs released *The Soul Assassins* ♫♫♫♫ (Columbia, 1997, prod. Muggs), a compilation of excellent new tracks, over which a stellar cast (KRS-One, Goodie Mob, RZA and GZA, MC Eiht, and, especially, Wyclef) gives solid performances.

influences:

◀◀ Public Enemy, the Bomb Squad, N.W.A., Ice Cube, 7A3, the Beastie Boys, Rammellzee & K-Rob

▶▶ Wu-Tang Clan, Call O' Da Wild, Mista Grimm, Total Devastation, House of Pain, Funkdoobiest

Jeff "DJ Zen" Chang

D

Da Brat

Born Shawntae Harris, in Chicago, IL.

It figures that the first female rapper to strike solo platinum would have to act like one of the guys. Or didn't you know that rap has long been a man's world, with only a handful of femcees asserting their femininity—and all within the past few years? Forceful, foul-mouthed, and almost comically hardcore, Da Brat was no Lauryn Hill or Bahamadia, instead coming off like Snoop Doggy Dogg without the Y chromosome on her *Funkdafied* debut as Svengali-producer Jermaine Dupri capably answered Dr. Dre's concise G-funk with a loose, airy variation on the same sonic theme. But by the follow-up, *Anuthatantrum*,

Da Brat's tomboy act had worn thin; her lyrics (about fame, fortune, 40s, and fatties) were highly cliched, and Dupri's too-consistent Southern-fried production touch was beginning to sound stale. Not that any of those factors scared away fans of the Windy City's most popular rap export, who got her start guesting on the Dupri-produced Kris Kross album *Da Bomb*.

what to buy: Comprised of the ear-candy singles "Funkdafied," "Fa All Y'All," and "Give It 2 You" and just seven other tracks, *Funkdafied* 🎵🎵🎵 (Chaos/Columbia, 1994, prod. Jermaine Dupri) is a tight and tidy debut.

the rest:
Anuthatantrum 🎵🎵 (So So Def/Columbia, 1996)
Anuthafunkdafiedtantrum 🎵🎵🎵 (So So Def/Columbia, 1996)

influences:
◀◀ Snoop Doggy Dogg, Ice Cube, Kris Kross, Conscious Daughters, Bo$$

▶▶ Lil' Kim, Passion, Suga T, Marvalless

Josh Freedom du Lac

Da Bush Babees
Formed in Brooklyn, NY.

Mr. Man, vocals; Lee Major/Babe-Face Kaos, vocals; Light/Y-Tee, vocals.

Like the Jungle Brothers and A Tribe Called Quest before them, Da Bush Babees draw heavily upon the conflicting imagery of African tribal griots trapped in the gritty urban jungle. Hailing from the tarmac-encrusted outback of Flatbush, Brooklyn, Mr. Man, Lee Major, and Light dish out a manic blend of rhyme and rhythm and are the newest members of the reunited Native Tongues Posse (De La, Tribe, Jungle Brothers, etc.).

what to buy: The group's sophomore album, *Gravity* 🎵🎵🎵 (Warner Bros., 1996, prod. the Ummah, Posdnous, Mr. Man, others), is a more mature and tightly woven effort than the debut. It's smoother and more relaxed, too, thanks to the likeminded producers (Q-Tip and Ali Shaheed Muhammad, De La's Posdnous, and Rahzel from the Roots). The title track sets the tone, what with its ethereal ambiance and gentle piano fills. Of course, while the beats supplied by the elders are solid, it's actually the group's own Mr. Man who creates the most seductive and captivating sound ("Wax," "Maybe").

what to buy next: On the debut, *Ambushed* 🎵🎵🎵 (Reprise, 1994, prod. Jermaine Dupri, Ali Shaheed Muhammad, others), the trio unleashes clever verses delivered in a frantic, multi-pitched tones, their voices all delirious vocal schizophrenia with raps

fluctuating between Pee Wee Herman screeches, rugged raggamuffin growls, and rapid-fire, hyper-active lyrical discharges. "Swing It" suggests a group of speed freaks doing a doubledutch routine; other tracks, such as "Pon De Attack" and "Put It Down," maintain the high level of energy with gritty dancehallisms, G-force deliveries, and deep bass grooves.

influences:
◀◀ De La Soul, A Tribe Called Quest, Jungle Brothers

Spence D.

Da Lench Mob
Formed 1990, in Los Angeles, CA.

T-Bone, vocals; J-Dee, vocals (1990–94); Shorty, vocals; Maulkie, vocals (1994–present).

Best known as Ice Cube's support crew, T-Bone, J-Dee, and Shorty first appeared in skits on Cube's seminal *Amerikkka's Most Wanted* album. The trio's musical vibe was a result of Ice Cube's work with the Bomb Squad and represented a brilliant cohesion of East Coast slam and West Coast bump.

what to buy: Under the guidance of Cube, Da Lench Mob delivered the potent and brilliant *Guerillas In Tha Mist* 🎵🎵🎵 (Street Knowledge/EastWest, 1992, prod. Ice Cube, T-Bone, others). Full of menacing lyrics set to equally dark and brooding music, the album is infused with spoken-word snippets and full-tilt gangsta boogie. "Freedom Got An A.K." sets the street-soldier motif into high gear, and is continued on "Lost In Tha System' (a hardcore black-men-in-lockdown rumination) and "You and Your Heroes," which elevates the group's hardline rhyme ethic by defaming every great white icon from Marilyn Monroe to Uncle Sam. The title track itself tramples negative black epithets under a thick sludge of chunky P-Funk. And who can dismiss "Ain't Got No Class," which features added nasal juice from Cypress Hill's high pitched hero, B-Real. Angry, funky, and hard as hell, *Guerillas In Tha Mist* is a slice of sonic glory from the Cube camp's most prolific and cutting-edge period.

what to buy next: While maintaining all of the lyrical rage and militancy of its predecessor, *Planet of the Apes* 🎵🎵🎵 (Priority, 1994, prod. Ice Cube, others) is more P-Funk-friendly, with "Chocolate City" and the title track slinking and swaying along to infectiously bouncy grooves; Bootsy Collins himself even checks in on "Mellow Madness." But the album, which features new member Maulkie in place of the newly imprisoned J-Dee, isn't all funk and games: The rumbling basslines and chaotic noise of the sinister "Cut Throats" conjure up apocalyptic images of the ghetto. Renegade funk of the highest grade.

influences:

⏪ Ice Cube, Low Profile, WC and the MAAD Circle

see also: *Kam*

Spence D.

Da Youngsta's /Illy Funkstas

Formed 1990, in Philadelphia, PA.

Qu'ran Goodman, vocals; Taji Goodman, vocals; Tarik Dawson vocals.

The sons and nephew of Pop Art Records co-owner Lawrence "L.G. the Teacher" Goodman, the Youngsta's (later rechristened the Illy Funkstas after passing puberty) were "discovered" by Goodman while serving as background singers for Pop Art artist Mentally Gifted on the tune "Something for the Youngsters." Hearing cash registers ringing in his head, Goodman took the trio's grammatically odd name from that track, assigned Mentally Gifted to pen lyrics for them and then thrust them onto the hip-hop scene full force with 1991's *Da Youngsta's*. Yet the group didn't attract much notoriety until 1993, when it released the single "Crewz Pop" featuring Naughty by Nature's Treach. With Treach's presence, the Illy Funkstas began to gain major attention in the rap world and released the albums *The Aftermath* and *No Mercy* in quick succession. Unable to rise above their mediocre performance skills and transform their sudden popularity into long-term success, however, Da Youngsta's never grew to stardom by any name, fading into obscurity by the mid-1990s.

what to buy: The helping hands of Treach and Mentally Gifted make *Da Youngsta's* 𝄢𝄢 (EastWest, 1991, prod. various) worth a listen. It's a decent album if you can get past the teenagers' contrived hardcore attitude. *The Aftermath* 𝄢𝄢𝄢 (EastWest, 1993, prod. various) is a step up from the group's first release production-wise, but the hardcore posturing wears thin very quickly. Despite the addictive, beat-happy walls of sound behind them, Da Youngsta's don't say anything that hasn't been said before—and better. *No Mercy* 𝄢𝄢 (EastWest, 1994, prod. various) features the single "Hip-hop Ride."

the rest:

I'll Make You Famous (Pop Art, 1995) 𝄢𝄢

influences:

⏪ Kris Kross, Run-D.M.C., Naughty by Nature

⏩ Junior M.A.F.I.A.

Andre McGarrity

Dana Dane

Born in New York.

What has plagued Dana Dane's career most is that his voice and rhyming style are so nearly identical to Slick Rick's. But Dane has an excuse: As a youngster, in the pre-"La Di Da Di" days of hip-hop, he and Rick were both in the Kangol Crew, developing and honing their vocal talents *together.* But Slick Rick achieved fame first, and Dane has been rapping in his considerable shadow ever since.

what's available: "Nightmares" is Dane's best-known song, but the rest of *Dana Dane with Fame* 𝄢𝄢 (Profile, 1987, prod. Hurby "Luv Bug" Azor) is difficult listening, mostly because it sounds so much like Slick Rick. Dane and Slick share the same vocal inflections, animated self-voiced samples and storytelling style. This is never more evident than on "Cinderfella Dana Dane," which could just be the lost verses to "La Di Da Di." Attempting to come back after an eight-year hiatus, the alumnus of New York's High School of Music and Art issued the forgettable *Rollin' with Dana Dane* 𝄢 (Maverick/Warner Bros., 1995, prod. DJ Battlecat, others). While Battlecat's production is notable, Dane now lacks any sort of identity at all and is a cliche of the hardcore rapper.

influences:

⏪ Spoonie Gee, Slick Rick

⏩ Slick Rick

Jazzbo

D'Angelo

Born Michael D'Angelo Arthur, 1975, in Richmond, VA.

Along with Maxwell, Erykah Badu, and Tony Rich, D'Angelo is leading R&B back to the future. Moving forward while respecting the traditions of Marvin Gaye, Stevie Wonder, Curtis Mayfield, Prince, and a host of other seminal soulsters, the Southern-born auteur's music sounds of a piece with today's hip-hop heavy chartbusters but goes much deeper thanks to D'Angelo's musicality—he's not quite a one-man band, but damn near, and he's also gone to school on the blues, gospel, and cool jazz. The son and grandson of preachers, D'Angelo's ministry is the dance floor, where his bump 'n' grind anthems and smooth, sexy vocals are manna from heaven.

what to buy: A debut almost as auspicious as that of the artist then known as Prince, *Brown Sugar* 𝄢𝄢𝄢𝄢 (EMI America, 1995, prod. D'Angelo, Ali Shaheed Muhammad, Bob Power, Raphael Saadiq) is a tour de force of retro soul power, driven by swirling harmonies and trippy, erotic rhythms. Throughout, D'Angelo's got seduction on his mind, offering a menage a trois on the provocative title track, then thinking better of it, deciding to "hit it solo/Hope my niggaz don't mind." He's also in mack mode on "Alright," "Me and Those Dreamin' Eyes of Mine," "Lady," "Smooth," and an ultra-smooth take on Smokey Robinson's "Cruisin'." He gets burned by a best buddy in the vengeful "Sh*t, Damn, Motherf*cker," but gets over it by album's end, a churchy return to his gospel roots. Altogether a remarkable and remarkably consistent effort.

influences:

◀◀ Stevie, Smokey Robinson, Marvin Gaye, Prince

Daniel Durchholz

Terence Trent D'Arby

Born March 15, 1962, in New York, NY.

Known for bringing the original grit of soul and funk back to popular music during the mid-1980s, D'Arby—an American and former journalist who moved to England around that time—scored quickly with his first album, *Introducing the Hardline According to Terence Trent D'Arby*, but then encountered difficulties. Fans and reviewers were put off by his overwhelming arrogance and, later, by his misguided musical experiments. Still—following the spirit of headstrong R&B greats Prince and Marvin Gaye—D'Arby continues to do things his own way despite the continual lack of commercial triumphs.

what to buy: *Introducing the Hardline According to Terence Trent D'Arby* ♫♫♫♫ (Columbia, 1987, prod. Martyn Ware, Terence Trent D'Arby) is a remarkable document of D'Arby's expansive range and sonic breadth. Highlights include the urgent "If You Let Me Stay," the cool "Wishing Well," and the mournful "Let's Go Forward."

what to buy next: Despite the critical and commercial disregard, D'Arby continued to put out solid, interesting material after his popular debut. *Neither Fish Nor Flesh* ♫♫♫ (Columbia, 1989, prod. Terence Trent D'Arby) contains several moving and innovative tracks, including "This Side of Love" and "To Know Someone Deeply Is To Know Someone Softly." Likewise, *Symphony Or Damn* ♫♫♫ (Columbia, 1993, prod. Terence Trent D'Arby) features many fiery soul cuts, including the immaculate "Do You Love Me Like You Say?" and "Wet Your Lips."

what to avoid: While still bolstered by Terence Trent D'Arby's vast creative vision, *Vibrator* ♫♫ (Work, 1995, prod. Terence Trent D'Arby) suffers a distinct lack of focus. Songs such as

"Supermodel Sandwich" and "Surrender" simply don't pack the same appeal as past works.

worth searching for: The Bruce Springsteen bootleg *New York City Night* ♫♫♫♫ (Crystal Cat, 1993) features D'Arby—who was rudely booed by the crowd at this 1993 benefit concert—joining the Boss for some inspired duets.

influences:

◀◀ Stevie Wonder, Marvin Gaye, Prince, the Rolling Stones, the Jackson 5

▶▶ Lenny Kravitz, Seal, Living Colour, Maxwell

Aidin Vaziri

Bobby Darin

Born May 14, 1936, in the Bronx, NY. Died December 20, 1973, in Los Angeles, CA.

Bobby Darin was never supposed to have lived past 17. The sheer variety of his achievements suggests a brash ambition, and his raw versatility belies his consummate showmanship. It very possibly could have been the congenital heart defect that filled him with the gnawing desire to defy categorization with wild, genre-lunging career moves between rock, Vegas, and folky political manifestos (with a secondary acting career thrown in for good measure). Short, pudgy, balding singers don't usually become teen idols, and they're rarely seen as sex symbols, yet these are what he was after he made his first hit with the indelible "Splish Splash" in 1958. The simple catchiness and ensuing success of that song—and "Dream Lover" which followed—only deepened Darin's thirst to be heard as a serious singer, not merely a belter of teenage ditties. Perhaps sensing his own physical frailties, he quickly donned a tux and charged into the Vegas spotlight to align his pipes with more "adult" music. The big band success of "Mack the Knife" and "Beyond the Sea" certainly validated his assumption that he was more than just a teen idol. His next and final move into mid-1960s folk took him out of the black ties and put him into blue jeans. Off came the toupee, out came the facial hair and acoustic guitars, and Darin was off once again, this time singing leftist politcal tunes and covering the likes of Tim Hardin and Bob Dylan. The hits stopped coming, but Darin himself never stopped believing, not even when he his heart finally did give out during surgery in 1973.

what to buy: At four discs, *As Long as I'm Singing: The Bobby Darin Collection* ♫♫♫♫ (Rhino, 1995, prod. various) is stuffed

with every facet from his ever-shifting musical journey. Listening to the hits and the unreleased tracks, and reading the excellent booklet, one gets the sense that Darin did not blindly jump from style to style but was solidly in charge as a writer, producer, and arranger. Both *Mack the Knife: Best of Bobby Darin, Vol. 1* 𝄞𝄞𝄞 (Atco, 1991) and *Mack the Knife: Best of Bobby Darin, Vol. 2* 𝄞𝄞𝄞𝄞 (Atco, 1991) are sturdy representations of Darin's oeuvre, offering ample portions of his early rock 'n' roll and big band days while mainly eschewing his folk leanings.

what to buy next: If it's only a brief handshake you want, *The Ultimate Bobby Darin* 𝄞𝄞𝄞 (Warner Special Products, 1986) hits on the hits and nothing but.

what to avoid: Like most Curb reissues, *Best of Bobby Darin* 𝄞 (Curb, 1990, prod. various) is far too skimpy to compete with the abundance of best-ofs on the market.

the rest:
Bobby Darin 𝄞𝄞𝄞 (Atlantic, 1958/1994)
That's All 𝄞𝄞𝄞𝄞 (Atlantic, 1959/1994)
25th Day of December 𝄞𝄞 (Atco, 1960/1991)
This Is Darin 𝄞𝄞𝄞 (Atlantic, 1960/1994)
Bobby Darin Story 𝄞𝄞 (Atlantic, 1989)
Bobby Darin: Capitol Collectors Series 𝄞𝄞𝄞 (Capitol/EMI, 1989)
Bobby Darin 1963–1973 𝄞𝄞 (Motown Records, 1989)
Best of Bobby Darin 𝄞𝄞𝄞 (Curb, 1990)
Bobby Darin/Johnny Mercer: Two of a Kind 𝄞𝄞𝄞 (Atlantic, 1990)
Spotlight on Bobby Darin 𝄞𝄞 (Capitol/EMI, 1995)

worth searching for: The confidence of his performance skills are in no short supply on *Darin at the Copa* 𝄞𝄞𝄞 (Atco, 1960, prod. Ahmet Ertegun, Nesuhi Ertegun), which hints that maybe above all his artistic claims, Darin was at his heart a crowd pleaser.

influences:
◀◀ Frank Sinatra, Bill Haley, Tim Hardin
▶▶ Frankie Avalon, Brian Setzer, Harry Connick Jr.

Allan Orski

Dark Sun Riders
Featuring Brother J

See: X-Clan

Terence Trent D' Arby (© Ken Settle)

Das EFX
/Bobby Sichran

Formed 1991, at Virginia State University, VA.

Krazy Drayz, vocals; Skoob, vocals.

Pop culture on PCP most appropriately describes this Brooklyn-based crew with the penchant for nonsensical rhymes. Adding "diggedy," "bliggedy," and "bum-stiggedy" to the vocabulary of modern rap may be the lasting achievement for the duo, whose divine inspiration comes from television, B-movies, and other factories of late-night pop culture. Having scored a record deal during a talent show judged by EPMD, the pair went on to define a brief era of unrestricted freestyle vogue. While hardly enlightening, Das EFX are at least enjoyable tour guides through the underworld of New York's psychological sewers.

what to buy: *Dead Serious* 𝄞𝄞𝄞𝄞 (EastWest, 1992, prod. Das EFX, EPMD, others) is a virtual encyclopedia of the last five decades of American pop culture. Hip-hop has always been a genre that cross-references the larger cultural geography, but Das EFX push the envelope. On this seminal work, phrases like "I diggedy dropped the jam and now I'm slammin' like Madonna/I gave a crew cut to Sinead O'Connor" are unearthed with each subsequent review.

what to buy next: *From a Sympathetical Hurricane* 𝄞𝄞𝄞 (Columbia, 1994, prod. various) is the debut from Bobby Sichran, a former Das EFX stagehand who supplied guitar on two *Dead Serious* cuts, later pursuing his own career as a solo blues rapper. The title cut is a representative melding of his blues-rock sensibilities and hip-hop influence that creates an experimental breeding ground also evidenced by Ben Harper.

the rest:
Straight Up Sewaside 𝄞𝄞 (EastWest, 1993)
Hold It Down 𝄞𝄞 (EastWest, 1995)

worth searching for: Ice Cube, the eminent preacher of Westside pride, teamed up with these idiosyncratic East Coasters on 1992's memorable, summer-shaking "Check Yo Self." First set to an amalgam of old soul sounds, the song garnered even more attention when a remix (Priority, 1993) reached back to "The Message" for its musical backdrop.

influences:
◀◀ EPMD
▶▶ Redman, Common, Mystikal, Fu-Schnickens

Corey Takahashi

Sammy Davis Jr.

Born December 8, 1925, in New York, NY. Died May 16, 1990, in Beverly Hills, CA.

Sammy Davis Jr. began singing and dancing at the age of three and became a cabaret/vaudeville star during the early 1950s with the Will Mastin Trio. He recorded for Capitol Records in 1949, then signed with the Decca label in 1954. (It was right around that time that he lost an eye in a car accident.) He recorded the hit "Hey There" that year, and "Something's Gotta Give" in 1955. But it wasn't until 1972 that he hit #1 with the catchy, "Willy Wonka & the Chocolate Factory"-inspired pop tune "The Candy Man" on MGM. Davis's association with Rat Pack lounge performers Frank Sinatra and Dean Martin opened many doors for the diverse entertainer. He made a record, *The Wham of Sam,* on Sinatra's newly-founded Reprise Records in 1961, and it is argued that equal booking for Davis and his popularity with both blacks and whites were breakthroughs in the color barriers in the entertainment business. But despite his successes with his fellow Vegas swingers, Davis continually took on new ventures, starring in Broadway musicals and working with jazz greats Count Basie and Mel Torme. He also found his way onto the silver screen in a film version of *Porgy and Bess* (1959), *Ocean's 11* (1969) with Martin and Sinatra, *The Three Penny Opera* (1962), and a string of movies as varied as *Cannonball Run* and its sequel during the early 1980s, *Tap* (1989), and his last film, *The Kid Who Loved Christmas,* (1990). Shortly before his death he was touring with Sinatra and Dean Martin, who was later replaced by Liza Minnelli.

what to buy: *The Wham of Sam: Sammy Davis Jr.* ♫♫♫♫ (Warner Archives, 1994, prod. various) is an excellent example of what Davis could do as a jazz vocalist. *I've Gotta Be Me* ♫♫♫♫ (Reprise Archives, 1996, prod. various) features more sides of Davis, with sweeping liner notes by author Will Friedwald and 15 tracks of songs from Davis's Broadway performances and his extensive repertoire of pop/jazz. Highlights include "Here's That Rainy Day" with Laurindo Almeida from *Carnival in Flanders,* a fine rendition of Mel Torme's "A Stranger in Town," and the track "Yes I Can" from the out-of-print album *If I Ruled The World.*

what to buy next: *Sammy Davis Jr.: Greatest Hits* ♫♫♫ (Garland, 1988, prod. various), a nostalgic collection of songs selected by Davis himself, includes digitally remastered works from several Decca, Warner/Reprise, and MGM recordings in the 1954–73 era.

the rest:
Greatest Hits, Volumes I & II ♫♫♫♫ (DCC, 1990)

The Decca Years (1954–1960) ♫♫♫♫ (MCA, 1990)
Greatest Hits Live ♫♫♫ (Curb, 1995)
All The Things You Are ♫♫♫ (Pair, 1996)

worth searching for: The out-of-print *If I Ruled The World* ♫♫♫♫ (Reprise, 1965) is one of Davis's high water marks during his Reprise years.

influences:

◄◄ Bill "Bojangles" Robinson, Sam Davis Sr., Al Jolson

►► James Brown, Jackie Wilson, Otis Redding, Marvin Gaye

Norene Cashen

Tyrone Davis

Born 1938, in Greenville, MS.

Like his first idol Bobby Bland, Tyrone Davis is an underacknowledged, underrecognized giant of American popular music. During the period of his greatest popularity, beginning with his first hit for Dakar in 1968 ("Can I Change My Mind") and extending into the early 1980s, Davis scored hit after chart-topping hit. Yet despite both the commercial success and the unparalleled artistry of his classy Chicago-soul recordings, Davis remains far less well known than many of his less-successful and less-talented peers. Davis's obscurity, like Bland's, may stem from the mature sensibility of his music. The narrative role that Davis adopted in "Can I Change My Mind"—the contrite lover whose impetuosity has left him on the streets facing the cold Chicago wind and longing to return to the comforts of home—was not readily adoptable by rock 'n roll bands and singers, whose attention might have validated Davis's reputation. Tyrone Davis was no Hoochie Coochie Man; he was a warm, vulnerable, articulately expressive stylist who enveloped songs in his big, deep baritone and delivered them with passion and finely honed craft. What the men may not have known, the women always understood: Davis's core audience has always comprised mostly females.

A big reason for the success of Davis's 1970s recordings is that they exploited the talents of the cream of the Chicago studio recording community. Producer Willie Henderson and arranger Tom Washington, and later Leo Graham and James Mack, surrounded Davis's songs with big, tight, brassy arrangements, sometimes sweetened with strings and background vocals, to create one of the most exciting new sounds of the decade. Writer Robert Pruter describes Davis's touring band during the mid-1970s: ". . . the Tyrone Davis band during those years was the most magnificent-sounding in any form of music, be it rock, blues, or soul. I have seen Al Green, the Rolling Stones, the Band, Bruce Springsteen and numerous others at the height of their careers, and only the James Brown aggregation had a band that could equal the live Davis band in rhythmic fury and overall flash and tightness of sound." After leaving Dakar in 1976, Davis and his producer Graham extended the Tyrone Davis sound with major-label support from Columbia Records. At Columbia, Davis made his lushest recordings, the best of which were exquisite ballads such as "In the Mood," "Close to You," and "Heart Failure." After leaving Columbia, Davis and Graham produced a dizzying array of discs on various labels, scoring one major hit with the novelty song "Mom's Apple Pie" (1991). Although Davis's first recording for Malaco Records of Jackson, Mississippi, *Simply Tyrone Davis* (1996), was disappointing, there is reason to hope that the last of the great soul labels will be able to energize Davis's career as it has the careers of Z.Z. Hill, Bobby Bland, Johnnie Taylor, Shirley Brown, Little Milton, and many others.

what to buy: Davis's Dakar hits are collected on *Greatest Hits* ♪♪♪♪ (Rhino, 1992, prod. various). A subset of this collection is also available as the budget-priced *Turn Back the Hands of Time* ♪♪♪ (Rhino, 1996, prod. various).

what to buy next: *In the Mood: Best of Tyrone Davis* ♪♪♪♪ (Sony, 1996, prod. various) is a beautifully packaged and well annotated retrospective of the best of Davis's Columbia recordings. *Best of the Future Years* ♪♪♪ (Ichiban, 1992, prod. various) collects some of Davis's better recent recordings for Ichiban.

the rest:
Tyrone Davis ♪♪ (Highrise, 1982)
Man of Stone ♪♪ (Timeless, 1987)
Pacifier ♪♪ (Timeless, 1987)
Flashin' Back ♪♪ (Future, 1988)
I'll Always Love You ♪♪♪ (Ichiban, 1991)
Something's Mighty Wrong ♪♪♪ (Ichiban, 1992)
You Stay On My Mind ♪♪♪ (Ichiban, 1994)
Simply Tyrone Davis ♪♪ (Malaco, 1997)

worth searching for: Available in LP only, *Our Shining Hour* ♪♪♪♪ (Polydor, 1983) is a collaboration with the Count Basie band that presents Davis in an entirely new context. Any Tyrone Davis LP on Dakar or Columbia—there were lots of them—is sure to contain at least two or three gems that are not available on the CD greatest hits packages. This is an artist who sorely deserves a "complete works of" box set, but isn't likely to ever get one.

influences:
◀◀ Bobby "Blue" Bland, Elvis Presley, Little Milton, Freddie

King, Wilson Pickett, Jerry Butler, Otis Clay, Johnny Sayles, Harold Burrage

▶▶ Maurice White, Luther Vandross

Bill Pollak

Morris Day
See: The Time

Taylor Dayne
Born Leslie Wunderman, March 7, 1963, in Baldwin, NY.

Raised by a rare coin dealer and an aspiring actress on Long Island, Dayne's powerful voice and love for classic soul overcame her suburban upbringing, creating the perfect package for

> ## word up!
>
> I'Ve looked at many other artists, and they seem to have a notoriety in ways I wish I had. That gives me the extra--not anger--but the drive, the ambition to keep pushing and going and driving and going and pushing. There are things I have to prove musically to myself, to my peers, to, OK, the critics. I feel like it gives me an added edge. That's my makeup, anyhow.
>
> **Taylor Dayne**

crossover success from the dance world to the pop charts. A performer from age six, she kicked around in rock and pop bands after graduating high school—first working under the name Leslee and eventually changing to her current moniker on advice of friend Dee Snider of Twisted Sister. Before long, Dayne joined forces with producer Ric Wake to create a percolating dance version of a ballad called "Tell It To My Heart," culled from a bunch of throwaway tunes sent over by Chappel Music. That single became Dayne's first Top 10 hit, paving the way for an album that fused her powerhouse blue-eyed soul vocal licks to full-throttle 1980s-style disco grooves. The result was a string of seven Top 10 singles through the end of the decade. But the downturn in crossover success that dampened many a dance diva's career during the early 1990s crippled Dayne's own work—a problem that wasn't helped by her participation in the soundtrack for the ill-fated film, *The Shadow*. Like fellow MTV creation Paula Abdul, Dayne has sought career refuge in acting, contributing a bit part to the Warren Beatty movie *Love Affair* and a low budget independent film, *Fools' Paradise.*

what to buy: Like all great dance divas, the appeal of Dayne's work lies mostly in her singles—making her career ripe for a good greatest hits record. And there is one—*Taylor Dayne: Greatest Hits* 𝄢𝄢𝄢 (Arista, 1995, prod. various), which sandwiches classic Dayne cuts such as the spastic "Tell It To My Heart" and frenetic "Don't Rush Me" next to her remake of Barry White's "Can't Get Enough of Your Love."

what to buy next: For those who can stand the singer's formula—teen-friendly lyrics about love, love, and more love set to a mindless, mechanical dance/pop groove—her debut album, *Tell It To My Heart* 𝄢𝄢 (Arista, 1987, prod. Ric Wake) sums up this approach most effectively, offering four of her biggest hits and the least amount of filler among her catalog.

what to avoid: On her last original-music album, *Soul Dancing* **woof!** (Arista, 1993, prod. various), they hired every hitmaker in sight to save Dayne's career from the ash heap of pop music history that had already claimed such luminaries as Tiffany, Debbie Gibson, and Shanice Wilson. Alas, all they could do was prolong the inevitable with a bunch of pop tunes no one cared to hear.

the rest:
Can't Fight Fate 𝄢𝄢 (Arista, 1989)

worth searching for: Dayne collectors take note—Arista actually made two different versions of the singer's debut album, redesigning the cover layout once the first pressing sold out.

influences:
◀◀ Madonna, Janet Jackson, Donna Summer

▶▶ Celine Dion, Mariah Carey

Eric Deggans

The Dayton Family
Formed 1990, in Flint, MI.

Ira Dorsey, vocals; Raheen Peterson, vocals; Matt Hinkle, vocals; Eric Dorsey, vocals (1992–present).

Most hardcore rappers just talk about gangbanging, dope dealing, and run-ins with the law, but these gangsta rappers from Michigan have lived it. Three of the group's four members are—or have been—in prison, mostly on drug charges. Since all but Peterson have been incarcerated at one time or another since they signed with Relativity in 1993, the group's promotional appearances and touring have been limited. The die was cast in the early '90s with an inexpensively recorded five-song cassette which included "Fuck Being Indicted," a song that named some of the Flint cops with whom the members have had brushes. Anti-social behavior aside, the group members—especially the imprisoned Ira Dorsey—are technically gifted rappers who chronicle urban decay from a brutal, often harrowing inside-looking-out perspective. Their future, however, remains as uncertain as their rough ghetto environment.

what to buy: *F.B.I.* 𝄢𝄢𝄢 (Relativity, 1995, prod. Stevie Pitts) needlessly exploits the group's underground notoriety with a staged photo of the members being led to jail. But the raps, which flow to fluid beats and tricky keyboard loops, are truly arresting, with plenty of murder, misogyny, and they're-out-to-get-us paranoia to satisfy the most hardcore of gangsta rap tastes. And it's real. There's also a little remorse mixed in (check out "Ghetto").

the rest:
What's On Your Mind 𝄢𝄢 (Relativity, 1993)

worth searching for: Released independently in 1991, the original *F.B.I.* 𝄢𝄢𝄢 was more crude, more graphic, and more harsh than the somewhat sanitized version that appears on the 1995 reissue of the same name. The local references won't mean much to outsiders, but themes of distrust and lust (sexual and financial) will.

influences:
◀◀ N.W.A., Ice Cube, M.C. Breed

▶▶ MC Eiht, Spice 1, Top Authority

Doug Pullen

The Dazz Band

Formed late 1970s, in Clevenad, OH.

Bobby Harris, alto & tenor sax; Wayne Preston, alto sax (1978–80); Les Thaler, trumpet (1978–80); Edward Myers, III, trombone (1978–80); Sennie "Skip" Martin, III, trumpet, vocals (1980–88); Pierre DeMudd, trumpet, flugelhorn, vocals (1980–88); Isaac Wiley Jr., drums, vocals (1978–88); Michael "Ferocious" Wiley, bass, vocals; Reggie Stewart, electric & acoustic guitars (1978–80); Michael Calhoun, guitars, vocals (1979–81); Eric Fearman, guitars (1980–88); Marlon McClain, guitar (1985–present); Kevin Frederick, keyboards (1980–82); Steve Cox, keyboards (1982–88); Keith Harrison, keyboards (1983–88); Kenny Pettus, percussion, vocals (1978–88); Terry Stanton, lead vocals (1993–present); Nate Phillips, bass, vocals (1993–present); Michael Norfleet, keyboards, vocals (1993–present); Niles McKinney, keyboards (1993–present); Derek Organ, drums (1993–present).

The Dazz Band started its journey through the groove as Bell Telefunk, a Cleveland funk band under the leadership of gifted young reedsman Bobby Harris. Harris, who comes from a musical family (his father, Robert Harris, is also a sax player who owned a music club), always had his ears open for new sounds; the night Harris saw Rahsaan Roland Kirk's trio Three Blind Mice and then stumbled upon a club hosting Blood, Sweat & Tears a couple of blocks away would present an important fork in the road for Harris and Bell Telefunk. So moved was he by BST's blend of jazz and pop, he dropped the Bell from the group's name and took the group in a distinct jazz/funk direction. Its live sets of Billy Cobham and Chick Corea covers quickly evolved into original material, which landed the band a deal at 20th Century Records. The group—now called Kinsman Dazz after the street that Harris's dad's club was on (Kinsman Avenue) and the contraction of "danceable jazz"—released two albums on the 20th Century imprint. When 20th Century closed its record division in 1979, the band was scooped up by Motown. It was there that the group—now called the Dazz Band—hit its stride, issuing seven LPs and 12 charting singles, and receiving multiple gold-record sales awards and a Grammy. In 1985, the Dazz Band left Motown for Geffen, where it issued the *Wild and Free* album. When its association with Geffen failed to produce the kind of success it enjoyed at Motown, the group moved on again—to RCA—but that new partnership also failed to generate a smash. Always one who would give out before he gave up, Bobby Harris assembled a new collective of musicians and continues to tour with this new incarnation of the Dazz Band.

word up!

WIth 'Let It Whip,' we found the sound everybody loved. It had a techno-pop ring to it, and the vocals were smooth. It was somewhere between funk and hard rock. The white bands are sounding like the black bands, and the black bands have white rock elements in them now. The white kids are dancing like black kids, and vice versa. It's changing the music, that's for sure.

Bobby Harris (of the Dazz Band)

what to buy: *Funkology: The Definitive Dazz Band* 🎵🎵🎵🎵 (Motown Master Series, 1994, prod. various) is just what the subtitle says. *Funkology* collects the best of its Motown output, including extended single versions of "Let It Whip" (the Grammy winner) and "Joystick" plus "I Might as Well Forget about Loving You" and "Catching Up on Love," the two Kinsman Dazz hits for 20th Century, along with three new songs and a new megamix. The album's title is its only flaw, as the record itself contains more than its fair share of ballads. Nevertheless, great songs are great songs, and tracks such as "Let It Whip," "Swoop (I'm Yours)," and "Keep It Live (on the K.I.L.)" swing.

what to buy next: *Under the Streetlights* 🎵🎵🎵 (Streetwise, 1995), a 13-track album of mostly new material plus and ironic cover of the Brick hit "Dazz" and three of the four new songs that debuted on *Funkology*. *Streetlights* is a fun album that shows Harris & Co. still got it. "Tryin' to Get My Groove On," a song crafted in the style of *One Nation Under a Groove*-era Funkadelic (replete with Bootsy Collins and *One Nation* references), is simultaneously cheesy and wonderfully nostalgic. The rest of the album takes on more of a modern R&B flavor which, in the context of the group's past material, is dynamically unchallenging. But there are moments, more often than not, that are sparks of brilliance—the reason you bought the *Keep It Live* album in the first place once upon a time.

what to avoid: *Greatest Hits* ♫♫ (Motown, 1986, prod. various) and *Motown Legends* ♫♫ (PolyGram Special Markets, 1993, prod. various) are each 10-12 track collections that are rendered redundant by the full-length *Funkology*.

worth searching for: *Keep It Live* ♫♫♫ (Motown, 1982) provides proof that the Dazz Band could do it on stage, too.

influences:

◀◀ Blood, Sweat & Tears, Rahsaan Roland Kirk, Ronnie Laws & Pressure, Earth, Wind & Fire

▶▶ Incognito

Dana G. Smart

DC Talk

Formed 1987, in Washington, DC.

Toby McKeehan; Michael Tait; Kevin Smith.

Religion has long been a part of hip-hop (Five Percenters surely accounted for more than five percent of the late-'80s rap world), but hip-hop hasn't necessarily been a big part of religion. Particularly not Christianity. DC Talk, however, tried to change that: with 1988's *DC Talk*, the group introduced hip-hop to the Christian music ranks, fusing it with traditional pop and rock—and, of course, messages of faith. In the process, DC Talk was anointed as the leader of Christian music's new guard. Formed by McKeehan and Tait, the name DC Talk was originally a nod to the pair's hometown; but their record label, ForeFront, suggested that it stand for "decent Christian talk." Whatever the meaning of the moniker, DC Talk's message has always remained constant: you've got to have faith. Even so, the group has recently (and unsuccessfully) tried to rid itself of the "Christian" label, making a controversial video that featured burning crosses, and repeatedly telling interviewers: "Courtney Love and Tina Turner are Buddhists, but you wouldn't call them "Buddhist rock." So?

what to buy: Hip-hop, fuzzy guitars, and synthesizers fill *Jesus Freak* ♫♫♫ (ForeFront/Virgin, 1995, prod. Toby McKeehan, John Painter), upping DC Talk's mainstream potential. With the group tackling the stereotype of Christian bands by mixing hard-driving guitars with pop-styled raps, the album sold more than 85,000 copies in its first week and had the highest-ever debut for a Christian act on *Billboard*'s pop album charts. Although more subtle than previous DC Talk releases, *Jesus Freak* still shows the musicians placing a premium on message; the lyrics tell you why you need Jesus in your life ("Like It, Love It, Need It"), why you need to confess ("Between You and Me"), and why racism needs to end ("What Have We Become," "Colored People").

the rest:

DC Talk ♫♫ (ForeFront, 1988)
Nu Thang ♫♫ (Heartwarm, 1991)
Free At Last ♫♫♫ (ForeFront, 1992)

influences:

◀◀ PM Dawn, Vanilla Ice, Seal, Beck, Nirvana

▶▶ All-Star United, Jars of Clay

Christina Fuoco and Josh Freedom du Lac

De La Soul

Formed 1985, in Amityville, NY.

Psdnous, vocals; Trugoy the Dove, vocals; P.A. Pasemaster Mase, vocals.

De La Soul single-handedly paved a new direction for hip-hop, away from a dead-end urban street of violence, misogyny, and tired rhymes. With producer Prince Paul, the trio of suburban high school friends crafted a new, no-holds-barred bed for their thoughtful, funny, laid-back rhymes. Everything was game—French instruction records, Hall and Oates beats, and even a Turtles song (which caused the '60s band to sue). With its flowers and primary colors, psychedelic swirl of sound, and promotion of "The D.A.I.S.Y. Age (Da Inner Sound Y'all)," De La Soul's debut, *3 Feet High and Rising*, had people talking about their hippie-hop. And while the album produced a couple of hits in "Me Myself and I" and "Buddy," the band felt it had to retreat and act tougher on subsequent releases to maintain street credibility. A spotty live act, De La Soul was loosely associated, on and off, with other articulate and committed East Coast acts—including A Tribe Called Quest, the Jungle Brothers, and Queen Latifah—in the Native Tongues Posse. By 1996, declaring on wax that the Native Tongues had been "officially reinstated," De La found itself recording without the eccentric turns of Prince Paul and, instead, was rapping over funk provided by a live band.

what to buy: *3 Feet High and Rising* 𝄢𝄢𝄢𝄢 (Tommy Boy, 1989, prod. Prince Paul, De La Soul) is a hip-hop classic that is still as fresh and fun to listen to as when it came out.

what to buy next: Most De La Soul albums hold their listenability over the years, and the multi-faceted messages are worth rehearing. But *Stakes Is High* 𝄢𝄢𝄢 (Tommy Boy, 1996, prod. De La Soul), the group's first album without Prince Paul, is strikingly direct. The rhymes are still surprising, but De La has matured, with fewer jokey asides.

the rest:
De La Soul Is Dead 𝄢𝄢𝄢𝄡 (Tommy Boy, 1991)
Buhloone Mindstate 𝄢𝄢𝄢𝄡 (Tommy Boy, 1993)

worth searching for: The seven-track CD single for "Ego Trippin' (Part Two)" (Tommy Boy, 1993) is, at more than 30 minutes, longer than some albums used to be.

influences:
◀◀ KRS-One, Ritz Brothers, Stetsasonic, Jungle Brothers, Biz Markie

▶▶ Jungle Brothers, A Tribe Called Quest, Digable Planets, Brand Nubian, Black Sheep, PM Dawn, Dream Warriors, Common, Da Bush Babees, Camp Lo, Boogie Monsters, Freestyle Fellowship, Hieroglyphics

Roger Catlin

DeBarge
/El DeBarge

Formed 1978 in Grand Rapids, MI.

Eldra DeBarge, vocals (1978–86); Bunny DeBarge, vocals; Mark DeBarge, vocals, trumpet, saxophone; James DeBarge, vocals, keyboards; Randy DeBarge, bass, vocals

A family act from the Midwest signs up with Motown, moves to Los Angeles . . . we've heard this one before. But in this case it's the DeBarge family, not the Jacksons, a talented sibling aggregate that enjoyed only modest success and never quite lived up to its billing as the label's savior. Coming from a talented clan of 10, the DeBarge members sang in church together before taking it to the professional level. Older brothers Bobby and Tommy were in the Motown band Switch, but Jermaine Jackson was the group's patron at the label, introducing them to his then father-

in-law Berry Gordy Jr. DeBarge came to the label with no small expectations; despite its ballyhooed 25th anniversary celebration, Motown was bereft of young hitmakers—and desprate enough for them that the label, known for maintining control over its artists—gave the fledgling band creative control. Its 1981 debut stiffed, but its sophomore effort, *All This Love*, yielded hits in the title track and "I Like It." *In a Special Way* did even better, but it was an outside writer—Diane Warren—who came up with "Rhythm of the Night," the group's biggest and most enduring hit, which was also used as a theme for the film *Berry Gordy's The Last Dragon*. El DeBarge left in 1986 for a solo career that never really caught fire, and nothing was the same for the DeBarges after that. Bunny DeBarge and another brother, Jonathan "Chico" DeBarge, recorded solo albums, too. But mostly the family made more turbulent headlines: El's no-contest plea for allegedly assaulting a Grand Rapids woman in 1986; Chico and Bobby's arrest and imprisonment for cocaine trafficking in 1988; James's elopement and subsequent annulment with Janet Jackson. The siblings are still making music individually and collectively (Chico was expected to release an album called *Long Time No See* on Universal Records in late 1997), and the hip-hop community has sampled its share of material from the DeBarge catalog. But their story remains one of talent and ambition sadly unfulfilled.

what to buy: *The Ultimate Collection* 𝄢𝄢𝄢𝄢 (Motown, 1997, prod. various) provides a fine overview of the music the family made, including solo tracks from El, Bunny, and Chico.

what to buy next: *In a Special Way* 𝄢𝄢𝄢 (Motown, 1983/1989, prod. El DeBarge) is the group's best outing, boasting a guest appearance by Stevie Wonder. El's *Heart, Mind and Soul* 𝄢𝄢𝄢 (Warner Bros., 1994, prod. Babyface) is his only solo album in print, with another cameo by Wonder and sympathetic production and songwriting from longtime admirer Babyface.

the rest:
Greatest Hits 𝄢𝄢𝄢 (Motown, 1986)

worth searching for: Besides his solo albums, El DeBarge contributed guest vocals to a number of albums. One of his better guest spots is on "After the Dance" for the all-star jazz-pop band Fourplay's debut album, *Fourplay* (Warner Bros., 1991).

influences:
◀◀ Marvin Gaye, the Sylvers, the Five Stairsteps, Earth, Wind & Fire, Stevie Wonder

▶▶ The Jets, Menudo, Babyface, Mary J. Blige

Gary Graff

Deee-lite

Formed 1988, in New York, NY.

Lady Miss Kier Kirby, vocals; Super DJ Dmitry, programming, various instruments; DJ Towa Tei, turntables (1988–92); DJ On-e, turntables (1992–present).

Deee-Lite was the perfect antidote to the dreary music of the late 1980s. Rising out of New York's club scene, the multi-cultural trio not only made music that combined influences like house, hip-hop, and disco, but topped off its image with a good dose of 1960s idealism, style, and positivity. Singer Lady Miss Kier Kirby, Soviet emigre DJ Dmitry, and Japanese mixmaster Jungle DJ Towa Towa Tei quickly became icons for the new decade, with their platform heels and the impossibly catchy grooves of their debut single "Groove Is in the Heart" and its accompanying album *World Clique*. The spell didn't last, however, as the group's focus shifted towards politics and club kid credibility with later albums—with disastrous results. Tei set out for a solo career mid-way through the completion of Deee-Lite's third album *Dewdrops in the Garden*, and the group has since filled its time by making solo cameo appearances at various raves.

what to buy: The creative success of Deee-Lite's debut album, *World Clique* 𝄫𝄫𝄫𝄫 (Elektra, 1990, prod. Deee-Lite), may have been a fluke, but it changed the landscape of popular music indefinitely. Its funky grooves and rosy sentiments perfectly captured the optimism of the new decade, while its mix of club, jazz, and hip-hop influences reflected the ever-expanding regression of stylistic barriers.

what to buy next: *Dancefloor Oddities & Sampladelic Relics—Deee Remixes* 𝄫𝄫𝄫 (Elektra, 1996, prod. Deee-Lite) presents the group with the opportunity to redeem itself and breathe new life into its predominantly irrelevant newer material. Even though the hits—"Groove Is in the Heart," "Runaway"—only get minor rewrites, a majority of Deee-Lite's more limber material benefits from potent junglist meltdowns and breakbeat deconstructions, particularly "Call Me" and "I Had a Dream I Was Falling Thru a Hole in the Ozone Layer."

what to avoid: Deee-Lite's initial burst of creative energy didn't last long. The group's positive vibes were crushed by the cynicism ushered into popular music by the big angst explosion of 1992. Instead of embracing the dark side with further wicked grooves and pointed insanity, like they should have, Deee-Lite disintegrated into a generic club act and released a pair of utterly forgettable follow-up albums with the politically bogged-

down *Infinity Within* 𝄫𝄫 (Elektra, 1992, prod. Deee-Lite) and the bloodless *Dewdrops in the Garden* 𝄫 (Elektra, 1994, prod. Super DJ Dmitry).

solo outings:
DJ Towa Tei:
Future Listening 𝄫𝄫𝄫𝄫 (Elektra, 1995)

influences:

◀◀ Sly and the Family Stone, Parliament-Funkadelic, Larry Heard, Donna Summer

▶▶ Bjork, Arrested Development, Betty Boo, Brand New Heavies

Aidin Vaziri

The Deele

See: Babyface

Def Jam

Where would hip-hop have gone without Rick Rubin and Russell Simmons? While there were certainly other important rap labels both before and after N.Y.U. student Rubin and New York party promoter Simmons teamed up to form Def Jam Records in 1984, none had the impact of Def Jam, which broke new rap ground by aligning itself with a major label (Columbia), then ushered hip-hop's new school right to the top of the charts, becoming the most successful new label of the 1980s in the process. Hip-hop's answer to Motown and Sun, Def Jam's first artist was a brash, young LL Cool J, whose "I Need a Beat" 12-inch kicked off the label in 1984 and wound up selling a cool 100,000 copies. Cool J would become Def Jam's most consistent draw, but there certainly were others, too, as rock lover Rubin and marketing maven Simmons assembled an amazing roster of New York talent that included everyone from Public Enemy and Slick Rick to the 3rd Bass and the Beastie Boys—whose Rubin-produced *Licensed to Ill* album in 1986 cemented hip-hop's foothold with white suburban youth.

what to buy: The Def Jam story is told through the vital music of those and other artists and excellent liner notes by former publicist Bill Adler on the *Def Jam Music Group 10th Anniversary Box Set* 𝄫𝄫𝄫𝄫 (Def Jam, 1995, prod. various), a four-disc, 59-track collection whose only fault is its haphazard, non-

Lady Miss Kier of Deee-Lite (© Ken Settle)

chronological sequencing. Virtually every Def Jam single that mattered (and a few that didn't) is included here. And some of the label's newest-schoolers are featured, too, including Method Man and Warren G—artists whose success is a testament to the staying power of the most important label in the history of rap.

Josh Freedom du Lac

Def Jef

Born Jeffery Fortson, in Harlem, NY.

Melding tangible hip-hop consciousness with a jazz- and soul-based approach, East Coast transplant Def Jef became a seminal part of the late-'80s hip-hop scene. Once considered one of the smoothest MCs, his accessible demeanor made him a frequent ambassador on albums by legendary artists from Etta James to Patti LaBelle.

what to buy: Accentuated by the early production efforts of now-famous Dust Brothers and songs like "Droppin' Rhymes on Drums," *Just A Poet with Soul* 𝄞𝄞𝄞𝄞 (Island, 1989, prod. Dust Brothers, Def Jef, others) sets the table for hip-hop's burgeoning Afrocentric and jazz-infusion movements.

what to buy next: The follow-up, *Soul Food* 𝄞𝄞𝄞 (Delicious Vinyl, 1991, prod. Def Jef, DJ Mark the 45 King, others), is vibrant and engaging, with songs like "Soul Provider" earning Def Jef a reputation as the Big Daddy Kane of the West Coast. A five-minute rhyme orgy over an instrumental supplied by the Brand New Heavies, "BNH Freestyle" inspired the Brand New Heavies to collaborate with other MCs on their 1993 album *Heavy Rhyme Experience, Volume 1.*

influences:

◀◀ Big Daddy Kane, Jungle Brothers

▶▶ Dream Warriors, Pharcyde

Jazzbo

Defunkt

Joseph Bowie, vocals, trombone, percussion; John Mulkerin, trumpet; Bill Bickford, guitar; Kenny Martin, drums; Kim Clarke, bass.

Growing out of an edition of James Chance's Contortions, this became the funkiest band of the 1980s, bar none, though few outside of New York City realized it. The original lineup focused on leader Joe Bowie's writing collaborations with lyricist Janos Gat, which produced a gleefully cynical and seamy view of 1980s urban life. When bassist Kim Clarke replaced Melvin Gibbs (who

formed several groups of his own and is currently in the Rollins Band) and was soon joined by drummer Kenny Martin, the most limber funk rhythm section since James Brown's bands was in place, laying down deep grooves that were never mechanical. With various changes in the guitar chairs, this edition of the band lasted into the 1990s, with time out during the mid-1980s while Bowie dealt with a substance abuse problem (at which point Bell departed, forming his group Kelvynator). But by the time long-time members Mulkerin, Bickford, and Kenny Martin left for Liquid Hips (a more modern outfit with hard rock leanings), and Clarke also departed, playing with Bickford in an uncategorizable jazz trio with drummer Bruce Ditmas, the band was past its prime. The subsequent addition of ex-JJ Jumpers vocalist Kelli Sae suggested a possible path for the group—her soulful, Chaka Khan-derived emoting mixed power and fervor with some subtle touches. But Bowie's increasingly uninspired vocals continued to dominate, and the new instrumentalists were less elastic and tended towards simpler beats. Mulkerin, Bickford, and Clarke's songwriting was also missed, and with Gat also absent, most tracks tripped over prosaic, uncompelling language, perhaps suggesting why the group began using more covers. Though there was no announced breakup, the group has not been active for several years now.

what to buy: *Defunkt* 𝄞𝄞𝄞𝄞 (Hannibal, 1980, prod. Byron Bowie, Janos Gat) was the band's debut album and the only one with the original lineup. Highlights include "In the Good Times," which takes off from Chic's disco classic "Good Times," but instead of feel-good optimism it explores the sordid joys of shooting up.

what to buy next: The title track of *In America* 𝄞𝄞𝄞 (Antilles, 1988, prod. Gene Kraut) is a biting denunciation of presidential policies from the 1960s onward, though most of the criticism seems inspired by Reaganism. The band's comeback found more shared writing credits, with Mulkerin and Bickford contributing excellent material, and Clarke and Martin credited on some fine collaborations. New guitarist Ronnie Drayton replaced Bell magnificently. *Avoid the Funk . . . a Defunkt Anthology* 𝄞𝄞𝄞 (Hannibal, 1988, prod. various) has the 12" version of "Razor's Edge" and the 4:27-long 7" version of "Stranglin' Me with Your Love (revisited)," plus two previously unreleased live recordings from 1983 along with four album tracks, three (though hardly the best three) from the out of print *Thermonuclear Sweat* (see below).

what to avoid: *Defunkt Special Edition: A Blues Tribute* 𝄞 (Enemy, 1994, prod. Michael Knuth) is a joint tribute to Muddy Waters and Jimi Hendrix that flounders on Bowie's vocal inaptness in comparison to both. The only redeeming quality is guitarist Jean-Paul Bourelly's spirited and imaginative extension of their legacies.

the rest:

Heroes 𝄢𝄢𝄢 (DIW, 1990)
Live at the Knitting Factory 𝄢𝄢 (Knitting Factory Works, 1991)
Crisis 𝄢𝄢𝄢 (Enemy, 1992)
Cum Funky 𝄢𝄢 (Enemy, 1993)

worth searching for: Defunkt's second album, *Thermonuclear Sweat* 𝄢𝄢𝄢𝄢 (Hannibal, 1982, prod. Joe Boyd, Joe Bowie) was the first to feature the Kim Clarke/Kenny Martin rhythm section and also includes Living Colour's Vernon Reid on six of the eight tracks, sharing guitar chores with Bell. Bowie's bitter disillusion with love and life produces some powerful songs, and the band's grooves were never deeper than on this shamefully out of print masterpiece; look for the LP. "Razor's Edge"/ "Stranglin' Me with Your Love (revisited)" (Hannibal, 1981, prod. Joe Boyd) is a killer 12-inch single. It features the excellent non-LP A-side and an epic remake of a *Defunkt* song, with Clarke on bass and a formidable horn section that features Bowie's brothers Lester (Art Ensemble of Chicago) and Byron, as well as alto saxophonist Luther Thomas.

solo outings:

Bigfood:
Semi-Precious Metal 𝄢𝄢𝄢 (Tutu/Enja, 1990)

influences:

◀◀ Charlie Parker, Roswell Rudd, Jimi Hendrix, James Brown, Tower of Power, Contortions

▶▶ Living Colour, Eye & I

Steve Holtje

Desmond Dekker

Born July 16, 1941, in Kingston, Jamaica.

One of reggae's seminal forces, Dekker started out with famed producer Leslie Kong in a group called the Aces. It was the release of the startling "The Isrealites" that brought Dekker to international fame. A pioneering, herky-jerky Biblical song that sold more than a million copies and went to #1 in Britain, it still stands as one of the more memorable songs in reggae history.

what to buy: *Rockin' Steady: The Best of Desmond Dekker* 𝄢𝄢𝄢𝄢 (Rhino, 1992, prod. Leslie Kong) contains his first single, "Honour Your Mother and Father," his first hit, "007 (Shanty Town)"—which helped further the "rude boy" image—and "The Isrealites."

what to buy next: *Shanty Town Original* 𝄢𝄢𝄢 (Drive Archive, 1994) contains "You Can Get It If You Really Want It," written for him by Jimmy Cliff, who later had bigger success with it on *The Harder They Come* soundtrack.

influences:

◀◀ Delroy Wilson, Toots and the Maytals, the Melodians

▶▶ Bob Marley, Bunny Wailer, Jimmy Cliff

Allan Orski

Del Tha Funkee Homosapien /Souls of Mischief /Casual /Extra Prolific

Just as the West Coast appeared to be in danger of producing nothing but gangsta derivatives, Del came from beyond the left-field fence to save the day. While in high school in Berkeley, California, Del, the cousin of seminal gangsta rapper Ice Cube, got together with a group of bright, like-minded student-rappers to form the formidable Hieroglyphics crew. Determining that lyrics, not image, should be the focus of hip-hop, the Hieroglyphics brought back to life the standards of the battle and freestyle MC that had seemingly been lost. A quirky, almost troll-like MC, Del knew he would be signed to a record deal once Cube earned success; in turn, he promised the other Hieroglyphics members that he would eventually help them out. Within two years of the release of Del's debut, the Souls of Mischief also had an album out, as did group members Casual and Extra Prolific. As such, the Hieroglyphics had established themselves as one of the most prolific crews in hip-hop. But in 1996, disappointed by poor record sales, all of the artists lost their label deals, and Extra Prolific was asked to leave the fold. Since then, Del and the rest of the Hieroglyphics crew have started their own independent label from which to make and distribute their music. And the crew members have remained committed to developing their minds: Soulsman Tajai is attending Stanford, Del is learning Japanese, and Soulsman Opio is taking courses in the humanities and arts.

what to buy: Those expecting Del to be Ice Cube Jr. must have been surprised when they heard his debut, *I Wish My Brother George Was Here* 𝄢𝄢𝄢𝄢 (Elektra, 1991, prod. Ice Cube, Boogiemen, Del Tha Funkee Homosapien). The album—whose title is a passing allusion to George Clinton—mixes the Boogiemen's layered, boombastic sound with Del's deep-voiced

the delfonics

eccentricities, making for neo-funk on songs like "Mista-dobalina," "Ahonetwo, Ahonetwo," and "Sunny Meadowz." The first Souls of Mischief album, *'93 Til Infinity* 🎜🎜🎜🎜 (Jive, 1993, prod. Domino, Souls of Mischief) spawned a bevy of rappers who tried to imitate the dizzying words-upon-words-upon-words style of delivery. The album's fresh musical approach and cogitative musings live up to its name.

what to buy next: Del's second album, *No Need for Alarm* 🎜🎜🎜🎜 (Elektra, 1993, prod. Del, Domino, Hieroglyphics), is a dark—if not mean-spirited and cynical—collection of raps. Curiously, all of the songs are roughly the same length and follow the same format, making it somewhat of a tedious listen from beginning to end. But it's hard not to appreciate a song like "Worldwide," in which Del raps with someone named Unicron (who, it turns out, was actually Del with a studio-altered voice). On Casual's *Fear Itself* 🎜🎜🎜 (Jive, 1993, prod. Domino, Casual), the rapper is hampered by spotty breath control and too many choruses. But the moments when he does find a groove ("Thoughts of the Thoughtful," "That's How It Is") fully warrant the comparisons to a young LL Cool J.

what to avoid: The Souls seemed to struggle with their identity on their sophomore album, making *No Man's Land* 🎜🎜 (Jive, 1995, prod. Domino, Souls of Mischief) a terse, indigestible volume of songs that tries to avoid the problem of making the Souls sound like their imitators. That Extra Prolific is no longer with the crew is perhaps an act of efficiency; his only album, *Like It Should Be* 🎜 (Jive, 1994, prod. Domino, Extra Prolific), is simple-minded and sounds like a Hieroglyphics misconception.

worth searching for: Some of the Hieroglyphics crew's best work came on Del's B-sides. "Burnt," the B-side to "Mista-dobalina" (Elektra, 1992), is legendary for launching the Souls of Mischief. And the B-side to "Dr. Bombay" (Elektra, 1991) features "Eye Examination," regarded as Del's best song.

influences:
◀◀ LL Cool J, George Clinton, Freestyle Fellowship, Leaders of the New School, Brand Nubian, Native Tongues,

▶▶ Pharcyde, Saafir/Hobo Junction, B.U.M.S.

Jazzbo

The Delfonics

Formed as the Four Gents, 1965, in Philadelphia, PA.

Randy Cain, vocals (1965–71); Wilbert Hart, vocals; William Hart, vocals; Ritchie Daniels, vocals (1965–68); Major Harris, vocals (1971–73, rejoined late 1980s).

Discovered and renamed by former Dell Vikings member Stan Watson, this vocal group first recorded for the Cameo and Moonshot labels before meeting musician-producer Thom Bell. They became his lab experiment, a prototype for his lush Philly soul sound epitomized by their first hit together, 1968's "La La Means I Love You." Bell and the Delfonics collaborated on a series of popular singles—"Break Your Promise," "You Got Yours and I'll Get Mine," "Didn't I (Blow Your Mind This Time)"—before Bell moved on to the Stylistics. William Hart became the group's creative director, but the Delfonics never again hit the peaks they achieved with Bell. After Cain left, the Delfonics became home for Major Harris prior to his solo career; with those releases out of print, he's since returned to the band.

what to buy: *La La Means I Love You: The Definitive Collection* 🎜🎜🎜🎜 (Arista Masters, 1997, prod. various) is all that's in print but also all that you need, collecting all the Bell hits and some of the more interesting material from Hart's turn at the helm.

influences:
◀◀ The Dell Vikings, the Miracles, the Drifters

▶▶ The Stylistics, the Dramatics, the Spinners, New Edition, Boyz II Men

Gary Graff

Delinquent Habits

Formed in Los Angeles, CA.

Ives, vocals; Kemo, vocals; O.G. Style, vocals.

Delinquent Habits are proteges of Sen Dog, the barker from hip-hop's most notorious stoner group, Cypress Hill. So it was surprising to hear Habits' anti-drug message, "Another Fix," near the end of their self-titled debut. That the Spanglish-language group had already earned a reputation as a fun, playful crew with its breezy summer-ready single, "Tres Delinquentes," made the serious musical pill even more difficult to swallow.

what's available: *Delinquent Habits* 🎜🎜🎜 (Loud/RCA, 1996, prod. Sen Dog, others) starts off promisingly, with the delightfully catchy opener, "Tres Delinquentes," and its Herb Alpert riff. But after getting the party started right, the Habits can't sustain the funky-good tempo. Their latest is called *Here Come the Horns* N/A (Loud/RCA, 1997).

The Dells (© Peter Amft/Ken Settle)

1 6 2

the dells

influences:

 Cypress Hill, Frost, Mellow Man Ace, Lighter Shade of Brown

Josh Freedom du Lac

The Dells

Formed 1952 as the El Rays, in Harvey, IL. Became the Dells in 1956.

Johnny Funches, lead vocals (1952–59); Johnny Carter, lead vocals (1959–present); Marvin Junior, first tenor; Verne Allison, second tenor; Mike McGill, baritone; Chuck Barksdale, bass.

No group made the transition from the doo-wop of the 1950s into the soul sounds of the 1960s and 1970s better than the Dells. They've racked up an astounding 43 R&B hits, with 24 of them crossing over to the pop charts. Initially known as the El Rays, the group made its first record for Checker Records (a Chess subsidiary) in 1954. The disc was a messy-sounding flop, and they were dropped by the label. They became the Dells after signing with Vee-Jay Records in 1956. Producer Calvin Carter had Harvey Fuqua and the Moonglows coach the Dells on how to get the most from their sound and encouraged the group to write and seek out its own material. Their first Vee-Jay releases, "Tell the World" and "Dreams of Contentment," were dramatic improvements over their Chess single, but became only regional hits. Irked by their lack of success, the Dells split up by the time their third single "Oh What a Night" was released, and didn't know they had a hit until they were congratulated by members of Moonglows. The Dells continued to write and record dreamy, romantic doo-wop songs, but only a few singles such as "Why Do You Have to Go," "Distant Love," and "Pain In My Heart" registered on the charts. In 1958, a car crash put the group out of commission, and lead singer Funches quit. The members were all working day jobs when a chance meeting with ex-Flamingos lead singer Johnny Carter resulted in the re-forming of the Dells. Under the tutelage of voice coach Curt Stewart, the group began a lucrative side career as backup singers on recordings for Jerry Butler, Etta James, Dinah Washington, Barbara Lewis, and many others. During the early 1960s, a complex legal arrangement allowed the Dells to make records for both Vee-Jay and Chess, but only an early version of "Stay In My Corner" hit nationally. Once Vee-Jay collapsed, the Dells recorded full-time for Chess's Cadet label, where Bobby Miller's production and Charles Stepney's vocal arrangements gave their records a fresh context of rich gospel soul. After solid R&B hits with "O-O, I Love You," "There Is," and "Wear It On Our Face," a new, six-minute long LP version of "Stay In My Corner" became a crossover smash. In 1969, at the height of

the oldies craze, the Dells re-cut "Oh What A Night" with a spoken introduction, and it outsold the original. After re-making several classic doo-wop tunes into hits in its new soul style, the group peaked with the million selling "Give Your Baby A Standing Ovation." The Dells left Chess in 1975 but continued to hit the R&B charts for the Mercury, 20th Century, ABC, and Private I labels through the mid-1980s. The 1991 film *The Five Heartbeats,* which was based on the Dells' story, furnished them with their last big hit, "The Heart Is the House of Love." The Dells are still one of the best vocal groups in the world.

what to buy: You can build yourself an instant library of hits from all phases of the Dells' fabulous career with *Dreams of Contentment* 𝄢𝄢𝄢𝄢 (Vee-Jay, 1992, prod. Calvin Carter), *On Their Corner: The Best of the Dells* 𝄢𝄢𝄢𝄢 (MCA, 1992, prod. various), *Bring Back the Love: Classic Dells Soul* 𝄢𝄢𝄢𝄢 (Chess, 1996, prod. various), and *Passionate Breezes: The Best of the Dells 1975–1991* 𝄢𝄢𝄢 (Mercury, 1995, prod. various). Select an era and dig in.

what to buy next: If you can't get enough of that Chicago Vee-Jay sound, *Oh What A Night* 𝄢𝄢𝄢 (Black Tulip, 1997, prod. Calvin Carter) has 28 tracks from that era, many not available on the big hits sets.

the rest:
There Is 𝄢𝄢𝄢𝄢 (Cadet, 1968/Chess, 1989)
The Dells 𝄢𝄢𝄢𝄢 (Chess, 1987)
Second Time 𝄢𝄢𝄢 (Urgent, 1988)
Oh What A Night 𝄢𝄢𝄢𝄢 (MCA Special Products, 1994)
The Dells vs. The Dramatics 𝄢𝄢𝄢 (MCA Special Products, 1997)
Oh What a Night: The Great Ballads 𝄢𝄢𝄢𝄢 (MCA, 1997)

worth searching for: *I Salute You—40th Anniversary* 𝄢𝄢𝄢 (Zoo/Volcano Records, 1992, prod. various) is positive proof that one of the greatest vocal groups of all-time hasn't lost a step.

influences:
 The Clovers, the Flamingos, the Moonglows

▶▶ Parliament, the Impressions, Boyz II Men

Ken Burke

Des'ree

Born Des'ree Weeks, 1968, in London, England.

Born to West Indian parents, Des'ree lived in London until age 10, then went with her family when they returned to their native Barbados for three years. When she returned to London at age 13, she began writing music (her first effort, "Love Is Here," appeared on her second album). In 1992 her "Feel So High," the demo of which prompted Sony to sign her, was a hit in the U.K.

and Europe, though in the U.S. it ended up not on her first album, released that year, but on her second. Her debut, *Mind Adventures*, earned her an opening slot on tour with Simply Red but made little impression on the American market. *I Ain't Movin'* had considerably more impact thanks to her first U.S. tour (opening for Seal) and to the spring 1995 radio success of the positive-thinking "You Gotta Be" (#5 on the *Billboard* charts), which sums up her smooth style well: highly tuneful, relaxed neo-soul, keyboard-based with strings sweetening the sound, but tinged with softened hip-hop rhythms. While she was making *I Ain't Movin'*, she also recorded a duet with Terence Trent D'Arby, "Delicate," which was a Top 10 U.K. hit. Des'ree writes or co-writes all her material, which sometimes has a mildly political slant. As she's explained: "A song is just an expression of my feeling—sometimes as a U.K. black woman, sometimes as a human being." Her sexily husky singing can strongly recall Tracy Chapman, but when Des'ree extends her vocal range for the soulful climaxes, it's clear her style comes out of R&B and not folk.

what to buy: The range and connections of *I Ain't Movin'* 🎵🎵🎵🎵 (Epic, 1994, prod. Ashley Ingram, Des'ree, others) are perfectly expressed by the cover art: on the front, the artist sits on a rock looking pensive yet self-assured; on the back is a relief sculpture of Africa constructed from rocks. If the music is less than ambitious, it's also immediately appealing, with not a weak track to be heard.

what to buy next: *Mind Adventures* 🎵🎵🎵 (Epic, 1992, prod. Phil Legg, others) is more stylistically diverse (including a bit of reggae rhythm and a dollop of rock guitar) but lacks the distinctiveness she developed later. Still, her singing and writing are enough to carry the record.

worth searching for: Terence Trent D'Arby's *Symphony or Damn* 🎵🎵🎵 (Columbia, 1993, prod. Terence Trent D'Arby) includes the D'Arby/Des'ree duet "Delicate." Des'ree also has otherwise unavailable songs on two soundtracks: the Spike Lee movie *Clockers* 🎵🎵 (MCA, 1995, prod. various) includes "Silent Hero," while *William Shakespeare's Romeo + Juliet* 🎵🎵🎵 (Capitol, 1996, prod. various) contains "Kissing You (Love Theme from *Romeo + Juliet*)," produced by Nellee Hooper of Soul II Soul.

influences:

◀◀ Joan Armatrading, Stevie Wonder, Bob Marley, Tracy Chapman

▶▶ Erykah Badu

Steve Holtje

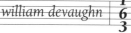

MInd Adventures was songs written by a teenager, I suppose, looking at the world from a very cozy place. I had no responsibilities, no pressure. There was pressure from school and studies, but no worldly pressures. Whereas *I Ain't Movin'* was written by the same person who is becoming an adult, who has left the nest of parental guidance and is out there taking a chance, taking a risk on her own.

Des'ree

William DeVaughn

Born 1948, in Washington, DC.

The wispy-thin former government employee with a voice to match could legitimately be categorized as a one-hit wonder, but oh, what a hit it was! In a lilting, reflective tone suggestive of Curtis Mayfield, DeVaughn soared up both the R&B and pop charts in the summer of 1974 with the incongruous "message" song, "Be Thankful for What You Got." Backed by famous Philly soul ensemble MFSB and using the metaphor of "a great big Cadillac" for the unattainable object that sparks desire and envy, DeVaughn sang a love-song-to-Detroit verse couplet that children of the 1970s can still recite today: "Diamond in the back/Sunroof top/Diggin' the scene/With a gangster lean." The Jehovah's Witness never again saw success anywhere near that #1 R&B single, but did have another brief moment in the sun with his follow-up tune, "Blood Is Thicker Than Water." De-Vaughn's style of feel-good funk turned out to be short-lived, however: by the time of his third single, "Give the Little Man a Great Big Hand," nobody did.

what to buy: It might as well be a 12-inch single, since *Be Thankful for What You Got* ♫♫♫ (Collectables, 1993, prod. various) really has only one song worth cherishing. But the CD version of DeVaughn's 1974 LP also contains his almost-hits and that plaintive, tremulous tenor that's still memorable decades later.

influences:

◄◄ The Drifters, Frankie Lymon, Little Anthony & the Imperials, Curtis Mayfield, MFSB

►► Roland Gift, El DeBarge, Maxwell

Jim McFarlin

Dexy's Midnight Runners /Kevin Rowland & Dexy's Midnight Runners

Formed 1979, in Birmingham, England.

Kevin Rowland, vocals; Billy Adams, banjo and guitar; Giorgio Kilkenny, bass; Micky Billingham, accordion, piano, organ; Seb Shelton, drums; Big Jimmy Patterson, trombone; Paul Speare, flute, tin whistle, saxophone; Brian Maurice, saxophone.

When New Wave raised its ugly commercial voice in 1980, punk singer Rowland answered back with Dexy's Midnight Runners, a high-octane mix of traditional Irish music, soul, and rock. Although Rowland's vision was inevitably short-sighted (he burned bridges with his first label and abused journalists and band members), he managed to find success producing honest, hard-working soul music at a time when it was anything but the fashion. For the group's 1982 hit album *Too-Rye-Ay*, and its hit "Come On Eileen," Rowland re-configured Dexy's as dungaree-clad Celtic rock group, featuring two-piece fiddle section, vocal trio, and the occasional horn backup. After a poor 1988 solo showing, Rowland has remained out of sight and ear shot. There's no word yet on his next move.

what's available: Sadly, Dexy's catalog is out of print in the U.S.; all that remains here is the spirited but sloppy *BBC Radio One Live in Concert* ♫♫♫ (Griffin, 1995) taken from a 1982 concert.

worth searching for: Of the imports, *Searching for the Young Soul Rebels* ♫♫♫♫ (EMI U.K., 1980, prod. Kevin Rowland, others)

is a foot-stomping rave-up of earnest soul tributes, while *Too-Rye-Ay* ♫♫♫ (Mercury U.K., 1982, prod. Kevin Rowland, others) isn't as focused but has some great moments shifting between rustic folk-rock ("The Celtic Soul Brothers"), to blazing soul (a cover of Van Morrison's "Jackie Wilson Said"), and rollicking pop (the international hit "Come On Eileen"). *Geno* ♫♫♫ (Old Gold UK, 1983, prod. various) is a worthwhile compilation of early singles.

influences:

◄◄ Van Morrison, MFSB, Gamble & Huff

►► The Waterboys, Clannad, Longpigs

Christopher Scapelliti

The Diablos

Formed 1950, in Detroit, MI.

Nolan Strong, lead vocals; Juan Guiterriez, tenor; Willie Hunter, baritone; Quentin Eubanks, bass; Bob "Chico" Edwards, guitar.

Fronted by the soaring, haunting falsetto of Nolan Strong, the Diablos came out of Detroit with a style some say was the precursor of the Motown sound. They debuted in 1954 on Fortune Records, Detroit's first black R&B label, and their second release that year, "The Wind," became an R&B classic even though it didn't dent the national charts the first time around. The next year they scored a solid R&B hit with "The Way You Dog Me Around," and in 1962, the re-released original of "The Wind" proved strong enough to make a showing on *Billboard*'s pop charts. Even into the early 1960s, it is said that Berry Gordy was intent on buying out Strong's Fortune contract and making him head producer and arranger for his label, without success. Although the Diablos did not experience great success in their recording career, "The Wind" captured both a mood and a moment for young lovers, and the group was heard and admired by many—most notably by a young Detroit teenager named Bill who was determined to capture the Nolan Strong sound in his own singing voice. That teenager later became known as Smokey Robinson.

worth searching for: A latter-day version of the Diablos is touring the oldies circuit, but in the main their music is gone and, sadly, almost forgotten. The 1960s Fortune Records compilations *Fortune of Hits, Vol. 1* and *Fortune of Hits, Vol. 2* have yet to make the transition to CD, but if you can find copies hidden in oldies bins or record shows, snatch them up for the transcendent high tenor of Nolan Strong alone, and see where Smokey Robinson got his inspiration.

influences:

◄◄ The El Dorados, the Moonglows, Clyde McPhatter and the Drifters, Ray Charles

►► The Orioles, the Kool Gents, the Fortunes, Jackie Wilson, Smokey Robinson and the Miracles, the Dramatics, Michael Jackson, Terence Trent D'Arby

Michael Kosser

Diamond D

Born Joe Kirkland in the Bronx, NY.

With the volume of key production work Diamond D has done, it almost seems as if his own albums are inconsequential. Born and raised in the Boogie Down Bronx, Diamond D has been one of the most sought-after beat-creators in hip-hop since he grabbed the hip-hop world's attention by supplying backing tracks for Lord Finesse. In addition to creating rock-solid rhythms for his Diggin' In the Crates crew (Showbiz and A.G., Lord Finesse, Fat Joe, Big L), Diamond has lent his production touch to everybody from the Pharcyde, Tha Alkaholiks, and Brand Nubian to House of Pain, KRS-One, and the Fugees.

what to buy: Diamond D, who made his public rhyming debut on A Tribe Called Quest's "Show Busines," would likely be the first to admit that he isn't the world's most gifted lyricist. But as demonstrated on his (actually, Diamond D and the Psychotic Neurotics') first album, *Stunts, Blunts and Hip-Hop* ✧✧✧✧ (Chemistry/Mercury, 1992, prod. Diamond D, Showbiz, DJ Mark the 45 King, others), Diamond's simplified rhymes are merely there to add texture to his crisp, block-rockin' beats. His production style on the album, whose title plays off the sex, drugs, and rock 'n' roll slogan, is very similar to that of Showbiz, as both like to create faster-paced tunes guided by fondled basslines and punctuated drum kicks. But on the follow-up, *Passion, Hatred and Infidelity* ✧✧✧ (Mercury, 1997, prod. Diamond D), Diamond's work is evolving, as he's relying on changing melodies rather than just loops. While the album is without any lasting hits (see the earlier "Sally Got a One Track Mind" and "Best Kept Secret"), Diamond has stepped up his writing and rhyming ("The Hiatus," "JD Revenge") to better match his musicianship.

influences:

◄◄ Jazzy Jay, Lord Finesse

►► Showbiz and A.G., Fat Joe

Jazzbo

Manu Dibango

Born February 10, 1934, in Cameroon, Africa.

From the 1940s through the 1950s, jazz gained popularity throughout Africa as a result of prized recordings and the visits of Louis Armstrong, Duke Ellington, and Dizzy Gillespie. Numerous jazz bands from Algiers to Johannesburg sprang up, but it wasn't until 1960, when an exciting alto saxophonist named Manu Dibango propelled the African Jazz band out of Zaire, that respect was gained. Within six years, Dibango was playing to a small but loyal following of natives and expatriates in Paris. In 1972, Atlantic released his album *Soul Makossa* in the U.S. The title tune instantly became an anthem, dominating America's pop/soul airwaves as well as the discotheques. "Soul Makossa" was truly massive; though more of a jazz-funk jam than Cameroonian makossa beat, the song also had a major influence on the emerging Puerto Rican salsa scene (check him out with the Fania All Stars on their 1976 album *Live at Yankee Stadium, Vol 2*). Since Dibango's 1974 Atlantic swan song *Makossa Man*, he has played jazz festivals, toured the world many times, and released more than 20 albums on both import and domestic record labels (scoring another international hit with 1985's "Abele Dance"). Today, the seemingly ageless Manu Dibango is still performing on the global stage, and his retirement seems a blessedly long way off.

what to buy: *Soul Makossa* ✧✧✧✧ (Atlantic, 1972) is Dibango's global move. In addition to the burning title tune, it boasts exotic moods and grooves aplenty ("New Bell" is a funky example). *Gone Clear* ✧✧✧✧ (Mango, 1980, prod. Geoffrey Chung) is a beguiling mix of African, R&B, and reggae grooves thanks to the prescence of folks such as like Sly & Robbie, Jocelyn Brown, Crusher Bennett, and Randy Brecker.

what to buy next: *Electric Africa* ✧✧✧ (Celluloid, 1985, prod. various) includes "Abele Dance" and is Manu *al electrique*, kinda like electro-computer makossa funk. *Live 91* ✧✧✧ (Stern, 1991, prod. Manu Dibango) is a bumping set recorded at Paris's legendary Olympia. From the spirited cover of Serge Gainsborough's reggafied "Le Marsaillaise"-spoof, "La Javanaise," to MC Mello's hip-hop freestyle flow on "Jam Rap Makossa," Dibango and crew are on fire.

what to avoid: The guest list on *Wakafrika* ✧✧ (Giant, 1994, prod. George Acogny) is impressive—Peter Gabriel, Youssou N'Dour, Sinead O'Connor, Ladysmith Black Mambozo—but they steal too much focus from Dibango's performance.

the rest:

Afrijazzy ✧✧✧ (Enemy, 1994)

Bao Bao 🎵🎵🎵 (MIL Multimedia, 1996)

worth searching for: Dibango's outstanding guest appreance on the Fania All Stars' 1976 release *Live At Yankee Stadium, Vol 2*. He also makes a worthwhile guest appearance on Angelique Kidjo's *Logozo* (Mango, 1991/1992).

influences:

◀◀ Wes Montgomery, John Handy, Junior Walker

▶▶ Fela Kuti, Eddie Palmieri, Hugh Masekela

Tom Terrell and Gary Graff

Bo Diddley

Born Elias Bates, December 30, 1928, in McComb, MS.

Unarguably one of the most-influential musicians in rock 'n' roll, Diddley's distinctive "chunka, chunka" rhythm guitar riff is the stuff of which rock's bedrock was made. Born near the Mississippi Delta, Diddley was raised by sharecroppers and earned his nickname in school. The family that adopted him—and changed his last name to McDaniel—moved to Chicago, where Diddley began making his guitars and playing them on the street and in small clubs. He signed with Checker Records during the mid-1950s and released a string of albums and singles through the mid-1960s that would influence countless rockers, from Elvis Presley and Buddy Holly to the Rolling Stones and Jimi Hendrix. Diddley's recorded output since then has been erratic, and most of what he has released has been either uninspired, ill-advised, or both—though the star-studded 1996 *A Man Amongst Men*, his first for a major label in 25 years, showed there's life in the old man yet. Diddley, a member of the Rock and Roll Hall of Fame, has stayed active on the concert trail, his rectangular guitars and Coke-bottle glasses as familiar to generations of admirers as that gritty voice and gut-bucket guitar sound.

what to buy: *Bo Diddley/Go Bo Diddley* 🎵🎵🎵🎵 (Chess, 1958 and 1959/1987) capture the primal "Bo Diddley Beat" in all its fever. Some of Diddley's greatest songs appeared on these records, including "Bo Diddley," "I'm a Man," "Who Do You Love," and "Crackin' Up." *His Best* 🎵🎵🎵🎵 (MCA/Chess, 1997, prod. various) is a solid, 20-song overview.

what to buy next: If you're willing to shell out a few more bucks, check out *The Chess Box* 🎵🎵🎵🎵 (Chess, 1990, comp. Andy McKaie), an exhaustive warehouse of Diddley's early and influential work for the famous Chicago label. All his most pop-

ular and important work is here, as well as worthwhile obscurities and previously unreleased material.

what to avoid: Just about anything Diddley did for the small Triple X Records label, most of them well-intentioned but poorly executed attempts to make Diddley relevant. Among them: *Breakin' Through the B.S.* 🎵 (Triple X, 1989, prod. Scott Free); *The Mighty Bo Diddley* 🎵🎵 (Bokay Productions, 1985), and *This Should Not Be* 🎵 (Triple X, 1993, prod. Scott Free).

the rest:

Bo Diddley 🎵🎵🎵🎵 (Chess, 1958)
Bo Diddley Is a Gunslinger 🎵🎵🎵 (Chess, 1960)
In the Spotlight 🎵🎵🎵 (Chess, 1960)
(With Chuck Berry) *Two Great Guitars* 🎵🎵🎵 (Chess, 1964)
(With Muddy Waters and Little Walter) *Superblues* 🎵🎵🎵 (Chess, 1967)
(With Muddy Waters and Howlin' Wolf) *The Super Super Blues Records* 🎵🎵🎵🎵 (Chess, 1968)
The London Bo Diddley Sessions 🎵🎵🎵 (Chess, 1973)
His Greatest Sides, Vol. 1 🎵🎵🎵 (Chess, 1986, cassette only)
Rare and Well Done 🎵🎵🎵 (Chess, 1991)
A Man Amongst Men 🎵🎵 (Code Blue/Atlantic, 1996)

worth searching for: Completists just have to track down one of Diddley's most opportunistic albums, *Surfin' with Bo Diddley* 🎵 (Chess, 1963) a record that proved that Bo knows trends, but doesn't always know when to avoid them.

influences:

◀◀ Louis Jordan, Muddy Waters, John Lee Hooker

▶▶ The Rolling Stones, Eric Burdon, Jimi Hendrix, Buddy Holly, Elvis Presley, Bow Wow Wow, U2

Doug Pullen

Digable Planets

Formed 1991, in Washington, DC.

Butterfly, vocals; Doodlebug/Knowledge, vocals; Ladybug/Mecca, vocals.

Revolutionary in song and soul, this gender-mixed trio helped revitalize rap during one of its most daunting stages of stagnation. But it wasn't necessarily that the Digable Planets did something new. In fact, in classic hip-hop tradition, their genius comes in doing something *old*. In the early 1990s, that meant integrating be-bop flavor into an increasingly fragmented

Manu Dibango (© Jack Vartoogian)

music scene. Digging into the crates for jazz samples and adopting '60s communitarianism while articulating it all to hip-cat syncopation, the Digable Planets earned a Grammy and briefly diverted attention away from hip-hop's creative slump. The group, which was conceived while its members were still college students, had found both a modern way to make Miles Davis important, and, to the surprise of some, a receptive audience spanning the rap savant to the average MTV viewer. A year after their debut, they dropped a less experimental follow-up, favoring nationalism and spartan soundscapes. The catchy loops and hooks that made their first effort so accessible were lost in the face of a decidedly message-oriented project. Nevertheless, an aura of progressive '60s coolness—mainly lyrical—emanates from the Brooklyn-based clan so artistically ahead (and behind) the times.

what to buy: *Reachin' (A New Refutation of Time and Space)* 𝄞𝄞𝄞𝄞 (Pendulum/Elektra, 1993, prod. various) brings the Digable Planets—and, thereby, jazz-hop—into the national spotlight with a coffee-house anthem built around samples of Art Blakey and the Jazz Messengers. "Rebirth of Slick (Cool Like Dat)" orders a call for change—musically through buoyant horns, and verbally through beatnik rhymes, which accurately boast "the Puba of the styles, like Miles, my man" over a descending bass riff. Most of the album follows stylistic suit, with rhymes either celebrating community pride or drifting into politics. "La Femme Fetal" even offers a hip-hop perspective on the pro-life lobby.

the rest: *Blowout Comb* 𝄞𝄞𝄞𝄞 (Pendulum/EMI, 1994)

influences:
◀◀ Miles Davis, Gang Starr, De La Soul, A Tribe Called Quest, Dream Warriors

▶▶ Fugees, Camp Lo

Corey Takahashi

Digital Underground
Formed 1988, in Oakland, CA.

Shock G, vocals; Humpty Hump, vocals; Money B, vocals; DJ Fuze, DJ; Chopmaster J, percussion.

The emergence of Digital Underground in 1990 made it official: the Mothership had landed once again. Picking up where George Clinton and company left off, the Bay Area crew brought the P-Funk for a whole new generation, this time communicating in the hip-hop tongue. Digital Underground emu-

lated many aspects of the Parliament/Funkadelic days: as the brainchild of smooth-tongued Shock G, DU was—like Clinton's cronies—a band of loose-grooved, odd personalities. Shock G had his many incarnations (e.g. MC Blowfish), and there was short, freaky, and freckle-faced Money B, the ever-silent DJ Fuze, and, of course, Humpty Hump, the brash and nasal-voiced star of "Doowutchyalike." Others affiliated with the group included Tupac Shakur (who launched his career with the Digital Underground), the Piano Man, Goldfingers, Saafir, and the Luniz. In true P-Funk style, the Digital Underground members even created caricatures of themselves and crammed their album covers and inserts with animated snapshots; they also perfected the art of the live show, as lively tales of the legendary summer tours will attest to. But perhaps Digital Underground is indicative of a simpler time, as its popularity on the musical front has decreased steadily since its inception.

what to buy: Part hyperbole, part rated-R fantasy, and part unadulterated funk (think 2 Live Crew-meets-De La Soul), *Sex Packets* 𝄞𝄞𝄞𝄞 (Tommy Boy, 1990, prod. Digital Underground) is considered a classic in many circles. Nobody dug through the Parliament/Funkadelic treasure-trove quite like Digital Underground did, opening the door for the G-Funk sound that followed in the early '90s. Even the virtual-reality concept of "sex packets" was ahead of its time (see: "cybersex"). "The Humpty Dance" and "Doowutchyalike" are venerable anthems, and "Freaks of the Industry" slows enough for Money B and Shock G to show off a freaky side. Within a few months came the release of *This Is an EP Release* 𝄞𝄞𝄞𝄞 (Tommy Boy, 1990, prod. Digital Underground), a collection of four new songs and two remixes that includes the national debut of Tupac Shakur, who clowns around with the underground on "Same Song" and a remix of "The Way We Swing." Even in 1990, Tupac posesses remarkable charisma, albeit with a lot more innocence.

what to buy next: Digital Underground never really matched its initial enthusiasm with subsequent albums. *Sons of the P* 𝄞𝄞𝄞 (Tommy Boy, 1991, prod. Digital Underground) is hardly *Sex Packets*, even if it does score some points for the charming "Kiss You Back" single. That same year brought the birth of Raw Fusion, a DJ Fuze-Money B side project that debuted with *Live from the Styleetron* 𝄞𝄞 (Hollywood BASIC, 1991, prod. Raw Fusion). Although Money B's voice is a smooth intoxicant that many feel they can never get sick of, the project is ill-conceptualized, satisfying the MC's dancehall infatuation more than providing a dose of *real* Money B. Still, "Throw Your Hands in the Air" offers a glimpse of what should have been the album's focus. With the P-Funk vibe considered played out, but Digital

Underground still decidedly on it, *Body Hat Syndrome* 🎵🎵 (Tommy Boy, 1993, prod. D-Flo, Digital Underground) received little attention. Although it marks the recording debut of Saafir's now-trademark colloquialism, the album suffers from decreasing group chemistry. That the group's relationship with Tommy Boy came to a halt was not a surprise; how the group rebounded, with the future funk of *Future Rhythm* 🎵🎵 (Crtique/BMG, 1996, prod. Digital Underground) was.

what to avoid: Raw Fusion is in a bad funk on *Hoochified Funk* 🎵 (Hollywood BASIC, 1994, prod. Raw Fusion). Simply a mistake.

influences:

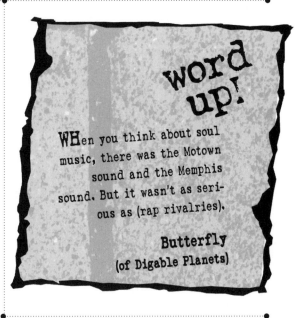

◀◀ Parliament/Funkadelic, Doug E. Fresh, Public Enemy, Too $hort, EPMD

▶▶ Force One Network, 2Pac, Saafir, Gold Money

Jazzbo

Dion

Born Dion DiMucci, July 18, 1939, in the Bronx, NY.

Training on street corners, DiMucci and his band the Belmonts won national acclaim with the hit "I Wonder Why" in 1959; the group was also the fourth-billed act for the tour on which Buddy Holly died. But unlike the innumerable doo-wop stars of the era that came and went in a flash, Dion showed staying power by forging a solo career. Effectively beginning in 1960 with the #1 hit "Runaround Sue," he continued into various styles of rock 'n' roll and R&B. Maintaining a streetwise soulfulness, he has remained a figure in the fickle music industry for more than 30 years.

what to buy: *Runaround Sue* 🎵🎵🎵 (Laurie, 1961/The Right Stuff, 1993, reissue prod. Eli Okun), his early 1960s solo break, is highlighted by the title track, "The Wanderer," "The Majestic," and "Little Star." Classic stuff.

what to buy next: From 1962–65, Dion branched out to sing blues, gospel, and country, and the best songs of that period are found in sterling sound quality, accompanied by informative liner notes, on *Bronx Blues: The Columbia Recordings* 🎵🎵🎵🎵 (Columbia/Legacy, 1991, comp. Greg Geller). *The Road I'm On* 🎵🎵🎵 (Legacy, 1997, prod. various) is a fascinating look at Dion's "lost" era, 1962–68, when he explored various styles such as blues and folk.

what to avoid: Steer clear of *When You Wish Upon a Star* 🎵🎵 (Collectables, 1983/1960)—it has absolutely crappy sound.

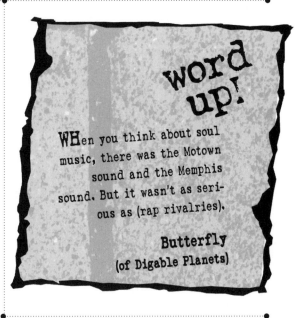

word up!

WHen you think about soul music, there was the Motown sound and the Memphis sound. But it wasn't as serious as (rap rivalries).

Butterfly (of Digable Planets)

the rest:
Lovers Who Wander 🎵🎵🎵 (Laurie, 1962/The Right Stuff, 1993)
Dion 🎵🎵🎵 (Columbia, 1968/The Right Stuff, 1994)
The Return of the Wanderer 🎵🎵🎵🎵 (Lifesong, 1978/DCC, 1990)
Velvet and Steel 🎵🎵🎵 (Columbia, 1986/1991)
Yo, Frankie 🎵🎵🎵 (Arista, 1989)
Reunion: Live at the Madison Square Garden 1972 🎵🎵🎵 (Rhino, 1993)

worth searching for: *The Fabulous Dion* 🎵🎵🎵🎵 (Ace) is a solid import greatest hits collection with "Runaround Sue" and "The Wanderer."

influences:

◀◀ The Orioles, the Cadillacs, the Dell Vikings

▶▶ Lou Reed, Billy Joel, Paul Simon

Allan Orski

Dirty Dozen Brass Band

Founded 1975, in New Orleans, LA.

Gregory Davis, trumpet (1975–present); Efrem Jones, trumpet (1978–present); Kevin Harris, tenor sax (1975–present); Roger Lewis, baritone and soprano sax (1975–present); Charles Joseph, trombone (1975–90); Kirk Joseph, sousaphone (1975–92); Jenell Marshall, snare drum (1975–95); Benny Jones, bass drum (1975–84); Lionel Batiste, bass drum (1985–95); Raymond Webster, drums (1991–96); Keith Anderson, sousaphone and trombone (1993); Revert Andrews, trombone (1996); Julius McKee, sousaphone and basses (1996); Richard Knox, keyboards (1996); Terence Higgins, drums (1996).

Of the masses of musical traditions that flow through New Orleans, one of the deepest is the brass marching band. The Dirty Dozen Brass Band spurred a new generation of players and audiences that give life to this immediate predecessor and midwife of jazz. But rather than rest as a historical repertory band, members of the Dirty Dozen have put their own imprint on the music by composing titles with more modern approaches and covering bebop, R&B, and pop titles. But as much fun and as great as they can be live, the recordings seldom elicit the same emotional response. Still, with solicitous use of such guests as Danny Barker, Eddie Bo, Dr. John, Elvis Costello, David Bartholomew, and others, the Dirty Dozen has managed to keep the records varied and entertaining (though they lay in the same groove much of the time). The band made a sharp turn in 1996, dropping the Brass Band label and changing instrumentation for a more conventional sound with trap drums and keyboards in addition to a guest guitarist on several pieces.

what to buy: The band burst onto the recording scene with *My Feet Can't Fail Me Now* &&&& (Concord Jazz, 1984, prod. Quint Davis), featuring a novel lineup and sound. This record set the tone that the band has seldom gone beyond, and tells you exactly what Dirty Dozen music is all about. The Dozen then came up with an excellent vehicle for its skills with *Jelly* &&&& (Columbia, 1993, prod. Scott Billington), a tribute to the incomparable Jelly Roll Morton. Interspersed with octogenarian Danny Barker's reminiscences of the self-proclaimed creator of jazz, the songs maintain the loose group feel of Morton's ensembles and the Spanish tinge so important to the New Orleans sound. Lewis's soprano saxophone work on "The Pearls" is a highlight.

what to buy next: The band's biggest change of pace came on *ears to the wall* &&&& (Mammoth, 1996, prod. the Dirty Dozen), which tosses out the traditional beats for a modern funky sound close to that of Maceo Parker. All the tunes here are originals, and the remake of "My Feet Can't Fail Me Now" from the first album shows the group slicker but still willing to have fun.

what to avoid: Though it holds up on its own, *Voodoo* &&& (Columbia, 1989, prod. Scott Billington) finds the band reworking territory they've pretty much covered before, despite appearances by Dizzy Gillespie and Branford Marsalis.

the rest:
Live: Mardi Gras at Montreux &&&& (Rounder, 1986)

The New Orleans Album &&&& (Columbia, 1990)
This is Jazz #30 &&&& (Columbia, 1997)

influences:
◀◀ Olympia Brass Band
▶▶ Rebirth Brass Band

Lawrence Gabriel

Disposable Heroes of Hiphoprisy /Spearhead

Formed 1990, in Oakland, CA. Disbanded 1990. Spearhead formed 1993 in Oakland, CA.

Disposable Heroes: Michael Franti, vocals; Rono Tse, DJ, percussion. Spearhead: Michael Franti, vocals; Mary Harris, vocals (1993–95); Le Le Jamison, keyboards; Keith McArthur, bass; David James, guitar; James Gray, drums; Sub Commander Ras I Zulu, vocals.

Singer-rapper Franti gained attention—first with the Beatnigs, and then with the more visible Disposable Heroes of Hiphoprisy—for his confrontational but articulate political rapping, which owed a massive debt to Gil Scott-Heron and the Last Poets. The Disposables, who sought to replace the boasting and misogyny of mainstream rap with substantive argument, essayed such topics as U.S. foreign policy, homophobia, and the corrosive effects of television. Franti's tract-like rhymes were placed in a sonic collage influenced by punk and free jazz more than R&B. The result, though admirable in its intent, was too mired in political correctness and in-your-face indie cred to be very enjoyable. As with the Beatnigs before them, Franti dissolved the Heroes after one release and returned in 1994 with something entirely different—and better. Spearhead allowed him to mingle the political and the personal in a powerful new way, and instead of samples and *musique concrete,* his new musical context was a band that played warm, emotionally powerful soul and funk. Unable to capture the gangsta-loving rap audience, Spearhead was marketed to the alternative rock crowd audience with some success, thanks in part to its insinuating single and video "Hole in the Bucket." Despite the departure of the band's other main vocalist, Mary Harris, after the release of the debut *Home*, the group remained together to record a second album—a first for Franti.

what to buy: On Spearhead's *Home* &&&& (Capitol, 1994, prod. Joe Nicolo), Franti stretches out lyrically and displays a surprisingly effective singing voice. Harris, meanwhile provides powerhouse accompaniment and a wry, sly counterpoint to Franti's sincere persona.

the rest:
Disposable Heroes of Hiphoprisy:
Hiphoprisy Is the Greatest Luxury 🎵🎵🎵 (4th &Broadway, 1992)

Spearhead:
Hole in the Bucket 🎵🎵🎵 (Capitol EP, 1995)
Chocolate Supa Highway 🎵🎵🎵 (Capitol, 1997)

worth searching for: Franti's first group, the Beatnigs, lasted for just one hard-to-find recording. But what an album. *The Beatnigs* 🎵🎵🎵🎵 (Alternative Tentacles, 1988, prod. the Beatnigs) is the most interesting and innovative album any of Franti's three groups has made, loaded with sonic twists and turns (buzzsaws! chains whipped against tire rims!). Despite the industrial album's strong political bent, though, Franti generally manages to avoid the sort of pedantry that too often marks similar groups. Like, say, the Disposable Heroes of Hiphoprisy.

influences:
⏪ Gil Scott-Heron, Last Poets, Einsturzende Neubautenesque, Public Enemy, Bob Marley, Stevie Wonder, Marvin Gaye

⏩ Paris, Consolidated

Simon Glickman and Josh Freedom du Lac

Divine Styler

Divine Styler and his Scheme Team crew made a significant impact on hip-hop upon their arrival in 1989, but the group's historical significance seemed to be unjustly erased when Divine began to dabble in the Southern California black music scene that included such multi-faceted players as Fishbone, Bronx Style Bob, Pop's Cool Love, and Justin Warfield. Long considered AWOL (there's even a Canadian 'zine called In Search of Divine Styler), Divine resurfaced recently, working with House of Pain, while Scheme Team member Cockni O' Dire appeared on albums by Freestyle Fellowship and the Angel.

what to buy: Though it now sounds slightly dated, Divine Styler's debut album, *Word Power* 🎵🎵🎵🎵 (CBS/Columbia, 1989, prod. Afrika Islam, Divine Styler) best captures the rapper's lyrical wordplay and oft-twisted concepts, especially on the title track and "Divine Stylistics."

what to buy next: *Spiral Walls Containing Autumns of Light* 🎵🎵🎵 (Giant/Reprise, 1992, prod. Divine Styler) is a 180-degree turn from Divine's first album. Though it features the fully charged "Grey Matter," the album's live instrumentation (Divine played most of the instruments himself, including guitars and bass) and acid-like, aural psychedelica hit hip-hop's re-

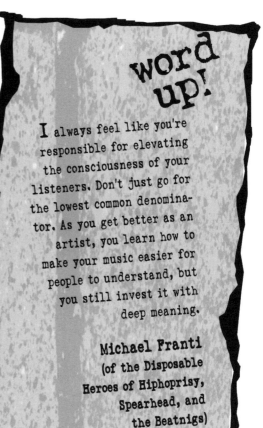

word up!

I always feel like you're responsible for elevating the consciousness of your listeners. Don't just go for the lowest common denominator. As you get better as an artist, you learn how to make your music easier for people to understand, but you still invest it with deep meaning.

Michael Franti
(of the Disposable Heroes of Hiphoprisy, Spearhead, and the Beatnigs)

stricted tastes like shrapnel. But if you can appreciate this rather bizarre music, the album's worth checking out.

influences:
⏪ Ice-T, Kool G Rap

⏩ Jungle Brothers, Bronx Style Bob

Jazzbo

DJ Honda

Even in its nascency, hip-hop always had an international presence. Japan's recent infatuation with hip-hop culture has led the country to export some of its best DJs to U.S. shores, and that includes DJ Honda. The guitarist-turned-turntablist made an impressive American debut when he tore up the one-and-twos in the 1990 DJ Battle for World Supremacy, but he actually earned even more respect when he finished second in the competition in 1992's heated battle.

what's available: Honda's foray into beat-making and producing culminated in his self-titled U.S. debut, *DJ Honda* 🎵🎵🎵 (Relativity, 1996, prod. DJ Honda). The album mimics the classic New York style of heavy rhythmic loops—an obvious and understandable influence—while employing the talents of rappers like Redman, Guru, Sadat X, Grand Puba, and Tha Alkaholiks. The most entertaining entry on the album, though, is Biz Markie's "Biz Freestyle."

influences:
◀◀ Grandmaster D.ST

Jazzbo

D.J. Jazzy Jeff & the Fresh Prince /Will Smith

Formed 1986 in South Philadelphia, PA.

Fresh Prince/Will Smith (born Willard Smith, September 25, 1968), vocals; D.J. Jazzy Jeff (born Jeffrey A. Townes, January 22, 1965), DJ.

While still in their teens, D.J. Jazzy Jeff & the Fresh Prince became the Martin and Lewis of rap music, parlaying their comical fusion of outlandish rap stories and South Philly hip-hop beats into across-the-board commercial acceptance and multimillion-dollar success—and achieving a succession of entertainment firsts in the process. The pair's debut album, *Rock the House*, got mad play on black radio with its combination of Jazzy's groundbreaking mix of samples and scratching and the humor-filled anecdotes by Prince (a nickname bestowed on Smith by his teachers at Philadelphia's Overbrook High due to his courtly, smooth-talking manner; he added the "Fresh" on his own). But it wasn't until 1988's *He's the D.J., I'm the Rapper* that the two attracted the true crossover audience needed to take them to #1 on the charts, selling 2.5 million copies along the way. In what seemed like an overnight phenomenon, Jeff and the Fresh Prince became superstars, making countless TV appearances, selling out major venues, and earning the first Grammy ever awarded to rap musicians. Heady with their momentum, the duo wasted no time releasing *And In This Corner* a year later, centering around the single "I Think I Can Beat Mike Tyson." Though it sold respectably, the LP lacked the bite to live up to massive fan expectations: instead of fresh and funny,

it came off as canned and corny. But Smith's personal popularity soared unabated: The first rap artist to make the transition to TV star, Smith took the title role in the situation comedy *The Fresh Prince of Bel-Air*. Based on the real-life experiences of Warner Bros. Records executive Benny Medina, the show ran for six successful seasons on NBC, and Smith eventually brought on his homeboy Townes as a co-star. Subsequently featured in hit movie (*Six Degrees of Separation, Bad Boys*) after hit movie (*Independence Day, Men In Black*), Smith made the ultimate transformation from rapper to box-office megastar; there's even talk of him playing Muhammad Ali in an upcoming biopic. While D.J. Jazzy Jeff & the Fresh Prince have never officially broken up, they haven't released a song together since 1993, and Smith (now using his given name) has signed a long-term solo deal with Columbia. The Artist Formerly Known As The Fresh Prince made his solo debut with two songs on *Men In Black: The Album*, including the silvery-smooth "Men In Black," which updates Patrice Rushen's "Forget Me Nots." It's unlikely, then, that Jazzy Jeff and the Fresh Prince will ever *Rock the House* in the same hilarious way again.

what to buy: The duo's first release, *Rock the House* 🎵🎵🎵 (Jive, 1987, prod. Jazzy Jeff) is jam-packed with lighthearted and irresistibly catchy tracks like "Girls Ain't Nothing But Trouble," "Just One of Those Days," and "Don't Even Try It"—songs that burned up urban airwaves in the summer of '87. Recording in hip-hop's pre-sample-clearance heyday, Jazzy Jeff skillfully reworks everything from James Brown funk to the *I Dream of Jeannie* theme to make this LP the epitome of good, clean hip-hop fun.

what to buy next: *He's the D.J., I'm the Rapper* 🎵🎵🎵 (Jive, 1988, prod. Bryan "Chuck" New, Pete Q. Harris) delivers an even smoother, tastier portion of the pair's hysterical hip-hop antics with songs including the mainstream breakthrough "Parents Just Don't Understand."

what to avoid: While Jeff's production work is admirable on *Code Red* 🎵🎵 (Jive, 1993, prod. Jazzy Jeff), it can't mask the fact that the Fresh Prince now sounds stale and worn out, showing no signs of the charismatic wit his earlier rhymes possessed. Instead, this lackluster LP is bogged down with a seriousness which ironically makes Smith come off like a Hollywood actor attempting to portray an angry young rapper.

the rest:
Homebase 🎵🎵🎵 (Jive, 1991)
And In This Corner 🎵🎵 (Jive, 1989)

solo outings:
Will Smith:
Big Willie Styles N/A (Columbia, 1997)

influences:

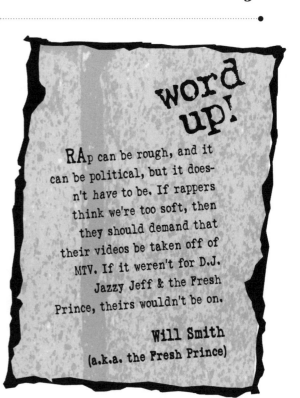

◀◀ Rufus Thomas, Pigmeat Markham, Kurtis Blow, Fat Boys, Slick Rick, Dana Dane

▶▶ Kid 'n Play, Da Youngsta's, Doctor Dre and Ed Lover, Coolio, Three Times Dope, Cash Money and Marvelous, the Roots

Andre McGarrity

DJ Kool

Born in Washington, DC.

There is no clearer lineage between hip-hop and black roots than the call-and-response routine an MC engages in with an audience during a live show. DJ Kool—a 38-year old, 10-year veteran of the DC go-go and hip-hop scene—parlayed that energy into several independent recordings that earned him regional success and eventually led to a major-label deal.

what's available: Originally a regionally popular independent recording, *Let Me Clear My Throat* ♪♪♪ (American/CLR, 1996/97, prod. DJ Kool, DJ Mark the 45 King, Funkmaster Flex) was reissued nationally and instantly became a club and video favorite. The catchy, dynamic tune—which uses the familiar 45 King break from "900 Number" as its bedrock—captures the live hip-hop element vividly. But aside from an "Old School Reunion Mix" that features Biz Markie and Doug E. Fresh, this EP isn't anything more than an exaggerated single.

influences:

◀◀ Rare Essence, Doug E. Fresh, Biz Markie

Jazzbo

DJ Krush

While DJ Shadow was making noise stateside with a decidedly progressive brand of abstract hip-hop, his eventual MoWax labelmate DJ Krush was doing likewise in Japan, although Krush's warm soundscapes lean on jazz much harder than Shadow's moody breakbeat collages.

what to buy: Guest appearances by jazz-minded MCs C.L. Smooth, Guru, and the Roots's Black Thought and Malik B. are a nice touch, but *Meiso* ♪♪♪♪ (MoWax, 1996, prod. DJ Krush) is clearly Krush's show, as he concocts a series of soothing, dynamic ambient soundscapes that rarely meander. Fellow abstract hip-hop heavyweight DJ Shadow emerges from the album's shadows, too, for the stunning "Duality."

> # word up!
>
> RAp can be rough, and it can be political, but it doesn't have to be. If rappers think we're too soft, then they should demand that their videos be taken off of MTV. If it weren't for D.J. Jazzy Jeff & the Fresh Prince, theirs wouldn't be on.
>
> **Will Smith (a.k.a. the Fresh Prince)**

what to buy next: Old-school beats and older-school horn lines mark the improvisational *DJ Krush* ♪♪♪♪ (Shadow, 1995, prod. DJ Krush), on which Krush is joined by capable Japanese jazz musicians.

the rest:

MiLight N/A (MoWax/ffrr/London, 1997)

influences:

◀◀ DJ Premier, Ali Shaheed Muhammad

▶▶ DJ Honda

Josh Freedom du Lac

DJ Quik

Born David Blake, in Compton, CA.

Quik has been labeled a gangsta rappper, but his lyrics are more about sex-trippin' than set-trippin'. Like a rapping version of Steve "Wild Man" Gallon or Rudy Ray Moore, Quik tells raunchy, explicit tales of sexual conquests past and future, setting them to self-produced music that blends taut, hard-hitting beats with both the sweaty, sanctified wah-wah swagger of Stax/Volt and the sweet dance-funk grooves of Parliament. For instance: "Sweet Black Pussy," "I Got That Feelin'," "Skankless," "Mo Pussy," "Me Wanna Rip Your Girl," and "Let Me Rip Tonite." Of course, Quik does have other lyrical concerns, rapping proudly about his neighborhood ("Born and Raised in Compton," "Jus Lyke Compton"), flexing his gangsta muscle ("Deep"), paying tribute to alcohol ("8 Ball"), and celebrating marijuana ("Tha Bombudd," although elsewhere, he shows that creativity supercedes consistency, declaring, "I hope you know I'd rather be dope than use it"). The songs are rated-G, all right, but not in the Disney sense. And O.G. Quik knows it: In his debut, he actually anticipates—then matter-of-factly shrugs off—the criticism his songs would eventually attract, saying, "Now, in my lyrics, I kick the shit that the critics debate to/But I can create the shit that the brothers relate to." A recent cameo on a radio-safe Tony! Toni! Tone! hit aside, expect the criticism to get louder now that Quik has joined the controversial Death Row stable.

what to buy: Quik's debut, *Quik Is the Name* ♪♪♪♪ (Profile, 1991, prod. DJ Quik) stands as his finest moment, partially because he hadn't yet become completely obsessed with raunch—but mostly because of his deft and confident production touch. "Tonite" rumbles and pops like a misplaced Dr. Dre track; the mesmerizing "Deep" hits it on the one (a la James Brown); the head-snapping "Born and Raised In Compton" inventively loops a riff from "Hyperbolicsyllabicsesquedalymistic" over a boisterous kick-drum foundation; the spiraling, left-right-left rhythmic punch of "Quik Is the Name" is drop-dead dizzying; and the too-short, guitar-driven "Quik's Groove" is a sweet funk instrumental that wouldn't sound out of place in a Stax/Volt set.

what to buy next: *Way 2 Fonky* ♪♪♪ (Profile, 1992, prod. DJ Quik) and *Safe & Sound* ♪♪♪ (Profile, 1995, prod. DJ Quik, G-One, others) generally lack the sonic bravado and freshness of Quik's debut, and the increasingly explicit and raunchy pseudo-comedic lyrics threaten to turn Quik into a joke himself. But the two albums are still decent examples of G-funk, with latter's standout "Jus Lyke Compton" certainly worth checking out.

the rest:
(With 2nd II None) *2nd II None* ♪♪♪ (Profile, 1991)

influences:
◀◀ Rodney O and Joe Cooley, 2 Live Crew, Too $hort, N.W.A., EPMD, Stax/Volt

▶▶ Tha Dogg Pound, Paperboy, M.C. Breed, AMG

Josh Freedom du Lac

DJ Red Alert

Although not a recording artist or on-the-town celebrity per se, there were few people more loved and influential in the New York hip-hop world of the 1980s than Kool DJ Red Alert. After starting out in the Bronx River Projects DJing parties with Afrika Bambaataa and the Cold Crush Brothers, among others, Red Alert became one of rap's pioneering radio DJs. Starting in the early 1980s, his Friday and Saturday night radio shows on New York's Kiss FM grew to be ridiculously popular, bringing the underground sounds of rap—which were thought to be too rough for the station's daytime format—to an audience that hung on every note. Aside from his buoyant on-air personality, the programming on his show was perfect for the times and for the music. Indeed, the hundreds of promo spots that were done by everyone who was anyone in the rap world are a testament to the power that Red Alert had at the time. And his support of groups such as the Jungle Brothers, Boogie Down Productions, and the Ultramagnetic MC's, to name a few, catapulted them to fame that never would have happened without it. Capitalizing on his popularity and influence, Red Alert has teamed up with various record labels over the years to release compilations of music representative of his shows, even down to the promos that previously were available only to his devoted listeners in New York. Red Alert no longer works at Kiss FM, though, as the station switched its format during the mid-1990s and abruptly released the DJ. Funkmaster Flex, the new ruler of hip-hop radio in New York, has taken over Red's throne with a show that frankly couldn't have existed without Red's pathbreaking work. Red's place in the overall history of hip-hop—although not as strong outside of New York as within the tri-state area—is indisputable.

what to buy: *Let's Make It Happen* ♪♪♪♪ (Next Plateau, 1990) is the third collection released with Red's name on the marquee and is a great compilation that shows off the DJ's inimitable style, selection and flair. The tracks here are 100 percent mid-school classics, from De La Soul's "Buddy" and Poor Righteous Teachers' "Rock Dis Funky Joint" to Chill Rob G's "The Power" and the Jungle Brothers' "J. Beez Comin' Through." The best thing about this record, though, is that it's laid out exactly like a real Red Alert radio show, mixing promos from DJ Premier, Total Control, Bizzy Boys, and Supreme DJ Nyborn with Red's groundbreaking live cutting and mixing. This is a great example of Red in his prime and an important historical document, not to mention a mind-bogglingly good party record.

worth searching for: The first two Red Alert compilations, *Red Alert Goes Berserk* (Let's Go, 1987) and *We Can Do This* (Next Plateau, 1988), are both out of print. Perhaps even more difficult to find is the "Hip-hop On Wax" 12-inch series (Vintertainment, 1984) and "Red Alert (Criminal Minded Mix)," which is included on Boogie Down Productions' "Man & His Music" (B-Boy, 1988).

influences:

◀◀ Pete DJ Jones, Kool Herc, Jocko Henderson, Afrika Bambaataa, Grandmaster Flash, Grandwizard Theodore, DJ Hollywood

▶▶ Marley Marl, Funkmaster Flex, Kid Capri, Sway, Ultramagnetic MC's, Jungle Brothers, King Tech, almost every other radio DJ in New York City and elsewhere who emerged after 1983

Brian Coleman

DJ Shadow

Born Josh Davis.

DJ Shadow's star has been on the rise since his initial remix work for Hollywood BASIC's Lifer's Group ("The Real Deal/Lesson 4") and Zimbabwe Legit ("Legitimate Mix") in 1992. When his impressive sides "In/Flux" (on the trendsetting U.K. label Mo Wax) and "Entropy" (on the American label, SoleSides) both arrived in 1993, they almost single-handedly heralded the new realization of the music that has become known as trip-hop—a term Shadow himself shuns. And although densely constructed and evocative soundscapes are what Shadow is chiefly known for, he is also one of the most interesting straight-up hip-hop producers in the worldwide rap underground: through his work with the Bay Area artists Blackalicious, Lyrics Born, and Lateef, he has brought his love of obscure breakbeat science to some of the more compelling and innovative rap recordings to have emerged in recent years—all of which have appeared on SoleSides, which Shadow partially owns. Although his influence has yet to show up on a large scale (in pop terms, anyway), the impact made by his 1996 full-length debut album, *Entroducing . . .*, has certainly been felt (and heard) by both fans and producers alike. Indeed, although no Shadow clones have stepped out of his considerable shadow, almost every artist who has heard him takes a little piece of what he's done and makes it a part of their own sound. Seemingly more concerned with making beats than magazine

covers, Shadow's image is one of the shy guy thrust into the spotlight. He smiles because he has to, but he really would rather be where the lights are less bright, and probably where there is a turntable and a sampler nearby.

what to buy: *Entroducing . . .* 🎵🎵🎵🎵🎵 (Mo Wax/ffrr, 1996, prod. DJ Shadow) was a long time coming but well worth the wait. And as the liner notes state: "This album reflects a lifetime of vinyl culture." Produced in the dangerous confines of San Francisco's Glue Factory (where Dr. Octagon's 1996 opus was conceived), the music on the album tends more toward aural introspection and compositional depth than the cavernous drums that his hip-hop productions benefit from. Of course, the cut-n-paste brilliance of "The Number Song" makes a serious exception, but "Building Steam with a Grain of Salt," "Midnight in a Perfect World," and "What Does Your Soul Look Like" show that the album is about blending sampled sounds and textures into entirely new entities. As a pure hip-hop album, *Entroducing . . .* is so far from the current status quo that it almost isn't fair comparing it. But Shadow's sampling mastery and respectful love for DJing and the art of making tracks are as real and as important as any other branch on hip-hop's family tree.

worth searching for: If you can find them, get Shadow's 12-inch singles "In/Flux" (Mo Wax, 1993) and "Entropy" (SoleSides, 1993), the Chief Xcel-DJ Shadow 12-inch "Fully Charged On Planet X"/"Hardcore Hip-Hop" (SoleSides, 1996), and the Lateef-Lyrics Born CD *Latyrx* (SoleSides, 1997, prod. DJ Shadow, others).

influences:

◀◀ Grandmaster Flash, Afrika Bambaataa, Grandwizard D.ST, Grandwizard Theodore, DJ Red Alert, DJ Cash Money, DJ Chuck Chillout, Frank Zappa, Brian Eno

Brian Coleman

The D.O.C.

Born Tray Curry, in Dallas, TX.

The D.O.C.'s story is one of the more tragic in hip-hop. After getting his start as a songwriter for N.W.A., the artist recorded his own album, *No One Can Do It Better*, for Eazy-E's Ruthless label in 1989. Graced by the ever-evolving production touch of Dr. Dre and featuring the D.O.C.'s clean, authoritative and occasionally raggae-tinged vocals, the album had fans shooting their gats in the air in celebration of the arrival of a new hardcore star. But the D.O.C.'s larynx was crushed in a car accident shortly after the release of the album, effectively ending his highly promising career as a performer. Or so everybody thought. The D.O.C. surprisingly resurfaced via brief guest appearances on Dre's *Chronic* and Snoop Doggy Dogg's *Doggystyle* before bitterly leaving Dre's Death Row camp in a dispute over money and, then, recording a new album of his own. Included on the grating recording is an ill-advised update of the D.O.C.'s seminal single, "It's Funky Enough," on which he sadly sounds like Froggy or, worse, an Onyx reject.

what to buy: The D.O.C. makes a pretty bold statement with the title of *No One Can Do It Better* 𝄢𝄢𝄢𝄢 (Ruthless, 1989, prod. Dr. Dre), especially given that he's joined on the album by the entire N.W.A. clan, which actually *does* do gangsta rap better. But this is still a West Coast hardcore classic, with Dre's taut, economical funk beats matching up well with the D.O.C.'s lyrics, delivered crisply and with occasional reggae inflections. "The Formula" and "It's Funky Enough" are particularly noteworthy, though the album loses points for an annoying piss-break interlude.

what to avoid: On *Helter Skelter* **woof!** (Giant, 1996, prod. D.O.C., others), the D.O.C. tarnishes his legacy by attempting to bring his classic "It's Funky Enough" back to life as "Return of Da Livin' Dead." He no longer has the voice to make it work, and he clearly misses Dre's production. This D.O.C. sounds like a quack.

influences:

◀◀ N.W.A., Dr. Dre

▶▶ RBX

Josh Freedom du Lac

Dr. Dre

Born Andre Young, February 18, 1965, in Compton, CA.

Dr. Dre is to '90s rap what Phil Spector was to '60s pop. While Spector's Wall of Sound production style changed the face of pop in the early '60s, upping the creative stakes and spawning a wave of imitators, Dre's pioneering G-funk sound similarly altered the course of rap. Largely because of Dre's success (every album he has produced has either gone either gold or platinum, and he's had massive success producing singles, too), countless other producers have tried to duplicate his trademark blend of concise, Parliament/Funkadelic beats; thick, rolling basslines; seductive samples; melodic choruses; and minor-key synth lines. Indeed, immediately following the release of Dre's sonically brilliant post-N.W.A. solo debut, *The Chronic*, G-funk became the commercially dominant style in rap, with even Dre's half-brother, Warren G, copping his style.

what to buy: Dig underneath Dre's glittering production work on *The Chronic* 𝄢𝄢𝄢𝄢 (Death Row/Interscope, 1992, prod. Dr. Dre), and you'll find two things: he's only an average lyricist, at best; and his gangstacentric thematic concerns—so groundbreaking when his former group, N.W.A., debuted in the late '80s—are now worn out. Then again, the appeal of the album (as with the one Dre produced for protege Snoop Doggy Dogg) is not in what Dre's saying, but in *how* he's saying it. By providing a soothing, almost easy-listening musical foundation for his surprisingly cool-sounding words, he's managed to make the killing fields of Compton sound sexy and alluring. That's no small feat. Certainly, it's a major departure from Dre's work on N.W.A.'s gangsta classic, *Straight Outta Compton*, which can sound as dangerous as any punk record.

what to avoid: Before Dre turned his attention to the gangsta lifestyle and joined N.W.A., he was a member of the HiNRG Los Angeles DJ collective known as the World Class Wreckin' Cru. Although the music sounds severely dated now, that didn't stop Wreckin' Cru's Grandmaster Lonz (Lonzo Williams) from slapping several of that group's songs together for the haphazard, quasi-anthologies *Concrete Roots* 𝄢𝄢 (Triple X, 1994, prod. Dr. Dre, DJ Yella, Lonzo Williams, others) and *First Round Knockout* 𝄢𝄢 (Triple X, 1996, prod. Dr. Dre, Lonzo Williams, others). At least the two collections show the breadth of Dre's production work; in fact, they might have even suceeded as a singlular album, what with the inclusion of songs Dre produced for the likes of the D.O.C. ("The Formula," "It's Funky Enough"), Michel'le ("Nicety," "No More Lies") and Snoop Doggy Dogg ("Deep Cover"). Too bad.

the rest:
Dr. Dre Presents . . . The Aftermath 𝄢𝄢𝄢 (Aftermath/Interscope, 1996)

influences:

◀◀ Jonzun Crew, Uncle Jamm's Army, World Class Wreckin' Cru

▶▶ Warren G, Domino, DJ Quik, Dove Shack, the Twinz, Jermaine Dupri, Snoop Doggy Dogg, Tha Dogg Pound, RBX, 2Pac, Notorious B.I.G., Lady of Rage

Josh Freedom du Lac

Doctor Dre and Ed Lover

Formed in New York, NY.

Doctor Dre (born Andre Brown); Ed Lover (born James Roberts).

Dre and Ed Lover got their start on the New York radio scene, but it wasn't until hosting *Yo! MTV Raps* that the two became

Dr. John **(© Ken Settle)**

nationally known as the Abbot and Costello of hip-hop. While Ed Lover (the tall one) got his own dance ("The Ed Lover," set to DJ Mark the 45 King's "900 Number"), Dre (the rotund one) had to deal, at least early on, with the constant confusion between him and the other Dr. Dre who was making noise on the West Coast. Since *Yo!* went to a rotating VJ format, Dre and Ed Lover have returned to their radio roots.

what's available: The notoriety the two jesters earned on MTV allowed them to make everything from insurance commercials to their own full-length feature film, *Who's the Man.* Can't fault anyone for seizing an opportunity, but the duo's album, *Back up off Me* **woof!** (Relativity, 1994, prod. Marley Marl, DJ Mark the 45 King, others), is gimmicky and exploitive. Or did you really enjoy "Recognize" and "Tootin' on the Hooters"?

worth searching for: Before teaming up with Ed Lover, Dre was a member of the group Original Concepts, whose *Straight from*

the Basement of Kooley High 🎵🎵🎵 (Def Jam, 1988) is certainly worth the hunt.

influences:
◀◀ D.J. Jazzy Jeff & the Fresh Prince

Jazzbo

Dr. John

Born Malcolm John "Mac" Rebennack Jr., November 21, 1940, in New Orleans, LA.

With his spooky, voodoo-drenched debut as The Night Tripper in 1967 and his guided tour of New Orleans roots music on *Dr. John's Gumbo* in 1972, Dr. John paved the way for America's discovery of the Crescent City's rich musical heritage. It was Dr. John who led listeners to legendary New Orleans artists such as Professor Longhair and Huey "Piano" Smith. And his 1973 hits "Right Place, Wrong Time" and "Such A Night" helped bring national attention to regional stars such as the Meters and Allen Toussaint. Born and raised in New Orleans, Rebennack already was performing and recording in his teens, mainly as a guitarist. But it was his funky piano and distinctive, gravelly drawl that made him a star with the release of the *In the Right Place* album in 1973. Financial and drug problems plagued him well into the 1980s, but the growing popularity of New Orleans music helped him regain his stride. Today, he reigns as the acknowledged master of the New Orleans sound; no one has done more to popularize it.

what to buy: *Mos' Scocious* &&&& (Rhino, 1993, prod. various) is the definitive Dr. John anthology—a two-CD set that begins with rare early sides cut with local bands such as Ronnie & the Delinquents, then marches on through more than 30 years of the doctor's finest. A virtual encyclopedia of the New Orleans sound. *The Very Best of Dr. John* &&&& (Rhino, 1995, prod. various) is a single CD collection that skims the cream of *Mos' Scocious*. *Dr. John's Gumbo* &&&& (Atlantic, 1972, prod. Jerry Wexler, Harold Battiste) is Dr. John's landmark tribute to the Crescent City's R&B roots—while, a year later, *In the Right Place* &&&& (Atco, 1973, prod. Allen Toussaint) gave him a hit. (Both *Gumbo* and *In the Right Place* are combined on a Mobile Fidelity Sound Lab 24K disc.)

what to buy next: *Goin' Back to New Orleans* &&&& (Warner Bros., 1992, prod. Stewart Levine) is another fine reflection of his early influences, with lots of stellar guest artists. *In a Sentimental Mood* &&&& (Warner Bros., 1989, prod. Tommy LiPuma) is Rebennack's career-reviving take on standards such as "Makin' Whoopee" (a Grammy-winning duet with Rickie Lee Jones) and "Accentuate the Positive." And have your mojo hand ready should you fall under the hoodoo spell of The Night Tripper on *Gris Gris* &&& (Atco, 1968).

what to avoid: *At His Best* && (Special Music Co., 1989) is a set that's been rendered redundant by the several more complete best-ofs.

the rest:
The Ultimate Dr. John &&& (Warner Bros., 1987)
At His Best && (Special Music Co., 1989)
The Brightest Smile in Town &&& (Clean Cuts, 1989)
Afterglow &&& (Blue Thumb, 1995)

worth searching for: An import CD of formative, loose-limbed 1960s sessions, *Cut Me While I'm Hot* (Magnum America) is well worth finding.

influences:
◀◀ Professor Longhair, James Booker, Tuts Washington, Joe Liggins, Huey (Piano) Smith

▶▶ The Neville Brothers, Marcia Ball, the Radiators

Doug Pippin

Tha Dogg Pound
Formed 1993, in Los Angeles, CA.

Dat Nigga Daz, vocals; Kurupt, vocals.

Controversy does not always sell records. If it did, then Sister Souljah would've gone multiplatinum to not long after then-presidential hopeful Bill Clinton took her to task for suggesting that blacks kill whites in retribution for slavery. As it was, nobody cared about Souljah's music, mostly because it wasn't any good. People cared about Tha Dogg Pound, of course, but not because of C. DeLores Tucker's Dogg-hunting expedition. Indeed, while the anti-rap crusader was busy targeting Tha Pound and its then-unreleased debut entre, *Dogg Food*, calling the group "the filthiest of them all" long before anybody had even heard a note of the album, the rap world was buzzing loudly about the duo's promising cameo on Snoop Doggy Dogg's *Doggystyle* and its memorable entry on the *Murder Was the Case* soundtrack, "What Would U Do?" Not surprisingly, when *Dogg Food* was finally served in late 1995, rap fans ate it up—Tucker's crusading be damned.

what's available: "Welcome," a horror-movie voice booms in the intro to *Dogg Food* &&& (Death Row, 1995, prod. Daz, Kurupt, DJ Pooh). "We have been expecting you. Dogg Pound. Are you (expletive) ready?" Well, of course we (expletive) were; we'd been (expletive) expecting you, too. Ultimately, though, Tucker's "filthiest-of-them-all" bark proved louder than Tha Dogg Pound's bite, as not even *Dogg Food*'s dirtiest, most misogynistic songs ("If We All Fuck," "Some Bomb Azz Pussy") came close to, say, Funkdoobiest's worst. But filth isn't what Daz and Kurupt specialize in. Rather, Tha Pound makes its mark on *Dogg Food* with confident, street-wise, and occasionally street-wary pass-the-mike raps, and thumping, cleanly produced, Funkadelic-inspired tracks that creep and bounce along like a '64 Chevy Impala in a speed-bump zone, a la obvious influence Dr. Dre. Still, there's no single song on *Dogg Food* that's as explosive as the *Murder Was the Case* soundtrack entry "What Would U Do?"

worth searching for: In other words, U might be better off picking up a copy of *Murder Was the Case* (Death Row/Interscope, 1994, prod. various) simply to hear what is, pound for pound, the group's best song.

influences:
◀◀ Dr. Dre, Snoop Doggy Dogg, Warren G

▶▶ Lady of Rage

see also: *Snoop Doggy Dogg*

Josh Freedom du Lac

Domino

Born Shawn Ivy, in St. Louis, MO.

Because Domino is neither a good singer nor a good rapper, he goes half way, delivering his vocals—mostly about getting paid and laid—in a decidedly West Coast singsong drawl. But Domino's vocals lack the danger, tension, and (misleading) playfulness that make, say, Snoop Doggy Dogg's lyrics compelling. As such, the focus turns to his backing music, an often languid Parliament-Ohio Players-Zapp hybrid that blends horn blasts, piano and organ vamps, rhythm-guitar riffs, synth squiggles, electro-funk fuzz, and loose-and-airy beats and comes off sounding like low-rent Dr. Dre.

what's available: *Domino* ✍✍ (OutBurst, 1993, prod. DJ Battlecat) is notable mostly for two ear-candy singles: "Sweet Potato Pie" (which updates the Stones's "Brown Sugar" recipe) and "Getto Jam" (a sweet summer groove that contains some surprising jazz-like scats). The rest of the material pales, although the use of a Hi Records-type Hammond loop does makes the grossly materialistic "Money Is Everything" somewhat worthy, sonically. On *Physical Funk* ✍✍ (OutBurst, 1996, prod. Domino), Domino sounds as if he's resting on all two of his past hits: "Hennessy" could be re-titled "(Back to the) Getto Jam," and "So Fly" might be "(Another Slice of) Sweet Potato Pie." Domino even seems to point out that his best songs might already be behind him, saying: "Now look into my past and see the work I've done/I'm up in *Billboard*, six weeks at #1." Not anymore, you aren't.

influences:

◀◀ Das EFX, Dr. Dre, Snoop Doggy Dogg

▶▶ Ahmad, Bone Thugs-N-Harmony, Da Brat, Warren G, the Twinz, Dove Shack, L.B.C. Crew

Josh Freedom du Lac

Fats Domino

Born Antoine Domino, February 26, 1928, in New Orleans, LA.

Not only is Domino responsible for an astounding 63 charted singles and more than 65 million in record sales, but he did it with nothing more than pure musical charm. A short-statured man of ample girth, Domino possessed none of the titillating antics or wild personality traits of contemporaries such as Little Richard and Chuck Berry. Instead, he smiled and let the rolling triplets of his piano and his warm New Orleans drawl steer his never-ending string of self-penned hits. Nearly everything the man recorded has a rollicking charm and gentleness, and they retain their impact and innocence to this day. He cut his first hit, "The Fat Man," in 1949, predating both Bill Haley and Elvis Presley by several years and therefore making it arguably the first rock 'n' roll song. From that point on, Domino's influence and importance as a musical force cannot be overstated.

what to buy: The four-disc box set *They Call Me the Fat Man* ✍✍✍✍ (EMI, 1991, prod. Dave Bartholomew) chronicles his stay at the Imperial label and renders almost every other release redundant with hits such as "Blueberry Hill," "Ain't That a Shame," "Walkin' to New Orleans," "I'm Walkin'," and "Whole Lotta Lovin'." *My Blue Heaven* ✍✍✍✍ (EMI, 1990, prod. Dave Bartholomew) is a fine introductory single-disc sampler to the warm Creole sound of the Fat Man.

what to buy next: *Antoine "Fats" Domino* ✍✍✍✍ (Tomato, 1992, prod. Kevin Eggers, Robert G. Vernon) is a vivacious live document, recorded when Domino was 61 and still in full possession of all his friendly energy. Plus, it offers a good version of "Red Sails in the Sunset."

what to avoid: *Christmas Is a Special Day* ✍✍ (The Right Stuff/EMI, 1993, prod. Fats Domino). Yes it is. So buy the box set and leave the caroling to cardigan-clad setsters such as Perry Como.

the rest:
The Best of Fats ✍✍✍ (Pair, 1990)
All-Time Greatest Hits ✍✍✍ (Curb, 1991)
Best of Fats Domino Live Vol. 1 ✍✍✍ (Curb, 1992)
Best of Fats Domino Live Vol. 2 ✍✍✍ (Curb, 1992)
Fats Domino: The Fat Man, 25 Classics ✍✍✍✍ (EMI, 1996)
That's Fats! A Tribute to Fats Domino ✍✍✍ (EMI, 1996)

worth searching for: *Out of New Orleans* ✍✍✍✍ (Bear Family, 1993) is an eight-disc import set that presents the complete Imperial recordings, along with unedited alternate takes and a 72-page book containing extensive liner notes and a complete sessionography.

influences:

◀◀ Big Joe Turner, Louis Jordan, Professor Longhair

▶▶ Van Morrison, Paul Simon, Billy Joel, Bruce Hornsby, the Neville Brothers, Allen Toussaint

The Dominoes

Formed in 1950. Disbanded 1961.

Billy Ward, piano; Clyde Ward (a.k.a. Clyde McPhatter), lead tenor (1950–53); Jackie "Sonny" Wilson, lead tenor (1953–57); Eugene Mumford, lead tenor (1957–61); Charlie White, second tenor (1950–52); James Van Loan, second tenor (1952–61); Joe Lamont, baritone; Milton Merle, baritone; Bill Brown, bass (1950–56); David Mc-Neil; Cliff Graves; Milton Grayson.

Billy Ward's Dominoes were one of the most influential groups in 1950's R&B. Their use of gospel pyrotechnics on decidedly secular material was unique for its time, and the group was a launching pad for two of the genre's greatest vocalists—Clyde McPhatter and Jackie Wilson. Ward assembled his group from the choirs he coached around Harlem, and he played piano and arranged the songs he wrote or chose for his teenaged singers. After a successful appearance on CBS's "Arthur Godfrey's Talent Scouts," the Dominoes became the first act signed by Federal Records (a subsidiary of King) in 1950. "Do Something for Me" was a Top 10 R&B hit, but the Dominoes really made a splash in 1951 with the overtly sexual "Sixty Minute Man," which crossed over to the upper regions of the pop charts. Other great R&B hits followed, such as "Have Mercy Baby," "I Am with You," and "That's What You're Doing to Me." The group's main attraction, both on record and in person, was Clyde McPhatter, and he knew it. His high tenor gave the group's records their distinctive hook, and his on-stage histrionics (sliding knee-drops, splits, sobbing) drove women wild. Ward, a control freak who insisted on overseeing every aspect of the Dominoes' personal behavior and grooming, fired McPhatter in 1953 after several ego clashes. McPhatter was immediately snapped up by Atlantic, where he formed the Drifters, and Ward hired young Jackie Wilson to take his place. The group's Wilson era was not as successful as the McPhatter days, but it still scored good-sized hits with reworked standards such as "Rags to Riches" and "These Foolish Things Remind Me of You," and on stage Wilson was one of the all-time greats. The Dominoes continued with modest success on King and Federal for a time, then recorded two singles that went nowhere for Jubilee. A drastically reshuffled line-up of the group signed with Decca Records in 1956, where it scored its biggest hit in three years, "St. Therese of the Roses." Shortly after, Wilson left the group to start his solo career and was replaced by Eugene Mumford. Ward kept the Dominoes going, though the records they made sounded more pop than R&B, and he had stopped writing in favor of reworking standards. At Liberty Records in 1957, the Dominoes cut a lush, heavily or-chestrated version of "Star Dust," and it became their biggest pop hit. So-so renditions of "Deep Purple" and "Jenny Lee" charted strongly, but their old label, Federal, undercut the group by glutting the market with their previously unreleased recordings. Soon their career momentum was lost entirely. A few final singles for ABC-Paramount and Ro Zan were artistic as well as commercial failures. Ward disbanded the Dominoes just as the gospel-based soul sounds he helped pioneer (and later abandoned), began to dominate the R&B charts.

what to buy: *Sixty Minute Men: The Best of Billy Ward & the Dominoes* ✍✍✍✍ (Rhino, 1993, comp. James Austin) is the best of the many hits compilations out. The 20 digitally remastered tracks feature all the big hits for Federal, such as "Have Mercy Baby," "Sixty Minute Man," "Can't Do Sixty Anymore," "Do Something for Me," and the underrated Eugene Mumford's great vocal on "Star Dust."

what to buy next: *All Their Hits* ✍✍✍ (King, 1995, prod. various) and *Greatest Hits* ✍✍✍ (Deluxe, 1988, prod. various) have all the hits from the Federal era, but little worthwhile annotation. *Greatest Hits* ✍✍✍ (King, 1994. prod. various) is an eight-song budget set. *Clyde McPhatter* ✍✍✍ (King, 1994, prod. various), despite being a deceptively labeled budget reissue of McPhatter's work with Billy Ward's Dominoes, is good stuff. *The Dominoes Featuring Clyde McPhatter, Vol. 2: 18 Hits* ✍✍✍ (King, 1996, prod. various) is a similar compilation with more tracks.

what to avoid: You don't need *Dominoes Meet the Ravens* ✍✍ (Sequel, 1995, prod. various), unless you want tracks by the Ravens in place of a full LP by the Dominoes.

the rest:
21 Original Greatest Hits ✍✍✍ (Deluxe, 1988)
Billy Ward & the Dominoes ✍✍✍ (King, 1994)
Sixty Minute Man ✍✍✍ (Charly, 1994)
Vol. 1: 14 Hits ✍✍✍ (King, 1996)
Vol. 3: 14 Hits ✍✍✍ (King, 1996)
Vol. 4: 21 Hits ✍✍✍ (King, 1996)

worth searching for: *Billy Ward with Jackie Wilson* ✍✍✍ (Decca, 1977, prod. various) contains Jackie Wilson's last recordings with Ward & the Dominoes, including the hit "St. Therese of the Roses."

influences:
◀◀ The Ravens, the Orioles
▶▶ The Drifters, the Moonglows, the Falcons

Ken Burke

Lee Dorsey

Born Irving Lee Dorsey, December 24, 1924, in New Orleans, LA. Died December 1, 1986.

Lee Dorsey is one of the most underrated R&B/soul singers of the 1960s. His laconic vocals ably expressed troubles, humor, and sexuality without resorting to screaming. Before becoming a singer, Dorsey was a journeyman professional boxer known as Kid Chocolate (not the featherweight champ of the 1930s) and worked in an auto wrecking yard. Dorsey was brought to producer Harold Battiste of Fury Records by legendary songwriter/arranger Allen Toussaint. Dorsey's Fury sides were smartly crafted New Orleans R&B with catchy small band arrangements and goofy, double entendre songwriting. His first major hit was 1961's "Ya Ya," a jivey novelty that works as both a nonsense ditty and an ode to sensual frustration. It was a Top 10 pop record and a million seller. His follow-up, "Do Re Mi," was a solid Top 20 hit, but the Fury label soon folded and Dorsey's career lost momentum. In 1965, Marshall Sehorn and Allen Toussaint brought Dorsey with them to Amy Records (a subsidiary of Bell Records). Together they recorded a string of danceable, funny pre-funk hits such as "Ride Your Pony," "Get Out of My Life Woman," "Confusion," and the crossover smash "Working in a Coalmine." (The chorus of "Coalmine" once again invited speculation that Dorsey was singing of something more salicious than just troubles at work.) "Holy Cow," "My Old Car," "Go Go Girl," and 1969's "Everthing I Do Gohn Be Funky (from Now On)" were equally fine recordings but made gradually less impact on the charts. After his critically acclaimed (but low-selling) 1970 Polydor LP *Yes We Can*, Dorsey semi-retired to his auto repair business. A 1976 guest appearance on Southside Johnny & the Asbury Juke's first LP led to a final disc on ABC-Paramount and, by request, Dorsey toured with the Clash in 1980. (Who knew the Clash had such cool tastes, eh?) Dorsey died of emphysema in 1986, leaving behind dozens of recordings that continue to raise sly, knowing smiles while people move their feet.

what to buy: *Wheelin' and Dealin': The Definitive Collection* ♪♪♪♪ (Arista Masters, 1997, prod. various) presents 20 of Dorsey's favorites, remastered from the original tapes and in the most sparkling sound quality available yet. *Ya Ya* ♪♪♪♪⁷ (Relic, 1994, prod. various) is 16-track reproduction of Dorsey's first LP filled with danceable novelties such as "Do Re Mi," "Yum Yum," "Great Googa Mooga," and the title track.

what to buy next: *Golden Classics* ♪♪♪♪ (Collectables, 1993, prod. various) contains his big hits from the early and mid-1960s. *Lee Dorsey* ♪♪♪♪ (Pickwick, 1995, prod. Allen Toussaint) is a 16-track greatest hits compilation at a budget price.

what to avoid: *Night People* ♪♪ (ABC, 1978, prod. Allen Toussaint) is Dorsey's last LP. It's not a bad disc, but Dorsey sounds tired, and the material is erratic. For completists only.

the rest:
Yes We Can . . . and Then Some ♪♪♪ (Polydor, 1970/1993)
Great Googa Mooga ♪♪♪ (Charly, 1991)
Get Out of My Life Woman ♪♪♪♪ (Essential Gold, 1995)

worth searching for: *Am I That Easy to Forget?* ♪♪♪♪ (Charly, 1987, prod. various) contains Dorsey's biggest hits, several interesting LP tracks, some uncharacteristic cover versions of "If I Were a Carpenter" and "Before the Next Teardrop Falls," and two Coca Cola commercials. *Can You Hear Me* ♪♪♪♪ (Charly 1987, prod. Allen Toussaint) has 22 tracks from Dorsey's hot mid-1960s run, featuring his big hits on the Amy label.

influences:
◀◀ Huey "Piano" Smith, Dave Bartholemew
▶▶ The Pointer Sisters, Southside Johnny

Ken Burke

Double XX Posse

Although the quartet was once the flagship of the Big Beat Records roster, the hip-hop climate changed dramatically, moving from ruffneck tendencies to gangsta mentalities. And Double XX couldn't—or wouldn't—alter itself accordingly.

what to buy: The hip-hop music of 1992 was a mix of dance-like grooves and slower, rumbling songs set at lower bpms. Indicative of the latter was "Headcracker" from the Double XX debut, *Put Ya Boots On* ♪♪♪ (Big Beat, 1992, prod. T. Ray, Double X). That style seemed to be the group's forte, though it did score a minor hit with "Not Gonna Be Able to Do It," a relatively upbeat song that relied on T. Ray's upright-bass manipulation and a jumpy, reciteable chorus for its hook.

the rest:
Ruff, Rugged and Raw ♪♪ (Big Beat/Atlantic, 1994)

influences:
◀◀ EPMD, JVC Force

Jazzbo

Dove Shack

Formed 1993, in Long Beach, CA.

2-Scoop, vocals; Bo-Rock, vocals; C-Knight, vocals.

Named after a garage-turned-hangout, the trio's humble roots

Will Downing (© Jack Vartoogian)

show in its down-home raps. For the most part, the rhymes are simple, straight-forward reflections of the Long Beach they know and love. It's not rap for analysis, but, rather, rap for rap's sake—something so appropriate as background music for a barbecue, party, or freeway cruise. However, less creative than Snoop, with less G-funk than Warren, and less verbal versatility than the Twinz, the Dove Shack ultimately has a tough time standing out among a more talented group of peers.

what's available: *This Is The Shack* ♪♪♪ (Def Jam, 1995, prod. Warren G, others) is a collection G-funk-flavored cruising tunes and Cheech and Chong-like skits. Although the Shack can come off hardcore and sexist, the trio shines when setting good-time rhymes to lazy Long Beach grooves (as on "The Shack" and the hit, "Summertime in the LBC").

influences:

◄◄ Warren G, Above the Law, Domino, Dr. Dre

Corey Takahashi

Will Downing

Born in New York, NY.

Will Downing has yet to receive the kind of respect he so richly deserves, primarily because his vocal style is so hard to classify. Is it jazz or is it R&B? Actually, it's a unique combination of both, and Downing bridges the gap between the two genres beautifully, with a style more often associated with female vocalists such as Anita Baker. Downing began his musical career during the mid-1980s as a background session singer, lending his velvety vocals to albums by artists such as Kool & the Gang, Stephanie Mills, Jennifer Holliday, and Billy Ocean. After singing lead on some projects for New York DJ/producer Arthur Baker, Downing signed as a solo artist with Island Records. Though successful in the U.K. right from the start, he's still relatively unknown in the U.S. despite constant touring and five quality albums. If Will Downing's music fit nicely into any one radio format, he'd be a superstar in no time. Until then, he'll remain one of music's best kept secrets.

what to buy: *A Dream Fulfilled* 𝄞𝄞𝄞𝄞𝄞 (Island, 1991, prod. Will Downing, Barry J. Eastmond, Onaje Allan Gumbs, Zane Mark, Wayne Brathwaite) is a splendid fusion of jazz and R&B. Downing—backed by such jazz luminaries as Jonathan Butler, Omar Hakim, and Kevin Eubanks—shines on "I'll Wait" and the classic Angela Bofill tune "I Try." His take on War's "The World Is a Ghetto" alone is worth the price of the CD. The magic continues on *Love's the Place to Be* 𝄞𝄞𝄞𝄞𝄞 (Mercury, 1993, prod. Will Downing, Barry J. Eastmond, Ronnie Foster, Bob Baldwin, Rex Rideout), which features a great cover of the Stylistics' "Break Up to Make Up" and a moving duet with Rachelle Ferrell ("Nothing Has Ever Felt Like This").

what to buy next: In the liner notes for *Moods* 𝄞𝄞𝄞𝄞 (Mercury, 1995, prod. Will Downing, Rex Rideout, Ronnie Foster, Onaje Allan Gumbs), Downing confesses that he temporarily lost his passion for singing in early 1994. The result of a "rollercoaster of emotions," this collection is Downing's most personal to date, as evidenced by his having written or co-written seven of the album's 13 tracks.

the rest:
Will Downing 𝄞𝄞𝄞 (Island, 1988)
Come Together as One 𝄞𝄞𝄞 (Island, 1989)
Invitation Only N/A (Mercury, 1997)

worth searching for: Downing and Mica Paris cover the Donny Hathaway-Roberta Flack duet "Where Is the Love" on Paris's *So Good* 𝄞𝄞 (Island, 1989) album. The remake will almost make you forget the original. On the lighter side, Downing and his son, Will Jr., make a guest appearance on Sesame Street's *Splish Splash: Bath Time Fun* 𝄞𝄞𝄞 (Sony Wonder, 1995, prod. Christopher Cerf).

influences:
◀◀ Donny Hathaway, Nat "King" Cole, Luther Vandross, Ray Charles, Marvin Gaye, Aretha Franklin, Anita Baker

Dean Dauphinais

Downtown Science

Formed 1991, in New York, NY. Disbanded 1992.

Sam Sever, DJ; Bosco Money, vocals.

The most controversial topic in 1991 rap was the existence of the white rapper. With Vanilla Ice being criticized by 3rd Bass, which itself was never exactly safe from racial criticism, Ken "Bosco Money" Carabello seemed an odd choice as an MC for Sam Sever, who had produced the majority of the two 3rd Bass albums. Once people heard the music, though, all was at ease,

as Downtown Science had managed to capture the mood of the times—and summertime New York—perfectly.

what to buy: *Downtown Science* 𝄞𝄞𝄞 (Def Jam/Columbia, 1991, prod. Downtown Science) remains the duo's only album: in spite of such winning songs as "Room to Breathe," "This Is a Visit," and "Topic Drift," which feature some of Sam Sever's best production work, the group broke up the following year.

influences:
◀◀ 3rd Bass, Prince Paul
▶▶ Kurious

Jazzbo

The Dramatics

Formed early 1960s as the Dynamics, in Detroit, MI.

Ron Banks, lead vocals; L.J. Reynolds, lead vocals and second tenor (early 1972–80, 1986–present); Larry Demps, baritone vocals; Willie Ford, bass vocals; Lenny Mayes, second tenor; William Howard, vocals (1968–73); Elbert Wilkins, vocals (1968–73); Craig Reynolds, lead vocals and second tenor (1980–86).

Detroit during the 1960s had more talent than its record companies could handle. Since not all of the city's most gifted vocal groups could be accommodated by Motown, the Dynamics—the act that would become known as the Dramatics—initially recorded for a series of small labels before ending up on Wingate Records. When Motown purchased the Wingate label, Motown staff producer Don Davis went south to Stax/Volt and took the group, by this time renamed the Dramatics, with him. The quintet scored major R&B hits right out of the gate with "Whatcha See Is Whatcha Get," which made the Top 20 on both the R&B and pop charts, and the #1 soul ballad "In the Rain." The group then suffered through a spate of growing pains before settling into its permanent lineup, fronted by original member Ron Banks and later recruit L.J. Reynolds. Davis chose to curtail his production pace to pursue other business opportunities, enabling several others—among them Tony Hester, who penned "Whatcha See Is Whatcha Get," as well as Banks and Reynolds—to assume production reins. A splinter act eventually surfaced featuring original members Elbert Wilkens and Willie "Wee Gee" Howard, so in order to avoid confusion the group began billing itself as "The Dramatics featuring Ron Banks." Reynolds left in 1980 to concentrate on a solo career that never quite jelled, only to return in 1986. A lack of significant chart action during latter years has never deterred this durable unit, which continues to perform concert dates with clockwork regularity. Superstar rapper Snoop Doggy Dogg recently provided a huge and unlikely boost to the Dramatics' popularity among a new generation of fans by featuring them on his recordings and including them prominently in his music videos.

what to buy: The Dramatics are one of the most underrated vocal aggregations of all time, and *The Best of the Dramatics* ♪♪♪♪ (Volt, 1986, prod. various) shows just how powerful this group could be. Its signature hit "Whatcha See Is Whatcha Get," with its Latin-tinged groove, anchors this 16-song set, along with the haunting "In the Rain" and the message song "The Devil Is Dope," the latter showing more than a hint of the Temptations influence inevitable for any Detroit-based vocal group of this period. Ensemble singing is elevated to a new level on *Dramatically Yours* ♪♪♪ (Volt, 1973, prod. Don Davis), and although Banks and Reynolds carry most of the leads, all of the fellas get a chance to shine. Willie Ford's baritone punctuates "Toast to the Fool," and the lyrical interplay on "Highway to Heaven" glides with an "Under the Boardwalk" feel. The reissue *Me and Mrs. Jones* ♪♪♪♪ (MCA, 1994, prod. various) consolidates some of the Dramatics' best work ever, the highlight being a reworking of the Billy Paul megahit which actually eclipses the original. Also represented are "Be My Girl" from the group's *Joyride* LP and "Shake It Well," the title song from a 1977 ABC effort.

what to buy next: There's no absence of emotion on *Drama V* ♪♪♪♪ (ABC, 1975, prod. Don Davis), beginning with the stirring "Dramatic Theme" instrumental overture leading into "Treat Me Like a Man," on which everyone takes a turn on the lead. *The Dramatics Live* ♪♪♪ (Stax, 1988, prod. various) was recorded primarily in 1972 with the original lineup but also features cuts from a 1973 performance after the arrival of L.J. Reynolds. *The Dells vs. The Dramatics* ♪♪♪ (Cadet, 1974) teams the Dramatics with an equally outstanding vocal group, combining their talents for a 10-voice tour de force on the tracks "I'm in Love" and "Love Is Missing from Our Lives."

what to avoid: *Somewhere in Time* ♪♪ (Fantasy, 1986) falls far short of the Dramatic standard, mostly due to the absence of Reynolds. His replacement, Craig Jones, a fine singer in his own right, isn't capable of taking the material to the level of his predecessor.

the rest:
A Dramatic Experience ♪♪♪♪ (Volt, 1973)
The Dramatic Jackpot ♪♪♪ (ABC, 1975)
Joyride ♪♪♪♪ (MCA, 1976)
Shake It Well ♪♪♪♪ (ABC, 1977)

Do What You Wanna Do ♪♪♪ (ABC, 1978)
Anytime, Anyplace ♪♪ (MCA, 1979)
10.5 ♪♪♪♪ (MCA, 1980)
Positive State of Mind ♪♪♪♪ (Volt, 1989)

solo outings:
L.J. Reynolds:
Travellin' ♪♪♪ (Capitol, 1982)
Lovin' Man ♪♪ (Mercury, 1984)
Tell Me You Will ♪♪♪ (Fantasy, 1987)

Ron Banks & L.J. Reynolds:
Two of a Kind ♪♪ (Life, 1994).

influences:

◀◀ The Moonglows, Little Anthony and the Imperials, the Temptations

▶▶ Ready for the World, New Edition, Boyz II Men

Matt Lee

Dream Warriors

Formed in Canada.

Capitol Q; King Lou.

Along with Gang Starr, A Tribe Called Quest, and the Young Disciples, the Dream Warriors (Capitol Q and King Lou) were one of the driving forces behind hip-hop's early-'90s jazz infusion. But after a three-year hiatus, which saw the addition of two more members, and thanks to the fickleness of the hip-hop audience, the group fell out of favor with a once-adoring public.

what to buy: *And Now the Legacy Begins* ♪♪♪♪ (4th and B'Way, 1991, prod. Dream Warriors) is one of the seminal albums from hip-hop's *Rebirth of Cool* jazz era. "My Definition of a Boombastic Jazz Style" samples the brassy kitsch of an old Canadian game show and makes for a new way of creating music. You'd think the album might sound dated now, but the glowing innocence of songs like "Wash Your Face In My Sink" still resonate with optimism.

what to avoid: Three years is a lifetime in hip-hop, and waiting that long before releasing the follow up, *Subliminal Simulation* ♪ (EMI/Pendulum, 1994, prod. Dream Warriors) ultimately cost the group a shot at longevity. Of course, the group's attempt at publicizing its newfound, quasi-spiritual, cafe-induced intellectualism through promotional comic books and indecipherable liner notes didn't help, either.

worth searching for: In the early '90s, 4th and B'Way's U.K. division began issuing a series of *Rebirth of Cool* compilations focusing on contemporary soul, jazz, and jazz-inspired hip-hop. *Rebirth of Cool: Volume 2* 𝄞𝄞𝄞𝄞 (4th and B'Way UK, 1992, prod. various) features the spellbinding, UK-only single "I've Lost My Ignorance (and Don't Know Where to Find It)," which matches the Dream Warriors with Gang Starr. While the song also appears on *Subliminal Simulation*, this version is better.

influences:

◀◀ De La Soul, Gang Starr

▶▶ Arrested Development, Digable Planets

Jazzbo

The Drifters

Formed 1953, in New York, NY.

Key Lead Vocalists: Clyde McPhatter (1953–54); David Baughan (1954–55); Johnny Moore (1955–57, 1964–65); Bobby Hendricks (1957–58); Ben E. King (1959–60); Rudy Lewis (1961–64).

The Drifters are to doo-wop what Elvis Presley is to rock 'n' roll; it could have existed without them, but a big ol' chunk would be missing. The Drifters were actually two different groups of two different eras—the classic doo-wop of the McPhatter-Moore group of 1953–58 and the more pop-oriented lineups led by Ben E. King, Rudy Lewis, and Johnny Moore between 1959–64. Both incarnations were giants of their time; few groups, after all, could have survived the departure of a talent such as McPhatter, who sang lead on hits such as "Money Honey," "Honey Love," and "White Christmas." But the harmony lineup of the group proved they could go on, backing Moore on "Adorable," "Ruby Baby," and "You Promise to Be Mine." Manager George Treadwell disbanded the group in 1958 and signed the Five Crowns to perform as the Drifters. First King led the group on "There Goes My Baby," "This Magic Moment," and "Save the Last Dance for Me." Then Lewis took the lead for "Sweets for My Sweet," "Under the Boardwalk," and "On Broadway." Finally, Moore returned to the group in time for "Up on the Roof." Since about 1967, the Drifters have been more a name than a group, with makeshift lineups packaged to play the supper club and hotel circuit. At times there were two so-called Drifters groups playing at the same time, a sad way to carry on a truly legendary legacy.

what to buy: The Drifters that most will remember come through on *1959–1965 All-Time Greatest Hits and More* 𝄞𝄞𝄞𝄞𝄞 (Atlantic, 1988, prod. Bob Porter, Kim Cook), a compilation that's been re-engineered to put a new sheen on the group's immaculate harmonies. The other side of the coin gets its due on *Let the Boogie Woogie Roll* 𝄞𝄞𝄞𝄞 (Atlantic, 1988, prod. various) covering the harmony heavy doo-wop of the 1950s.

what to buy next: There are lots of crummy collections of the same rehashed songs available, but the three-disc set *Rockin' and Driftin': The Drifters Box* 𝄞𝄞𝄞𝄞 (Atlantic & Atco Remasters, 1996, prod. various) is excellent, rightly emphasizing the McPhatter years (and his solo work) and featuring a booklet full of great photos.

what to avoid: *Up on the Roof, Under the Boardwalk, and On Broadway* 𝄞𝄞𝄞 (Rhino, 1993, prod. various) trades on the title tunes, but after those three there's not a lot to recommend.

the rest:

16 Greatest Hits 𝄞𝄞𝄞𝄞 (Deluxe, 1987)
Greatest Hits 𝄞𝄞𝄞 (Hollywood/Rounder, 1987)
Live at Harvard University 𝄞𝄞 (Rose, 1993)
Save the Last Dance for Me 𝄞𝄞𝄞 (Avid, 1995)

worth searching for: *The Very Best of the Drifters* 𝄞𝄞𝄞𝄞 (Rhino, 1993, prod. Mike Stoller) compiles the hits and only the hits for those who just want to dance and not delve into the intricacies of doo-wop.

influences:

◀◀ The Ink Spots, the Orioles, the Ravens

▶▶ The Temptations, the Four Tops, the Parliaments, Boyz II Men

see also: *Clyde McPhatter, Ben E. King*

Lawrence Gabriel

D.R.S. (Dirty Rotten Scoundrels)

Formed late 1980s, in Sacramento, CA. Disbanded 1994.

Pick, vocals; Indo, vocals; Jail Bait, vocals; Deuce Deuce, vocals; Blunt, vocals.

Well before anybody had heard of Nate Dogg, L.V., or the rest of the gangsta crooners, the Dirty Rotten Scoundrels were already enjoying the view from atop the R&B charts, pouring out a little liquor for their dead homies in 1993's million-selling lost-ones lament "Gangsta Lean." Singing about gritty inner-city life from a decidedly insider's perspective, the all-male vocal group had previously caught the ears of both Hammer and Eazy-E, with Hammer helping the group nail a deal with Capitol. But after one hit—and one album—D.R.S. disbanded.

Creative mastermind Pick went on to form the Jackers with Indo, but the R&G group's long-completed debut has still yet to see release.

worth searching for: The lone D.R.S. album *Gangsta Lean* is no longer in print, but you can find the hit title track on the two-disc collection *Black Entertainment Television's 15th Anniversary Music Celebration* 🎵🎵🎵 (Rhino, 1996).

influences:

◀◀ Donny Hathaway, Marvin Gaye, N.W.A.

▶▶ L.V., Nate Dogg, Michael Speaks, Bone Thugs-N-Harmony

Josh Freedom du Lac

Dru Down

Coming straight from the pimp- and playa-filled streets of The East O (Oakland, California), Dru Down is cast in a similar mold as Oakland's nasty, master pimp-daddy, Too $hort. Like $hort, Dru Down and partner Chris Hicks started their own record label (C-Note) and began selling CDs and tapes out of their trunks. No fools, Relativity Records caught wind of the rising indie star and repackaged, retitled, and re-released his *Fools from the Streets* album a year later.

what to buy: The reissue, *Explicit Game* 🎵🎵🎵 (Relativity, 1994, prod. Ant Banks, others) is classic Oakland mack-hop. Thanks to some bumpin' production from the (regionally) legendary Ant Banks, Dru's "Pimp of the Year" became a popular street anthem and rejuvenated the East Oakland supafly ambiance Too $hort had sparked back in the '80s. The album also introduces the Luniz to the world.

what to buy next: Dru is still vying for pimp of the year honors, so *Can You Feel Me* 🎵🎵🎵 (Relativity, 1996, prod. DJ Fuze, others) is more of the same. The now-established Luniz check back in ("Freaks Come Out"), and master blaster Bootsy Collins lends his manic charm to "Baby Bubba."

worth searching for: The original version of Dru Down's debut, *Fools from the Streets* 🎵🎵🎵 (C-Note Records, 1993, prod. Ant Banks, others) contains several tracks that were ommited from the Relativity reissue.

influences:

◀◀ Ant Banks, Dangerous Dame, Richie Rich, Too $hort

▶▶ Luniz

Spence D.

Dru Hill

Formed 1993, in Baltimore, MD.

Mark "Sisqo" Andrews, vocals; James "Woody" Green, vocals; Tamir "Nokio" Ruffin, vocals; Larry "Jazz" Anthony Jr., vocals.

Contemporary R&B is littered with vocal groups who oversing and are undersexed. Dru Hill could easily fall into that trap if its four members didn't have such strong, restrained voices. Thinks Boyz II Men, or a tamer Jodeci. Taking its name from a historic district in its native Baltimore (Druid Hill), the group's confectionary sound can be traced to the fudge shop where they met, formed, and entertained the clientele. Originally a gospel group, Dru Hill went on to win several talent shows, including third place in the Apollo Theater's national competition. The quartet signed with Island Records, better known for European rock acts like U2 and various World Music groups, and tasted success out of the box with its first single, "Tell Me," which bumped former BLACKstreet singer David Hollister's version off the *Eddie* soundtrack.

what's available: The debut album, *Dru Hill* 🎵🎵🎵 (Island, 1996, prod. various), features the slow-building followup hit "In My Bed" and a radio-savvy production from a team that included New Jack innovator Keith Sweat, rap's Tim Dawg, Daryl Simmons, manager A. Haqq Islam, and member Nokio Ruffin.

influences:

◀◀ Boyz II Men, Jodeci, New Edition

Doug Pullen

Duice

L.A. Sno, vocals; Creo-D, vocals.

Booty hop isn't just about dropping bass; it's also about, well, *booty*. Duice's "Dazzey Duks," then, is prime booty hop, with its uptempo, bottom-heavy thump and, of course, bottom-obsessed lyrics. The 1992 song sold two million copies—mostly in the Southeast—before Duice ducked out of the spotlight.

worth searching for: The full-length *Dazzey Duks* 🎵🎵 album is out of print, but so what? A goofy ode to the sort of women's short shorts favored by TV's Daisy Duke, the "Dazzey Duks" single (Bellmark, 1992) is all the Duice you'll ever need.

influences:

◀◀ 2 Live Crew, Magic Mike, Afro Rican

▶▶ 95 South, 69 Boyz, 12 Gauge, Tag Team, A-Town Players, Ghost Town DJs, Quad City DJ's

Josh Freedom du Lac

George Duke
/The Clarke/Duke Project

George Duke (born January 12, 1946, in San Rafael, CA), keyboards, percussion, vocals; Stanley Clarke (born June 30, 1951, in Philadelphia, PA), acoustic and electric bass, vocals.

The most famous jazz Duke since Ellington, George Duke is one of the most prolific and eclectic musicians of his generation, continually redefining his range as a keyboardist, songwriter, singer, and producer. In addition to making his own trendsetting fusion LPs, both as a solo artist and partnered with preeminent bass master Stanley Clarke, his outside musical involvements have been so diverse—he toured with Frank Zappa and the Mothers of Invention, produced three LPs for Jeffrey Osborne, and played on Michael Jackson's *Off the Wall* album—that some jazz purists have accused him of abandoning his roots. But Duke is a jazz cat at his core: he often tells the story of how his mother took him to see Ellington in concert when he was four, an experience which sent him racing around his house yelling, "Get me a piano!" Heavily influenced by giants such as Miles Davis, Les McCann, and Cal Tjader, he graduated from the San Francisco Conservatory of Music and formed his first jazz combo with a young singer named Al Jarreau. Duke went on to blaze new trails in jazz with violinist Jean-Luc Ponty in his George Duke Trio; tour with sax great Cannonball Adderley and drummer Billy Cobham; and enjoy a series of successful solo funk-fusion LPs beginning in 1976 with *From Me to You*. Turning his interests to producing, Duke made his first vocal album with singer Dee Dee Bridgewater, then earned his breakthrough with the group A Taste of Honey when his production on their album yielded a #1 single on the R&B, pop, and AC charts in "Sukiyaki," selling over two million copies. He has since worked as producer and/or musician for many of popular music's brightest stars, ranging from Sarah Vaughan, Anita Baker, and Gladys Knight to the Winans, Keith Washington, and his cousin, Dianne Reeves. Duke joined forces with bassist Stanley Clarke—an accomplished musician in his own right as a sideman with such stars as Stan Getz and Pharoah Sanders, a founding member of Return to Forever, and a standout solo artist—in the funk duo the Clarke/Duke Project, and wrote and produced their #1 pop single, "Sweet Baby." Duke won a 1989 Grammy for producing the late Miles Davis's album *Tutu*; Clarke has shifted his focus in recent years to writing movie scores, including the 1992 Wesley Snipes blockbuster *Passenger 57*.

what to buy: The obvious choice here would be *The Best of George Duke* 🎵🎵🎵🎵 (Epic, 1996, prod. various), and it is a won-

drous work, assembling "Dukey Stick," "Reach for It," "Sweet Baby," and other key tracks from his solo albums and work with the Clarke/Duke Project. However, for a sensational example of Duke's dedication to and innovation within the jazz idiom, check out *Muir Woods Suite* 🎵🎵🎵🎵 (Warner Bros. 1996, prod. George Duke), a brilliant composition recorded live at the Montreaux Jazz Festival which glides between intimate jazz trio (with Clarke and drummer Chester Thompson) and full orchestra with electrifying interplay between the two.

what to buy next: The first of the three albums from *The Clarke/Duke Project* 🎵🎵🎵🎵 (Epic, 1981, prod. Stanley Clarke, George Duke) is arguably still the best, with the breath of new collaboration and experimentation inspiring such cuts as "Winners" and "Touch and Go" in addition to the duo's best-known hit, "Sweet Baby."

what to avoid: Of Duke's many pop-jazz confections, *Rendezvous* 🎵🎵 (Epic, 1995) is the most lightweight and disposable.

the rest:
Dream On 🎵🎵🎵 (Epic, 1982)
Don't Let Go 🎵🎵🎵🎵 (Legacy, 1990)
Stanley Clarke/George Duke 3 🎵🎵🎵 (Epic, 1990)
Reach for It 🎵🎵🎵 (Legacy, 1991)
Snapshot 🎵🎵🎵🎵 (Warner Bros., 1992)
Three Originals 🎵🎵 (Verve, 1993)
A Brazilian Love Affair 🎵🎵🎵🎵 (Legacy, 1994)
Clarke/Duke Project II 🎵🎵🎵🎵 (Epic, 1995)
Guardian of the Light 🎵🎵 (Epic, 1995)
Illusions 🎵🎵🎵 (Warner Bros., 1995)
Is Love Enough? 🎵🎵🎵🎵 (Warner Bros., 1997)

solo outings:
Stanley Clarke:
School Days 🎵🎵🎵 (Epic, 1976)
Let Me Know You 🎵🎵 (Epic, 1982)
Find Out! 🎵🎵🎵 (Epic, 1985)
Hideaway 🎵🎵🎵 (Portrait, 1986)
If This Bass Could Talk 🎵🎵🎵🎵 (Portrait, 1988)
Stanley Clarke 🎵🎵🎵🎵 (Epic, 1989)
Time Exposure 🎵🎵🎵 (Epic, 1989)
Journey to Love 🎵🎵🎵 (Epic, 1989)
Live 1976–1977 🎵🎵 (Epic, 1991)
Rocks, Pebbles and Sand 🎵 (Columbia, 1991)
Passenger 57: Original Soundtrack 🎵🎵 (Slamm Dunk, 1992)
East River Drive 🎵🎵 (Epic, 1993)
I Wanna Play for You 🎵🎵🎵 (Epic, 1994)
Children of Forever 🎵🎵 (One Way, 1994)
Live at the Greek 🎵🎵🎵🎵 (Slamm Dunk, 1994)
At the Movies 🎵🎵🎵 (Epic Soundtrax, 1995)
The Rite of Strings 🎵🎵🎵🎵 (Gai Saber, 1995)

influences:

◀◀ Cannonball Adderley, Miles Davis, Les McCann, Cal Tjader, Frank Zappa, Sonny Rollins, Chick Corea

▶▶ Al Jarreau, Jaco Pastorius, Patrice Rushen, Everette Harp, Dianne Reeves, Arrested Development

Stacey Hale

Dyke & the Blazers

Formed 1966, in Phoenix, AZ. Disbanded 1971.

Arlester "Dyke" Christian (born 1943, in Brooklyn, NY. Died March 13, 1971, in Los Angeles, CA.).

Dyke & the Blazers, though little remembered and never played on oldies R&B radio, are elemental in the canon of funk for being one of the first to slow the rhythm and emphasize the syncopation as early as 1966. Dyke began his career singing backing vocals and playing bass for the Blazers, the O'Jays' backing band, during their 1965 tour. Dyke and some other members of the Blazers were stranded in Phoenix when the O'Jays couldn't afford to bring the band back East. In order to make money, they enlisted local musicians to fill out the band and started playing the Phoenix club circuit. They were soon discovered by a couple of producers who cut a track that would secure the Blazers' place in history: "Funky Broadway—Pts. 1 & 2." Following the success of "Funky Broadway" (both the Blazers' original and Wilson Pickett's cover), the group cut an album of the same title. Mixing Pickett's Southern-fried sound and mid-1960s James Brown, Dyke created a ruff 'n' ready, raw, proto-funk soul that's as danceable as it is aggressive. Dyke and Original Sound president Art Laboe thought it beneficial to have Dyke record the follow-up records to the *Funky Broadway* album in L.A. The Los Angeles sessions featured members of the Soul Runners, a group that would back Charles Wright as the Watts 103rd Street Rhythm Band: bassist Melvin Dunlap, guitarist Al McKay (who went on to join Earth, Wind & Fire), and drummer James Gadson (who played on many of Motown's early Los Angeles-era sessions). In L.A., the raw groove became nastier and punchier, producing hits such as "We Got More Soul" and "Let a Woman Be a Woman—Let a Man Be a Man." Despite the groundbreaking music Dyke was creating in L.A., he always returned home to Phoenix, and it was in Phoenix that Dyke was shot and killed on March 13, 1971, on the street where he used to hang out.

worth searching for: As a fitting tribute to Dyke & the Blazers' contributions to funk, Kent Records issued *So Sharp!* 🎵🎵🎵🎵

(Kent/Ace U.K., 1991, prod. various), an exceptional compendium of hits, album tracks, and B-sides. The collection includes "Funky Broadway—Pts. 1 & 2," "We Got More Soul," and "Let a Woman Be a Woman—Let a Man Be a Man," but the accomplishments are the lesser-known cuts such as "Shotgun Slim," the 10-minute jam "The Wrong House," "Runaway People" (about the Blazers' inital stranding in Phoenix), and a version of the Isley Brothers' "It's Your Thing" that's as dangerous as a street fight. It's impossible to understand the evolution of funk without this collection of vital embryonic grooves.

influences:

◀◀ James Brown, Wilson Pickett, the O'Jays

▶▶ James Brown, Tower of Power, Charles Wright & the Watts 103rd St. Rhythm Band

Dana G. Smart

E

E-40 and the Click

Formed in Vallejo, CA.

E-40 (born Earl Stevens), vocals; Suga T, vocals; B-Legit, vocals; D-Shot, vocals.

One of the most infallible empires in hip-hop isn't based in Brooklyn or the Bronx or the gritty metropolises of Houston, Atlanta, or Los Angeles. Instead, you'll find it in the Northern California city of Vallejo, a previously little-known suburb that E-40 and his family-turned-crew the Click (brother B-Legit, sister Suga T, and cousin D-Shot) have transformed into the headquarters of their multi-million dollar enterprise in a story that would make even Horatio Alger proud. It began in 1987 when E-40 and B-Legit performed in an alumni talent show at Grambling State University (under the moniker the Intellectual Drifters). Music had always been a part of E-40's family, but the warm reception he and his brother encountered after the performance inspired the two to continue. D-Shot was just getting into rapping, and he, too, was interested in creating a rap group. So the three formed the Most Valuable Players. One year and one independent single under the MVP guise later, the three renamed themselves the Click, mapped out a new strategy and started the independent record label Sick Wid' It. The label's first release was the EP *Less Side*, which sold over

20,000 copies in the Bay Area. The members of the crew now readily admit that they dabbled in drug-dealing, saying that their collective desire to leave behind that illegal life increased exponentially when they realized how much money they could make in the music business. Eventually, the Click earned enough money—or, "scrilla" as E-40 likes to say—to record and manufacture their full-length debut, *Down and Dirty*, which sold an astonishing 300,000 (or so) copies. While successful on their own, the Click went national in 1994, signing with Jive what is believed to be one of the most lucrative distribution contracts in hip-hop history. With the deal, E-40 and the Click established a business franchise that's since been used as the model by burgeoning rap entrepreneurs all over the country.

what to buy: E-40 and the Click have sold millions of rap records, yet they remain outside the public's typical definition of what *real* hip-hop is, largely because their intoxicating organic, home-grown funk owes more to artists like the Temptations and Harold Melvin than the traditional rap resources. The crew has made a franchise out of keyboard-laced cruising music, with over a dozen records attributed to E-40, the Click, and their progenies. The record that started it all, the Click's *Down and Dirty* ♫♫♫♪ (Sick Wid' It/Jive, 1991/1994, prod. Studio Ton Capone, Mike Mosely, others), served as a blueprint for the music of other rappers in the region, but what really put E-40—and, thus, the Click—on the map was his solo EP, *The Mailman* ♫♫♫♪ (Sick Wid' It/Jive, 1993/1994, prod. Sam Bostic, Studio Ton, Mike Mosely, others). The song "Captain Save a Hoe" brought instant recognition to the Bay Area unit, as did E-40's mix of humor, realism, and musicianship. The song also shows off E-40's two most distinguishable traits: his liquid, lightning-fast rhyming style and knack for making up new words, which, together, can make his words sound like a river's soothing babble.

what to buy next: E-40's subsequent albums, *In a Major Way* ♫♫♫♪ (Sick Wid' It/Jive, 1995, prod. Mike Mosely, Studio Ton, others) and *Hall of Game* ♫♫♫♪ (Sick Wid' It/Jive, 1996, prod. Ant Banks, Studio Ton, others) provide a much tighter take on the same formula; on the two albums, it's evident E-40 is both comfortable with the music he's making and extremely canny, knowing exactly what people want to hear. As the other members of the Click released their albums individually—with Suga T being the most popular, partly due to her radiant looks—it seemed to make the whole unit exponentially better. An incredibly smooth and playful record, the group's latest, *Game Related* ♫♫♫♪ (Sick Wid' It/Jive, 1996, prod. Tone Capone, Mike Mosely, others), suggests that the crew can do no wrong.

the rest:
E-40:
Federal ♫♫♫♪ (Sick Wid' It/Jive, 1992/1994)

D-Shot:
Call Me on the Unda ♫♫♫♪ (Sick Wid' It, 1994)

B-Legit:
Trying to Get a Buck ♫♫♫♪ (Sick Wid' It/Jive, 1994)
Hemp Museum ♫♫♫♪ (Sick Wid' It/Jive, 1996)

Suga T:
Paper Chase ♫♫♫♪ (Sick Wid' It/Jive, 1996)

influences:
◀◀ Too $hort, KRS-One, Geto Boys, Spice 1

▶▶ JT the Bigga Figga, Celly Cel, Mac Mall, Young Lay

Jazzbo

Earth, Wind & Fire /Maurice White

Formed 1969, in Chicago, IL. Disbanded 1984. Re-formed 1987.

Maurice White, drums, vocals, kalimba; Philip Bailey, vocals, percussion (1972–present); Verdine White, bass; Donald Whitehead, keyboards (1969–72); Wade Felmons, vocals, keyboards (1969–72); Michael Beal, guitar, harmonica (1969–72); Yackov Ben Israel, percussion (1969–72); Chet Washington, tenor sax (1969–72); Alex Thomas, trombone (1969–72); Sherry Scott, vocals (1969–72); Larry Dunn, keyboards (1972–83); Ralph Johnson, percussion (1972–83); Roland Bautista, guitar (1972, 1981–84); Ronnie Laws, sax, flute (1972); Jessica Cleaves, vocals (1972); Andrew Woolfolk, soprano sax, flute (1973–present); Al McKay, guitar (1973–81); Sheldon Reynolds, guitar (1987–present); Johnny Graham, guitar (1973–83); Freddie White, drums (1974–75).

One of the most successful groups of the 1970s, EWF is a smooth funk band that plays songs, not just grooves. Anchored by blues/soul drummer Maurice White—a former Chess Records session drummer and a member of Ramsey Lewis's trio—and his brother Verdine on bass, the band soared on Philip Bailey's angelic falsetto and a series of well-written and sumptuously crafted singles that made the most of the group's formidable instrumental skills. Embellishing the catchy tunes and propulsive rhythms is a nebulous but colorful Afrocentric cosmology, a motif that also enlivens the album covers and the concerts, which are vast communal affairs of astonishing precision and compelling impact. The group adjusted easily to disco, but further developments in R&B left it behind as it was unwilling to jettison elements that had worked so well for so long. Bailey already had a florishing solo career by the time the group broke up in 1984, and the 1987 come back album sounded more like vintage EWF than subsequent efforts. The group continues to tour, with either Maurice White or Bailey (whose falsetto, though still impressive, isn't what it used to be) acting as frontman and Verdine usually on bass, and remains an impressive concert experience. The band's first new studio album in four years, *In the Name of Love*, finally manages a slight accomodation with rap that isn't too awkward, and marks a dramatic upturn in song quality and the players' apparent enthusiasm.

what to buy: The big hit on *Spirit* ✍✍✍✍ (Columbia, 1976, prod. Maurice White, Charles Stepney) was "Getaway," but it's the album's seamlessness that stands out—as well as Bailey's greatest vocal performance, "Imagination." *All 'n' All* ✍✍✍✍ (Columbia, 1977, prod. Maurice White) has "Serpentine Fire" (one of the most original funk tracks EWF made), a strong Brazilian flavor (Paulinho da Costa, Eddie Del Barrio, and Deodato contribute) and "Fantasy." *The Eternal Dance* ✍✍✍✍ (Columbia Legacy, 1992, prod. various) is a nicely packaged three-CD box with not only all the pop-chart hits (if far from all the band's good tracks) but also 14 previously unreleased items.

what to buy next: *Head to the Sky* ✍✍✍✍ (Columbia, 1973, prod. Joe Wissert) is great except for the long closing instrumental, with "Keep Your Head to the Sky" and "Evil" pointing toward the group's future sound. *Open Our Eyes* ✍✍✍✍ (Columbia, 1974, prod. Earth, Wind & Fire) doesn't have many hits, but is a wonderfully coherent yet also varied album. *That's the Way of the World* ✍✍✍✍ (Columbia, 1975, prod. Sig Shore) boasts the seminal hits "Reasons" and "Shining Star," while *I Am* ✍✍✍✍ (ARC/Columbia, 1979, prod. Maurice White) moved smoothly into the disco era with "Boogie Wonderland," "In the Stone," and the slow groove "After the Love Is Gone."

what to avoid: *Last Days and Time* ✍ (Columbia, 1972, prod. Joe Wissert) misfires with covers of "Where Have All the Flowers Gone" and "Make It with You," and the originals are even less memorable. *Faces* ✍ (ARC/Columbia, 1980) is rather faceless; bland and overlong are a bad combination. *Heritage* ✍ (ARC/Columbia, 1990, prod. various) uses a wide variety of producers in a desperate effort to seem contemporary and relevent. Two guest spots by M.C. Hammer are particularly pathetic.

the rest:
Earth, Wind & Fire ✍✍ (Warner Bros., 1971/1996)
The Need of Love ✍✍ (Warner Bros., 1971/1996)

Gratitude ✍✍✍✍ (Columbia, 1975)
The Best of Earth, Wind & Fire, Vol. 1 ✍✍✍ (ARC/Columbia, 1978)
Raise ✍✍✍ (ARC/Columbia, 1981)
Powerlight ✍✍ (ARC/Columbia, 1983)
Electric Universe ✍✍✍ (ARC/Columbia, 1983)
Touch the World ✍✍ (ARC/Columbia, 1987)
The Best of Earth, Wind & Fire, Vol. 2 ✍✍ (ARC/Columbia, 1988)
Millenium ✍✍ (Reprise, 1993)
Elements of Love: The Ballads ✍✍✍✍ (Columbia, 1996)
Let's Groove: A Dance Collection ✍✍✍ (TriStar, 1996)
Greatest Hits Live ✍✍✍ (Pyramid/Rhino, 1996)
In the Name of Love ✍✍✍ (Pyramid/Rhino, 1997)

worth searching for: The Ramsey Lewis album *Sun Goddess* ✍✍✍ (Columbia, 1974, prod. Teo Macero, Ramsey Lewis, others) puts EWF members in his fusiony pop-jazz context on a number of tracks, and they play as a group on the title track, which Maurice White produced.

solo outings:
Maurice White:
Maurice White ✍✍ (Columbia, 1985)

influences:

◀◀ James Brown, Sly & the Family Stone, the Ohio Players

▶▶ The Brothers Johnson, Brand New Heavies, Incognito, Kim Pensyl

Steve Holtje

Sheena Easton

Born Sheena Shirley Orr, April 27, 1959, in Bellshill, near Glasgow, Scotland.

To look at this petite, fair-skinned Scottish beauty, one would be hard pressed to believe she'd even be *reading* an R&B music guide, much less be included in one. But the 5-foot-nothing, 1980s phenom, unlike other white women of recent vintage who have attained their musical fame in rhythm & blues (Teena Marie, Lisa Stansfield), ascended to soul prominence not by the emotion of her voice, but by the enterprise of her producers. Learning to sing without her thick brogue by imitating classic Motown singles imported from America, Easton started down her road to success while studying at the Royal Scottish Academy of Music and Drama, where she was chosen to be the focus of a BBC documentary called *The Big Time,* about the making of a pop recording star. Moving her base of operations from Scotland to London after graduation, Easton's widespread TV exposure helped her land a contract with EMI Records and subsequently become the first artist to have two Top 10 singles in the U.K. ("Modern Girl" and "Nine to Five") at the same time since Ruby Murray in 1956. She released her debut U.S. album, *Sheena Easton*, in 1981 to even greater success, selling over a million copies, hitting #1 on the singles charts with "Morning Train (Nine to Five)" (renamed to avoid confusion with Dolly Parton's movie theme), and claiming the Grammy as Best New Artist. She was invited to sing the title song on the James Bond movie *For Your Eyes Only*, the only singer ever to have her face shown during the opening credits of a Bond blockbuster. Her popularity skyrocketing, from 1982 to 1985 Easton headlined a worldwide concert tour; recorded #1-charting duets with Kenny Rogers (the Bob Seger classic "We've Got Tonight") and Mexican crooner Luis Miguel; starred in her own NBC-TV special, *Sheena Easton . . . Act One*; won an Emmy award; released four albums, none selling less than gold; earned a Grammy for Best Mexican-American Performance (for the Miguel duet "Me Gustas Tal Como Eres" on her Spanish language LP *Todo Me Recuerda A Ti*—a remarkable accomplishment considering she didn't know Spanish); and became the only artist in history to score Top 5 singles on the R&B, Pop, Country, AC, and Dance charts. In her spare moments, she found time to take on Tipper Gore's Family Resource Center over the blushingly suggestive lyrics of her Artist-Then-Known-as-Prince-penned hit, "Sugar Walls." That single gave her acceptance in America's R&B community, and her sudden celebrity in the genre enticed her to experiment even further by recruiting producers like Narada Michael Walden and working with Prince on several more projects, including the Grammy-nominated duet "U Got the Look" and her appearance in the concert movie *Sign O' the Times*. Refusing to rest on her musical laurels, Easton used her early dramatic training to establish TV, film, and theater careers with the Broadway plays *Man of LaMancha, Les Miserables,* and *Grease*, a five-year recurring TV role as Don Johnson's wife in *Miami Vice* and film work in *Indecent Proposal* and *All Dogs Go to Heaven 2*. The diminutive dynamo still shows no signs of slowing down, constantly writing songs for her music publishing company Skye Heart, releasing albums all over the world, acting, and spending QT with her two adopted children, Jake and Skylar.

what to buy: Of her decidedly R&B-flavored LPs, *The Lover in Me* ♪♪♪ (MCA, 1990, prod. Prince) displays Easton's most concentrated effort in the form. Standout songs like the title track and "101" (another Prince composition) demonstrate just how versatile this pint-sized powerhouse can be. For a more comprehensive overview of the singer, *Sheena Easton: Greatest

word up!

THe Creator gave us all something great. It's just a matter of tapping into that greatness, taking the time, taking a good look. . . . It's very easy to discover. That's what I've been trying to share in the music all these years.

**Maurice White
(of Earth, Wind & Fire)**

Hits ♪♪♪ (CEMA Special Products, 1997, prod. various) contains more than enough Sheena for any newcomer; in fact, since it includes the lusty hits "Sugar Walls" and "Strut," it could be too much for novices to handle.

what to buy next: *No Strings* ♪♪♪ (MCA, 1993, prod. Patrice Rushen) is a pleasant divergence from Easton's usual dance-pop presentation. The Scottish sexpot turns chanteuse here, caressing a collection of jazz and American show tunes to reinforce her desire to be regarded as one of the more versatile vocalists of our time.

what to avoid: *My Cherie* ♪♪ (MCA, 1995, prod. various), an album that catches Easton in transition between Prince puppet and classic songstress, has little quality material to offer as a result.

the rest:
Best of Sheena Easton ♪♪♪ (EMI America, 1989)
What Comes Naturally ♪♪♪♪ (UNI/MCA, 1991)
Sheena! ♪♪♪ (CEMA Special Products, 1992)
The World of Sheena Easton: The Singles ♪♪♪ (EMI America, 1993)

worth searching for: The Japanese import *No Sound But a Heart* ♫♫♫ (1997) contains material so far unreleased in the States and signals an even deeper maturation of Easton's vocal skills.

influences:

◄◄ Aretha Franklin, Diana Ross & the Supremes, Martha & the Vandellas, Little Eva, Lulu, Teena Marie, Barbra Streisand, Prince

►► Taylor Dayne, Celine Dion, Toni Braxton, Lisa Stansfield

Andre McGarrity

Eazy-E

Born Eric Wright, September 7, 1963, in Compton, CA. Died March 26, 1995.

Many of Eazy-E's songs about inner-city street life were full of violence and rage, but Eazy himself was full of something else (no, not *that*). Contradictions. Consider: Eazy often lashed out against the police in his music, especially on the highly controversial N.W.A. song "Fuck tha Police." But on his own, he decided to make statements on behalf of Theodore J. Briseno, one of the Los Angeles police officers charged with beating motorist Rodney King. The short rapper, who fancied himself an anti-establishment street soldier in song, also paid $2,490 to join the Republican Senatorial Inner Circle in 1991, a move that allowed him to attend a luncheon speech by then-President Bush, who wasn't exactly a fan of gangsta rap. Still, Wright, who was 31 when he died of AIDS-related pneumonia, will not be remembered for his inconsistencies. Instead, he'll be remembered as a pioneer—the unofficial leader of N.W.A., one of the most influential rap groups ever. Ironically, though, Eazy was probably the least-talented member of the seminal West Coast gangsta group. He didn't write lyrics (that was left to Ice Cube and MC Ren, plus associate D.O.C.). He didn't produce the music (see Yella and, especially, Dr. Dre). And his whiny, high-pitched voice was easily the least tolerable of the bunch. But Eazy still played an important role in N.W.A., bankrolling its early recordings and starting up Ruthless Records to distribute them. And his marketing savvy was instrumental in making N.W.A. one of the more successful independent acts in hardcore rap.

what to buy: Though Eazy's voice becomes grating in large doses, the posthumous best-of collection *Eternal E* ♫♫♫ (Priority, 1995, prod. Dr. Dre, DJ Yella, Eazy-E, Naughty by Nature, Cold

Sheena Easton (© Ken Settle)

187um, others) is still an album that every fan of West Coast gangsta rap should have. Rough and raunchy, furious and funny, gross and graphic, the utterly unapologetic recording includes just the right amount of material from Eazy's career, opening with the early N.W.A. classic "Boyz-N-the Hood" and including the solo tunes "We Want Eazy," "Nobody Move," and "Niggaz My Height Don't Fight." Steer clear, though, of the so-misogynist-they-hurt tracks "I'd Rather Fuck You" and "Automobile."

what to avoid: After all the Ice Cube diss songs N.W.A. recorded after the talented writer-vocalist left the group, you'd think that Eazy might have finally washed that bitter, vindictive taste out of his filthy mouth. Nope. On the EP *It's On (Dr. Dre) 187Um Killa* **woof!** (Ruthless, 1993, prod. Cold 187um, Yella, others), Eazy finds himself obsessed with the latest N.W.A. runaway, Dr. Dre, "dedicating" the album to him and firing off "Real Muthaphuckkin' Gs," which isn't anywhere near as effective as Dre's Eazy diss, "Dre Day."

the rest:

Eazy-Duz-It ♫♫ (Ruthless/Priority, 1988)
5150 Home 4 tha Sick ♫ EP (Ruthless/Priority, 1992)
Str8 Off Tha Streetz of Muthaphukkin Compton ♫ (Ruthless/Relativity, 1996)

influences:

◄◄ N.W.A., Ice Cube

►► Bushwick Bill, Bone Thugs-N-Harmony, Above The Law, Kokane, BG Knoccout

see also: *N.W.A.*

Josh Freedom du Lac

Ed O.G. and Da Bulldogs

Formed in Boston, MA.

Ed O.G. (born Edward Anderson), vocals.

As one of the first rappers to put Boston's Roxbury borough on the map, Ed O.G. and his crew, Da Bulldogs, represent a simpler time in hip-hop, when lyrics delivered observation rather than fiction.

what's available: Ed O.G.'s first album, *Life of a Kid in the Ghetto* ♫♫ (Mercury, 1991, prod. Awesome 2) has several songs that fans of hip-hop radio shows and early *Yo! MTV Raps* should remember: "Be a Father to Your Child," "I Got to Have It," and the irreverent "Bug-A-Boo." On *Roxbury 02119* ♫ (Chemistry/Mercury, 1994, prod. Awesome 2, Diamond D, Prince Rakeem), Ed is just another rapper (insincerely) trying to sound harder than he really is. The album does, however, feature "Love Comes and Goes" (a heartfelt classic that's closer to Ed's original style) and "As Long as You Know" (one of the first tracks Prince Rakeem the RZA produced outside the Wu-Tang fold).

worth searching for: The "Love Comes and Goes" single (Chemistry/Mercury, 1994) includes "Easy Comes and Goes," an otherwise unreleased song featuring Last Poet Umar Bin Hassan reciting verse over a swaying, jazz-tinged groove. Find it if you can.

influences:

◀◀ Craig G, Masta Ace

▶▶ Special Ed

Jazzbo

Dennis Edwards

See: The Temptations

Eightball & MJG

Formed in early 1990s in Houston, TX.

Eightball, vocals; MJG, vocals.

If the sun rises in the East but sets in the West, as Ice Cube so joyfully noted, then what happens in that vast space in between? Something crazy's going on out there, for sure, because toughened rap artists have been leaping onto the national map from all spots in between in the past few years, from Cleveland's Bone Thugs-N-Harmony and Chicago's Crucial Conflict to the Big Easy's Mystikal and Houston's Eightball & MJG. Of course, hardcore rappers from the Lone Star State are nothing new. The Geto Boys put Texas on the rap map in 1990 by kicking frightening rhymes about the Fifth Ward while also kicking up a shitstorm of controversy, and junior g's have been filtering from the state ever since. Few of the post-Geto boys have had as much success, though, as Eightball & MJG, who released two regional hit albums for the Houston label Suave before their appropriately titled third recording, *On Top of the World*, debuted at #8 on *Billboard*'s national pop albums chart and at #2 on the R&B chart in late 1995.

what to buy: Those looking for a sonic reference point could consider sub-dubbing the duo Houston's Most Wanted featuring (MC) Eightball, but that would be overstating 8's contributions while grossly downplaying MJG's. *On Top of the World* 𝄢𝄢𝄢𝄢 (Suave/Relativity, 1995, prod. various), for instance, shows the brooding duo at its mike-passing peak, laying intricately weaved air-tight ghetto rhymes over southern-fried funk grooves and beats. In both the old and new schools, they call this sort of vocal magic "chemistry." And although a nice sales point, guest spots from the Bay Area's E-40 and Mac Mall and fellow Texas gangstas South Circle and Big Mike simply interrupt the vocal interplay.

the rest:

Comin' Out Hard 𝄢𝄢 (Suave/Relativity, 1993)
On the Outside Looking In 𝄢𝄢 (Suave/Relativity, 1994)

influences:

◀◀ Geto Boys, Compton's Most Wanted featuring MC Eiht, N.W.A., South Circle

▶▶ Tela, 3-2, UGK, 5th Ward Boyz, Crime Boss

Josh Freedom du Lac

The El Dorados

Formed 1952, in Chicago, IL.

Pirkle Lee Moses Jr., first lead and tenor; Louis Bradley, second lead and tenor; Jewel Jones, tenor and baritone; James Maddox, baritone; Robert Glasper, bass. Subsequent members included: John McCall, tenor; Douglas Brown, second tenor; Arthur Bassett, baritone; Teddy Long, baritone; Richard Nickens, bass; John Carter, bass.

A quintet of teenagers on the South Side of Chicago attracted the attention of the custodian in their high school, not because they were vandalizing the halls, but because the harmonies they created while singing in those hallways were mesmerizing. The custodian, Johnny Moore, became their manager, and for a while they were called the Five Stars, even after they grew to have six members. They changed their name to the El Dorados (adapting the name of a popular Cadillac model) and won a local talent show, thereby earning themselves a recording deal with Chicago's powerhouse Vee-Jay Records. In September 1955, the El Dorados' third single for Vee-Jay, "At My Front Door," became one of the great doo-wop jump tunes of all time, a #1 R&B hit that crossed over to #17 on the *Billboard* pop chart (earning them an appearance on *The Ed Sullivan Show*) and might well have risen higher had Pat Boone not rushed to cover the song and ride it to #7 himself. Nevertheless, the song became both an R&B and rock standard. The El Dorados' follow-up, "I'll Be Forever Loving You," was the group's only other national chart record (#10 R&B); though they released nearly a dozen more singles on Vee-Jay, they never came close to approaching the success of "At My Front Door." The El Dorados had much tighter harmony than most doo-wop groups of the era, made some great records, and stirred the hearts and ears of many fans during their memorable recording life.

what to buy: The 25-song compilation *Bim Bam Boom* ♫♫♫♫ (Vee-Jay, 1992, prod. Calvin Carter)—named after a 1956 jump tune the El Dorados cut to imitate their own record, an earlier single called "A Fallen Tear"—collects virtually all of the group's significant songs (a few lesser B-sides, like "A Rose for My Darling," are absent but not missed), with previously unreleased versions of "Annie's Answer" with female singer Hazel McCollum, "She Don't Run Around," and "Rock 'n' Roll's for Me." Their underrated ballad "I Began to Realize" is one of the most beautiful and textured slow songs of the era. To hear the El Dorados in the context of their times, "I'll Be Forever Loving You" is included in the exceptional Rhino box set *The Doo Wop Box II: 101 More Vocal Group Gems from the Golden Age of Rock 'n' Roll* ♫♫♫♫ (Rhino, 1995, prod. Bob Hyde, Walter DeVenne).

influences:

◀◀ The Soul Stirrers, the Midnighters, the Five Blind Boys, the Dominoes, the Orioles

▶▶ The Spaniels, the Flamingos, the Kool Gents, the Dells, the Chi-Lites, the Five Echoes, Johnnie Taylor

Michael Kosser

Electro Funk

Aside from Afrika Bambaataa, electro funk artists haven't received much recognition from hip-hop historians. But for a time during the mid-1980s, electro was the music of choice of West Coast breakdancers, with Cybotron's "Clear," Twighlight 22's "Electric Kingdom," Jonzun Crew's "Pack Jam," Newcleus's "Jam On It," Planet Patrol's "Play at Your Own Risk," and Egyptian Lover's "Egypt Egypt" all in heavy rotation on street-corner boom boxes, or anywhere else there was a piece of linoleum on the floor and a group of kids sporting nylon Puma suits and fat-laced shoes and getting ready to throw down.

what to buy: All of these tracks are included on *Street Jams: Electric Funk, Parts 1–4* ♫♫♫♫ (1996, prod. various), a fascinating and exhaustive anthology that's brimming with digitized vocals, creative rhythmic foundations, burbling synthesizers, and furious turntable antics. The Afrika Bambaataa classics "Planet Rock" and "Looking for the Perfect Beat" are included here, too, along with a host of other tracks you wouldn't have heard of unless you were there on the corner, busting a Kurt Thomas. Of course, if this set doesn't play like a thrilling flashback to you, the four discs are available individually, with the first two stronger than

the others. And about that historical import? Just know that that there'd also be no Miami bass without electro funk.

Josh Freedom du Lac

Duke Ellington

Born Edward Kennedy Ellington, April 29, 1899, in Washington, DC. Died May 24, 1974, in New York, NY.

If you haven't heard of Duke Ellington, you were obviously placed in suspended animation in the 19th century and were unfrozen only yesterday. Even people who listen to Muzak all day long and never know the names of the composers who penned the pasteurized tunes know who Duke Ellington is. Ellington is quite possibly the greatest musician and composer of the 20th century—certainly one of the top five. As a composer, he wrote thousands of songs and arranged and rearranged those and others his whole life. He wrote his songs for the individual musicians in his orchestra and not for "sections." As a bandleader, he performed nearly constantly for most of his career. As a musician, he was a giant, considered one of the best pianists of his era. And unlike most of his contemporaries, he was able to update his work, modernizing it to blend into the sound of the decade in which he was creating. Ellington's orchestra was his main vehicle, and he worked with "his" orchestra—though it changed constantly—throughout his career, recording more than 200 albums, currently available, with more collections and newly reissued work coming out annually, as if he hadn't died in 1974. He started studying the piano at the age of seven, adopting the nickname "Duke" around the same time. Every one of his family friends knew he was destined to be great. Drawn by the ragtime music of the time, he became a musician. Ellington joined the music world in 1917 with the biggest ad in the telephone yellow pages and a desire to be a bandleader despite his then-limited repertoire. The ad worked, and he was soon heading up several Washington, D.C.-area bands. He worked on his technique by analyzing fingering from slowed-down piano rolls. In 1923, he ventured to New York and soon formed the Washingtonians with friends. He landed the band a job at the Hollywood Club, where they began to play regularly and where Bubber Miley helped Ellington create the "jungle sound" that made his group distinct. After some struggles to find the right sound or breakthrough music, Duke Ellington and His Orchestra was born around 1926 with hot numbers like "East St. Louis Toodleoo" and "Birmingham Breakdown." The very next year, the group scored its break, earning a permanent spot at the Cotton Club on the strength of numbers such as "Black and Tan Fantasy" and "Creole Love Call." From there, Ellington and crew began radio broadcasts and became famous throughout the country. By the time the Great Depression struck, Ellington had found the road to success so that hardship did not really affect him. He never again lacked work or suffered through hard times. He was a celebrity and one of the greatest performers in the world. During the 1930s, he built his band up with eight soloists—most bands didn't even have three—and left the Cotton Club in 1931 for greener pastures. The Ellington Orchestra hit the road and became a big act throughout the country and soon throughout the world, touring Europe and Sweden in 1933 and 1939. By 1940, Duke Ellington's Orchestra was the greatest in the world, featuring newly acquired musicians like Ben Webster on tenor sax, Jimmy Blanton on bass, and Billy Strayhorn as an arranger and composer—all of whom, like many of the musicians who worked with Ellington, would go on to become some of the greatest names in jazz music. His 1940–42 band was one of his best, and Ellington added many songs to his repertoire during those years that would become lifelong standards—"Take the 'A' Train," "Perdido," and "The 'C' Jam Blues," among others. Ellington gave his first performance at Carnegie Hall in 1943, debuting "Black, Brown and Beige." As the 1940s killed the big bands and bebop rose to prominence, Ellington continued to perform, tour, and record with his orchestra. The 1950s is considered his "slump" decade, even though his artistic output was never stronger, and it was simply the illusion of waning commercial success. In 1956, Duke soared back into the spotlight at the Newport Jazz Festival. During the 1960s, Duke dabbled in religious music and collaborated with jazz greats who had not started under his wing, including Charles Mingus, Max Roach, Count Basie, John Coltrane, and Louis Armstrong. Ellington continued to tour and record extensively throughout the 1960s despite his age and received the recognition he so richly deserved. He outlasted many of his closest working partners, including Billy Strayhorn and Johnny Hodges, and he continued making music despite the deaths of his associates and friends, updating the orchestra and persevering until 1974 when, stricken with cancer, he died a month after his 75th birthday. With Duke Ellington's passing, one of the greatest musicians of the 20th century was lost to the world. Ironically, though he is one of the most widely known artists, there is still much that is unknown about the man personally. He was reticent to speak about his life, and he is conspicuously absent as a character in his own autobiography, *Music Is My Mistress*. Ellington was an even-tempered man, some said almost saintly in demeanor. Even in the face of obvious prejudice—for example, when the Pulitzer Prize committee of 1965 denied him a special lifetime achievement award, overruling its own official judges—Ellington was unphased, saying, "Fate doesn't want me to be famous too young." He was 66 years old when he said that.

what to buy: Ellington and his orchestra performed all over the world, thousands of times. And though each performance couldn't be the greatest ever, there were nights when the crew reached a unique level of inspiration and craft. *All Star Road Band Vol. 2* ♪♪♪♪ (Signature, 1957/CBS Special Products, 1990) is one such occasion. At a dance one evening in Chicago in 1964, Ellington and his orchestra rocked the hall and tried out some new arrangements of the standards. He got superb solo work from trumpeters Cootie Williams and Cat Anderson, trombonists Lawrence Brown and Buster Cooper, and the entire saxophone section. This is a great one. Ellington revitalized his career with *Ellington at Newport* ♪♪♪♪ (Columbia, 1956/1987, prod. George Avakian), a big commercial comeback for the musician. "Diminuendo and Crescendo in Blue" was one of the concert's most intense tunes, and the 27-chorus blues marathon solo by Paul Gonslaves drove the audience wild, so much so that there was nearly a riot. Ellington made worldwide news as a result and was back on top of the music world.

what to buy next: *All Star Road Band* ♪♪♪♪ (Signature, 1964/1989) is not as wild as Vol. 2, but it's enjoyable and fun and includes Ellington's best standards, such as "Take the A Train," "Mood Indigo," and "Sophisticated Lady." This is an all-star orchestra and an all-star performance. Then, if you're looking for a good sampler of the Duke's works, try *Compact Jazz: And Friends* ♪♪♪♪ (Verve, 1987, prod. Norman Granz), a hot collection with a variety of the best of jazz and blues musicians working with Ellington, including Ella Fitzgerald, Ben Webster, Johnny Hodges, Oscar Peterson, and Dizzy Gillespie. *The 1952 Seattle Concert* ♪♪♪♪ (RCA, 1954/1995, prod. Jack Lewis) is another fine live recording, with great back-up and impressive versions of "Skin Deep," "Sultry Serenade," "Sophisticated Lady," and "Perdido," not to mention a sublime rendering of "Harlem Suite."

what to avoid: There's really no bad Ellington. But when it comes to collections, there are some that are clearly not the best places to start. *16 Most Requested Songs* ♪♪♪♪ (Columbia/Legacy, 1994, prod. various) is just too incomplete to serve as an introduction to his career.

best of the rest:
Duke Ellington Presents . . . ♪♪♪♪♪ (Bethlehem, 1956/1995)
Ellington Jazz Party ♪♪♪♪♪ (Columbia, 1959)
The Great Paris Concert ♪♪♪♪♪ (Atlantic, 1963/1989)

(With Ray Brown) *This One's for Blanton—Duets* 🎵🎵🎵🎵 (Original Jazz Classics, 1972/1994)

Duke's Big Four 🎵🎵🎵🎵 (Pablo, 1973/1988)

Duke Ellington: The Blanton-Webster Band, 1939–1942 🎵🎵🎵🎵🎵 (Bluebird, 1986)

(With Coleman Hawkins) *Duke Ellington meets Coleman Hawkins* 🎵🎵🎵🎵🎵 (MCA, 1986)

(With Johnny Hodges) *Side by Side* 🎵🎵🎵🎵🎵 (Verve, 1986)

Money Jungle—1962 🎵🎵🎵🎵🎵 (Blue Note, 1986)

(With Count Basie) *First Time: The Count meets the Duke—1961* 🎵🎵🎵🎵🎵 (Columbia, 1987)

Uptown—Early 1950s 🎵🎵🎵🎵🎵 (Columbia, 1987)

The Duke Ellington Orchestra: Digital Duke 🎵🎵🎵🎵 (GRP, 1987)

Walkman Jazz/Compact Jazz 🎵🎵🎵🎵 (Verve, 1988)

Black, Brown, & Beige 1944–46 🎵🎵🎵🎵 (Bluebird, 1988)

Blues in Orbit—1960 🎵🎵🎵🎵🎵 (Columbia, 1988)

Duke Ellington & John Coltrane 🎵🎵🎵🎵🎵 (MCA/Impulse, 1988)

The Piano Album 🎵🎵🎵🎵🎵 (Capitol, 1989)

Braggin' in Brass: The Immortal 1938 Year 🎵🎵🎵🎵 (Portrait Masters, 1989)

Ellington Indigos: Sept–Oct. 1957 🎵🎵🎵🎵🎵 (Columbia, 1989)

The Private Collection, Vols. 1–4 🎵🎵🎵🎵🎵 (Saja, 1989)

The Private Collection, Vol. 5: "The Suites" 1968 🎵🎵🎵🎵🎵 (Saja, 1989)

The Private Collection, Vols. 6-10: Dance Dates, California, 1958 🎵🎵🎵🎵🎵 (Saja, 1989)

The Best of Duke Ellington 🎵🎵🎵🎵 (Signature, 1989)

New Mood Indigo 🎵🎵🎵🎵 (Signature, 1989)

Solos, Duets, & Trios 🎵🎵🎵🎵 (Bluebird, 1990)

The Jungle Band: The Brunswick Era, Vol. 2 (1929–1931) 🎵🎵🎵🎵 (Decca Jazz, 1990)

The Intimacy of the Blues 1967 & 1970 🎵🎵🎵🎵 (Fantasy, 1991)

1924–1927 🎵🎵🎵🎵🎵 (Classics, 1991)

Up in Duke's Workshop—1969–1972 🎵🎵🎵🎵 (Fantasy, 1991)

The Essence of Duke Ellington: I Like Jazz 🎵🎵🎵🎵 (Columbia, 1991)

Duke Ellington's My People 🎵🎵🎵🎵 (Red Baron, 1992)

Sophisticated Lady: Masters of the Big Bands 🎵🎵🎵🎵🎵 (Bluebird, 1992)

Duke Ellington & His Orchestra: Jazz Cocktail: 1928–1931 🎵🎵🎵🎵 (ASV Living Era, 1992)

Live at the Blue Note—1952 🎵🎵🎵🎵 (Bandstand, 1992)

Duke Ellington Vol. 4: 1928 🎵🎵🎵🎵 (MA Recordings, 1992)

The Pianist 1966, 1970 🎵🎵🎵🎵🎵 (Fantasy, 1992)

1937 w/Chick Webb 🎵🎵🎵🎵 (Classics, 1993)

Original Hits, Vol. 1: 1927–31 🎵🎵🎵🎵🎵 (King Jazz, 1993)

Original Hits, Vol. 2: 1931–38 🎵🎵🎵🎵🎵 (King Jazz, 1993)

The Great London Concerts—1964 🎵🎵🎵🎵 (MusicMasters, 1993)

Duke Ellington and His Orchestra—1938, Vol. 2 🎵🎵🎵🎵 (Classics, 1993)

Duke Ellington and His Orchestra—1938, Vol. 3 🎵🎵🎵🎵 (Classics, 1993)

In the Twenties—Jazz Archives No. 63 🎵🎵🎵🎵🎵 (EPM, 1993)

Things Ain't What They Used to Be 🎵🎵🎵🎵🎵 (LRC, 1993)

Things Ain't What They Used to Be/S.R.O. 🎵🎵🎵🎵🎵 (LRC, 1993)

Live at the Rainbow Grill 🎵🎵🎵🎵 (Moon/FTC, 1993)

Mood Indigo 🎵🎵🎵🎵🎵 (EPM Musique, 1994)

Live at the Blue Note 🎵🎵🎵🎵🎵 (Roulette Jazz, 1994)

Black, Brown, & Beige—Mastersound Series 🎵🎵🎵🎵🎵 (Columbia, 1994)

Duke Ellington, 1938–1939 🎵🎵🎵🎵🎵 (Classics, 1994)

Duke Ellington, Vol.2: Swing 1930–1938 🎵🎵🎵🎵🎵 (ABC Music, 1994)

Duke Ellington & His Orchestra Live at Newport—1958 🎵🎵🎵🎵🎵 (Columbia/Legacy, 1994)

Uptown Downbeat w/His Orchestra: Cotton Club, Jungle Band 1927–1940 🎵🎵🎵🎵🎵 (Empire/Avid, 1995)

Satin Doll, 1958–1959 🎵🎵🎵🎵🎵 (Jazz Time, 1995)

Duke Ellington, 1924–1930—Box Set 🎵🎵🎵🎵🎵 (Classics 6, 1995)

From the Blue Note—Chicago 1952 🎵🎵🎵🎵 (Musicdisc, 1995)

In a Mellotone—1940–1944 🎵🎵🎵🎵🎵 (RCA, 1995)

70th Birthday Concert—Nov. 1969 🎵🎵🎵🎵🎵 (Blue Note, 1995)

Live at the Whitney: April 10, 1972 🎵🎵🎵🎵🎵 (MCA/Impulse, 1995)

The Cornell University Concert—December 1948 🎵🎵🎵🎵🎵 (Musicmasters, 1995)

New York Concert: In Performance at Columbia University—1964 🎵🎵🎵🎵🎵 (MusicMasters, 1995)

Duke Ellington & His Great Vocalists 🎵🎵🎵🎵🎵 (Legacy, 1995)

The Best of Duke Ellington 🎵🎵🎵🎵🎵 (Blue Note, 1995)

Duke Ellington & John Coltrane with Jimmy Garrison, Aaron Bell etc., Recorded September 1962 🎵🎵🎵🎵🎵 (MCA/Impulse, 1995)

Duke Ellington: Greatest Hits 🎵🎵🎵🎵🎵 (RCA, 1996)

Ellingtonia 🎵🎵🎵🎵 (Fat Boy, 1996)

This Is Jazz 🎵🎵🎵🎵 (Columbia, 1996)

Vol. 4: The Mooche, 1928 🎵🎵🎵🎵🎵 (EPM Musique, 1996)

Vol. 5: Harlemania, 1928–1929 🎵🎵🎵🎵🎵 (EPM Musique, 1996)

Vol. 6: Cotton Club Stomp 🎵🎵🎵🎵 (EPM Musique, 1996)

Vol. 9: Mood Indigo—1930 🎵🎵🎵🎵🎵 (EPM Musique, 1996)

Vol. 10: Rockin' in Rhythm, 1930–31 🎵🎵🎵🎵🎵 (EPM, 1996)

Sophisticated Lady—1941–1949 🎵🎵🎵🎵🎵 (Vocal Jazz, 1996)

Ellington at Basin Street East: The Complete Concert of 14 January 1964 🎵🎵🎵🎵🎵 (Music & Arts, 1996)

Rockin' In Rhythm, 1958–1959 🎵🎵🎵🎵🎵 (Jazz Hour, 1996)

Duke Ellington at the Cotton Club—1938, Band Remotes from Harlem 🎵🎵🎵🎵🎵 (Sandy Hook)

1941: The Jimmy Blanton/Ben Webster transcriptions 🎵🎵🎵🎵🎵 (VJC)

Duke Ellington & His Famous Orchestra: Fargo, North Dakota, Nov. 7, 1940 🎵🎵🎵🎵🎵 (VJC)

Duke Ellington & His Famous Orchestra: Hollywood, CA—Jan-Dec. 1941 🎵🎵🎵🎵🎵 (VJC)

The Complete Capitol Recordings of Duke Ellington, 1953–1955 🎵🎵🎵🎵🎵 (Mosaic)

Second Sacred Concert—1968 🎵🎵🎵🎵🎵 (Prestige)

New Orleans Suite—1970 🎵🎵🎵🎵🎵 (Atlantic)

Lullaby of Birdland 🎵🎵🎵🎵🎵 (Intermedia)

(With Billy Strayhorn) *Great Times* 🎵🎵🎵🎵 (Fantasy)

worth searching for: Ellington didn't do very much work with the movies, but his out-of-print soundtrack for *Anatomy of a Murder* 🎵🎵🎵🎵🎵 (Anadisq, 1959/Rykodisc, 1987) fit the story and movie perfectly and is one of the very best soundtracks of the era, as well as a good stand-alone album. Dave Grusin's *Homage to Duke* ⍟⍟⍟⍟ (GRP, 1993) is a great collection of different interpretations of Ellington tunes by one of the masters of contemporary light jazz.

influences:

◀◀ Fats Waller, James P. Johnson, Sidney Bechet, Willie "The Lion" Smith

▶▶ Thelonius Monk, Cecil Taylor, Count Basie, Quincy Jones, Gil Evans, Fletcher Henderson, Sun Ra, Maurice White

Chris Tower

The Emotions

Formed 1968, in Chicago, IL. Disbanded late 1980s.

Wanda Hutchinson, lead vocals; Sheila Hutchinson, vocals; Jeanette Hutchinson, vocals (1968–70, 1978–late 1980s); Theresa Davis, vocals (1970–mid-1970s); Pamela Hutchinson, vocals (mid-1970s–1978).

The Emotions did the bulk of their work either with Isaac Hayes and David Porter at Stax or with Maurice White of Earth, Wind & Fire—not bad company at all, which assured a higher caliber of songwriting, arrangement, and production than many of their contemporaries were getting at the time. Sisters Wanda, Sheila, and Jeanette Hutchinson started their own gospel group, the Hutchinson Sunbeams, when they were youngsters, and it was at Pops Stapels suggestion that they auditioned for Stax Records in Memphis. With Hayes and Porter guiding them, the trio scored hits such as "So I Can Love You" and "Stealin' Love," among others. After Stax folded, they moved on to White's ARC label and not only made their own albums—and the #1 smash "Best of My Love"—but also backed Earth, Wind & Fire on its 1979 hit "Boogie Wonderland." As the 1980s wore on, the singers moved to a variety of labels, including Motown, before calling it quits to raise their families. Still, they continued to sing backups for Earth, Wind & Fire and gospel singer Helen Baylor, and there are rumblings about an eventual return to action.

what to buy: *Best of My Love: The Best of the Emotions* ⍟⍟⍟⍟ (Legacy, 1996, prod. Maurice White) collects the best of their time spent with White, including the title track, spiritual fare such as "Blessed" and "Rejoice," and EW&F's "Boogie Wonderland." *Chronicle: Greatest Hits* ⍟⍟⍟⍟ (Stax, 1991, prod. Isaac Hayes, David Porter) completes the picture of their key decade of music-making.

what to buy next: The spiritual tip implied by the title of *Rejoice* ⍟⍟⍟⍟ (Columbia, 1977/1990, prod. Maurice White) makes this the best of the Emotions' individual albums to own.

what to avoid: *45 All-Time Greatest Love Songs* ⍟⍟ (K-Tel, 1995) has too many covers and feels like an ill-conceived project.

the rest:

So I Can Love You/Untouched ⍟⍟⍟⍟ (Stax, 1969 and 1971/1996)
Flowers ⍟⍟⍟ (Columbia, 1976)
Sunshine ⍟⍟⍟⍟ (Stax, 1977/1995)
Sunbeam ⍟⍟⍟ (ARC, 1979/RSI, 1997)

worth searching for: EW&F's *Heritage* ⍟⍟⍟ (Columbia, 1990, prod. various) features backing vocals by Wanda and Jeanette.

influences:

◀◀ The Staple Singers, Aretha Franklin, the Soul Stirrers, Mahalia Jackson, Martha & the Vandellas

▶▶ SWV, TLC, the Braxtons

Gary Graff

En Vogue

Formed 1988, in Oakland, CA.

Terry Ellis, vocals; Cindy Herron, vocals; Maxine Jones, vocals; Dawn Robinson, vocals (1988–97).

Assembled by superstar producers Denzil Foster and Thomas McElroy (Club Nouveau, Tony! Toni! Tone!), the members of En Vogue barely knew each other before winning a series of auditions to join the pair's latest venture. At first called U-4 and then Vogue, the quartet sang on Foster and McElroy's solo record *FM2* before landing a deal with Atlantic. Marketed as a 1990s-style Supremes with fashion model looks, soul singer vocal chops, and rump-shaking, hip-hop inspired backing beats, the group's 1990 debut album turned heads—starting with an a capella version of Smokey Robinson's "Who's Loving You" leading into their first hit, "Hold On." But it wasn't until their sophomore album that En Vogue rose to superstar status, with a multiplatinum record that soared into the Top 10. Though the quartet always professed a sisterly loyalty—acting on TV shows such as *Roc* and *A Different World* together—the group wound up taking a break for Terry Ellis to record a solo venture in 1995, two years before Robinson would leave the group for good, announcing a deal with rap producer Dr. Dre's Aftermath Entertainment label.

what to buy: On their second album, *Funky Divas* ⍟⍟⍟ (East-West, 1992, prod. Denzil Foster, Thomas McElroy), En Vogue finally nails the formula that makes them truly unique—melding 1990s style New Jill Swing with classic soul/gospel vocal licks and a sultry, sexy visual appeal. From the poppy allure of "My Lovin' (You're Never Gonna Get It)" to the rock-tinged "Free Your Mind," En Vogue proved a versatile, talented studio creation.

what to avoid: Released as a stopgap following the explosive success of *Funky Divas*, the EP *Runaway Love* **woof!** (EastWest, 1993, prod. Denzil Foster, Thomas McElroy) is notable only for the title track and the group's collaboration with rappers Salt-N-Pepa, "Whatta Man." Only the heartiest of fans will be running to this one.

the rest:
Born to Sing 🎵🎵🎵 (Atlantic, 1990)
Remix to Sing 🎵🎵🎵 (EastWest, 1991)
EV3 🎵🎵🎵 (EastWest, 1997)

worth searching for: The soundtrack to the film *Set It Off* (Elektra, 1996) offers a kicking En Vogue cut, "(Don't Let Go) Love."

solo outings:
Terry Ellis:
Southern Gal 🎵🎵🎵 (EastWest, 1995)

influences:
◀◀ The Supremes, Guy, Janet Jackson
▶▶ TLC, Jade

Eric Deggans

Enchantment

Formed 1967, in Detroit, MI.

Bobby Greene, vocals; Joe "Jobie" Thomas, vocals; David Banks, vocals; Emanuel "EJ" Johnson, vocals, strings, piano, keyboards, harpsichord, clavinet; Edgar "Mickey" Clanton, vocals.

EJ Johnson and David Banks, two high school friends, began formulating what would become Enchantment while still in school. Inspired by gospel and Motown alike, Johnson and producer Michael Stokes set to writing romantic, fairly mid-tempo R&B. In the studio, full-scale productions set the tone, with teams of horns and back-up singers, adding even the Detroit Symphony Orchestra at times. Not exactly the most down home experience, but Johnson does engage one's interest as a kind of gruff Phillipe Wynne of the Spinners. Inconsistency perhaps, such as plopping junk dance numbers next to inspired gospel-like calls to action, spelled out the group's brief recording career. Enchantment still tours today, as Johnson is quick to point out.

what to buy: Nearly every thing you'll need to hear (and it's nearly everything it recorded) can be found on the recent *If You're Ready: The Best of Enchantment* 🎵🎵🎵 (EMI, 1996, prod. Michael Stokes). Taken almost solely from *Enchantment* and *Once Upon a Time*, the compilation is a hodgepodge of winners like "Sunshine" and throwaways like "Dance to the Music" (not the Sly Stone song).

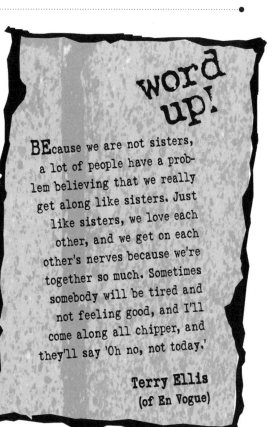

word up!

BEcause we are not sisters, a lot of people have a problem believing that we really get along like sisters. Just like sisters, we love each other, and we get on each other's nerves because we're together so much. Sometimes somebody will be tired and not feeling good, and I'll come along all chipper, and they'll say 'Oh no, not today.'

Terry Ellis (of En Vogue)

the rest:
Golden Classics 🎵🎵 (Collectables, 1991)

influences:
◀◀ Stevie Wonder, Smokey Robinson and the Miracles, Jackie Wilson, the Soul Stirrers
▶▶ The Spinners, the Jackson 5, Michael Jackson, the O'Jays

Allan Orski

EPMD

Formed 1986, in Long Island, NY. Disbanded 1992. Reunited 1997.

Erick Sermon, vocals; Parrish Smith, vocals.

Making it clear with their name exactly what their agenda was, Erick Sermon and Parrish Smith teamed up in 1986 to form

EPMD—or, Erick and Parrish Makin' Dollars—and took just two years to fulfill their mission: a dazzling collection of pure, phunkalistic samples, pounding beats and edgy, marble-mouthed rhymes, the duo's debut LP, *Strictly Business*, went gold in just six weeks, topping the R&B chart in the process. The album, which featured the hit singles "You Gots to Chill," "It's My Thing," and "Strictly Business," was a major triumph (especially for a debut), but EPMD wasn't quite done making dollars: three subsequent albums (*Unfinished Business*, *Business As Usual*, and *Business Never Personal*) each dramatically outperformed their predecessor. At the height of their partnership, EPMD discovered and launched such acts as Redman and Das EFX and elevated themselves to the top of hip-hop's creative community. Unfortunately, after the release of *Business Never Personal* in 1992, the pair took their differences personally and parted ways on less-than-friendly terms. Both rappers went on to issue solo LPs, but only Sermon remained truly successful in the music business, becoming a much-sought-after songwriter and producer for everyone from George Clinton to Ice Cube. The hip-hop world rejoiced in 1997, though, when word got out that Erick and Parrish were finally back together, working on a new album. It was expected to be released in the fall of 1997.

what to buy: With samples ranging from Parliament to War, from rock to reggae, and featuring tracks such as the classic "You Gots to Chill," *Strictly Business* ✧✧✧✧ (Fresh/Sleeping Bag, 1988, prod. EPMD) is the definitive EPMD album. Even though the production is not as polished or intricate as on the subsequent EPMD releases, the raw funk and grimy rap rhetoric still sparkles, forcing listeners to bob their heads in rhythmic agreement.

what to buy next: *Unfinished Business* ✧✧✧ (Fresh/Sleeping Bag, 1989, prod. EPMD) and *Business as Usual* ✧✧✧ (Def Jam, 1991, prod. EPMD) are both variations on the same EPMD thing, with several standouts (including "Gold Digger").

what to avoid: Although it contains the interesting "Crossover," *Business Never Personal* ✧✧ (RAL/Def Jam, 1992, prod. EPMD) is an uneven LP that suffers from lazy rhymes and haphazard production. The widening musical gulf and personal tensions between the two can almost be felt between the grooves, as what once was an inspired creative whole becomes two conspicuously separate parts, each waiting for his solo departure.

Maxine Jones of En Vogue (© Ken Settle)

solo outings:
Parrish Smith:
(As PMD) *Shade Business* ✧✧ (BMG, 1994)
Bu$ine$$ I$ Bu$ine$$ ✧✧ (Relativity/Combat/Ruthless, 1996)

Erick Sermon:
No Pressure ✧✧✧ (Def Jam/Rush, 1993)
Double or Nothing ✧✧✧✧ (Def Jam/Rush, 1995)
Insomnia: The Erick Sermon Compilation ✧✧✧ (Interscope, 1996)

influences:

◀◀ Parliament/Funkadelic, Roger/Zapp, Run-D.M.C., Eric B. & Rakim

▶▶ Redman, Keith Murray, Das EFX, JVC Force, Black Moon, MC Breed, Digital Underground

Andre McGarrity

Eric B. & Rakim

Formed 1985, New York City, NY. Disbanded 1992.

Eric B. (born Eric Barrier), DJ; Rakim (born William Griffin Jr.), vocals.

For years after Eric B. & Rakim blew up, folks still thought the rapper's name was Eric B. The duo may have emerged back when DJ's names were still billed first, but after people heard Rakim, there was no question the MC belonged in the limelight. His golden tone and flow was as monumental to hip-hop as Bird's was to jazz; he possessed a drummer's instinct for the breaths and fills that turn an ordinary beat into an extraordinarily funky one. But, unlike a drummer, Rakim also had words to work with—words that epitomized racial pride and street pragmatism, New Jack militance and spacey spirituality. He took your gold, then meditated. He was of the streets, but seemed to float above them. No one, not even self-proclaimed metaphysician KRS-One, would ever bridge the stoop and the stars as easily again; no one better summarized for an entire generation what it meant to be a B-boy or B-girl.

what to buy: *Paid In Full* ✧✧✧✧✧ (4th & Broadway/Island, 1987, prod. Eric B. & Rakim) is the seminal New Jack document. Gucci and gold drape the cover as if to refute Run-D.M.C.'s black-on-black asceticism. The breakbeats, computer drums, and turntable cuts are spare and echoing, as if designed to fill urban canyons. Rakim's graffiti-written rhymes roll back and forth over the beat with an astonishing polyrhythmic ease, anticipating the denser sonics that Public Enemy's Bomb Squad would later bring. And the imagery is all progressive B-boy myth—a music fiend energized by drum roll blasts, a poet imprisoned by his rhymes, a rapper conquering the fear of his

own magnetizing microphone, a word-slinger eliminating seven MCs at a time, a studious scientist whose alchemy controls your soul. If the first album charts Rakim's journey into self-esteem, *Follow the Leader* 𝄢𝄢𝄢𝄢 (Uni, 1988, prod. Eric B. & Rakim) takes the voyage spiraling outwards. Eric B. (assisted by Ced Gee of the Ultramagnetic MC's) adds edgy and airy textures to the mix; the effect is a much more tense and propulsive tone. Rakim's breathless delivery on the title track alone leaves the listener to sort out whirlwind allusions to intergalactic travel, third-rail subway electroshocks, street-corner politics, and Five Percent Nation metaphysics in one of the craftiest battle rhymes ever written.

what to buy next: Eric B. moves to rawer funk on *Let the Rhythm Hit 'Em* 𝄢𝄢𝄢𝄢 (MCA, 1990, prod. Eric B. & Rakim). While the sound is more complex than ever, the density of some of the tracks actually tends to detract from Rakim's lyrics. But the music doesn't get in the way of the simple "In the Ghetto"; a prayer moving through meanings on many levels, it is perhaps Rakim's finest moment. Then there's "Mahogany," Rakim's first love song and an ominous sign. *Don't Sweat the Technique* 𝄢𝄢𝄢𝄢 (MCA, 1992, prod. Eric B. & Rakim) actually leads with "What's on Your Mind," the group's biggest pop hit to date. Rakim's lyrics are less (gratifyingly) obtuse; he's playing other people's superheroes on "The Punisher" and the 007 turn on "Rest Assured." But Large Professor's (largely uncredited) production touch and the second half of the LP, including nuggets like "Relax with Pep," "Know the Ledge," and the title track, balance the disappointments. Splitting shortly thereafter, Eric B. went on to make bass records, while Rakim occasionally emerged from retirement for the odd track.

influences:

◄◄ Marley Marl, Ced Gee

►► The entire new school

Jeff "DJ Zen" Chang

Gloria Estefan /Miami Sound Machine

Born Gloria Fajardo, September 1, 1957 in Havana, Cuba.

Simply put, Estefan has terrific pipes that were co-opted—willingly—away from Miami's Cuban dance scene into the blander

Gloria Estefan (© Ken Settle)

> I was so shy when I started out. I remember I used to stand there and clutch the microphone and close my eyes and look down. I tried to be as inconspicuous as possible--with a spotlight on me. I'd videotape myself, and I hated it. I used to sit on the sofa and look through my fingers at the tape and just cringe.
>
> **Gloria Estefan**

but phenomenally successful realm of middle-of-the-road pop. The Cuban native, who fled that country's revolution with her family and moved to the U.S. when she was two, started out fronting the Miami Sound Machine, a former wedding band led by husband Emilio Estefan Jr., whose South of the Equator polyrythms provided an interesting mainstream pop alternative during the mid-1980s. It didn't last long; as Estefan's voice grew from chirpy to assured, the Miami Sound Machine moniker gradually disappeared from the album covers in order to showcase the singer. During 1990, Estefan's tour bus was hit by a tractor-trailer, and she fractured one of her vertebrae; but a year later, she was back in action, singing the #1 hit "Coming Out of the Dark," a song inspired by the accident. Give Estefan this much: she's no producer's tool, writing many of her own lyrics and checking off on the creative decisions. If only one of those decisions would be a return to the those irresistible club grooves. . . .

what to buy: *Eyes of Innocence* ♫♫♫ (Epic, 1984/1989, prod. Emilio and the Jerks) had only the minor hit, "Dr. Beat," but the Miami Sound Machine's debut is an intoxicating blend of Caribbean rhythms. You won't find anything from that album on *Greatest Hits* ♫♫♫ (Epic, 1992, prod. Emilio Estefan), but you do get her best, a largely upbeat collection that includes "Conga," "Rhythm Is Gonna Get You," and "Get on Your Feet."

what to avoid: There are lots of songs Estefan can probably sing very well. Why'd they pick these for *Hold Me, Thrill Me, Kiss Me* ♫ (Epic, 1994, prod. various)?

the rest:
Into the Light ♫♫ (Epic, 1981)
Primitive Love ♫♫♫ (Epic, 1985)
Let it Loose ♫♫♫ (Epic, 1987)
Cuts Both Ways ♫♫♫ (Epic, 1989)
Mi Tierra ♫♫♫ (Epic, 1993)
Christmas through Your Eyes ♫♫ (Epic, 1993)
Abriendo Puertas ♫♫ (Epic, 1995)
Destiny ♫♫ (Epic, 1996)

worth searching for: Estefan's guest vocal on the song "Africa" from Arturo Sandoval's *Dayon* ♫♫♫ (GRP, 1994, prod. Arturo Sandoval, Richard Eddy) is worth checking out.

influences:

◀◀ Carmen Miranda, Tito Puente, Herb Alpert & the Tijuana Brass, Aretha Franklin, Donna Summer

▶▶ Debbie Gibson

Gary Graff

E.U. (Experience Unlimited)
Formed 1970, in Washington, DC.

The second oldest Go Go band (after Chuck Brown & the Soul Searchers), Experience Unlimited—formed by bassist Gregory "Sugar Bear" Elliot—is one of Washington, D.C.'s oldest pop bands, period. A sweaty covers group, E.U. started off in the direction of the funky black rock of Sly Stone and the Bar-Kays. By the mid-1970s, E.U. was knee deep in the Go Go, and in 1976 the group released the Chocolate City-certified seminal straight-up Go Go record, "Hey You," on the House of Peace label, co-written by Go Go svengali Maxx Kidd. In 1978, E.U. released its debut LP, *Free Yourself*, on the local Black Fire Records label. A wacky blend of black 1970s consciousness, conflicting calls to party sedately and rock hard, and a fairly lethal level of funkativity, *Free Yourself* documents a band in the process of discovering that its true calling was in the Go Go. Their 1979 double-A side "Rock Your Butt/E.U. Groove" and "Party Time" marked a

groundbreaking Go Go/rap collaboration with Kurtis Blow that spotlights Sugar Bear's phat bass and the percolating percussion of Ju Ju House. Four years later, E.U. was the scene's top dawg. During this period, E.U. dropped a series of 12-inch singles—"E.U. Freeze," "Ooh La La La," "Computer Funk," "Somebody's Ringing That Doorbell"—which are some of the most powerful Go Go ever waxed. In 1985, Island Records signed several Go Go bands after a New Musical Express article about the scene triggered a mini Go Go frenzy in London's trendy club world. Island released E.U.'s major label debut, *E.U. Live: Two Places at the Same Time,* in 1986. Easily one of the lamest recordings of an awesome live band, the LP was an apt metaphor for the label's brief, ill-advised adventure with Go Go. The next year, at a show at the 930 Club, E.U.'s future was forever changed. At a party in the club celebrating the screening of his debut film, *She's Gotta Have It,* then-fledgling director Spike Lee was caught up in the band's groove. He met E.U. after the show and said he'd keep in touch. He did; the band played its song "Da Butt" in his next film, 1988's *School Daze.* Before the year was out, thanks to the film's soundtrack and a video directed by Lee, "Da Butt" was the first Go Go record to make an impact with the pop mainstream. In 1989, E.U. grabbed the gold donut by signing with Virgin. Though they released three albums for the label, their debut *Livin' Large* is the only one where they really kicked it. E.U. had its last taste of gold when it guested on Salt-N-Pepa's 1988 hit "Shake Your Thang." Today they still rock the Go Go back home and abroad.

what to buy: *Free Yourself* ♫♫♫ (Black Fire Records, 1977, prod. Jimmy Gray) is a weird record, but worth checking (see above). Order from Black Fire Music, 4409 Douglas St., N.E., Washington, DC, 20019.

worth searching for: *Livin' Large* ♫♫♫♫ (Virgin, 1989) is as good as an E.U. studio album is going to get. Look for it in cutout bins everywhere.

influences:

◀◀ Chuck Brown & the Soul Searchers, Sly Stone, the Bar-Kays

▶▶ Benny & the Masters, DJ Kool, Salt-N-Pepa

Tom Terrell

Eurythmics
Founded 1980, in London, England. Disbanded 1990.

Dave Stewart, guitar, keyboards; Annie Lennox, vocals, flute, keyboards.

The Eurythmics: Dave Stewart (l) and Annie Lennox (© **Ken Settle**)

Emerging from the ashes of British folk/psychedelic/New Wave rockers the Tourists, members Annie Lennox and Dave Stewart became the oddest of couples—breaking up as lovers before forming the Eurythmics together. They met in a London eatery where Lennox was waiting tables and Stewart was dining with fellow musician and future Tourist Peet Coombes. Lennox was a classically-trained child of working class parents inspired by Joni Mitchell and Stevie Wonder, while Stewart was a former jock who dug Mississippi John Hurt and Robert Johnson. The pair lived together while in the Tourists, which connected with a cover of "I Only Want to Be with You" before the group disbanded during 1980. No longer lovers but still musical partners, the two made a batch of eight-track demos in a London warehouse that became their first album—melding New Wave synthpop sounds with Lennox's amazing 1960s soul vocal influences. Tired of the baby doll blonde image she'd fostered in the Tourists, Lennox dyed her hair orange, appeared in men's suits, and occasionally dressed as Elvis Presley during the group's early years. As synth-pop began to take a back seat on the

charts, Stewart leavened the group's sound with garage rock and earthier soul touches—teaming up with soul queen Aretha Franklin in 1985, for instance—only to try a return to techno form just before the duo went on indefinite hiatus in 1990.

what to buy: The pair's breakthrough record, *Sweet Dreams (Are Made of This)* ♫♫♫♫ (RCA, 1983, prod. Dave Stewart), provides a neat summation of the group's appeal. Stewart's eerily emotionless, synthesizer-bred arrangements stand in stark contrast to Lennox's expressive vocals—making the hit title track, along with the driving dance cut "Love Is a Stranger," sizzle with the friction. With full band backing, *Be Yourself Tonight* ♫♫♫♫ (RCA, 1985, prod. Dave Stewart) enjoys an energetic live group flavor with the charging "Would I Lie to You?," the soulful midtempo hit "It's Alright (Baby's Coming Back)," and Lennox's muscular duet with Aretha Franklin, "Sisters Are Doin' It for Themselves."

what to buy next: For an overview of the duo's biggest commercial triumphs, it's hard to beat *Greatest Hits* ♫♫♫ (Arista,

1991, prod. Dave Stewart, Jimmy Iovine), a collection of the group's 14 best-selling songs—excerpting material from the disastrous *1984* soundtrack. The best 1990s-era representation of the Eurythmics' sound turns out to be Lennox' first solo album, *Diva* 𝄞𝄞𝄞 (Arista, 1992, prod. Stephen Lipsom), a record that blends the updated synth-pop of "Legend in My Living Room" with the pop/rock of "Walking on Broken Glass"—a potent reminder why we liked the group so much in the first place.

what to avoid: As a film soundtrack that even the director denounced publicly, *1984* **woof!** (RCA, 1984, prod. Dave Stewart) upsets Eurythmics' delicate stylistic balance, drowning Lennox's evocative vocals in an oppressive flood of downbeat techno-pop.

the rest:
In the Garden 𝄞𝄞 (RCA U.K., 1981)
Touch 𝄞𝄞𝄞 (RCA, 1983)
Revenge 𝄞𝄞 (RCA, 1986)
Savage 𝄞𝄞 (RCA, 1987)
We Too Are One 𝄞𝄞 (Arista, 1989)
Live 1983–1989 𝄞𝄞𝄞 (Arista, 1993)

worth searching for: Get *Rough and Tough at the Roxy* 𝄞𝄞𝄞 (RCA, 1986), a promotional EP sporting four live cuts recorded with Eurythmics best-ever touring band.

solo outings:
Annie Lennox:
Medusa 𝄞𝄞𝄞 (Arista, 1995)

Dave Stewart:
Lily Was Here 𝄞𝄞 (soundtrack) (Anxious, 1989)
Dave Stewart and the Spiritual Cowboys 𝄞𝄞𝄞 (Arista, 1990)
Honest 𝄞𝄞 (Arista, 1991)
Greetings from the Gutter 𝄞𝄞 (EastWest, 1995)

influences:
◀◀ Lene Lovich, Aretha Franklin, Kraftwerk, Can

▶▶ Garbage, Roxette

Eric Deggans

Everything but the Girl

Formed 1983, in London, England.

Tracey Thorn, vocals; Ben Watt, guitar, keyboards, vocals.

Naming themselves after a London boutique claiming to sell "everything but the girl" behind the counter, Ben Watt and former Marine Girls singer Tracey Thorn joined Sade and Matt Bianco as the most visible proponents of London's early 1980s jazz-pop movement. Although their engaging sound—a sensitive, savvy blend of Stan Getz-inspired Brazilian jazz and acoustic guitar-driven pop—won over U.K. audiences, Americans enamored of the chanteuse-like Sade weren't as quick to embrace Everything but the Girl's dour outlook and moody, often mopey image. So it was black-clad teens with Bauhaus T-shirts and Smiths albums who first recognized the alternately soothing and aching beauty of Thorn's cool but emotive alto. However, after 10 years of vainly cramming everything from orchestras to dance rhythms onto their subtle sound, EBTG scaled the *Billboard* charts with the groove-enhanced remix of "Missing," a late-blooming single from 1994's *Amplified Heart* album that made them one of pop's oldest overnight success stories and introduced a style they'd carry into their next album, *Walking Wounded*. Sometimes there is justice in the world.

what to buy: *Amplified Heart* 𝄞𝄞𝄞𝄞 (Atlantic, 1994, prod. Ben Watt, Tracey Thorn) deftly blends every style that the duo has experimented with into a cool, cohesive whole—it's beautiful music in every sense of the phrase. The beat-heavy followup, *Walking Wounded* 𝄞𝄞𝄞 (Atlantic, 1996, prod. Ben Watt, Spring Heel Jack), builds upon the house remixes of "Missing" and Thorn's collaborations with trip-hop group Massive Attack for a seductive, sonically captivating work. *Love Not Money* 𝄞𝄞𝄞 (Sire, 1985, prod. Robin Millar) forsakes the heavy jazz leanings of their debut album for jangling pop with a social conscience that includes a lovely cover of the Pretenders' "Kid."

what to buy next: Thorn's interpretive skills are spotlighted on *Acoustic* 𝄞𝄞𝄞 (Atlantic, 1992, prod. Tracey Thorn, Ben Watt), which includes covers of Elvis Costello's "Alison," Cyndi Lauper's "Time After Time," and Bruce Springsteen's "Tougher Than the Rest."

what to avoid: *Language of Life* 𝄞𝄞 (Atlantic, 1990, prod. Tracey Thorn, Ben Watt, Tommy LiPuma) teams them with LiPuma, the late Stan Getz, and several American jazz session players—but the result is all surface and little substance.

the rest:
Everything but the Girl 𝄞𝄞𝄞 (Sire, 1984)
Baby, the Stars Shine Bright 𝄞𝄞𝄞 (Sire, 1986)
Idlewild 𝄞𝄞𝄞 (Sire, 1988)
Worldwide 𝄞𝄞 (Atlantic, 1991)

worth searching for: Thorn's pre-EBTG solo album, *A Distant Shore* 𝄞𝄞𝄞 (Cherry Red, 1982), offers a gorgeous reading of the Velvet Underground's "Femme Fatale" that shames all other covers.

Ben Watt:
North Marine Drive ♪♪♪ (Cherry Red, 1983)

influences:
◀◀ Astrud Gilberto, Stan Getz, Massive Attack
▶▶ Eddi Reader, Tanita Tikaram

David Okamoto

The Falcons

Formed 1959, in Detroit, MI. Disbanded late 1960s.

Members have included: Eddie Floyd, lead; Joe Stubbs, tenor; Wilson Pickett, tenor; Tom Shelter, baritone; Bonny Mack Rice, baritone; Willie Schoefield, bass; Bob Marando, first tenor; Arnette Robinson, first tenor; Lance Finnie, first tenor.

The musical career of the Falcons perfectly embodied doo-wop's transformation into soul music. Initially an integrated quintet like the Dell Vikings, they cut several fine doo-wop singles that sold well around the Detroit area for the Mercury, Silhouette, Falcon, and Kudo labels before Bob Marando and Tom Shelter left the group for the Army. Once Joe Stubbs took over the lead chores, the Falcons' sound became churchier and less poppy. In 1959, on their manager Robert West's Flick label, the Falcons scored a crossover market smash with the classic "You're So Fine." A quirky leasing and distribution deal with United Artists, by way of Chess Records, failed them on subsequent releases. Solid offerings such as "Just for Your Love" and "The Teacher" were only minor R&B hits, and deserving releases such as "You Must Know That I Love You," and "Working Man's Song" failed to chart. In 1962, Stubbs left the Falcons to sing with the Contours, the Originals and occasional stints with his brother Levi's group, the Four Tops. He was replaced by 19-year-old Wilson Pickett, whose lead vocals on the beautiful soul ballad "I Found a Love" helped propel the Falcons (this time on West's LuPine label) back into the R&B Top 10. After singles leased to Atlantic failed to click and founding member Willie Schoefield was drafted, the Falcons broke up in 1963. In 1964, West hired members of the Fabulous Playboys (Johnny Alvin, Frank Holt, James Gibson, and Charles "Sonny" Monroe) to record and tour as the Falcons. They recorded for LuPine and

later for Big Wheel records, where their single "Standing on Guard" was a minor soul hit in 1966. Of the original Falcons, Eddie Floyd and Wilson Pickett went on to great careers as solo artists, and Bonny Mack Rice reemerged as Sir Mack Rice and had a minor hit with the self-penned "Mustang Sally" (which Pickett later covered). Though the group has been dormant for decades, "You're So Fine" by the Falcons is alive and well on oldies radio stations everywhere.

what to buy: *You're So Fine* ♪♪♪♪ (Relic, 1991, prod. various) features their late 1950s doo-wop style with Joe Stubbs singing lead on the classic title track, plus "Just for Your Love" and "The Teacher." *I Found A Love* ♪♪♪♪ (Relic, 1991, prod. Robert Bateman) contains tracks from Pickett's short, energizing stint with the group.

influences:
◀◀ The Dominoes, the Moonglows
▶▶ The Four Tops, the Fabulous Playboys, the Contours

Ken Burke

Fat Boys

Formed 1983, in Brooklyn, NY.

Prince Markie Dee, vocals; Kool Rock-ski, vocals; Darren "Buffy" Robinson (the Human Beat Box), vocals and percussion.

Like the Three Stooges of hip-hop without a diet plan, the Fat Boys were all about fun. The rotund trio's songs—celebrating women (or the lack thereof), parties, beat-heavy music and, of course, food—were all delivered with a surprisingly appealing mix of tongue-in-cheek humor and canny street sensibility. Busting out of a New York neighborhood as the Disco 3, the group entered the Coca-Cola/Tin Pan Apple rap contest at Radio City Music Hall in 1983 and summarily blew away the competition, claiming a recording contract on Sutra Records as top prize. But as a preview of the warped mentality that would later define their music, the threesome was upset over not winning the second prize of a stereo—it was their inability to afford a turntable that prompted member Darren "Buffy" Robinson to perfect the art of making percussion noises with his mouth, leading to his nickname of "The Human Beat Box." It wasn't long, though, before Markie Dee, Kool Rock-ski, and the late, great Human Beat Box were able to afford their own stereo—not to mention all the all-you-can-eat meals they could ever possibly need—achieving monstrous commercial success that lead to a string of music awards, commercials, and even two feature films (*Krush Groove* and *Disorderlies*). Though the

The Falcons (© Jack Vartoogian)

Fat Boys were practically household names in the mid-'80s, the three artists went their separate ways after their peculiar popularity burned out—due in great part to the threesome's (or their record label's) insistence on recording cover versions of such '50s and '60s party songs as "Louie Louie" and "Wipe-out." Prince Markie Dee fared far better than either of his former partners, working behind the boards for Father MC, among others. Kool Rock-ski, meanwhile, attempted a solo LP, but his misguided effort couldn't keep pace with the ever-changing rap scene. Just prior to his heart attack in 1996, Robinson had been standing on a chair, huffing and puffing in search of the perfect backbeat.

what to buy: The 18-song CD compilation *All Meat, No Fillah! The Best of Fat Boys* 🎵🎵🎵 (Rhino, 1997, prod. various) should be more than enough to satisfy those who may have a hunger to hear these rollicking rappers at the peak of their hefty form. Containing all of the group's hits, the album serves as a goofy flashback to hip-hop's jolliest era.

solo outings:
Prince Markie Dee:
Love Daddy 🎵🎵🎵 (Motown, 1995)

influences:
◄◄ Sugarhill Gang, Kurtis Blow

►► Kid 'N' Play, D.J. Jazzy Jeff & the Fresh Prince, M.C. Hammer, Coolio, Biz Markie, Heavy D.

Andre McGarrity

Fat Joe Da Gangsta
Born Joseph Cartagena.

One look at Fat Joe Da Gangsta's resume tells you almost everything you need to know about the Bronx rapper, who's lent his verbal skills to albums by everybody from the Hispanic R&B group the Barrio Boyz, to the legendary Bronx MC KRS-One. Joe himself is part Puerto Rican and part Cuban, but definitely 100 percent Bronx bomber, coming off hardcore like KRS-One without the social conscience or agenda.

what to buy: On *Jealous One's Envy* 𝄞𝄞𝄞 (Violator/Relativity, 1995, prod. Diamond D, L.E.S., DJ Premier, Fat Joe, others), Joe showcases his forceful delivery and pure lyrical skills to good effect, with subject matter ranging from said skills to borough pride. The album suffers, though, from inconsistent production. And, curiously, the standout isn't even a new song, as DJ Premier checks in with a primo remix of the previous album's "Shit Is Real."

the rest:
Represent 𝄞𝄞𝄞 (Violator/Relativity, 1993)

influences:
◀◀ Boogie Down Productions, Lord Finesse
▶▶ Big L, Frankie Cutlass

Josh Freedom du Lac

Fatback Band /Fatback

Formed 1970.

Johnny King, guitar; Johnny Flippin, bass; Bill Curtis, drums; Earl Shelton, saxophone; George Williams, trumpet; George Adam, flute; Saunders McCrae, keyboards; Richard Cromwell, trombone; Wayne Woolford, congas; Michael Walker, vocals; Fred Demery, saxophone; George Victory, guitar; Wild Sugar, backing vocals.

At the core of funk and disco music is the desire for a good time, and that's just what we got from the Fatback Band. Or did you think that songs such as "Wicky-Wacky," "Yum Yum (Gimme Some)," "King Tim III (Personality Jock)," and "(Are You Ready) Do the Bus Stop" were rife with social commentary? Fatback was started in 1970 by producer Bill Curtis, who wanted to put together a session band—*a la* Motown's Funk Brothers—to back a roster of artists he hoped to assemble. That never happened, but Fatback started rolling out the dance floor hits, making an impact in the U.S. but enjoying even more success in Great Britain. The group changed its name officially to Fatback in 1977, just in time for its first U.S. Top 10 hit, "I Like Girls." Fatback continued recording into the mid-1980s, and it still pops up occasionally on the oldies circuit.

what to buy: *The Fattest of Fatback* 𝄞𝄞𝄞𝄞 (Rhino, 1997, prod. various) feeds the feet more than the head, but it has all the tracks you need to set a house party rockin'.

the rest:
XII 𝄞𝄞𝄞 (IMS, 1979/Southbound, 1997)
Gigolo 𝄞𝄞𝄞 (Spring, 1981/Southbound, 1996)
The Perception of Years 𝄞𝄞𝄞 (Collectables, 1996)
Bright Lights 𝄞𝄞𝄞 (Southbound, 1996)

worth searching for: *On the Floor* 𝄞𝄞𝄞 (Spring/Southbound, 1982) is an import reissue of one of Fatback's best albums, which includes the tracks "Fatback" and "She's My Shining Hour."

influences:
◀◀ Edwin Starr, Parliament, Sly & the Family Stone
▶▶ Brick, BT Express, Brass Construction, LTD, Zapp

Gary Graff

Rachelle Ferrell

Born in Philadelphia, PA.

A professional singer since the age of 13, Rachelle Ferrell has an unusual, two-label recording contract. She records R&B for Capitol and jazz for Blue Note, and no matter what she's singing, her multi-octave vocals are a joy to listen to. Ferrell—who accompanys herself on keyboards and is also a classically trained violinist—attended the Berklee College of Music with Branford Marsalis and later taught music for the New Jersey State Council of the Arts with Dizzy Gillespie. In fact, it was Gillespie who once told Ferrell's parents that she would be a "major force" in the music industry. For such a prolific composer, Ferrell records relatively infrequently (two albums in seven years), something her devoted fans hope changes in the not too distant future.

what to buy: *Rachelle Ferrell* 𝄞𝄞𝄞𝄞 (Capitol/Manhattan, 1992, prod. George Duke, Michael J. Powell, Barry J. Eastmond, Rachelle Ferrell, Erik Zobler) is Ferrell's R&B/pop album. Her powerful vocals and songwriting abilities—she wrote or co-wrote 10 of the album's 13 cuts—helped keep this collection on the R&B charts for almost three years. Highlights include "With Open Arms," "Nothing Has Ever Felt Like This" (a duet with Will Downing), and the gospel-tinged "Peace on Earth."

what to buy next: Originally released only in Japan in 1990, *First Instrument* 𝄞𝄞𝄞𝄞 (Somethin' Else, 1990/Blue Note, 1995, prod. Hitoshi Namekata, Lenny White) showcases Ferrell's incredible range as a jazz vocalist. Backed by the likes of Stanley Clarke, Lenny White, Wayne Shorter, and Terrence Blanchard, Ferrell glides effortlessly through standards like "Bye Bye Blackbird" and "What Is This Thing Called Love," with a couple

of original compositions thrown in for good measure. One of those, "Don't Waste Your Time," is the disc's finest track.

worth searching for: Okay, so it's not a CD; it's a videotape. Nevertheless, *Manhattan Project* is worth checking out. It features the live recording of "Autumn Leaves" from *First Instrument*, allowing one to see, as well as hear, the talented Ferrell in action.

influences:

◀◀ Billie Holiday, Betty Carter, Shirley Horn, Anita Baker

Dean Dauphinais

The Fifth Dimension

Formed 1966, in Los Angeles, CA.

Marilyn McCoo, lead vocals; Billy Davis Jr., lead vocals; LaMonte McLemore, baritone vocals; Florence LaRue Gordon, alto vocals; Ron Towson, bass vocals.

The preeminent adult pop-vocal group of the late 1960s and early 1970s, the Fifth Dimension floated to a string of seven gold LPs and five gold singles during their heyday by bridging the gap between the star-crossed hippie rock idealism of one decade and the glossy, antiseptic, "champagne soul" of the next. While doing so, the quintet introduced songs written by many of America's consummate pop composers of the day, including their original arranger/conductor Jimmy Webb ("Up, Up, and Away"), Laura Nyro ("Stoned Soul Picnic"), Ashford & Simpson, Neil Sedaka, and Bacharach & David. The Fifth Dimension derived from a quartet called the Hi-Fi's, formed by fashion model McCoo and fashion photographer McLemore, that toured with Ray Charles. When their singing mates Harry Elston and Floyd Butler departed (later to form the Friends of Distinction), McCoo recruited fellow "Miss Bronze Grand Talent Award" winner Florence LaRue and McLemore drafted gospel singers Ron Towson and Billy Davis Jr. Originally called the Versatiles, they produced a minor hit on the West Coast with "I'll Be Loving You Forever" on the Soul City label, owned by singing star Johnny Rivers. Changing their name to the Fifth Dimension, they earned national attention with the Mamas and the Papas tune "Go Where You Wanna Go," but became household names with the airy Webb classic "Up, Up, and Away," which earned the group four Grammy Awards. Hits like "Stoned Soul Picnic" and "Sweet Blindness" quickly followed. Then, after seeing the

Broadway production of *Hair* in 1969, they were inspired to join together two of the musical's songs, "Aquarius" and "Let the Sunshine In (The Flesh Failures)"; the resulting single soared to #1 on the pop charts and stayed there for six weeks, while the accompanying album sold nearly two million copies. Possibly intoxicated by their great success, McCoo and Davis married, as did LaRue and manager Marc Gordon. But "Aquarius/Sunshine" was the Fifth Dimension's pinnacle of success, and they never again experienced such popularity. They managed only an occasional hit after 1969, trading on past glory to expand their appearances in nightclubs, on television, and at the White House during the Nixon administration. McCoo and Davis left the group in 1975 to make three albums (one yielding the #1 single "You Don't Have to Be a Star") before splitting entirely in 1980. McCoo went on to co-host the syndicated TV program *Solid Gold*. In the 1990s, the Fifth Dimension, with Greg Walker and Phyllis Battle replacing Davis and McCoo, toured with their stage version of the musical *Ain't Misbehavin*. Buoyed by its success, the group attempted a full-fledged comeback in 1995 with the LP *In the House*, which opened with Dick Clark jubilantly proclaiming that "The Fifth Dimension is *IN . . . THE . . . HOUSE!*" That effectively sounded the death knell for this group to recapture any glimmer of its past greatness.

what to buy: The song "Aquarius/Let the Sunshine In" was the Fifth Dimension's shining moment, and it's featured prominently on their *Greatest Hits on Earth* ♪♪♪♪ (BMG/Arista, 1987/1972, prod. Bones Howe), surrounded by such memorable Top 40 tracks as "Wedding Bell Blues," "(Last Night) I Didn't Get to Sleep at All," and, of course, "Up, Up, and Away." Though the album showcases the seamless, delicate harmonies of the male-female ensemble, it also spotlights over a dozen musicians and vocalists prominent in the 1960s and 1970s.

what to buy next: For the whole nine yards on the Fifth Dimension, *Up, Up & Away—The Definitive Collection* ♪♪♪ (BMG/Arista, 1997, prod. various) assembles every one of the group's 30 chart singles on the Soul City and Bell labels from 1967–1975. It's a good representation of their best work, although the package is somewhat flawed by the inclusion of early, weaker album cuts that never received any airplay. It covers the group's first album *Up, Up and Away*, released by Soul City in 1967, the 1969 LP *The Age of Aquarius,* and liner notes that attempt to place the group in a historical context.

what to avoid: It's really a shame when musical acts that have had much more than their 15 minutes of fame don't have the

Rachelle Ferrell (© Jack Vartoogian)

common courtesy to retire gracefully and never be heard from again. Instead, the public is too often assaulted by things like *In the House* **woof!** (Click, 1995, prod. Ollie E. Brown), an attempt by an overhauled Fifth Dimension to cash in on a 30-year-old reputation. Disco killed their silken harmonies, but maybe no one told them since they felt that covering the Bee Gees's "How Deep Is Your Love" was a wise idea. This nostalgia trip is about as hip as Barry Manilow wearing a nose ring.

solo outings:
Marilyn McCoo and Billy Davis Jr.:
The Two of Us ♫♫ (Columbia, 1977)
Marilyn and Billy ♫♫ (Columbia, 1978)
I Hope We Get to Love in Time ♫♫ (Razor & Tie, 1996)

influences:

◀◀ The Platters, Ray Charles, the Mamas and the Papas, Johnny Rivers, Dionne Warwick

▶▶ Friends of Distinction, Hues Corporation, Earth, Wind & Fire, Jimmy Webb, Peaches & Herb, the Carpenters, Lionel Richie, Rita Coolidge

Chris Tower

Fine Young Cannibals

Formed 1983, in Birmingham, England.

Andy Cox, guitar; David Steele, bass, keyboards; Roland Gift, vocals.

From the wake of the English Beat, former members Andy Cox and David Steele hooked up with actor/singer Roland Gift to form the more mainstream pop-leaning Fine Young Cannibals. Crafty dance-pop smarts and the human element of Gift's exotic looks and romantic cawing made for a debut of engaging singles and effective covers. Alas, machines won out, hamstringing any jumpy rhythms into a grating groove and dominating the group's massive-selling *The Raw and the Cooked*. The increasingly apparent pseudo-soul of the band and Gift himself, ultimately mannered and dour, became more of a white-washed soul vacuum than a 1980s answer to Motown. The band stalled after its sophomore album and, presumably, hung it up, unable to complete a worthy third.

what to buy: *Fine Young Cannibals* ♫♫♫ (IRS, 1985, prod. Robin Millar, Mike Pela, Fine Young Cannibals) was a promising mix of R&B accents and rich pop in a decidedly modern setting, with Gift doing justice to "Johnny Come Home" and Elvis Presley's "Suspicious Minds."

what to buy next: Besides highlighting the hits, *The Finest* ♫♫♫ (MCA, 1996, prod. various) offers the winning moments from

Raw ("Don't Look Back," "Tell Me What"). In accentuating its singles strength, the pervading lifelessness that seeps across *Raw* is kept to a minimum.

what to avoid: Had the Cannibals bothered to hire in a live drummer instead of relying on programmed drum machines to piffle out inert bass kicks, *The Raw and the Cooked* ♫♫ (IRS, 1989, prod. Jerry Harrison, Fine Young Cannibals) may have attained some of Motown's sprightly qualities. Song quality notwithstanding, the robotic grooves that lead the arrangements lead only to rhythmic monotony.

the rest:
The Raw and the Remix ♫♫ (MCA, 1990)

influences:

◀◀ Smokey Robinson, Elvis Presley, the Temptations, English Beat

▶▶ Terrence Trent D'Arby, Mighty Mighty Bosstones

Allan Orski

Fishbone

Formed 1980, in Los Angeles, CA.

John (Norwood) Fisher, bass vocals; Phillip Dwight (Fish) Fisher, drums; Kendall Rey Jones (1994–present), guitar, vocals; Angelo Christopher Moore, vocals, saxophone; Christopher Gordon Dowd, trombone, keyboards; Walter Adam Kibby, trumpet; John Bigham, guitar, keyboards (1990–present).

Without benefit of mainstream radio play, Fishbone has built its fan base on the strength of blistering live performances. Were the band able to bring some focus to its hyper blend of punk, ska, hardcore, and funk long enough to sufficiently focus, Fishbone might achieve the transcendence it's been threatening for quite some time. Instead, the music is most often a supercharged hodgepodge of styles and social messages, which creates an air of rootlessness covered up by fiery chops.

what to buy: *The Reality of My Surroundings* ♫♫♫♫ (Columbia, 1991, prod. Fishbone, David Kahne) is arguably the band's best and is certainly its most ambitious effort, one that won over modern rock fans with the tunes "Everyday Sunshine" and "Sunless Saturday." *Fishbone 101 . . .* ♫♫♫ (Legacy, 1996, prod. various) is a generous overview of the group's work on Columbia.

what to buy next: *Truth and Soul* ♫♫♫ (Columbia, 1988, prod. David Kahne) is another mixed bag, featuring a steroid take on Curtis Mayfield's "Freddie's Dead" and scorchers such as "Bonin' in the Boneyard" mixed in with some forgettable riff-o-

Fishbone (© Jack Vartoogian)

ramas. *In Your Face* ♪♪♪ (Columbia, 1986, prod. David Kahne) is a slicked-up bid for commercial play, but it *is* Fishbone at its most accessible as the band keeps (more or less) a ska-inflected backbeat to "A Selection" and "Cholly."

what to avoid: *Give a Monkey a Brain and He'll Swear He's the Center of the Universe* ♪♪ (Columbia, 1993, prod. Terry Date, Fishbone) is as obtuse as the title, overreaching, schizophrenic, and frustrating.

the rest:
Fishbone ♪♪♪ (Columbia EP, 1985)
It's a Wonderful Life (Gonna Have a Good Time) ♪♪♪ (Columbia EP, 1987)
Bonin' in the Boneyard ♪♪♪ (Columbia EP, 1990)
Chim Chim's Badass Revenge ♪♪♪ (Rowdy, 1996)

worth searching for: *Singles* ♪♪♪♪ (Sony, 1993, prod. various) is a Japanese collection of some of Fishbone's best tracks, highlighted by a handful of fiery live performances.

influences:
◀◀ Curtis Mayfield, Rush, James Brown, Sly Stone
▶▶ Living Colour, Weapon of Choice

Allan Orski

Ella Fitzgerald

Born April 25, 1917, in Newport News, VA. Died June 14, 1996, in Beverly Hills, CA.

Many critics consider Ella Fitzgerald "The First Lady of Song," the best female jazz singer ever, though in her customary modesty Fitzgerald hailed Sarah Vaughan as the finest vocalist of all time. Regardless, there can be no debate that Ella—the first name is all that's required—belongs in that select pantheon of incomparable voices (Vaughan, Billie Holiday) that could transform the weakest material into a masterpiece, making any song uniquely her own. She could swing with the best of them, is credited with creating the free-form singing style known as "scat," and interpreted every number with spectacularly clear diction and a powerful, versatile voice. The perpetually cheerful lilt in that voice stood in sharp contrast to an early life spent in abysmal poverty; she was a homeless 16-year-old in 1933, but turned her fortunes around the following year. Ella showed up at an amateur talent contest at Harlem's Apollo Theater and won the $25 first prize by singing an impromptu version of "Judy" in the style of her main influence, Connee Boswell. Jazz great Benny Carter was in the audience and soon landed Fitzgerald a spot singing with Chick Webb's orchestra; by 1937, she was the featured attraction. Her first successful recordings included "Love and Kisses," "Undecided," and "A-Tisket, A-Tasket"—created, the legend goes, as a nonsensical ditty to lift the spirits of Webb, who was critically ill. Webb died in 1939, and Fitzgerald took over as leader of his orchestra until 1941 when she broke up the band to go solo. In the '40s, Ella collaborated with acts like the Ink Spots and the Delta Rhythm Boys, eventually finding a home with Norman Granz's Jazz at the Philharmonic. She began performing more jazz and bop numbers, teaming with Dizzy Gillespie and doing raucous, scat-filled numbers in her sets. She hit the charts with "Lady Be Good" and "Flying Home," married bassist Ray Brown in 1948 (a union that would last only four years), appeared in the films *St. Louis Blues* and Jack Webb's *Pete Kelly's Blues,* and made many TV appearances starting in the '50s and continuing throughout her career. All these events were concurrent with Ella's signing to Granz's Verve label and beginning her project of making her seminal and very popular "songbook" recordings. She achieved the pinnacle of her career in 1960 with her European concert tour, notably the Berlin show featuring her scat-heavy spoof of "Mack the Knife." Fitzgerald's radiance lost some luster in the late '60s as she tried to cash in on the popular music of the day, but she rebounded with live recordings in the '70s, working with Count Basie, Oscar Peterson, and Joe Pass. In the 1980s, however, Ella began to fade. Her health declined and she lacked the "verve" she had displayed so effortlessly in her younger years. Heart and eye trouble prevented her from performing or recording for long stretches. Ella was, interestingly, at once shy and yet not given to introspection. Consequently, she was never self-conscious as an artist and, thus, never prone to self-imitation. She was simply an extraordinary singer. She didn't merely sing; she played herself like a musical instrument. By 1994, she had completely retired. Ella Fitzgerald died in the spring of 1996, though her legacy lives on in more than 100 available recordings and a reputation that has made her name synonymous with great singing, great jazz, and scat coolness.

what to buy: In 1956, Fitzgerald signed with Verve Records and undertook a massive project: A series of "songbooks" featuring the works of the greatest composers of the 20th century. Though not her finest jazz performances, the best of these albums is *The Cole Porter Songbook* ����� (Verve, 1956, prod. Norman Granz, or as the gold disc DCC, 1995), and it serves as a wonderful introduction to Ella if you prefer not to drop a quarter of a grand for *The Complete Ella Fitzgerald Song Books* ����� (Verve, 1993, prod. Norman Granz). Her Porter offering was the best-received of all the "songbooks," and features Fred Astaire, Bing Crosby, Marlene Dietrich, Billie Holiday, Gene Kelly, Judy Garland, Ethel Merman, and Porter himself teaming with her talent. A solid companion piece to the Porter disc is Fitzgerald's *The Complete Duke Ellington Songbook* ����� (Verve, 1956, prod. Norman Granz), though this Verve offering is a two-volume box set and priced accordingly. If the Porter set is Fitzgerald at her vocal best, the Ellington sessions find Ella at her jazz singing best, backed by jazz music's best: Dizzy Gillespie, Johnny Hodges, Oscar Peterson, Billy Strayhorn, and, of course, Sir Duke. Predictably, a flood of new recordings and reshuffled compilations have hit the market since Ella's death. The wide-ranging collection *The Best of the Songbooks* ���� (Verve, 1996) is certainly worthy, but has the disadvantage of moving the songs far away from their original context.

what to buy next: By 1960, Fitzgerald had reached the pinnacle of her dazzling career. She carried the experience 30 years of singing brings, along with the energy and intensity she had when she began. *Mack the Knife: The Complete Ella in Berlin Concert* ����� (Verve, 1993, prod. Phil Schaap) is an example of Ella at her best. Her hilarious and legendary take on "Mack the Knife" made this concert perhaps her most memorable. This disc combines the concert tracks with several rare and previously unreleased recordings, as Ella sparkles on her rendition of Sarah Vaughan's "Misty," her own scat-filled "How High the Moon," and standards like "The Lady Is a Tramp" and "Too Darn Hot." For all-around collections, there are none better than *75th Birthday Celebration* ����� (Decca, 1993, compilation prod. Orrin Keepnews). It's a two-CD set which charts 39 songs from the first half of her career. Ella swings and scats here as both a big band and jazz vocalist.

what to avoid: There's nothing inherently wrong with K-Tel, except that their TV ads are annoying. But *Ella Fitzgerald* � (K-Tel, 1996, prod. various) is just a weak assortment compared to all the others competing with it. Should you get the urge to order by phone at 3 a.m., strap yourself in bed until you can get to the CD store the next day and purchase a truly good compilation.

the rest:

Swingin' NBC Radio 1940 Big Band Remotes ✍✍✍✍ (Sandy Hook, 1940)

Gershwin Songbook ✍✍✍✍ (Verve, 1950)

Ella & Louis ✍✍✍ (Laserlight, 1956)

Ella Fitzgerald & Jazz at the Philharmonic ✍✍✍ (Tax, 1957)

Ella Fitzgerald Sings the George & Ira Gershwin Songbook ✍✍✍✍ (Verve, 1959)

Ella & Basie ✍✍✍✍ (Verve, 1963)

The Johnny Mercer Songbook ✍✍✍ (Verve, 1964)

Ella & Louis ✍✍✍✍ (Verve, 1972)

Ella in London ✍✍✍✍ (Pablo, 1974)

Dream Dancing ✍✍ (Pablo, 1978)

Ella Fitzgerald & Joe Pass: Speak Love ✍✍✍✍ (Pablo, 1983)

Silver Collection: The Songbooks ✍✍✍ (Verve, 1984)

The Jerome Kern Songbook ✍✍✍✍ (Verve, 1985)

These Are the Blues ✍✍✍✍✍ (Verve, 1986)

Ella Fitzgerald at the Opera House ✍✍✍ (Verve, 1986)

The Irving Berlin Songbook Vols. 1 & 2 ✍✍✍✍✍ (Verve, 1986)

Fine and Mellow ✍✍✍ (Pablo, 1987)

Ella Fitzgerald & Louis Armstrong, "Compact Jazz" series ✍✍✍✍ (Verve, 1988)

The Harold Arlen Songbook Vol. 1 ✍✍✍ (Verve, 1988)

The Harold Arlen Songbook Vol. 2 ✍✍✍ (Verve, 1988)

Fitzgerald And Pass . . . Again ✍✍✍✍ (Pablo, 1988)

Ella Fitzgerald/Count Basie/Joe Pass: Digital III at Montreux ✍✍✍✍✍ (Pablo)

Ella Fitzgerald & Count Basie: A Classy Pair ✍✍✍✍✍ (Pablo, 1989)

Ella Fitzgerald & Joe Pass: Easy Living ✍✍✍✍ (Pablo, 1989)

Ella Fitzgerald & Count Basie: A Perfect Match ✍✍✍✍ (Pablo, 1989)

Ella Fitzgerald/Tommy Flanagan, Montreux 1977 ✍✍✍✍ (Original Jazz Classics, 1989)

Ella Fitzgerald & Duke Ellington: The Stockholm Concert Feb. 7, 1966 ✍✍✍✍✍ (Pablo, 1989)

Clap Hands, Here Comes Charlie ✍✍✍✍✍ (Verve, 1989)

Ella: Things Aren't What They Used to Be: And You Better Believe It ✍✍✍✍✍ (Reprise, 1989)

The Best of Ella Fitzgerald ✍✍✍✍ (Pablo, 1989)

The Intimate Ella ✍✍✍✍✍ (Verve, 1990)

Ella and Louis Again ✍✍✍✍✍ (Verve, 1990)

Ella A Nice ✍✍✍✍✍ (Original Jazz Classics, 1990)

Ella Live! ✍✍ (Verve)

Ella Fitzgerald/Count Basie/Benny Goodman Jazz Collector Edition Vol. 2 ✍✍✍✍✍ (Laserlight, 1991)

Ella Fitzgerald & Joe Pass: Take Love Easy ✍✍✍✍ (Pablo, 1991)

Returns to Berlin ✍✍✍ (Verve, 1991)

Like Someone in Love ✍✍✍ (Verve, 1991)

Ella Fitzgerald & Oscar Peterson: Ella and Oscar ✍✍✍✍ (Pablo, 1991)

Ella Swings Lightly ✍✍✍✍ (Verve, 1992)

The Essential Ella Fitzgerald: The Great Songs ✍✍✍ (Verve, 1992)

Ella Swings Gently with Nelson ✍✍✍✍✍ (Verve, 1993)

Ella Swings Brightly with Nelson ✍✍✍✍✍ (Verve, 1993)

At the Montreux Jazz Festival, 1975 ✍✍✍✍ (Original Jazz Classics, 1993)

First Lady of Song ✍✍✍✍✍ (Verve, 1993)

Compact Jazz—Ella & Duke ✍✍✍ (Verve, 1993)

The Best of Ella Fitzgerald ✍✍✍✍ (Curb, 1993)

The Best of Ella Fitzgerald: First Lady of Song ✍✍✍✍ (Verve, 1994)

The Best of the Songbooks: The Ballads ✍✍✍✍ (Verve, 1994)

Jazz 'Round Midnight ✍✍✍✍ (Verve, 1994)

Jazz 'Round Midnight Again ✍✍✍✍ (Verve, 1994)

The War Years ✍✍✍✍ (Decca Jazz, 1994)

Pure Ella ✍✍✍ (Decca Jazz, 1994)

The Concert Years ✍✍✍✍✍ (Pablo, 1994)

Verve Jazz Masters 6 ✍✍✍✍ (Verve, 1994)

Verve Jazz Masters 24 ✍✍✍✍ (Verve, 1994)

The Jazz Sides: Verve Jazz Masters 46 ✍✍✍✍ (Verve, 1995)

Ella: The Legendary Decca Recordings ✍✍✍✍✍ (Decca Jazz, 1995)

Live from the Roseland Ballroom-New York 1940 ✍✍✍✍ (Musicdisc, 1995)

Newport Jazz Festival/Live at Carnegie Hall ✍✍✍✍ (Classics, 1995)

Ella Fitzgerald/Billie Holiday/Dinah Washington, Jazz 'Round Midnight: Three Divas ✍✍✍✍ (Verve, 1995)

The Early Years Pt. 1 & 2 ✍✍✍✍ (Decca Jazz, 1995)

Let No Man Write My Epitaph ✍✍✍✍✍ (Classic, 1995)

Lady Time ✍✍✍✍ (Pablo, 1995)

Dreams Come True ✍✍✍ (Drive Archive, 1995)

Daydream: The Best of the Duke Ellington Songbook ✍✍✍✍ (Verve, 1995)

Love Songs: Best of the Verve Songbooks ✍✍✍✍✍ (Verve, 1996)

The Best of Ella Fitzgerald w/Chick Webb and his Orchestra ✍✍✍✍ (Decca Jazz, 1996)

Oh, Lady Be Good! Best of the Gershwin Songbook ✍✍✍✍ (Verve, 1996)

Ella & Friends ✍✍✍ (Decca Jazz, 1996)

Sunshine of Your Love ✍✍ (Verve, 1996)

Ella Fitzgerald ✍✍ (Dove Audio, 1996)

Bluella: Ella Fitzgerald Sings the Blues ✍✍✍ (Pablo, 1996)

You'll Have to Swing It ✍✍✍ (Eclipse, 1996)

Rock It for Me ✍✍✍ (Eclipse, 1996)

The Best Is Yet to Come ✍✍✍✍✍ (Pablo, 1996)

Sings the Rodgers & Hart Songbook ✍✍✍✍✍ (Verve, 1997)

Rhythm & Romance ✍✍✍ (Living Era, 1997)

A-Tisket, A-Tasket ✍✍✍✍ (ITC Masters, 1997)

The Best of Ella Fitzgerald & Louis Armstrong on Verve ✍✍✍✍✍ (Verve, 1997)

The Complete Ella Fitzgerald & Louis Armstrong on Verve ✍✍✍✍✍ (Verve, 1997)

Ella Fitzgerald/Sarah Vaughan/Carmen McRae: Ladies of Jazz ✍✍✍✍ (Laserlight, 1997)

Ella Fitzgerald with the Tommy Flanagan Trio ✍✍✍ (Laserlight, 1997)

Priceless Jazz Collection ✍✍✍✍ (GRP, 1997)

worth searching for: Christmas albums are not always easy to find, since they're usually only big in the bins during the season to be jolly. But Fitzgerald's Christmas offerings, *Ella Fitzgerald's*

Christmas 🎵🎵🎵 (Capitol/EMI, 1996, prod. Ron Furmack, Rob Furmack) and *Wishes You a Swinging Christmas* 🎵🎵🎵 (Verve, 1993, prod. Norman Granz) are worth tracking down. Once you get in the spirit, you'll be jolly to have Ella's swinging versions of timeless Christmas standbys.

influences:

◀◀ Maxine Sullivan, Connee Boswell, Billie Holiday, Bessie Smith

▶▶ Sarah Vaughan, Lena Horne, Betty Carter, Mel Torme, Carmen McRae, Joe Williams, Shirley Horn, Diana Ross, Whitney Houston, Gladys Knight, Bette Midler, Barbra Streisand

Chris Tower

The Five Keys

Formed 1949, in Newport News, VA.

Maryland Pierce, lead vocals; Dickie Smith, vocals (1949–53); Rudy West, vocals (1949–53, 1955–present); Bernard West, vocals; Ripley Ingram, vocals; Ulysses K. Hicks, vocals (1953–present); Ramon Loper, vocals (1953–present).

The Five Keys were a great vocal group that had some major R&B hits, but most important, they were the first R&B group in the modern rock 'n' roll era to cut a series of hits for a major record label. Originally known as the Sentimental Four in Virginia, they started recording for Aladdin Records in 1951 and had over a dozen releases with them, including their signature tune "The Glory of Love," a #1 R&B hit in the fall of 1951—plus one on RCA's Groove label before signing with Capitol Records in 1954. Their first single on Capitol, "Ling Ting Tong," crossed over and zipped to #28 on the pop charts in 1954; its signature background lick, "Tie-sa-moke-um-bood-a-yay," was picked up in the 1960s by potheads who insisted that the song was about smoking dope. It wasn't, but the notion boosted its popularity immeasurably. Their next two singles, "Close Your Eyes" and "The Verdict," released in 1955, were among their all-time best sellers, yet did not chart pop; another 1955 release, "Gee Whittakers," might have done well had it not been covered by that ubiquitous copycat, Pat Boone. The following year, they put out two more classic R&B ballads, "Out of Sight, Out of Mind," and "Wisdom of a Fool." They continued to record for Capitol through 1958, then moved over to King Records and recorded for the Cincinnati-based label into the 1960s. They survived in various configurations for many years thereafter, but it is their 1950s records that influenced countless R&B and pop artists who came after.

what to buy: Getting the full picture on the Five Keys' career is impossible with any single release still available on the group. *The Five Keys: The Aladdin Years* 🎵🎵🎵 (Collectables, 1995, prod. various) offers their biggest hit, "The Glory of Love," but nothing from the mid-1950s on; *Golden Classics* 🎵🎵🎵🎵 (Collectables, 1994, prod. various) has their memorable later hits, "The Verdict," "Close Your Eyes," "I Wish I'd Never Learned to Read," "Out of Sight, Out of Mind," "Wisdom of a Fool," "My Pigeon's Gone" (love that title!), and, of course, "Ling Ting Tong," but nothing early. Obviously, the Collectables label would like you to purchase both discs. For true fans of doo-wop, the Five Keys are featured prominently in both the Rhino Records compilations *The Doo Wop Box: 101 Vocal Group Gems from the Golden Age of Rock 'n' Roll* 🎵🎵🎵🎵 (Rhino, 1994, prod. Bob Hyde, Walter DeVenne) and *The Doo Wop Box II* 🎵🎵🎵🎵 (Rhino, 1995, prod. Bob Hyde, Walter DeVenne); "Ling Ting Tong" is included in Set Two.

influences:

◀◀ The Ink Spots

▶▶ The Five Blue Notes, the Five Thrills, the Spaniels, the Gems, the Parliaments, George Clinton, the Temptations, the Chi-Lites, the Dells, Frankie Valli & the Four Seasons

Michael Kosser

The "5" Royales

Formed late 1940s, in Winston-Salem, NC. Disbanded 1965.

Lowman Pauling, vocals, guitar; Jimmy Moore, vocals; Johnny Tanner, vocals; Obadiah Carter, vocals; Johnny Holmes, vocals; Otto Jeffries, vocals.

Often—despite its name—a sextet, this great 1950s vocal group was innovative and revered at the time, but is now mostly remembered for the success Lowman Pauling's songs had in later cover versions: "Think" (James Brown), "Tell the Truth" (Ray Charles), and, most famously, "Dedicated to the One I Love," a hit for both the Shirelles and the Mamas & the Papas. But Charles, Brown, Hank Ballard & the Midnighters, Eric Clapton, and Steve Cropper are just a few of the acts significantly influenced by the group's tight, gospel-derived harmonies or Pauling's stinging guitar leads and obbligatos. He was the only group member to play an instrument; hired sidemen, including tenor saxophonist Charlie Ferguson, filled out the lineup. Tenor Johnny Tanner took most of the lead vocals, with his brother Eugene, also a tenor, taking some leads, including "Dedicated to the One I Love." Their intense styles anticipated soul, while the group interaction was the inspiration for James Brown's Famous Flames. The Royal Sons were a gospel group of shifting membership formed during the early 1940s and including Lowman's brother, Clarence Pauling (who, as Clarence Paul, later wrote and produced for Motown and became the label's assistant director of A&R). Lowman and Johnny Tanner joined later, and the group became known as the Royal Sons Gospel Quintet. After recording a single for the Apollo label, they moved to New York in 1951 to be close to the label. The group became the "5" Royales a year later after it began recording secular pop. In 1952, "Baby, Don't Do It," their third secular single, stayed at #1 on the *Billboard* R&B charts for three weeks, and the follow-up, the gospel-fueled "Help Me Somebody," spent five weeks at #1 in 1953. After several more R&B Top 10 hits, they switched to King Records, claiming that Apollo had not been forthcoming with royalties. Apollo sued to retain the group, but eventually it was allowed to go to King in 1955. It took two years for them to recover their chart momentum. In 1957 they had two R&B Top 10 hits, with "Think" even reaching #66 on the pop chart. They also recorded "Dedicated to the One I Love" and released it at the end of the year; it didn't chart at the time, though in 1961 King reissued it after the Shirelles' version became a hit, with the original only then slipping up to #81 on the Hot 100. At a time when albums were much less common than singles, especially in the R&B vocal-group market, King released three LPs compiling the group's singles. These all became collectors' items. But the group had peaked commercially and was overtaken by those building on its innovations. Pauling left the group for a while in 1960 and then rejoined; though its records weren't charting, the group remained a concert draw for years based on past hits. After 1959 it switched, with no sales success, to a variety of other record labels, putting out just a few singles, and finally broke up in 1965. Only Lowman Pauling remained in music, working as a guitarist for artists including Ben E. King and Sam & Dave until his death in 1974. In a genre in which reunions are rife regardless of the number of living members, the "5" Royales have been an exception, with lead vocalist Johnny Tanner refusing to sing non-religious material.

what to buy: The two-CD collection *Monkey Hips and Rice: The "5" Royales Anthology* 🎵🎵🎵🎵 (Rhino, 1994, prod. various) provides a solid overview of this seminal R&B group. It starts with a Royal Sons Quintet gospel track for perspective, then covers the Apollo period with 10 songs. The King period is documented with 29 of the 51 tracks recorded for that label, and a Vee-Jay single from 1962 closes the set. The liner notes and discographical info are thorough, and this set firmly establishes the "5" Royales' place in history.

what to buy next: The documentation is thin and sometimes misleading, and the group's name is misspelled on the cover and the CD, but there are so many songs not on the Rhino set among the 23 tracks on *The Apollo Sessions* 🎵🎵🎵 (Collectables, 1995) that it's definitely worth acquiring for a more complete view of the group's R&B work for Apollo.

what to avoid: Stay away from various cheapie, fly-by-night collections not listed here, as they duplicate this material in skimpy programs.

the rest:
Dedicated to You 🎵🎵🎵 (King, 1957)
The "5" Royales Sing for You 🎵🎵🎵 (King, 1959)
The "5" Royales 🎵🎵🎵 (King, 1960)

influences:

◄◄ The Golden Gate Quartet, the Soul Stirrers, the Five Blind Boys of Alabama

►► Hank Ballard & the Midnighters, Jackie Wilson, James Brown, the Falcons/Wilson Pickett, Eric Clapton, Steve Cropper

Steve Holtje

Roberta Flack

Born February 10, 1939, in Asheville, NC.

Roberta Flack became a singer as an alternative to teaching music, then went on to teach millions about vocal nuance and melodic sophistication in a career spanning 30 years. The daughter of a church organist, Flack began her own musical education learning the piano as a child in Arlington, Virginia, displaying so much ability that she received a music scholarship to Washington D.C.'s Howard University at the age of 15. After earning her degree and student teaching, she began performing at D.C.'s Tivoli Club playing piano for singers. Eventually she started singing blues and R&B herself at clubs throughout the city, developing her own elegant style with romantic, light-jazz ballads. It wasn't long before she was discovered by Les McCann, who signed her to a contract with Atlantic Records. Flack's first two LPs, *First Take* and *Chapter Two*, started slowly, but then Clint Eastwood chose the Ewan MacColl song "The First Time Ever I Saw Your Face" for his 1972 movie *Play Misty For Me.* Flack's haunting rendition of the tune was an instant success, shooting the single straight to #1 on the pop charts and keeping it there for six weeks. She began working with singer-songwriter Donny Hathaway, whom she knew from Howard, and scored big hits with "Killing Me Softly with His

Roberta Flack (© Jack Vartoogian)

Song" in 1973 and the chart-topping "Feel Like Makin' Love" the following year. Flack slowed down after her 1974 triumph, continuing to record but taking time off from the performing circuit. She scored several more hits in the mid-to-late 1970s, with and without Hathaway, but none matched the enormous popularity of her early songs. Then in 1979, Hathaway fell to his death at a New York hotel. The loss of her partner was emotionally crushing for Flack, but she rebounded in 1980 to team with Peabo Bryson, tour, and continue to perform. She recorded a memorable duet with Bryson in 1983, "Tonight, I Celebrate My Love." Though Flack continues to perform into the 1990s, her days of 1970s superstardom are past. She has collaborated with Luther Vandross, Miles Davis, and Sadao Watanabe, and scored her last Top 10 single in 1991, the duet "Set the Night to Music," with Maxi Priest.

what to buy: Produced by Burt Bacharach, *Softly with These Songs: The Best of Roberta Flack* ♫♫♫♫ (WEA/Atlantic, 1993, prod. various) is a superb entry into Flack's world of light jazz,

restrained passion, smooth crooning, and urban romance. All her biggest hits are included, plus some of her lesser-known but quality material recorded after 1980. Also, for lovers of commercial jazz, this "Best of" features some of the best of the genre, like David Sanborn, Earl Klugh, Luther Vandross, and Lee Ritenour.

what to buy next: The remastered *First Take* ♫♫♫♫ (WEA/Atlantic, 1969, prod. Joel Dorn) is step two in advanced Flack education. In retrospect, her first album may still be her best, and includes the introductory airing of "The First Time Ever I Saw Your Face." Though not her best work, *Roberta Flack: Featuring Donny Hathaway* ♫♫♫♫ (WEA/Atlantic, 1972, prod. Roberta Flack, Eric Mercury) is her most beloved, most popular album. Both "You've Got a Friend" and "Where Is the Love" were big hits in 1972, the latter for the entire year.

what to avoid: Most of Flack's work is exceptional, but of all her albums, *Set the Night to Music* ♫♫♫ (WEA/Atlantic, 1991, prod.

Arif Mardin) is by far the weakest. It includes a cover of "Unforgettable" with Maxi Priest that came out the same year as the Natalie Cole version, which was the big hit of that year. Coincidence? Can you say, "cashing in?"

the rest:
Chapter Two ✍✍✍ (Atlantic, 1970)
Quiet Fire ✍✍✍ (WEA/Atlantic, 1971)
Killing Me Softly ✍✍✍ (WEA/Atlantic, 1973)
Feel Like Makin' Love ✍✍✍ (WEA/Atlantic, 1975)
Blue Lights in the Basement ✍✍✍ (WEA/Atlantic, 1977)
I'm the One ✍✍✍ (WEA/Atlantic, 1982)
Oasis ✍✍✍ (WEA/Atlantic, 1988)
Roberta ✍✍✍ (WEA/Atlantic, 1994)
The Classic Mix EP ✍✍ (Atlantic, 1996)
The Christmas Album N/A (Angel, 1997)

influences:
◄◄ Sarah Vaughan, Ella Fitzgerald, Carmen McRae, Billie Holiday, Bessie Smith, Maxine Sullivan, Shirley Horn, Lena Horne

►► Natalie Cole, Brenda Russell, Melba Moore, Luther Vandross

Chris Tower

Flatlinerz
Formed in New York.

Graveravin', vocals; Tempest, vocals; Redrum, vocals.

Following the success of the Gravediggaz, the Flatlinerz capitalized on a sub-genre dubbed "horrorcore," which mixed judicious images of the macabre, slasher flicks, and nightmare visage.

what's available: *U.S.A.* ✍✍✍ (RAL/Def Jam/PLG, 1994, prod. Tempest, others) is filled with dense rhythms and aggressive vocal patter, as the trio delivers rhymes in a style similar to that of labelmates Onyx: Part growl, part snarl, and part top-of-the-lungs yelling. Lyrical devices include stark imagery on loan from the *Friday the 13th* franchise, with song titles running the gamut from "Good Day to Die" to "Rivaz of Red" and, of course, "Satanic Verses." And on the guest (rapper) list: The Headless Horseman and Omen.

worth searching for: The video for *Live Evil* ✍✍✍—a song that's filled with demonic chanting and eerie piano strokes and whisper-to-a-scream synth lines—is an atmospheric black-and-white affair that's loaded with disturbing images of lynchings, zombies, and grave robbers.

influences:
◄◄ Gravediggaz, Art of Origin, Onyx

Spence D.

Eddie Floyd
Born June 25, 1935, in Montgomery, AL.

Calling Eddie Floyd a second-rate talent amongst his Stax peers is a bit like chiding the sluggishness of a Carrera next to a Ferrari. He simply had the historical misfortune of being a very good singer-songwriter on a label with artists who made the earth move. That's not to say his signature song, "Knock on Wood," doesn't jar the Richter scale; it does, and the countless cover versions that have abounded over the years are further testaments to its power. But Floyd simply didn't reach those dazzling results with the same frequency of Otis Redding or Sam & Dave. Not too shabby at all.

what to buy: *Rare Stamps* ✍✍✍ (Stax/Fantasy, 1993, prod. Steve Cropper) compiles two 1960s albums—*I Never Found a Girl* and *Rare Stamps*—into a stunning 25-track disc. Backed by the peerless Booker T. and the MG's, Floyd kicks out his best material, including "Knock on Wood," a lively version of Sam Cooke's "Bring it on Home to Me," and the pre-metal lament "Big Bird." The reissue also contains two hot duets with Mavis Staples.

what to buy next: *Knock on Wood* ✍✍✍ (Stax, 1967/Rhino, 1991, reissue prod. Yves Beauvais) is Floyd's strongest studio album, highlighted by the title track, "634-5789" and the sublime "I've Just Been Feeling Bad." *Chronicle: Greatest Hits* ✍✍✍ (Stax, 1991, prod. various) collects some of the *Rare Stamps* material along with "My Girl" and the Memphis funk of "Soul Street."

what to avoid: *Baby Lay Your Head Down* ✍✍ (Stax, 1973, prod. Eddie Floyd, Al Bell, Dale Warren, Al Jackson Jr.) contains the weakest material of his career.

the rest:
California Girl/Down to Earth ✍✍✍ (Stax, 1996)

worth searching for: *You've Got to Have Eddie* (Stax, 1969), *Soul Street* (Stax, 1974) and *Experience* (Malaco, 1977) are all out of print (*Soul Street* is available on cassette). These albums' highlights are available on the aforementioned collections, but they're still worth hearing in their entirety.

influences:
◄◄ Sam Cooke, Lou Rawls, Otis Redding

$$\frac{2}{2}$$
0

force m.d.'s

▶▶ The Commodores, Rick James, Bruce Springsteen, Toots and the Maytals, Eric Clapton

Allan Orski

Force M.D.'s
Formed 1979, in Staten Island, NY.

Stevie D., vocals; T.C.D., vocals; Jesse Lee Daniels, vocals (1979–87; 1992–present); Trisco Pearson, vocals (1979–90); Mercury, vocals (1979–90); Khalil, vocals (1990–present); Shaun Waters, vocals (1990–present).

The Wu-Tang Clan may be credited with being the first major hip-hop crew to emerge from Staten Island, but long before the Wu ruled everything around the island—and, for that matter, New York in general—a group of hip-hop inspired singers from Staten Island was already proving itself to be a major force in the marketplace. Anticipating by more than a decade the hip-hop doo-wop trend that would star the likes of Boyz II Men and Color Me Badd, the Force M.D.'s scored several hits with their shimmering hip-hop harmonies, including "Tears," "Love Is a House," and the Jimmy Jam–Terry Lewis smash, "Tender Love," which was featured on the soundtrack of the embarrassing rap film *Krush Groove*. Ironically, as hip-hop doo-wop began to take off in the early 1990s, the Force M.D.'s saw their own popularity decrease and eventually parted ways with longtime label Tommy Boy. The group remained active, though, as various members served as producers for other artists or attempted to start up solo careers, and in 1994, the Force M.D.'s returned with an album that, unfortunately, confirmed that the group was no longer a force, either artistically or commercially.

what to buy: *For Lovers and Others* ♫♫♫ (Tommy Boy, 1992, prod. various) collects the group's best ballads, though much of the material sounds dated in an old-but-not-really-classic-soul sort of way.

what to avoid: *Get Ready* ♫♫ (PolyGram, 1994): see above. 'Nuf sed.

the rest:
Love Letters ♫♫♫ (Tommy Boy, 1984)
Chillin' ♫♫ (Tommy Boy, 1986)
Touch and Go ♫♫♫ (Tommy Boy, 1987)
Step to Me ♫♫ (Tommy Boy, 1990)

worth searching for: The Force M.D.'s joined forces with their rapper labelmates, Stetsasonic, to recast the Floaters' "Float On" as a rap song (Tommy Boy, 1989). The single is out of print, but worth the search.

influences:
◀◀ Planet Patrol
▶▶ Color Me Badd, Boyz II Men, New Edition

Josh Freedom du Lac

The Four Seasons
See: Frankie Valli

The Four Tops
Formed 1954, in Detroit, MI.

Levi Stubbs, vocals; Abdul "Duke" Fakir, vocals; Lawrence Payton, vocals; Renaldo "Obie" Benson, vocals.

One of Motown's two mightiest male vocal groups, the Four Tops held power by remaining intact, while individual Temptations, by contrast, came and went. The gruff authority of Stubbs's voice has been a wondrous thing, celebrated in songs by other artists years later. As a group, few in Motown exemplified the real powerhouse of the label—the songwriting of Holland-Dozier-Holland and the power of the in-house band—as the Tops did. Amid a flurry of mid-1960s hits, the highlight may have been "Reach Out I'll Be There," which kicked off with its heralding flutes and military drumbeats; few songs of support and solidarity have been so grippingly recorded. The group relied more on its strong vocals and less on dancing, *a la* the Tempts, with whom the Tops staged a friendly rivalry at various song "showdowns." But the Tops didn't enjoy a second run of psychedelic hits as did their Motown rivals; in fact, when Holland-Dozier-Holland left the label, so did Stubbs and company. The Tops came back quickly with a couple of quick hits in "Keeper of the Castle" and "Ain't No Woman (Like the One I've Got)" in 1972 but had little else on the pop charts afterwards. The 1990 Rock and Roll Hall of Fame inductees continue to tour—often with the Temptations—showing remarkable durability for a group consigned to the oldies circuit. Underlying the close-knit solidarity of the group, Stubbs, Fakir, and Benson opted not to replace Lawrence Payton following his death from liver cancer in June 1997. They now perform as The Tops. A boxed set is due imminently.

what to buy: The double-length *Anthology* ♫♫♫♫♫ (Motown, 1989, prod. various) spans the Top's hits on Motown and other labels, showcasing the group's awesome run of hits.

what to buy next: For a more intense rush of the group's hey-day, the silver-covered *Greatest Hits* 𝄞𝄞𝄞𝄞 (Motown, 1967/1987, prod. Holland-Dozier-Holland) is relentless. *Until You Love Someone: More of the Best* (Rhino, 1993, prod. various) 𝄞𝄞𝄞 is worthwhile for those who want to delve deeper than the hits. *Keepers of the Castle: Their Best 1972–1978* 𝄞𝄞𝄞 (MCA, 1997, prod. various) captures the best of the group's immediate post-Motown era.

what to avoid: The group's latest, *Four Tops Christmas* 𝄞 (Motown, 1995, prod. Four Tops) is a lame holiday effort in which each of the members produces his own selection and nothing but a visit from Aretha Franklin helps them.

the rest:
Four Tops 𝄞𝄞𝄞 (Motown, 1965)
Second Album 𝄞𝄞𝄞𝄞 (Motown, 1966)
On Top 𝄞𝄞𝄞 (Motown, 1966)
Live 𝄞𝄞𝄞𝄞 (Motown, 1967/1991)
Four Tops Reach Out 𝄞𝄞𝄞𝄞 (Motown, 1967/1983)
Yesterday's Dreams 𝄞𝄞𝄞 (Motown, 1968)
Four Tops Now 𝄞𝄞𝄞 (Motown, 1969)
Soul Spin 𝄞𝄞𝄞 (Motown, 1969)
Still Waters Run Deep 𝄞𝄞 (Motown, 1970/1982)
Changing Times 𝄞𝄞 (Motown, 1970)
(With the Supremes) *The Magnificent Seven* 𝄞𝄞𝄞𝄞 (Motown, 1970)
(With the Supremes) *The Return of the Magnificent Seven* 𝄞𝄞𝄞 (Motown, 1971)
(With the Supremes) *Dynamite* 𝄞𝄞𝄞 (Motown, 1972)
Nature Planned It 𝄞𝄞 (Motown, 1972)
Greatest Hits (1972–76) 𝄞𝄞𝄞 (MCA, 1982/1987)
Back Where I Belong 𝄞𝄞 (Motown, 1983)
Great Songs 𝄞𝄞𝄞𝄞 (Motown, 1983/89)
Magic 𝄞𝄞 (Motown, 1985)
Ain't No Woman . . . 𝄞𝄞𝄞 (MCA, 1987/1994)
Indestructible 𝄞𝄞 (Arista, 1988)
When She Was My Girl 𝄞𝄞 (Mercury, 1992)
Motown Legends 𝄞𝄞𝄞 (ESX Entertainment, 1994)
The Ultimate Collection 𝄞𝄞𝄞𝄞 (Motown, 1997)

worth searching for: The soundtrack for the film version of *Little Shop of Horrors* 𝄞𝄞𝄞 (Geffen, 1986, prod. Bob Gaudio), which features Stubbs as the wickedly soulful voice of the man-eating plant, is worth getting if you find it.

influences:
◀◀ The Orioles, the Drifters, the Moonglows

▶▶ The Temptations, Darius Rucker/Hootie and the Blowfish, Boyz II Men

Roger Catlin

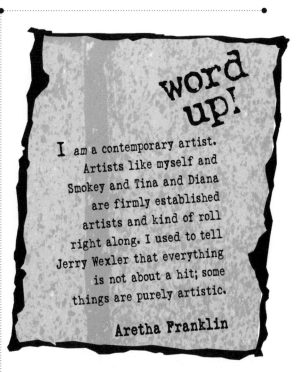

word up!

I am a contemporary artist. Artists like myself and Smokey and Tina and Diana are firmly established artists and kind of roll right along. I used to tell Jerry Wexler that everything is not about a hit; some things are purely artistic.

Aretha Franklin

Aretha Franklin

Born March 25, 1942, in Memphis, TN.

For the daughter of the famous Detroit preacher C.L. Franklin, gospel was second nature. Having achieved young stardom in the gospel world, her first venture to the secular world was an uneasy one at Columbia Records. But Atlantic's Jerry Wexler pursued her after her contract ran out. Together they made an astounding string of classics during the late 1960s that not only defined soul music but also crowned Aretha "Queen of Soul" for life. Besides being a joy to hear, Franklin's work was also culturally significant, helping to define black self-awareness at a time when a little bit of R-E-S-P-E-C-T was much needed. Franklin's success seems tied to her various recording companies; none could match Atlantic, but she enjoyed odd bouts of success once more on Arista during the early 1980s. Her love for gospel remains strong, and she continues to be an ambassador for soul music from her home in the Detroit area.

what to buy: *I Never Loved a Man (the Way I Loved You)* 𝄞𝄞𝄞𝄞𝄞 (Atlantic, 1967, prod. Jerry Wexler) is a startling achievement. There's no way her Atlantic debut could have been more electri-

fying. With the Muscle Shoals backing and Jerry Wexler producing, the album includes her searing "Respect" as well as the enduring "Do Right Woman, Do Right Man" and "Dr. Feelgood."

what to buy next: If your billfold is thick enough, the opulently packaged box set *The Queen of Soul* &&&&& (Rhino/Atlantic, 1992, prod. various) has it all—the hits, the surprises, the achievements of her career. In an economic pinch, *30 Greatest Hits* &&&&& (Atlantic, 1985, prod. various) distills the hit period. *Lady Soul* &&&& (Atlantic, 1968, prod. Jerry Wexler) is also from her greatest period. *Amazing Grace* &&&&& (Atlantic, 1972, prod. Jerry Wexler, Arif Mardin, Aretha Franklin) is her triumphant return to gospel. *Aretha's Greatest Hits (1980–1994)* &&&& (Arista, 1994, prod. various) shows she's still able to sing with soul even when the material is uneven.

what to avoid: On *La Diva* & (Atlantic, 1979), Lady Soul gets stuck in the disco period.

the rest:
Aretha && (Columbia, 1961)
The Electrifying Aretha Franklin &&& (Columbia, 1962)
Laughing on the Outside &&& (Columbia, 1963)
The Tender, the Moving, the Swinging Aretha Franklin && (Columbia, 1963)
Unforgettable: A Tribute to Dinah Washington &&& (Columbia 1964)
Running Out of Fools && (Columbia, 1964)
Yeah! Aretha Franklin in Person && (Columbia, 1965) *Soul Sister* &&& (Columbia, 1966)
Greatest Hits &&& (Columbia, 1967)
Take It Like You Give It && (Columbia, 1967)
Take a Look &&& (Columbia, 1967)
Aretha Arrives &&&& (Atlantic, 1967)
Aretha Now &&&& (Atlantic, 1968)
Aretha in Paris &&&& (Atlantic, 1968)
Greatest Hits, Vol. 2 &&& (Columbia, 1968)
Soul '69 &&&& (Atlantic, 1969)
Aretha's Gold &&&&& (Atlantic, 1969)
This Girl's in Love with You &&&& (Atlantic, 1970)
Spirit in the Dark &&&&& (Atlantic, 1970)
Live at the Fillmore West &&&& (Atlantic, 1971) *Greatest Hits* &&&& (Atlantic, 1971)
Young, Gifted and Black &&&& (Atlantic, 1972)
Hey Now Hey (The Other Side of the Sky) &&& (Atlantic, 1973)
The First Twelve Sides && (Columbia, 1973)
The Best of Aretha Franklin &&&& (Atlantic, 1973)
Let Me in Your Life &&&& (Atlantic, 1974)

With Everything I Feel in Me && (Atlantic, 1974)
You && (Atlantic, 1975)
Sparkle &&&& (Atlantic, 1976)
Ten Years of Gold &&&& (Atlantic, 1976)
Sweet Passion &&& (Atlantic, 1977)
Almighty Fire && (Atlantic, 1978)
Love All the Hurt Away &&&& (Arista, 1981)
Jump to It &&&& (Arista, 1982)
Sweet Bitter Love && (Columbia, 1982)
Get It Right &&&& (Arista, 1983)
Aretha's Jazz && (Columbia, 1984)
Who's Zoomin' Who &&&& (Arista, 1985)
Aretha Sings the Blues &&& (Columbia, 1985)
Aretha && (Arista, 1986)
After Hours && (Columbia, 1987)
One Lord, One Faith, One Baptism &&&& (Arista, 1987)
Through the Storm &&& (Arista, 1989)
What You Get Is What You Sweat &&& (Arista, 1991)
Jazz to Soul &&&& (Columbia Legacy, 1992)
Love Songs &&& (Atlantic & Atco Remasters/Rhino, 1997)

worth searching for: *The Gospel Sound of Aretha Franklin* &&&& (Checker, 1956) captures Aretha tearin' it up in church at age 14.

influences:
◀◀ Celia Ward, Ruth Brown, the Rev. C.L. Franklin, Sam Cooke
▶▶ Whitney Houston, Anita Baker, Chaka Khan

Roger Catlin

Kirk Franklin & the Family
Formed 1991, in Ft. Worth, TX.

Kirk Franklin, vocals, piano, synthesizer; Jeannette Johnson, vocals; Keisha Grandy, vocals; Yolanda "Yo" McDonald, vocals; Sheila "Mother" Brice, vocals; Tamela "Biscuit" Mann, vocals; Stephanie "Chicken" Glynn, vocals; David "Big Daddy" Mann, vocals; Dalon "Big Love" Collins, vocals; Theresa Young, vocals; Terri Pace, vocals; Demetrice Clinkscale, vocals; Bryon Cole, vocals; Carrie "Mousey" Young Davis, vocals; Jon "J.D." Drummond, vocals; Darrell Blair, vocals; Chris "Sweetie" Simpson, vocals.

If you don't believe in the power of God and faith, you could not possibly have heard of Kirk Franklin. Abandoned by his mother as a baby in 1971, never knowing his father, and spending his teen years running the inner city's mean streets with gangs and drugs, Franklin found an outlet for his instinctive musical gifts in the church. Miraculously, he turned his life around, bursting out of nowhere to become the Garth Brooks of gospel—the most popular, successful young artist of his genre. His 1993

Aretha Franklin (© Jack Vartoogian)

debut LP *Kirk Franklin and the Family*, recorded on the struggling, unknown independent label Gospo-Centric, spent 100 weeks topping the *Billboard* gospel charts while crossing over to urban, pop, and Contemporary Christian audiences. The stately song "Why We Sing" from that LP, actually a clever reworking of the inspirational classic "His Eye Is on the Sparrow" performed by his 17-voice choir of longtime friends called the Family, became a hit on urban contemporary stations (even though it was never released as a single), placing Franklin and gospel in the R&B limelight simultaneously. His second effort, *Christmas*, entered the gospel charts at #1 and went on to sell over a million copies; the only other million-selling gospel LPs in history belong to Aretha Franklin and Elvis Presley. Franklin (no relation) has exhibited an uncanny ability to put the real-life struggles and emotions of the African American community into a hip, relatable context that has helped bring young people back to the church, a talent possibly developed through his own experience. Raised and adopted by his great aunt Gertrude, a deeply religious woman who scraped together money for his piano lessons, Kirk demonstrated the ability to sight-read music and play by ear; by 11, he was conducting the adult choir at Mt. Rose Baptist Church in Ft. Worth. Yet he rebelled against his strict upbringing, using drugs and hanging with gang members until, at 15, his good friend Eric Pounds was accidentally shot and killed. The incident shocked the grief-stricken Franklin into immersing himself in the church. He has faced and overcome other obstacles—fathering a child while in his teens and, in 1996, falling off a stage in Memphis during the "Tour for Life" and sustaining serious injuries—while maintaining a single-minded focus on his musical mission. Franklin is making gospel sexy, accessible, and streetwise, and his passion to spread the Good News to the mainstream has found him singing on the movie soundtracks to *Don't Be a Menace to South Central While You're Drinking Your Juice in the Hood* and *The Preacher's Wife* and contributing to the 1995 album of R&B singer-producer R. Kelly. Franklin's blockbuster 1997 LP, *God's Property from Kirk Franklin's Nu Nation*, pairs the conductor-composer with the 50-member youth choir from God's Property, an arts and educational foundation.

what to buy: The phenomenal debut LP *Kirk Franklin & the Family* ♫♫♫ (Gospo-Centric, 1993, prod. Rodney Frazier, Arthur Dyer) is gospel for the next millennium. Firmly rooted in religious tradition, Franklin still brings a tough urban sensibility to the music, taking dead aim at the hearts and souls of R&B audiences who may not have heard the message otherwise. The majestic "Why We Sing"—which caused people to line up at

record stores requesting the song when it became a radio favorite—is reason enough to buy this album.

what to buy next: Recorded live from Atlanta to Los Angeles in 1994 but released two years later, *Whatcha Lookin' 4?* ♫♫♫ (Gospo-Centric/Sparrow, 1996, prod. Kirk Franklin, Buster & Shavoni) proved to be worth the wait. The Grammy-winning LP shows Franklin's musical formula polished to a high gloss, moving effortlessly from contemporary to traditional and back again through outstanding production. Working New Jack, jazz, and funk in unison with gospel and giving much of his spotlight over to the Family, Franklin creates a heartfelt outpouring of praise you can feel emanating from every track. The urban-flavored ballad "Conquerors" and "Mama's Song," dedicated to Franklin's late mother, are standouts.

the rest:
Christmas ♫♫♫ (Gospo-Centric, 1995)
God's Property from Kirk Franklin's Nu Nation ♫♫♫♫ (Interscope Records, 1997)

worth searching for: While formulating the Family, Franklin honed his conducting and arranging skills under his mentor Milton Biggham with the DFW (Dallas-Ft. Worth) Mass Choir. Either of the DFW albums *Another Chance* ♫♫♫ (Savoy, 1993) or *I Will Let Nothing Separate Me* ♫♫♫ (Savoy, 1991) give some aural insights to the maturation of a gospel prodigy.

influences:
◀◀ Andrae Crouch, Edwin Hawkins, the Winans, Sounds of Blackness

Andre McGarrity and Tim A. Smith

Freestyle Fellowship

Formed 1991, in South Central, Los Angeles, CA. Disbanded 1994.

J-Sublimi, vocals (1991–93); Mikah Nine/Microphone Mike, vocals; Self-Jupiter, vocals; Aceyalone, vocals; Peace/Mtulazaji, vocals (1993–94).

Discussions of '90s West Coast hip-hop center on so-called gangsta rap, but for those who really know, the experimental edge of the Los Angeles underground has been as influential as it has been overlooked. All roads begin at an ongoing series of open-mic nights organized in the early '90s by cafe owner and community activist Bea Hall at her South Central site called the Good Life. Attracting a wildly talented group interested in pursuing poetic and rhythmic complexity, these artists worked with the same intensity and dogma of late-'60s free jazzers. The similarities don't end there. While they blew down all kinds of artistic borders, they would be received by the public in much the same way—derided, especially, by East Coast critics and fans who favored simplicity and directness. Their innovations would be taken into the mainstream by much less committed artists in the most ironic way: although they were post-gangsta in spirit, the artists' tricky cadences would gain credibility and transform street rap through groups like Bone Thugs-N-Harmony and Crucial Conflict. Although the L.A. rappers' commitment to jazz was strictly in line with their deep understanding of African American music, their quest to make hip-hop more complex would be short-circuited by Kerouac-reading, goateed acid jazz hipsters.

what to buy: By 1991, a loosely configured federation of Good Life alumni calling themselves the Freestyle Fellowship was committing itself to wax on its self-released *To Whom It May Concern* ♫♫♫♫ (Sun, 1991, prod. various). The record took on mythic status in some quarters, as much for what it represented as for what it did and said musically. Taking seriously the collectivist vibe of the Native Tongues Movement, vibrant local scenes based around college radio, fanzines, and small open-mic cafes were springing up across the nation. Hip-hop that experimented with jazz structures was the emerging sound of choice. Freestyling—the improvisation of lyrics in shifting rhythmic patterns—was the new standard. Nostalgia for long microphone sessions was chic. Anti–major label independence, articulated by A Tribe Called Quest on *The Low End Theory*'s "Check the Rhime," presented the first sustained Do-It-Yourself move by hip-hop artists. *To Whom It May Concern* manifests all of these trends, along with a respect for diversity of sound. This diversity makes the album exciting. There are J-Sumbi's political attacks on government on "Legal Alien" and on wack East Coast rhymers on "Sunshine Men." There's Mikah Nine's (here as "Microphone Mike") leaps into rap-scatting and horror-flick psychedelia ("Five O'Clock Follies," "Seventh Seal"); the off-center word experiments of Self-Jupiter ("Jupiter's Journey"); and the Langston Hughes B-boy rebel style of Aceyalone ("My Fantasy," "Here I Am"). Down to Mikah Nine, Self-Jupiter, Aceyalone, and new member Peace, the Fellowship refines its attack on *Inner City Griots* ♫♫♫♫ (Island, 1993, prod. Earthquake Brothers, Freestyle Fellowship). The group's musical mission is nothing less than to show that Louis Armstrong, Eddie Jefferson, Art Blakey's Jazz Messengers, and John Coltrane all belong in a deconstructed version of hip-hop. Their approach and their lyrics seem to summon entropy, even while proclaiming "Everything's Everything." Undeniably, tracks like "Hot Potato" and "Cornbread" are hip-hop. But the Freestyle Fellowship forces the listener to answer the question

How? To those in 1993 for whom hip-hop had become wallpaper music, the challenge was too much. Ignored by everyone except a sizable cult following, the artists went their own ways in 1994—and in Self-Jupiter's tragic case, to jail.

what to buy next: Aceyalone's *All Balls Don't Bounce* ♫♫♫♪ (Capitol, 1995, prod. Aceyalone, others) is somewhat of a disappointment. A whimsical personality of protean poetic strength on the first two Fellowship albums, Acey is less cohesive over a wide-ranging solo record. There are moments of brilliance, however (the exciting microphone session with Abstract Rude and Mikah Nine of "Knownots," the engaging beat politics of "Headaches and Woes," the spraycan rhythms of "Arhythmaticulas," the deadpan delivery of "I Think") that are insistent enough for all but the most jaded to be hopeful about a hip-hop alternative.

the rest:
Project Blowed ♫♫♫♪ (Afterlife, 1994/1995)

worth searching for: The underground is always churning with live bootlegs, demos, and rumors of Freestyle Fellowship tracks. One of the more rewarding finds is Abstract Rude's 1996 promotional single, *Oooo I'ma Getcha/Left Hand Sided/Shogun* ♫♫♫♫ on Grand Royal.

influences:

◀◀ Watts Prophets, De La Soul, Ultramagnetic MC's, Organized Konfusion

▶▶ Bay Area hip-hop underground, Abstract Rude, Bone Thugs-N-Harmony, Crucial Conflict, Busta Rhymes, Wu-Tang Clan, Chino XL, the Nonce, Volume 10

Jeff "DJ Zen" Chang

Doug E. Fresh
Born Douglas Davis, September 17, 1966, in New York, NY.

Doug E. Fresh knows how to put on a show, all right. In 1985, the self-proclaimed "original human beatbox" teamed up with rapper MC Ricky D. to record the left-field classic "The Show," in which Ricky served up lyrical (a)musings while Doug E. Fresh let loose a symphony of mouth beats and sound effects. Although the Biz Markie and the Fat Boys' Human Beat Box might have quibbled with Doug's claim of originality, there was no denying that he raised the stakes for vocal percussionists everywhere. Ricky D. established himself with the song, too, and immediately split with Fresh for a solo career as Slick Rick. Sometime between the release of "The Show" and the completion of his largely disappointing 1986 full-length debut, *Oh, My*

The Fugees (© Jack Vartoogian)

God!, Fresh found his God, and it showed, with the beatboxing rapper suddenly more excited about exploring religion ("All the Way to Heaven") than trying to recapture the rhythmic spark of "The Show." On the 1988 follow-up, *The World's Greatest Entertainer*, Fresh hardly lived up to his own billing, although "Keep Risin' to the Top" did become a major hit. After a four-year absence, Doug E. Fresh returned on Hammer's Bust It label with an uninspired Rick James cover, "Bustin' Out (On Funk)." Undeterred, he returned again in 1995 with the decent *Play*, which produced the minor singles "I-ight" and "Where's Da Party At?" but was more notable for "The Original Old School" and its cast of hip-hop legends (DJ Hollywood, Cold Crush Four, Love Bug Starski, Furious Five).

what to buy: *The Greatest Hits, Vol. 1* 🐾🐾🐾 (Bust It/Capitol, 1996, prod. various) features the seminal Doug E. Fresh track, "The Show," which is still a delightful sonic rush after all these years and all these copycats (including the "Show Stoppa," an answer song by a young version of Salt-N-Pepa). Also included

here is the oft-referenced "La Di Da Di" and the Fresh one's last notable hit, "Keep Risin' to the Top." Annoyingly, though, the album is padded with some worthless new tracks recorded with Sean "Puffy" Combs.

the rest:
Play 🐾🐾 (Gee Street/Island, 1995, prod. Doug E. Fresh, Easy Mo Bee, Todd Terry, Frankie Cutlass, Da Beatminerz, others)

influences:
◀◀ Biz Markie, Human Beat Box
▶▶ Digital Underground, Slick Rick, Salt-N-Pepa, Rahzel

Josh Freedom du Lac

Friends of Distinction

Formed 1969, in Los Angeles, CA. Disbanded in late 1970s.

Floyd Butler, vocals; Harry Elston, vocals; Jessica Cleaves, vocals; Barbara Love (a.k.a. Charlene Gibson), vocals; Leaveil Degree, vocals.

The Fifth Dimension with attitude, the pop-soul singing group called Friends of Distinction was created in the shadow of their more famous counterparts and shares at least three things in common with them: gliding, pinpoint harmonies; an L.A. mailing address; and a little-remembered quartet called the Hi-Fi's, which contributed two members to each act (Elston and Butler to the Friends, Marilyn McCoo and LaMonte McLemore to the Fifth). The quintet—three women and two men, the reverse of the Fifth Dimension format—cobbled a short string of legitimate hits in their own right, beginning in 1969 with a zingy vocal version of trumpeter Hugh Masekela R&B instrumental "Grazin' in the Grass." They went on to make the charts with the moody, memorable ballad "Going in Circles" and the dramatic "Love Me or Let Me Be Lonely." The five went their separate ways by the mid-1970s: Jessica Cleaves went on to record a couple of LPs with Earth, Wind & Fire, while Barbara Love, a mezzo soprano, returned to teaching and singing opera. Luther Vandross covered "Going in Circles" on his 1994 album, *Songs*.

what to buy: Of the two "greatest hits" collections currently available on the Friends of Distinction, the CD compiled by the group's former home label, RCA, *Best of the Friends of Distinction* 🎵🎵🎵 (RCA, 1996, prod. various) is of infinitely greater value. Among its 20 cuts, all recorded between 1968 and 1973, the obvious inclusions are surrounded by the group's time-capsule cover versions of "It Don't Matter to Me" and "Ain't No Woman (Like the One I've Got)," and their own subordinate but interesting tracks "Crazy Mary," "Lonesome Mood," and "I Really Hope You Do." If there had been no Fifth Dimension, the FOD would be hailed as one of its era's most talented ensembles; as it is, they're still highly listenable.

the rest:
Golden Classics 🎵🎵 (Collectables, 1991, prod. various)

influences:
◀◀ Nancy Wilson, Billy Eckstine, Manhattan Transfer, the Fifth Dimension, Leontyne Price, the Chi-Lites

▶▶ Minnie Riperton, Earth, Wind & Fire, Will Downing, Moments, the Commodores, Rachelle Ferrell, Take 6

Stacey Hale

Fugees
Formed 1989, in South Orange, NJ.

Nel Wyclef Jean, vocals, guitar, keyboards, bass; Lauryn Hill, vocals; Prakazrel Michael, vocals, keyboards.

The group's name is short for refugees, a reminder of the Hait-

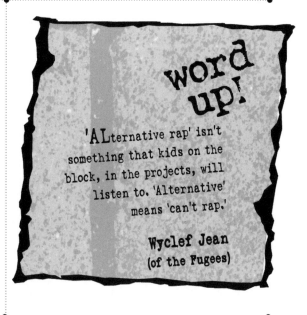

'ALternative rap' isn't something that kids on the block, in the projects, will listen to. 'Alternative' means 'can't rap.'

**Wyclef Jean
(of the Fugees)**

ian heritage of cousins Clef and Pras. While their brand of hip-hop is musical and conscious, the Fugees are no sucker MCs: in their struggle to keep it both positive and real, their music falls squarely between the hardcore jeep beats of gangsta rap and the trippier alternarap of Arrested Development and De La Soul. With two of their three principals being instrumentalists, the group emphasizes musicality as well as grooves. On the mic, they earn extra points for according Hill as much—and perhaps even more—time out front as Clef and Pras, a rare act of equality in the rap game. Even better, she's up to the task, turning in smooth sung vocals and a cool measured rap flow. More than almost any other hip-hop act, the Fugees set their goals high and then took well-measured steps toward achieving them.

what to buy: Alternarap's long-awaited breakthrough, *The Score* 🎵🎵🎵 (Ruffhouse/Columbia, 1996, prod. Fugees, Diamond D, others) moves hip-hop forward even as it looks back to pay tribute to seminal influences such as Bob Marley and Roberta Flack. The covers of Marley's "No Woman, No Cry" and Flack's "Killing Me Softly" are less than revelatory, but the original tracks "Fu-Gee-La," "Ready or Not," and "Family Business" prove that the Fugees are worthy successors to their heroes. Equally impressive is the album's almost cinematic quality, combining occasionally noirish grooves, compelling and sometimes uplifting tales from the 'hood and the only funny skit to grace a rap album in recent memory. The multiplatinum disc deservedly won the 1997 Grammy Award for Best Rap Album.

what to buy next: Distinguishing himself as the group's true visionary, Wyclef followed *The Score* with the *Wyclef Jean Presents the Carnival* ♪♪♪♪ (Ruffhouse/Columbia, 1997, prod. Wyclef Jean, others), an astonishingly adventurous and wide-reaching solo album on which he receives more than a little help from his musically gifted friends (i.e., Celia Cruz, the 62-piece New York Philharmonic Orchestra, the Neville Brothers, and, of course, Pras and Hill). Although it features the same sort of righteous undertones and thoughtful, albeit paranoid, lyrics that highlighted *The Score*, musically, the album is in a different world, throwing in a Bee Gees sample or sweet soprano vocalist here, remaking a Cuban folk tune there. On four newly composed songs, Clef even dares to throw in French patois as he sings about Haitian pride and politics. If the hip-hop headz only knew.

the rest:
Blunted on Reality ♪♪♪ (Ruffhouse/Columbia, 1994)
Bootleg Versions ♪♪♪ EP (Ruffhouse/Columbia, 1996)

influences:
◀◀ Bob Marley, Roberta Flack, De La Soul, Neneh Cherry, Arrested Development

Daniel Durchholz

Full Force

Formed mid-1970s, in Brooklyn, NY.

B-Fine, vocals; Paul Anthony George, vocals; Bow Legged Lou, vocals; Curt-t-t, guitar; Baby Gerry, keyboards; Shy Shy, bass

Full Force first got busy as the force behind Lisa Lisa & Cult Jam, assembling and producing the group and appearing on many of its hits, including its biggest, 1986's "All Cried Out." Full Force also worked in the studio with everyone from U.T.F.O. and Patti LaBelle to James Brown and Cheryl "Pepsi" Riley, but the group wasn't just a behind-the-scenes force, as it performed on its own, amusingly answering Lisa Lisa's "I Wonder If I Take You Home" with the less-successful "Girl If You Take Me Home" before faring better with singles such as "Temporary Love Thing," "Love Is for Suckers (Like Me and You)" and "All In My Mind." The group also had prominent roles in the first two *House Party* films. Most recently, Full Force appeared on the posthumous release by the slain Tejano star Selena.

what's available: The only Full Force title still in print actually isn't a Full Force title. It's appropriate, given that, as a recording entity, Full Force was never quite able to match the success it had in production and songwriting with other artists. *Lisa Lisa & Cult Jam with Full Force* ♪♪ (Columbia, 1985, prod. Full Force) contains the dated-sounding hits "I Wonder If I Take You Home" and "All Cried Out," plus the rap ditty "Take Me Home."

influences:
◀◀ The Jonzun Crew, Kurtis Blow
▶▶ Lisa Lisa & Cult Jam, U.T.F.O.

Josh Freedom du Lac

Funkdoobiest

Formed 1991, in Los Angeles, CA.

Sondoobie, vocals; Tomahawk Funk, vocals; Ralph M., DJ.

Part of the renewed, post-N.W.A. Los Angeles hip-hop scene, Funkdoobiest was also an extension of the Soul Assassins family (House of Pain, Cypress Hill), giving them access to the supreme beat manipulations of the Hill's DJ Muggs. After debuting on House of Pain's "House of the Rising Sun," then popping up on militant rapper Paris's indie debut, the oft-sophomoric group finally sparked its own joint in 1993.

what to buy: Propelled by Muggs's tweaked beats and Sondoobie's trippy cadence, *Which Doobie U B?* ♪♪♪ (Immortal/Epic, 1993, prod. DJ Muggs) is packed with no less than four hip-hop smashes: "The Funkiest" (which is propelled by high-pitched horns and thick, hollow drums); "Bow Wow Wow" (a polyrhythmic sub-woofer blow-out); "Freak Mode" (which moves quickly from lounge horns to minimalistic piano lines); and, finally, "Wopbabalubop" (a twisted Little Richard-infused romp that features a guest shot from similarly nasal-voiced B-Real).

what to buy next: Whereas the debut sounds like the Son of Cypress Hill (musically speaking), *Brothas Doobie* ♪♪♪ (Immortal/Epic, 1994, prod. DJ Muggs, others) showcases a different sound and tighter lyrical flow. Although Muggs is again on board, he bypasses his traditional grit-n-grime sound for soulful, smoothed-out funk, especially on "Rock On" and "What's the Deal." Best known for his bizarre cadence, love of pornographic movies, and penchant for bringing cartoon dialogue and nursery rhymes into his lyrics, Sondoobie shows a more serious side on "Dedicated," lovingly acknowledging family and dead friends. On the other hand: "Super Hoes," "Pussy Ain't Shit," and "XXX Funk."

influences:

◀◀ Cypress Hill

▶▶ Pharcyde

Spence D.

Funkmaster Flex

Born in the Bronx, NY.

With mix shows on New York's Hot 97, Chicago's 106 Jamz, and L.A.'s Power 106—as well as frequent guest spots on England's BBC1 and Japan's Bay FM—Funkmaster Flex essentially owns the hip-hop airwaves. Numerous projects and DJ gigs have established Flex and his crew the Flip Squad (Biz Markie, Doo Wop, Big Kap) as hip-hop's premier DJ ensemble.

what's available: Featuring a continuous mix of hip-hop singles, freestyles (Method Man, KRS-One, Busta Rhymes, etc.), and even a few original cuts (two produced by Flex), *Funkmaster Flex Presents the Mix Tape Volume 1: 60 Minutes of Funk* ♪♪♪ (Loud/RCA, 1995, prod. Funkmaster Flex) is notable for being the first commercially available mix "tape." So say revisionist-history-loving publicists, although Kid Capri would surely disagree. Clocking in at 71 minutes, *The Mix Tape Volume II: 60 Minutes of Funk* ♪♪♪ (Loud/RCA, 1995, prod. Funkmaster Flex) isn't as strong as its predecesor, (no) thanks to lackluster freestyles from Lil' Kim, Das EFX, and PMD. The album does, however, feature an interesting intro by model/journalist/sex pot Veronica Webb.

influences:

◀◀ DJ Red Alert, Chuck Chillout, Kid Capri

▶▶ Sway and Tech

Jazzbo

Fu-Schnickens

Poc; Moc; Chip Fu.

Having embraced a Kung-Fu motif—even down to the outfits—the Fu-Schnickens should now look back on their 15 minutes of fame with a bit of embarrassment. While each possessed some semblance of talent (Chip Fu could rap at unbelievable speeds—and backwards, too), the group's approach was gimmicky and limiting. Of course, basketball star Shaquille O'Neal did say they were his favorite group.

what's available: The Fu-Schnickens arrived with a hip-hop version of the Tenor Saw classic "Ring the Alarm," and followed that with a relatively acceptable album, *F.U. Don't Take It Personal* ♪♪♪ (Jive, 1991, prod. A Tribe Called Quest, Dres, Fu-Schnickens, others). Even with its somewhat dated sound, the songs can be digested in small doses; but as a whole, it's bound to cause headaches. Unless you want to hear the debut of the world's tallest rapper, Shaq-Fu, on "What's Up Doc?!?," don't break down and buy *Nervous Breakdown* ♪ (Jive, 1994, prod. Fu-Schnickens, Diamond D, others).

influences:

◀◀ A Tribe Called Quest, Special Ed

▶▶ Das EFX, Shaquille O'Neal

Jazzbo

G

G. Love & Special Sauce

Formed 1993, in Boston, MA.

G. Love (born Garrett Dutton), vocals, guitar, harmonica; Jeffrey Clemens, drums, backing vocals; Jimmy Prescott, stand-up bass.

Straight out of a coffee house, G. Love & Special Sauce sold fans on its fusion of rag-mop, blues, rap, and swing with the release of its self-titled debut. G. Love, in his fire-engine red silk suits and Elvis-like stage presence, sings of shooting hoops, hanging out on the street, and enjoying a refreshing drink. The group did something that has traditionally eluded blues artists—bringing to radio hook-laden odes like the back porch raps, an approach that makes it abundantly refreshing in its own right.

what to buy: The group's sophomore effort, *Coast to Coast Motel* ♪♪♪♪ (Okeh, 1995, prod. Jim Dickinson, G. Love & Special Sauce), serves up healthy portions of funk ("Sweet Sugar Mama"), New Orleans R&B groove ("Kiss and Tell" and "Bye Bye Baby") and stripped-down acoustic sounds ("Coming Home").

the rest:

G. Love & Special Sauce ♪♪♪ (Okeh, 1994)
Yeah, It's That Easy N/A (Epic, 1997)

influences:

◀◀ Bob Dylan, Eric Clapton

Christina Fuoco

Warren G

Born Warren Griffin III, in Long Beach, CA.

If it weren't for his obligatory sex boasts, Warren G might be an artist your mother could learn to like. And not because he's a doughboy rapper or palatable in the PG-ways of the old M.C. Hammer. Long Beach's boy-next-door is simply a down-home G-funk architect whose strength comes in bridging that eternal gap between harmony and street. For that he owes thanks, no doubt, to the influence of step-brother Dr. Dre and early years spent as a DJ with Snoop Doggy Dogg and Nate Dogg. Only a few years removed from that trio, 213, his songs continue to emanate a feel-good vibe at a time when rap is several decades removed from the heyday of neighborhood park jams. You also can thank Warren for being one of the few contemporary artists who makes radio cuts that don't sound overproduced, glossy or fake (see: "Regulate" and "This D.J." from his debut). Rather, his energy and vision generates funk-rooted songs that offer a soundtrack for the sunny days of lounging in the LBC. As the CEO of G-Funk Music, he couldn't have it any other way.

what to buy: *Take a Look over Your Shoulder (Reality)* ♫♫♫♫ (G-Funk Music/RAL, 1997, prod. Warren G) provides the high point in Warren's career, an album that sounds as if it were completely guided by his creative compass and G-funk dreams. From the narrative "Annie Mae" (featuring gangsta crooner Nate Dogg) to the summertime cookout cut, "Smokin' Me Out" (featuring Ronald Isley), the melodies are fresh, simple and entertaining. Even when Warren takes on law enforcement on the revamped "I Shot the Sheriff," the result is a light-hearted jam built for a summertime cruise down the Long Beach Freeway.

what to buy next: *Regulate . . . G-Funk Era* ♫♫♫ (Violator/RAL, 1994, prod. Warren G) contains the rapper's two biggest hits: "This DJ" and the Michael McDonald-sampling platinum breakthrough, "Regulate."

worth searching for: Prior to leading the G-funk revolution, Warren wrote, produced, and guest-starred on Mista Grimm's unforgettable weed-themed track, "Indo Smoke," which appears on the soundtrack for *Poetic Justice* (Epic Soundtrax, 1993, prod. various). Later—and more established in his career—he teamed up with sex-starved soulstress Adina Howard, flipping Tina Turner's "What's Love Got to Do with It?" with a '90s twist that depicts shady relationships with women and the record industry. That one is on the soundtrack from *Supercop* (Interscope, 1996, prod. various).

influences:

◀◀ Dr. Dre, Snoop Doggy Dogg, DJ Quik, Above the Law

▶▶ The Twinz, Dove Shack, Domino, Tha Dogg Pound

Corey Takahashi

Rosie Gaines

Born in Pittsburg, CA.

Soul singer and keyboardist Rosie Gaines, long a talented fixture on California's East Bay club scene, failed to make any sort of impression with her first album in 1985, due in part to turmoil at her record label. That may have been a blessing, because not long after that she hooked up with Prince and joined his band, the New Power Generation. With mighty pipes able to conquer both the whispers of soft ballads and screams of her beloved funk music, Gaines became, for a while, the vocal counterpoint that Prince had lacked in other partners. Although she made her mark on his album *Diamonds and Pearls*, she quit the band after a disagreement with Prince—leaving behind a recorded but unreleased solo album. She released her second solo album, *Closer to Home*, on Motown to critical but not popular fanfare. *Arrival*, her third album, was made available only on the Internet via her own label. Its release curiously coincided with a resurgence in interest in the U.K. for a dance remix of the title cut from *Closer Than Close*, making her one more in a long list of soul artists who have had to leave the U.S. to find an audience hungry for their work.

what to buy: Although she has labelled the album as too tame, *Closer Than Close* ♫♫♫♫ (Jive, 1995, prod. various) mixes smart mid-tempo soul, with deeply personal and often political lyrics to make a solid, and greatly overlooked, package.

what to buy next: Produced, written and performed almost entirely by Gaines in her home studio, *Arrival* ♫♫♫♫ (Dredlix, 1997, prod. Rosie Gaines) is a soul treasure that finally displays the true diversity and fire within Gaines—though it suffers when she throws restraint to the wind.

worth searching for: "Nothing Compares 2 U," her live, nearly spiritual duet with Prince from his compilation *The Hits 1* ♫♫♫♫ (Paisley Park, 1993, prod. Prince), is by itself almost as good a catch as *Caring* ♫♫♫ (Epic, 1985, prod. Rosie Gaines), her debut album.

influences:

◀◀ Tina Turner, Aretha Franklin, Mavis Staples

▶▶ Oleta Adams, Mary J. Blige, Tracy Chapman

Franklin Paul

Gang Starr

Formed in 1988, in Brooklyn, NY.

Guru, vocals; DJ Premier, DJ.

Although the hip-hop one-two punch of Guru and DJ Premier use the moniker Gang Starr, the two aren't gangstas: Guru's consciousness-raising lyrics recall KRS-One more than Spice 1, while the gritty, jazzbo-cool backing music supplied by Premier is miles closer to "Doo Bop"–era Miles than "Fuck Tha Police"–era Dre. Influenced by jazz at least as much as any other hip-hop group, Gang Starr understands better than the rest the correlation between jazz and rap—two black art forms with similar cadences that thrive on spontaneous innovation. The group's songs typically feature jazzy basslines, horn riffs, and obscure jazz samples laid out over loose hip-hop beats; many could probably work as instrumental tracks. Yet Guru's conversational, laconic vocals weave perfectly through Premier's raw, soulful, and simple constructions, with neither music nor lyrics fighting for attention. How refreshing. Outside of the Gang Starr format, one-time computer science major Premier has become one of the most sought-after producers in East Coast rap, working with the likes of KRS-One, Nas, Jeru the Damaja and Group Home. Meanwhile, Guru has coordinated two jazz-meets-rap projects under the moniker Jazzmatazz.

what to buy: The minimalist *Daily Operation* ✍✍✍✍ (Chrysalis, 1992, prod. DJ Premier, Guru), which samples artists from Mingus to Byrd, is Gang Starr's best, most consistent album, with the thoughtful "Soliloquy of Chaos" (which warns against the cycle of violence) and the tender, respectful "Ex Girl to the Next Girl" serving as antidotes to the killing and misogyny of the day's dominant style, gangsta-(c)rap. On the racially concerned "Conspiracy," Guru also attacks the shady side of the rap business—an appropriate topic, perhaps, given that he graduated from Morehouse College with a degree in business. *Guru's Jazzmatazz: Vol. I* ✍✍✍✍ (Chrysalis, 1993, prod. Guru) falls on the other side of the jazz-hop fence, using live contributions from jazz legends (Roy Ayers, Donald Byrd, Lonnie Liston Smith) and comers (Ronny Jordan, N'Dea Davenport, Carleen Anderson) instead of old, dusty samples. It also swings more than any Gang Starr album.

what to buy next: The upbeat *No More Mr. Nice Guy* ✍✍✍♪ (Wild Pitch/EMI, 1989, prod. DJ Premier, Guru) features the tone-setting history lesson, "Jazz Thing," based on a poem by the longtime jazz publicist Elliot Horne. Also included is the hip-hop classic, "Manifest," which makes excellent use of a Dizzy Gillespie sample. On *Hard to Earn* ✍✍✍ (Chrysalis/ERG, 1994, prod.

DJ Premier, Guru), Premier strips away much of the jazz influence to reveal old-school hip-hop roots. Yet Guru's cautionary tone of "Tonz 'O' Gunz" is decidedly '90s.

the rest:

Step in the Arena ✍✍✍ (Chrysalis, 1990)
Jazzmatazz Vol. II: The New Reality ✍✍ (Chrysalis/EMI, 1995)
Guru Presents Ill Kid Records ✍✍✍ (Payday, 1995)
Moment of Truth N/A (Noo Trybe/Virgin, 1997)

influences:

◀◀ Miles Davis, Jungle Brothers, Eric B. & Rakim, Poor Righteous Teachers

▶▶ Buckshot LeFonque, the Roots, Ronny Jordan, Bahamadia, Digable Planets, Us3, A Tribe Called Quest, Jeru the Damaja, Dream Warriors, Black Moon

Josh Freedom du Lac

Gap Band

Formed 1967, in Tulsa, OK.

Charlie Wilson, lead vocals, keyboards, drums, percussion, background vocals; Robert Wilson, bass, percussion, background vocals; Ronnie Wilson, vocals, trumpet, flugelhorn, keyboards, percussion, background vocals.

Taking their band's name from the initials of the streets that formed Tulsa's business hub—Greenwood, Archer and Pine—brothers Charlie, Robert, and Ronnie Wilson emerged from roots as choirboys in their father's Pentecostal church in Tulsa, Oklahoma, to become kings of funk/R&B in the 1980s with a string of platinum and gold albums, as well as numerous R&B and pop hits. Just as appealing as their bottom-heavy grooves was lead singer Charlie Wilson's unabashed and charming sex-appeal, a presence that moved one writer to call him "the first funk love-god and its premier front man" and "the de-facto father of New Jack." Cultivating sexuality would prove to be a key factor in their presentation and success, with desire and fun leaping out of their music videos—a largely unused tool for the time, which they worked to their advantage. As bits of their more famous riffs come alive in the hip-hop soundtrack of the 1990s (Da Brat and Notorious B.I.G. among the more well-known culprits), the Gap Band remain poised at the top of our booty-shaking consciousness. (Also, Charlie Wilson stepped out to guest and co-write two songs on Eurythmics' 1989 album *We Too Are One*, and, as Snoop Doggy Dogg's uncle, he guested with the rapper during the 1997 Lollapalooza tour.)

what to buy: As much as best-of compilations tend to gloss over a band's career or try to make them look as if they were more popular than they were, the numerous Gap Band collections, including *Gap Gold/Best of Gap Band* 𝄞𝄞𝄞𝄞 (Mercury, 1985, prod. various), are lots of fun. Hits such as "You Dropped A Bomb On Me," "Party Train," "Burn Rubber On Me," "Outstanding," "I Don't Believe You Want To Get Up And Dance (Oops!)" may all sound similar, yet are always fun tunes—the Gap Band at their high-octane best. Ditto *Best of Gap Band* 𝄞𝄞𝄞𝄞𝄞 (Mercury Funk Essentials, 1994, prod. various).

what to buy next: While almost all of their records are worth hunting down just to check the fly-gear of the day, *Gap Band VI* 𝄞𝄞𝄞𝄞 (Total Experience, 1984, prod. Lonnie Simmons) characterizes the spirit of the mid-1980s with "Video Junkie" and "Beep A Freak"—era politics with extra sexy bump.

what to avoid: *Ain't Nothing But a Party* 𝄞𝄞 (Capitol, 1995, prod. Lonnie Simmons, Charlie Wilson) kind of leaves you feeling sorry for the band not really evolving beyond party crew mentality. Yes, that's what made them, but you'd hope they would become more well-rounded over the years.

the rest:
Magician's Holiday 𝄞𝄞𝄞𝄟 (Shelter, 1974)
The Gap Band 𝄞𝄞𝄞𝄟 (Tattoo, 1977)
The Gap Band II 𝄞𝄞𝄞 (Mercury, 1979)
The Gap Band III 𝄞𝄞𝄞 (Mercury, 1980)
Gap Band IV 𝄞𝄞𝄞𝄟 (Total Experience, 1982)
Gap Band V—Jammin' 𝄞𝄞𝄞𝄞 (Mercury, 1983)
Gap Band VII; The 12" Collection 𝄞𝄞𝄞 (Mercury, 1986)
Straight from the Heart 𝄞𝄞𝄞 (Total Experience, 1987)
Round Trip 𝄞𝄞𝄞 (Capitol, 1989)
Testimony 𝄞𝄞𝄞𝄞 (Rhino, 1994)

solo outings:
Charlie Wilson:
You Turn My Life Around 𝄞𝄞𝄞 (Bon Ami, 1992)

influences:
◀◀ Parliament-Funkadelic, Bootsy Collins, Leon Russell

▶▶ Yarbrough and Peoples, Bobby Brown, Notorious B.I.G., R. Kelly

Tamara Palmer

Marvin Gaye

Born Marvin Pentz Gay Jr., April 21, 1939, in Washington, DC. Died Sept. 1, 1984, in Los Angeles, CA.

A moody, mercurial soul who always seemed to be searching for some elusive happiness but reveled in—and sometimes seemed to invent—his own personal miseries, Gaye was Motown's most ambivalent pop star. His real desire, so he said, was to be a crooner along the lines of Frank Sinatra and Nat King Cole. But his fame—and, indeed, his best music—came from his early pop hits and his socially conscious spiritual journeys, culminating in the 1971 masterpiece *What's Going On*. Gaye came to Motown via the Marquees (a group that enjoyed the patronage of Bo Diddley) and the Moonglows; it was during one of the latter's performances in Detroit that Berry Gordy Jr. heard Gaye and signed him to his burgeoning label. Starting as a session drummer and marrying Gordy's sister Anna (their breakup would be the focus of his harrowing 1978 album *Here, My Dear*), Gaye began his string of hits in 1962 with "Stubborn Kind of Fellow," a run that would last into the mid-1970s. Gaye also established himself as a generous duet partner, scoring hits with Mary Wells, Kim Weston, Tammi Terell, and Diana Ross. Gaye's biggest solo hit, "I Heard It through the Grapevine" in 1968, signaled a shift into deeper material—and darker subject matter; he fought hard to get Motown to release *What's Going On*, an epic song cycle on which Gaye took total control and weaved his observations about inner city youth, the ecology, and race relations. He followed that with *Let's Get It On*, an immersion in eroticism that remained a focus through his last big hit, 1982's "Sexual Healing." Addled by drugs and depression, Gaye was in the midst of a career comeback when his father fatally shot him after an argument. His has been one of the most lamented of the Motown passings, commemorated every year in Detroit with a special ceremony or concert.

what to buy: You have to ask? *What's Going On* 𝄞𝄞𝄞𝄞𝄞 (Motown, 1971, prod. Marvin Gaye) is not just a great Gaye album but is one of the great pop albums of all time. (Splurge and get the deluxe edition.) *The Master, 1961–1984* 𝄞𝄞𝄞𝄞𝄞 (Motown, 1995, prod. various) is one of those rare box sets that sustains its quality over the course of four discs. *Superhits* 𝄞𝄞𝄞𝄞𝄟 (Motown, 1970/1991, prod. various) isn't the most comprehensive of Gaye's collections, but it was *the* Gaye album to own at the time and is still worth having for its cheesy superhero caricature on the cover.

what to buy next: *Let's Get It On* 𝄞𝄞𝄞𝄞 (Motown, 1973, prod. Marvin Gaye) offers the visceral desire of a man in serious heat. *Midnight Love* 𝄞𝄞𝄞𝄞 (Columbia, 1992, prod. Marvin Gaye) is much the same, though it's a little softer and just a touch more subtle. *Marvin Gaye & His Girls* 𝄞𝄞𝄞𝄞𝄞 (Motown, 1969/1990, prod. various) is a nice collection of his duets with Wells, Weston, and Terell, missing only Diana Ross to make it a complete overview.

what to avoid: *Dream of a Lifetime* 𝄞 (Columbia, 1985, prod. Marvin Gaye, Gordon Banks, Harvey Fuqua), a posthumous release of material Gaye was working on at the time of his death, is as bald a violation of his artistry as the releases that came out after Jimi Hendrix's death.

the rest:

Together with Mary Wells 🎵🎵🎵 (Motown, 1964/1991)

A Tribute to the Great Nat King Cole 🎵🎵🎵 (Motown, 1965/1989)

The Soulful Moods of Marvin Gaye 🎵🎵🎵 (Motown, 1966/1994)

I Heard It through the Grapevine 🎵🎵🎵 (Motown, 1968/1989)

Trouble Man 🎵🎵🎵🎵 soundtrack (Motown, 1972/1989)

Live 🎵🎵🎵🎵 (Motown, 1974)

I Want You 🎵🎵🎵 (Motown, 1976)

Greatest Hits 🎵🎵🎵🎵 (Motown, 1976/1989)

Live at the London Palladium 🎵🎵🎵 (Motown, 1977)

Here, My Dear 🎵🎵🎵🎵 (Motown, 1978/1994)

In Our Lifetime: The Final Motown Sessions 🎵🎵 (Motown, 1981/1994)

Every Great Motown Hit 🎵🎵🎵🎵 (Motown, 1983)

Great Songs & Performances That Inspired Motown 25 🎵🎵🎵 (Motown, 1983)

Romantically Yours 🎵🎵 (Columbia, 1985/1989)

A Musical Testament 🎵🎵🎵 (Motown, 1988)

The Marvin Gaye Collection 🎵🎵🎵🎵 (Motown, 1990)

The Last Concert Tour 🎵🎵🎵 (Giant, 1991)

Adults 🎵🎵 (Hollywood/Rounder, 1992)

Seek and You Shall Find: More of the Best 🎵🎵🎵 (Rhino, 1993)

The Norman Whitfield Sessions 🎵🎵🎵🎵 (Motown, 1994)

Motown Legends 🎵🎵🎵🎵 (ESX, 1994)

Classics Collection 🎵🎵🎵🎵 (Motown, 1994)

When I'm Alone I Cry 🎵🎵🎵 (Motown, 1994)

Anthology 🎵🎵🎵🎵🎵 (Motown, 1995)

Vulnerable 🎵🎵 (Motown, 1997)

worth searching for: In 1986, Motown put both *What's Going On* and *Let's Get It On* on a single CD. The fidelity isn't quite up to the standards of later CD releases, but it's still a wonderful trip to slap it on and hear two of Gaye's finest albums flow back-to-back.

influences:

◄◄ Nat King Cole, Frank Sinatra, Billie Holiday, Ray Charles, Clyde McPhatter, Little Willie John, Rudy West, the Orioles, the Capris

►► Stevie Wonder, Frankie Beverly, Rick James, Terence Trent D'Arby, Barry White, Al B. Sure!, Keith Sweat, El DeBarge

Gary Graff

Gloria Gaynor

Born September 7, 1949, in Newark, NJ.

It is the height of irony that Gloria Gaynor's signature hit, the smash 1979 single titled "I Will Survive," still survives with a life of its own far beyond her own soul music heyday. The song remains a frequently sampled empowering anthem for countless women and gays on and off the dance floor, and earned Gaynor the title of "First Lady of Disco" in the 1980s. Beginning her career in 1965 by fronting a band called the Soul Satisfiers, Gaynor was "discovered" at the Wagon Wheel in New York in the early 1970s. Teaming with engineer Tony Bongiovi and eccentric producer/arranger Meco, she notched her breakout solo hit in 1975, a swirling, uptempo remake of the Jackson 5's "Never Can Say Goodbye" on MGM records. Arriving on the leading edge of a musical trend, the tune elevated Gaynor to the status of the first Disco Diva, leading to a string of dance-oriented hits like "How High the Moon" and her reworking of the Four Tops' "Reach Out I'll Be There" in the mid-1970s. But the Disco Queen truly came of age in 1979 with "I Will Survive," a #1 hit for three of its 17 consecutive weeks on the pop music charts. Through that record and several subsequent releases, Gaynor helped to popularize the "segue" or "extended mix" recordings that came to define the disco era. She signed on as the opening act for the Village People on the first nationwide arena tour for disco, playing major stadiums. After suffering severe injuries when she fell off a stage and damaged her spine, Gaynor turned to drugs and alcohol for relief before reclaiming her life through religion. As a born-again Christian, Gaynor redirected her career and began to thrive again in Europe, where she hosted a gospel program for the BBC in Great Britain and continues as a significant force in devotional music to this day. One of her last pop appearances was singing a duet with Engelbert Humperdinck on the title track of Humperdinck's 1991 LP, *Love Is the Reason*.

what to buy: Gaynor's *Greatest Hits* 🎵🎵🎵🎵 (1982, Polydor, prod. various) is a total experience of the Disco Diva. It contains the trademark "I Will Survive," her first hit "Never Can Say Goodbye," plus some tasty covers of true soul classics like "Casanova Brown," "Walk On By," and "Reach Out I'll Be There."

what to buy next: *I'll Be There* 🎵🎵🎵 (1995, Radikal, prod. Jurgen Korduletsch, Don Oriolo) features duets with Isaac Hayes ("You're the First, the Last, My Everything") and Earl Young & The Tramps ("Mighty High").

the rest:

I Am What I Am 🎵🎵 (ZYX, 1993)

worth searching for: *I Will Survive* 🎵🎵🎵 (1990, PolyGram) surrounds the hit with a captivating collection of songs. It's currently out of print in the United States, but if you can get it, get it.

influences:

◀◀ Diana Ross & the Supremes, Aretha Franklin, Maxine Brown, Gwen McCrae

▶▶ Kristine W., Loletta Holloway, Robin S., CeCe Peniston, Taylor Dayne, Teena Marie, Corona

"Lisa Lisa" Orlando

J. Geils Band /Bluestime

Formed 1967, in Boston, MA. Disbanded 1985.

J. (Jerome) Geils, guitar; Peter Wolf, vocals (1967–83); Seth Justman, keyboards, vocals (1968–85); Magic Dick, harmonica; Danny Klein, bass; Stephen Jo Bladd, drums. Bluestime includes J. Geils and Magic Dick.

Part barroom blues ensemble, part soul revue, part arena rabble rousers, the J. Geils Band was a quintessentially American rock 'n' roll band, drawing from sources that stretched from Mississippi Delta blues to Motown to the Rolling Stones. During its 18 years together, the Geils gang was always painfully inconsistent, and for a minute—with 1981's multi-million selling *Freeze-Frame*—it was the hottest band in the land. The inconsistency was always frustrating for fans, because Geils had a loaded arsenal of talent—the motor-mouthed histrionics of former disc jockey Wolf, the sharp melodic sense of Justman, the truly enchanting harp skills of Magic Dick. When it clicked, few could beat Geils, and its concerts were usually 'til-we-all-drop marathons. The bottom fell out when the group was at the top, when Wolf left in 1983. The Geils chemistry was never the same without him, and a break-up was inevitable. Wolf has had a middling solo career, while Geils and Magic Dick went on to form the rootsier group Bluestime. There's periodic talk of a Geils reunion, but it has yet to transpire.

what to buy: The two-CD *Houseparty: The J. Geils Band Anthology* &&&& (Atlantic & Atco Remasters/Rhino, 1993, prod. various) nails it, housing all the truly great Geils moments (though we'd rather have the full-length version of the 1970s hit "Give It to Me"); it's essential either on its own or as a guide for future purchases. *Monkey Island* &&& (Atlantic, 1977, prod. J. Geils Band) and *Love Stinks* &&& (EMI, 1980, prod. Seth Justman) are the best of the studio sets, both of them marked by adventurous sonic forays that don't abandon the group's melodic roots.

what to buy next: *Freeze-Frame* &&& (EMI, 1981, prod. Seth Justman) was Geils's smash and remains entertaining, if not as consistently fresh as *Love Stinks*. No Geils collection is com-

plete without a live recording; *Blow Your Face Out* &&& (Atlantic, 1976/Rhino, 1993, prod. Allen Blazek, Bill Szymczyk, the J. Geils Band) is the choice there, a rowdy representation of the group's onstage charisma, including Wolf's stream-of-consciousness raps.

what to avoid: *Hotline* & (Atlantic, 1975/1990, prod. Bill Szymczyk, Allen Blazek) is typical of the ineffectual studio work Geils proliferated during the early and mid-1970s.

the rest:
The J. Geils Band &&& (Atlantic, 1970)
The Morning After &&& (Atlantic, 1971)
Full House &&& (Atlantic, 1972)
Bloodshot &&& (Atlantic, 1973)
Ladies Invited && (Atlantic, 1973)
Nightmares . . . and Other Tales from the Vinyl Jungle && (Atlantic, 1974)
Sanctuary &&& (EMI, 1978)
The Best of the J. Geils Band &&& (Atlantic, 1979)
You're Getting Even While I'm Getting Odd && (EMI, 1984)
Flashback: The Best of the J. Geils Band &&&& (EMI, 1985)

worth searching for: Available only as an import, the live *Showtime!* &&& (EMI, 1982/BGO, 1995, prod. Seth Justman) isn't quite as definitive as *Blow Your Face Out*, but it catches an exuberant Geils stand at the end of its triumphant *Freeze-Frame* tour.

solo outings:
Bluestime:
Bluestime &&& (Rounder, 1994)
Little Care of Blues &&& (Rounder, 1996)

influences:

◀◀ James Brown, Jackie Wilson, the Yardbirds, John Mayall, the Rolling Stones, John Lee Hooker, Motown, Stax, Bill Haley & the Comets

▶▶ Aerosmith, Bruce Springsteen and the E Street Band, Michael Stanley Band, the Iron City Houserockers, Blues Traveler

see also: *Peter Wolf*

Gary Graff

Genius/GZA

See: Wu Tang Clan

Gerardo

Born Gerardo Mejia III, April 16, 1965, in Guayaquil, Ecuador.

With the rap world in dire need of a Latin playboy with a hairless chest and not a lot of talent, Gerardo gladly presented his

"Rico Suave" calling card—and got the job. Putting himself in inane videos that showed off his pectoral muscles (plus plenty of scantily clad muchachas), the Spanglish-language artist became a success in 1991, as "Rico Suave" went gold and the Parliament-ary "We Want the Funk" charted, too. After the Los Angeles–based Ecuadorian transplant saw his popularity plummet and his image skewered by Weird Al Yankovic ("Taco Grande"), he became a Spanish-language artist. Still didn't put on his shirt, though.

what to buy: If you must, *Mo'Ritmo* ♫♫ (Interscope, 1991, prod. various) contains the "essential" Gerardo hits "Rico Suave" and "We Want the Funk," as well as "Latin Till I Die (Oye Como Va)." More entertaining, though, is the goofy *Behind the Scenes with the Latin King* video ♫♫ (A*Vision Entertainment, 1991).

the rest:
Asi Es ♫♫♫ (Capitol/EMI Latin, 1994)
Derrumbe ♫♫ (EMI Latin, 1995)

influences:
◄◄ Mellow Man Ace, Menudo, NKOTB, Marky Mark, M.C. Hammer, Kid Frost, 7A3

►► Right Said Fred, Spice Girls, LSOB, Puff Daddy

Todd Inoue

Geto Boys

Formed 1986, in Houston, TX.

Scarface, vocals; Willie D, vocals (1986–92, 1996–present); Bushwick Bill, vocals; Ready Red, DJ; Big Mike, vocals (1992–96).

What the 2 Live Crew did for sex in hip-hop, the Geto Boys did for violence, all but destroying the boundaries of what's acceptable—and driving prominent critics (Tipper Gore, Bob Dole) up the wall in the process. The Geto Boys were the first examples of "horrorcore," which aptly describes their most controversial song, the self-explanatory "Mind of a Lunatic." The song was included on their self-titled 1990 major-label debut for Def American, but parent company Geffen Records—which later distributed such pussycats as Guns N' Roses—refused to release the album. Many of the group's lyrics deserve the criticism they've received for gratuitous violence; the Boys' beating-an-old-horse defense that they're "just rapping about reality" is no excuse for songs like "Chuckie," which say nothing except "killing is scary." But every now and then they unveil the mojo hand—"Mind Playing Tricks on Me" (a #23 hit in 1991) is one of the best hip-hop singles ever recorded: Scarface, Willie D, and Bushwick Bill's monologues go even beyond stark

description of life on the streets. Their voices are scared, vulnerable, and they sound like they're trembling in anticipation of inevitable death. In the end, the entire story about fighting with a frightening murderer (the devil?) turns out to be a reality-warping illusion. All three original Geto Boys employ forceful rapping styles, like Public Enemy's Chuck D. if he'd gone to prison instead of college, and they have a devastating knack for the perfect underlying old-school funk sample. After replacing Willie D with Big Mike, the band broke up in 1993; it turned out to be a lucrative decision, as all three founders—most notably, the multiplatinum-selling Scarface—became superstar solo artists. Having liberated gangsta rap from its boundaries (Snoop Doggy Dogg and Dr. Dre regularly get away today with saying stuff that's just as bad as anything on 1990's *Geto Boys*), the original threesome reunited in 1996.

what to buy: *We Can't Be Stopped* ♫♫♫♫ (Rap-A-Lot, 1991, prod. Scarface, Willie D, Bushwick Bill, others) pronounces itself something scary and different simply with the explicit cover photo of Jamaican-born dwarf Bushwick Bill, shot in the eye in 1991, clutching a cellular phone as the other Boys wheel him down a hospital hallway. Inside, the music has incredible moments of dramatic power: "Mind Playing Tricks on Me" could be a Robert Johnson song, and the anti-Grammys "Trophy" and anti–Gulf War "F— a War" forcefully (and humorously) get their points across.

what to buy next: Try sampling each original member's solo career. Scarface's hit *The Diary* ♫♫♫ (Rap-a-Lot, 1992, prod. various) contains a less-potent version of "Mind Playing Tricks on Me," and it slurs and rambles a bit too incoherently, but it's still solid overall gangsta rap. Willie D's *I'm Goin' Out Lika Soldier* ♫♫♫ (Rap-a-Lot, 1992, prod. various) isn't as distinctive, but the beats are strong. And Bushwick Bill's *Little Big Man* ♫♫ (Rap-a-Lot, 1992, prod. various) proves his Jamaican-inflected voice has always relied on the power boost of his cronies.

what to avoid: The controversial major-label debut, *Geto Boys* ♫♫♫ (Def American, 1990, prod. various) is generally worth owning only for curiosity purposes; it was, after all, the first rap album to be rejected by its own record label, setting in motion a weird trend (see Ice-T's *Body Count*, Paris, the Boo-Yaa T.R.I.B.E. and, most recently, Insane Clown Posse).

the rest:
Uncut Dope ♫♫ (Rap-a-Lot, 1992)
Till Death Do Us Part ♫♫ (Rap-a-Lot, 1993)
The Resurrection ♫♫♫ (Rap-a-Lot/Virgin, 1996)

worth searching for: Their early albums, *Making Trouble* 𝄢𝄢 (Rap-a-Lot, 1988, prod. various) and *Grip It! On That Other Level* 𝄢𝄢 (Rap-a-Lot, 1988, prod. various), got lost in the shuffle when the Boys' homegrown Rap-a-Lot hooked up with big Virgin Records.

solo outings:
Big Mike:
Somethin' Serious 𝄢𝄢𝄢 (Rap-a-Lot, 1994)
Still Serious 𝄢𝄢𝄢 (Noo Trybe, 1997)

Scarface:
Mr. Scarface Is Back 𝄢𝄢𝄢 (Rap-a-Lot, 1991)
The World Is Yours 𝄢𝄢𝄢 (Rap-a-Lot, 1993)
The Untouchable 𝄢𝄢𝄢 (Rap-a-Lot, 1997)

Willie D:
Controversy 𝄢𝄢𝄢 (Rap-a-Lot, 1989)
Trouble Man 𝄢𝄢𝄢 (Wize Up/Wrap, 1993)
Play Wicha Mama 𝄢𝄢 (Wize Up/Wrap, 1994)

Bushwick Bill:
Phantom of the Rapra 𝄢𝄢𝄢 (Rap-a-Lot, 1995)

influences:
◄◄ Public Enemy, Ice-T, N.W.A., Isley Brothers, James Brown, George Clinton, Last Poets, Gil Scott-Heron, Schoolly D

►► Snoop Doggy Dogg, Dr. Dre, 2Pac, Flatlinerz, Gravediggaz, Sir Mix-a-Lot

Steve Knopper

Ghost Face Killa

See: Wu Tang Clan

Johnny Gill

See: New Edition

Goats

Formed 1990 in Philadelphia, PA.

Swayzack, vocals; Madd, vocals; Oatie Kato, vocals.

Specializing in tight, original funk breaks and beats under highly charged political verses, the Goats aren't so much rappers as they are purveyors of alternative political discourse. Addressing injustices (to indigenous people, women, and other so-termed minorities), the artists even refer to themselves as political raptivists.

what to buy: *Tricks of the Shade* 𝄢𝄢𝄢𝄢 (Ruffhouse/Columbia, 1992, prod. Joe "The Butcher" Nicolo, Oatie Kato) is quite pos-

sibly the first hip-hoperetta, a concept album following in the vein of the Who's *Tommy* and Genesis' *Lamb Lies Down on Broadway.* As the album opens, we're introduced to the lead character/hero, Chicken Little, and his younger brother, Hangerhead. (Really.) The album then follows the pair as they search for the single mother who abandoned them at birth. Their travels ultimately bring them to Uncle Scam's Federally Funded Welfare and Freak Show, where the Goats cleverly and blatantly utilize the carnival theme as a metaphor for Amerikkka (!) and her glorious political past; along the way, our two anti-heroes bump into Columbus, Noriega, Leonard Peltier, Daryl Gates, the (George) Bush babees, Roe v. Wade, and, finally, at the album's end, Uncle Scam himself. The sociopolitical content is scathing, covering everything from police brutality and abortion to racism and other injustices. There's also some musicality: Madd, Swayzack, and Oatie fluidly pass the mic as their six-piece backup band (female vocalist, drummer, bassist, keyboardist, guitarist, DJ) shows off its funky chops. The mixture of live instrumentation and sampling wizardry is used to good effect, with DJ 1 Take Willie even paying homage to hometown legend Schooly D with plentiful Schooly scratches. Although some have dismissed the Goats as semi-angry youths armed with tired, re-worked political slogans, the group has actually created a musically and conceptually challenging piece of hip-hop that demands to be heard.

the rest:
No Goats No Glory 𝄢𝄢𝄢 (Ruffhouse/Columbia, 1994)

influences:
◄◄ Urban Dance Squad, Beastie Boys

Spence D.

Goodie Mob

Formed mid-1990s, in Atlanta, GA.

T-Mo, vocals; Cee-Lo, vocals; Khudjo, vocals; Gipp, vocals.

Heralds of a new Southern sound in the late '90s, the Goodie Mob (or, the Good Die Mostly Over Bullshit) followed their homeys OutKast like a set of related X-Files brought to light. If OutKast focused on supernatural occurrences, then Goodie Mob focused on the conspiracies behind them. What separated their themes of paranoia and suspicion from that of an average "gangsta" rapper was an earnest effort to universalize their situation, and thereby manifest a real rebellion.

what's available: *Soul Food* 𝄢𝄢𝄢𝄢 (LaFace, 1995, prod. Organized Noize) is a tour-de-force. Taking its musical cue from the claustrophobic sonics of producers like Dr. Dre, Organized Noize slows down and strips out his warm and dense mid-range, leaving a sound with minimal piano color and bass on the bottom to complement the raw Southern textures of Goodie Mob's rappers. During a period in which regional street rhymers achieved new audiences hooked on close-ended stories of revenge, apocalypse, and decay, the Goodie Mob refreshingly focuses on the external threat and the internal dilemma. "Cell Therapy," with its scratchy dub, Louis Armstrong groans, and gripping piano, evokes a world of black helicopters, gated neighborhoods, racial wars, and ubiquitous surveillance—and was more real than most "reality"-based raps that year. "Listen up young brother, I'm talking to you!" they command. Topical, smart and street, the Goodie Mob provides promise for those interested in seeing rap take a turn back toward social commentary.

influences:

◀◀ Scarface, Geto Boys, Dr. Dre, Poor Righteous Teachers, OutKast

▶▶ PA

Jeff "DJ Zen" Chang

Cuba Gooding
See: The Main Ingredient

Berry Gordy Jr.
Born December 28, 1929, in Detroit, MI.

When Berry Gordy was a boy, he dreamed of being "somebody." He was so inspired by his first hero, Joe Louis, that he seriously considered a boxing career during his early adult life. But pop history shows that his visionary energies were better spent scouring the streets of Detroit for funding and musical talent for his record labels, especially the legendary Motown empire. In 1959, sometime after his 3D Record Mart went bankrupt, Gordy first wrote songs for Jackie Wilson, then established Motown Studio A and Hitsville USA in a renovated house on West Grand Boulevard in Detroit. There he played manager, songwriter, and A&R man to a long roster of soon-to-be preeminent R&B artists of the 1960s and early 1970s: Smokey Robinson & the Miracles, Diana Ross & the Supremes, Martha & the Vandellas, Marvin Gaye, the Four Tops, the Temptations, Stevie Wonder, the Jackson 5, and others. Gordy's venture was a tremendous, trend-setting success, and Motown grew, inspiring artists around the world with its music and African Americans in general with its success in the white-dominated enter-

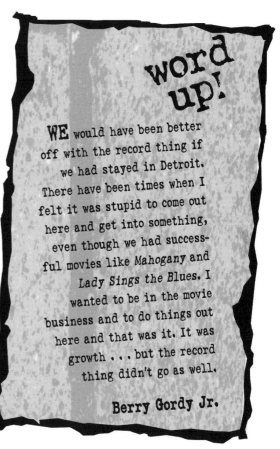

word up!

WE would have been better off with the record thing if we had stayed in Detroit. There have been times when I felt it was stupid to come out here and get into something, even though we had successful movies like *Mahogany* and *Lady Sings the Blues*. I wanted to be in the movie business and to do things out here and that was it. It was growth . . . but the record thing didn't go as well.

Berry Gordy Jr.

tainment industry. The label was moved to Los Angeles in 1972. By the mid-1980s financial and corporate pressures weighed heavily on Gordy's enthusiasm. Keeping Motown afloat as a multi-media giant was a struggle for the label founder, who seemed to thrive on the creative collaborations and challenges of earlier years. On June 29, 1988, he sold Motown to MCA for $61 million. Letting go of his dream was a difficult move for Gordy and a disappointment for African Americans who drew inspiration from his success. But he held on to his publishing company Jobete (though he sold a large piece of it in 1997) and rejoined the Motown board when PolyGram acquired the company from MCA. Though he was never a recording artist in his own right, Gordy was a competent singer and pianist, and he wrote and co-wrote many of the songs that contribute to the Motown legend, including: "Shop Around" with Smokey Robinson; "This Heart of Mine" with Rob Johnson; the Jackson 5's "ABC"; and "To Be Loved," which became the title of his autobiography.

what to buy: On the audiocassette version of *To Be Loved* 𝄞𝄞𝄞𝄞 (Time Warner Audio Books, 1994), Gordy not only reads two hours' worth of his autobiography but also performs some of the songs he talks about. A much more ambitious endeavor than most audio books.

influences:

◀◀ Phil Spector, Sam Phillips, Phil Chess, Leonard Chess

▶▶ Kenny Gamble, Leon Huff, Prince, Rick Rubin, James "Jimmy Jam" Harris III, Terry Lewis, Kenneth "Babyface" Edmonds, L.A. Reid

Norene Cashen

Graham Central Station /Larry Graham

Formed 1973, in Oakland, CA. Disbanded 1980. Re-formed 1994.

Larry Graham (born August 14, 1946, in Beaumont, TX), vocals, bass; Patryce "Chocolate" Banks, vocals, percussion; Hershall "Happiness" Kennedy, keyboards; Robert "Butch" Sam, keyboards; David "Dynamite" Vega, guitar; Willie "Wild" Sparks, drums.

Larry Graham rewrote the vocabulary of the bass with his work with Sly & the Family Stone. Originally a guitar player who switched to bass—temporarily, he thought—Graham developed his revolutionary signature pluck-and-thump finger-picking style while working in a duo with his mother, which is where disc jockey Sylvester Stewart (a.k.a. Sly Stone) found him. In Graham Central Station, Graham showed he learned many lessons from Sly Stone but pursued a more streamlined, heavy funk sound. His basso profundo vocals gave a rich, resonant sheen to the songs, while the band stayed in deep groove overdrive behind him. Bursting out of the Bay Area club scene in 1973, Graham Central brought a powerful sense of ensemble instrumental prowess to the growing funk world and, while he frequently indulged in some of the worst cornball mannerisms of the genre, Graham could also be counted on to rouse audiences at the time with the kind of antics and theatrics that were more commonplace in rock band arena shows. He re-formed the group with most of the original members in 1994, although he still lives in a Jehovah's Witness compound in Jamaica.

what to buy: The band's first album, *Graham Central Station* 𝄞𝄞𝄞 (Warner Bros., 1973, prod. Larry Graham, Russ Titleman),

captures the excitement of the band's pumping nightclub show, especially on the modestly successful single of the set, "Can You Handle It?" and the ripping Al Green cover, "It Ain't No Fun To Me."

the rest:

Release Yourself 𝄞𝄞 (Warner Bros., 1974)
The Best of Larry Graham and Graham Central Station . . . Vol. 1 𝄞𝄞𝄞 (Warner Bros., 1996)

worth searching for: Graham's first solo album, *One in a Million You* 𝄞𝄞𝄞 (Warner Bros., 1980, prod. Larry Graham), was one of his most commercially successful outings, launching his only Top 10 single with the title track.

influences:

◀◀ Billy Eckstine, Al Hibbler, Sly Stone

▶▶ Bootsy Collins, the Ohio Players, Brothers Johnson, Flea (Red Hot Chili Peppers)

see also: *Sly & the Family Stone*

Joel Selvin

Grand Daddy I.U.

Born in Long Island, NY.

This Strong Island native was discovered by the legendary Biz Markie and subsequently signed to the influential Cold Chillin' label (home to the Biz, Big Daddy Kane, M.C. Shan, and the rest of the Juice Crew). Grand Daddy's 1990 debut spawned three Top 10 hits, but the rapper fell silent for four . . . long . . . years (an eternity in rap time) before finally releasing his sophomore effort.

what to buy: The debut, *Smooth Assassin* 𝄞𝄞𝄞𝄞 (Cold Chillin', 1990, prod. Biz Markie, Cutmaster Cool V), is a classic slab of Cold Chillin' wax that features precisely what the title suggests: Smooth, killer tracks and tight, deadly rhymes. Grand Daddy possess a rich, sugary baritone (not unlike Big Daddy Kane's) that melts in your ears. He's simultaneously suave and forceful. The three hits alone ("Something New," "Sugarfree," "This Is a Recording") are worth the price of admission, but don't overlook the mellow madness of "The U Is Smooth," the sped-up poetry of "Pick Up the Pace" and the slow, devastating "Mass Destruction."

what to avoid: By *Lead Pipe* 𝄞𝄞 (Cold Chillin', 1994, prod. various), Grand Daddy has ditched the smooth, jazzy hustle that made *Smooth Assassin* such a killer, replacing it with the fist-waving, repeated-chorus Uptown Harlem style that dominated East Coast rap in the mid-'90s. The crime imagery is increased, too, and Grand Daddy is now forcing his words, rather than letting them flow out slowly. This one's hardly worth its weight in lead.

influences:

◄◄ Eric B. & Rakim, Big Daddy Kane, Biz Markie

Spence D.

Grandmaster Flash & the Furious Five /Melle Mel & the Furious Five

Formed 1977, in New York, NY. Disbanded 1983. Re-formed 1987. Disbanded 1987.

Grandmaster Flash (born Joseph Sadler), vocals; Melle Mel (born Melvin Glover), vocals; Kidd Creole, vocals; Scorpio/Mr. Ness, vocals; Rahiem, vocals; Cowboy, vocals.

Is the pioneer the one who invents it or the one who becomes known for it? Was the Sugarhill Gang really a pioneering group, or was it simply a case of being in the right place at the right time armed with just the right amount of luck? (Hint: Try the latter.) Consider, though, the cases of Grand Wizard Theodore and Grandmaster Flash. Theodore may have invented the art of scratching as a teenager during the 1970s, but as the first DJ to break out of the New York underground and into the mainstream, it was Flash who wound up exposing the music-buying world to "the zhigga-zhigga," not to mention back-spinning (manually rewinding record, then repeating the break or groove) and phasing (record-speed manipulation). Flash, however, was no Wonder Mike-come-lately; like Theodore, he, too, was a pioneer, introducing the world to punch phrasing, a technique that was a precursor to sampling and, therefore, ultimately more important than scratching. (Flash, who had studied electronics in school, also earned a footnote in rap history for essentially building the first hip-hop-era mixing board out of spare parts and glue.) After earning legendary status for his innovative techniques in the underground, where he had performed since the mid-'70s with various rappers (including Kurtis Blow), Flash and his new rap accompanists, the Furious Five, took the plunge into the realm of recorded music with 1979's long-lost "Superrappin" and, then, 1980's better-known "Freedom." But it was 1981's groundbreaking side, "The Adventures of Grandmaster Flash on the Wheels of Steel," that finally introduced the world to the previously unheard (on record) DJ techniques that had become so popular at New York parties and clubs. Loaded with breaks and bits from Chic's "Good Times,"

Queen's "Another One Bites the Dust," a children's recording, and Blondie's "Rapture" (on which noted Flash fan Deborah Harry chants "Flash is bad" over and over), the layered, adventurous collage was endlessly rewarding and fascinating. Of course, while the technically accomplished Flash got then-customary top billing, he wouldn't be the only star of his records: the Furious Five, led by Cowboy and one of rap's first great lyricists, Melle Mel, also earned an important place in the hip-hop pantheon, introducing groundbreaking vocal routines and harmonizing on 1982's "Flash to the Beat." The Furious Five also occasionally moved away from the lightweight party themes that were so typical in their day: the edgy, apocalyptic 1982 single, "The Message," for instance, focused on social decay and despair in the black inner cities, and 1983's "White Lines (Don't Don't Do It)" addressed the destructive nature of cocaine while also examining racial and socioeconomic injustice. After recording "White Lines," however, Grandmaster Flash & the Furious Five splintered into two groups, with Flash, Rahiem and Kidd Creole going one way, and Melle Mel, Scorpio and Cowboy another. Although Mel's post-Flash trio confusingly retained the Furious Five name, with Mel adding "Grandmaster" to his own moniker, Flash's group (which now included the forgettable likes of Larry Love, Lavon, Mr. Broadway, and Shame) also billed itself as the Furious Five—until Flash lost a lawsuit against Sugar Hill Records. Not that it mattered: Mel had more success taking a solo guest turn on Chaka Khan's 1984 hit "I Feel for You" than either Furious Five camp would with any of their group projects. After recording several poor-selling, poor-quality albums each, the two sides reunited for a 1987 charity concert and a new album. Ironically, though, the sampling and production technology that Flash had anticipated with his pioneering mixing techniques had already passed the group by; the rappers' suddenly old-school lyrical deliveries didn't fare much better, either. That didn't stop Melle Mel from becoming an in-demand guest artist, though, appearing in the 1990s on albums by everybody from the Last Poets and Bootsy Collins to EBN and Duran Duran before dropping an "L" from his name and releasing a new playa-era recording with Cowboy in 1997.

what to buy: Aside from a few greatest-hits collections, all of the Grandmaster Flash and Grandmaster Melle Mel albums are out of print. That, however, isn't a bad thing, since the Grandmasters and their Furious friends come from the singles-oriented rap era. The best bet is *Message from the Beat Street: The Best of Grandmaster Flash, Melle Mel & the Furious Five* 🎵🎵🎵 (Rhino, 1994, prod. various), which includes most of the group's key songs—"Freedom," "The Message," "White Lines

(Don't Don't Do It)," "Scorpio," and "Beat Street"—plus the amusing "Showdown," which pits the Furious Five against the studio-created Sugarhill Gang.

what to buy next: *The Adventures of Grandmaster Flash, Melle Mel & the Furious Five: More of the Best* ✍✍✍ (Sugar Hill/Rhino, 1996, prod. various) is worth buying simply for the otherwise impossible-to-find "The Adventures of Grandmaster Flash on the Wheels of Steel." A Grandmaster Flash remix of "Style (Peter Gunn Theme)" and one of the better post-Flash Melle Mel tracks, "Internationally Known," are also worth noting here.

the rest:
The Message ✍✍✍✍ (Sugarhill, 1982)
Greatest Messages ✍✍✍ (Sugarhill, 1983)
On the Strength ✍✍ (Elektra, 1988)
Greatest Hits ✍✍✍ (Sugarhill, 1989)

worth searching for: Melle Mel's *White Lines '89* 12-inch ✍✍✍ (New Day, 1989) updates the original message for the crack era and almost comes off like Eric B. & Rakim.

solo outings:
Grandmaster Flash:
They Said It Couldn't Be Done ✍ (Elektra, 1985)
The Source ✍✍ (Elektra, 1986)
Ba-Dop-Boom-Bang ✍✍ (Elektra, 1987)

Grandmaster Melle Mel & the Furious Five:
Work Party ✍✍ (Sugarhill, 1984)
Stepping Off ✍✍ (Sugarhill, 1985)

Grandmaster Melle Mel & Scorpio:
Right Now ✍✍ (Str8 Game, 1997)

influences:
◄◄ Grand Wizard Theodore, Kool DJ Herc, Grandmaster Flowers, Pete Jones
►► All of hip-hop

Josh Freedom du Lac

Dobie Gray
Born Leonard Victor Ainsworth, July 26, 1942, in Brookshire, TX.

The hit song "Drift Away" may have been Dobie Gray's most memorable moment. But his stirring blend of country, rock, and soul music inspired many more. He first emerged during the mid-1960s with his version of the Ramsey Lewis Trio hit "The 'In' Crowd." After the single, Gray experienced a lull in his musical career and turned to acting—including a stint in *Hair*—before joining a band called Pollution in 1969. His comeback as a

solo artist seemed effortless when he made three albums for MCA with Mentor Williams (who penned "Drift Away") and Troy Seals: *Drift Away* and *Loving Arms* in 1973 and *Hey Dixie* in 1974. All three albums were produced by Williams, the brother of songwriter Paul Williams—with whom Gray had been cutting demos just after his stint with Pollution. Gray moved to the Capricorn label in 1975, then to Infinity in 1979, where he had a disco hit "You Can Do It," which put him back in the charts. He returned to his country roots and to his partnership with Seals, making *The Dark Side of Town* in 1986 on Capitol. Gray's famous "Drift Away" has been covered by Rod Stewart and Michael Bolton, among others, and is considered a pop classic.

what to buy: *Drift Away with Dobie Gray: His Greatest Hits* ✍✍✍✍ (Razor & Tie, 1996, prod. various) is a career-spanning collection of Gray's work including collaborations with Williams and Seals.

worth searching for: *Drift Away* ✍✍✍ (Decca, 1973, prod. Mentor Williams) is Gray's best individual album, a solid showcase of his skill with a broad range of approaches.

influences:
◄◄ Mentor Williams, Paul Williams, Otis Redding, Sam Cooke
►► Rod Stewart, Michael Bolton, Maxwell, Roachford

Norene Cashen

Al Green
Born April 13, 1946, in Forrest City, AK.

When soul music began to shifting gears as the 1960s became the 1970s, a new voice emerged with a sweetness and hoist not quite heard since Sam Cooke's death in 1964. Green brought a freshness and tradition to soul music that had otherwise attempted to get harder or funkier or jump into the pools of psychedelia. With superb, subtle production by Willie Mitchell and a crack Memphis band, Green made enduring classics celebrating love's exuberance and pain throughout the 1970s, even as he made his way back to gospel in the latter part of the decade. His unbridled joy and soulful instincts made his sacred material worth a listen, and when he returned more solidly to the secular world with new work during the 1990s, it was as if he hadn't gone away. In a way he hadn't; as a singer who grew up in the church, he frequently included praise to Jesus even during his

Al Green (© Linda Vartoogian)

most sexy soul workouts, and he sang of romance in the middle of his gospel work. Even after becoming a minister of his own church, Green continues to administer the gospel of soul, with most of his best-loved albums back in print.

what to buy: If you can afford it, the four-CD *Anthology* 🎵🎵🎵🎵 (The Right Stuff, 1997, prod. Palmer James, Curtis Rodgers, Willie Mitchell, Robert Mugge, Al Green, Kaname Tajima) is the essential Al Green. It contains all the hits, previously-unreleased live tracks, alternate takes, and interview excerpts. *Greatest Hits* 🎵🎵🎵🎵 (Hi, 1975/The Right Stuff, 1995, prod. Willie Mitchell, Al Green), a superb collection of the hit singles, was made even better in its latest incarnation by adding later recordings "L-O-V-E" and "Belle" to what was already one of the great romantic soul albums of all times.

what to buy next: For a one-album slice of how wonderful Green can be, you can do no better than *Call Me* 🎵🎵🎵🎵 (Hi, 1973/The Right Stuff, 1994, prod. Willie Mitchell, Al Green). In addition to the hits "You Ought to Be with Me," "Here I Am (Come and Take Me)," and the title song, this record explores Green's love for country in versions of Hank Williams's "I'm So Lonesome I Could Cry" and Willie Nelson's "Funny How Time Slips Away," which Green would re-record 20 years later with Lyle Lovett. There's also a powerful gospel workout, "Jesus is Waiting." *One in a Million* 🎵🎵🎵🎵 (Word/Epic, 1991, prod. Al Green, James Bullard, Bill Cantrell, Quinton Claunch) compiles the best of his gospel recordings.

what to avoid: On *White Christmas* 🎵🎵 (Word/Epic, 1983/1991, prod. Moses C. Dillard Jr.), when he was deep in his gospel period, Green failed to infuse sufficient cheer into these seasonal standards.

the rest:
Al Green Gets Next to You 🎵🎵🎵🎵 (Hi, 1970)
Let's Stay Together 🎵🎵🎵🎵 (Hi, 1971)
I'm Still in Love with You 🎵🎵🎵🎵 (Hi, 1972/The Right Stuff, 1993)
Livin' for You 🎵🎵🎵🎵 (Hi, 1973)
Al Green Explores Your Mind 🎵🎵🎵🎵 (Hi, 1974/The Right Stuff, 1994)
Al Green Is Love 🎵🎵🎵 (Hi, 1975/The Right Stuff, 1994)
Full of Fire 🎵🎵🎵 (Hi, 1976/The Right Stuff, 1994)
The Belle Album 🎵🎵🎵🎵 (Hi, 1977/The Right Stuff, 1995)
Tokyo . . . Live 🎵🎵🎵🎵 (Cream, 1978/The Right Stuff, 1994)
Precious Lord 🎵🎵🎵 (Myrrh, 1982)
I'll Rise Again 🎵🎵🎵 (Myrrh, 1983, Word/Epic, 1991)
Soul Survivor 🎵🎵🎵 (A&M Records, 1987)
Your Heart's in Good Hands 🎵🎵🎵🎵 (MCA, 1995)
Greatest Hits, Vol. 2 🎵🎵🎵🎵 (The Right Stuff, 1997)

worth searching for: *Love Ritual: Rare and Previously Unreleased, 1968–76* 🎵🎵🎵🎵 (MCA, 1989, prod. Colin Escott) features leftover tracks from sessions originally produced by Green and Mitchell, dating from his first single (a surprising cover of the Beatles' "I Want to Hold Your Hand") to an alternate mix of "Love Ritual" from the *Al Green Is Love* sessions and an astounding 15-minute track, "Beware."

influences:
◀◀ Sam Cooke, Otis Redding, Clyde McPhatter
▶▶ Luther Vandross, Prince, Otis Clay, Terence Trent D'Arby

Roger Catlin

Groove Theory
Formed 1991, in New York, NY.

Amel Larrieux, vocals; Bryce Wilson, keyboards, production.

With its artful, moody, often topical sound, the duo Groove Theory has set itself apart from the formulaic wasteland that is contemporary R&B. Producer and keyboardist Bryce Wilson is formerly one-half of the late 1980s rap duo Mantronix, which cut a few records for Capitol. Frustrated by his lack of creative control in the group, Wilson split, bought a keyboard, and began exploring a jazzier, more melodic style of music. His sultry rhythms and shuffling beats retain some of hip-hop's street freshness while providing fitting backdrops for singer Amel Larrieux's soft, soaring soprano.

what to buy: On *Groove Theory* 🎵🎵🎵 (Epic, 1995, prod. Bryce P. Wilson, Jimmy Henchmen), the enigmatic Larrieux is a beauty with a beautiful voice who weaves topical themes—"10 Minute High" is an ode to a dead crack user, "Boy at the Window" is a touching look at poverty—with tales of love and lust. She turns Todd Rundgren's song about love from a distance, "Hello It's Me," into a five-minute seduction.

influences:
◀◀ Sade, Donny Hathaway, Roberta Flack, A Tribe Called Quest

Doug Pullen

Group Home
Formed in Brooklyn, NY.

Lil' Dap, vocals; Malachi, vocals.

Lil' Dap and Malachi were actually two solo MCs down with Gang Starr before they joined forces at the behest of Guru. Before they had their own recording home, Dap debuted on the infamous "I'm the Man" from Gang Starr's *Daily Operation*, while Malachi's premiere Starr turn came on *Hard To Earn*.

what's available: It's fair to say that Group Home's debut album, *Livin' Proof* 𝄞𝄞𝄞 (Payday/London, 1995, prod. DJ Premier) earned more accolades for the crafty production work of DJ Premier than for the simple (if not undeveloped) lyrical abilities of Lil' Dap and Malachi. Though their purpose is essentially to add gritty texture to Premier's pristine beats, Dap and Malachi can be unbearably bad.

worth searching for: The bootleg album of *Livin' Proof* instrumentals is a must-have for Premier completists.

influences:

◀◀ Gang Starr

Jazzbo

Guy

Formed 1985, in New York, NY. Disbanded 1991.

Teddy Riley, vocals, keyboards, various instruments; Aaron Hall, vocals, keyboards; Timmy Gatling, vocals (1985–89); Damion Hall, vocals (1989–91).

It's nearly impossible to overestimate Teddy Riley's impact on the current urban-music milieu. Since the late 1980s, the Harlem-born wunderkind has produced a slew of hit-making heavies, including Keith Sweat, Bobby Brown, Patti LaBelle, Heavy D. & the Boyz, Wreckx-N-Effect, Kool Moe Dee, and even Michael Jackson (1991's sextuple-platinum *Dangerous*). And as the cynosure of the hip-hop quartet BLACKstreet, Riley's artistic currency in today's R&B marketplace can hardly be questioned. The root of Riley's phenomenal success lies in his pioneering work as a founding member of the seminal trio Guy, where he cross-pollinated classic soul grooves with hip-hop's electro-rhythmic infrastructure and engendered "New Jack Swing"—and with it, the sonic blueprint for the next decade of commercial urban music.

what to buy: A tightly wound, meticulously processed 10-song tour de funk, the debut album *Guy* 𝄞𝄞𝄞𝄞 (Uptown/MCA, 1988) sets singer Aaron Hall's gospel-inflected melisma to Riley's pristine synthscapes. Edifices of fortified funk such as "Groove Me," "You Can Call Me Crazy," "Spend the Night," and especially "I Like" (which reached #2 on the R&B charts) are veritable house parties unto themselves. Conversely, the album's slower numbers—"Piece of My Love" and "Goodbye Love"—showcase Hall's facility for sweet-talking seduction.

the rest:
The Future 𝄞𝄞𝄞 (Uptown/MCA, 1990)

solo outings:
Aaron Hall:
The Truth 𝄞𝄞𝄞 (Silas/MCA, 1993)

Damion Hall:
Straight to the Point 𝄞𝄞 (Silas/MCA, 1994)

influences:

◀◀ The Temptations, the Jackson 5, Stevie Wonder, the Gap Band, Prince

▶▶ Keith Sweat, Bobby Brown, Heavy D. & the Boyz, Michael Jackson, Janet Jackson, Boyz II Men, Mary J. Blige

Greg Siegel

Buddy Guy

Born George Guy, July 30, 1936, in Lettsworth, LA.

With a gigantic grin and inventive electric guitar riffs played so fast you can barely focus on one at a time, Buddy Guy has come to symbolize traditional Chicago blues more than any of his contemporaries. Until 1991 he was, amazingly, still an undiscovered talent by most of the world; he ran his downtown Chicago nightclub, Buddy Guy's Legends, and showed off his immense charisma and talent on the national blues circuit. But still, despite opening gigs for the Rolling Stones and other blues-rock performers during the early 1970s, few outside Chicago and the national blues community had really heard of him. Then came a marketing break: his comeback album, *Damn Right, I've Got the Blues*—with a new version of the old standard "Mustang Sally" and guest cameos by Mark Knopfler and Eric Clapton—worked like a charm. It sold well, earned a Grammy, established Guy as a blues celebrity along with B.B. King and John Lee Hooker, and eventually opened the doors for a lucrative Reebok television commercial with White Sox slugger Frank Thomas. Guy's career beginnings paralleled those of many other bluesmen, from mentors Muddy Waters and King to contemporaries Otis Rush and Junior Wells. Born in Lettsworth, Louisiana, to a sharecropping family, Guy picked cotton until blues songs on the radio inspired him to pick up a guitar. After playing local roadhouses, he moved to Chicago's thriving, blues-friendly South Side and, despite his young age, gained renown in "head-cutting" competitions against Rush and Magic Sam. Following Howlin' Wolf, Little Walter, Waters, and so many others to the legendary Chess Records, Guy recorded his trademark songs, including 1960 versions of Eurreal Montgomery's

"First Time I Met the Blues" and Willie Dixon's "Let Me Love You Baby." During the 1960s, he was one of the few nationally recognized bluesmen who wasn't old enough to be a rock 'n' roller's father, so he started to cross over into the rock audience. But the blues revival died down in the 1970s, and despite a creatively rich partnership with harpist Junior Wells, Guy had trouble translating the energy of his long, heavy-jamming songs to record. He eked out a living in Chicago as owner of the Checkerboard Lounge before opening Legends, befriending the hero-worshiping Stevie Ray Vaughan (he played at the guitarist's final show before his death) and recording *Damn Right, I've Got the Blues*. He continues to tour, play festivals, sell out 20 or 30 consecutive Legends appearances every January, and serve as Chicago's reigning blues hero.

what to buy: True to its reputation, *Damn Right, I've Got the Blues* ⅃⅃⅃ (Silvertone, 1991, prod. John Porter) pretty much captures Guy's fiery performances, although you miss things like watching him walk from the stage to the bathroom while continuing to play the guitar. Despite overwillingness to please non-blues fans—"Mustang Sally" is included just for familiarity, not because it adds anything to the original, and the guest stars sometimes crowd the singer—Guy's voice is at top soul power. His best album is *Stone Crazy* ⅃⅃⅃⅃ (Alligator, 1981, prod. Didier Tricard), with a hot Chicago four-piece rhythm section and Guy's soaring-and-smashing electric riffs. Before that, the closest Guy came to matching his live power was his debut, *A Man and the Blues* ⅃⅃⅃⅃ (Vanguard, 1968/1987, prod. Samuel Charters), with killer versions of "Mary Had a Little Lamb" and "Money (That's What I Want)." To complete the set, you'll need one of several Chess compilations, such as *Buddy's Blues* ⅃⅃⅃⅃ (Chess/MCA, 1997, prod. various), and at least one Junior Wells collaboration, most notably *Alone and Acoustic* ⅃⅃⅃⅃ (Alligator, 1991, prod. Didier Tricard), a spontaneous 1981 Paris session including Hooker's "I'm in the Mood," Guy's "Sweet Black Girl," and the rock classic "High Heel Sneakers."

what to buy next: An early linking up with Clapton, who once called Guy the world's greatest living guitar player, produced the nice but not-so-explosive *Buddy Guy & Junior Wells Play the Blues* ⅃⅃⅃ (Atlantic, 1972/Rhino, 1992, prod. Eric Clapton, Ahmet Ertegun, Tom Dowd, Michael Cuscuna). While Chess/MCA has mined Guy's early hits on many indistinguishable compilations, *I Was Walkin' Through the Woods* ⅃⅃⅃ (Chess, 1970). *Feels Like Rain* ⅃⅃⅃ (Silvertone, 1993, prod. John Porter), the slower followup to *Damn Right*, is especially worth buying for Guy's soulful vocals—but not for the Travis Tritt and Paul Rodgers cameos.

what to avoid: Beware: Chess Records has driven a long way on the strength of its classic 1950s and 1960s singles; if you buy the newer *Buddy's Blues*, you won't need the more thorough but redundant *The Complete Chess Studio Recordings* ⅃⅃⅃ (Chess/MCA, 1992, prod. various). *Live! The Real Deal* ⅃⅃⅃ (Silvertone, 1996, prod. Buddy Guy, Eddie Kramer), with the pompous pony-tailed guitarist G.E. Smith and his "Saturday Night Live" band, captures a lackluster performance, with typically good Guy solos but very little else.

the rest:
I Left My Blues in San Francisco ⅃⅃⅃ (Chess, 1967/MCA, 1987)
This Is Buddy Guy ⅃⅃⅃ (Vanguard, 1968)
Hold That Plane! ⅃⅃⅃ (Vanguard, 1972)
Live in Montreaux ⅃⅃⅃ (Evidence, 1977/1992)
(With Junior Wells) *Drinkin' TNT and Smokin' Dynamite* ⅃⅃⅃ (Blind Pig, 1982)
The Best of Buddy Guy ⅃⅃⅃ (Rhino, 1992)
My Time after Awhile ⅃⅃⅃ (Vanguard, 1992)
Slippin' In ⅃⅃⅃ (Silvertone, 1994)
Southern Blues 1957–1963 ⅃⅃⅃ (Paula, 1994)

worth searching for: The import-only JSP series captures Guy smoking, with his great 1970s band (including brother Phil on rhythm guitar). The best of these hard-to-find CDs are *D.J. Play My Blues* ⅃⅃⅃ (JSP, 1994), *Breaking Out* ⅃⅃⅃⅃ (JSP, 1993) and *Live at the Checkerboard Lounge* ⅃⅃⅃ (JSP, 1979/1995).

influences:
◀◀ Muddy Waters, Magic Sam, Otis Rush, Junior Wells, T-Bone Walker, Guitar Slim, B.B. King, Albert King

▶▶ Eric Clapton, Stevie Ray Vaughan, Son Seals, Jonny Lang, Kenny Wayne Shepherd, Tinsley Ellis, Luther Allison, the Rolling Stones, Jeff Beck

Steve Knopper

Bill Haley

Born July 6, 1925, in Highland Park, MI. Died February 9, 1981, in Harlingen, TX.

It's kind of cute how the history books depict Haley's "Rock Around the Clock" as inciting teenagers to riot, rip up theater seats, flash knife blades, you name it. Try imagining the chunky singer, with his goofy ever present grin and greased curly-Q hair, putting fear in the hearts of the religious right today. On the contrary, he'd be lauded as wholesome family entertainment. But in 1954, the former country & western singer's lumpen tunes were at the helm of rock 'n' roll's birth and thus brought with them the air of revolution. His songs were plodding, his arrangements barely existent, he was fat and already 30, yet still managed to drive the kids nuts. Why? Because there was no one else on the playing field. When the sex-drenched Elvis Presley and the lunatic Little Richard burst upon the American public, Haley was revealed as the square he always was and lost his teenage cachet as quickly as he found it. As a country singer with a fondness for cutting R&B songs, Haley first dabbled in cultural miscegenation with a 1951 recording of the Jackie Brenston R&B hit "Rocket 88"; he was Bill Haley and the Saddlemen then. The first record by the renamed Bill Haley and the Comets, "Crazy Man Crazy," on the independent Essex Records label became the first rock 'n' roll record to make the nationwide Top 20. After signing to Decca Records in 1954, he recorded the epochal "Rock Around the Clock," which failed on its initial release but scorched up the charts after a film, "The Blackboard Jungle," used the song as a theme the following year. Haley's records tended toward the cutesie ("Skinny Minnie") and novelty ("Mambo Rock"), but Decca producer Milt Gabler, a savvy veteran, sagaciously styled Haley's sound after another one of his charges, the rollicking Louis Jordan, and came up with some stunning, under-rated pieces. Haley's "Rip It Up," for instance, may actually out-rock the Little Richard original. Ultimately, however, his career amounted to little more than "Rock Around the Clock," and he spent many years living in Mexican exile before settling in Texas, where a bitter, deranged Haley would show strangers his driver's license to prove who he was.

what to buy: All compilations on the market have nearly identical song listings, but *From the Original Master Tapes* ♫♫♫ (MCA, 1985, prod. Milt Gabler) is the most thorough and provides adequate detail for most libraries. A good boost in sound quality finds the congenial Haley remastered for the modern age.

what to buy next: Haley's evolution from a country singer to the first rock and roll star is examined in fine-point detail on *Rock the Joint! The Original Essex Recordings, 1951–1954* ♫♫♫ (Schoolkids, 1994), an historic 24-song collection that hews closely to Haley's developing rock and roll style.

what to avoid: An unilluminating late 1960s interview with Haley, interspersed with snatches of music, *The Haley Tapes* **woof!** (Jerden, 1995), does not make an interesting or rewarding CD.

the rest:
Rock & Roll ♫ (Orfeon)
Greatest Hits ♫♫♫ (MCA, 1968/1991)
Shake, Rattle and Roll ♫♫♫ (Drive Archive, 1994)
Los Grandes Hits De Haley ♫ (Orfeon, 1996)

worth searching for: The German reissue specialists, Bear Family, produced a five-disc boxed set called *The Decca Years & More* ♫♫♫ (Bear Family, 1990, prod. Milt Gabler, others), although that may be overkill in this case.

influences:

◀◀ Big Joe Turner, Bob Wills, Louis Jordan

▶▶ Pat Boone, Bruce Springsteen, the Ramones

Joel Selvin and Allan Orski

Daryl Hall & John Oates

Formed 1972, in Philadelphia, PA.

Daryl Hall (born Daryl Franklin Hohl, October 11, 1948, in Pottstown, PA), vocals, keyboards, guitar; John Oates (born April 7, 1949, in New York, NY), vocals, guitar.

The most commercially successful duo in rock history, Hall & Oates have had 29 Top 40 hits, six of them #1, and have come to epitomize the term "blue-eyed soul" (in other words, they're white guys who sound black, or at least soulful). They did this not by playing it safe, but by sometimes innovating and thus creating trends in popular music. The two singers met at Temple University after growing up in the Philadelphia suburbs, and Oates joined Hall's failed group Gulliver in 1969, just before it fell apart. They then went separate ways but reunited and signed with Atlantic. Atlantic never quite knew what to do with them, and they bounced from near-folk to soul to rock. Their sole Atlantic hit, "She's Gone," charted only after they'd switched to RCA, riding the coattails of the hit from their first RCA album, "Sara Smile." For several years after that, though they charted, their experimental tack dampened their commercial success; in fact, RCA long refused to issue Hall's first solo album, an adventurous effort produced by Robert Fripp. Hall & Oates recovered from their commercial slump not by going along with the record company, but by producing their 1980 album *Voices* themselves. Inventing a perky pop style particularly distinctive for its bouncy, percolating electric keyboard parts, but with plenty of room for Hall's virtuosic vocal fillips and melismas, it yielded four Top 40 hits, including the #1 "Kiss on My List." That launched a four-year string during which Hall & Oates dominated radio playlists, pop charts, and even MTV.

Daryl Hall (l) and John Oates (© Ken Settle)

But by the late 1980s, the duo was, if not over, at least spent. These days they work together intermittently, and their music—together and apart—no longer causes the stir it once did.

what to buy: *Voices* 𝄞𝄞𝄞𝄞 (RCA, 1980, prod. Daryl Hall, John Oates) and *Private Eyes* 𝄞𝄞𝄞𝄞𝄞 (RCA, 1981, prod. Daryl Hall, John Oates) have far more good tunes than could go on any compilation, and the production style has held up well over the years. Hall's *Sacred Songs* 𝄞𝄞𝄞𝄞𝄞 (RCA, 1980, prod. Robert Fripp) in a way proved RCA right; it isn't even slightly commercial, or even pop. But its chilly contrast to his passionate vocal style makes it great, and it's not an offputting listen.

what to buy next: How convenient that practically all the duo's good tracks for Atlantic were all on one album. *Abandoned Luncheonette* 𝄞𝄞𝄞 (Atlantic, 1973, prod. Arif Mardin) is most notable for "She's Gone" but is tuneful throughout. *Along the Red Ledge* 𝄞𝄞𝄞𝄞 (RCA, 1978, prod. David Foster) exhibited the first fruits of Hall's adventurous recasting of the group's sound, and

while the (slight) hit was "It's a Laugh," the highlights are the haunting "Melody for a Memory" and "I Don't Wanna Lose You."

what to avoid: The debut *Whole Oats* **woof!** (Atlantic, 1972, prod. Arif Mardin) is lame singer-songwriter mellowness having nothing to do with the duo's later strengths. On Daryl Hall's bloated *Three Hearts in the Happy Ending Machine* 𝄞 (RCA, 1986, prod. Daryl Hall, David A. Stewart, Tom "T-Bone" Wolk), he just never knows when to stop—all the songs go on forever, with the overdubs piled on way past the point of overkill.

the rest:
War Babies 𝄞𝄞𝄞 (Atlantic, 1974)
Daryl Hall & John Oates 𝄞𝄞𝄞 (RCA, 1975)
Bigger Than Both of Us 𝄞𝄞𝄞 (RCA, 1976)
Beauty on a Back Street 𝄞𝄞𝄞 (RCA, 1977)
Livetime 𝄞𝄞𝄞 (RCA, 1978)
X-Static 𝄞𝄞𝄞 (RCA, 1979)
H2O 𝄞𝄞𝄞𝄞 (RCA, 1982)
Rock 'n Soul Part 1 𝄞𝄞𝄞𝄞 (RCA, 1983)

Bigbamboom 🎵🎵🎵🎶 (RCA, 1984)
Live at the Apollo 🎵🎵🎶 (RCA, 1985)
Ooh Yeah! 🎵🎵🎶 (Arista, 1988)
Change of Season 🎵🎵 (Arista, 1990)
Marigold Sky 🎵🎵🎵 (Push, 1997)

worth searching for: The ultimate H&O best-of is no longer the 12-song *Rock 'n Soul Part 1*, though completists will still want its live version of "Wait for Me"). The new king is the two-CD, 32-track *Greatest Hits* 🎵🎵🎵🎵🎵 (Razor & Tie/BMG Direct Marketing, 1997, prod. various), which can be found via mail-order only at 1-800-633-9577. It only covers the RCA years but does so with admirable thoroughness, containing every RCA Top 40 hit except the live Motown medley from the Apollo concert album and throwing in such key albums tracks as "Every Time You Go Away" and "I Don't Wanna Lose You." Fanatics will want to look for an import of dubious legitimacy, *Really Smokin'* 🎵🎶 (Magnum, 1993) which contains not only 1970–71 Hall demos but also some 1970 Gulliver material.

solo outings:
Daryl Hall:
Soul Alone 🎵🎶 (Epic, 1993)

influences:

⏪ The O'Jays, Gamble & Huff, Sam & Dave, the Temptations

⏩ Charles & Eddie, Boyz II Men, Go West

Steve Holtje

Hammer
See: M.C. Hammer

Herbie Hancock
Born Herbert Jeffrey Hancock, April 12, 1940, Chicago, IL.

Sticking keyboardist Herbie Hancock's musical output in one category is downright impossible. His reach spans the entire spectrum, from free jazz to funk, from cool jazz/blues to trendsetting hip-hop. He was even doing techno before techno was cool, to borrow a phrase. On his 1983 smash "Rockit," Hancock not only brought scratching and hip-hop beats to mainstream Top 40, he also used robotics in a totally new way for his accompanying video. Even before that hit, Hancock was considered one of the major pioneers of jazz fusion and is listed alongside Miles Davis, Charlie Mingus, and John Coltrane as one of the giants of new jazz. Hancock was, in fact, one of Davis's sidemen during the 1960s, along with Ron Carter and Tony Williams—both of whom Hancock used on *Maiden Voyage*. The oft-covered "Watermelon

Man" is a Hancock composition; "Chameleon" was a disco staple. (Both appear on one of Hancock's classic albums, 1973's *Head Hunters*, though "Watermelon Man" was a hit 10 years earlier.) Even more remarkable than his ability to cross over into so many modern genres is the fact that he started out as a classical prodigy, performing a Mozart concerto movement with the Chicago Symphony Orchestra at age 11. He also studied engineering, which may have helped fuel his interest in electronic instruments. In a career as prolific and varied as Hancock's, there's bound to be heated discussion about his output. His enormous success—e.g. between 1973–84, 17 Hancock albums showed up on the *Billboard* charts—has earned him his share of detractors; i.e. people who whine that his genre-hopping commercialism is tantamount to selling out. He's largely told these elitists where to go and continues to do what he pleases (including things like his former Showtime music series "Coast To Coast") with class and intelligence.

what to buy: *Maiden Voyage* 🎵🎵🎵🎵 (Blue Note, 1965, prod. Alfred Lion), often called the definitive Blue Note Hancock, features Ron Carter on bass and Tony Williams on drums; together with Hancock, the Miles Davis bandmates also have been referred to as the definitive rhythm section of the era. (Horn players George Coleman and Freddie Hubbard rounded out the quintet.) It's a concept album, with each song thematically related to the sea. *Empyrean Isles* 🎵🎵🎵🎵 (Blue Note, 1964/1985; prod. Alfred Lion) once again features Hubbard, Carter, and Williams, an unbeatable combination that dominated jazz-funk both together and individually for many years.

what to buy next: *Head Hunters* 🎵🎵🎵🎶 (Columbia, 1973/1992, prod. David Rubinson, Herbie Hancock), Hancock's attempt to find more funk, worked quite well; his disco-flavored "Chameleon" helped give this disc platinum sales. But there's a softer side as well, on the lyrical, delicate "Vein Melter." *Sound-System* 🎵🎵🎵🎵 (Columbia, 1984, prod. Bill Laswell/Material, Herbie Hancock), is full of heavily layered and catchy funk that employs scratching, Fairlight programming, and other then-innovative electronic instruments. Among its players are Wayne Shorter, Anton Fier, Bernard Fowler, and Aiyb Dieng.

what to avoid: *Monster* 🎵🎵 (Columbia, 1980/1994, prod. David Rubinson & Friends Inc., Herbie Hancock) is plodding, formulaic, repetitive funk. In-between, it's filled with Lite FM ballads that offer little serious soul.

the rest:
Takin' Off 🎵🎵🎵🎵 (Blue Note, 1962/1987)
My Point of View 🎵🎵🎵 (Blue Note, 1963/1996)

2/4/8 *herbie hancock*

Herbie Hancock (© Jack Vartoogian)

Inventions and Dimensions (a.k.a. *Succotash* 𝄞𝄞𝄞) (Blue Note/Pausa, 1963)

Blow-Up 𝄞𝄞𝄞𝄞 (MGM, 1966/1992)

Speak Like a Child 𝄞𝄞𝄞 (Blue Note, 1968/1988)

The Best of Herbie Hancock: The Blue Note Years 𝄞𝄞𝄞𝄞 (Blue Note, 1968/1988)

Fat Albert Rotunda 𝄞𝄞𝄞𝄞 (Warner Bros., 1969)

The Prisoner 𝄞𝄞𝄞𝄞 (Blue Note, 1969/1996)

Mwandishi 𝄞𝄞𝄞𝄞 (Warner Bros., 1970/1994)

Crossings 𝄞𝄞𝄞𝄞 (Warner Bros., 1971)

Sextant 𝄞𝄞 (Columbia, 1972)

Treasure Chest 𝄞𝄞𝄞 (Warner Bros., 1974)

Death Wish 𝄞𝄞𝄞 (Columbia, 1974)

Thrust 𝄞𝄞𝄞𝄞 (Columbia, 1974)

Man-Child 𝄞𝄞𝄞 (Columbia, 1975/1987)

Herbie Hancock 𝄞𝄞𝄞 (Blue Note, 1976)

Secrets 𝄞𝄞 (Columbia, 1976/1988)

(With V.S.O.P.) *Live Under the Sky* 𝄞𝄞𝄞𝄞 (Columbia, 1976)

(With V.S.O.P.) *V.S.O.P.* 𝄞𝄞𝄞𝄞 (Columbia, 1976)

(With Chick Corea) *An Evening with Chick Corea & Herbie Hancock In Concert* 𝄞𝄞𝄞𝄞 (Columbia, 1978/1988)

Feets Don't Fail Me Now 𝄞𝄞 (Columbia, 1978/1987)

Mr. Hands 𝄞𝄞𝄞𝄞 (Columbia, 1980/1994)

Magic Windows 𝄞𝄞 (Columbia, 1981)

Quartet 𝄞𝄞𝄞𝄞 (Columbia, 1981/1987)

(With V.S.O.P.) *V.S.O.P. Vol. 2* 𝄞𝄞𝄞𝄞 (Columbia, 1981)

Lite Me Up 𝄞𝄞 (Columbia, 1982)

Future Shock 𝄞𝄞𝄞 (Columbia 1983)

Village Life 𝄞𝄞𝄞 (Columbia, 1985)

Perfect Machine 𝄞𝄞𝄞 (Columbia, 1988)

Best of Herbie Hancock 𝄞𝄞 (Columbia, 1988)

A Jazz Collection 𝄞𝄞𝄞𝄞𝄞 (Columbia, 1991)

Cantaloupe Island 𝄞𝄞𝄞 (Blue Note/Capitol, 1994)

Collection 𝄞𝄞𝄞 (Griffin Music, 1994)

Dis Is Da Drum 𝄞𝄞 (Mercury, 1995)

Jazz Portrait 𝄞𝄞𝄞𝄞 (Tristar Music Imports, 1996)

Sunlight 𝄞𝄞𝄞 (Verve, 1996)

The New Standard 𝄞𝄞𝄞 (Verve, 1996)

worth searching for: Hancock does some fine playing on the wonderful soundtrack to the movie *Round Midnight* 𝄞𝄞𝄞𝄞𝄞 (Columbia, 1986, prod. Herbie Hancock). The soundtrack won an

Academy Award and features such jazz legends as Dexter Gordon, Chet Baker, Ron Carter, and Wayne Shorter. A "sequel" to that album, *The Other Side of Round Midnight* 𝒲𝒲𝒲 (Blue Note, 1987, prod. Herbie Hancock) features music that didn't make the original disc.

influences:

◀◀ Bill Evans, Oscar Peterson, George Shearing, Gil Evans, John Coltrane, Miles Davis, Clare Fischer, Robert Farnon, Sly & the Family Stone, James Brown, Stevie Wonder

▶▶ Red Hot Chili Peppers, Harry Connick Jr., Lyle Mays, Chick Corea, Kenny Kirkland, Bobby McFerrin, Us3

Lynne Margolis

Ben Harper

Born October 28, 1969, in Pomona, CA.

Ben Harper made quite an initial critical splash, partly because it's still unusual nowadays for a young black man to sing reflective, bluesy acoustic folk-rock. Given the political bent of some of Harper's lyrics, it would be easy to tag him as a male version of Tracy Chapman, but his voice is less distinctive and his sound more so, making particular use of the Weissenborn, a rare Hawaiian guitar with a thin but singular tone. With a small but avid international following, Harper would seem to have a solid, and lengthy, career ahead of him, especially given his reputation as a dynamic, committed live performer. Whether he will be able to develop into new areas as a recording artist remains to be seen.

what to buy: Harper's debut album, *Welcome to the Cruel World* 𝒲𝒲𝒲𝒲 (Virgin, 1994, prod. Ben Harper, J.P. Plunier), remains his best. Highlights range from the funny, reggae-ish "Mama's Got a Girlfriend Now," to the surprisingly upbeat "How Many Miles Must We March?," to the dreamy "I'll Rise." He and his main collaborator/producer J.P. Plunier keep the instrumental arrangements simple but cleverly nuanced throughout, often adding choir-like backing vocals.

what to buy next: *Fight for Your Mind* 𝒲𝒲𝒲 (Virgin, 1995, prod. Ben Harper, J.P. Plunier) gets more electric on a few numbers, but mostly it sticks to the same Bob Marley- and Neil Young-influenced folk-rock. Occasionally he gets too ambitious for his own good, adding a string quartet to the already dark "Power of the Gospel" and winding up with something tedious instead of stirring. Still, "Ground on Down" is powerful, damning stuff. His most recent effort, *The Will to Live* 𝒲𝒲𝒲 (Virgin, 1997, prod. J.P. Plunier), was promoted as a sudden shift from acoustic to electric, but most of it remains in the same old mode. The Sly Stone-like "Mama's Trippin'" and the stinging blues shuffle "Homeless Child" are potent tracks, but the haunting "Widow of a Living Man," in which Harper's voice speaks for a beaten, but not defeated, woman, is the real standout. The lyrics get cliched in spots, but he remains an artist with integrity, and these days, that's something special.

influences:

◀◀ Richie Havens, Taj Mahal, Curtis Mayfield

Bob Remstein

Major Harris
See: The Delfonics

Wynonie Harris

Born August 24, 1915, in Omaha, NE. Died June 14, 1969, in Los Angeles, CA.

The rowdy jump blues and smoky vocal bravado of Wynonie Harris clearly set the stage for rock 'n' roll. Between 1945–52, no blues shouter (not even Harris's idol and mentor, Big Joe Turner) rocked harder or scored more R&B hits. Harris began his career as a comedian and hoofer (he danced in the film *Harlem Hit Parade 1943*) before he taught himself to play drums and formed his own band. Harris's big break as a vocalist came with Lucky Millender's Orchestra in 1944. Their Decca recordings of "Hurry Hurry" and "Who Threw the Whiskey In the Well" were solid hits, but Harris was unsatisfied with the financial arrangements and quickly departed. As a free agent, he recorded the hits "Wynonie's Blues," "That's the Stuff You Gotta Watch," "Playful Baby," and "Young & Wild" for the Philo (later Aladdin), Apollo, Bullet, and Hamp-Tone labels before settling in for a long run at King Records, beginning in 1947. The following year, Harris's incendiary reworking of Roy Brown's "Good Rockin' Tonight" established him as a major star. (The Sun Records-era Elvis Presley would record this song and feature "That's the Stuff You Gotta Watch" in his stage show.) Though most of Harris's King hits were about sex ("All She Wants to Do Is Rock," "I Like My Baby's Puddin'," "Lovin' Machine") or liquor ("Rot Gut," "Don't Take My Whiskey Away," "Drinkin' Wine Spo-Dee-Oh-Dee"), artistically Harris was more than just a whiskey-guzzling sex fiend. (Off-stage is another story, however.) On songs such as "Grandma Plays the Numbers," "I Feel Old Age Coming On," and others, he displays comic timing unique among blues shouters. Harris, quite a songwriter early in his career, had an ear for good songs too, no matter the source. His transformation of Hank Penny's C&W hit "Bloodshot Eyes" into a delightful R&B stomper is not only one his best remembered recordings but also a daring cross-cultural move that would later influence the creative method of early rockers such as Chuck Berry, Fats Domino, and Elvis Presley. After 1952, smoother, less suggestive sounds began to rule the R&B charts, and Harris's string of hits ended. He continued to make good, occasionally great records for the King, Atco, Roulette, and Cadet labels, but nothing hit the charts. During his glory years, trade publications denounced the music of Wynonie "Mr. Blues" Harris as vulgar. Nowadays, they refer to these same recordings as classics.

what to buy: *Bloodshot Eyes—The Best of Wynonie Harris* 𝄞𝄞𝄞𝄞 (Rhino, 1994, comp. James Austen) features 18 of Harris's biggest pre-rock hits from 1945–55. Essential.

what to buy next: *Everybody Boogie* 𝄞𝄞𝄞 (Delmark, 1996, prod. various) contains tracks from Harris's first year of recording, including the hits "Playful Baby" and "Young & Wild." Rock 'n' roll started right here, folks.

what to avoid: *Battle of the Blues* 𝄞𝄞𝄞 (King, 1986), *The Battle of the Blues, Vol. 2* 𝄞𝄞𝄞 (King, 1989), and *Battle of the Blues* 𝄞𝄞𝄞 (King, 1989), unless you want tracks by Roy Brown mixed in with Harris's.

the rest:
Good Rockin' Tonight 𝄞𝄞𝄞 (Charly, 1989)
Laughing But Crying 𝄞𝄞𝄞 (Route 66, 1991)
Mr. Blues Is Coming to Town 𝄞𝄞𝄞 (Route 66, 1991)
1944–45 𝄞𝄞𝄞 (Classics, 1996)

worth searching for: *Women, Whiskey, & Fishtails* 𝄞𝄞𝄞 (Ace Records, 1993, prod. various) contains 21 previously unreleased tracks and alternate takes from Harris's fertile King records period.

influences:
◀◀ Louis Jordan, Big Joe Turner, Jimmy Rushing

▶▶ Roy Brown, Screaming Jay Hawkins, Elvis Presley

Ken Burke

Donny Hathaway
Born October 1, 1945, in Chicago, IL. Died January 13, 1979, in New York, NY.

Had Donny Hathaway decided against leaping from the 15th floor of the Essex House, he may have surpassed even the most pre-eminent musicians of his era. At the time of his death, his skills as an arranger, producer, and composer were electri-

fying his own music as well as that of Roberta Flack, Aretha Franklin, and the Staple Singers. A formally trained musician, Hathaway drew on both his Howard College education (his teachers would often turn the class over to him, such were his abilities on the piano) and his time spent with his grandmother, a professional singer on the gospel circuit. His keening voice paired him with former classmate Flack throughout his career in successful MOR duets, but it is his solo work that leaves the greatest impression. Working out the elaborate arrangements that ran through his mind, Hathaway created a truly communal and joyous ensemble of sound, reflecting a decidedly positive ghetto atmosphere.

what to buy: His last studio album, *Extension of a Man* 𝄞𝄞𝄞𝄞 (Rhino, 1973/1993, prod. Arif Mardin, Jerry Wexler), was a major achievement. Comprising a complex song cycle, the album employs intricate arrangements for full orchestra and emits a hypnotic blend of experimental and romantic soul.

what to buy next: Hathaway burst out with *Everything Is Everything* 𝄞𝄞𝄞 (Atlantic, 1970/1995, prod. Donny Hathaway, Ric Powell), an inclusive and sprawling debut. The funky togetherness of the title track and the uplifting "The Ghetto" are as wide open as soul gets, loosely encompassing both tradition and his own ambitions.

the rest:
Donny Hathaway 𝄞𝄞𝄞 (Rhino, 1971/1993)
A Donny Hathaway Collection 𝄞𝄞𝄞 (Atlantic, 1990)

influences:
◀◀ Nina Simone, Ray Charles

▶▶ Stevie Wonder, Roberta Flack, Herbie Hancock, Lalah Hathaway

see also: *Roberta Flack*

Allan Orski

Lalah Hathaway
Born 1969, in Chicago, IL.

Although discouraged early from becoming a singer, the daughter of legendary soul man Donny Hathaway settled on a musical career and released her debut at 21, shortly after graduating from Boston's Berklee School of Music. It would be both unfair and off base to compare her to Donny, a soul genius whose foundation was the gospel music upon which he was raised. Lalah, whose name means "music of the night" in Arabic, felt her calling from the jazz tradition. Though her first album toed the contemporary R&B line, it showcased her breathy, often dark voice and chilling ability to mine the lower register. Though the producers tried to tailor her second album more towards Janet Jackson's young, music video-watching crowd, Hathaway showed a more sophisticated, jazzy inclination. She further explored her jazz jones as a guest vocalist on albums by Grover Washington Jr., Marcus Miller, and Gerald Albright before signing to Motown's now-defunct MoJAZZ label in 1996.

what to buy: *A Moment* ♫♫♫ (Virgin, 1994, prod. various) is a jazz-soul hybrid, rich with moody harmonies, provocative lyrics, and live instruments in the tradition of Anita Baker and Chaka Khan. Its songs—the type that will weather time—disappoint only when the tempo rises above that of a vigorous toe tap.

the rest:
Lalah Hathaway ♫♫♫ (Virgin, 1990)

worth searching for: "Love Like This," from Grover Washington Jr.'s *Next Exit* ♫♫♫♫ (Columbia, 1992, prod. Grover Washington Jr.) places Hathaway right where she belongs: awash in strings, horns, and a smooth tempo under the guidance of Philadelphia's favorite saxophonist.

influences:
◄◄ Anita Baker, Sarah Vaughan, Regina Belle

Franklin Paul

Richie Havens

Born January 21, 1941, in Brooklyn, NY.

Though he first established himself as a folk singer on the New York coffee house circuit, Richie Havens's rich and craggy voice, and his prowess as an interpreter of others' material, gained him national recognition during the late 1960s. His first couple of albums stiffed, but subsequent releases for MGM/Verve—notably *Mixed Bag*—encapsulated the humanistic, progressive mood of the time. Almost distinctive as his clarion vocals was Havens's powerful guitar playing, which involved hooking his thumb over the open-tuned strings and strumming furiously. His moment of greatest visibility came with his extended improvisation on the old spiritual "Motherless Child" at the Woodstock festival in 1969. He scored several hit singles during the next few years, recording memorable renditions of songs by Bob Dylan and the Beatles, as well as his own material. After a decade-long hiatus from recording, he began turning out albums again in 1987 and has appeared frequently with other 1960s pop veterans at nostalgic reunion concerts. Aside from his musical endeavors, Havens has long worked as an environmental activist and done commercial voice-over work (he's best known in this regard as the singer of the Amtrak train jingle), as well as some film acting.

what to buy: *Resume: The Best of Richie Havens* ♫♫♫ (Rhino, 1993, comp. Johanan Vigoda) is a generous anthology that draws from his best original songs and covers.

what to buy next: *Mixed Bag* ♫♫♫♫ (Verve, 1967, prod. Johanan Vigoda) is an early peak, boasting the anti-war classic "Handsome Johnny" and his versions of Dylan's "Just Like a Woman" and the Beatles' "Eleanor Rigby."

what to avoid: *Mixed Bag II* ♫♫ (Verve, 1974, prod. Johanan Vigoda) is, like so many sequels, inferior to the original.

the rest:
A Richie Havens Record ♫♫♫ (Douglas, 1965)
Electric Havens ♫♫♫ (Douglas, 1966)
Something Else Again ♫♫♫ (Verve, 1968)
Richard P. Havens ♫♫♫ (Verve, 1969/1983)
Stonehenge ♫♫♫ (Stormy Forest, 1970)
State of Mind ♫♫♫ (Verve, 1971)
Alarm Clock ♫♫♫ (Verve, 1971)
Great Blind Degree ♫♫♫♫ (Verve, 1971)
Richie Havens on Stage ♫♫♫ (Verve, 1972)
Portfolio ♫♫♫ (Verve, 1973)
Richie Havens ♫♫♫ (Polydor, 1975)
The End of the Beginning ♫♫ (A&M, 1976)
Mirage ♫♫ (A&M, 1977)
Connections ♫♫ (Elektra, 1980)
Common Ground ♫♫♫ (EMI, 1984)
Simple Things ♫♫♫ (RBI, 1987)
Now ♫♫♫ (Solar/Epic, 1991)
Cuts to the Chase ♫♫♫ (Forward, 1994)

worth searching for: *Richie Havens Sings the Beatles and Bob Dylan* ♫♫♫♫ (Rykodisc, 1986, prod. Douglas Yeager, Richie Havens) is an album full of covers from Havens's favorite songwriters.

influences:
◄◄ Bob Dylan, the Beatles, Sam Cooke, Leadbelly, Robert Johnson, Muddy Waters

►► Tracy Chapman, Ben Harper, Hootie and the Blowfish

Simon Glickman

The Edwin Hawkins Singers

Formed 1968, in Berkeley, CA.

Edwin Hawkins will take his rightful place in music history as the man whose inspired choral visions—crystallized by his universal hit song "Oh Happy Day"—motivated millions to turn their thoughts to matters spiritual by introducing them to the world of gospel. Actually, it was while serving as the organist and choir director for the Ephesians Church of God In Christ in Berkeley, California, that a young Hawkins recorded his first "live" album, *Let Us Go Into the House of the Lord*, with the Northern California State Youth Choir. The LP became a huge seller, due to the unexpected crossover appeal of the straightforward, exhilarating "Oh Happy Day." Ironically, Hawkins' updated arrangement of the age-old tune first took off on secular radio stations, then took the entire nation, and then the world, by storm. Today it stands as a pop music classic. Off that song's popularity, the Northern California State Youth Choir—now renamed the Edwin Hawkins Singers—received the opportunity to tour the U.S. and Europe extensively, appear on such television programs as *The Ed Sullivan Show*, and sign a recording contract in 1969 with the mainstream music label, Buddah Records. Almost all those events were unheard of for gospel acts at that time. Today, Hawkins heads up the Edwin Hawkins Music and Arts Seminar, an organization that assists young artists in furthering their careers in gospel music. Each seminar usually culminates with a live recording.

what to buy: Since it's still available, the best place to begin with the Edwin Hawkins Singers is at the beginning, with *Oh Happy Day* 🎵🎵🎵🎵 (Buddah, 1996, prod. LaMont Bench). Released on CD in 1996, the 1969 recording has lost none of the vibrancy or magnificent texture and sensitivity that caused "Oh Happy Day" to become a breakout musical sensation. Feel the sweeping dynamics of "Jesus, Lover of My Soul," or the rollicking spirit of "To My Father's House," and you may wonder why only one song emerged from the album as a single.

what to buy next: "Oh Happy Day" is sure to be included in any Hawkins greatest-hits anthology, but *The Best of the Edwin Hawkins Singers* 🎵🎵🎵 (The Right Stuff, 1997, prod. various) fills the rest of the disc with a convincing collection of songs displaying Hawkins' mastery for bringing out the contemporary elements of a choir without straying totally from traditional gospel structures. Noteworthy are his full choir interpretations of Bill Withers' "Lean on Me" and Bob Dylan's "Blowin' in the Wind."

what to avoid: Because it's seasonal, because it's not his best recorded work, and because you can find more arresting holiday music elsewhere, the *Edwin Hawkins Christmas Album* 🎵🎵 (Special Music Company, 1994, prod. various) can be the last addition to your Edwin Hawkins catalog.

the rest:
Kings & Kingdoms 🎵🎵🎵 (Intersound, 1994)
All Things Are Possible 🎵🎵🎵 (Bellmark, 1995)
Imagine Heaven 🎵🎵 (Lection, 1989)
Music & Arts Seminar Mass Choir, Dallas 🎵🎵🎵 (Harmony, 1997)

worth searching for: Hawkins lent his polished production skills to an amazing all-star Christmas CD—leagues better than his own Yuletide album—called *Joyous Christmas* 🎵🎵🎵🎵 (Columbia, 1994), featuring performances by Lou Rawls, Patti LaBelle, Commissioned, Nancy Wilson, and Peabo Bryson, among others. The CD was a benefit for the Children's Defense Fund.

influences:

◀◀ Andrae Crouch, James Cleveland, Thomas A. Whitfield

▶▶ John P. Kee, Kirk Franklin, Richard Smallwood, the Winans, Sounds of Blackness

Tim A. Smith

Screamin' Jay Hawkins

Born Jalacy Hawkins, July 18, 1929, in Cleveland, OH.

Primarily known as one of early rock's great showmen, Hawkins found fame promoting himself as a rock 'n' roll lunatic—appropriate for both Wolfman Jack and Dr. Demento. A former Golden Gloves boxing champion, he embarked on a musical career working small clubs with an energetic R&B revue show that often found him carried onstage in a flaming coffin, using flash powder, or waving spears with skulls on them at the audience. His work was attacked by the usual authorities; early singles, particularly the classic "I Put a Spell on You" (reportedly cut by a dead-drunk Hawkins), featured so much of his wild moaning and vocal thrashing that they were banned from some radio stations and therefore, sold little. A surprising cameo in Jim Jarmusch's 1989 cult film *Mystery Train*, as well as a song for *The X-Files* album project, *Songs in the Key of X*, were enthusiastically received and led to a minor resurgence of interest in his career.

what to buy: *Portrait of a Man* 🎵🎵🎵 (Demon, 1995, prod. various) compiles his crucial tracks, with all the great histrionics of near-misses and should've-beens such as "The Whammy" and "Little Demon."

the rest:
Voodoo Jive: The Best of Screamin' Jay Hawkins 🎵🎵🎵 (Rhino, 1990)
Cow Fingers and Mosquito Pie 🎵🎵🎵 (Epic/Legacy, 1991)

influences:
◀◀ Howlin' Wolf, Muddy Waters

▶▶ Bobby Boris Pickett

Todd Wicks

Ted Hawkins

Born 1936, in Biloxi, MS. Died Jan. 1, 1995, in Los Angeles, CA.

Singer-songwriter Ted Hawkins was one of the rawest and most unschooled musicians to ever record, yet he was able to convey deep emotions through his rudimentary vocal and guitar skills. Unknown for most of his life—though he recorded as early as 1971—Hawkins attracted attention as a street singer in the Venice Beach area near Los Angeles during the early 1980s. His style is that of a country bluesman with a little city soul thrown in. He was on the verge of breaking big, with a new major label deal, when he died in 1995.

what to buy: Some of Hawkins' best work is on *Happy Hour* ♫♫♫♪ (Rounder, 1986/1993, Rounder, prod. Bruce Bromberg, Dennis Walker), where his vocals and guitar highlight such original tunes as "Bad Dog," "Revenge of Scorpio," and the title song, which should be a country-western standard with its barroom-worthy heartbreak lyrics. Hawkins also kicks it out pretty good on *Songs from Venice Beach* ♫♫♫♪ (Evidence, 1995, prod. H. Thorp Minister III), a spare solo outing where he puts the country soul touch on such Motown classics as "Too Busy Thinking" and "Just My Imagination," and shows the Sam Cooke side of his heart on other songs.

the rest:
Watch Your Step ♫♫♫♫ (Rounder, 1982/1993)
The Next Hundred Years ♫♫♫ (DGC, 1994)

influences:
◀◀ Sam Cooke, Otis Redding, Robert Johnson, Wilson Pickett, Curtis Mayfield

▶▶ Chris Isaak, Robert Cray

Lawrence Gabriel

Isaac Hayes

Born August 6, 1938, in Covington, TN.

Along with partner David Porter, Hayes was one of the pre-eminent and most successful songwriters at Stax records, churning out hits for Sam & Dave, Johnnie Taylor, Carla Thomas, and Mable John. But Hayes truly made his mark with his own recordings. His sweaty, epic productions featured extended sides of influential soul orchestration and ushered R&B into the concept album era; and his work on the Oscar- and

> **TH**e record companies and radio stations didn't want to play oldies, and they put people like myself and Barry White and Bobby Womack out into the pasture. They were throwing away something of value. These kids need to know about us. . . . They need to know the history of black music in this country. There should not be a breakage in the chain.
>
> **Isaac Hayes**

word up!

Grammy-winning *Shaft* soundtrack paved the way for similar blaxploitation artists such as Curtis Mayfield and Marvin Gaye. Through his albums and performances, the shirtless, bald-headed, sunglass-wearing basso profundo transformed himself into the sexually charged Black Moses; his groundbreaking half-sung, half-spoken pillow-talk monologues became standard practice for 1970s soul. Quickly, though, Hayes seemed to run out of creative gas, as the quality of his recordings began to decrease at an astonishing rate. Hayes also ran out of luck: in 1976, he declared bankruptcy. By the 1980s, he had become seemingly more interested in Hollywood than Memphis, his acting credits (*Escape from New York, I'm Gonna Git You Sucka, Robin Hood: Men in Tights, It Could Happen to You*) accumulating more rapidly than his album sales. Hayes, who now works as a DJ at a New York radio station, also became active in the Church of Scientology. In 1995, he attempted a comeback with two albums, one of which included his first songwriting collaboration with Porter since the pair split during the late 1960s.

what to buy: The seminal Hayes concept album, *Hot Buttered Soul* 🎵🎵🎵🎵 (Enterprise, 1969/Stax, 1987, prod. Al Bell, Marvell Thomas, Allen Jones) contains just four songs, including the sprawling, nearly 19-minute interpretation of Jimmy Webb's "By the Time I Get to Phoenix," a loping, 12-minute cover of Burt Bacharach's "Walk on By," and the essential high-hat groove, "Hyperbolicsyllabicsesquedalymistic." For a slightly more traditional album, the soundtrack *Shaft* 🎵🎵🎵🎵 (Enterprise, 1971, prod. Isaac Hayes) features several shorter cuts, including the classic title track and a series of instrumentals. Yet it also features a lengthy workout, the nearly 20-minute vocal ramble, "Do Your Thing." While the soundtrack does not address social concerns, *a la* Curtis Mayfield's *Superfly*, it still grooves hard. Both *Hot Buttered Soul* and *Shaft* feature a crack rhythm section, the Bar-Kays.

what to buy next: *The Isaac Hayes Movement* 🎵🎵🎵🎵 (Enterprise/Stax, 1970, prod. Isaac Hayes) features more orchestral, string-heavy soul, including a tremendous reading of Jerry Butler's "I Stand Accused" and the 12-minute cover of the Beatles' "Something." *Double Feature* 🎵🎵🎵🎵 (Enterprise, 1974/Stax, 1993, prod. Isaac Hayes) features the underheard soundtracks from *Truck Turner* and *Tough Guys*.

what to avoid: Hayes's work is best digested whole; taking songs out of context can lessen their impact, particularly when they've been trimmed for commercial-radio purposes. As such, *Best of Isaac Hayes, Vol. 1* 🎵🎵 (Stax, 1986, prod. various), *Best of Isaac Hayes, Vol. 2* 🎵🎵 (Stax, 1986, prod. various), and *Greatest Hit Singles* 🎵🎵 (Stax, 1991, prod. various) should be avoided, as seminal songs are edited down and sequenced haphazardly, making for a poor introduction to Hayes's work.

the rest:

Presenting Isaac Hayes 🎵🎵🎵 (Enterprise/Stax, 1967)
To Be Continued 🎵🎵🎵 (Enterprise/Stax, 1970)
Black Moses 🎵🎵 (Enterprise, 1971)
Live at the Sahara Tahoe 🎵 (Enterprise/Stax, 1973)
Joy 🎵🎵 (Enterprise, 1973)
Hotbed 🎵 (Stax, 1978)
Don't Let Go 🎵🎵 (PolyGram Special Products, 1979)
Enterprise: His Greatest Hits 🎵🎵 (Stax, 1980)
Love Attack 🎵🎵 (Columbia, 1988)
Branded 🎵🎵 (Pointblank, 1995)
Wonderful 🎵🎵🎵 (Stax, 1995)
Movement: Raw and Refined 🎵🎵 (Pointblank, 1995)

Soul Essentials: The Best of the Polydor Years 🎵🎵🎵 (Polydor/Chronicles, 1996)

worth searching for: *Branded/Raw & Refined Sampler* 🎵🎵🎵 (Pointblank, 1995) is a one-disc distillation of Hayes's two 1995 albums—which creates, in effect, the single disc set these works should have been in the first place.

influences:

◀◀ Henry Mancini, Nat King Cole, Burt Bacharach, Brook Benton, Rufus Thomas, Wilson Pickett, Percy Sledge, Motown

▶▶ Gamble and Huff, Barry White, Teddy Pendergrass, DJ Quik, Cypress Hill, Marvin Gaye, Al Green, Lenny Kravitz, Terence Trent D'Arby

Josh Freedom du Lac

Roy Head

Born January 9, 1943, in Three Rivers, TX.

Roy Head is a top-notch blue-eyed country/soul singer whose 1965 hit "Treat Her Right" is still being played on oldies radio. Besides being a convincing soul vocalist, Head's good looks and dynamic sense of showmanship made him a popular club attraction. (Once Head participated in an eight-hour show where he more than held his own with the great Jerry Lee Lewis.) Head's first recordings with his band the Traits raved and rocked, but they sold poorly outside of Texas. After he signed with Back Beat Records, Head wrote and recorded "Treat Her Right," as convincing a soul record as anything on Stax-Volt. The single hit #2 on both the pop and soul charts, and he performed the number on ABC-TV's *Shindig*; the network's censors commanded him to substitute the word "kissin'" for "lovin'." Yeeesh! Head followed up with a strong reinterpretation of Roscoe Gordon's "Just a Little Bit" and his own "Apple of My Eye." Both registered in the lower regions of the pop Top 40, but none of his subsequent singles did as well. Head kept recording and made LPs for Dot, Dunhill, ABC, T.M.T., and Elektra. In 1977, Head shifted his focus from soul to country music. His biggest country hits were duets with Janie Fricke on "Tonight's the Night" (a remake of the Rod Stewart hit) and "In Our Room." Though Head's country career dried up during the early 1980s and none of his LPs from that period remain in print, interest in his early hits remains strong.

what to buy: *Treat Her Right: The Best of Roy Head* 🎵🎵🎵🎵 (Varese Vintage, 1995, prod. various) contains all of his hits ("Treat Her Right," "Just a Little Bit," "Apple of My Eye,"

"Teenage Letter") from the Backbeat Records era, plus three fine tracks that were previously unreleased.

what to buy next: *Slip Away—His Best Recordings* 🐾🐾 (Collectables Records, 1993) is short on hits, liner notes, and other information, but it contains enjoyable blue-eyed soul versions of "Before You Accuse Me," "Bring It to Jerome," and "Money."

worth searching for: *Treat Me Right* 🐾🐾🐾 (Bear Family, 1988) features no hits, but Head and his group the Traits rip-it-up and rave, bar-band style, on 10 pre-"Treat Her Right" recordings. Vinyl only.

influences:

◀◀ James Brown, the Righteous Brothers

▶▶ Tony Joe White, Delbert McClinton

Ken Burke

The Heartbeats /Shep & the Limelites

Formed as the Hearts, 1954, in Jamaica, Queens, NY. Disbanded 1959. Shep & the Limelites formed 1961, in Queens, NY. Disbanded 1966.

The Heartbeats: James "Shep" Sheppard, lead vocals (died 1970); Albert Crump, tenor; Robby Tatum, tenor; Vernon Seavers, baritone; Wally Roker, bass. Shep & the Limelites: James "Shep" Sheppard; Clarence Bassett, vocals; Charles Baskerville, vocals.

James "Shep" Sheppard was a silky-voiced singer who fronted two doo-wop groups that had lasting, though shared, legacies. First formed as the Hearts in the high schools of Queens, New York, the Heartbeats got their big break after bass singer Wally Roker's encounter with saxophone great Illinois Jacquet led to a recording session. Success followed in 1956 with "A Thousand Miles Away," which Sheppard wrote when his girlfriend moved to Texas. That story became the touchstone of Sheppard's repertoire: even when ego and musical concerns forced him to leave the group and form Shep & the Limelites—one of doo-wop's few trios—he continued the storyline with "Daddy's Home," an even bigger hit, and at least three other songs following the couple through the stages of love. The Limelites recorded from 1961–63 and disbanded during the mid-1960s. Sheppard was robbed, beaten, and killed on the Long Island Expressway in 1970.

what to buy: *The Best of the Heartbeats* 🐾🐾🐾🐾 (Rhino, 1990, prod. various) contains the best of Sheppard's recordings, 14 by the Heartbeats and five by Shep & the Limelites. The groups' arrangements are distinguished by the nearly always present celesta (much like a vibraphone), which lent an air of classy romance. The album also collects the "Thousand Miles Away"/"Daddy's Home" saga, though slightly out of order (1961's "Daddy's Home" immediately precedes the Heartbeats' 1957 "500 Miles to Go" in the sequencing).

worth searching for: The European import *Daddy's Home* 🐾🐾🐾🐾 (Remember, 1992) has a few different tracks, but most of the material also appears on *The Best of the Heartbeats*. Fanatics will want to search out the two-disc *For Collectors Only* 🐾🐾🐾🐾 (Collectables, 1992), which contains 40 tracks, four of which were previously unreleased.

influences:

◀◀ The Flamingos, the Five Keys, the Moonglows

▶▶ The Jive Five, the Dells

Brian Mansfield

Heatwave

Formed 1975, in Germany.

Johnnie Wilder, vocals; Keith Wilder, vocals; Jesse Whitten, guitar (1975–77); Roy Carter, guitar (1977–present); Eric Johns, guitar; William Jones, guitar; Rod Temperton, keyboards (1975–78); Calvin Duke, keyboards (1978–present); Mario Mantese, bass (1975–78); Derek Bramble, bass (1978–present); Ernest Berger, drums; Keith Harrison, guitar (1978–present); J.D. Nicholas, touring vocalist (1979–82).

Formed by Dayton, Ohio-bred brothers Johnnie and Keith Wilder while they were in the U.S. Army and stationed in Germany, Heatwave was designed to be a slamming R&B outfit with strong song sensibilites and equally strong grooves to keep 'em dancing in the discos. It succeeded spectacularly, thanks mostly to the presence of keyboardist/arranger Rod Temperton—who, after he left the band in 1978, scored a batch of hits with Michael Jackson, Aretha Franklin, George Benson, Jeffrey Osborne, and others. Meanwhile, the multi-national Heatwave introduced itself with "Boogie Nights" and "Too Hot to Handle," and the rest of the 1970s found DJs spinning hits such as "The Groove Line" and "Always and Forever." Tragedies have plagued the band: guitarist Jesse Whitten was stabbed to death during a visit in Chicago; Johnnie Wilder and original bassist Mario Mantese were both paralyzed in auto accidents. Heatwave has soldiered on, though, and while the hits have stopped coming, the group still tours, keeping the groove line going around the world.

what to buy: *Always and Forever: The Best of Heatwave* 🎵🎵🎵 (Legacy, 1996, prod. various) lives up to its title, with some of the best dance club singles of the 1970s.

the rest:
Too Hot to Handle 🎵🎵🎵 (Epic, 1976/1989)
Central Heating 🎵🎵🎵 (Epic, 1977/1995)
Greatest Hits 🎵🎵🎵 (Epic, 1984)

influences:
◀◀ Parliament, B.T. Express, Earth, Wind & Fire
▶▶ The Fatback Band, Michael Jackson, Wild Cherry, Slave

Gary Graff

Heavy D. & the Boyz
Formed 1984, in Mount Vernon, NY.

Heavy D. (born Dwight Arrington Meyers, May 24, 1967, in Jamaica, West Indies), vocals; Eddie F., DJ; Trouble T-Roy, dancer; G-Whiz, stylist.

Heavy D. was never anybody's candidate to become one of the most durable artists in hip-hop. Def Jam impresario Russell Simmons even famously passed on signing the rapper because he figured nobody would buy records by a rotund, fair-skinned, not-too-hot, part-Jamaican loverman. But by embracing New Jack production and (jokingly) feasting on women in a polite, gentlemanly way, the self-styled overweight lover has established himself as a consistent hip-pop hitmaker, both on wax and on TV (see the funky theme to the now-defunct show *In Living Color* that he penned). Heavy has also established himself as a businessman, first running Uptown Records (Mary J. Blige, Jodeci, Soul for Real, etc.), and then becoming a vice president of the parent Universal Music Group—even as he continued to make new music of his own. Declaring that "The Overweight Lover's in the House" and calling himself "Mr. Big Stuff," Heavy D. told the world exactly who he thought he was on his 1986 debut, *Living Large*, which takes a more suave and adult approach to the Fat Boys' schticky concept. Some called him gimmicky, but the ever-savvy Heavy minded his own thing, proving himself a formidable heavyweight contender with the back-to-back platinum-selling albums, *We Got Our Own Thang* and *Big Tyme*. To date, none of Heavy's albums has sold less than gold.

what to buy: After growing serious, sensitive, and introspective in his early 1990s albums, Heavy D.'s jazzy, frolicsome *Nuttin' But Love* 🎵🎵🎵🎵 (Uptown/MCA, 1994, exec. prod. Heavy D., James Earl Jones Jr.) is the LP that brought him back to his successful beginnings while at the same time transforming him from Heavy D. the novelty rapper to Heavy D. the established

recording artist. With samples ranging from James Brown ("The Payback") to Diana Ross ("Love Hangover"), and a guest list that includes Spike Lee and Martin Lawrence, his street-sure morality and romantic charisma float above the brawny beats of tunes like "Got Me Waiting" and "Spend a Little Time on Top."

what to buy next: The album that introduced Heavy D. & the Boyz to the world, *Living Large* 🎵🎵🎵 (MCA, 1987, prod. Marley Marl), is also the album that established his unique mix of playfulness, social consciousness, self-deprecation, and world music roots, containing such Heavy-D-fining, trademark tracks as "The Overweight Lover's in the House," "Chunky But Funky," "Mr. Big Stuff," and "Moneyearnin' Mount Vernon."

the rest:
Big Tyme 🎵🎵🎵 (MCA, 1989)
Peaceful Journey 🎵🎵🎵🎵 (MCA, 1991)
Blue Funk 🎵🎵🎵 (Uptown, 1992)
Waterbed Hev 🎵🎵🎵🎵 (Universal/Uptown, 1997)

influences:
◀◀ Marley Marl, Fat Boys
▶▶ Fat Joe, Father MC, Chubb Rock

Andre McGarrity

Bobby Hebb
Born July 26, 1938, in Nashville, TN.

Best known for having written and sung the 1966 million-seller "Sunny," Bobby Hebb forged a fascinating career that left its mark on the worlds of vaudeville, country music, Chicago blues, and even the Beatles. The Nashville native was a song-and-dance prodigy who began performing at the age of three, eventually becoming adept on spoons, guitar, trumpet, and piano. After working street corners, trolley cars, private parties, and local vaudeville shows, he landed a spot on a WSM-TV program and from there was hired by Roy Acuff to play spoons in Acuff's band, the Smoky Mountain Boys. As a teenager during the early 1950s, Hebb worked the Grand Ole Opry with Acuff for several years, and in 1960 he cut an R&B version of the Acuff hit "Night Train to Memphis" for deejay John "John R" Richbourg's Rich label. After moving to Chicago in 1955, Hebb met and befriended Bo Diddley and has said that he played spoons on the Chess recording of "Diddley Daddy." He later returned to Nashville, where he played studio guitar on some Excello sessions, then moved to New York where he worked and recorded with Sylvia Robinson (under the name Bobby & Sylvia) after the breakup of the Mickey & Sylvia duo. Signed as a solo act to the Philips label,

Hebb cut "Sunny" and a full album with the same name. Among other things, the song's success earned him a slot on the Beatles' final American tour of 1966. He continued to record commercially well into the 1970s and remains an active songwriter today.

worth searching for: You'll have to search for everything because none of Hebb's individual albums is in print right now. Besides the Rich and Philips labels, Hebb's material has appeared on Epic (a 1970 album), Scepter, and Laurie Records, among others. Though no Hebb reissue is currently available, his "Night Train to Memphis" and "A Satisfied Mind," the followup hits to "Sunny," are to be included in a boxed set of African American country music produced by the Country Music Foundation for the Warner Bros. label, tentatively scheduled for release in early 1998.

influences:

◀◀ Roy Acuff, Porter Wagoner, O.C. Smith

▶▶ Joe Simon, Dobie Gray, Al Green, Charlie Pride, Clive Francis

Daniel Cooper

Heltah Skeltah

Formed in Brooklyn, NY.

Rock, vocals; Ruck, vocals.

There's nothing Beatlesque about Heltah Skeltah: yet another crew with Boot Camp Clik affiliations, the grimy, rugged duo's rhymes and beats feature the Clik's trademark ghetto-dub style.

what to buy: It doesn't take long for Heltah Skeltah to set the tone of its debut, *Nocturnal* 🎵🎵🎵 (Priority, 1996, prod. Buckshot, Da Beatminerz, others): the mellow, shuffling introductory urban chant, "Here We Come," tells you exactly where the shadowy, red-eyed album is going. Although the album's centerpiece is the underground classic "Leflaur Leflah Eshkoshka" (featuring O.G.C.), the mystic harp and hazy snares of the masterfully moody final track, "Operation Lockdown," shouldn't be overlooked.

influences:

◀◀ Black Moon, Smif-N-Wessun

▶▶ O.G.C.

Spence D.

Michael Henderson

Born 1951, in Mississippi.

A musically precocious teenager could not have found a better environment in which to grow up than Detroit in the 1960s.

After Michael Henderson relocated from Mississippi to the Motor City, he began playing bass guitar at 13 for a Who's Who of Motown acts, eventually landing in the touring band of another young prodigy, Stevie Wonder. It was while he was on the road with Wonder that jazz icon Miles Davis recruited Henderson, offering him as much money per show as the bassist was making in a week as a Motown sideman. When Henderson informed the great trumpeter that he had never played jazz before, Davis assured him it would work out fine. As he had done before, Miles retooled the framework of his own music and consequently revolutionized the direction of jazz (once again). Henderson would remain a constant in Davis's various groups for the next seven years, helping to lay the groundwork for much of the modern jazz and fusion that continues to influence musicians of all stripes. After leaving Miles in 1975, Henderson hooked up with drummer/producer Norman Connors, who recruited him to sing vocals for Connors' signature tune, "You Are My Starship," and gave him the chance to record songs Henderson had written. One of his originals, a duet with Jean Carne called "Valentine Love" from the *Saturday Night Special* album, became an R&B hit. His success with Connors led to a solo deal with Buddah Records in 1976 and a string of moderately successful records, including a pairing with the late jazz singer Phyllis Hyman for the ballad "Can't We Fall in Love Again." One of the few musicians who can move effortlessly between jazz and soul circles, Henderson has been relatively inactive in recent years but has concentrated on jazz when he does perform.

what to buy: Henderson's only gold-selling album, *In the Night Time* 🎵🎵🎵🎵 (Buddah, 1978, prod. Michael Henderson) opens with his biggest hit single, "Take Me I'm Yours," a duet with singer Rena Scott which remains a staple on "Quiet Storm" radio formats. For his jazz fans, the funky instrumental "Happy" blends influences of Billy Preston (with whom Henderson played briefly during his Motown years) and Sly Stone.

what to buy next: *Slingshot* 🎵🎵🎵 (Buddah, 1981, prod. Michael Henderson, Chuck Jackson), perhaps best remembered for Henderson's nearly naked photo on the LP cover, was an blatant attempt to promote his image as a sex symbol; the title cut owes so much to his former employee, Stevie Wonder, that one would swear the Motown legend made a guest spot on the song—but no, it's Henderson, sounding just like Stevie! Meanwhile, the ballad with Phyllis Hyman, "Can't We Fall in Love Again," soars with a decidedly Philly sound.

the rest:

Solid 🎵🎵🎵 (Buddah, 1976)
Goin' Places 🎵🎵🎵 (Buddah, 1977)

Do It All 🎵🎵🎵 (Buddah, 1979)
Bedtime Stories 🎵🎵🎵 (EMI America, 1986)

worth searching for: Available only on British import, *Wide Receiver* 🎵🎵🎵 (Buddah, 1980) is one of Henderson's best overall creations.

influences:

◀◀ James Jamerson, Miles Davis, Norman Connors, Stevie Wonder, Billy Preston

▶▶ Larry Graham, Bootsy Collins, the Tony Rich Project

see also: *Norman Connors*

Matt Lee

Jimi Hendrix

Born James Marshall Hendrix, November 27, 1943, in Seattle, WA. Died September 18, 1970, in London, England. (Some sources report his birthname as Johnny Allen Hendrix, which was later changed to James Marshall by his father.)

Considering Jimi Hendrix's work in an R&B context, rather than in its more familiar rock milieu, isn't as farfetched as it may sound. Though his incendiary guitarwork is regarded as the epitome of psychedelic-era rock 'n' roll, and remains a vital influence and source of inspiration for contemporary musicians, the evidence of his roots is right there in his feedback-drenched excursions into string- and mind-bending tonalities. A quick check of his resume is instructive; it lists stints with Curtis Mayfield, Sam Cooke, Jackie Wilson, Little Richard, the Isley Brothers, and Ike & Tina Turner. Hendrix's own output was abundantly influenced by R&B. The clues can be heard in "Fire" and "Foxy Lady" on *Are You Experienced?*, his first effort with the Jimi Hendrix Experience (his previous band was the short-lived Jimmy James & the Blue Flames). Hendrix's R&B sensibility blossomed in various psychedelic ways on *Axis: Bold As Love*; the song "You Got Me Floatin'," sung by Experience bassist Noel Redding, is probably the most straightforwardly R&B tune on the album—and it's as funky as anything Sly & the Family Stone were up to at the time (though less flamboyant). If more testimony regarding his pedigree is needed, listen to the gentle falsetto opening to the title tune of *Electric Ladyland*, the album many consider his masterpiece; or the funky bass in "Crosstown Traffic"; or "Long Hot Summer Night," with its hints of doo-wop Philly streetcorner harmony; or the Hammond organ and guitar interplay of the sultry "Rainy Day, Dream Away." The latter strongly conveys Hendrix's jazz leanings, as solid a base as any for explorations of R&B. Many of his arrangements contain classic R&B/gospel call-and-response, in both vocal and instrumental phrasing. Worth seeking out is Hendrix's funkified, anthemic version of Bob Dylan's "Like a Rolling Stone" on the Monterey International Pop Festival box set, or the oozing-soul vocal of Buddy Miles on "They Don't Know" from Hendrix's *Band Of Gypsys* (the man was known for his guitar playing, not his spelling). This live album contains some of Hendrix's funkiest, groove-laden playing available—remarkable considering that the band was a trio, with only Hendrix on guitar, Miles on drums, and Billy Cox on bass. In 1997, Hendrix's family took control of the catalog that had been ravaged and exploited since his death, and under the Experience Hendrix moniker began a series of top-notch remastered reissues.

what to buy: On *Axis: Bold As Love* 🎵🎵🎵🎵 (Reprise, 1967/Experience Hendrix/MCA, 1997, prod. Chas Chandler), Hendrix's melodic explorations come to the fore through the oft-covered "Little Wing" and other sensual delights. *Are You Experienced?* 🎵🎵🎵🎵 (Reprise, 1967/Experience Hendrix/MCA 1997, prod. Chas Chandler), Hendrix's first release with the Jimi Hendrix Experience, features "Hey Joe," "The Wind Cries Mary," and the suggestive come-on of "Foxy Lady," as well as the classic "Purple Haze."

what to buy next: *Electric Ladyland* 🎵🎵🎵🎵 (Reprise, 1968/Experience Hendrix/MCA 1997, prod. Jimi Hendrix) is, for rock fans, the disc to buy first; but R&B fans might argue the point. True fans should own all three of these discs. In addition to the aforementioned songs, *Ladyland* includes "Crosstown Traffic" and his cover of Bob Dylan's "All Along the Watchtower."

what to avoid: Many of the posthumous albums contain material that Hendrix was working on before his death in 1970. However, he never got the chance to mix this material himself, nor did he, in many cases, even finish recording all the tracks he wanted. Thus, an album like *Voodoo Soup* 🎵🎵 (MCA, 1994, prod. Alan Douglas), even though it claims to be Hendrix's great unfinished masterpiece, sounds just that—unfinished. A much better choice, one that gives a tantalizing glimpse of the direction Hendrix was headed in, is *First Rays of the New Rising Sun* 🎵🎵🎵🎵 (Experience Hendrix/MCA, 1997). This album, which contains songs that have appeared on other inferior compilations, was remastered from the original tapes by Hendrix's long-time engineer and studio collaborator Eddie Kramer; the remastering process was supervised by Hendrix biographer John McDermott and the Hendrix family, preserving and conforming as closely as possible to the musician's intentions. Here's proof that Hendrix was laying the foundation for what became '70s funk.

the rest:
Band of Gypsys ✍✍✍ (Capitol, 1970/1994)
Live at Winterland ✍✍✍ (Rykodisc, 1987)
Radio One ✍✍✍ (Rykodisc, 1988)
Woodstock ✍✍✍ (MCA, 1994)
South Saturn Delta ✍✍✍ (Experience Hendrix/MCA, 1997)

worth searching for: *The Monterey International Pop Festival* ✍✍✍✍ (Rhino, 1992, Stephen K. Peeples, Geoff Gans, Lou Adler) offers a sample of the set that put Hendrix on America's musical radar. Like a greatest hits package, it includes favorites such as "Hey Joe," "Foxy Lady," "The Wind Cries Mary," "Purple Haze," and "Wild Thing," as well as "Like a Rolling Stone." *The Essential Jimi Hendrix* ✍✍✍✍ (Reprise 1978, prod. various), a double-disc compilation of greatest hits, is a good primer for those still willing to own vinyl or track down the deleted CD.

influences:

◀◀ Miles Davis, Billy Butler, Charlie Christian, Buddy Guy, the Isley Brothers, Bob Dylan, the Beatles, Robert Johnson, Howlin' Wolf, Chuck Berry, Freddie King

▶▶ Miles Davis, Stevie Ray Vaughan, Eddie Van Halen, Lenny Kravitz, Prince, Robin Trower, Carlos Santana, Eric Clapton, Sly Stone, Johnny Lang, Kenny Wayne Shepherd, Eric Johnson

Lynne Margolis

Nona Hendryx

Born August 18, 1945, in Trenton, NJ.

Nona Hendryx spent 15 years with two groups—Patti LaBelle & the Bluebells and LaBelle, eventually becoming the latter's songwriter. After the very successful LaBelle broke up in 1976, Hendryx switched from R&B to rock; with disco then peaking, neither labels nor radio could sell a black woman singing aggressive rock. But Hendryx's talents and refusal to be pigeonholed found a sympathetic milieu in the downtown Manhattan scene. Her backing vocals became an integral part of Talking Heads' sound (she's on the albums *Remain in Light, The Name of This Band Is Talking Heads*, and *Speaking in Tongues*) and was a strong visual presence at T-Heads concerts. But the collaboration that would most influence Hendryx's career was with Material. She sang on its 1981 club hit "Bustin' Out" and its album *One Down*, and the Material production team (Bill Laswell, Michael Beinhorn) then resurrected her solo career with *Nona* and *The Art of Defense*, bringing her back on the R&B charts with "Keep It Confidential," "Transformation," "I Sweat," though it's the rock and reggae tracks that hold up

best. Since then, Hendryx has recorded sporadically, continuing as a studio vocalist while further expanding the stylistic range of her music and collaborations.

what to buy: *Female Trouble* ✍✍✍✍ (EMI America, 1987, prod. various) combines excellent material, a freshly percolating sound and exciting guests (Peter Gabriel, Bernie Worrell, George Clinton, Mavis Staples, and members of the Time). Every track is strong, particularly "I Know What You Need (Pygmy's Confession)," the hit "Why Should I Cry?," the title track, and "Baby Go-Go," penned by Prince under the pseudonym J. Coco.

what to buy next: *Nona* ✍✍✍ (RCA, 1983, prod. Material, Nona Hendryx) may have benefitted from a long gap between albums. The high quality of the songwriting suggests Hendryx had a large stockpile of songs and could choose the best, while the Material production gives coherence to a broad stylistic range.

what to avoid: Hendryx's forceful vocals are stranded amid dry backing on *The Art of Defense* ✍ (RCA, 1984, prod. Material, Nona Hendryx), with drum tracks that are downright boring.

the rest:
Nona Hendryx ✍✍ (Epic, 1977)
The Heat ✍✍ (RCA, 1985)
Skindiver ✍✍✍ (Private, 1989)
(With Billy Vera) *You Have to Cry Sometime* ✍✍✍ (Shanachie, 1992)

worth searching for: The attraction on the *Why Should I Cry* ✍✍✍ 12-inch (EMI, 1987, prod. various) is neither the club-oriented extended version of the *Female Trouble* single nor the even longer "dub version/a capella" mix. It's the non-album track "Funkyland," produced by Hartman and Hendryx.

influences:

◀◀ Eurythmics, Mavis Staples

▶▶ Lisa Lisa & Cult Jam, Tasmin Archer, Neneh Cherry

Steve Holtje

Herm

Born Andre Lewis, in San Francisco, CA.

An ex-San Quentin inmate-turned-ghetto griot, Herm created a regional hip-hop craze in Northern California with his San Franciscocentric 1993 compilation *Trying to Survive In the Game*. Following in his footsteps, just about every other rapper with clout—from Money B to Master P—released a compilation featuring (mostly) unsigned rappers from the area. Herm's compilations stood out, though, because he was able to bring together a wide array of rappers from the rival neighborhoods, and because he delivered spoken word passages that urged kids to pursue legitimate money-making avenues.

what to buy: *Trying to Survive In the Ghetto* ♫♫♫ (Black Power Productions, 1993, prod. various) represents the hard-edged, rival San Francisco districts, with well-known locals RBL Posse, I.M.P., Rappin' 4-Tay, and JT the Bigga Figga kicking the slow-n-low funk flavor. But there's more to the collection than just established artists, as a bevy of newcomers (Fly Nate, Suga Bear, Cold World Hustlers) rise above curbside hustler status. Herm, too, steps up to the mic, providing a verbal bookend by laying down some ghetto-beat poetry on the album's intro- (and outro-) ductions.

what to buy next: *Still Trying to Survive In the Ghetto* ♫♫♫ (Black Power Productions, 1995, prod. various) again showcases a few known names (11/5, Dre Dog, Tabb Doe), plus a lot of unknown ones (Hitman, Female Fonk, 3-Deep, Terribly Real, West Mob, Black C, 187 Mob).

influences:

◄◄ Rappin' 4-Tay, I.M.P., Last Poets

►► West Coast Bad Boyz, D-Shot Presents Boss Ballin', Get Low Playaz, Primo, T-Lowe

Spence D.

Howard Hewett

Born October 1, 1955, in Akron, OH.

Few R&B voices were as pretty, passionate, and recognizable in the 1980s as crooner Howard Hewett. His career began at 12 as a gospel singer in Ohio, and he eventually toured with gospel acts like the Five Blind Boys and the Staple Singers. He joined the pop-soul trio Shalamar in 1978 and led the group to several big hits before going solo in 1985, years after the other popular group members had already quit. His solo career paled in comparison to his previous success, however, due to albums that were thin on quality material. But along the way, he has recorded many hits with other artists, including Anita Baker, Dionne Warwick, Brenda Russell, and Stacy Lattisaw.

what to buy: Nearly a decade after leaving Shalamar, and three years after his last major label album, Hewett took creative control and released *It's Time* ♫♫♫ (Calibre, 1995, prod. Howard Hewett, Monte Steward). A certain hearty emotion missing from his other works results, as is evinced by his stunning rendition of Marvin Gaye's classic, "Just to Keep You Satisfied."

what to buy next: The rest of his body of work is very similar in level of quality, but *I Commit to Love* ♫♫♫ (Elektra, 1986, prod. Howard Hewett) excels primarily due to his exquisite gospel cut, "Say Amen."

the rest:
Forever & Ever ♫♫♫ (Elektra, 1988)
Howard Hewett ♫♫♫ (Elektra, 1990)
Allegiance ♫♫♫ (Elektra, 1992)

worth searching for: Of Hewett's many collaborations, few were as perfectly matched as "Heaven Sent You," from fusion bassist Stanley Clarke's *Time Exposure* ♫♫♫ (Epic, 1984, prod. Stanley Clarke).

influences:

◄◄ Marvin Gaye, Jeffrey Osborne, Luther Vandross

►► Christopher Williams, JOE, Babyface

see also: *Shalamar*

Franklin Paul

Hi Records

It's hard to be an R&B label in Memphis and not be Stax-Volt. But Hi Records held its own, producing hits by a stable of artists that included Al Green, Ann Peebles, Otis Clay, Syl Johnson, and Willie Mitchell. Hi was actually founded by Ray Harris, Quinton Claunch, and Bill Cantrell, refugees from nearby Sun Records. The trio found five other investors from the local business community, and one of them—Joe Coughi, a co-owner of Memphis Popular Tunes record store—quickly moved to assume control of the label. Hi's first success was "Smokie Part 2," billed to the Bill Black Combo (named for Elvis Presley's former sideman) but also featuring input from musician-songwriter-producer-arranger Willie Mitchell. Mitchell had some hits of his own ("Soul Serenade," "30-60-90") and assumed control of Hi following Coughi's death in 1970. It was Mitchell's artistic vision—lush, polished but moody arrangements—that put Hi on the map, particularly with its leading lights Green and Peebles. Others, such as Johnson, Clay, and O.V. Wright, made a grittier sound, while Mitchell's Hi Rhythm Section was a crack unit that made its own mark with "Superstar." Hi began to falter during the mid-1970s, however, and it was sold to Cream Records in 1977. Mitchell left two years later, which foreshad-

Howard Hewett (© Ken Settle)

$\frac{2}{6}$ *hi-five*
$\frac{2}{6}$

owed the label's eventual closing. Hi was eclipsed by Stax and Motown even during its heyday, but time has been kind, and Green's continued success along with the propers paid the label by young artists such as Maxwell, D'Angelo, and Tony Rich are gradually giving the imprint its due.

what to buy: *Hi Times/Hi Records: The R&B Years* 🎵🎵🎵🎵 (Hi/The Right Stuff, 1995, prod. various) is a three-volume box set that features every notable song from the label—starting with "Smokie Part 2" and offering generous selections from the catalogs of Green, Peebles, Mitchell, Clay, Johnson, and Wright. As essential as any Motown or Stax collection.

Gary Graff

Hi-Five

Formed 1989, in Waco, TX.

Tony Thompson, vocals; Marcus "Mac" Sanders, vocals; Roderick "Pooh" Clarke, vocals; Russell Neal, vocals; Toriano Easley, vocals (1990–92); Treston Irby, vocals (1992–present).

Hi-Five arrived on the music scene at the right time—just as New Edition, the reigning Jackson Five replacements, had begun to splinter. Armed with teen-idol faces and bubblegum voices, and flanked by a team of hot producers, the quintet was centered around lead singer "Little Tony" Thompson, a talent-contest winner from Oklahoma City. His voice became a signature for the group, much like forebears Ralph Tresvant and Michael Jackson. But Hi-Five failed to distinguish itself despite several early hits such as Teddy Riley's "I Like the Way (The Kissing Game)" and "Quality Time." Whether or not it was poor material or a backlash against bubblegum that turned buyers against the group is hard to say. A "grown-up," 19-year-old Thompson dropped a solo album in 1995 to lukewarm response. He was recently linked with urban mogul Sean "Puffy" Comb's label, Bad Boy Entertainment.

what to buy: *Greatest Hits* 🎵🎵🎵 (Jive, 1994, prod. various) neatly packages all of the group's hits and some now-dated popular album cuts.

what to buy next: The group seemed to be at a crossroads on *Keep It Goin' On* 🎵🎵🎵 (Jive, 1992, prod. various), which showcases its appeal to the popcorn crowd ("She's Playing Hard to Get") and a more mature audience ("Quality Time," which was penned by a then-unknown R. Kelly).

what to avoid: *Faithful* **woof!** (Jive, 1993, prod. various), a do-nothing set that suffered in comparison to better singers (Boyz II Men) and sexier performers (Johnny Gill, Jodeci).

the rest:
Hi-Five 🎵🎵🎵 (Jive, 1990)

solo outings:
Tony Thompson:
Sexsational 🎵🎵🎵 (Giant, 1995)

influences:
⏪ New Edition, the Jackson 5
⏩ 112, H-Town

Franklin Paul

Jessie Hill

Born December 9, 1932, in New Orleans, LA.

Jessie Hill was not one of New Orleans' leading lights, but he did crank out one party classic, 1960's frenetic "Ooh Poo Pah Doo," which has the timeless, celebratory quality of a "Louie Louie" or "Wild Thing"—with production by the usually more refined Allen Toussaint. Hill began his career as a drummer, playing with his band the House Rockers as well as with N'awlins legends Professor Longhair and Huey "Piano" Smith. He switched from the drum chair to center stage during the late 1950s, just before recording "Ooh Poo Pah Doo." He went on to work behind the scenes in Los Angeles, writing material for Ike & Tina Turner, among others.

what to buy: *Golden Classics* 🎵🎵🎵 (Collectables, 1989, prod. various) has the essential "Ooh Poo Pah Doo" as well as some other spirited material from the late 1950s and early 1960s.

worth searching for: Hill makes a strong showing on James Booker's *The Lost Parmount Tapes* (DJM, 1995/1997).

influences:
⏪ Allen Toussaint, Fats Domino, Professor Longhair, Huey "Piano" Smith, Chuck Berry, Little Richard
⏩ Ike Turner, Richard Berry, Sylvia Robinson

Gary Graff

Z.Z. Hill

Born September 30, 1935, in Naples, TX. Died April 7, 1984, in Dallas, TX.

Z.Z. Hill had been a journeyman soul singer for nearly 20 years before the world caught wind of his 1960s-based R&B. While he began his musical career with the gospel group the Spiritual Five, it wasn't until he signed with the R&B label Kent that his secular side began to bud. Kent's production, at odds with Hill's more traditional approach, kept the singer from wider success.

He did record two somewhat bizarre, disco-tinged albums for Columbia during the 1970s, prior to his signing with the independent Malaco label in 1980. At Malaco he finally won more of a mainstream audience, and his 1982 album *Down Home* remained on the charts for nearly two years. It was a brief respite, however, as Hill was felled in his driveway two years later by a heart attack.

what to buy: Maybe the realization of his life's work, *Down Home* 𝄞𝄞𝄞𝄞 (Malaco, 1981, prod. Tommy Couch) established Hill as a major artist. It's also his most traditional blues-based work.

what to buy next: Both of his Columbia albums are compiled on *Love Is So Good When You're Stealing It* 𝄞𝄞𝄞 (Ichiban, 1996, prod. Bert deCoteaux), which finds the singer at the height of the disco craze struggling vainly to maintain some degree of roots while remaining contemporary.

influences:

◄◄ Sam Cooke, Otis Redding, the Chi-Lites

►► The Temptations, Clarence Carter, David Ruffin

Allan Orski

Billie Holiday

Born Eleanora Harris, April 7, 1915, in Baltimore, MD. Died July 17, 1959, in New York, NY.

Billie Holiday's voice—sweet, sexy, pulsing with blues feeling—could chill a soul or warm it like a fireplace of emotion. Born to teen-age parents, Sadie Harris and Clarence Holiday, the singer was raped at the age of 10 and, thanks to the sexual double standard of the day, was sent to a home for wayward girls as a result. Her father, a jazz guitarist with Fletcher Henderson, abandoned her. Today, mental-health professionals believe such abuse will shape and shadow the rest of a victim's life, and Holiday's life did seem to play out with the predestination of a Greek tragedy. Her music rescued her from her teen-age careers as a house servant and hooker, but it did not stop her from ravaging herself with drugs, which in her final years took away all but a remnant of her voice. Known affectionately as "Lady Day," a name she was given by Lester Young, she brought the breadth of her worldly experience to the stage and recording studio with a vulnerability that—like all the best blues—didn't just speak of being a victim, but spoke of self-worth betrayed (by the world, a lover, or the singer herself). That's not to say that all her songs were sad, but that even her happy tunes had an edge. She seemed in those happier songs to want to overindulge in every appetite to gird herself for the hard times. Offstage, she was dependent on a succession of not-quite-Svengalis, who acted as lovers and father figures. In "God Bless the Child," she sings what one reviewer called a whiny lyric (her own) about how people court a person who's successful but ignore the same person when "money's gone." Yet she doesn't sound whiny at all. Instead, she's having a gentle laugh at the weakness of human nature. Talent scout John Hammond found her all but irresistible in live performance, so he advocated her to the top people in jazz. Benny Goodman led her first session in 1933. Teddy Wilson followed. When she hit the peak of her form in the late '30s, the presence of—and her interplay with—Buck Clayton and Lester Young underscored just how much her singing resembled the playing of an instrumentalist. She sang slowly and "behind the beat" and trailed off her voice for emotional punctuation. (Her influence shows up in the work of many singers who followed, possibly most notably in Frank Sinatra.) Her fluid phrasing and the rasp in her voice were reminiscent of Louis Armstrong. Although she sang very few actual blues tunes, the blue feeling in her voice descended directly from Bessie Smith. Holiday melded these influences into a completely distinctive sound.

Despite her submissiveness to her lovers, she was strong-willed and moody, which often hindered her career. Yet her landmark 1939 recording, "Strange Fruit," a protest against lynchings, was a triumph of determination. Columbia, to which she was signed for the bulk of the 1930s, would not record the tune, so she secured a contract that put her on loan to Milt Gabler's Commodore label for a single session. Gabler later signed her to Decca. In this period of the late '30s and early '40s, she gradually abandoned the jazz settings of her earlier recordings for grander pop orchestrations. Her voice was at its peak, and her version of "Lover Man" defines her style. By the '50s, when she signed up with Norman Granz, after serving a late '40s prison term for heroin possession, she was on a downward spiral. Although her voice faded in the late stages of her life thanks to her indulgences, she retained her expressive capabilities. So nearly all of her recordings are of interest (although sometimes that interest can be of a rather morbid variety).

what to buy: Holiday's work is documented on more than 80 CDs and collections, but thanks to the archival genius of the CD age, it's very easy to reduce that number to a core, must-have collection. First of all, the title of Columbia's nine-volume retrospective series, *The Quintessential Billie Holiday* 𝄞𝄞𝄞𝄞 (Columbia, 1987/1991, prod. John Hammond, Bernie Hanighen, reissue prod. Michael Brooks), is not far off the mark. A chrono-logical series of her work for the Columbia, Brunswick, and Vo-calion labels, even the most dispensible set *Volume 1, 1933–1935* contains great performances—"Miss Brown to You," "If You Were Mine"—as the new recording artist finds her sea legs. By the last CD, *Volume 9, 1940–1942*, Holiday's char-acter and style are completely formed and she sings with ab-solute certainty on such definitive numbers as "God Bless the Child," "Solitude," and "Gloomy Sunday." For listeners who want to delve deeply into her creative process in the studio, *The Complete Commodore Recordings* ৶৶৶৶ (GRP, 1997, origi-nal prod. Milt Gabler, reissue prod. Orrin Keepnews, Joel Dorn) is a two-CD set full of alternate takes (including a second take of "Strange Fruit") and gives insight into her evolution from the jazz-band-oriented style to full-blown pop. *The Complete Decca Recordings* ৶৶৶৶ (GRP, 1991, original prod. Milt Gabler, reis-sue prod. Steven Lasker, Andy McKaie) covers Holiday's best performing period on just two CDs. She recorded only 36 sides for the label, and the definitive "Lover Man" sets the collec-tion's tone. It includes a number of alternate takes but isn't as heavy with them as the Commodore collection. This is the most satisfying and consistent listening experience in Holiday's cata-log. After her vacation in the reformatory, producer Norman Granz returned her to jazz-oriented sessions. Her voice was raspier, and sometimes you can hear her struggle for the breath to finish a phrase, but there's a soulfulness that the rav-ages of abuse bring out in her voice that makes her stint with Granz nearly as memorable as her Decca years. Hence, the 10-CD *The Complete Billie Holiday on Verve 1945–1949* ৶৶৶৶ (Verve, 1995, original prod. various, reissue prod. Phil Schaap) is an indispensible collection of the work she did as she col-lapsed upon herself, including "Lady Sings the Blues," the tune written to capitalize on the title of her autobiography.

what to buy next: *Lady in Satin* ৶৶৶৶ (Columbia, 1986, orig. prod. Ray Ellis, reissue prod. Michael Brooks) is based on the template of the original 1958 album that paired Holiday, at her request, with the easy-listening orchestral sounds of Ray Ellis. Technical wizardry creates a stereo take of "The End of a Love Affair," which previously existed only in a mono master. The juxtaposition of her soulful but nearly shot voice and Ellis's ex-tremely sweet strings gives the project a character it couldn't have had when she was younger. *Billie's Blues* ৶৶৶৶ (Blue Note, 1988) features Holiday's top concert recording, from a 1954 date in Europe.

what to avoid: *Last Recordings* ৶ (Verve, 1988, prod. Ray Ellis), recorded early in 1959, is another date with Ellis, absent the tri-

umph of *Lady in Satin*. Besides, you have the complete Verve set already, don't you?

best of the rest:

Solitude ৶৶৶ (Verve, 1952)
All or Nothing at All ৶৶৶ (Verve, 1955)
Lady Sings the Blues ৶৶৶ (Verve, 1956)
The Essential Billie Holiday: Carnegie Hall Concert ৶৶৶ (Verve, 1956)
Songs for Distingue Lovers ৶৶৶ (Verve, 1957)
Masters of Jazz, Vol. 3 ৶৶৶ (Storyville, 1987)
At Storyville ৶৶৶ (Black Lion, 1988)
Fine and Mellow ৶৶৶ (Collectables, 1990)
Lady in Autumn: The Best of the Verve Years ৶৶৶ (Verve, 1991)

worth searching for: *Live and Private Recordings in Chronolog-ical Order* ৶৶৶ (New Sound Planet Jazz Up, prod. various) fills in a number of gaps. This set of 12 CDs features Holiday's only recording with Duke Ellington, "Big City Blues (The Saddest Tale)," plus recordings from radio and television and other sources such as private parties.

influences:

◀◀ Bessie Smith, Louis Armstrong

▶▶ Frank Sinatra, Betty Carter, Anita Baker, Erykah Badu

Salvatore Caputo

Holland, Dozier & Holland

Brian Holland (born February 15, 1941, in Detroit, MI); Lamont Dozier (born June 16, 1941, in Detroit, MI); Eddie Holland (born October 30, 1939, in Detroit, MI).

Lamont Dozier first came aboard at Motown as a performer and songwriter. Berry Gordy signed him to the Motown subsidiary label Anna in 1960, and Dozier debuted with "Let's Talk It Over" under the name Lamont Anthony. But his recording career took a back seat after he combined creative forces with brothers Brian and Eddie Holland. Holland-Dozier-Holland, a very tal-ented production and songwriting team, became essential to the success of artists on the Motown label during the 1960s. They wrote and produced numerous hits for Marvin Gaye, the Four Tops, Martha & the Vandellas, and others. But nothing surpassed their song collaborations with the Supremes, which included "Where Did Our Love Go?" (1964), "Baby Love" (1964), "Stop in the Name of Love" (1965), and "You Can't Hurry Love" (1966). HDH sued Motown for song rights in 1968, then made a break from the label and started their own Invic-tus and Hot Wax labels in Detroit, working with the Chairmen of the Board, Freda Payne, Honeycone, and others. The team split up in 1973, and Dozier went on to produce and write for many soul and pop performers, including Aretha Franklin, Ben E. King, Simply Red, Eric Clapton, Z.Z. Hill, and Phil Collins. But Dozier's desire to sing his own songs never died. In 1974, he recorded *Out Here on My Own* and charted with the singles "Fish Ain't Bitin'" and "Trying to Hold on to My Woman." *Back Black* came the following year with the hit "Let Me Start Tonite." He signed with Warner Bros. in 1976 and made the critically acclaimed album *Peddlin' Music on the Side*. Dozier proved to be a capable and prolific recording artist who was perhaps overlooked. He released *Bigger Than Life* on his own Megaphone label in 1983 and the less impressive *Inside Seduction* on Atlantic in 1991. (Dozier's recordings are currently out of print). HDH reunited during the early 1980s to work with the Four Tops at Motown and were inducted into the Rock and Roll Hall of Fame in 1990.

what to buy: *The Picture Never Changes* ✍✍✍✍ (HDH) features some of the top material recorded for the trio's Invictus and Hot Wax labels during the 1970s, proof that their talents as writers and producers did not depend strictly on the Motown stable.

worth searching for: On the other hand, *The Composers Series: Holland-Dozier-Holland* ✍✍✍✍ (Motown) shows that their mid-'60s run at Motown was one of the most prolific exhibitions of great pop music making in history.

influences:

◄◄ Rogers and Hammerstein, Smokey Robinson, Rodgers and Hart, Burt Bacharach and Hal David

►► James "Jimmy Jam" Harris III and Terry Lewis, Kenneth "Babyface" Edmonds and Antonio "L.A." Reid, Michael Bivins, Maurice Starr, Prince

Norene Cashen and Gary Graff

Jennifer Holliday

Born October 19, 1962, in Houston, TX.

A member of a touring production of *A Chorus Line* discovered the 17-year-old Jennifer Holliday at a production in her native Houston and brought her to New York, where she won the lead in a Broadway revival of "Your Arms Too Short to Box with God." In 1981, at the age of 21, she won a starring role in *Dreamgirls,* where she sang her signature song, "And I Am Telling You I'm Not Going." She earned a Tony and a Grammy award the next year. Yet, despite possessing a vocal range that allowed her to effortlessly belt out grand show tunes as well as gritty, blues-y tunes, and winning another Grammy in 1986, she never quite recreated the success of her stage career in the

word up!

YOU know, I remember being a daydreamer when I lived in Detroit, and all my teachers . . . used to tell me that if I didn't stop daydreaming, my life is going to slip away. But I knew what I wanted to be--an international celebrity, another Cole Porter or one of those people. And I've been able to make a lot of those dreams come true.

Lamont Dozier
(of Holland, Dozier
& Holland)

recording world. She continues to perform in the theater, but has promised to record only gospel albums in the future.

what to buy: *The Best of Jennifer Holliday* ✍✍✍✍ (Geffen, 1996, prod. various) puts it all together: the Broadway gems, the treasured album cuts, and her hit singles. It also includes two new songs—a remix of Holliday's 1985 hit "No Frills Love" and "Someday," a track recorded in 1983, but never before released.

what to buy next: Holliday promised to give up recording R&B albums upon the release of *On & On* ✍✍✍ (Intersound, 1994, prod. O'landa Draper), her thrilling return to the gospel arena. The album was made amid a period of personal tragedy: her mother had recently passed away and she and her husband were headed for divorce.

what to avoid: *Say You Love Me* 🎵🎵 (Geffen, 1985, prod. various) is Holliday's weakest effort, easily skippable.

the rest:
Feel My Soul 🎵🎵🎵 (Geffen, 1983)
I'm on Your Side 🎵🎵🎵🎵 (Arista, 1991)

worth searching for: *Get Close to My Love* 🎵🎵🎵 (Geffen, prod. various) is far from her best album. But it does contain one of her most chilling performances—"Giving Up," Van McCoy's tune popularized by Gladys Knight & the Pips and Donny Hathaway. Holliday digests the song's essence and spits out a dark, gut-wrenching ode to loneliness.

influences:

◀◀ Patti Austin, Aretha Franklin, Patti LaBelle

▶▶ Vesta, Regina Belle, Oleta Adams

Franklin Paul

John Lee Hooker

Born August 22, 1920 (some sources say 1922), in Clarksdale, MS.

Hooker is a giant of the blues and one of its most distinctive voices; he's also the father of the boogie, which makes him one of rock 'n' roll's great antecedents. Hooker's deep, primitive rhythms and his dark, growly, hypnotic vocals have inspired innumerable performers over his 50-plus year career. A semi-transient street musician from the age of 15, Hooker moved to Detroit in 1943. His recording career began in 1948 with "Boogie Chillen," a blues classic that topped the R&B charts in 1949. He was a raw, undisciplined musician who seldom played a song the same way twice, yet he managed to record prolifically through the 1950s on a number of labels. His output—under such names as Johnny Lee, John Lee Booker, John Lee Chance, Birmingham Sam, Delta John, Texas Slim, Boogie Man, and John Williams—is second only to that of Lightnin' Hopkins. His songs "Dimple" and "Boom Boom" made waves on the 1960s British blues scene, and he went acoustic during the blues revival and played the hippest clubs in the U.S. and Europe. During the 1970s, Hooker went electric and did records with Canned Heat, Elvin Bishop, Van Morrison, and other rockers. The aging Hooker faded into semi-retirement during the 1980s, but 1989's *The Healer*, featuring Bonnie Raitt, Carlos Santana, Robert Cray, and George Thorogood, won a Grammy and put Hooker back at center stage. He's managed to remain there with two more solid albums since then. Although Hooker tends to recycle tunes, such classics as "Crawlin' King Snake," "I'm In the Mood," "One Bourbon, One

Scotch, One Beer," "Little Wheel," "Boogie with the Hook," and "I'm Bad Like Jesse James" all bear re-telling. In 1997, B.B. King is the only living bluesman with the same stature as Hooker, and there are but a handful of others, period. His spots in the Rhythm and Blues Foundation's Hall of Fame and in the Rock and Roll Hall of Fame—among other honors—are well deserved.

what to buy: *The Ultimate Collection, 1948–1990* 🎵🎵🎵🎵🎵 (Rhino, 1991, comp. James Austin) lives up to its title, with 31 of Hooker's best-known cuts and a bevy of guests such as Jimmy Reed, Willie Dixon, and Raitt. The septuagenarian Hooker seems to boogie effortlessly on *Chill Out* 🎵🎵🎵🎵 (Point Blank, 1995, prod. Roy Rogers), and with Santana adds a Latin edge to his mantra-like boogie on "Chill Out (Things Gonna Change)."

what to buy next: Hooker is clearly having fun on *The Healer* 🎵🎵🎵🎵 (Chameleon, 1989, prod. Roy Rogers), the record that sprung him back into the limelight with friends like Raitt and Cray helping out.

what to avoid: Hooker may have presaged the funk, but the slick 1970s edge on *Free Beer and Chicken* 🎵🎵 (ABC, 1974, prod. Ed Michel) just didn't fit, regardless of the rock 'n' roll heavies in tow.

the rest:
Endless Boogie 🎵🎵🎵 (MCA, 1971)
Never Get Out of These Blues Alive 🎵🎵🎵 (Pickwick, 1978) *Real Folk
    Blues* 🎵🎵🎵🎵 (MCA, 1987)
Simply the Truth 🎵🎵🎵 (One Way, 1988)
Mr. Lucky 🎵🎵🎵🎵 (Charisma, 1991)
I Feel Good 🎵🎵🎵 (Jewel, 1995)
Boom Boom 🎵🎵🎵🎵 (Capitol, 1995)
Alone 🎵🎵🎵🎵 (Blues Alliance, 1996)
Don't Look Back 🎵🎵🎵 (Point Blank, 1997)
His Best 🎵🎵🎵🎵 (Chess/MCA, 1997)

worth searching for: *Hooker 'N' Heat* 🎵🎵🎵🎵 (Liberty, 1971/EMI, 1991 prod. Skip Taylor, Robert Hite Jr.) was the equivalent of *The Healer* 20 years earlier. Though it's a rougher-edged affair, Hooker's collaboration with Canned Heat made the rock crowd take notice.

influences:

◀◀ Robert Johnson, Charley Patton

▶▶ James Brown, George Clinton, Bonnie Raitt, John Mayall, Savoy Brown, Canned Heat, Robert Cray, George Thorogood

Lawrence Gabriel

Hot Chocolate

Formed 1970, in London, England.

Errol Brown, vocals; Patrick Olive, guitar, bass, percussion; Larry Ferguson, keyboards; Harvey Hinsley, guitar; Ian King, drums (1970–73); Tony Wilson, bass (1970–75); Tony Connor, drums (1973–present).

Hot Chocolate enjoyed chart success here and in Europe during the mid-1970s, thanks to hits such as the quirky "You Sexy Thing" and "Disco Queen." The group's hybrid sound of Caribbean, R&B, funk, rock, and pop might be considered World Beat today, especially given the social and political themes of some of their songs (the anti-racism song "Brother Louie" was a #1 hit in 1973 for the group Stories). Most of its founding members were from Caribbean nations such as Jamaica and Trinidad, but they met in London, where rock 'n' roll was exploding. Brown and Wilson wrote most of the material, with Brown assuming the lion's share when Wilson left for a solo career during the mid-1970s. Most recently, the Talking Heads spin-off group the Tom Tom Club brought "You Sexy Thing" back onto the radio.

worth searching for: None of Hot Chocolate's more than half-dozen albums is currenlty in print domestically, though a 1993 hits compilation, *Everyone's a Winner* 🎵🎵🎵 (EMI America, 1993, prod. Mickie Most) has only been out of print for a few years. It's an adequate collection of the band's American hits.

influences:

◀◀ James Brown, the Temptations, the Beatles

▶▶ Brick, Brass Construction, the Trammps, the Tom Tom Club

Doug Pullen

House of Pain

Formed 1990, in Los Angeles, CA.

Everlast, vocals; Danny Boy, vocals; DJ Lethal, DJ.

Unlike many white acts that perform rap, House of Pain is no mere novelty. The trio's old-school rhymes, combined with a dense soundscape littered with heavy jeep beats and shrill effects (thanks, in part, to producer DJ Muggs from Cypress Hill) makes for a heady brew. And if you're buying, make theirs a Guinness Stout. The L.A. rappers wear their Irish heritage proudly (even if not all of them are actually Irish!), singing a snippet of "Danny Boy" here, and claiming "I never eat pig, but I can fuck up a potato" there. The group flirted with going pop on its debut, but since then has turned toward a more hardcore posture—albeit without any sign of breakthrough success.

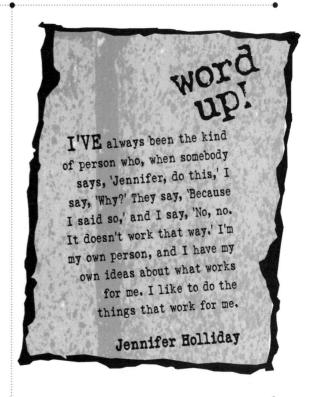

word up!

I'VE always been the kind of person who, when somebody says, 'Jennifer, do this,' I say, 'Why?' They say, 'Because I said so,' and I say, 'No, no. It doesn't work that way.' I'm my own person, and I have my own ideas about what works for me. I like to do the things that work for me.

Jennifer Holliday

what to buy: It's tough to recommend *House of Pain* 🎵🎵🎵 (Tommy Boy, 1992, prod. DJ Muggs, DJ Lethal), if only because of how easily it gives in to hip-hop's worst tendencies: its lyrics are laced with homophobia, misogyny, racism, and pointless posturing. Which is too bad, because it's tough to deny the irrepressible romps "Jump Around" and "Top o' the Morning to Ya."

the rest:
Same As It Ever Was 🎵🎵 (Tommy Boy, 1994)
Truth Crushed to Earth Shall Rise Again 🎵🎵🎵 (Tommy Boy, 1996)

worth searching for: Alternarock stalwart Butch Vig's raucous rock remix of "Shamrocks and Shenanigans," featuring guitar parts by Steve Marker (who would later form Garbage with Vig), is an excellent fusion of rock and rap and is available on the "Who's the Man"/"Shamrocks and Shenanigans" import single (XL UK, 1993).

solo outings:
Everlast:
Forever Everlasting 🎵🎵 (Warner Bros., 1990)

DJ Lethal:
(With Limp Bizkit) *Three Dollar Bill, Y'all$* ♫♫♫ (Flip/Interscope, 1997)

influences:

◀◀ Beastie Boys, Black Flag, Ice-T, Cypress Hill

▶▶ Funkdoobiest

Daniel Durchholz

Son House

Born Eddie James House Jr., March 21, 1902, in Riverton, MS. Died October 19, 1988, in Detroit, MI.

One measure of Son House's influence as a Delta blues player in the 1920s and 1930s is the fact that he taught and inspired a young man named Robert Johnson. House lived most of his childhood in New Orleans, where he recalled listening to church music and Louis Armstrong. He returned to Mississippi in his mid-twenties and learned to play bottleneck slide guitar. When he wasn't driving a tractor on the cotton plantation where he was employed, the bluesman was playing in rough "juke joints" with friend and fellow guitarist Willie Brown. True to the blues requirement for tragedy and legend, House spent time in prison for shooting and killing a man in Mississippi, but he only served a few years. In 1929 he met Charlie Patton, who got him a recording deal with Paramount, where he made three two-part 78s including the well-known blues standard "Preachin' the Blues." Patton also introduced House to Blind Lemon Jefferson, who heavily influenced his guitar style. These recordings led blues archivist Alan Lomax to the music of Son House; Lomax caught up with him in 1941 and recorded House for his Library of Congress collection. For more than two decades after that, House was but a blues legend who no longer made music. He was rediscovered in 1965, however. That year he played Carnegie Hall and, with the help of Alan Wilson (guitarist for Canned Heat), he recorded again for Columbia. The revival was short-lived, though, as Alzheimer's and Parkinson's diseases left him unsteady and suffering severe memory loss. He quit performing during the mid-1970s and moved to Detroit, where he resided until his death in 1988, eight years after his induction into the Blues Foundation Hall of Fame.

what to buy: Son House, *Father of the Delta Blues: The Complete 1965 Sessions* ♫♫♫ (Columbia/Legacy, 1992, prod. various) is a definitive two-CD collection recorded during House's

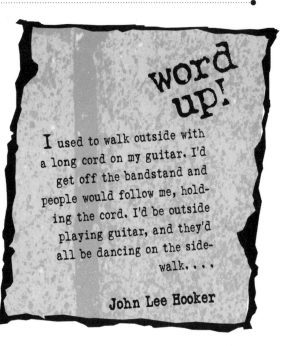

word up!

I used to walk outside with a long cord on my guitar. I'd get off the bandstand and people would follow me, holding the cord. I'd be outside playing guitar, and they'd all be dancing on the sidewalk. . . .

John Lee Hooker

resdicovery period. The equally important *Delta Blues* ♫♫♫♫ (Biograph, 1991, prod. Alan Lomax) also features Willie Brown.

worth searching for: Well worth listening to are import versions of the Lomax sessions, including *Son House and the Great Delta Blues Singers* ♫♫♫ (Document, 1990, prod. Johnny Parth) and Son House's cuts on *Masters of the Delta Blues: The Friends of Charlie Patton* ♫♫♫♫ (Yazoo, 1994).

influences:

◀◀ Blind Lemon Jefferson, Charley Patton

▶▶ Robert Johnson, Muddy Waters

Norene Cashen

Whitney Houston

Born August 9, 1963, in Newark, NJ.

The daughter of soul and gospel singer Cissy Houston and cousin of pop vocalist Dionne Warwick, Whitney Houston's success may just be a matter of genetics. But you don't have to call cousin Didi's Psychic Friends Network to know that, in strong contrast to Houston's voice—one of the most powerful, yet supple instruments in all of pop music—her albums have

Whitney Houston (© Ken Settle)

been less than spectacular, thanks to vapid material and cheesy 1980s synth-pop production that have not aged as well as Houston herself. Like Michael Jackson, Houston is more interesting as a phenomenon than as an artist; her albums have sold in the tens of millions worldwide, and along with Jackson, Houston helped break the racial barriers that once kept black performers off of MTV. Unlike the gloved one, however, Houston's success has spilled over onto the silver screen, where she has starred in a trio of successful films, *The Bodyguard, Waiting to Exhale,* and *The Preacher's Wife.* She also has enjoyed massive non-album hits with "One Moment in Time," the theme to the 1988 Summer Olympics, and her Super Bowl rendition of "The Star Spangled Banner," which rode a wave of Desert Storm patriotism all the way to the bank. As impressive as her past has been, Houston's future remains a question mark. It's been eons since she made a non-soundtrack pop album, and her career has been waylaid by the birth of a daughter, several miscarriages, and her turbulent marriage to pop singer/miscreant Bobby Brown.

what to buy: *Whitney Houston* 𝄽𝄽𝄽𝄽 (Arista, 1985, prod. L.A. Reid) rocketed the young singer to superstardom almost instantly, and not without reason. Houston demonstrates her astonishing talent as a balladeer on "Saving All My Love for You" and "You Give Good Love." "The Greatest Love of All" may be a little over the top in terms of it's vapid self-help message, but Houston delivers it sincerely. And while it's only a bit of fluff, "How Will I Know" is Houston's most infectious single ever. After its release, copies of *The Bodyguard* 𝄽𝄽𝄽 soundtrack (Arista, 1992, prod. various) were issued upon entrance to a shopping mall, or so it seemed at the time. Still, much of the attention was deserved. The album contains Houston's best vocal performance ever, a triumphant take on Dolly Parton's "I Will Always Love You" that you probably still haven't dislodged from your memory. The album also contains five other Houston performances along with contributions by Kenny G and Aaron Neville, Lisa Stansfield, Joe Cocker, and others.

what to buy next: The problem with *Whitney* 𝄽𝄽𝄽 (Arista, 1987, prod. Narada Michael Walden, Jellybean, Michael Masser, Kashif) is that Houston attempts to be all things to all formats. With so many producers, the albums lacks a cohesive feel. Still, the hits are there, including the pop ditty "I Wanna Dance with Somebody (Who Loves Me)," the dance-floor friendly "So Emotional," and the wrung-out ballads "Didn't We Almost Have It All" and "Where Do Broken Hearts Go."

what to avoid: *I'm Your Baby Tonight* 𝄽𝄽 (Arista, 1990, prod. L.A. Reid, Babyface, Narada Michael Walden, Luther Vandross, Ste-

vie Wonder, Michael Masser, Whitney Houston, Rickey Minor) is a mess, thanks to its crazy quilt of producers and the fact that, for a star of Houston's magnitude, the material is extraordinarily weak. The sole standout is the bombastic "He's All the Man I Need," which refers to God, in case you were wondering.

the rest:
Waiting to Exhale 𝄽𝄽𝄽 (Arista, 1995)
The Preacher's Wife 𝄽𝄽𝄽 (Arista, 1996)

influences:

◀◀ Aretha Franklin, Cissy Houston, Dionne Warwick, Chaka Khan, Diana Ross

▶▶ Toni Braxton, Mariah Carey, Brandy

Daniel Durchholz

Howlin' Wolf

Born Chester Arthur Burnett, June 10, 1910, in West Point, MS. Died January 10, 1976, in Hines, IL.

With all due respect to Willie Dixon and Muddy Waters, there was something *fearsome* about Howlin' Wolf and the particular kind of blues he created at Chess Records during the 1950s. Maybe it's the name, a formidable handle even by gangsta rap standards. Maybe it was his size, a hulking 6-foot-3, 300-some pounds. Or maybe it was his performances, which were down, dirty, and tough—"Spoonful," "Smokestack Lightnin'," "Little Red Rooster," "I Ain't Superstitious," "Killing Floor," "Back Door Man." You'll recognize those titles from lots of rock albums during the 1960s and the 1970s, and it's true—Wolf was perhaps *the* most seminal blues influence on rock 'n' roll, a performer whose ferocity spoke directly to the hearts of the proteges who were trying to create an even bigger noise. (Some of them repaid the debt in 1971 by backing him up on *The London Howlin' Wolf Sessions*.) The young Burnett was raised on a cotton plantation and learned to play guitar when he was a child. He soaked up influences from around the Mississipi Delta, particularly his half-sister's husband, Sonny Boy Williamson. His journeys north took him first to Memphis, where he recorded for Sun Records. Sun then leased those tapes to Chess, and Howlin' Wolf became part of that city's immense blues heritage. Simply put, there's practically nowhere in R&B and rock 'n' roll where Wolf's influence isn't felt; even artists who don't convey an overt blues influence reflect some of his performance standards.

what to buy: *The Chess Box* 𝄽𝄽𝄽𝄽 (Chess, 1991, prod. various) fills three discs with Wolf's best. It's pricey. And long. But you won't be wasting a penny, or a minute. *His Best* 𝄽𝄽𝄽𝄽

(Chess/MCA, 1997, prod. various) is a good, 20-song overview of his very best.

what to buy next: The twofer *Howlin' Wolf/Moanin' in the Moonlight* 𝄞𝄞𝄞𝄞 (Chess, 1987) pairs two of his best albums for another captivating listening experience. *Cadillac Daddy* 𝄞𝄞𝄞𝄞 (Memphis Recordings, 1952/Rounder, 1989) offers a selection of Wolf's pre-Chess days. The *Real Folk Blues* 𝄞𝄞𝄞𝄞𝄞 (Chess, 1966/1988) and *More Real Folk Blues* 𝄞𝄞𝄞𝄞 (Chess, 1967/1988) albums are akin to audio texts on the form. *The London Howlin' Wolf Sessions* 𝄞𝄞𝄞 (Chess, 1971/1994) is flawed—Eric Clapton, Steve Winwood, and the rest seem a bit awed and timid to be recording with their hero—but Wolf still manages a winning performance.

what to avoid: *Live and Cookin'* 𝄞𝄞 (Chess, 1972/1992) catches Wolf late in the game, when failing health was beginning to take a toll on his skills.

the rest:
The Back Door Wolf 𝄞𝄞𝄞𝄞 (Chess, 1973/1995)
Change My Way 𝄞𝄞𝄞𝄞𝄞 (Chess, 1975/1992)
Live in Cambridge 𝄞𝄞𝄞 (NRR, 1992)
Wolf Is at Your Door 𝄞𝄞 (NRR, 1992)
Howlin' Wolf Rides Again 𝄞𝄞𝄞𝄞 (Virgin, 1993)
Ain't Gonna Be Your Dog, Vol. 2 𝄞𝄞𝄞 (Chess, 1994)
Chicago Blue 𝄞𝄞𝄞𝄞 (Rhino, 1995)
Blues Master 𝄞𝄞𝄞 (Chess, 1996)
Highway 49 𝄞𝄞𝄞𝄞 (1996)

worth searching for: On *The Howlin' Wolf Album* 𝄞𝄞𝄞𝄞 (Chess, 1969) the music is great, but the cover—with its simple legend: "This is Howlin' Wolf's new album. He doesn't like it. He didn't like his electric guitar at first either."—speaks volumes about the man.

influences:

◀◀ Sonny Boy Williamson, Robert Johnson, Charley Patton, Willie Dixon

▶▶ Eric Clapton, Cream, John Mayall, the Yardbirds, Jeff Beck, Led Zeppelin, the Doors, the rest of this book . . .

Gary Graff

Hues Corporation

Formed 1969, in Los Angeles, CA. Disbanded in 1980s.

H. Ann Kelley, vocals; Bernard Henderson, vocals; Fleming Williams, vocals (1969–74); Tommy Brown, vocals (1974–75); Karl Russell, vocals (1975–present).

Neither as successful nor as enduring as its Fortune 500

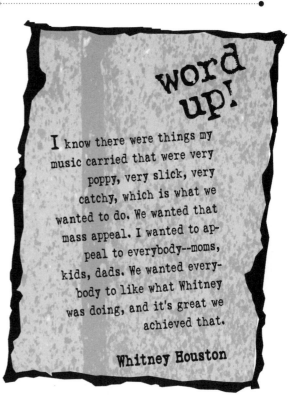

word up!

I know there were things my music carried that were very poppy, very slick, very catchy, which is what we wanted to do. We wanted that mass appeal. I wanted to appeal to everybody--moms, kids, dads. We wanted everybody to like what Whitney was doing, and it's great we achieved that.

Whitney Houston

namesake, the Hues Corporation recorded one of the most sensitive and evocative ballads of the 1970s, "Freedom for the Stallion." But the three-member singing group didn't find its niche until the arrival of disco. They were one of the first acts to hit #1 on the *Billboard* pop charts with a pure disco song, the monster 1974 single "Rock the Boat." They have been referred to many times as "one-hit-wonders," but the Hues Corporation actually had five chart hits in the U.S., including "Stallion" and "Rockin' Soul." Frequent changes in personnel and record labels spelled the beginning of the group's demise, but their minor music legacy lives on from having one of the first true disco classics.

what's available: The only Hues Corporation collection currently in print, *Rock the Boat: Golden Classics* 𝄞𝄞𝄞 (Collectables, 1993, prod. various) features the extended "disco mix" (a.k.a. 12-inch) versions of "Rock the Boat" and "Rockin' Soul," as well as "Freedom for the Stallion" and two lesser-known but worthy tracks, "All Goin' Down Together" and "One Good Night Together."

influences:

◄◄ The Miracles, Tony Orlando & Dawn, Honey Cone, MFSB, the Three Degrees

►► Average White Band, the Captain and Tennille, KC and the Sunshine Band, A Taste of Honey, Culture Club, Wham!, LaBouche, Fun Factory

"Lisa Lisa" Orlando

Ivory Joe Hunter

Born October 10, 1914, in Kirbyville, TX. Died November 8, 1974, in Memphis, TN.

Ivory Joe Hunter was sneaking elements of country music into his jazzy ballads and jump blues as far back as the 1940s. His big hits during the 1950s sold as well to white audiences as black, and performers such as Elvis Presley and Pat Boone scrambled to record cover versions of them. Initially a piano boogie artist in the Fats Waller mode, Hunter leased recordings from his own Ivory and Pacific labels, his 1948 #1 R&B hit "Pretty Baby Blues" among them. He signed with King Records in 1949 and had an enviable string of mostly self-written hits with "Guess Who," "Don't Fall In Love with Me," "Landlord Blues," "I Quit My Pretty Mama," and many others. During his King period, Hunter banged out lots of first rate boogie, but on songs such as "Jealous Heart" he embraced country sounds years before Fats Domino, Chuck Berry, or Solomon Burke did. Moving to MGM in 1950, Hunter scored one of his signature hits, "I Almost Lost My Mind," which was a blues but sounded pretty country for its time. "S.P. Blues" and "I Need You So" were solid follow-ups. In 1954, Hunter signed with Atlantic, where he was to have his greatest commercial success. "A Tear Fell" and "You Mean Everything to Me" were modest sellers, but the romantic rock-a-ballad "Since I Met You Baby" was a major pop and R&B smash. "Empty Arms" b/w "Love's a Hurting Game" was a two-sided hit, though not as big. Atlantic accentuated Hunter's velvety country vocals with slick orchestration and choral arrangements (an approach Ray Charles would get credit for during the 1960s), but the formula did not score many more hits. "Yes I Want You" was his last chart success before leaving Atlantic. Hunter's final entry on the pop charts was his rendition of country singer Bill Anderson's "City Lights" on Dot Records. Through the 1960s and into the 1970s he recorded extensively for labels such as Vee-Jay, Smash, Capitol, Veep, Paramount, Lion, Strand, and Home of the Blues; but, though his talent was undiminished, his days as a hitmaker were over. During the 1960s, Hunter worked as a staff producer at Motown and secured a regular spot on the Grand Ol' Opry

(cool dichotomy, eh?). Hunter remained a well-respected, well-reviewed artist until his death from lung cancer in 1974. He was R&B's smoothest innovator.

what to buy: *Since I Met You Baby: The Best of Ivory Joe Hunter* ♫♫♫♫♫ (Razor & Tie, 1994, comp. Dave Booth) is a fabulous collection of 20 tracks culled from the MGM and Atlantic years. "I Almost Lost My Mind," "S.P. Blues," "Empty Arms," and many other goodies are here. Go for it.

what to buy next: *Sings 16 of His Greatest Hits* ♫♫♫ (King, 1994, prod. various) is a fine, more boogie-oriented set of his earliest hits for the King label, including "Guess Who" and "Landlord Blues."

what to avoid: *Since I Met You Baby* ♫♫♫ (Mercury, 1988, prod. various) is one of those sets of greatest hits re-recordings that Smash/Mercury had all established artists do once they joined their label. It's not bad, but the originals are tough to beat.

the rest:
I'm Coming Down with the Blues ♫♫♫ (Collectables, 1991)

worth searching for: *7th Street Boogie* ♫♫♫♫ (Route 66, 1991, prod. various), an import that features 16 tracks from the Pacific, 4 Star, and King labels, featuring some jumpin' blues and early attempts at his ballad style. This guy could *cook* when he wanted to.

influences:

◄◄ Fats Waller, Duke Ellington

►► Charles Brown, Fats Domino, Chuck Willis

Ken Burke

Willie Hutch

Born Willie McKinley Huntchinson, 1946, in Los Angeles, CA.

Willie Hutch's only problem was timing. Hutch was an excellent singer/songwriter/performer/producer/arranger at Motown when the label had not one but two supremely gifted singer/songwriter/performer/producer/arrangers in Marvin Gaye and Stevie Wonder. Hutch released a couple of sides for RCA before joining Motown in the midst of the label's move West. He made his first impression as part of the writing team—with Berry Gordy, Bob West, and Hal Davis—of "I'll Be There," the fourth in a string of four back-to-back #1 hits for the Jackson 5. He continued to work behind the scenes, producing records for the Four Tops, the Temptations, G.C. Cameron, Syreeta, and, most notably, Smokey Robinson, directing his first album after leaving the Miracles. By 1973, Hutch found a project that would take him out from behind the boards: the original score and soundtrack to the black action film *The Mack,* followed by another soundtrack, for the film *Foxy Brown.* Like Quincy Jones around this same time, Hutch quickly established himself as a potent creative force in film scoring. While Motown has yet to issue Hutch's non-theatrical works of the time, such as *Mark of the Beast,* these two soundtracks best exemplify Hutch as a gifted multi-talented musician.

what to buy: On *The Mack* ♫♫♫ (Motown Master Series, 1973/1996, prod. Willie Hutch) you can appreciate Hutch's gift for crafting cinematic soul with his lush, layered guitars, floating backing vocals, and swirling strings. Tracks such as the soaring "I Choose You," the sly and wicked "Slick," the viciously funky "Mack Man (Got to Get Over)," and the tour de force anthem "Brother's Gonna Work It Out" secured *The Mack*'s placement alongside the other great soundtracks of the era—Isaac Hayes's *Shaft,* Curtis Mayfield's *Superfly,* and labelmate Marvin Gaye's *Trouble Man.*

what to buy next: Having found an idiom that he worked well in, Hutch returned the next year with the score and soundtrack to the film *Foxy Brown* ♫♫♫ (Motown Master Series, 1974/1996, prod. Willie Hutch). Though not as cinematic as *The Mack,* *Foxy Brown* is a wonderfully orchestrated album with a huge drum sound and great funk jams of almost *Fresh*-era Sly Stone proportions.

influences:

◄◄ Jackie Wilson, Smokey Robinson, Marvin Gaye, Johnny Rivers, Junior Waler, Ray Charles

►► Tony Rich, D'Angelo, Maxwell

Dana G. Smart

Hyenas in the Desert

Formed mid-1990s, in Long Island, NY.

Kendo, vocals; plus three unnamed performers.

Pointman Kendo is surrounded by three mysterious, nameless cohorts, but the group's claim to fame isn't found on its own roster, anyway. Rather, the Hyenas are notable for their label ties, as their debut, *Die Laughing,* was the first release from Public Enemy frontman Chuck D.'s Slam Jamz label.

what's available: Adhering to Chuck D.'s Slam Jamz philosophy of only releasing 12-inch recordings and EPs, the dark and brooding *Die Laughing* ♫♫♫ (Slam Jamz/Columbia, 1996, prod. Gary G-Wiz) contains just six songs, plus an intro and a few in-terludes. Kendo's verbal delivery is forceful and steelo-hard, and the beats (from the Bomb Squad's Gary G-Wiz) are appropriately minimalist, rugged, and edgy, with tracks ranging from the atonal mysticism of "Can You Feel It" and the lumbering throb of "Wild Dogs" to the wispy, mournful "Why Me," wherein Kendo drops an autobiographical, back-in-the-day saga of growing up.

influences:

◄◄ Public Enemy, Mobb Deep, M.O.P.

Spence D.

Phyllis Hyman

Born July 6, 1950, in Pittsburgh, PA. Died June 30, 1995, in New York, NY.

Phyllis Hyman got her start singing with Norman Connors in 1976. She went on to a solo career, signing to Buddah Records in 1977, where she made her first record, *Phyllis Hyman. Somewhere in My Lifetime,* her Arista debut, came the following year. From R&B songstress to jazz singer to soulful balladeer, Hyman constantly exhibited her flexibility as a vocalist. She has performed with Pharoah Sanders, Barry Manilow, Grover Washington, and a long list of diverse artists. Hyman's second record for Arista, *You Know How to Love Me,* went gold in 1979. She was nominated for a Tony Award in 1981 for her performance in the Broadway musical *Sophisticated Ladies.* In 1990, Hyman hit #1 on the R&B charts with "Don't Wanna Change the World," a position she would not see enough throughout her lifetime. The world can only speculate about whether coming so close to great commercial success without ever reaching it contributed to Hyman's troubled mind during the last two decades of her life. She left Arista after *Goddess of Love* in 1983 and signed to Philadelphia International Records. She debuted on the label with the poignant album *Living All Alone.* Unfortunately, her bouts with manic depression kept her from promoting it. Hyman made another record for Philadelphia in 1991, strangely titled *Prime of My Life,* in tumultuous times. During the final stages of making *I Refuse to Be Lonely* in 1995, Hyman committed suicide in her Manhattan apartment by overdosing on pills. It was just a week before her 45th birthday, and she was scheduled to appear at the Apollo theater later that evening.

what to buy: There are plenty of greatest hits packages, but *The Legacy of Phyllis Hyman* ♫♫♫♫ (Arista, 1996, prod. various) is an excellent selection of hits and favorites from 1977–91, with chart positions in the liner notes.

what to buy next: *I Refuse to Be Lonely* 🎵🎵🎵 (Zoo/Philadelphia International Records, 1995, prod. various) is a sad but compelling series of songs that take off with "Waiting for the Last Tear to Fall." Most of the uncompleted record was produced by Nick Martinelli, Keith Gamble, and Dexter Wansel.

the rest:

Under Your Spell: Greatest Hits 🎵🎵🎵 (Arista, 1990)

Prime of My Life 🎵🎵🎵 (Zoo/Volcano, 1991)

Loving You, Losing You: The Classic Balladry of Phyllis Hyman 🎵🎵🎵🎵 (RCA, 1996)

influences:

⏪ Minnie Riperton, Nancy Wilson, Billie Holiday, Sarah Vaughan, Ella Fitzgerald

⏩ Whitney Houston, Toni Braxton, Erykah Badu, D'Angelo, Maxwell

Norene Cashen

Ice Cube

Born O'Shea Jackson, June 15, 1969, in Los Angeles, CA.

It didn't take long for Ice Cube to set the tone of his post-N.W.A. career. Indeed, just a few seconds into his brilliant solo debut, *AmeriKKKa's Most Wanted*, the soon-to-be-mock-executed rapper offers what are supposed to be his last words to the world. "Fuck all y'all," he says. Of course, Cube would have much more to say beyond that, but those three words neatly sum up Cube's worldview: he's mad as hell at the world (for years and years of oppression, among other things)—and, frankly, he's not interested in taking it any more. Throwing verbal daggers at whatever target happens to pop into his head, Cube has managed to offend just about everybody during his productive solo years, be it Koreans, Jews, blacks, cops, women, East Coast rappers, homosexuals or even former bandmates. He's also managed to establish himself as one of the most durable hitmakers in hip-hop, as well as the genre's most successful actor (*Boyz 'N the Hood, Friday, Higher Learning, Anaconda, Trespass*, etc.). While his acting credits have piled up, Cube's music has declined, and his songs don't quite carry the same impact as they once did. With Cube becoming more and more concerned with West Coast rap superiority (especially with the all-star Westside Connection) and less interested in casting his angry eye at societal problems and perceived racial injustices, he's lost his status as *AmeriKKKa's Most Wanted*.

what to buy: Ferocious, funny, intelligent and incendiary (but not always all at once), *AmeriKKKa's Most Wanted* 🎵🎵🎵🎵 (Priority, 1990, prod. the Bomb Squad, others) is one of the most powerful albums in 1990s music—genre-classification be damned. With the Bomb Squad supplying the dense, funky, and occasionally frightening soundtrack of chaotic urban America and Cube taking a star turn as "The Nigga You Love to Hate," the album is hard-hitting as hell, both musically and lyrically. Cube doesn't just dish it out, though, as the crowd in the ingenious chorus of "The Nigga You Love to Hate" repeatedly chants "Fuck you Ice Cube." Yo Yo—Bonnie to Cube's Clyde—plants a few on Cube's chin, too, on "It's a Man's World." An essential classic.

what to buy next: The Bomb Squad is missing on *Death Certificate* 🎵🎵🎵🎵 (Priority, 1991, prod. Sir Jinx, Ice Cube, others), but Cube's unflinching, unforgiving attitude isn't as he harshly examines life as an embattled young black man. Not only is Cube the one you love to hate, he's now also the "Wrong Nigga To Fuck Wit." And how. Although he can come off as racist, homophobic, and misogynistic (see this visceral album's "Black Korea," "No Vaseline," "Givin' Up the Nappy Dug Out," and "Look Who's Burnin'"), Cube always forces you to think. No harm there—even when you don't agree with him, as with the justification he wields along with his gun: "Bustin' caps in the mix/Rather be judged by 12 than carried by six."

what to avoid: On *Lethal Injection* 🎵🎵 (Priority, 1993, prod. Sir Jinx, QD III, Ice Cube, others), it's clear that Cube is no longer the creative force he was just a few years earlier.

the rest:

Kill At Will 🎵🎵🎵 EP (Priority, 1990)

The Predator 🎵🎵🎵 (Priority, 1992)

Bootlegs & B-Sides 🎵🎵 (Priority, 1994)

(With Westside Connection, WC, and Mack 10) *Bow Down* 🎵🎵🎵 (Priority, 1996)

influences:

⏪ Public Enemy, Ice-T, George Clinton

⏩ Mack 10, WC & the MAAD Circle, Da Lench Mob, Kam, Homicide, Yo Yo Kausion, K-Dee, Comrads

see also: *N.W.A.*

Josh Freedom du Lac

Ice Cube (© Ken Settle)

Ice-T

Born Tracy Morrow, 1959, in Newark, NJ.

If South Central Los Angeles gangbanger-turned-rapper Ice-T didn't father gangsta rap, he was likely present in the delivery room. Adapting his name from ghettocentric pulp-fiction author Iceberg Slim, the former Tracy Marrow has accurately described himself as a hoodlum who happened to become a rapper, a rare instance in which a gangsta MC actually experienced first-hand the lifestyle of guns, dope, and sex he exploits in rhyme. His seminal gangsta track, "6 in the Mornin'," now sounds quaint by the standards of the shock-rappers that followed him, but Ice-T paved their way. He brought his inner-city tales to a mass audience by rapping the title song in *Colors,* the 1988 movie directed by Dennis Hopper about Los Angeles street gangs. And he drew the wrath of the political left with his insensitive rhymes about women and gays, and that of right-wingers who objected to his explicit language and insisted that his albums come equipped with parental warning stickers. The rapper became the center of a major free-speech battle when his thrash-metal group Body Count issued a track called "Cop Killer" in 1992, and he was villified by then-President George Bush. Time-Warner, Ice-T's label, eventually ordered the track removed from the album (replaced by a free speech rant from punker Jello Biafra), and then refused to release his subsequent hip-hop album, *Home Invasion.* Ice-T has survived the ruckus, however, by continuing to issue hard-hitting albums and maintaining a credible career as a Hollywood actor, usually in roles not far removed from his street hustler origins.

what to buy: *O.G. Original Gangster* 🎵🎵🎵🎵 (Sire, 1991, prod. Ice-T, others) is a hip-hop classic, gangsta or otherwise. All but gone are the misogynist sex rhymes and tired boasts that marred previous releases. In their place is hard-hitting music about escaping the ghetto minefield of gangs, guns, and drugs. In "Mind Over Matter," Ice-T talks about the thrill of putting words to paper—one of the more effective advertisements for literacy any rock or rap star has ever made—while the title track is a bravura performance about individuality in a cookie-cutter age. The disc also marks the debut of Ice-T's metal group, Body Count.

what to buy next: Declaring "My lethal weapon's my mind," Ice-T was among the first gangsta rappers to sprinkle his bloody, bawdy urban vignettes with political and social content. His *Iceberg/Freedom of Speech . . . Just Watch What You Say* 🎵🎵🎵 (Sire, 1989, prod. Ice-T, Afrika Islam) is more than just an assault on political correctness; it's also a thought-provoking essay on what it means to be the member of a minority in America.

what to avoid: *Body Count* 🎵🎵 (Sire, 1992, prod. Ice-T, Ernie C.), Ice-T's initial foray into thrash metal with guitarist and boyhood chum from Crenshaw High in South Central, Ernie C., is redeemed by its over-the-top novelty, its parody of nastiness, but subsequent releases *Born Dead* 🎵🎵 (Virgin, 1994, prod. Ernie C., Ice-T) and *Violent Demise: The Last Days* 🎵🎵 (Virgin, 1997, prod. Howard Benson) hardly expand the formula.

the rest:
Rhyme Pays 🎵🎵🎵 (Sire, 1987)
Power 🎵🎵🎵 (Sire, 1988)
Home Invasion 🎵🎵🎵🎵 (Rhyme Syndicate/Priority, 1993)
The Classic Collection 🎵🎵🎵 (Rhino, 1993)
VI: Return of the Real 🎵🎵🎵 (Rhyme Syndicate/Priority, 1996)
Cold as Ever 🎵🎵🎵 (Hitman, 1996)
The Ice Opinion N/A (Ichiban, 1997)

worth searching for: The original version of *Body Count* 🎵🎵🎵 (Sire, 1992, prod. Ice-T, Ernie C.) containing "Cop Killer" is a collector's item.

influences:

◀◀ Iceberg Slim, Run-D.M.C., Slayer, Kool DJ Herc, Black Flag, Dead Kennedys

▶▶ N.W.A., Ice Cube, MC Eiht, Geto Boys, Too $hort, Frost, Boogie Down Productions, Boo Yaa Tribe, Divine Styler, WC and the MAAD Circle, House of Pain

Greg Kot

Ill Al Skratch

Formed 1993, in Brooklyn, NY.

Ill, vocals; Al Skratch, vocals, scratching.

Most prominent for their contributions to the albums of other hip-hop artists—especially for coming off the bench to dish assists to NBA/rap star Shaquille O'Neal—Ill Al Skratch, like Run-D.M.C., is a hybrid name for the two New York rappers who combined to form the act, Ill and Al Skratch. The "Brooklyn Uptown Connection," as the duo is also known, managed to curry favor among both hardcore underground fans and R&B listeners on their 1994 debut album *Creep Wit' Me,* primarily on the strength of two singles: "Where My Homiez?" an aggressive hip-hop demand, and "I'll Take Her," featuring the romantic vocals of popular labelmate Brian McKnight. In the intervening years between that release and their ensuing 1996 disc *Keep It Movin',* Ill Al Skratch contributed to the movie soundtrack for *New Jersey Drive,* appeared in the Whoopi Goldberg film *Eddie,* and performed on O'Neal's *Shaq-Fu: Da Return* and *Best of Shaquille O'Neal* LPs and albums by J. Quest and Gina Thompson.

what to buy: The hauntingly beautiful voice of Brian McKnight on the runaway hit "I'll Take Her" is reason enough—some might say the only reason—to commend *Creep Wit' Me* 🎵🎵🎵 (Mercury, 1994, prod. various); though less polished than Ill Al Skratch's second LP, it is precisely their raw street energy and unpredictability that make the album palatable.

what to buy next: The follow-up *Keep It Movin'* 🎵🎵 (Mercury, 1997, prod. various), conversely, tries too hard to repeat the successful formula. If McKnight's appearance elevated *Creep Wit' Me*, they apparently reasoned, why not have a studio full of cameo performers for the next project? Drop-ins by Crystal Waters, Gina Thompson, Christopher Williams, Big E, Big Mike, Kid Capri, and Greg Nice make the LP feel as cluttered and stifling as an all-night underground party, resulting in overproduced tracks and forced concepts.

influences:

◀◀ Run-D.M.C., Pete Rock & C.L. Smooth, Wu-Tang Clan, Kid Capri

▶▶ Shaquille O'Neal, Def Jef

Andre McGarrity

Illegal
/Jamal

Formed 1993, in New Jersey. Disbanded 1995.

Jamal Phillips, vocals; Malik Edwards, vocals.

Troubled youths Jamal and Malik were brought together by TLC's Left Eye and producer Dallas Austin and managed to secure for their debut a team of top-flight producers (Erick Sermon, Diamond D, Lord Finesse, Biz Markie). The two microphone prodigies used the star backing to good effect, as their breakout single, "We Getz Buzy," won the 1993 *Billboard* Award for Best Rap Single. Two years later, though, the rappers split up, with Jamal becoming the more productive of the two, releasing a full-length album, guesting on records by Keith Murray, Busta Rhymes, and Junior M.A.F.I.A., and contributing a song to the *Panther* soundtrack. Malik, meanwhile, has released just one 12-inch to date, 1995's "Malik Goes On."

what to buy: Jamal was a cool 16 when he recorded *Last Chance, No Breaks* 🎵🎵🎵 (Rowdy, 1995, prod. Erick Sermon, Redman, Easy Mo Bee, others), but he has a mature, commanding voice that delivers raps in a solid, crisp flow that complements the booming ghetto-dub beats well. Although rife with references to guns, weed, and "bitch-ass-niggas," the lyrics occa-

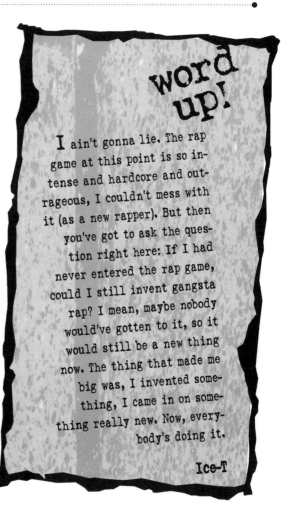

word up!

I ain't gonna lie. The rap game at this point is so intense and hardcore and outrageous, I couldn't mess with it (as a new rapper). But then you've got to ask the question right here: If I had never entered the rap game, could I still invent gangsta rap? I mean, maybe nobody would've gotten to it, so it would still be a new thing now. The thing that made me big was, I invented something, I came in on something really new. Now, everybody's doing it.

Ice-T

sionally display a depth that reaches far beyond Jamal's young years—particularly on "Keep It Live," which recounts Jamal's journey from New Jersey to Philadelphia to Atlanta, from reform-school pupil to rap superstar. Jamal's rapography is replete with nods to his grandmother, as he exclaims: "I never forgot that my No. 1 plot was for me to rock the crowd and make my granny proud."

what to avoid: One of the more disturbing movements in '90s hip-hop is the whole underaged-MCs-rockin'-lyrics-about-drinkin'-40s-and-slappin'-bitches-and-carressing-9MMs thing.

To that end, Illegal's well-produced *The Untold Truth* ♫♫ (Rowdy, 1993, prod. Erick Sermon, Diamond D, Lord Finesse, Biz Markie, others) is lyrically annoying. It doesn't help that the rappers' 14-year-old voices begin to grate after a few listens.

influences:

◀◀ Chi-Ali, Kris Kross

Spence D.

Immature

Formed 1991, in Los Angeles, CA.

Marques "Batman" Houston, lead vocals; Jerome "Romeo" Jones, vocals; Kelton "Little Drummer Boy" Kessee, beats and vocals.

With nicknames like "Romeo," "Batman," and "Little Drummer Boy," and a group name like Immature, the three teenage members of this West Coast trio had better walk it like they talk it. And they do, in a teeny-bopper, cocky-little-brother kind of way. The first successful R&B "kiddie" act to emerge after the New Edition/New Kids on the Block wave of the 1980s faded, this audacious act is the brainchild of its L.A.-based manager/producer/Svengali Chris Stokes, created to feed the demand for urban pin-up boys and *Right On!!* magazine heart-throbs among squealing, hormonal teenage girls. Led by lead singer Houston, with his runaway hairstyles and Michael Jackson worship, and eyepatch-wearing Romeo, the group was signed to Virgin Records and released its 1992 debut album *On Our Worst Behavior* to generally lukewarm response. The LP, filled with such tracks as "Mom's Illin'" and "Da Munchies," ultimately targeted a far too narrow preteen audience with its preoccupation with bubblegum topics. Doing its homework quickly, Immature moved to MCA and broke through its self-imposed confines the following year with the CD *Playtyme Is Over*. As the title implies, this album marked a calculated move toward a more adult, soulful sound and a growth spurt toward their dream of mass-appeal stardom. Propelled by a #1 single in "Never Lie," the trio staged a sudden media blitz, appearing together in the movie *House Party 3* as Batman landed a feature TV role in the WB network's teen sitcom *Sister, Sister*. Their slow jam "Feel the Funk" was included in the *Dangerous Minds* movie soundtrack in 1995, providing an added boost to their third album, the modestly titled *We Got It*. Immature's mounting popularity has become almost cultish among younger (and female) fans but appears to be spreading throughout a broad age spectrum, as evidenced by the fact that the group has signed to shoot its own WB TV series pilot for 1998, described as a sitcom version of *The Wonder Years*.

what to buy: The best Immature album to date, *We Got It* ♫♫♫ (MCA, 1995, prod. Chris Stokes) captures the trio's ever-evolving talent and musical maturity. The funky title track proves they've got what it takes to keep even hardcore hip-hop listeners interested, while the smooth, provocative "Baby Please Don't Go," perhaps the LP's strongest track, shows off Batman's Michael Jacksonesque vocal range while diving into deeper emotional wells. It's Exhibit A that the explosive success of *Playtyme Is Over* was no childhood prank.

what to buy next: Focusing on contemporary songs with universal themes, *Playtyme Is Over* ♫♫♫ (MCA, 1994, prod. Roy "Dog" Pennon) delivers on the assertion of its title. It catapulted Immature from the ranks of juvenile funksters to legitimate R&B contenders by making them palatable to adult audiences. The album's even blend of mainstream pop, R&B, hip-hop, and funk, dominated by the emotional burners "Never Lie" and "Constantly," elevated the group to the next level.

the rest:

On Our Worst Behavior ♫♫ (Virgin, 1992)
The Journey ♫♫♫ (MCA, 1997)

worth searching for: The movie soundtrack to *House Party 3* (Select Street, 1994), already out of print, features the flavorful Immature track "Wakes You Up (House Party)."

influences:

◀◀ Michael Jackson, the Jackson 5, New Edition, New Kids on the Block, Smooth

▶▶ GYRL, K-Ball

Andre McGarrity

The Impressions

Formed 1957, in Chicago, IL.

Jerry Butler, vocals (1957–59); Curtis Mayfield, vocals, guitar, musical director (1957–70); Arthur Brooks, vocals (1957–62); Richard Brooks, vocals (1957–62); Fred Cash, vocals (1958–present); Sam Gooden, vocals; Leroy Hutson, vocals (1970–73); Ralph Johnson, vocals (1973–76); Reggie Torian, vocals (1973–present); Nate Evans, vocals (1976–present).

Led by the multi-talented Curtis Mayfield, the Impressions were Chicago R&B's most successful vocal group of the 1960s. Like William "Smokey" Robinson in nearby Detroit, Mayfield was the prime creative force in Chicago R&B during the 1960s and 1970s. The Impressions showcased Mayfield's wide array of talents—his warm, expressive singing, sophisticated songwriting, and fluid, melodic guitar playing—and provided the vehicle by which Mayfield profoundly influenced the R&B of the 1960s and 1970s. The Impressions' first hit record, "For Your Precious Love," set the tone for their later work. Sung by their first lead vocalist, Jerry Butler, in a deep, reverential baritone backed by the group's ethereal harmonies, the record's references to the sound and feel of gospel music set it apart from other vocal group records of the late 1950s; it sold more than 150,000 copies during the two weeks following its 1958 release and launched Butler's solo career (with Mayfield's blessings and assistance). Although much softer and more pop-oriented than the recordings of the gospel quartets, the Impressions' subsequent recordings for ABC-Paramount were infused with the attitude and approach of gospel music. Beginning with "It's All Right" in 1963, the pared-down Impressions—Mayfield, Cash, and Gooden—departed from the lead-vocalist-backed-by-group style of singing that was typical of 1950s doo-wop. Instead, the Impressions adopted a style more typical of gospel quartets such as the Soul Stirrers and the Dixie Hummingbirds, with Mayfield, Cash, and Gooden all singing lead alternately throughout the song. The Impressions' love songs—"I'm So Proud," "I've Been Trying," "I Loved and I Lost"—have a distinctly spiritual quality, reflected in the dramatic gravity of the vocal delivery and the musical settings crafted by arranger Johnny Pate.

Most important, though, many of Mayfield's 1960s compositions for the Impressions, including "Keep On Pushing" in 1964 and "We're a Winner" in 1968, explicitly promoted African American identity and pride, anticipating themes that would dominate the R&B of the 1970s. This application of the black Christian church's didacticism to a secular context was Mayfield's greatest achievement. After he left the Impressions in 1970 to establish a solo career, Mayfield's recordings for his own Curtom label were even more consistently message oriented than his work with the Impressions had been. The Impressions soldiered on after Mayfield left. For Mayfield's Curtom label, where the Impressions had moved in 1968, the group made two unsuccessful LPs with Leroy Hutson as lead vocalist. Later, though, the group re-formed around new lead singers Ralph Johnson and Reggie Torian, and released a number of excellent hit records produced by Ed Townsend, including "Finally Got Myself Together," "Sooner or Later," "Loving Power," and "Same Thing It Took." In 1976, Curtom attempted to form a new group, Mystique, around Johnson, an outstanding gospel-style vocalist. But Mystique's only LP failed to make any commercial noise. Meanwhile, the remaining Impressions,

word up!

IT was a little hard. The public thought the Impressions was a band. But, Jerry moving on, that was a blessing in disguise. It put me in a position to write and be a lead singer. Playing for him allowed me to save enough money to bring the Impressions back.

Curtis Mayfield
(formerly of
the Impressions)

with Nate Evans replacing Johnson, recorded for Cotillion and for Carl Davis's Chi-Sound label without much success. In 1990, Mayfield was the victim of a freak accident when a stage-lighting scaffold fell on him, leaving him paralyzed and permanently bound to a wheelchair. Two separate tribute collections, in which well-known recording artists interpret Mayfield's songs, appeared in 1993 and 1994, reflecting the high esteem in which Mayfield is held by his peers.

what to buy: *The Anthology, 1961–1977: Curtis Mayfield and the Impressions* 𝄞𝄞𝄞𝄞 (MCA, 1992, prod. various) is the definitive two-CD set of Mayfield's work, with the emphasis on his work with the Impressions. Only his essential recordings as a solo artist are included.

what to buy next: *Keep On Pushing/People Get Ready* 𝄞𝄞𝄞𝄞 (ABC-Paramount, 1964/ABC-Paramount, 1965/Kent, 1996, prod. Johnny Pate) collects two of the early 1960s Impressions' finest LPs on a single CD, filling in some of the holes from *The Anthology*. The same can be said of *The Impressions/Never Ending Impressions* 🎵🎵🎵 (ABC-Paramount, 1963/ABC-Paramount, 1964/Kent, 1996, prod. Johnny Pate), although *Never Ending Impressions*, the group's second ABC LP, was somewhat thin on material. *This Is My Country/Young Mods Forgotten Story* 🎵🎵🎵 (Curtom 1968/Curtom 1969/Sequel, 1996, prod. Curtis Mayfield) collects two of the three Curtom LPs that Mayfield recorded with the group before his departure and contains some great moments. *The Very Best of the Impressions* 🎵🎵🎵 (Rhino, 1997, prod. various) is a single-CD collection of the biggest of the Impressions' hits.

what to avoid: *Check Out Your Mind/Times Have Changed* 🎵🎵 (Curtom 1970/Curtom 1972/Sequel, 1996, prod. Curtis Mayfield) combines what was originally two albums. *Check Out Your Mind*, the last Impressions album with Mayfield, contains some strong material. *Times Have Changed*, however, was the first post-Mayfield album, with Leroy Hutson replacing Mayfield, and it failed both commercially and artistically. *Preacher Man* **woof!** (Curtom, 1973, prod. Rich Tufo) was Hutson's last LP with the Impressions.

the rest:
For Your Precious Love 🎵🎵🎵 (Vee-Jay, 1964)
One by One 🎵🎵🎵 (ABC-Paramount, 1965)
Impressions Greatest Hits 🎵🎵🎵 (ABC-Paramount, 1965)
Ridin' High 🎵🎵🎵 (ABC-Paramount, 1966)
Fabulous Impressions 🎵🎵🎵 (ABC-Paramount, 1967)
We're a Winner 🎵🎵🎵 (ABC-Paramount, 1968)
Best of the Impressions 🎵🎵🎵 (ABC-Paramount, 1968)
Versatile 🎵🎵 (ABC-Paramount, 1969)
Best Impressions 🎵🎵 (Curtom, 1969)
16 Greatest Hits 🎵🎵🎵 (ABC-Paramount, 1970)
Early Years 🎵🎵 (Probe, 1973)
Three the Hard Way 🎵🎵 (Curtom, 1974)
It's About Time 🎵🎵 (Cotillion, 1976)
Originals 🎵🎵🎵 (ABC, 1976)
Collection 🎵🎵🎵 (ABC-Paramount, 1976)
Come to My Party 🎵🎵 (20th Century, 1979)
Fan the Fire 🎵🎵 (20th Century/Chi-Sound, 1981)
Greatest Hits 🎵🎵🎵 (MCA, 1982)
Right on Time 🎵🎵🎵 (Charly, 1983)
Complete Vee-Jay Recordings 🎵🎵🎵 (Vee-Jay, 1993)
It's All Alright 🎵🎵🎵 (MCA, 1995)
All the Best 🎵🎵🎵 (Pickwick, 1995)
Further Impressions: More Soulful Classics 🎵🎵🎵 (HIPP, 1996)

worth searching for: The LPs *Finally Got Myself Together* 🎵🎵🎵 (Curtom, 1974, prod. various), *First Impressions* 🎵🎵🎵 (Curtom, 1975, prod. various), and *Loving Power* 🎵🎵🎵 (Curtom,

1975, prod. various) showcase the vocals of the highly underrated Ralph Johnson. Some of this material is available on *Lasting Impressions* 🎵🎵🎵 (Ichiban/Curtom, 1989, prod. Ed Townsend). Also worth hearing is *Mystique* 🎵🎵🎵 (Curtom, 1976, prod. various), by the Johnson-led group of the same name.

influences:

◀◀ Jerry Butler, the Swan Silvertones, the Dixie Hummingbirds, the Soul Stirrers

▶▶ The Esquires, the Van Dykes, Enchantment, Earth, Wind & Fire, New Edition, Boyz II Men, the Stylistics, the Delfonics, the O'Jays, the Manhattans, the Masqueraders, the Originals, the Mad Lads, the Temprees

see also: *Jerry Butler, Curtis Mayfield*

Bill Pollak

Incognito

Formed 1980, in London, England.

Jean-Paul "Bluey" Maunick, guitar, lead vocals, various instruments; Paul "Tubbs" Williams, bass (1980–91); Maysa Leak, vocals (1991–94, 1996–present); Christopher Ballin, vocals (1996–present); Imani, vocals (1996–present); Graham Harvey, keyboards; Fayyaz Virji, trombone; Kevin Robinson, trumpet.

The dream group for club DJ mixers the world over, Incognito has been variously described as everything from a 1970s-style pop-funk troupe to a futuristic Latin jazz ensemble, so diverse and constantly changing is its sound. However, Jean Paul "Bluey" Maunick, co-founder and creative genius of the loosely constructed group, will forever be hailed as the man who almost singlehandedly kept Britain's dynamic "acid jazz" scene alive after it all but collapsed in the mid-1980s. Born on the island of Mauritius, off Africa's east coast, but raised in London, Maunick and musical partner Paul "Tubbs" Williams enjoyed moderate success in the late 1970s with their band Light of the World (LOTW) and the U.K. hits "Swinging" and a cover version of "I Shot the Sheriff." Gaining a large cult following but little commercial acceptance, Maunick and Williams started over in 1980 with a new concept called Incognito. A 12-inch single, "Parisienne Girl," and the debut album *Jazz Funk* followed, after which Bluey and Tubbs reappeared in 1982 under yet another name, The Warriors, for a one-shot LP titled *Behind the Mask*, which yielded the British funk-jazz classic "Destination." For nearly a decade following that release, the two immersed themselves in other music projects and placed Incognito on the back burner; it wasn't until famous London DJ Gilles Peterson heard a demo Bluey was working on in 1991 and signed him to his new Talkin' Loud label for PolyGram that Incognito fully took flight. The "new" Incognito resurfaced with the 1992 LP *Inside Life* and their best-known dancefloor staple, a bristling remake of Ronnie Laws's "Always There" featuring Jocelyn Brown on vocals. After that triumphant return, the group reshuffled again and was without a lead singer; then Bluey met former Stevie Wonder backup singer Maysa Leak, and the search was over. Propelled by Maysa's powerhouse vocals and majestic diva presence, Incognito dominated Contemporary Jazz charts with the LPs *Tribes, Vibes + Scribes* and *Positivity* and a CD re-release of *Jazz Funk*. When Maysa left in 1994 to pursue a solo career, Maunick didn't miss a beat, shifting to string-dominated compositions on the 1995 album *100 Degrees and Rising*. Maysa returned the following year on the Incognito release *Beneath the Surface*; in the interim, Bluey allowed top DJs from around the world to fulfill their fantasy by inviting them to remix their own versions of Incognito songs for the innovative "greatest hits" album, *Remixed*. Despite an ever-shifting roster of players and Bluey's immersion in new projects and production work for others (George Benson, Ramsey Lewis), Incognito keeps bouncing back with richer sounds and funkier grooves, making the group a certainty to be around—in some form—making inspired fusion music for a long time to come.

what to buy: With the maturity and effortless swing of Maysa's voice at full power and Bluey's production values at peak form, *Positivity* 𝄞𝄞𝄞 (Verve, 1994, prod. Jean-Paul Maunick) is the Incognito concept at its very best. Bouncing between the James Brown-inspired soul shout of "Talkin' Loud" and the sinewy, landmark acid-jazz track "Deep Waters," if you like funk in your jazz with a dash of salsa whipped in, there's no way you can't dig this. Ironically, after wrapping herself in *Positivity*, Maysa then left the group for a two-year solo experiment.

what to buy next: The first merger of Maysa's voice and Maunick's verve, *Tribes, Vibes + Scribes* 𝄞𝄞𝄞𝄞 (Verve, 1993, prod. Jean-Paul Maunick) is the album that established Incognito as a stellar attraction in the States. A tight, spotless creation that leaves virtually no room for improvement, the disc is highlighted by Maysa's rendition of her former boss Stevie Wonder's classic, "Don't You Worry 'Bout a Thing."

the rest:
Jazz Funk 𝄞𝄞𝄞 (Chrysalis, 1980)
Inside Life 𝄞𝄞𝄞 (Verve, 1992)
100 Degrees and Rising 𝄞𝄞𝄞 (Verve, 1995)
Remixed 𝄞𝄞𝄞 (Verve, 1996)
Beneath the Surface 𝄞𝄞𝄞𝄞 (Verve, 1997)

worth searching for: Any Japanese release of the above albums includes several bonus tracks. And the all-instrumental 1997 LP *Blue Moods* was initially released in Southeast Asia, with promotional copies only available in the U.S.

solo outings:
Maysa Leak:
Maysa 𝄞𝄞𝄞 (Blue Thumb, 1995)

influences:

◄◄ James Brown, Stevie Wonder, Earth, Wind & Fire, Lonnie Liston Smith, Roy Ayers, George Benson, Parliament-Funkadelic, Donny Hathaway, Chuck Mangione, Herbie Hancock, Tower of Power, Marvin Gaye, Level 42, Roberta Flack, Weather Report, Sade

►► Jocelyn Brown, Sister Sledge, Maxi Priest, MC Solar, Turnaround, R. Kelly, Brand New Heavies

Andre McGarrity

James Ingram

Born February 16, 1953, in Akron, OH.

Though famous for his silky smooth voice, Ingram paid his dues during the early 1970s as a songwriter and keyboardist with his Ohio band Revelation Funk, and, after moving to L.A., as a member of touring bands for Ray Charles and the Coasters. While looking for music for a Patti Austin album, Quincy Jones discovered Ingram and invited him to sing on Jones's landmark 1980 album, *The Dude*. Ingram sang the title song, "Just Once," and "One Hundred Ways," for which he won a Grammy Award in 1981, making him the first pop artist to win the award without having a solo release of his own. Ingram continued to thrive as a writer, co-writing both "P.Y.T." for Michael Jackson's *Thriller* and Jones's "We Are the World." But his solo albums never matched the level of success he had enjoyed and has since achieved as a guest artist. His 1982 debut *It's Your Night* was a strong start, sporting a diverse style and scoring another Grammy with the Michael McDonald duet "Yah Mo B There." Successive albums, however, were more popular with late-night "Quiet Storm" radio formats than the populace. Yet, his soundtrack duets remained top notch, including "Somewhere Out There" with Linda Ronstadt from *An American Tail,* and Carol Bayer Sager's "When You Love Someone," with Anita Baker, from *Forget Paris*. Ingram left Warner Bros. in 1995 and has since been rumored to be recording an album of duets with Jeffrey Osborne.

what to buy: To appreciate the breadth of Ingram's work, the best choice is his collection package, *The Power of Great Music* ♪♪♪♪ (Warner Bros., 1992, prod. various). *It's Your Night* ♪♪♪ (Qwest/Warner Bros., 1983, prod. Quincy Jones) is a playground for Ingram's smooth tenor. He excels when he sings signature Jones-produced tunes like "There's No Easy Way" and "Whatever We Imagine."

what to buy next: The overlooked *Never Felt So Good* ♪♪♪ (Qwest, 1988, prod. Maurice White, Thom Bell) is a testament to Ingram's songwriting skills but also hints at a certain sameness in his style.

what to avoid: Producer Teddy Riley tried unsuccessfully to draft Ingram into the New Jack Swing ranks on *It's Real* ♪♪ (Warner Bros., 1989). Thankfully, the disc's best ballads can be found on *The Power of Great Music*.

the rest:
Always You ♪♪♪ (Warner Bros., 1993)

worth searching for: Ingram, the collaborative crooner, can be found on many works beyond his own. Check out *West Side Story* (RCA Victor, 1996, prod. David Pack) for a chilling rendition of "Maria" with Michael McDonald and Pack. For something completely different, there's *America, the Dream Goes On* ♪♪♪ (Philips Records, 1987), with the Boston Pops Orchestra, an album of American classics ranging from "New York, New York," to "The Battle Hymn of the Republic." Lastly, there's the tune "Love's Calling," a song he recorded in 1981 on fly-by-night label Wheel Records that released it under the phantom name Zingara.

influences:
◄◄ Jeffrey Osborne, Lionel Richie, Donny Hathaway

►► Johnny Gill, Kenny Latimore, Tony Terry

Franklin Paul

Luther Ingram

Born November 30, 1944, in Jackson, MS.

Luther Ingram will go down as an R&B immortal on the strength of one song—his tortured 1972 rendition of "If Loving You Is Wrong (I Don't Want to Be Right)," one of the purest and most-copied examples of country-fried soul ever recorded—but his noteworthy achievements in the genre extend even farther. Raised singing gospel in Mississippi church choirs, he moved to New York and was signed to Smash Records, a Mercury subsidiary; his first hit, "I Spy for the FBI," became a classic R&B

novelty song, later covered with greater success by Jamo Thomas. At Stax, Ingram went on to cut a string of R&B heartbreakers, including "Pity for the Lonely," "Missing You," and "To the Other Man" before striking the motherlode with "If Loving You Is Wrong." Along the way, he co-wrote yet another classic-in-waiting, "Respect Yourself" for the Staple Singers. Unfortunately, Ingram was rounding into prime form at precisely the time the great Stax Records hit machine was beginning its tragic downward spiral, leading to its eventual closure in 1976. Even more unfortunate, Ingram's manager, Johnny Baylor, was a key figure in helping to accelerate the label's demise.

what to buy: Ingram's choice 1970s material is today contained on two best-of collections, *Luther Ingram's Greatest Hits* ♪♪♪♪ (The Right Stuff, 1996, prod. various) and *If Loving You Is Wrong, I Don't Want To Be Right* ♪♪♪ (Collectables, 1993, prod. various). The selections are similar—almost identical, in fact—but the first compilation is preferable due to production quality and packaging.

influences:
◄◄ The Staple Singers, O.C. Smith, Percy Sledge, Ray Charles, Ben E. King, Bobby Womack, Johnnie Taylor

►► Lionel Richie, Bill Withers, Sweet Pea Atkinson/Was (Not Was), Teddy Pendergrass, Keith Sweat

Jim McFarlin

The Ink Spots

Formed 1931, in Indianapolis, IN.

Original members: Deek Watson, tenor (1931–45); Jerry Daniels, tenor (1931–36); Bill Kenny, tenor (1936–52); Billy Bowen, tenor (1945–53); Charlie Fuqua, baritone; Orville "Hoppy" Jones, bass; Herb Kenny, bass (1945–53).

Though their styles could not have been more different, the two great, seminal vocal groups in all of recorded music were the Mills Brothers and the Ink Spots. Whereas the Mills Brothers were distinguished by their flawless four-part harmonies, the Ink Spots cast the spotlight on their soloists—quivering tenor Bill Kenny and bass singer Hoppy Jones, who was best known for his mid-song recitations—in laying the foundation for the doo-wop phenomenon of the 1950s. The group started out in 1930s Indianapolis with Deek Watson, Charlie Fuqua (the uncle of Moonglows lead singer Harvey Fuqua) and Jerry Daniels, performing first as the Swingin' Gate Brothers, then as King, Jack and Jester. That name had to go, too, because there was already a group singing with bandleader Paul Whiteman called the King's Jesters, so the group's new manager, Moe Gale, came up with "Ink Spots." By the mid-1930s the group had acquired Jones, and in January 1935 they cut their first record, "Swingin' on Strings" b/w "Your Feet's Too Big." Trademark tenor Kenny replaced Daniels in 1936, and the Ink Spots did plenty of touring, both in the U.S. and abroad, while putting out 10 records on the Decca label. Yet the business continued to be a struggle for them until the 1939 release of "If I Didn't Care": that satiny, melodramatic romantic ballad introduced the world to the distinctive Ink Spots sound—the low background "oohs" and "aahs" behind Kenny's soaring solos and Jones's rumbling bass—and reached #2 on the *Billboard* charts, selling more than a million copies. Throughout World War II, the group released one Top 10 hit after another, including the standards-to-be "Maybe," "My Prayer," "When the Swallows Come Back to Capistrano," "I Don't Want to Set the World on Fire," and "Don't Get Around Much Anymore." But nothing this good lasts forever: in 1944, Watson left and tried to form his own Ink Spots, but the courts wouldn't let him (he called his group the Brown Dots instead); that same year, Jones died. Yet the group continued to record throughout the 1940s, drawing huge draws wherever they appeared. In the early 1950s, however, the Ink Spots did split up. Amazingly, the name had become so popular that instead of disappearing, Ink Spots groups began to proliferate (notwithstanding periodic lawsuits). Even into the 1990s, there were dozens of acts calling themselves the Ink Spots performing across the country.

what to buy: The number of Ink Spots compilations is almost as vast as the number of counterfeit Ink Spots groups still at work. (There is, for example, a 1994 cassette release on the Bainbridge label called *I'll Still Be Loving You* on which the group that disbanded in the 1950s performs its versions of "Three Times a Lady" and "Purple Rain"!) The original is almost always the best, and *Greatest Hits: The Original Recordings 1939–1946* ♫♫♫♫ (MCA, 1989, prod. various) captures the group in its peak form from the 1939 breakthrough of "If I Didn't Care" through the departures of Watson and Jones. Included are "I'll Never Smile Again," "We Three (My Echo, My Shadow and Me)," "I Don't Want to Set the World on Fire," and "Someone's Rocking My Dreamboat."

what to buy next: While many of the obligatory "best of" cuts are also included, the tracks are generally more diversified on *Whispering Grass* ♫♫♫ (Pearl, 1991, prod. various), adding the humorous "That Cat Is High," "Stompin' at the Savoy," "Don't Let Old Age Creep Up on You," and the original single, "Your Feet's Too Big."

what to avoid: The collection *Truck Stop Country* ♫♫ (Jewel, 1996)—you have to ask?

the rest:
I'll Never Smile Again ♫♫ (Orfeon)
Ink Spots ♫♫ (K-Tel, 1956)
Best of the Ink Spots ♫♫♫♫ (MCA, 1980)
On the Air ♫♫♫ (Sandy Hook, 1986)
Java Jive ♫♫♫ (Laserlight, 1992)
Encore of Golden Hits ♫♫♫ (Juke Box Treasures, 1994)
18 Hits ♫♫♫ (King, 1996)
Swing High, Swing Low ♫♫♫♫ (Eclipse, 1996)
Golden Memories ♫♫♫ (ITC Masters, 1997)

worth searching for: Both of pop music's greatest vocal ensembles are available for comparison and contrast on the Ella Fitzgerald album *Ella & Friends* ♫♫♫ (Decca Jazz, 1996, prod. various) as both the Ink Spots and the Mills Brothers share guest-artist honors with the First Lady of Song. Add in duet appearances by Louis Jordan and Louis Armstrong, and you get a complete crash course in black music for the first half of the 20th century.

influences:

◀◀ Cab Calloway, the Harmonizing Four, the Delta Rhythm Boys

▶▶ Louis Jordan, the Platters, the Five Royales, the Clovers, the Coasters, the Temptations, Boyz II Men, BLACKstreet

Michael Kosser

Insane Clown Posse

Formed 1992, in Detroit, MI.

Shaggy 2 Dope, vocals; Violent J, vocals.

Forget the Bible; the Insane Clown Posse knows exactly when the world will end: each of the group's albums is a joker's card, and by the time the sixth card is drawn, the world will end. "Final judgment will be passed, with all those who were evil in life suffering eternal torment," ICP's press kit says. Where, then, will that leave executives at Disney-owned Hollywood Records, who pulled the horrorcore group's fourth album from stores just hours after its release because of "inappropriate" lyrics? Instead of deeming them evil, perhaps Shaggy 2 Dope and Violent J should thank the executives behind the unprecedented action; by recalling *The Great Milenko*, they instantly turned the regionally popular act into a nationally known commodity. As of press time, the group—which favors sexually explicit, occasionally shocking lyrics and demented, demonic, clown-on-PCP voices and noises—was trying to wrangle ownership of its shelved album away from Hollywood, and several labels were standing by with contracts in hand. Even before the controversy, ICP was planning to launch a line of action figures—perhaps in homage to one of its chief influences, KISS.

what to buy: Although the album was officially recalled by Hollywood Records, many retailers refused to return their original copies of *The Great Milenko* &&& (Hollywood, 1997/Island, 1997, prod. Mike Clark). Not only is the original version a collector's item, it's also ICP's strongest and hardest-hitting album, thanks in part to guest guitarist Slash. The album was subsequently rereleased by Island, with three additional songs Hollywood had trimmed from its version.

the rest:
Carnival of Carnage && (Psychopathic, 1994)
Ringmaster && (Psychopathic, 1994)
Riddle Box &&& (Psychopathic/Zomba/Jive, 1995)

influences:
◀◀ Geto Boys, Beastie Boys, KISS, Alice Cooper
▶▶ Flatlinerz, Gravediggaz

Christina Fuoco

Intelligent Hoodlum /Tragedy

Born Percy Chapman, in Queensbridge, Brooklyn, NY.

One of the few rappers who's widely recognized by two different recording names, Intelligent Hoodlum a.k.a. Tragedy (and a.k.a. the lesser-known handle, MC Jade) is a former felon who was once considered the wild child of Marley Marl's Juice Crew. The Intelligent Hoodlum moniker captured Tragedy's style perfectly: a ruff-and-rugged lyricist who was never at a loss for thoughtful ideas and opinions.

what's available: Tragedy's last album, *Tragedy: Saga of a Hoodlum* &&& (A&M/Tuff Break, 1993, prod. Marley Marl, K-Def, others), is a solid album that's slightly overproduced. Although such songs as "Grand Groove" and "Street Life" echo Tragedy's earlier work, they didn't capture the attention of hip-hop fans.

worth searching for: The rapper's out-of-print debut, *Intelligent Hoodlum*, features the underground classic "Arrest the President."

influences:
◀◀ Lord Finesse, Kool G Rap, Masta Ace
▶▶ Dred Scott, Nas, Mobb Deep

Jazzbo

The Intruders

Formed 1960, in Philadelphia, PA. Disbanded 1975.

Phil Terry, vocals; Robert Edwards, vocals; Samuel Brown, vocals; Eugene Daughtry, vocals.

Better known as an early Gamble & Huff project than as a functioning artistic vocal force in its own right, the Intruders nonetheless enjoyed a string of successful and engaging singles during the latter half of the 1960s. With an easygoing stride and Brown's untutored lead vocals, the group found a balance between slick pop and funky grit. In their offhand interplay, members would often break down and start a dialogue between themselves in the middle of a song, predating rap by several years. Hip-hop foundations aside, the Intruders were not sharp enough to stay abreast of later Philly soul giants such as the O'Jays and the Spinners. By the time of its demise in 1975, those bands had eclipsed it to the point where its break-up went largely unnoticed.

what to buy: *Cowboys to Girls: The Best of The Intruders* &&&& (Sony Legacy, 1995, comp. Leo Sacks) collects everything you'd need to hear starting with "A Love That's Real" and the breakthrough "Cowboys to Girls," which has a fondly nostalgic air. From novelty toss-offs ("Love Is Like a Baseball Game") to more credible street corner numbers ("I'll Always Love My Mama"), it's all that remains from the band's skimpy recorded output.

influences:
◀◀ The Spinners, Sam Cooke, Otis Redding, Major Lance
▶▶ The O'Jays, Boyz II Men, New Edition, the Trammps

Allan Orksi

Isley Brothers

Formed 1957, in Cincinnati, OH.

Ronald Isley, vocals; Rudolph Isley, vocals (1957–86, 1990–present); O'Kelly Isley, vocals (1957–86, died March 31, 1986); Ernie Isley, guitar, drums (1969–84, 1996); Marvin Isley, bass (1969–84); Chris Jasper, keyboards (1969–84).

The Isley Brothers started out as a gospel group but didn't enjoy much success until—following the death of brother Vernon, who was killed in a 1955 bicycle accident—they brought gospel to the soul sound during the early 1960s (during which a sideman named Jimi Hendrix played guitar for them) and then added hard rock in the 1970s. The 1959 single "Shout," featuring their church organist, put the Isleys on the charts and remains one of the most popular party anthems of all time. Sporadic success during the 1960s, including a stint at Motown, left them bouncing from label to label until the band hit its stride in 1969 after reviving their own T-Neck label and releasing the funky "It's Your Thing." The Isleys enjoyed considerable success throughout the 1970s, particularly after younger brothers Ernie and Marvin and cousin Chris Jasper joined, adding a harder rock edge to the sound. An acrimonious split with the younger trio yielded the moderately successful Isley-Jasper-Isley project, while the older brothers soldiered on as a regular presence on the R&B charts. The group successfully sued pop star Michael Bolton for plagiarizing their song "Love Is a Wonderful Thing" for his hit of the same name. Since O'Kelly's death in 1986, the group has spotlighted Ronald with moderate success.

what to buy: Black rock music took a step forward with *3 + 3* 🎵🎵🎵🎵 (T-Neck, 1973, prod. Isley Brothers), which featured Ernie Isley's screaming electric guitar on "That Lady" and acoustic, soulful treatments of folk-rock tunes such as "Don't Let Me Be Lonely Tonight" and "Summer Breeze." The Isleys crossed the line into funk with *The Heat Is On* 🎵🎵🎵🎵 (T-Neck, 1975, prod. Isley Brothers) and its hit "Fight the Power," though they also turned down the lights and crooned the sensual "For the Love of You."

what to buy next: *The Isley Brothers Story, Vol. 1: Rockin' Soul* 🎵🎵🎵🎵 (Rhino, 1991, comp. Bill Inglot) gathers the harmonies of the Isleys' 1960s output on tunes such as "This Ol' Heart of Mine" and "Shout."

what to avoid: *In the Beginning . . .* 🎵🎵 (T-Neck, 1972, prod. Isley Brothers) is a compilation that tries to capitalize on Jimi Hendrix's short stint with the band during 1964–65. Neither Hendrix nor the Isleys had really broken into their signature styles at this point.

the rest:
Get Into Something 🎵🎵🎵 (T-Neck, 1969/Legacy, 1997)
The Brothers: Isley 🎵🎵🎵🎵 (T-Neck, 1969/Legacy, 1997)
Givin' It Back 🎵🎵🎵 (T-Neck, 1971/Legacy, 1997)
Brother, Brother, Brother 🎵🎵🎵 (T-Neck, 1972/Legacy, 1997)
Harvest for the World 🎵🎵🎵🎵 (T-Neck, 1976)
Winner Takes All 🎵🎵🎵🎵 (Epic, 1979)
Go All the Way 🎵🎵🎵🎵 (Columbia, 1980)
Between the Sheets 🎵🎵🎵🎵 (Epic, 1983)
Smooth Sailin' 🎵🎵🎵🎵 (Warner Bros., 1987)
Spend the Night 🎵🎵🎵 (Warner Bros., 1989)
The Isley Brothers Story, Vol. 2: The T-Neck Years 🎵🎵🎵🎵 (Rhino, 1991)
Greatest Hits and Rare Classics 🎵🎵🎵🎵 (Motown, 1991)
Tracks of Life 🎵🎵🎵 (Warner Bros., 1992)
The Isley Brothers Live 🎵🎵🎵 (Elektra, 1993)
Beautiful Ballads 🎵🎵🎵🎵 (Legacy, 1994)

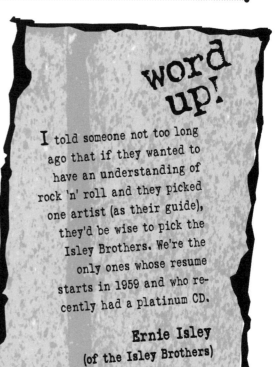

word up!

I told someone not too long ago that if they wanted to have an understanding of rock 'n' roll and they picked one artist (as their guide), they'd be wise to pick the Isley Brothers. We're the only ones whose resume starts in 1959 and who recently had a platinum CD.

Ernie Isley
(of the Isley Brothers)

Funky Family 🎵🎵🎵 (Legacy, 1995)
Mission To Please 🎵🎵🎵 (Island, 1996)

worth searching for: Get an idea of where the Beatles learned their harmony style on *Twist and Shout* 🎵🎵🎵🎵 (Sundazed, 1993, comp. Bob Irwin), which also features "Rubber Leg Twist," "Spanish Twist," and "Twistin' With Linda."

solo outings:
Isley-Jasper-Isley:
Caravan of Love 🎵🎵🎵 (Epic Associated, 1985)

Ernie Isley:
High Wire 🎵🎵🎵🎵 (Elektra, 1990)

influences:
◀◀ The Drifters, Sam Cooke, James Brown, Jimi Hendrix, Sly & the Family Stone

▶▶ Funkadelic, Bone Maxwell, Boyz II Men, Mother's Finest

Lawrence Gabriel and Gary Graff

J

Jackson 5
/The Jacksons

Formed 1964, in Gary, IN.

Jackie Jackson, vocals; Tito Jackson, guitar, vocals; Marlon Jackson, vocals; Jermaine Jackson, vocals, bass (1964–76, 1984–present); Michael Jackson, vocals (1964–85); Randy Jackson, vocals (1975–present); Janet Jackson, vocals; Maureen Jackson, vocals; and LaToya Jackson, vocals (mid-1970s).

Although the recent years of infighting and controversy have eclipsed this family group's musical output, the Jacksons remain among the most successful vocal soul-pop groups ever. Schooled (some claim brow-beaten) by father Joe Jackson, the five oldest Jackson boys became a tight, slick performing unit when they were just adolescents and teenagers, with Michael demonstrating a stylistic maturity unfathomable for his age. Signed to Motown in 1969, the group became a sensation right away—four #1 hits in a row that injected fresh energy into the label, which was suffering from the graying of some of its most popular acts. The Jackson 5 became a Saturday morning cartoon and lunch box caricatures, though the formula was tapped out by the mid-1970s. A move to Epic—after much legal wrangling and Jermaine's departure to stay with Motown and his father-in-law, Berry Gordy Jr.—gave the newly christened Jacksons a chance to modernize, which they did as Michael and Randy in particular exercised more control over the writing and production. But at the beginning of the 1980s, Michael's *Off the Wall* gave him a solo career even more successful than that of the group's, irreparably altering the chemistry of the clan and the band. The 1984 "Victory" tour was an arm-twisting last gasp in the wake of Michael's *Thriller* triumph, and the rest of the Jacksons faded into the background as Michael and Janet took off for the pop stratosphere.

what to buy: *The Ultimate Collection* ♫♫♫♫♫ (Motown, 1995, prod. various) offers a crackling overview of Motown's last great singles group; the sheer exuberance of "ABC," "The Love You Save," and "I Want You Back" are hard to argue with, as is Michael's early solo stuff like "Rockin' Robin." The 82-song box set *Soulsation! The 25th Anniversary Collection* ♫♫♫♫ (Motown Records, 1995, prod. various) goes even deeper; it even has one of *Jackie's* solo cuts!

what to buy next: *Destiny* ♫♫♫ (Epic, 1978, prod. the Jacksons) marks the brothers' first attempt at the production/songwriting helm, and they come up triumphant with ace hits such as "Blame It on the Boogie" and "Shake Your Body (Down to the Ground)." *Triumph* ♫♫♫ (Epic, 1980, prod. the Jacksons) may be even more consistent, with a new element of tense foreboding that would crop up to even better effect on Michael's *Thriller.*

what to avoid: *The Jacksons: An American Dream* ♫♫ , (Motown, 1992) an uneven live celebration of the group that adds nothing significant to the Jackson catalog.

the rest:
Diana Ross Presents the Jackson 5 ♫♫♫ (Motown, 1969/1989)
ABC ♫♫♫♫ (Motown, 1970/1989)
Third Album ♫♫♫♫ (Motown, 1970/1989)
Christmas Album ♫♫ (Motown, 1970/1986)
Maybe Tomorrow ♫♫♫ (Motown, 1971/1989)
Greatest Hits ♫♫♫♫ (Motown Records, 1971)
Skywriter ♫♫ (Motown, 1973/1990)
Anthology ♫♫♫♫ (Motown Records, 1976)
The Jacksons ♫♫♫ (Epic, 1976)
Goin' Places ♫♫♫ (Epic, 1977)
Victory ♫♫♫ (Epic, 1984)
2300 Jackson Street ♫♫♫ (Epic, 1989)
Great Songs and Performances ... ♫♫♫ (Motown, 1991)
Pre-History: The Lost Steeltown Recordings ♫♫♫ (Brunswick, 1996)

worth searching for: Led by the disco favorite title track—which approaches the vivaciousness of "ABC"—the now-deleted *Dancing Machine* ♫♫♫♫ (Motown, 1974) marks a strong finish of the Jackson's Motown era.

solo outings:
Jermaine Jackson:
Greatest Hits & Rare Classics ♫♫♫ (Motown Records, 1991)

LaToya Jackson:
You're Gonna Get Rocked ♫ (Private I, 1988)

influences:

◀◀ The Temptations, Smokey Robinson, Frankie Lymon, James Brown, Jackie Wilson

▶▶ Boyz II Men, New Edition, Jodeci

see also: *Michael Jackson, Janet Jackson*

Allan Orski and Gary Graff

Chuck Jackson

Born July 22, 1937, in Winston-Salem, SC.

Journeyman soul singer Chuck Jackson may have fared better had his fame peaked at the height of the R&B explosion of the late 1960s. He instead had the misfortune of having all his chart hits fall during the early part of the decade, missing the boat by a few years. Although he did start with a stint in the Dell Vikings and nabbed a slew of solo singles written by top-notch writing teams such as Leiber and Stoller, Goffin and King, Bacharach and Hilliard, and Ashford and Simpson, Jackson was eclipsed during the next few years by an avalanche of performers coming out of Stax, Muscle Shoals, and Motown. He quickly joined Motown himself in 1967, but was soon label jumping with only minor hits every few years. Like so many other aging soul singers, Jackson's main ticket has been a near constant touring schedule, which has kept the seats pretty well full, especially in the U.K., where he still has a loyal following.

what to buy: It may be more than you need, but *Best Of* ✍✍✍ (Tomato, 1995) is by far the most complete Jackson anthology, including his signature hit "Any Day Now (My Wild Beautiful Bird)" as well as his other charters, "I Don't Want To Cry," "I Wake Up Crying," and "I Keep Forgettin'." A plethora of lesser-known material, such as his version of "Stand By Me," is thrown in as well. For a more concise and affordable compilation, *The Very Best of Chuck Jackson 1961–1967* ✍✍✍ (Varese Vintage, 1997) has all Jackson's better-known material contained on one disc.

the rest:
Greatest R&B Hits ✍✍ (King, 1995)
Greatest Hits ✍✍ (Curb, 1996)
Golden Classics ✍✍ (Collectables, 1991)
I Don't Want to Cry/Any Day Now ✍✍✍ (Kent, 1993)

influences:
◀◀ Ben E. King, Dell Vikings, Sam Cooke
▶▶ Elvis Presley, Edwin Starr, Stevie Wonder

Allan Orski

Freddie Jackson

Born October 2, 1956, in New York, NY.

Along with Luther Vandross, Alexander O'Neal, and Peabo Bryson, Freddie Jackson was one of the new soul romeos of the 1980s. His tone was smooth and sultry, his demeanor that of a man totally engrossed in and devoted to the woman he was singing to. True, he's not quite up there (or, more appropriately, down there) with Barry White, but Jackson's expressive pipes have often bailed him out of the mediocre material that's kept him from becoming a crossover superstar. Raised in Harlem, Jackson met Nicholas Ashford and Valerie Simpson while

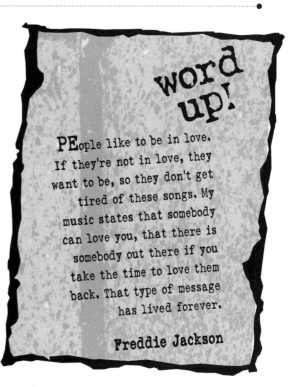

word up!

PEople like to be in love. If they're not in love, they want to be, so they don't get tired of these songs. My music states that somebody can love you, that there is somebody out there if you take the time to love them back. That type of message has lived forever.

Freddie Jackson

singing in the White Rock Baptist Church Choir. He was in the groups LJE and Mystic Merlin before singing backup for Evelyn King and Melba Moore, and it was Moore's managers who helped Jackson secure his own recording contract. Jackson started strong with *Rock Me Tonight*, which peeled off three hits—including the Top 20 title track and "You Are My Lady." After that, however, Jackson began a quick fade, and these days he seems something of an also-ran, a fine singer to whom nobody is paying quite enough attention.

what to buy: *For Old Times Sake: The Freddie Jackson Story* ✍✍✍ (EMI, 1996, prod. various) is a solid compilation that has almost all the right tracks, including his duet with Melba Moore on "A Little Bit More."

what to buy next: Even though *Rock Me Tonight* had the big hits, Jackson's sophomore effort, *Just Like the First Time* ✍✍✍ (Capitol, 1986/EMI, 1996, prod. various) is his most consistent outing. The debut's success gave him his pick of material, and he came up with aces such as "Have You Ever Loved Somebody," "Jam Tonight," and the lengthy "Tasty Love."

what to avoid: On *Private Party* ♫ (Scotti Bros., 1995, prod. various), Jackson sounds like he's floundering and trying to find a place for himself amidst the New Jacks.

the rest:
Don't Let Love Slip Away ♫♫♫ (Capitol, 1988/EMI, 1996)
Do Me Again ♫♫♫ (Capitol, 1990/EMI, 1996)
Time for Love ♫♫♫ (Capitol, 1992/EMI, 1996)
At Christmas ♫♫ (Orpheus, 1994)
The Greatest Hits of Freddie Jackson ♫♫♫♫ (Capitol/EMI, 1994)
Just Like the First Time ♫♫ (EMI, 1996)

worth searching for: *A Little Bit Moore: The Magic of Melba Moore* ♫♫♫♫ (EMI, 1997, prod. various) features Jackson's ace duet on "I Can't Complain."

influences:
◀◀ Marvin Gaye, Barry White, Luther Vandross, Jeffrey Osborne
▶▶ Maxwell, Eric Benet, D'Angelo

Gary Graff

Janet Jackson

Born Janet Damita Jackson, May 16, 1966, in Gary, IN.

Growing up the youngest daughter in the mega-successful Jackson clan, Janet stepped into the shadow of a monumental dynasty when she began performing with her brothers during the mid-1970s. Indeed, it seemed at first that this Jackson's future lay in television, as she found minor success with roles in the sitcoms "Good Times" and "Diff'rent Strokes." But family patriarch Joe Jackson had other ideas, encouraging Janet to deliver her mostly forgettable self-titled solo debut. A subsequent album produced by Time guitarist Jesse Johnson also stiffed, signaling what seemed the end of a vapid recording career. But then A&M executives got the idea to pair Janet with former Time members James "Jimmy Jam" Harris III and Terry Lewis, resulting in the singer's first blockbuster success, *Control*. Backed by her producers' cutting edge dance grooves and a series of hyperkinetic videos choreographed by Paula Abdul, Jackson became a major star. Taking the tone of her breakthrough record to heart, she jettisoned her father as manager and plowed into *Rhythm Nation 1814*—a further distillation of the percolating dance formula, with Janet, Harris, and Lewis tackling social issues. This 1989 record's suc-

cess shot her into the pop culture stratosphere occupied by stars like Madonna and her brother, Michael—allowing the singer to negotiate a new, $32-million deal with Virgin Records and to star in a 1992 movie with doomed rapper Tupac Shakur, *Poetic Justice*. The album *janet.*, the first product of Virgin's deal, also did massive business, emphasizing the singer's smoldering sexuality while trafficking in the dance pop grooves of the day. By 1996, brother Michael was asking his sister for help—musically, she joined in the duet "Scream" to get attention for his *HIStory* album, while conducting select interviews and appearances to aid him in fending off child molestation allegations.

what to buy: No record in her limited catalog matches the impact of *Control* ♫♫♫♫ (A&M, 1986, prod. Janet Jackson, James Harris III, Terry Lewis, Monte Moir), an album that virtually redefined the world of dance-oriented R&B. Fresh from work with R&B stalwarts the S.O.S. Band, Harris and Lewis were ready to re-write the rules for contemporary soul—they just needed a good-looking, videogenic singer to help them do it. From the mechanized funk of the title track to the percolating, sultry groove of "Nasty" and the sassy hit single "What Have You Done for Me Lately," the trio welds artsy, funky percussion grooves to slashing keyboard sounds and Jackson's breathy, insubstantial voice. The world of hi-tech funk would never be the same.

what to buy next: Jackson's sophomore record, *Rhythm Nation 1814* ♫♫♫♫ (A&M, 1989, prod. Janet Jackson, James Harris III, Terry Lewis, Jellybean Johnson), pushed their patented dance formula even further—nicking bits of an old Sly Stone tune for the title track's avalanche of percussive sounds. Forget about the clumsy lyrical references to ill-defined social problems such as homelessness and racism; what matters here are the grooves—from the direct, near-industrial flavor of the hit single "Miss You Much" to the rock-tinged "Black Cat" and frothy pop of "Escapade," every tune here will either make you want to hit the dance floor or the bedroom. And after all, isn't that what good dance jams are all about?

what to avoid: Jackson's pre-Harris/Lewis solo record *Dream Street* **woof!** (A&M, 1984, prod. Jesse Johnson) reeks of formulaic pandering. Bereft of memorable cuts, it came before the days when a good MTV video could make anyone a star, so even Jackson's talents as a videogenic dance diva couldn't save the day.

the rest:
janet. ♫♫♫♫ (Virgin, 1993)
Design of a Decade: 1986–1996 ♫♫♫ (A&M, 1996)
The Velvet Rope ♫♫♫♫ (Virgin, 1997)

Freddie Jackson (© Jack Vartoogian)

worth searching for: Jackson's potency as a performer can't really be judged until you see her in action—the involved choreography with a lone chair in the "Pleasure Principle" video; her army of military-style dance recruits in the "Rhythm Nation" clip; her sensuously curvy body moves in "That's the Way Love Goes." That's why she's gathered video clips from every album onto separate anthologies—there are actually two for *Control*—and it's also why fans worth their weight in 12-inch remix records will buy them.

influences:

Michael Jackson, Prince, Madonna, Diana Ross

Paula Abdul, Karyn White, Jody Watley

Eric Deggans

J.J. Jackson

Born in New York, NY.

J.J. Jackson was mostly a one-hit wonder with his 1966 R&B dance cut, "But It's Alright"—but what a hit it was. Muscular and horn-filled, with Jackson's Otis-Redding-meets-Al-Green vocals, it was a perfect party tune for the Naugahyde-filled rumpus rooms of teenage America and is still included on 1960s-era dance compilations. As with Jimi Hendrix, Jackson's greatest fame in the U.S. occurred after he crossed the ocean to England. "But It's Alright" was recorded in the U.K. with session musicians, though it sounds authentically Stax/Volt. Before scoring his own hit, Jackson arranged music for Jack McDuff and Jimmy Witherspoon, and he's credited with co-writing "Long Live Our Love" with Sidney Barnes, a 1966 hit for the Shangri-La's. He also wrote the Pretty Things' 1960s proto-punk cut "Come See Me," later recording his own version as well. Other Jackson tunes credited as hits are "I Dig Girls" and "Four Walls." In keeping with the consciousness-raising of the era, Jackson turned to more socially aware lyric-writing, but unlike his contemporaries, he never made a mark as a thought-provoking soul man, and his girth—300-plus pounds—most likely prevented him from cultivating a sex-symbol image. Eventually, Jackson became a disc jockey in Los Angeles (not, as many believe, one of the original VJs on music video channel MTV). He can, however, be seen on video—that is, if you can find a copy of the film *Car Wash,* in which he had a cameo that reportedly has been sampled by several rap artists.

Janet Jackson (© Ken Settle)

what to buy: *The Great J.J. Jackson* (Warner, 1966; reissued 1989 as *See For Miles* ♫♫♫; prod. Miki Dallon) includes "But It's Alright," "Come See Me," and "I Dig Girls." A mix of party tunes and soul-filled ballads, it's a good exhibit of Jackson's pop-soul talents.

the rest:

With the Greatest Little Soul Band ♫♫♫ (Strike, 1967)
The Greatest Little Soul Band in the Land ♫♫♫ (Congress/MCA, 1968)
J.J. Jackson's Dilemma ♫♫ (Perception, 1970)

worth searching for: *The Best of Loma Records: The Rise and Fall of a 1960s Soul Label* ♫♫♫ (Warner Bros., 1995, prod. various) contains three Jackson cuts, including "But It's Alright."

influences:

Otis Redding, Jimmy Witherspoon, Jack McDuff

Huey Lewis & the News, Tower of Power, Rick James

Lynne Margolis

Mahalia Jackson

Born 1911, in New Orleans, LA. Died January 27, 1972.

The most famous gospel singer of all time, the late Mahalia Jackson will be remembered throughout the world as inspirational music's first bonafide superstar. A dark, mountainous woman with an alto voice to match, Jackson grew up in New Orleans idolizing legendary blues singer Bessie Smith. "Bessie was my favorite, but I never let people know I listened to her," Jackson is quoted as saying in a Smith compilation album. "Her music haunted you even when she stopped singing." Though many music purists believe Jackson could have been the greatest blues singer since Smith, she opted to remain true to her spiritual roots. Moving to Chicago in 1927, Jackson served a 10-year stint as a member of the Johnson Gospel Singers. When the group disbanded in the mid-1930s, Jackson went solo, cutting her first record for the Decca label in 1937. Around this time Jackson met Thomas Dorsey, the acknowledged "Father of Gospel Music," who asked her to serve as his song demonstrator, a position she didn't accept until some nine years later. But their eventual 14-year union would help to shape and propel the gospel music tradition celebrated today. Jackson didn't record again until 1946, when she signed with the small New York–based label Apollo Records. Her recordings for Apollo brought her national attention: her third album, *Move On Up a Little Higher,* sold over a million copies. In 1954, Jackson signed a lucrative major-label deal with Columbia Records, which mounted a huge publicity campaign for its new star that included appearances on *The Ed Sullivan Show* and other major television programs as well as a cover story in *Life* magazine, unheard-of fanfare for a gospel singer at that time. One of Jackson's most memorable performances was her emotionally charged rendition of the hymn, "Soon I Will Be Done with the Troubles of the World," in the classic 1959 film *Imitation of Life*, but she also was the featured vocalist prior to Dr. Martin Luther King's immortal "I Have a Dream" speech in Washington, D.C., and sang "Take My Hand, Precious Lord" at King's funeral in 1968. As the decade of the 1960s came to a close, failing health began to take its toll on Jackson. In 1971, after flying to Europe for a scheduled tour, she returned almost immediately, gravely ill. The "Queen of Gospel" died in January, 1972.

what to buy: For gospel lovers who want all the good news delivered in one edition, *The Best of Mahalia Jackson* 🎵🎵🎵 (Columbia Legacy, 1995, comp. Nedra Olds-Neal) stands as a superb legacy to an incomparable talent. Containing all of the top hits from her Columbia recordings, the disk is a must for record collectors, fans whose LPs may be scratchy from years of playing and, most important, anyone who may be too young to have been properly introduced to the music of this legendary figure. Other highlights include guest performances by Duke Ellington and his Orchestra and live recordings of "How I Got Over" and "He's Got the Whole World in His Hands." (Note: eight of the 17 tracks were originally recorded in mono.)

what to buy next: To experience a different dimension to Jackson's gospel interpretations, pick up *Live at Newport, 1958* 🎵🎵🎵 (Columbia Legacy, 1994, prod. Cal Lampley). Nine of the 15 tracks on this must-get LP, recorded in concert at the Newport Jazz Festival, July 6, 1958, are previously unreleased (including an electrifying "When the Saints Go Marching In"), and Ellington and his orchestra are back to provide accompaniment. All the cuts have been digitally remastered, as part of the Columbia Jazz Masterpieces series.

the rest:
Apollo Years 🎵🎵 (Collectables, 1996)
Gospel at Its Best 🎵🎵🎵 (Queen, 1996)
Silent Night, Holy Night 🎵🎵🎵 (Sony Special Music Products, 1995)
Mahalia Sings Songs of Christmas! 🎵🎵🎵 (Legacy, 1995)
16 Most Requested Songs 🎵🎵🎵🎵, (Columbia, 1996)
Queen of Gospel 🎵🎵🎵 (Special Music, 1996)
The World's Greatest Gospel Singer 🎵🎵🎵🎵 (Sony Special Music Products, 1993)
The Essence of Mahalia Jackson 🎵🎵🎵 (Legacy, 1994)
I'm Going to Tell God 🎵🎵 (MCA Special Products, 1992)
Apollo Sessions 1946–1951 🎵🎵🎵🎵 (ESX Entertainment, 1994)

Apollo Sessions Volume II 🎵🎵🎵 (Pair, 1995)
Amazing Grace 🎵🎵🎵 (MCA Special Products, 1988)
Christmas with Mahalia Jackson 🎵🎵 (Special Music Company)
Mahalia Jackson: Gospels, Spirituals and Hymns 🎵🎵🎵🎵 (Legacy, 1991)
Mahalia Jackson: Volume 2 🎵🎵🎵 (Legacy, 1992)
Silent Night: Gospel Christmas with Mahalia Jackson 🎵🎵🎵 (Laserlight)
Go Tell It on the Mountain 🎵🎵🎵 (Arrival, 1993)
Mahalia Jackson's Greatest Hits 🎵🎵🎵 (Columbia, 1988)
Mahalia Jackson Sings America's Favorite Hymns 🎵🎵🎵 (Columbia, 1989)

worth searching for: To hear Jackson's personal reflections as well as her magnificent voice, find the cassette-only *I Sing Because I'm Happy* 🎵🎵🎵🎵 (Smithsonian Collection Recordings, 1995, prod. Jules Schwerin), a collection of excerpts from interviews dating back to 1952 combined with her renditions of four songs. The tape was originally released in 1992 as the audio companion to Schwerin's fine Jackson biography, *Got to Tell It.*

influences:

◀◀ Bessie Smith, Thomas Dorsey, Ma Rainey

▶▶ Clara Ward, Aretha Franklin, Dottie Peoples, Della Reese, Tramaine Hawkins

Tim A. Smith

Michael Jackson

Born Michael Joseph Jackson, August 29, 1958, in Gary IN.

While others have worked years to win worldwide fame in the music business, for superstar Michael Jackson, it must have seemed a birthright. A founding member of the Jackson 5, he was bringing his powerful contralto vocals to bear as lead singer for the group at age four. By age 10, he was touring the country with the group, opening for respected Motown acts such as Gladys Knight & the Pips and the Temptations. At age 11, he came to national attention as the Jackson 5's hit "I Want You Back" exploded onto the charts. Groomed by Motown mogul Berry Gordy Jr., Michael was encouraged to go solo in 1972, reportedly as an answer to Donny Osmond's rising popularity. His first solo record, like all of his early and mid-1970s solo efforts, veered between schmaltzy ballads aimed at the pop audience and bits of lightweight fluff aimed at the teenybopper crowd. Though Jackson found some success during these times, his work always seemed guided by older, more domineering hands and overshadowed both by his brother Jermaine's ascent as a teen idol and by his continuing work with the Jacksons (as they were re-christened in 1976, after leaving Motown). It wasn't until 1979's *Off the Wall*—co-produced by Quincy Jones, who Jackson met while filming "The Wiz"—that the singer's own creative instincts began to emerge. Fusing an unerring pop sensibility with up-to-date R&B grooves and solid songs, this record set the stage for Jackson's greatest triumph: 1982's *Thriller*. At more than 40 million records sold, *Thriller* stands as the most successful album ever, a phenomenon fed by Jackson's creative use of videos—from the dance showcase of the "Billie Jean" clip to the *West Side Story* take-off of "Beat It" and the horror movie special effects extravaganza for the title track. It made him the most popular performer on the planet, hands down.

But Jackson's tremendous success was dogged by speculation about his private life; acquiring most of the Beatles' songwriting catalog proved a good business move, but reports of severe plastic surgery, alleged use of hyperbaric oxygen chambers and, later, his insistence on being called the King of Pop portrayed him as eccentric at best, disturbed at worst. His next record, *Bad*, attempted to refute a bit of his goody-goody image with some funkier material, while still reaching out to pop audiences, with mixed results. Again, a powerful series of videos saved the day. Jettisoning Jones, Jackson enlisted the aid of hitmaking R&B producer Teddy Riley for several songs on his next album, *Dangerous*, strengthening the techno-funk strains in his work. Both records were (wrongly) considered failures for not matching the benchmark set by *Thriller*. The shine really came off Jackson's star in 1993, when a 13-year-old boy accused the star of molesting him. Pepsi-Cola canceled a decade-long endorsement deal as police raided his Los Angeles home, and the star eventually admitted an addiction to painkillers. Interest in Jackson faded to the point where his two-CD set of new and old material, *HIStory: Past, Present and Future, Book 1*—attacked for anti-Semitic lyrics in one song—fizzled in the amount of time it took to announce both his wedding and, later, divorce from Elvis Presley's daughter, Lisa Marie. Never one to admit defeat, Jackson in 1996 wed Debbie Rowe, the secretary to his longtime plastic surgeon, fathering a child born Feb. 13, 1997. Early 1997 also brought an induction into the Rock and Roll Hall of Fame with his brothers in the Jackson 5, and a collection of eight remixed tunes from *HIStory* with five new songs called *Blood on the Dance Floor: History in the Mix*—which also fizzled into a quick oblivion.

what to buy: In this case, it's a no-brainer. The most artistically satisfying record of Jackson's career also happens to be his most successful, *Thriller* ♫♫♫♫ (Epic, 1982, prod. Michael Jackson, Quincy Jones). From the simmering funk of "Billie Jean" to the rock-tinged "Beat It" (complete with guitar solo by Eddie Van Halen) and the epic title track, Jackson and Jones create a

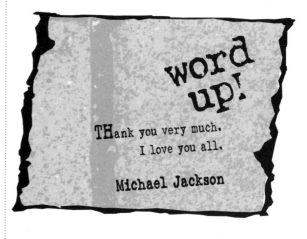

word up!

THank you very much. I love you all.

Michael Jackson

perfect fusion of commercial R&B and pop sensibilities—with the good luck to release it at a time when such naked ambition wasn't yet considered uncool.

what to buy next: As the record that first showed Jackson's promise as a solo artist, *Off the Wall* ♫♫♫ (Epic, 1979, prod. Michael Jackson, Quincy Jones) lets the singer stretch beyond his teenybopper image. "Rock with You" is a slick, sensual R&B-tinged pop package, while "Wanna Be Starting Something" seems tailor-made for the kind of adult-oriented dance clubs that wouldn't get near a Jackson 5 single. Best of all, by welding impressive, inventive production with solid songs, the pair showed hints of what a mature Michael Jackson might be capable of.

what to avoid: In a bald-faced attempt to cash in on Jackson's explosive mid-1980s success, Motown assembled a bunch of unreleased tracks from 1975 on the album *One Day in Your Life* **woof!** (Motown, 1981, prod. various), proving that sometimes, when material goes unreleased, there's a good reason why.

the rest:
Got to Be There ♫♫♫ (Motown, 1972)
Ben ♫♫♫ (Motown, 1972)
Music and Me ♫♫ (Motown, 1973)
The Best of Michael Jackson ♫♫♫ (Motown, 1975)
Anthology ♫♫♫ (Motown, 1976)
Bad ♫♫♫♫ (Epic, 1987)
Dangerous ♫♫♫♫ (Epic, 1991)
HIStory: Past, Present and Future, Book I ♫♫♫♫ (Epic, 1995)
Blood on the Dance Floor: History in the Mix ♫♫♫ (Epic, 1997)

worth searching for: Three Jackson classics don't appear on any of his solo albums: the title track of the Jackson 5 album *Dancing Machine* ✍✍✧ (Motown, 1974) which offers a peek at the sleek hit machine that would emerge on *Off the Wall*; "Heartbreak Hotel," a moody, complex gem from the Jacksons' *Triumph* ✍✍✍✍ (Epic, 1980, prod. the Jacksons); and "State of Shock" from *Victory* ✍✍✧ (Epic, 1984, prod. the Jacksons), which became an oddly danceable hit on the strength of Jackson's duet with Rolling Stones frontman Mick Jagger.

influences:

⏪ Jackie Wilson, Diana Ross, Gene Kelly, James Brown

⏩ Janet Jackson, Tevin Campbell, El DeBarge

see also: The Jackson 5

Eric Deggans

Millie Jackson

Born July 15, 1943, in Thompson, GA.

The "Queen of Extreme" is one of R&B's bawdiest and most misunderstood singers. Jackson racked up a string of gold albums during the 1970s with her raunchy missives about sex and philandering men. Her husky voice and blinding hip-grind act can threaten and seduce the very males she's lampooning, while emboldening the women in her audience who know only too well the trials and tribulations about which she sings. Yet there's more to Jackson than meets the crotch. A talented singer and songwriter, Jackson's work has been covered by Luther Vandross, and she has branched out over the years into record production, artist management, and publishing. Raised by her preacher grandfather until she ran away from home at age 14, Jackson has been the model of self-sufficiency, even when her songs often portray her as vulnerable and in need of male companionship. The teen-aged Jackson settled in New York, where she modeled for confession magazines and occasionally acted. She sang in a club on a dare and cut her first single for the MGM label in 1969. She had a minor hit in 1972 with "A Child of God (It's Hard to Believe)," the first glimpse into a woman who, like Prince, reveres both the sexual and the spiritual. A string of hits followed, and by 1974 she recorded her first conceptual album, *Caught Up*, which chronicled a love triangle. Jackson's star faded during the 1980s, despite early flirtations with rap and collaborations with Isaac Hayes (their "Royal Rappin'" is no longer in print) and Elton John. After a series of raucous gold albums, the mouthy singer (who's been known to eat bananas suggestively onstage) switched gears—to country. The one-album foray flopped and Jackson, stuck in

her sex groove, disappeared for a few years. She changed record labels, recording for a time with Jive while making a couple of stabs at legit pop stardom. But her raw, lusty nature kept clawing back—and keeping her off mainstream radio. In recent years, Jackson helped create and tour in the musical "Young Man, Older Woman," a hit on the black theater circuit from 1993–95. With her recent move to the Atlanta independent label, Ichiban, Jackson began blending her gutsy R&B/soul sound with rock and pop.

what to buy: With most of her material from the 1970s out of print and only available on import (see below), her best recordings are either too costly or too much trouble to track down. But her 1990s stuff isn't bad, either, and the move to Ichiban in 1993 didn't hurt. *Rock 'n' Soul* ✍✍✍✧ (Ichiban, 1994, prod. Brad Shapiro, Douglas Smith, Betty Wright, Millie Jackson), is the best album Tina Turner didn't make. It reteams Jackson with 1970s collaborator Shapiro, features a very Tina-like "Love Quake" (the album's first single) and a collaboration with kindred spirit Betty Wright on "Check in the Mail."

what to buy next: Jackson's late 1980s tenure on Jive is rounded up on *The Very Best of Millie Jackson* ✍✍✧ (Jive, 1994, prod. various), a somewhat uneven collection from an uneven period that includes the vivacious "Hot! Wild! Unrestricted! Crazy Love!," "Young Man, Older Woman," and a live version of "Will You Love Me Tomorrow."

what to avoid: *Young Man, Older Woman: The Cast Album* ✍✍ (Ichiban, 1993, prod. Douglas Knyght-Smith, PJaye Scott) was recorded early in the show's successful two-and-a-half-year run in theaters across the country and features dialogue from the show and appearances by cast members such as Reynaldo Rey, who plays Jackson's philandering hubbie, and daughter Keisha Jackson. But it's only adequately recorded and doesn't put across Jackson's humor or lustiness. A poor substitute for the real thing.

the rest:

An Imitation of Love ✍✍✧ (Jive, 1986)
The Tide Is Turning ✍✍ (Jive, 1988)
Back to the Shit ✍✍✧ (Jive, 1989)
Young Man, Older Woman ✍✍✧ (Jive, 1991)
It's Over!? ✍✍✧ (Ichiban, 1995)
Totally Unrestriced! The Anthology ✍✍✧ (Rhino, 1997)

worth searching for: Though mild by today's standards, Jackson's X-rated boldness was considered lewd, even shocking during the let-it-all-hang-out 1970s. But she not only changed our expectations about a woman's sexual attitudes, she made some good music, which audiences lapped up. All of those titles are out of print in the United States, but virtually all but her live album are available as imports on the SouthBound label, including *Feelin' Bitchy* ♫♫♫ (SouthBound, 1977, prod. Brad Shapiro), the conceptual *Caught Up* ♫♫♫ (SouthBound, 1974, prod. Brad Shapiro), and its successor, *Still Caught Up* ♫♫♫ (SouthBound, 1975, prod. Brad Shapiro).

influences:

◀◀ Ruth Brown, Mahalia Jackson, Etta James

▶▶ Betty Wright, Denise LaSalle, Tina Turner

Doug Pullen

Walter Jackson

Born March 19, 1938, in Pensacola, FL. Died June 20, 1983.

Walter Jackson comes from the uptown side of Chicago soul. He was influenced more by pop crooners such as Billy Eckstine, Arthur Prysock, Al Hibbler, Joe Williams, and Nat "King" Cole than by gospel-style singers, and he frequently expressed disapproval of attempts to place him in rock 'n' roll and R&B musical settings. His technical proficiency as a singer made a strong impression on everyone who ever heard or worked with him, and no less an authority than Luther Vandross has stated that Jackson was his favorite singer. Yet Jackson never quite achieved the success warranted by his prodigious vocal skills. Jackson was permanently disabled by childhood polio and performed on crutches. A fearsomely strong-willed man, however, Jackson never treated himself nor allowed himself to be treated as a handicapped person. His career began as a member of the Velvetones vocal group. In 1962, Okeh Records A&R director Carl Davis brought Jackson to the label after hearing him sing in a Detroit piano bar. Davis and Curtis Mayfield, two of the primary forces in Chicago R&B during the 1960s, co-produced Jackson's earliest recordings for Okeh, a combination of standards such as "Moonlight in Vermont" and R&B songs aimed at contemporary R&B radio, including several Mayfield compositions ("That's What Mama Said" in 1963 and "It's All Over" in 1964). This recording pattern continued through later productions for Okeh by Ted Cooper; Jackson straddled the fence between pop R&B and supper-club crooning. When the combination clicked, the results were magnificent: "Funny (Not Much)" (1964), "Speak Her Name" (1967), "It's an Uphill Climb to the Bottom" (1967), and especially "Welcome Home" (1965). The hits stopped coming after "My Ship Is Comin' In" in 1967, and Jackson recorded unsuccessfully for several labels (the lone exception

was "Anyway You Want Me" for Cotillion in 1969) before Carl Davis resurrected his career at his new Chi-Sound label in 1976. Jackson's Chi-Sound material was more pop- and mainstream-oriented than his Okeh recordings had been, and he succeeded with lushly produced covers of pop songs such as Morris Albert's "Feelings" (1976) and Peter Frampton's "Baby I Love Your Way" (1977). His last hit, two years before his death, was "Tell Me Where It Hurts" (1981).

what to buy: *The Best of Walter Jackson: Welcome Home—The Okeh Years* ♫♫♫♫ (Sony, 1996, prod. various) contains most of Jackson's hit records during his most productive period.

what to buy next: *Feelings* ♫♫♫ (Collectables, 1994, prod. various) collects Jackson's Chi-Sound recordings. Jackson would sound good singing almost anything, but much of his Chi-Sound material puts this statement to a challenging test. The Chi-Sound remakes of Jackson's Okeh recordings are worth listening to, but most fans of hard-core R&B and soul will have a hard time with the schlockier material on this CD. Those who wish to dip a toe in the water of the Chi-Sound material without the risk of drowning could try *A Celebration of Soul: The Chi-Sound Records Collection, Volume One* ♫♫♫ (Varese Sarabande, 1996, prod. various) and *A Celebration of Soul: The Chi-Sound Records Collection, Volume Two* ♫♫♫ (Varese Sarabande, 1996, prod. various). In addition to some selections by Jackson, these discs include late 1970s and early 1980s recordings by the Chi-lites featuring Eugene Record, the Dells, Gene Chandler, the Impressions, Manchild, Windy City, and Paris. *Curtis Mayfield's Chicago Soul* ♫♫♫♫ (Sony, 1995, prod. various) documents Mayfield's work as a writer and producer with Chicago artists including Jackson, the Opals, Gene Chandler, Major Lance, the Artistics, and Billy Butler & the Enchanters.

what to avoid: *Send in the Clowns* ♫ (20th Century, 1979, prod. Carl Davis) is a disappointment.

the rest:

Feeling Good ♫♫ (Chi-Sound, 1976)
I Want to Come Back as a Song ♫♫ (Chi-Sound, 1977)
Good to See You ♫♫ (United Artists, 1978)
It's Cool ♫♫♫♫ (Charly)
Walter Jackson's Greatest Hits ♫♫♫♫ (Epic, 1987)
Greatest Hits ♫♫♫♫ (Sony, 1991)

worth searching for: Jackson's three Okeh LPs comprise his output during the period of his greatest artistic and commercial success: *It's All Over* ♫♫♫♫ (Okeh, 1964, prod. Carl Davis, Curtis Mayfield); *Welcome Home* ♫♫♫♫ (Okeh, 1965, prod. Carl Davis,

Curtis Mayfield); and *Speak Her Name* 🎵🎵🎵 (Okeh, 1967, prod. Ted Cooper).

influences:

◀◀ Jerry Butler, Curtis Mayfield, Arthur Prysock, Billy Eckstine, Al Hibbler, Joe Williams, Nat "King" Cole, Dionne Warwick, Johnny Mathis

▶▶ Luther Vandross, Freddie Jackson, Jeffrey Osborne

Bill Pollak

Jade

Formed 1991, in Los Angeles, CA.

Tonya Kelly, vocals; Joi Marshall, vocals; Diana "Di" Reed, vocals.

Of the slew of R&B groups that mushroomed in the wake of the success of Boyz II Men and TLC during the early 1990s, Jade stood apart. Pieced together by producer Vassal Benford, the trio—Chicago's Kelly and Marshall and Houston-bred Reed—debuted on the soundtrack to the movie *A Class Act,* with the catchy "I Wanna Love You." But it was the street jam "Don't Walk Away" from their freshman album, *Jade to the Max,* that became the trio's biggest hit. Lurking beneath the made-for-video cuts was a capable blend of harmonic voices that drew on the group's jazz and gospel backgrounds. Its second album expounded on these harmonic sensibilities, but it failed to draw an audience. Though the group's future is still in limbo, it was recently sighted on the soundtrack of the film *The 6th Man* (Hollywood, 1997), singing "Keep on Risin'."

what to buy: *Mind Body and Song* 🎵🎵🎵 (Giant, 1994, prod. various) displays a mature, gelled Jade singing a diverse range of soul tunes. More than a show of growth, it displayed the trio's willingness to be more than birds chirping on cue for their producers.

what to buy next: *Jade to the Max* 🎵🎵🎵 (Giant, 1992, prod Vassal Benford) is prefab and filled with empty calories, but it does sport a taste of the group's more mature potential, particularly on the monogamy anthem "One Woman" and its cover of the Emotions' "Don't Ask My Neighbor."

the rest:

BET's Listening Party 🎵🎵🎵 (Giant, 1993)

influences:

◀◀ Boyz II Men, the Emotions

▶▶ SWV, Xscape

Franklin Paul

Jimmy Jam & Terry Lewis

Producing partnership began 1982, in Minneapolis, MN.

Friends since meeting at a high school youth program at the University of Minnesota, James "Jimmy Jam" Harris III and Terry Lewis have evolved into one of the most successful production teams in modern R&B, bringing a signature style to blockbuster albums by Janet Jackson, Michael Jackson, New Edition, Boyz II Men, the Human League, and many others. The pair first became musical partners in Flyte Tyme, a popular Minneapolis group that proved the only competition for a young Prince and his group, Grand Central. When Prince drafted a band to back his friend Morris Day, Jam and Lewis were recruited for the Time. Feeling stifled by Prince's insistence on recording all the music for Time records himself, the two began producing an up-and-coming R&B outfit, the S.O.S. Band, in 1983. When a snowstorm kept the two from making a scheduled gig with the Time after recording with the S.O.S. Band, they were fired from the Time—just in time to see S.O.S.'s hit "Just Be Good to Me" climb the charts. Steady work followed for R&B stars such as Gladys Knight, Cheryl Lynn, and Klymaxx, but it was Janet Jackson's 1985 album *Control* 🎵🎵🎵🎵 (A&M, 1986, prod. Janet Jackson, James Harris III, Terry Lewis, Monte Moir) that established Jam and Lewis as A-level pop producers. Fueled by their unique blend of percolating keyboards, sinewy basslines, and slamming drum tracks, *Control* rose to #1 and earned Jam and Lewis a Grammy for Producer of the Year. Work resuscitating—briefly—the careers of the Human League and trumpeter Herb Alpert followed before Jackson's 1989 record *Rhythm Nation 1814* 🎵🎵🎵 (A&M, 1989, prod. Janet Jackson, James Harris III, Terry Lewis, Jellybean Johnson), which brought five #1 R&B hits and sold even better than *Control.* During the next few years, the pair would start their own record label, Perspective Records; build a multi-million-dollar studio facility for their company, Flyte Tyme Productions; and produce superstar singer Karyn White, who Lewis married in 1990. Jackson's 1993 record with the pair, *janet.* 🎵🎵🎵 (Virgin, 1993, prod. Janet Jackson, James Harris III, Terry Lewis, Jellybean Johnson), entered the pop charts at #1, paving the way to another Grammy, a star on the Hollywood Walk of Fame, and work with Jackson's mega-superstar brother, Michael, on the siblings' 1995 duet "Scream."

Eric Deggans

Elmore James

Born Elmore Brooks, January 27, 1918, in Richland, MS. Died May 24, 1963.

In Elmore James's raunchy voice and buzzing electric slide-guitar riffs, you can hear the Chicago blues dissolving into early rock 'n' roll. Best known for "Dust My Broom" (which he borrowed from Robert Johnson and souped up), "Shake Your Money Maker," and "Madison Blues," James's licks became as much part of blues and rock standard practice as Bo Diddley's beat and Chuck Berry's lyrics. James, who, like Muddy Waters, was born in Mississippi and moved to Chicago to make his name, built his entire career on the electric boogie riff that pulses through his best hits. He also had the Broomdusters, the smokingest band this side of Waters's legendary combo in the early 1950s. He influenced generations of bluesmen and rockers, from B.B. King and Jimmy Reed to the Rolling Stones, Jimi Hendrix, George Thorogood, Stevie Ray Vaughan, and every band that picked up guitars and cranked up the amp volume.

what to buy: James recorded so many sessions with so many different record labels—he put out countless versions of "Dust My Broom," for example—that until 1992 it was tough to compile a definitive collection. _The Sky Is Crying: The History of Elmore James_ ↙↙↙↙ (Rhino, 1993, prod. Robert Palmer, James Austin) solved that problem, collecting the best versions of "Dust My Broom," "The Sky Is Crying," "Shake Your Moneymaker," and the explosive "Rollin' and Tumblin'." Song completists will probably want _The Complete Elmore James Story_ ↙↙↙↙ (Capricorn/Warner Bros., 1992, prod. various), which has many more songs but starts to drown you with slide after a while.

what to buy next: _The Complete Fire and Enjoy Sessions, Parts 1–4_ ↙↙↙↙ (Collectables, 1989, prod. Bobby Robinson) are overwhelming but establish James as a crucial guitar pioneer whose wailing slide was as powerful as Howlin' Wolf, the Rolling Stones, or anybody who has dabbled in the blues. _Street Talkin'_ ↙↙↙↙ (1975/Muse, 1988) also features bluesman Eddie Taylor.

what to avoid: Some of the early compilations—_Anthology of the Blues: Legend of Elmore James_ ↙↙↙ (Kent, 1976), _Anthology of the Blues: Resurrection of Elmore James_ ↙↙↙ (Kent, 1976), _Red Hot Blues_ ↙↙ (Quicksilver, 1982), _The Classic Early Recordings, 1951–1956_ ↙↙↙ (Atomic Beat, 1994)—are solid, but have been trumped by the superior Rhino and Capricorn collections, so they're for blues completists and James aficionados only.

the rest:
Blues Masters, vol. 1 ↙↙ (Blues Horizon, 1966)
Tough ↙↙ (Blues Horizon, 1970)
The Sky Is Crying ↙↙ (Sphere Sound, 1971)
I Need You ↙↙ (Sphere Sound, 1971)

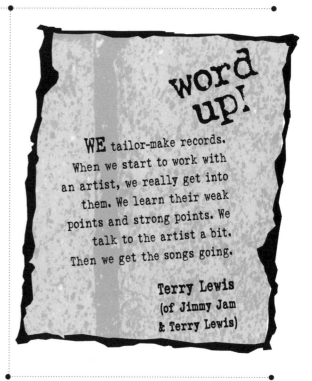

word up!

WE tailor-make records. When we start to work with an artist, we really get into them. We learn their weak points and strong points. We talk to the artist a bit. Then we get the songs going.

Terry Lewis
(of Jimmy Jam & Terry Lewis)

worth searching for: _Whose Muddy Shoes_ ↙↙↙↙ (1969; Chess/MCA, 1991) contains songs by James and the obscure-but-great Chicago bluesman John Brim.

influences:

◄◄ Robert Johnson, Sonny Boy Williamson, Muddy Waters, Robert Nighthawk

►► The Rolling Stones, B.B. King, Jimi Hendrix, Stevie Ray Vaughan, George Thorogood, the Allman Brothers, Johnny Winter

Steve Knopper

Etta James

Born Jamesetta Hawkins, January 25, 1938, in Los Angeles, CA.

Is it heresy to suggest that it is Etta James—not schmaltzy, Vegasified Aretha Franklin—who rules as Queen of Soul these days? Not only does she come from the lineage—from her days as a 1950s R&B teen queen through her time as a 1960s soul shouter—but James has matured into one of the grand dames of R&B. She always sang with a great, intense passion, but the

years only seem to have added depth of character and subtle, rich color and emotion. Her first record was a simple answer to a popular Hank Ballard record, "Roll with Me Henry," that landed James on the road in 1954, where she has stayed for the rest of her life. She made one of the great gospel soul records, "Something's Got a Hold on Me," in 1961, and by 1967 she could be found putting the fiery lead vocals on one of the landmarks of Southern soul, "Tell Mama." By 1994, she could assay material some thought indelibly linked with Billie Holiday for *Mystery Lady*, an album that was at once a tribute to her earliest source of inspiration and a personal liberation. Through her own relentless determination and stubborn artistic strength, Etta James steered her own course through the rapid waters of the music's ever-changing path, relying always on instincts and bald-faced honesty. And the years have apparently only strengthened her resolve.

what to buy: A double-disc retrospective of her 1960–74 tenure at Chicago's Chess Records, *The Essential Etta James* 𝄞𝄞𝄞𝄞 (Chess/MCA, 1993, prod. various) collects the backbone of her illustrious career.

what to buy next: *Mystery Lady* 𝄞𝄞𝄞𝄞𝄞 (Private, 1994, prod. J. Snyder) is a leap from her vernacular soul and blues into a realm of pure personal expression. With jazz pianist Cedar Walton at the bandstand, the resulting work defies easy categorization and gives James a platform to just be herself in a stunning triumph that finally earned her a Grammy award.

what to avoid: Even her most paltry recent effort, *Stickin' to My Guns* 𝄞𝄞 (Island, 1990), a largely unsuccessful attempt to incorporate rap and hip-hop into a more traditional R&B context, is more of an aberration than an artistic misstep.

the rest:
The Second Time Around 𝄞𝄞𝄞𝄞 (Chess, 1961)
Tell Mama 𝄞𝄞𝄞𝄞 (Chess, 1968)
Come a Little Closer 𝄞𝄞 (Chess, 1974)
Deep in the Night 𝄞𝄞𝄞 (Bullseye Blues, 1978)
(With Eddie "Cleanhead" Vinson) *Blues in the Night* 𝄞𝄞 (Fantasy, 1986)
R&B Dynamite 𝄞𝄞𝄞𝄞 (Flair, 1986)
(With Eddie "Cleanhead" Vinson) *The Late Show* 𝄞𝄞 (Fantasy, 1987)
Seven Year Itch 𝄞𝄞𝄞 (Island, 1989)
The Right Time 𝄞𝄞𝄞𝄞 (Elektra, 1992)
How Strong Is a Woman: The Island Sessions 𝄞𝄞𝄞 (Polydor, 1993)
These Foolish Things: The Classic Balladry of Etta James 𝄞𝄞𝄞 (MCA, 1995)

Etta James (© Ken Settle)

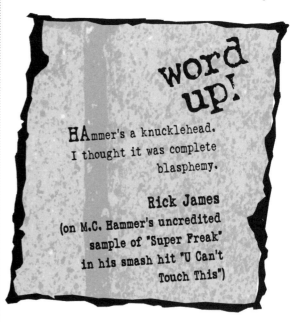

word up!

HAmmer's a knucklehead. I thought it was complete blasphemy.

Rick James
(on M.C. Hammer's uncredited sample of "Super Freak" in his smash hit "U Can't Touch This")

Live in San Francisco 𝄞𝄞𝄞 (On the Spot, 1994)
Time after Time 𝄞𝄞 (Private, 1994)
Her Best 𝄞𝄞𝄞𝄞 (MCA/Chess 1997)
Love's Been Rough on Me 𝄞𝄞𝄞 (Private, 1997)

worth searching for: *Etta James Rocks the House* 𝄞𝄞𝄞𝄞 (Chess, 1964) is an early album that more than lives up to its title.

influences:

◀◀ Billie Holiday, Hank Ballard, Big Mama Thornton, Bessie Smith

▶▶ Tina Turner, Janis Joplin

Joel Selvin

Rick James
Born James Johnson Jr., February 1, 1948, in Buffalo, NY.

After a decade of trying to make it—including a period in Toronto, Canada with roommate Neil Young in the Mynah Birds, which recorded unreleased material for Motown in 1968—James cracked through in 1977 when he formed the Stone City Band (featuring the Mary Jane Girls) and signed with Motown. With his "funk 'n' roll" sound patterned after Funkadelic, James traded in a raunchy rock that delighted in easy pre-AIDS era sex and drug use. By 1981, he was at the top of the charts with such naughty novelties as "Super Freak" and "Give It to Me Baby." He also produced the hit 1983 LP for his sexy back-up singers, the Mary Jane Girls. James managed to keep his hand in things during the 1980s, producing Eddie Murphy's hit "Party All the Time" in 1985. His influence was clear when M.C. Hammer grabbed James's "Super Freak" bass riff for his own smash, "U Can't Touch This." James, however, has been on ice since 1991, when drug addictions led to him being jailed on assault charges. He was released in 1996 and resumed touring and recording the following year.

what to buy: The super freaky *Street Songs* ♫♫♫♫ (Motown, 1981, prod. Rick James) revels in the hedonism of the times with a self-satisfied smirk. In addition to the big hits, "Ghetto Life" and "Below the Funk" are top-flight songs that convey realistic ghetto scenes. James's debut, *Come Get It* ♫♫♫♫ (Motown, 1978, prod. Rick James), brought tracks such as "You and I" and "Mary Jane" that competed with Parliament-Funkadelic for the R&B limelight.

what to buy next: *The Flag* ♫♫♫ (Motown, 1986, prod. Rick James) doesn't have the fine-honed street sense of his earlier work, but the hard-driving funk grooves are intact. *The Ultimate Collection* ♫♫♫ (Motown, 1997, comp. Amy Herot) is a good primer for the uninitiated.

what to avoid: *Throwin' Down* ♫♫ (Motown, 1982, prod. Rick James) seems lyrically uninspired next to *Street Songs*, though the grooves are strong—if a bit redundant.

the rest:
Cold Blooded ♫♫♫ (Motown, 1983)
Reflections ♫♫♫♫ (Motown, 1984)
Bustin' Out! The Very Best of Rick James ♫♫♫♫ (Motown, 1994)
Motown Legends: Give It to Me Baby—Cold Blooded ♫♫♫ (ESX, 1994)
Urban Rhapsody ♫♫♫ (Private I/Mercury, 1997)

worth searching for: *Bustin' Out of L7* ♫♫♫♫ (Motown, 1979, prod. Rick James) showed James on the way to *Street Songs* and had its own hits in "Bustin' Out" and "High on Your Love Suite."

solo outings:
Mary Jane Girls:
Only Four You ♫♫♫♫ (Motown, 1985)

influences:
◀◀ Parliament-Funkadelic, James Brown, Sly & the Family Stone

▶▶ Prince, 2 Live Crew, Jodeci

Lawrence Gabriel

Jamiroquai

Formed 1989, in London, England.

Jason Kay, vocals; Toby Smith, keyboards; Stuart Zender, bass; Derrick McKenzie, drums; Simon Katz, guitar; Wallis Buchanan, digeridoo.

Jason Kay, leader of Jamiroquai, does not normally inspire high regard from the music press. He is persistently written off as a white guy playing black music, a hapless Stevie Wonder clone, and the walking embodiment of the simple-minded, New Age hippie. It didn't help that his outfit's first two albums—1993's *Emergency on Planet Earth* and 1994's *The Return of the Space Cowboy*—were centered around such pedestrian themes as rain forests, romance, and The Man. But the criticism only helped the Brit streamline his craft. Jamiroquai's third disc, *Traveling without Moving,* finally broke the band in America.

what to buy: Jamiroquai's second album, *The Return of the Space Cowboy* ♫♫♫♫ (Columbia, 1994, prod. Jason Kay), shows the band's primary strengths. Funky to the hilt and unbearably bodacious, it is an absolute stormer. It maintains the momentum set out by the band's energetic debut, all the while charting a new course for the group with the sweet, soaring chorus of "Stillness in Time," the liquid bassline of "Half the Man" and the assured soul bite of "Light Years." Its predecessor, *Emergency on Planet Earth* ♫♫♫♫ (Columbia, 1993, prod. Jason Kay), is a lush groove-laden affair, packed with momentous melodies and miles of soul-wrenching crooning. Even though critics were quick to chastise the band, it is hard to discredit the sheer disco sunshine of songs like "When You Gonna Learn" and "Too Young to Die," or an album that invokes Earth, Wind & Fire, Roy Ayers, and Marvin Gaye's finest moments.

what to buy next: With *Traveling without Moving* ♫♫♫♫ (Work, 1997, prod. Jason Kay), Kay has abridged the wide-eyed politics, tightened-up the band's nervous musical inertia, and matured with grace. He still upholds the lustrous funk of the 1970s, pumping up the album with elaborate and infectious tunes that incorporate elements of straight soul, modern funk, and electro, as well as lyrics that deal with more intricate subject matter than previous efforts.

influences:
◀◀ Stevie Wonder, Earth, Wind & Fire, Blackbyrds, Roy Ayers

Aidin Vaziri

Al Jarreau

Born April 12, 1940, in Milwaukee, WI.

During the mid-to-late 1960s, Al Jarreau was a rehabilitation counselor by day (with a master's degree in psychology) and the ultimate professional amateur singer (parties, open mike nights, weddings, talent shows) by night. He even managed to cut a few local LPs of pop tunes and jazz standards that, while ordinary, have since become collector's items. As the decade waned, Jarreau expanded his night moves beyond the hometown crowd and developed into quite a songwriter. Moving to San Francisco, the budding vocalist barnstormed the left coast, eventually hooking up with master agent Patrick Rains. Soon, Warner Bros. and Tommy LiPuma came a-callin', the result being his 1975 debut *We Got By*. A stunning jazzy/folk compendium of self-penned tunes of love, melancholy, and life, *We Got By* was a showcase for Jarreau's fully matured channeling of Johnny Mathis, Tony Bennett, and Jon Hendricks that was, for that time, unique for an African American male. Immediately placed on tour with Dionne Warwick, Jarreau became The Man with urban audiences as well as the new flavor on the radio. His preeminence was solidified with 1976's *Glow* (it won a German Grammy) and *Look to the Rainbow*, the live document of his 1977 European tour. His next release, *All Fly Home* in 1978, found Jarreau in a pop crossover mode (his true colors). The next two releases, *This Time* and *Breakin' Away* (1980 and 1981, respectively) went gold and platinum, but they also lost his soul. Now a perennial Grammy nominee and winner, Jarreau managed to win and lose simultaneously. Still recording today, Jarreau is just a brand name, a footnote, when he coulda been a contendah. *C'est la Vie.*

what to buy: *We Got By* ♪♪♪♪♪ (Warner Bros., 1975, prod. Al Schmitt) is a great album and a bittersweet epitaph for a legend that should have been. Not enough vocalists have been able to write and sing the hell out of classics like "Sweet Potato Pie," "Susan's Song," and the title track. *Look to the Rainbow* ♪♪♪♪♪ (Warner Bros., 1977, prod. Al Schmitt, Tommy LiPuma) is the only live evidence of Jarreau's mishandled gifts. Backed by all-stars such as Tom Canning (keyboards), Joe Correro (drums), Abraham Laboriel (bass), and Lynn Blessing (vibes), Jarreau kills, especially on a twisting "Take Five," "Rainbow in Your Eyes," and his own "Burst in with the Dawn" and "You Don't See Me."

what to buy next: *Breakin' Away* ♪♪♪♪ (Warner Bros., 1981, prod. Tommy LiPuma) is pretty much sweet urban pop with a dollop of jazz ("Blue Rondo A La Turk"). This is the best example of the tracks of his tears, and the last time you may care about him.

what to avoid: *Jarreau* ♪♪ (Warner Bros., 1983, prod. Jay Graydon) takes an unfortunate cue from *Breakin' Away* and further

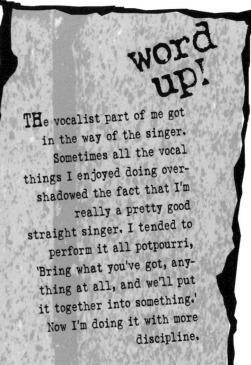

word up!

THe vocalist part of me got in the way of the singer. Sometimes all the vocal things I enjoyed doing overshadowed the fact that I'm really a pretty good straight singer. I tended to perform it all potpourri, 'Bring what you've got, anything at all, and we'll put it together into something.' Now I'm doing it with more discipline.

Al Jarreau

dilutes Jarreau's sound to appeal to the mainstream pop crowd. A waste of tremendous vocal talent.

the rest:
Glow ♪♪♪♪ (Warner Bros., 1976)
All Fly Home ♪♪♪♪ (Warner Bros., 1978)
This Time ♪♪♪ (Warner Bros., 1980)
High Crime ♪♪♪ (Warner Bros., 1984)
Live in London ♪♪♪ (Warner Bros., 1984)
L is for Lover ♪♪ (Warner Bros., 1986)
Heart's Horizon ♪♪♪ (Warner Bros., 1988)
1965 ♪♪♪ (Bainbridge, 1990)
Heaven and Earth ♪♪♪ (Reprise, 1992)
Ain't No Sunshine ♪♪♪♪ (Warner Bros., 1992/Starportrait 11, 1996)
Tenderness ♪♪♪ (Reprise, 1994)
The Best of Al Jarreau ♪♪♪ (Warner Bros., 1996)
Lean on Me ♪♪♪ (ITC, 1997)

worth searching for: Jarreau is a relaxed and welcome guest on Inner Voices' *Christmas Harmony* 𝄞𝄞𝄞 (Rhino, 1990).

influences:

◀◀ Jon Hendrix, Johnny Mathis, Nat King Cole, Bill Withers

▶▶ Bobby McFerrin, Kurt Elling, Joni Mitchell

Tom Terrell and Gary Graff

Miles Jaye
See: Village People

Jay-Z
Born Shawn Cartee.

Leave it to a Brooklynite to embody the finest traditions of smooth flow and engaging braggadocio. If that's what you're looking for, Jay-Z's the man, constantly telling you how great a rapper he is and backing it up with a steady delivery. Surprisingly, the rapper keeps you convinced for 55 minutes on an album whose criminalistic, materialistic, and hedonistic themes only could sound unique to someone who hasn't heard rap in the past decade. Suffice it to say, the self-styled Big Willie doesn't have much when it comes to lyrical originality.

what's available: *Reasonable Doubt* 𝄞𝄞𝄞 (Roc-A-Fella, 1996, prod. Clark Kent, DJ Premier, others) is an impressive debut that doesn't burn too fast or lag too slow. Released on Jay-Z's own label, the album is a solid mix of mid-tempo cuts, sleek production, and complementary crooning from female vocalists (Mary J. Blige on "Can't Knock the Hustle," jazz-hop singer Mecca on "Feelin' It"). The ultimate pairing, however, comes on "Ain't No Nigga," an anthem for adultery and scheming in the same vein as Naughty by Nature's "O.P.P." While sure to enrage the likes of C. DeLores Tucker, this standout cut insightfully narrates a dysfunctional '90s relationship in which a woman praises a lover who sleeps around, but "gives me a lot." Jay-Z and sex-charged microphonemate Foxy Brown play off one another's strengths, each threatening to steal the show. Similar friendly competition runs deep on "Brooklyn's Finest," featuring the late Notorious B.I.G. ("Jay-Z and Biggie Smalls/Make ya shit ya drawers"). *In My Lifetime* N/A (Rock-A-Fella/Def Jam, 1997) is Jay-Z's second album.

influences:

◀◀ LL Cool J, Nas, Notorious B.I.G.

Corey Takahashi

Al Jarreau (© Jack Vartoogian)

Jazzmatazz
See: Gang Starr

Blind Lemon Jefferson
Born reportedly as Lemon Jefferson, July 11, 1897, in Couchman, TX. Died December 1929, in Chicago, IL.

Blind Lemon Jefferson roamed thousands of miles and packed 100 recordings into his abbreviated 32 years, enough to establish himself as the first great male blues star of the 1920s and a man whose success set the standard for generations who followed. Corpulent, blinking out at the world through wire-rimmed spectacles, Jefferson's unmistakable keening voice and odd, stop/start strumming reportedly sold thousands of copies of Paramount 78s. The record company issued 43 records, rare for a blues artist of that time. Jefferson was such an admired figure among his peers that blues titans like Leadbelly and T-Bone Walker talked reverently about leading Jefferson around Dallas for street performances. Titles and stanzas from his songs have found their way into the blues lexicon for decades. Among the most familiar: "That Black Snake Moan"; "Matchbox Blues" (later a standard for Albert King and Carl Perkins); "Easy Rider Blues"; and the solemn "See That My Grave Is Kept Clean" (adapted by Bob Dylan). Little is known about Jefferson's early years; he seemed to have appeared out of nowhere, a fully-formed bluesman, on the streets of Dallas. Described by other musicians as an independent sort who equipped himself with both a cane and a gun, Jefferson could reportedly identify paper bills by feeling them in his hands. Brought to Paramount's attention by a Dallas retailer in 1925, Jefferson was an overnight success. Paramount treated him the way big labels now pamper gangster rappers, buying him a new Ford equipped with a chauffeur. Jefferson had the repertoire to back up their confidence in him, able to trot out Texas specialties like "Mean Jumper Blues" or cover Leroy Carr's "How Long How Long." Commuting between Dallas and Chicago, where he recorded, Jefferson apparently found work as a porter during lean times. He was in Chicago for the harsh winter of 1929, dying under mysterious circumstances in the middle of a snowstorm. Some accounts maintain he froze to death; others insist he collapsed of a heart attack in his car and was abandoned there by his chauffeur. However he died, Jefferson left a motherlode of recordings and some of the most influential songs ever recorded.

what to buy: The four discs of *Blind Lemon Jefferson: Complete Works 1926–1929* 𝄞𝄞𝄞𝄞 (Document, 1991, produced by Johnny Parth) contain all of Jefferson's known efforts. Most are surprisingly clear-sounding, considering the fact that most Paramount

78s tended to scratch and wear out quickly. It is hard to choose a favorite among the four, but the third disc, which covers 1928, has better sound than the earlier volumes and a wide variety of fine performances, including "Grave." *Blind Lemon Jefferson* 🎵🎵🎵🎵 (Milestone, 1992, prod. Orrin Keepnews) is the best single-disc representation of Jefferson's work, ranging from 1926 to 1929 and including "Black Snake Moan," "Matchbox Blues," and 23 other cuts. The sound is as good as early-1990s technology can provide.

what to avoid: *Penitentiary Blues* 🎵🎵 (Collectables, 1994) offers stingy sampling of Jefferson with mushy sound and haphazard notes. An afterthought.

the rest:
King of the Country Blues 🎵🎵🎵🎵 (Yazoo, 1990)

influences:
⏪ Mamie Smith, Bessie Smith

⏩ T-Bone Walker, Lightnin' Hopkins, Albert King, B.B. King, Carl Perkins, Bob Dylan

Steve Braun

Garland Jeffreys

Born mid-1940s, in Brooklyn, NY.

Though critically acclaimed, singer-songwriter Jeffreys never seemed to catch on with the masses with the exception of the single "Wild in the Streets" in 1977. By and large, Jeffreys's low-key rock and thematic tour of the life's downside didn't work in the disco and funk-crazed 1970s. He first appeared on the New York music scene during the mid-1960s, where he palled around with Lou Reed and Eric Burdon. He later assembled the band Grinder's Switch, which recorded an eponymous LP in 1969. Jeffreys went solo in 1970 and recorded several albums through the early 1980s, picking up a reggae influence along the way. Most of his albums are obscure or out of print.

what to buy: *Matador and More* 🎵🎵🎵🎵 (A&M, 1992, prod. David Spinozza) features a few of his songs that did get notice. The single "Matador," with its gospel reggae feel, was a hit across Europe.

worth searching for: His best album, *Escape Artist* 🎵🎵🎵🎵 (Epic, 1981, prod. Garland Jeffreys, Bob Clearmountain) rides on several tales of twisted love and includes one of Jeffreys's rare cover efforts with "96 Tears."

influences:
⏪ ? and the Mysterians, Van Morrison, Sam Cooke, Wilson Pickett, Levi Stubbs (the Four Tops), Arthur Lee (Love), Meat Loaf

⏩ Terence Trent D'Arby, Ben Harper, Dave Matthews Band

Lawrence Gabriel

Jeru the Damaja

Born Kendrick Jeru Davis, in Brooklyn, NY.

Jeru's deep, dexterous flow over a Charles Mingus bassline on Gang Starr's "I'm the Man" made an indelible imprint on the minds of underground hip-hop heads. So when his cutting, dungeon-esque DJ Premier–produced "Come Clean" was released on the first *Ill Kids* collection released by Gang Starr's Guru, it became more than just a hit record; it (eventually) blew up into one of hip-hop's last true classics. Since he came clean, Jeru has commandeered a nouveau consciousness in music, championing the causes of intelligence, spirituality, and dignity in hip-hop. Jeru, however, hasn't been absent from controversy, scuffling with journalists and engaging in lyrical battles with the Fugees. Still, the self-styled guardian of hip-hop remains one of the few MCs who, once on the microphone, actually has something to say.

what to buy: Released a year after "Come Clean" hit the underground, Jeru's debut album, *The Sun Rises in the East* 🎵🎵🎵🎵 (Payday/ffrr, 1994, prod. DJ Premier) rose above the hip-hop heap not only on the strength of its ideas and rhymes, but also with the help of DJ Premier's beat creation. (Considered to be at his creative pinnacle, Premier actually outdid himself on the closing track "Static" by rocking a loop out of the revolving static found at the end of a record.) Lyrically, Jeru created such hip-hop mainstays as "Mind Spray" and "Can't Stop the Prophet," a superhero battle between Jeru and personified villains like Jealousy and Ignorance.

what to buy next: *The Wrath of the Math* 🎵🎵🎵 (Payday/ffrr, 1996, prod. DJ Premier) is a creative letdown, as the majority of the songs are either "sequels" or tracks that were previously on compilations ("Frustrated Nigga," "Invasion"). Many of the songs aren't too compelling, but those that do work do so tremendously: in "Black Cowboy," Jeru engages in some verbal sparring with a few other rappers, and in "One Day," he rescues hip-hop from those who have kidnapped it. Jeru also denounces rappers he thinks are superficial and materialistic on "Ya Playin' Ya Self" as Premier cleverly flips the bassline and cowbell used in Junior M.A.F.I.A.'s "Player's Anthem," leaving no room to guess exactly who is being indicted.

worth searching for: Originally assembled for the soundtrack to Spike Lee's *Crooklyn,* the all-star Crooklyn Dodgers trio returned with an all-new lineup for Lee's *Clockers*. The resultant song, "Return of the Crooklyn Dodgers" (MCA, 1995), features one of Jeru's most poignant verses, along with the resurrection of Chubb Rock and a contribution from the always rock-steady OC.

influences:

◀◀ Gang Starr, KRS-One

Jazzbo

The Jets

Formed early 1980s, in Minneapolis, MN.

Leroy Wolfgramm; Eddie Wolfgramm; Eugene Wolfgramm; Haini Wolfgramm; Rudy Wolfgramm; Kathi Wolfgramm; Elizabeth Wolfgramm; Moana Wolfgramm.

The epitome of 1980s cheese pop, The Jets—children of Tongese emigres—landed a string of hits throughout the 1980s. All of the Jets' albums are out of print now, but fans who look hard enough may be able to find them in record stores' $1.99 bins.

worth searching for: The best bet is to find *The Best of the Jets* ♫♫ (MCA, 1990, prod. various), which includes the hits "Crush on You" and "Make It Real."

influences:

◀◀ The Jackson 5, the Osmond Brothers, the DeFranco Family

▶▶ The Boys, Hanson, the Backstreet Boys

Christina Fuoco

J.J. Fad

Formed 1987 in Los Angeles, CA.

MC J.B., vocals; Juanita Lee, vocals; Fatima Shaheed, vocals; Baby-D, vocals; Lady Anna, DJ.

What was "J.J. Fad," anyway? To quote the group's famous "Supersonic" single: the "J" was for Juana; the other for Juanita. "F" was for Fatima. And the "D" was for Dania. On the turntables was Lady Anna; mixing and scratching she was a sho'nuff jammah. And so on. Of course, there's a more concise J.J. Fad meaning: Just Jammin' Fresh and Def. With its incessant N.W.A./"Something 2 Dance 2" beat and raindrop sample, they, indeed, jammed fresh and def on their gold hit, "Supersonic," melding HiNRG and rap to make a point about "nosey people." After the subsequent "Way Out" (and "Anotha Hoe," on which the group disses Salt-N-Pepa, the Real Roxanne, Rox-

anne Shante, and Sparky D hard—with nursery rhymes, no less!), the Fad faded away.

what to buy: The only available J.J. Fad recording is *Supersonic* ♫♫♫ (Atco, 1988, prod. Dr. Dre, others), which is just about all you need, anyway, since it features the hit title track. A better bet, however, may be *Queens of Rap* ♫♫♫♫ (Priority, 1989, prod. various), a compilation that features "Supersonic," plus entries from the sisterly likes of MC Lyte ("10% Dis"), Real Roxanne ("Respect"), Big Lady K ("Don't Get Me Started"), Salt-N-Pepa ("Shake Your Thang"), and Roxanne Shante ("Have a Nice Day"). Go, girls.

worth searching for: Besides the hit itself, the "Supersonic" 12-inch (Dream Team, 1988) contains two versions of "Anotha Hoe," plus a picture of the group's members striking a classic rap pose in Lotto sweats.

influences:

◀◀ N.W.A., World Class Wreckin' Cru, Salt-N-Pepa, Roxanne Shante, Cheryl the Pearl

▶▶ L'Trimm, Spice Girls,

Todd Inoue

Jodeci

Formed 1991, in Charlotte, NC.

Joel "Jo-Jo" Hailey; Cedric "K-Ci" Hailey; Dalvin "Mr. Dalvin" DeGrate; Donald "DeVante Swing" DeGrate.

With the soulful ballad "Cherish" off their debut album, *Forever My Lady*, Jodeci—a savagely sexy quartet consisting of two sets of brothers, Jo Jo and K-Ci Hailey and Devante and Mr. Dalvin, who combined their first names for the group's title—burst into the pop music spotlight with an upstart bad-boy brazenness that soon became their trademark. While "Cherish" opened the door, "Come and Talk to Me," their first "official" airplay single, was the song that welcomed them in the house. "Come" stayed at #1 on the national R&B charts for 30 weeks and #11 on the pop charts for 28, propelling the group into the ranks of New Jack superstars. The sound that was uniquely Jodeci blended the powerhouse vocal sensuality of Jo Jo and K-Ci, calling to mind the animal magnetism of Gaye or Pendergrass, with the heady musical panorama of hip-hop, R&B, funk, pop, and sex by resident songsmith Devante. That inherent passion and energy was noticeably lacking by the 1995 release of their third LP, the life-on-tour concept album *The Show, the After Party, the Hotel*, possibly due to the group's abundant side projects. Along with opening two separate production companies, Jo-Jo and K-Ci (both alone and together) spent time contributing their much sought-after vocals to several movie soundtracks as well as duets with such artists as the late Tupac Shakur and K-Ci's girlfriend, Mary J. Blige. Meanwhile, DeVante and Mr. Dalvin turned to developing untapped new talent. In 1997, Jodeci decided to make those hobbies their primary focus: though the group has not officially separated, they have drifted apart on friendly terms. The Hailey brothers released a duet LP in 1997, *Love Always*, dominated by surprisingly mature lyrics and odes to romance and monogamy. Maybe they've started to grow up.

what to buy: The first Jodeci album, *Forever My Lady* ♪♪♪♪ (MCA, 1991, prod. Donald DeGrate, Al B. Sure), is also the best. This is hip-hop soul to the fullest, highlighted by the transcendent jams "Cherish," "Come and Talk to Me," "Play Thang," and the title track. No (obvious) gimmicks, no ego-indulged flights of fancy, and no mess—just great R&B.

what to buy next: Jodeci strayed from their successful formula on their sophomore effort, *Diary of a Mad Band* ♪♪♪ (Uptown/MCA, 1993, prod. Donald DeGrate), experimenting with an LP top-heavy in funk, but didn't change so much as to lose any fans. *Diary*, in fact, outsold *Forever My Lady*, though it was not a better album. Dripping with the newly-inflated egos the group carries throughout the tracks, original songs like "Ride and Slide" emphasized the foursome's darker side of soul. The album's redeeming grace is their remake of the Stevie Wonder classic "Lately," which reaffirmed their standing as new kings of the group ballad: "Lately" soared to #1 and stayed there for months, becoming so popular that Jodeci released a live studio version and two videos of the song.

the rest:
The Show, the After Party, the Hotel ♪♪♪ (Uptown/MCA, 1996)

solo outings:
Jo-Jo & K-Ci:
Love Always ♪♪♪ (MCA, 1997)

influences:
◄◄ Marvin Gaye, the Jackson 5, Teddy Pendergrass, Mick Jagger, New Edition, Prince, New Kids on the Block

►► Silk, Shai, Dru Hill, 112

Andre McGarrity

Joe

Born Joe Thomas, in Brooklyn, NY.

Joe Thomas—just Joe to his fans—is a singer-songwriter for whom "going to the movies" became a shrewd career strategy.

Despite not releasing an album for four years after his credible 1993 freshman effort *Everything*, he managed to keep his voice in the minds and ears of R&B followers and maintain a presence in the music industry by using the alternative of movie soundtrack LPs to superb advantage. Joe was able to notch two Top 10 R&B singles from the soundtracks of urban-oriented films during his absence from the album charts—"All the Things (Your Man Won't Do)" from *Don't Be a Menace to South Central While You're Drinking Your Juice in the 'Hood* and "Don't Want to be a Player" from *Booty Call*—ironically reinforcing his staying power and hitmaking abilities until his 1997 followup LP, *All That I Am*, could arrive. Joe's voice, melodic yet unremarkable, doesn't seem to bring anything unique to the musical table at first listen. But by crafting sumptuous ballads that celebrate monogamy and romance at a time when many of his R&B contemporaries are drooling over infidelity and sex, Joe has carved out a large niche of admirers—mostly female—who will probably keep going to the CD stores, or movie theaters, to advance his career.

what's available: Building an effective bridge between old-school soul foundations and smooth hip-hop flavored R&B, *Everything* ♪♪♪ (Mercury, 1993, prod. Joe, J. Dibbs, Dave Hall) is an impressive debut album. Both it and the followup, *All That I Am* ♪♪♪ (Mercury, 1997, prod. Joe, J. Dibbs, Dave Hall), endeavor to explore the male-female relationship in all its facets through textured vocals and lyrics sweeter than a box of bonbons; the hit singles "All the Things (Your Man Won't Do)" and "Don't Want to be a Player" are contained on the latter LP.

influences:
◄◄ Marvin Gaye, Isaac Hayes, Teddy Pendergrass, Stevie Wonder, Brian McKnight

Andre McGarrity

Johnnie Johnson

Born July 8, 1924, in Fairmont, WV.

Turnabout, as they say, is fair play, and it is sweet irony to note that the career of rock and roll piano legend Johnnie Johnson is flourishing these days, and that he is receiving the recognition he so richly deserves, while his former employer, Chuck Berry, can't get arrested (figuratively speaking, that is). For if Berry is the father of rock 'n' roll—or, more accurately, its deadbeat dad—then Johnson should be accorded credit as its stepfather at the very least. Berry may have been the crucible in which the blues, R&B, and country gave birth to a new form which was further shaped by his wit and poetic sense, but it was Johnson who led his band and who wrote—uncredited—the music for some of the songs that are the very cornerstone of rock. Gracious to a fault, Johnson is willing to let bygones be bygones and let his music speak for itself. In recent years, Johnson has recorded with Eric Clapton, Buddy Guy, and Bo Diddley, and played the summer tour circuit with ex-Grateful Dead guitarist Bob Weir's band Ratdog.

what to buy: *Johnnie B. Bad* 𝄢𝄢𝄢 (Elektra Nonesuch American Explorer Series, 1991, prod. Terry Adams, Keith Richards) is Johnson's best album overall, thanks in part to an all-star cast including Keith Richards, Eric Clapton, and members of NRBQ. "Tanqueray" and "Stepped in What!?" are Johnson's first vocal performances ever, and while far from spectacular, they capture perfectly his gentle, self-effacing personality.

what to buy next: *Johnnie Be Back* 𝄢𝄢𝄢 (Musicmasters, 1995, prod. Jimmy Vivino) is another all-star affair, with Phoebe Snow, Buddy Guy, Al Kooper, John Sebastian, and Max Weinberg all lending a hand. There's still plenty of room for Johnson to shine, though. *Rockin' Eighty-Eights* 𝄢𝄢𝄢 (Modern Blues, 1991, prod. Daniel Jacoubovitch) teams Johnson with two other St. Louis piano greats, Clayton Love, who played with Ike Turner during the 1950s, and Jimmy Vaughn, who played with Albert King, Little Milton Campbell, and Ike Turner, among others. The album is an interesting compendium of Midwestern postwar blues styles. Of special note is Johnson's smoking take on "Frances," an instrumental track named for his wife.

the rest:
Blue Hand Johnnie 𝄢𝄢𝄢 (Pulsar, 1988/Evidence, 1993)
(With the Kentucky HeadHunters) *That'll Work* 𝄢𝄢𝄢 (Elektra Nonesuch American Explorer Series, 1993)

worth searching for: Of course, you'll want to have some of his work with Berry. We suggest the single disc collection *His Best* 𝄢𝄢𝄢𝄢 (Chess/MCA, 1997), 20 strong songs that, if you're paying attention, tell you much about Johnson's role in Berry's sound.

influences:
◀◀ Earl "Fatha" Hines, Count Basie, Bud Powell

▶▶ Anyone who's ever played piano in rock 'n' roll or R&B

Daniel Durchholz

Marv Johnson

Born October 15, 1938, in Detroit, MI. Died May 16, 1993.

The thrill of Marv Johnson's voice and talent may have faded from memory, but the Detroit-born singer will always hold a niche in history as the first artist selected by Berry Gordy for development in what would become the Motown Records production line. After discovering Johnson in a Detroit record store, Gordy collaborated with the tenor on a tune called "Come to Me" in 1959. After Gordy received a family loan of $800, he first released the song on his own Tamla label. After the record became a local hit, Gordy realized he lacked the promotional machine to exploit it fully and leased the record to well-established United Artists. The success of this song and a few others helped provide the seed money to launch Motown Records; as the saying goes, the rest is history. Johnson scored followup hits on UA with "You've Got What It Takes" and "I Love the Way You Love," released overseas on the London label. Recording for Motown's Gordy label during the mid-1960s, Johnson's stature with the company was eclipsed by other acts; his final release for Motown was "So Glad You Chose Me" in 1970. Johnson's relationship with Berry Gordy and his company was often acrimonious, but he later held various administrative positions within the Motown ranks.

what's available: Little of Johnson's work is available today; the best examples are found on the compilation *Marv Johnson* 𝄢𝄢𝄢 (Golden Classics, 1991, prod. various), which includes much of his early work recorded in Detroit.

worth searching for: After an 18-year hiatus from recording, Johnson—always very popular in England—hooked up with millionaire R&B enthusiast and producer Ian Levine. This collaboration can be heard on the import *Come to Me* 𝄢𝄢𝄢 (Motor City, 1990, prod. Ian Levine). Sadly, after relocating from Detroit to Columbia, S.C., Johnson suffered a fatal heart attack in May 1993.

influences:
◀◀ Louis Jordan, Big Joe Turner, Nat King Cole, Jackie Wilson

▶▶ Marvin Gaye, Dennis Edwards, Stevie Wonder, Frankie Beverly, Michael Jackson

Matt Lee

Robert Johnson

Born May 8, 1911, in Hazlehurst, MS. Died August 16, 1938, in Greenwood, MS.

More has been written about, and more mythology surrounds, Robert Johnson and his 29 recorded songs than any other bluesman and his music—more than almost any other music, period. That thin, smoldering sheaf of songs, his edgy, high moaning voice, the fecund paucity of details about his life, and the unusual circumstances of his death (apparently poisoned by a jealous husband at a country roadhouse gig)—leavened with the rumors of Johnson's pact with the devil—have made him one of the most legendary figures in American culture of the twentieth century. Despite the deluge of hype over the last few years, listening to *King of the Delta Blues Singers* is still the scariest thing next to spending the night alone at a crossroads in Coahoma County under a full moon. The ironies have proliferated: one of the youngest of a generation of Delta acoustic bluesmen, Johnson was nearly an anachronism by the time he was recorded (although who knows what he could have done with electricity coursing through his guitar?); producer John Hammond came looking for Johnson for his "From Spirituals to Swing" black revue—several months after his death; he didn't make the *Billboard* charts until a half century after he died; no one is sure where he's buried, though at least two cemeteries have markers for him. Except for those fortunate enough to buy the few 78s that were distributed during his lifetime (or to get the bootleg tapes made from them), Johnson's music was pretty much unavailable until more than 20 years after his death. Research has lifted some of the clouds from his life just as it seemingly has obscured others. But beyond the myth, it's those existential songs—"Hellhound on My Trail," "Stones in My Passway," "Love in Vain," "32-20 Blues"—and that tightly strung, slightly scared, tormented voice—that burn right through the decades and the scratches, pointing the way to the future. Recent advances in studio technology have attempted to make those scratchy recordings more clear. But no matter how remastered a version of "Hellhound on My Trail" you wind up with, you'll still have to squint a little to see that big devil dog in the shadows behind paranoid Bob's hunched back.

what to buy: There is no let-up on *King of the Delta Blues Singers* ♫♫♫♫ (Columbia, 1961, prod. Don Law, Frank Driggs), which introduced Johnson to the world at large, heavily influencing a generation of superstars, including Keith Richards and Eric Clapton. Johnson sometimes sounds like a band, and the connection between his voice and guitar is complete—they sound like one instrument. (There's even a gold disc version of this one available.) And it's an album, not a greatest-hits collection. If you're interested in hearing the full sessions in chronological order, pick up *Robert Johnson: The Complete Recordings* ♫♫♫♫ (Columbia, 1990, prod. Don Law, Frank Driggs, Stephen LaVere), the two-disc set which landed old Bob in the pop charts and on *Entertainment Tonight.*

what to avoid: For some inexplicable reason there's a "new" compilation, *Robert Johnson: King of the Delta* ♫♫♫ (Columbia/Legacy, 1997), which, since all tracks have been released before—most of them twice—there is no reason to own.

the rest:
King of the Delta Blues Singers Vol. 2 ♫♫♫♫ (Columbia, 1970)

worth searching for: For more on Johnson's life we heartily recommend reading *Deep Blues* ♫♫♫♫ (Viking, 1981), Robert Palmer's groundbreaking book that makes the connection between the acoustic Delta blues of Johnson and the electric version that Muddy Waters conceived in Chicago. Also worth watching is *The Search for Robert Johnson* ♫♫♫♫ (Sony video, 1992), in which narrator John Hammond travels the Delta in a convertible, stopping to talk to historians and scholars and former Johnson girlfriends and contemporaries (including Honeyboy Edwards, who was there the night Johnson was poisoned).

what to avoid: Except for a short, sepia-toned opening segment, steer way clear of Walter Hill's totally inept 1986 film, *Crossroads,* which stars Ralph Macchio as a blues kid who winds up in a guitar "duel" with a heavy-metal devil played (strikingly, you have to admit) by Steve Vai. Really!

influences:
◀◀ Lonnie Johnson, Tommy Johnson, Charley Patton, Willie Brown, Son House

▶▶ Muddy Waters, Eric Clapton, Keith Richards, Robert Jr. Lockwood

Leland Rucker

Syl Johnson
Born Sylvester Thompson, July 1, 1936, in Holly Springs, MS.

Soul music is a language. The satisfaction that we derive from a great soul performance comes from our sense that the feelings that the singer is expressing could not have been expressed as well in any other language. That's why a great soul performance means so much more than just a combination of music and lyrics; the message is in the singer's delivery—the subtleties of nuance, pacing, emphasis, phrasing, and attitude. It follows that the greatest soul singers are those most skilled at communicating subtle messages through the medium of their voices; skill as a soul singer has more to do with communication than with vocal ability per se. By this standard, Syl Johnson is a master of the soul genre. It's as if Johnson has a cry that permanently resides in his voice box, lending a disorienting, world-weary sadness to even the most innocuous lyrics ("Come On Sock It To Me," "Different Strokes") and a sense of desperate urgency to expressions of joy and celebration ("We Did It," "Back for a Taste of Your Love," "I'm Gonna Take You Home to See Mama"). In his more substantive songs—"Anyway the

Wind Blows," "Wind, Blow Her Back My Way," "Please Don't Give Up On Me," "I Let a Good Girl Go," "Concrete Reservation"—Johnson's expressions of pain and despair through the medium of his achingly thin, frayed tenor/falsetto is chillingly precise and deeply compelling. Another of Johnson's great artistic strengths is his ability to synthesize disparate threads of music—blues, gospel, R&B, country, and dance music—into a sound that is at once firmly rooted in tradition and entirely unique. For example, Johnson entered the soul pantheon by way of Chicago blues, enabling him to inform his soul singing with that music's jagged edges. Over the years he recorded for Federal, Twilight (later Twinight), and Hi Records. At Twilight/Twinight, Johnson dominated the label as both a hit-maker and a producer of other artists such as the Notations and the Radiants. Like other black songwriters of the late 1960s—Marvin Gaye, Curtis Mayfield, and Norman Whitfield to name a few—Johnson's Twilight/Twinight period also explored themes of African American identity and social problems ("Is It Because I'm Black" and "Concrete Reservation" among others). At Hi, Johnson often toiled in Al Green's shadow, but he did cut magnificent material such as "Back for a Taste of Your Love" and "Take Me to the River." After the Hi years ended, Johnson produced two worthy LPs for his own Shama label, the latter of which (1982's *Ms. Fine Brown Frame*) was picked up for distribution by Boardwalk Records and produced Johnson's last hit single, the title cut. After dropping out of the music business to operate a chain of fish restaurants in Chicago, Johnson reemerged on Delmark Records in 1995, along with the Hi Rhythm Section, with a great comeback disc, *Back in the Game*.

what to buy: *Best of the Hi Records Years* 🎵🎵🎵🎵 (Capitol/The Right Stuff, 1995, prod. Willie Mitchell) is a good introduction to some of the high points of Johnson's peak period in Memphis.

what to buy next: *Twilight & Twinight—Masters Collection* 🎵🎵🎵🎵 (Collectables, 1996, prod. various) documents the raw exuberance of Johnson's first soul recordings. This is pure, stripped-down soul music that goes straight for the heart. *Is It Because I'm Black?* 🎵🎵🎵🎵 (Charly, 1994, prod. various) covers much of the same ground. *Music to My Ears* 🎵🎵🎵🎵 (Hi, 1991, prod. Willie Mitchell) is another great collection of singles and album cuts from the Hi years. *Back For a Taste of Your Love/Diamond in the Rough* 🎵🎵🎵🎵 (Hi 1973 and 1974/Hi, 1995, prod. Willie Mitchell) is a CD collection of the first two Johnson LPs on Hi. The other two Hi LPs, one great and one awful (see below) are collected on *Total Explosion/Uptown Shakedown* 🎵🎵🎵 (Hi 1975 and 1979/Hi, 1995, prod. Willie Mitchell, Jerry Barnes). On Johnson's comeback disc with the Hi Rhythm Section, *Back In*

the Game 🎵🎵🎵🎵 (Delmark, 1995, prod. Pete Nathan), he sings as well as he ever did and the musicians are in top form; and this album may contain the best version ever of the much-recorded Al Green song "Take Me To the River."

what to avoid: Johnson's final album on Hi, *Uptown Shakedown* **woof!** (Hi, 1979, prod. Jerry Barnes) is abominable. It was recorded after Mitchell's relationship with Hi had ended and solely to fulfill Johnson's contract to Cream Records, the label that had inherited ownership of Hi. Its only achievement is to capture on one record everything that was awful about disco— including the demeaning "Otis Redding Medley." *This Time Together by Father and Daughter* 🎵 (Twinight, 1995, prod. Syl Johnson) gives some low-budget disc time to Syl's daughter Syleena, who also sings with him on *Back in the Game*.

the rest:
A-Sides 🎵🎵🎵🎵🎵 (Hi, 1994)
Take Me to the River 🎵🎵🎵🎵 (Capitol Special Products, 1994)

worth searching for: *Twinight's Chicago Soul Heaven* 🎵🎵🎵🎵🎵 (Kent, 1996, prod. various) is a retrospective of the label for which Johnson was the prime creative force as its most successful recording artist and producer of many of its other records. This blistering set of hard-core Chicago soul includes a few cuts by Johnson. *Brings Out the Blues in Me* 🎵🎵🎵 (Shama, 1980, prod. Syl Johnson) is an exuberant, if somewhat noisy (too many guitars!), return to Johnson's Chicago blues roots with guest stars such as his brother, Mac Thompson, and James Cotton. *Ms. Fine Brown Frame* 🎵🎵🎵🎵 (Boardwalk, 1982, prod. Syl Johnson) provides more evidence of Johnson's eclecticism, as he pulls off a surprisingly successful amalgamation of disco, blues, and soul.

influences:

◄◄ Billy Boy Arnold, Magic Sam, Elmore James, Jimmy Reed, Junior Wells, Howlin' Wolf, Muddy Waters, Willie Dixon, Freddie King, James Brown, Donny Hathaway, Mahalia Jackson, Sister Rosetta Tharpe

►► Tyrone Davis, Robert Cray, the Subdudes, Jonny Lang, Earth, Wind & Fire

Bill Pollak

Glenn Jones

Born 1961, in Jacksonville, FL.

Despite being blessed with a strong, distinguished voice and impressive range, Glenn Jones remains an unsung R&B talent after scattering a handful of hits during the mid-1980s and early 1990s. But he shined in the first leg of his first career, as a teenage gospel singer. At 14, the precocious Jones created the gospel group the Modulations and recorded two albums under the direction of the Rev. James Cleveland. He cut his first secular recording at 19 with RCA and scored a big hit in 1983 with the ballad "Show Me." Each of his albums showcased his confidence and energy, and each contained at least one popular R&B song, like "I Am Somebody," "We've Only Just Begun (The Romance Is Not Over)," and "I've Been Searchin' (Nobody Like You)." But he, like other artists catering to a mature audience, was too often saddled with uptempo cuts that did not fit his style, and did not wrest creative control until the early 1990s. He is remembered by many as the voice accompanying Dionne Warwick on the theme song for the 1984 television series *Finder of Lost Loves.*

what to buy: Jones hit his stride with *Here I Go Again* 🎵🎵🎵 (Atlantic, 1992, prod. various), a tight work rich with ballads and mid-tempo grooves that evidenced his greater creative control.

what to buy next: *Best of Glenn Jones* 🎵🎵🎵 (Jive, 1992, prod. various) captures Jones on out-of-print albums recorded by RCA. It includes the songs "Finesse," "Take It from Me," and "Everybody Loves a Winner."

what to avoid: Despite sporting the hit "Stay," *All for You* **woof!** (Jive, 1990, prod. various) is formulaic and lacks originality.

the rest:
Glenn Jones 🎵🎵🎵 (Atlantic, 1987)
Here I Am 🎵🎵🎵 (Atlantic, 1994)

worth searching for: Pick up *James Cleveland Presents the Modulations* (Savoy, 1975, prod. James Cleveland) to hear Jones at the beginning of his gospel careeer.

influences:
◀◀ Donny Hathaway, Bobby Womack, Luther Vandross
▶▶ Joe, Tony Terry, Johnny Gill

Franklin Paul

Grace Jones

Born May 19, 1952, in Spanishtown, Jamaica.

Haughty fashion model turned haughty chanteuse, Grace Jones started as a disco diva, then moved into rock without abandoning her dance roots. She has enjoyed success on the R&B charts, though she has never managed to cross over to the pop Top 40 despite some visually stunning videos on MTV. Her tough, ultravixen image (she slapped around a British TV host in 1980 during a live program!) was vastly magnified by the arty cover photos and videos of Jean-Paul Goude, to whom she was married for a while. Jones has also done some film acting, most notably in *Conan the Destroyer* (Arnold Schwarzenegger reportedly complained she hit too hard in fight scenes), the James Bond flick *A View to a Kill,* and the Eddie Murphy vehicle *Boomerang.* Jones's music career started as more image than substance. Purveying a persona that appealed to the gay disco audience, she got over despite a distinct lack of singing ability, and in spite of producer Tom Moulton's by-the-numbers disco productions on her first three albums. *Fame*'s mellow disco version of "Autumn Leaves," partly in the original French (and with the tackiest rhythm track imaginable, like a setting on a cheap organ bought at the Wurlitzer shop in the local mall), demonstrates just how bad Jones's vocals could be. She has endured through a couple of hiatuses and a cocaine problem, though her musical output has slowed singificantly. Her only output during the 1990s has been a cover of the Sheep on Drugs song "Sex Drive," and she was recently on the road in a touring production of *The Wiz.*

what to buy: *Inside Story* 🎵🎵🎵🎵 (Manhattan, 1986, prod. Nile Rodgers, Grace Jones) is Jones's most consistent, coherent album as well as her most personal. Her lyrics draw on her experiences and work in an unpretentious, often wistful way, with complementary musical arrangements that are often stripped down for the more casual numbers.

what to buy next: *Island Life* 🎵🎵🎵🎵 (Island, 1986, prod. various) is far from an adequate survey of the first two phases of her career, missing many crucial tracks but still offering a taste of Jones's particular *elan.*

what to avoid: *Muse* 🎵 (Island, 1979, prod. Tom Moulton) features a lyrically overwrought, musically faceless sidelong concept/morality play medley—"Sinning/Suffer/Repentance (Forgive Me)/Saved"—with a pseudo-gospel section that is unintentionally hilarious. Some tracks strain Jones way past whatever tiny degree of legitimate vocal technique she possessed.

the rest:
Portfolio 🎵🎵 (Island, 1977)
Fame 🎵🎵 (Island, 1978)
Warm Leatherette 🎵🎵🎵🎵 (Island, 1980)
Nightclubbing 🎵🎵🎵 (Island, 1981)

Living My Life ⚌⚌⚌ (Island, 1982)
Slave to the Rhythm ⚌⚌ (Manhattan/Island, 1985)
Bulletproof Heart ⚌ (Capitol, 1989)
Sex Drive ⚌⚌ (Island, 1993)

worth searching for: On *So Red the Rose* ⚌⚌ (Capitol, 1985, prod. Alex Sadkin, Arcadia), the only album by Arcadia—a side project of Duran Duran members Roger Taylor, Nick Rhodes, and Simon LeBon—Jones guests on the first track, "Election Day." The soundtrack for *Dancehall Queen* ⚌⚌ (Island Jamaica, 1997, prod. various) includes "My Jamaican Guy" in a remake by Jones and Bounty Killer with a much-modernized rhythm track and his added vocal.

influences:

◀◀ Gloria Gaynor, Andrea True, the Pretenders, the Normal

▶▶ David Bowie, Black Box, Wally Badarou, Joan Armatrading, Fine Young Cannibals, Robert Palmer

Steve Holtje

Linda Jones

Born January 14, 1944, in Newark, NJ. Died March 14, 1972 in New York, NY.

Linda Jones is an acquired taste, and too much will give you indigestion and bad dreams. Jones had a minor hit with "Hypnotized" in 1967 for Loma, a subsidiary of Warner Bros., in which her vocal idiosyncracies were toned down. Later in her career, however, she let it all loose—a warbling display of vocal gymnastics unlike anything you've ever heard. The best example was "Not On the Outside," recorded for Turbo Records in Newark, perhaps the most over-the-top vocal performance ever released. Jones makes Tina Turner sound like Judy Collins, achieving a level of intensity in the first 10 seconds that is well beyond what most singers ever attempt. *Your Precious Love*, a collection of her Turbo recordings, carries a disclaimer attributing the poor sound quality to the fact that CDs enhance defects in the original analog recordings. It's hard to imagine any recording equipment—analog or digital—that would *not* have been distorted by Jones's voice. She died shortly after a performance at the Apollo Theatre in New York, from complications with diabetes at the age of 28.

what to buy: *For Your Precious Love* ⚌⚌⚌ (Turbo/Sequel, 1988, prod. various) . . . you simply have to hear it. As music, this is not as good as her earlier work for Loma and other labels, and the sound quality is truly abysmal, but as pathology—well, you have to hear it. Jones invented five or six unique and totally off-

the-wall vocal licks, and she throws them in with predictable regularity on all 19 songs on this disc. Despite the tedium of it, there are some truly incredible moments.

what to buy next: *Hypnotized—20 Golden Classics* ⚌⚌⚌ (Collectables, 1994, prod. various) covers material from throughout Jones's too-brief career, including her outstanding version of the O'Jays' "I'll Be Sweeter Tomorrow," which was released as a 45 on Neptune.

what to avoid: All of it should be avoided if you have any known medical problems.

the rest:
Hypnotized ⚌⚌⚌ (Loma, 1967)

worth searching for: *The Best of Loma Records: The Rise and Fall of a 1960's Soul Label* ⚌⚌⚌ (Warner Bros., 1994, prod. various) has five fine selections by Jones as well as some excellent recordings by J.J. Jackson, Ike & Tina Turner, Lorraine Ellison, the Enchanters, the Marvellos, and others. If you buy this disc, you don't want to put your CD player on random play mode; Linda Jones and Lorraine Ellison back-to-back could be dangerous.

influences:

◀◀ Jackie Wilson, Inez Andrews

▶▶ Gladys Knight, Patti LaBelle, Chaka Khan, Mariah Carey

Bill Pollak

Quincy Jones

Born March 14, 1933, in Chicago, IL.

Believe it or not, there are some people who criticize Quincy Jones—primarily for applying his vast wealth and reputation to further the popularity of R&B, rap, and pop rather than jazz. Those critics point out that long before the man known as "Q" ever conceived of becoming one of the world's most renowned record producers, composers, and entertainment entrepreneurs, he started his career as a jazz trumpeter, forming a band with Ray Charles at the age of 14 and playing with Lionel Hampton before he was old enough to drive. But those detractors obviously aren't aware that Jones has given back to jazz, founding the Qwest Records label in 1980 and building it into one of the most important proving grounds for young jazz artists as well as a home for all-time greats like Milt Jackson and Sonny Simmons. Despite this laudable achievement and his numerous contributions to jazz, Jones is probably still best known as the man who gave Michael Jackson his *Thriller* and the only man respected enough by his peers to have pulled off the "We Are the

World" studio session. After winning a scholarship in his teens and attending Boston's Berklee School Music, he was invited to write arrangements for Oscar Pettiford and began hobnobbing with the likes of Miles Davis, Charlie Parker, Dizzy Gillespie, and Thelonious Monk. In the mid-1950s, he lived in Paris and played Europe with Dizzy and Lionel. He studied classical music in Paris and earned awards for arranging and composing. Ever on the lookout for ways in which modern trends in music could be fused with the great traditions of jazz, Jones became the first contemporary conductor-arranger to record with a Fender bass guitar, according to his autobiography. Returning to New York in 1961, he became one of the first African Americans to become a music industry executive, as a vice president for Mercury Records. He began producing and playing on other people's sessions and continued to arrange, winning Grammy Awards for his 1963 arrangement of the Count Basie Orchestra's "I Can't Stop Loving You" and Frank Sinatra's "Fly Me to the Moon." His solo work also won him Grammys for the LPs *Walking in Space* and *Smackwater Jack* during the time he was married to Peggy Lipton of TV's *The Mod Squad* (whom he later divorced), and he composed such memorable TV themes as *Ironside* and *Sanford and Son*. His preeminence as a producer was cemented in the '70s with his work for Aretha Franklin and the Brothers Johnson, the *Roots* mini-series soundtrack, and Michael Jackson's monster hit *Off the Wall*; it was magnified with Jackson's followup, *Thriller*, in 1982, the album for which Jones won five Grammys for producing and arranging. Jones has been at the center of some of the most important projects of the '80s, producing "We Are The World" as well as Steven Spielberg's film *The Color Purple*. In the 1990s, Jones was honored with a Grammy Legend Award; saw the release of his film biography, *Listen Up: The Lives of Quincy Jones*; produced the hit TV sitcom *Fresh Prince of Bel-Air*; launched the hip-hop music magazine *Vibe* and a spinoff television version; and released *Miles and Quincy Live at Montreux*, a document of Miles Davis's final recording. On an astounding variety of fronts, "Q" continues to prove that he is one of the essential cogs of the entertainment industry machine.

what to buy: Of Jones's several "greatest hits" packages, *The Best of Quincy Jones* (A&M, 1981, prod. Quincy Jones) is the standout, combining his best efforts for A&M ("Killer Joe," "Smackwater Jack") with key tracks off his blistering pop albums, like 1974's *Body Heat*. It omits his album sides with some of jazz music's greats, but still serves as a fine overall introduction to his singular genius. *Pawnbroker/Deadly Affair* (Verve, 1996, prod. Quincy Jones) is a recently re-released

double dip soundtrack that features some scintillating Quincy Jones compositions, particularly "Main Theme to *The Pawnbroker*." The 1965 Sidney Lumet film was Jones's first movie soundtrack and the beginning of a pursuit that would eventually bring him an Academy Award for *In the Heat of the Night*.

what to buy next: The best feature of *Back on the Block* (Qwest, 1989), like many projects from Quincy the Great, is a guest list that reads like a Who's Who of the music world: Sarah Vaughan, Dionne Warwick, George Benson, Ray Charles, Miles Davis, Ella Fitzgerald, Dizzy Gillespie, Luther Vandross, Ice-T, Sheila E, Take 6, Chaka Khan, James Moody, and Kool Moe Dee. Some nitpicky music critics with horns for brains complain that "Q" steers clear of jazz and instead puts together a buffet of run-of-the-mill urban pop. What do they know? The LP was still a huge, Grammy-winning hit and features some the best work Jones has ever done. Want to take a decidedly unique look at Jones' work? *The Best, Vol. 2* (Rebound, 1988) celebrates "Q's" TV themes, like the streetwise *Sanford and Son* music and the kooky "Hikky-Burr" scat from *The Bill Cosby Show*. By no means the greatest Jones collection, it still hits a higher level than most routine "Best of" packages (especially the first volume in this series).

what to avoid: Too much of a good thing can sometimes be a bad thing, and *Q's Jook Joint* (Qwest, 1995) proves that adage true. Sure, Jones can assemble a bevy of musicians at the drop of a hat that any hip pleasure-monger would love to have as guests at his party. But this dispassionate rehashing of old formulas shows that "Q" must constantly guard against letting that power spin out of control. This one's all over the place, like a Grateful Dead fan at a patchouli factory. There are brief cameos by literally hundreds of superstar performers, the voices of Miles Davis, Dizzy Gillespie, Charlie Parker, and others, and an introduction to a great vocal talent in Tamia—even a visit by the cast of *Stomp!*. But all that's not enough to keep *Jook* from being a gyp.

the rest:
This Is How I Feel about Jazz (UNI/Impulse, 1957/1992)
Live at the Alhambra, 1960 (Jazz Music Yesterday)
Vol.1—Swiss Radio Days Jazz Series (TCB Music, 1960)
Body Heat (A&M, 1974)
Sounds . . . and Stuff Like That! (A&M, 1978)
Roots (A&M, 1977/1997)
The Dude (A&M, 1981)
The Quintessence (MCA Jazz/Impulse, 1986)
Quincy Jones: Compact Jazz Series (Verve, 1989)
Sarah Vaughan/Quincy Jones, "Misty" (Mercury, 1990)

Miles Davis & Quincy Jones Live At Montreux ♫♫♫ (Warner Bros., 1993)
Pure Delight: The Essence of Quincy Jones and His Orchestra, 1953–1964 ♫♫♫ (Razor & Tie, 1995)
Q Live In Paris Circa 1960 ♫♫♫ (Qwest, 1996)
Greatest Hits ♫♫♫ (A&M, 1996)
Jazz 'Round Midnight ♫♫♫ (Verve, 1997)

worth searching for: With Jones at his artistic and career peak, the out-of-print *Walking In Space* ♫♫♫♫ (A&M, 1969) is a return to the big-band styles with contemporary flair that resurrected "Q's" rep as a bandleader and artist after a long spell of hacking for Hollywood. Mindful of the modern era, Jones merges old styles with new, blending in electric instruments and pop music while making a sizzling version of "Hair" (from the hit Broadway show) the album's hallmark. At the same time, he gathered some of the best jazz musicians of his age—Freddie Hubbard, Roland Kirk, Hubert Laws, J.J. Johnson, Jimmy Cleveland—to add their expertise; the superior sound quality does them all justice.

influences:

◄◄ Clark Terry, Dizzy Gillespie, Ray Charles, Lionel Hampton

►► Thad Jones, Gil Evans, Benny Carter, Mel Lewis, the Brothers Johnson, George Benson, Michael Jackson, James Ingram, Patti Austin, Patrice Rushen, Luther Vandross, Prince, Maxwell

Chris Tower

Janis Joplin
/Big Brother
& the Holding Company

Born January 19, 1943, in Port Arthur, TX. Died October 4, 1970, in Hollywood, CA.

Big Brother members: Sam Andrew, vocals; James Gurley, guitar; Peter Albin, bass; David Getz, drums.

The cloudy glass jar filled with dead 1960s icons, which pop culture pushes to the front shelf decade after decade, leaves quite an impression—so much so that it's hard to remember that the public life of most of these musicians was a scant few years. And if Janis Joplin's career is the least celebrated of these fallen idols, it's because hers was not only the shortest but the most fitful. It was barely three years between her volcanic career-making performance at the Monterey Pop Festival and the discovery of her needle-tracked body in a Hollywood hotel. And in between? Disastrous relationships, devoured pharmaceuticals, and a screeching blues mutation whose desperate passion gave her howling a reverberating intensity. When Joplin left the nurturing fold of Big Brother & the Holding Company, she turned into a commodity. Her early recordings with the San Francisco ballroom band capture a raw Joplin, enmeshed in the passionate throes of an equally untamed band. Ambition was her true weapon of self-destruction, not the drugs and ill-fated romances. She left behind a frustrating glimpse of something powerful enough to ignite her enduring legend. Joplin exploded all over the crowd at the historic 1967 Monterey Pop Festival; in a single show she established her reputation. At that very moment, she also sowed the seeds of eventual departure from her helpless communal colleagues in Big Brother. The very week their *Cheap Thrills* album hit #1, she announced her intention to go solo to her unsurprised bandmates. As a solo artist, she was a disaster. She made her debut performance after a mere two days rehearsal, headlining an authentic soul show to an indifferent audience at an annual Memphis black fundraiser. Her first band never jelled and, although the Full Tilt Boogie Band, which she used by the time she cut her second solo album, represented an improvement, she didn't have time to build up a substantial enough body of work to support her looming posthumous stature. She was dead at age 28 in 1970 before even finishing that final, second solo album. Attempts by producer Paul Rothchild to cast Joplin in the pop-R&B vein then popularized by Chips Moman and his American Group productions of Memphis resulted in her posthumous hit album, "Pearl," but her insufficiencies as a soul singer undermined even this sleek effort. There are currently two film biographies in the works, one of which is slated to star contemporary Joplin protege Melissa Etheridge.

what to buy: Even a quarter-century later, *Cheap Thrills* ♫♫♫♫ (Columbia, 1968, prod. John Simon) still sounds nervy, rich, and radical. The album rips along, high-voltage electricity charging every number, until it reaches its climax—"Ball and Chain," which Joplin turns into one of the highpoints of personal expression in rock history.

what to buy next: Although the band's debut album, *Big Brother and the Holding Company* ♫♫♫ (Mainstream, 1967, prod. B. Shad) was a shoddy and hasty affair made in a few days, the record nevertheless captured the warm, sloppy atmosphere of the band and some precious Joplin vocals. Joplin's posthumously released *Pearl* ♫♫♫♫ (Columbia, 1971) is a bloodletting reminder that Joplin was on the rebound. "Me and Bobby McGee" is effortless country while "Cry Baby" is an ear-shredding wail that cements her place as the most exciting white blues singer of her generation. The odd assortment of studio tracks and outtakes doesn't make for a handy introduction, but *18 Essential Songs* ♫♫♫♫ (Columbia, 1995, comp. and prod. Bob Irwin) is an interesting toss-up of studio stunners ("Down on Me"), previously unavailable live tracks (a ripping "Ball and Chain" from Monterey), and home tapes ("Trouble in Mind," with Jefferson Airplane's Jorma Kaukonen), all drawn from the *Janis Joplin* box set.

what to avoid: *I Got Dem Ol' Kozmic Blues Again Mama!* (Columbia, 1970, prod. Gabriel Meckler) is a sprawling, awful mess of a pseudo-soul album that sounded forced and shrill at the time and which the years have not treated kindly.

the rest:
Joplin in Concert ♫♫♫ (Columbia, 1972)
Farewell Song ♫♫♫ (Columbia, 1982)
Janis Joplin ♫♫♫♫ (Columbia, 1993)

worth searching for: For hard-core collectors, the import-only *Cheaper Thrills* ♫♫♫ (Made to Last, 1982, prod. David Getz) offers a particularly raw early live performance of the unruly and exciting Big Brother crew.

influences:
◄◄ Memphis Minnie, John Coltrane, Lightnin' Hopkins, Howlin' Wolf

►► Melissa Etheridge, Mariah Carey, Liz Phair, Bette Midler, Courtney Love

Joel Selvin and Allan Orski

Louis Jordan

Born July 8, 1908, in Brinkley, AK. Died February 4, 1975, in Los Angeles, CA.

Yes, Louis Jordan's jumping novelty music bridged the gap from old-school R&B and big-band music to Little Richard and Chuck Berry's fast-paced rock 'n' roll. But more importantly, today his songs still swing—maybe that's why the musical *Five Guys Named Moe*, loosely based on Jordan's life and music, has had so much staying power around the world. Among Jordan's classics, which are both party-happy and aware of poverty, racism, and other social problems: "Caldonia," "Let the Good Times Roll," "Beans and Corn Bread," "What's the Use of Getting Sober (When You're Gonna Get Drunk Again)." The son of an Arkansas bandleader, Jordan left town in his 20s to play in Philadelphia with Charlie Gaines and in Harlem with drummer-bandleader Chick Webb and then-unknown singer Ella Fitzgerald. Soon, after Webb's sudden death, the alto sax player built on his musical talent and fun-loving sense of humor to create a more popular, accessible version of Louis Armstrong and Duke Ellington's jazz. "What makes your big head so hard?" he wondered of "Caldonia," the subject of which also had "great big feet." On "Beans and Corn Bread," a subtly disguised social commentary about racial conflict, the beans fight at a party with the corn bread. Countless artists, from Ray Charles to B.B. King, heard Jordan's records on the radio and tried to copy his style. Years after Jordan's peak, Chuck Berry stepped up the old blues beat, added humorous lyrics about dances and teenagers and sounded uncannily like Jordan's famed seven-member Tympani Five—only with guitar solos where the sax bits used to be. In 1981, British rocker Joe Jackson's *Jumpin' Jive* paid further homage.

what to buy: *The Best of Louis Jordan* ♫♫♫♫ (MCA, 1975, prod. Milt Gabler) has all his 1940s hits, including "Choo Choo Ch'-Boogie," "Caldonia," and "School Days (When We Were Kids)," and it remains the most thorough Jordan retrospective.

what to buy next: Slowly, the rest of Jordan's material has seeped into other sets: though it's not essential, fans will find different, jazzier perspectives on *I Believe in Music* ♫♫♫ (Evidence, 1973/Classic Jazz, 1980, prod. various) and *Just Say Moe! Mo' of the Best of Louis Jordan* ♫♫♫ (Rhino, 1992, prod. Milt Gabler). *Rock 'N' Roll* ♫♫♫ (Mercury, 1989, prod. various), with re-recorded 1956–57 versions of older hits, features conductor-arranger Quincy Jones.

what to avoid: *No Moe!: Decca Recordings* ♫♫ (MCA, 1992, prod. various) is deceptively advertised; despite a few original Jordan tracks, the bulk of it is actors' versions of songs from *Five Guys Named Moe*. *Rock 'n' Roll Call* ♫♫ (RCA Bluebird, 1993, prod. John Snyder) reissues Jordan's 1950s recordings even though they sound just as good on earlier collections.

the rest:
One Guy Named Louis ♫♫♫ (Blue Note, 1954)
No Moe!: Louis Jordan's Greatest Hits ♫♫♫ (Verve, 1992)

worth searching for: *At the Cat's Ball—the Early Years* ♫♫♫ (JSP, 1991, prod. various), an import, is a nice historical look into the big-band swing sound that led up to Jordan's seminal 1940s recordings.

influences:
◄◄ Louis Armstrong, Duke Ellington, Bessie Smith, Charlie Christian, Cab Calloway

►► Elmore James, Chuck Berry, B.B. King, Ray Charles, Robert Jr. Lockwood, Joe Jackson, Royal Crown Revue, Squirrel Nut Zippers

Steve Knopper

Montell Jordan

Born in Los Angeles, CA.

The rap that opens his sophomore album, *More . . .*, introduces Montell Jordan as "the king of hip-hop soul," a claim that, at this point, is still wishful thinking. Still, there's nothing wrong with having ambitions, though in the realm of soul/funk lovermen, latter-day contenders such as Jordan should be happy if they can even make prince. Jordan is an imposing presence, both because of his size (he's 6-foot-8) and his talent, which recalls the silky-smooth plaints of Marvin Gaye and Teddy Pendergrass (whose "Close the Door" Jordan covers on his debut). But Jordan's music is contemporary, not retro, and his slammin' tracks prove he knows from hip-hop production techniques. With a lyrical bent that splits between hitting on the honeys, giving praise to God, and dealing with being a positive black male role model, there's a lot going on in Jordan's world that bears listening to.

what to buy: With only a couple of rhythmic exercises ("Bounce 2 This" and "All I Need") and one shout-out to God ("I Say Yes"), *More . . .* &&&& (Def Jam, 1996, prod. various) throws down one slow jam after another, each of them positing Jordan as the most sensitive superloverman since Marvin and Teddy. They're almost all convincing, especially "Falling," "What's On Tonight," and "Never Alone." The album could do with a little tempo variation, but seldom has singlemindedness paid off so well. *More . . .* made less of a splash than Jordan's dynamic debut, but where that album merely boasts, his latest delivers the goods.

the rest:
This Is How We Do It &&& (PMP/RAL, 1995)

influences:
◀◀ Luther Vandross, Stevie Wonder, Marvin Gaye, Teddy Pendergrass

Daniel Durchholz

Margie Joseph

Born 1950, in New Orleans, LA.

Margie Joseph's career is a perfect example of the capricious nature of fame, of the thin line that separates superstardom from the chitlin circuit. A beautiful, enchanting singer with an exceptional voice seasoned in New Orleans church choirs, Joseph was encouraged by a disc jockey to record some sides for the local Okeh label. Those cuts eventually landed her a contract with Stax, for whom she recorded a pair of albums with unremarkable results. Released there, Joseph was picked up in 1973 by Atlantic Records, a major-label hotbed for soul music at the time, and assigned to celebrated producer Arif Mardin. It appeared that her career couldn't be on a more positive track, but Mardin tried to mold Joseph into a poor-man's imitation of her labelmate Aretha Franklin, and Joseph had neither the vocal power nor the inclination to pull it off. The effect was devastating. Though she continued to record for Atlantic and its subsidiary label Cotillion well into the 1980s, and created one memorable LP (*Hear the Words, Feel the Feeling* on Cotillion) and a signature ballad in "Words (Are Impossible)" (which, in fairness, was produced by Mardin), she was never considered more than a second-tier artist. Her career never seemed to receive the kick start it needed to truly explode. Adored by small pockets of fans familiar with her rapturous voice, Joseph may be forever regarded as a magnificent talent with potential unfulfilled.

what to buy: The 1994 collection *The Atlantic Sessions: The Best of Margie Joseph* &&&& (Soul Classics, 1994, prod. various) is all that's left of Joseph's recorded material on CD. The title is a misnomer because some of her earliest work on Stax (including an interesting cover of the Supremes' "Stop! In the Name of Love") is worth having for Josephiles. But "Words" is here, as is her remake of Al Green's "Let's Stay Together," her wonderful Lamont Dozier-produced album title track "Hear the Words, Feel the Feeling," and cuts produced by Norman Harris and Johnny ("Hang On In There, Baby") Bristol.

influences:
◀◀ Irma Thomas, Gladys Knight, Aretha Franklin, Minnie Riperton, Roberta Flack

▶▶ Brenda Russell, Oleta Adams, Miki Howard, Regina Belle

Jim McFarlin

JT the Bigga Figga

Born 1950, in San Francisco, CA.

It's hard to tell whether JT the Bigga Figga is primarily a musician or an entrepreneur. At the tender age of 21, the rapper already had four albums, one hit single, and a long list of production credits under his belt; he also had ownership of two record companies (Straight Out the Labb Records and Get Low Records). Go figga.

what to buy: JT's third album, *JT's Playaz in the Game* &&&▽ (Get Low, 1993, prod. JT the Bigga Figga), features the popular, oft-imitated "Game Recognize Game" and establishes the impresario's lush, live instrumental sound and playa-like flow.

the rest:
Dwellin' in the Lab ⨍⨍⨍⨎ (1995, Straight Out The Labb/Priority)

worth searching for: Fans of JT's smooth funk sound should pick up *Legal Dope* ⨍⨍⨎ (Straight Out The Labb/Priority, 1995, prod. various), a compilation that features JT plus many of his progenies and other similar Northern California rappers.

influences:
◄◄ E-40, Too $hort, Rappin' 4-Tay
►► Seff tha Gaffla, San Quinn, Get Low Playaz

Jazzbo

Jungle Brothers

Formed 1986, in Brooklyn, NY.

Mike G, vocals; Afrika Baby Bambaataa, vocals; Sammy B, DJ.

It's been nearly 10 years since the Jungle Brothers debuted on wax, and what a tumultuous period it's been: once revered as one of the most influential rap groups of all-time, the JBs began to lose their clout when they started making tweaked-out psychedelic music instead of the organically creative beats and rhymes that helped bring Afrocentric consciousness into hip-hop. Rappers Afrika Baby Bam and Mike G met while attending high school in Manhattan, and the group was born when the pair recruited Sammy B to be their DJ for a performance in a school talent show. With the help of Mike G's uncle, the famed New York DJ Red Alert, the Jungle Brothers cultivated a strong underground following before landing a record deal, releasing a groundbreaking debut and creating the free-thinking, loose-knit Native Tongues collective—an inventive, vibrant crew of hip-hop artists (A Tribe Called Quest, De La Soul, Queen Latifah, etc.) who shared a common ideology and mutual respect. But the growing cynicism in hip-hop, the rise of gangsta rap, the decline of the consciousness movement, and the dissolution of the Native Tongues made the Jungle Brothers tentative during a four-year layoff between their second and third LPs; the latter features tripped-out recording that seems to push the group toward obscurity. But after another long hiatus (three years), the group re-emerged with a new outlook and repaired relationships within the Native Tongues clique. The group, however, couldn't find a remedy for their musical malaise.

what to buy: The first two Jungle Brothers albums are classics. *Straight Out the Jungle* ⨍⨍⨍⨎ (Warlock, 1988, prod. Jungle Brothers) introduced the world to the "tribe vibe," an ideology of pro-blackness expressed through good, undeniably funky music. Afrika Baby Bam and Mike G have just the right type of rhymes—the right cadence, the perfect voices, and a premium command of rhythm—to rock a party any time, anywhere. The album would open up the eyes and ears of many young rappers, suggesting that intelligent music could be made to sound good. The opening title cut, "Jimbrowski," and "The Promo" are all part of hip-hop's musical lore, as is "Black Is Black," the song that featured the debut of a young Q-Tip from A Tribe Called Quest. The follow up, *Done by the Forces of Nature* ⨍⨍⨍⨍ (Warner Bros., 1989, prod. Jungle Brothers) is just as inspirational, just as classic, and, perhaps, even a little more refined. The songs use artfully crafted beats that feature heavier drums and instruments from flute to guitars. "Doin' Our Own Dang" is one of the few Native Tongue posse cuts to feature almost everyone in the crew (including newcomer Monie Love). With these two records, the Jungle Brothers established themselves as one of the most important groups in hip-hop.

what to buy next: Most stringent hip-hop fans wouldn't recommend *J.Beez Wit the Remedy* ⨍⨎ (Warner Bros., 1993, prod. Jungle Brothers, Bob Power, Material), as it's a bizarre, acidic trip into a different musical dimension that, upon its release, only faintly resembled anything the rap nation had ever heard; like Divine Styler's second album, it represented the avant-garde. While a third of the record will resonate with hip-hop heads ("Book of Rhyme Pages," "I'm in Love with Indica"), the rest is very much like "Man Made Material" and the kind of chaotic sound Bill Laswell is known for. Indeed, fans of, say, Archie Shepp or Laswell's various incarnations will appreciate *J.Beez Wit the Remedy*. By the time the overproduced *Raw Deluxe* ⨍⨍⨎ (Gee Street, 1997, prod. Jungle Brothers, the Roots, Roc Raider, others) was released, the JBs seemed to be almost irrelevant to the hip-hop world, although fans of the old Native Tongues sound thrived on "How You Want It" (featuring De La Soul and A Tribe Called Quest) and "Brain" (featuring live beats from the Roots).

worth searching for: Even though they seemed to be on a wholly different planet, the JBs occasionally gave signs that they weren't totally lost. The B-side to *My Jimmy Weighs a Ton* ⨍⨍⨍⨍⨎ (Warner Bros., 1993) features a slick, soulful remix with Q-Tip that's quintessential Jungle Brothers and one of their strongest recordings ever.

influences:
◄◄ Afrika Bambaataa, Cold Crush Brothers, Treacherous Three, Red Alert, Divine Styler

▶▶ De La Soul, Roots, Leaders of the New School, KMD, A Tribe Called Quest, Common, X-Clan, Black Sheep

Jazzbo

influences:

◀◀ Stevie Wonder, Marvin Gaye, Curtis Mayfield

▶▶ Loose Ends, Soul II Soul, Young Disciples, Sade, Incognito

Tom Terrell

Junior

Born Junior Giscombe, mid-1960s, in London, England.

As a people, the British have been a lot of things—colonizers, warriors, loyal subjects of the Crown, class enforcers, race car drivers—but perhaps their greatest role has been as gifted cultural anthropologists. Rock 'n' roll was initially introduced to that nation's youth by American soldiers stationed there; the anarchic energy of the music and its rebel pioneers (Little Richard, Chuck Berry, Elvis, Gene Vincent) created a social upheaval, and the fruits of this malaise were the rock stars of the first British Invasion. Meanwhile, thanks to Motown and Stax, the homefront love for R&B (the roll of rock 'n' roll, after all) became an obsession for the masses of working class youth. During the late 1970s, the U.K. struck gold with the Average White Band and Hot Chocolate. In the early 1980s New Wave era, crypto-white soul acts such as David Bowie, ABC, Culture Club, and Spandau Ballet carried the torch until a soul-struck young black club kid from Clapham named Junior Giscombe walked into a studio in mid-1981 and recorded "Mama Used to Say," single-handedly creating Brit Soul. Ironically, the single became a massive urban radio/club hit in the U.S. first, though the U.K. fell in line by the year's end. To capitalize on "Mama"'s success, Junior rushed out his LP debut, *Ji*. While subsequent singles ("Too Late," "Communication Breakdown," "Oh Louise") and albums (*Inside Lookin' Out*, *Acquired Taste*) gained Junior a following in America, he was ignored by an England preoccupied with the real soul of African America. Aside from a freak U.K. Top 10 hit with Kim Wilde (1987's "Another Step Closer to You"), Junior's run ended in 1990 with the doomed *Step in the Right Direction*. A true prophet dishonored in his homeland, Junior's influence can be heard in the sounds of Brit Soulsters such as Loose Ends, Soul II Soul, Sade, and Incognito. Today, Junior is working on a self-produced love and life triology—stay tuned.

what's available: *Funk Essentials: The Best of Junior* ♫♫♫♫ (Mercury Chronicles, 1995, prod. various) is a convincing reevaluation of Junior's oeuvre. This compilation is a vibrant testimony to his creativity, consistency, and funkativity. Sadly, all of his albums are out of print in the U.S.

Junior M.A.F.I.A. /Lil' Kim

Formed 1995, in Brooklyn, NY.

Little Kim/Lil' Kim (born Kimberly Jones), vocals; Klepto, vocals; Trife, vocals; Larceny, vocals; Little Caesar, vocals; Chico, vocals; Nino Brown, vocals.

Cronyism is the hip-hop way. Get a hit record, and you're expected to help your friends and family do likewise. Enter, then, the late Notorious B.I.G. and his merry (ad hoc) band of proteges, Junior M.A.F.I.A. Comprised of two soloists (Little Kim and Klepto) and two groups (Trife and Larceny, a.k.a. the Snakes; and Little Caesar, Chico, and Nino Brown, a.k.a. the Sixes), the collective issued an album on the heels of B.I.G.'s big debut that was entirely average—save for the forceful, confident performances of Little Kim, who eventually shortened her name and parlayed her spotlight-stealing role into a lucrative solo career. Tough, forceful, and thoroughly raunchy, the self-styled "Queen B" just as easily could have nicknamed herself "Queen X" instead, posing like a soft-porn star on the cover of her attention-grabbing solo debut *Hard Core* and proving that she had the dirty thoughts to match. Indeed, the little B.I.G. woman kicked shocking rhymes about everything from anal sex to masturbation, and when she flatly declared "I'll do things to you Vanessa del Rio be ashamed to do," nobody doubted her.

what to buy: A dynamic rapper whose lyrical concerns range from gunplay and foreplay to street business and between-the-sheets business, Lil' Kim comes across on *Hard Core* ♫♫♫♫ (Undeas/Atlantic, 1996, prod. Sean "Puff Daddy" Combs, Notorious B.I.G., Stretch Armstrong, Jermaine Dupri, others) like a female cross between her favorite Brooklyn hustler, Notorious B.I.G., and the freak-nasty Too $hort. Which either makes the unladylike rapper the anti-Lauryn Hill or simply one of the most interesting gender-role-twisting rappers ever. Or both.

what to buy next: M.A.F.I.A. supposedly stands for Masters At Finding Intelligent Attitudes, but there's really nothing masterful—or intelligent, for that matter—about the Junior M.A.F.I.A. debut *Conspiracy* ♫♫♡ (Undeas/Atlantic, 1995, prod.

Lance "Un" Rivera, Daddy-O, Notorious B.I.G., DJ Clark Kent, EZ Elpee, Special Ed, others). Still, "Player's Anthem" became just that and helped launch Little Kim's career, and the funky "Get Money," too, got noticed—at least on the underground. Not surprisingly, B.I.G. has a big presence on the album, taking the requisite mentor-star turn in "Player's Anthem," among others.

worth searching for: Tapes containing a few rough tracks from Kim's *Hard Core* sessions were leaked by her record company well in advance of the album's completion. Some of these include a meandering version of "Queen Bitch" in which Kim disses B.I.G.'s estranged wife, Faith Evans, and makes an allusion to her rumored affair with B.I.G.'s rival, 2Pac. The song was apparently changed after 2Pac was killed.

influences:

◀◀ Notorious B.I.G., Adina Howard, Too $hort, 2 Live Crew, Da Brat

▶▶ Jay-Z, Foxy Brown

Josh Freedom du Lac

Just Ice

The self proclaimed "original gangster of hip-hop," Just Ice rose to fame as a gruff-tongued Bronx Bomber in the early days of hip-hop via his four albums on the legendary Fresh Records imprint. The rapper has one of those voices that can make even a children's nursery rhyme rock, putting him in the company of such rap icons as Run-D.M.C., Chuck D., and KRS-One. He's also got some of the most influential teeth in hip-hop, as he was one of the first rappers to sport the gold fronts that Flava Flav and the Wu-Tang Clan, among others, later embraced. Along with occasional collaborator KRS-One, Just Ice was also one of the first New York rappers to bring reggae dancehall slang to hip-hop.

what to buy: *Kill the Rhythm (Like a Homicide)* ♪♪♪ (Sleeping Dawg/In-A-Minute, 1995, prod. KRS-One, Mark V, Prince Ice, others) marks a slight departure for the bona fide East Coast rap legend: while tracks like "Bad Boy Back (In Town)" and "Cenci" team him up with longtime cohort KRS-One, the other half of the album takes a West Coast approach. Not quite a Just Ice classic.

the rest:
Masterpiece ♪♪♪ (Fresh, 1990)
Gun Talk ♪♪♪ (Savage, 1993)

worth searching for: On the other hand: Just's out-of-print debut, *Back to the Old School* ♪♪♪♪ (Fresh, 1986, prod. Mantronix) is especially noteworthy for the switch-backed rhythm workouts and techotronic Roland excursions of Mantronix, plus the crazy human beatbox antics of DMX. KRS-One instilled both *Kool and Deadly (Justicizms)* ♪♪♪♪ (Fresh, 1987, prod. KRS-One) and *The Desolate One* ♪♪♪♪ (Fresh, 1988, prod. KRS-One) with sparse, raw beats that accurately complement Just Ice's raspy verbal buckdowns. Whether it's the old-school flashback "Going Way Back" or the KRS/Just Ice tag-team romp "Moshitup," Ice just plain wrecks shop on *Kool and Deadly*. *The Desolate One* is just as meaty. "Welfare Recipients" is a scathing examination of the system; and who can forget the jagged reggae vibe of "Na Touch Da Just," which constantly flips the beat with plenty of selector switchback.

influences:

◀◀ Boogie Down Productions, Mantronix

▶▶ Busta Rhymes, Method Man, Nine, Onyx

Spence D.

K

K7

Born Louis "Kayel" Sharpe, in New York, NY.

K7 made his first impression on the music scene in the late 1980s under the name Kayel, a singer in the Latino dance-pop-R&B trio TKA. In 1993 he reinvented himself as the solo act K7, offering an infectious, barrio-inspired blend of hip-hop, swing, salsa, and classic R&B. He parlayed his crossover single "Come Baby Come"—a huge smash in the U.K.—and a hunger for success into a respectable album, *Swing Batta Swing*. K7 didn't make any musical breakthroughs, but the combination of his call-and-response vocals with his background trio Swing Kids Project (Prophet LOS, Non-Stop, and Tre Deuce), carefully selected funk samples, and an original singing style he calls "Popeye Talk" manage to put a refreshingly upbeat face on the usually dark and gloomy image of urban street hip-hop. Romantically linked briefly to fellow New Yorker Rosie Perez, K7's other notable brush with stardom was the appearance by the late legendary bandleader Cab Calloway as his father in the K7 music video to "Hi De Ho," which borrowed heavily from Calloway's trademark songs "Minnie the Moocher" and "Zaz Zu Zaz."

what to buy: Refusing to take himself too seriously, K7 makes *Swing Batta Swing* ♫♫♫ (Tommy Boy, 1994, prod. Joey Gardner) an invigorating change from most of the depressing hip-hop music favored by his contemporaries. Borrowing freely from all the rap, soul, and Latin influences permeating his home streets, his songs—particularly the standouts "Come Baby Come," "Zunga Zeng," "Move It Like This," and his cover of the Johnny Bristol standard "Hang on in There Baby"—are spirited fun, filled with the kind of hooks you catch yourself humming subconsciously throughout the day.

the rest:
(With TKA) *Scars of Love* ♫♫♫ (Tommy Boy, 1987)
(With TKA) *Louder Than Love* ♫♫♫ (Tommy Boy, 1990)

influences:

⏪ Afrika Bambaataa, Cab Calloway, C+C Music Factory, Latin Rascals, Cold Crush, Doug E. Fresh

⏩ DLG (Dark Latin Groove), Poyecto Uno

Andre McGarrity

Kam

Born Craig A. Miller, in Watts, CA.

As a tangential member of the Lench Mob, Kam steered Ice Cube towards the Nation of Islam. But while Cube flirted with the message and moved on to more commercial considerations, Kam remained serious about his role as a messenger.

what to buy: If Kam is remembered for only one record, let it be the incredible "Peace Treaty," a 1992 single that captured all the cathartic exuberance and ominous foreboding of the short-lived unity amongst L.A.'s warring gangs during the summer following the so-called Rodney King riots. A West Coast classic. It's included on the subsequent debut LP, *Neva Again* ♫♫♫ (East West, 1993, prod. DJ Pooh, others), which borrows Cube's P-Funk groove for a hard-hitting manifesto. "Drama" and "Stereotype" establish Kam as both a keen-eyed storyteller and a cutting, articulate didacticist.

what to buy next: *Made in America* ♫♫♫ (East West, 1995, prod. Battle Cat, DJ Quik, Warren G, others) is less engaging politically, but more varied sonically.

influences:

⏪ Ice Cube

Jeff "DJ Zen" Chang

Kashif

Born Michael Jones, 1959, in Brooklyn, NY.

A musician's musician, Kashif made more guest appearances and has more writing and producing credits than he has music of his own. And, to be honest, he's better at collaborating and at helping others find their sound, which may be why his own career never really took off. The former Michael Jones began his career as the keyboardist for B.T. Express from 1976–79, leaving first to work with the Four Tops and then to form Mighty M production company with Paul Lawrence Jones and Morrie Jones. There Kashif wrote songs for Melba Moore, Evelyn "Champagne" King, and the Average White Band, and he produced songs by Moore, Whitney Houston, George Benson, and Kenny G, among others. His own solo career began during 1983, and his four releases were drenched with guests—including virtually all the folks he was writing for or producing. The songwriting was usually strong, but his voice never conveyed his material as well as the aces with whom he was associated. As an artist, Kashif has been quiet for quite a few years, though he continues to work behind the-scenes.

what's available: None of his own albums are readily available. But many of his collaborations with Moore, Meli'sa Morgan, and George Benson are still in print. He co-produced and guested on King's *Get Loose* ♫♫♫ (RCA 1982/1994), which might be the best way to hear him in his behind-the-scenes capacity.

worth searching for: Kashif's second album, *Send Me Your Love* ♫♫♫ (Arista, 1984) is the best of his lot, with strong songs such as "Call Me Tonight," "Are You the Woman," and "Edgartown Groove," a duet with Al Jarreau.

influences:

⏪ Al Jarreau, George Benson, Dionne Warwick, Smokey Robinson, Melba Moore

⏩ Howard Hewitt, Kenneth "Babyface" Edmonds, Tony Rich

see also: *B.T. Express*

Gary Graff

KC & the Sunshine Band

Formed 1973, in Hialeah, FL.

Harry Wayne Casey, vocals, keyboards; Richard Finch, bass; Jerome Smith, guitar; Robert Johnson, drums; Fermin Coytisolo, congas; Ronnie Smith, trumpet; Denvil Liptrot, saxophone; James Weaver, trumpet; Charles Williams, trombone.

KC's funky party strut in many ways typified the feel-good vibe pumping through Miami's dance floors during the polyester-cloaked 1970s. After the jittery noises flashing out from Sly Stone, the O'Jays, and Stevie Wonder during the early part of the decade, the Sunshine Band's harmonious horns were, at least in part, an answer to that pervading sense of dread. In place of backstabbers, riots, and superstition, Casey rallied like a pre-*Saturday Night Fever* Travolta. His call to arms? Shaking your booty. A low-risk proposition to be sure, and the band's massive crossover appeal in the R&B and pop charts suggested a public's thirst for a party with no strings attached (if you doubt that, remember that this was the first group since the Beatles in 1964 to rack four #1 singles in a year). The songwriting team of Casey and Finch had a way with a catchy phrase, owing more to pop than Parliament, and they kept a stream of instant dance jingles on the lips and hips of boogie children everywhere. The momentum was stopped only by a serious auto wreck Casey had during the early 1980s. After a lengthy convalescence, he rebounded in 1984 with the pure pop of "Give It Up," but all follow-ups have failed to recapture his former glories. Casey, less mane, more gut, can be found with his latest incarnation of the Sunshine Band shaking their paunchy booties on the oldies circuit.

what to buy: *The Best of KC & the Sunshine Band* 🎵🎵🎵🎵 (Rhino, 1989, prod. Harry Casey and Richard Finch) offers all the singles in a row, and it is an infectious bunch—starting with "Sound Your Funky Horn" and "Get Down Tonight," leading to the inevitable "(Shake, Shake, Shake) Shake Your Booty," "That's the Way I Like It," and "Keep It Comin' Love." The pull toward the dance floor is still there, even if you leave your white patent leather shoes at home.

what to buy next: *Part 3 . . . and More* 🎵🎵🎵 (Rhino, 1994, prod. Harry Casey and Richard Finch) is the band's strongest studio album, augmented by eight bonus tracks on CD—many featuring KC sans Sunshine. The Spanish reading of "Please Don't Go" is a dubious treat.

the rest:
Get Down Live 🎵🎵 (Intersound International, 1995)
Greatest Hits, Vol. 1 🎵🎵🎵 (Hollywood/Rounder)
Greatest Hits, Vol. 2 🎵🎵🎵 (Hollywood/Rounder)

worth searching for:

influences:
◀◀ The Spinners, the Temptations, Donna Summer
▶▶ C+C Music Factory, Gloria Estefan

Allan Orski

Ernie K-Doe

Born Ernest Kador Jr., February 22, 1936, in New Orleans, LA.

For all his gospel influences and professional training as a teen member in groups such as Zion Travellers, the Moonglows, and the Flamingos, K-Doe has but one single that he's remembered by. Lucky for him "Mother-In-Law" is a winner that shot to #1 on both the pop and R&B charts, gaining a wider audience for the good-humored New Orleans R&B style in the process. When it hit in 1961, the doo-wop bassline naming the nagging tormentor struck a chord with every married guy in America (who probably said a silent "thank you" to K-Doe every time they heard it). But it boasts more than just funny put-downs, as famed arranger Allen Touissant's concise production brings the novelty tune to jaunty heights. Although his subsequent singles failed to generate the same attention (he also released albums during the 1970s that are out of print), K-Doe remained an energetic stage presence well into the 1990s on the New Orleans club circuit.

what to buy: "Mother-In-Law" can be found on numerous oldies compilations, two of which, *All Time Greatest Hits of Rock 'n' Roll* 🎵🎵🎵 (Curb, 1990) and *Only Rock 'n' Roll 1960–1964 #1 Radio Hits* 🎵🎵🎵 (JCI, 1996, prod. various) are inexpensive and compact samplers of 1960s pop.

the rest:
I'm Cocky but I'm Good 🎵🎵 (Dejan, 1996)

influences:
◀◀ The Coasters, Sam Cooke, Fats Domino
▶▶ Allen Touissant, Zachary Richard

Allan Orski

John P. Kee

Born John Prince Kee, 1962, in Durham, NC.

The gifted, unconventional singer-choirmaster proclaimed the "Prince of Gospel Music," John P. Kee has created his own unique fusion of inspirational and urban sounds labeled "Sunday Hip-Hop" by his swelling legion of fans. A child prodigy who studied at the Yuba Conservatory of Music and performed with such mainstream music notables as Cameo and Donald Byrd & the Blackbyrds while still in his teens, Kee is a former cocaine addict and dealer who literally operated out of the church; he turned his life over to God and gospel music after experiencing the drug-related death of a close friend. From there, Kee went on to form the New Life Community Choir, an energetic group of young singers from the inner city of Char-

lotte, North Carolina, which has already made a lasting impression on the gospel landscape while doubling in street ministry and community activism. Kee is also the inspiration behind the Victory in Praise Music and Artist Seminar, an annual gathering highlighted by a live recording featuring a V.I.P. Mass Choir. Whether he's leading the chorus, singing with his own rugged power, or sharing his personal testimony of overcoming drugs to young gang members, John P. Kee—the man "who can make the babies dance"—is definitely a gospel music revolutionary.

what to buy: Nothing short of an absolute jam, *Show Up!* ♪♪♪♪ (Verity, 1994, prod. John P. Kee), under the imprint of The New Life Community Choir featuring John P. Kee, is the most musically consistent and well rounded of all Kee's albums. The spirit moves with electrifying passion on a slammin' remix of "Made Up Mind," featuring Kee and guest Vanessa Bell Armstrong wailing like never before over the thumping bass licks of Fred Hammond.

what to buy next: Although Kee's music can at times sound one dimensional, the V.I.P. Music and Arts Seminar Mass Choir LP *Stand!* ♪♪♪♪ (Verity, 1996, prod. John P. Kee) proves he can deliver the gospel goods in a variety of tempos, moods, and attitudes, appealing to a broad spectrum of listening tastes. Armstrong is listed as choir director on the LP, but Kee produced the disc and wrote all the songs. Think it represents his vision?

the rest:
Wash Me ♪♪♪ (Verity/Tyscot, 1991)
We Walk by Faith ♪♪♪ (Verity/Tyscot, 1992)
Colorblind ♪♪♪♪ (Verity/Tyscot, 1994)
Yes Lord ♪♪♪ (Verity, 1994)
Just Me This Time ♪♪♪ (Verity, 1994)
Wait on Him ♪♪♪ (Jive, 1994)
(With Yolanda Adams, Daryl Coley, Fred Hammond) *There Is Hope* ♪♪♪ (Verity, 1994)
A Special Christmas Gift ♪♪♪♪ (Verity, 1996)
Thursday Love ♪♪♪♪ (Verity, 1997)

worth searching for: Kee has the talent to inspire any choir under his practiced hand. The Inner City Mass Choir release *Heaven* ♪♪♪♪ (GCI, 1996), produced by Kee, doesn't have his name on it, but songs like "Shine Your Light" and "God of Mercy (Rain on Us)" have his spirit in them.

influences:
◀◀ Rev. James Cleveland, Donald Byrd, Edwin Hawkins, Cameo, Rance Allen, Marvin Winans

Ernie K-Doe (© Jack Vartoogian)

word up!

IT's sort of like if a comedian could sing, they would sing a song like 'You Remind Me of Something.' Just to make people smile or laugh. A woman doesn't remind me of a Jeep literally, you know. So I wouldn't want the woman to take her brain and boggle it like that once they hear that song. Just think of it as an entertainment piece.

R. Kelly

▶▶ Vanessa Bell Armstrong, Doug Williams, Inner City, Surrender

Tim A. Smith

R. Kelly

Born Robert Kelly, 1970, in Chicago, IL.

Street-performer-turned-R&B-star R. Kelly has made his Chicago-based studio into a hit factory in the 1990s with production and songwriting work on records by his teenage bride Aaliyah ("Back and Forth"), Michael Jackson ("You Are Not Alone"), and countless others. Kelly the performer has emerged as the most flamboyant of the New Jack Swingers, combining pleading, gospel-drenched vocals with streetwise beats and lusty lyrics on three sexually explicit albums. It was 1993's salacious *12 Play*, on which Kelly slides from tender seductions to sexist aggression and back again, that made him a star. But in early 1997, Kelly startled his audience by announcing on a Chicago stage that he had embraced Christianity, which cast his 1996 hit "I Believe I Can Fly," from the *Space Jam* movie, in an unlikely but nonetheless inviting spiritual glow that he reprised with "Gotham City" from the "Batman and Robin" soundtrack.

what to buy: With the self-titled *R. Kelly* ♫♫♫ (Jive, 1995, prod. R. Kelly), the singer plays the randy pimp again on "You Remind Me of Something" and "Hump Bounce," but also displays a deeper personal richness that eluded him in the past. If *12 Play* was about a night of pursuit and conquest, *R. Kelly* tracks such as "Down Low" and "I Can't Sleep Baby" dwell in the land of the morning after, of consequences and responsibilities. At times it isn't clear whether Kelly is talking to his lover, his late mother, or God, and the ambiguity is haunting, particularly on *Religious Love.*

the rest:
Born into the 90s ♫♫♫ (Jive, 1991)
12 Play ♫♫♫ (Jive, 1993)

influences:
◀◀ Donny Hathaway, Isley Brothers, Marvin Gaye, Keith Sweat
▶▶ Aaliyah, Montell Jordan

Greg Kot

Eddie Kendricks
See: The Temptations

Chaka Khan
See: Rufus

Kid Capri
Born David Anthony Love, 1968, in New York, NY.

Known mostly for his turntable and production work on other people's records, Kid Capri got his start in the basement and street parties of his Bronx hometown, rockin' the wheels of steel at the tender age of eight. By age 18, he was putting his master mixes on tapes he sold streetside, earning a huge reputation as an underground master of the DJ arts. High-profile stints on WBLS-FM's evening mix show and as the house DJ for HBO's *Def Comedy Jam* raised Capri's profile to the point where everyone from KRS-One to Heavy D., Nas, and Grand Puba was tapping his skills, both as a producer and top-notch record scratcher.

what to buy: Capri's only album, *Kid Capri: The Tape* ♫♫♫ (Cold Chillin', 1991, prod. Biz Markie) captures those skills at their

height, offering a commercialized pastiche of the mix-tape sounds that earned his initial reputation.

influences:
▶▶ Funkmaster Flex

Eric Deggans

Kid Creole & the Coconuts /Dr. Buzzard's Original Savannah Band
Formed 1974, in New York, NY.

Kid Creole (1980–present): Thomas August "Kid Creole" Darnell Browder, vocals; Andy "Coati Mundi" Hernandez, vibes, percussion (1980–87); Peter Schott, keyboards; Cheryl Poirier, vocals. Dr. Buzzard's Original Savannah Band (1974–80, 1984): Stoney Browder Jr., guitar, piano (1974–79, 1984); Thomas August "Kid Creole" Darnell Browder, bass (1974–79); Mickey Sevilla, drums (1974–79, 1984); Sugar Coated Andy Hernandez, vibes, marimba, accordion (1974–79); Corey Daye, vocals (1974–79, 1984); Don Armando Bonilla, percussion (1974–76); Mark Josephsberg, vibes (1984); Michael Almo, horns (1984); Roland Prince, guitars (1984); Michael Boone, bass (1984); Mark Radice, bass (1984).

Before swing music became hip during the late 1990s, Dr. Buzzard's Original Savannah Band brought 1930s big band sounds to the disco era with a witty edge, scoring a hit with "Cherchez La Femme" on 1976's *Dr. Buzzard's Original Savannah Band*, and enjoyed moderate success for a few years. The group broke up in 1980, although it resurfaced in 1984, minus Darnell and Hernandez, for the badly conceived *Calling All Beatniks.* Kid Creole, on the other hand, based its sound in disco, with Latin and Caribbean rhythms added. That unique mixture was enhanced by Darnell's often tongue-in-cheek lyrics and his Caribbean Cab Calloway image, as well as the party hearty stage show featuring the beautiful Coconuts as backup singers and break dancing by Coati Mundi. With a sound that defies categorization, Kid Creole's is more of a cult following, although the music itself presaged salsa's popularity in U.S. pop circles. The band enjoyed some greater exposure when it backed Barry Manilow on a cut from his 1987 release *Swing Street*, and it's been featured in the films "Against All Odds," "Car 54 Where Are You," and "The Forbidden Dance." Darnell has also distinguished himself as a producer.

what to buy: *In Praise of Older Women and Other Crimes* ♫♫♫♫ (Sire, 1985, prod. August Darnell) finds the band in funky and fun form with "Endicott," a cry of independence from a hen-pecked husband and the group's best-known tune stateside. The cry becomes the coo of doo wop on "Particul'y Interested," and soulful on "Name It." The band even takes a break from its usual party mode for musically successful stabs at social concerns on "Caroline Was a Dropout" and "Dowopsalsaboprock (We're Fighting Back)." In an earlier Caribbean party mode, *Wise Guy* ♫♫♫ (Sire, 1982, prod. August Darnell) landed Top 10 hits in the U.K. with "Annie, I'm Not Your Daddy" and "I'm a Wonderful Thing, Baby."

what to buy next: Both of these bands feature strong musicianship and production, and *Dr. Buzzard's Original Savannah Band* ♫♫♫ (RCA, 1976, prod. Sandy Linzer) is a well-played, disco-style delight.

what to avoid: *Calling All Beatniks* **woof!** (Passport, 1984, prod. Sandy Linzer) features bad 1950s-style rock by Dr. Buzzard minus Darnell and Hernandez. It proves the fire in this group really came from Darnell.

the rest:
Kid Creole & the Coconuts:
Fresh Fruit in Foreign Places ♫♫♫ (Sire, 1981) *Doppelganger* ♫♫♫♫ (Sire, 1983)
I, Too, Have Seen the Woods ♫♫♫♫ (Sire, 1987)
You Should Have Told Me You Were . . . ♫♫♫ (Columbia, 1991)
Kid Creole Redux ♫♫♫♫ (Sire, 1992)
To Travel Sideways ♫♫♫♫ (Atoll, 1994)

Dr. Buzzard's Original Savannah Band:
Dr. Buzzard's Original Savannah Band Meets King Penett ♫♫♫ (RCA, 1978)

worth searching for: *Off the Coast of Me* ♫♫♫♫ (Antilles, 1980, prod. August Darnell) is the transitional album from Dr. Buzzard to the Coconuts. The Kid steps out front with his humor, but he hasn't dropped the big band feel yet.

solo outings:
The Coconuts:
Don't Steal My Coconuts ♫♫♫ (EMI, 1983)

influences:
◀◀ Machito and His Afro-Cubans, Cab Calloway, Ricky Ricardo
▶▶ Gloria Estefan, Buster Poindexter, Squirrel Nut Zippers

Lawrence Gabriel

Kid Frost
Born Arturo Molina Jr., May 31, 1962, in Los Angeles, CA.

Proudly declaring that "this is for la raza," Kid Frost and his simply titled 1990 Hispanic-pride anthem, *La Raza*, heralded the arrival of an L.A. rap brown-out, as fellow SoCal Latin lingoists from Mellow Man Ace and Cypress Hill to Lighter Shade of Brown would make their marks within two years. None of the artists, though, was as interested in—or capable of—doing cultural and societal good with their rhymes as Frost, who followed the infectiously cool *La Raza* with album tracks that implored his people to "Come Together." Subsequently, a coalition of like-minded Spanglish-language rappers did just that.

what to buy: On Kid Frost's sophomore album, *East Side Story* ♫♫♫♫ (Virgin, 1992, prod. Kid Frost, others), the rapper tells the disturbing tale of a Hispanic who's causing panic with the police with his ethnicity alone, getting pulled over by racist cops and then going to the pen, where there ain't no sunshine—only sorrowful Bill Withers samples. Frost, who figures he's got it "Bad 'Cause I'm Brown," ultimately cross-breeds the first album's two best tracks for "Raza Unite" before taking pause to review his crazy life in "Mi Vida Loca." The bass-age production is hardly groundbreaking, but it's effective enough to help Frost tell his jagged but well-meaning tale.

the rest:
Hispanic Causing Panic ♫♫♫ (Virgin, 1990)
(With Latin Alliance) *Latin Alliance* ♫♫♫ (Virgin, 1991)
Smile Now, Die Later ♫♫♫ (Ruthless, 1995)
When Hell.A. Freezes Over ♫♫♫ (Ruthless, 1997)

influences:
◀◀ Ice-T, Grandmaster Flash & the Furious Five
▶▶ Mellow Man Ace, Delinquent Habits, Lighter Shade of Brown, Tha Mexakinz

Josh Freedom du Lac

Kid 'n Play
Formed 1988 in Queens, NY.

Kid (born Christopher Reid), vocals; Play (Christopher Martin), vocals.

Neither Kid nor Play was a very talented lyricist, but the duo gained a big following anyway by presenting the perfect video-age package of wholesome, family-friendly raps, go-go-inspired production, state-of-the art dance moves, and a unique look, featuring Kid's towering seven-inch 'do and Play's self-made outfits. Starring in the *House Party* film series and getting their own *Kid 'n Play* cartoon series didn't hurt the duo's popularity, either, although it did kill their street cred.

worth searching for: All of the Kid 'n Play albums are out of print, but those in need of a pop-rap flashback might consider hunting for *2 Hype* 🎵🎵🎵 (Select, 1988, prod. various), if only for the giddy go-go rush of "Rollin' with Kid 'n Play." The title track is fairly hype, too.

influences:

◀◀ Salt-N-Pepa, Fat Boys, D.J. Jazzy Jeff & the Fresh Prince

▶▶ Kris Kross, Immature

Josh Freedom du Lac

Kid Rock

Born Bob Ritchie, January 17, 1971, in Dearborn, MI.

Ritchie began rapping and DJing when he was the same age as most of his fans: in high school. Still, by his debut, the young rapper with the strange, vertical hairdo had clearly already hit puberty, as many of his amusing songs matched Too $hort's in sex-crazed spirit.

what to buy: The highlight of the underappreciated *Grits Sandwiches for Breakfast* 🎵🎵🎵 (Zomba/Jive/RCA, 1990, prod. Kid Rock, Mike Clark, Too $hort, others) is "Yo-Da-Lin in the Valley," a wickedly funny (and funky) song in which Rock doesn't really yodel, but instead calls oral sex with a woman "a delicious break from potatoes." Too $hort, too, checks in for a quickie. Elsewhere, the heavy bass and stop-start music of "New York's Not My Home" recalls *Raising Hell*–era Run-D.M.C.

what to buy next: Proving why he's called Kid Rock, and not Kid Rap, Rock kicks out the metallic jams on *The Polyfuze Method* 🎵🎵🎵 (Continuum, 1993, prod. Kid Rock, Mike Clark, others), including the hard-hitting single, "You Don't Know Me."

the rest:
Fire It Up 🎵🎵🎵 (Continuum, 1994, prod. Andy Nehra and Mike Nehra)
Early Morning Stoned Pimp 🎵🎵🎵 (Top Dog, 1996, prod. Kid Rock)

influences:

◀◀ Beastie Boys, Too $hort

▶▶ Jesse Jaymes, Insane Clown Posse

Christina Fuoco

King Curtis

Born Curtis Owsley, February 7, 1934, in Ft. Worth, TX. Died August 14, 1971, in New York, NY.

Although he only rarely achieved fame on his own, King Cur-

tis probably was the most influential R&B/rock saxophone player of his time. He began playing in Texas during the 1940s, hooked up with Lionel Hampton in 1952, and later became one of New York's most desired session players. As leader of Atlantic Records' house R&B band during the 1950s and 1960s, Curtis played some of the most famous sax breaks in pop music, among them the Coasters' "Yakety Yak" and Aretha Franklin's "Respect." Curtis also backed Nat "King" Cole, Buddy Holly, Sam Cooke, and John Lennon, among many, many others. But Curtis, who came from the tradition of hard-blowing Texas blues saxophonists, also had his own hits. Three of his instrumental records crossed over to the pop Top 40: "Soul Twist" in 1962 and "Memphis Soul Stew" and "Ode to Billy Joe" in 1967. Curtis was stabbed to death outside his New York City apartment in 1971 at age 37.

what to buy: *Instant Soul: The Legendary King Curtis* 🎵🎵🎵🎵 (Razor & Tie, 1994) is an excellent compilation that covers 1956–70 but concentrates on the recordings he made with the Muscle Shoals Rhythm Section. The 23 tracks include all three of his Top 40 pop hits.

what to buy next: During the live session captured on *King Curtis & Champion Jack Dupree: Blues at Montreux* 🎵🎵🎵 (Atlantic, 1973/1992, prod. King Curtis and Joel Dorn), Curtis is at his loosest, with a band that includes Cornell Dupree on guitar and Jerry Jemmott on bass.

what to avoid: The thankfully out-of-print *Soul on Soul* 🎵🎵 (Pickwick, 1972) is a cheapie posthumous compilation from Curtis's Capitol period, issued as part of Pickwick's "Harlem Hitparade" series. *Best of King Curtis* 🎵🎵 (Collectables, 1996) doesn't nearly cover the claim of its title.

the rest:
The New Scene of King Curtis 🎵🎵🎵 (New Jazz-Prestige, 1960/Original Jazz Classics, 1992)
Soul Meeting 🎵🎵🎵 (Prestige, 1960/1995)
Trouble in Mind 🎵🎵🎵 (Tru-Sound, 1961, Fantasy/OBC, 1988)
It's Party Time with King Curtis 🎵🎵🎵 (Tru-Sound, 1962/Ace)
Instant Groove 🎵🎵🎵 (Atco, 1969/Pinnacle)
Soul Twist & Other Golden Classics 🎵🎵🎵 (Collectables)
Enjoy . . . The Best of King Curtis 🎵🎵🎵 (Collectables, 1991)
Soul Serenade 🎵🎵🎵 (JCI, 1991)
Home Cookin' 🎵🎵🎵 (Point/Zillion, 1992)
Didn't He Play 🎵🎵 (Drive, 1995)
Night Train 🎵🎵🎵 (Prestige, 1995)
Piping Hot 🎵🎵🎵 (Relic, 1995)
Old Gold/Doing the Dixie Twist 🎵🎵🎵 (Ace, 1995)

Trouble in Mind/It's Party Time ✍✍✍ (Ace, 1995)
Best of King Curtis ✍✍✍ (Blue Note, 1996)

worth searching for: *Live at the Fillmore West* ✍✍✍✍ (Atco, 1971, prod. King Curtis and Arif Mardin) captures a hot set when Curtis opened a Bay Area stand for Aretha Franklin, who recording her own live album of the same name (with Curtis's band backing her). The box set *Blow Man, Blow!* ✍✍✍✍ (Bear Family, 1992) compiles Curtis's recordings for Capitol from 1962–65 on three CDs and includes 16 previously unreleased cuts.

influences:

◀◀ Illinois Jacquet, Earl Bostic, Arnett Cobb

▶▶ Clarence Clemons, Leroi Moore (Dave Matthews Band)

Brian Mansfield

King Sun

Born Todd Turnbow, February 23, 1967.

Representing both Uptown and the Bronx, King Sun came to prominence with a mixture of hardcore Afrocentrism, gold-chain braggadocio, and even syrupy love raps. Indeed, despite his commanding stature and mad microphone finesse, King Sun is best known for his 1989 love-jam duet with D-Moet, "Hey Love."

what to buy: King Sun's debut, *XL* ✍✍✍✍ (Profile, 1989, prod. DJ Mark The 45 King, others) is filled with the uptempo rhythms of the day, plus some genuinely funky loops and breaks. The DJ Mark The 45 King–produced "Fat Tape" is, indeed, phat. And on the other hand: "Hey Love," Sun's dip into Barry White (or pajama-era Big Daddy Kane) territory. A mere year later, Sun dropped *Righteous but Ruthless* ✍✍✍✍ (Profile, 1990, prod. Tony D, others), an album loaded with gems from "Be Black" and "Big Shots" to "Stunts" and "The Gods Are Taking Heads," on which fellow Five Percenters Poor Righteous Teachers take a guest turn.

what to avoid: After releasing two albums in two years, King Sun dropped from sight, only to re-emerge four years later with a new name (the Jeweler Sundulah) and a new title (winner of Clark Kent's Superman MC Battle for World Supremacy). He also had a new EP, *Strictly Ghetto* ✍✍ (Cold Chillin', 1994, prod. various), which didn't come close to matching the brilliance of his earlier work.

influences:

◀◀ Big Daddy Kane

Spence D.

King Tee

Los Angeles' King Tee may never have enjoyed the platinum sales of peers like Ice Cube or the plaudits of proteges like Tha Alkaholiks, but there's no doubt he's the genuine article. For over a decade, the party's been wherever he's at. Like Biz Markie to East Coast fans, King Tee is beloved on the Westside for his clown-prince antics and his humorous brand of story-telling. Unlike the Biz's *Going Off*, though, Tee has no start-to-finish classic. No one better deserves a retrospective anthology.

what to buy: Any definitive King Tee compilation would have to begin with 1987's "Payback's A Mutha" and "Bass," Tee's incredible indie singles. Both make their appearance on his major-label debut *Act a Fool* ✍✍✍ (Capitol, 1988, prod. D.J. Pooh). But when placed against the East Coast records of the same period (EPMD's *Strictly Business*, Eric B. & Rakim's *Paid in Full*), the album sounds dated. Plus, King Tee's earthy concerns (drinking, flirting, battle rhyming) never fit the stark, minimal Los Angeles sound pioneered by such Tee cronies as Ice-T. *At Your Own Risk* ✍✍✍ (Capitol, 1990, prod. D.J. Pooh, others) is much better, featuring King Tee's third classic, the irrepressible "Ruff Rhyme (Back Again)." On such vignettes as "Skanless," "Jay Fay Dray," and the turntable showcase for Tha future Alkaholik, "E Gets Swift," Tee starts flowing like the Old English he's tapping. At the same time, there are the embarrassing New Jack swing-isms on the horrible "On the Dance Tip" and "Diss You." By *Tha Triflin Album* ✍✍✍✍ (Capitol, 1993, prod. D.J. Pooh, Tha Alkaholiks, Marley Marl, others), things are finally coming together. A virtual prototype for Tha Alkaholiks' debut later that year, the music and pacing are catching up to Tee's quick wit. With its screaming car-alarm hook, Tha Liks' debut on "I Got It Bad Y'All" is unforgettable. Even Tee's classic Saint Ides commercial appears here as "King Tee's Beer Stand." Still, there are questionable inclusions: Marley Marl's remix of "At Your Own Risk" is redundant, and the post-riot "Black Together Again" sticks out like a red bow-tie in the album's casual party atmosphere. Call *IV Life* ✍✍✍ (MCA, 1994, prod. Broadway, D.J. Pooh, E-Swift, others) the morning after. The tempos are slower, the rhymes less frenetic, and the vibe is chill; see "Dippin'" for that Sunday-afternoon feel. Pick "Super Nigga" and "Free Style Ghetto" to fill out the imaginary compilation, and let us know when the next party's jumping off.

influences:

◀◀ Slick Rick, World Famous Supreme Team, Rakim

▶▶ Tha Alkaholiks, Madkap, Nefertiti, Xzibit

Jeff "DJ Zen" Chang

B.B. King (© Jack Vartoogian)

Albert King

Born April 25, 1923, in Indianola, MS. Died December 21, 1992, in Memphis, TN.

Never as well-known as his like-named contemporary, B.B., Albert King was nonetheless almost as big an influence. More rock guitarists, notably Jimi Hendrix, Cream-era Eric Clapton, and Stevie Ray Vaughan, have copped directly from Albert than from any other bluesman. Standing an imposing six feet five inches and weighing in at 250 pounds, the left-handed former bulldozer driver played with brute force, bending the strings on his upside-down Gibson Flying V with a ferocity that could be downright frightening. King made his first recordings in the early 1950s and cut some fantastic sides for Bobbin and King from 1959–63, but he really hit his stride when he signed with Stax in 1966 and began working with Booker T and the MG's and the Memphis Horns. His collaborations with them worked as well as they did because, for all his toughness, King's music swung, a fact well-documented on the excellent live albums, where he re-

captures the Stax albums' drive backed by a horn-less quartet. He was also a fantastic, if not particularly flexible, singer.

what to buy: King's Stax debut, *Born under a Bad Sign* 𝄢𝄢𝄢𝄢 (Atlantic, 1967, prod. Al Jackson), is an undisputed classic. The two-disc compilation, *The Ultimate Collection* 𝄢𝄢𝄢𝄢 (Rhino, 1992) offers a fine career overview. Any of the three live albums recorded at San Francisco's Fillmore West Auditorium in 1968, all produced by Al Jackson, capture the full power of Albert King onstage: *Live Wire/Blues Power* 𝄢𝄢𝄢𝄢 (Stax, 1968); *Wednesday Night in San Francisco* 𝄢𝄢𝄢𝄢 (Stax, 1990); and *Thursday Night in San Francisco* 𝄢𝄢𝄢𝄢 (Stax, 1990).

what to buy next: *Let's Have a Natural Ball* 𝄢𝄢𝄢𝄢 (Modern Blues, 1989) collects King's late 50s/early 60s sides backed by a hard-charging horn section. *I'll Play the Blues for You* 𝄢𝄢𝄢𝄢 (Stax, 1972, prod. Allen Jones and Henry Bush) includes the killer title track as well as "Little Brother," perhaps King's most tender moment. Soul-blues never got much better than this.

what to avoid: *Red House* ♫♫ (Castle, 1991, prod. Joe Walsh and Alan Douglas) is a misguided, probably well-intentioned attempt to help the great bluesman by modernizing his sound. Ugh. Somebody got really excited when they discovered long-missing tapes of King jamming with John Mayall. Then Fantasy released *The Lost Session* ♫♫ (Stax, 1986), and it became painfully clear why the tapes got shoved into the warehouse in the first place.

the rest:

Jammed Together: Albert King, Steve Cropper, Pops Staples ♫♫♫ (Stax, 1969)
Years Gone By ♫♫♫♫ (Stax, 1969)
Lovejoy ♫♫♫ (Stax, 1970)
I Wanna Get Funky ♫♫♫ (Stax, 1973)
The Pinch ♫♫♫ (Stax, 1977)
New Orleans Heat ♫♫♫♫ (Tomato, 1979)
Montreux Festival ♫♫♫ (Stax, 1979)
Blues for Elvis ♫♫ (Stax, 1981)
Crosscut Saw: Albert King in San Francisco ♫♫♫♫ (Stax, 1983/1992)
I'm in a Phone Booth Baby ♫♫♫ (Stax, 1984)
Blues at Sunrise ♫♫♫♫ (Stax, 1988)

influences:

◀◀ B.B. King, Jimmy Reed, T-Bone Walker

▶▶ Otis Rush, Eric Clapton, Jimi Hendrix, Stevie Ray Vaughan, Buddy Guy, Billy Gibbons, Joe Louis Walker, Kenny Wayne Shepherd

Alan Paul

B.B. King

Born September 16, 1925, near Itta Bena, MS.

No other blues artist has ever entered mainstream American culture quite like B.B. King. He is the only one to step inside from the commercial cold that has long been the bluesman's fate, to receive presidential citations and honorary degrees and star in commercials for the likes of Wendy's and Northwest Airlines. He has become so omnipresent that it's easy to forget *why* he's so revered: He fundamentally changed the way the electric guitar is played. The roots of any blues-based electric guitarist can be traced back to B.B. King, whether they know it or not. King took single-string electric lead guitar playing, pioneered by Charlie Christian and T-Bone Walker, and coated it with Mississippi grit. The result was a highly personalized style—marked by stinging finger vibrato, incredible economy, and uncannily vocal-like phrasing—which had tremendous impact on virtually every electric blues guitarist to follow, includ-

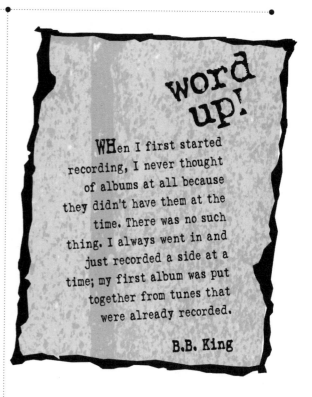

word up!

WHen I first started recording, I never thought of albums at all because they didn't have them at the time. There was no such thing. I always went in and just recorded a side at a time; my first album was put together from tunes that were already recorded.

B.B. King

ing Buddy Guy, Albert King, Freddie King, and Otis Rush. These players, in turn, inspired countless rock guitarists, notably Jimi Hendrix, Eric Clapton, and Stevie Ray Vaughan.

what to buy: The emergence of King's groundbreaking style can be heard on *The Best of B.B. King, Vol. One* ♫♫♫♫ (Flair/Virgin, 1991), an essential collection of 50s recordings that includes his original versions of standard-bearers like "Three O'Clock Blues," "You Upset Me Baby," and "Every Day I Have the Blues." B.B.'s vocal-like guitar playing is part and parcel of his rare ability to communicate intimately with an audience, a powerful rapport that is perfectly captured on *Live at the Regal* ♫♫♫♫ (MCA, 1971, prod. Johnny Pate), a 1964 performance considered by many to be not only his finest recording but the greatest album in all modern blues. This treasure trove of sophisticated-yet-down-home music includes such staples as "It's My Own Fault," "Every Day I Have the Blues," and "Sweet Little Angel." *Completely Well* ♫♫♫♫ (MCA, 1969, prod. Bill Szymczyk) contains King's only Top-20 hit, "The Thrill Is Gone," and is solid through and through.

$\begin{matrix}3\\3\\0\end{matrix}$ *ben e. king*

what to buy next: Sooner or later, you'll probably want the four-CD boxed set, *King of the Blues* ✍✍✍✍ (MCA, 1992, prod. Andy McKaie), an excellent summary of King's career. *Live at San Quentin* ✍✍✍✍ (MCA, 1990) and *Blues Summit* ✍✍✍✍ (MCA, 1993), which features a host of guest stars, are King's best recent efforts, both showing that he still had plenty of sting in his vibrato and ideas in his head.

what to avoid: *B.B. King in London* ✍✍ (MCA, 1971) is the usual pointless hook-the-blues-guy-up-with-well-meaning-rockers-who-love-him-but-can't-play-his-stuff-half-as-well-as-his-own-band exercise. Also, his 70s and 80s records are virtually all burdened by over-production. Tread carefully.

the rest:
Blues Is King ✍✍✍✍ (MCA, 1967)
Lucille ✍✍✍✍ (MCA, 1968)
The Electric B.B. King—His Best ✍✍✍✍ (MCA, 1968)
Live & Well ✍✍✍✍ (MCA, 1969)
Incredible Soul of B.B. King ✍✍✍✍ (MCA, 1970)
Indianola Mississippi Seeds ✍✍✍✍ (MCA, 1970)
Live in Cook County Jail ✍✍✍✍ (MCA, 1970)
Back in the Alley: The Classic Blues of B.B. King ✍✍✍✍ (MCA, 1973)
The Best of B.B. King ✍✍✍✍ (MCA, 1973)
To Know You Is to Love You ✍✍✍ (MCA, 1973)
Friends ✍✍✍ (MCA, 1974)
B.B. King and Bobby Bland: Together for the First Time Live ✍✍✍✍ (MCA, 1974)
Lucille Talks Back ✍✍✍ (MCA, 1975)
B.B. King & Bobby Bland: Together Again Live ✍✍ (MCA, 1976)
King Size ✍✍✍✍ (MCA, 1977)
Midnight Believer ✍✍✍ (MCA, 1978)
Take It Home ✍✍ (MCA, 1979)
Live at Ole Miss ✍✍✍ (MCA, 1980)
Great Moments with B.B. King ✍✍✍ (MCA, 1981)
There Must Be a Better World Somewhere ✍✍✍ (MCA, 1981)
Love Me Tender ✍✍✍ (MCA, 1982)
Blues 'n' Jazz ✍✍✍ (MCA, 1983)
Six Silver Strings ✍✍ (MCA, 1985)
Do the Boogie: Early 50's Classics ✍✍✍✍ (Flair/Virgin, 1988)
King of the Blues 1989 ✍✍✍ (MCA, 1989)
There Is Always One More Time ✍✍✍ (MCA, 1991)
The Fabulous B.B. King ✍✍✍✍ (Flair/Virgin, 1991)
Singin' the Blues/The Blues ✍✍✍✍ (Flair/Virgin, 1991)
Live at the Apollo ✍✍✍ (GRP, 1991)
Sweet Little Angel ✍✍✍✍ (Flair/Virgin, 1992)

influences:
◀◀ Blind Lemon Jefferson, T-Bone Walker, Django Reinhardt, Lonnie Johnson, Clarence "Gatemouth" Brown

▶▶ Buddy Guy, Eric Clapton, David Gilmour, Albert King, Otis Rush, Albert Collins

Alan Paul

Ben E. King
Born September 23, 1938, in Henderson, NC.

With its reverberating, four-note bass line, "Stand by Me" is a Hall of Fame song before King even starts singing; when he wraps his smooth tenor around the lyrics, it becomes a hymn for the ages. It's one of the most covered songs on the planet, and it enjoys regular boosts in popularity thanks to TV commercials and movies—most notably Rob Reiner's 1986 film of the same name. It's hardly all King has to offer, though. As one of the many fine lead singers in The Drifters' revolving door of frontmen, he sang lead on "There Goes My Baby," "Save the Last Dance for Me," and "I Count the Tears," and his solo career boasts "Spanish Harlem" and a handful of other pop-R&B gems.

what to buy: *The Ben E. King Anthology* ✍✍✍✍ (Rhino, 1993, prod. various) covers all the aforementioned—plus non-album singles—across a remastered, double-length, and nicely annotated package. It's what you need; the rest of the available titles are mostly second-rate compilations.

what to avoid: A couple of the aforementioned inferior collections that remain available—*The Best of Ben E. King* ✍ (Curb, 1993) and *The Best of Ben E. King and the Drifters* ✍ (Dominion, 1993)—are not worth acquiring.

the rest:
The Ultimate Collection ✍✍✍ (Atlantic, 1987)

influences:
◀◀ The Drifters, Sam Cooke, Chuck Jackson

▶▶ Ted Hawkins, Paul Rodgers, Bruce Springsteen, Terence Trent D'Arby

Allan Orski

Evelyn "Champagne" King
Born June 29, 1960, in the Bronx, NY.

As she grew older, Evelyn King grew to loathe the bubbly nickname placed on her early in her career, but it was exactly her effervescent style and sparkling voice that made her the teen queen of the disco era in the 1970s. Born into a musical family (her father had been a member of the doo-wop groups The Orioles and The Harptones), King turned professional in 1976, singing in the booming club circuit around Philadelphia. A year later, legend has it, she was discovered while subbing for her sister as a cleaning woman at Philadelphia's Sigma Studios, when producer Theodore Life heard her singing Sam Cooke's "A Change Is Gonna Come." Signed by Life to RCA in 1978, King recorded a string of hits for the label over the next eight years. Her saucy debut single, "Shame," is one of the definitive dance songs of the disco age and vaulted King into prominence. Her 1979 follow-up, the midtempo groove "I Don't Know If It's Right," became her second consecutive Top 10 hit, followed by the #1 R&B sensations "I'm in Love" and "Love Come Down," her vocals on the latter two songs elevating good arrangements into great ones. Her final hit for RCA was "Betcha She Don't Love You" in 1982; in 1988, King moved to EMI-Manhattan Records where her single "Flirt," revealing a tougher and more sophisticated King but a disappointment from her earlier works, never crossed over to the pop charts.

what to buy: Produced by Theodore Life and aided by the production talents of Andre Cymone and Leon Sylvers, *Love Come Down: The Best of Evelyn "Champagne" King* 𝄢𝄢𝄢𝄢 (RCA, 1993, prod. Theodore Life) catalogs King's career in 15 gleaming cuts, including, of course, all the big hits: "Shame," "I Don't Know If It's Right," "I'm in Love," and the title track.

what to buy next: Featuring a brilliant group of supporting vocalists, including Freddie Jackson and Lillo Thomas, *Get Loose* 𝄢𝄢𝄢𝄢 (RCA, 1994, prod. Morrie Brown) is as much showcase for King as it is for the talents of singer-songwriter Kashif: not only does the former B.T. Express star join in the harmonies, but he wrote or co-wrote every song on the album except "I'm Just Warmin' Up."

worth searching for: Ah, youth. King's teenage exuberance and sheer joy permeate through virtually every track of *Smooth Talk* 𝄢𝄢𝄢𝄢 (RCA, 1977), her out-of-print first album and true collector's item of the disco years.

influences:

◄◄ Donna Summer, Dionne Warwick, Anita Ward, Gwen McCrae

►► Melba Moore, Stacy Lattisaw, Irene Cara, Paula Abdul, Janet Jackson, Vanessa Williams, Spice Girls, Miisa, Toni Braxton

"Lisa Lisa" Orlando

Freddie King

Born September 30, 1934, in Gilmer, TX. Died December 28, 1976, in Dallas, TX.

Not possessing the towering presence on ghetto jukeboxes of his namesake B.B. King or the sweeping influence of his Chicago blues elders Muddy Waters and Howlin' Wolf, Freddie King nevertheless eventually emerged as one of the great electric bluesmen. His melodic, driving shuffles struck a resonant chord with a younger generation of white blues-rock guitarists, who passed around his rare, out-of-print albums like sacred scriptures. His 1961 instrumental hit, "Hideaway," provided King with a nationwide reputation, although none of his subsequent singles appeared on even the R&B charts after that year. But the blues boom of the late 1960s rescued him from obscurity and he made a pair of modest albums under the aegis of saxophonist King Curtis and a series of more successful albums produced by Leon Russell. His stinging attack on loping instrumentals laid one of the cornerstones of modern blues guitar vocabulary. Although his reputation rests with his guitar, King also sang with an underrated, powerful style. His lasting influence has led Freddie King to be recognized as one of the great post-war blues masters.

what to buy: The best available overview of his long career, *Hideaway: The Best of Freddie King* 𝄢𝄢𝄢𝄢 (Rhino, 1993), includes three cuts from his later recording but concentrates on the fruitful abundance of his King Records years (1961–66).

what to buy next: A recently discovered tape, *Live at the Electric Ballroom 1974* 𝄢𝄢𝄢𝄢 (Black Top, 1995, exec. prod. Hammond Scott), mixes a rare pair of acoustic numbers recorded at a radio show with a blasting, ripping concert appearance.

what to avoid: The two albums King recorded with the customarily savvy King Curtis, *Freddie King Is a Blues Master* 𝄢𝄢 (Cotillion, 1969) and *My Feeling for the Blues* 𝄢 (Cotillion, 1970), both lean heavily on thin accompaniment, little guitar, and reedy vocals.

the rest:

17 Hits 𝄢𝄢𝄢𝄢 (Federal, 1987)
1934–1976 𝄢𝄢𝄢𝄢 (Polydor, 1993)
King of the Blues 𝄢𝄢𝄢 (EMI, 1995)

worth searching for: All of his original King Records albums remain highly prized, desirable collector's items, but his especially enduring debut album, *Freddy King Sings* 𝄢𝄢𝄢𝄢 (King, 1961), one of the great modern blues albums, was remixed and released for the first time in stereo on CD by Modern Blues Recordings (1989).

influences:

◄◄ Otis Rush, Eddie Taylor, Robert Jr. Lockwood

►► Eric Clapton, Jimi Hendrix, Stevie Ray Vaughan

Joel Selvin

3
3 *earl klugh*
2

Earl Klugh

Born September 16, 1954, in Detroit, MI.

The most important thing to know about Earl Klugh is that though you will usually find him in the jazz section of your music store, he does not consider himself a jazz artist. He lists Chet Atkins as his biggest influence and considers himself an acoustic guitarist. Pulling a guitar into his hands for the first time as a three-year-old, Klugh was playing on an album with jazzman Yusef Lateef by the age of 15 and began to earn a reputation for his remarkable instrumental skills while working with George Benson. He played with Benson throughout the early 1970s (most notably on Benson's 1971 *White Rabbit* LP), was briefly a member of Return to Forever in 1974, then worked as a sideman with Chick Corea. Klugh began forging his solo musical path by the late 1970s, becoming famous for mixing funk beats with a strong melody line from which he rarely strays. His music is seldom surprising, but it's consistently listenable and comforting. He has collaborated with Bob James, Hubert Laws, and George Benson, among others, since setting out on his own.

what to buy: For years, Earl waited to be Klugh less accompaniment: solo, one-man-one-guitar, no frills. In 1989 he fulfilled the dream with *Solo Guitar* 🎸🎸🎸🎸 (WEA/Warner Bros., 1989, prod. Earl Klugh). Though he keeps the cuts in the three-minute range, Klugh plays each composition beautifully, with delicate and supple grace. On some tracks, he approaches a fluid groove reminiscent of the great jazz guitarists of the 1930s, like Joe Pass.

what to buy next: The title of *Soda Fountain Shuffle* 🎸🎸🎸🎸 (WEA/Warner Bros., 1984, prod. Earl Klugh) says it all. Soda fountains, indeed. This album is laced with synthesizer droning and drum machines *kerthunking*. It's spacy and light, easy listening and tightly packaged. While Klugh fans love this one, it's not his best effort.

what to avoid: Need to fulfill an album contract, and quick? Collect as many romantic ditties as you can from 20 years of music making and call it *Ballads* 🎸🎸 (EMD/Manhattan, 1993, comp. prod. Steven Schenfeld). If you want nothing more than fluffy background music, this is it. The songs drift into one long, languid pastiche: nothing stands out, breaks new ground, or intrigues, but every cut is pretty.

the rest:
Living Inside Your Love 🎸🎸🎸 (EMD/Capitol, 1977)
Finger Paintings 🎸🎸🎸 (EMD/Capitol, 1977)
Dream Come True 🎸🎸🎸 (EMI, 1979)

(With Bob James) *Two of a Kind* 🎸🎸🎸🎸 (Manhattan, 1982)
Life Stories 🎸🎸🎸 (WEA/Warner Bros., 1986)
Midnight in San Juan 🎸🎸🎸 (WEA/Warner Bros., 1989)
Whispers & Promises 🎸🎸🎸 (WEA/Warner Bros., 1989)
Earl Klugh Trio, Vol. 1 🎸🎸🎸 (WEA/Warner Bros., 1991)
Best Of 🎸🎸 (EMD/Capitol, 1991)
Best of—Vol.2 🎸🎸🎸 (EMD/Capitol, 1992)
Sound and Visions, Vol. 2 🎸🎸🎸 (Warner Bros., 1993)
Late Night Guitar 🎸🎸🎸 (Liberty, 1993)
Move 🎸🎸 (WEA/Warner Bros., 1994)
Crazy for You 🎸🎸🎸🎸 (Blue Note, 1996)
Love Songs 🎸🎸 (EMD/Capitol, 1996)
Magic in Your Eyes 🎸🎸🎸 (One Way, 1996)
Sudden Burst of Energy 🎸🎸🎸🎸 (Warner Bros., 1996)
The Journey 🎸🎸🎸 (Warner Bros., 1997)

worth searching for: Years after Klugh played behind George Benson, he played beside him as equal partner on the duet album *Collaboration* 🎸🎸🎸 (Warner Bros., 1987, prod. Tommy LiPuma). Produced by Benson's main man, Tommy LiPuma, the LP is a keepsake of two guitar geniuses feeding off each other's musical energy, in a spectrum of music ranging from the funk-fueled "Brazilian Stomp" to the haunting "Love Theme from Romeo and Juliet."

influences:

◄◄ Chet Atkins, Les Paul, Wes Montgomery, Jose Feliciano, George Benson

►► Pat Metheny, Lee Ritenour, Michael Hedges, Liona Boyd, Julian Bream

Chris Tower

KMD

Formed in Brooklyn, NY.

Subroc, vocals; Zevlove X, vocals; Onyx, vocals.

KMD's intoxicating hip-hop elixir was a heady mix of soul and jazz-based beats, charming and smooth lyrical deliveries, and an unwavering sense of black pride; along with their peers—Leaders of the New School, Brand Nubian, 3rd Bass, De La Soul—Subroc, Zevlove X, and Onyx represented all that was good in hip-hop. But the story of KMD could very well be one of the most heartbreaking in hip-hop. Friends since childhood, the three rappers saw their careers launched with the help of neighborhood cronies 3rd Bass. During the making of the group's second album, though, Subroc was accidentally killed by a driver on the streets of New York. Still feeling the pangs of loss, Zev and Onyx managed to complete the album, but a heartless Elektra Records dropped the group from its roster shortly before the record's release, using the poor excuse that its cover—a symbolic picture of a black "Sambo" figure being hung—was too controversial. The one-two punch seemed to all but end the careers of Zevlove X and Onyx.

what to buy: The crew's debut, *Mr. Hood* ♫♫♫ (Elektra, 1991, prod. KMD, Stimulated Dummies), is centered around a bumbling, ignorant man named Mr. Hood whom KMD leads through the album, educating him along on the way. The songs are like chapters in the story, weaving fresh breakbeats with Subroc's downy lyricism, with a few *Sesame Street* interludes on the way. "Peachfuzz" is a sweet serenade that became the downtempo hip-hop song of the summer, while other songs like "Humrush" are just innocent fun.

worth searching for: The B-side to "Nitty Gritty" (Elektra, 1991) was "Plumskinz," an even smoother song than its "Peachfuzz" prequel; it's one of the best KMD songs ever made. Another item worth the search is a (bootleg) copy of the unreleased second album, *Black Bastards*. It's haunting to hear Subroc posthumously, and just plain sad to hear Zevlove X's post-tragedy verses. KMD is a group that truly didn't deserve its fate.

influences:

◄◄ 3rd Bass, De La Soul, Brand Nubian, A Tribe Called Quest

►► Leaders of the New School, Hieroglyphics, Blood of Abraham

Jazzbo

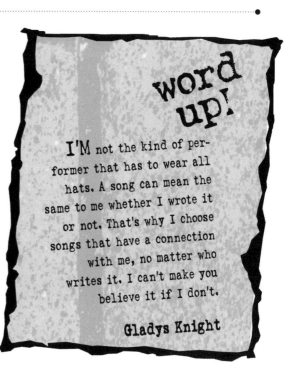

word up!

I'M not the kind of performer that has to wear all hats. A song can mean the same to me whether I wrote it or not. That's why I choose songs that have a connection with me, no matter who writes it. I can't make you believe it if I don't.

Gladys Knight

Gladys Knight & the Pips

Formed 1952, in Atlanta, GA.

Gladys Knight (born May 28, 1944, in Atlanta, GA), lead vocals; Merald "Bubba" Knight, vocals; William Guest, vocals; Brenda Knight, vocals (1952–59); Eleanor Guest, vocals (1952–59); Langston George, vocals (1959–62); Edward Patten, vocals (1959–present).

Starting her performing career as a child when she, her brother Merald, and two cousins formed a youth gospel quartet that would become the standard bearer for modern rhythm and blues, Gladys Knight, along with the Pips, inspired many of the singing groups that became popular in the 1950s, 1960s, and 1970s, yet they never reached the full superstardom they deserved. At the age of seven, Gladys won the grand prize on *Ted Mack's Original Amateur Hour,* and many other television appearances followed. Her solo success sparked the formation of Gladys Knight & the Pips in 1957; their first gig was at a birthday party for Merald Knight (Gladys's brother), after which they began to tour and record. They finally scored their first Top 20 hit on Atlanta's Huntom label in 1961 with the Johnny Otis tune "Every Beat of My Heart," but by that time original group members Eleanor Guest and Brenda Knight had been replaced by cousins Edward Patten and Langston George, the latter leaving in the early 1960s. The group faded in the 1960s when Gladys had a child, and the group worked as backup vocalists for other artists. Signing with Motown Records later in the decade jumpstarted their career with a string of hits, but Motown never fully appreciated the act's potential. Gladys Knight & the Pips proved their star value as soon as they left Motown and signed with Buddah, where they landed their biggest hit in 1973, "Midnight Train to Georgia." They followed that success with many others, as Motown continued to release albums under their name without paying them royalties. Subsequent lawsuits kept Gladys from recording for three years, though the group continued to perform live. But the entanglements stalled their momentum and caused the group's popularity to decline. During this period, Gladys recorded a solo album and appeared in a movie and on television. She and the Pips reunited in 1980 and made a resurgence with many more hits, earning a Grammy for

"Love Overboard" in 1988. The group officially "suspended" after Gladys released a solo LP in 1991, but she went on to record many best-selling singles on her own, such as "It's Gonna Take All Our Love," "License to Kill," (from the James Bond film), and "Men." In 1986, she won a Grammy with Elton John, Dionne Warwick, and Stevie Wonder for the AIDS-benefit record *That's What Friends Are For.*

what to buy: Though they had been performing together for more than a decade when they signed with Motown, *All the Great Hits* ✧✧✧✧ (PGD/Motown, 1974, prod. various) affirms that Gladys Knight & the Pips really came into their own when they began to work with the label. Aided by producer Norman Whitfield, the group created classics in the distinctive Detroit/Motown groove, including "Everybody Needs Love," "I Heard It through the Grapevine," "Friendship Train," and, later, "If I Were Your Woman" and "Neither One of Us (Wants to Be the First to Say Goodbye)." Though this is only a 30-minute sample, it's still a wonderful introduction to Knight and Pips-ology.

what to buy next: The first album they recorded after leaving Motown, *Imagination* ✧✧✧✧✧ (Buddah, 1974/The Right Stuff, 1997) captures a group rejuvenated by its newfound status as a label's showcase attraction. Even though they rushed this LP to the streets, Knight sounds exhilarated and celebratory, singing with depth and emotion. Many argue that this is the group's finest album.

what to avoid: Though more musicians, singers, and engineers worked on this album than on a Hollywood movie soundtrack, *All Our Love* ✧✧ (MCA Special Products, 1988) is a random collection of trendy, vacuous saccharine. It features Knight's voice and her chameleon-like versatility, but neither her passion nor her trademark intensity.

the rest:
That Special Time of Year ✧✧✧ (Sony, 1971)
Best of: Columbia Years ✧✧✧ (Sony, 1974)
I Feel a Song ✧✧✧✧ (Buddah, 1975/The Right Stuff, 1997)
The One & Only/Miss Gladys Knight ✧✧✧ (Sequel, 1978/1994)
Touch ✧✧✧✧ (Sony, 1981/1993)
Christmas Album ✧✧✧ (Special Music, 1989)
Soul Survivors: The Best of Gladys Knight & the Pips 1973–1983 ✧✧✧✧ (Rhino, 1990)
Greatest Hits ✧✧✧✧ (Curb/Warner Brothers, 1990)
Room in Your Heart ✧✧ (Drive Archive, 1994)
The Best of Gladys Knight & the Pips: Anthology ✧✧✧✧ (Motown, 1995)
Blue Lights in the Basement ✧✧✧ (RCA, 1996)
The Lost Live Album ✧✧✧✧ (Buddah, 1996)
The Ultimate Collection ✧✧✧✧ (Motown, 1997)

worth searching for: Rereleased under an obscure label made specially for those preoccupied by the past, *Letter Full of Tears/Golden Classics* ✧✧✧ (Collectables, 1961) is an album of unique perspective. It's a collection of Gladys and Pips pre-Motown material recorded in the early 1960s for the Fury label. Though they became a more polished act in later years, this album spotlights Knight's talents well, especially on the title track cut when the singer was only 12 years old. And, though currently out of print, *Neither One of Us* ✧✧✧✧ (Motown, 1973) is the last of the Motown recordings for Gladys Knight & the Pips, at the peak of their skills as recording artists. The title cut is Gladys Knight at her finest, supported by striking backup vocals. The LP is also a testament to the reason why the act left Motown: they were never properly promoted by the company, and proved as much to the world as soon as they left.

solo outings:
Gladys Knight:
Good Woman ✧✧✧✧ (MCA, 1991)
Just for You ✧✧✧ (MCA, 1994)

influences:

◀◀ The Platters, the Flamingos, Dinah Washington, Mary Wells, Sam Cooke, Jackie Wilson, Van McCoy

▶▶ Dionne Warwick, Betty Wright, Anita Baker, Deniece Williams, Toni Braxton, Cornelius Brothers & Sister Rose, Brand New Heavies

Chris Tower

Jean Knight

Born June 26, 1943, in New Orleans, LA.

Jean Knight is a one-hit wonder, but that one hit was big stuff—"Mr. Big Stuff," to be exact. Recorded for Stax-Volt, Knight rode that taunting call-out to #2 on the pop charts in 1971, and it remains her sole claim to fame. But there's more to her story than that. Before that, Knight worked with producer Huey P. Meux, without great success. And after "Mr. Big Stuff," she had a modest revival with her 1985 cover of Rockin' Sidney's zydeco standard "My Toot Toot." And just when you were ready to consign her to the history books, Knight emerged with a new album in 1997.

what's available: *Mr. Big Stuff* ✧✧✧ (Stax, 1991) is a spirited effort, though there's nothing as distinctive as the title cut. *Shaki De Boo-Tee* ✧✧✧ (Ichiban, 1997) won't launch a comeback, but it shows Knight's still got her chops and also includes live versions of "Mr. Big Stuff" and "My Toot Toot."

influences:

◀◀ Ann Peebles, Curtis Mayfield, Charles Wright, Carla Thomas, Tina Turner

▶▶ Teena Marie, Millie Jackson, Madonna

Gary Graff

Kool & the Gang

Formed 1964, in Jersey City, NJ.

Robert "Kool" Bell (a.k.a. Muhammad Bayyan), bass, vocals; Ronald Bell (a.k.a. Khalis Bayyan), trumpet, sax; Dennis "D.T." Thomas, sax, flute; George "Funky George" Brown, drums; Robert "Spike" Mickens, trumpet; Charles Smith, guitar; Clifford Adams, trombone (1976–present); James "J.T." Taylor, vocals (1979–89, 1995–present); plus more than two dozen other players over the years.

Although bassist Robert "Kool" Bell is the leader in name of this veteran group, it was actually his brother, Ronald Bell, who shaped the Kool and the Gang sound. After forming first as an African percussion outfit, the group changed in 1966 to the Jazziacs, influenced by the holy trinity—John Coltrane, Miles Davis, and Thelonious Monk. The group played local club dates with jazz giants such as Pharoah Sanders and McCoy Tyner occasionally sitting in. Two years later, the group changed its course once again, this time to an upbeat, predominantly instrumental party-funk sound that was anchored by musical director Ronald Bell's punchy, jazz-grounded horn blasts. Calling itself the Soul Music Review, then the New Dimensions, then Kool and the Flames, and finally Kool and the Gang, the group recorded a few minor singles during the late 1960s and early 1970s. In 1973, the group broke big with two crossover hits, "Jungle Boogie" and "Hollywood Swinging," beginning a run as one of the most successful funk outfits of the 1970s and 1980s. In 1979, after disco temporarily pushed its taut, jazz-informed funk off the dance floor, Kool and the Gang rebounded by adding its first lead vocalist (Taylor) and teaming up with jazz-funk producer Eumir Deodato for a more pop-oriented approach. Those moves led to two of the group's biggest songs, "Ladies Night" and "Celebration," which became a welcome-home anthem for the American hostages returned from captivity in Iran, a theme for sports teams, and a staple at weddings and graduations. Although Kool and the Gang was still enjoying chart success, by the mid-1980s its watered-down pop sound wore thin. In 1988, Taylor, who had become the face of Kool and the Gang, left to pursue a mildly successful solo career; he returned in 1995, but nobody seemed to notice.

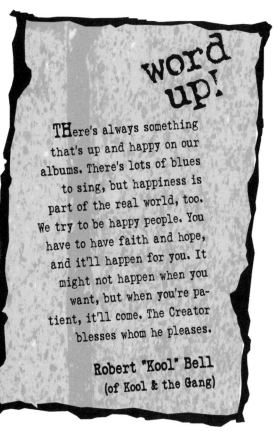

word up!

THere's always something that's up and happy on our albums. There's lots of blues to sing, but happiness is part of the real world, too. We try to be happy people. You have to have faith and hope, and it'll happen for you. It might not happen when you want, but when you're patient, it'll come. The Creator blesses whom he pleases.

**Robert "Kool" Bell
(of Kool & the Gang)**

what to buy: With many of the group's early albums out of print, *The Best of Kool and the Gang 1969–1976* ♫♫♫♫♫ (Mercury/Chronicles, 1993, prod. various) is the best place to go hear the group in its pre-pop prime, as most of the key pre-Taylor tracks are included here ("Jungle Boogie," "Hollywood Swinging," etc.). The funked-up set will come as a revelation to those who only know of the group from its "Celebration" era.

what to buy next: Many of Kool and the Gang's later albums were loaded with filler, so *Everything's Kool and the Gang: Greatest Hits* ♫♫♫♪ (Mercury, 1988, prod. various) is the best way to examine the most noteworthy songs from the J.T. Taylor era. Still, the music pales in comparison to the early- and mid-1970s output.

what to avoid: The title of *Emergency* ♪♪ (De-Lite/Mercury, 1984) expresses the artistic dire straits the group is on with this release.

the rest:
Kool and the Gang Spin Their Top Hits ♪♪♪ (De-Lite/Mercury 1978)
Celebrate! ♪♪ (De-Lite/Mercury, 1980)
Celebration: The Best of Kool & the Gang 1979–1987 ♪♪♪♪ (Mercury/Chronicles, 1994)
Kool Jazz ♪♪♪♪ (Mercury Chronicles, 1997)

worth searching for: *Wild and Peaceful* ♪♪♪♪ (De-Lite, 1973)—out-of-print like most of the Gang's catalog—is a funky good throw-down marked by the hits "Funky Stuff" and "Hollywood Swinging."

solo outings:
J.T. Taylor:
Master of the Game ♪♪ (MCA, 1989)
Feel the Need ♪♪♪ (MCA, 1991)
Baby, I'm Back ♪♪ (MCA, 1993)

influences:
◀◀ Rahsaan Roland Kirk, Horace Silver, Miles Davis, Manu Dibango, Sly and the Family Stone, Mandrill, Isley Brothers, Marvin Gaye

▶▶ Digable Planets, Con Funk Shun, Living Colour, Slave, the Time, the Dazz Band

Josh Freedom du Lac

Kool Ass Fash

See: Beatnuts

Kool G Rap and D.J. Polo

Formed 1986 in Queens, NY. Disbanded 1992.

Kool G Rap (born Nathaniel Wilson), vocals; D.J. Polo, DJ.

The duo's 1986 debut single, "It's a Demo," captivated the hip-hop nation with its sheer intensity. Never before had a rapper asserted himself with such cool, confident lyrical ferocity as the Kool Genius of Rap. He was a rapper's rapper, one who assembled so many styles and techniques in his delivery that aspiring MCs would use the songs as textbooks in rhyming. Subsequent records cemented the pair's legendary status, and songs like "Talk Like Sex," "Poison," and "Streets of New York" will forever be embedded in the hip-hop consciousness. Inspired by the twisting ebb and flows of Fantasy 3 MC Silver Fox, Kool G Rap (with Polo in tow) sought out the production expertise of Marley Marl and both were invited to join Marley's Juice Crew, with G.

Rap subsequently featured on the now-classic "The Symphony" from Marley's *In Control*. But G. Rap's relationship with fellow Juice Crew member Big Daddy Kane soon became strained. G. Rap claimed that Kane had stolen his style for the classic "Ain't No Half Stepping," using a roll-off-the tongue rhyme pattern G. Rap said he'd introduced to Kane during a private, late-night freestyle session. G. Rap's relationship with Polo also ended, in 1992, after six years together. That it lasted that long at all is surprising, since Polo didn't seem to contribute much after the first album (with most of the later releases featuring outside producers). G. Rap has continued his career, and Polo (sort of) has, too: he recently released an embarrassing single called "Freak of the Week," featuring porno star Ron Jeremy.

what to buy: Album after album seemed to produce hit after hit for G. Rap and Polo. The group's second, *Wanted Dead or Alive* ♪♪♪♪ (Cold Chillin'/Warner Bros., 1990, prod. Kool G Rap, D.J. Polo, Large Professor, Eric B., others), is loaded with such songs as "Streets of New York," "Money in the Bank," and "Talk Like Sex," making it one of the stronger hip-hop records released between 1989 and 1992. In many ways, G. Rap can be considered one of the original gangsta rappers, since he was a master of vivid narratives that were unrelentingly rigid and gritty. The third album, *Live and Let Live* ♪♪♪ (Cold Chillin', 1992, prod. Sir Jinx, Kool G Rap, others) goes even further, with "Ill Street Blues," "On the Run," and "Live and Let Live" depicting dark, unapologetic scenarios. The album was originally supposed to be released via Warner Bros., but the music industry hip-hop witch hunt instigated by Ice-T's "Cop Killer" meant Cold Chillin' was on its own.

what to buy next: G. Rap's first album since he officially went solo, *4,5,6* ♪♪♪ (Cold Chillin'/Epic Street, prod. Buckwild, others), is signature Kool G Rap, but it doesn't really carry much musical impact. The choice of beat-makers seems to be at fault here, though the album does have a few nice cuts ("It's a Shame," "Fast Life," the title track).

worth searching for: Kool G Rap and D.J. Polo's first album, *Road to the Riches* ♪♪♪♪ (Cold Chillin', 1988, prod. D.J. Polo, Marley Marl, others) is as raw as it gets. It's certainly a classic worth finding, with tracks including "It's a Demo" and "Poison," which introduced G. Rap's battle-rhyming-just-to-prove-a-point style. Also worth the search is the "On the Run" remix single (Hoppoh/Columbia), which includes a better version of the song using a nasty, old soul beat.

influences:
◀◀ Fantasy 3, Kool Moe Dee, Schoolly D, Spoonie Gee, Juice Crew All Stars

▶▶ Ice Cube, Notorious B.I.G., Naughty by Nature, Nas, Wu-Tang Clan, Mobb Deep

Jazzbo

Kool Keith
/Dr. Octagon

Born Keith Thornton.

While LL Cool J is the model of hip-hop longevity, Kool Keith is the genre's version of the Phoenix, showing that hip-hop has developed enough staying power for artists to enjoy second— or, in the case of Keith's ever-expanding roster of alter-egos, third and fourth—lives. One of rap's most accomplished freestylers and arguably its most colorful eccentric, Keith first turned up as a member of the legendary Ultramagnetic MC's. Following that group's breakup, Keith drifted, landing for a spell in the hospital to battle depression before finally resurfacing in 1995 with a series of underground 12-inch sides under the pseudonyms Big Willie Smith, the Cenubites, and, finally, Dr. Octagon. In 1996, Keith hit pay dirt when Bulk Records expanded his Dr. Octagon persona into a self-titled album, which proved to be one of the most deliriously inventive and relentlessly bugged hip-hop releases ever. With Dan "The Automator" Nakamura supplying the space-age beats, Keith assumed the guise of a demonic gynecologist, born on Jupiter sometime in the third millennium. The near-epic scope of Keith's impressionistic musings ("Earth People," "Blue Flowers") and loony freestyles turned *Dr. Octagon* into an underground sensation, earning Keith an audience among the growing post-alternative rock crowd. Now calling himself Keith again, his next release, *Sex Style*, ditched Octagon's space talk for an over-the-top sojourn into the world of adult entertainment. Here, Keith plays the leering freak, doing it doggy style with porn starlets while wearing a cape and mask, occasionally dipping into his bag of non-sequiturs ("we pull the drawers off girls/we look out windows and stare" he raps on the delightful "Sly We Fly").

what to buy: Keith's bugged-out flow is in full effect on Ultra's seminal *Critical Beatdown* album, but on his own, the best bet is *Dr. Octagon* 𝄞𝄞𝄞𝄞 (Bulk, 1996/Dreamworks, 1997, prod. The Automator), which is a feast for fans of lyrical madness.

what to buy next: Keith's *Sex Style* 𝄞𝄞𝄞𝄞 (Funky Ass, 1997, prod. Kutmasta Kurt and T.R. Love) is an expansion of the sex-maddened "Big Willie Smith" persona first debuted on the "Keep It Real" 12-inch.

worth searching for: Some of Keith's most *out-there* work has come on the 12-inch tip: "So Intelligent" by Sir Menelik, featuring Kool Keith and the Cenubites' "Fondle 'Em," for instance. Other projects include the *Big Time* LP with Tim Dog (under the Ultra heading; Our Time, 1997) and producer Automator's *Better Tomorrow* EP on Ubiquity, on which Keith appears as Sinister 6000.

influences:

◀◀ Ultramagnetic MC's

▶▶ Organized Konfusion, Chino XL, Freestyle Fellowship, Ras Kass

see also: *Ultramagnetic MC's*

Logan Creed

Kool Moe Dee

Born Mohandas Dewese, in New York, NY.

Although most of the world only got to know Kool Moe Dee as a mid-1980s/early 1990s solo artist, the Harlem rapper had actually been a major player in the *original* old school, as the leading voice in the long-lost Treacherous Three. The underappreciated trio split up in the early 1980s after issuing a series of mild-selling 12-inch singles ("The New Rap Language," "Body Rock," etc.) on the indie Enjoy label, never having enjoyed the sort of success that pioneering peers such as Kurtis Blow and Grandmaster Flash & the Furious Five had. On his own, though, Moe Dee finally gained the music world's attention, first with a decent self-titled solo debut, but even more so with the next two powerhouse recordings, *How Ya Like Me Now* and *Knowledge Is Power*. Working with Teddy Riley, who was in the midst of perfecting his layered, funk-laden New Jack Swing formula, Moe Dee tossed off boasts with speed and precision, his crisp, authoritative baritone one of the more distinctive voices in rap. Apparently, though, Moe Dee thought that another rapper was beginning to sound a bit too much like him. So with the Jeep-running-over-a-red-Kangol cover art and the hard-hitting title track of *How Ya Like Me Now*, he kicked off a recorded debate with LL Cool J that would go several bloody rounds, with Cool J firing back with "Jack the Ripper," Moe Dee returning with the next album's "Let's Go" (in which he decides that "LL" stands for "lousy lover," among other things), and so on. As the rivalry petered out, so too did Moe Dee's star. After issuing his fourth solo album, *Funke Funke Wisdom*, he remained silent for three long years, finally resurfacing in 1994 with the sub-par solo album, *Interlude*, and, more surprisingly, a new Treacherous Three full-length, *Old School Flava*. As with the group's early efforts, though, the new Treacherous Three recording received little attention, despite both the reunion of Moe with LA Sunshine and Special K and the inclusion of other old-schoolers, including Melle Mel and Grandmaster Caz.

what to buy: Lyrically, *Knowledge Is King* 🎵🎵🎵 (Jive, 1989, prod. Teddy Riley, Mohandas Dewese, others) isn't much different from the other Moe Dee albums, although the title track and the closing "Pump Your Fist" do convey previously unheard Islamic-influenced messages of black pride. What separates the album from the others the most, though, is Riley's synth- and percussion-heavy New Jack production, which is now at its peak, especially on "I Go to Work."

what to buy next: Of course, Riley's work on *How Ya Like Me Now* 🎵🎵🎵 (Jive, 1987, prod. Mohandas Dewese, Teddy Riley, others) isn't bad, either, and Moe Dee himself is in peak form, deftly carrying a Cool J–sized chip on his shoulder during the winning title track, and reaffirming his pioneering, older-than-old status on "Wild Wild West" and "Way Way Back."

the rest:
Kool Moe Dee 🎵🎵🎵 (Jive, 1986)
Funke Funke Wisdom 🎵🎵🎵 (Jive, 1991)
Greatest Hits 🎵🎵🎵🎵 (Jive, 1993)
Interlude 🎵🎵 (Wrap/Ichiban, 1994)
(With Treacherous Three) *Old School Flava* 🎵🎵🎵 (Ichiban, 1994)
The Jive Collection Series Vol. 2 🎵🎵 (Jive, 1995)

influences:
◀◀ Kurtis Blow, Furious Five, Grandmaster Caz
▶▶ Kurtis Blow, Furious Five, LL Cool J

Josh Freedom du Lac

Lenny Kravitz

Born Leonard Albert Kravitz, May 26, 1964, in New York, NY.

As the son of Jewish television producer Sy Kravitz and an African American actress—the late Roxie Roker of *The Jeffersons*—Kravitz seemed assured of a career in show business, a fate compounded by high school classmates such as Slash of Guns n' Roses and Lone Justice's Maria McKee. Still, when Kravitz married *Cosby Show* actress Lisa Bonet in 1987 and announced plans to release a record, critics snickered, calling him "Mr. Bonet." But his first album, featuring Kravitz himself on nearly every instrument (including drums) played live, silenced many naysayers. Even though his sound proved highly derivative of 1960s and 1970s influences, there was an unmistakable talent emerging; like Prince and Sly Stone before him, Kravitz loots a wide range of rock and R&B influences in service of his soul-drenched pop tunes. After collaborating with Madonna on her 1990 hit "Justify My Love" (Kravitz was later sued by Prince protege Ingrid Chavez, who claimed to have co-written the tune, and rappers Public Enemy, who said a sample of their work used in the song was not licensed), he recorded an all-star version of the John Lennon hit "Give Peace a Chance" during the Gulf War. By 1991, his marriage with Bonet had ended (not before they had a daughter, Zoe), but his career kept going. His own solo output veered between overt Jimi Hendrix, Curtis Mayfield, and Led Zeppelin influences, selling well enough to keep him in the public eye but never enough to bring blockbuster fame.

what to buy: Though he continues to wear his influences on his sleeve, *Circus* 🎵🎵🎵 (Virgin, 1995, prod. Lenny Kravitz) has proved his most consistent outing yet, mimicking Led Zep in the hit single "Rock and Roll Is Dead" without losing any of his own conviction.

what to buy next: As a blueprint of where *Circus* would eventually end up, *Are You Gonna Go My Way?* 🎵🎵🎵 (Virgin, 1993, prod. Lenny Kravitz) is an intriguing album, fired up by the Hendrix-inspired titled track and other numbers that trace his fascination with long-gone musical styles.

what to avoid: Sabotaged mostly by petulant lyrics detailing the 1991 disintegration of his marriage to Bonet, *Mama Said* 🎵🎵 (Virgin, 1991, prod. Lenny Kravitz) is Kravitz's most inconsistent work, despite the presence of two appealing singles, "It Ain't Over 'til It's Over" and "Always on the Run." And while it's good to see him toss aside his hippie influences for psychedelic rock, here the artistic thievery is so bad, it's hard to overlook.

the rest:
Let Love Rule 🎵🎵🎵 (Virgin, 1989)

worth searching for: Look for Kravitz's collaboration with Madonna, "Justify My Love"—if only to marvel that Chavez had the guts to claim credit for lyrics this awful. It's available on Madonna's hits set, *The Immaculate Collection* (Sire, 1990, prod. various).

influences:
◀◀ Led Zeppelin, Jimi Hendrix, Sly & the Family Stone, Living Colour, Prince
▶▶ Self, Beck, Maxwell

Eric Deggans

Lenny Kravitz (© Ken Settle)

Kris Kross

Formed 1991, in Atlanta, GA.

Mack Daddy, vocals; Daddy Mack, vocals.

Growing up isn't easy in the music industry. Artists who start out in the kiddie ranks often end up stuck there, their careers dying somewhat prematurely (so to speak). Kris Kross tried hard to break the chains of youth that strangled the likes of New Kids on the Block and the Bay City Rollers, but the Atlanta rap duo—which scored big in 1992 with a childish, backwards fashion sense and the exuberant kiddie-rap anthems "Jump," "Warm It Up," and "I Missed the Bus"—had serious growing pains. Indeed, after a splashy debut, the duo twice attempted to reach some level of maturity, via hardcore posturing and lyrics about women and money. Both albums, however, were creative failures, and neither matched the commercial success of the *Totally Krossed Out* debut, either, suggesting that it might be time to totally cross out the notion of longevity where Kris Kross is concerned.

what to buy: The youthful exuberance of "Warm It Up" and, especially, "Jump," plus producer-Svengali Jermaine Dupri's layered funk, make *Totally Krossed Out* ♬♬♬ (Ruffhouse/Columbia, 1992, prod. Jermaine Dupri) worth jumping for.

the rest:
Da Bomb ♬♬♬ (Ruffhouse/Columbia, 1993)
Young, Rich & Dangerous ♬♬ (Ruffhouse/Columbia, 1995)
The Best of Kris Kross Remixed '92 '94 '96 ♬♬♬ (Ruffhouse/Columbia, 1996)

influences:
◄◄ Chi-Ali
►► Da Youngsta's, Da Brat, Illegal

Josh Freedom du Lac

Kurious

A half-Puerto Rican, half-Cuban product of New York who adopted his moniker from the children's literary character Curious George, Kurious handled the microphone with such smooth and savvy locution, he attracted the support of several heavy hitters in the hip-hop industry. But while influential radio host Bobbito Garcia, proven A&R executive Dante Ross, and former 3rd Bass-man-turned-music-executive Pete Nice all tried to get Kurious's work out, the rapper never really found the right musical vehicle for his style beyond the occasional song or cameo.

what's available: Curiously, Kurious's sole album, *A Constipated Monkey* ♬♬ (Hoppoh/Columbia, 1994, prod. Beatnuts, Pete Nice, others), was held up for almost two years following the release of his debut single, the quirky and enigmatic "Walk Like a Duck." By the time the album was finally released, the uptempo production and Kurious's jocularity made the album sound terribly dated.

worth searching for: Kurious's best work comes on "Mansion and a Yacht," the B-side to "I'm Kurious" that features Sadat X (of Brand Nubian) and Mike G (of the Jungle Brothers) in a smooth, old-school throwdown.

influences:
◄◄ 3rd Bass, KMD, Downtown Science, Powerule

Jazzbo

Kwest Tha Madd Lad

Born Thomas St. John.

Though his cartoon logo portrays Kwest Tha Madd Lad as an MC in diapers, his sexual appetite and obsession are anything but infantile. Juvenile in attitude perhaps, but definitely "adult" in content. While not unique, Kwest's path through the recording industry was noticeably protracted: his first single, "Lubrication," came out on now-defunct Ill Labels in 1993; after a year, he showed up on American with "101 Things to Do When I'm with Your Girl" (and you can bet that taking her to Sunday Mass isn't one of them); and, finally, two years later, the album *This Is My First Album* arrived. Unfortunately, the three-year wait didn't help Kwest mature much. The portrait of Kwest we're left with, then, is of an MC who's just past puberty, still riding out the hormone rush.

what's available: *This Is My First Album* ♬♬ (American, 1996, prod. Kwest, Da Baka Boyz, Tony D, others) is a long album that's hit and miss, with some amusing punchlines and decent beats, but too many familiar samples and styles. First released in 1993, "Lubrication" and the freestyle "Blase Blah" are the brightest spots on the album. "Lubrication" jazzes it up with a funky keyboard sample laid over a strong bassline and ride cymbals as Kwest professes his "slickness" (hence "lubrication") in the realm of sexual exploits. And on "Blase Blah," Kwest shows promising flashes of creativity with a freestlye over an old funk loop. But the rest of the album is monotonous, with track after track of sexual braggadocio that just packages the same themes in different clothing.

worth searching for: A promo copy of "What's the Reaction" (American, 1996) features a bonus remix (complete with new lyrics) that's better than at least half of *This Is My First Album*. Commercial copies of the single don't contain the remix, though, and the promos are scarce.

influences:

◄◄ Biz Markie, Luke

                                        Oliver "O-Dub" Wang

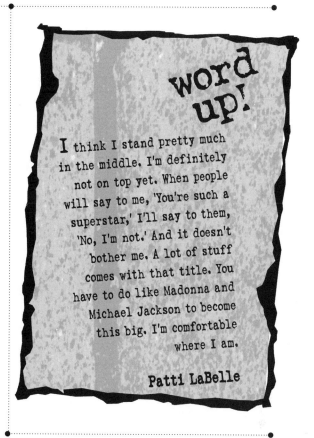

word up!

I think I stand pretty much in the middle. I'm definitely not on top yet. When people will say to me, 'You're such a superstar,' I'll say to them, 'No, I'm not.' And it doesn't bother me. A lot of stuff comes with that title. You have to do like Madonna and Michael Jackson to become this big. I'm comfortable where I am.

Patti LaBelle

Patti LaBelle
/Patti LaBelle & the Blue Belles
/LaBelle

Born Patricia Louise Holt, May 24, 1944, in Philadelphia, PA.

Of all the words that could be used to describe Patti LaBelle, diva is by far the most fitting. But unlike others who lay claim to this title in R&B, LaBelle embodies it without the negative connotations. Onstage and off, she has a reputation of being pleasant and loving to all who meet her, often cooking meals for her friends and fans. It's hard to believe that the booming voice that entrances audiences around the world was almost nonexistent when she was a child growing up in southwest Philadelphia. Though LaBelle sung in the church choir as a girl, she rarely spoke. And the outgoing performer who now sells out major concert halls spent so much time alone while she was growing up that her mother would pay her to go outside and play. By 1961, LaBelle had shed enough of her shyness to form an all-girl vocal group called the Blue Belles with Nona Hendryx, Sarah Dash, and Cindy Birdsong. After meeting producer Bobby Martin through a local talent show, the Blue Belles signed with Newton Records. The following year the group had its first Top 20 hit with a remake of the Four Sportsmen's song "I Sold My Heart to the Junkman." Soon after, Martin elevated Patti Holt to lead singer and christened her Patti LaBelle. The quartet had moderate success, but by the 1970s their momentum had ground to a halt and Birdsong left to replace Diana Ross in the Supremes (during this time the remaining trio sang backup for the late Laura Nyro's *It's Gonna Take a Miracle*). It was then that Vicki Wickham, a U.K. expatriate, took on the roll of manager for the group, revamping the look, the

sound, and even the name of the group—now known simply as LaBelle. Despite all the tweaking, the trio did not make a significant impression on the music world until 1974, when they donned their futuristic space suit costumes and released the now-classic song, "Lady Marmalade," putting the song's keynote French come-hither phrase on the lips of tittering adolescents who could never ask the same question in plain English. For the next two years, LaBelle would rule the disco clubs in both the U.S. and Great Britain.

Though seemingly on a meteoric rise, the group unexpectedly broke up in 1976. Now a solo artist, LaBelle went back to her soul roots, releasing a self-titled LP on Epic Records in 1977. But in keeping with the up-and-down pattern of her career, her next wave of success didn't come until 1985, when she recorded the powerhouse track "New Attitude" for the Eddie Murphy film *Beverly Hills Cop*. She followed that resurgence the next year with "On My Own," a duet with Michael McDon-

ald off her #1 R&B album *Winner in You*. Looking to repeat the quick-hit mass exposure that "New Attitude" gave her, LaBelle launched a stream of film soundtrack singles, including "Something Special" (from *Outrageous Fortune*), "Just the Facts" (*Dragnet*), and "If You Asked Me To" (*License to Kill*), which Celine Dion turned into an international smash. Following a U.S. tour, charity concerts (Live Aid), playing the Acid Queen in the Who's all-star 1989 version of *Tommy*, sitcoms (a recurring role in NBC's *A Different World*), and a host of awards, LaBelle returned to the top of the charts with the 1991 album *Burnin'*, which featured songs by Jimmy Jam and Terry Lewis and The Artist Formerly Known as Prince ("I Hear Your Voice"). Focusing more on her acting career, she starred in her own short-lived sitcom, *Out All Night*, in 1992. In 1994, LaBelle contributed her voice to the critically-acclaimed album *Rhythm, Country & Blues*, released her 11th solo LP, *Gems*, and sang with Frank Sinatra on his *Duets II* disc. Never one to slow down, she recorded the chart-topping "My Love, Sweet Love" from the megaplatinum *Waiting to Exhale* soundtrack in 1996, then wrote the touching, insightful autobiography *Don't Block the Blessing*. LaBelle followed the book's success with the 1997 LP *Flame*, featuring a song that shares the book's title. Not bad for a little girl in Philly whose mother had to pay her to go outside.

what to buy: *Burnin'* ♪♪♪♪ (MCA, 1991, prod. various) is the best of her solo albums, not long on hits but consistently strong from start to finish. *Something Silver* ♪♪♪♪ (Warner Archives, 1997, prod. various) is a solid compilation of the LaBelle group's best material.

what to buy next: Of two greatest hits collections, *The Best of Patti LaBelle* ♪♪♪ (Epic, 1982) and *Patti LaBelle's Greatest Hits* ♪♪♪♪ (MCA, 1996), the latter is by far the superior.

what to avoid: *The Spirit's In It* ♪♪ (Philadelphia International, 1981/The Right Stuff, 1993), one of the slightest of her solo albums.

the rest:
Patti LaBelle & the Blue Belles:
Down the Aisle ♪♪♪♪ (Relic, 1992)
Sleigh Bells, Jingle Bells & Bluebelles ♪♪♪ (Relic, 1992)
Golden "Philly" Classics ♪♪♪♪♪ (Collectables, 1993)
Merry Christmas to You ♪♪♪ (Collectables, 1993)
Over the Rainbow: The Atlantic Years ♪♪♪♪ (Soul Classics, 1994)
At the Apollo ♪♪♪♪ (Collectables, 1995)

Patti LaBelle (© Jack Vartoogian)

LaBelle:
Nightbirds ♪♪♪ (Epic, 1974)
Chameleon ♪♪♪ (Epic, 1989)
Lady Marmalade: The Best of Patti & LaBelle ♪♪♪♪♪ (Legacy, 1995)

Patti LaBelle:
Patti LaBelle (Epic, 1977/1989)
Winner In You ♪♪♪♪ (MCA, 1986/MCA Special Products, 1986)
Be Yourself ♪♪♪ (MCA, 1989)
Patti LaBelle Live! ♪♪♪♪ (MCA, 1992)
I'm In Love Again ♪♪♪ (The Right Stuff, 1993)
Gems ♪♪♪♪ (MCA, 1994)
Flame ♪♪♪ (MCA, 1997)
You Are My Friend: The Ballads ♪♪♪♪ (Epic, 1997)

worth searching for: *The Early Years* ♪♪♪♪ (Ace, 1995), a British import, does a nice job summarizing the Blue Belle and pre-"Lady Marmalade" period.

influences:

◀◀ Mahalia Jackson, Ella Fitzgerald, Sarah Vaughan, Billie Holiday, Aretha Franklin, Gamble & Huff

▶▶ Mariah Carey, the Pointer Sisters, Salt-N-Pepa, the Supremes, Chaka Khan, the Emotions, Deniece Williams, Nona Hendryx, Candi Staton, Michael Karyn White, Thelma Houston, Whitney Houston, En Vogue, SWV

Andre McGarrity

Lady of Rage
Born Robin Allen, in Farmville, VA.

The Lady of Rage is the embodiment of everything girls are supposed to be: sugar and spice. The sweet-looking, big-bodied Southerner with the afro-puffs is tame upon first glance; but get her on the microphone, and she becomes one of today's fiercest lyricists. Rage was raised in Farmville, Virginia, but moved to New York at 17 with dreams of becoming a music and acting star. There, she recorded a song for the LA Posse compilation album, and hooked up with various members of the rap community, including Chubb Rock, Nikki D, and Leaders of the New School. Still, Rage had hardly made it, and for nearly a year, she was homeless, living on the sofa at famed Chung King Studios. Out of the blue, however, Dr. Dre—who had heard Rage on the LA Posse album—called her up and asked her to be a part of his new label, Death Row. She subsequently made cameos on Dre's *The Chronic* and Snoop Doggy Dogg's *Doggystyle*, and finally became a recognized MC with her effort on the *Above the Rim* soundtrack, the Dre-produced "Afro Puffs."

what's available: Rage's debut album, *Necessary Roughness* ✍✍✍✍ (Death Row, 1997, prod. Dat Nigga Daz, DJ Premier, Kenny Parker, others), was nearly four years in the making, a delay caused by both Death Row's full-capacity roster and the untimely (and unamicable) departure of label co-founder Dr. Dre. Upon Dre's exit, all of his preliminary sessions with Rage were scrapped, and the rapper started over with an all-new team of producers. It's too bad, because Dre seemed to provide the perfect context for Rage's bending lyricism. Nonetheless, such songs as "Sure Shot" and "Some Shit," as well as the title track, are good examples of Rage's style, though her album didn't quite materialize as the classic many people had thought it would be. Still, a very compelling album from one of the best MCs out today.

influences:

◄◄ Queen Latifah, Dr. Dre, Snoop Doggy Dogg

Jazzbo

Lakeside

Formed 1969, in Dayton, OH. Disbanded 1987.

Tiemeyer McCain, vocals; Thomas Shelby, vocals, percussion; Stephan Shockley, guitar, synthesizer, vocals; Otis Stokes, guitar, bass, vocals; Mark Adam Wood Jr., piano, vocals; Marvin Craig, bass, vocals; Fred Alexander Jr., drums, vocals; Fred "Timbales" Lewis, percussion, synthesizer, vocals; Norman Beavers, keyboards.

A formidable and versatile nine-piece outfit, Lakeside couldn't managed to separate itself from the faceless funk pack of the 1970s, languishing on the second tier with groups such as Brick and B.T. Express while Parliament-Funkadelic, Earth, Wind & Fire, and others took the spotlight. For such a big band, Lakeside's music could be surprisingly compact and light in spots, as focused on melody as on the grooves. Vocals were never a strongpoint, however, with leads and harmonies that seemed tame amidst the group's more stratospheric peers. The 1980 album *Fantastic Voyage* was Lakeside's commerical zenith, even sailing into the Top 20 of the pop charts while the title track made a minor crossover impact. The group soldiered on well into the 1980s, but it ultimately stands as a strong and under-appreciated also-ran in a particularly fertile scene. And the group's performance of "Fantastic Voyage" is featured on Coolio's mid-1990s remake of the song.

what to buy: *Fantastic Voyage* ✍✍✍ (Solar, 1980/The Right Stuff, 1996, prod. Lakeside, others), one of just two Lakeside albums in print, is a good indication of the group's strength—a mix of perky post-disco funk and airy, lush love songs that

showcased solid musicianship and, on this album, the best vocal delivery of Lakeside's output.

the rest:
Shot of Love ✍✍✍ (Solar, 1978/The Right Stuff, 1997)
Invasion N/A (Intersound, 1997)

worth searching for: *The Best of Lakeside* ✍✍✍ (Solar, 1989, prod. various) offers a good sampling of all of Lakeside's music, making it slightly preferable to *Fantastic Voyage*.

influences:

◄◄ The Temptations, Parliament, Earth, Wind & Fire, Mandrill, the Ohio Players

►► Shalamar, Chapter 8

Gary Graff

Major Lance

Born April 4, 1939, in Winterville, MS. Died September 3, 1994, in Decatur, GA.

Growing up in Chicago with fellow stars-to-be Curtis Mayfield and Jerry Butler (they all went to the same high school), this slim, handsome R&B singer parlayed a job as a dancer on a local TV show into a single deal on Mercury. The Mayfield-penned songs didn't take off, but three years later, Lance's smooth, caressing voice began making him a regular presence on the R&B charts. He specialized in mid-tempo plaints ("Crying in the Rain," "Gotta Right to Cry," "It Ain't No Use," "Ain't It a Shame," "I'm So Lost," "You Don't Want Me No More") with an undercurrent of happy buoyancy. His biggest hit by far (Billboard Pop Chart #5, 1963), and one of the greatest R&B songs ever, was Mayfield's "Um, Um, Um, Um, Um, Um," the story of a man so overwhelmed that the title was all he could say. Mayfield's "The Monkey Time," a jumping party tune, charted almost as high (Pop #8, 1963). After some label hopping, Lance's luck ran out, and he was convicted in 1978 of selling cocaine. He returned to performing after his release in 1982 and died of heart failure at age 55.

what's available: The two-CD compilation *Everybody Loves a Good Time!* ✍✍✍✍ (Legacy/Epic, 1995, prod. Carl Davis, others) is currently Lance's only domestically available album. Since he was primarily a singles artist, its 40 tracks do justice to his peak period with Okeh Records (1962–68), with all six of his pop hits and five previously unreleased tracks.

worth searching for: Though it's no match for Lance's classic material, *Now Arriving* ✍✍✍ (Soul/Motown, 1978, prod. Major Lance, Otis Leavill, Kent Washburn, William Bickelhaupt) finds him in good voice in an odd but appealing soul-disco hybrid setting. There's even a Mayfield track for old times' sake, "Wild & Free."

influences:

◀◀ Sam Cooke, Jerry Butler

▶▶ Marvin Gaye, Curtis Mayfield

Steve Holtje

Denise LaSalle

Born Denise Allen, July 16, 1939, in Belzoni, MS.

Big, bold, and sassy, Denise LaSalle belts out her blues with equal portions of soul, gospel, and pop. Her favorite subjects include good for nothing men, women who stand up for themselves, and love in all its heady and horny incarnations. Raised in rural LeFlore County, Mississippi, LaSalle didn't have to look far for her influences. She started singing gospel in church. She lived across the street from a juke joint. Both locales and the music associated with them have played a part in LaSalle's brassy, often humorous music, much of which she wrote. Trying to differentiate between the blues and R&B influences in her sound is like finding a needle in a haystack. As a youngster, LaSalle assimilated the vocal styles of Ruth Brown and LaVern Baker. She moved to Chicago in her early 20s and signed with, but never officially recorded for, the legendary blues label Chess Records. She was 28 when her first single, "A Love Reputation," began to spread her own rep. A move to Westbound Records led to her first major hit, "Trapped by a Thing Called Love," which topped the R&B charts and crossed over to pop in 1971. A move to ABC during the mid-1970s, which eventually became MCA Records, saw LaSalle lean toward pop and even disco, a period she says she'd rather forget. A formidable songwriter whose songs have been covered by a wide variety of artists, from country's Barbara Mandrell to fellow soulster Z.Z. Hill, LaSalle took control of her career in the early 1980s, signing with the Mississippi-based traditional R&B label Malaco, where she has churned out a steady stream of music that rarely veers from the soul/blues/R&B/gospel she has mined successfully, yet without much recognition from white audiences, over the years.

what to buy: LaSalle hung up her disco shoes and returned to her roots—and the South—with her first Malaco album, *Lady in the Street* ⅃⅃⅃⅃ (Malaco, 1983, prod. Tommy Couch, Wolf Stephenson, Denise LaSalle), an inspired mix of country blues, Southern gospel, and soul that showcased her soaring vocals, streetwise femininity, and warm sense of humor. It set the standard for her future releases.

what to buy next: *Hittin' Where It Hurts* ⅃⅃⅃ (Malaco, 1988, prod. Tommy Couch, Wolf Stephenson, Denise LaSalle) and *Love Me Right* ⅃⅃⅃ (Malaco, 1992, prod. Tommy Couch, Wolf Stephenson, Denise LaSalle) update the classic LaSalle sound with better-than-average songs, and, on the latter, a growing awareness of social ills.

what to avoid: LaSalle mistakenly tried to compete with disco during the late 1980s, thus the ill-advised *Do Ya Think I'm Sexy?* ⅃ (MCA Special Products, 1980, prod. various), which takes its title from the Rod Stewart disco grinder. It's available on cassette only.

the rest:

Right Place, Right Time ⅃⅃⅃ (Malaco, 1984)
Love Talkin' ⅃⅃⅄ (Malaco, 1985)
Rain & Fire ⅃⅃⅄ (Malaco, 1986)
It's Lyin' Time Again ⅃⅃⅄ (Malaco, 1987)
Still Trapped ⅃⅃ (Malaco, 1990)
Feel Bad ⅃⅃⅄ (Malaco, 1994)
Smokin' in Bed ⅃⅃⅃ (Malaco, 1997)

influences:

◀◀ Ruth Brown, LaVern Baker, Dinah Washington

▶▶ Tina Turner, Millie Jackson, Betty Wright, Patti LaBelle

Doug Pullen

Last Poets

Formed 1967, in Harlem, NY.

Jalal Nuriddin/Alfia Pudim/Lightnin' Rod, vocals (1967–75, 1985–present); Abiodun Oyewole, vocals (1967–71); Umar Bin Hassan, vocals (1967–72, 1992); Nilija, percussion (1967–73); Sulieman El-Hadi, vocals (1972–75, 1985–present).

Backed only by sparse percussion, the Last Poets rode the beat and lived for the music and the power of the word. Black nationalist to the bone, the seminal urban griots were, by the mid-'70s, the first and last word in political raptivism. Their spoken-word aggression has been manifested in the form of more than 12 albums spanning more than two decades. Despite the seemingly spare output, the group's influence has been astounding, as their music and words have inspired and influenced generations of rappers, including Afrika Bambaataa, Chuck D., Ice Cube, the X-Clan, Paris, Michael Franti, and even Too $hort. If nothing else is said about Poets, know that they are unquestionably the Godfathers of modern-day rap. Abiodun Oyewole, Jalal Nuriddin, Umar Bin Hassan, and Nilaja formed the nucleus of the group, which dropped a bomb of a self-titled debut (in the most explosive sense, of course) in 1970. Nuriddin has been the main fixture since, with the group continually splintering around him (the departure of Oyewole, Bin Hassan's comings and goings). Two versions of the Poets exist today: The Nuriddin/Sulieman El-Hadi lineup and the pairing of Oyewole and Bin Hassan. Even without the confusion, though, getting an accurate bead on the Poets' body of work might be rather tricky, since many of the group's records are out of print. And much of their later work is available only as Japanese imports and in various re-release adaptations on the French label On the One. Still, the group's seminal early recordings—originally released by the long-defunct Douglas label—have been reissued several times on CD. Just about any album in the catalog is worth purchasing, but the ones featuring Oyewole and Bin Hassan are your best bet.

what to buy: Originally released in 1970, *Last Poets* ♫♫♫♫ (Celluloid, 1984) is a poetical, political tour de force that blasts away at racism and oppression (while, nevertheless, also attacking Jews and homosexuals) and contains the seminal "Niggers Are Scared of Revolution," a song sampled 20 years later at the end of Too $hort's hit "The Ghetto." Originally released in 1973, *Hustler's Convention* ♫♫♫♫ (Celluloid, 1984) is credited to one "Lightnin' Rod," who in reality is just Nuriddin. With the help of greasy chops served up by Kool & the Gang, the album is a funky ode to pimps, playas, and macks everywhere. While the sleeve lists 12 tracks, it's really just one long game-related rhyme that would become a classic blueprint for the likes of Too $hort, Dru Down, Ice-T, and all the other modern-day hustlers. After almost 20 years of silence, original poet Bin Hassan returned to the studio and unleashed *Be Bop or Be Dead* ♫♫♫♫ (Axiom, 1993, prod. Bill Laswell). Laswell adds the music of Bootsy Collins, Bernie Worrell, Buddy Miles, Foday Musa Suso, and a host of other prominent musicians from around the globe, placing Bin Hassan's urban street poetry into a global jazz-funk-hard bop context. Tunes like "Pop" revolve around Middle Eastern raga-tinged rhythms, and "Love" is beefed up by thick Hammond organ vamps and some deep jazz drum work. In addition to new material, the album reworks a couple of Last Poets classics: 1972's "This Is Madness" is given a metallic facelift and is transformed into a hectic aural melee, and 1970's "Niggers Are Scared of Revolution" is given a '90s makeover, thanks to a fast paced drum track, a thrombobulating bass, and some subdued noize.

what to buy next: Originally issued in 1971, *This Is Madness* ♫♫♫♫♫ (Celluloid, 1984) is the first Last Poets release without Oyewole. Despite his absence, though, the album still contains plenty of sparks, including the scathing "White Man's Got a God Complex." Bin Hassan left before the 1972 follow-up *Chastisement* ♫♫♫♫ (Celluloid, 1992), and the mediocre Sulieman El-Hadi was brought to fill shoes that were simply too big. The album also features more instrumental accompaniment than the first two. But Nuriddin (here as Pudim) is still a commanding oratorial force. Oyewole retrofitted the 1970 anthem "When the Revolution Comes" for his 25th anniversary celebration *25 Years* ♫♫♫♫ (Black Arc/Rykodisc, 1995, prod. Bill Laswell, others). A tight mixture of intercoastal funk, smoother grit blues, and dusted dubphonics, the album shows that Oyewole hasn't lost any of his verbal tenacity or grace. Yet another Laswell-enhanced update, *Time Has Come* ♫♫♫♫ (Mouth Almighty/Mercury, 1997, prod. Bill Laswell, others) once again shows Oyewole and Bin Hassan working their verbal magic, this time interacting with some of hip-hop's frontiersmen (Chuck D., Keith Shocklee, DXT, etc.). New rappers Jamal Whatley and Khalil Muhammad Hassan flex righteously alongside the elder statesmen on "Kings of Pain," demonstrating how the words (and mic) are passed from generation to generation. And the now-venerable Poets disciple, Chuck D., matches his baritone with the legends on "Down to Now." Quite possibly a minor modern classic.

what to avoid: *Oh My People* ♫♫ (Celluloid, 1985, prod. Bill Laswell) shows the Poets (Nuriddin and El-Hadi, anyway) in decline, with lackluster lyrics and musical accompaniment. And the frequent excursions into electro-rhythm just don't work. The disjointed *Freedom Express* ♫♫ (Celluloid, 1991) isn't much better—a musical mixture of mediocre jazz, Caribbean shuffles, and just plain cheese with Nuriddin and El-Hadi sounding more like leftovers from the '60s as opposed to inspired poets.

the rest:
Delights of the Garden ♫♫♫ (Celluloid, 1985)
Retrofit ♫♫♫ (Celluloid, 1992)
Holy Terror ♫♫♫ (Black Arc/Rykodisc, 1993/1995)

worth searching for: Gylan Kain's *The Blue Guerrilla* ♫♫♫♫ (Collectibles, 1990) is a bit of pre-Last Poets wordology. Check the track "Constipated Monkey." Billed as an "exploration into inner-self for the listener," *Right On!* ♫♫♫♫ (Collectibles, 1990) is a raw, unfiltered "soundtrack" to the film of the same name.

influences:

◄◄ Iceberg Slim, Stokely Carmichael, H. Rapp Brown, Malcolm X, Martin Luther King Jr.

►► All of hip-hop

Spence D.

Bill Laswell
/Material

Born February 12, 1955, in Salem, IL.

You can almost tell from his willingness to mix genres and defy stereotypes that Laswell grew up in Detroit, where funk and punk exist side-by-side. He's one of the busiest producers in music, not just because he's in demand (his credits include Herbie Hancock, Mick Jagger, Motorhead, Iggy Pop, and scores of others) but because he's got such an overflow of ideas he needs to enact. He works steadily for a number of labels, several of them his own to varying degrees. The band Material first consisted of Laswell (an exceptional bassist), drummer Fred Maher, and synthesizer/keyboardist/tape processor Michael Beinhorn working on their own or with a small coterie of fellow avant-gardists. The three found success as a production team on modern urban R&B projects, and the breadth of Material's music began increasing. When vast numbers of guest performers were brought in for 1982's *Memory Serves*, the group's future modus operandus was set; an ever-shifting array of performers has kept the group mutating, and Laswell has increased the use of world music artists over the years, particularly from Africa and Asia. Laswell also started experimenting with ambient music long before it was popular and has always pursued his own path in that area, though he's also collaborated with the most interesting members of that genre—from Peter Namlook and Terre Thaemlitz to Jah Wobble and the Orb. His ambient and techno projects incorporate a range of music, often drawing on the bountiful vaults of his labels and completely recontextualizing the performances. He has also nurtured a stable of performers (such as Brain, Bootsy Collins, and the young guitarist Buckethead). He retains a special affection for the funk heroes of his youth, in some cases giving them much-needed work and respect. On the other hand, he always keeps up with trends, and leaped feet-first into the British drum 'n' bass craze on *Oscillations*, where he worked with Ninj and Transonic.

what to buy: Material's *Memory Serves* ♫♫♫♫ (Celluloid/Elektra Musician, 1982, prod. Material, Martin Bisi) was the group's first album to take the guest star approach to the extreme, and it worked fantastically, with the cream of New York's avant/jazz legends (Sonny Sharrock, Billy Bang, Fred Frith, Henry Threadgill, George Lewis, Charles K. Noyes, Olu Dara) concocting music unlike anything ever heard before. But the greatest moment is Laswell's unearthly combination of instrumental virtuosity and timbral imagination on "Silent Land," where he coaxes uncanny harmonics from his bass.

what to buy next: Material's *One Down* ♫♫♫♫ (Celluloid/Elektra, 1982, prod. Material) is Laswell at his funkiest and most commercial (the CD bonus track, "Busting Out," was a club hit). The guests range from jazzers to avant types to R&B players, but the most startling performance is "Memories," with '60s jazz great Archie Shepp playing impassioned solos and a pre-superstar Whitney Houston soaring on a performance she's never equalled on her own. Axiom Ambient's *Lost in the Translation* ♫♫♫♫ (Axiom, 1994, prod. Bill Laswell) is labeled "Sound Sculptures by Bill Laswell with contributions from Terre Thaemlitz, the Orb, Tetsu Inoue" and represents something of an ambient all-star team. Laswell reshapes performances from Eddie Hazel, Sharrock, Sanders, Nicky Skopelitis, Jah Wobble, Bernie Worrell, Buckethead, Collins, Ginger Baker, Liu Sola, and more into abstract art music with incredible sensitivity to sonic textures. The two-CD, mid-line-priced *Deconstruction: The Celluloid Recordings* ♫♫♫♫ (Metrotone/Restless, 1993) is the fastest way to get an idea of the amazing breadth of Laswell's many 1980s projects. Besides lots of Laswell and Material items, it includes tracks by Timezone, Massacre, Jalal Nuriddin & D.ST, Manu Dibango, Peter Br'tzmann & Laswell, Deadline, the Last Poets, Fela Kuti, Ginger Baker, Mandingo, Fab Five Freddy, Shango, Last Exit, and Toure Kunda, all Laswell-led or -produced acts.

what to avoid: Material's *Live from Soundscape* ♫ (DIW, 1991, prod. Verna Gillis) is rambling, episodic free-form improvisation with nothing more to offer than isolated moments of instrumental wizardry. Valis I's *Destruction of Syntax* ♫♫ (Subharmonic, prod. Bill Laswell) is a brave but flawed attempt to meld ambient and hip-hop.

the rest:
Bill Laswell:
Baselines ♫♫♫♫ (Celluloid/Elektra Musician, 1983)
Hear No Evil ♫♫♫♫ (Venture/Virgin, 1988)
Silent Recoil: Dub System One ♫♫♫ (Low, 1996)
Oscillations ♫♫ (Subharmonic, 1996)
City of Light ♫♫♫ (Sub Rosa, 1997)

Material:
Temporary Music ♫♫♫ (Celluloid, 1981)
Red Tracks ♫♫♫ (Red, 1985)
Seven Souls ♫♫ (Virgin, 1989)
The Third Power ♫♫♫ (Axiom, 1991)
Live in Japan ♫♫♫ (Restless, 1993)
Hallucination Engine ♫♫♫ (Axiom, 1994)

Massacre:
Killing Time ♫♫♫♫ (Celluloid, 1982)

Laswell, Ryuichi Sakamoto, and Yosuke Yamashita :
Asian Games ♫♫♫ (Verve, 1994)

SXL:
Live in Japan 🎵🎵🎵 (CBS/Sony Japan, 1987)
Outlands 🎵🎵🎵 (Celluloid/Pipeline, 1988)

Deadline:
Down By Law 🎵🎵🎵 (Celluloid, 1985)

Arcana:
The Last Wave 🎵🎵🎵🎵 (DIW, 1996)

Praxis:
Transmutation 🎵🎵🎵🎵 (Mutatis Mutandis) (Axiom, 1992)
Sacrifist 🎵🎵🎵 (Subharmonic, 1993)
Metatron 🎵🎵🎵 (Subharmonic, 1994)

Shango:
Shango Funk Theology 🎵🎵🎵🎵 (Celluloid, 1984)

Divination:
Distill 🎵🎵🎵🎵 (Submeta, 1996)

Bill Laswell & Terre Thaemlitz:
Web 🎵🎵🎵 (Subharmonic)

Bill Laswell & Peter Namlook:
Psychonavigation 🎵🎵🎵🎵 (Subharmonic)

Sacred System:
Chapter One: Book of Entrance 🎵🎵🎵🎵 (ROIR, 1996)

Chaos Face:
Doom Ride 🎵🎵 (Subharmonic)
Outland 🎵🎵🎵 (PW, 1996)

M.J. Harris & Bill Laswell:
Somnific Flux 🎵🎵🎵🎵 (Subharmonic, 1995)

Bill Laswell and Nicholas James Bullen:
Bass Terror 🎵🎵🎵 (Sub Rosa, 1995)

Somma:
Hooked Light Rays 🎵🎵🎵 (Low, 1996)

Bill Laswell & Jonah Sharp:
Visitation 🎵🎵🎵 (Subharmonic, 1996)

Equations of Eternity:
Equations of Eternity 🎵🎵🎵 (Word Sound, 1996)

influences:

◀◀ John Coltrane, Sonny Sharrock, Jimi Hendrix, Mad Professor, Parliament-Funkadelic/George Clinton

▶▶ The Orb, Ben Neill, Mitchell Froom, DJ Spooky, Nona Hendryx, Arthur Baker, Golden Palominos

Steve Holtje

Latimore

Born Benjamin Latimore, September 7, 1939, in Charleston, TN.

The veteran blues-soul balladeer with the silver mane and the bedroom voice put tiny Florida label Glades Records (a subsidiary of TK Records, best remembered as the home of KC & the Sunshine Band) on the big-time music map in 1974 with the #1 R&B single "Let's Straighten It Out," a tortured plea for romantic reconciliation that remains his trademark theme to this day. Latimore's vocals bear an earnestness developed from early years spent singing in Southern church choirs and various gospel and soul groups in high school and college. When he decided to pursue a professional music career while a student at Tennessee State University, he joined a Nashville-based band called Louis Brooks and the Hillstoppers (originally billed as Benny Latimore), which eventually brought him to Miami. There, he signed a solo contract with Glades in 1974 and immediately went to work churning out distinctive, blues-drenched melodies. He followed the success of "Let's Straighten It Out" with the singles "Stormy Monday," "Keep the Home Fires Burning," "Something 'Bout 'Cha," "I Get Lifted," and "There's a Red Neck in the Soul Band." When he wasn't making his own records, Latimore doubled as house pianist for the parent label, TK. In 1982, Latimore moved to the Malaco label (where he still records) and released six LPs. Noted for selecting songs with unconventional lyrics, he has also written numerous songs for such Malaco labelmates as Shirley Brown, Little Milton, and Johnnie Taylor.

what to buy: Latimore is a lot like Spanish peanuts: once you start enjoying the flavor, it's hard to get enough. But *Straighten It Out: The Best of Latimore* 🎵🎵🎵🎵 (Rhino, 1995, prod. Bob Fisher) is a wonderful starter set for sampling the work of this sensuous Southern blues growler. With a guest list including Al Kooper, Betty Wright, and both the McCraes—Gwen and George—Rhino's fine 17-track compilation highlights his work from 1973–79, including the title track, the other prominent hits mentioned above and the comic piece "Discoed to Death."

what to buy next: Perhaps nowhere is Latimore's bent for choosing offbeat material to challenge his smoky, suggestive voice more evident than on *Catchin' Up* 🎵🎵🎵 (Malaco, 1993, prod. Tommy Couch). The disc, which also contains "Something 'Bout 'Cha" and the Barry White hit "Your Sweetness Is My Weakness," also favors listenable tunes entitled "Meet Me in the Middle of the Bed," "Feed Your Hungry Man," and "Skinny Little White Girl."

the rest:
The Only Way Is Up 🎵🎵🎵🎵 (Malaco, 1991)
Slow Down 🎵🎵 (Malaco, 1995)

Everyway but Wrong ♫♫ (Malaco, 1995)
Good Time Man ♫♫♫ (Malaco, 1995)
Turnin' Up the Mood ♫♫♫ (Malaco, 1996)
Singing in the Key of Love ♫♫♫♫ (Malaco, 1996)
I'll Do Anything for You ♫♫♫ (Malaco, 1996)

influences:

◀◀ Johnnie Taylor, Little Milton, Barry White, Ray Charles, Z.Z. Hill, Bobby "Blue" Bland, Clarence Carter

▶▶ Teddy Pendergrass, Keith Sweat, Will Downing

Jim McFarlin

Stacy Lattisaw

Born November 25, 1966, in Washington, DC.

Stacy Lattisaw is the last of a breed—the overworked, overexposed pop child artist. Blessed with a strong, sweet voice, she was a talent-show circuit veteran by the time she turned 11. At 12, she recorded her debut album, *Young and In Love*, a collection of mostly oldies. It failed, so her label switched producers and generated big hits with "Dynamite," a disco hit, and "Let Me Be Your Angel," a simple but impressive big-voiced ballad penned by Narada Michael Walden. By 13, Lattisaw was on the road with Smokey Robinson and the Spinners. But she never settled into an identity, nor did she outgrow the little girl label, despite her able chops. She plugged away for a decade, recording 10 albums—some made in less than a week's time— but scoring few hits, save for duets with Johnny Gill like "Perfect Combination" in 1984 and "Where Do We Go from Here" in 1990. In recent years, lacking a recording contract, she swore off secular music, choosing to perform gospel locally instead. However, in 1996 she made a cameo appearance on "That's the Way of the World," a remake of the Earth, Wind & Fire favorite, performed on *Spuraddict*, by jazz group Spur of the Moment.

what to buy: *Perfect Combination* ♫♫♫ (Cotillion, 1984, prod. Narada Michael Walden) is the only one of her albums stores tend to stock (though others are in print), thanks to the appearance of Johnny Gill, Lattisaw's high school friend.

what to buy next: Again, it's her chemistry with Gill that powers *What You Need* ♫♫ (Motown, 1989), her last album, which includes the energetic duet (and her last hit) "Where Do We Go From Here."

what to avoid: Most of her albums, unfortunately, are forgettable, particularly *Sneakin' Out* ♫ (Cotillion, 1986, prod. Narada Michael Walden), *Personal Attention* ♫ (Motown, 1988, prod. Narada Michael Walden), and *Young and In Love* **woof!** (Cotillion, 1979, prod. Van McCoy).

the rest:

Let Me Be Your Angel ♫♫ (Cotillion, 1980)
With You ♫♫ (Cotillion, 1981)
Sixteen ♫ (Cotillion, 1983)
I'm Not the Same Girl ♫ (Cotillion, 1985)
Take Me All the Way ♫♫ (Motown, 1986)

worth searching for: Check out that cameo appearance on "That's the Way of the World," the remake of Earth, Wind & Fire's hit, on *Spuraddict* (Pinnacle, 1996, prod. Spur of the Moment).

influences:

◀◀ The Jackson 5, Frankie Lymon

▶▶ New Edition, Debbie Gibson, Monica

Franklin Paul

Leaders of the New School /Busta Rhymes

Charlie Brown; Dinco D; Cut Monitor Milo; Busta Rhymes.

Created out of the same mold as legendary rhyme crew the Cold Crush Brothers, Leaders of the New School were a spectacle to behold. While their harmonizing and rhapsodized rhyming was exciting, it was also their spastic live performances that energized listeners. Four friends from around the way, the group's relationship eventually became turbulent and the Leaders disbanded backstage at a taping of *Yo! MTV Raps*, literally minutes before going on—the culmination of months of tension that began while recording their sophomore album. After taking time to pursue other opportunities—including a successful solo career for Busta Rhymes—the LONS rekindled their initial bond and are apparently working on a third album.

what to buy: The Leaders' first album, *A Future without a Past* ♫♫♫♫ (Elektra, 1991, prod. Leaders of the New School, Eric Sadler, SD50s, others) was part of a creative renaissance in hip-hop that was spurred by the likes of Brand Nubian, the Native Tongues posse, and Main Source. "Case of the PTA," "Sobb Story," and "International Zone Coaster" mark the group as irreverent and loose, without being campy or obnoxious. The heavy layers of jazz-inspired beats (accentuated by Bomb Squad producer Eric Sadler, who was also responsible for Public Enemy's loud sound), showcased each MC's unique personality—especially the lion-like growls and suave confidence of stand-outs Busta Rhymes and Charlie Brown, respectively.

what to buy next: While *T.I.M.E. The Inner Mind's Eye* ♫♫♫ (Elektra, 1993, prod. Leaders of the New School, Backspin, Sam Sever, others) was created amidst fraying relationships, it's still worth having if only for Busta Rhymes's ever-increasing exuberance on "Connections." More conceptual—and in some cases, a lot smoother and jazzier than its predecessor—the album highlighted the improved craftsmanship of Dinco D. But after the group's break-up, the only member to actually release anything was Busta Rhymes. Replete with millennium undertones, *The Coming* ♫♫♫♪ (Elektra, 1996, prod. the Ummah, Easy Mo Bee, Busta Rhymes, others) features Busta at his most boombastic. Flashing back to the Sugarhill Gang's "8th Wonder," the single "Woo Hah! Got You All In Check" is a cartoonish, euphonious anthem that rocked clubs from coast to coast, cementing Busta's status as the premier MC of the quartet. While songs like "Do My Thing" and "Ill Vibe" (featuring Q-Tip) revel in their lavishness, the LONS's reunion on "Keep It Movin" induces the biggest dose of nostalgia. Busta also released *When Disaster Strikes* N/A (Elektra, 1997) in late 1997.

influences:

◀◀ Cold Crush Brothers, Treacherous Three, Public Enemy

▶▶ Pharcyde, Freestyle Fellowship, Onyx

Jazzbo

Tracey Lee

Reality (rap) never used to be a friend of Lee's, who uses his real name as his MC moniker and gets the party started right with his head-noddin' hit "The Theme (It's Party Time)." It's difficult to accept Lee's sincerity, though, since he drops every good-life cliche in the book (cars, girls, champagne). Not surprisingly, he comes from the commercial-minded Bad Boy production camp.

what's available: *Many Facez* ♪ (Universal, 1997, prod. Tracey Lee, others) has the kind of simplistic, catchy grooves and smoothly delivered "now" lyrics that can get any party bouncin'. Then again, those are the same qualities that may make this an outdated, cut-out bin specialty come tomorrow.

influences:

◀◀ Craig Mack, Busta Rhymes, Puff Daddy

Jazzbo

Levert

Formed 1986, in Cleveland, OH.

Gerald Levert, lead vocals, various instruments, programming; Sean Levert, vocals; Marc Gordon, vocals, various instruments.

It was inevitable that brothers Gerald and Sean Levert would achieve success as R&B musicians. Their primary influence was living right in their home—father Eddie Levert, legendary lead singer of the O'Jays. Gerald began by imitating his father's distinctive voice, and by the age of 12, he and Dad were singing duets at home. The senior Levert encouraged the fledgling professional career of his then-teenage sons and nephew Marc Gordon. Honing their skills around the Cleveland club scene, the trio drew from their rich musical knowledge and heritage in molding their sound: at a time when every other young group was jumping on the hip-hop and New Jack Swing bandwagons, they hopped aboard the soul train, reviving the classic R&B structures of the 1960s and 1970s and infusing them with a modern edge. Levert released its debut album, *I'm Still*, on Harry Coombs's independent label in 1985, carving a niche for itself with tender rhythm-and-blues ballads and street-smart harmonies as the title track reached #60 on the R&B charts. The group's next two albums, *Bloodline* and *The Big Throwdown* scored a number of hits including "(Pop, Pop, Pop, Pop) Goes My Mind" and "Casanova"—an instant classic with its fresh "new" old-school sound. Since then, Levert has taken up residence in R&B's Top 40 regions with such songs as "Baby I'm Ready." Taking a break from each other, the brothers embarked on solo outings that were equally successful. Gerald, the chief lyricist for Levert, has become a respected songwriter and producer through his collaborations with Anita Baker, Barry White, Keith Sweat, the Winans, New Edition—and the O'Jays. He is also a some-time actor, appearing on TV's *New York Undercover* and the definitive 1991 film *New Jack City*. At the height of their momentum, Levert discovered and produced a singing duo called Men at Large (after their massive physical attributes); using the same formula that worked for them, they led the group to moderate success with their debut LP, *Men at Large* ♫♫ (EastWest America, 1994, prod. Gerald Levert).

what to buy: Levert's second album, *The Big Throwdown* ♫♫♫ (Atlantic, 1987, prod. various), is an essential disc for R&B lovers to have in their collections. Their maturity and confidence can be heard throughout, but nowhere as clearly as on the smash tune "Casanova," a piece of pure pop candy touted as one of the first hits in the "New Jack" category. The LP, which also features the masterful "Sweet Sensation" and "Love the Way U Love Me," earned the trio a Grammy nomination.

what to buy next: While *Bloodline* ♫♫♫ (Atlantic, 1986, prod. various) provided Levert with its first #1 single in "(Pop, Pop, Pop, Pop) Goes My Mind" and established the trio as young kings of romance with the Barry White-esque "I Start You Up, You Turn Me On" and "Kiss and Make Up," it was *Just Coolin'* ♫♫♫ (Atlantic, 1988, prod. Gerald Levert, Marc Gordon) that helped to shape a new direction in pop music. The title track, featuring Heavy D., became one of the first songs to combine traditional R&B with powerful hip-hop influences. Gordon says that Levert isn't just about R&B ballads, it's about music. That's certainly true with *The Whole Scenario* ♪♪♪ (Atlantic, 1997, prod. various), which incorporates viola, violin, cello, harp, oboe, and French horn. The trio continues its homage to hip-hop by trading vocals with rappers Yo-Yo and Queen Pen, and the guest appearances by rapper/writer Missy Elliott and Mad Lion.

the rest:

Rope a Dope Style ♪♪♪ (Atlantic, 1990)
For Real Tho' ♪♪ (Atlantic, 1993)

solo outings:

Gerald Levert:

Private Line ♪♪♪ (EastWest America, 1991)
Groove On ♪♪ (EastWest America, 1994)
(With Eddie Levert) *Father and Son* ♪♪♪ (EastWest America, 1995)
(With Keith Sweat and Johnny Gill) *Levert. Sweat. Gill.* N/A (EastWest America, 1997)

Sean Levert:

The Other Side ♪♪♪ (Atlantic, 1995)

influences:

◀◀ The O'Jays, Eddie Levert, Cameo, the Ohio Players, the Spinners

▶▶ R. Kelly, Jodeci, Al B. Sure!

Christina Fuoco and Andre McGarrity

Ramsey Lewis

Born May 27, 1935, in Chicago, IL.

From that moment way back in 1956 when Ramsey Lewis released *Consider the Source* (his debut for the Chess label), he has been the most commercially successful pop-jazz pianist. Coming up during a time when aces of the caliber of Erroll Garner, Oscar Peterson, and Ahmad Jamal ruled, Lewis's singular blend of crescendo, ostinato, bop, gospel, R&B, airy funk, and romantic pop melodies rendered in a jazz trio setting found a new audience. Lewis became the cat for people who weren't jazz heads but who wanted more than just regular mainstream pop. Lewis trudged on for years in this underground limbo until he hit crossover paydirt in 1965 with his two Chess LPs, *In Crowd* and *Hang On Ramsey*. Both albums spawned two *Billboard* chart-topping covers (Dobie Gray's "The In Crowd" and the McCoys' "Hang On, Sloopy," respectively), resulting in Lewis's overnight success. After upgrading to concert halls, TV, and pop radio, the pianist consolidated his ascension with his

dance version of the spiritual "Wade In the Water" (also the title of his massively successful 1966 album). However, all was not groovy in Lewis's camp; his longtime sidemen Eldee Young (bass) and Red Holt (drums) acrimoniously split to form their own hit-making machine, Young-Holt Unlimited. Undaunted, Lewis enlisted new cats (Cleveland Eaton on bass, a pre-Earth, Wind & Fire Maurice White on drums) and continued on his increasingly jazz-lite way to record 10 more albums for Chess until his departure in 1971. Since his platinum peak with *Sun Goddess* in 1974, Lewis has recorded and toured prolifically. Now recording for GRP, he's added regular stints on radio and cable TV (NPR and BET, respectively) to his ever-evolving resume.

what to buy: *Maiden Voyage (and More)* ♪♪♪♪ (Chess, 1968/GRP, 1994, prod. Charles Stepney) is better than a greatest hits package from that period. Culled from two 1968 LPs, *Maiden Voyage* and *Mother Nature's Son*, this compilation finds Lewis at his style-stretching best, embellishing and transmuting Charles Stepney's exalted arrangements of his own tunes and songs by Burt Bacharach, Aretha Franklin, and the Beatles. *Sun Goddess* ♪♪♪♪ (Columbia, 1974/1987, prod. Charles Stepney) features the whole EWF crew on various cuts. It is the paradigm for jazz-funk.

what to buy next: *The In Crowd* ♪♪♪♪ (Chess, 1965/1990) and *Consider the Source* ♪♪♪♪ (Chess, 1956/1996) are classic works from Lewis and his trio's Chess era.

what to avoid: *His Greatest Sides* ♪ (Chess) is a thin collection of Lewis's time at Chess. You're better off with the individual albums.

the rest:

Best of Ramsey Lewis ♪♪♪ (Columbia, 1972)
Greatest Hits ♪♪♪ (Columbia, 1973/1989)
Tequila Mockingbird ♪♪♪ (Columbia, 1977)
(With Nancy Wilson) *The Two of Us* ♪♪♪♪ (Columbia, 1984)
Keys to the City ♪♪♪ (Columbia, 1987)
A Classic Encounter ♪♪♪ (Columbia Masterworks, 1988)
Urban Renewal ♪♪♪♪ (Columbia, 1988)
(With Billy Taylor) *We Meet Again* ♪♪♪ (Columbia Masterworks, 1989)
The Greatest Hits of Ramsey Lewis ♪♪♪ (Chess, 1989)
Electric Collection ♪♪♪♪ (Legacy, 1991)
Ivory Pyramid ♪♪♪ (GRP, 1992)
Sky Islands ♪♪♪ (GRP, 1993)
Between the Keys ♪♪♪♪ (GRP, 1996)
This Is Jazz #27 ♪♪♪♪ (Sony, 1997)

worth searching for: *Gentleman of Swing* ♪♪♪♪ (Argo, 1958) is a jazzy masterwork that finds Lewis playing convincingly in the swing format.

influences:

◀◀ Oscar Peterson, Erroll Garner, Ray Bryant, Nat King Cole

▶▶ George Duke, Joe Sample, Lonnie Liston Smith, Bruce Hornsby

see also: *Young-Holt Unlimited*

Tom Terrell and Gary Graff

Lifers Group

Organized by Funken-Klein, the former head of eclectic Hollywood BASIC Records, this was one of hip-hop's more interesting projects, as the group was comprised of actual life-sentenced prisoners from Rahway Prison in New Jersey. On the one hand, the project was viewed as a legitimate attempt to give the prisoners both a voice to preach prevention and an artistic outlet; on the other, it was regarded as nothing but a gimmick for a fledgling label.

what's available: Now, while the rappers featured in the Lifers Group weren't horribly bad, they weren't necessarily Rakims either. The first album, *Lifers Group* ⅃ (Hollywood BASIC, 1991, prod. Phase 5, Dr. Jam), is a novelty that's really only worth it for its instrumentals. Starring a new set of prisoner-rappers, *Living Proof* ⅃ (Hollywood BASIC, 1993, prod. Phase 5, Dr. Jam) actually sounds more refined than the first album, but is still nothing incredibly compelling. Onetime labelmates Organized Konfusion do check in, though, with a version of "Short Life of a Gangsta," one of their trademark dark, bass-manipulating productions.

worth searching for: The Lifers Group's first single, "The Real Deal" (Hollywood BASIC, 1991) features a remix by DJ Shadow, marking the heralded DJ's debut. The vinyl-only promotional copy of that same single features Shadow's "Lesson 4" on the B-side; it's a stunning breakbeat collage created as a tribute to Double D and Steinski.

influences:

◀◀ Scarface, Geto Boys

▶▶ Bloods and Crips

Jazzbo

Lighter Shade of Brown (LSOB)

Formed early 1990s, in Los Angeles, CA.

ODM, vocals; DTTX, vocals.

If Kid Frost represented the KRS-One of the West Coast's early 1990s Hispanic hip-hop movement, and Cypress Hill was the

Schoolly D, then Lighter Shade of Brown must've been the D.J. Jazzy Jeff & the Fresh Prince. Indeed, the duo made its mark with wholesome, engaging hip-pop that featured smooth beats, recognizable samples, and pleasant rhymes about low riders, weekend parties in the park, and the homeboys.

what's available: On *Hip-hop Locos* ⅃⅃ (Pump, 1993, prod. DTTX, others), War's "Spill the Wine" is cleverly recast as "Spill the Rhyme," and Cypress Hill's Muggs checks in with an interesting remix of same. "Viva Zapata" seems out of place in the context of this otherwise good-time album, the biggest hit of which is "Homies." The follow-up, *Layin' In the Cut* ⅃⅃⅃ (Mercury, 1994, prod. Lighter Shade of Brown, others), works better and plays like a thumping soundtrack that might just be perfect for a Whittier Boulevard cruise, with DTTX and ODM eschewing violence for such simpler topics as parties and cars and homies who're just "Doin' the Same Thing."

influences:

◀◀ Kid Frost, Mellow Man Ace

Josh Freedom du Lac

Lil' Kim
See: Junior M.A.F.I.A.

Lipps, Inc.
Formed late 1970s, in Minneapolis, MN.

Steve Greenberg, instruments; Cynthia Johnson, vocals.

Taking its beep-beep synthesizer sound from the "Star Wars" character R2D2 (not really, but they sure sound alike), Lipps, Inc.'s "Funkytown" was the monster dance hit of 1980, proof that disco wasn't dead yet and that—particularly during the summer—a fun pop ditty is the ticket. Lipps, Inc. was a studio project rather than a band; Steve Greenberg, wrote, produced, arranged, and played everything, while Cynthia Johnson, Miss Black Minnesota U.S.A. of 1976, provided the vocals. Lipps, Inc. never came near the top again, and it's been installed in its rightful place in pop music history—in the One Hit Wonders exhibit at the Rock and Roll Hall of Fame and Museum in Cleveland.

what's available: It would be nice to report that *Funkyworld: The Best of Lipps, Inc.* ⅃⅃ (Casablanca/Mercury, 1992, prod. Steve Greenberg) inspires a re-evaluation of Lipps, Inc.'s accomplishments. But that's not true. Mostly it serves to show that after "Funkytown"—available on plenty of decent disco compilations—there's little else of interest.

influences:

◄◄ *Star Wars*, Kraftwerk, Chic

►► Paula Abdul, Ace of Base, Nu Shooz

Gary Graff

Lisa Lisa & Cult Jam

Formed 1985, in New York, NY.

Lisa Lisa (born Lisa Velez), lead vocals; Alex "Spandor" Mosely, guitar, bass, keyboards; Mike Hughes, percussion, timbales.

Originally a spinoff project for Full Force, Lisa Lisa & Cult Jam arrived on the R&B scene in 1987 with their hit song "Head to Toe." Though the group was composed of three members, it was clear from the start that Lisa Lisa was the focal point—perhaps not so much for her musical attributes as for her physical ones. Born and raised in New York's Hell's Kitchen, Lisa Lisa was a hot Latin bombshell whose beauty and charisma more than made up for her limited vocal range. Lisa Lisa & Cult Jam were one of the first groups to delve into what would later become known as hip-hop R&B. Primarily produced by Full Force for their first couple of albums, Cult Jam enjoyed respectable R&B success, but they did not gain mass crossover appeal until they collaborated with the then-unknown David Cole and Robert Clivilles—later to become the core of C+C Music Factory—in 1991. Cole and Clivilles gave Lisa Lisa & Cult Jam their biggest hit with "Let the Beat Hit 'Em." After riding on that success, the group moved further and further away from their R&B roots. Songs like "You + Me = Love" and "Little Jackie Wants to Be a Star" were pop hits, but they found little response from R&B fans. In the late 1980s, Lisa Lisa & Cult Jam faded from the music scene, but Lisa Lisa would later reappear as a solo artist. Her solo albums reflected more of the music from her Hell's Kitchen roots, delivering a potpourri of salsa and R&B with a rock backdrop that gained her a measure of success. However, Lisa Lisa could not keep up with the changing sounds of the 1990s. The vast number of female solo artists and groups that were taking over the music charts at the time—Janet Jackson, En Vogue, and Mariah Carey, to name just a few—quickly knocked her out of the running and she fell off the music charts once and perhaps forever more.

what to buy: *Super Hits* ♫♫♫♪ (Columbia, 1997, prod. Full Force, others) is a respectable hits collection. It's all the Lisa Lisa & Cult Jam you really need.

what to avoid: Steer clear of Lisa Lisa's solo LP, *LL77* ♪ (Pendulum, 1993, prod. Giovanni Salah). What was she thinking?

the rest:
Lisa Lisa & Cult Jam with Full Force ♫♫♫ (Columbia, 1985)
Spanish Fly ♫♫♫♪ (Columbia, 1987)
Straight Outta Hell's Kitchen ♫♫♫ (Columbia, 1991)
Past, Present and Future ♫♫♫♪ (Thump, 1996)

influences:
◄◄ Full Force

►► Club Nouveau, Cheryl "Pepsi" Riley

Andre McGarrity

Little Eva

Born Eva Narcissus Boyd, June 29, 1945, in Bell Haven, NC.

Little Eva's is one of the great overnight success stories of early rock 'n' roll. Cookies singer Earl-Jean McCrea introduced teen-aged Eva Boyd to songwriter Carole King; the introduction led to jobs as King's live-in babysitter and as an alternate member of the Cookies; she sang on Ben E. King's "Don't Play That Song for Me (You Lied)." Little Eva eventually got her own single, "The Loco-Motion," a bright explosion of drums, horns, guitar, and Cookies harmonies that was one of the essential dance hits of the early 1960s (and of the mid-1970s in the hands of hard rockers Grand Funk Railroad). Little Eva nearly matched the success of "The Loco-Motion" with one other record, "Keep Your Hands Off My Baby," but soon fell into recording silly dance retreads like "Let's Turkey Trot" and "Old Smokey Locomotion."

what to buy: *Best of* ♫♫♫ (Collectables, 1991) covers roughly the same ground as the more concise and more easily accessible *The Loco-Motion* ♫♫♫♪ (Rhino, 1996), which contains "The Loco-Motion" and "Keep Your Hands Off My Baby," as well as Eva's versions of "Will You Love Me Tomorrow," "Breaking Up Is Hard to Do," and "Swinging on a Star," recorded with Big Dee Irwin.

the rest:
Back on Track ♫♫ (San Francisco Sound, 1989)

influences:
◄◄ Mahalia Jackson, LaVern Baker, Carole King

►► Linda Ronstadt, Kylie Minogue

see also: *The Cookies*

Brian Mansfield

Little Milton

Born Milton Campbell, September 7, 1934, in Inverness, MS.

Little Milton is perhaps most famous for his fusion of blues, soul, and R&B, but he always seemed to return to the blues and kept his influences (B.B. King and T-Bone Walker, among others) evident in his music. He moved around the country quite a bit early in his career. When he was in Memphis he met Ike Turner, who was talent-scouting for the Sun label. Turner signed him in 1953, and Milton proceeded to record his most undiluted blues. By the time Milton moved on to the Bobbin label in St. Louis, he was scouting for talent as well as recording. He discovered local artists Albert King and Oliver Sain and signed them to the label, and they would become frequent collaborators. Milton finally settled in Chicago, where he began recording for the Chess/Checker label. His hit "Blind Man" was released in 1964. The R&B-tinged superhit arranged by Donny Hathaway, "We're Gonna Make It," followed. Milton climbed the charts in 1969 again with "Grits Ain't Groceries," but he left Chess soon after the death of label founder Leonard Chess that same year. Milton's willingness to use the popular lure of soul and R&B were obvious once again when he signed with Stax in 1971 and released a string of catchy R&B songs which included "Walking the Back Streets and Crying" (1972) and a cover version of Charlie Rich's "Behind Closed Doors" (1974). After Stax filed for bankruptcy in 1975, Milton made one album for MCA in 1983. He then moved to the Malaco label and recorded several purely blues albums, *Strugglin' Lady* (1992) and *I'm a Gambler* (1994) among them. Milton continues to record and tour, making many club and blues festival appearances.

what to buy: Either *Little Milton's Greatest Hits* ♪♪♪♪ (Chess, 1997, prod. various), put out as part of the Chess Records 50th Anniversary Series, or *Welcome to the Club: The Essential Chess Recordings* ♪♪♪♪ (Chess, 1994, prod. various) is a good place to start getting familiar with Little Milton. Both offer a full range of the Chess-era hits recorded between 1961–69.

what to buy next: *The Sun Masters* ♪♪♪♪ (Rounder, 1990, prod. Sam Phillips), with Ike Turner on piano, shows a more diverse and experimental Milton. His *Greatest Hits* ♪♪♪♪ (Malaco, 1996, prod. various) offer Milton at his slow-blues best.

what to avoid: *His Greatest Sides* ♪♪♪ (Chess/MCA, 1984, prod. various) offers a mediocre mix of material that is less than definitive of any part of Milton's career.

the rest:
Walkin' the Back Streets ♪♪♪ (Stax, 1981)
The Blues Is Alright! ♪♪♪♪ (Evidence, 1993)
I'm a Gambler ♪♪♪♪ (Malaco, 1994)
Live at Westville Prison ♪♪♪ (Delmark, 1995)

influences:

◀◀ B.B. King, Charley Pride, Bobby Bland, T-Bone Walker

▶▶ Albert King, Oliver Sain, Roosevelt "Booba" Barnes, Lucky Peterson, Lester Bowie

Norene Cashen

Little Richard

Born Richard Penniman, December 5, 1935, Macon, GA.

Not just the king of rock 'n' roll, but the queen, too, Little Richard drove his music with the maniacal energy of an androgenous but unambiguous raw sexuality. He blasted the path for rock 'n' roll, his 1955 hit "Tutti Frutti" shattering the tame tempos of the Eisenhower era. For all his extraordinary impact, Little Richard spent something like a mere 72 hours total over in the recording studio compiling his towering legacy. He cut some sessions in a Roy Brown vein for RCA Victor during 1951–52 and did a couple of R&B sides with producer Johnny Otis on the Texas-based Duke label. But it wasn't until he hooked up with producer Bumps Blackwell in New Orleans and made "Tutti Frutti" for Specialty Records that Little Richard forever changed the course of pop music history. A man as tall in life as legend, at the height of his popularity he quit show business to study for the ministry and disappeared off the scene. When he returned to rock 'n' roll performances several years later in Europe, his opening acts included some band called the Beatles. He continues to record to this day, almost catching a comeback hit off the 1986 *Down and Out in Beverly Hills* soundtrack with "Great Gosh A'Mighty." He has cut some interesting records, everything from gospel to children's records, but nothing he ever committed to tape again would surpass the handful of records he made for Specialty in the 1950s.

what to buy: The current owners of the Specialty catalog have made the 25 greatest Little Richard recordings available on *The Georgia Peach* ♪♪♪♪ (Specialty, 1991, prod. Bumps Blackwell) and, if that isn't enough, an additional 24 lesser known pieces and alternate takes of hits on *Shag On Down By the Union Hall* ♪♪♪♪ (Specialty, 1996, prod. Bumps Blackwell).

what to buy next: For the truly ambitious, there's a three-disc boxed set, *The Specialty Sessions* ♪♪♪ (Specialty, 1989, prod. Bumps Blackwell) abridged from a five-disc British predecessor.

Little Richard (© Jack Vartoogian)

what to avoid: His gospel recordings turn up from time to time on various labels, including *Sings the Gospel* **woof!** (MCA, 1995). Although his powerful rock 'n' roll singing might lead one to reasonably suspect a great gospel singer lies beneath, Richard records deliberately tame, unexciting ballads sung without any flair or color.

the rest:
Well Alright 𝄢𝄢𝄢 (Specialty 1970)
The Essential Little Richard 𝄢𝄢𝄢𝄢 (Specialty, 1985)
18 Greatest Hits 𝄢𝄢𝄢𝄢 (Rhino 1988)

worth searching for: His 1965 Okeh Records jived-up "live" album that was actually recorded in the studio—Club Okeh, get it?—captures the wild, extravagant personality of the man himself, along with some impossibly intense vocal performances, and was released on a budget-priced CD, *Little Richard's Greatest Hits* 𝄢𝄢𝄢𝄢 (Epic, 1988, prod. Larry Williams). This is one of the greatest live performances in music's history, an underrated masterwork that easily ranks with better known landmarks such as James Brown's *Live At the Apollo* and Otis Redding's *Live In Europe*.

influences:
◀◀ Roy Brown, Cab Calloway

▶▶ Paul McCartney, Otis Redding, John Fogerty, Prince, Michael Jackson

Joel Selvin

Little Steven /Little Steven & the Disciples of Soul

Born Steven Van Zandt, November 22, 1950, in Boston, MA.

Little Steven, a.k.a. "Miami" Steve Van Zandt, came out of the same New Jersey music scene that produced Bruce Springsteen and Southside Johnny. Van Zandt frequently played with both singers, producing writing for Southside Johnny's early albums and joining Springsteen's E Street Band from 1975–82. Van Zandt adopted the Little Steven moniker after leaving Springsteen and forming the Disciples of Soul, which included former Young Rascals drummer Dino Dannelli. Little Steven has also produced albums for Lone Justice, Gary "U.S." Bonds, Nigerian singer Majek Fashek, and Hanoi Rocks' singer Michael Monroe.

what's available: The songs Van Zandt wrote for Southside Johnny included some white-soul cult classics, and Little Steven & the Disciples of Soul's *Men without Women* 𝄢𝄢𝄢 (EMI America, 1982/Razor & Tie, 1991, prod. Miami Steve) continued in the same vein and produced one minor hit, "Forever." Subsequent albums, *Voice of America* 𝄢𝄢 (EMI, 1984/Razor & Tie, 1991, prod. Little Steven) and *Freedom No Compromise* 𝄢𝄢 (Manhattan, 1987, prod. Little Steven), were released simply under the name Little Steven, mixing rock anthems, hip-hop, reggae, and politically slanted lyrics that produced occasional flashes of musical heat but grew increasingly polemical and less soulful. *Freedom No Compromise* even came with its own reading list.

worth searching for: Little Steven has never come closer to his vision of cross-cultural rock 'n' roll than on the Artists United Against Apartheid protest record *Sun City* 𝄢𝄢𝄢 (Manhattan, 1985/Razor & Tie, 1991, prod. Little Steven), which he orchestrated. "Sun City" was perhaps the greatest protest single ever produced, with artists as disparate as Springsteen, Miles Davis, George Clinton, Grandmaster Melle Mel, U2's Bono, and the Who's Pete Townshend railing against South Africa's institutionalized racism.

influences:
◀◀ Bruce Springsteen, Gary "U.S." Bonds, Motown, Stax, Chess

see also: *Southside Johnny & the Asbury Jukes*

Brian Mansfield

Little Willie John

Born William J. Woods, November 15, 1937, in Cullendale, AK. Died in May 26, 1968, in Walla Walla, WA.

Little Willie John stood tall in the R&B world of the 1950s. His intensity brought his vocal performances to the edge of hysteria. John was a constant presence on the R&B charts for six years, beginning with his 1955 King Records debut, "All Around the World." John suffused his signature song, "Fever," with vivid eroticism. He sounded desolate beyond description moaning, "I Need Your Love So Bad." Whatever he sang, John put the full weight of his feelings behind it. Offstage he was a wild, untamed character who came to a sorry end, dying of a heart attack in Washington State Prison, where he was serving a 20-year sentence for manslaughter after being convicted of stabbing a man to death in a nightclub argument. Though he's not well-known these days, Little Willie John inspired and influenced a generation of black musicians whose names became household words. The owner of Harlem's famed Apollo Theater, who ought to know, believes John was the best male vocalist he ever heard. And the Rock and Roll Hall of Fame gave him some long overdue notice with an induction in 1996.

what to buy: After years of being impossible to find, John's music finally received the long overdue treatment it deserves with *Fever: The Best of Little Willie John* 𝄞𝄞𝄞𝄞 (Rhino, 1993, prod. H. Glover), a 20-song collection that details his glory years at King Records.

what to buy next: Two of his original albums have also been reissued on CD—*Mister Little Willie John* 𝄞𝄞𝄞 (King, 1958, prod. H. Glover) and *Sure Things* 𝄞𝄞𝄞 (King, 1961, prod. H. Glover).

influences:

◀◀ Johnny Otis, Willie Dixon, John Lee Hooker

▶▶ James Brown, Smokey Robinson, Edwin Starr, Otis Redding

Joel Selvin

Living Colour
Formed 1983, in Brooklyn, NY. Disbanded 1995.

Corey Glover, vocals; Vernon Reid, guitar; Muzz Skillings, bass (1983–92); William Calhoun, drums; Doug Wimbish, bass (1992–95).

Convened by Reid after stints in Ronald Shannon Jackson's Decoding Society and Defunkt, Living Colour remained a curiosity of the downtown New York rock scene until Rolling Stones frontman Mick Jagger produced a demo tape of two songs by the group in 1987. Though originally marketed as an all-black metal band, the group's brainy, politicized lyrics and razor-sharp instrumental chops showed it had much more to offer. But the MTV support that made its first album a hit never returned, and subsequent forays into subjects of racial pride and social injustice seemed to fly over the heads of many rock fans. By 1992, Skillings had left the group, replaced by former Sugarhill Gang member Doug Wimbish, and by 1995 tensions between Glover and Reid had blown the band apart for good.

what to buy: The group's sophomore record, *Time's Up* 𝄞𝄞𝄞𝄞𝄞 (Epic, 1990, prod. Ed Stasium) stakes its ground with a muscular mix of songs, from the sorta bluesy, sorta fusion vibe of "Love Rears Its Ugly Head" to the heavy metal funk of "Elvis Is Dead" and the bruising punk of the title track. One listen and it's obvious: no other band in history could have made this record.

what to buy next: Living Colour's last statement as a band, *Stain* 𝄞𝄞𝄞𝄞 (Epic, 1993, prod. Ron Saint Germain, Andre Betts, Living Colour), also turned out to be among its best, as Wimbish's bionic bass sounds prove the final link in pushing the band toward new sonic territory. Balancing almost punky rockers like "Go Away" and "Mind Your Own Business" with the

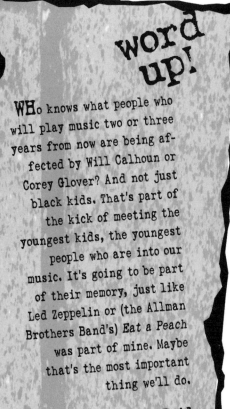

word up!

WHo knows what people who will play music two or three years from now are being affected by Will Calhoun or Corey Glover? And not just black kids. That's part of the kick of meeting the youngest kids, the youngest people who are into our music. It's going to be part of their memory, just like Led Zeppelin or (the Allman Brothers Band's) *Eat a Peach* was part of mine. Maybe that's the most important thing we'll do.

Vernon Reid
(of Living Colour)

tongue-in-cheek rumination "Bi" and the dreamy "Wall," the album offers a tantalizing look at what might have been.

what to avoid: Released when the band couldn't get an album together in time, the collection of live tracks and unreleased tunes that fills the six-song *Biscuits* **woof!** (Epic EP, 1991, prod. Ed Stasium, Living Colour) probably did more harm than good—exposing the public to uninspired playing and half-done compositions far below the standard set by the previous album. Sometimes, there's a reason why tracks are unreleased.

the rest:
Vivid 𝄢𝄢𝄢♩ (Epic, 1988)
Pride (Greatest Hits) 𝄢𝄢𝄢 (Epic, 1995)

worth searching for: The fiery Japanese live album *Dread* 𝄢𝄢𝄢𝄢
(Epic, 1995) provides proof of Living Colour's onstage acumen.

solo outings:
Vernon Reid:
Mistaken Identity 𝄢𝄢♩ (Sony 550, 1996)

influences:

◀◀ Jimi Hendrix, Parliament-Funkadelic, Bad Brains, Mother's
Finest, Fishbone

▶▶ Fugees, Me'Shell Ndegeocello, I Mother Earth

Eric Deggans

LL Cool J

Born James Todd Smith, August 16, 1968, in Queens, NY.

Hip-deep in the rap scene after a relative bought him DJ gear at
the age of 9, LL Cool J came to the attention of then-New York
University student Rick Rubin via a self-made demo sent to his
dormitory. By age 13, the rapper was featured on the first release of Def Jam, the legendary rap label Rubin co-funded with
Public Enemy manager Russell Simmons and ran out of his NYU
dorm room. At age 16, LL had his first aboveground hit, a frenetic ode to his Samsonite-sized boom box called "I Can't Live
without My Radio" (also featured in the film *Krush Groove*). It's
the perfect example of his rap style—upfront drum machine
beats, spiced with synthesized horn blasts and scratches, with
LL's aggressive, adept lyrical style pushing the beat in your
face. Over the next few albums, he would push his ladykilller
image (his stage name, after all, stands for Ladies Love Cool
James), appearing as a pinup boy for young girls and a threatening superior to other guys. After five years at the top, LL
began to lose touch with his audience, releasing laid-back, almost experimental singles and looking ready for a hard fall. So
it was a huge surprise when he bounced back with a record
crafted by old school producer Marley Marl—coming back so
hard, he featured one tune with insults directed at Ice-T, M.C.
Hammer, and longtime nemesis Kool Moe Dee. But even as he
landed roles in the films *Toys* and *The Hard Way,* performed at
President Clinton's inauguration, and became the first rapper

Vernon Reid of Living Colour **(© Ken Settle)**

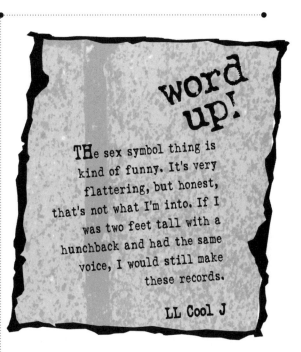

word up!

THe sex symbol thing is
kind of funny. It's very
flattering, but honest,
that's not what I'm into. If I
was two feet tall with a
hunchback and had the same
voice, I would still make
these records.

LL Cool J

to perform on MTV's *Unplugged,* LL was losing his artistic way
again, struggling for a way to stay hard in the face of increasingly explicit gangsta rap. A starring role on the sitcom *In the
House* kept LL in the public eye—seemingly a last resort for
aging rap stars—until he rebounded yet again, first with a
verse on a hit Craig Mack remix, then with *Mr. Smith* and its
three hits (the sappy "Hey Lover," the steamy "Doin' It" and the
ubercool "Loungin").

what to buy: LL's *first* comeback album, *Mama Said Knock You
Out* 𝄢𝄢𝄢𝄢 (Def Jam/Columbia, 1990, prod. LL Cool J, Marley
Marl), is his most consistent, impressive record yet. The visceral wallop of the furious title track will, indeed, knock you
out. And, filled with producer Marl's thumping tracks, songs
such as the hit "Boomin' System" provide a perfect soundtrack
for hip-hop cruising, while the funky, in-your-face groove "To
Da Break a Dawn" takes on West Coast rivals with lines like
"That right/A little kick for that crap/'Cause your old gym
teacher ain't supposed to rap." Several of *Mama Said*'s better
songs are featured on *All World* 𝄢𝄢𝄢♩ (Def Jam Music Group,
1996, prod. Marley Marl, Rick Rubin, others), which is among
the sturdiest, most essential greatest-hits set in hip-hop—perhaps rating behind only Run-D.M.C.'s *Together Forever.* The col-

lection documents LL's phenomenal run with 16 tracks, from his raw debut single, "I Need a Beat," to his latest million-selling single, "Loungin."

what to buy next: A breath of fresh air on the newly emerging rap scene, LL's debut, *Radio* ₡₡₡₡ (Def Jam, 1985, prod. Rick Rubin), sets new standards in recorded hip-hop, offering tunes with recognizable verses and choruses, as well as pointed insults and muscular street jams.

what to avoid: Despite featuring one of his best singles ever—the testosterone-fueled workout "I'm Bad"—*Bigger and Deffer* ₡₡ (Def Jam, 1987, prod. various) fails to live up to its name. One reason is the sugary sweet ballad "I Need Love." Another, the uneven collection of songs that miss more often than they hit.

the rest:
Walking with a Panther ₡₡₡ (Def Jam, 1989)
14 Shots to the Dome ₡₡₡ (Columbia, 1993)
Mr. Smith ₡₡₡₡ (Def Jam/RAL/Island, 1995)
Phenomenon N/A (Def Jam/Mercury, 1997)

worth searching for: It's not a particularly great film, but *Krush Groove* (Warner Home Video, 1985) does contain at least one triumphant, noteworthy moment: full-of-himself LL walking into an office, plopping his suitcase-sized jambox on the desk, and belting out "I Can't Live without My Radio."

influences:
◀◀ Run-D.M.C., Whodini, Kurtis Blow
▶▶ Big Daddy Kane, Notorious B.I.G.

Eric Deggans

Lord Finesse

An undisputed king of braggadocio and freestyle liquidity, Lord Finesse has been a constant fixture on the New York rap scene since he first emerged in the early '90s backed by DJ Mike Smooth.

what to buy: The debut platter, *Funky Technician* ₡₡₡₡ (Wild Pitch/EMI, 1990/1992, prod. Diamond D, DJ Premier, Showbiz, others), is marked by laid-back production and Finesse's strictly butter flow and mesmerizing wordplay. Indeed, few can touch Finesse's boasting: "Using bad words/Pronouns and adverbs/Puttin' English together just like a mad nerd/MCs I stomp and scare/I make 'em lose their hair/I rip the mic and take it home as a souvenir." The album also marks the rapping debut of Andre the Giant (a.k.a. A.G.).

what to buy next: The first half of the follow-up, *Return of the Funky Man* ₡₡₡ (Warner Bros., 1992, prod. Lord Finesse, Diamond D, Showbiz, others), is hard on the hit, with flavorful pieces of funk like "Show 'Em How We Do Things," "Save That Shit," and "Hey Look at Shorty." Side two, too, starts off with a bang, slamming you with "Isn't He Something." The sonic vibe of *The Awakening* ₡₡ (Penalty, 1996, prod. Lord Finesse, others) is considerably darker. While Finesse still possesses the gift of gab, the down-tempo, hardcore, extra-sparse beats all but erase the upbeat, funky ambiance that made his earlier records so likeable.

worth searching for: The cassette version of *Return of the Funky Man* (Warner Bros., 1992) contains the mad-crazed bonus jam, "Hands in the Air, Mouth Shut."

influences:
◀◀ Gang Starr, Eric B. & Rakim, Chill Rob G
▶▶ Diamond D, Showbiz & A.G., Percee P

Spence D.

Lords of the Underground

Formed 1991, in Raleigh, NC.

Doitall; Mr. Funky; Lord Jazz.

If Lords of the Underground had existed at the time Spike Lee made his 1988 film *School Daze,* they probably would have been in it as the band at the school dance. They're so ambitious that they would not have taken "no" for an answer—and besides, college life is their paradigm. Originally hailing from Cleveland and New Jersey, the individual Lords convened at North Carolina's Shaw University, where they caught a break when Marley Marl's cousin signed on as their manager. That led to Marl's involvement with their two recordings.

what to buy: The debut, *Here Come the Lords* ₡₡₡ (Pendulum, 1993, prod. Marley Marl, Kevin "K-Def" Hansford), portrays the Lords as both clean-cut and hardcore. The Lords' pep rally shoutalongs mesh well with Marl's dense wall of sound, a combination that would yield three hit singles ("Funky Child," "Chief Rocka," and the title track).

what to buy next: Perhaps the success of *Here Come the Lords* went to the Lords' heads: the follow-up, *Keepers of the Funk* ₡₡₡ (Pendulum, 1994, prod. Marley Marl, Kevin "K-Def" Hansford, Lords of the Underground) isn't as effective—in part because the group's careerist ambitions are a bit too transparent. The album has repeated references to the "gold and platinum" the rappers insist will soon be theirs, which would be fine except it ain't backed up with much.

influences:
◀◀ Run-D.M.C., Eric B. & Rakim

David Menconi

Lordz of Brooklyn
Formed in Brooklyn, NY.

ADMoney; Scotty Edge; Dino Botz; Paulie Two Times; Kaves.

The five Lordz are spraycan-artists-turned-mic-wielders who spent their collective childhood running the tracks, taggin' up the A-Trains, and generally livin' like Tony Manero before becoming purveyors of what they term "goombah rap." Representing the Bay Ridge section of Brooklyn, the Lordz come from the wild, white-boy ruffian school of rap: while the beats are uncut funk, the rap delivery borderlines on post-punk angst.

what's available: While the lyrical delivery on *All In the Family* ✦✦✦ (Ventrue/American, 1995, prod. ADMoney, others) can be a bit edgy and even a tad rough on the ears, the Lordz have the beats to stain the sheets. Their use of the Guess Who's "American Woman" on their ode to Brooklyn, "Saturday Nite Fever," is a stroke of twisted genius. So, too, are the acoustic guitar stylings of "American Made." The rest of the album is packed with break-ya-kneecap beats and third-rail bravado, manifested to the fullest in the graf-inspired "Tales from the Rails" and "Out Ta Bomb."

influences:
◀◀ Beastie Boys, House of Pain, Onyx

Spence D.

Lost Boyz
Formed in Queens, NY.

Mr. Cheeks, vocals; Pretty Lou, vocals; Spigg Nice, DJ; Freaky Tah, vocals.

New York rap is becoming increasingly more polarized, with minimalism-favoring hardcore realists sitting on one side and excess-loving fantasyland materialists on the other. Although the Lost Boyz rap about both the gritty streets and the glamorous "Lifestyles of the Rich and Shameless," they really don't fit into either category, largely because they're most concerned with throwing positive musical parties that never spin out of control. Of course, while their two albums, *Legal Drug Money*

and *Love, Peace and Nappiness*, did go gold on the strength of their good-time party jams, the Lost Boyz have hardly ignored just how ghetto-unfabulous life on the streets can be. *Legal Drug Money*'s standout is the poignant "Renee," about a girlfriend lost to senseless, random violence, and a similar sense of loss and self-mortality also runs through the otherwise upbeat *Love, Peace and Nappiness*—brought on, no doubt, by the recent murders of two of hip-hop's biggest stars. "When will this shit stop?" Mr. Cheeks wonders sorrowfully. "We lost two ill niggas: B-I-G and 2Pac." Unlike too many rappers, the Lost Boyz go beyond mere observational mode, issuing a fan challenge at the end of *Love, Peace and Nappiness*: "Instead of bringing crime ills and senseless wars/You clowns need to expand, buy land, open stores," the group chants. "You talk of revolution, but you're very much afraid/Take the chip off your shoulder, let's all get paid."

what to buy: All melodic basslines, infectious beats, catchy choruses, and interweaved vocals, *Love, Peace and Nappiness* ✦✦✦ (Universal, 1997, prod. Easy Mo Bee, Clark Kent, others) is the better of the Boyz' two albums, but only by a hair. The string-fueled "Me & My Crazy World" is the standout, with Cheeks getting personal with the hilarious first line: "Now I'm in love with these two chicks/I don't know which one to pick."

what to buy next: The debut *Legal Drug Money* ✦✦✦ (Universal, 1996) features the underground hits "Jeeps, Lex Coups, Bimaz & Benz," "Lifestyles of the Rich and Shameless," and "Renee," the crew's best song.

influences:
◀◀ Whodini, Onyx
▶▶ Almighty RSO

Josh Freedom du Lac

Love Unlimited Orchestra /Love Unlimited
Love Unlimited Orchestra formed early 1970s, in Los Angeles, CA. Love Unlimited formed as the Croonettes, late 1960s, in San Pedro, CA.

Love Unlimited: Glodean James, vocals; Linda James, vocals (late 1960s–78); Diane Parsons, vocals.

The Love Unlimited entities are inextricably tied to Barry White, who put together both of them as he began his solo career (even though the Love Unlimited vocal group had begun performing as the Croonettes in high school). Together they all rode an early and mid-1970s R&B wave that put a premium on

Darlene Love (© Jack Vartoogian)

lush, romantic arrangements and love-to-love-ya tunesmithery. White's golden touch extended to these projects as well: Love Unlimited hit the charts with "It May Be Winter Outside (But in My Heart It's Spring)" and "Walkin' in the Rain (With the One I Love)"; while the 40-piece Orchestra—which at one time included a 17-year-old Kenny G—flexed some commercial muscle with "Love's Theme," "My Sweet Summer Suite," and "Rhapsody in Love." Both groups still exist, though mostly at this juncture to serve White's needs. Glodean James, who married White in 1974, now fronts a different incarnation of Love Unlimited since her sister Linda moved to Switzerland and Diane Parsons died of cancer.

what to buy: *The Best of Love Unlimited* ♪♪♪♪ (Mercury Chronicles, 1997, prod. Barry White, Harry Weinger) sets up the vocal trio as a post-1960s girl group, employing a unison approach to power over the dense backdrop of the Orchestra. *The Best of Barry White's Love Unlimited Orchestra* ♪♪♪ (Mercury, 1995, prod. Barry White) mixes vocal and instrumental selections

with extended 12-inch versions of "My Sweet Summer Suite," "Brazilian Love Song," and the theme from *King Kong*.

the rest:
Love Unlimited:
He's All I've Got ♪♪♪ (Priority, 1976)
Love Is Back ♪♪ (Priority, 1980)
Rise ♪♪♪ (Priority, 1983)
From a Girl's Point of View ♪♪♪ (Varese Vintage, 1995)

worth searching for: Love Unlimited raises eyebrows with a guest appearance on, of all things, the Barry Manilow album *Summer of '78* ♪♪♪ (Arista, 1996). Both parties reportedly survived intact.

influences:
◄◄ The Shangri-Las, the Ronnettes, the Supremes
►► En Vogue, SWV, the Sylvers

see also: *Barry White*

Gary Graff

Darlene Love

Born Darlene Wright, July 26, 1938, in Los Angeles, CA.

When compiling any roster of the 1960s most distinctive and in-fluential songstresses, Darlene Love's name undoubtedly ranks alongside those of Diana Ross and Aretha Franklin. However, because she seemed content to toil as a mere back-up singer, or in the case of several Phil Spector hits, go totally uncredited for her work, Love's contributions have cruelly gone unrecognized and, to all but the keenest students of pop and R&B, largely un-noticed. Along with sister Edna (later a member of the chart-topping Honey Cone) and friends Fanita James and Gracia Nitzsche, Love formed the Blossoms in 1957, which made sev-eral records for Capitol, Challenge, and Okeh before settling into a successful career as Los Angeles's back-up singers of choice. It was in this capacity that Phil Spector hired them in 1962 to record the classic "He's a Rebel," although he released this #1 hit under the name of his Philles Records act the Crys-tals, not the Blossoms. Sufficiently impressed by Love's voice, however, Spector released six singles by her over the next two years, but ironically none of these sold as well as the Crystals' follow-up "He's Sure the Boy I Love" and a version of the Disney standard "Zip-A-Dee-Doo-Dah" (released under the name Bob B. Soxx & the Blue Jeans), both of which again featured Love's uncredited lead vocals. The Blossoms spent the remainder of the 1960s performing behind myriad acts in the studio, on tele-vision (the landmark *Shindig* series), and on stage (they were the vocal support behind Elvis Presley's Vegas comeback). Love then spent the ensuing decade vocalizing behind Nancy Sinatra, Dionne Warwick, and Cher, although she seldom stepped into the recording studio under her own name (one bizarre exception being a 1977 single which reunited her with the increasingly er-ratic Spector). Love pursued an acting career during the 1980s, appearing in all three *Lethal Weapon* films and even the Royal Shakespeare Company's co-production of Stephen King's *Carrie,* and in 1993 she returned to television on the soap opera *An-other World.* It was at this time, however, that Love *finally* began to receive the attention and, yes, credit she'd so long deserved for her contributions to some of the greatest records ever made: her role in the Broadway musical *Leader of the Pack* led to her very own long-running show at the Bottom Line in New York City, *Portrait of a Singer,* in which Love was at last being hailed as one of the most important voices of the 1960s. Not only is recognition finally hers, but a successful suit against Spector will enable her for the first time to collect the royalties she's long been due for her work on his records. Love is currently completing her autobiography, with plans being made already to adapt it for the motion picture screen.

what to buy: Proudly setting the record straight at last, *The Best of Darlene Love* ♪♪♪♪ (Abkco, 1992, prod. Phil Spector) collects 15 of her greatest Crystals, Bob B. Soxx, and—oh, yeah!—Darlene Love releases on one concise and illuminating disc. The hits are all here, of course, but so are the equally en-joyable misses ("Not Too Young to Get Married") and even that lone 1977 release ("Lord, If You're a Woman") that demon-strates just how fully Spector's gifts had by then abandoned him. Not to worry though: Love *still* sounded absolutely fabu-lous on it.

what to buy next: Spector's infamous *A Christmas Gift for You* ♪♪♪♪ (Philles, 1963/Abkco, 1990, prod. Phil Spector) includes Love's blistering "Christmas (Baby, Please Come Home)," spec-tacular Yuletide work she recently continued on the soundtrack for *Jingle All the Way* ♪♪ (TVT Soundtrax, 1996, prod. various), accompanied by the Brian Setzer Orchestra.

worth searching for: Friends both old (Paul Butterfield, sister Edna) and new (Tom Petty, Joan Jett) provide able if occasion-ally bombastic support on *Paint Another Picture* ♪♪♪ (Colum-bia, 1990, prod. various), but the true highlight of this over-looked gem is Love's soaring, practically *a capella* rendition of "You'll Never Walk Alone."

influences:

◄◄ Arlene Smith, Raelettes

►► Tina Turner, Bill Medley, Whitney Houston

see also: *The Crystals, Phil Spector*

Gary Pig Gold

L.T.D.
/Jeffrey Osborne

Jeffrey Osborne born March 9, 1948, in Providence, RI. L.T.D. formed 1968, in Greensboro, NC. Disbanded 1982.

Robert Santiel, drums, (1974–76); Toby Wynn, saxophone (1974–76); Jeffrey Osborne, vocals, drums (1970–80); Billy Osborne, vocals, organ; Carle Wayne Vickers, trumpet; Jake Riley, trombone; A.J. "Onion" Miller, saxophone; Lorenzo Carnegie, saxophone; Jimmie Davis, piano; John McGhee, guitar; Henry Davis, guitar; Melvin Webb, drums; Alvino Bennett, drums (1979–82); Andre Ray, vocals (1980–82); Leslie Wilson, vocals (1980–82).

L.T.D.—which stands for Love, Tenderness, and Devotion—is a member of a special class of late 1970s bands and performers that had no problem diversifying between knee-deep funk and lyrically-intense ballads. Formerly named Love Men Ltd., the band found its niche behind its potent horn section and behind the powerful voice of lead singer and sometimes-drummer Jeffrey Osborne. The group scored several major hits, including "Love Ballad." Feeling creatively stifled, Osborne, who joined the group as a teenager, left in 1980 at the age of 29. The band, devastated by his departure and reeling from the death of long-time producer Bobby Martin, managed to record one more hit album in 1981 before it disbanded in 1982. Osborne, himself a diverse talent, moved on to a brilliant solo career. He scored on many occasions with smooth, commercial ballads like "You Should Be Mine (the Woo Woo Song)" and "On the Wings of Love," but he also stayed true to his funk roots on some of his album cuts.

what to buy: L.T.D.'s *Greatest Hits* ♪♪♪♪ (A&M, 1996, prod. various) compiles most of the band's standout songs, and shows off its ability to diversify between hard-driving funk grooves and sensitive slow jams, with Osborne out in front in both cases. Osborne's *Stay with Me Tonight* ♪♪♪♪ (A&M, 1983) is his best solo album available and includes the hits "Don't Get So Mad" and the title track.

what to buy next: Thick with funk tunes such as "We Party Hearty," and ballads like "Won't Cha (Stay with Me)," L.T.D.'s *Something to Love* ♪♪♪♪ (A&M, 1977, prod. Bobby Martin) captures the vitality of the funk genre at the time, even as disco was taking over.

what to avoid: *Love Magic* ♪♪♪ (A&M, 1981, prod. various) had one last hit single, but the band had by then already lost its spark.

the rest:
L.T.D.:
Love to the World ♪♪♪ (A&M, 1976)
Devotion ♪♪♪ (A&M, 1979)
Shine On ♪♪♪ (A&M, 1980)

Jeffrey Osborne:
Jeffrey Osborne ♪♪♪ (A&M, 1982)

worth searching for: It's curious that *Togetherness* ♪♪♪♪ (A&M, 1978, prod. Bobby Martin), the group's biggest selling album, remains out of print, despite the recent reissue of most of the band's catalog. Similarly strange is the fact that none of the album's songs, which include hits such as "Concentrate on You" and "We Both Deserve Each Other's Love," appear on the *Greatest Hits* package, or that no "Best of" product exists for Osborne, whose albums are also mostly out of print.

influences:
◀◀ Parliament, Earth, Wind & Fire
▶▶ Mint Condition, Atlantic Starr, S.O.S. Band

Franklin Paul

L'Trimm
Formed in Miami, FL.

Tigra, vocals; Bunny D., vocals.

They liked the cars, the cars that go "boom"—they're Tigra and Bunny and, well, they turned that love of the boomin' systems into a popular hit that was played at just about every nightclub and in-the-gym school dance in the latter half of 1988. Atco's answer to Salt-N-Pepa, L'Trimm was almost obsessed to the point of distraction with the "Push It" queens, attempting to serve them on several tracks ("Rock the Beat," "Grab It," "Better Yet L'Trimm"). But while Salt-N-Pepa remained on top, Tigra and Bunny soon saw their careers go "boom."

what to buy: It's not a L'Trimm album per se, but the compilation *This Is Bass* ♪♪♪ (Hot Productions, 1989, prod. various) does star the group's big hit, "Cars with the Boom." The 1989 collection also includes several other well-known booty hop songs from its time, including Gucci Crew II's "Sally (That Girl)," Afro Rican's "Give It All You Got," and 2 Live Crew's "Throw the D." If nothing else, *This Is Bass* serves as a recorded reminder that the Afrocentrics and gangstas didn't entirely rule the late 1980s rap scene—even if they did make most of the significant music of the era.

the rest:
Grab It ♪♪♪ (Atco, 1988)
Drop That Bottom ♪♪ (Atco, 1989)

influences:
◀◀ Salt-N-Pepa, J.J. Fad, Cookie Crew, Wee Papa Girl Rappers, Weather Girls, B.W.P., H.W.A.
▶▶ Lil' Kim, Foxy Brown, Spice Girls

Todd Inoue

Lucas
Born Lucas Secon, in Copenhagen, Denmark.

Although the *keep-it-real* set will never admit this Scandinavian-American MC into its ranks, it's refreshing that a rapper like Lucas can make hip-hop his own, twisting it in so many genre-defying ways. Popular inclination seems to lump him with alternarappers, but it's just as well to call him a rap, jazz, and ragtime artist who doesn't care much for boundaries. Perhaps it has something to do with his background: being born in Copenhagen, experimenting with breakdancing and DJing, then getting into rap in his early teens. His conscious immersion in hip-hop culture, if not indigenous to his European roots, is a fact that Lucas celebrates with all the vigor of the old guard of New York, the city to which he moved at the age of 18.

what to buy: *Lucacentric* ✍✍✍ (Big Beat/Atlantic, 1994, prod. Lucas) is a plate full of jazz-funk spontaneity wholly constructed by this rapper, songwriter, and producer. The standout cut, "Lucas with the Lid Off," is an extended metaphor, describing, in upbeat bursts of verse, the freedom that comes with tapping a creative subconscious. Drawing aural influences from big-band and dancehall, the tune offers an unprecedented summit of sound. On other musical tangents, Lucas probes dense funk ("CityZen"), while also running off with a contemplative jazz keyboard groove on "The Statusphere."

the rest:
To Rap My World Around You ✍✍ (Uptown, 1991)

influences:
◀◀ Clifford Brown, Benny Goodman, Digable Planets, M.C. Shan
▶▶ Us3

Corey Takahashi

Luniz
Formed 1990, in Oakland, CA.

Yukmouth, vocals; Knumskull, vocals.

Sophomoric rappers without much new to say, the Luniz are nevertheless noteable for their weed anthem "I Got 5 On It." Aside from Cypress Hill, few rappers have built their reputations more singularly around a discussion of "the fat crispy" than these endearing class clowns. However, had they not acquired a gift for ganja celebration, these newcomers from the East Bay may have had precious little else to offer. Oakland, after all, is home to competitive ranks of pimps and independents, two traditions that the Luniz embody but don't define. In their stylistically versatile raps, they can be degrading hustlers (Too $hort) just as well as they can be humorous nuts (Del Tha Funkee Homosapien). The most important thing they fail to be, though, is unforgettable.

what's available: *Operation Stackola* ✍✍✍ (Noo Trybe, 1995, prod. Shock G, EA-Ski, others) debuts the duo's distinct flow and tiresome subjects. It may be a telling fact that the Luniz

shine most when accompanied by super-polished production on the sleek, radio-friendly "I Got 5 On It." With its hypnotic sampling, which draws heavily from Club Nouveau's "Why You Treat Me So Bad," the song enabled the Luniz enough summertime glory to justify writing their next best cut, "Playa Hata," a finger-pointing dedication to jealous punks. Although most of the album lacks topical depth, "Blame a Nigga" craftily pokes fun at America's propensity to do just that while giving voice to some plausible conspiracy theories.

influences:
◀◀ Dru Down, the Beatnuts, Richie Rich, Souls of Mischief, Rappin 4-Tay

Corey Takahashi

Luscious Jackson
Formed 1992, in New York, NY.

Jill Cunniff, bass, vocals; Gabrielle Glaser, guitar, vocals; Vivian Trimble, keyboards; Kate Schellenbach, drums.

Named after a sports announcer's mispronunciation of NBA star Lucius Jackson's name, this group grew from the duo of friends Jill Cunniff and Gabby Glaser, with Vivian Trimble and Kate Schellenbach joining during the making of the debut EP. Schellenbach drummed in an early version of the Beastie Boys (as well as with Lunachicks and Wench), while Trimble has been involved in the New York music scene, working with dance companies. The group's style suggests an all-female take on the funky sound of the Beastie Boys' *Check Your Head*. However, five years on the quartet has failed to continue developing that sound in interesting directions.

what to buy: *In Search of Manny* ✍✍✍✍ (Grand Royal/Capitol, 1992) is a seductively catchy, 24-minute, seven-track EP which sounded fresh and new on its release and retains its impact even now.

what to buy next: *Natural Ingredient* ✍✍✍ (Grand Royal/Capitol, 1994, prod. Jill Cunniff, Gabby Glaser, Tony Mangurian) develops the EP's sound, perhaps too tightly since it's much less startling.

the rest:
Fever In Fever Out ✍✍✍ (Grand Royal/Capitol, 1996)

worth searching for: The otherwise electronica-oriented soundtrack to the Val Kilmer movie *The Saint* ✍✍ (Virgin, 1997, prod. various) includes "Roses Fade," apparently an outtake from *Fever In Fever Out* but more striking than anything either

$\frac{3}{6}$
$\frac{6}{6}$ l.v.

therein or on the rest of the soundtrack, thanks to its flamenco-tinged rhythm and a bit more melodic shape.

influences:

◀◀ Beastie Boys, De La Soul

▶▶ Cibo Matto, Poe

Steve Holtje

L.V.

Born Larry Sanders.

Like the overweight lover Heavy D., L.V. is a sentimental man in the midst of madness. Although lending a sweet voice to gritty topics is a tradition that goes back at least as far as Marvin Gaye, several Los Angeles-area artists have mastered a new sound that accommodates soul, R&B, and rap in a way that hasn't been challenged since rappers started raiding Isley Brothers' samples. In short, the smooth retro soul of Long Beach's Nate Dogg and South Central's L.V. (short for "Large Variety"), along with Sacramento's now-defunct DRS, is paving the route for a rugged rhapsodized form termed R&G (that is, rhythm and gangsta). L.V., who got his start with the South Central Cartel and B.G. Knoccout & Dresta, is one of the most promising talents leading this pack.

what to buy: *I Am L.V.* ♪♪♪ (Tommy Boy, 1996, prod. various) is a collection of kicked-back gangsta soul with a West Coast bounce that's just perfect for the barbecue. Although L.V. may have made his biggest splash on Coolio's "Gansta's Paradise," the gem here proves to be his own version, void of rap but equally poignant in an assured O.G. croon. "Throw Your Hands Up" and "Heaven Must Be Like This" show his ability to switch from the party to slow jam and not miss a beat.

influences:

◀◀ Curtis Mayfield, Marvin Gaye, Charlie Wilson, Aaron Hall, Michael Speaks, DRS

▶▶ Nate Dogg

Corey Takahashi

Frankie Lymon & the Teenagers

Formed 1955, in New York, NY. Disbanded 1956. Reunited 1965.

Frankie Lymon (born September 30, 1942, in New York, NY; died February 28, 1968), lead vocals; Joe Negroni, baritone vocals; Herman Santiago, first tenor vocals; Jimmy Merchant, second tenor vocals.

One of the sweetest voices in all of doo-wop, 13-year-old Frankie Lymon brought the Teenagers massive acclaim with the 1956 smash "Why Do Fools Fall in Love?" An enduring paean that has not aged one whit, it showcased Lymon's wise-be-yond-his-years delivery, thus spawning a number of kid groups and influencing legions of later superstars such as Michael Jackson, Smokey Robinson, Marvin Gaye, and Diana Ross. That was about all she wrote, as Lymon soon left for a disappointing solo career hampered by drug addiction, which killed him at age 26. Nasty legal battles among surviving band members over authorship of the hit and over his estate cast a greedy shadow over an already tragic tale.

what to buy: *The Best of Frankie Lymon & the Teenagers* ♪♪♪♪ (Rhino, 1990) offers classic New York doo-wop and has all the essential songs recorded by the child prodigy.

what to buy next: *At the London Palladium* ♪♪♪ (Collectables, 1991) captures a performance in front of an ecstatically ex-cited crowd.

worth searching for: *Complete Recordings* ♪♪♪♪ (Bear Family) is a five-disc import set for hard-core collectors.

influences:

◀◀ The Harlemaires, the Premiers, Bobby Day, Dell Vikings

▶▶ Michael Jackson, Smokey Robinson, Marvin Gaye, Maze

Allan Orski

Cheryl Lynn

Born March 11, 1957, in Los Angeles, CA.

Cheryl Lynn owns a footnote in pop culture history as the only artist to get her start on *The Gong Show* and remain credible. Instead of being gonged, she was flooded with record offers. Ultimately signing with Columbia Records in 1978, Lynn's debut LP featured the thrilling, exultant track "Got to Be Real," which topped the R&B charts. Her soaring, often captivating voice and tremendous range were showcased on several other great dance hits in the late 1970s and early 1980s. Lynn ended up charting three songs—"Got to Be Real," "Star Love" (the fol-low-up, a Top 20 R&B hit), and "Shake It Up Tonight"—in 1981. She teamed up with Luther Vandross for a brilliant remake of "If This World Were Mine" in 1982, then ruled the charts again the following year with "Encore." She remained with Columbia Records until 1987, then moved to the Manhattan label. In re-cent years, she has appeared as a background vocalist on al-bums by Luther Vandross (*Your Secret Love*), Richard Marx (*Paid Vacation*), and Lenny Williams.

what to buy: All you'll need to appreciate the full range of Lynn's remarkable vocal skills is *The Best of Cheryl Lynn: Got to*

Be Real 🎵🎵🎵🎵 (Legacy Records, 1996, prod. various). It features the original single version of "Got to Be Real," the extended disco version of "Star Love," "Shake It Up Tonight," "Encore," and her most powerful duets—with Luther Vandross ("If This World Were Mine") and, shockingly, Toto (the disco version of "Georgy Porgy"). Producers climbed over each other to work with Lynn's amazing voice early in her career, and her impressive cast of studio magicians includes Ray Parker Jr. and Vandross, as well as Jimmy Jam and Terry Lewis.

what to buy next: If you have *The Best of* you'd only want *Cheryl Lynn* 🎵🎵🎵 (Columbia, 1978) for nostalgia's sake—and for her gorgeous rendition of "Daybreak (Storybook Children)." Her voice is at its best here, in her first album.

influences:

◀◀ Mary Wells, Roberta Flack, Gladys Knight, Patti LaBelle & the Blue Belles

▶▶ Wild Orchid, CeCe Peniston, Lonnie Gordon, Gabrielle, Chantay Savage, Crystal Waters

"Lisa Lisa" Orlando

M

Mac Mall

Born Jamal Darocker.

Mac Mall comes from a straight-game hip-hop bloodline: he's related to mob-styled rap mastermind E-40. The Vallejo rapper hit the Bay Area with a vengeance in 1993 with slinky, funk-laced tracks and an infectiously youthful exuberance.

what to buy: Mac Mall's debut, *Illegal Business* 🎵🎵🎵 (Young Black Brotha, 1993, prod. Khayree) is a prime example of Vallejo rap, with Khayree's air-tight production on tracks like "Sic Wit Tis" and "Pimp Shit" filled with squiggly swerve and luminous bump.

what to buy next: Mac Mall's sophomore outing, *Untouchable* 🎵🎵🎵 (Relativity, 1996, prod. Khayree, Mike Mosely, Tone Capone, Cold 187um, Ant Banks), presents a thicker, more ominous sound.

influences:

◀◀ E-40, Mac Dre, Spice 1, Rappin' 4-Tay, JT the Bigga Figga

▶▶ Young Lay

Spence D.

Mack 10

Born August 9, 1971, in Inglewood, CA.

Mack 10 pulled away from the crowded West Coast gangsta field by sounding a lot like one of its biggest stars, Ice Cube—and doing so with the seminal rapper's blessings. Indeed, Cube produced Mack 10's 1995 self-titled debut and appeared on the album's "Westside Slaughterhouse" along with WC. The collaboration would hardly be the trio's last, though, as they got together a year later to record a full-length album as the regionally minded Westside Connection.

what's available: Some have argued that Mack 10 isn't just another Ice Cube clone, and in a way, they're right: on *Mack 10* 🎵🎵🎵 (Priority, 1995, prod. Ice Cube, others), the rapper does a fair imitation of Ice Cube, but without going for the rage and unflinching attitude that made Cube so vital in the first place.

influences:

◀◀ WC, Ice Cube

▶▶ Comrads

see also: *Ice Cube*

Josh Freedom du Lac

Mad Lion

Like a fierce jungle cat, Mad Lion has a roar that can be heard for miles. The London-born, Jamaican-raised, Brooklyn-living ragamuffin MC sprang up from the Boogie Down Productions camp and quickly captured the hip-hop scene with the song "Shoot to Kill" (which so aptly used the slick backing track from KRS-One's "Black Cop"). Originally called Medallion, Mad Lion got his new name from Super Cat, whom he met while visiting Super Power Records in Flatbush, Brooklyn. It was at that same store where Mad Lion met KRS-One, which led to his BDP membership. Even while releasing albums and underground singles, Mad Lion also found time to earn his Certified Public Accountant's degree—just in case his career as a musician roars to a close.

what to buy: After the B-side single "Shoot to Kill" infected the underground rap-club scene, Mad Lion released the dark and menacing "Take It Easy" (another KRS-One production) and it looked as if he could do no wrong. Unfortunately, his debut album, *Real Ting* 🎵🎵🎵 (Weeded, 1994, prod. KRS-One), couldn't sustain that same raw energy for its entirety, though Mad Lion did come through with notable songs like the title track and "Double Trouble."

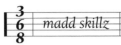

the rest:
Ghetto Gold and Platinum Respect N/A (Nervous, 1997)

influences:
Super Cat, Nicodemus, Shabba Ranks, KRS-One

Jazzbo

Madd Skillz

Born Shaquan Lewis.

While the majority of hip-hop's partisans come from metropolises like New York, Los Angeles, Atlanta, San Francisco, Philadelphia, and Chicago, it wasn't until Madd Skillz came onto the hip-hop landscape that Richmond, Virginia, was represented on the map. Mad Skillz created a buzz for himself by placing second in the New Music Seminar Battle for Rap Supremacy in 1993, but it was his freestyle (with Q-Tip) on New York radio's *Stretch and Bobbito Show* the following year that catalyzed his recording career (and also found itself on mix tapes from coast to coast).

what's available: Considering the hype that preceded Madd Skillz, his debut album, *From Where???* 𝄞𝄞 (Big Beat/Atlantic, 1995, prod. Beatnuts, Buckwild, Q-Tip, Large Professor, others) is somewhat disappointing. The first, pre-album single, "The Nod Factor," only heightened expectations with its rhythmic purity; the rapper's cavalier delivery and the backing track's bass hook made it look like Madd Skillz could do no wrong. But aside from a few cuts, including "Extra Abstract Skillz" with Q-Tip and Large Professor, the album's biggest shortcoming is a lack of real ingenuity from song to song.

influences:
Nas, Lord Finesse

Jazzbo

Madonna

Born Madonna Louise Veronica Ciccone, August 16, 1958, in Bay City, MI.

From the moment her street-urchin image and pop-drenched dance hits first began to affect America's consciousness, Madonna knew how to push society's buttons. Born in Michigan to a family of six, Madonna lost her mother when she was six years old. Studying dance and drama in high school, she spent brief periods in a few colleges before heading to New York in 1978, where she studied for a time with the Alvin Ailey dance troupe. Living hand to mouth in the big city, Madonna spent time in a group called the Breakfast Club before working up

tunes on her own with a former boyfriend, drummer Steve Bray. These demos caught the ear of DJ Mark Kamins from the Manhattan nightspot Danceteria, who got the singer her first record deal with Sire Records and produced her first single as a solo artist. A self-titled album quickly followed, produced by legendary New York DJ John "Jellybean" Benitez, yielding two Top 10 hits, a couple of controversial videos, and lots of media exposure. At first, her use of revealing stage outfits garnered the most attention, but with her second album *Like a Virgin*—produced by ex-Chic guitarist Nile Rodgers—critics began looking at her lyrical messages as well. Turning her MTV-friendly image into movie work with the 1984 film *Desperately Seeking Susan,* Madonna finished the year with hit songs from that and *Vision Quest,* in which she made a cameo, as well as her first #1 smash, "Like a Virgin," and a sophomore record that sold more than seven million copies. As other dance divas such as Janet Jackson and Paula Abdul began following her lead, Madonna stepped ahead of the curve again, first marrying actor Sean Penn in 1986, and then releasing her third record, *True Blue,* titillating the public with a leadoff single about an unwed mother who keeps her baby ("Papa Don't Preach"). Work in another forgettable movie, "Who's That Girl," followed in 1987, and by 1988 her marriage to Penn was history. Her 1989 single "Like a Prayer" featured a video full of racially charged imagery, including stigmata and intimacy with a black Jesus, which prompted censure by the Vatican, the loss of a Pepsi commercial, and a new round of explosive publicity. The next year brought a role in the film *Dick Tracy* with new boyfriend Warren Beatty and a hit based on the gay dance craze ("Vogue"). By 1991, a no-holds-barred documentary of her Blonde Ambition Tour called *Truth or Dare,* combined with the controversial success of a racy hit co-written with Lenny Kravitz ("Justify My Love"), made it seem as if Madonna was everywhere. A 1992 deal with Time Warner allowed her to release films, books, and album projects under her production company, Maverick. At first it seemed her erotic book, *Sex,* was a misstep—featuring titillating photos with another ex-boyfriend, NBA star Dennis Rodman—but it merely set the stage for her success as a record company mogul, releasing albums by artists such as Me'Shell Ndegeocello, Alanis Morissette, and Candlebox. Her albums in 1992 and 1994 also did well, leading to a role in a 1996 film version of the musical *Evita,* released just after the birth of her first child (fathered by her boyfriend, trainer Carlos Leon), Lourdes Maria Ciccone.

what to buy: Blasting through your stereo speakers with a funky, furious mix, *Like a Virgin* 𝄞𝄞𝄞𝄞 (Sire, 1984, prod. Nile Rodgers) marries Madonna's emerging boy toy image with

Madonna (© Ken Settle)

funky musicianship and catchy pop tunes. She would acheive much the same result with a more electronic approach on *True Blue* 𝄢𝄢𝄢𝄢 (Sire, 1986, prod. Madonna, Patrick Leonard, Stephen Bray), which gets a bone just for the thick, funky bassline powering her ode to single motherhood, "Papa Don't Preach." Her greatest hits album, *The Immaculate Collection* 𝄢𝄢𝄢𝄢 (Sire, 1990, prod. various), is a potent compilation.

what to buy next: Combining crafty sonic samples with slinky, sinewy grooves, *Bedtime Stories* 𝄢𝄢𝄢𝄢 (Maverick, 1994, prod. Madonna, Nellee Hooper, Kenneth "Babyface" Edmonds, Dallas Austin, Dave "Jam" Hall) remains her most underrated work, percolating along on potent, understated jams. As her foray into the world of ambient/techno, *Erotica* 𝄢𝄢𝄢 (Maverick, 1992, prod. Madonna, Shep Pettibone) stands as alluring evidence of her pop savvy, exploring a genre it would take the rest of the pop world four or five more years to appreciate.

what to avoid: As the worst in a long string of bad soundtrack recordings, the songs for her lackluster film *Who's That Girl?*

woof! (Sire, 1987, prod. various) seemed a potent argument for keeping Madonna out of the film game for life.

the rest:
Madonna 𝄢𝄢𝄢 (Sire, 1983)
You Can Dance 𝄢𝄢 (Sire, 1987)
Like a Prayer 𝄢𝄢𝄢 (Sire, 1989)
I'm Breathless 𝄢𝄢𝄢 (Sire, 1990)
Something to Remember 𝄢𝄢𝄢 (Maverick/Sire, 1995)
Evita 𝄢𝄢𝄢 (Warner Bros., 1996)

worth searching for: Check out Sonic Youth's bizarre and hilarious sendup of mostly Madonna tunes, *The Whitey Album* 𝄢𝄢𝄢𝄢 (Blast First, 1989, prod. Ciccone Youth) credited to Ciccone Youth, a sly parody of Madonna's surname.

influences:
◀◀ Diana Ross, Teena Marie, Michael Jackson, Cyndi Lauper

▶▶ Janet Jackson, Paula Abdul, TLC, Alanis Morissette, Gwen Stefani

Eric Deggans

Taj Mahal

Born Henry Sainte Claire Fredricks, May 17, 1942, in New York, NY.

Singer-instrumentalist Taj Mahal emerged during the mid-1960s as a bluesman in the tradition of Mississippi John Hurt and Sleepy John Estes. He's always held onto the blues as his root, but over the years he's added reggae, calypso, African, and pop elements. Taj has a powerful gospel voice and vocal timing that alternately drags out notes and then squeezes many into a short space. His Caribbean forays sometimes evidence a beautiful blending of acoustic fingerpicking, soprano saxophone, and steel pan playing. Taj's shows usually include a solo set even when he has a band, and these portions range through *a cappella* singing to accompanying himself on pennywhistle, kalimba, handclaps, guitar, conch shell, banjo, harmonica, piano, and more.

what to buy: Which Taj Mahal do you want? For the bluesman, try the double-length *Giant Step/De Ole Folks at Home* 𝄞𝄞𝄞𝄞 (Columbia, 1969, prod. David Rubinson), which covers the country and urban sides. *Giant Step* features Taj backed by bass, drums, and guitar doing his unique takes on standards such as "Good Morning Little Schoolgirl" and his own songs. *De Ole Folks* . . . is Taj acoustic and alone on a series of work songs, blues, and rags; "Fishin' Blues" and "Annie's Lover" are exquisite. On the Caribbean side, *Mo' Roots* 𝄞𝄞𝄞𝄞 (Columbia, 1974, prod. Taj Mahal) marks a revelatory change in his music. From "Johnny Too Bad," through "Cajun Waltz" and "Clara (St. Kitts Woman)," each song drips with genuine island charm.

what to buy next: The 1966–71 years are well represented on *The Taj Mahal Anthology* 𝄞𝄞𝄞𝄞 (Columbia, 1977, prod. David Rubinson), which caters to the blues crowd. *World Music* 𝄞𝄞𝄞𝄞 (Columbia, 1993, prod. various) has most of the *Mo' Roots* album with a few other West Indian revelations.

what to avoid: *Taj* 𝄞 (Gramavision, 1986, prod. Taj Mahal) has Taj all slicked up for the pop market. And he doesn't slick up well.

the rest:
The Natch'l Blues 𝄞𝄞𝄞𝄞 (Columbia, 1969)
Happy Just to Be Like I Am 𝄞𝄞𝄞𝄞 (Columbia, 1971)
The Real Thing 𝄞𝄞𝄞𝄞 (Columbia, 1971)
Recycling the Blues (And Other Related Stuff) 𝄞𝄞𝄞𝄞 (Columbia, 1972)
Oooh So Good 'n' Blues 𝄞𝄞𝄞𝄞 (Columbia, 1973)
Satisfied 'n' Tickled Too 𝄞𝄞𝄞 (Columbia, 1976)
Music Fuh Ya' 𝄞𝄞𝄞𝄞 (Warner Bros., 1977)
Mule Bone 𝄞𝄞𝄞 (Gramavision, 1991)
Taj's Blues 𝄞𝄞𝄞𝄞 (Legacy, 1992)

Dancing the Blues 𝄞𝄞𝄞 (Private Music, 1993)
Phantom Blues 𝄞𝄞𝄞𝄞 (Private Music, 1996)
An Evening of Acoustic Music 𝄞𝄞𝄞𝄞 (Ruf, 1996)
Senor Blues 𝄞𝄞𝄞 (Private Music, 1997)

worth searching for: There's proof that Taj is still worth listening to on *Like Never Before* 𝄞𝄞𝄞𝄞 (Private Music, 1991, prod. Skip Drinkwater) with the real R&B of "Don't Call Us" and the boogie woogie of "Big Legged Mamas Are Back in Style."

influences:
◀◀ Sleepy John Estes, Mississippi John Hurt
▶▶ Keb' Mo, Vinx

Lawrence Gabriel

The Main Ingredient

Formed as the Poets, 1964, in New York, NY. Disbanded 1975. Re-formed 1980.

Donald McPherson, vocals (1964–71); Luther Simmons Jr., vocals (1964–89); Tony Sylvester, vocals; Cuba Gooding, vocals (1971–present); Jerome Jackson, vocals (1989).

O.K., show us the . . . whoops, that's the other Gooding—Cuba Jr., not the singer of the salad days of this New York soul group. The Main Ingredient actually recorded first as the Poets, cutting an album in 1965 for the Red Bird label and enjoying a modest hit with "She Blew a Good Thing" the following year. In 1969 they became the Main Ingredient, while Donald McPherson's death from leukemia in 1971 brought the elder Gooding in as his replacement. The trio went on to score a series of hits, including "Everybody Plays the Fool" in 1972, "Just Don't Want to Be Lonely" in 1974, and "Happiness Is Just Around the Bend" that same year. The trio disbanded mid-decade, and Gooding tried a solo career with Motown. The Main Ingredient re-formed in 1980, though Simmons, who had become a stock broker in the meantime, returned to Wall Street shortly thereafter. The comeback went nowhere, though Gooding had a modest British hit with a re-recorded version of "Happiness Is Just Around the Bend" in 1973. You're still likely to see them pop up at an oldies show, and Cuba Gooding Jr. carries on the family name with his film work in *Boyz in the Hood* and *Jerry Maguire*.

what to buy: *All-Time Greatest Hits* 𝄞𝄞𝄞𝄞 (RCA, 1989, prod. various) shows off the group's smooth, soulful harmonies and some of the most seamless arrangements you'll find in all of R&B. *A Quiet Storm* 𝄞𝄞𝄞 (RCA, 1996, prod. various) is another good compilation that skips some of the more obvious hits in favor of audience and group favorites.

what to avoid: *Golden Classics* ♫♫ (Collectables, 1991), a slight set that pales before *All-Time Greatest Hits.*

influences:

◀◀ The Miracles, the Drifters, the Impressions

▶▶ Luther Vandross, the Stylistics, Boyz II Men, All-4-One, SWV, the Braxtons

Gary Graff

Main Source /Large Professor

Formed in New York.

Large Professor/Extra P (born William Paul Mitchell), vocals; Sir Scratch, DJ; K-Cut, DJ; Mikey D, vocals.

By the age of 18, New York rapper/producer prodigy Large Professor (a.k.a. Extra P) was already hooking up unforgettable tracks for Kool G Rap, Eric B. & Rakim, Biz Markie, and Intelligent Hoodlum. With his crew, including two brother turntablists from Canada, he made his own classic LP and the future looked bright. Then the crew split acrimoniously—Extra P accusing the McKenzies' mother-manager of withholding royalties—and left fans to forever wonder what might have been. Sir Scratch and K-Cut tried again with veteran Brooklyn rapper Mikey D before being unceremoniously dropped from their label. Extra P, meanwhile, became the subject of a heated bidding war. After signing with DGC/Geffen in 1995, he dropped two decent singles in "Mad Scientist" and "Ijuswannachill," but at press time still had fans wondering if he'd ever deliver another full-length album.

what to buy: *Breaking Atoms* ♫♫♫♫ (Wild Pitch, 1991, prod. Large Professor, others) is a must-have. The tour-de-force "Peace Is Not the Word to Play" deploys a ton of them, beginning with a quick cutting of disparate beats and scratches, moving into a single rapped verse under which the driving music shifts incessantly, and culminating in a bold illustration of the dynamic possibilities of the two-DJ format. If this were rock, this kind of pushing of the limits of song structure would be called progressive, even arty. Call Large Professor the Frank Zappa or Robert Fripp of hip-hop. But the pleasures aren't merely intellectual. "Looking Out the Front Door" and "Snake Eyes" demonstrate Extra P's brand of crisp, humorous storytelling. "Just a Friendly Game of Baseball" is an extraordinary extended metaphor and a cutting examination of race relations. "Live at the Barbecue" is simply the best posse session ever cut, the world's introduction to Nasty Nas.

what to buy next: After Extra P left, Mikey D came aboard for the forgettable single "What You Need" b/w "Merrick Boulevard." The full-length LP *Fuck What You Think* never made it to stores, although seven tracks from the record showed up on the Japanese import-only double-LP, *The Best of Main Source* (Mary Joy/Wild Pitch, 1996, prod. various). Of them, the only cut worth mentioning is "Hellavision," which cynics may argue has Mikey D trying hard to sound like the Prof. The compilation also includes the fine Large Professor single "Fakin' the Funk," recorded for the soundtrack of *White Men Can't Jump.*

worth searching for: In fact, "Fakin' the Funk" was so promising that rumors of Extra P's post-*Breaking Atoms* tracks keep the bootleg market abuzz. The only rumored song that's surfaced to date is "How My Man Went Down in the Game" on *Wild Pitch Classics* (Wild Pitch, 1994), reportedly an unfinished demo. As for pre-Wild Pitch recordings, a compilation of Canadian crews entitled *Cold Front* (Attic, 1991) features the early single "Atom." Rarest of all is the first single, "Think"/"Watch Roger Do His Thing" on Actual Records. It's also worth noting that the 12-inch remixes of "Just Hanging Out" and "Peace Is Not the Word to Play" are excellent—and highly collectable. Of Large Professor's long list of guest productions and notable remixes, Kool G Rap & D.J. Polo's seminal *Wanted Dead or Alive* and the radio promo-only version of Nas's "It Ain't Hard to Tell" stand out from a formidable pack.

influences:

◀◀ Paul C, Ultramagnetic MC's, Marley Marl, Biz Markie, A Tribe Called Quest

▶▶ Nas, Akinyele, Nikki D

Jeff "DJ Zen" Chang

Mandrill

Formed 1968, in Brooklyn, NY. Disbanded 1982.

Carlos D. Wilson, flute, trombone, guitar, percussion, vocals; Louis Wilson, trumpet, flugelhorn, congas, percussion, vocals; Ric Wilson, M.D., tenor sax, percussion, vocals; Claude "Coffee" Cave, organ, piano, vibes, percussion, vocals; Omar Mesa, lead guitar, percussion, vocals; Bundie Cenas, bass, percussion, vocals; Fudgie Kae, bass, percussion, vocals; Wilfredo "Wolf" Wilson, bass, congas, percussion, vocals; Charles Padro, drums, percussion, vocals; Neftali Santiago, drums, percussion, vocals.

As the 1970s dawned, black pop music experienced a wrenching metamorphosis from the caramel soul of Motown to the jazz-laced, planet funk of Curtis Mayfield, Gil Scott-Heron,

Funkadelic, Earth, Wind & Fire, Santana, Roy Ayers, and Mandrill. Of all these bands, Mandrill was the most unique. While the others looked to Hendrix, Miles, Sly, and James Brown for the grail, Mandrill alone went for the grooves south of the border. Boasting a revolving lineup of players from Panama, Cuba, Puerto Rico, and the Virgin Islands as well as the U.S., Mandrill's music was a potent, unique marinade of guauancos, mambos, guajiros, funk, soca, soul, rock, blues, street chant, and pastoral jazz. Although the group only cracked the Top 20 once during its nine-year existence (with "Fencewalk" in 1973), Mandrill matters because of its high output of seminal, genre-bending cuts such as "Git It All," "Polk Street Carnival," and "House of Wood." Looming large over both Latin and black pop, Mandrill's influence has been aped by everyone from Eddie Palmieri to the Fugees.

what to buy: The breadth and depth of Mandrill's sonic range is fully displayed on *Fencewalk: The Anthology* ♬♬♬♬ (Chronicles, 1997, comp. Harry Weinger). A fairly astute evaluation of the band's best work, this collection is full of the shapes of grooves to come (but sadly, no "Polk Street Carnival").

what to buy next: *Best of Mandrill* ♬♬♬ (Polydor, 1994) is tasty, but again, no "Polk Street Carnival."

worth searching for: A recording of Santana motifs, Mahavishnu guitar, Afro-Cuban time, and dirty doo-wop soul, the two-LP vinyl copy of *Mandrilland* (Polydor, 1974, prod. Mandrill) is worth the hunt for "House of Wood" alone, in all its slow-grinding, analog splendor.

influences:

◄◄ Santana, Joe Bataan, Sly & the Family Stone, Charlie Palmieri

►► Maze, War, India, Brooklyn Funk Essentials, Fugees

Tom Terrell

The Manhattans

Formed 1960, in Newark, NJ.

Richard Taylor (1960–85); Kenneth Kelly; Gerald Alston (1972–88); Edward "Sonny" Bivins; Winfred "Blue" Lovett; George "Smitty" Smith (1960–71).

During the 1960s and 1970s, as in many other periods in the history of R&B, the male vocal group sound was a distinct and conservative thread that tied contemporary music to its recent past. Groups such as the Dells, the Temptations, the O'Jays, the Impressions, and the Spinners were all either part of the 1950s

doo-wop scene or directly descended from it. Whereas the disco era of the 1970s destroyed the careers of many great soul vocalists of the 1960s, many of these same vocal groups were able to thrive into and beyond the radical stylistic changes that disco initiated. This must be because the male vocal group sound is easily adaptable to a wide variety of musical settings. Since the days of the Ravens, the Ink Spots, and the Mills Brothers, vocal group music has always affirmed values such as showmanship, choreography, precision, presentation, style, and class—another indication of the music's inherent conservatism. During the 1960s, other vocal groups were always measured against the standard of the Temptations, with their neatly pressed sharkskin suits, precise choreography, and the chilling vocals of the two coolest humans on the face of the earth, Eddie Kendricks and David Ruffin.

At least in the New York/New Jersey/Connecticut area, however, there were many fans who believed that the Manhattans were as good or better. On stage with their matching suits and trademark white gloves, the Manhattans were every bit as smooth, precise, and explosive as the Tempts. What's more, they too were fronted by two outstanding lead singers, Winfred "Blue" Lovett and George "Smitty" Smith. Lovett was the group's leader and an outstanding songwriter whose compositions with producer Joe Evans and fellow Manhattan Sonny Bivins gave the group a string of hit records on Carnival Records during the mid-1960s. As lead vocalist on the group's more straightforward pop/soul recordings, Lovett's baritone projected a warm, relaxed persona in hits such as "I Wanna Be," "The Boston Monkey," and "Baby, I Need You." The Manhattans' more memorable early recordings, however, were sung by Smith, a distinctive stylist whose readings of songs such as "Can I," "I'm the One That Love Forgot," and "Follow Your Heart" conveyed a discomforting sense of anguish and despair. Particularly in live performance, Smith's voice seemed to be directly wired to the spines of his listeners.

When Smith died of an illness suddenly in 1971, the Manhattans' survival seemed unlikely. Yet they were able to replace Smith with Gerald Alston (nephew of Shirley Alston of the Shirelles), another fine singer whose style paid obvious homage to Sam Cooke. More of a pop singer than either Smith or Lovett, Alston's incorporation into the group enabled the Manhattans to break well beyond their status as the standard-bearers for the New York doo-woppers and achieve major national success. With Alston handling all lead vocals and Lovett relegated to providing spoken introductions *a la* Barry White, the Manhattans moved to Columbia Records in 1973, where producers Bobby Martin—a former colleague of Kenny Gamble and Leon Huff in Philadelphia—and, later, Leo Graham, who also produced Tyrone Davis, helped the Manhattans craft an impressive string of elegant pop/soul hit ballads; most notably "Kiss and Say Goodbye," a platinum-selling #1 pop and R&B hit in 1976. Despite their high gloss and pop pedigree, however, these recordings always maintained continuity with the original Manhattans sound through strong, doo-wop influenced ensemble singing. Alston left the Manhattans in 1988 and went on to pursue a solo career on Motown, with moderate success.

what to buy: Taking nothing away from the Manhattans' great Columbia recordings of the 1970s, the Carnival recordings represent their most original and transcendent work. These are available in a number of collections: *Dedicated to You/For You and Yours* ♪♪♪♪ (Kent/UK, 1993, prod. Joe Evans); *Dedicated to You: Golden Carnival Classics, Pt. 1* ♪♪♪♪♪ (Collectables, 1991, prod. Joe Evans); *For You and Yours: Golden Carnival Classics, Pt. 2* ♪♪♪♪♪ (Collectables, 1991, prod. Joe Evans).

what to buy next: *Best of the Manhattans: Kiss and Say Goodbye* ♪♪♪♪ (Sony, 1995, prod. various) is a fine retrospective of their Columbia recordings. *Back to Basics* ♪♪♪♪ (Columbia, 1986, prod. various) is notable for the production contributions of the great Bobby Womack. This was Alston's final recording with the group and also featured the vocals of Regina Belle, who went on to a very successful solo career after debuting with the Manhattans here. "Where Did We Go Wrong," a lovely Alston/Belle duet, was the hit from this disc.

what to avoid: It speaks volumes about the Manhattans' talent that even its weakest effort, *Sweet Talk* ♪♪ (Valley Vue, 1989, prod. Leo Graham, Gary Taylor) still has a good share of worthwhile performances.

the rest:
Dedicated to You ♪♪♪♪♪ (Carnival, 1966)
For You and Yours ♪♪♪♪♪ (Carnival, 1967/1982)
There's No Me without You ♪♪♪♪♪ (Columbia, 1973)
Summertime in the City ♪♪♪♪ (Columbia, 1974)
That's How Much I Love You ♪♪♪♪ (Columbia, 1974)
The Manhattans ♪♪♪♪ (Columbia, 1976)
I Wanna Be Your Everything ♪♪♪♪♪ (DJM, 1976)
It Feels So Good ♪♪♪♪ (Columbia, 1977)
There's No Good in Goodbye ♪♪♪♪ (Columbia, 1978)
Love Talk ♪♪♪ (Columbia, 1979)
After Midnight ♪♪♪ (Columbia, 1980)
Greatest Hits ♪♪♪♪ (Columbia, 1980)
Follow Your Heart ♪♪♪♪♪ (Solid Smoke, 1981)
Best of the Manhattans ♪♪♪♪ (Embassy, 1981)

Black Tie (Columbia, 1981)
Forever by Your Side (Columbia, 1983)
Heart & Soul of the Manhattans ♪♪♪♪ (Castle, 1992)
Collection ♪♪♪♪ (Castle, 1993)
One Life to Live ♪♪♪♪ (Sony Special Products, 1995)

worth searching for: The Manhattans recorded two LPs for Deluxe, a subsidiary of Starday-King of Nashville, between their Carnival and Columbia recordings. *With These Hands* ♪♪♪ (Deluxe, 1970, prod. Buddy Scott) was George Smith's last LP with the group and includes such uncharacteristic material as "Georgia on My Mind" and "By the Time I Get to Phoenix." *A Million to One* ♪♪♪♪ (Deluxe, 1972, prod. various) was the first LP with Alston. "One Life to Live," from this LP, was one of their best.

influences:
◄◄ The Moonglows, the Dells, the Flamingos, Sam Cooke, Johnnie Taylor

►► Boyz II Men

Bill Pollak

The Marcels

Formed 1959, in Pittsburgh, PA.

Cornelius Harp, lead vocals (1959–62, 1975); Ronald Mundy, tenor vocals (1959–61); Gene Bricker, tenor vocals (1959–61); Richard Knauss, baritone vocals (1959–61); Fred Johnson, bass vocals; Alan Johnson, baritone vocals (1961–64); Walt Maddox, second tenor vocals (1961–present); Richard Harris, vocals (1964–present); William Herndon, vocals (1964–present).

A racially mixed doo-wop group named after lead singer Cornelius Harp's hairstyle, the Marcels hit the airwaves in 1961 with a crazed version of the Rodgers/Hart standard "Blue Moon" that featured a bass "bomp-ba-ba-bomp" intro against which all other bass lines before and since are measured. According to myth, New York DJ Murray the K liked the song so much he played it 26 times in one show. White tenors Richard Knauss and Gene Bricker left the group in the summer of 1961, and an all-black lineup recorded "Heartaches," the only other single that would come close to duplicating the success of "Blue Moon." The Marcels cut a number of sides for their label, Colpix Records, during 1961 and 1962; versions of the group also recorded as the Fabulous Marcels during the mid-1970s, and as Walt Maddox and the Marcels during the early 1980s.

what to buy: The Marcels specialized in uptempo doo-wop versions of R&B and Tin Pan Alley standards, so *The Best of the Marcels* ♪♪ (Rhino, 1990) contains songs such as "That

Old Black Magic," "Summertime," "Over the Rainbow," even "My Melancholy Baby." A gimmick that worked fabulously once with "Blue Moon" obviously wasn't enough to sustain a career, and while these are strong performances, they're only mildly interesting.

what to buy next: *Summertime* ✍✍✍ (Relic, 1992) comes mostly from early demos that the group recorded around the time they signed with Colpix. One of the most fascinating tracks is an *a cappella* cover of the Cadillacs' "Zoom" that served as a prototype for the group's version of "Blue Moon." Most of the other tracks are *a cappella* or have only minimal accompaniment, though a few fully arranged tracks come from as late as 1975.

what to avoid: At more than twice the length of the Rhino collection, *Complete Colpix Sessions* ✍✍✍ (Sequel, 1993) gives all but the most obsessed doo-wop fans more Marcels than they could possibly need.

influences:

◀◀ Little Anthony and the Imperials, the Dell Vikings, the Cadillacs, the Five Keys, the Moonglows, the Drifters, the Dominoes

▶▶ The Jarmels, the Rivingtons, Sha Na Na

Brian Mansfield

Teena Marie

Born Mary Christine Brockert, March 5, 1957, in Santa Monica, CA.

With a family full of music lovers supporting her, young Mary Brockert began performing at age eight, eventually taking her nickname—Teena Marie—as her stage name. While in college, she was spotted by Motown Records chief Berry Gordy and signed to the label; as legend goes, R&B superstar Rick James heard her singing in a studio and offered to produce her first record. Before long, the industry and fans were buzzing about this white girl who could sing funk and soul with convincing passion. From 1979–81, she found success with Motown and James, gradually taking over more of her own songwriting and production responsibility as she became the most successful white artist ever to work at Motown. Moving to Epic Records during the early '80s after a royalty dispute with Motown, Marie truly spread her creative wings, refining the rock/funk mix Prince, Cameo, and James were successfully spreading while adding her own unique touches. Enjoying her biggest hit in the 1984 single "Lovergirl," Marie crossed into the pop territory that Mariah Carey would later stumble into. But it was a success she would never duplicate again. Releasing a series of

ever more ambitious albums that failed to find an audience, she lost her record deal in 1991—around the time she gave birth to her daughter, Alia Rose Noelle.

what to buy: For an album that balances Marie's talents as a multi-instrumentalist, producer, and performer, none stands taller than her most successful record, *Starchild* ✍✍✍✍ (Epic, 1984, prod. Teena Marie). Besides offering her biggest hit, the pop/funk number "Lovergirl," this record has a touching tibute to Marvin Gaye, "My Dear Mr. Gaye," and a scorching ballad, "Out on a Limb." This is one of the funkiest records in a year known for landmark funk efforts. Marie's records for Motown had a different flavor, shaped less by the Minneapolis influence of Prince than by the grittier Detroit-bred funk of her funk mentor, Rick James. The best album from this period is *It Must Be Magic* ✍✍✍✍ (Gordy, 1981, prod. Teena Marie), a record where she experiments with Latin-tinged funk numbers such as "Portugese Love" and straight-up funk grooves like "Square Biz."

what to buy next: Because no one's yet waded through the legal morass that envelops much of her work, you'll have to buy two greatest hits packages to get the best from her entire, amazing career. Motown's *Greatest Hits* ✍✍✍✍ (Motown, 1985, prod. Teena Marie, Rick James, Art Stewart, Richard Rudolph) features the James-penned smash "I'm a Sucker for Your Love"—Marie's first, breakthrough single—along with the surprise disco smash "Behind the Groove," as well as "I Need Your Lovin'" and her other classic hits. *Lovergirl: The Teena Marie Story* ✍✍✍✍ (Epic Legacy, 1997, comp. Leo Sacks) boasts her less impressive, post-Motown work.

what to avoid: Coming after the powerhouse success of *Starchild*, the ambitous, experimental funk of *Emerald City* **woof!** (Epic, 1986, prod. Teena Marie) seemed like a jagged left turn. For the first time, she committed the unpardonable R&B sin of forgetting her target audience—offering a host of rock and jazz-influenced compositions that fell on deaf ears.

the rest:

Wild and Peaceful ✍✍✍ (Gordy, 1979)
Lady T ✍✍✍ (Gordy, 1980)
Irons in the Fire ✍✍✍ (Gordy, 1980)
Robbery ✍✍✍✍ (Epic, 1983)
Naked to the World ✍✍✍ (Epic, 1988)
Ivory ✍✍✍ (Epic, 1990)

worth searching for: *Passion Play* ✍✍✍ (Sarai Records/Valley Vue, 1994, prod. Teena Marie), Marie's sexually-charged, 14-cut offering on her independent label, shows she still has a gift for singing, writing, and production even after a seven-year absence.

influences:

◀◀ Aretha Franklin, Rick James, Prince, Sly & the Family Stone, Janis Joplin

▶▶ Mariah Carey, Lisa Stansfield, Madonna, Wendy & Lisa

Eric Deggans

Marky Mark

Born Mark Wahlberg, June 5, 1971, in Boston, MA.

Wahlberg was originally a member of his brother Donnie's group, New Kids on the Block, but when the New Kids moved from rap to schlocky bubble-gum love songs ("I'll Be Loving You Forever," etc.), Wahlberg decided that he wouldn't love staying with the New Kids forever and teamed up with a DJ (Terry Yancey) and five dancers to form Marky Mark and the Funky Bunch. After scoring two gold singles, "Good Vibrations" and "Wildside," muscle-bound Mark scored a golden contract as the underwear model for Calvin Klein and starred in a massive ad campaign that included TV commercials and billboards.

what to buy: The high-energy, dance-inspired *Music for the People* &&& (Interscope, 1991, prod. Donnie Wahlberg) borrows heavily from past musical people: the #1 pop hit "Good Vibrations" samples disco diva Loleatta Holloway's "Love Sensation" and the Top 10 "Wildside" rework's Lou Reed's "Walk on the Wild Side." The catchy numbers—plus Mark's rippling muscles—appealed to hordes of teen-age girls. Unlike the even more popular New Kids, though, Mark steers away from love songs, focusing instead (in spots) on social issues and the troubles of growing up in inner-city Boston.

what to avoid: *You Gotta Believe* && (Interscope, 1992, prod. Donnie Wahlberg, Mark Wahlberg, Danny Wood, others) was an unbelievably weak effort. Thankfully, Wahlberg has since traded his music career for one in the movies, where he's shown enough promise—in *The Basketball Diaries* and *Fear*—to land the high-profile role of porn legend John Holmes.

influences:

◀◀ Vanilla Ice

Christina Fuoco

The Mar-Keys

Formed 1957, in Memphis, TN.

Steve Cropper, guitar; Charlie Freeman, guitar; Donald "Duck" Dunn, bass; Terry Johnson, drums; Jerry Lee "Smoochie" Smith, piano; Packy Axton, saxophone; Wayne Jackson, trumpet; Don Nix, saxophone.

Bearing distinction as the first house band at the Stax-Volt label, back when the label was known as Satellite, the Mar-Keys nonetheless had only one Top 10 single in its career. The Steve Cropper-formed band got its start providing support for both Rufus and Carla Thomas as well as releasing singles of its own. The first, 1961's "Last Night," went gold, but constantly shifting personnel and the emergence of Booker T. & the MG's (which contained Cropper and Dunn) eventually led to a nearly undetected fadeaway. Various members have had successful ventures since, including Wayne Jackson with the Memphis Horns, Freeman with the Dixie Flyers, and Don Nix as a solo artist.

what to buy: The music on the twofer *Damifiknow/Memphis Experience* &&& (Stax, 1994/1972, prod. various) foreshadows Booker T. & the MG's penchant for reworking other artist's material, with the Mar-Keys' versions of "Mustang Sally," "Knock on Wood," "Soul Man," "Reach Out I'll Be There," and "Let It Be."

the rest:

The Great Memphis Sound &&&& (Rhino, 1991/1966)
Back to Back &&&& (Rhino, 1991/1967)

influences:

◀◀ Rufus Thomas, Carla Thomas, Cannonball Adderley

▶▶ Booker T. & the MG's, the Bar-Keys, Memphis Horns, Dixie Flyers

Allan Orski

Marley Marl

Born Marlon Williams, September 30, 1962, Queens, NY.

A former radio DJ on New York's famed *Mr. Magic's Rap Attack*, producer Marley Marl significantly shaped hip-hop's (and music's) history as one of the most prolific producers during the mid- and late-'80s. Marley organized the formidable, since-dissolved Juice Crew, bringing together Big Daddy Kane, Kool G Rap, Masta Ace, Intelligent Hoodlum, Biz Markie, Craig G, Roxanne Shante, and M.C. Shan, and his recordings with those artists, plus the likes of Eric B. & Rakim (*Eric B. for President*) and LL Cool J (*Mama Said Knock You Out*) are classics, forever part of the hip-hop narrative.

what to buy: Most hip-hop heads should already have the albums of the Juice Crew members and other Marley-produced groups, but those who don't should purchase the recently issued *Marley Marl's House of Hits* &&&& (Cold Chillin', 1995, prod. Marley Marl). The greatest-hits package boasts a number of hip-hop classics: Kool G Rap & D.J. Polo's "Poison," Biz Markie's "Make the Music with Your Mouth Biz," M.C. Shan's "The Bridge," Roxanne Shante's "Roxanne's Revenge," and, of course, "The Symphony," the seminal posse cut featuring Ace, Kool G Rap, Kane, and Craig G. The collection also includes Lords of the Underground's "Chief Rocka," one of Marley's later production efforts—and certainly not one of his best.

what to buy next: Marley Marl was one of the first producers to put out his own album. Named after his radio show, *The In Control Rap Show*, the second installment, *In Control Volume 2* 𝒶𝒶𝒱 (Cold Chillin/Warner Bros., 1991, prod. Marley Marl) is a collection of up-tempo New York-flavored hip-hop beats that fits easily with a DJ's mix. Although tantalizing in theory, "The Symphony Pt. II"—featuring the original four rappers, plus Kane progeny Little Daddy Shane—doesn't quite live up to its predecessor. Except for the sleeper, "Cheatin' Days Are Over," starring Mike Nice, the other songs feature unspectacular newcomers. Tuff City Records, now relying on its aging catalog, recently released *Marley Marl: The Queensbridge Sessions* 𝒶𝒶𝒱 (Old Skool Flava/Tuff City, 1996, prod. Marley Marl), a collection of (mostly) demo outtakes and instrumentals from 1985–87 that had been buried in the vaults. There are hidden gems, though, like Grandmaster Caz's "I'm the Judge" and the Poet's "Beat You Down."

worth searching for: *In Control Volume I* (Cold Chillin', 1988, prod. Marley Marl) isn't in print, but there are certainly copies floating around. The collection's highlight, of course, is what could arguably be called the greatest posse cut of all time, and Marley's most famous production, "The Symphony."

influences:

◀◀ Mr. Magic, Grandmaster Flash

▶▶ Buckwild, Masta Ace, Large Professor, Juice Crew All Stars, Tragedy, Heavy D. & the Boyz, Eric B. & Rakim, Kool G Rap, Pete Rock & C.L. Smooth, Real Live, Lords of the Underground

Jazzbo

Bob Marley & the Wailers
Formed 1963 as the Wailin' Wailers, in Kingston, Jamaica.

Robert Nesta Marley (died May 11, 1981 in Miami, FL), vocals, guitar; Peter Tosh, vocals, keyboards, guitar (1963–73); Bunny Wailer, vocals (1963–73); Rita Marley, vocals (1973–81); Judy Mowatt, vocals (1973–81); Marcia Griffiths, vocals (1973–81); Carlton Barrett, drums (1963–81); Ashton Barrett, bass (1963–81); Touter, keyboards (1972–74); Tyrone Downie, keyboards (1975–81); Al Anderson, guitar (1972–81); Alvin Patterson, percussion (1972–81); Julian "Junior"

Marvin, guitar (1972–81); Earl "Wire" Lindo, keyboards (1978–81); Earl Smith, guitar (1974–76).

Marley's is the one name most associated with reggae worldwide, though the original Wailin' Wailers was a more-or-less equal partnership between him, Tosh, and Wailer. The Wailers were a moderately successful harmony singing group in Jamaica when they signed with Island records in 1972. The two seminal albums, *Catch a Fire* and *Burnin'*, put reggae and rastas, Jamaica and ganja on the international music map with their hard-edged music and uncompromising, socially and spiritually conscious lyrics. When the trio broke up in 1973, Marley took over, added the I-Threes as background singers, and embraced a more rock-oriented sound. Marley's raw charisma and brilliant songwriting led to international superstar status no other reggae musician has equalled, though his biggest hit would come in another's hands—Eric Clapton's 1973 cover of "I Shot the Sheriff." Marley became the revolutionary standard bearer rock musicians of the 1960s had been. He was given the United Nations Peace Medal in 1978, the same year he coaxed feuding Jamaican presidential candidates to join hands on stage at a concert. Marley died of cancer in 1981, at age 36.

what to buy: *Burnin'* 𝒶𝒶𝒶𝒶 (Island, 1973, prod. Chris Blackwell, the Wailers) features the Wailers' classic harmonies on some of their best material: "Get Up, Stand Up," "I Shot the Sheriff," and "Burnin' and Lootin'" took the world by storm. *Legend* 𝒶𝒶𝒶𝒶 (Tuff Gong/Island, 1984, prod. various) is a tightly compiled greatest hits set with "No Woman No Cry," "Is This Love," and the lovely acoustic "Redemption Song."

what to buy next: *Babylon by Bus* 𝒶𝒶𝒶𝒱 (Island, 1978, prod. Chris Blackwell, Jack Nuber) captures the Marley charisma at various concerts over a three-year period, particularly on a killer version of "War."

what to avoid: It's not actually bad, but *Kaya* 𝒶𝒶𝒱 (Island, 1978, prod. Bob Marley & the Wailers) is comprised of some of Marley's most forgettable tunes, except for "Easy Skanking" and "Is This Love."

the rest:
Natty Dread 𝒶𝒶𝒶𝒶 (Island, 1974)
Live 𝒶𝒶𝒶𝒱 (Island, 1975)
Rastaman Vibration 𝒶𝒶𝒶𝒱 (Island, 1976)
Exodus 𝒶𝒶𝒶𝒱 (Island, 1977)
Survival 𝒶𝒶𝒶 (Island, 1979)
Uprising 𝒶𝒶𝒶𝒱 (Island, 1980)
Confrontation 𝒶𝒶𝒱 (Island, 1983)
Rebel Music 𝒶𝒶𝒶𝒱 (Island, 1986)
Talkin' Blues 𝒶𝒶𝒶𝒱 (Tuff Gong/Island, 1991)

One Love 𝄢𝄢𝄢 (Heartbeat, 1991)
Songs of Freedom 𝄢𝄢𝄢𝄢 (Tuff Gong/Island, 1992)
Natural Mystic 𝄢𝄢𝄢 (Tuff Gong/Island, 1995)
Dreams of Freedom: Ambient Translations of Bob Marley in Dub 𝄢𝄢 (Island, 1997)

worth searching for: *The Birth of a Legend* 𝄢𝄢𝄢 (Calla, 1976, prod. C.S. Dodd) features some of the Wailers' 1960s work at the legendary Studio One, including the 1964 Jamaican hit "Simmer Down."

influences:

◄◄ Skatalites, Desmond Dekker

►► Ziggy Marley & the Melody Makers, UB40, English Beat, Lucky Dube, Tricky

Lawrence Gabriel

Ziggy Marley & the Melody Makers

Formed 1979, in Kingston, Jamaica.

David "Ziggy" Marley, vocals, guitar; Stephen Marley, vocals, percussion; Cedella Marley, vocals; Sharon Marley Prendergast, vocals.

Bearing a striking resemblance, both physically and vocally, to his father—reggae icon Bob Marley—has likely been as much a burden as a boon to Ziggy Marley. But he's borne up under it amazingly well, leading a group including his brother and two sisters. Their father wrote and produced a single for the group, "Children Playing in the Streets," but the Melody Makers' first two albums suffered from their general lack of seasoning and from their record company's focus on making Ziggy a solo star. After moving to Virgin, Ziggy was still out front, but his family's influence grew on each successive album. While the group leans decidedly toward the pop side of reggae, with considerable influence from American R&B and hip-hop, its lyrics continue in the vein of their late father—cautionary, righteous, but ever optimistic.

what to buy: The group's years on Virgin, certainly its most fertile period, is well summed up on *The Best Of (1988–1993)* 𝄢𝄢𝄢𝄢 (Virgin, 1997, prod. various), a 17-track compilation. In terms of individual releases, though, *Conscious Party* 𝄢𝄢𝄢𝄢 (Virgin, 1988, prod. Chris Frantz, Tina Weymouth) fulfills both parts of its title, with lyrics extolling Rastafarianism and liberation, and grooves that just won't quit. The title track and "Tomorrow People" promote awareness and uplift, while "Lee and Molly" recounts the strife encountered by an interracial couple.

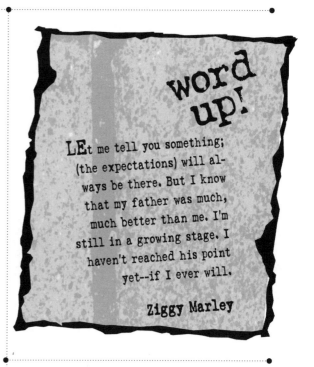

word up!

LEt me tell you something; (the expectations) will always be there. But I know that my father was much, much better than me. I'm still in a growing stage. I haven't reached his point yet—if I ever will.

Ziggy Marley

The production by Weymouth and Frantz doesn't get in the way of the songs, and it certainly makes some of them more palatable to American ears with the Talking Heads-style keyboard textures on "Have You Ever Been to Hell," for example. The group's reggae/hip-hop/rock synthesis is picked up again on *Free Like We Want 2 B* 𝄢𝄢𝄢𝄢 (Virgin, 1995, prod. the Melody Makers), which finds the family's involvement at an all-time high. Backup vocalists Cedella and Sharon (along with Erica Newell) take the lead on "Today," and Stephen steps to the fore on a number of tunes, including "Tipsy Dazy," "Keep On," and "Bygones." Ziggy's presence is still strong, especially on the title track and "Power to Move Ya."

what to buy next: *Jahmakya* 𝄢𝄢𝄢 (Virgin, 1991, prod. the Melody Makers, Glenn Rosenstein) is perhaps the group's first truly mature album, with a nod to reggae's past, but with an eye more on creating a sound of their own, incorporating riddim-heavy hip-hop and dancehall influences, and adding a harder rock edge to boot. "Raw Riddim," "Kozmik," and "So Good So Right" are standouts.

what to avoid: *Time Has Come . . . The Best of Ziggy Marley & the Melody Makers* 𝄢𝄢 (EMI America, 1988, prod. Rita Marley)

captures the best of a developmental period, a treat for the devout fan but few others.

the rest:
One Bright Day 🎝🎝🎝 (Virgin, 1989)
Joy and Blues 🎝🎝🎝 (Virgin, 1993)
Fallen Is Babylon 🎝🎝🎝 (Elektra, 1997)

worth searching for: Die-hard fans or collectors can scour the racks for the original Melody Makers releases: *Children Playing* 🎝🎝 (EMI America, 1984, prod. Steve Levine), *Play the Game Right* 🎝🎝 (EMI America, 1985, prod. Grub Cooper, Tyrone Downie, Ricky Walters, David Marley), and *Hey World* 🎝🎝🎝 (EMI America, 1986, prod. David Marley, Tyrone Downie, Grub Cooper, Ricky Walters).

influences:
◀◀ Bob Marley, the Wailers, Curtis Mayfield, Earth, Wind & Fire
▶▶ Fugees, Spearhead, Big Mountain

Daniel Durchholz

Martha & the Vandellas
Formed 1962, in Detroit, MI.

Martha Reeves, lead vocals; Annette Beard, vocals (1962–63); Rosalind Ashford, vocals (1962–69); Betty Kelly, vocals (1963–67); Lois Reeves, vocals (1967–73); Sandra Tilley, vocals (1969–73).

A more emotionally forthright alternative to their chief rivals, the Supremes, the Vandellas were led by Reeves's no-nonsense vocals, making it one of the toughest sounding girl groups of the 1960s. Possessing an earthy soulfulness and a street-sass charm, the group recorded a string of propulsive dance hits ("Heatwave," "Dancin' in the Streets," "Quicksand") that stand among some of Motown's finest achievements. Reeves locked horns with Motown and left for a solo career in 1974, though she still performs with different combinations of Vandellas, including Beard and Ashton. The Vandellas were inducted into the Rock and Roll Hall of Fame in 1995.

what to buy: *Motown Milestones* 🎝🎝🎝🎝 (Motown, 1995, prod. various) is condensed, definitive, and cheap, an 18-track collection with all the essential hits—including "Jimmy Mack," "Nowhere to Run," "Heatwave," and "Dancin' in the Streets."

what to buy next: *Live Wire! The Singles 1962–1972* 🎝🎝🎝🎝 (Motown, 1993, prod. various) is an excellent two-disc package that has numerous B-sides and non-hit singles in addition to the obvious hits.

what to avoid: *Motown Superstar Series, Vol. 2* 🎝🎝 (Motown, 1981, prod. various) is a skimpy 11-track sampler.

the rest:
Heatwave 🎝🎝🎝 (Motown, 1963)
Come and Get These Memories 🎝🎝🎝 (Motown, 1963/1994)
Greatest Hits 🎝🎝🎝 (Motown, 1966)

worth searching for: *Martha Reeves: The Collection* 🎝🎝🎝 (Object Enterprises, 1986) gathers some of her later, though inferior, material.

influences:
◀◀ Della Reese
▶▶ The Supremes, the Pointer Sisters, Salt-N-Pepa, TLC, En Vogue

Allan Orski

> **word up!**
>
> I heard (Barrett Strong's) 'Money,' and we all needed money. I'd clap my hands, snap my fingers, stomp my feet, because there were no synthesizers at the time. I supplemented that $35 (as a Motown secretary) to a point where I could afford to work there.
>
> **Martha Reeves (of Martha & the Vandellas)**

Martha Reeves of Martha & the Vandellas (© Ken Settle)

The Marvelettes

Formed 1960, in Inkster, MI. Disbanded 1971.

Katherine Anderson, vocals; Gladys Horton, vocals (1960–68); Georgeanna Tillman, vocals (1960–66); Juanita Cowart, vocals (1960–65); Georgia Dobbins, vocals (1960–61); Wanda Young, vocals (1961–71); Anne Bogan, vocals (1968–71).

The only Motown act that could safely be slipped into the "girl group" genre, the Marvelettes's lack of an identifiable front-person and frequent inter-group shake-ups denied them their fair share of the spotlight during the image-conscious mid-1960s. History, however, records that despite these draw-backs, they produced a most solid, creditable body of work which easily holds its own against that of their more colorful Motor City counterparts. Gathering around her a group of friends already adept at vocalizing in local church choirs and talent shows, Gladys Horton formed the initial quintet while still in high school, and it was at a contest there that a scout from the newly-formed Motown label first heard them perform (under the name the Marvels; a previous moniker, the Casinyets, as in "can't sing yet," had already been discarded). Advising the group to seek out new and original material, Dobbins helped re-work a song her neighbor—yes, a letter carrier—had composed, and "Please Mr. Postman" not only se-cured The Marvelettes a contract with Motown, but became the label's very first #1 R&B *and* pop hit in December 1961. The group continued to score successes the following year with "Playboy" and "Beechwood 4-5789," but in 1963 it turned down the chance to record a new Holland-Dozier-Holland com-position entitled "Baby Love." Snapped up by the Supremes, this song quickly launched *their* career, and it can be safely ar-gued that the lack of attention afforded the Marvelettes dur-ing the ensuing years by Berry Gordy Jr. effectively, and ir-reparably, stalled their momentum. Nevertheless, it was dur-ing this comparatively fallow period, sales-wise, that the group cut some of its very best material, thanks to brilliant songwriting and production assists from Smokey Robinson, Marvin Gaye, Ashford & Simpson, and Van McCoy. Reduced to a trio by 1967, falling victim to both changing musical times and continuing inattention from Motown, the group struggled gallantly onwards before unceremoniously calling it a day dur-ing the early 1970s. Sadly, Tillman succumbed to sickle-cell anemia in 1980, and subsequent efforts by Horton to reform the group have all been unsuccessful.

what to buy: Their definitive career overview remains *The Mar-velettes Deliver: The Singles, 1961–1971* 🎵🎵🎵🎵 (Motown, 1993,

comp. Cary E. Mansfield), a 42-track, double-CD parade of hits, B-sides, key album tracks, and rarities which not only amply showcase the lead vocals of Horton and Young, but demon-strate yet again the absolute wealth of talent operating under Berry Gordy at the time (for example, that's Marvin Gaye play-ing drums on "Please Mr. Postman"!).

what to buy next: For a closer look, *Marvelettes/Sophisticated Soul* 🎵🎵🎵 (Motown, 1977, prod. various) reissues two of the group's best original LPs for listeners eager to uncover hidden gems from their most creative, if least high-profile years.

the rest:

Please Mr. Postman 🎵🎵🎵 (Motown, 1961)
Playboy 🎵🎵🎵 (Motown, 1962)
Marvelous Marvelettes 🎵🎵🎵 (Tamla, 1963)
Greatest Hits 🎵🎵🎵🎵 (Motown, 1966)
Marvelettes 🎵🎵🎵🎵 (Motown, 1967)
Sophisticated Soul 🎵🎵🎵🎵 (Motown, 1968)
Compact Command Performances 🎵🎵🎵 (Motown, 1986)
Motown Legends 🎵🎵🎵🎵 (Motown, 1994)
Beechwood 4-5789 🎵🎵🎵 (Motown, 1995)
Motown Milestones 🎵🎵🎵🎵 (Motown, 1995)
Best of the Marvelettes 🎵🎵 (Hot Productions, 1996)

influences:

◀◀ The Chantels, the Shirelles, Smokey Robinson

▶▶ The Supremes, Tammi Terrell, Deborah Harry

Gary Pig Gold

Massive Attack /Protection

Formed 1988, in Bristol, England.

3D; Daddy G; Mushroom; Shara Nelson, vocals (1988–91); Tricky (1988–91).

Strong influences from dub reggae, hip-hop, and classic soul brought Massive Attack to its beginning points, and the fusion resulted in a brand new sound that shot the band to the fore-front of the British urban soul movement. It arose out of the Wild Bunch, a loose collective of graffiti artists, breakdancers, and musicians based in Bristol that once featured acclaimed producer Nellee Hooper (Soul II Soul, Madonna). The collective made its first splash in 1991 with the debut album *Blue Lines*, which launched three U.K. hits ("Unfinished Sympathy," "Safe from Harm," and "Daydreaming") and scored strong under-ground support in America, which would be solidified in the pop world with 1995's follow-up album *Protection*. Relishing their role as behind-the-scenes producers and music lovers, the Massive Attackers formed their own record label, Melankolic, in 1997. Its initial releases feature longtime pal Horace Andy and reputed English newcomers Ariel. Among the more interesting points in Massive Attack history: having to briefly change their band name to Massive following the eruption of the Gulf War in order to maintain British radio airplay; remixing "Mysterious Ways" for U2; collaborating with Everything But the Girl; and seeing their early anthems resurface as theme music for Nike tennis shoe commercials.

what to buy: Massive Attack's seminal *Blue Lines* ⚜⚜⚜⚜ (Wild Bunch/EMI, 1991, prod. Massive Attack) is an extraordinarily polished debut album. Shara Nelson's vocals on "Unfinished Sympathy" and "Safe from Harm" are breathtaking and unforgettable, while Tricky's smoldering delivery on "Daydreaming" foreshadows his later successes as a solo artist. Everything But the Girl's Tracey Thorn, who appears on *Protection* ⚜⚜⚜ (Virgin, 1995, prod. Massive Attack), successfully rekindled her career—and her band's—with her stunning performances on both the title track and "Better Things," while Horace Andy's distinctive voice lends "Light My Fire (Live)" and "Spying Glass" their special edge. More linear than *Blue Lines*, *Protection* has fewer memorable moments than the debut but is definitely a worthwhile selection.

what to buy next: Mad Professor vs. Massive Attack's remix album *No Protection* ⚜⚜⚜⚜ (Caroline, 1996, prod. Mad Professor, Massive Attack) reworks *Protection* into a dub delight. The mark of a remixer without an ego complex, Mad Professor makes his distinct mark on each track without disturbing the essence of Massive Attack. Songs are stripped down to their most minimal elements and then processed through the dementia of the Professor, which generally means a lot of reverb, delay, random funny sound effects and a real sense of the value of sparse production. Excellent.

solo outings:
Tricky:
Maxinquaye ⚜⚜⚜⚜ (Island, 1995)
Nearly God ⚜⚜⚜ (Island, 1996)
Tricky Presents Grassroots ⚜⚜ (Payday, 1996)
Pre-Millennium Tension ⚜⚜⚜ (Island, 1996)

Horace Andy:
Skylarking: The Best of Horace Andy (Melankolic, 1997)

Shara Nelson:
What Silence Knows ⚜⚜⚜⚜ (Chrysalis/ERG, 1994)
Friendly Fire ⚜⚜⚜ (Cooltempo/UK, 1995)

influences:
◀◀ Horace Andy, Soul II Soul, Jamaican sound systems
▶▶ Nicolette, Erykah Badu, Groove Theory

Tamara Palmer

Masta Ace
Born in Brooklyn, NY.

Once regarded as the posterchild for artistic integrity, Masta Ace found himself on the outside looking in when critics accused him of simplifying his musicianship and lyricism to find mass appeal. Nonetheless, nobody can argue that, for at least two-thirds of his career (thus far), Ace has been one of hip-hop's most cherished MCs. He began his recording career after a rap contest he won awarded him six hours in the studio with influential producer Marley Marl. After recording two songs ("Simon Says" and "Keep Your Eyes on the Prize"), Marl was impressed enough with the Ace to include him as a member of the Juice Crew on the now-classic cut "The Symphony." Always known for his love of the rebellious arts (graffiti, tagging, etc.), Ace eventually followed his passion for cruising and created a style of music he dubbed "Brooklyn Bass."

what to buy: Hip-hop purists should already have Ace's debut *Take a Look Around* ⚜⚜⚜ (Cold Chillin/Reprise, 1990, prod. Marley Marl, DJ Mista Cee, Masta Ace); any fan of the early Juice Crew sound who doesn't, should. Underground favorites like "Music Man" and "Me and the Biz" (in which Ace gives a "cameo" impersonation of Biz Markie), and such unsung gems as "Brooklyn Battles" and the Gil Scott-Heron-like title track, distinguish Ace as an astute observer of everyday life. Ace's second album, *Slaughtahouse* ⚜⚜⚜ (1993, Delicious Vinyl, prod. Masta Ace), finds Ace being more critical of his peers and introducing his on-beat/off-beat lyrical style. "A Walk through the Valley" is quintessential poetic Ace, while "The Mad Wunz" and "Jeep Ass Niguh" became favorites.

what to buy next: The remix to the single "Jeep Ass Niguh" manipulated an obscure beat by the group Original Concept (which Ace found in the dollar rack at his local record shop) into "Born to Roll," a bass-heavy cruising anthem that went on to become Ace's biggest-selling record. That song's success inspired him to create the "Brooklyn Bass" sound—lots of tight, reverberating dub sounds cast in hip-hop context—on *Sittin' On Chrome* ⚜⚜ (Delicious Vinyl, 1995, prod. Masta Ace). Essentially an album full of "Born to Rolls," longtime fans hated Ace for the switch, complaining that it made his music sound diluted.

worth searching for: Two collaborations really defined Ace as a modern-day griot. One was with the Young Disciples, a new-jazz group from the UK, on "Talkin' What I Feel"—a poignant, cerebral song on the outstanding *Road to Freedom* 𝄞𝄞𝄞𝄞 (Talkin' Loud/Mercury, 1993, prod. Young Disciples). The other was with the Brand New Heavies for their *Heavy Rhyme Experience Volume 1* 𝄞𝄞𝄞𝄞 (Delicious Vinyl, 1992, prod. Brand New Heavies). The song, "Wake Me When I'm Dead," solidified Ace's status as the go-to poet in the burgeoning acid jazz and new-soul scene.

influences:

◀◀ Kool G Rap, Big Daddy Kane

▶▶ Lord Digga, Paula Perry

Jazzbo

Master P

Born Percy Miller, in New Orleans, LA.

The rap world has turned into a pop-culture marketing circus, and Master P stands out as prime example of how self-promotion can overcome lukewarm artistic vision. His No Limit Records label, originally a record store in California, has expanded into one of the most successful black-owned businesses in the country, earning P a well-deserved reputation as one of the most ingenious commercial strategists on the hip-hop planet. Despite churning out releases at a breakneck pace, No Limit's projects rarely sell under six figures, thanks largely to P's record retail experience, which taught him two things: that low-riding, funk-powered West Coast style is as popular with Southerners as it is on the left coast; and nothing sells like excess. That helps explain the success of P's gangstacentric material, then, with its unabashed tales of drug dealing and violence, often delivered with a bare minimum of rapping skill. P's approach—rivaled only by Luke's for sheer over-the-top shamelessness—at times approaches the comic. The inside of 1995's *99 Ways to Die*, for instance, advertises a 1-900 number where you can "talk live to fine ass No Limit bitches." And P's penchant for remakes (Aaliyah's "If Your Girl Only Knew" got the P-fun cover treatment while the original was still on the charts) prompted one rival crew to dub him the Weird Al Yankovic of rap. But when it comes down to record sales and the resultant cash infusion, P has always had the last laugh. Indeed, long after the deaths of Notorious B.I.G. and 2Pac had turned hardcore rap into hip-hop's ultimate liability, P's No Limit players, including Mia X, Tru, and Kane and Abel, were still bringing in the dollars, while his own low-budget, straight-to-video movie *I'm Bout It* was selling at a CD pace, threatening to make P the Rudy Ray Moore of the 1990s.

what to buy: Master P's formula rarely changes. As such, there's nothing particularly new or interesting about his contributions to his compilation *West Coast Bad Boyz II* 𝄞𝄞𝄞 (No Limit/Priority, 1997, prod. various). The album, though, gives you just enough P while balancing the attack with contributions from artists from P's inner circle and from the West Coast gangsta underground.

the rest:

The Ghetto's Tryin to Kill Me! 𝄞𝄞 (No Limit, 1994)
99 Ways to Die 𝄞𝄞𝄞 (No Limit, 1995)
Ice Cream Man 𝄞𝄞𝄞 (No Limit, 1996)
Ghetto D 𝄞𝄞𝄞 (No Limit/Priority, 1997)

influences:

◀◀ Herm, E-40, Too $hort, Eazy-E

▶▶ TRU, Mia X, Skull Dugrey, Silkk, Kane and Abel

Logan Creed

Johnny Mathis

Born September 30, 1935, in San Francisco, CA.

If Frank Sinatra is the Chairman of the Board, Johnny Mathis must be the CEO. Mathis is not just one of the world's most successful male vocalists: he is a living bronze institution. His *Greatest Hits* LP spent over *nine years* on the best-selling album charts. The wiry crooner with the tremulous, distinctively clipped phrasing is also commonly believed to be one of the first African American millionaires, which is ironic because Mathis grew up around wealth—his parents worked as domestic help for the upper crust of San Francisco. Though he began taking opera lessons at the age of 13, Mathis was determined to become a physical education teacher; quite an athlete in his own right, he was invited to the 1956 Olympic track and field trials. But Mathis made it neither to the Olympics nor the gymnasium. His vocal talent simply could not be overlooked, and while singing at San Francisco's 440 Club he was discovered by a Columbia Records executive and signed to a recording contract. He went to New York in 1956 and began his career doing jazz, but Columbia A&R chief Mitch Miller (yes, *that* Mitch Miller) convinced him to switch to the material that would ultimately make him famous: romantic pop ballads. That did the trick. A year later, Mathis scored three consecutive hits, including his unforgettable #1 "Chances Are." Mathis soon was considered the crown prince of pop music, right alongside King

Frankie. Mathis landed the rest of his hits in the 1950s and 1960s, then stopped being a popular radio sensation and transformed into a cultural icon. He sold millions and millions of albums around the world and became the undisputed champion of bedroom balladry. He returned to the charts in 1978 with Deniece Williams in the duet "Too Much, Too Little, Too Late," a #1 R&B hit, and shortly thereafter joined Williams again to record "Without Us," which became the theme of the TV series *Family Ties*. His subsequent rock and dance adventures were dismal failures, sending him back to his familiar ballad turf. Mathis continues to ply his craft in Atlantic City, Las Vegas, New York, and other large venues, to sellout crowds. He and his catalog of timeless romantic rhapsodies have fused into the American fabric like baseball, apple pies, or making out in the back seat of a convertible while the car stereo plays "The Twelfth of Never."

what to buy: You want romance? You want love ballads to make you—or better yet, your lover—swoon? Then you must have the ultimate Johnny Mathis collection, *Johnny's Greatest Hits* 𝕃𝕃𝕃𝕃 (Columbia, 1958/1988, prod. various). An aural aphrodisiac, the swing and groove of this album supply the sultry tones of such *Mathisiosity* as "Chances Are," "It's Not For Me To Say," "Wonderful, Wonderful," and "The Twelfth of Never." Pure, unadulterated splendor.

what to buy next: Though he is the ultimate crooner and king of makeout music, some people only can handle so much Mathis on his own. Double your pleasure, then, with *Better Together—The Duet Album* 𝕃𝕃𝕃𝕃 (Sony, 1991, prod. various), compiling his best male-female harmonies with Regina Belle, Patti Austin, Dionne Warwick, and Angela Bofill, among others. The million-selling blockbuster "Too Much, Too Little, Too Late" is here, as are great Mathis-Williams pairings like "Love Won't Let Me Wait" and the Mathis-Austin inspiration "You Brought Me Love." It's not all Mathis, but it's all good. For a penetrating view of Mathis alone, particularly in the formative stages of his career, the *40th Anniversary Limited Edition Collectors' Set* 𝕃𝕃𝕃𝕃 (Columbia, 1996, prod. various) is highly recommended. The box contains his early LPs *Johnny Mathis, Good Night, Dear Lord* (backed by the Percy Faith Orchestra), and *I'll Buy You a Star*, with Mathis himself providing the liner notes. It's warm, it's intimate, it's a bearskin rug and a bottle of champagne. *Open Fire, Two Guitars* 𝕃𝕃𝕃𝕃 (Sony Master Sound/Legacy, 1959/1994) is a standout Mathis release because of its wonderful simplicity and understatement. It's just melodic guitar work by Al Caiola and Tony Mottola, the bass of Milt Hinton and Frank Carroll, and Mathis singing.

what to avoid: Steer clear of *Love Songs* 𝕃 (Columbia, 1988, prod. various), which, by the way, is a needless and misleading title. EVERY Mathis hit is a love song, and he's recorded far better ones than the motley batch assembled here.

the rest:
Johnny Mathis 𝕃𝕃𝕃 (Columbia/Legacy, 1957/1996)
Good Night, Dear Lord w/ Percy Faith Orchestra 𝕃𝕃𝕃𝕃 (Columbia, 1958/1996)
More Johnny's Greatest Hits 𝕃𝕃𝕃 (Columbia, 1959/1989)
I'll Buy You A Star 𝕃𝕃𝕃𝕃 (Columbia, 1961/1996)
Johnny w/Don Costa & Orchestra 𝕃𝕃𝕃𝕃 (Columbia, 1963/1996)
That's What Friends Are For w/Deniece Williams 𝕃𝕃𝕃 (Columbia, 1978)
Best Days of My Life 𝕃𝕃𝕃𝕃 (Columbia, 1979/1989)
The Best of Johnny Mathis 1975–1980 𝕃𝕃 (Columbia, 1980)
Silver Anniversary Album: The First 25 Years 𝕃𝕃𝕃 (Columbia, 1981)
Friends in Love 𝕃𝕃 (Columbia/Legacy, 1982/1991)
Johnny Mathis Live 𝕃𝕃𝕃𝕃 (Columbia, 1983)
A Special Part of Me 𝕃𝕃𝕃 (Columbia, 1984)
Hollywood Musicals w/Henry Mancini 𝕃𝕃𝕃 (Columbia, 1986)
16 Most Requested Songs 𝕃𝕃𝕃𝕃 (Columbia/Legacy, 1987)
You Light Up My Life 𝕃𝕃 (Columbia, 1988)
Once in a While 𝕃𝕃𝕃 (Columbia, 1988)
Heavenly 𝕃𝕃𝕃𝕃 (Columbia, 1989/1959)
16 Most Requested Songs: Encore! 𝕃𝕃𝕃𝕃 (Sony, 1989)
In the Still of the Night 𝕃𝕃𝕃𝕃 (Sony, 1989)
In a Sentimental Mood: Mathis Sings Ellington 𝕃𝕃𝕃𝕃 (Columbia, 1990)
How Do You Keep the Music Playing? 𝕃𝕃𝕃𝕃 (Sony, 1993)
The Music of Johnny Mathis: Personal Collection 𝕃𝕃𝕃𝕃 (Sony, 1993)
This Heart of Mine 𝕃𝕃 (Columbia Special Products, 1993)
The Essence of Johnny Mathis 𝕃𝕃𝕃 (Columbia/Legacy, 1994)
Heavenly/Greatest Hits/Live 𝕃𝕃𝕃𝕃 (Columbia, 1995)
All About Love 𝕃𝕃 (Columbia, 1996)
The Global Masters 𝕃𝕃𝕃𝕃 (Sony, 1997)

worth searching for: The second-best time to seek out Mathis music? December 25th. Johnny's voice has become as traditional a part of Christmas as trees, stockings, and fat men in red suits, and when sleigh bells ring you can find him on *Christmas Eve with Johnny Mathis* 𝕃𝕃𝕃 (Columbia, 1986), *Merry Christmas* 𝕃𝕃𝕃𝕃 (Columbia, 1960), *For Christmas* 𝕃𝕃 (Columbia), *The Christmas Music of Johnny Mathis: A Personal Collection* 𝕃𝕃𝕃𝕃 (Legacy, 1993), *Christmas with Johnny Mathis* 𝕃𝕃𝕃 (Columbia), and *Give Me Your Love for Christmas* 𝕃𝕃𝕃 (Columbia). He's never met a carol he didn't like—or record.

influences:

◄◄ Clyde McPhatter, Little Anthony & the Imperials, Nat "King" Cole, Sam Cooke, Frank Sinatra, Brook Benton

Michael Bolton, Barry Manilow, Barbra Streisand, Tom Jones, Englebert Humperdink, Paul Anka, Neil Diamond

Chris Tower

Maxwell

Born 1973, in Brooklyn, NY.

Growing up in a hardscrabble Brooklyn neighborhood, the part-Puerto Rican, part-West Indian Maxwell—a self-described "shy, lonely, straight up nerd"—first began tinkering with songwriting by plugging away on a beat-up Casio keyboard. Hooking up with noted author and critic Nelson George to provide vocal sounds to back his film *To Be a Black Man,* Maxwell also caught the ear of executives at Columbia, which eventually released his debut record—a soul music masterwork that established him as one of the hot newcomers as R&B approached the millenium.

what to buy: Employing an old school soul sound that features lots of live instruments, Maxwell traces the evolution of a single relationship on *Maxwell's Urban Hang Suite* ♪♪♪ (Columbia, 1996, prod. Maxwell), a vibrant, emotional record that features the help of players such as Sade's Stuart Matthewman, Marvin Gaye collaborator Leon Ware, and ex-Barry White guitarist Wah Wah Watson. Providing much of the keyboard, guitar, and programming work himself, Maxwell vaults from the swirling, moody funk of "The Urban Theme" to the flashy funk of "Sumthin' Sumthin'" and the propulsive rhythms of "Ascension (Don't Ever Wonder)." Buoyed by such quality funk and Maxwell's own magnetic, MTV-ready presence—complete with mile-wide, dreadlocked afro—it's no wonder this disc went on to sell more than a million copies.

the rest:
MTV Unplugged ♪♪♪ (Columbia, 1997)

influences:
Marvin Gaye, Teddy Pendergrass, Barry White, Sam Cooke

Eric Deggans

Curtis Mayfield

Born June 3, 1942, in Chicago, IL.

Curtis Mayfield got his chance to lead the Impressions and made the best of it when Butler left the group in 1959 after a

Curtis Mayfield (© Jack Vartoogian)

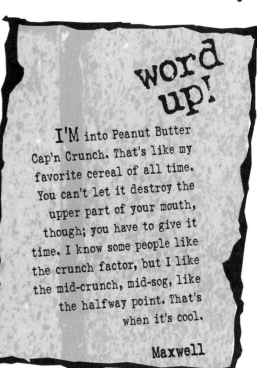

word up!

I'M into Peanut Butter Cap'n Crunch. That's like my favorite cereal of all time. You can't let it destroy the upper part of your mouth, though; you have to give it time. I know some people like the crunch factor, but I like the mid-crunch, mid-sog, like the halfway point. That's when it's cool.

Maxwell

handful of hits such as "For Your Precious Love." Mayfield's songwriting, engaging vocals, and spare arrangements led the group to an early and mid-1960s peak with hits such as "Gypsy Woman" and "I'm So Proud." Unlike many soul artists during the early part of the decade, Mayfield's themes embraced civil rights sentiments; "People Get Ready" and "Choice of Colors" set a musical agenda long before its artists forced Motown to address social issues. Mayfield started his own Curtom label in 1968 for Impressions releases and wrote hits for Major Lance, Jerry Butler, and others. He left the Impressions for a solo career in 1970, though he continued to manage the group, and reached the height of fame with his score for the 1972 movie *Superfly*—a gritty souladelic tour de force that yielded the hits "Freddy's Dead," "Pusherman," and the title track. Mayfield even performed in the movie as the leader of a local bar band. Though he began to lose form in the mid-1970s, Mayfield the songwriter, singer, arranger, producer, and label owner stands as a giant of soul music. His performing career ended tragically in 1990, when some stage lights fell on him and left him a quadriplegic, though he's made a triumphant return to recording in recent years.

what to buy: Mayfield was never better than on *Superfly* 🎵🎵🎵🎵 (Curtom, 1972/Rhino, 1997, prod. Curtis Mayfield), where his falsetto cut through visions of ghetto life like a stiletto blade in a street fight. The wah-wah guitar that drives through this album is exemplary proto-funk. The Rhino reissue is a deluxe, two-disc set, complete with previously unreleased music from the movie, studio outtakes, radio spots, and exclusive interview excerpts. Mayfield's tenure with the Impressions—as well as some of his solo highlights—are captured on *Curtis Mayfield and the Impressions: The Anthology 1961–1977* 🎵🎵🎵🎵 (MCA, 1992, prod. various).

what to buy next: The three-disc boxed set *People Get Ready* 🎵🎵🎵🎵 (Rhino, 1996, prod. various) covers the whole spectrum, from the Impressions to 1970s hits such as "Kung Fu" and "Billy Jack." The liner notes include reflections from proteges such as Stevie Wonder, Don Cornelius, and George Clinton, in addition to an interview with Mayfield.

what to avoid: Taking on longer forms and conceptual compositions didn't serve Mayfield well on *There's No Place Like America Today* 🎵🎵 (Curtom, 1975, prod. Curtis Mayfield), which features preachy raps on themes not conducive to partying.

the rest:
The Impressions Greatest Hits 🎵🎵🎵🎵 (MCA, 1965)
Groots 🎵🎵🎵🎵 (Curtom, 1971)
Curtis in Chicago 🎵🎵🎵 (Charly, 1973)
Of All Time 🎵🎵🎵🎵 (Curtom, 1974)
Do It All Night 🎵🎵🎵 (Curtom, 1978)
Living Legend: Heartbeat 🎵🎵🎵🎵 (Curtom, 1979/1995)
Curtis Mayfield's Chicago Soul 🎵🎵🎵🎵 (Legacy, 1995)
New World Order 🎵🎵🎵 (Warner Bros., 1996)
The Very Best of Curtis Mayfield 🎵🎵🎵🎵 (Rhino, 1997)

worth searching for: *Heartbeat* 🎵🎵🎵🎵 (Curtom, 1979, prod. various) finds Mayfield in a disco mode with dance floor grooves such as "Tell Me, Tell Me (How Ya Like to Be Loved)."

influences:

◀◀ The Drifters, the Soul Stirrers

▶▶ Seal, Maxwell, D'Angelo, Tony Rich

see also: *The Impressions*

Lawrence Gabriel and Aidin Vaziri

Percy Mayfield

Born August 2, 1920, in Linden, LA. Died August 11, 1984.

Percy Mayfield's legacy is the songs he wrote rather than the music he performed. He moved to Los Angeles during the 1940s and began writing for a variety of artists, but he was recording blues and R&B for Specialty Records when he began writing songs for Ray Charles—the biggest of which was "Hit the Road, Jack." Charles repaid the favor by signing Mayfield to his Tangerine label, for which Mayfield recorded the modest hit "River's Invitation." Mayfield went on to record for Brunswick and RCA, but with little success.

what to buy: *Memory Pain* 🎵🎵🎵 (Specialty, 1992, prod. Art Rupe) is a solid 25-song collection that shows Mayfield was capable of good work and that on certain numbers—such as the title track, "Please Send Me Someone to Love," "My Heart," and "Hit the Road, Jack"—he had the potential to be a first-tier artist.

the rest:
Poet of the Blues 🎵🎵🎵 (Specialty, 1980)
Hit the Road Again 🎵🎵 (Timeless, 1982/1990)
Live 🎵🎵🎵 (Winner, 1992)

influences:

◀◀ Louis Jordan, Big Joe Turner, Leadbelly, Muddy Waters

▶▶ Jimmy Witherspoon, Ray Charles

Gary Graff

Maze

Formed as Raw Soul, c. 1971, in Philadelphia, PA. Became Maze c. 1976.

Frankie Beverly, lead vocals, rhythm guitar; William Bryant, keyboards, synthesizers; Robin Duhe, bass; Ronald "Roame" Lowry, congas, background vocals; Ron Smith, lead and rhythm guitars; McKinley "Bug" Williams, percussion, background vocals; Philip Woo, keyboards, synthesizers; Mike White, drums. Other members have included Wayne Thomas; Sam Porter; Joe Provost; Billy "Shoes" Johnson; Ahaguna G. Sun.

A vastly underrated soul/R&B/funk band, Maze has been fronted by Frankie Beverly since its inception. Beverly—one of the smoothest soul singers ever to pick up a microphone—grew up in Philadelphia and was inspired by the sounds of vocal groups such as Frankie Lymon & the Teenagers, the Moonglows, and the Dells. (Given the name Howard at birth, Beverly was so enamored with the music of Frankie Lymon that he later changed his own name to Frankie.) After stints with various local groups, Beverly put together Raw Soul—the immediate predecessor to Maze—and relocated to Oakland, California. The band's big break came when the sister-in-law of the legendary Marvin Gaye caught its act at a San Francisco club. She passed the word on to Gaye, and days later Gaye was checking the group out for himself. At Gaye's urging, the band changed its name to Maze and soon joined the Motown star on the road as his opening act. More than 20 years and 12 albums later, Maze is still going strong, developing a loyal core of fans who have come to appreciate Beverly's brilliant singing and songwriting skills and the band's spectacular live performances. The fact that Beverly and Maze still remain relatively unknown to the masses is puzzling, especially in this day and age of the crossover soul ballad. But their anonymity doesn't seem to bother them one bit. Capable of playing the softest of ballads, as well as rough and tumble funk, Maze just goes on selling out shows worldwide and making R&B albums that stand the test of time.

what to buy: One would be hard pressed to find a better collection of soul than *Anthology* ✍✍✍✍ (The Right Stuff, 1996, comp. Tom Cartwright), which compiles Maze's best work from their years with Capitol. All the big hits are on this 20-track, two-disc set, including "Joy and Pain," "Feel That You're Feelin'," "Southern Girl," and "Back In Stride." While the arrival of *Anthology* made *Lifelines Volume I: The Greatest Hits of Maze* ✍✍✍✍ (Capitol, 1989, prod. Frankie Beverly) pretty much expendable, its remixed version of "Joy and Pain"—featuring a rap by Kurtis Blow—is way cool. If you'd rather have a single-disc hits package, you can't miss with this one.

what to buy next: *Live in New Orleans* ✍✍✍✍ (Capitol, 1981/1987, prod. Frankie Beverly) does a terrific job of capturing the electricity of a Maze concert. Believed by many to be one of the finest live soul albums of all-time, it also features some studio material, including the hit "Running Away." *Silky Soul* ✍✍✍✍ (Warner Bros., 1989, prod. Frankie Beverly) was the band's first album for Warner Bros. and contains moving tributes to both Gaye (the title track) and Nelson Mandela ("Mandela").

what to avoid: Unhappy with its relationship with Capitol, Maze more or less released *Live in Los Angeles* ✍ (Capitol, 1986/Gold Rush, 1997, prod. Frankie Beverly) to complete its contractual obligation with the label. Like *Live in New Orleans*, this album features both live and studio tracks. Unfortunately, five of the nine live tracks on this set were also recorded live for the New Orleans album. There's no need to waste your money on this classic case of too much of a good thing.

word up!

I was aware of the influence the Impressions had (on 1960s-era reggae artists) simply because Bob Marley used to put his own name on many of my songs. I began to find this out after he died; I began to pick up pieces of his and I'd hear my music. He even used 'People Get Ready.' I wish he was still here so I could sue him! (Laughs.) At least he'd still be here, too.

Curtis Mayfield

the rest:
Inspiration ✍✍✍ (Capitol, 1979/Razor & Tie, 1995)
Joy and Pain ✍✍✍✍ (Capitol, 1980/Razor & Tie, 1995)
Can't Stop the Love ✍✍✍ (Capitol, 1985/Razor & Tie, 1995)
Back to Basics ✍✍✍ (Warner Bros., 1993)
Southern Girl ✍✍✍ (Capitol Special Products, 1996)

worth searching for: A few of Maze's albums—*Maze Featuring Frankie Beverly* ✍✍✍ (Capitol, 1976, prod. Frankie Beverly), *Golden Time of Day* ✍✍✍ (Capitol, 1978, prod. Frankie Beverly), and *We Are One* ✍✍✍✍ (Capitol, 1983, prod. Frankie Beverly)—have yet to see the light of day on CD. If you still have your turntable, you might want to check your local used record store for the vinyl versions.

influences:
◀◀ Frankie Lymon & the Teenagers, the Moonglows, the

Dells, the Dell Vikings, Sam Cooke, Sly & the Family Stone, Marvin Gaye

▶▶ Prince, Anita Baker, Toni Braxton, Gerald Levert

Dean Dauphinais

MC Breed & the DFC

Formed early 1990s, in Flint, MI.

MC Breed (born Eric Breed); Alpha Breed; T-Double.

For an artist who is relatively unknown and largely unheralded in his sphere of music, MC Breed has the resume of a seasoned rap star. When Breed first started rocking the microphone during the 1980s, there were few if any rappers of significance coming out of the Midwest. Despite the lack of doors (and minds) open to urban poets between the East and West Coasts, he managed to achieve national recognition from his first and most recognizable single, "Ain't No Future In Yo' Frontin'." This was a remarkable accomplishment, considering that many denizens of the hip-hop nation consider the place their performers represent to be as important as the music they make and that Flint-bred Breed couldn't even claim bragging rights to a major Midwestern city like Detroit. After battling around Flint with his arsenal of laid-back rhymes and bass-heavy beats, Breed eventually made his way down to the club scenes of Detroit, Chicago, and Toledo, and with its irresistible funk (on loan from the Ohio Players' "Funky Worm") and catchy chorus, 1991's "Frontin" soared to the top of radio playlists in those cities, becoming such a runaway underground hit that established rappers like Daddy-O and LL Cool J were moved to work the "Flintian" slogan into their records, giving Breed the credit. Despite the breakout success of his subsequent single, "Gotta Get Mine," plus myriad guest appearances on other well-known artists' LPs and a prolific production schedule (at least one album a year since the 1991 debut *MC Breed & the DFC*), Breed has never been able to make it to the next plateau.

what to buy: Breed's most musically developed album, *Funkafied* ♫♫♫♫ (Wrap/Ichiban, 1994, prod. Brett Ski) receives a major boost from the great God of P-Funk himself, George Clinton, who makes a guest appearance. Every song is textured with real instruments and jolted with old-school funk; many of the tracks even sound as if they should be included in a classic 1970s R&B compilation. Breed can do no wrong on this LP.

what to buy next: Though it seems extremely pretentious for an artist who's still largely anonymous to release a greatest hits album, *The Best of MC Breed* ♫♫♫♫ (Wrap/Ichiban, 1995, prod.

various) delivers as promised. The seamless, compelling presentation features Breed's hit collaboration with the late 2Pac ("Gotta Get Mine") and a bevy of other memorably funky tracks.

what to avoid: Despite a few interesting tracks, *One Puff Music/MC Breed Saucy Vol. 1* ♫♫ (Ichiban, 1997, prod. various) fails to live up to Breed's own lofty standards. This is really little more than an assortment of unknown Ichiban acts, highlighted by Breed's early backup ensemble, DFC (Da Funk Clan).

the rest:
Mc Breed:
MC Breed & the DFC ♫♫♫ (Wrap/Ichiban, 1991)
20 Below ♫♫♫ (Wrap/Ichiban, 1992)
The New Breed ♫♫♫ (Wrap/Ichiban, 1993)
Big Baller ♫♫♫♫ (Wrap/Ichiban, 1995)
To Da Beat Ch'all ♫♫♫♫ (Wrap/Ichiban, 1996)

DFC:
Things in Tha Hood ♫♫ (Assault, 1994)
The Whole World Is Rotten ♫♫♫ (Penalty, 1997)

influences:
◀◀ George Clinton, EPMD

▶▶ Dayton Family, Rappin 4-Tay, DFC, MC Brainz, Jamal

Andre McGarrity

MC Eiht /Compton's Most Wanted

MC Eiht is one of hip-hop's most underrated, underrecognized MCs. Compton's Most Wanted made original "gangsta rap" when it was still a clear, expressive portrayal of the cold realities in the inner city and not a get-rich-quick construct, and Eiht was a modern-day griot using words to create vivid images of that landscape. Eiht, DJ Slip, and the Unknown DJ came together to form CMW, but after three albums, Eiht and the Unknown DJ had a falling out. Though the make-up of the group was pretty much the same, the name became MC Eiht featuring Compton's Most Wanted (perhaps because Eiht was beginning to make a name for himself as an actor, playing the critically acclaimed role of A-Wax in the film *Menace II Society*).

what to buy: Believe it or not, gangsta rap didn't all used to sound the same. In fact, some of hip-hop's most musically creative songs have come from the albums of N.W.A., Ice Cube, and Compton's Most Wanted. By far, CMW's best album is its third, *Music to Driveby* ♫♫♫♫ (Orpheus/Epic, 1992, prod. MC

Eiht, Unknown DJ, Slip, Mike T). Eiht's concise and gritty lyricism is backed by a soundtrack of dark, edgy jazz beats. It's narcotic—especially the "Hit the Floor" introduction—and songs such as "Hood Took Me Under" and "Compton 4 Life" evoke more emotion in their completeness than a dozen of today's imitators.

what to buy next: The group's sophomore album, *Straight Checkn 'Em* ✂✂✂ (Orpheus/Epic, 1991, prod. Unknown DJ, Mike T, Slip) features a lot of posturing and despairing attitudes in its songs, but is unquestionably one of the better albums of the gangsta rap genre. "Compton's Lynchin," "Growin' Up in the Hood," and "Mike T's Funky Scratch" should be familiar to any rap fan who was living in California at the beginning of the decade. The sheer number of artists making gangsta rap made it difficult to discern many differences, and the group's (or, rather, MC Eiht featuring CMW's) subsequent releases, *We Come Strapped* ✂✂ (Epic, 1994, prod. MC Eiht, DJ Slip, Ric Roc) and *Death Threatz* ✂✂ (Epic, 1996, prod. MC Eiht, DJ Slip, others), simply didn't carry the impact of their predecesors. *We Come Strapped* may be most notable for being the first album to come strapped with two warning stickers: The usual "Parental Advisory" label and a larger, more noticeable one placed on the album by Epic that declared, "The lyrical content contained on this album solely expresses the views of the artist."

worth searching for: CMW's first album, *It's a Compton Thang* ✂✂✂✂ (Orpheus, 1990, prod. Unknown DJ, Mike T, Slip) is a true original. Now out of print, it introduced Eiht's trademark, drawn-out "ghyeeeaaahh" phrase, and included the two most recognizable CMW songs, "Def Wish" and "Duck Sick" (of which Eiht continues to make sequels).

influences:

◀◀ N.W.A., Too $hort

▶▶ Scarface, Dr. Dre, N.O.T.R.

Jazzbo

M.C. Hammer

Born Stanley Kirk Burrell, March 30, 1963, in Oakland, CA.

A kid from the projects who became one of the biggest-selling stars in '80s pop, Hammer is now regarded as the ultimate example of an artist who had it all, then lost it. Struck early in life with twin passions for baseball and music, Stanley Burrell turned a gig dancing for change in the parking lot of the Oakland A's ballclub into work as a batboy and unofficial team mas-

cot. Nicknamed "Little Hammer" for his resemblance to legendary ballplayer "Hammerin'" Hank Aaron, the entertainer eventually started his own record label with money borrowed from wealthy ballplayer friends. Success in the Bay Area as M.C. Hammer led to a contract with Capitol Records, which advanced the artist $750,000. Bursting onto the music scene with a raft of sampled Parliament and James Brown songs disguised as rap records, M.C. Hammer nevertheless gained a growing reputation for his amazing dance prowess and well-choreographed shows. But it wasn't until his second album, *Please Hammer Don't Hurt 'Em*, that M.C. Hammer became a pop star. Backed by an unauthorized sample of the Rick James hit, "Super Freak"—for which the rapper was later forced to pay some fees and list James as a co-writer—the song "U Can't Touch This" became a pop phenomenon, and *Please Hammer* was perched at #1 for a staggering 21 weeks. A tour with a 30-member entourage followed, as did high-profile endorsement deals with Pepsi and Kentucky Fried Chicken and a kiddie cartoon, *Hammerman*. But even as other rappers denounced his slick, pop appeal and flashy genie pants, the artist's fortunes were unraveling. Even after Hammer ditched the "M.C." from his name, a third record, *Too Legit to Quit*, failed to catch fire, undone by the ascension of gangsta rap and fans insisting on more realistic stars. Investments in a horse breeding business, sprawling mansions, and his ever-growing entourage drained his finances, along with a fourth record that stalled in 1994. Two years later, while trying to hitch his star to gangsta rap mogul Suge Knight's Death Row Records, Hammer was forced to declare bankruptcy. He named $13.7 million in debts, including $500,000 owed to star athlete Deion Sanders and $613,000 owed as a settlement payment to a woman who claimed members of the rapper's entourage gang raped her. *People* magazine soon featured Hammer on its cover with the headline "Going Broke on $33 Million a Year." Now desperate to prove that the final nail hasn't been hammered into the coffin that houses his career, Hammer has made a film for Showtime and recorded a new album.

what to buy: Never a very accomplished rapper, Hammer nevertheless brings breathtaking energy to his major-label debut, *Let's Get It Started* ✂✂✂✂ (Capitol, 1988, prod. M.C. Hammer, Felton Pilate), cramming together James Brown and P-Funk samples into an intoxicating, hip-shaking stew. It may have been amateurish in spots—despite co-production by Con Funk Shun's Felton Pilate—but few rap fans could listen to such powerhouse jams as "Turn This Mutha Out" and "They Put Me in the Mix" without shaking their groove thang at least a little.

what to avoid: Well aware that his nice-guy, churchgoing, pop-oriented image wouldn't cut it with '90s-era rap fans, Hammer tried to reposition himself as a harder-edged rapper with *The Funky Headhunter* **woof!** (Giant, 1994, prod. Hammer, Tha Dogg Pound, Teddy Riley, others). Unfortunately, the guy who gave us the rap anthem "Pray" just doesn't sound right dissing his fellow MCs from the East Coast. The processed jams on this record can't help matters, drowning what little lyrical prowess Hammer can muster in a flood of cliched rap/soul shadings.

the rest:
Feel My Power 🎵🎵 (Bust It, 1988)
Please Hammer Don't Hurt 'Em 🎵🎵🎵 (Capitol, 1990)
Too Legit to Quit 🎵🎵🎵 (Capitol, 1991)

worth searching for: Hammer's true value always lay in his MTV-ready image and spot-on dance moves, so a look at the video collection *Here Comes the Hammer* (Capitol, 1991) should offer a glimpse of the onstage energy and charisma that sealed his legend.

influences:

◀◀ James Brown, Michael Jackson, Prince

▶▶ Oaktown 3-5-7, Bobby Brown

Eric Deggans

MC Lyte

Born Lana Moorer, October 11, 1971, in Queens, NY.

One of the first female rappers to cultivate a rough-n-tumble image, Queens-born, Brooklyn-raised MC Lyte got her start at age 12, busting rhymes with her half-brother Milk and his Audio Two partner in rhyme, Gizmo. Four years later, the threesome released "I Cram to Understand You (Sam)"—a biting account of its namesake's crack habit—on their father Nat Robinson's newly formed First Priority label. On her first two full-length releases, *Lyte as a Rock* and *Eyes on This*, Lyte came out swinging like a B-girl scorned (and with something to prove), taking on everyone from game-show bimbo Vanna "Whyte" and rival rapper Roxanne Shante to nameless dope-dealing hustlers and sex-scamming homeboys. Beginning with 1991's *Act Like You Know* and continuing on an album-by-album basis thereafter, Lyte strove to keep pace with the times (and her own restless

tastes) by willfully tweaking her no-frills, street-savvy style. The results sounded by turns ambitious and desperate. Throughout her career, Lyte has been an outspoken social and political activist, recording public service announcements for the Rock the Vote organization and contributing her time and likeness to the fight against AIDS.

what to buy: Set against a spartan backdrop of syncopated scratching and primeval beatbox clatter, Lyte turns loose her best collection of raps on her sophomore outing, *Eyes on This* 🎵🎵🎵🎵 (First Priority/Atlantic, 1989, prod. King of Chill, others). Among them: "Cha Cha Cha" (penned by King of Chill), "Not Wit' a Dealer," and "Cappuccino," a brilliant tale of frothy coffee and deadly crossfire.

what to buy next: *Lyte as a Rock* 🎵🎵🎵 (First Priority/Atlantic, 1988, prod. various) introduced the world to high-school student Lana Moorer's husky voice, tough-as-nails attitude, and lickety-split spritzes in such songs as "10% Dis," "Paper Thin," and the title track. Widely regarded as her return to hardcore, Lyte's fourth album, *Ain't No Other* 🎵🎵🎵 (First Priority/Atlantic, 1993, prod. Audio Two, others), isn't as much a reclamation of roots as a co-opting of the day's reigning street style, gangsta rap. Still, with its phalanx of hard-ass beats and expletive-intensive rhymes (and Top 40 hit "RuffNeck"), *Ain't No Other* rocks the house, Ice Cube-style.

what to avoid: Although not without its merits ("Search 4 the Lyte," "Big Bad Sister"), *Act Like You Know* 🎵🎵 (First Priority/Atlantic, 1991, prod. various) is largely a hapless foray into urban pop led by Bell Biv DeVoe svengalis Wolf and Epic. Suffice it to say Lyte is no New Jill Swing. Following the ferocious frontal assault of 1993's *Ain't No Other*, Lyte recast herself as a slow-jam soul sista on *Bad as I Wanna B* 🎵🎵 (First Priority/Elektra, 1996, prod. Jermaine Dupri, R. Kelly, others). Containing a lean 10 tracks—one of which is a remix of the album opener "Keep On, Keepin' On"—*Bad as I Wanna B* smacks of artistic exhaustion. Indeed, it's not without a certain longing for glories past that Lyte, in "TRG (The Rap Game)," delivers the bittersweet lines: "I remember when I hit the scene/It was the second phase/Rope chains, two finger rings/Those were the days."

worth searching for: The 1988 First Priority various-artists compilation *Basement Flavor* includes three otherwise-unavailable Lyte tracks: the original mix of "Survival of the Fittest," "I'm Not Having It" (featuring Positive K), and "Victory Is Calling" (featuring Michie Mee and L.A. Luv).

M.C. Hammer **(© Ken Settle)**

influences:

◀◀ KRS-One, LL Cool J, Run-D.M.C., Roxanne Shante, Salt-N-Pepa

▶▶ Queen Latifah, Yo Yo, Da Brat, Positive K, Missy Elliot, Bahamadia, Bo$$

Greg Siegel

MC 900 FT Jesus

Formed 1988, in Dallas, TX.

Mark Griffin, vocals; DJ Zero, DJ.

A onetime classical trumpeter with a weird sense of humor and a cool, bratty rap style reminiscent of the Beastie Boys, Mark Griffin has helped push hip-hop into funky unknown territory. Quirky early songs such as the rambling "Truth Is Out of Style," with turntable whiz DJ Zero, won the hearts of college radio DJs. After that, MC 900 FT Jesus—his name came from an offhand Oral Roberts comment—smoothed out his production sound, found a mildly literary voice, and added elements of jazz, Indian, and Latin rhythms. *Welcome to My Dream* is most notable for its excellent songwriting, such as the spooky, gangsta-worthy, first-person "Killer Inside Me." After signing to the big American Records, Griffin rediscovered his loopy instincts and managed to push the lighthearted "If I Only Had a Brain" (with equally fun rolling-down-the-street-in-a-box video) onto MTV. He's not exactly a musical visionary, and his songs are often too clunky for fun and too weird to be taken seriously, but his heart is always worth the attention.

what to buy: *One Step Ahead of the Spider* ⚜⚜⚜ (American, 1994, prod. Mark Griffin) contains some of Griffin's best songwriting, notably the hit "If I Only Had a Brain" and the *Confederacy of Dunces*-inspired "New Year's Eve," and uses a full band for the first time (with Indian percussion and horns, no less).

what to buy next: *Welcome to My Dream* ⚜⚜⚜ (Nettwerk/I.R.S., 1991, prod. Mark Griffin), Griffin's encounter with the dark side (check the titles: "Dali's Handgun," "Hearing Voices In One's Head," "Killer Inside Me," "Falling Elevators"), matches the gloom with nice literary devices and slick funk.

what to avoid: Despite the fun bratty rap "Truth Is Out of Style" and some nice DJ Zero mixmastering, *Hell with the Lid Off* ⚜⚜ (Nettwerk/I.R.S., 1990, prod. Mark Griffin) is frequently tedious and unmemorable.

worth searching for: The four-song EP *Too Bad* ⚜⚜⚜ (Nettwerk, 1989, prod. Mark Griffin) includes one of the few good *Hell with the Lid Off* songs ("Too Bad") and a better version of "Shut Up."

influences:

◀◀ Beastie Boys, Sly & the Family Stone, Minutemen, Eric B. and Rakim, D.J. Jazzy Jeff & the Fresh Prince, Dead Milkmen, Red Hot Chili Peppers

▶▶ Sublime, Bloodhound Gang, Lucas, Fun Lovin' Criminals

Steve Knopper

M.C. Shan

Born Shawn Moltke, in Queens, NY.

M.C. Shan is one of the original Queens MCs, and his association with master producer Marley Marl during the mid-1980s helped his star rise considerably. Starting off with singles such as "Beat Biter" and "Marley Marl Scratch," Shan's confident, nasal vocal style worked to keep him on top of the growing rap scene in New York City. With Marl's blessing, Shan quickly joined Big Daddy Kane, Biz Markie, Roxanne Shante, and Kool G Rap & D.J. Polo in an exclusive group of Queensbridge rappers dubbed the Juice Crew All Stars. Mostly recording for the Cold Chillin' label, an imprint which benefited greatly from a major-label buyout by Warner Bros. in 1987, the crew was one of the more popular, prolific, and progressive in the history of hip-hop, helping to bring rap music from the streets of New York to the rest of America. Besides benefiting from his association with this Queensbridge clique, Shan also incurred the wrath of Bronx-based rapper KRS-One in 1987, which resulted in a famous rivalry. KRS's "The Bridge Is Over," a direct response to Shan's "The Bridge," created quite a stir in the rap world, which, as some may remember, actually once was about battling rival crews that tried to outdo (but not outgun) each other. Shan released several albums after his Marl-produced 1987 debut, *Down By Law*, many without Marl's production help, though he never achieved the popularity that he had at the Juice Crew's height. During the early 1990s, Shan discovered white reggae-pop toaster Snow and wound up managing Snow's career and producing his hit debut album, *12 Inches of Snow*. After all is said and done, though, Shan's most important legacy will be as a crucial player in rap's transition from its modest indie-label beginnings to the multi-million dollar industry that it is today.

what's available: *Down By Law* ⚜⚜⚜⚜ (Cold Chillin'/Warner Bros., 1987, prod. Marley Marl), Shan's debut and only album still in print, is full of old-school classics and stands as one of Marl's best production efforts. With beats and samples that are considered old now—but were revolutionary a decade ago—Marl's musical work jumps out of the speakers and grabs the listener, and Shan himself is the perfect MC for the tracks. From classics such as "The Bridge," "Down By Law," "Kill That Noise," and "Left Me—Lonely" to more playful fare such as "Jane, Stop This Crazy Thing" and "M.C. Space," the album is full of tracks that suggest the rapper and his producer were standing at the edge of a void, coloring in the lines as they went along. This is a great album and an important document of what came out of the New York City rap scene that burst at the seams in the mid-1980s.

worth searching for: "Beat Biter" (Bridge Records, 1985), "Marley Marl Scratch" (Nia, 1986), and "Juice Crew All Stars" (Cold Chillin', 1987) are all important (if not essential) 12-inch singles.

influences:

◀◀ Melle Mel, Spoonie Gee, Cold Crush Brothers, Marley Marl, Juice Crew All Stars

▶▶ N.W.A., Nas, Lord Finesse, Lucas

Brian Coleman

MC Solaar

Born Claude M'Birali, in France.

Within the global context of hip-hop, MC Solaar is a transcontinental legend. Solaar, along with producer/DJ Jimmy Jay, has been creating smooth, jazzy masterpieces that showcase his liquescent flow since 1990. In fact, it is his uniquely French interpretation of the New York-bred art form that has won him universal praise. The way his words and inflections fit the music provided by Jimmy Jay is uncannily infectious. His rich, mellow baritone is seductive and captivating—whether you understand French or not—and Jimmy Jay's sonic concoctions are tailored to fit Solaar's words like a skin-tight glove. Even though his 1991 French release, *Qui Seme Le Vent Recolte Le Tempo*, achieved multi-platinum status overseas, Solaar didn't actually make an impact stateside until his 1992 duet with Guru on Guru's Jazzmatazz track "Le Bien, Le Mal."

what's available: *Prose Combat* ♪♪♪♪ (Cohiba/Island, 1993, prod. Jimmy Jay) is Solaar's second full-length endeavor, his first to be released in the United States. While rapping solely in his native tongue, Solaar manages to draw on a wide range of lyrical influences (Nietzsche and John Wayne, to name a few) and tackles a variety of subjects and styles, ranging from the

effect of American culture on the rest of the world ("Noveau Western") to his French twist on the standard N.Y.C.-styled battle rhyme ("A Dix De Mes Disciples").

worth searching for: MC Solaar's first album is much jazzier and more laid back than *Prose Combat*. Available as a French import, *Qui Seme Le Vent Recolte Le Tempo* ♪♪♪♪ (Polydor France, 1991, prod. Jimmy Jay) roughly translates to "Who Sows the Wind Receives the Tempo." The title couldn't be more poetically precise, as every track—from the rolling, hypnotic soul jazz of the title cut to the silky seductiveness of "Victime De La Mode"—is brilliant, proving that Solaar is an MC to be reckoned with. Jimmy Jay released a compilation album, *Jimmy Jay presente Les Cool Sessions* ♪♪♪♪ (Virgin France, 1993, prod. Jimmy Jay), which showcases many of France's top MCs, including La Funk Mob, Les Sages Poetes De La Rue, and Lucien, who was immortalized stateside in A Tribe Called Quest's 1990 track "Luck of Lucien."

influences:

◀◀ A Tribe Called Quest, De La Soul, Gang Starr

▶▶ La Funk Mob

Spence D.

Van McCoy

Born January 6, 1944, in Washington, DC. Died July 6, 1979, in Englewood, NJ.

His legacy still honored at virtually every wedding reception and office party in America, producer/composer Van McCoy is best remembered as the man who supplied the music for the defining dance of the disco 1970s, "The Hustle." But McCoy enjoyed a lengthy career in R&B and dance music, with experience dating back to the 1950s when he sang with the groups the Marylanders and the Starlighters. He became an A&R (artist and repertoire) executive for Scepter/Wand Records in 1961, and during his three-year stint there wrote songs for the Shirelles and Jackie Wilson ("Get the Sweetest Feeling") and produced sessions for the Drifters and Gladys Knight & the Pips. He worked as an arranger for Leiber & Stoller, owned MAXX records in the mid-1960's, created Van McCoy Productions in 1968 (working with artists such as Aretha Franklin, David Ruffin, and Stacy Lattisaw), and formed the pop-soul group Faith, Hope & Charity before becoming a solo artist. Signing with Avco Records, his first single, "The Hustle," exploded to a #1 hit on both the pop and R&B charts in 1975, quickly turning gold. McCoy also had a Top 10 R&B hit with "Change with the Times," and his biggest album, *Disco Baby* (with its slinky, seductive female dancer on the cover), became regulation issue for every club DJ in the country. But McCoy's true gift was as a songwriter and producer, crafting tunes for Knight, Franklin, Wilson, Lattisaw, Melba Moore, Barbara Lewis, and the Stylistics before falling victim to a heart attack in 1979.

what's available: Including both the original version and the "Super Hustle Mix" of his personal greatest hit, *The Hustle and the Best of Van McCoy* ⚡⚡⚡ (Amherst, 1995) celebrates "The Hustle" along with his other chart notable, "Change with the Times," and the "Theme from Star Trek."

influences:

◀◀ The Supremes, the 5th Dimension, Love Unlimited Orchestra, Chic, Sister Sledge

▶▶ Bunny Sigler, Meco, Lipps Inc., M, Kool & the Gang, Jaydee, Todd Terry, Daft Punk

"Lisa Lisa" Orlando

McFadden & Whitehead

Formed early 1970s, in Philadelphia, PA.

Gene McFadden, vocals; John Whitehead, vocals.

Friends and collaborators since their teens, Gene McFadden and John Whitehead were pursuing a career as performers—in bands such as the Epsilons (once managed by Otis Redding) and Talk of the Town—when Philadelphia International's Kenny Gamble and Leon Huff put them to work as writers, arrangers, and producers. The duo came up with "Backstabbers" for the O'Jays, "I'll Always Love My Mama" for the Intruders, and other compositions for Archie Bell & the Drells, Harold Melvin & the Blue Notes, and others before recording their own album in 1979. "Ain't No Stoppin' Us Now" was a Top 20 hit, but McFadden and Whitehead were soon back to working behind-the-scenes during the early 1980s.

what's available: Just the duo's debut, *McFadden & Whitehead* ⚡⚡⚡ (Philadelphia International, 1979/The Right Stuff, 1993, prod. John Whitehead), is in print. It's got "Ain't No Stoppin' Us Now" and some other first-rate songs that show the duo's material was best delivered by others.

influences:

◀◀ Sam & Dave, Otis Redding, the Four Tops

▶▶ Daryl Hall & John Oates, Simply Red, Lisa Stansfield, Culture Club

Gary Graff

Brian McKnight

Born June 5, 1969, in Buffalo, NY.

When Brian McKnight finally decided he wanted to take the leap into the music business, he considered joining his older brother Claude in the celebrated R&B-gospel group Take 6. He even followed Claude to Oakwood College, the small Alabama Christian school where Take 6 got its start. But Brian's stay at the college wasn't as propitious: he got caught with a girl in his room as a sophomore and was kicked out of school. (Besides, it would have meant renaming the group Take 7.) Brian's preoccupation with romance would go on to serve him well in a solo career launched in 1990, as his classic, old-school soul balladeering stands in sharp contrast to the raunchy, trendy "freakin' you" lyrics which dominate the world of 1990s R&B. His 1992 debut LP, *Brian McKnight*, released three years after his signing to Mercury Records, introduced a silky tenor gliding over love sonnets with an ease and maturity that belied his young years. Casting himself in the role of hopeless romantic and supported by the talents of Take 6 and Vanessa Williams, his LP yielded a breakthrough R&B single, "One Last Cry." Perhaps best known currently for his Top 3 duet in 1993 with Williams, "Love Is," and the Emmy-nominated theme "Every Beat of My Heart" for the TV soap *As the World Turns* from his second album *I Remember You*, Brian is turning prolific as a producer and guest artist. He has given his angelic voice to the recordings of Boyz II Men, Quincy Jones, and rappers Ill Al Skratch, appeared on the movie soundtracks to *Addams Family Values* and *When We Were Kings*, and produced works by Take 6 (of course), UNV, Vesta, and Christopher Williams.

what to buy: An all-around captivating mix of hip-hop attitude ("On the Down Low"), jazz-influenced soul, and the lush romanticism of songs like "Crazy Love" and "I Can't Go for That," *I Remember You* ⚡⚡⚡⚡ (Mercury, 1995, prod. Brian McKnight), McKnight's sophomore effort, is simply outstanding. NBA power forward and respectable jazz bassist Wayman Tisdale (whose 1995 LP *Power Forward* was produced by Brian) guests on several tracks.

what to buy next: Establishing himself as a vulnerable male lover of the first rank, *Brian McKnight* ⚡⚡⚡ (Mercury, 1992, prod. various) is full of impassioned ballads and smooth grooves that massage the ears in wave after tender wave.

influences:

◀◀ Nat King Cole, Marvin Gaye, Take 6, Donny Hathaway, Stevie Wonder, Bobby McFerrin, James Ingram, Mighty Clouds of Joy, Gino Vannelli, Keith Washington

▶▶ Joe, Eric Benet, Kenny Latimore

Andre McGarrity and Andy Ernst

Clyde McPhatter

Born Clyde Lensey McPhatter, November 13, 1933, in Durham, NC. Died June 13, 1972, in Teaneck, NJ.

Clyde McPhatter's high gospel tenor brought a fresh and vastly influential sound to 1950s R&B and early rock 'n' roll. In 1950, the 17-year-old McPhatter recorded with Billy Ward & the Dominoes for Federal Records. His soaring tenor can be heard above the choruses of their big hits "Sixty Minute Man," "Have Mercy Judge," and others. After Ward fired the cocky young singer in 1953 (Jackie Wilson was his replacement), Ahmet Ertegun signed him to Atlantic Records, where he formed a new group, the Drifters. Immediately they scored with major R&B hits such as "Money Honey," "Such a Night," "Honey Love" (which McPhatter co-wrote), and their doo-wop version of "White Christmas." McPhatter's sound was so popular that a two-year stint in the U.S. Army barely affected his career. On periodic leave, he not only recorded hits with the Drifters and Ruth Brown, but also his first solo hit, "Seven Days." McPhatter's post-Army Atlantic recordings remain his finest, most consistent work. Whether singing catchy pop songs for teens ("Lovey Dovey," "A Lover's Question"), tender ballads ("Treasure of Love") or pre-Roy Orbison operatic pop ("Without Love"), he made them all into hits. McPhatter also appeared in the Alan Freed teen-flick *Mr. Rock 'n' Roll* (1957), stiffly lip-synching the lesser hits "Rock & Cry" and "You'll Be There." McPhatter's career began a slow downward spiral when he left Atlantic and signed with MGM Records in 1959. "I Told Myself a Lie," "Let's Try It Again," and "Think Me a Kiss" achieved respectable chart positions, but the MGM material was weak and Atlantic confused his public by releasing Drifters tracks from 1953 as new recordings by Clyde McPhatter. The move to Mercury records in 1960 yielded his last classic hit, "Lover Please," and several minor chart records such as "Ta Ta," "I Never Knew," "Deep in the Heart of Harlem," and a cover version of "Little Bitty Pretty One." Mercury recorded McPhatter extensively until his contract expired during the mid-1960s. Wracked with drug and alcohol addictions, McPhatter recorded a disappointing final LP with Decca in 1970, and made a disastrous tour of Europe. According to Ruth Brown's autobiography, McPhatter then begged Atlantic Records to help him stage a comeback, and their refusal broke his spirit. He suffered a fatal heart attack in 1972.

what to buy: *Deep Sea Ball: The Best of Clyde McPhatter* 🎵🎵🎵🎵 (Atlantic, 1991, prod. Ahmet Ertegun, Jerry Wexler) is a 19-track collection of McPhatter's seminal solo work for Atlantic, featuring big hits and gospel oriented goodies such as "Rock & Cry" and "Whatcha Gonna Do."

what to buy next: *Rock 'n' Roll Radio* 🎵🎵🎵🎵 (Radiola, 1978) is a still-in-print live Alan Freed broadcast that features McPhatter singing a luminescent version of "Treasure of Love" as well as equally interesting cuts by LaVern Baker, the Drifters, the Charms, Gene Vincent, Chuck Berry, and others. *Greatest Hits* 🎵🎵🎵🎵 (Curb Records, 1991. prod. various) contains McPhatter's biggest hits both as a Drifter and a solo artist from the Atlantic, MGM, and Mercury labels. An excellent place to start.

what to avoid: *Live at the Apollo* 🎵🎵 (Mercury, 1965/Collectables, 1996) was McPhatter's way of getting around the label's policy of having established artists re-record their greatest hits. McPhatter is in only fair voice, and the audience sounds canned.

the rest:
Let the Boogie Woogie Roll 1953–1955 🎵🎵🎵🎵 (Atlantic, 1988)
Clyde McPhatter 🎵🎵🎵🎵 (King, 1994)
The Dominoes Featuring Clyde McPhatter, Vol. 2: 18 Hits 🎵🎵🎵🎵 (King, 1996)

worth searching for: *Love Ballads* 🎵🎵🎵 (Sequel, 1996, prod. Ahmet Ertegun, Jerry Wexler) is an import reissue of McPhatter's second LP for Atlantic and features the hits "Come What May" and "Long Lonely Nights," as well as some solid album tracks.

influences:
◀◀ Billy Ward, Gerhart Thrasher
▶▶ Dee Clark, Sam Cooke, Jackie Wilson

Ken Burke

Me Phi Me

Born Laron Wilbur, in Flint, MI.

The hardcore rap crowd didn't care much for Me Phi Me and his thoughtful, folksy hippie-hop, but alternative kids were more than willing to join his Fraternity of One—at least for one engaging recording. They may have remained there, too, had Me Phi Me not disappeared after releasing his one and only album, *One*.

worth searching for: Me Phi Me's appropriately titled debut, *One* 🎵🎵🎵🎵 (RCA, 1992, prod. Chris Cuben-Tatum), is out of print but definitely worth the hunt. Combining insightful, pro-black lyrics with hand-clapping acoustic roots music that might fare better at a folk festival than a block party, Me Phi Me blissfully ignores any and all genre gaps, dipping into everything from African pop (via Ladysmith Black Mambazo) to funk (samples of James Brown and Sly Stone) and even introducing the 12-string Rickenbacker to an unsuspecting—and, ultimately, unimpressed—hip-hop nation. Those who long for a return to meaningful Afropop, though, might not find much better in the 1990s than this album's delightful "Sad New Day" and "Pu' Sho Hands 2Getha." Also worth noting is the "Poetic Moment" in three parts: "The Dream," "The Streets," and "The Light."

influences:

Sly & the Family Stone, De La Soul, PM Dawn, Arrested Development

OMC, Basehead

Josh Freedom du Lac

Mellow Man Ace

Born Ulpiano Sergio Reyes, April 12, 1967, in Cuba.

The half-black, half-Hispanic MC Mellow Man Ace was born in Cuba but grew up in the tough Southgate area of Los Angeles, finding his youthful thrills on Cypress Hill with his gang member brother Senen. While Sen went on to form the paranoid, violence-obsessed, and perpetually stoned hardcore rap group Cypress Hill, Ace took a safer, more mellow approach, churning out musically and lyrically accessible songs that were mostly about women. Brilliantly dipping into both his black and Hispanic heritages, Ace scored biggest when he brought Latin lingo to rap vocals about a lying woman, then laid it out over the Latin-infused rock of Santana ("Evil Ways"). The resultant "Mentirosa" went gold and, with Kid Frost's anthemic declaration of Hispanic pride, "La Raza," marked the start of a Latin rap movement. Ace and Frost eventually joined forces under the umbrella of the Latin Alliance coalition, appearing with War in a decent remake of "Low Rider."

worth searching for: All of Ace's work is out of print, but you can find his essential Spanglish hit "Mentirosa" on the haphazardly assembled *Latin Lingo: Hip-Hop from the Raza* (Rhino, 1995, prod. various), which inexplicably contains only one track by Kid Frost and none by the ad hoc group, Latin Alliance.

influences:

Santana, 7A3, Kid Frost

Lighter Shade of Brown, Cypress Hill, Proper Dos, Gerardo

Josh Freedom du Lac

Harold Melvin & the Blue Notes

Formed 1954, in Philadelphia, PA.

Lawrence Brown, bass; Jerry Cummings, first tenor/lead-tenor (1974–77); Harold J. Melvin, first tenor/manager (1954–97, died March 24, 1997); Lloyd Parks, first tenor/lead-tenor (1972–74); Theodore D. "Teddy" Pendergrass, lead-baritone (1972–76); Bernard Wilson, baritone/arranger/choreographer (1972–77); Sharon Paige, vocals (1975–80); David Ebo, vocals (1977–80); Dwight Johnson, vocals (1977–97); William Spratelly, vocals (1977–97). Current members: vocalists Rufus Thorne; Anthony Quarterman; Dwight Johnson; William Spratelly.

The Blue Notes of Philadelphia, Pennsylvania, led by original lead vocalist Harold Melvin, began their career in 1954, recording a handful of records for small labels. Not until 1972, however, when drummer Theodore "Teddy Bear" Pendergrass became their lead vocalist, did they begin to make their mark. Supported by the high-gloss production and songwriting of Kenny Gamble and Leon Huff of Philadelphia International Records and propelled by the crack TSOP (The Sound of Philadelphia) rhythm section, Pendergrass's muscular, impassioned baritone was equally effective on lush ballads ("If You Don't Know Me By Now," "I Miss You"), uptempo pop/soul songs ("Where Are All My Friends," "Satisfaction Guaranteed"), and extended disco/funk workouts ("Bad Luck," "The Love I Lost"). The recordings of Harold Melvin & the Blue Notes, along with those of the O'Jays, represent the artistic pinnacle of Gamble and Huff's legacy. Despite their 1970s success, however, a group whose musical focal point (Pendergrass) took second billing to its leader (Melvin) proved inherently unstable. Pendergrass left the Blue Notes to launch a solo career on Philadelphia International in 1976 and achieved brief status as a macho heartthrob before a tragic 1982 automobile accident left him paralyzed from the neck down. Meanwhile, Melvin & the Blue Notes continued to record with other lead vocalists, including David Ebo and Sharon Paige, without achieving the artistic or commercial success that they enjoyed with Pendergrass.

what to buy: Despite the fact that there are fewer songs on *Collector's Item* (Sony, 1976, prod. Kenneth Gamble, Leon Huff) than on the 1995 "Best of" collection on Sony, *Collector's Item* alone contains one of Teddy Bear's deepest and most intense performances—"Be for Real"—making this disc the place to start.

what to buy next: *If You Don't Know Me By Now—Best of* (Sony, 1995, prod. Kenneth Gamble, Leon Huff) contains all of the big hits, though it's demoted for its bizarre and irrelevant liner notes. Yet another largely overlapping package is *Greatest Hits* ♪♪♪ (Philadelphia International, 1977/Sony, 1985/Columbia, 1990, prod. Kenneth Gamble, Leon Huff) which, unfortunately, contains only Part 1 of four of the group's extended workouts, which isn't enough.

what to avoid: *Don't Leave Me This Way* ♪ (Embassy, 1978, prod. Harold Melvin); *Blue Album* ♪ (Valley Vue, 1980, prod. Harold Melvin, Sharon Paige); *Reaching for the World* ♪ (MCA, 1977, prod. Harold Melvin); *All Things Happen in Time* (MCA, 1981, prod. Harold Melvin) —all are post-Pendergrass recordings that are of little interest.

the rest:
Harold Melvin & the Blue Notes ♪♪♪♪ (Philadelphia International, 1972)
Black & Blue ♪♪♪♪ (Philadelphia International, 1974)
To Be True ♪♪♪♪♪ (Philadelphia International, 1975)
Wake Up Everybody ♪♪♪♪ (Sony, 1975)
All Their Greatest Hits ♪♪♪♪♪ (Philadelphia International, 1976)
Now Is the Time ♪♪♪ (ABC, 1977)

influences:

◄◄ Mighty Clouds of Joy, the Dells, the Four Tops, Williams Brothers, the O'Jays

►► Boyz II Men, Simply Red

see also: *Teddy Pendergrass*

Bill Pollak

The Meters
Formed 1967, in New Orleans, LA. Disbanded 1977. Re-formed 1990.

Art Neville, keyboards, vocals; Leo Nocentelli, guitar; George Porter Jr., bass; Zig Modeliste, drums (1967–77); Cyril Neville, percussion, vocals (1975–77); David Russell Baptiste, drums (1990–present).

The Meters cooked up some of the most intoxicating grooves in the history of funk, adding the flavor of the syncopated rhythms of the group's hometown, New Orleans. Under the leadership of organist Neville—overseen by impressario Allen Toussaint—the quartet assembled during the late 1960s as the house band for Toussaint's and Marshall Sehorn's label, Josie. Between studio sessions for a panoply of New Orleans soul artists and grueling live work, the Meters honed a funky chemistry that surfaced most distinctively on the instrumental tracks the group cut toward the end of the decade. A few of these recordings became R&B hits, notably "Sophisticated Cissy," "Cissy Strut," "Looka-Py-Py," and "Chicken Strut." After signing with Reprise during the early 1970s, the Meters moved into rock-soul territory, with

vocals provided by Neville. While none of the band's albums achieved the success of its leaner 1960s instrumentals, the Meters have been widely influential and frequently sampled, with a track record of backing up other acts such as Dr. John, Paul McCartney and Wings, the Pointer Sisters, and Robert Palmer. The band broke up in 1977 but have reunited in different configurations into the 1990s; legal disputes involving the name of the band and the rights to their recordings were mostly resolved by the middle of that decade. Neville's main gig is with the Neville Brothers, a troupe that has enjoyed some of the commercial success that the Meters never found.

what to buy: The two-CD anthology *Funkify Your Life* ♪♪♪♪ (Rhino, 1995, prod. various) collects most of the group's important tracks, with one disc devoted to its work for Josie and the other sifting the wheat of the Reprise years from the substantial chaff.

what to buy next: The best album-length collection of Meters instrumentals, *Looka Py-Py* ♪♪♪♪ (Josie, 1969/Rounder, 1990, prod. Allen Toussaint, Marshall Sehorn) captures the band at its grooving peak.

what to avoid: The band's first farewell album, *New Directions* ♪♪ (Reprise, 1977, prod. David Rubinson, others) dilutes its greasy funk with soggy rock tropes and is a far cry from the economy of its best work.

the rest:
The Meters ♪♪♪♪ (Josie, 1969)
Struttin' ♪♪♪♪ (Josie, 1970)
Cabbage Alley ♪♪♪ (Reprise, 1972)
Fire on the Bayou ♪♪♪ (Reprise, 1975)
Trick Bag ♪♪♪ (Reprise, 1976)
Good Old Funky Music ♪♪♪ (Rounder, 1990)
Funky Miracle ♪♪♪♪ (Charly, 1991)
The Meters Jam ♪♪♪ (Rounder, 1992)
Uptown Rulers: The Meters Live on the Queen Mary ♪♪♪ (Rounder, 1992)

worth searching for: The hard-to-find *Rejuvenation* ♪♪♪♪ (Reprise, 1974, prod. Allen Toussaint, the Meters) has a few vital tracks that didn't make it to the Rhino anthology.

influences:

◄◄ James Brown, Booker T. & the MG's, Allen Toussaint, Professor Longhair

►► Parliament-Funkadelic, the Neville Brothers, Prince, Red Hot Chili Peppers, Beastie Boys, De La Soul

see also: *The Neville Brothers*

Simon Glickman

Method Man

See: Wu-Tang Clan

MFSB

Formed 1971, in Philadelphia, PA. Disbanded early 1980s.

Norman Harris, guitar; Bobby Eli, guitar; T.J. Tindall, guitar; Reginald Lucas, guitar; Roland Chambers, guitar; Larry Moore, bass; Lenny Pakula, keyboards; Zach Zachary, alto saxophone; Tony Williams, saxophone, flute; Eddie Green, piano; Harold Williams, piano; Leon Huff, piano; Vince Montana, vibraphone; Ronnie Baker, bass; Anthony Jackson, bass; Earl Young, drums; Karl Chambers, drums; Norman Farrington, drums; Larry Washington, percussion; Michael Fuentes, drums; Quinton Joseph, drums; the Three Degrees, vocals.

Philadelphia's version of Motown's famous Funk Brothers session band, MFSB (Mother, Father, Sister, Brother) got to do what that Detroit aggregetation never had a chance to—make hit records under its own name. Besides playing the lush sweep of Kenny Gamble and Leon Huff's songs for the O'Jays, Harold Melvin & the Blue Notes, Teddy Pendergrass, the Spinners, and others, the ensemble also made a series of records on its own. Its biggest hit, "T.S.O.P. (The Sound of Philadelphia)" was a #1 pop and R&B hit and became the *Soul Train* theme song as well as a favorite for sports TV broadcasts. MFSB had other hits as well—"T.L.C." in 1975, "Mysteries of the World" in 1980—but the group was too large to keep active for its own purposes, and it disintegrated as the Philadelphia International label flagged during the early 1980s.

what to buy: *The Best of MFSB: Love Is the Message* 𝄢𝄢𝄢𝄢 (Legacy, 1995, prod. various) is all that's left in print from the Philly International days, but its 16 tracks tell you all you'll need to know about the group's majestic R&B approach, from the big hits ("T.S.O.P.," "T.L.C.") to its instrumental re-castings of the O'Jays "Back Stabbers" and Elton John's "Philadelphia Freedom."

what to buy next: The group's last album, *Mysteries of the World* 𝄢𝄢𝄢 (T.S.O.P., 1980/The Right Stuff, 1993), shows that it was still formidable at the turn of the decade.

influences:

◄◄ The Funk Brothers, the Glenn Miller Orchestra, Duke Ellington, Nelson Riddle

►► Love Unlimited Orchestra, Daryl Hall & John Oates, Elton John, the Average White Band

Gary Graff

Mic Geronimo

Born in Queens, NY.

Discovered by producer DJ Irv at a talent show, Flushing's Mic Geronimo introduced himself to the hip-hop nation in 1993 with his independently released single "Shit's Real," a heavy-handed song that chronicled life in his native Queens. Hip-Hop Darwinism dictates that only a few out of every hundred artists will actually turn a Do-It-Yourself release into a career, but Mic G's record quickly became the choice cut of influential New York radio DJs Funkmaster Flex and Red Alert, giving the artist the break he needed.

what to buy: Much like the Roy Hobbes swing in the baseball novel of the same name, *The Natural* 𝄢𝄢𝄢 (Blunt/TVT, 1995, prod. Da Beatminerz, DJ Irv, Buckwild, others) is a graceful, unassuming, instinctive artistic swing for the fences. Done in thick, dark, bass-rich strokes, the sparse production highlights Mic's verbal skills. Mic G has been compared to a young Nas because of the effortless ease he has in commanding the microphone, as demonstrated on the title cut and "Wherever You Are."

influences:

◄◄ Mobb Deep, Nas

Jazzbo

George Michael /Wham!

Formed 1981, in London, England. Disbanded 1986.

George Michael (born Georgios Kyriacos Panayiotou, June 25, 1963 in London, England), vocals; Andrew Ridgely, vocals, guitar.

When lightweight British pop bands started storming the American charts during the early 1980s, it was George Michael's talent that set Wham! apart from its competition. In a glut of synthesizers and hairstyles, it was the songs the honey-voiced singer authored for Wham's brief string of albums that gave the duo's music uncommon appeal, with a sound that clinched the American R&B tradition and set it to a contemporary pop beat. Wham's exhaustive success caused Michael to disband the group at the height of its popularity in 1986 and head forth with a solo career that initially proved more lustrous though has since bogged down in high-minded denouncements of pop

George Michael (© Ken Settle)

music marketing and an unsuccessful lawsuit against his old record company.

what to buy: George Michael did not come into his creative prime until *Listen without Prejudice: Vol. 1* 𝄞𝄞𝄞𝄞 (Columbia, 1990, prod. George Michael), an album filled with melancholy lyrics and lush, soaring melodies that recalled the great pop and soul hits of the 1960s. As Michael's commanding artistic statement, it gave the former teen idol uncharacteristic depth, inspiring comparisons to everyone from Stevie Wonder to Elton John.

what to buy next: Michael's solo debut *Faith* 𝄞𝄞𝄞𝄞 (Columbia, 1987, prod. George Michael) sold nearly 15 million copies worldwide and represented an artistic leap from the pre-fab pop Wham!, balancing soulful ballads ("Kissing a Fool") with hard-hitting dance numbers ("Monkey," "I Want Your Sex").

what to avoid: Michael's talentless Wham! partner Andrew Ridgely made a dismal attempt at a solo singing career with *Son of Albert* **woof!** (Epic, 1990), which deservingly slipped through the cracks unnoticed.

the rest:
George Michael:
Older 𝄞𝄞𝄞 (DreamWorks, 1996)

Wham!:
Fantastic 𝄞𝄞 (Columbia, 1983)
Make It Big! 𝄞𝄞𝄞 (Columbia, 1984)
Music from the Edge of Heaven 𝄞𝄞𝄞 (Columbia, 1986)

worth searching for: Paying tribute to Queen's late singer Freddy Mercury, Michael joined the surviving members of the British group on-stage at Wembley Stadium with special guest Lisa Stansfield. The resultant EP, *Five Live* 𝄞𝄞𝄞 (Hollywood, 1992) features several remarkable covers by the assemblage, including a take on Seal's "Killer."

influences:
◀◀ Elton John, Aretha Franklin, Stevie Wonder
▶▶ Seal, Take That, Babyface

Aidin Vaziri

Lee Michaels

Born November 24, 1945, in Los Angeles, CA.

Lee Michaels's organ-heavy soul-rock was an anomaly in guitar-happy California during the mid-1960s. Michaels worked with a number of inconsequential bands until moving to San Francisco during 1965 and coming under the influence of the Jefferson Airplane (Michaels had formerly worked with Airplane

drummer John Barbata). A talented producer, Michaels became enamored of overdubbing and began playing all the instruments on his records shortly after garnering a contract. His eponymous third album, a jam between Michaels and drummer Frosty (Bartholomew Eugene Smith-Frost), gave Michaels his first large-scale public notice, and he remained a draw for the next few years, scoring a major hit, "Do You Know What I Mean?," in 1971. When Michaels lost drummer Keith Knudsen to the Doobie Brothers in 1973, he retired for a short while before returning to a lower rung on the music biz ladder.

what to buy: Most of what you want to hear from him can be found on *The Lee Michaels Collection* 𝄞𝄞𝄞 (Rhino, 1992).

worth searching for: *5th* 𝄞𝄞𝄞𝄞 (A&M, 1971, prod. Lee Michaels) has "Do You Know What I Mean?"

influences:
◀◀ Ray Charles, Booker T. Jones, Huey "Piano" Smith
▶▶ James Taylor Quartet, Sly Stone

Lawrence Gabriel

Midnight Star

Formed 1976, in Cincinnati, OH. Disbanded early 1990s.

Reggie Calloway, flute, percussion, trumpet, vocals; Vincent Calloway, flute, percussion, trombone, trumpet, keyboards; Kenneth Gant, trombone, guitar, keyboard; Melvin Gentry, guitar, percussion, drums, guitar, vocals; Belinda Lipscomb, vocals; Bobby Lovelace, drums, vocals; Jeffrey Cooper, Guitar, keyboards; Bo Watson, synthesizer, keyboards; Bill Simmons, percussion, drums, saxophone, vocals.

Midnight Star was the synth-funk, electronic keyboard-heavy contingent of the crop of hot R&B bands that popped up during the late 1970s and early 1980s, many of which appeared on Solar Records. The group was formed by brothers Reggie and Vincent Calloway, who are credited with founding the so-called Cincinnati Sound and helping to spark the careers of groups including the Deele, whose membership included Antonio "L.A." Reid and Kenneth Edmonds before he became Babyface. A thriving live band with no real lead vocalist, the nine-member Midnight Star scored its biggest hits with fun, dance-floor oriented grooves with silly themes, including "No Parking on the Dance Floor" and "Body Snatchers," although it also enjoyed hits with ballads such as the Babyface-penned "Slow Jam." By the mid- to late 1980s, with neo-disco dance fads fading, the group's appeal began to dim, partially due also to that lack of a marquee vocalist. The band tried to stay alive after the Calloway brothers went solo during the late 1980s, but the two albums it generated were neither critical nor popular successes. The brothers, under the name Calloway, did not fare much better but managed to score one huge chart-topper, "I Wanna Be Rich."

what to buy: All of the group's best tunes can be found on the collection *Very Best of Midnight Star* 🎵🎵🎵🎵 (Castle, 1996, prod. Reggie Calloway), including "Wet My Whistle" and "Freak-a-Zoid." The cuts are still funky, but the relatively primitive computers used then to make the music gives some of the songs a dated feel.

what to avoid: Despite the fact that it went gold and had a solid hit in "Midas Touch," *Headlines* 🎵🎵 (Solar, 1986) found the group at the end of its creative run. The Calloway brothers must have felt so, too—they left the group after this album.

the rest:
No Parking on the Dance Floor 🎵🎵🎵 (Solar/EMI, 1983)
Planetary Invasion 🎵🎵🎵 (Solar/EMI, 1984)

solo outings:
Calloway:
All the Way 🎵🎵 (Solar, 1990)
Let's Get Smooth 🎵🎵 (Solar, 1992)

influences:
◀◀ Funkadelic, Shalamar, Zapp
▶▶ Lakeside, Starpoint, Klymaxx

Franklin Paul

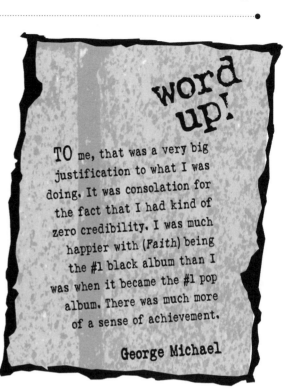

word up!

TO me, that was a very big justification to what I was doing. It was consolation for the fact that I had kind of zero credibility. I was much happier with (Faith) being the #1 black album than I was when it became the #1 pop album. There was much more of a sense of achievement.

George Michael

Amos Milburn

Born April 1, 1927, in Houston, TX. Died January 3, 1980, in Houston, TX.

Amos Milburn stomped out the piano-boogie and sang the virtues of whiskey and sex in an unashamed, seductive manner. After signing with Aladdin Records in 1946, Milburn began recording his great string of drinking records ("Bad Bad Whiskey," "One Scotch, One Bourbon, One Beer," "Let Me Go Home, Whiskey"), influential and danceable boogie songs ("Down the Road Apiece," "Chicken Shack Boogie," "Let's Rock Awhile," "Roomin' House Boogie"), smooth, emotive blues ("Walkin' Blues," "Empty Arms Blues") and intimate R&B ballads ("Bewildered," "Tears, Tears, Tears"). As a pianist, Milburn could bang the boogie hard like Cecil Gant or tinkle the ivories light and jazzy like Johnnie Johnson, and his band the Chicken-Shackers could play burbling hot or icy cool behind him. As a vocalist, he could be velvety smooth like his friend Charles Brown (with whom he cut a few duets) or playful like Louis Jordan. As good as Milburn was, his music was too adult in nature to make it out of the R&B joints into the teen-oriented rock 'n'

roll scene of the mid-1950s—which is probably why it sounds so good today. After 1954's "Good Good Whiskey," Milburn's string of hits ended, though he kept a high professional profile, playing top night spots and appearing in the films *Harlem Jazz Festival* (1955), *Rhythm & Blues Revue* (1955), and *Basin Street Revue* (1956). Milburn's last legitimate shot at a comeback came with Motown in 1962; Berry Gordy Jr. tried hard to update Milburn's sound, but their LP *Boss of the Blues* flopped. Always a heavy drinker, Milburn's health went sour during the 1960s, but he played club dates until a series of strokes and the amputation of one of his legs retired him from the business. His last recordings were weak affairs made for the Blues Spectrum label, not long before he died in 1980. It's better to remember Milburn through his early sides, which helped set the stage for the joyous, soulful throb we all came to know as rock 'n' roll.

what to buy: *The Best of Amos Milburn—Down the Road Apiece* 🎵🎵🎵🎵 (EMI, 1993, comp. Ron Furmanek) contains a generous sampling of Milburn's greatest boogie anthems, whiskey tributes, and romantic ballads. Essential.

what to buy next: *Blues Barrelhouse & Boogie Woogie* 🎵🎵🎵🎵 (Capitol/EMI, 1996, comp. Pete Welding) contains 66 songs over three discs from his hot period on the Aladdin label. *All* the hot boogie, hits, and drinking songs are here.

what to avoid: *Johnny Otis Presents . . .* 🎵 (LaserLight, 1993, prod. Johnny Otis, Tom Morgan) features remakes of big hits by Milburn, Joe Turner, Joe Liggins, Charles Brown, and Louis Jordan cut over the years for Otis's Blues Spectrum label. Milburn could only play with one hand at this point in his career (Otis played the other parts), and Milburn doesn't sound like he's in very good shape. Sad.

the rest:
Ace Story, Vol. 2 🎵🎵🎵 (Ace Records, 1994)
Motown Years 1962–64 🎵🎵🎵 (PolyGram, 1996)

worth searching for: *The Complete Aladdin Recordings of Amos Milburn* 🎵🎵🎵🎵 (Mosaic, 1994, prod. various) is a seven-CD, 155-song compilation that includes every decent note Milburn laid down at Aladdin. If you've got the bucks, this is in the import shops.

influences:

◀◀ Charles Brown, Louis Jordan

▶▶ Ivory Joe Hunter, Fats Domino

Ken Burke

Buddy Miles

Born September 5, 1946, in Omaha, NE.

At his height, he was playing the back line next to Jimi Hendrix in the legendary supergroup Band of Gypsies. At his nadir, he was living in the body-search line next to some guy named Bubba while serving a prison sentence. In between, Buddy Miles has been a buffoonish, occasionally brilliant drummer/singer/bandleader who has shifted easily between hard rock and R&B genres since the 1960s. Learning his heavy-handed, bottom-end drum style as a child, playing his first professional gig with his father's Omaha jazz combo at the age of 12, Miles attracted the interest of touring soul and doo-wop groups and joined Wilson Pickett's live revue while in his teens. Becoming one of the most sought-after session musicians in the business while working with the Wicked One, he was approached in 1967 by guitarist Michael Bloomfield to join a new psychedelic rock band called Electric Flag. That group made one memorable LP before splitting the following year, whereupon Miles formed his own band, the Buddy Miles Express. Renewing a friendship with Hendrix, whom he had met while play-ing the Monterey Pop Festival, Miles joined him in the studio to collaborate on Jimi's groundbreaking *Electric Ladyland* album and lay down a thick blues backbeat for the tunes "Still Raining, Still Dreaming" and "Rainy Day, Dream Away." (Hendrix repaid the favor by writing the liner notes to the Miles LP *Expressway to Your Skull* and producing cuts on the subsequent Express release *Electric Church*.) When the Jimi Hendrix Experience broke up in 1969, Hendrix recruited Miles for what would become a landmark moment in rock music history: over the objections of his management, Hendrix formed the power trio Band of Gypsys with Miles on drums and Billy Cox on bass, in essence the first true "black rock" group. In their historic 1970 concert recording at Bill Graham's Fillmore East, the trio performed the propulsive, prophetic Miles tune "Them Changes," which would become his trademark hit. Since that milestone event, "Booger Bear" (the nickname divulged on a Miles album title) has dabbled in a variety of performing aggregations, and his session playing can still be found in almost every corner of the record store. He has worked with Carlos Santana, the Monkees—he even has a drum credit on the Priority LP *The California Raisins Sing the Hits*.

what to buy: While none of Miles's albums with the Buddy Miles Express are still in print, the 1997 compilation *The Best of Buddy Miles* 🎵🎵🎵 (Mercury, 1997, prod. various) is a representative assortment of his best moments. "Them Changes" is here, of course, as are his other noteworthy hits: "Wholesale Love," "Dreams (to Remember)," "Memphis Train," "Midnight Rider"—awash in Buddy's melodramatic, over-the-top soul vocals—and the pulsating, previously unreleased "69 Freedom Special."

what to buy next: Trying to recapture the Band of Gypsys magic, Miles entered into a stunning but uneven alliance with P-Funk legend Bootsy Collins and guitarist Stevie Salas as a power trio called Hardware on the LP *Third Eye Open* 🎵🎵🎵 (Rykodisc USA, 1994, prod. Bill Laswell). Eccentric, eclectic producer Bill Laswell never seems to quite get a handle on this threesome or where he wants it to go, though the playfulness of "I Got a Feeling" and Buddy's piledriving R&B on "Hard Look" and "Love Obsession" hold promise.

the rest:
Greatest Christmas Hits 🎵 (Priority, 1991)
Hell and Back 🎵🎵🎵 (Rykodisc USA, 1994)
(With Carlos Santana) *Carlos Santana/Buddy Miles Live* 🎵🎵🎵 (Legacy, 1994)

worth searching for: Though their focus is clearly on the star, two 1997 Jimi Hendrix reissues do give the drummer some spotlight time, featuring Miles at the peak of his energetic prowess. *Electric Ladyland* ♪♪♪♪ (MCA, 1997) is a remastered version of the 1968 classic with Miles on drums when Mitch Mitchell is not, and *First Rays of the New Rising Sun* ♪♪♪♪ (MCA, 1997), the first Hendrix LP released under the direct supervision of the Hendrix family, finds Miles as one of myriad guest artists including Steve Winwood, Stephen Stills, and the Ronettes.

influences:

◄◄ James Brown, Gene Krupa, Wilson Pickett, Michael Bloomfield, Buddy Rich, Jimi Hendrix, Mitch Mitchell, George Clinton

►► Bus Boys, Maze featuring Frankie Beverly, Fat Boys, Afros

Jim McFarlin

Marcus Miller

Born June 14, 1959, in Brooklyn, NY.

Long known as one of the most innovative jazz/R&B bassists around, Marcus Miller has also distinguished himself as a world-class composer and producer, puting together landmark works for artists such as David Sanborn, Luther Vandross, and Miles Davis. Inspired by his father, an amateur jazz pianist and church organist, he picked up the clarinet at age 10 and later learned piano and bass, landing gigs with flutist Bobbi Humphrey and keyboardist Lonnie Liston Smith by age 16. A graduate of New York's legendary High School of Music and Art, Miller landed a spot in the backing band for the TV show *Saturday Night Live,* making connections that led to work as an ace session player, holding the bottom end for artist such as Aretha Franklin, Roberta Flack, and Sanborn. Tapped by Davis to join his band in 1981, Miller also handled production work and playing on attention-getting records for Sanborn and Vandross. But it wasn't until Davis's groundbreaking, hi-tech 1986 record "Tutu"—on which Miller played nearly all the instruments and wrote most of the material—that his talent for composition really shone through. Though his solo career started with a couple of ignominious R&B records, his later projects would mine jazzy funk flavor with flair and razor sharp playing. Along the way, he also found time to establish a funk band with pal/jazz drummer Lenny White called the Jamaica Boys, serve as musical director for Sanborn's short-lived late night music show "Sunday Night," and write material for soundtracks to the movies *School Daze, House Party, Boomerang,* and *The Great White Hype.*

what to buy: Serving up a potent combination of evocative material and mind-blowing instrumental chops, Miller's third solo album, *The Sun Don't Lie* ♪♪♪♪ (PRA, 1993, prod. Marcus Miller) marks an aspicious occasion: the moment a consummate backing player finally finds his own distinctive voice. Heads and shoulders above the vapid R&B that filled his two previous solo records, this one melds jazz with funk grooves on a sensitive tribute to Stevie Wonder called "Steveland" and a ferocious take on Jaco Pastorius's classic tune "Teen Town."

what to buy next: Not as groundbreaking as *The Sun Don't Lie,* Miller's *Tales* ♪♪♪ (PRA, 1995, prod. Marcus Miller) nevertheless continues his winning formula, unfolding as a dialogue between older and younger musicians. Bolstered with sampled anecdotes from Joe Sample, Bill Withers, Roberta Flack, and Q-Tip, this album serves as a powerful showcase for Miller's ever-growing playing and compositional skills.

what to avoid: The bassist makes two deadly mistakes on his first solo record *Suddenly* **woof!** (Warner Bros., 1983, prod. Marcus Miller). First, he crafts R&B material dull enough to disappoint both his musician fans and funk afficionados. Next, he tries to sing—proving there are times when even the best bass players should learn to stay in the background.

the rest:
Marcus Miller ♪♪♪ (Warner Bros., 1984)
Live and More ♪♪♪ (Dreyfus Jazz, 1996)

worth searching for: Miller nails his funk songwriting and production chops on the Jamaica Boys' second album, *J-Boys* (Reprise, 1990); he crystallizes Luther Vandross's simmering R&B loveman charisma into a potent sonic stew on *The Night I Fell In Love* (Epic, 1985); and his synth-drenched jazz style moved to a new level with Miles Davis's late-period signature album *Tutu* (Warner Bros., 1986).

influences:

◄◄ Larry Graham, Stevie Wonder, Stanley Clarke, Jaco Pastorius

►► Victor Bailey, Victor Wooten, Levi Seacer Jr.

Eric Deggans

Milli Vanilli

Formed 1988, in Munich, Germany.

Rob Pilatus, vocals; Fabrice Morvan, vocals.

Milli Vanilli almost went down in pop history as one of the most successful—albeit artistically insignificant—groups of the video era. Instead, the duo has become the biggest punchline in pop. After scoring five Top 5 hits (including the consecutive #1's "Baby Don't Forget My Number," "Girl I'm Gonna Miss You," and "Blame It on the Rain"), selling more than seven million copies of its debut album, and capturing a Grammy for Best New Artist, it was discovered that Pilatus and Morvan hadn't sung a single note on their record. Instead, the vocals were handled by Charles Shaw, John Davis, and Brad Howe. But Milli Vanilli mastermind Frank Farian—the German producer known for his work with Boney M—wanted an attractive look to go with his lightweight dance-pop, so he hired former breakdancers Pilatus (from Munich) and Morvan (from Paris) to become the faces of Milli Vanilli. The dreadlocked, bare-chested men, who had met at a Los Angeles club during the mid-1980s, appeared on the album cover, in videos, and on stage (lip-synching, of course) and were described by *The New York Times* as "exotically sexy." The duo also conducted interviews as Milli Vanilli, with Pilatus telling a writer at one point: "Musically, we are more talented than any Bob Dylan. We are more talented than Paul McCartney, Mick Jagger . . . I'm the new Elvis." Following the revelations that they weren't quite ready to build their own Gracelands, Pilatus and Morvan were stripped of their Grammy, while their record company was ordered to give partial refunds to anybody who bought Milli Vanilli recordings or attended concerts believing that the duo was actually singing. Ironically, after Pilatus and Morvan sang *a capella* at a press conference, a voice coach said the duo sounded better than the men who actually were recorded. In 1991, a despondent Pilatus attempted suicide; five years later, he was charged on eight counts of allegedly attacking and threatening two people in separate incidents. Under court order, he later entered a drug treatment facility.

what to avoid: *Girl You Know It's True* **woof!** (Arista, 1989), *Quick Moves: The Remix Album* 🎵🎵 (Arista, 1990), and *Rob and Fab* **woof!** (Taj, 1993) all make better Frisbees than they do albums. Avoid them like the plague.

Josh Freedom du Lac

The Mills Brothers

Formed 1925, in Piqua, OH.

Herbert Mills (born April 2, 1912, in Piqua, OH, died April 12, 1989, in Las Vegas, NV), tenor; Donald Mills (born April 29, 1915, in Piqua, OH), tenor; Harry Mills (born August 19, 1913, in Piqua, OH, died June 28, 1982, in Los Angeles, CA), baritone; John Mills Jr. (born October 19, 1910, in Piqua, OH, died January 24, 1936 in Bellefontaine, OH), bass; John H. Mills Sr. (born February 11, 1882, in Bellefonte, PA, died December 8, 1967 in Bellefontaine, OH), bass (1936–67); John H. Mills II (born 1956 in Los Angeles, CA) (1983–present).

Originally billing themselves as "Four Boys and a Kazoo," the Mills Brothers—Herb, Don, Harry, and John Jr.—toured the Midwest theater circuit and tent shows around their Ohio hometown as children with an act in which they imitated musical instruments with their voices. As the history of popular music later confirmed, the quartet's genetically-matched voices could create the kind of seamless pop-swing harmonies no instruments could match. The group, by now advanced to "Four Boys and a Guitar," moved from Cincinnati's WLW Radio to New York City, becoming a top attraction on national radio broadcasts by the 1930s as the Mills Brothers and recording their first major hit, "Glow Worm." They continued to release successful singles as one of the first African American vocal acts to achieve mainstream pop acceptance and were featured in several movie musicals (including *The Big Broadcast* of 1932), but suffered a severe blow when John Jr. died of tuberculosis in 1936. Their father, John Sr.—a concert vocalist and the man who taught the boys to sing—stepped in as a replacement and the quartet persevered. From the time of their signature recording, "Paper Doll," in 1942, the Mills Brothers became synonymous with buoyant, effortless harmonies that crossed generational lines of taste and popularity for more than a half-century. Since 1983, Donald, the last surviving brother, has toured in concert with his son, John H. II, in keeping the Mills Brothers name alive; an octogenarian, Donald suffered a broken hip in a fall at LAX Airport in 1997, but John H. II says he and his father plan to resume performing.

what to buy: The epitome of class, style, and smooth sophistication, the Mills Brothers and their special musical aura are deliciously preserved in the 1995 box set *The Mills Brothers: The Anthology (1931–1968)* 🎵🎵🎵🎵 (MCA, 1995, prod. various), a digitally-remastered life achievement award compiling 48 songs recorded over a three-decade span, from their first million-seller "Tiger Rag" to their last Top 40 tune "Cab Driver," and including their collaborations with Ella Fitzgerald, Bing Crosby, Louis Armstrong, Count Basie, and Al Jolson, among others. A sparkling gem.

what to buy next: There are so many Mills Brothers "greatest hits" LPs—approximately 17, at last count—basically covering the same material ("Glow Worm," "Paper Doll," "Up a Lazy River") that the trick becomes finding discs that actually add songs to the collector's inventory. The British label JSP has reissued all of the brothers' earliest recordings from 1931–39 on six separate CDs titled *Chronological, Vol. 1* through *Chronological, Vol. 6* 𝅘𝅥𝅮𝅘𝅥𝅮𝅘𝅥𝅮𝅘𝅥𝅮 (JSP, 1996, prod. various) which fill in many of the sequential gaps most compilations leave blank. The same can be said of *Essential Mills Brothers: Four Boys and a Guitar* 𝅘𝅥𝅮𝅘𝅥𝅮𝅘𝅥𝅮𝅘𝅥𝅮 (MCA, 1995, prod. various). *50th Anniversary/Country Music's Greatest Hits* 𝅘𝅥𝅮𝅘𝅥𝅮𝅘𝅥𝅮 (Ranwood, 1972, prod. various), actually two old albums on one CD, finds the Millses crooning country in such rare and atypical tunes as "Red River Valley," "Tennessee Waltz," and "El Paso" and placing their distinctive stamp on barbershop standards like "My Gal Sal" and "Nevertheless (I'm in Love with You)."

what to avoid: *Best of the Mills Brothers and the Ink Spots* 𝅘𝅥𝅮𝅘𝅥𝅮 (Juke Box Treasures, 1994, prod. various) is a jumbled, directionless assortment that does little to celebrate either act, while the anthology *Mills Brothers* 𝅘𝅥𝅮 (Pearl Flapper, 1994, prod. various) is simply an undersized waste of time.

the rest:
Greatest Hits 𝅘𝅥𝅮𝅘𝅥𝅮𝅘𝅥𝅮 (MCA, 1958)
Best of the Mills Brothers 𝅘𝅥𝅮𝅘𝅥𝅮𝅘𝅥𝅮 (MCA, 1965)
16 Great Performances 𝅘𝅥𝅮𝅘𝅥𝅮 (UNI/MCA, 1972)
Lazy Bones 𝅘𝅥𝅮 (Golden Stars)
22 Great Hits 𝅘𝅥𝅮𝅘𝅥𝅮𝅘𝅥𝅮 (Ranwood, 1985)
Sweeter Than Sugar 𝅘𝅥𝅮𝅘𝅥𝅮 (ASV/Living Era, 1985)
Close Harmony 𝅘𝅥𝅮𝅘𝅥𝅮𝅘𝅥𝅮 (Ranwood, 1990)
Louis Armstrong/Mills Brothers Greatest Hits 1932–1940 𝅘𝅥𝅮𝅘𝅥𝅮𝅘𝅥𝅮𝅘𝅥𝅮 (EPM/Jazz Archives)
Paper Doll 𝅘𝅥𝅮𝅘𝅥𝅮𝅘𝅥𝅮 (MCA Special Products, 1995)
Essential 𝅘𝅥𝅮𝅘𝅥𝅮𝅘𝅥𝅮 (Collector's Edition, 1996)
Country Music's Greatest Hits 𝅘𝅥𝅮𝅘𝅥𝅮𝅘𝅥𝅮 (Ranwood, 1996)
Best of the Decca Years 𝅘𝅥𝅮𝅘𝅥𝅮𝅘𝅥𝅮𝅘𝅥𝅮 (UNI/MCA, 1996)
All Time Greatest Hits 𝅘𝅥𝅮𝅘𝅥𝅮𝅘𝅥𝅮𝅘𝅥𝅮 (UNI/MCA, 1997)

worth searching for: The video documentary *The Mills Brothers Story* 𝅘𝅥𝅮𝅘𝅥𝅮𝅘𝅥𝅮𝅘𝅥𝅮 (Kultur, 1993), a 52-minute history that traces the four Mills offspring from their earliest moments caught on film to their innovative triumphs as movie and recording stars. The video clips include renditions of "Paper Doll," "Glow Worm," and the foursome's other timeless hits.

influences:
⏪ Duke Ellington, the Ink Spots, the Orioles, Bing Crosby, Billy Ward & the Dominoes

⏩ The Crows, Hank Ballard & the Midnighters, the Commodores, Harold Melvin & the Blue Notes, Boyz II Men

Jim McFarlin

Stephanie Mills

Born March 22, 1957, in Brooklyn, NY.

Stephanie Mills had all the makings of a superstar soul music singer early in her life. She began by singing at her mother's church when she was seven and, after winning the Apollo Theater's Amateur Night contest eight weeks in a row, graduated, at nine, to Broadway, and the play *Maggie Flynn*. Her career stalled until she released her debut album in 1973 and, at 17, returned to Broadway as Dorothy in the Broadway production of *The Wiz* for what became a career-defining five-year stint. What followed was a prolific, decade-long string of gold albums and singles, ranging from energetic early 1980s dance classics to sophisticated ballads, including popular duets with Teddy Pendergrass. A handful of disappointments in her life, including Diana Ross's selection as Dorothy for the movie of *The Wiz*, and a few failed marriages, never interfered with her powerful sound. In 1995, she returned to her roots with a gospel album.

what to buy: Unfortunately, Mills's body of work is split between record labels. A collection of her early hits can be found on *In My Life: Greatest Hits* 𝅘𝅥𝅮𝅘𝅥𝅮𝅘𝅥𝅮 (Casablanca, 1985, prod. various), while standouts from after 1985 are contained on *Greatest Hits* 𝅘𝅥𝅮𝅘𝅥𝅮𝅘𝅥𝅮 (MCA, 1996, prod. various).

what to buy next: Although the gospel album *Personal Inspirations* 𝅘𝅥𝅮𝅘𝅥𝅮𝅘𝅥𝅮 (Gospo-Centric, 1995, prod. Donald Lawrence) is a departure from Mills's typical form, it is a pleasant showcase of her vocal ability, and includes a cover of Curtis Mayfield's "People Get Ready."

what to avoid: Mediocre material hurts *Something Real* 𝅘𝅥𝅮𝅘𝅥𝅮 (1992, MCA, prod. various), which suffers from way too many wannabe-New Jack uptempo cuts and uninspired ballads.

the rest:
For the First Time 𝅘𝅥𝅮𝅘𝅥𝅮 (Motown, 1976)
What Cha Gonna Do with My Lovin'? 𝅘𝅥𝅮𝅘𝅥𝅮𝅘𝅥𝅮 (20th Century, 1979)
Sweet Sensation 𝅘𝅥𝅮𝅘𝅥𝅮𝅘𝅥𝅮 (20th Century, 1980)
Stephanie 𝅘𝅥𝅮𝅘𝅥𝅮𝅘𝅥𝅮 (20th Century, 1981)
Tantalizingly Hot 𝅘𝅥𝅮𝅘𝅥𝅮 (Casablanca, 1982)
Merciless 𝅘𝅥𝅮𝅘𝅥𝅮 (Casablanca, 1983)
I've Got the Cure 𝅘𝅥𝅮𝅘𝅥𝅮 (Casablanca, 1984)
Stephanie Mills 𝅘𝅥𝅮𝅘𝅥𝅮 (MCA, 1985)
If I Were Your Woman 𝅘𝅥𝅮𝅘𝅥𝅮𝅘𝅥𝅮 (MCA, 1987)
Home 𝅘𝅥𝅮𝅘𝅥𝅮𝅘𝅥𝅮 (MCA, 1989)
Christmas 𝅘𝅥𝅮𝅘𝅥𝅮𝅘𝅥𝅮 (MCA, 1991)

worth searching for: Get *The Wiz—Original Cast Album* 𝅘𝅥𝅮𝅘𝅥𝅮𝅘𝅥𝅮 (Atlantic, 1975, prod. Jerry Wexler) for the original version of her classic "Home" and to get a flavor for the singer while she was still raw.

influences:

◀◀ Patti LaBelle, Aretha Franklin, Teddy Pendergrass

▶▶ Angela Winbush, Regina Belle

Franklin Paul

Mint Condition

Formed 1986, in Minneapolis, MN.

Stokely Williams, drums, vocals; Larry Waddell, keyboards; Jeff Allen, saxophone; Homer O'Dell, guitar; Chris "Daddy" Dave, drums; Ricky Kinchen, bass; Keri Lewis, keyboards.

Drawing on the funk and soul legacy left by Earth, Wind & Fire, the Time, and Cameo, this group of Minnesota natives is an abnormality—a self-contained R&B band, one that writes, performs, and produces its own music. With the exception of Chicagoan Kinchen, the band met in high school and played around the Twin Cities area until they were discovered in 1989 by former Time members James "Jimmy Jam" Harris III and Terry Lewis, who signed the group to their young Perspective Records. Though popular mostly for their ballads, Mint Condition's albums contain a full range of sounds, from electrically charged rock tunes to jazz interludes to steel pan-flavored reggae. Their unbalanced debut album had a test-the-waters feel to it, with hyperactive funk tunes pitted against sensitive love songs, like their first breakthrough hit "Breakin' My Heart (Pretty Brown Eyes)." Their next two albums found a comfortable middle ground, where their impressive instrumentality meshed with their clever, sensitive lyrics and hip-hop-era charisma, forming a style that puts them head and shoulders above the crowd.

what to buy: Alternately exciting and cool, *From the Mint Factory* ♫♫♫♫ (Perspective/A&M, 1993, prod. Mint Condition) is a near-complete work that revives the spirit of all the group's influences to make an R&B sound that is as familiar and fun as it is innovative.

what to buy next: *Definition of a Band* ♫♫♫ (Perspective/A&M, 1996, prod. Mint Condition) takes fewer chances and finds the group members still using vignettes to prove that they play instruments. That said, they create funk here that would make George Clinton proud, and sweetly sing the caliber of mature love songs last seen on the lips of EW&F's Phillip Bailey nearly two decades earlier.

the rest:

Meant to Be Mint ♫♫♫ (Perspective/A&M, 1991)

worth searching for: Two examples of the group's diversity are "My Dear," a moody Prince-inspired tune on the soundtrack to the film *Mo' Money* (Perspective, 1992), and "If Trouble Were Money," a straight up blues duet with Albert Collins from the soundtrack to *Jason's Lyric*.

influences:

◀◀ Earth, Wind & Fire, the Time, L.T.D., Cameo, Prince

▶▶ Toni! Tony! Tone!

Franklin Paul

Mobb Deep

Formed early 1990s in Queensbridge, Queens, NY.

Havoc, vocals; Prodigy, vocals.

Like the Wu-Tang Clan and the late Notorious B.I.G., Mobb Deep rose to fame with the revival of hardcore New York reality rap. Although the hardcore genre seemed headed toward a Los Angeles monopoly, the Rotten Apple snatched back its share—thanks, in large part, to this gothic duo and their wicked turn of the phrase. While conceptually unoriginal, the creative essence of Havoc and Prodigy lies in the medium of their message, not the message itself. Icy, unflinching deliveries chronicle common ghetto tales, which they amplify with rapid wordplay and rugged backdrops. Add to their songs a preoccupation with Italian Mob bosses, and you begin to understand why they consistently are equated with the darkest mental alleyways of their native Queens.

what to buy: *Hell On Earth* ♫♫♫♫ (Loud/RCA, 1996, prod. Havoc) marks the continuation of the duo's hardcore sound on an enhanced CD-ROM that features video clips and a hidden track. Although the album lacks standout singles, such as past classics "Shook Ones Pt. II" and "Hit It from the Back," it nonetheless illustrates Mobb Deep's ability to keep an entire project consistently intense. "Animal Instinct" and "G.O.D. Pt. III" offer the signature Mobb Deep sound, and other cuts get help from lyrical big guns Raekwon, Method Man, and Nas.

the rest:

Juvenile Hell ♫♫ (4th & Broadway, 1993)
The Infamous ♫♫♫♪ (Loud/RCA, 1995)

influences:

◀◀ Schoolly D, Rakim, EPMD, RZA, Black Moon, Kool G Rap

▶▶ The Firm, Big Noyd, Cella Dwellas, Youngstas, Group Home

Corey Takahashi

The Moments

See: Ray, Goodman & Brown

Monie Love

Born Simone Johnson, July 2, 1970, in London, England.

With her irresistible little-sister vibe, Monie Love wooed and won over the hip-hop world for a brief fling in the late 1980s and early 1990s. Even before signing her first record deal, she already had made a sizable name for herself by doing vocal cameos on songs by such established artists as Queen Latifah ("Ladies First"), De La Soul ("Buddy"), and the Jungle Brothers ("Doin' Our Own Dang"). The Brooklynite-by-way-of-London would soon join the Native Tongues posse formed by those acts, and was signed by Warner Bros. largely on the strength of the buzz generated by her guest appearances. Her trademark first single, "Monie in the Middle," was released in 1990, a light, party confection produced by Andy Cox and David Steele of the British group Fine Young Cannibals that successfully integrated the two most popular sounds at the time, rap and Euro-dance. Love's first album, *Down to Earth*, followed in 1991, and the favorable response it generated from fans and critics alike allowed the former high school classmate of MC Lyte to stay afloat in the turbulent waters of the rap music industry for a full two years thereafter. But by the arrival of her second LP, 1993's *In a Word or 2*, fickle rap followers had clearly started to lose interest in the London lyricist. The album's key single, "Born to B.R.E.E.D." (as in: Build Relationships where Education and Enlightenment Dominate), was produced by The Artist Formerly Known as Prince, but even the participation of the Purple One ultimately could not bring record buyers to Love again. Though most of the members of Native Tongues (especially A Tribe Called Quest) managed to sustain their individual popularity, the collective lost the cohesiveness it had enjoyed in the past and Monie fell victim to its demise. In 1994 Love made the switch from full-time recording artist to part-time radio DJ, hosting a weekend show on New York's Hot 97. While she has put her recording career on the back burner, a Native Tongue reunion album is said to be in the works, which could bring Monie right back into the middle of the limelight.

what to buy: There's nothing quite like a British accent filtered through a Brooklyn upbringing, and the fizzy uniqueness of Monie's voice on her debut outing *Down to Earth* 🎵🎵🎵 (Warner Bros., 1991, prod. Afrika Baby Bambaataa, F.Y.C.) exudes pure energy and fun. "Monie in the Middle" and the smart Spinners remake, "It's a Shame (My Sister)," are perfect examples of

Love's brand of energetic party rap and would be a delightful addition to any hip-hop collection.

the rest:
In a Word or 2 🎵🎵 (Warner Bros., 1993)

influences:
◀◀ MC Lyte, Salt-N-Pepa, Queen Latifah, Jungle Brothers, Marley Marl, De La Soul

▶▶ Spice Girls

Andre McGarrity

The Moonglows /Harvey Fuqua

Formed as the Crazy Sounds in 1951. Became the Moonglows in 1952. Disbanded 1960, with periodic reunions by different incarnations since.

Harvey Fuqua (born July 17, 1924), baritone vocals; Bobby Lester, lead vocals; Pete Graves, vocals; Alexander Walters, tenor vocals; Prentiss Barnes, bass vocals; Billy Johnson, guitar.

Among 1950s doo-wop groups, the Moonglows were one of the most admired by their peers. Bobby Lester's aching vibrato lead, Harvey Fuqua's jazzy baritone, and the group's amazing ability to write and arrange its own material set a high standard for this genre. Initially billed as the Crazy Sounds, the group's big break came in 1952, when disc jockey Alan Freed heard them over the phone, singing in a club. Freed signed them to his own Champagne Record label and renamed them the Moonglows. Though Champagne went out of business just as their first single, "I Just Can't Tell No Lie," was getting airplay, Freed enthusiastically promoted the group throughout their career. Yet he extracted a high price for his patronage; a great many songs written by Fuqua were listed as being written or co-written by Freed—just one of many forms of payola the famous DJ set up in exchange for airplay. The following year, the group signed with Ewart Abner's Chance label, where its ballad "Baby Please" hit regionally. But "Just a Lonely Christmas," a remake of Doris Day's "Secret Love," and the jumping "Ooh Rockin' Daddy" broke nationally. Chance folded in mid-1954, and the Moonglows moved on to Chess Records with the doo-wop classic "Sincerely," a Fuqua composition that was shut out of the pop market by the McGuire Sisters' cover version. However, the beautifully executed "Most of All" defied cover versions, and the Moonglows finally gained a share of the pop market. More hits led to appearances in two Alan Freed teen flicks, *Rock Rock Rock* (1956) and *Mister Rock 'n' Roll* (1957). During this period, Chess caused much dissension within the group by occasionally releasing records credited to Bobby Lester & the Moonglows. Lester sang lead on their last big hit of the 1950s, the romantic doo-wop prayer "Ten Commandments of Love," but at that point the billing read Harvey & the Moonglows. After the group splintered, Fuqua appeared solo (simply billed as Harvey) in Freed's *Go Johnny Go* (1958) and put together a new Moonglows line-up featuring young Marvin Gaye as lead singer. Neither approach was successful, and by 1960, the Moonglows had officially disbanded. Fuqua went on to start the Tri Phi and Harvey labels and recorded with a new act, the Spinners. During the mid-1960s, Fuqua became a producer and A&R man for his brother-in-law, Berry Gordy Jr., at Motown. Through the years, several incarnations of the Moonglows have recorded for labels such as Lana, Times Square, and Crimson. In 1972, Fuqua reunited with Lester and Graves to cut an LP for RCA, which featured a quasi-funk remake of "Sincerely," the group's final chart appearance. Though new line-ups of the Moonglows appear on the oldies circuit, none come close to capturing the magic conjured by the originals.

what to buy: You can't go wrong with *Their Greatest Hits* ♫♫♫♫ (Chess/MCA, 1997, prod. various), which features all their big hits for Chess and some great B-sides.

what to buy next: If you want it all at once, including some of the Chance sides plus previously unreleased tracks, *Blue Velvet—The Ultimate Collection* ♫♫♫♫ (Chess, 1993, comp. Andy McKaie) is an amazing two-disc, 44-track anthology still available in many record shops.

what to avoid: You should know that *On Stage* ♫♫ (Relic, 1992, prod. Walter DeVenne) is a live recording from 1978 featuring only one original Moonglow, Bobby Lester.

the rest:
Moonglows Hits ♫♫♫♫ (Jukebox Treasures, 1996)
Encore of Golden Hits ♫♫♫♫ (Jukebox Treasures)
Moonglows Acapella ♫♫♫ (Jukebox Treasures, 1996)

worth searching for: If you're on a budget, *Look, It's The Moonglows* ♫♫♫♫ (Chess, 1989, prod. Phil Chess, Leonard Chess) is an exact reproduction of the Moonglows best LP and is still around if you look.

influences:
◀◀ The Dominoes, Five Royales, the Orioles, the Ravens

▶▶ The Dells, Marvin Gaye, the Spinners

Ken Burke

Chante Moore

Born in San Francisco, CA.

Once people stopped staring at the tiny black dress she wore in her early music videos and began concentrating on her voice, beautiful Chante Moore leaped to the forefront of the next generation R&B divas. The daughter of a jazz-loving minister in San Francisco, the young soprano grew up heavily influenced by gospel music while setting her own poetry to the instrumental jams of Lee Ritenour and George Duke (now one of her producers and studio musicians). After a few fits and starts breaking into the music business—including almost signing away all of her songwriting and publishing rights to an unscrupulous Bay Area promoter—Moore landed a deal with Silas Records (affiliated with MCA) and launched her 1992 debut album, *Precious*, to overwhelming response. Filled with light, jazzy midtempo grooves and breathy love appeals, the LP quickly went gold and spawned two Top 5 R&B singles in "Love's Taken Over" and "It's Alright." Hailed as the year's "Best Album" by Britain's Blues & Soul magazine, *Precious* led to Moore being hailed "Best Female Vocalist" and "Most Promising Newcomer" by that same publication, performing at the 1992 Montreux Jazz Festival and starring in BET's first-ever hourlong solo music special, *Candlelight and You: Chante Moore Live*. A supple, multi-octave vocalist frequently compared to Diana Ross but possessing Mariah Carey's glass-shattering abilities, Moore encored in 1994 with the album *A Love Supreme*, and has since appeared on LPs by Toni Braxton (*Secrets*) and Prince (*Emancipation*), as well as the *Beverly Hills Cop III* and *Waiting to Exhale* film soundtracks. She has a daughter with actor Kadeem Hardison.

what's available: Of Moore's two albums to date, the first, *Precious* ♫♫♫♫ (Silas/MCA, 1992, prod. various) is overall the more appealing, showing more diversification in its jazz-oriented backgrounds and a singer eager to show off her angelic, stratospheric range and emotion. *A Love Supreme* ♫♫♫ (Silas/MCA, 1994, prod. various), conversely, is a touch too coy. She co-wrote 14 of the LP's 16 tracks, and may not be the best creator of her own material; the uptempo "Searchin'," for example, sounds too much like a Madonna outtake. Moore records cover tunes for the first time as well, and does little to redefine Deniece Williams's "Free," the Commodores' "Sail On," or Alicia Myers's "I Want to Thank You." However, the best moments of *A Love Supreme*—"I'm What You Need," "Am I Losing You?," and the sensuous "Old School Lovin'"—are exceptional.

Chante Moore (© Ken Settle)

worth searching for: Not too hard to find is the ubiquitous *Waiting to Exhale* ♫♫♫ (BMG/Arista, 1995, prod. Babyface) movie soundtrack and a chance to hear her sing the unconventional tune "Wey U." Tougher to locate, but perhaps more worth the effort, is Moore's effort on the sweeping "Inside My Love," a song from the soundtrack to the TV series *New York Undercover* ♫♫♫ (UNI/MCA, 1995, prod. various).

influences:

◀◀ BeBe Winans, CeCe Winans, Barron Peeler, Minnie Riperton, Diana Ross, George Duke, Deniece Williams, Roberta Flack, Sade, Mariah Carey, Toni Braxton

▶▶ Brandy, Donna Lewis, LaBouche

Andre McGarrity

Melba Moore

Born Melba Hill, October 29, 1945.

Melba Moore entered the R&B realm with a reputation already well in place; she had starred on Broadway, her versatile, multi-octave voice winning rave notices in *Hair* and *Purlie,* the latter of which earned her a slew of awards, including a 1970 Tony for best supporting actress in a musical. Moore entered the recording realm shortly thereafter, singing with Mercury, Buddah, Epic, and Arista with only modest success; there seemed to be no place for this talented vocalist amidst the plethora of funk and disco outfits that dominated the 1970s. Moore also intimidated the male-dominated music industry by joining her husband, Beau Higgins, in running her own production and management company—which helped to start the career of soul crooner Freddie Jackson. When she moved to Capitol during the early 1980s, however, the times caught up with her, and the payoff included a string of high-tech R&B hits such as "Living for Your Love," "It's Been So Long," and (for Capitol corporate cousin EMI) "Love's Comin' at Ya." Her peak came in 1986, with two R&B #1 songs—"Falling" and a duet with Jackson, "A Little Bit More"—and "Love the One I'm With (A Lot of Love)" with Kashif. During the early 1990s she battled Higgins, whom she divorced, over control of the production company, but she remains active, most recently recording jazzier fare with the Lafayette Harris Jr. Trio.

what to buy: *A Little Bit Moore: The Magic of Melba Moore* ♫♫♫♫ (EMI, 1997, prod. various) showcases Moore's successful 1980s recordings with Capitol, the commercial zenith of her career so far. *This Is It: The Best of Melba Moore* ♫♫♫♫ (Razor & Tie, 1995, prod. various) captures the cream of her earlier

recordings. The original cast recording of *Purlie* ♫♫♫♫ (RCA Victor, 1970/1990) is her career highlight, on which she sings alongside established TV and film actors Sherman Hemsley and Cleavon Little.

the rest:
This Is It ♫♫♫ (Buddah, 1976/1996)
(With the Lafayette Harris Jr. Trio) *Happy Together* ♫♫♫ (Muse, 1996)

worth searching for: Moore is among the voices on the original cast recording of *Hair* (Atco, 1969).

influences:

◀◀ Ann Peebles, Martha Reeves, Tina Turner, McFadden & Whitehead

▶▶ Mary J. Blige, Madonna, Paula Abdul, Janet Jackson, R. Kelly

Gary Graff

Van Morrison

Born August 31, 1945, in Belfast, Ireland.

More than anyone's except maybe that of Jerry Lee Lewis or Little Richard, the mercurial music of Van Morrison explores that most elusive of dichotomies: the tension between the sacred and the profane, the spiritual and the worldly, sex and chastity. Alternately pious and lascivious, Morrison's best albums explore the most tenuous and volatile of life's conflicts. He has lurched all over the emotional and musical landscape in his search. As a teen-ager in Them, Morrison screamed lustily, emulating hard-bitten American bluesmen and scoring hits with the proto-rock/blues of "Baby, Please Don't Go" and his own "Gloria," still a garage-band mainstay. After the pop-heavy (but controversial) "Brown-Eyed Girl," which revealed a seemingly endless capacity for hit records, Morrison's first real solo record, *Astral Weeks*, veered away from the mainstream, introducing an inquisitive, introspective, and self-absorbed obsession with folk/jazz, all banging acoustic guitars, strings, impressionistic lyrics, and a grunting, growling scat that would differentiate his voice from all others. He embraced the poetry and mysticism of William Blake and William Butler Yeats with the same enthusiasm as the lyrics of Jackie Wilson or Huddie Ledbetter. His early solo records for Warner Bros., especially the warm country/soul of *Moondance, His Band and Street Choir, Tupelo Honey,* and *St. Dominic's Preview* reflect the rural hippie aesthetic of the period and his Woodstock, N.Y., surroundings. After a brief hiatus between 1974–77, his later Warners albums seemed to tilt further in favor of the mystic and spiritual, most notably on *Beautiful Vision* and *Into the*

Music. Since moving to Polydor in the mid-1980s, Morrison's music has matured even more but has retained—some would probably say re*gained*—its edge. For all his accomplishments and influence, Morrison remains something of a (large) cult artist, and his aversion to show business mechanisms has been well-documented. Eschewing fashion in favor of his muse, wherever it takes him, Morrison displays a rare honesty, tenacity, and willingness for growth and exploration without consideration for commercial trends or fashion. It can be a bumpy ride at times, but none of his albums has been completely without merit. Morrison seems forever trapped at the junction of the path of righteousness and the highway to hell, and he's brought us along as he makes up his mind which way he's heading. It's a trip well worth taking.

what to buy: Choosing the best from someone as prolific and challenging as Morrison is difficult at best, but his first three solo records are absolute musts. *Astral Weeks* 𝄢𝄢𝄢𝄢 (Warner Bros., 1968, prod. Lewis Merenstein) is a song cycle that sounds like a concept album, even if it isn't, as it meanders through the alleys and back streets of London's pre-punk Notting Hill Gate with sleazy eccentrics like the unforgettable icon "Madame George." *Moondance* 𝄢𝄢𝄢𝄢 (Warner Bros., 1970, prod. Van Morrison) and *Van Morrison His Band and the Street Choir* 𝄢𝄢𝄢𝄢 (Warner Bros., 1970, prod. Van Morrison) would have made an extraordinary double album, with numerous youthful examples of the Morrison acoustic soul magic including "Into the Mystic," "Caravan," "Crazy Love," "Domino," "Blue Money," and "Call Me Up in Dreamland." *Hymns to the Silence* 𝄢𝄢𝄢𝄢 (Polydor, 1991, prod. Van Morrison), a lengthy double set, is one of his more recent triumphs. Disc one, with a couple of wry show-biz rants ("Professional Jealousy" and "Why Must I Always Explain") and a masterful version of "I Can't Stop Loving You," is especially listenable.

what to buy next: You'll also want to have *St. Dominic's Preview* 𝄢𝄢𝄢𝄢 (Warner Bros., 1972/Polydor, 1997, prod. Van Morrison, Ted Templeman), with wonderful songs like "Jackie Wilson Said (I'm in Heaven When You Smile)," "Almost Independence Day," and the epochal "Listen to the Lion." *Irish Heartbeat* 𝄢𝄢𝄢𝄢 (Mercury, 1988, prod. Van Morrison, Paddy Maloney), a collaboration with the Chieftains, is an inspired collection of traditional music. *A Night in San Francisco* 𝄢𝄢𝄢𝄢 (Polydor, 1994, prod. Van Morrison) is a two-disc extended live set that does justice to his current high-energy, big-band performances and includes amazing medleys that place his music in context. *Too Long in Exile* 𝄢𝄢𝄢𝄢 (Polydor, 1993, prod. Van Morrison)

finds a loose Morrison in a bluesy mood, relaxing on alto saxophone, electric guitar, and harmonica and reprising "Gloria" for his middle age. Neophytes can't go wrong with *The Best of Van Morrison* 𝄢𝄢𝄢𝄢 (Polydor, 1990, prod. various) and *The Best of Van Morrison Vol. 2* 𝄢𝄢𝄢𝄢 (Polydor, 1993, prod. various), with 35 distinct tracks between them that will have to do until the inevitable boxed set comes along.

what to avoid: *Inarticulate Speech of the Heart* 𝄢 (Warner Bros., 1983, prod. Van Morrison), which is as confusing as the title would suggest, is synthesized New Age blather. Not surprisingly it was his last record for Warner Bros.

the rest:
(With Them) *Them* 𝄢𝄢𝄢 (Parrot/Decca, 1965)
Them Again 𝄢𝄢𝄢 (Parrot/Decca, 1966)
Blowin' Your Mind 𝄢𝄢𝄢 (Bang, 1967)
Best of Van Morrison 𝄢𝄢𝄢 (Bang, 1970)
Tupelo Honey 𝄢𝄢𝄢𝄢 (Warner Bros., 1971/Polydor, 1997)
T.B. Sheets 𝄢𝄢𝄢 (Bang, 1972)
Them Featuring Van Morrison 𝄢𝄢𝄢𝄢 (Parrot/London, 1972)
Hard Nose the Highway 𝄢𝄢 (Warner Bros., 1973/Polydor, 1997)
It's Too Late to Stop Now 𝄢𝄢𝄢𝄢 (Warner Bros., 1974/Polydor, 1997)
Veedon Fleece 𝄢𝄢 (Warner Bros., 1974/Polydor, 1997)
A Period of Transition 𝄢𝄢𝄢 (Warner Bros., 1977/Polydor, 1997)
Wavelength 𝄢𝄢𝄢𝄢 (Warner Bros., 1978/Polydor, 1997)
Into the Music 𝄢𝄢𝄢 (Warner Bros., 1979)
Common One 𝄢𝄢𝄢 (Warner Bros., 1980)
Beautiful Vison 𝄢𝄢𝄢𝄢 (Warner Bros., 1982)
A Sense of Wonder 𝄢𝄢𝄢 (Mercury, 1985)
Live at the Grand Opera House Belfast 𝄢𝄢𝄢𝄢 (Mercury, 1985)
No Guru, No Method, No Teacher 𝄢𝄢𝄢𝄢 (Mercury, 1986)
Poetic Champions Compose 𝄢𝄢𝄢 (Mercury, 1989)
Avalon Sunset 𝄢𝄢𝄢𝄢 (Mercury, 1989)
Enlightenment 𝄢𝄢𝄢𝄢 (Mercury, 1990)
Bang Masters 𝄢𝄢𝄢 (Epic, 1991)
Days Like This 𝄢𝄢𝄢𝄢 (Polydor, 1995)
(With Georgie Fame) *How Long Has This Been Going On* 𝄢𝄢𝄢 (Verve, 1996)
(With Georgie Fame and Ben Sidran) *Tell Me Something: The Songs of Mose Allison* 𝄢𝄢𝄢𝄢 (Verve, 1996)
The Healing Game 𝄢𝄢𝄢𝄢 (Polydor, 1997)

worth searching for: Morrison's infrequent live sets are generally considered the best way to experience the Belfast Cowboy, as witnessed by his three excellent, authorized live albums. There are literally dozens more available in bootleg form, and since Morrison rarely does the same show twice, many of them are worth the effort. *Can You Feel the Silence?* 𝄢𝄢𝄢𝄢 (Great Dane) captures a 1982 show and includes a great Morrison rant about "Idiot Wind" that tries to explain why he's playing at a rock festival. *Van Morrison Gets His Chance to Wail Vols. 1 & 2* ♪♪♪♪ (Gold Standard) puts you in the studio during 1969–71, with Van on acoustic guitar as he works out demo versions of "Ballerina," "Domino," "And It Stoned Me," "Wild Night," "Caravan," and many more.

influences:

◀◀ Sonny Boy Williamson, Leadbelly, Muddy Waters, John Lee Hooker, Sam Cooke, Slim Harpo, Solomon Burke, James Brown, Ray Charles, Sonny Terry and Brownie McGhee, Jackie Wilson, Bo Diddley, Curtis Mayfield and the Impressions, Johnny and the Pirates, Alexis Korner, Mose Allison, Bob Dylan

▶▶ Counting Crows, Graham Parker & the Rumour, Dexy's Midnight Runners, Sinead O'Connor, U2, the Band, Elvis Costello, Rod Stewart, Mark Knopfler, Bob Seger, John Mellencamp, Bruce Springsteen, Joan Armatrading, Rickie Lee Jones

Leland Rucker

Mother's Finest

Formed 1970, in Dayton, OH. Disbanded 1983. Re-formed 1989.

Joyce Kennedy, vocals; Garry Moore (a.k.a. Moses Mo), guitar; Glenn Murdock, vocals; Jerry Seay (a.k.a. Wizzard), bass; Barry Borden (a.k.a. B.B. Queen), drums; Mike Keck, keyboards.

Starting with the Chicago-bred vocal partners Joyce Kennedy and Glenn Murdock, Mother's Finest emerged as the pair toured through Dayton, Ohio and later Miami. Though renowned for incendiary live shows and the Chaka Khan-style power of vocalist Kennedy, the band melded old-school soul vocals to a riff-laden, bombastic rock approach. This was a tough way to go during the 1970s, when the openness that allowed Sly & the Family Stone to play on the same bill as Creedence Clearwater Revival fell victim to a more segregated music industry. It also didn't help that Mother's Finest was never really able to properly present its formula in the studio. Despite the success of sultry funk tunes such as "Baby Love" and "Love Changes," the band broke up in 1983, with Kennedy moving on to a solo career and drummer Barry Borden playing with Molly Hatchet. Though the group re-formed in 1989, it had the same problems reaching audiences—prompting the irreverent title of its last record, *Black Radio Won't Play This*.

what to buy: If Mother's Finest came off a little stiff in the studio, it made up for it on the firey concert album, *Live* ♪♪♪♪

(Epic, 1979, prod. Jimmy Iovine), which showcased the group's booty kicking stage presentation.

what to buy next: *The Very Best of Mother's Finest: Not Your Mother's Funk* ♪♪♪ (Razor & Tie, 1997, prod. various) is a top-notch compilation and a fine introduction to a sadly underappreciated group.

the rest:
Black Radio Won't Play This ♪♪♪ (RCA, 1992)

influences:

◀◀ Sly & the Family Stone, Rufus, Jimi Hendrix, Funkadelic

▶▶ Living Colour, Red Hot Chili Peppers, the Black Rock Coalition

Eric Deggans

Motown

Berry Gordy Jr. was writing songs for Jackie Wilson ("Reet Petite," "To Be Loved") and came to realize he probably wasn't making the kind of money he should for the hits. His answer: start his own record company. So with a loan of $800 from his family, Gordy launched the Motown empire in 1959 with the appropriately titled Barrett Strong single "Money (That's What I Want)." That's what Motown got, too, as the company went through the roof during the 60s with an unstoppable string of hits by the likes of Smokey Robinson & the Miracles, Martha & the Vandellas, the Marvelettes, Mary Wells, the Supremes, the Temptations, the Four Tops, Marvin Gaye, Stevie Wonder, Junior Walker & the All-Stars—a veritable hall of fame of popular music. And that's not counting other groups, such as the Spinners, the Isley Brothers, and Gladys Knight & the Pips, that schooled at Motown on their way to bigger things; heck, Motown even had Neil Young for a minute, in a group called the Mynah Birds, as well as Meat Loaf's first recording. Coming as the civil rights movement was kicking into gear, Motown gave voice to the hopes and aspirations of black Americans at a crucial time, and while the company always treaded lightly in the political arena, it did release such crucial statements as Marvin Gaye's *What's Going On*, Edwin Starr's hit "War," and the Temptations' "Message from a Black Man," as well as releasing recordings of the Rev. Martin Luther King Jr.'s speeches. Gordy withstood charges of inequitable promotion and financial mismanagement—though several of his acts went elsewhere over the years—and he eventually set his sights on the show biz empire and moved Motown to Los Angeles during the 70s, where it got into the movie business (*Lady Sings the Blues, Ma-*

hogany, *The Wiz*). Recent years have seen its cadre of hitmakers diminish (Boyz II Men is the leading light these days, and they don't record that often). Still, Motown remains a formidable brand name, with a burgeoning back catalog and a restaurant chain, the Motown Cafe.

what to buy: *Hitsville U.S.A.: The Motown Singles Collection 1959–1971* 𝄢𝄢𝄢𝄢 (Motown, 1992) is a supreme (ar, ar) four-CD anthology of all the label's seminal hits, featuring not only the obvious superstars but also important pieces of the Motown picture such as Barrett Strong, the Contours, the early Spinners, and the Velvelettes. *Hitsville U.S.A., Vol. 2: The Motown Singles Collection 1972–1992* 𝄢𝄢𝄢𝄢 (Motown, 1993), another four-CD set, is just a touch less essential; the first couple of discs are as non-stop great as its predecessor, but the rest of the set—like the label itself—gets a little thin as it goes on. *Every Great Motown Song, Vol. 1: The 1960's* 𝄢𝄢𝄢𝄢 (Motown, 1986) and *Every Great Motown Song, Vol. 2: The 1970's* 𝄢𝄢𝄢𝄢 (Motown, 1984) overlap the box sets but are great to toss on for parties.

what to buy next: The label's *Motown Year by Year: The Sound of Young America* series—12 individual volumes released during 1995, each in the 𝄢𝄢𝄢 to 𝄢𝄢𝄢𝄢 range—combines hits with rarities for a solid historical overview.

what to avoid: The three-part series *Baddest Love Jams* 𝄢𝄢 (Motown, 1996) is proof that you *can* have too much of a good thing.

worth searching for: Worth finding is the out-of-print two-volume set *20 Hard to Find Motown Classics* 𝄢𝄢𝄢𝄢 (Motown, 1986), which gathers hits by some of those Motowners (Shorty Long, Barbara Randolph, the Elgins, R. Dean Taylor) that have fallen between the cracks.

Gary Graff

Alison Moyet
/Yaz
/Yazoo

Born Genevieve Alison-Jane Moyet, June 18, 1961, in Basildon, Essex, England.

Yaz (Yazoo in England)—singer Moyet and Depeche Mode refugee Vince Clarke on keyboards—made an argument for synthesizer music with its remarkably emotional pop created in the often vacuous techno landscapes of the early 1980s. Much of the duo's vibrancy belonged to Moyet's rich, passionate voice, a sultry blend of R&B and nervy energy. Her singing, matched with Clarke's quirky keyboard pop, lifted the group's

songs to a more resonant level above many of their peers. After only a year and a half with Yaz, Clarke went on to form Erasure, while Moyet carved out a successful solo career that has seen her moving quickly into American mainstream.

what to buy: Yaz's *You and Me Both* 𝄢𝄢𝄢𝄢 (Sire, 1983), the group's second and final release, is a romantic overture of defiance and desperation with a little joyous bounce thrown in to lighten the load. Moyet has yet to come up with material as strong as "Nobody's Diary," "Good Times," and "Walk Away From Love." Moyet's *Hoodoo* 𝄢𝄢𝄢𝄢 (Columbia, 1991, prod. Pete Glenister) was a commercial flop, but its diversity creates a better stage for her blazing honesty than any of her previous solo efforts.

what to buy next: Yaz's *Upstairs at Eric's* 𝄢𝄢𝄢 (Sire, 1982, prod. E.C. Radcliffe, Yaz) is the group's ambitious and experimental debut that hits sonic warm spots ("Only You" and "Don't Go") as well as horrendous left-field ditches ("I Before E Except After C").

what to avoid: Moyet's *Raindancing* 𝄢 (Columbia, 1987, prod. Jimmy Iovine) is smothered by formula pop production. And titles such as "I Grow Weak in the Presence of Beauty" add insult to injury.

the rest:
Alison Moyet:
Alf 𝄢𝄢𝄢 (Columbia, 1984)
Essex 𝄢𝄢𝄢 (Columbia, 1994)
Singles 𝄢𝄢𝄢 (Columbia, 1995)

influences:

◀◀ Aretha Franklin, Billie Holiday, Depeche Mode, Kraftwerk, Joy Division

▶▶ Erasure, Blue Nile, Eurythmics, Annie Lennox

Allan Orski

Maria Muldaur

Born Maria D'Amato, September 12, 1943, in New York, NY.

When Maria Muldaur started her solo career, she rode her distinctive, sweet voice to the pop stratosphere with the single "Midnight at the Oasis." As usual with overnight successes, she had worked for a long time. Through the 1960s, she was part of the Even Dozen Jug Band and then the Jim Kweskin Jug Band (with whom she recorded a great early version of her solo hit, "I'm a Woman"). After the Kweskin band broke up, she and Kweskin bandmate/husband Geoff Muldaur recorded together before they divorced in 1972. She released her self-titled solo debut in 1973 and enjoyed a quick rise and fall on the pop charts. During the 1980s, she became a born-again Christian and recorded some gospel and a contemporary Christian album. During the 1990s, Muldaur has enjoyed good success on the blues and roots-music circuit.

what to buy: There's no question that Muldaur's best album is her first. *Maria Muldaur* 𝄞𝄞𝄞𝄞 (Reprise, 1973/Warner Archives, 1993, prod. Lenny Waronker, Joe Boyd) came out at a time when the pop scene was ready to enjoy the eclecticism of American music. She hit swing with "Walking One and Only," sexy radio pop with "Midnight at the Oasis" (that song, for good or ill, set a standard for the come-on pop songs of the 1970s), country with "Tennessee Mountain Home," and more. The follow-up, *Waitress in a Donut Shop* 𝄞𝄞𝄞𝄟 (Reprise, 1974/Warner Archives, 1993, prod. Lenny Waronker, Joe Boyd), was just as broad and excellently performed but didn't hang together as well. It featured her rock 'n' rolling on "I'm a Woman" (her second and last chart hit), as well as two cuts led by jazz great Benny Carter—"Sweetheart" and "It Ain't the Meat (It's the Motion)."

what to buy next: On *Sweet and Slow* 𝄞𝄞𝄞𝄞 (Tudor, 1983/Stony Plain, 1993, prod. David Nichtern) Muldaur sings with her old fire for Nichtern, who wrote "Midnight at the Oasis," with bands led by Dr. John and Kenny Barron. *Jazzabelle* 𝄞𝄞𝄞𝄞 (Stony Plain, 1995, prod. Maria Muldaur) is a jazz effort that finds Muldaur just as sharp with a huskier voice. *Louisiana Love Call* 𝄞𝄞𝄞𝄟 (Black Top, 1992, prod. Hammond Scott) and *Fanning the Flames* 𝄞𝄞𝄞𝄟 (Telarc, 1996, prod. John Snyder, Maria Muldaur, Elaine Martone) don't capture the pop moment the way her earlier albums did, but Muldaur certainly gives her all vocally.

what to avoid: Generally speaking, you can't go wrong with a Muldaur album, but if you're rummaging through remainder bins of old vinyl, avert your eyes and close your wallet if you see *Southern Winds* 𝄞𝄞 (Reprise, 1978, prod. Christopher Bond) and *Open Your Eyes* 𝄞 (Reprise, 1979, prod. Patrick Henderson, David Nichtern), which sound totally tired.

the rest:
There Is a Love 𝄞𝄞𝄞 (Myrrh, 1982)
On the Sunny Side 𝄞𝄞𝄞 (Music for Little People, 1992)
Meet Me at Midnite 𝄞𝄞𝄞𝄟 (Black Top, 1994)

worth searching for: Geoff and Maria Muldaur's fine *Pottery Pie* 𝄞𝄞𝄞 (Reprise, 1967/Hannibal, 1993, prod. Joe Boyd) points the way toward Muldaur's first solo outing. Out of print, her third solo outing—*Sweet Harmony* 𝄞𝄞𝄞𝄞 (Reprise, 1976, prod. Lenny Waronker)—was just a tad less interesting than her first two.

influences:
◀◀ Billie Holiday, Bessie Smith, Dolly Parton
▶▶ Wendy Waldman, Linda Ronstadt

Salvatore Caputo

Shirley Murdock
Born in Toledo, OH.

Shirley Murdock ended a successful career singing gospel when she joined Roger Troutman's funk outfit Zapp during that group's 1984 tour. Under Troutman's tutelage, she began her solo career with a huge hit, "As We Lay," a provocative ballad about adultery that wed her bold-yet-smooth voice with his trademark groove. Murdock, who married songwriter and producer Dale DeGroat when both were in Zapp, then had a curious string of hits with infidelity themes, like "Husband" and "Go on without You." Despite diminishing popularity after her first album, her storytelling style, ability to personalize songs, and heavenly voice set her apart from her peers.

what to buy: Troutman's somewhat stifling authority can still be felt on *Let There Be Love!* 𝄞𝄞𝄞𝄞 (Elektra, 1991, prod. Roger Troutman, Shirley Murdock), but first-time co-writer and co-producer Murdock leaves the soap opera topics behind this time and crafts a work that fully meshes the best aspects of her gospel and secular influences.

the rest:
Shirley Murdock 𝄞𝄞𝄞 (Elektra, 1985)
Woman's Point of View 𝄞𝄞𝄞 (Elektra)

worth searching for: A de facto member of Zapp, Murdock adds color and fire to more than half of the cuts on *Roger & Zapp, The Compilation: Greatest Hits II and More* 𝄞𝄞𝄞 (Reprise, 1996, prod. Roger Troutman), a package of new and previously released works.

influences:
◀◀ Betty Wright, Jennifer Holliday, Anita Baker

see also: *Zapp*

Franklin Paul

Eddie Murphy
Born April 3, 1961, in Hempstead, NY.

Doing a good Stevie Wonder impression does not necessarily mean you can be a good musician yourself. Otay? That was the lesson for Eddie Murphy, the gifted *Saturday Night Live* alumnus, stand-up comic, and film actor who tried to take the next step into the music biz and, excepting a #2 hit in 1985 with "Party All the Time," he failed. It's not hard to figure out why; Murphy's voice is reedy and thin, and though he had the formidable help of superstars such as Wonder, Rick James, Garth Brooks, Paul McCartney, B.B. King, En Vogue, Heavy D., Michael Jackson, and Amy Grant, there was no real vision to do anything spectacular with it. His comedy albums are much more appropriate to his talents.

what's available: *So Happy* ♪ (Columbia, 1989, prod. Nile Rodgers) is the only one of his three albums in print—curious, because it's probably the least notable. Pass.

influences:

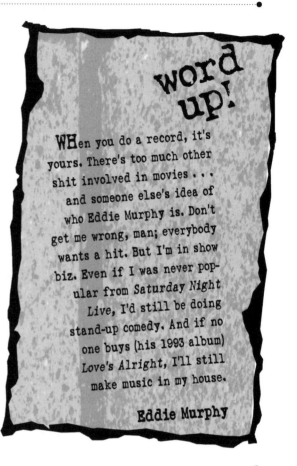 Stevie Wonder, Rick James, Chic, Brick, Parliament-Funkadelic

Gary Graff

Keith Murray

Born 1972, in Long Island, NY.

The youthful progeny of Erick Sermon's Def Squad, Murray first came to light dropping smokey, syrupy rhymes on Sermon's *No Pressure*. One thing led to another, and Murray—one of the few artists in hip-hop whose nom de CD is actually his given name—scored himself a solo deal with Jive.

what's available: *The Most Beautifulest Thing in This World* ♪♪♪♪ (Jive, 1994, prod. Erick Sermon, Busta Rhymes, others) sees Murray continuing to serve up the smoky-smooth vibes he first delivered on *No Pressure*. True to Def Squad form, the beats rumble like twisted ghetto dub, and the groove packs plenty of low-end boom and sharp, minimalistic samples. Murray controls the mic with hazy confidence, rapping in a smooth but raspy baritone that's simultaneously thick and liquescent. His lyrical delivery is abstract and purely stream-of-consciousness, making for a mesmerizingly enigmatic listen. The cornerstone of this release is the titular single, which rides a smoothed-out R&B undertow thanks to the Boosty Collins, Isley Brothers, and Edie Brickell samples. Also notable are Murray's ode to weed, "Get Lifted," "How's That" (which features Sermon and Redman), and the bonus "Green-Eyed Remix" of "The Most Beautifulest Thing in This World." Tracks on Murray's follow-up, *Enigma* ♪♪♪ (Jive, 1996, prod. Erick Sermon, the Ummah, others), range from the swirling "The Rhyme—The Slum Village Remix" and the eerie "Call My Name" to the dusted blues guitar lingo of "What's Happenin'." The album's highwater mark

comes in the form of the fluid posse cut "Yeah," a tight jam featuring the bugged rambunction of Busta Rhymes, the thick-mouthed smoothness of Sermon, the hazy gruffness of Redman, and the Illegal verbal maneuvers of Jamal. (Most of the crew is also featured on Busta's own *The Coming*, with Murray, Redman, Jamal, Busta, and Rampage dropping wicked verses on "Flipmode Squad Meets Def Squad.")

influences:

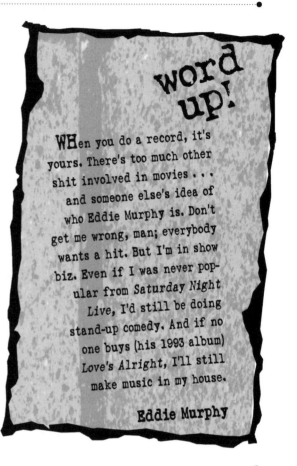 EPMD/Erick Sermon, Redman, Busta Rhymes

Spence D.

Alicia Myers

See: One Way

---

word up!

WHen you do a record, it's yours. There's too much other shit involved in movies . . . and someone else's idea of who Eddie Murphy is. Don't get me wrong, man; everybody wants a hit. But I'm in show biz. Even if I was never popular from *Saturday Night Live*, I'd still be doing stand-up comedy. And if no one buys (his 1993 album) *Love's Alright*, I'll still make music in my house.

Eddie Murphy

Mystikal

Born in New Orleans, LA.

When it comes to music, New Orleans is best known as the home of jazz and blues, but Mystikal helped to put the Big Easy on the rap map with the 1994 release of his eponymous indie debut. Mystikal, who alternately comes off like an herb-smokin' dancehall chat master or the rapid-fire verbalizer Spice 1, further secured a place in the hip-hop history books by both performing at the rap-unfriendly New Orleans Jazz and Heritage Festival and becoming the first rapper ever to headline at the original House of Blues.

what's available: Mystikal's major-label debut, *Mind of Mystikal* ♫♫♪ (Big Boy/Jive, 1995, prod. L. "Precise" Edwards), is essentially a beefed-up re-release of his self-titled, regionally released indie debut, with five additional tracks, a couple of remixes, and a bonus cut ("Out That Boot Camp Clicc"). Although he occasionally sounds like a weird, agro-ragga ruffian, Mystikal works best when he's flowing smooth—the better to match the slinky, almost NorCal-styled beats. The overall sonic mix is a little bit East, a little bit West, and a whole lotta South, which may leave some listeners in a mild state of schizophrenia. But one thing is clear: the inclusion of some overtly misogynistic lyrical anger ultimately makes the album little more than an average hip-hop excursion.

influences:
◀◀ E-40, Das EFX

Spence D.

N2Deep

Formed in Vallejo, CA.

Johnny Z, producer; "Jay Tee" Trujillo, vocals; "TL" Lyon, vocals.

The hip-hop world may now equate Vallejo with E-40, but two years before the quirky-voiced one took his Sick Wid' It empire national and "saved a hoe," V-Town's own N2Deep was already bringing its own female friends "Back to the Hotel." Along the way, the group also made a pit stop in the pop Top 15. Previously known as the indie single "Telly," "Back to the Hotel" was given a new title and a shot at broad exposure in 1992 with the help of Profile Records, which helped usher the single to gold status. Of course, Wreckx-N-Effect built its own song ("Rump Shaker") around "Back to the Hotel" and summarily went double-platinum; but who's counting?

what to buy: *Back to the Hotel* ♫♫♪ (Profile, 1992, prod. Johnny Z) features not only the hit title track, but also a slew of other sex-crazed party songs ("Toss-Up," "Weekend," etc.).

the rest:
The Golden State ♫♫♪ (Swerve, 1997)

influences:
◀◀ 2 Live Crew
▶▶ Wreckx-N-Effect

Josh Freedom du Lac

Nas

Born Nasir Jones, in New York, NY.

Heralded as the new Rakim, Nas is the latest urban bard to embody the spirit of East Coast hip-hop in his decidedly New York rhymes. The rapper snatched notoriety with his 1994 debut, *Illmatic*, and has since influenced countless MCs and ushered in a host of new talents from his clique the Firm (Foxy Brown, AZ, Cormega). On both his albums, straight-forward street themes dominate rugged audioscapes, which allow the narrator to spin parables of ghetto economics, moral ordeals, and poverty's influence on community life. In a distanced, nearly omniscient tone, this MCs' MC concentrates his energy on speed, spontaneity, and the clarity of his lyrics. Nas's well-crafted verses and wide-ranging vocabulary simultaneously point to his love of the English language as well as his keen ability to subvert it.

what to buy: *Illmatic* ♫♫♫♪ (Columbia, 1994, prod. Large Professor, DJ Premier, Pete Rock, Q-Tip, others) had New Yorkers singing praises as Nas dropped complicated street rhymes reminiscent of the heyday of rugged New York City rap. Showing a restraint that doesn't bless most young artists, Nas keeps the album to 10 tight tracks, each ringing with an immediacy that make him sound as if every verse he raps will be his last. Particularly compelling are "Life's a Bitch," "It Ain't Hard to Tell," and "N.Y. State of Mind," on which the rapper breaks down an honest self-analysis: "I got so many rhymes, I don't think I'm too sane/Life is parallel to hell but I must maintain."

what to buy next: *It Was Written* ♫♫♫♪ (Columbia, 1996, prod. Havoc, Dr. Dre, TrackMasters, others) represents an artist who has matured enough to move past mere reportage and on to social judgment. While "Affirmative Action" and "If I Ruled the

World (Imagine That)" show the album's variety—from Godfather grooves to hip-hop pop, respectively—the total package is burdened by the fact that Nas has eased his intensity on the mic, sounding disturbingly more comfortable and less creative than he did on his debut. Under the wing of Large Professor, "Nasty Nas" dropped his recorded lyrical debut on Main Source's exceptional pass-the-mic posse cut "Live at the Barbeque" (Wild Pitch, 1991), which foreshadows the Nas's vocal virility and stands as one of the most memorable group efforts on wax.

influences:

◀◀ Rakim, Raekwon, Large Professor, Schoolly D, Kool G Rap, Chill Rob G, M.C. Shan

▶▶ Foxy Brown, AZ, Cormega, A+

Corey Takahashi

Johnny Nash

Born August 19, 1940, in Houston, TX.

Best known for his 1972 chart-topper "I Can See Clearly Now," Johnny Nash was one of the first artists to popularize reggae outside of the Caribbean. Nash had an early reggae hit with "Hold Me Tight" in 1968, but it was through his association with Bob Marley that Nash would make his greatest contribution to the music form. During the late 1960s, Nash worked with, was influenced by, and got a recording contract for a then-unknown Marley. Nash's own breakthrough effort, *I Can See Clearly Now*, features the Wailers and four of Marley's songs. Born in Houston, Nash was something of a child prodigy, serving as the lead singer in his Baptist choir and performing on television by age 13. He recorded several pop songs during the late 1950s and early 1960s, including the Top 40 hit "A Very Special Love" (1957). In 1965, Nash scored an R&B hit with "Let's Move and Groove Together," which was recorded on Joda, one of two labels he started with partner/promoter Danny Sims (Jad being the other). A trip to Jamaica in 1967 made a lasting impact on Nash's musical interests and ultimately led to a string of reggae hits, including "Hold Me Tight," "Guava Jelly," and the epochal "I Can See Clearly Now," which has been cited by the ASCAP as one of the most recorded songs of all time. In addition to performing, Nash writes and produces music for himself and others, and he has appeared in several films.

what to buy: *I Can See Clearly Now* 𝄞𝄞𝄞𝄞 (Epic, 1972, prod. Johnny Nash) features the now-classic title song along with faithful renditions of Bob Marley's "Stir it Up," "Guava Jelly,"

"Comma, Comma," and others. With backing from the Wailers, the album displays a purity unmatched by the rest of his work.

what to buy next: *The Reggae Collection* 𝄞𝄞𝄞 (Epic, 1993, prod. Johnny Nash, Arthur Jenkins, Roy Halee, Ken Khoury, Sonny Limbo, Mickey Buckins) is a worthy collection of 20 reggae offerings, eight of which were previously unreleased. Though some of the tracks are decidedly tepid, others are among his best, including "Stir It Up," "Hold Me Tight," "Cupid," and an alternate version of "I Can See Clearly Now."

what to avoid: *Very Best of Johnny Nash* 𝄞𝄞 (Black Tiger, 1995) doesn't provide a representative sampling of his work.

the rest:
Hold Me Tight 𝄞𝄞𝄞 (Jad, 1968)
Best of Johnny Nash 𝄞𝄞𝄞𝄞 (Columbia, 1996)

worth searching for: *My Merry-Go-Round* 𝄞𝄞𝄞 (Epic, 1973) was Nash's only other charting album and featured modest hits in the title track and "Loving You."

influences:

◀◀ Sam Cooke, Bob Marley & the Wailers

▶▶ Jimmy Cliff, Desmond Dekker, Black Uhuru, Seal

Jim Kamp

Naughty by Nature

Formed in East Orange, NJ.

Treach, vocals; Vinnie, vocals; Kay Gee, DJ.

From their first song—the irresistibly catchy "O.P.P.," which freaked the Jackson 5's "ABC" groove—Naughty by Nature has achieved a consistent commercial success that few groups have matched. Rapper Vinnie and DJ Kay Gee had previously formed a group called New Style, before pulling in Treach (as in treacherous) as their lead MC. The group impressed fellow Jersey MC and Flavor Unit Management head Queen Latifah so much that she helped them get a deal with her own label, Tommy Boy. The gargantuan success Naughty by Nature eventually enjoyed with their singles and albums opened the door to other opportunities, such as acting roles for Treach (*Juice*, *Jason's Lyric*), a production company for Kay Gee with basketball star Chris Webber (though it was short lived), and the group's own Illtown entertainment empire (Illtown Records, Illtown Films, and Naughty Gear clothing). Illtown, incidentally, is the 18th Street block of Orange, New Jersey, that the three members call home.

what to buy: Naughty's debut album, *Naughty by Nature* ♫♫♫ (Tommy Boy, 1991, prod. Naughty by Nature, Luis Vega), came at a time when commercial singles were more difficult to distinguish from just plain good songs. Because of that the group didn't really upset anybody with the likes of the double-platinum hit "O.P.P.," "Everyday All Day," and "Guard Your Grill." On the contrary, they made their strongest album.

what to buy next: Naughty's second album, *19NaughtyIII* ♫♫ (Tommy Boy, 1993, prod. Naughty by Nature), features one major hit single surrounded by a bevy of hardcore tracks. The hit, "Hip-hop Hooray," became an anthem for some, but to underground hip-hop heads was a joke because of its cheesy simplicity. Instead, it was on such songs as the title track and "The Hood Comes First" where Treach shined. Though it features the hit "Feel Me Flow," *Poverty's Paradise* ♫♫ (Tommy Boy, 1995, prod. Naughty by Nature, Minnesota, others) isn't as cohesive or as interesting as the group's other efforts.

influences:

◀◀ Freddie Foxxx, Queen Latifah, Art of Origin, Big Daddy Kane

▶▶ Fugees, Lords of the Underground, Chino XL, Rottin Razkals

Jazzbo

Me'Shell Ndegeocello

Born August 29, 1969, in Berlin, Germany.

In a way, it may be best to think of Me'Shell Ndegeocello as a modern Patrice Rushen: a child prodigy schooled in music, becoming an accomplished composer, arranger, producer, vocalist, and multi-instrumentalist (bass being primary) who signs to a small label—Madonna's Maverick Recordings—because of the assurances of artistic and creative freedom. And like Rushen, Ndegeocello refuses to follow the claustrophobic course of one specific genre. She blends soul, funk, jazz, rock, pop, and hip-hop (and various hybrids of all of those) to create a sound that's the future of R&B, but a future that thankfully—and unashamedly—knows its past. Me'Shell Ndegeocello has, in a very short period of time, shown herself to be one of the most—if not *the* most—important and vibrant forces in modern R&B. It is clear that she has learned a lot and is more than willing to share that knowledge with us. We'd be wise to pay attention.

what's available: Her debut, *Plantation Lullabies* ♫♫♫ (Maverick, 1993, prod. Bob Power, Andre Betts, David Gamson), is a

mosaic of black music styles over which she addresses—quite candidly—drugs, love, lust, poverty, and race. *Lullabies* is a showcase of Ndegeocello's talents: she co-produced many of the album's tracks; played guitar, keyboards, and bass; and sang all the vocals. The album overflows with the youthful exuberance of a wunderkind, an aural assault driven by Ndegeocello's approach to the bass. She doesn't play the bass—she attacks it, firing off riffs and figures that force you to stop and take notice. It's clear from tracks such as "I'm Diggin' You (Like An Old Soul Record)" and "Dred Loc" that Ndegeocello knows how to bring black music's past into the present and mold an enticing future from it. Having made her point on *Lullabies*, Ndegeocello allows herself to relax on the follow-up, *Peace Beyond Passion* ♫♫♫♫ (Maverick, 1996, prod. David Gamson). She loosened her grip and allowed a host of talented people to share her Revolutionary Jazz vision. With David Gamson, one of *Lullabies*' co-producers, at the controls, Ndegeocello was able to focus exclusively on her music. She enlisted a do-no-wrong group of musicians—including guitar funkmeister Wah Wah Watson, organ grinder Billy Preston, reedsman Joshua Redman, former Revolution guitarist Wendy Melvoin, and concertmaster Gene Page—to bring *Peace Beyond Passion* to fruition. The album is a raw and subtle funk tour de force, a suite of 12 songs (eleven originals and one cover) that shows how Ndegeocello has matured as a composer and performer.

worth searching for: The mass pop audience knows Ndegeocello via her spunky (it's the only word for it) duet with John Mellencamp on Van Morrison's "Wild Night." It can be found on Mellencamp's album *Dance Naked* ♫♫♫♫ (Mercury, 1994).

influences:

◀◀ Marvin Gaye, Teena Marie, Charles Mingus, Bootsy Collins, Prince, George Clinton, Millie Jackson

▶▶ Ambershower, Erykah Badu

Dana G. Smart

Ann Nesby

Born in Joliet, IL.

Nesby, the powerful former lead singer of the Minnesota ensemble Sounds of Blackness, is more than just a big voice. A vocal child prodigy, this preacher's daughter was convinced she would have a career in music after watching a performance in Chicago by the Edwin Hawkins singers. A fateful visit to her sister in Minneapolis led to her joining Sounds. She's probably best known for her gospel-tinged work with the ensemble, such as "Optimistic," "The Pressure," and "I Believe." But

Treach of Naughty by Nature (© Ken Settle)

she's written songs that have been performed by the likes of Gladys Knight and Patti LaBelle, and the two-time Grammy winner uses her solo album to touch on themes more about relationships rather then straight-up gospel.

what's available: Nesby's strong, gorgeous voice makes *I'm Here for You* ♪♪♪ (Perspective, 1996, prod. James "Jimmy Jam" Harris III, Terry Lewis) one of the most complete and pleasurable packages ever put together by Jam and Lewis—even if it is a bit long (71 minutes).

influences:

◀◀ Aretha Franklin, Patti LaBelle, Shirley Caesar

see also: *Sounds of Blackness*

Franklin Paul

The Neville Brothers

Formed 1977, in New Orleans, LA.

Art Neville, keyboards, vocals; Charles Neville, saxophone, vocals, percussion; Aaron Neville, vocals, percussion; Cyril Neville, percussion, vocals.

The Neville Brothers formed in New Orleans in 1977, though various incarnations of the group had been performing and recording since the early 1960s. Indeed, keyboardist Art Neville formed his first band, the Hawketts, in the preceding decade and later achieved some success with the soul/funk quartet the Meters, which had backed up brother Aaron on his solo sides and on some records made under the Neville Sounds moniker. The group's debut as the Neville Brothers came out in 1978, after the brothers had gotten together for their uncle George "Big Chief Jolly" Landry's *Wild Tchoupitoulas* project. The Nevilles's following increased during the 1980s, mostly on the strength of the group's fiery live shows. Aaron's success both as a solo artist and in a series of high-profile, Grammy-winning duets with pop singer Linda Ronstadt and country singer Trisha Yearwood brought the group's name to a larger following. Its upbeat, grooving, often syncopated soul and Mardi Gras vibe owe much to the Meters, though the Nevilles streamlined the sound with pop and, of course, Aaron's sweet, soaring pipes.

what to buy: *Treacherous: A History of the Neville Brothers* ♪♪♪♪ (Rhino, 1988, prod. various) is, hands-down, the best collection of the group's strongest work.

Me'Shell Ndegeocello (© Jack Vartoogian)

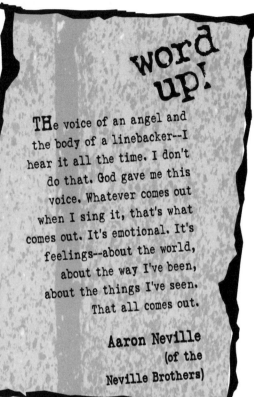

what to buy next: *Yellow Moon* ♪♪♪♪ (A&M, 1989, prod. Daniel Lanois) is an impressive, mature album that boasts a kinetic rendition of Link Wray's "Fire and Brimstone."

what to avoid: On Aaron's *Soulful Christmas* ♪♪ (A&M, 1993, prod. Steve Lindsey), the fine singer makes lite R&B mush of over-recorded seasonal favorites.

the rest:
The Neville Brothers ♪♪♪ (Capitol, 1978)
Fiyo on the Bayou ♪♪♪♪ (A&M, 1981)
Neville-Ization ♪♪♪♪ (Black Top, 1984)
Live at Tipitina's ♪♪♪ (Spindletop, 1985)
Uptown ♪♪♪ (EMI America, 1987)
Brother's Keeper ♪♪♪ (A&M, 1990)
Treacherous Too! ♪♪♪♪ (Rhino, 1991)
Family Groove ♪♪♪ (A&M, 1992)

Ricky Bell (l) and Michael Bivins of New Edition and Bell Biv DeVoe (© Ken Settle)

Live on Planet Earth 🎵🎵🎵 (A&M, 1994)
Mitakuye Oyasin Oyasin (All My Relations) 🎵🎵🎵🎵 (A&M, 1996)

worth searching for: *The Wild Tchoupitoulas* 🎵🎵🎵 (Island, 1976, prod. Allen Toussaint, Marshall Sehorn), the Nevilles's soulful collaboration with their older relatives, mines a soulful vein of Louisiana musical history.

solo outings:
Aaron Neville:
Greatest Hits 🎵🎵🎵 (Curb, 1990)
My Greatest Gift 🎵🎵🎵 (Rounder, 1991)
Warm Your Heart 🎵🎵 (A&M, 1991)
The Grand Tour 🎵🎵 (A&M, 1993)
The Tattooed Heart 🎵🎵🎵 (A&M, 1995)
To Make Me Who I Am 🎵🎵🎵 (A&M, 1997)

Art Neville:
His Specialty Recordings, 1956–58 🎵🎵🎵 (Specialty, 1992)
That Old Time Rock 'n' Roll 🎵🎵🎵 (Specialty, 1993)

Cyril Neville:
Fire This Time 🎵🎵🎵 (Iguana, 1995)

Charles Neville:
(With Songcatchers) *Moving in Color* 🎵🎵🎵🎵 (A&M, 1994)

influences:
◀◀ Mahalia Jackson, Andrae Crouch, Professor Longhair, Ray Charles, Lee Dorsey, the Meters

▶▶ Daniel Lanois, Elton John, Black Crowes, Angelo, Boyz II Men

Simon Glickman

New Edition
Formed 1981, in Boston, MA.

Ralph Tresvant, vocals; Ronnie DeVoe, vocals; Michael Bivins, vocals; Ricky Bell, vocals; Bobby Brown, vocals (1981–86); Johnny Gill, vocals (1986–present).

Bound by friendships forged growing up in one of Boston's more notorious ghettos, New Edition hit the road to stardom when producer/manager Maurice Starr caught the vocal quartet performing at one of his talent shows. Crafting a sound much like a

1980s update of the classic Jackson 5 singles, Starr packaged the group around Tresvant's eerily high, Michael Jackson-style lead vocals. In 1984, the group dumped Starr as manager/producer/Svengali, two years before Bobby Brown left for an uneven solo career. The group floundered for a few years, until Stacy Lattisaw protege Johnny Gill replaced Brown and the group enlisted Janet Jackson producers James "Jimmy Jam" Harris III and Terry Lewis to handle their comeback record—which hinted at the mixture of soul power and hip-hop flavor (also called New Jack Swing) that would fuel each member's future solo success. After a successful fifth record, the group splintered, with Gill, Tresvant, and Brown all scoring major solo hits riding the New Jack wave, while DeVoe, Bivins, and Bell joined forces in Bell Biv DeVoe. But the quickly changing face of contemporary R&B made their late 1980s shtick passe, forcing all of the bandmembers to team up for yet another comeback project in 1996. Though the record debuted at #1, the reunion tour—marred by ego clashes, absences by Brown, the death of Tresvant's mother, and a car accident involving Bivins—raised doubt as to whether this get-together would survive for long.

what to buy: As a group, New Edition's *Heart Break* ♫♫♫♪ (MCA, 1989, prod. James Harris III, Terry Lewis) reveals the talented foursome as an entertaining, aggressive urban vocal quartet. Presaging the fusion of hip-hop fashion with R&B style by years, this record emphasizes lush, percolating soundscapes while giving the best singers in the band—Gill and Tresvant—plenty of room to strut their stuff. On the solo tip, the albums that best took advantage of the New Jack explosion were Brown's *Don't Be Cruel* ♫♫♫♪ (MCA, 1988, prod. Bobby Brown, Antonio "L.A." Reid, Kenneth "Babyface" Edmonds, Gene Griffin, Louil Silas Jr., Larry White, Gordon Jones) and Bell Biv DeVoe's *Poison* ♫♫♫♪ (MCA, 1990, prod. Ricky Bell, Michael Bivins, Ronnie DeVoe, Timmy Gatling, Hank Shocklee, Eric "Vietnam" Sadler, Keith Shocklee, Dr. Freeze, Carl E. Bourelly). Each was loaded with hits, injecting the energy of hip-hop into the smooth tones of mainstream R&B.

what to buy next: As the only record that jams together both their Jackson 5 and New Jack periods, *Greatest Hits, Vol. 1* ♫♫♫ (MCA, 1991, prod. Louil Silas Jr.) offers every notable single from the group's first five albums, including "Cool It Now," "If It Isn't Love," and a new cut, "Boys To Men." Solo-wise, Gill's *Johnny Gill* ♫♫♫ (Motown, 1990, prod. James Harris III, Terry Lewis, Kenneth "Babyface" Edmonds, Antonio "L.A." Reid, Kayo, Daryl Simmons, Nat Adderly Jr., Pebbles, Randy Ron) managed to eke a few hits of its own—"My, My My" and "Fairweather Friend"—while showcasing the singer's gritty, soulful vocals.

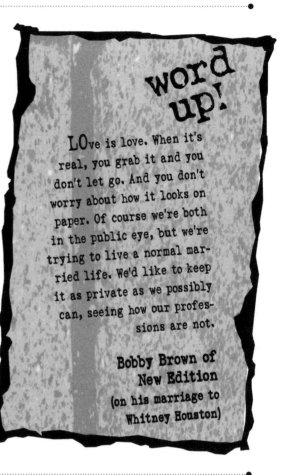

word up!

LOve is love. When it's real, you grab it and you don't let go. And you don't worry about how it looks on paper. Of course we're both in the public eye, but we're trying to live a normal married life. We'd like to keep it as private as we possibly can, seeing how our professions are not.

Bobby Brown of
New Edition
(on his marriage to
Whitney Houston)

what to avoid: These guys could barely handle contemporary soul, so hearing them sing music from the 1950s and 1960s on *Under the Blue Moon* woof! (MCA, 1986, prod. Freddie Perren) is an exercise in endurance. For unintended giggles, listen as they gamely fail to hit the low notes in "Duke of Earl." On the solo front, no New Edition alumnus has yet produced an effort as embarrassing as Brown's *King of Stage* woof! (MCA, 1987, prod. Larry Blackmon), a record so generically toothless it's hard to imagine how his career survived it to get to *Don't Be Cruel.*

the rest:
Candy Girl ♫♫♫ (Streetwise, 1983)
New Edition ♫♫♪ (MCA, 1984)
Christmas All Over the World ♫♫ (MCA, 1985)
All for Love ♫♫♪ (MCA, 1985)
Home Again ♫♫♫ (MCA, 1996)

worth searching for: To actually see the transformation of New Edition from a bunch of parachute pants-wearing, Jhery curl-sporting pre-teens to self-assured, hip-hop-influenced young men, consult the video anthology *Past to Present,* boasting clips from the full length of the group's career.

solo outings:
Bobby Brown:
Dance! . . . Ya Know It! ♫♫♫ (MCA, 1990)
Bobby ♫♫♡ (MCA, 1992)
Forever N/A (MCA, 1997)

Johnny Gill:
Perfect Combination ♫♫♡ (Cotillion, 1983)
Chemistry ♫♫♡ (Atlantic, 1985)
Provocative ♫♫♡ (Motown, 1993)
Let's Get the Mood Right ♫♫♡ (Motown, 1996)
(With Gerald Levert and Keith) *Levert. Sweat. Gill.* N/A (EastWest America, 1997)
Greatest Hits N/A (Motown, 1997)

Ralph Tresvant:
Ralph Tresvant ♫♫♡ (MCA, 1990)
It's Goin' Down ♫♫ (MCA, 1993)

Bell Biv DeVoe:
WBBD—Bootcity! ♫♫♫ (MCA, 1991)
Hootie Mack ♫♫♡ (MCA, 1993)

influences:
◀◀ The Jackson 5, the Four Tops, Janet Jackson
▶▶ H-Town, Solo, New Kids on the Block

Eric Deggans

New Kids on the Block
Formed 1985, in Boston, MA. Disbanded 1994.

Jordan Knight, vocals; Donnie Wahlberg, vocals; Joe McIntyre, vocals; Danny Wood, vocals; Jon Knight, vocals.

There was no middle ground with teen sensations New Kids on the Block during the late 1980s and early 1990s: you either loved 'em or hated 'em. And although prepubescent girls seemed to be the only ones who loved them, that was apparently enough. At its peak, the ubiquitous New Kids had their own line of Hasbro dolls and were named the world's highest-paid entertainers by Forbes, earning $115 million in 1990 and 1991. More a marketing ploy than a musical force, the group was formed and controlled by writer-producer-manager Maurice Starr, who wanted to replace his suddenly departed black teen group, New Edition, with a similar group that would appeal to a broader (read: white) au-

dience. One of his original recruits was Mark Wahlberg, who later decided to pursue a career in rap as Marky Mark instead. However, Wahlberg's brother, Donnie, signed up and was eventually joined by three of his schoolmates (Wood and the Knight brothers) plus McIntyre. The group, which was originally called Nynuk, broke through in 1988 with its chart-topping second album, *Hangin' Tough,* winning over legions of adoring, squealing teenyboppers through boyish looks and hook-laden, R&B-influenced, bubble-gum pop. Its 1990 tour was one of the biggest-grossing in the history of the concert business, bringing in $74.1 million, but the group was greeted with hard skepticism and intense loathing by nearly everybody over the age of 15, particularly pop critics. During the Milli Vanilli scandal, a disgruntled associate producer for the New Kids accused the group of similar fraudulent practices, saying that Starr and his brother did most of the singing on the New Kids' albums. The group eventually appeared on *The Arsenio Hall Show* to sing *a capella* and prove its detractor wrong. After a four-year hiatus from studio work and a split with Starr, the group attempted to reposition itself in 1994 as tougher and more mature, appearing with facial hair and a changed name, NKOTB. But New Kids simply could not shake the past. (Hey, whatever they call themselves, they're still L-A-M-E, said David Letterman.) They broke up later that year.

what to buy: Although it sounds grossly dated now, if you must see what the New Kids fuss was about, the breakthrough *Hangin' Tough ♫♫* (Columbia, 1988, prod. Maurice Starr) is the best place to go with its abundance of hits, including the innocent teen ballads "I'll Be Loving You (Forever)," "Please Don't Go Girl," and the quasi-funk title track, as well as "You Got It (The Right Stuff)" and "Cover Girl."

what to buy next: Hip-hop-informed New Jack production values and tight, layered harmonies make *Face the Music ♫♫♫* (Columbia, 1994, prod. Teddy Riley, Donnie Wahlberg, Narada Michael Walden, Walter Afanasieff) the most current and vibrant-sounding album in the New Kids catalog, although the group's street-style stance is a bit tough to digest after three albums of sugar-sweet pop.

the rest:
New Kids on the Block ♫ (Columbia, 1986)
Merry, Merry Christmas **woof!** (Columbia, 1989)
Step By Step ♫♡ (Columbia, 1990)
No More Games: The Remix Album ♫♡ (Columbia, 1990)

influences:
◀◀ New Edition, Bay City Rollers, the Jackson 5
▶▶ Milli Vanilli, Marky Mark

Josh Freedom du Lac

New Kingdom

Formed 1987.

Sebastian, vocals; Nosaj, vocals.

New Kingdom has barely registered a blip on the hip-hop radar, but that has more to do with the closed minds of the majority of rap fans than it does with the talents of Sebastian and Nosaj (Jason backwards—duh!). Yes, New Kingdom is way out, but an undeniable B-boy mentality races through the duo's psychedelic veins. Sebastian and Jason met while working at a clothing warehouse in Brooklyn, and their mutual love of hip-hop, punk rock, and just about everything else out there drew them into a musical union that reverberates with influences from Jimi Hendrix to the Jungle Brothers to the Misfits.

what to buy: Underneath the thick bass, dusted rhythms, and Sebastian and Jason's scraggly vocal tones, New Kingdom posseses a strong rock 'n' roll aesthetic. The duo's debut, *Heavy Load* 𝅘𝅥𝅮𝅘𝅥𝅮𝅘𝅥𝅮 (Gee Street/Island, 1994, prod. the Lumberjacks, Del Tha Funkee Homosapien) mashes up sample after sample, mixing in live instrumentation with dynamic turntablism. Though most people can get with the instrumentals—especially for the Del-produced "Good Times"—many find the vocals abrasive. Still, this album is adventurous and unapologetically intriguing. (Fans of the Tricky sound should peep "Mighty Maverick").

what to buy next: *Paradise Don't Come Cheap* 𝅘𝅥𝅮𝅘𝅥𝅮𝅘𝅥𝅮 (Gee Street/Island, 1996, prod. the Lumberjacks) is a little more daring—and a little harder to swallow. "Mexico or Bust" fared better with skate and ska kids than hip-hop heads, though, again, there's an underlying element throughout the album that's inviting to old school hip-hop fans.

influences:

◀◀ Del Tha Funkee Homosapien, the Jungle Brothers

▶▶ Tricky

Jazzbo

New Power Generation

Formed 1991, in Minneapolis, MN.

Prince, vocals and all instruments; Rosie Gaines, vocals; Levi Seacer Jr., rhythm guitar; Tommy Barbarella, keyboards; Michael Blands, drums; Sonny T., bass; Kirk Johnson, dancer, percussion; Tony M., rap vocals; Damon Dickson, percussion; Mayte Garcia, tambourine and Egyptian vibe; Torra Torra (a.k.a. Prince, in group's third incarnation from 1993–95), vocals, all instruments; Mr. Hayes, organ (1993–95);

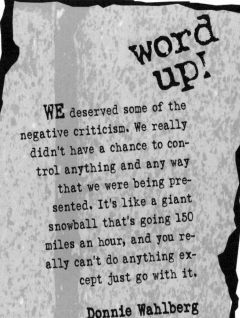

word up!

WE deserved some of the negative criticism. We really didn't have a chance to control anything and any way that we were being presented. It's like a giant snowball that's going 150 miles an hour, and you really can't do anything except just go with it.

**Donnie Wahlberg
(of New Kids
on the Block)**

Rhonda S., bass (1996–present); Karen Dyson, rhythm guitar (1996–present); Eric Leeds, saxophone, flute; the NPG Horns, brass accompaniment.

If Parliament-Funkadelic had a star child, its name would be the New Power Generation. Conceived in a typical burst of creative energy by Prince (before he became The Artist Formerly Known as Same), the NPG was formed from musicians who performed on the soundtrack to his 1990 movie *Graffiti Bridge* primarily as a vehicle for Prince to release his less mainstream material. The new ensemble earned its chops by backing Prince on his 1991 Paisley Park album, *Diamonds and Pearls*. But like Clinton's P-Funk legions, the massive band has more than established an identity of its own despite its constantly changing membership. Even more than Prince's most famous backup band, the Revolution—especially given the fact that the Revolution never recorded a solo album—NPG has made its musical voice heard by giving birth to some of the rawest, nastiest funk any Artist-spinoff group has dropped since the Time unleashed its *What Time Is It?* LP in 1982. Whether you're a true funkateer or merely an F.I.T. (Funkateer In Training), you have to check this band out. Note: virtually all LPs by Prince satellite bands are out of circulation to the general public (except for those releases by the Time) and available only through Prince's 1-800-NEW-FUNK number.

what to buy: You can purchase the NPG's CD single *Good Life* 𝄞𝄞𝄞 (WEA/Warner Bros., 1995, prod. NPG) at your local music shop, but if you venture to order any album over the Funkphone, it must be *Exodus* 𝄞𝄞𝄞𝄞 (Warner Bros./NPG, 1995, prod. NPG). Released only in Europe, *Exodus* is nothing short of a classic P-Funk jam for the millennium, with songs ranging from Motownesque ballads to underground voodoo funk ("The Exodus Has Begun") and hypnotic, psychedelic retro soul ("Hallucination Rain"). Be warned, however, that this LP was made during Prince's bitter feud with Warner Bros., and nearly every song is filled with anger, attitude, and obscenities (even the ballads). This is not an album for the weak of heart.

what to buy next: The sloppy rapping of Tony M. and strained hip-hop efforts like "Call the Law" make *Gold Niggaz* 𝄞𝄞𝄞 (Warner Bros., 1993, prod. NPG) an album that takes time to warm up to, despite the fact that its funk pedigree is undeniably purebred. Truth is, the waiting for the wonderment is the hardest part for most listeners.

influences:

◄◄ The JBs, the Ohio Players, the Time, Parliament-Funkadelic, Prince

►► Mint Condition

see also: *Prince, Rosie Gaines*

Andre McGarrity

Newcleus

Formed 1976, in Brooklyn, NY. Disbanded mid-1980s.

Ben "Cozmo D" Cenad, keyboards, programming, vocals; Bob "Chilly B" Crafton, bass, keyboards, vocals; Yvette Cenad, vocals; Monique Crafton, vocals.

Newcleus may have singlehandedly kept manufacturers of vocorders and other voice manipulation devices in business during the early 1980s, thanks to a batch of singles that featured Bob "Chilly B" Crafton's "munchkin" vocals. Newcleus is the mid-point between Sugarhill Gang and the Prodigy; the quartet—plus additional backing musicians—merged the sensibilities of 1970s funk bands and early rappers with technology-minded production that made use of repeating sonic motifs be-

fore the world came to know them as tape loops. Newcleus came out of the post-disco hip-hop scene, staking out its turf in the parks and block parties of Brooklyn; among their stiffest competition was the duo that would go on to become Whodini. Newcleus had its moment in the sun with "Jam on the Revenge (The Wikki-Wikki Song)," a novelty of sorts that hit #9 on the *Billboard* R&B charts and sold more than 300,000 copies. A handful of other singles and two albums later, however, Newcleus was over, its good-timey funk surpassed by edgier hip-hop stylists. Crafton and Ben "Cozmo D" Cenad continue to work behind the scenes in the music business, and there's even talk of re-forming Newcleus in the near future.

what's available: *Jam on This: The Best of Newcleus* 𝄞𝄞 (Rhino, 1987, prod. various) unfortunately shows Newcleus to be an outfit of little substance. "Jam on the Revenge" is a cute novelty but doesn't have much staying power, and the rest of the songs are equally unmemorable.

influences:

◄◄ Parliament-Funkadelic, Kraftwerk, Afrika Bambaataa, Sugarhill Gang

►► Public Enemy, D.J. Jazzy Jeff & the Fresh Prince, Chemical Brothers, Beck

Gary Graff

Nice & Smooth

Formed late 1980s, in New York City.

Gregg Nice (born Greg Mays), vocals; Smooth Bee (born Darryl Barnes), vocals.

It's not easy to escape the contagious party grooves of Nice & Smooth. The duo's unique blend of hip-hop, soul, and New York City funk long has been a staple for rap connoisseurs of all persuasions. Emerging in the late 1980s, the light-hearted, self-proclaimed hip-hop junkies were able to reach a hip-hop community that needed a license to party after the political exhaustion accompanying groups like Public Enemy. With cheeky samples (the Partridge Family and the Monkees!) and boisterous rhymes that sometimes touched on ghetto survival, Nice & Smooth kept their groove funky, upbeat, and danceable.

what to buy: *Jewel of the Nile* 𝄞𝄞𝄞 (Rush Associated Labels, 1994, prod. Showbiz, others) is a sleek, sometimes silly, endeavor that shows Gregg Nice and Smooth Bee as the out-for-fun MCs that they are. Not shy to experiment, the duo plays with a nursery-rhyme loop and extemporaneous lyrics on "Doin' Our Own Thang" while proving to be "back with a brand new sound" on the horn-driven "Old to the New." Most of the album showcases the seamless way in which the duo swaps verses, although Slick Rick upstages both his hosts on "Let's All Get Down." Worse yet, on "Cheri," Smooth Bee attempts a half-baked ballad, saved only by backup vocals from Jo-Jo of Jodeci.

what to buy next: *Ain't a Damn Thing Changed* ♫♫♫ (Rush Associated Labels, 1991) features the best appropriation of a Tracy Chapman melody in hip-hop history on the "Fast Car"-driving hit "Sometimes I Rhyme Slow."

the rest:
Nice & Smooth ♫♫♫ (Fresh, 1989)

influences:
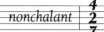 Run-D.M.C., Rob Base and DJ E-Z Rock
▶▶ Black Sheep

Corey Takahashi

Nine
Born September 19, 1969.

Gravel-timbred New York rapper Nine burst onto the hip-hop scene when he dropped ruff verbal ruggedness on Funkmaster Flex's 1993 underground hit, "Six Million Ways to Die." Predictably, the underground buzz lead to a deal for Nine, who takes his name from his birthdate (9/19/1969).

what's available: The New York-centric production on *Nine Livez* ♫♫ (Profile, 1995, prod. Rob Lewis, others) is solid, and Nine's got the lyrics; but his scratchy voice eventually wears you out. Still, there are a few bright moments ("Da Fundamentalz," "Fo' Eva Blunted"), and "Whutcha Want?" is a catchy, rugged gem of a hit single, what with its taut snares, rumbling bass, '70s strings, and a shouted chorus that's punctuated by *I Dream of Jeannie*-type horns and turntable scratches. On *Cloud 9* ♫♫♫ (Profile, 1996, prod. Rob Lewis, others), producer Lewis elevates the sonic backdrop, favoring strings and twisted classical elements, and Nine's vocals are smoother, burbling over the lush tracks like lukewarm lava. The fluttering strings and eerie vibes on "Tha Product" and Nine's flow over the chamber orchestration of "Uncivilized" are simply brilliant.

worth searching for: The import 12-inch of "Wutcha Want?" (Profile, 1995) contains several moody reworkings of Nine's hit. Foremost among them is the Portishead mix, by the acclaimed British trip-hop group.

influences:
◀◀ Busta Rhymes, KRS-One, Method Man, Onyx

Spence D.

The Nonce
Formed in Los Angeles, CA.

Nouka Base, vocals; Yusef Afloat, vocals.

Two veterans of South Central's Good Life Cafe scene, Nouka Base and Yusef Afloat made their debut on the fabled underground compilation *Project Blowed* (which starred the Freestyle Fellowship) just as they were being signed to Wild West Records. Their understated rhymes and spare but warm textures provided a compelling alternative to the Hollywoodized big-screen version of gangsta rap that was simultaneously making its way up the charts.

what's available: *World Ultimate* ♫♫♫ (Wild West, 1993, prod. the Nonce) captures the muted ambition of the Los Angeles underground, a scene borne in the same streets as the G-funk of Domino or Warren G, but with much different aims. Where the G-funksters went for champagne-sweet crossover indulgence, the freestylers celebrated competition and asceticism. Where G-funksters partied like it was 1999, the freestylers struggled for recognition. *World Ultimate* is full of nostalgia for simpler days in the "Bus Stops," "Eighty Five," and "Mix Tapes," but there's also the confrontation of the hard realities of the rappin' biz in "On the Road Again." Ultimately, the gentility of Nouka and Yusef make the burden easy to bear, bringing the listener a memorable and lingering look into the process of B-boys growing into men.

influences:
◀◀ Freestyle Fellowship, Native Tongues

Jeff "DJ Zen" Chang

Nonchalant
Born Tanya Pointer, in Washington, DC.

Nonchalant's decision to rap about community issues and relationships—rather than Versace and one-night stands—is no small step, given the current hip-hop Zeitgeist. In an era of microphone sexpots (see Lil' Kim and Foxy Brown), artists like Nonchalant have a hard time getting respect, not to mention recording contracts. It's an unfortunate fact because, although Nonchalant can sound like a street-edged high school principal, she also is a down-to-earth rapper fit to inspire the young. In honest terms she lays out her goals, rapping: "I'm not here to scold but rather shape and mold the young black mind." Equally responsible when talking about romance, she stands in contrast to her peers' polished hedonism and materialistic values.

what's available: *Until the Day* ♫♫♫ (MCA, 1996, prod. various) is a consistent mix of positive lyrics packaged in street-pop beats. Nonchalant's controlled lyrical skills give her authority, while her play with street vernacular presents a sassy side. If songs like "Crab Rappers" sound more like cheers at a pep rally than qualified raps, "Lights N' Sirens" and "5 O'Clock" are real enough, denouncing drug dealers, abusive police officers, and other urban tyrants not held accountable for their actions.

influences:

◀◀ Queen Latifah, MC Lyte

Corey Takahashi

Notorious B.I.G.

Born Christopher Wallace, May 21, 1972, in Brooklyn, NY. Died March 9, 1997, in Los Angeles, CA.

Hip-hop may have been born and raised in New York, but for several post-N.W.A. years, the faraway West Coast was the genre's commercial center, with California rappers from Ice Cube and Dr. Dre to 2Pac and Snoop Doggy Dogg earning more attention and, of course, money than their Rotten Apple counterparts. In 1993 and 1994, though, a new wave of New York MCs helped shift the spotlight back to the East by ending the left coast's commercial domination of rap. Leading the charge was Notorious B.I.G., a 6-foot-3, 300-(or-so)-pound former drug dealer with a big, booming, marble-mouthed voice who first appeared on the Mary J. Blige album *What's the 411?—The Remixes*. Although B.I.G.'s first three big singles of his own were the gold-selling daydream "Juicy" and the platinum loverman-hustler anthems "Big Poppa" and "One More Chance," other songs on his debut, *Ready to Die*, were less happy, covering everything from stickups to beat-downs while also exploring B.I.G.'s rare-for-rap feelings of vulnerability and self-worthlessness. On the closing track, "Suicidal Thoughts," B.I.G. even commits suicide after declaring "When I die, fuck it, I wanna go to hell/'Cause I'm a piece of shit, it ain't hard to fuckin' tell" and noting that "my mother wish she got a fuckin' abortion." The confused, thumping, occasionally tortured album became a critical and commercial smash, one of New York rap's first multimillion-sellers in several years. Following the success of his debut, B.I.G. never left the spotlight, making high-profile appearances on hit albums by everybody from Total, 112, and Jay-Z to Junior M.A.F.I.A., R. Kelly, and Michael Jackson. He also made headlines as one of the key players in the media-driven East-West rap rivalry, which heated up after his former friend 2Pac accused him of being somehow involved in a shooting and robbery of 2Pac in New York in 1994. Anticipation of B.I.G.'s sophomore album, *Life After Death*, was high, but soared through the roof when the rapper was murdered outside of a music-industry party in Los Angeles shortly before the record's release. Eerily, the double-album featured grainy photos of B.I.G. standing in a graveyard and, as with the debut, showed a rapper who was obsessed with his own death. But the chart-topping, slickly produced album was generally much happier in tone than *Ready to Die*, with B.I.G. no longer dreaming about success (a la "Juicy"), but celebrating it. Although the recording closed with the bitter (and ironic) "You're Nobody (Til Somebody Kills You)," B.I.G. had known otherwise, becoming one of the most celebrated and successful rap stars of the 1990s while earning a spot in the genre's history books as one of the key players in the resurgence of New York rap.

what to buy: *Ready to Die* ♪♪♪♪ (Bad Boy/Arista, 1994, prod. Easy Mo Bee, Sean "Puffy" Combs, DJ Premier, Lord Finesse, others) is a conflicted, emotionally rich, beat-driven recording that opens with birth and ends with B.I.G.'s self-inflicted death. In between, B.I.G. explores rough life on the streets ("Warning," "Gimme the Loot," "Everyday Struggle," the title track) while also taking pause to, um, celebrate women ("Me & My Bitch," "One More Chance") and reminisce about his days as a young rap fan who dreamed of one day achieving superstardom ("Juicy"). Mission accomplished.

what to avoid: On the posthumously released *Life After Death* ♪♪♪ (Bad Boy/Arista, 1997, prod. Sean "Puffy" Combs, RZA, DJ Premier, Easy Mo Bee, Buckwild, Havoc, Clark Kent, others), B.I.G. appears to be obsessed with providing something for everybody, wandering all over the thematic and stylistic map with his lyrics and backing himself with production that ranges from radio-friendly, sample-driven hip-pop ("Mo Money Mo Problems," which borrows heavily from Diana Ross) to gritty New York minimalism (courtesy of Wu-Tang's RZA). The album has its moments, for sure, but success seems to have spoiled B.I.G., as the album is missing much of the tension and tough self-questioning that made *Ready to Die* so vital.

influences:

◀◀ 2Pac, Dr. Dre, Kool G Rap

▶▶ Puff Daddy, Foxy Brown, Jay-Z, Lil' Kim/Junior M.A.F.I.A., Shaquille O'Neal

Josh Freedom du Lac

N.W.A.

Formed 1986, in Compton, CA. Disbanded 1991.

Eazy-E, vocals; Ice Cube, vocals (1986–90); Dr. Dre, vocals, producer; DJ Yella, vocals, DJ; M.C. Ren, vocals.

Although the pages of hip-hop's still-brief history book are littered with so-called major turning points and seminal albums, there is little doubt that N.W.A.'s *Straight Outta Compton* in 1989 deserves its spot in rap history as one of the most important, influential, and essential recordings ever. None of the gangsta rap artists who preceded N.W.A. (Ice-T, Schoolly D, or even Boogie Down Productions) packed the punch on their recordings that *Straight Outta Compton* did. Full of violent, angry, misogynistic lyrics that were neatly garnished with attractive rhythms and rolling basslines, the album painted a disturbing—but generally realistic and undoubtedly well-crafted—portrait of inner-city street (or "gangsta") life in South Central, Los Angeles. The stark content of *Straight Outta Compton*—which offered brutal tales of street warfare, drug use, womanizing, and anti-establishment and anti-police uprisings—shocked the unsuspecting mainstream and whipped up a firestorm of controversy. The FBI's assistant director for public affairs even wrote a letter to N.W.A.'s record label, saying that "advocating violence and assault is wrong, and we in the law enforcement community take exception to such action." Not since the early days of punk had music appeared so dangerous. Despite a decided lack of radio exposure, *Straight Outta Compton* found a broad audience, selling more than two million copies (including many in suburban America) and paving the multiplatinum way for future gangsta rap artists from Snoop Doggy Dogg and Tupac Shakur to Notorious B.I.G. and Bone Thugs-N-Harmony. In a genre that has historically refused to sit still, plowing through sounds, styles, and lyrical bents with stunning regularity, gangsta rap has managed not only to endure, but it's become rap's most commercially successful subgenre. If it wasn't for N.W.A., mainstream America probably would never have discovered gangsta rap. It may not have realized, either, that there were artists outside of New York making vital rap music. *Straight Outta Compton* caused a seismic shift in the hip-hop landscape that is still producing aftershocks. But the group slid straight downhill after *Straight Outta Compton*. Shortly after that album came out, N.W.A.'s most talented writer and lyricist, Ice Cube, left in a bitter dispute, creating a huge void that was apparent on N.W.A.'s next release, 1990's *100 Miles and Runnin'*. With Cube gone, Eazy-E's whiny, high-pitched voice now dominated. The result was grating. The disappointing EP, which pushed the group into a misogynistic rut, was actually a sign of things to come. When 1991's *Efil4Zaggin* (*Niggaz4Life*, in reverse) came out, it was clear that N.W.A. no longer made music that mattered. The album said everything about gangsta life that N.W.A. had said before—only this time, it didn't sound frightening. It sounded more like a joke. Still, *Efil4Zaggin* sold nearly a million copies

during its first few weeks of release and became the first hardcore rap album ever to top the *Billboard* Top 200. The group celebrated its success by breaking up.

what to buy: OK, so maybe Ice Cube was oversimplifying things a bit when he declared that "life ain't nothing but bitches and money." On *Straight Outta Compton* 🎵🎵🎵🎵 (Ruthless, 1989, prod. Dr. Dre, Yella), life's also about raging against the machine and offering a thrilling peak at the gangsta lifestyle via songs like "Fuck Tha Police" and "Gangsta Gangsta," which are both thrilling and terrifying on the lyrical front but somehow alluring on the musical end. And in the end, here, it's either comforting or totally disturbing to note that N.W.A. can go through such a furious song cycle and then party it all off with the closing "Something 2 Dance 2."

what to avoid: The EP *100 Miles and Runnin'* **woof!** (Priority, 1990) is thankfully out of print. How the group could follow the brilliantly visceral *Straight Outta Compton* with such a flat, lazy-sounding, sex-obsessed dud is a mystery—until you remember that Cube had already left the building. If you see *100 Miles and Runnin'* in a record store, run the other way.

the rest:
N.W.A. and the Posse 🎵🎵🎵 (Macola/Priority, 1987)
Efil4Zaggin 🎵🎵 (Ruthless/Priority, 1991)
Greatest Hits 🎵🎵🎵🎵 (Ruthless, 1996)

solo outings:

M.C. Ren:
Kizz My Black Azz 🎵🎵 EP (Priority, 1992)
Shock of the Hour 🎵🎵🎵 (Ruthless/Relativity, 1993)
The Villain In Black 🎵🎵 (Ruthless/Relativity, 1996)

Yella:
One Mo Nigga Ta Go 🎵🎵 (Scotti Brothers, 1996)

influences:
◀◀ Watts Prophets, Ice-T, Uncle Jamm's Army, World Class Wreckin' Cru, Boogie Down Productions, Rakim

▶▶ All gangsta rappers

see also: *Dr. Dre, Ice Cube, Eazy-E*

Josh Freedom du Lac

Laura Nyro

Born Laura Nigro, October 18, 1947, in the Bronx, NY. Died April 8, 1997, in Danbury, CN.

One of the best and brightest songwriters of the late 1960s, Nyro is essential listening for anyone seeking out the roots of rock's singer-songwriter movement. Nyro was a mere 18 years old when she recorded her first album, *More Than a New Discovery*, a remarkable debut that showcased her prodigious musical talent and gutsy, swooping voice. Throughout a 30-year career, Nyro has written and released a sterling catalog of angst-bearing, confessional music inflected with R&B, soul, and gospel touches. While she has had only one recording reach the Top 100 (her cover of the Drifters' "Up on the Roof" in 1970), her own songs have been major hits for artists such as Barbra Streisand ("Stoney End"), the 5th Dimension ("Wedding Bell Blues"), Blood, Sweat & Tears ("And When I Die"), and Three Dog Night ("Eli's Coming"). With her 1971 album *Gonna Take a Miracle*, Nyro became one of the first rock-era songwriters to release an album of cover material in tribute to past mentors. Tragically, Nyro died from ovarian cancer at the age of 49, just as new compilation and tribute albums were signalling revived interest in her artistry.

what to buy: *The Best of Laura Nyro: Stoned Soul Picnic* ♪♪♪♪ (Sony/Legacy, 1997, prod. various) offers a good point of entry into Nyro's considerable and diverse catalog. True to its name, the two-CD set is a well-stocked portfolio of her strongest and most eclectic material. Those wishing to dive deeply into Nyro's emotional netherlands should check out *The First Songs* ♪♪♪♪♪ (Columbia, 1973, prod. Milton Okun), Nyro's stellar debut which was recorded when she was all of 18. Featuring numerous songs that later became hits for other artists ("Wedding Bell Blues," "And When I Die," "Flim Flam Man," and "Stoney End"), the album spins out a continuous stream of first-class, introspective music. Another bona fide classic. *New York Tendaberry* ♪♪♪♪♪ (Columbia, 1969, prod. Laura Nyro, Roy Halee) is the culmination of the style Nyro began developing on her debut, a dramatic *noir* journey through love and its loss. Supporting her expressive vocal work with piano and delicate instrumental accompaniment, Nyro explores a vast spectrum of human emotions with music that memorably touches the core of expression.

what to buy next: *Eli & the 13th Confession* ♪♪♪♪ (Sony, 1968, prod. Charlie Calello, Laura Nyro) is a mini-progression from *The First Songs*. Nyro is more soulful and more introspective, presenting a stellar collection of memorable songs that range from R&B ("Stoned Soul Picnic") to gospel ("Poverty Train") and powerful ballads ("Lonely Women"). Nyro changed the pace on her fourth album, *Gonna Take a Miracle* ♪♪♪♪ (Sony, 1971, prod. Kenny Gamble, Leon Huff), teaming with soul-funk group La-Belle for joyful and inspired readings of 1960s R&B hits such as "Jimmy Mack," "Spanish Harlem," and "Nowhere to Run."

what to avoid: Although Nyro's work can never be considered weak, *Mother's Spiritual* ♪♪ (Line, 1984, prod. Laura Nyro) is not among her best works. The urgent passion of her earlier music is replaced here by a cooler, more politically attuned sensibility that's respectable but not compelling.

the rest:
Smile ♪♪♪ (Sony, 1976)
Season of Lights ♪♪♪♪ (Columbia, 1977)
Live at the Bottom Line ♪♪♪ (Cypress, 1990)
Walk the Dog & Light the Light ♪♪♪ (Columbia, 1993)

worth searching for: Given Nyro's considerable influence on contemporary female artists, it only seems fitting that 14 of them (including Suzanne Vega, Rosanne Cash, Phoebe Snow, and Jonatha Brooke) should pay her tribute with *Time and Love: The Music of Laura Nyro* ♪♪♪ (Astor Place, 1997, prod. Peter Gallway). Recorded just prior to Nyro's death, the album reinterprets her best-known songs in rock, country, blues, and spoken-word. Few of the entries are as compelling as the originals, but anyone looking for fellowship in Nyro devotion should look no further than here.

influences:

◄◄ Joan Baez, Leonard Cohen, Bob Dylan, LaBelle, Carole King, Judy Collins, Joni Mitchell, Aretha Franklin

►► Todd Rundgren, Barbra Streisand, Carole King, the 5th Dimension, Blood, Sweat & Tears, Randy Newman, Rickie Lee Jones, Carly Simon, Chaka Khan, Des'ree, Alanis Morissette, Sarah McLachlan, Fiona Apple, Joan Osborne

Christopher Scapelliti

O'Bryan

Born O'Bryan Burnett II, 1961, in Sneads Ferry, NC.

Just a gigolo, just a gigolo. . . . O'Bryan Burnett was almost just "The Gigolo," his 1982 hit that was all the rage in 1982, when disco and New Wave were vying for the attention (and money) of the masses. But he managed to produce a series of R&B chart hits, including "I'm Freaky" and "Lovelite." O'Bryan had moved from North Carolina to Southern California and was singing in a choir when he met Ron Kersey, a Philadelphia International veteran who was forming a new group on the left coast. That didn't work out, but Kersey introduced O'Bryan to *Soul Train* host Don Cornelius, who recommended the singer to Capitol Records. O'Bryan stayed there through the late 1980s and hasn't been heard from since.

what's available: *The Best of O'Bryan* 🎵🎵🎵 (The Right Stuff, 1996, prod. various) is all that's in print, but it does show O'Bryan had more to offer than "The Gigolo." Had he come along during the 1970s rather than the rock- and pop-oriented early 1980s, he might have made a greater impact.

influences:

◀◀ Prince, Atlantic Starr, Midnight Starr, the Brothers Johnson

▶▶ Terence Trent D'Arby, Bobby Brown, Tevin Campbell

Gary Graff

O.C.

"Of course we got to pay rent, so money connects/But I'd rather be broke and have a whole lot of respect." With lines like these from his first single, "Time's Up," it's easy to see how O.C. was anointed posterchild for hip-hop purists everywhere. While many artists vocalized their desires for money and material goods, O.C. talked the good talk, rapping about integrity, principle, and personal triumphs. Prophetically, however, the former plumbing student's steadfast words earned him massive amounts of respect, but little financial fortitude. Still, rich with highly regarded hip-hop friends, O.C., who considers both Queens and Brooklyn home, recently helped form the Diggin' in the Crates Crew with Diamond D, Show and A.G., Lord Finesse, Fat Joe, Buckwild, and Big L. The crew independently released a single ("Day One") in early 1997, with an EP expected in the summer and an album by fall.

what to buy: O.C. got his first start with his mentor-friends Organized Konfusion, who featured him on their song "Fudge Pudge." It took O.C. about a year to complete his own debut single, "Time's Up," and the Buckwild-produced beat was originally meant to be used by Organized Konfusion; but when all was said, done, and rapped, the manifesto became a classic. The rest of O.C.'s album, *Word Life* 🎵🎵🎵🎵 (Wild Pitch/EMI, 1994, prod. Buckwild, Organized Konfusion, Lord Finesse), showcases his reflective, emotionally rich lyricism more, with compositions that are deeply personal. The sincerity and exposed artistic risk are the biggest reasons O.C. endeared himself to his fans.

what to buy next: On *Jewelz* 🎵🎵🎵 (Payday, 1997, prod. DJ Premier, Lord Finesse, Da Beatminerz, others), all seems to be forgotten. O.C.'s focus on his rhyming swagger and ability to rock parties with the cadence of his voice (as on "Dangerous" and "My World") now take precedence over anything else espoused on his debut. For the first time, O.C. has exposed some creative weaknesses. Still, it's hard to hate him, since few MCs possess his command on the mic.

worth searching for: The otherwise gluttonous soundtrack to *New Jersey Drive* (Tommy Boy, 1994) includes "You Won't Go Far," a collaboration between O.C. and Organized Konfusion.

influences:

◀◀ Organized Konfusion, Lord Finesse, Gang Starr

Jazzbo

Billy Ocean

Born Leslie Sebastian Charles, January 21, 1950, in Trinidad.

Billy Ocean was a hitmaker in England before he landed on U.S. shores in 1984 with his Top 10 single "Caribbean Queen (No More Love on the Run)." It began an impressive run as he garnered six more Top 10 hits during the next four years. His albums are best remembered for their hits, however, not for the adjoining tracks. That's a pity, since Ocean produced some seamless recordings, deftly incorporating soul, pop, and dance material into each. His knack for crossover success made him a bigger star in pop than R&B, but during the 1990s he seems to have pulled a disappearing act. With his talent and soulful, expressive voice, don't count him out.

what to buy: *Greatest Hits* 🎵🎵🎵 (Jive, 1989, prod. various) includes all of them—his lovely and passionate ballad "What Is the Color of Love," his pumped-up dance track "Get Outta My Dreams, Get Into My Car," and his huge soundtrack hit "When the Going Gets Tough, the Tough Get Going," plus a couple of new tracks.

the rest:

Nights (Feel Like Getting Down) 🎵🎵 (Epic, 1981)
Suddenly 🎵🎵🎵 (Jive, 1984)
Love Zone 🎵🎵 (Jive, 1986)
Tear Down These Walls 🎵 (Jive, 1988)

influences:

◀◀ Bob Marley, Desmond Dekker, Sam Cooke, Lionel Richie

▶▶ Maxwell, Eric Benet, Julian Marley, Damian Marley

Patrick McCarty

O.G.C. (Originoo Gun Clappaz)

Formed in Brooklyn, NY.

Starang Wondah, vocals; Louieville Sluggah, vocals; Top Dog Da Big Kahuna, vocals.

As the fourth crew to emerge from the Boot Camp Clik collective, the Originoo Gun Clappaz serve up the sort of duck-down mellow madness that can only come from denizens of Crooklyn, New York.

what's available: With the release of *Da Storm* ♫♫♫♪ (Priority, 1996, prod. DJ Evil D, Mr. Walt, Buckshot, others), the O.G.C. solidified the Boot Camp Clik's status as one of hip-hop's most formidable regimes, rivaled only by the Wu-Tang Clan and E-40's Sick Wid' It posse in terms of sheer output. Boot Camp drill sergeant and former Black Moon leader Buckshot proves that he's as adept behind the boards as he is on the mic with his bass-heavy production work on "God Don't Like Ugly," and knob-twisters Mr. Walt and DJ Evil D add some productive sparkle of their own on "Hurricane Starang" and the title track, respectively. Among the album's more gleefully stormy tracks is "Wild Cowboys In Bucktown," in which Brand Nubian's Sadat X pits his piercing nasal voice against the O.G.C.'s low-end flow.

influences:

◄◄ Black Moon, EPMD, Gang Starr, Heltah Skeltah, Smif-N-Wessun

Spence D.

The Ohio Players

Formed 1969, in Dayton, OH.

Leroy "Sugar" Bonner, guitar, vocals; James "Diamond" Williams, drums, percussion (1974–present); Marvin Pierce, trumpet (1972–80); Billy Beck, keyboards (1974–88); Clarence "Satch" Satchell, saxes (1972–80); Marshall "Rock" Jones, bass (1968–80); Ralph "Pee Wee" Middlebrooks, trombone, trumpet (1968–80); Walter "Junie" Morrison, keyboards (1970–74); Greg Webster, drums (1968–74); Clarence "Chet" Willis, rhythm guitar, vocals (1974–present); Robert "Kuumba" Jones, percussion (1988–present); Darwin Dortch, bass, vocals (1988–present).

Created as an instrumental group, the Ohio Players started as the Ohio Untouchables before lucking into a stint backing the Falcons (with lead singer Wilson Pickett) during 1962. Though they were recording on their own that year, it took them until the early 1970s to make their mark—fusing hardcore funk sensibility with Sly Stone-style adventurousness to create ambi-tious, fun funk such as the singles "Funky Worm," "Fire," and "Love Rollercoaster." Once they had moved from the Westbound record label to Mercury, their hitmaking career began in earnest. Chart-toppers like "Fire," "Skin Tight," and "Love Rollercoaster" came during this time, along with a string of outrageous album covers featuring scantily-clad women (for the *Honey* album, the woman was draped only in honey, and so on) that made the band R&B stars. But as disco began to push out the classic funk bands, the Players' albums became increasingly more predictable. Hoping to ride out the disco craze, they attempted to change their sound to meet the new commercial priorities and only succeeded in killing the band's career. A shadow version of the band released forgettable records for obscure labels through most of the 1980s, while Williams, Willis, and Beck formed the band Shadow. A 1988 "reunion" with Williams and Willis produced an uninspired album; another eight years would pass before the Players would record their first-ever live album—which also vanished from the R&B charts without a trace.

what to buy: To collect their greatest triumphs in one basket, *Ohio Players Gold* ♫♫♫♫ (Mercury, 1976, prod. the Ohio Players) does the trick nicely. Serving as a compilation of tracks from the band's most successful and best-constructed records—*Skin Tight*, *Fire*, and *Honey*—this collection of unforgettable tracks, from "Sweet Sticky Thing" to the ballad "I Want to Be Free," offers a compelling view of the band's best work ever.

what to buy next: You can't do better than the albums themselves, including *Skin Tight* ♫♫♫♫ (Mercury, 1974, prod. the Ohio Players) and *Honey* ♫♫♫♫ (Mercury, 1975, prod. the Ohio Players)—records chock full of nasty funk grooves and slick, emotive soul ballads. Each album has its own special charms, but both are also R&B classics that will remain notable for years to come.

what to avoid: Released after the band had officially broken up, *Jass-Ay-La-Dee* (Mercury, 1978, prod. the Ohio Players) was their worst album in a string of late 1970s mishaps that led to the group's decline. Filled with uninspired songs and shameless trend-hopping, this record shows the awful fate that befell some funk bands who dared try competing with disco.

the rest:

Pain ♫♫♫ (Westbound, 1972)
Ectasy ♫♫♪ (Westbound, 1973)
Pleasure ♫♫♫♪ (Westbound, 1973)
Climax ♫♫♪ (Westbound, 1974)
Rattlesnake ♫♫♪ (Westbound, 1976)
Contradiction ♫♫♪ (Mercury, 1976)

Mr. Mean 🎵🎵 (Mercury, 1977)
Angel 🎵🎵 (Mercury, 1977)
Ohio Players 🎵🎵🎵 (Trip, 1977)
Everybody Up 🎵🎵 (Arista, 1979)
Young and Ready 🎵🎵 (Accord, 1980)
Tenderness 🎵🎵 (Boardwalk, 1981)
Ouch 🎵🎵 (Boardwalk, 1982)
Graduation 🎵 (Boardwalk, 1983)
Back 🎵🎵 (Track, 1988)
Orgasm: The Very Best of the Westbound Years 🎵🎵🎵 (Westbound, 1993)
Funk On Fire: The Mercury Anthology 🎵🎵🎵🎵 (Mercury, 1995)
School 🎵🎵🎵 (Intersound, 1996)
Jam 🎵🎵🎵 (Mercury, 1996)

worth searching for: Check out the future Ohio Players backing Wilson Pickett and the Falcons on that group's seminal recording "I found a Love," which kicks off the Pickett compilation *A Man and a Half* 🎵🎵🎵🎵🎵 (Rhino/Atlantic and Atco Remasters, prod. various).

solo outings:
Leroy "Sugar" Bonner:
Sugar 🎵🎵 (Warner Bros., 1985)

Shadow:
Love Lite 🎵🎵 (Elektra, 1979)
Shadow 🎵🎵🎵 (Elektra, 1980)
Shadow in the Streets 🎵🎵 (Elektra, 1981)

influences:
◀◀ Sly & the Family Stone, the Bar-Kays, the JBs, the Isley Brothers

▶▶ Cameo, Guy, the Time, Prince, 2 Live Crew

Eric Deggans

The O'Jays

Formed 1958, in Canton, OH.

Bobby Massey, vocals (1958–72); Walter Williams, vocals; Eddie Levert, vocals; Bill Isles, vocals (1958–65); William Powell, vocals (1958–76); Sammy Strain, vocals (1976–91); Nathaniel Best, vocals (1991–93).

During the early 1970s, waves of jittery, almost paranoid R&B music could be heard from car radios throughout America. Like Stevie Wonder and Sly Stone, the O'Jays made twitchy crossover hits—such as "Backstabbers"—that enjoyed success in the same marketplace that inspired the material. During the group's peak years (1972–78), it managed the trick of crafting socially conscious songs you could dance to, culminating in a staggering eight #1 singles. Smooth harmonies, augmented

by Levert's impassioned growls and the high-powered production of Gamble and Huff, earmark the group's heyday. Unlike many of their peers, the O'Jays have remained intact, releasing engaging albums throughout the 1980s and into the 1990s, touring often with Levert's sons Gerald and Sean and their group, Levert.

what to buy: *Back Stabbers* 🎵🎵🎵🎵 (Philadelphia International, 1972/Legacy, 1996 prod. Kenny Gamble, Leon Huff, comp. Leo Sacks) is the band at its most searing. A complex document of groove-laced R&B that features its two best songs, "Backstabbers," a slinky finger-pointer, and the rolling joy of the album closer "Love Train." *Love Train: The Best of the O'Jays* 🎵🎵🎵🎵 (Epic/Legacy, 1994, prod. Kenny Gamble, Leon Huff, comp. Leo Sacks) is a concise but meaty intro for the uninitiated. Several of their inspirational singles, culled from the glory years, are here, making for a barrel-chested overview of Philly soul.

what to buy next: *Give the People What They Want* 🎵🎵🎵🎵 (Epic/Legacy, 1995, prod. Kenny Gamble, Leon Huff, comp. Leo Sacks) delivers a street-shuffle of 11 politically minded tracks from the 1970s. The slower paced sizzle makes it the next logical step from *Love Train*.

what to avoid: *Serious* 🎵🎵 (EMI America, 1989) is not worthless, but the dabbling with New Jack production may shock the unprepared.

the rest:
In Philadelphia 🎵🎵🎵 (Philadelphia International, 1969/Legacy, 1994)
Ship Ahoy 🎵🎵🎵🎵 (Philadelphia International/CBS, 1973)
Survival 🎵🎵🎵🎵 (Columbia, 1975) (cassette only)
Family Reunion 🎵🎵🎵 (Philadelphia International/CBS, 1975)
Message in the Music 🎵🎵🎵 (Philadelphia International, 1976/The Right Stuff, 1993)
So Full of Love 🎵🎵🎵 (Philadelphia International, 1978/The Right Stuff, 1993)
Collector's Items 🎵🎵🎵 (Philadelphia International, 1978/CBS, 1989)
Love Fever 🎵🎵🎵 (Philadelphia International/CEMA Special Products, 1985)
Greatest Hits 🎵🎵🎵 (Columbia, 1989)
Home for Christmas 🎵🎵 (EMI America, 1991)
Emotionally Yours 🎵🎵🎵 (EMI America, 1991)
Heartbreaker 🎵🎵🎵 (EMI America, 1993)
From the Beginning 🎵🎵🎵🎵 (MCA Special Products, 1994)
Let Me Make Love to You 🎵🎵🎵🎵 (Epic/Legacy, 1995)
In Bed with the O'Jays 🎵🎵 (EMI, 1996)
Love You to Tears 🎵🎵🎵 (Global Soul/Volcano, 1997)

influences:
◀◀ The Mascots, the Drifters, Sam Cooke, Jackie Wilson

▶▶ The Spinners, Isley Jasper Isley, Boyz II Men, Keith Sweat, New Edition, Levert

see also: *Levert*

Allan Orski

Ol' Dirty Bastard
See: Wu-Tang Clan

One Way
/Alicia Myers
Formed 1979, in Detroit, MI.

Al Hudson, vocals; Dave Roberson, guitar, keyboards, vocals; Kevin McCord, bass, vocals (1979–84); Alicia Myers, vocals (1979–80); Leroy Hyter, keyboards (1979–80); Greg Green, drums (1979–85); Brenda Wiley, vocals (1979); Jonathan "Corky" Meadows, keyboards (1980–present); Cortez Harris, guitar, vocals (1980–83); Denise Cleveland, vocals (1980); Candyce Edwards, vocals (1981–84); John Brooks, percussion, vocals (1983); Jack Hall, keyboards (1983); Tony Lippitt, vocals (1985–86); Curtis Dudley, bass (1985–86); Ewana Wilson, vocals (1985); Valdez Brantley, keyboards (1986); Jeanette Mack, vocals (1986); Cliff Stevens, drums (1986); Yasmina Tiku, vocals (1986); Lori Tice, vocals (1988).

One Way emerged from the remnants of the 1970s group Al Hudson & the Soul Partners. Formed by a trio of childhood friends (Hudson, Dave Roberson, and Kevin McCord), One Way produced 11 albums during the 1980s that provided proof that quality R&B was coming out of post-Motown Detroit. One Way took James Brown-style grooves and added ballad-friendly harmonies to achieve a unique balance between a group that could funk with Rick James and doo-wop with the O'Jays. Its 1979 debut has the hit singles "Now That I've Found You" and the disco hit "You Can Do It." Hudson's voice is best described as having a range from a rappin' baritone to an anguished tenor. His falsetto stands out on tunes such as "Something in the Past," "My Lady," and the 1982 smash "Cutie Pie," though his tenor makes him sound like a totally different vocalist on hits such as "Now That I've Found You," "Don't Think about It," and "Pop It." After "Cutie Pie"— from One Way's top-selling album *Who's Foolin Who*—won the group a larger audience, its successor, 1984's *Lady*, was #1 on the *Billboard* R&B chart for three weeks before it was knocked out by Prince's *Purple Rain*. Subsequently the group went through numerous personnel changes, and although there were more hit singles to follow, it never equaled those

successes. The title of 1988's *A New Beginning* was ironic, since it turned out to be One Way's last album. Alicia Myers, who sang on One Way's first two albums, had moderate success but seemed to be a victim of bad timing. Just as Myers began to make her mark, another Detroiter, Anita Baker, broke out with her *Rapture* album. It seemed there was only room enough for one Detroit diva at that time, and Baker exploded while Myers seemed to fade.

what to buy: *The Best of One Way featuring Al Hudson and Alicia Myers* ♪♪♪♪ (MCA, 1996, prod. various) is a well-chosen collection, though only one song features Myers with the band—there are, however, two of her solo selections and one by Al Hudson & the Soul Partners.

the rest:
Cutie Pie ♪♪♪ (MCA Special Products)

worth searching for: Myers's first solo album, *Alicia Myers* ♪♪♪ (MCA, 1981, prod. Kevin McCord) contains her biggest hits, "I Want to Thank You" and "If You Play Your Cards Right." One Way's *Who's Foolin' Who* ♪♪♪♪ (MCA, 1982, prod. ADK, Irene Perkins) was the group's largest-selling album, with "Cutie Pie" and the title track among its standouts.

influences:
◀◀ James Brown, Al Green, the Ohio Players, Frankie Beverly & Maze

Jonathan "Corky" Meadows and Gary Graff

Alexander O'Neal
Born November 15, 1953, in Natchez, MS.

Of all the singers to emerge from the deep stables of producers James "Jimmy Jam" Harris III and Terry Lewis during the 1980s, O'Neal owned the most striking voice—a hearty tenor capable of both great, Marvin Gaye-style tenderness and gruff, Bobby Womack-like grit. He was recruited to be the lead singer of the Time after singing with a handful of groups in the Minneapolis area—including Sounds of Blackness—just as the region was gaining popularity. But Prince fired the brawny crooner before the group gained a recording contract. Jam and Lewis, also eventually fired by Prince, showed off their production talents and O'Neal's range on his 1985 debut, from the techno-dance hit "Innocent" to the sensitive ballad "A Broken Heart Can Mend." His breakthrough second release, along with "Saturday Love," his popular post-disco duet with frequent-collaborator Cherrelle, put O'Neal on the brink of crossover stardom. But fame never came, at least not in the U.S. Ultimately, despite a break with Jam and Lewis, a fruitless two-and-a-half year deal with Motown Records, and a public battle with substance abuse, O'Neal achieved superstar status in Europe, the only place that his last album was released.

what to buy: While packaged as a party album, *Hearsay* &&&& (Jive, 1994, prod. James Harris III, Terry Lewis), O'Neal's biggest selling album, runs the gamut from sensitive ("Sunshine") to slick ("Fake"), with his compelling voice as the constant.

what to buy next: *All True Man* &&&& (Tabu, 1991, prod. James Harris III, Terry Lewis), easily his most underrated work, finds O'Neal cranking out funk jams and tender ballads as if this was the last time he'd work with Jam and Lewis. And it was.

what to avoid: The remix project *All Mixed Up* && (Tabu, 1988, prod. various) is just what the title says and appeals neither to the soul audience or the dance crowd.

the rest:
Alexander O'Neal &&& (Tabu, 1985)
My Gift to You &&& (Tabu, 1988)
Love Makes No Sense &&& (Tabu, 1993)
The Best of Alexander O'Neal &&&& (Tabu, 1995)

worth searching for: O'Neal fans will find the most value in the hard-to-find British import *Lovers Again* &&& (One World/EMI Premier, 1996, prod. various), which, sadly, finds O'Neal struggling to overcome mediocre material.

influences:

◀◀ Marvin Gaye, Otis Redding, Jeffrey Osborne

▶▶ Aaron Hall, Jeff Redd

Franklin Paul

Shaquille O'Neal
Born March 6, 1972, in Newark, NJ.

If Ice Cube and a host of other MCs can dream (in song) about slam dunking like Shaquille O'Neal, then why can't lifelong hip-hop fan O'Neal live out his dream of rapping? O'Neal, who grew up on a steady rap diet that included everything from "Planet Rock" to "Roxanne, Roxanne," became the biggest grown kid in hip-hop's candy store when he landed a recording deal with Jive after befriending Jive's own Fu-Schnickens (his then-favorite group) and cutting the song "What's Up Doc? (Can We Rock)" with them. While Shaq actually dueted with Rakim, he hardly proved himself to be the next Rakim. Yet he fared better on the microphone than the rest of the athlete-rappers (Deion Sanders, Jason Kidd, Cedric Ceballos, etc.), actually managing not to embarrass himself much through three studio albums.

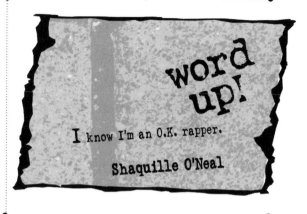

word up!

I know I'm an O.K. rapper.

Shaquille O'Neal

what to buy: Shaq has never really established his own vocal style, instead opting to tailor his delivery and lyrical concerns to fit the collaborators around him, be it the Fu-Schnickens, Erick Sermon, Fat Joe, or Notorious B.I.G. On his debut, *Shaq Diesel* &&& (Jive, 1993, prod. Def Jef, Erick Sermon, Ali Shaheed Muhammad, others), O'Neal tries on a handful of styles and, really, sounds happy to just be here in hip-hop world, sampling the Cold Crush Brothers, referencing Biz Markie and Pharcyde and eventually saying: "Never mind a whore/I wanna do a fat tour." With the album, Shaq also became the only hip-hop artist to sample NBA Commissioner David Stern, who announces the hoop star as the #1 pick in the league's draft. *Shaq Fu—Da Return* &&& (Jive, 1994, prod. RZA, Warren G, Erick Sermon, Redman, others) is notable mostly for its better production and vocal guests, including Redman, Keith Murray, Ill Al Skratch, Warren G, Sermon, and Wu-Tang's RZA and Method Man. O'Neal actually gets topical, too, with "Biological Didn't Bother," a song critical of his invisible biological father. Shaq shoots a major airball, though, with "Shaq's Got It Made," an ill-advised remake of the Special Ed classic.

the rest:
The Best of Shaquille O'Neal &&& (Jive, 1996)
You Can't Stop the Reign &&& (T.W.IsM/Interscope, 1996)

influences:

◀◀ Fu-Schnickens, Def Jef, A Tribe Called Quest, Erick Sermon, Wu-Tang Clan, Warren G, Ill Al Skratch, Notorious B.I.G., Fat Joe, Mobb Deep, Rakim, Lord Tariq

▶▶ B-Ball's Best Kept Secret

Josh Freedom du Lac

Onyx

Formed in Jamaica, NY.

Stickyfingaz, vocals; Fredro Star, vocals; Suave Sonny Caesar, vocals; Big D.S., vocals.

Originally a crew of breakdancers, Onyx transformed themselves into roughnecks and soon found platinum success. Kids loved them because they brought slam-dancing back to hip-hop, they had a cool logo, and they were all bald. Stickyfingaz actually had some great lines, and Fredro was the kind of guy who could steal your girl. It's when they got serious that the problems started.

what to buy: *Bacdafucup* 🎧🎧🎧 (JMJ/RAL, 1993, prod. Chyskillz, Jam Master Jay) deserves props for the title alone. No doubt, it gave chain-store buyers nightmares. As for the album itself, it's an unrelenting locker-room testosterone maximizer, with such subtly titled tracks as "Blac Vagina Finda," "Bichasniguz," and "Da Mad Face Invasion." Although they called it "grimy," Jam Master Jay and Chyskillz's production is bright and bumping, and when Onyx brings the teenage shout-alongs, it's either join in or leave. This formula works to instantly memorable effect on the platinum hit, "Slam" (where the Mohawks' "Champ" gets its funniest treatment yet); not so well on "Throw Ya Gunz."

what to buy next: B-b-but wait, it gets worse. *All We Got Iz Us* 🎧🎧 (JMJ/RAL, 1995, prod. Fredro, Stickyfingaz) takes a turn towards the topical—*a la* Mobb Deep—but with none of the vivid stories or musical snap. Shock is nothing without the surprise. Nothing shocking here.

influences:
◀◀ Lords of the Underground
▶▶ Kris Kross

Jeff "DJ Zen" Chang

Organized Konfusion

Formed in Queens, NY.

Pharoahe Monch, vocals; Prince Poetry, vocals.

Groups that regard hip-hop solely as a business, concentrating on making commercial hits and records that cater to the lowest common denominator, are detrimental to hip-hop's functionality as an expressive art form. Rather than take risks and attempt innovation, those rappers find safety in "keeping it real." Pharoahe Monch and Prince Poetry of Organized Konfusion, on the other hand, are true creators. With three albums and a handful of productions, the jazz- and improvisation-loving Queens duo (originally called Simply 2 Positive) is constantly stretching the bounds of hip-hop through genius lyricism, symbolism, concepts, and beats. By staying true to themselves in the wake of a lack of mass appeal and furthering hip-hop's parameters with their creations, Organized Konfusion has become the bastion of experimental hip-hop, particularly in New York, a region that sometimes is too "real" for its own good.

what to buy: Organized Konfusion will forever be a group that can be relied upon to make thought-provoking hip-hop that captures the imagination of anybody attached to a pair of headphones. *Organized Konfusion* 🎧🎧🎧🎧 (Hollywood BASIC, 1991, prod. Organized Konfusion) is a luminous debut that features a variety of styles for everybody: the smooth funk of "Fudge Pudge," the luscious, soulful emotions of "Walk Into the Sun," or the Rakim-like hallucinatory metaphors of "Releasing Hypnotical Gases." The latter is typical of OK songs: it's music that can be read or deciphered like the best literature. Only Organized could create a song like "Stray Bullet" from *Stress: The Extinction Agenda* 🎧🎧🎧🎧 (Hollywood BASIC, 1994, prod. Buckwild, Organized Konfusion). The song is rapped from the perspective of a stray bullet on a destructive, violent path that runs through both innocent and intended victims of a community. The album was made as both members were going through emotional turmoil, including the death of Monch's father. As a result, the album takes a very personal, dark tone that makes it an infallible piece of art. The opening "Intro" and "Stress" make for a brilliant introduction to the album, and Monch's otherworldly verse on "Bring It On" could very well be one of hip-hop's best ever.

what to buy next: Using the concept of duality and equity represented in the album's title, *The Equinox* 🎧🎧🎧 (Priority, 1997, prod. Buckwild, Organized Konfusion, Showbiz) is a conceptual release that tells the story of two characters named Life and Malice. The song is narrated by an older Life reflecting back on his own travails, with the songs acting as story background ("Move"), plot advancements ("In Vitro"), or manifestations of the characters' own emotions ("Hate"). On the latter, Pharoahe and Prince take the perspectives of young white supremacists to make powerful, potentially offensive commentary on their own black community.

worth searching for: In making remixes for the single "Fudge Pudge" b/w "Walk Into the Sun" (Hollywood BASIC, 1991), Organized created two wholly new songs that are definitely worth getting. "Decisions," from the *America Is Dying Slowly* (EastWest America, 1996) AIDS benefit compilation, is one of their more soulful, pensive songs and is worth it for Monch's lyricism alone.

influences:

◀◀ Gang Starr, Eric B. & Rakim, Ultramagnetic M.C.'s, Paul C, Large Professor

▶▶ Freestyle Fellowship, O.C., Ras Kass

Jazzbo

Osibisa

Formed 1969, in London, England.

Teddy Osei, tenor sax, flute, African drums, vocals; Sol Amarfio, drums, percussion, fontonfrom; Mac Tontoh, trumpet, flugelhorn, percussion; Spartacus R., bass, percussion; Wendell Richardson, lead guitar, vocals; Robert Bailey, organ, piano, timbales; Loughty Lasisi Amao, tenor/baritone sax, flute, congas, fontonfrom.

The world's first true Afropop band, Osibisa emerged out of London's African expatriate underground scene. A veritable Middle Passage crew composed of cats from Ghana, Nigeria, Antigua, Grenada, and Trinidad, Osibisa was a hothouse of hip-shaking, polyrhythmical flow. Their unique mix of Fela Kuti beats, jazz atmospherics, griot-wisdom soundbites, carnival mas, and skydog guitars secured them a recording contract with Decca—the first such band to be signed to a major British label. At the beginning of 1971, Osibisa released its self-titled debut album; before the year was out, the band also released *Woyaya*. On a roll, Osibisa toured the U.K. and Europe extensively. In 1972, Osibisa released *Heads*, which proved so popular among black college students that the band played several successful shows on that circuit during its 1972 U.S. tour. Since that high point, the band has drifted from label to label and to ever-shrinking prominence. Osibisa still exists today, gigging in the U.K. and Europe, sadly overlooked in the World Music/Afropop scene. Nonetheless, their page in music history is guaranteed.

what to buy: *Woyaya* 🎵🎵🎵🎵🎵 (MCA, 1971/AIM, 1993, prod. Tony Visconti) is Osibisa's masterpiece. From the ancestral spirits channeling through "Beautiful Seven" to the Nevilles-meet-War-at-the-intersection-of-Horace Silver take on Rahsaan Roland Kirk's "Spirit Up Above," *Woyaya* is a worldpop fusion that no one—not even Osibisa itself—has equaled since.

the rest:
Celebration: The Best of Osibisa 🎵🎵🎵 (AIM, 1993)
Ojah Awake 🎵🎵🎵 (AIM, 1995)
African Flight 🎵🎵 (AIM, 1995)
Welcome Home 🎵🎵🎵 (Songhai Empire, 1995)

worth searching for: The out-of-print LP versions of *Osibisa* (Decca, 1971), *Woyaya*, and *Heads* (Decca, 1972) all have great gatefold cover art, the first two with surreal flying elephant imagery by Roger Dean and the latter with humorous elephant imagery by Mati Klarwein.

influences:

◀◀ E.T. Mensah, Guy Warren, Fela Ransome Kuti, Rahsaan Roland Kirk

▶▶ Mandrill, O.J. Ekomede, Santana, Toure Kunde

Tom Terrell

Johnny Otis

Born John Veliotes, December 28, 1924, in Vallejo, CA.

Orchestra leader Johnny Otis contributed substantially to the development of R&B during the 1940s and 1950s—more than just his hit, "Willie & the Hand-Jive." His skills as a talent scout were unmatched; among his discoveries were Hank Ballard, Little Willie John, Etta James, and Jackie Wilson. Besides playing on sessions with jazz greats Charlie Parker, Lester Young, and Art Tatum, Otis produced and played drums on Big Mama Thornton's original recording of "Hound Dog" and played vibes on Johnny Ace's "Pledging My Love." Otis's band has featured the likes of Mel Walker, Jimmy Rushing, Bill Doggett, Big Jay McNeely, Little Esther Phillips, and the Robins (who would later become the Coasters). Otis signed with Savoy Records in 1945; the following year he had a solid hit with the jazzy "Harlem Nocturne." Otis and his Rhythm & Blues Caravan (later renamed the Johnny Otis Show), had 15 more R&B hits between then and 1952, among them "Double Crossing Blues," "Mambo Boogie," "Rockin' Blues," and "Gee Baby." In the mid-1950s Otis started his own label (Dig Records), hosted his own R&B flavored radio and TV shows in the Los Angeles area, and his orchestra consistently played to huge crowds at weekend dance parties. Otis signed with Capitol Records in 1957, where he wrote and recorded his sole Top 10 pop hit, "Willie & the Hand-Jive" (later featured in the 1959 teen-flick *Jukebox Rhythm* and covered by George Thorogood, Eric Clapton, and dozens of others). He followed with lesser chart offerings such as "Crazy Country Hop," "Castin' My Spell," "Mumblin' Mosie," and "Ma, He's Makin' Eyes At Me." (Otis has disavowed much of this work.) After leaving Capitol, Otis went on to record many inventive and danceable sides for the King, Dig, and Kent labels, but the market for his brand of R&B had shrunk, and there were no new hits. When the rock 'n' roll revival blossomed during the late 1960s, Otis was rediscovered by college audiences. "Country Girl" was a fair-sized hit for him in 1969, and it led to a strong-selling live LP on Epic Records. Always willing to reinvest in the music, he started up the Blues

Spectrum label in 1974, which recorded Otis and many of his famous friends live and in the studio. Since then, Otis has recorded and toured with new editions of his orchestra (featuring his son Shuggie Otis, a top-notch slide guitar player) on Alligator Records, written *Upside Your Head* (his second book), and kept his music alive through various leasing deals. In 1994, Otis was voted into the Rock and Roll Hall of Fame as a "non-performer," which in light of all the music he's played seems ill-informed.

what to buy: *The Original Johnny Otis Show* 🎵🎵🎵🎵 (Savoy, 1995, prod. Ralph Bass, reissue prod. Bob Porter) features the best of Otis and his orchestra backing Jimmy Rushing, Little Esther, and the Robins on "Harlem Nocturne," "Deceiving Blues," "Mambo Boogie," "Rockin' Blues," and others.

what to buy next: *The Capitol Years* 🎵🎵🎵 (Capitol/EMI, 1989, prod. Tom Morgan, Ben Vaughn, comp. Ben Vaughn, Johnny Otis) contains 24 tracks from Otis's hit years at Capitol, including "Willie & the Hand-Jive," "Crazy Country Hop," and "Castin' My Spell."

what to avoid: *Johnny Otis Presents . . .* 🎵 (LaserLight, 1993, prod. Johnny Otis, Tom Morgan) features remakes of big hits cut over the years for Otis's Blues Spectrum label by Amos Milburn, Joe Turner, Joe Liggins, Charles Brown, and Louis Jordan. Thus, although this five-disc set is cheap, it features none of the superior original material and is recommended for completists only.

the rest:
Live at Monterey 🎵🎵🎵 (Epic, 1970/Legacy, 1970/1993)
The New Johnny Otis Show 🎵🎵🎵 (Alligator, 1981)
Good Lovin' Blues 🎵🎵🎵 (Ace, 1990)
Let's Live It Up 🎵🎵🎵 (Charly, 1991)
Spirit of the Black Territory Bands 🎵🎵 (Arhoolie, 1992)
Live in Los Angeles 1970 🎵🎵🎵 (Wolf, 1994)
Too Late to Holler 🎵🎵🎵 (Night Train, 1995)

worth searching for: *Creepin' with the Cats . . . Dig Masters Vol.1* 🎵🎵🎵 (Ace, 1993, prod. various) contains 22 tracks ("Ali Baba's Boogie," "Hey Hey Hey," etc.) and 10 previously unreleased cuts from 1956–75.

influences:
⏮ Count Basie

⏭ Shuggie Otis, Lucky Otis

Ken Burke

Shuggie Otis
Born 1953, Los Angeles, CA.

If anybody fits the profile of the quintessential cult musician better than guitarist/composer Shuggie Otis, let us know. The son of R&B pioneer Johnny Otis, Shuggie was a stage-trunk baby, spending his formative years in the backstage wings, hypnotized by the shenanigans of his father's traveling roadshow. Enthralled by the guitar pyrotechnics of artists like Johnny "Guitar" Watson as well as the stage moves of stars such as Little Esther Philips and Eddie "Cleanhead" Vinson, Shuggie began his apprenticeship in his pop's band at the tender age of 13. Word of this teen phenom eventually reached New York and the ears of blues aficionado/rock producer (Blood, Sweat & Tears) Al Kooper, who signed and produced Otis's debut, *Al Kooper Introduces*, for Columbia Records in 1969. Well-received at the time, in retrospect the record is a competent yet so-so blues record—the best anyone could expect from a 26-year-old neophyte. Otis's sophomore disc, *Here Comes Shuggie Otis* (1970), is a much improved balance of originals and standards in a Buddy Guy mode. The guitarist took a giant step the next year with his magnum opus, *Freedom Flight*. A Hendrixian future blues piece, *Freedom Flight* was perhaps too black and audacious for the marketing crew at Epic Records; it died an unnatural death, though the Brothers Johnson vindicated it during the late 1970s with their huge cover hit of *Freedom Flight*'s "Strawberry Letter No. 23." In 1975, Otis released his swan song *Inspiration Information*. A prescient melange of guitar, keyboards, Linn drum programming, cheesy rhythm box beats, and yearningly romantic lyrics, *Inspiration Information*'s original vision would not find favor until the debut five years later of a kid from Minneapolis named Prince. Dropped by the label the next year, a somewhat disillusioned Otis returned to the safe harbor of his father's blues revue; his last recorded appearance would be with his father on the 1982 Alligator LP *The New Johnny Otis Show*. Today, Johnny Otis is retired, an artist more acclaimed for his rootsy folk art work than his music. And Shuggie is, well, MIA. Will he surface one more time? Let's hope so.

what's available: *Shuggie's Boogie: Shuggie Otis Plays the Blues* 🎵🎵 (Legacy, 1994, prod. various) is an inadequate collection of Otis's CBS blues output and only worthwile because all of his records are out of print.

worth searching for: The search for *Freedom Flight* 🎵🎵🎵🎵 (Epic, 1971) and *Inspiration Information* 🎵🎵🎵🎵 (Epic, 1975), no matter how arduous, will prove to be totally worth the energy spent.

influences:
⏮ T-Bone Walker, Jimi Hendrix, Esther Phillips

⏭ Prince, Eric Clapton, Nona Hendryx

Tom Terrell

OutKast

Formed 1993, in Atlanta, GA.

Big Boi, vocals; Dre, vocals.

If a single city deserves credit for flipping the script on Southern stereotypes, then applause goes to Atlanta, home of the ever-evolving OutKast. By staying grounded in hip-hop innovation and swaying clear of the booty bass plague that afflicts their peers, OutKast manages compelling songs that defy geographical boundaries while maintaining a connection to deep-fried funk, lyrical pimpin', and other Southernisms, such as endlessly rhyming about Cadillacs. Formed at Tri-Cities High School, a performing arts school also attended by members of Xscape, the duo is one of the South's few hopes for gaining respect within a rap scene that not-so-subtly looks at music with bi-coastal blinders. If the Geto Boys represented the untamed psychosis of the South, OutKast brings social analysis as well as elevated party tunes.

what to buy: *ATLiens* ✍✍✍ (LaFace, 1996, prod. Organized Noize) is a diverse yet cohesive collection of new-school sound with down-home lyrics. Older and wiser than on their debut, the crew's topics range from immorality ("Jazzy Belle") to resistance ("Mainstream") to coming of age in the '90s ("Babylon"). The crew also is enjoyable when just rapping for rap's sake and drawing connections that bring them closer to their fans. On "Elevators (Me & You)," Dre raps, "I live by the beat like you live check to check/If you don't move your feet, then I don't eat, so we like neck to neck."

what to buy next: *Southernplayalisticadillacmuzik* ✍✍✍✍ (LaFace, 1994, prod. Organized Noize) debuts the group's Southern repertoire with the blaxploited "Player's Ball" and an anthem for self-determination, "Git Up, Git Out."

influences:

◀◀ Das EFX, Hieroglyphics, Geto Boys

▶▶ Goodie Mob

Corey Takahashi

Robert Palmer

Born Alan Palmer, January 19, 1949, in Bately, England.

Robert Palmer started off in a series of forgettable British groups before going solo during the mid-1970s. With a knack for picking the right cover tunes and an intriguing mix of rootsy, soul-tinged, Caribbean-influenced rock compositions (early albums featured members of the Meters and Toots & the Maytals), Palmer carved out a healthy niche as an eclectic, progressive pop artist. Still, it wasn't until his brief stint with supergroup the Power Station—which featured members of Duran Duran and Chic—that the singer became a bona fide pop star. Leaving the group after one record (his refusal to tour was the reported stumbling block), Palmer snagged the group's production team for his own work, rafting a metallized rock/soul sound that brought his biggest solo hits yet. But an unfortunate turn toward the Tin Pan Alley standards of his youth brought commercial disaster—a fate from which he has yet to recover.

what to buy: As one of the few Palmer albums that doesn't sabotage its great material with equally confusing and eclectic indulgences, *Secrets* ✍✍✍ (Island, 1979, prod. Robert Palmer) contains classics such as his rocking cover of Moon Martin's "Bad Case of Lovin' You (Doctor, Doctor)" along with a sensitive, soulful take on Todd Rundgren's "Can We Still Be Friends?" Almost as impressive is his solo debut, *Sneakin' Sally through the Alley* ✍✍✍ (Island, 1974, prod. Steve Smith). Featuring the Allen Toussaint–written title cut backed by both Little Feat and the Meters, the record is about as close to New Orleans soul as any British guy will ever get.

what to buy next: For a consistently engaging taste of his 1980s pop star incarnation, no album touches all the bases better than his breakthrough, *Riptide* ✍✍✍ (Island, 1986, prod. Bernard Edwards). With a well-crafted, edgy production style courtesy of Power Station mate (and Chic principal) Edwards, and with songs ranging from the hormone-addled hit "Addicted to Love" to a synthesizer-laden remake of the blues tune "Trick Bag," Palmer turns in his most creative, confident album in years. To sample the best of his 1970s and early 1980s work, the hits collection *Addictions, Volume Two* ✍✍✍ (Island, 1992, prod. various) isolates highlights such as his inspired cover of the System's funky "You Are in My System" and the dreamy, reggae-tinged ballad "Every Kind of People."

what to avoid: As a tribute to the jazzy pop standards of the 1940s, *Ridin' High* **woof!** (EMI, 1992, prod. Teo Macero, Robert Palmer) falls flat—mostly due to Palmer's emotionless, bionic delivery.

the rest:

Pressure Drop ✍✍✍ (Island, 1975)

Robert Palmer (© Ken Settle)

Some People Can Do What They Like 🎧🎧🎧 (Island, 1976)

Double Fun 🎧🎧🎧 (Island, 1978)

Clues 🎧🎧🎧♪ (Island, 1980)

Maybe It's Live 🎧🎧🎧 (Island, 1982)

Pride 🎧🎧 (Island, 1983)

(With Power Station) *The Power Station* 🎧🎧🎧🎧 (Capitol, 1985/Gold Rush, 1997)

Heavy Nova 🎧🎧 (EMI, 1988)

Addictions, Volume One 🎧🎧🎧 (Island, 1989)

Don't Explain **woof!** (EMI America, 1990)

Honey 🎧🎧♪ (EMI America, 1994)

The Very Best of Robert Palmer 🎧🎧🎧♪ (Guardian, 1995)

(With Power Station) *Living In Fear* 🎧🎧🎧 (Guardian, 1997)

worth searching for: *Simply Palmer* (EMI, 1988) is a promotional interview CD that has a smooth, suave James Bond quality.

influences:

◀◀ James Brown, Wilson Pickett, Tony Bennett, Mel Torme, Billie Holiday, Nina Simone, Ronald Isley

▶▶ Toto, Mr. Mister, Nina Simone

Eric Deggans

Paperboy
Born M. Johnson, in Los Angeles, CA.

Paperboy delivered a catchy, funky, million-selling hip-pop ditty in 1993 called, simply, "Ditty" and based on a sample of Zapp's "Do Wa Ditty (Blow That Thing)." But Paperboy faded just as quickly, suggesting that the route *from* stardom is a short one, too.

what's available: *The Nine Yards* 🎧🎧 (Next Plateau, 1993, prod. Rhythm D) features all the "Ditty" you'll need, opening with the original version and closing with the "Ditty (Divine Street Mix)." Nothing else on the album matches the joyful funk of the hit, although "Bumpin' (Adaptation of Humpin')" tries, taking the song from Gap Band to rap band. His follow-up album, *City to City* 🎧🎧 (Next Plateau, 1996), fell short.

influences:

◀◀ Candyman, DJ Quik

Josh Freedom du Lac

Paris

Born Oscar Jackson, October 29, 1967, in San Francisco, CA.

Paris quickly rose from a college radio DJ at UC-Davis, where he studied economics, to one of the brightest stars in Bay Area hip-hop. Combining a Rakim-meets-Chuck D. style (note his D.-favored Pittsburgh Pirates cap on the cover of *Sleeping with the Enemy*) with tremendous samples and scratches, Paris is notable for being both listenable and topical. Generally eschewing the nature of gangsta rap, but not the violence of it, Paris combines Black Panther rhetoric with Nation of Islam doctrine in an aggressive—albeit occasionally confusing—manner. His cop-killing fantasy "Coffee, Donuts & Death" and the presidential-assassination fantasy "Bush Killa" followed Ice-T's lead and helped get Paris dropped by Warner Bros., thus forcing him to release his second album on his own Scarface label.

what to buy: The first album, *The Devil Made Me Do It* ♪♪♪♪ (Tommy Boy, 1989/90, prod. Paris) slams from "Intro" to the bonus remixes of "Break the Grip of Shame" and "The Devil Made Me Do It." This CD is truly a stand-back-or-you-might-get-hurt compendium of dope beats, violent, tireless scratching, and angry, pro-black lyrics. Paris cunningly combines car-stereo-testing tracks with wordplay that cannot be ignored.

what to buy next: Avoiding a sophomore slump, Paris returned with *Sleeping with the Enemy* ♪♪♪♪ (Scarface, 1992, prod. Paris). Despite irritating interludes that include the too-long-to-unfold fantasy shooting of then-President George Bush and a played-out telephone conversation bit, *Sleeping with the Enemy* is a fine effort, highlighted by "Make Way for a Panther" and "Conspiracy of Silence." Guest appearances by Sundoobie (of Funkdoobiest) and a still-unknown DJ Shadow serve to bring both humor and variety to the mix.

what to avoid: What the hell happened here? *Guerilla Funk* ♪♪ (Scarface/Priority, 1994, prod. Paris) would have just been a mildly whack album by another artist, but from Paris, it is an unexpected turd. Why hadn't he spent as much time on the music as he had on the packaging, with its lame and disgusting photos? Watered down G-funk and lyrical water-treading make this effort very avoidable. Maybe this finally explains his inexplicable production of the generally horrible Conscious Daughters.

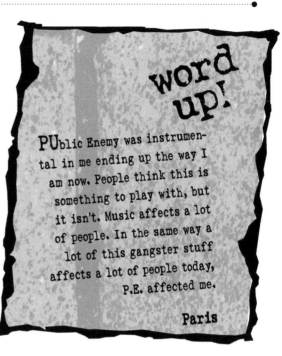

word up!

PUblic Enemy was instrumental in me ending up the way I am now. People think this is something to play with, but it isn't. Music affects a lot of people. In the same way a lot of this gangster stuff affects a lot of people today, P.E. affected me.

Paris

worth searching for: Completists will want to pick up Consolidated's *Play More Music* (Nettwerk, 1992), which contains a slightly industrialized version of the second album's "Guerrillas in the Mist."

influences:

◀◀ Public Enemy, Ice-T, Rakim

▶▶ Conscious Daughters, DJ Shadow

Barry M. Prickett

Mica Paris

Born Michelle Warren, April 27, 1969, in London, England.

As the 1980s became the 1990s, British soul watchers had their eyes trained on Lisa Stansfield; they should have kept a closer watch on Mica (MEE-sha) Paris, a prodigy who incorporated jazz and gospel touches for one of the most unique voices to come out of her homeland. A member of the gospel troupe the Spirit of Watts at age 16, Paris was recruited by Hollywood Beyond to be part of that group's touring lineup. By the late 1980s, Paris had her own deal and her first British hits, though there was a curious disinterest from U.S. audiences. Paris has never given up, however, and these days she's still working and is an in-demand guest on others' albums.

what to buy: *Whisper a Prayer* 🎵🎵🎵♪ (Island, 1993, prod. Rod Temperton) brings a guest appearance from Alex Acuna as well as a nice variety of material that includes ballads and hip-hop-laced uptempo tunes.

the rest:
So Good 🎵🎵🎵 (Island, 1989)
Contribution 🎵🎵🎵♪ (Island, 1990)

worth searching for: Of her many guest appearances, Paris particularly shines on *Jazzmatazz Vol. II: The New Reality* 🎵🎵🎵🎵 (Chrysalis, 1995).

influences:
◀◀ Aretha Franklin, Dinah Washington, Anita Baker, Chaka Khan, Donna Summer

Gary Graff

Maceo Parker

Born February 14, 1943, in Kinston, NC.

The public became aware of funk-jazz saxophonist Maceo Parker when he joined James Brown's band during the mid-1960s. His sympathetic ear and playing—rhythms, accents, and countermelodies to Brown's voice—was instrumental in defining the JB sound on tunes such as "It's a Man's, Man's, Man's World," "Money Won't Change You," and "Say It Loud." Along with trombonist Fred Wesley, Parker helped develop the choppy horn-section style that was more rhythmic than melodic and powerfully in sync. The JBs stepped out on their own in 1972 with *Food for Thought*, an album regularly sampled by modern rappers. Parker and Wesley switched to the P-Funk Mob in 1975 and helped define that group's sound during its hottest years. Parker still works with George Clinton and in recent years has recorded jazz-funk albums as a bandleader himself.

what to buy: Parker's been around a long time and played all kinds of stuff, but deep down it's the music on *Mo' Roots* 🎵🎵🎵🎵 (Verve, 1991 prod. Steve Meyner, Maceo Parker) that's in his heart—a little jazz, a little soul, a little gospel, and the eight-minute "Chicken," which bumps along on a bass line while the horns stretch out with the groove. *Roots Revisited* 🎵🎵🎵🎵 (Verve, 1990 prod. Steve Meyner, Maceo Parker) hangs with some jazzy arrangements and the seldom-heard Charles Mingus piece

"Better Get Hit in Your Soul." A nice reading of the Impressions' "People Get Ready" shows the soulful side of the package.

what to buy next: *Life on Planet Groove* 🎵🎵🎵🎵 (Verve, 1992, prod. Steve Meyner, Maceo Parker) gets a little more modern and into stretchy funk, but "Shake Everything You've Got" is 16 minutes of soloists taking it to the limit.

what to avoid: *For All the King's Men* 🎵🎵🎵 (4th and Broadway/Island, 1990, prod. Bill Laswell, Bootsy Collins) is all P-Funked up and has little identity outside that arena.

worth searching for: *Southern Exposure* 🎵🎵🎵🎵 (Novus, 1994, prod. Steve Meyner, Maceo Parker) features Parker, along with the Rebirth Brass Band and the Meters, serving up a big helping of Crescent City funk.

influences:
◀◀ Ray Charles, John Coltrane, Charlie Parker
▶▶ The Brecker Brothers, Tower of Power, Clarence Clemons

Lawrence Gabriel

Ray Parker Jr.

Born May 1, 1954, in Detroit, MI.

Not to say he was ambitious, but by the time he was 16, Ray Parker Jr. was playing guitar at sessions for Motown greats such as Stevie Wonder as well as for the songwriting/production team of Holland-Dozier-Holland, who had recently split from the label. Parker went on to have a strong career as a session player, working with a wide array of artists including Boz Scaggs, Barry White, Earl Klugh, Donna Summer, Marvin Gaye, Patti Labelle, Stephen Bishop, Najee, Alphonse Mouzon, and New Edition. Parker's first hit as a writer was Rufus's "You Got the Love" in 1974, which helped finance his own Ameraycan recording studio as well as the early days of his group, Raydio. The sextet scored a batch of hits during the late 1970s and early 1980s, including "Jack and Jill," "You Can't Change That," and "A Woman Needs Love (Just Like You Do)." Parker went solo in 1981, scoring a few hits of his own, including "The Other Woman" and the theme for the film *Ghostbusters*; the latter resulted in a lawsuit in which rocker Huey Lewis successfully accused Parker of plagiarizing his hit "I Want a New Drug." In recent years Parker has left the spotlight, returning to session work and writing.

Maceo Parker (l) and fellow James Brown horn man
Pee Wee Ellis (© Jack Vartoogian)

4
4
4 *passion*

what's available: A skimpy collection called *Greatest Hits* ♪♪ (Arista, 1982, prod. various) has just 10 songs and was released before *Ghostbusters*.

worth searching for: Parker's *Chartbusters* ♪♪♪ (Arista, 1984, prod. various), a cash-in on the *Ghostbusters* success but a far better representation of his work. All the Raydio material is out of print, too, but either *Raydio* ♪♪♪ (Arista, 1977) or *Rock On* ♪♪♪♪ (Arista, 1979) are worthwhile.

influences:

◀◀ Stevie Wonder, Marvin Gaye, Holland-Dozier-Holland, Parliament, Rare Earth

▶▶ Prince, R. Kelly

Gary Graff

Passion

Formed early 1990s.

Women in rap was one of the genre's bigger stories in 1996, but, apparently, somebody forgot to include the Oakland, California, femcee Passion in the press release. Of course, Passion likely didn't garner nearly as much attention as the likes of Lil' Kim, Foxy Brown, and Bahamadia simply because she's neither as shocking or as well-produced as sex-crazed commercial darlings Kim and Brown, or as gifted as the more thoughtful critical darling Bahamadia. Then again, it could just be that she had the, um, balls to title a song "Keep It Real" with a straight face when the keep-it-real backlash was in full effect.

what's available: Hangin' tough like a hard-ass, cliche-wielding cousin of the Conscious Daughters or something, the rapper-singer gets very unladylike on her debut, *Baller's Lady* ♪♪ (MCA, 1996, prod. various), tossing about the B-word like Too $hort with a sex change (see "B.I.T.C.H."). Perhaps that's what it takes to earn membership to the playa's club; still, it hardly makes for a compelling recording.

influences:

◀◀ Too $hort, Rappin 4-Tay, Conscious Daughters

Josh Freedom du Lac

Billy Paul

Born Paul Williams, December 1, 1934, in Philadelphia, PA.

It took Billy Paul 20 years of recording to land a hit single, but when he finally did, it became the kind of rare masterpiece that stands the test of time for another 20 years and beyond. Paul's classic, bluesy 1972 ode to infidelity, "Me and Mrs. Jones," shot to the #1 position on both the R&B and pop music charts, becoming a multimillion seller and a ballad that would be perpetually covered by crooners and rappers alike. Paul, who attended the West Philadelphia Music Academy as a child and was singing on the radio by the age of 12, began his recording career on the Jubilee label and worked both as a solo vocalist and with his own trio. He never duplicated the international phenomenon of "Me and Mrs. Jones," but Paul enjoyed a solid run of success in the 1970s with the Top 10 single "Thank You for Saving My Life" and the memorable tunes "Am I Black Enough for You," "Let's Make a Baby," and his cover of Paul McCartney's "Let 'Em In." Paul announced his retirement in London in 1989, but has since resurfaced for occasional nightclub dates in the U.S. and abroad.

what to buy: An R&B hero not heralded in his homeland, Paul's existing material on CD is mostly available only on imports. The only widely distributed U.S. release, *360 Degrees of Billy Paul* ♪♪♪♪ (Columbia, 1988), does contain the essential cut, however—"Me and Mrs. Jones," with its full-bodied instrumental richness, along with "Am I Black Enough for You" and engaging covers of "Let's Stay Together" and "Your Song." It's a proper introduction to a noteworthy R&B-blues interpreter.

what to avoid: A mismatched assortment of lounge-singer cover tracks like "Takin' It to the Streets" and "The Times of Our Lives," the German import *Only the Strong Survive* ♪♪ (Philadelphia International, 1995) is a must-miss in the line of Billy Paul acquisitions.

worth searching for: Of the import CDs, all from Germany, *Got My Head on Straight* ♪♪♪ (Philadelphia International, 1995) has the most to offer. It's a combination of his better second-rung tunes, like "July, July, July, July" and "Billy's Back Home," with a pair of interesting facing-one's-mortality tracks in "I've Got So Much to Live For" and "When It's Your Time to Go," and a tender remake of "Everything Must Change." Paul's greatest hit fits in marvelously on the compilation LP *Cheatin'—From a Man's Point of View* ♪♪♪♪ (Ichiban, 1995, prod. various). "Me and Mrs. Jones" is the centerpiece of a batch of well-chosen, equally delicious paeans to philandering like Clarence Carter's "Slip Away," Bill Withers's "Who Is He and What Is He to You," and, of course, Luther Ingram's "If Loving You Is Wrong (I Don't Want to Be Right)."

influences:

◀◀ Little Milton, Z.Z. Hill, Dinah Washington, Isaac Hayes, Jerry Butler, Johnnie Taylor, Lou Rawls, Bill Withers

▶▶ Philippe Wynne, William Bell, George Benson, Robert Cray

Jim McFarlin

Freda Payne

Born September 19, 1945, in Detroit, MI.

Before she struck gold with soul, Freda Payne studied voice, piano, and ballet. She sang in the chorus of a Pearl Bailey show and toured with Duke Ellington's band as a jazz singer and with Quincy Jones—a sophisticated early career for a woman who smoked the charts in 1970 with her passionate urgency and longing on "Band of Gold." One of the most memorable soul tracks from the 1970s, it launched an R&B career that was curiously brief. In the hands of legendary songwriters and producers Holland-Dozier-Holland, Payne had the material, sound, and backing to have a long run on the charts. But she had only a handful of hits ("Deeper and Deeper," "Cherish What Is Dear to You (While It's Near to You)," "Joy," and an anti-Vietnam War single, "Bring the Boys Back Home").

what's available: *Greatest Hits* ✍✍✍ (HDH, 1991) has all of them and a fine sampling of her other material.

influences:

◀◀ Pearl Bailey, Duke Ellington, Quincy Jones, Martha Reeves, Gladys Knight, Kim Weston

▶▶ Cher, Donna Summer, Gloria Gaynor, Tiffany, Debbie Gibson

Patrick McCarty

Peaches & Herb

Formed 1965, in Washington, DC.

Herb Fame, vocals; Francine Barker, vocals (1965–68); Marlene Mack (1968–69); Linda Greene (1977–83).

Herb Fame (born Herbert Feemster) met Francine Barker (born Francine Hurd) during the early 1960s when she was a member of a group called the Sweet Things. Fame had been with the Dreamtones and tried a solo career before forming Peaches & Herb. The soul duo signed with the CBS subsidiary Date, debuted with the hit album *Let's Fall in Love* in 1967, and had two hit singles, "Let's Fall in Love" and "Close Your Eyes." *For Your Love* came the following year, and a greatest hits package arrived in 1968. Marlene replaced Barker for just one year. Then the original duo signed with Columbia in 1970. But the hit-making machine had stalled, and they stopped recording. During the mid-1970s Fame worked as a police officer and released a

few singles on his own BS label. He made a full comeback, however, with new Peaches Linda Greene in 1977 and signed with Polydor, where P&H would have their best years. In 1978 their platinum *2 Hot!* went to #2 on *Billboard* charts, and the single "Reunited" went to #1. *Twice the Fire* went gold in 1979. The mildly successful *Worth the Wait* and *Sayin' Something* were their last records for Polydor. In 1983 they made *Remember* on Columbia, then stopped recording altogether.

what to buy: *The Best of Peaches & Herb* ✍✍✍ (Polydor, 1996, prod. Freddie Perren) features guest artists Jose Feliciano and Gary Hebrig. This album is part of Polydor's Soul Essentials series and shows the duo's second incarnation with Linda Greene. Its only #1 single, "Reunited," is included.

what to buy next: *Love Is Strange: The Best of Peaches & Herb* (Legacy, 1996, prod. various) ✍✍✍, captures the act's late 1960s and mid-1980s incarnations.

influences:

◀◀ Ashford & Simpson, Ike & Tina Turner

▶▶ Atlantic Starr, James Ingram

Norene Cashen

Pebbles

Born Perri McKissack, August 29, 1965, in Oakland, CA.

It would be easy to think of Pebbles as just another pretty face, as well as Cherelle's cousin. But throughout her career, she has shown signs that she is much more, first as a student of opera and classical ballet, then early in her career as writer with Con Funk Shun and Sister Sledge. Though she signed a production deal at 16 with jazz man Bill Summers, it wasn't until she was 23, and under the tutelage of emerging hitmakers Kenneth "Babyface" Edmonds and her husband, Antonio "L.A." Reid, that she dropped her first album. By 1989, Pebbles—a name given to her by her godfather—had scored two big hit singles and one husband Reid. She next focused on developing the group that would become the multi-platinum-selling trio TLC, whose achievement far overshadowed hers, despite a successful second album. Things fell apart during the mid-1990s, when she divorced Reid and sued his and Edmonds's label, LaFace Records, amid accusations they tried to steal TLC from her management firm. Then a bankrupt TLC sued her. Despite these hardships, she managed to release her finest work in 1995, a testament to her struggle and growth as a singer, songwriter, and producer.

what to buy: Pebbles flexes her creative muscles on *Straight from the Heart* 𝄞𝄞𝄞 (MCA, 1995, prod. various), after a messy break from Reid and Babyface. There are no hits here, but the CD as a whole finds Pebbles, like Sade, working material that fits her wispy voice, coloring the sound, rather than trying to power her way through.

what to buy next: An early classic, *Pebbles* 𝄞𝄞𝄞 (MCA, 1988, prod. various) sports several mid-to-uptempo winners, including Grammy-nominated "Girlfriend," which was originally to be recorded by Vanessa Williams.

the rest:
Always 𝄞𝄞𝄞 (MCA, 1990)

influences:
◀◀ Cherelle, Janet Jackson, Diana Ross

Franklin Paul

Ann Peebles

Born April 27, 1947, in St. Louis, MO.

Often overlooked in the vast shadow of Al Green's success, Ann Peebles's seven albums for Memphis-based Hi Records contain some of the finest music of the 1970s soul era. Like Green, Peebles's records were produced and arranged by Willie Mitchell, and they featured the same superb Hi Records house band. But while Green sang of "Love and Happiness," Peebles mined a darker vein of bitter loss, betrayal, and regret with tunes such as "I'm Gonna Tear Your Playhouse Down" and "Feel Like Breakin' Up Somebody's Home." And Mitchell's musical arrangements for Peebles were sparer, more intimate—emotionally attuned to a voice soaked in longing and pain. Her high point came with the 1974 album *I Can't Stand the Rain* and its oft-covered title tune. During the late 1970s, she abruptly retired from music to raise a family, though she was coaxed back into a Memphis studio for an excellent 1992 comeback record, *Full Time Love.*

what to buy: *The Best of the Hi Records Years* 𝄞𝄞𝄞𝄞 (The Right Stuff, 1996, prod. Willie Mitchell) is the only existing domestic-released overview of Peebles's Hi Records years. Containing all the essential hits, it's the place to start. Anyone who loves classic soul should own a copy of *I Can't Stand the Rain* 𝄞𝄞𝄞𝄞 (Hi, 1974/The Right Stuff, 1993, prod. Willie Mitchell).

what to buy next: *Full Time Love* 𝄞𝄞𝄞 (Bullseye Blues, 1992, prod. Ron Levy) is Peebles's long-overdue return to the studio, backed by many of the original Hi Records studio musicians.

Despite the absence of Mitchell's guiding hand, its high points (such as a brilliant version of Delbert McClinton's "Read Me My Rights") reach the level of her finest Hi recordings.

the rest:
Part Time Love 𝄞𝄞𝄞𝄞 (Hi, 1971/The Right Stuff, 1994)
Straight from the Heart 𝄞𝄞𝄞 (Hi, 1971/The Right Stuff, 1993)
Fill This World with Love 𝄞𝄞𝄞 (Bullseye Blues, 1996)
St. Louis Woman—Memphis Soul 𝄞𝄞𝄞 (Hi, 1996)

worth searching for: Most of Peebles's original Hi albums are only available now as imports. Look for *If This Is Heaven* 𝄞𝄞𝄞 (Hi U.K., 1978, prod. Willie Mitchell).

influences:
◀◀ Mahalia Jackson, Aretha Franklin, Sam Cooke
▶▶ Toni Braxton, Annie Lennox, Otis Clay

Doug Pippin

Teddy Pendergrass

Born March 26, 1950, in Philadelphia, PA.

March 18, 1982, wasn't the day the music died, but it was the night rhythm and blues suffered a critical injury. At the height of his career, Teddy Pendergrass—the prowling, growling, sensuous sex symbol of latter-day male soul singers—skidded his Rolls Royce off a Pennsylvania highway under questionable circumstances and incurred massive spinal cord damage, ending up paralyzed from the neck down. That Pendergrass survived is remarkable; that he returned from a two-year hiatus for recuperation to record gold-selling albums again is nothing short of miraculous. It's a testament to the inherent musical ability and inner faith of a man whose mother was a popular nightclub singer and who was immersed in gospel music as a child. He taught himself how to play the drums as a teenager and began performing with a local band called the Cadillacs, which was eventually invited to be the backup group for veteran Philly doo-wop singers Harold Melvin & the Blue Notes. When Melvin's lead vocalist, John Atkins, left the group in mid-tour in 1970, Pendergrass was asked to replace him as the Blue Notes' frontman. That sparked an association with Gamble and Huff's now-legendary Philadelphia International label and a five-year run of dazzling hit songs powered by Teddy's urgent baritone, including "The Love I Lost," "Bad Luck," "Wake Up, Everybody,"

Ann Peebles (© Linda Vartoogian)

and the quintessential ballad "If You Don't Know Me By Now." Emboldened by his popularity, Pendergrass embarked on a solo career in 1977, going platinum with his debut LP *Teddy Pendergrass* (featuring the single "I Don't Love You Anymore") and touring the world with his SRO "For Ladies Only" concerts backed by the Teddy Bear Orchestra, confirming his status as the virile young lion of vocal seduction. In 1979, Pendergrass won the American Music Award as Favorite Male Soul/R&B Artist. Then came the crash. Pendergrass regained partial movement after the accident, but didn't return to recording until 1984, making his comeback on the Asylum label with the gold LP *Love Language*. Pendergrass has since released a string of moderate to successful albums, founded the Pendergrass Institute for Music and Performing Arts in Pennsylvania, and in 1996 co-starred with Stephanie Mills and BeBe Winans in a touring production of the gospel musical *Your Arms Too Short to Box with God*.

what to buy: With most of Pendergrass's early albums out of print, the place to experience his first flush of success in the solo phase of his career—as well as to recall the electrifying energy and sexual tension of his live performances—is on the reissued *Teddy Live! Coast to Coast* 𝄞𝄞𝄞 (The Right Stuff, 1994, prod. Kenneth Gamble, others; reissue prod. Tom Cartwright). Originally released in 1979, the double-disc set captures Teddy in concert at Philadelphia's Shubert Theater and the Greek Theater in Los Angeles. Technically, it's not a great album, compromised by inconsistent production and studio-cut "live interview" segments, but it does contain live versions of the Teddy trademarks "Close the Door" and "Love TKO," and it's the best early Pendergrass domestically available.

what to buy next: Of his post-recovery LPs, *A Little More Magic* 𝄞𝄞𝄞 (Elektra, 1993, prod. Reggie Calloway) is arguably Teddy's strongest overall achievement, an undeniably positive and sensitively romantic record bolstered by a circle of support from guests Barry White, Patti LaBelle, Chuckii Booker, and Gerald Levert and highlighted by the Grammy-nominated single "Voodoo."

what to avoid: A clear case of too many producers (nine in all, including Pendergrass) spoiling the mix, *Workin' It Back* 𝄞𝄞 (Asylum, 1985, prod. various) lapses into uneven choices in both songs and interpretations.

the rest:
Love Language 𝄞𝄞𝄞 (Asylum, 1987)
Joy 𝄞𝄞𝄞 (Elektra, 1988)
Truly Blessed 𝄞𝄞𝄞 (Elektra, 1991)

Touch of Class 𝄞𝄞 (MSI, 1997)
You & I 𝄞𝄞𝄞 (Surefire, 1997)

worth searching for: Several German imports under the Repertoire label capture the Teddy Bear backstory brilliantly, especially *The Philly Years* 𝄞𝄞𝄞𝄞 (Repertoire, 1994, prod. various), a rapturous 32-song double CD set that blends his Blue Notes period and solo hits into a cohesive collection, including his seldom-heard covers "Is It Still Good to Ya" and "This One's for You" and the ultrafunky "Get Up, Get Down, Get Funky, Get Loose."

influences:

◀◀ Jackie Wilson, Sam Cooke, Brook Benton, Harold Melvin, Barry White, Gamble & Huff, Marvin Gaye, Luther Vandross, Isaac Hayes

▶▶ Babyface, BLACKstreet, Keith Sweat, Jodeci, Maxwell

see also: *Harold Melvin & the Blue Notes*

Andre McGarrity

The Penguins

Formed 1953, in Los Angeles, CA. Disbanded 1965.

Cleveland Duncan, tenor; Curtis Williams, baritone (1953–57); Bruce Tate, baritone (1953–54); Dexter Tisby, tenor (1953–62); Randy Jones, baritone (1954–62); Teddy Harper, baritone (1957–62).

If the Penguins had never recorded "Earth Angel," no one would be interested in them today. The vocal group's biggest hit was a monster, moving to #8 on the *Billboard* pop charts in 1954, which was pretty darn good for a group that was also charting in R&B. The mellow doo-wop single sold four million copies during the next decade. The Penguins' story could be a template for one-hit wonders, except that they recorded nearly 50 sides, some of them gems that were ignored in the marketplace. Curtis Williams was a member of the Hollywood Flames vocal group when he bumped into grammar-school pal Cleveland Duncan at a talent show in 1953. Williams was developing "Earth Angel" with the Flames (after a series of lawsuits, the song is now attributed to Williams, Jesse Belvin, and Gaynel Hodge, who was a fellow member with Williams of the Hollywood Flames). Williams and Duncan invited respective high school pals Bruce Tate and Dexter Tisby to form a new vocal quartet. They named the group after the penguin used in Kool cigarette ads—because the group was "cool." The quartet interested Walter "Dootsie" Williams of Dootone Records. "Earth Angel" was released on the flip side of their second single, "Hey Senorita," a relatively typical R&B number, in September 1954—so it took a while before people started paying attention to the song. As the song climbed the charts, Tate left the lineup in November and was replaced by the group's first real bass singer, Randy Jones. By the time the single was a hit, the group decided Williams was playing games with royalties and, under the wing of Platters' founder Buck Ram, bolted to Mercury Records in early 1955. That's when the lawsuits began. They recorded good tracks at Mercury, but with fortunes fading left for Atlantic in early 1956, where they recorded four tunes, producing the #15 rhythm and blues hit, "Pledge of Love." When Dootsie Williams won in court, the group returned to his fold in 1957. (Curtis Williams soon bowed out to be replaced by Teddy Harper.) By 1960, the dispirited quartet left Dootsie Williams again, and continued performing and recording until 1962. "Memories of El Monte," written by Frank Zappa about the big doo-wop shows at El Monte Legion Stadium, was credited to the Penguins in 1963 but was actually just Duncan with a group of hired guns. So was the final Penguins single, "Heavenly Angel," in 1965.

what to buy: Although the Penguins redid "Earth Angel" almost note-for-note for Mercury Records, there's a certain feeling missing from Cleveland Duncan's smooth vocal performance. The original Dootone version is the one to have, and that's available on *The Authentic Golden Hits of the Penguins* 𝄞𝄞𝄞𝄞 (Juke Box Treasures, 1993, prod. various). The collection features cuts from both stints with Dootone, including the demo "There Ain't No News Today" that became the group's first single. It's hard to understand why the Penguins' fortunes faded so quickly when you listen to *The Best of the Penguins—The Mercury Years* 𝄞𝄞𝄞𝄞 (Mercury, 1996, prod. various). The 21 selections include remakes of the Dootone numbers "Earth Angel," "Ookey Ook," "Love Will Make Your Mind Go Wild," and "Hey Senorita," plus any number of hit-worthy tunes, ranging in mood from the mellow "My Troubles Are Not at an End" to the raucous "Promises, Promises, Promises." The Penguins' sense of harmony is slightly off, but there's plenty of energy in these songs.

what to buy next: The true Penguins collector is going to want a copy of "Memories of El Monte," which features Duncan and his cohorts imitating some favorite oldies such as "Cherry Pie" and "Night Owl." The song hinges on this medley of doo-wop nostalgia, and it's featured in the multi-artist compilation *The Doo Wop Box II* 𝄞𝄞𝄞𝄞 (Rhino, 1996, prod. various).

what to avoid: Until someone does a cross-label collection of the Penguins' tunes (including the Atlantic sides and "Memo-

ries of El Monte"), the albums mentioned above should give all but the most rabid fans an excellent grasp of the group's career. Other available albums such as the import *Earth Angel* 𝄞𝄞𝄞 (Ace) just cover the same ground.

influences:

◀◀ Jesse Belvin, the Clovers, the Five Keys

▶▶ Boyz II Men, All-4-One

Salvatore Caputo

CeCe Peniston

Born September 6, 1969, in Dayton, OH.

The former "Miss Black Arizona" became a disco diva just as disco/house music surged back into the pop mainstream during the early 1990s. Peniston's big break came in 1991, when she sang background vocals on Phoenix rapper Overweight Pooch's album. Her vocals impressed a record label scout, who signed her. Her debut album went gold on the strength of the Top 10 pop hit "Finally" and the popular single "We Got a Love Thang." Follow-up works were greeted less warmly, despite her confident and competent talent. Seeking legitimacy as a soul singer and, possibly, crowded by a storm of female house singers, she took an R&B turn on her last album.

what to buy: While *Finally* 𝄞𝄞𝄞𝄞 (A&M, 1992, prod. Steve "Silk" Hurley) takes full advantage of dance music's resurgent popularity, it sparkles most when it blends thumping beats and Peniston's throaty voice with a classic R&B vibe, particularly on the ballads "Inside That I Cried," and "You Win, I Win, We Lose."

what to buy next: Peniston left her dance comfort zone and went for more of a smooth soul groove on *I'm Movin' On* 𝄞𝄞𝄞 (A&M, 1996, prod. various), which features her voice more prominently. Unfortunately, the album only found moderate success, far from the extent of her previous incarnation.

the rest:

Thought 'Ya Knew 𝄞𝄞𝄞 (A&M, 1994)

worth searching for: Although her role is limited, Peniston shows she has the chops to stand next to vocalists Albertina Walker, Thelma Houston, and Phoebe Snow on their collaborative gospel album, *Good News in Hard Times* 𝄞𝄞 (Warner Bros., 1995, prod. Jennifer Cohen)

influences:

◀◀ Madonna, Evelyn "Champagne" King, Lisa Stansfield

Franklin Paul

The Persuasions

Formed 1966, in Bedford-Stuyvesant, NY.

Jerry Lawson, lead vocals; Joseph "Jesse" Russell, tenor; Jayotis Washington, tenor; Herbert "Tubo" Rhoad, baritone (1966–88); Jimmy "Bro" Hayes, first tenor and bass.

To listen to the Persuasions is to be swept up in one of the most soulful vocal experiences you'll ever have. The *a capella* group specializes in taking songs—some famous and some not—and making them their own, their voices creating a symphony of sound that equals any full-blown instrumental band. Because this kind of singing comes from church, it's natural that the group gravitates toward spiritual fare (lots of Curtis Mayfield songs, in fact), but there's also social commentary ("Buffalo Soldier," "Hymn #9") and an admiring nod toward the Temptations; after all, the Persuasions' Jerry Lawson is a dead sonic ringer for the Tempts' Dennis Edwards. The charts have eluded them over the years, but the Persuasions remain active and produce as rich a sound now as they ever have.

what to buy: *Man, Oh Man: The Power of the Persuasions* 𝄞𝄞𝄞𝄞𝄞 (EMI, 1997, prod. various) compiles its 14 selections from the group's three most successful albums, recorded for Capitol Records during 1971–72. Their renditions of the Impressions' "People Get Ready," Bob Dylan's "Three Angels," Sam Cooke's "Good Times" and the amazing Temptations memories are seminal moments in vocal music.

what to buy next: *Right Around the Corner* 𝄞𝄞𝄞𝄞 (Bullseye Blues, 1994, prod. Jerry Lawson), recorded during a brief stint as a trio, and *Sincerely* 𝄞𝄞𝄞 (Bullseye Blues, 1996, prod. Jerry Lawson) offer assurance that the Persuasions still have it three decades later.

the rest:
We Came to Play 𝄞𝄞𝄞𝄞 (Capitol, 1972/Collectables)
Spread the Word 𝄞𝄞𝄞𝄞 (Capitol, 1972/Collectables, 1995)
Street Corner Symphony 𝄞𝄞𝄞𝄞 (Capitol, 1972/Collectables)
Chirpin' 𝄞𝄞𝄞 (Elektra, 1977/1990)
Good News 𝄞𝄞𝄞 (Rounder, 1988/1991)
No Frills 𝄞𝄞𝄞 (Rounder, 1989)
Comin' at Ya 𝄞𝄞𝄞 (Flying Fish, 1990)
Stardust 𝄞𝄞𝄞 (Relic, 1994)

worth searching for: The Persuasions offer some sweet vocals to both complement and counteract the avant skew on the Frank Zappa tribute *Zappa's Universe* (Verve, 1993).

influences:
◄◄ The Mills Brothers, the Dell Vikings, the Impressions, the Prisonaires, Joe South, the Temptations, the Four Tops

►► The Spinners, Ray, Goodman & Brown, New Edition, Boyz II Men

Gary Graff

Pete Rock & C.L. Smooth

Formed 1984, in Mount Vernon, NY. Disbanded 1994.

Pete Rock (born Peter Phillips), DJ; C.L. Smooth (born Corey Penn), vocals.

Hip-hop came to know the New York City suburb of "money earnin'" Mount Vernon thanks in large part to the popularity of Heavy D. But it was Heavy's younger cousin, producer-DJ Pete Rock, plus Rock's partner in rhyme, C.L. Smooth, who elevated the region's contributions to the hip-hop menagerie. Pete Rock and C.L. met during high school in your typical DJ-searching-for-MC scenario. Their big break came when Heavy D. introduced Pete Rock to his childhood hero, Marley Marl, and the rest of the New York radio community. Marley really took to Rock, hyping him on his show and even debuting some of his early material. With Pete Rock's supple funk creations and C.L.'s silky basso, the duo became one of the most revered groups in hip-hop. Rock was part of the DJ culture that lived and died by obscure soul, funk, and blues LPs and 45s, and the music he created certainly sounded like it was culled from dusty crates. One of the first DJs to supply interludes consisting of rare groove breakbeats—a codified by-product of his DJ/musicologist background—Rock's trademark style features thick soul-soaked basslines punctuated by slick and seductive horns; his concoctions were always noticeable, too, for the ad-libbed "yeahs," "oohs," and "uhhs" he parenthetically placed beneath the vocal tracks. In addition to two albums and an EP he made with C.L., Rock has produced innumerable tracks for other artists (Heavy D., Nas, Public Enemy) and has thrust himself into the upper echelon of hip-hop producers. (Rock also found time to rhyme, though his lines sounded forced and reminded listeners of what his *real* strength was.) Similarly, C.L. is regarded as one of the most consistent MCs around. Mixing confidence and intelligence with a dash of erotic smooth talk, C.L. made all the men want to be like him—and all the women want to be *with* him. Just like Marvin Gaye and Isaac Hayes, C.L. also established himself as a writer who could achieve a legitimate balance between musicianship and knowledge of self. Although Pete Rock and C.L. Smooth were regarded as brothers, they quietly (and sadly) decided to pursue other opportunities in 1994, just as they were promoting their second full-length album. Rock is now producing a group called INI (featuring his younger brother Grap Lover), while C.L. is working on his solo album to be produced by myriad DJs.

what to buy: Everything Pete Rock & C.L. Smooth recorded together was intoxicating. Their debut EP, *All Souled Out* ♪♪♪♪ (Elektra, 1991, prod. Pete Rock) features six solid, classically constructed hip-hop songs, including "The Creator" and "Go with the Flow." The EP introduced people to the concept of Mecca—a spiritual meeting of the minds derived from the Islamic site of the same name—and set the table for the duo's first full-length album, *Mecca and the Soul Brother* ♪♪♪♪ (Elektra, 1992, prod. Pete Rock). The duo with the fresh barber-shop fades could do no wrong with such creations as "For Pete's Sake" and "Lots of Lovin'." The album's best-known track is "They Reminisce over You (T.R.O.Y.)," a poignant song dedicated to Trouble T Roy, the dancer from Heavy D.'s crew who died after falling off a riser in preparations for a concert performance. *The Main Ingredient* ♪♪♪♪ (1994, Elektra Records, prod. Pete Rock) is an even better album; one song seems to ease into the other, creating extreme reluctance to press the stop button. To hear the title track or "I Got a Love" is to hear a tighter, more refined, and professional-sounding duo—but one that had remained amazingly consistent since its inception. Pete Rock and C.L.'s camaraderie and bond is clearly audible, which makes their break-up even more disappointing.

worth searching for: The "Lots of Lovin'" single (Elektra, 1993) features the otherwise unreleased B-side "It's Not a Game," one of the group's strongest songs.

influences:

◀◀ Heavy D., Queen Latifah, Marley Marl

▶▶ INI, Common, Dred Scott, Blackalicious

Jazzbo

Pharcyde

Formed early 1990s, in Los Angeles, CA.

Darky Boy, vocals; Bootie Brown, vocals; Slim Kid 3, vocals; Fat Lip, vocals (left group in 1997).

For the majority of its existence, the Pharcyde has been a group of pranksters in a world of gangsters. And whether it has been the thug mentality of fellow MCs or the thuggish record industry, the quartet has received a good deal of alienation for its stance and goofball antics. The Pharcyde's rhymes, after all, run a gamut, covering everything from masturbation to getting bullied by former classmates. As such liberated MCs, they serve up the alter-ego of Hip-hop Proper, giving a rare glimpse

of what the genre could look like without boundaries and incessant fronting.

what to buy: *Bizarre Ride II the Pharcyde* ♪♪♪♪ (Delicious Vinyl, 1992, prod. various) is a tour through a hip-hop carnival packed with soul-jazz samples and plenty of stream-of-consciousness lyrics. In a classic toast to the dozens, "Ya Mama" offers old and new insults aplenty, while self-deprecating cuts such as "On the DL" and "Oh Shit" address sexual frustrations ignored in the sphere of macho-man rap. "Passing Me By" harks back to the old school, dusting off a horn riff and delivering a jazzy, universal narrative about unrequited love and the folly of pursuing it. A distinctly more serious effort, *Labcabincalifornia* ♪♪♪♪ (Delicious Vinyl/Capitol, 1995, prod. various), picks up where the crew left off, citing experiences during the years since they first left the studio. Time and maturity give the follow-up a more somber, intelligent feel, and the group opts for backdrops grounded in hip-hop tradition rather than experimentation. "Devil Music" is an autobiographical attack on record industry exploitation, while "Runnin'" and "Moment in Time" offer coming-of-age stories that show the crew can stop laughing when the situation demands: the latter track is dedicated to "those who passed away far too young."

worth searching for: For the group's 1996 *Drop* video, noted director Spike Jonze filmed the members of Pharcyde rapping and moving backwards, then reversed the tape, making the footage look almost normal. But you'll notice some absurd things happening along the way: Balls bouncing up stairs, bicyclists going the wrong way, rappers leaping into the sky like superheroes. It's an amazingly bizarre ride.

influences:

◀◀ A Tribe Called Quest, De La Soul, Biz Markie, Jungle Brothers, Beastie Boys, Def Jef

▶▶ The Roots, Ahmad, Skee-Lo, Freestyle Fellowship, Souls of Mischief, Anotha Level

Corey Takahashi

Philadelphia International

The home of the "Philly sound," Philadelphia International was created in 1966 by songwriter-producers Kenneth Gamble and Leon Huff, a duo whose early successes with Jerry Butler, Wilson Pickett, Dusty Springfield, and Archie Bell & the Drells allowed them to finance their vision of an independent production house—a little like Motown and a little like Stax—that would allow them to have the lush but still groove-worthy sound that was their specialty. Gamble and Huff packed Philly International with a powerhouse roster—the O'Jays, Teddy Pendergrass, Harold Melvin & the Blue Notes, Billy Paul, the Intruders. They also recruited other producers and writers, including Thom Bell, Bobby Martin, Bunny Sigler, and the late Norman Harris, who in turn brought their own artists to town. And the house pound, MFSB (Mother, Father, Sister, Brother), not only provided stellar backing but also launched a career of its own with the 1973 smash "T.S.O.P. (The Sound of Philadelphia)." Philadelphia International closed just a decade after it opened, but in that short time it created more than its share of timeless pop and R&B, and it created a sonic template that's still imitated today.

what to buy: *The Philly Sound: Kenny Gamble, Leon Huff & the Story of Brotherly Love (1966–1976)* 𝄞𝄞𝄞𝄞 (Epic/Legacy, 1997, comp. Leo Sacks) is a wondrous three-volume set that starts with Gamble & Huff's early hits and traces the rise of Philadelphia International, particularly during the early 1970s. Besides an awesome collection of music, there are strong liner notes with pieces by Quincy Jones, Jerry Butler, Barry White, Curtis Mayfield, Michael Jackson, Public Enemy's Chuck D., Eddie Levert of the O'-Jays, Teddy Pendergrass, and others. An essential piece.

Gary Graff

Dewey Phillips

Born May 13, 1926, in Adamsville, TN. Died September 28, 1968, in Millington, TN.

Dewey Phillips was the white southern disc jockey who spun blues records on Memphis radio during the 1950s. Though he's now remembered as the answer to a trivia question (What DJ played Elvis Presley's first record?), Phillips's WHBQ show was an unparalleled regional phenomenon that probably had as much impact on early rock as the Sun Records label. An integral member of the Beale Street scene, Phillips was at his most engaging playing the up-tempo R&B and blues records of the early 1950s, but when rock 'n' roll came into prominence, he claimed it as his own. A canny self-promoter, his trademark catch phrase "Tell 'em PHILLIPS sent ya!" and zany rants during commercials ("If you can't drink it, freeze it and eat it") tickled teenagers almost as much as the incendiary new music he was playing. At his peak, Phillips hosted a top-rated Memphis TV show in addition to his highly popular stint on radio. When his on-air partner Harry Fritzius made lewd advances to a cardboard statue of Jayne Mansfield, the TV program was canceled instantly. A few months later, Phillips's own increasingly erratic behavior forced the cancellation of his radio program. He hung

on in the mid-South market, spinning discs at increasingly smaller stations. By 1964, Phillips's career and humor had gone sour. Though he remained a flamboyant radio presence, he was clearly out of his element playing British Invasion pop. He died in 1968, forgotten by the many artists (Elvis in particular) whose careers he helped make possible.

what's available: The *Dewey Phillips: Red, Hot, & Blue* 𝄞𝄞𝄞𝄞 (Memphis Archives, 1995, prod. Richard James Hite) disc contains air checks of Phillips speed-talking, singing along with the records by Amos Milburn, Little Milton, Piano Red, etc., cracking jokes, impersonating Dizzy Dean, messing up, and straightening out on his "Red, Hot & Blue" show for various stations from 1952–64. This CD is a stunning document, not just of the man but also of a style of entertainment that simply doesn't exist today. On top of that, it's a lot of fun.

influences:

◄◄ Alan Freed, Sleepy Eyed John

►► The Famous Coachman

Ken Burke

Esther Phillips

Born Esther Mae Jones, December 23, 1935, in Galveston, TX. Died August 7, 1984, in Carson, CA.

The youngest female singer ever to claim a #1 hit on the R&B charts, "Little" Esther Phillips grew up to have a long and versatile career that crossed easily between R&B, jazz, blues, and southern soul genres. Though never a jazz singer in the classic, Ella Fitzgerald sense, Phillips was blessed with an incredibly powerful voice that allowed her to embrace a variety of material and make it uniquely her own. Moving to L.A. from Texas in 1940, she sang in the sanctified church and competed in local talent shows, winning first prize in a contest at the Barrelhouse nightclub. From there, she joined the traveling Johnny Otis Rhythm and Blues Caravan Show, becoming nationally known for her recordings with the Otis orchestra. After topping the charts at age 15 with the single "Double-Crossing Blues," Esther went on to have a string of R&B hits in the early 1950s—"Mistrustin' Blues," "Misery," "Cupid's Boogie," and "Ring-a-Ding Doo," to name a few—many in duets with the Otis band's male lead vocalist, Mel Walker. Despite her tender years, she sang the blues with vigor and conviction and proved herself an extraordinary ballad heartbreaker. She performed with Otis until 1954, then moved back to Texas and put her career on hold. She made a remarkable comeback in 1962, signing with the Lenox label and notching a Top 10 R&B and pop single with her version of the country tune "Release Me." Meanwhile, she was seeking her own release from the drug problems that constantly interrupted her rise to stardom and kept her one of the most underrated vocalists of her time. Phillips enjoyed a renaissance in the 1960s on Atlantic Records, doing everything from Beatles covers to making a transcendent performance at the Newport Jazz Festival, recording a classic live LP in 1970, and tackling the disco era head-on with her hit dance-oriented remake of Dinah Washington's blues standard "What a Diff'rence a Day Makes." *Rolling Stone* magazine named her America's best blues singer in 1974. Continuing to make great music through the 1970s, Phillips died of liver and kidney failure in 1984.

what to buy: One of the few artists to be featured in jazz, blues, and R&B compilations, the box set *The Best of Esther Phillips 1962–1970* 𝄞𝄞𝄞𝄞 (WEA/Atlantic/Rhino, 1997, prod. various) displays all facets of this uncommon artist in one representative package. Unlike the earlier Sony collection *The Best of Esther Phillips* 𝄞𝄞 (Sony, 1990, prod. various), which contains none of her earliest blues work as "Little Esther" (but is notable for her reworkings of such familiar standards as "Do Right Woman, Do Right Man," "Such a Night," and her disco version of "What a Diff'rence a Day Makes"), the 1997 retrospective includes her first hit, "Double-Crossing Blues," as well as "Release Me" and the classic "Some Things You Never Get Used To" among its 40 tracks.

what to buy next: Fully living up to its title, *Confessin' the Blues* 𝄞𝄞𝄞𝄞 (WEA/Atlantic, 1990, prod. Nesuhi Ertegun, King Curtis) showcases Phillips in the genre she clearly loves best. Recorded live in Los Angeles, the LP includes a houserocking rendition of "C.C. Rider" and a riveting medley of "Blow Top Blues," "Jelly Jelly Blues," and "Long John Blues." Blues lovers, heaven must be like this.

the rest:
From a Whisper to a Scream 𝄞𝄞𝄞𝄞 (Sony, 1972)
What a Diff'rence a Day Makes 𝄞𝄞𝄞 (Sony, 1975)
Rising Sun Collection 𝄞𝄞 (Just a Memory, 1995)

worth searching for: Though no longer in print, the album *Burnin'—Live at Freddie Jett's Pied Piper, LA* 𝄞𝄞𝄞𝄞 (Roulette, 1969) is an amazing work, the recording some jazz purists still use as the standard against which all live solo LPs should be measured.

influences:

◀◀ Big Maybelle, Etta James, Dinah Washington, Johnny Otis, Ray Charles, Billie Holiday, Solomon Burke, LaVern Baker, Ruth Brown

▶▶ Aretha Franklin, Teena Marie, Phyllis Hyman, Patti Austin, Tracy Nelson, Lisa Stansfield

Jim McFarlin

Wilson Pickett

Born March 18, 1941, in Prattville, AL.

Among all of soul music's throat-shredding testifiers, none could match Pickett. From his earliest recordings as lead vocalist with the Falcons, Pickett's voice was unmistakable in its sheer, unsettling power. But until he was sent off to Memphis in 1965 by Atlantic Records, Pickett had not found the right instrumental backing for chart success. He most definitely found it there: using musicians from the Stax house band and from Muscle Shoals, Pickett unleashed a string of incomparable soul classics—"Mustang Sally," "In the Midnight Hour," and "Funky Broadway" among them. His combination of gospel urgency and sexual swagger earned him the nickname "The Wicked Pickett," as his singles ruled the dance floor. But despite a career-reviving stint with Kenny Gamble and Leon Huff's slicker Philadelphia sound during the early 1970s, the hits soon stopped coming. Though the wicked side of Pickett gets him more press these days than his music (he has a fondness for guns, it seems), he still stands as one of the soul era's greatest vocalists.

what to buy: Pickett's best has been thoroughly and admirably documented on the two-CD set *Wilson Pickett: A Man and a Half* 𝄞𝄞𝄞𝄞 (Rhino/Atlantic, 1992, prod. various). Beginning in 1961 with Pickett's vocalizing on "I Found a Love" by the Falcons, this collection offers a comprehensive journey through the Atlantic years and the Philadelphia sides and culminates with a live 1971 performance of "Funky Broadway" from a show in Ghana. And there are a few unreleased songs, alternate versions, and rare live cuts along the way. If you just want the hits and nothing more, *The Very Best of Wilson Pickett* 𝄞𝄞𝄞𝄞 (Rhino, 1993, prod. various) is where to find them on one tight CD.

what to buy next: Of the earlier Atlantic albums available on CD, *The Exciting Wilson Pickett* 𝄞𝄞𝄞𝄞 (Atlantic, 1966, prod. Jerry Wexler) and *The Sound of Wilson Pickett* 𝄞𝄞𝄞𝄞 (Atlantic, 1967, prod. Tom Dowd) are the best. *Wilson Pickett in Philadelphia* 𝄞𝄞𝄞𝄞 (Atlantic, 1970, prod. Kenny Gamble, Leon Huff) is the great soul shouter's final outstanding album.

what to avoid: On *Mr. Magic Man* 𝄞 (RCA, 1973) the voice is still there, but this is the beginning of Pickett's slide into uninspired mediocrity.

the rest:
In the Midnight Hour 𝄞𝄞𝄞𝄢 (Atlantic, 1965)
Wicked Pickett 𝄞𝄞𝄞𝄢 (Atlantic, 1966)
Wilson Pickett's Greatest Hits 𝄞𝄞𝄞𝄞 (Atlantic, 1973)

worth searching for: *American Soul Man* 𝄞𝄞𝄞 (Motown, 1987) is a brief stop at the legendary Detroit R&B label that finds Pickett in good voice—perhaps inspired by the hallowed surroundings.

influences:

◀◀ The Swan Silvertones, the Soul Stirrers, Hank Ballard & the Midnighters

▶▶ Bobby Womack, Teddy Pendergrass, the Commitments

see also: *The Falcons*

Doug Pippin

The Platters

Formed 1953, in Los Angeles, CA.

Tony Williams, lead vocals (1953–60); David Lynch, tenor vocals; Herbert Reed, bass vocals; Alex Hodge, baritone vocals (1953–54); Zola Taylor, contralto vocals (1954–61); Paul Robi, baritone vocals (1955–62); Sonny Turner, lead vocals (1961–65); Nate Nelson, baritone vocals (1962–65); Sandra Dawn, contralto vocals (1962–65).

From 1955–60, few vocal groups could touch the Platters' crossover appeal. Featuring Williams's heart-rending lead vocals, the group had several smash hits that are now inarguable classics of the genre. "Only You," "The Great Pretender," and "Smoke Gets in Your Eyes" remain piercing examples of head-over-heels romantic R&B. Williams's total emotional immersion in the material is nothing less than overwhelming. As the 1960s wore on, numerous member changes effectively stalled the former hit-makers. The 1970s were marked by court battles over ownership of the group's name; the rights are now held by Robi's widow. The group was inducted into the Rock and Roll Hall of Fame in 1990.

what to buy: *The Very Best of the Platters* 𝄞𝄞𝄞𝄞𝄞 (Mercury, 1991, comp. Bill Levenson) hits the highlights from these tremulous masters of melodrama in a single-disc package. It's the perfect introduction.

what to buy next: *The Magic Touch—An Anthology* 𝄞𝄞𝄞𝄞𝄞 (Mercury, 1991, comp. Harry Weinger) is a more complete two-disc set that includes many lesser-known tracks, making it a more definitive album for those already acquainted.

what to avoid: *Greatest Hits Vol. 2* 𝄞𝄞 (Curb Records, 1996, prod. various) is a skimpy collection devoid of the biggest hits.

the rest:
Christmas with the Platters 𝄞𝄞𝄞 (Mercury, 1994)
Greatest Hits 𝄞𝄞 (Special Music Company)
The Platters 𝄞𝄞 (King)
Golden Hits Collection 𝄞𝄞𝄞𝄞 (Pickwick, 1993)
The Musicor Years 𝄞𝄞𝄞 (Kent, 1994)

worth searching for: *Four Platters and One Lovely Dish* 𝄞𝄞𝄞𝄞𝄞 (Bear Family, 1994, prod. various) is a typical whole-hog, nine-disc set that should appeal to the ultra-completists.

influences:

◀◀ The Ink Spots, Bobby Bland

▶▶ New Edition, Boyz II Men, Huey Lewis & the News

Allan Orski

PM Dawn

Formed 1990, in Jersey City, NJ.

Prince Be, vocals; DJ Minutemix, DJ.

"Reality Used to Be a Friend of Mine" is one of the anthems that put PM Dawn on the map; it could also serve as a label for the duo's metaphysical raps and musings. Some take its hippy dippy attitude as an influence from De La Soul, which has since taken on a more hardcore image. But in music, the tent is big, and the otherworldly excursions of PM Dawn add another spoke to the wheel.

what to buy: *The Bliss Album . . . ? (Vibrations of Love and Anger and the Ponderance of Life and Existence)* 𝄞𝄞𝄞𝄞 (Gee Street/Island, 1993, prod. PM Dawn) proves to be inspired musicianship, whatever the genre, though "Beyond Infinite Affections," "Nocturnal Is in the House," and, especially, "Plastic" show the duo can throw down when the challenge arises (the latter song inspired by KRS-One's infamous on-stage assault of Prince Be).

what to buy next: Paradoxically, PM Dawn broke in during the height of gangsta rap with *Of the Heart, of the Soul and the Cross: The Utopian Experience* 𝄞𝄞𝄞 (Gee Street/Island, 1991, prod. PM Dawn), an album loaded with interesting samples—and one in which Prince Be croons bona fide soul between

Wilson Pickett (© Jack Vartoogian)

throwing down rhymes. Built around Spandau Ballet's "True," the breakthrough single "Set Adrift on Memory Bliss" is a glorious slice of dreamy pop. The group's poppish psychedelia begins to wear thin, though, by its third album, *Jesus Wept* ♫♫♫ (Gee Street/Island, 1995, prod. PM Dawn), even though "My Personal Gravity" did hit the airwaves with its haunting "What could be lonely 'bout you?" line. Reportedly, the final product isn't even close to the one PM Dawn wanted to release, (no) thanks to sample-clearance issues—a major problem for a group that thrives on sampling unlikely sources (Spandau Ballet, George Michael, Joni Mitchell, Hugh Masekela, Doobie Brothers).

influences:

◀◀ Prince, the Beatles, George Michael, De La Soul

▶▶ Me Phi Me, O.M.D.

Lawrence Gabriel

The Pointer Sisters

Formed 1971, in Oakland, CA.

Ruth Pointer, vocals; Anita Pointer, vocals; June Pointer, vocals; Bonnie Pointer, vocals (1971–78).

The Pointer Sisters trained to become the "So Excited" queens of early '80s pop-soul music in church. Both of their parents were ministers at the West Oakland Church of God in West Oakland, California, and the sisters, along with their two older brothers, all sang as part of the services. The youngest Pointers, Bonnie and June, were first to begin musical careers outside the church in 1969. Eventually Anita joined them, and the trio began singing backup for such acts as Boz Scaggs, Taj Mahal, and Esther Phillips. In 1972, Ruth left her job as a keypunch operator and the group quickly landed a recording contract. Making a name for themselves with their 1940s-era outfits and updated versions of nostalgic, big band/swing tunes, the Pointer Sisters scored hits with the songs "Yes We Can Can" and "Wang Dang Doodle" and became a star attraction within a year. They were the first African American women to perform at Nashville's Grand Old Opry and the first pop act ever to perform at San Francisco's Opera House. The Pointers won wide acceptance for their ability to excel in a variety of styles from pop and R&B to jazz and even country. Bonnie left for a solo career in 1978, just before the group really began rocketing up the pop charts: a cover of Bruce Springsteen's "Fire" the next year was the group's first Top 10 hit, followed in rapid succession by the likes of "He's So Shy," "Slow Hand," "Auto-

matic," "Jump (For My Love)," and "I'm So Excited." Though their career sagged in the early '90s, the Pointer Sisters have demonstrated a knack for reinventing themselves and changing their musical colors like chameleons, as evidenced by their teaming with country Clint Black on the single, "Rhythm, Country and Blues."

what to buy: With 19 albums in their 25-year-plus history, *Fire: The Very Best of the Pointer Sisters 1973–1986* ♫♫♫♫ (RCA, 1996, prod. various) is the best place to get one's feet wet experiencing the soulful melodies of the Pointer Sisters. Impressively covering the two decades of the group's best work, the LP collects the early material released on the Blue Thumb and Planet labels and includes the important hits "Fairy Tale," "Slow Hand," and "I'm So Excited," among others.

what to buy next: The Pointers went heavy metal—double platinum, that is—on *Break Out* ♫♫♫♫ (BMG/RCA, 1983, prod. Richard Perry), easily the biggest album of their career. Under Perry's canny production, this slick, well-balanced, quintessential pop disk included the unsurprising but spicy pop hits "Automatic," "Jump," and "Neutron Dance," and attracted many prominent modern musicians like guitarist Lee Ritenour.

what to avoid: The Pointer Sisters held court as one of the music industry's hottest acts in the early 1980s, then had trouble maintaining their status as queens of the pop world. *Sweet & Soulful* ♫♫ (BMG/RCA, 1992) failed to produce any hits or significant tracks and symbolizes the disappointing downturn of the group's career.

the rest:

Pointer Sisters ♫♫♫ (UNI/MCA, 1973/1990)
Black & White ♫♫♫♫ (BMG/RCA, 1981/1995)
Greatest Hits ♫♫♫♫ (BMG/RCA, 1982/1989)
Jump: Best of the Pointer Sisters ♫♫♫♫ (RCA, 1989)
Best of the Pointer Sisters 1978–81 ♫♫♫♫ (BMG/RCA, 1993)
Only Sisters Can Do That ♫♫ (EMD/Capitol, 1993)
New Cast Recording: Ain't Misbehavin' ♫♫♫ (RCA, 1996)
Yes We Can Can: The Best of the Blue Thumb Recordings ♫♫♫ (Hip-O, 1997)

worth searching for: Though available only on vinyl, the solo works by Bonnie and Anita Pointer are for the most part worth investigating. Bonnie's first two releases, *Bonnie Pointer* ♫♫♫ (Motown, 1978) and *Bonnie Pointer II* ♫♫ (Motown, 1979) placed well on the album charts and produced hits like "Free Me from My Freedom/Tie Me to a Tree (Handcuff Me)" and "Heaven Must Have Sent You." (Her last solo outing, however, *The Price Is Right* ♫♫ (Private, 1984), was extremely disappointing and delayed several times due to messy legal battles with Motown.) Anita has produced one solo work to date, without leaving the group like Bonnie, *Love for What It Is* 🎵🎵🎵 (RCA, 1987).

influences:

⏪ The Andrews Sisters, Aretha Franklin, the Staple Sisters, Boz Scaggs, Patti LaBelle, the Supremes

⏩ Janet Jackson, Michael Jackson, Manhattan Transfer, Madonna, Betty Wright, Sister Sledge, En Vogue, La Bouche

Chris Tower

Doc Pomus

Born June 27, 1925, in New York, NY. Died March 14, 1991, in New York, NY.

The first glimpse the world got of Doc Pomus was of the young man hobbling his obese, polio-stricken body onto smoky nightclub stages and singing his heart out for black audiences. Sensing the career limits a disabled Jewish blues singer would face, Pomus took to songwriting for Atlantic and became one of the most famed and respected songwriters in the R&B and pop world. A master of the three-minute slice of life, Pomus penned classic hits for everyone from Ray Charles ("Lonely Avenue") and the Coasters ("Youngblood") during the 1950s to the Drifters ("Save the Last Dance for Me," "I Count the Tears," "This Magic Moment," "Sweets for My Sweet") and Elvis Presley (who covered the most Pomus songs of anyone, including "Viva Las Vegas," "Little Sister," "Surrender," "A Mess of Blues") in the 1960s. A less-known facet of Pomus's enduring legacy is his loyalty and availability to artists themselves—not only the stars who covered his music but also struggling hacks who sought fundamental advice from him. Everyone concerned was free to call Pomus up (he remained listed in the phone book throughout his life) and pepper him with questions. Aside from songwriting, Pomus's other consuming passion was championing artists' rights and royalties, eventually setting up grants for artists in need. Bedridden with lung cancer, Pomus was writing songs on a laptop computer as little as two weeks before his death.

what's available: The tribute *Till the Night Is Gone* 🎵🎵🎵 (Forward, 1995, prod. various) isn't the embarrassment most albums of this nature are, nor is it the best representation of Pomus's work. The reworkings of his material—some inspired, some drastic—from fans as diverse as Los Lobos, Lou Reed, Dion, B.B. King, and Brian Wilson make for an engaging and quite illuminating listen.

influences:

⏪ Louis Jordan, Sammy Cahn, Duke Ellington, Cab Calloway, George & Ira Gershwin

⏩ Elvis Presley, the Drifters, Clyde McPhatter, Bruce Springsteen, Lou Reed

Allan Orski

Pooh-Man /M.C. Pooh

Born Lawrence Thomas.

Like Too $hort, Pooh-Man delivers nasty raps and loves the word "bitch." His lyrical flow is classic early-'90s East Oakland, a mid-pitched, laid-back drawl that slinks and slides over creamy funk licks. As of this writing, the former M.C. Pooh was serving time at San Quentin.

what to buy: Credited to M.C. Pooh, *Life of a Criminal* 🎵🎵🎵 (FBI, 1990, prod. Ant Banks) is an East Oakland classic, in which Pooh sounds like a cross between Too $hort and Eazy-E. Among the songs is "Fuckin' with Dank," which introduced to many a new term for weed. Now known as Pooh-Man, the rapper's *Funky As I Wanna Be* 🎵🎵🎵 (Jive, 1992, prod. Ant Banks) features "Don't Cost a Dime" (a duet with M.C. Breed) and "Racia," in which Pooh and Too $hort discuss the word "bitch." Interestingly, Pooh soon became rivals with $hort and producer Banks, with disses being exchanged on wax (Pooh would say about $hort "you ain't shit but a weak bitch").

the rest:

Judgement Day 🎵🎵🎵 (Scarface, 1993)
Ain't No Love 🎵🎵 (In-A-Minute, 1994)
The State vs. Poohman 🎵🎵🎵 (In-A-Minute, 1997)

influences:

⏪ Too $hort

⏩ Rappin' 4-Tay, JT the Bigga Figga, Seagram

Spence D.

Poor Righteous Teachers

Formed in Trenton, NJ.

Wise Intelligent, vocals; Culture Freedom, vocals; Father Shaheed, DJ.

The Poor Righteous Teachers' impact has been as much ideological as musical. Once Chuck D. and Public Enemy battered down the walls between Afrocentric politics and mainstream pop culture, the next wave of rappers was able to disseminate provocative and often controversial views through the powerful channels of pop music. As avatars of the Five Percent Nation, a youth-oriented sect of the Nation of Islam, the Poor Righteous Teachers—along with the likes of Rakim, King Sun, Paris, and Brand Nubian—transformed the language and worldview of an entire generation. Is it possible to imagine '90s debates over multiculturalism, Afrocentrism, and Ebonics on college campuses and local school boards without Five Percent rap? Perhaps—and perhaps not. At the least, there are not many acts that have created a catalog more notable in their blend of didacticism and booty-blessing beats than PRT.

what to buy: *Holy Intellect* ✍✍✍✍ (Profile, 1990, prod. Tony D and Eric "IQ" Gray) is a promising debut. Producer Tony D (a.k.a. Harvey Wallbanger) provides a clean, elastic funk for Wise Intelligent's stop-and-start-stutter flow, and the result is a consistently listenable conscious party. "Time to Say Peace," "Strictly Ghetto," "Rock Dis Funky Joint," and the title track jump off the record. Only Tony D's bizarre performance on "Can I Start This" prevents the record from being a coherent whole and a 5-bone record.

what to buy next: *Pure Poverty* ✍✍✍ (Profile, 1991, prod. Tony D, Father Shaheed) moves deeper into Five Percent territory, including a funky take on "The Nation's Anthem" and more dancehall-inflected grooves, such as the sublime "Easy Star." In particular, the group's take on dancehall/hip-hop fusion is much more organic than most attempts. Also solid are "Methods of Dropping Mental" and "Hot Damn I'm Great." *The New World Order* ✍✍✍ (Profile, 1996, prod. Culture Freedom, Ezo Brown, Father Shaheed, KRS-One, Clark Kent) is an interesting concept unexplored. Most of the science on *The New World Order* shows up on the cover sleeve and in tedious interludes, while most of the tracks comment on the prevalence of studio gangstaism. As if to hedge their bets, they invite a star-studded array of guests: the Fugees, KRS-One, MissJones, Junior Reid, Nine, Brother J, and Sluggy Ranks. But the standout tracks, "Word Iz Life" and "Wicked Everytime," are strictly PRT ventures with mostly battle rhymes that suggest a return to form.

the rest:
Black Business ✍✍ (Profile, 1993)

worth searching for: The 12-inch remix of "Rock Dis Funky Joint" (Profile, 1990) slams much harder than the album version.

solo outings:
Wise Intelligent:
Killin U . . . for Fun ✍✍ (Contract, 1996)

influences:
◀◀ Tony D, Public Enemy

▶▶ YZ, Naughty by Nature, Fu-Schnickens, Spearhead, Brand Nubian, Goodie Mob, Jeru the Damaja

Jeff "DJ Zen" Chang

Portrait

Formed early 1990s, in Los Angeles, CA.

Phillip Johnson, vocals (early 1990s–95); Irving Washington III, vocals; Eric Kirkland, vocals; Michael Angelo Saulsberry, vocals, keyboards; Kurt Jackson, vocals (1995–present).

This smooth-singing quartet was a cross-country concoction, with Johnson coming from Tulsa, Oklahoma, Washington from Providence, Rhode Island, and Kirkland and Saulsberry hailing from Los Angeles. Given to lush arrangements and love songs—plus inventive use of samples from songs such as Shuggie Otis's "Strawberry Letter 23," Seals & Crofts's "Summer Breeze," and Grover Washington Jr.'s "Paradise"—Portrait has scored a hit from each of its two albums: "Here We Go Again" from its 1993 debut and a re-make of the Bee Gees' "How Deep Is Your Love" from its follow-up. New member Kurt Jackson joined as Johnson's replacement after the second album's release.

what's available: Both *Portrait* ✍✍✍ (Capitol, 1992, prod. Portrait) and *All That Matters* ✍✍✍ (Capitol, 1995, prod. Portrait) are of a piece, and neither makes a definitive artistic statement. But the latter took some interesting new sonic turns that make sure we'll be listening for whatever they come up with next.

influences:
◀◀ The Chi-Lites, the Spinners, Gerald Albright, New Edition, Boyz II Men

Gary Graff

Positive K

Born Darryl Gibson.

Positive Knowledge Allah rapped with a sense of humor while also using Afrocentric and Islamic rhetoric and got himself a gold hit, "I Got a Man."

what's available: Positive K's only album, *The Skills Dat Pay Da Bills* ✍✍ (Island, 1992, prod. Blossette Kitson), is split into "The Skills Side" and the "Pay the Bills Side." The album is hooks-laden musically, but not lyrically. That doesn't mean that it can't be fun. "I Got a Man," a song about a guy who keeps getting dissed by women who allegedly have boyfriends, is the prize.

influences:

⏮ LL Cool J, Eric B. & Rakim

⏭ Father MC

Christina Fuoco

Billy Preston

Born September 9, 1946, in Houston, TX.

Best known for his distinctive bluesy keyboard work on the Beatles' *Let It Be* album, Billy Preston had already established himself on the gospel and R&B circuits before George Harrison pulled him into the Fab Four's fracturous recording sessions in 1969. A child prodigy, Preston played organ for gospel queen Mahalia Jackson and landed a role playing songwriter W.C. Handy as a boy in the movie *St. Louis Blues* (1958; Nat King Cole played the adult Handy). Throughout the early 1960s, Preston toured with Little Richard and Sam Cooke in Europe, where he first met the Beatles at Hamburg's Star Club. A spot as a backup musician on Britain's *Shindig* TV music program landed him a gig touring the continent with Ray Charles; on that tour, he again met up with Harrison, who promptly signed him to the Beatles' Apple label. Next to Badfinger, Preston was the best-known and most prolific artist in Apple's stable, and he was the only artist to receive a performance credit with the Beatles (the "Get Back" single is credited to "The Beatles with Billy Preston"). After the Beatles broke up, Preston worked with John Lennon on a number of his Plastic Ono Band albums and also recorded with Ringo Starr and Harrison. He performed at Harrison's Concert for Bangladesh in 1971, where his was among the concert's standout performances. Throughout the 1970s Preston enjoyed a string of hit singles ("Will It Go 'Round in Circles," "Outa-Space") while backing up such top acts as the Rolling Stones and Aretha Franklin. Preston continues to write and record, dividing his energies between gospel and secular recordings. Among rock keyboardists, he is an original, a true living legend.

what to buy: *The Best of Billy Preston* ♫♫♫♫ (A&M, 1988, prod. Billy Preston, George Martin) is an excellent retrospective of Preston's solo work, with all his pop hits along with the moving gospel-rocker "That's the Way God Planned It," originally recorded for Apple.

the rest:

Encouraging Words ♫♫♫ (Apple, 1970)
Minister of Music ♫♫♫ (Pepper Co. Music Group, 1995)

influences:

⏮ Ray Charles, Aretha Franklin, Little Richard, W.C. Handy

⏭ Stevie Wonder, Gregg Allman, Lee Michaels, the Beatles, James Taylor, Ben Folds

Christopher Scapelliti

Lloyd Price

Born March 9, 1933, in New Orleans, LA.

Lloyd Price began his career following the stylistic lead of Fats Domino and Roy Perkins. By the end of the 1950s, he was a top pop singer with a style all his own. As a teenager, Price incorporated "Lawdy Miss Clawdy!," a catch-phrase by WBOK disc jockey Okey Dokey, into a radio station jingle. After turning it into a full song, he auditioned for Art Rupe of Specialty Records and sang it so emotionally, Rupe thought Price was actually crying. Recorded with Fats Domino on piano, "Lawdy Miss Clawdy" was one of 1952's biggest R&B hits. (Most of Price's early recordings feature Domino's band.) He followed with "Restless Heart," "Ooh, Ooh, Ooh," and "Ain't It a Shame," which were fine performances but lesser hits. Price was drafted into the Army in 1953. When he returned to civilian life, his style of plaintive blues singing had gone out of favor. It was the age of rock 'n' roll, and his place at Specialty had been usurped by his friend Little Richard, whom Price had steered towards the label a few years earlier. After his last session, Specialty hired Price's pianist and valet, Larry Williams, to take his place on the roster. Late in 1956, Price and his partner Harold Logan formed KRC Records and leased "Just Because" to ABC-Paramount; the record hit #29 on the pop charts. Price signed with ABC-Paramount outright in 1958. Working with producer Don Costa, Price's music became more mainstream pop than the raw R&B of a few years earlier. Their first collaboration updated "Stack-O-Lee," the old folk blues about gambling and murder. Though the record was a major smash, Price was forced to cut an alternate version with a happy ending for "American Bandstand" and a few hypercritical radio stations. "Stagger Lee" was a #1 record for four weeks. Price's pop career peaked in 1959 with the bouncy New Orleans double-entendre of "Personality" and the teen lament "I'm Gonna Get Married." Price continued his hit streak into 1960, but his formula at ABC-Paramount soon wore out its welcome. His final hit record came late in 1969 with the socially conscious "Bad Conditions" on Turntable Records, another label he and Logan formed just before the latter was brutally murdered. Price went on to record for a number of other labels without much success, and though one music service listed him as dead, Price is very much alive and plays rock revival shows to very enthusiastic crowds with his old buddy Little Richard.

what to buy: *Greatest Hits* 🎵🎵🎵🎵 (MCA, 1994, comp. Bill Inglot) contains 18 tracks featuring his best ABC-Paramount recordings, two versions of "Stagger Lee," (the sanitized version has Billy and Stagger Lee parting friends), "Personality," "Where Were You On Our Wedding Day," "I'm Gonna Get Married," and a sharp remake of his own "Lawdy Miss Clawdy."

what to buy next: *Lawdy* 🎵🎵🎵🎵 (Specialty Records, 1991, prod. Art Rupe) is the best of Price's earlier, grittier work at Specialty. The original "Lawdy Miss Clawdy" and its sequel, "Forgive Me Clawdy," are here as well as other chart numbers and alternate takes recorded between 1952 and 1956.

what to avoid: *Personality* 🎵🎵🎵 (MCA Special Products, 1990, prod. Don Costa) has only eight of Price's ABC-Paramount hits. For a couple of extra dollars, you can get a lot more.

the rest:
Lloyd Price—His Originals 🎵🎵🎵🎵 (Specialty, 1959)
Greatest Hits 🎵🎵🎵🎵 (Curb, 1990)
Vol. 2—Heavy Dreams 🎵🎵🎵🎵 (Specialty, 1993)
Sings His Big Ten 🎵🎵🎵🎵 (Curb, 1994)
Walkin' the Track 🎵🎵🎵🎵 (Specialty, 1997)

worth searching for: *Greatest Hits* 🎵🎵🎵🎵 (Pair, 1991, prod. various) features some of Price's big ABC-Paramount hits, plus surprisingly effective cover versions of "I Count the Tears," "Shop Around," "He Will Break Your Heart," and others.

influences:

◀◀ Roy "Boogie Boy" Perkins, Fats Domino

▶▶ Larry Williams, Wilson Pickett

Ken Burke

Prince/ ♀

Born Prince Rogers Nelson, June 7, 1958, in Minneapolis, MN.

No matter what you call him—Prince, The Artist Formerly Known As Prince, The Artist, or that unpronounceable symbol you see above—there's no denying his stature as one of the most influential dance/funk artists in the history of popular music. Named after his father's jazz trio, Prince didn't attract much more than a cult following until after his fifth album, *1999*, was released in 1982, earning him Rock Artist of the Year honors from *Rolling Stone*. The semi-autobiographical movie *Purple Rain* and its soundtrack propelled Prince to the top of the charts and exposed one of music's best-kept se-

crets to the world. Frequently laced with sexually explicit lyrics and religious overtones, the sound of Prince encompasses a wide range of musical genres—pop, rock, dance, funk, soul, gospel, jazz, rap, world music, and more. The ability of "His Royal Badness" to mesh these many styles into his own unique sound is truly remarkable. Dubbed a musical genius by many, Prince writes all his own material, plays all the instruments on many of his albums, and has never been produced by anyone but himself. With the release of *Chaos & Disorder* in July 1995, Prince officially ended his longtime relationship with Warner Bros. Records. To celebrate the event he released *Emancipation*, an appropriately named three-disc collection that contains some of his best work since *Sign O' the Times*. Prince and Mayte Garcia—one of his backup singers—were married on Valentine's Day, 1996. In October of that year their son was born prematurely and died shortly after birth, reportedly from Pfeiffer syndrome type 2, an extremely rare skull deformity.

what to buy: *Sign O' the Times* 🎵🎵🎵🎵🎵 (Paisley Park/Warner Bros., 1987, prod. Prince) is a masterpiece that leads the listener on an incredible journey through the world according to Prince. This double-disc set is Prince at his diverse best and showcases his amazing range as an instrumentalist and singer. *1999* 🎵🎵🎵🎵🎵 (Warner Bros., 1982, prod. Prince) gave rockdom its first taste of Prince with the title track and "Little Red Corvette." It's a masterful mix of pop, rock, and funk, and was Prince's breakthrough project. *Dirty Mind* 🎵🎵🎵🎵🎵 (Warner Bros., 1980, prod. Prince) is perhaps the definitive funk/rock album (with a nasty theme) and contains the classics "When You Were Mine," "Uptown," and "Partyup." *Purple Rain* 🎵🎵🎵🎵🎵 (Warner Bros., 1984, prod. Prince) may be a bit too mainstream for some (it was #1 for 24 weeks), but this album put Prince over the top, and it's loaded with great dance/pop songs.

what to buy next: *The Hits/The B-Sides* 🎵🎵🎵🎵🎵 (Paisley Park/Warner Bros., 1993, prod. Prince) is chock full of hits, though they do lose some of their luster when listened to out of their original context. Nevertheless, this is the only album that contains such legendary Prince B-sides as "Erotic City," "Gotta Stop (Messin' About)," and "How Come U Don't Call Me Anymore." *Parade (Music from the Motion Picture Under the Cherry Moon)* 🎵🎵🎵🎵 (Paisley Park/Warner Bros., 1986, prod. Prince) is often dismissed as a failure, due largely in part to the lack of success of its companion movie. While "Kiss" may be its

most familiar track, it contains other great songs—"Girls & Boys," "Mountains," "Anotherloverholenyohead," and the haunting "Sometimes It Snows in April"—that were inexplicably left off the hits packages.

what to avoid: Prince was handpicked to do the *Batman Motion Picture Soundtrack* **woof!** (Warner Bros., 1989, prod. Prince) by one of the film's stars (and Prince fan), Jack Nicholson. That's one phone call Prince should've never answered. A couple of cuts ("The Future," "Partyman") aren't half bad, but the album as a whole is Prince's worst effort to date.

the rest:

For You ✍✍✍ (Warner Bros., 1978)

Prince ✍✍✍✍ (Warner Bros., 1979)

Controversy ✍✍✍✍ (Warner Bros., 1981)

Around the World in a Day ✍✍✍✍ (Paisley Park/Warner Bros., 1985)

Lovesexy ✍✍✍ (Paisley Park/Warner Bros., 1988)

(With others) *Music from Graffiti Bridge* ✍✍ (Paisley Park/Warner Bros., 1990)

Diamonds and Pearls ✍✍✍✍ (Paisley Park/Warner Bros., 1991)

⚥ ✍✍✍ (Paisley Park/Warner Bros., 1992)

The Hits 1 ✍✍✍✍✍ (Paisley Park/Warner Bros., 1993)

The Hits 2 ✍✍✍✍✍ (Paisley Park/Warner Bros., 1993)

The Black Album ✍✍✍ (Warner Bros., 1994; recorded in 1987 and originally available only as a bootleg)

Come ✍✍ (Warner Bros., 1994)

The Gold Experience ✍✍✍ (NPG/Warner Bros., 1995)

(With others) *Girl 6 Motion Picture Soundtrack* ✍✍✍✍ (Warner Bros., 1996)

Emancipation ✍✍✍✍ (NPG/EMI, 1996)

Crystal Ball N/A (NPG, 1997)

The Truth N/A (NPG, 1997)

worth searching for: *The White Album* ✍✍✍✍✍ (Neutral Zone, 1989), a bootleg live CD recorded in Germany in 1988, is 71 minutes of no-holds-barred funk, made even better by its surprisingly fine sound quality.

influences:

◀◀ Carlos Santana, Sly & the Family Stone, Jimi Hendrix, James Brown, the Beatles, the Rolling Stones

▶▶ The Time, Vanity 6, Tevin Campbell, Madonna, Terence Trent D'Arby

Dean Dauphinais

Professor Longhair

Born Henry Roeland "Roy" Byrd, December 19, 1918, in Bogalusa, LA. Died January 30, 1980, in New Orleans, LA.

Professor Longhair's music is important to a number of musical genres, not the least of which are rock 'n' roll, calypso, zydeco, and the New Orleans R&B with which he is most often associated. A piano player and singer of profound talent and innovative technique, 'Fess (as he was often called) has been cited by a number of prominent musicians, including Fats Domino, Dr. John, Allen Toussaint, Art Neville, and Huey "Piano" Smith, as a primary influence on their playing. Raised in New Orleans, 'Fess was a sponge for the city's diverse culture and rich musical heritage, especially the prevalent sounds of boogie woogie, blues, and calypso. His musical "gumbo" is best defined in his piano playing—a style often referred to as "rhumba-boogie," driven by propulsive left hand rhythms and intricate right hand chording. In addition to his piano playing, 'Fess was a gifted singer with a wide and idiosyncratic range; whoops, hollers, whistles, high screeches, and low growls were all in his repertoire. Though suffused with his ripe sense of humor, his vocals ran the gamut from heartsick longing to predatory sexuality to pure unbridled joy. Despite having more than enough talent to strike it rich during rock's gold rush years of the 1950s, a combination of mismanagement and his reluctance to tour extensively prevented the 'Fess's ascendancy to stardom. As a result, many of his proteges, notably Domino, surged ahead of him in popularity, and until his "rediscovery" in 1971, Longhair worked as a janitor and was frequently destitute. Popular support notwithstanding, Professor Longhair's contributions are now deemed irreplaceable, and he is today considered a cornerstone of New Orleans' rich musical tableau.

what to buy: Originally released in France, *Rock 'n' Roll Gumbo* ✍✍✍✍✍ (Barclay, 1974/Dancing Cat, 1985, prod. Philippe Rault, George Winston, Steve Hodge, Frosty Horton) is a veritable primer on Longhair's style. Recorded in three days in 'Fess's birthplace of Bogalusa, Louisiana, the album features a number of his regular sidemen (who, in the manner of James Brown's band, played *exactly* what the Professor told them to play) and legendary blues guitarist Clarence "Gatemouth" Brown. The tracks offer a sampling from across Longhair's career and include many Crescent City classics—"Rockin' Pneumonia," "Rum and Coke," "Tipitina," "Hey Now Baby." *Rock 'n' Roll Gumbo* epitomizes Longhair's contributions and expertly conveys the exhilaration that music brought to his life.

what to buy next: It's equally important to recognize the genesis of 'Fess's career, and *Mardi Gras in New Orleans* ✍✍✍✍ (Nighthawk, 1981) collects 'Fess's crucial recordings from the late 1940s and early 1950s, including "She Ain't Got No Hair," "Professor Longhair's Boogie," and the original versions of the title track and "Tipitina." The sound quality is less than desirable, but the fire of the performances is unforgettable.

what to avoid: Beware myriad cheap compilations from off-brand labels; the quality is almost always poor.

the rest:
Crawfish Fiesta 𝄢𝄢𝄢 (Alligator, 1980)
The Last Mardi Gras 𝄢𝄢𝄢𝄢 (Atlantic, 1982)
Houseparty New Orleans Style 𝄢𝄢𝄢 (Rounder, 1987)
New Orleans Piano: Blues Originals, Vol. 2 𝄢𝄢𝄢𝄢 (Atlantic, 1989)
'Fess: The Professor Longhair Anthology 𝄢𝄢𝄢𝄢 (Rhino, 1993)

worth searching for: A live recording from 1975, *Live on the Queen Mary* 𝄢𝄢𝄢 (Harvest, 1978), is scarce, but persistent hunters should find it with moderate effort. The album features 'Fess performing at a gala party hosted by Paul McCartney aboard the Queen Mary luxury liner.

influences:

◄◄ Albert Ammons, Meade Lux Lewis, Big Maceo, Pete Johnson, Jimmy Yancey

►► Fats Domino, Dr. John, Allen Toussaint, Art Neville, the Neville Brothers, Huey "Piano" Smith, Little Richard, Jerry Lee Lewis, Elvis Presley, James Booker, Bruce Hornsby, Jason D. Williams

David Galens

Professor X
See: X-Clan

Profile Records

Possibly the most important independent label in hip-hop history, Profile Records also became one of the most successful thanks to Run-D.M.C. Formed in 1981 by Corey Robbins and Steve Plotnicki, two veterans of the New York dance-club scene, Profile was responsibile for seminal sides like the Fresh 3 MC's "Fresh," Rammelzee vs. K-Rob's "Beat Bop" (produced by Jean-Michel Basquiat!), Pumpkin's "King of the Beat," Dana Dane's "Nightmares," and Word of Mouth's "King Kut," all of which are collected on *Diggin' in the Crates* 𝄢𝄢𝄢 (Profile, 1994, prod. various). Even Motown CEO Andre Harrell got his start in the industry as a hot-selling rapper for the label. But it was the crew from Hollis that ensured Profile's place in history. By dropping *Run-D.M.C.*, the first major hip-hop LP, in 1984, Profile proved that hip-hop could survive in the long-form artistically—and financially. Profile consolidated its strengths toward the end of its first decade, introducing the world to artists like

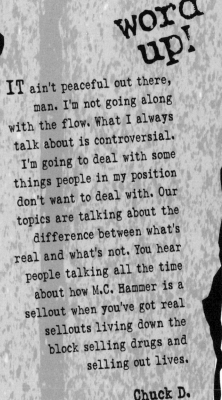

word up!

IT ain't peaceful out there, man. I'm not going along with the flow. What I always talk about is controversial. I'm going to deal with some things people in my position don't want to deal with. Our topics are talking about the difference between what's real and what's not. You hear people talking all the time about how M.C. Hammer is a sellout when you've got real sellouts living down the block selling drugs and selling out lives.

Chuck D.
(of Public Enemy)

Special Ed, DJ Quik, Poor Righteous Teachers, King Sun, Twin Hype, and even an early incarnation of Onyx. In the late 1980s, Profile also successfully merged the dancehall and hip-hop markets via essential sides like Asher D and Daddy Freddy's "Ragamuffin Hip-hop" and Frighty and Colonel Mite's "Life (Is What You Make It)," plus a series of crucial compilations entitled *Dancehall Stylee*. After a long and ugly legal split between partners Robbins and Plotnicki in the mid-1990s, though, the label's output dropped off somewhat in terms of both quantity and quality. But Profile recovered by going back to its stronghold—the New York underground—and issuing hits from Nine, Smoothe Da Hustler, and Camp Lo. Despite the fact that all of the other early 1980s hip-hop imprints such as Tommy Boy, Enjoy, Prism, and Sugar Hill had either folded, sold their catalogs, or merged with majors, Profile remained independent as it headed toward its second decade.

Jeff "DJ Zen" Chang

Public Enemy

Formed 1982, Long Island, NY.

Chuck D., vocals; Flavor Flav, vocals; Terminator X, DJ; Professor Griff, minister of information (1985–89, 1997–present).

In the late 1980s, Public Enemy seized the still-young hip-hop genre and transformed it from lighthearted, braggy dance music to politically potent bullhorn news broadcasting. Leader Chuck D.'s voice, always the equivalent of yelling "fire!" at a crowded concert, dismissed Elvis Presley as a racist, excoriated Hollywood as patronizing, and encouraged revolution. He was often brilliant but, as egotistical visionaries are wont to do, often shot himself in the foot. He embraced the anti-semitic Nation of Islam Minister Louis Farrakhan and hired, apologized for, and then reluctantly fired the even more anti-semitic "minister of information" Professor Griff (before finally bringing him back after eight years), and his lyrics distorted Biblical passages to hold Jews responsible for Christ's crucifixion. But none of that mattered when Public Enemy's songs came on: Chuck's voice, augmented by sidekick Flavor Flav's high-pitched "yeeaaaahhh booooyeeees" and the Bomb Squad production team's complex collage of funk samples, was as powerful as Johnny Rotten or Mick Jagger (but maybe not Howlin' Wolf) ever were. Public Enemy bestowed upon rap a political conscience and, more important, gave hip-hop music and culture a soul. Though Flav briefly went to jail for alleged domestic abuse and other altercations, and Chuck D. put out a soul-influenced solo album in 1996, the band stayed together, toured, and recorded an album (with the Bomb Squad's Hank Shocklee) set for release in the fall of 1997.

what to buy: *It Takes a Nation of Millions to Hold Us Back* ♪♪♪♪♪ (Def Jam, 1988, prod. Hank Shocklee, Carl Ryder) is the definitive political rap album, establishing Public Enemy's underground power with "Bring the Noise," the anti-media "Don't Believe the Hype," and the searing funk grooves of "She Watch Channel Zero" and "Black Steel (In the Hour of Chaos)." An undisputed classic. The follow-up, *Fear of a Black Planet* ♪♪♪♪ (Def Jam, 1990, prod. Hank Shocklee, Carl Ryder, Eric "Vietnam" Sadler, Keith Shocklee), has some filler, but the incendi-

ary "Fight the Power" (originally heard in Spike Lee's *Do the Right Thing*), "Who Stole the Soul?," and "Welcome to the Terrordome" are some of the most forceful songs ever recorded.

what to buy next: *Muse Sick-N-Hour Mess Age* ♪♪♪♪ (Def Jam, 1994, prod. Gary G-Wiz, Carl Ryder, Bomb Squad Production), with the wise-old-soul hit "Give It Up," is tremendously underrated. The first album, *Yo! Bum Rush the Show* ♪♪♪ (Def Jam, 1987, prod. Bill Stepheny, others), is not as complex as later Public Enemy stuff, but it contains the buzzing battle cry "Public Enemy No. 1." *Apocalypse '91 . . . The Enemy Strikes Black* (Def Jam, 1991, prod. Gary G-Wiz, Stuart Robertz, Cerwin "C-Dawg" Depper, the JBL) meanders with moral messages about the evils of drinking alcohol but is worth the price for the Public Enemy–Anthrax metal-rap collaboration, "Bring the Noise."

what to avoid: Professor Griff's solo albums, *Pawns in the Game* ♪ (Luke Records, 1990) and *Kao's II Wiz*7*Dome* **woof!** (Luke, 1991), are morally irritating.

the rest:
Greatest Misses ♪♪ (Def Jam, 1992)

worth searching for: Chuck D.'s improvised reading of the Charles Mingus poem "Gunslinging Bird (Or If Charlie Parker Were a Gunslinger, There'd Be a Whole Lot of Dead Copycats)" off the Mingus tribute album *Weird Nightmare* (Columbia, 1992) is simply brilliant.

solo outings:
Chuck D.:
The Autobiography of Mistachuck ♪♪♪ (Slam Jamz/Mercury, 1996)

Terminator X:
Terminator X and the Valley of the Jeep Beets ♪♪♪ (RAL, 1991)
Terminator X and the Godfathers of Threatt: Super Bad ♪♪ (RAL, 1994)

influences:
◄◄ James Brown, Gil Scott-Heron, Last Poets, Kurtis Blow, Boogie Down Productions, Anthrax

►► Rage Against the Machine, Geto Boys, Boo-Yaa T.R.I.B.E, Wu-Tang Clan, Tricky, X-Clan, Poor Righteous Teachers, Digital Underground, Brand Nubian, Native Tongues, Flavor Unit

Steve Knopper

Puff Daddy

Born Sean Combs, 1970, in Harlem, NY.

Shortly before he appeared on the cover of *Rolling Stone* magazine in the summer of 1997 (wearing designer underwear by

Versace, of course), Sean "Puff Daddy" Combs said that he was destined to become the most powerful and successful record mogul in pop history. While Tommy Mattola, Clive Davis, and David Geffen, among others, might have chuckled at the claim, this much is certain: Combs is in a hip-hop league of his own as a triple-threat producer/executive/artist. Working in the control room, he's been behind platinum hits for everybody from Mariah Carey ("Fantasy") to the late Notorious B.I.G. ("One More Chance"). Working in the board room, he's helped usher Jodeci and Mary J. Blige to stardom (as an A&R exec at Uptown) and has more recently shaped the fruitful careers of Total, Craig Mack, 112, Faith Evans, and Notorious B.I.G. (as the CEO of his own Bad Boy Entertainment empire). And working on the microphone, the ex-Howard University student has surprisingly become a recording star in his own right, scoring two consecutive #1 pop singles ("Can't Nobody Hold Me Down" and the B.I.G. tribute "I'll Be Missing You") and then a phenomenally successful #1 album (*No Way Out*). Not bad for a guy who can't really rap.

what's available: What's more annoying about *No Way Out* ⏯⏯ (Bad Boy/Arista, 1997, prod. Sean Combs, others) to the hip-hop purist? Is it the abundance of cliched lyrical references to Puff's favorite materialistic excesses (Versace, Rolex, Mercedes, Cristal) and his own record label, Bad Boy? Is it that Puffy acts as if the hip-hop production innovations of the last 18 years never happened as he returns to the "Rapper's Delight" era by building his songs almost exclusively on past pop hits ("Let's Dance," "Every Breath You Take," "The Message," etc.)? Or is it that he's risen to the top despite a decided lack of verbal skills (all undynamic monotone, all the time)? Of course, the masses outnumber the purists, and Puff Daddy has clearly appealed to the former with his lightweight party-ready beats and rhymes. On the bright side, at least he's not wearing genie pants.

influences:
◀◀ Hammer, Sugarhill Gang, Notorious B.I.G., Jay-Z, Lil' Kim
▶▶ Mase, Lox

Josh Freedom du Lac

Bobby and James Purify
Formed 1965.

James Purify (born May 12, 1944, in Pensacola, FL); Bobby Purify (born September 2, 1939, in Tallahassee, FL).

The Purify cousins made a cheery blip on the soul screen with "I'm Your Puppet" in 1966. While they had been singing to-gether for only a year, "Puppet" made for an undeniably congenial debut, hitting the Top 10 in both the pop and R&B charts. The true success of the song lies in the hands of co-writer and co-producer Dan Penn (who is the secret force behind a lion's share of southern soul hits of the 1960s). Paring down the Muscle Shoals team to a tinkling shimmer, Penn hits directly on the song's innate pop sense while the cousins add an airy fluffiness to keep it afloat. The duo had a few subsequent singles that did not fare as well, resulting in Bobby's departure in 1970.

what's available: As there are no albums available from the Purify boys, "I'm Your Puppet" can only be found on compilations. Of the many in print, *Muscle Shoals Sound* ⏯⏯⏯ (Rhino, 1993, prod. various) and *Soul Shots* ⏯⏯⏯ (Rhino, 1988, comp. Bill Inglot) are both handy samplers of 1960s soul, the latter offering a meatier selection than the streamlined mega-hits of the former.

influences:
◀◀ The Intruders, Sam Cooke
▶▶ Dan Penn

Allan Orski

Quad City DJ's
Formed 1996, in Jacksonville, FL.

Johnny "Jayski" McGowan, singer-producer; Lana LeFleur, vocals.

What the hip-hop purists don't know, the fatback understands. Indeed, the purists may openly despise Miami bass music, calling it shallow and overly simplistic. But there's no denying that the up-tempo, bass-heavy music packs 'em in on the dance floor. And, anyway, the genre that's also known as Southern bass (because all of the best-selling bass artists have come from the Southeast) and booty hop (because most of the records feature lyrics about booties) actually *is* marked by shallow and simplistic records; but therein lies the secret to the genre's success. The shallow lyrics—mostly about partying, dancing, sex, and the intersection of the three—may require little by way of analysis, but they're perfect for the dance floor. Likewise, the simple sing-along hooks. And Johnny "Jayski" Mc-Gowan seems to understand better than most that keeping it simple, stupid, can lead to bass-music success. Although the genre is notorious for producing one-hit wonders (anybody heard from Tag Team or 12 Gauge lately?), McGowan has managed to score three massive hits, producing 95 South's "Whoot, There It Is" and the 69 Boyz' "Tootsee Roll" with partner Nathaniel "C.C." Lemonhead before putting himself in the spotlight, performing and producing "C'Mon N' Ride It (The Train)" with female vocalist Lana LeFleur under the guise of the Quad City DJ's.

what's available: Bass music is a decidedly singles-driven genre, so any bass album is a risky proposition. The lone Quad City DJ's album, *Get on Up and Dance* ♫♫ (Big Beat/Atlantic, 1996, prod. "Jayski" McGowan, Thrill Da Playa), for instance, is truly notable for just one song: "C'Mon N' Ride It (The Train)," which features a layered retro-funk groove, an irresistible melody, LeFleur's vocal hook and some catchy "whoo-whoo" train sounds that remind you that there's no parking on the dance floor. Interestingly, the track—which seems to succeed in spite of McGowan's sometimes slurred quasi-rap—doesn't lean on the sort of dropping bass that booty hop is known for, relying instead on a driving, 150 bpm tempo for its kick. A more accurate representation of bass music can be found on the album's penultimate track, "Ride That Bass," a retooled version of "C'Mon N' Ride It" that features the 69 Boyz. And if that's not enough "C'Mon" for you, the song is also reprised here in house-remix form. Whoo whoo.

worth searching for: Although they're not Quad City DJ's tracks, 95 South's "Whoot, There It Is" (Wrap, 1993) and the 69 Boyz' "Tootsee Roll" (Rip-It, 1994) do owe much of their success to producer McGowan. The two singles, along with "C'Mon N' Ride It," would make a fine start to any best-of-bass compilation.

influences:

◀◀ Magic Mike, 95 South, 69 Boyz, 12 Gauge, Tag Team, A-Town Players

▶▶ Freak Nasty

Josh Freedom du Lac

Queen Latifah

Born Dana Owens, March 18, 1970, in Newark, NJ.

Latifah may be Arabic for "delicate and sensitive," but the key to understanding Jersey-born rapper Dana Owens's muse lies in the designation "Queen." Indeed, as the first—and best—hip-hop artist to consistently espouse both feminism and black power, Latifah's claim to mike-rockin' royalty is no empty boast.

She's also hip-hop's queen of diversification: while still a highly respected rapper, Latifah is also working as a film and TV actress (*Set It Off*, *Living Single*) and serving as CEO of Flavor Unit Records. At the time of this writing, she was in the studio, working on her fourth album.

what to buy: One of the most auspicious debuts in hip-hop history, *All Hail the Queen* ♫♫♫♫ (Tommy Boy, 1989, prod. Prince Paul, DJ Mark the 45 King, Daddy-O, KRS-One, Luis Vega) is a nearly flawless collection of righteous freestyling, fresh samplescapes, and inspired collaborations with everybody from fellow Native Tongues tribalists De La Soul ("Mama Gave Birth to the Soul Children") to KRS-One ("Evil That Men Do") and Stetsasonic's Daddy-O ("The Pros"). The album's most compelling duet, though, is "Ladies First," on which Latifah and Brit B-girl Monie Love set their sights on fem-baiting naysayers ("Some think that we can't flow/Stereotypes, they got to go") as they commandeer the cosmos ("I'm divine and my mind expands throughout the universe").

what to buy next: The gold-selling *Black Reign* ♫♫♫ (Motown, 1993, prod. Kay Gee, Tony D, Queen Latifah, others) yielded the Grammy-winning hit "U.N.I.T.Y." And if the album doesn't fully dispense with the commercial-R&B excesses that marred Latifah's sophomore outing, *Nature of a Sista'*, at least her flow feels revitalized, thanks in part to the incorporation of a little gangsta-du-jour attitude on "Rough," "Coochie Bang," and "Just Another Day" (an ironic move, given that Latifah bristled, in song, at the thought of Apache's hit "Gangsta Bitch"). It's hard to top a masterpiece, and Latifah's sophomore outing, *Nature of a Sista'* ♫♫ (Tommy Boy, 1991, prod. Queen Latifah, others) trades in its predecessor's vibrant funk workouts, house rave-ups, and ragamuffin riddims for the streamlined urban-contemporary jams. Not surprisingly, Latifah often sounds out of place in such velvety environs—most notably on "Fly Girl" (in which her highness lets smooth crooners Simple Pleasure ham it up in the choruses) and "How Do I Love Thee" (an embarrassing bedroom come-on so removed from her persona—and beneath her talents—it would have been unthinkable on *All Hail the Queen*). Only the title track, with its hearty James Brown-inflected kick, suggests the Queen hadn't yet abdicated her throne.

influences:

◀◀ James Brown, KRS-One, Public Enemy, MC Lyte, De La Soul, A Tribe Called Quest, Jungle Brothers

▶▶ Monie Love, Yo Yo, Sister Souljah, Mary J. Blige, Fugees

Greg Siegel

Ma Rainey

Born Gertrude Pridgett, April 26, 1886, in Columbus, GA. Died December 22, 1939, in Columbus, GA.

There is no doubt that Gertrude "Ma" Rainey was one of the biggest names in 20th-century music even before 1994. It was in that year, however, that she was bestowed an honor given only to a select few: her own U.S. postage stamp. Rainey is commonly regarded as the "Mother of the Blues" even though she was neither the first woman to sing nor to record blues music. Part of that reputation is due to her Southern-flavored, rural, and earthy brand of blues, performed at a time when most singers were trying to take blues out of the country and give it a big-city sound. Her style—which made her the first commercially successful black female blues singer in America—came from her roots. She was born in the Deep South and began singing in medicine and minstrel shows as a young girl. When she married "Pa," William Rainey, in 1904, she changed her professional name to "Ma" Rainey and began appearing with her spouse as "Rainey and Rainey, Assassinators of the Blues." By the 1920s, after years of touring, Ma Rainey had become an established headliner on the Theater Owners' Booking Association circuit. In 1923, she signed a recording contract with Paramount that would last only six years, but during that time she recorded over 100 songs with some of the blues and jazz masters of the era, like Louis Armstrong, Buster Bailey, and Coleman Hawkins. Like many other blues-belting mamas, Rainey spent years developing a repertoire of pop and minstrel tunes in addition to her great blues numbers, all of which remain classics to this day—"See See Rider," "Bo-Weevil Blues," and "Ma Rainey's Black Bottom," to name a few. Her recording career fell prey to the same "last hired, first fired" fate all African American performers suffered with the onset of the Great Depression, so Rainey made no other records after 1928. Still, as a Southern girl she was able to maintain her popularity in the South; even there, however, her notoriety began to wane in the early 1930s as blues audiences became less interested in seeing women sing the blues. Following the death of her mother, Rainey retired in 1933 to her hometown of Columbus, Georgia, at the age of 47. She would not have long to enjoy her golden years: she died of a heart attack in 1939. But in Ma Rainey's 20-plus years of performing and recording, she left a legacy of blues music that nearly every female singer who followed her has drawn upon as a touchstone. In fact, some argue

that Rainey is responsible not only for the roots of blues, but of rock 'n' roll and country music as well. Because of that enormous influence, she was inducted into the Blues Foundation Hall of Fame in 1983 and the Rock & Roll Hall of Fame in 1990.

what to buy: Fletcher Henderson's piano pounding and the slippery bass saxophone of Coleman Hawkins are just two of the dozens of reasons to experience *Ma Rainey* 𝄢𝄢𝄢𝄢 (Fantasy/Milestone, 1975), a hard-to-find collection of 1924–1928 recordings by one of the greatest voices in music. Rainey was no songbird, there are no flights of stratospheric high notes here. She was more of a bottom-feeder, dipping into earthy, murky tones and phrases that rumbled along just slightly faster than a dirge. This is not just some of the best blues of all time, but a fascinating glimpse of the tumultuous cultural stew of 1920s America, particularly of African American culture and its pioneering role in the emergence of new musical styles.

what to buy next: Same thing, different tunes on *Ma Rainey's Black Bottom* 𝄢𝄢𝄢𝄢 (Yazoo, 1975). This album inspired a Broadway musical featuring a montage of songs and moments from Rainey's life, and the CD captures her immeasurable talent along with the artistry of instrumental legends of the era like Buster Bailey, Charlie Dixon, Georgia Tom Dorsey, and Al Wynn.

the rest:
Ma Rainey, 1928 𝄢𝄢𝄢𝄢 (Document, 1993)
Complete Master Takes, Vol. 1, 1923–24 𝄢𝄢𝄢𝄢 (King Jazz, 1994)
Complete Master Takes, Vol. 2, 1924–26 𝄢𝄢𝄢𝄢 (King Jazz, 1994)
Complete Master Takes, Vol. 3, 1926–27 𝄢𝄢𝄢𝄢 (King Jazz, 1994)
Complete Master Takes, Vol. 4, 1927–28 𝄢𝄢𝄢𝄢 (King Jazz, 1994)

influences:
◀◀ Sara Martin, Mamie Smith, W.C. Handy, Blind Lemon Jefferson

▶▶ Bessie Smith, Lovie Austin, Alberta Hunter, Mahalia Jackson, Billie Holiday, Ida Cox, Dinah Washington, Ma Rainey II, Janis Joplin, Aretha Franklin, Ethel Waters, Carmen McRae, Sippie Wallace, Sarah Vaughan, Koko Taylor

Chris Tower

Rappin' 4-Tay

Born Anthony Forte, 1969, in San Francisco, CA.

San Francisco may be a city filled with musicians, but its well-known rappers are as numerous as, say, country singers in East Oakland. Crawling out from the shadows of the city's little-known MCing tradition, Rappin' 4-Tay is no boy wonder—but he's an improvement over what little existed before. It's no coincidence if his voice sounds vaguely familiar: 4-Tay debuted it on Too $hort's classic "Don't Fight the Feelin'" and continues to echo his comrades across the bay. What most obviously sets 4-Tay apart from the Oaktown school, however, is a style and flow that is decidedly, unapologetically '80s-sounding. Grounded in mid-tempo funk and soul samples, his raps intertwine odes to weed, sex, and hustling with moralistic discussions on friendships and the need to escape violence and negativity. Although offering little that's new when compared to what's come out of overproductive Oakland and Vallejo, 4-Tay's voice carries an upstart vigor that is able to earn San Francisco some hard-fought props.

what to buy: *Don't Fight the Feelin'* ♫♫♪ (EMI, 1994, prod. various) nationally debuted the talents of a rapper who can sound like a cross between the disparate personas of Hammer and Too $hort. On standouts such as the breakthrough "Playaz Club" and a remake of "I'll Be Around," 4-Tay etches a unique personality. But he quickly falls back under the influence of Too $hort on "She's a Sell Out."

the rest:
Off Parole ♫♫ (EMI, 1996)
4 Tha Hardway ♫♫ (Noo Trybe/Virgin, 1997)

influences:
◀◀ Too $hort, M.C. Hammer
▶▶ JT the Bigga Figga

Corey Takahashi

Rare Earth

Formed as the Sunliners, 1964, in Detroit, MI. Disbanded 1983. Reformed late 1980s.

Gil Bridges, reeds, vocals (1964–78); Pete Rivera, drums, vocals (1964–74, 1977–78); John Persh, bass, trombone, vocals (1964–72); Rod Richards, guitars, vocals (1969–70); Kenny James, keyboards (1969–70); Ray Monette, guitar (1971–76, 1978); Ed Guzman, percussion (1970–78); Mark Olson, keyboards, vocals (1971–74, 1978); Michael Urso, bass, vocals (1972–74, 1977–78); Roger McBride, bass, vocals (1975–76); Gabriel Katona, keyboards, vocals (1975); Jerry LaCroix, vocals, reeds (1975–76); Barry Eugene Frost, percussion (1975); Paul Warren, guitar, vocals (1975); Frank Westerbrook, keyboards (1976); Ron Fransen, keyboards (1977); Daniel Ferguson, guitar (1977).

For a long time Motown played around with rock 'n' roll, dabbling—with the Neil Young/Rick James-led Mynah Birds, for instance—but never really making a move until the label signed Rare Earth in 1968. Ironically, the group's first big hit was a re-

make of the Temptations' "Get Ready" in 1970; it was a workmanlike cover, but it was wholly unrepresentative of Rare Earth's original material, which blended touches of jazz and psychedelic pop. Crammed into the Motown machine, where its songs came from staff songwriters, Rare Earth fit somewhere between Parliament and Blood, Sweat & Tears, which made it a hard sell for any company, much less a label whose primary experience had been in the R&B and pop markets and was a virtual stranger to the newer—and growing—rock community. Rare Earth did hit the Top 20 again with "I Just Want to Celebrate" and "Hey Big Brother," both driven by soulful vocal chorales. But the group never really hit the mainstream in a big way, which has as much to do with the woozy focus of its music as it does with Motown's unfamiliarity with rock. Rare Earth is still around however, led by Bridges and Monette and enjoying particular favor in Europe.

what to buy: With 20 tracks, *Greatest Hits and Rare Classics* ♫♫♫♪ (Motown, 1991, prod. various) is a good introduction to this group's varied body of work.

what to buy next: If *Greatest Hits* really grabs you, go for the two-CD *Anthology* ♫♫♫ (Motown, 1995, prod. various), which is diffuse but provides a sonic smorgasbord for the various sounds being made in pop music as the 1960s became the 1970s.

what to avoid: *Earth Time: The Essential Rare Earth* ♫ (Motown, 1994, prod. various) is a misleadingly titled collection marked by long, ponderous live cuts and the unfair sense that these guys couldn't play a tightly constructed song.

the rest:
Get Ready ♫♫♪ (Rare Earth/Motown, 1969)
Ecology ♫♫ (Rare Earth/Motown, 1970)
In Concert ♫♫ (Rare Earth, 1971/Motown, 1989)
Different World ♫♫ (Koch International, 1993)

influences:
◀◀ The Temptations, Pink Floyd, Procol Harum, Sly & the Family Stone
▶▶ The Commodores, Was (Not Was), Funkadelic, Mother's Finest

Gary Graff

Ras Kass

Born John Austin, in Carson, CA.

Calling Ras Kass an enlightened gangsta doesn't do justice to the complexity of his category-defying style. But it's still tempting. One can't help but feel a tinge of guilt for enjoying a lyricist who so mercilessly offends every person and ideology in sight. From sucka MCs to bible-waving Christians, Ras Kass lampoons all enemies with a hear-me-now-catch-me-later wit that delves into history, religion, and philosophy for its ammunition. In such a way, the promising lyricist penetrates the listener's mind, sounding like a Ph.D. candidate who's studying the conceptual zone between doing dirt and dropping academic knowledge. Like fellow Los Angeles-area rapper Ice-T, who draws from the literature of Iceberg Slim, Ras Kass finds his spiritual mentor in vintage Eldridge Cleaver. By adopting themes from Cleaver's *Soul on Ice,* Ras Kass lyrically represents the confusion, contradictions, and chaos in urban black America. Original and insightful, he proves that hip-hop still has an intelligent edge; all it takes is an artist who can balance fury with humor and self-critique.

what's available: *Soul on Ice* ✍✍✍✍ (Priority, 1996, prod. various) is an album that plays like a good novel. Dealing with a variety of diverse issues, the work offers well-planned musical chapters bridged with ecstatically funny interludes. Although Ras Kass could sharpen his delivery, his content is definitely pointed. "Nature of the Threat" presents a harsh, well-studied critique of Eurocentrism and propagandist history, and cool-out cuts such as "Marinatin" and "Drama" illustrate his hustler essence. "Sonset," meanwhile, gives a productive analysis of the East/West MC debate, with Ras Kass paying homage to New York forefathers while demanding that skills—not area codes and nostalgia—be the current criteria for props. "I'm a rap fan who never saw Bam rock the park in the Bronx," he says of hip-hop pioneer Afrika Bambaataa. "But I still snap skulls in the dark."

worth searching for: Ras Kass first showcased his skills to a national audience on "Come Widdit" off the soundtrack to the film *Street Fighter* (VRS, 1994). Ras Kass steals the show on the esoteric cut, which pairs him with his apparently undermatched peers Ahmad and Saafir.

influences:

⏪ Ahmad, Kam, KRS-One, Chino XL, Paris, Saafir, Ultramagnetic MC's, Freestyle Fellowship, Organized Konfusion

Corey Takahashi

Lou Rawls

Born December 1, 1935, in Chicago, IL.

Lou Rawl's low-key croon, in all of its rich, smooth depth, has carried him through a career that has been both lackluster and captivating. His gospel background with the Pilgrim Travellers provided the seasoning to carry the trade-off vocal on Sam Cooke's "Bring It on Home to Me," which led to a contract with Capitol in 1962. However, his willingness to be buried under sprawling arrangements and cabaret schmooze robs many of his recordings of any punch, reducing his timbre to a workmanlike trade tool. There are instances when he catches fire, most notably the bruised lament of "Love Is a Hurtin' Thing" (1966), which exemplified his warm control and a perfectionist's sense of phrasing (not unlike Cooke's). The first of three Grammys came with "Dead End Street" (1967), a mix of spoken monologues and verse which became a staple of his live act. Although he had reached white audiences by this point, it wasn't until nearly a decade later that he enjoyed a true crossover smash with the disco-tinged ballad "You'll Never Find Another Love Like Mine." At the close of the 1980s, a relatively dormant period for him, he hooked up with the recently re-invigorated Blue Note label and returned to traditional blues with the likes of music archivist Billy Vera in a promising return to form.

what to buy: The Philly soul team of Kenny Gamble and Leon Huff bring out the best in Rawls on *All Things In Time* ✍✍✍✍ (Philadelphia International, 1976/The Right Stuff, 1993 prod. various), which includes his enduring "You'll Never Find Another Love Like Mine" and the swinging "Groovy People." Clearly, when given the proper material and setting, Rawls will rise to the occasion. For a concise document of his more inspired performances, *The Legendary Lou Rawls* ✍✍✍✍ (Blue Note, 1992, prod. various) contains "Dead End Street," "Love Is a Hurtin' Thing," "Tobacco Road," and a pairing with sax great Cannonball Adderley.

what to buy next: *Portrait of the Blues* ✍✍✍✍ (Manhattan, 1993, prod. Billy Vera) is the strongest of his more recent fare. Guests such as Joe Williams, Phoebe Snow, and Buddy Guy up the ante for Rawls, resulting in an album with more oomph than he's made in ages.

what to avoid: Like most live albums, *Lou Rawls Live* ✍✍✍ (Philadelphia International, 1978/The Right Stuff, 1994, prod. Kenneth Gamble, Leon Huff) leaves you feeling like you're left holding a still-life. The abundance of overly long medleys don't exactly tip the scales in the right direction either.

the rest:
Live at the Century Plaza ✍✍✍ (Rebound, 1973/1994)
When You Hear Lou, You've Heard It All ✍✍✍ (Philadelphia International, 1977/The Right Stuff, 1993)
Let Me Be Good to You ✍✍✍ (Epic, 1983/The Right Stuff, 1993)
At Last ✍✍✍✍ (Blue Note, 1989)
Stormy Monday ✍✍✍ (Blue Note, 1990)

It's Supposed to Be Fun 𝄞𝄞𝄞 (Blue Note, 1990)
Greatest Hits 𝄞𝄞 (Curb, 1991)
Christmas Is the Time 𝄞𝄞𝄞 (EMI, 1993)
For You My Love 𝄞𝄞 (Capitol, 1994)
Love Songs 𝄞𝄞 (CEMA, 1994)
Spotlight on . . . Lou Rawls 𝄞𝄞𝄞 (Capitol, 1995)
Love Is a Hurtin' Thing: The Silky Soul of Lou Rawls 𝄞𝄞𝄞 (EMI, 1997)

worth searching for: Rawls's late '60s work at Capitol broke him out of the Nat King Cole mold. His albums from that period, *Soulin'* 𝄞𝄞𝄞𝄞 (Capitol, 1966), *Too Much* 𝄞𝄞𝄞𝄞 (Capitol, 1967), and *That's Lou* 𝄞𝄞𝄞𝄞 (Capitol, 1967) are all worthy finds.

influences:

◄◄ Nat King Cole, Sam Cooke, Frank Sinatra, Joe Williams

►► Billy Vera, Peabo Bryson, Luther Vandross

Allan Orski

Ray, Goodman & Brown /The Moments

Formed late 1960s, in Hackensack, NJ.

Harry Ray, vocals; Al Goodman, vocals; Billy Brown, vocals.

In either of its incarnations, this vocal trio made sweet Philly soul-style music but lacked the distinctive production touch of a Thom Bell or others at the Philadelphia International label. Instead, the Moments sounded more like Philly wannabes, though they scored some hits for the Stang label—"Sexy Mama," "Love on a Two Way Street," "Look at Me (I'm in Love)." But the Moments lost credibility with their 1975 team-up with the Whatnauts on "Girls," which was so baldly and unapologetically chauvinistic that many U.S. radio stations refused to play it. Three years later they changed the group name to simply Ray, Goodman & Brown and scored hits with "Special Lady" and "My Prayer." Harry Ray's solo albums didn't meet with much success, and the group occasionally pops up on the oldies circuit.

what to buy: Two compilations—one for each entity—will provide your fill of the trio's music. *The Best of the Moments: Love on a Two-Way Street* 𝄞𝄞𝄞𝄞 (Sugarhill, 1996, prod. various) collects the Stang material, while *The Best of Ray, Goodman & Brown* 𝄞𝄞 (Polydor, 1996, prod. various) does the job for the group's latter incarnation. Both provide pleasant listening, but neither is essential.

the rest:
The Moments:
Greatest Hits 𝄞𝄞𝄞 (Chess)

influences:

◄◄ The Vipers, the Corvettes, the Four Tops, the Isley Brothers, Thom Bell

►► Hamilton, Joe Frank & Reynolds

Gary Graff

Ray J

Born Raymond Norwood, 1981 in McComb, MS.

After loading up the truck and moving to Beverly (Hills, that is) from Mississippi, Ray J—the younger brother of teen rap/sitcom superstar Brandy—began his own professional career by acting in commercials at the age of eight. By 1993, he had graduated to sitcom work as Sinbad's son on the short-lived FOX series *The Sinbad Show*. While his sister was working in a sitcom of her own (*Thea*) and releasing her first album, Ray J was busying himself as an actor in the HBO TV-movie *The Enemy Within* and the big-screen films *When We Were Colored, Mars Attacks,* and the superhero action movie *Steel* with Shaquille O' Neal, as well as appearing in several of Brandy's music videos. It wasn't until 1996 that Ray decided to fully capitalize on his Brandy connection by releasing his own album, *Everything You Want*, bringing much of the same exuberant, sassy adolescent vibe that his sister injected into the teen hip-hop market. Ray J immediately gained radio recognition with his first single, "Let It Go," and widespread praise as a rap child prodigy on the basis of his remarkably keen musical "ear" and raw but confident vocal dynamics that suggested a maturity beyond his years. Brandy, you're a fine girl, but Ray J has shown that he doesn't need any help from Big Sis to carve a strong niche of his own in the R&B music field, and seems poised to make bigger and better strides—as a recording artist as well as an actor—in the future.

what's available: *Everything You Want* 𝄞𝄞𝄞 (Elektra, 1996, prod. various) is a cool, self-assured blend of rap, R&B, funk, and pop that stands head and shoulders above other teen troubadours of the 1990s. Unlike his contemporaries, Ray J consciously chose not to have any sampling on his debut release, and to have live musicians in place of synthesized substitutes whenever possible. With songs as funky as "Let It Go" and as soulful as "Because of You" and "Thank You" (featuring—surprise!—Brandy), this maiden effort is sure to please kids and adults alike.

influences:

◄◄ Michael Jackson, Brandy, Prince, Jodeci, Snoop Doggy Dogg, Coolio, Immature, Da Brat, Bobby Brown, Whitney Houston

Andre McGarrity

RBX

One of hip-hop's first family feuds began to take shape when RBX bitterly left the Death Row camp in 1995, incensed that his long-promised solo project never materialized, even after he'd contributed to cousin Snoop Doggy Dogg's smash hit *Doggystyle*. When RBX finally did record and release his own album for a different label, the track that received the most attention was "A.W.O.L.," in which the gruff rapper summarily disses almost the entire Death Row camp—cousin Snoop Dogg included.

what's available: RBX proves to be far more thoughtful and fair than most of the Death Row crew, anyway, on his underappreciated debut, *The RBX Files* &&&&*V* (Premeditated, 1995, prod. Greg Royal).

influences:
◀◀ Dr. Dre

Josh Freedom du Lac

Ready for the World

Formed 1982, in Flint, MI.

Melvin Riley Jr., vocals; Gordon Strozier, guitar; Gregory Potts, keyboards; Willie Triplett, keyboards; John Eaton, bass; Gerald Valentine, drums.

Following in the dance steps of the Time and other Midwestern R&B bands of the period, Ready for the World took its brand of pop-influenced funk beyond the city limits of Flint, Michigan, by blending the electrified soul of the 1980s with sexuality and a European twist. The sextet's self-titled 1984 debut album spawned the first of their two #1 singles, "Oh Sheila," a whiny plea for commitment sung by Prince wannabe Riley. Initially many of the group's fans thought RFTW was a British act because Riley sung "Oh Sheila" with a pronounced accent; when asked why, the Michigan native replied that it was simply a sound the band felt was popular at the time. Ready for the World went on to achieve a Top 10 hit with the song "Digital Display," then reached #1 a second and final time with "Love You Down" from its second LP, *Long Time Coming*. The magic was too long in coming again for the group, which released a dismal effort called *Straight Down to Business* in 1991 and went straight down to obscurity shortly thereafter.

what to buy: You can find everything you need to hear from RFTW on *Oh Sheila—Ready for the World's Greatest Hits* &&&*V* (MCA, 1993, prod. various), since only about half its 12 hits are actually "greatest." When the band was good, as on "Can He

Do It (Like This, Can He Do It Like That)," "Digital Display," "Love You Down," and, of course, the title track, its hooks were distinctive and irresistible. But when your "Greatest Hits" album has filler material, you've got a problem.

what to buy next: The group's debut LP, *Ready for the World* &&*V* (MCA, 1984, prod. RFTW), is still in print, but who knows for how long? Its best moments are also on the *Oh Sheila* compilation, but if you're a speculator, you might pick it up as an investment—it might be worth some money someday.

what to avoid: Lead singer Melvin Riley resurfaced in 1994 with a solo effort called *Ghetto Love* &* (MCA, 1994, prod. Melvin Riley), a sad attempt to project himself as a sex symbol. With gratuitous obscenities in nearly every track and labored macho-player vocals, not even an assist from fellow Flint recording star MC Breed can save him. Moral: producing your own first solo LP is like going to court as your own attorney.

the rest:
Long Time Coming &&* (MCA, 1986)
Ruff 'N Ready &&*V* (MCA, 1988)

influences:
◀◀ The Time, Cameo, the Jackson 5, Prince and the Revolution, Parliament-Funkadelic, the Ohio Players
▶▶ Mint Condition, New Kids on the Block, Digital Underground, Tony! Toni! Tone!

Christina Fuoco and Andre McGarrity

Real Live

Larry Lar, vocals; K-Def, DJ.

Critics couldn't wait to pick on the duo when it released its debut single, "Real Live Sh*t." Although K-Def's ruff-n-rugged production was praised, naysayers sharpened their teeth on rapper Lar, ridiculing his simplistic flow and materialistic, violence-riddled Big Willie mentality. Conceptually, Real Live's fascination with Iceberg Slim and the whole pimp/playa image was a nostalgic nod to the ghettocentricity of the blaxploitation era that preceded by a year Camp Lo's similar (and more successful) obsession. The group has been fairly silent since the release of its 1996 debut, and it's unclear whether Larry Lar and K-Def will ever be seen together again as Real Live.

what's available: Although hardly a threat to the legions of better-skilled MCs, Larry Lar's vocal flow and tough voice are a good match for K-Def's hard-hitting beats on *The Turnaround: The Long Awaited Drama* &&&* (Big Beat, 1996, prod. K-Def, Marley

Marl). K-Def's use of short loops between songs may be more annoying than inspiring, but his overall production touch—especially the wicked beats, which feature powerful basslines and prominent drums—is what makes this album worthwhile. Although easily one of *Turnaround*'s highlights, K-Def's album-closing DJ turn is, strangely, unlisted and uncredited.

influences:

◄◄ Mobb Deep, Wu-Tang Clan, Marley Marl

►► Camp Lo

Oliver "O-Dub" Wang

Red Hot Chili Peppers

Formed 1983, in Hollywood, CA.

Flea, bass; Jack Irons, drums (1983–88); Anthony Kiedis, vocals; Hillel Slovak, guitar (1983–88, died 1988); Chad Smith, drums (1989–present); Jack Sherman, guitar (1983–85); Cliff Martinez, drums (1983–85); John Frusciante, guitar (1989–92); Jesse Tobias, guitar (1993); Dave Navarro, guitar (1993–present).

The Red Hot Chili Peppers began as post-punk novelties, like less funny, more funky Dead Milkmen, best known for such lunkheaded stunts as posing with socks on their private parts and lampooning the cover of the Beatles' *Abbey Road*. Gradually, thanks to tattooed, crewcutted underwear exhibitionist bassist Flea's growing technical skill, they became a legitimate band of good songwriters and accomplished musicians. Flea's bass, derived from a lifetime of listening to old P-Funk records, gave the funny songs a bottom funk, nurtured when they scored a coup and hired George Clinton himself as an early producer. Novelties gave way to hits, first with the 1989 singles "Knock Me Down" and Stevie Wonder's "Higher Ground," then with the breakthrough 1991 album *BloodSugarSexMagik*. By 1992, the Chili Peppers were one of the world's most popular rock bands, headlining Lollapalooza, dominating MTV, and helping create alternative-rock radio. Though their music became more serious—the smash "Under the Bridge" was a sad-eyed walk through the big city—they continued to undress onstage and performed at Woodstock '94 with giant light bulbs on their heads. They constantly struggled with personnel, from the time drummer Jack Irons left with personal problems and original guitarist Hillel Slovak died of a heroin overdose. The Peppers juggled lineups in 1993, settling on ex-Jane's Addiction guitarist Dave Navarro, and put out a hit album, *One Hot Minute*, which sounded disconcertingly like the Doobie Brothers.

what to buy: At more than 75 minutes, *BloodSugarSexMagik* ✒✒✒✒ (EMI, 1991, prod. Rick Rubin) is far too long and there's plenty of filler, but if you wade towards "Under the Bridge" and the explosively funky first single "Give It Away," it's an essential record. *Mother's Milk* ✒✒✒ (EMI, 1989, prod. Michael Beinhorn) is a strong transitional album, with good jokes ("Magic Johnson"), strong funk ("Higher Ground" and Jimi Hendrix's "Fire"), and powerful punk ("Nobody Weird Like Me"). *What Hits!?* ✒✒✒ (EMI, 1992, prod. various) completes a non-fanatic's essential collection; it summarizes the band's career up to *BloodSugarSexMagik*, and includes "Taste the Pain," "If You Want Me to Stay," and "Higher Ground."

what to buy next: Of the pre-superstar albums, *Freaky Styley* ✒✒✒ (EMI, 1985, prod. George Clinton) and *The Uplift Mofo Party Plan* ✒✒✒ (EMI, 1987, prod. Michael Beinhorn) are the funniest and most charming.

what to avoid: *Out in L.A.* ✒ (EMI, 1994, prod. Tom Cartwright, Vincent M. Vero) is a hodgepodge of nasty remixes.

the rest:
The Red Hot Chili Peppers ✒✒ (EMI, 1984)
Abbey Road ✒✒ (EMI, 1988)
One Hot Minute ✒✒✒ (Warner Bros., 1995)

worth searching for: *The Plasma Shaft* ✒✒✒✒ (Warner Music Australia, 1992) is a special edition of *BloodSugarSexMagik* with a second disc of singles, remixes, and live tracks.

solo outings:
John Frusciante:
To Clara ✒✒ (American, 1994)

influences:

◄◄ Parliament-Funkadelic, Stevie Wonder, Jimi Hendrix, Sex Pistols, Minutemen, Flipper

►► Primus, Rage Against the Machine, Fishbone, Anthrax, Onyx, Body Count, Pearl Jam

Steve Knopper

Otis Redding

Born September 9, 1941, in Dawson, GA. Died December 10, 1967, in Madison, WI.

Because his approach to 1960s soul music was more organic than that of his contemporaries, Otis Redding has endured and

Anthony Kiedis of the Red Hot Chili Peppers (© Ken Settle)

the appreciation of his music has even deepened in the years since his death at age 26. The prince of Memphis soul was blossoming into something only hinted at in his final recording, "(Sittin' On) The Dock of the Bay," recorded only three days before he died. He might not have bothered to learn all the lyrics to a song before recording—the most glaring example is his version of the Rolling Stones' "(I Can't Get No) Satisfaction)"—but close scrutiny of his live recordings or the available outtakes indicate it was exactly this spirit of improvisation, this enthusiasm for creativity, that illuminated all his work. From his earliest Little Richard-inspired efforts to the enormous body of work he compiled in four short years at Memphis's Stax/Volt, Redding dominated whatever he recorded with a vivid vision of himself; warm and whimsical, both cornpone and secretly wise.

what to buy: With ace Atlantic engineer Tom Dowd at the board, *Otis Blue* ♪♪♪♪ (Stax, 1965, prod. Jim Stewart) features a rich, resonant sound that, coupled with the single finest selection of songs of any Redding album, makes it one of the greatest soul albums of its era. *The Very Best of Otis Redding* ♪♪♪♪ (Rhino, 1992, prod. various) is a terrific compilation of the essential material.

what to buy next: The evergreen *Live In Europe* ♪♪♪♪♪ (Stax, 1967, prod. Jim Stewart), with Dowd at the controls again, commemorates Redding's greatness as a live performer and is one of the most historic live albums ever recorded.

what to avoid: Although compelling in its unvarnished honesty, *Good to Me* ♪♪ (Stax, 1993, prod. Al Jackson Jr.) is not really a very good album. Composed of scraps leftover from *Live at the Whiskey* and featuring Redding's unskilled—undoubtedly underpaid—road band stumbling through the songs, this is the least interesting of his many live recordings.

the rest:
Pain In My Heart ♪♪♪♪ (Stax, 1965)
The Great Otis Redding Sings Soul Ballads ♪♪♪♪ (Stax, 1965)
The Soul Album ♪♪♪♪ (Stax, 1966)
The Otis Redding Dictionary of Soul ♪♪♪♪ (Stax, 1966)
(With Carla Thomas) *King and Queen* ♪♪♪ (Stax, 1967)
The Dock of the Bay ♪♪♪♪ (Stax, 1968)
In Person at the Whiskey a Go Go (Stax, 1968) ♪♪♪♪
The Immortal Otis Redding ♪♪♪♪ (Stax, 1968)
Love Man ♪♪♪♪ (Atco, 1970)
Tell the Truth ♪♪♪ (Atco, 1970)
Remember Me ♪♪♪ (Stax, 1992)
The Very Best of Otis Redding, Vol. 2 ♪♪♪♪ (Rhino, 1995)

worth searching for: The three-disc box set *The Otis Redding Story* ♪♪♪♪ (Atlantic, 1987, prod. various), also released in a

six-LP edition, was replaced—but not improved upon—by a pricey, four-disc box, *Otis: The Definitive Otis Redding* ♪♪♪ (Rhino, 1993, prod. various).

influences:
◀◀ Little Richard, Sam Cooke, Solomon Burke
▶▶ Al Green, Janis Joplin, Mick Jagger, Maxwell

Joel Selvin

Redman
Born Reggie Noble.

Land of the Lost (New Jersey) refugee Redman was first brought to mass hip-hop attention by EPMD. As a member of the Hit Squad, he caught wreck on "Hardcore" and "Brothers on My Jock," both from EPMD's 1990 album, *Business as Usual*. His maniacal persona was barely contained within the deep funk confines of the track and beckoned to be released into the wilds of the hip-hop community.

what to buy: Redman's schizophrenic personality blossoms on *Whut . . . Thee Album* ♪♪♪♪ (RAL/CHAOS Records, 1992, prod. Erick Sermon, others). This is one of those albums that's like fine wine, getting better the longer it lays around. For his debut, the Noble one slings plenty of ill-styled verbal buckdowns and dishes out gruff, harsh vocals that remind you of Busta Rhymes on crack. He's strictly in your face, flexing his raw guttural growl over rich, minimal beats on such cuts as "I'm a Bad," "How to Roll a Blunt," "Da Funk," and "Rated R." Beats throughout (supplied by Erick Sermon) are fat and sticky, rolling over Redman's gritty vocals like a thick fog. And when he "freaks it in Korean" on "Blow Your Mind," you know the madness has just begun.

what to buy next: Redman's third outing, *Muddy Waters* ♪♪♪♪ (Def Jam, 1996, prod. Erick Sermon, Reggie Noble, Rockwilder), is even further out in the zone. "Iz He For Real" is drenched in weird, stoney swirls, "Whateva Man" is pure supercalafragalisticexpifunkadociousness and "Rock Da Spot" is deftly stripped down. "Soopaman Luva 3," meanwhile, is the third installment in a series about a hip-hop lothario, running along the same lines as EPMD's continuing "Jane" saga. Redman's second outing, *Dare Iz a Darkside* ♪♪♪ (Def Jam, 1994, prod. Erick Sermon, Reggie Noble, Rockwilder), starts off slowly, weighted down by a few too many ultra-short tracks and extrapolated skits. However, dig a little deeper and you'll find an album that covers similar terrain as Redman's debut, serving up some dusted funk. A few standouts emerge, including "Rockafella," "Sooperman Luva II," and "Green Island" (an ode to stinky weed that smuggles in some slack-key guitar).

influences:

◄◄ EPMD, Das EFX, Just-Ice

►► Diezzel Don & the Govener, Keith Murray, Ill Al Skratch

Spence D.

Jimmy Reed

Born Mathis James Reed, September 6, 1925, in Dunleith, MS. Died August 29, 1976, in Oakland, CA.

Jimmy Reed was the last of the archetypal blues primitives. His simple electric guitar lines, shrill harmonica playing, and understated vocals forged some of the most unique and enduring records of the 1950s and early 1960s. After a World War II hitch in the Navy, Reed moved to Indiana, worked in the steel mills, jammed with local bands, and occasionally played for tips on the street. In 1949, he teamed up with his childhood friend Eddie Taylor and began to work Southside Chicago nightclubs. Albert King directed Reed to the fledgling Vee-Jay label, and his first single, "High and Lonesome," was released on their Chance subsidiary. Reed moved to Vee-Jay full time in 1953, but didn't have his first national hit until late 1955 with "You Don't Have to Go." Over the next eight years, Reed scored nearly two dozen R&B hits, several of which crossed over to the middle regions of the pop charts. Reed, a functional illiterate who "made up" many of his best songs, needed his wife Mary (Mama Reed) to cue him by whispering forgotten lyrics while he sang live in the studio. Producer Calvin Carter cleverly turned this handicap into an irresistible facet of the Jimmy Reed sound, and soon Mama Reed was a regular feature of her husband's recordings. Reed's sideman Eddie Taylor (a great performer in his own right) continually added guitar fills and arrangement ideas that gave Reed's records their distinctive hooks. The early to mid-1960s was a peak time for Reed; besides his string of hits and acclaimed performance at Carnegie Hall, many of his songs were being covered with great success by the likes of Elvis Presley, the Animals, and the Rolling Stones. But by then, alcoholism and epilepsy were taking their toll. When the Vee-Jay label crumbled in 1964, Reed's manager Al Smith moved him to ABC-Bluesway. The loss of Calvin Carter behind the glass was a big blow and Reed seemed to dry up as a songwriter. With Al Smith (who wrote "Big Boss Man") producing and writing most of the songs, Reed's recordings developed a cleaner, more professional sound but somehow became a less compelling listening experience. Reed's last recordings mistak-

enly attempted to put him in the 1960s soul/1970s funk bag, and they were artistic disasters as well as commercial flops. Reed finally sobered up when he hit the comeback trail in 1976, but just as bookings were picking up, he died in his sleep after an attack of epilepsy. Reed's work has undergone a revival in the last few years, and several compilations of his Vee-Jay material attest that Reed sounded great in his time, but even better in ours.

what to buy: *Speak the Lyrics to Me Mama Reed* 𝄢𝄢𝄢𝄢 (Vee-Jay, 1993, prod. Calvin Carter) has 25 digitally remastered tracks, all the influential numbers that Reed made famous plus two previously unissued recordings. A nice starter set. *Best of Jimmy Reed* 𝄢𝄢𝄢𝄢 (GNP/Crescendo, 1990, prod. Calvin Carter), *Greatest Hits* 𝄢𝄢𝄢𝄢 (Charly, 1992, prod. Calvin Carter), *Big Boss Blues—Original Vee-Jay Recordings* 𝄢𝄢𝄢𝄢 (Charly, 1988, prod. Calvin Carter), and *Bright Lights, Big City—Charly Blues Masterworks Vol. 17* 𝄢𝄢𝄢𝄢 (Charly, 1992, prod. Calvin Carter) are equally good sets of hit Vee-Jay material if you're wiling to do without digitally remastered sound.

what to buy next: *The Classic Recordings* 𝄢𝄢𝄢𝄢 (Tomato, 1995, comp. Pete Welding) is a three-CD, 44-song set that features all of his Vee-Jay hits, some top B-sides and LP cuts, interesting liner notes, and an ugly cover painting. *Classic Recordings* 𝄢𝄢𝄢𝄢 (Rhino, 1995, prod. Calvin Carter) is a three-CD, 55-song compilation of Reed's Vee-Jay material with most of the hits (though "Honest I Do" is missing) and his best LP sides.

what to avoid: *Big Legged Woman* 𝄢 (Collectables, 1996), *Jimmy Reed Is Back* 𝄢 (Collectables, 1994), and *Cry Before I Go* 𝄢 (Drive Archives, 1995) are budget compilations of slickly over-produced later sides where much of Reed's charm is lost. Info is scarce, and the packaging is deceptive.

the rest:

Rockin' with Reed 𝄢𝄢𝄢 (Charly, 1987)
Ride 'Em On Down 𝄢𝄢𝄢 (Charly, 1989)
Jimmy Reed—1965 𝄢𝄢𝄢 (Paula/Jewel Records, 1991)
Greatest Hits 𝄢𝄢 (Hollywood/Rounder, 1992)
Heartaches and Troubles 𝄢𝄢 (MCA Special Products, 1995)
Rockin' with Reed 𝄢𝄢𝄢 (Eclipse, 1996)
Big Boss Man 𝄢𝄢𝄢 (Ronn, 1996)
New Jimmy Reed Album/Soulin' 𝄢𝄢𝄢 (See For Miles, 1997)
Big Boss Man/Down in Virginia 𝄢𝄢 (See For Miles, 1997)

worth searching for: *Jimmy Reed at Carnegie Hall* 𝄢𝄢𝄢𝄢 (Mobile Fidelity Sound, 1992, prod. Calvin Carter) is a tremendous sounding 23-track remastering of the original Vee-Jay double LP on a 24-k gold disc. Reed doesn't perform live at all on this, but he recreates his Carnegie Hall playlist with new recordings cut in 1961. The rest is Vee-Jays' LP *The Best of Jimmy Reed*, which has original versions of many of his 1950s hits and B-sides.

influences:

◀◀ Elmore James, Eddie Taylor

▶▶ Slim Harpo, Lonnie Brooks

Ken Burke

Della Reese

Born Delloreese Patricia Early Taliaferro, July 6, 1932, in Detroit, MI.

While Della Reese wasn't the most prolific or enduring singer of her day, she was a great influence on another generation of black female vocalists, especially Motown stars Diana Ross and Martha Reeves (the latter named the Vandellas in Reese's honor). Drawing her inspiration from the likes of Dinah Washington and Mahalia Jackson, Reese had her roots firmly planted in gospel and blues. During her early teens, she spent her summers touring as a back-up singer for Jackson. After high school Reese attended Wayne State University and majored in psychology. But music called her back; after her stint with the Detroit gospel group the Meditation Singers, she was discovered by a music publisher from Detroit named Al Green, who sent her on to a manager named Lee Magid in New York. Reese wowed Magid immediately with her potent, bluesy voice and uncontrived sensuality. He signed her to the Jubilee label, where she debuted with "In the Still of the Night" in 1957. The record sold half a million copies, allowing the sometimes campy yet grounded performer to move on to bigger and better things. She signed with RCA in 1959 and topped the charts that year with "Don't You Know" and the next with "Someday." Reese continued to make records for the ABC label in the sixties with dwindling success. In 1969 she landed her own TV variety show, *The Della Reese Show,* which only lasted a little more than a year. But that wasn't the last viewing audiences would see of Ms. Reese. She appeared on the big screen in several films, including *Psychic Killer* (1975), *Harlem Nights* (1989), *The Kid Who Loved Christmas* (1990), and *A Thin Line Between Love and Hate* (1996). Reese returned to television in the 70's sitcom *Chico and the Man* and currently plays "Tess" in the TV series *Touched By an Angel.*

what's available: *Della Reese: Voice of a Angel* 𝄢𝄢𝄢𝄢 (RCA, 1996, prod. various) includes remastered RCA recordings by Hugo and Luigi from August 5, 1959 to November 25, 1964. A great place to get to know the unique bluesy cabaret style that

made Reese a hit, even if only for a little while. *The Angel Sings* 𝄢𝄢𝄢𝄢 (Amherst, 1997, prod. Leonard Silver, Chris Biehler) is also a worthy compilation.

worth searching for: There are some import compilations and her performances with Duke Ellington that are well worth finding. One of the better imports is *All the Hits and More by Della Reese* 𝄢𝄢𝄢 (Marginal, 1995), arranged and conducted by Neal Hefti.

influences:

◀◀ Mahalia Jackson, Dinah Washington

▶▶ Diana Ross, Martha Reeves

Norene Cashen

Dianne Reeves

Born 1956, in Detroit, MI.

This versatile singer has upset some critics with her unwillingness to be pigeonholed stylistically, alternating R&B and jazz albums and occasionally mixing the two. Vocally she has a multi-octave range that's warm, dark, and magesterial on the bottom, and light and clear on top. She relies equally on R&B, jazz, and gospel phrasing and inflections, and is thus equally effective no matter what the style, mood, or tempo. Born in Detroit, Reeves moved with her family to Denver when she was two years old. After her high school band competed for and won the opportunity to perform at the annual National Association of Jazz Educators conference, she caught the attention of jazz trumpeter Clark Terry, with whom she performed even while she was attending the University of Colorado. She then moved to Los Angeles in 1976, where she started a long association with jazz pianist Billy Childs (in a cooperative group called Night Flight) and performed with a variety of bands, including the Latin-oriented Caldara, which included not only Eddie del Barrio, later her producer, but also one-time Earth, Wind & Fire keyboardist Larry Dunn. During the early 1980s she toured in the groups of Sergio Mendes and later Harry Belafonte, and recorded a pair of albums under her own name for the indie label Palo Alto. When Reeves signed to EMI, her producer was her uncle, George Duke. Her first album was mostly R&B but included a few tracks that tilt toward jazz (there are two jazz standards—"Yesterdays" and "I've Got It Bad and That Ain't Good"—and one song on which Herbie Hancock plays). However, it was the solidly R&B "Better Days" (also known as "the grandma song") that became a mild hit. Perhaps as a result, her second album stayed away from jazz and aimed for the pop charts (without much success), emphasizing her original material (though a cover of Rickie Lee Jones's "Company" was an effective album closer). At the same time this album was being recorded, she was also working on a strictly jazz album, *I Remember*, which ended up consisting of 1988 and 1990 sessions; the four later tracks feature her best singing yet, including a volcanic rendition of "Love for Sale." The pattern was set: her EMI albums were R&B, her Blue Note albums were jazz (she's never strictly one or the other though, and for a while it seemed as if the two were starting to converge). But then her 1996 release was not just jazz, but all-star jazz of a very traditional kind. If there is always a certain inconsistency to her albums, always something not quite right about a few tracks, she nonetheless has built up a fairly impressive body of work for a 40-year-old jazz singer with eclectic tendencies.

what to buy: *Art + Survival* 🎵🎵🎵 (EMI, 1994, prod. Eddie del Barrio, Terri Lyne Carrington) contains Reeves's greatest pop moment, the joyous, gospel-tinged "Come to the River." If some lyrics weren't so one-dimensionally preachy (women's issues, the environment, and a sort of new-agey spirituality), this would be an even better album. As it stands, it's by far the best integration on one record of her many styles.

what to buy next: Her major-label debut, *Dianne Reeves* 🎵🎵🎵 (EMI, 1987, prod. George Duke), is not among her best albums, as the production sounds dated. But from a strictly R&B point of view, it's a must-own for "Better Days," and some of the other material also stands up.

what to avoid: Drawn from her first two albums (plus a guest performance with the group Caldera), *The Palo Alto Sessions, 1981–1985* 🎵 (Blue Note, 1996, prod. various) is strictly for die-hard fans. At the beginning of her recording career, Reeves's voice was too far ahead of her interpretive abilities; too much of her singing consisted of vocal quirks unrelated to the songs at hand. By the second album, her singing had improved markedly, but this compilation selects much more heavily from the first album due to her expressed fondness for the songs themselves.

the rest:
Never Too Far 🎵🎵 (EMI, 1989)
I Remember 🎵🎵🎵 (Blue Note, 1991)
Quiet After the Storm 🎵🎵🎵 (Blue Note, 1995)
The Grand Encounter 🎵🎵🎵 (Blue Note, 1996)

worth searching for: *For Every Heart* 🎵🎵 (Palo Alto, 1984) shows Reeves starting to find her way vocally and will be of interest to the devoted.

influences:
◀◀ Sarah Vaughan, Carmen McRae, Flora Purim, Chaka Khan
▶▶ Nnenna Freelon

Steve Holtje

Rene & Angela
Formed 1977, in Los Angeles, CA.

Angela Winbush, vocals; Rene Moore, vocals.

When Angela Winbush, a former schoolteacher, and Rene Moore, an instructor at a classical education program in California, met in 1977, they had their sights set on becoming a writing team, akin to Ashford and Simpson. But they got a contract after a record label heard them singing on a demo tape of songs they had written. Several hits, ranging from funk tunes ("I'll Be Good") to string-laden ballads ("My First Love") followed between 1980 and 1985. Their distinct sound, built upon Moore's tenor and Winbush's soprano, complemented their diverse songwriting talent. At first it seemed as though they were singing these love tunes to each other, but a rocky breakup belied that notion. The bitter end came years after each had gone solo, when Moore won a suit against Winbush dealing with unpaid and uncredited writing work on the Isley Brothers' hit song, "Smooth Sailing." Winbush continued to write hit songs for other artists, and had a handful of solo hits of her own. Moore recorded a solo album, but it was poorly received by the public.

what to buy: The duo's early work, mostly out of print, is captured on *Best of Rene & Angela: Come My Way* 🎵🎵🎵🎵 (EMI, 1996, prod. various), with a particular bent towards ballads.

what to buy next: The latter stage of their work is highlighted on *Street Called Desire & More* 🎵🎵🎵🎵 (1997, Mercury/Chronicles), a remastered version of their most popular album, with a bonus bunch of extended versions of songs like "Your Smile" and "You Don't Have to Cry."

worth searching for: *Rene & Angela* 🎵🎵🎵 (Capitol, 1980) is an interesting time capsule of the last popular self-contained guy-gal duo, created just as disco ended and the age of the megastar appeared.

solo outings:
Rene Moore:
Destination Love 🎵🎵 (Polydor, 1988)

influences:
◀◀ Ashford and Simpson, Peaches and Herb

see also: *Angela Winbush*

Franklin Paul

Richie Rich

Oakland's Richie Rich first hit the (then-emerging) Bay Area rap scene in 1990 with the group 415. Comprised of Rich, D-Loc, D.J. Daryl, and executive producer JED, 415 released two albums, with both D-Loc and Rich going on to solo careers. The 415 albums introduced several classic tracks to the Bay Area rap pantheon, including "Snitches & Bitches," "41Fivin'," and the underground classic, "Side Show"; many of the cuts were written by Rich, whose smooth, creamy baritone stood out against the nasal tenors of other noted East Oakland rappers. Although 415's future seemed bright, Rich ran into (illegal) drug troubles and wound up serving time in Santa Rita County Jail from 1991 to 1992. While Rich was locked up, the rest of 415 released *Nu Niggaz on Tha Blokk* to little notice. Upon his release, Rich worked his way back into the rap game by contributing songs, production, and raps to albums by Too $hort, 2Pac, and the Luniz. Following the success of the artists, plus the release of Rich's own indie album on 41510 Records (the name is a nod to Oakland's area-code change, from 415 to 510), Def Jam got Rich quick.

what to buy: After an almost five-year absence from the mic, Richie Rich returned full force with *Half Thang* ₰₰₰₰ (41510, 1996, prod. DJ Daryl, others), an album that percolates with the thick trunk-o'-funk sound that made Oakland famous. The title track is packed with playa' bump and is a lyrical recollection of the coke-slangin' lifestyle Rich used to live. Rich's major-label debut, *Seasoned Veteran* ₰₰₰ (Def Jam, prod. DJ Darryl, Jermaine Dupri, others), keeps the funk on the down low, with its slinky verve and whoridin' aplomb. Rich's deep baritone doesn't miss a beat as he rolls smoothly over the midtempo grooves. Like-minded NorCal vets including E-40 show their guest-vocal love, making this album an East Bay Area pleaser.

what to avoid: With Richie Rich absent, the rest of the 415 crew released *Nu Niggaz on Tha Blokk* ₰₰ (Priority, 1991, prod. various). From the "KK" title to the cover photo of the crew in black gangsta garb, the album is a failed attempt at creating a new N.W.A. Sans Rich, though, the group has no real pizzaz.

worth searching for: Their first 415 album, *41Fivin'* ₰₰₰₰ (Big League, 1990) is the group's best. Such cuts as "Side Show" show that Richie Rich is bound for stardom and suggest that 415 is East Oakland's first rap supergroup. Rich's first solo effort, *Don't Do It* ₰₰₰ (Big League, 1990, prod. various), features the humourous "Rodney the Geek."

influences:
◀◀ Digital Underground, Too $hort

Spence D.

Tony Rich Project

Born in Detroit, MI.

Among the young generation of R&B performers who are taking the music into the future by paying attention to its past, look for Tony Rich to go the distance. A virtual one-man band who recorded the Project's debut album with only scant assistance (mostly from his brother, Joe), Rich's brand of soul music is understated, acoustic-based, and irresistible. A protege of famed production duo Antonio "L.A." Reid and Kenneth "Babyface" Edmonds, Rich—who was actually discovered by former Detroit Pistons star John Salley—clearly learned his lessons well, and his songs, especially the haunting ballad "Nobody Knows," stand shoulder-to-shoulder with Babyface's solo work. Lyrically, Rich recalls the more contemplative work of Stevie Wonder, Marvin Gaye, and Donny Hathaway. As if to prove Rich's talent transcends genre, "Nobody Knows" was also a hit on the country charts for singer Kevin Sharp. To be sure, there's more chart action in Rich's future.

what to buy: Rich's debut, *Words* ₰₰₰₰ (LaFace, 1995, prod. Tony Rich), deservedly won the 1997 Grammy Award for best R&B album, perhaps as much for what it's *not* as for what it is. Flying in the face of contemporary R&B's penchant for vocal histrionics and grandiose production, *Words* is a masterwork of understatement. The ballads "Nobody Knows" and "Missin' You," are stark yet smooth, led by Rich's unassuming vocals. And while those songs follow the genre's reliance on songs of heartbreak, the album also contains character studies ("Hey Blue," "Billy Goat"), inner-city laments ("Grass Is Green"), and even a missive from the afterlife ("Ghost"). Overall, Rich's sense of quietude and spirit of contemplation draws the listener in, making *Words* one of the most intimate albums in recent memory.

the rest:
This World of the Blue Butterfly N/A (LaFace/Arista, 1997)

influences:
◀◀ Babyface, Marvin Gaye, Donny Hathaway, Stevie Wonder

Daniel Durchholz

Lionel Richie

See: The Commodores

Righteous Brothers

Formed 1962, in Los Angeles, CA. Disbanded 1968. Subsequent re-unions in 1974 and throughout the 1980s and 1990s.

Bill Medley (born September 19, 1940, in Santa Ana, CA), vocals; Bobby Hatfield (born August 10, 1940, in Beaver Dam, WI), vocals.

The archetypal blue-eyed soul team, the Righteous Brothers churned out a steady procession of classic rock and roll—with "Little Latin Lupe Lu" at the apex—long before even meeting Wagnerian producer Phil Spector, who assured the duo pop immortality on their first collaboration, the epochal 1965 #1 hit "You've Lost That Lovin' Feelin'." By matching Medley's oozing baritone with Hatfield's ecstatic tenor, the pair could generate sparks with their furious, almost intuitive vocal tradeoffs. And, after splitting with Spector following a string of massive hits with Medley at the helm, the Brothers proved they learned their lessons well, etching a pop perfect recreation of the Spector sound, "(You're My) Soul and Inspiration," which also earned them a #1 hit. After splitting up and reforming—on a guest appearance on the Sonny and Cher television show, no less—the Righteous Brothers returned to the Top 5 in 1974 with "Rock 'n' Roll Heaven," a relatively cheesy piece of formula radio fodder fashioned for them by the songwriting-production team, Dennis Lambert and Brian Potter, who were experiencing similar Top 40 successes at the time with the Four Tops and the Tavares. The re-emergence of the Spector-produced "Unchained Melody" on the 1990 soundtrack of *Ghost* led to yet another reformation (Medley, in the meantime, scored a #1 hit on a duet with Jennifer Warnes with "(I've Had) The Time Of My Life" from the *Dirty Dancing* soundtrack), leaving the pair headlining oldies but goodies shows and casino main rooms with a slickly produced act honed to a fare-thee-well over four decades of performing.

what to buy: Released in the wake of the *Ghost* soundtrack, *Unchained Melody: The Very Best of the Righteous Brothers* ♫♫♫♫ (PolyGram, 1990, prod. various) covers the basics of the group's hit repertoire with little chaff amidst the wheat.

what to buy next: Before linking up with Spector, Medley and Hatfield combined on a succession of rollicking R&B-influenced sides collected on *The Moonglow Years* ♫♫♫ (PolyGram, 1991, prod. various).

what to avoid: The two-disc set *Anthology: 1962–1974* ♫♫♫♫ (Rhino, 1989, prod. various) contains more Righteous Brothers than is probably useful, given the almost gratuitous second disc. But the 16-track first disc thoroughly covers the duo's frat rock classics on the Moonglow label and culminates with five Spector epics.

the rest:
The Best of the Righteous Brothers ♫♫ (Curb, 1993)
The Best of the Righteous Brothers, Vol. 2 ♫ (Curb, 1993)

worth searching for: *Some Blue-Eyed Soul* ♫♫♫ (Moonglow, 1964) is the deepest and most consistent of the individual albums from the duo's peak period.

influences:
◀◀ Don and Dewey, Ray Charles
▶▶ The Walker Brothers, Daryl Hall and John Oates

Joel Selvin

Minnie Riperton

Born November 8, 1947, in Chicago, IL. Died July 12, 1979, in Los Angeles, CA.

Chicago during the 1960s was a hotbed of black pop rivaled only by Detroit and Memphis. In addition to a still-thriving blues scene on the South Side (Muddy Waters, Howlin' Wolf, Magic Sam), the town could boast of Ramsey Lewis, Gene Chandler, the Dells, Jerry Butler, the Five Stairsteps, and the Impressions, as well as top arrangers Johnny Pate and Charles Stepney. As a diminutive teenager with a huge, three-octave range, young Minnie Riperton dove into the deep amateur talent pool. After a series of false starts, her group the Gems were inked by the powerhouse Chess record label. The Gems never made it out of the home R&B circuit, but Chess saw a greatness in Riperton. In 1967 she joined the psychedelic soul-rock chorale project, Rotary Connection; the multi-racial group's radical re-arrangements of rock songs ("The Weight," "Burning of the Midnight Lamp") and Christmas hymns (the entire *Peace* LP) were the ideal vehicles for the singer's trademark stratospheric wails and girlish alto. Aside from a minor hit with its version of Aretha Franklin's "Respect," Rotary Connection never caught on, breaking up in 1970 (the tune "I Am the Black Gold of the Sun" from its last LP *Hey Love* was covered in 1997 on the jazz dance project Nuyorican Soul). Four years later, after a stint in Stevie Wonder's backing group Wonderlove, Riperton reemerged on Epic Records with *Perfect Angel*, a sublime cycle of life and love songs rendered exquisitely by her warm vocals.

By 1975's *Adventures In Paradise*, she had become a very popular R&B/pop singer with radio hits, a full concert schedule, and guest appearances on albums by Quincy Jones and Wonder. In 1979, poised on the precipice of superstardom, Riperton was diagnosed with cancer. *Minnie*, her final album, was released by Capitol shortly before her death.

what to buy: *Capitol Gold: the Best of Minnie Riperton* 𝄞𝄞𝄞 (Capitol, 1993, prod. various) is a pretty balanced collection of the singer's work, though not definitive. A proper anthology of Riperton s career is yet to be produced.

what to buy next: Once indoctrinated, seek out *Perfect Angel* 𝄞𝄞𝄞𝄞 (Capitol, 1974, prod. Richard Rudolph, Stevie Wonder), the quintessential Minnie Riperton Experience.

the rest:
The Chess Recordings N/A (MCA, 1997)

influences:
◀◀ Ivie Anderson, Betty Roche
▶▶ Linda Lewis, Joi, Mariah Carey

Tom Terrell

Roachford

Formed mid-1980s, in London, England.

Andrew Roachford, vocals, keyboards; Chris Taylor, drums; Michael Brown, guitar; Hawi Gondwe, guitar; Paul Bruce, bass; Derrick Taylor, bass.

One of the great shoulda-beens in rock and R&B, Roachford was discovered and championed by Terence Trent D'Arby, who got his label's sister act, Epic Records, to sign the upstarts and release three of their albums. The quartet plays a rockin' kind of soul, with big grooves, meaty vocal harmonies, and some exceptional songs. Sadly, Roachford never caught fire, though its 1995 release *Permanent Shade of Blue* shows it's still capable of compelling music. Listen up, already!

what's available: *Permanent Shade of Blue* 𝄞𝄞𝄞 (Epic, 1995, prod. Roachford, Martin Phillips, Gill Norton) isn't the group's strongest effort, but it's all that's available right now. And nobody with a taste for good rock-R&B fusion should be without a Roachford album.

worth searching for: *Roachford* 𝄞𝄞𝄞 (Epic, 1988, prod. Mike Vernon, Michael H. Brauer) is an exceptional debut, with a truly exciting performance from Andrew Roachford and his troupe. Find it.

influences:
◀◀ The Temptations, Sam & Dave, Garland Jeffries, Southside Johnny & the Asbury Jukes, Steve Winwood

Gary Graff

Smokey Robinson & the Miracles

Formed 1957, in Detroit, MI.

William "Smokey" Robinson (born February 19, 1940, in Detroit, MI), vocals (1957–72); Ronnie White, vocals; Bobby Rogers, vocals; Warren "Pete" Moore, vocals; Claudette Rogers, vocals (1957–64); William Griffin, vocals.

Berry Gordy Jr. owned Motown, but Smokey Robinson was the label's king. A singer and songwriter who befriended Gordy during the late 1950s, Robinson was Motown's go-to guy. He wrote the label's first #1 pop hit, "My Guy" for Mary Wells, and its biggest, "My Girl" for the Temptations. Sensing a theme here? As an artist, Robinson wrote and performed some of the sweetest and most poetic loves songs in pop music history. No less than Bob Dylan called him "America's greatest living poet," and the British band ABC celebrated Robinson in song with "When Smokey Sings." In his prime, Robinson was able to convey passion, pain, longing, and any other emotion with just a few words and his own flexible vocals—particularly his ability to sweep into an ear-clutching falsetto. The Miracles were no simple backup group, either; the others—particularly the late Ronnie White (who co-wrote "My Girl") and Bobby Rogers— served as creative foils, while Robinson and Claudette Rogers were married for nearly 25 years. On his own, Robinson coined a whole new pop music genre—the pillow-talk "Quiet Storm"— though his hits have become considerably more sporadic. He actually left Motown during the early 1990s, though he remains an occasional ambassador for the label.

what to buy: *Anthology: The Best of Smokey Robinson & the Miracles* 𝄞𝄞𝄞𝄞 (Motown, 1995, prod. Smokey Robinson) is a marvelous two-CD distillation that has all the hits—"Ooo Baby Baby," "Going to a Go-Go," "I Second That Emotion," "The Tears of a Clown"—plus some important album tracks. *A Quiet Storm* 𝄞𝄞𝄞𝄞 (Motown, 1975/1989, prod. Smokey Robinson) is a landmark solo album, a sexy, whispery affair that launched a whole new realm of music.

what to buy next: While some of the other Motown box sets have their share of filler, *The 35th Anniversary Collection* 𝄞𝄞𝄞𝄞 (Motown, 1994, prod. various) reminds us that with a talent like

Robinson on board, it's not hard to have four discs worth of wonderful music (including selections from his solo career and from the post-Smokey Miracles). Robinson's *One Heartbeat* 𝄢𝄢𝄢 (Motown, 1987, prod. various) is another fine solo album, a return to form after several fallow years with the hits "Just to See Her" and the title track. *The Ultimate Collection* 𝄢𝄢𝄢𝄢 (Motown, 1997, prod. various) is a suitable gathering of Robinson's solo hits.

what to avoid: *Motown Superstar Series Volume 18* 𝄢𝄢 (Motown) is, in this case, a useless redundancy.

the rest:
Smokey Robinson & the Miracles:
Cookin' with the Miracles 𝄢𝄢 (Motown, 1962/1994)
Christmas with the Miracles 𝄢𝄢𝄢 (Motown, 1963)
Going to a Go-Go 𝄢𝄢𝄢𝄢 (Motown, 1965)
Greatest Hits, Vol. II 𝄢𝄢𝄢𝄢 (Motown, 1968)
The Season for Miracles 𝄢𝄢𝄢 (Motown, 1970)
The Tears of a Clown 𝄢𝄢𝄢𝄢 (Motown, 1970)
Whatever Makes You Happy: More of the Best 𝄢𝄢𝄢𝄢 (Rhino, 1993)
Motown Legends: The Ballad Album 𝄢𝄢𝄢𝄢 (ESX, 1994)

Smokey Robinson:
Blame It on Love & All the Great Hits 𝄢𝄢𝄢𝄢 (Motown, 1983/1990)
Double Good Everything 𝄢𝄢 (SBK/EMI, 1991)
Cruisin'—Being with You 𝄢𝄢𝄢 (ESX, 1995)

worth searching for: Here's a true mark of Robinson's talents: his vocal on "We've Saved the Best for Last" actually makes a Kenny G album—*Silhouette* (Arista, 1988)—worth buying.

influences:
◀◀ Jackie Wilson, Clyde McPhatter, Sam Cooke

▶▶ Paul McCartney, Michael Jackson, Terence Trent D'Arby, Babyface

Gary Graff

word up!

THere was a long period when I was searching and being produced and written for by a lot of people other than myself. There have only been two times when that worked--when Brian Holland and Lamont Dozier cut 'Mickey's Monkey' on the Miracles and me, and the *One Heartbeat* album. Other than those two times in my life, I've never had enormous success with anything other than the stuff I've done myself.

Smokey Robinson

Rodney O & Joe Cooley
Formed mid-1980s, in Los Angeles, CA.

Rodney O (born Rodney Oliver), vocals; Joe Cooley, DJ; General Jeff (born Jeff Page), vocals.

Run-D.M.C. isn't the only hip-hop trio whose name ignores the third member. Rodney O & Joe Cooley, too, are three, although secondary rapper General Jeff has always been off the marquee. Unlike Run-D.M.C.'s Jam Master Jay, though, Jeff didn't have to worry much about losing out on household recognition; where Run-D.M.C. enjoyed massive, across-the-board success, Rodney O & Joe Cooley only fared well in the under-ground, especially in California, where their well-crafted, bass-heavy, Impala-ready funk productions earned converts with the hardcore crowd. The rest of the rap world did take notice when Rodney O & Joe Cooley answered Tim Dog's "Fuck Compton" with the 1992 album *Fuck New York*, but by that time, the trio was already past its peak.

worth searching for: N.W.A., DJ Quik, and MC Eiht may have earned the most national attention, but Rodney O & Joe Cooley were just as vital in the West Coast hardcore scene. The group's lyrics may say little, but its funk-for-the-trunk bass-beat combos resonated in more ways than one. The crew's albums are all out of print, but its best-known tracks are collected on *Everlasting Hits: Best of Rodney O & Joe Cooley* 𝄞𝄞𝄞 (React, 1995, prod. Rodney O & Joe Cooley), including "Everlasting Bass," "This Is for the Homies," "U Don't Hear Me Tho," "Cooley High," and "Humps for the Blvd.," all of which should be familiar to anybody who was cruising a boulevard somewhere in California in the late 80s or early 90s.

influences:

◀◀ World Class Wreckin' Cru, Uncle Jamm's Army, KDAY Mixmasters

▶▶ DJ Quik

Josh Freedom du Lac

The Rolling Stones

Formed 1962, in London, England.

Mick Jagger, vocals; Keith Richards, guitar, vocals; Brian Jones (died 1969), guitar (1962–69); Bill Wyman, bass (1962–94); Charlie Watts, drums; Mick Taylor, guitar (1969–74); Ron Wood, guitar (1974–present).

Before becoming the self-proclaimed world's greatest rock 'n' roll band, the Stones were a blues combo. Their initial flurry of releases is essentially an homage to the blues, soul, and R&B music that shook them from their youthful middle-class lethargy in London. During their first decade, the Stones would, of course, define the classic rock lineup—two guitars, bass, drums, and a little red rooster crowing out front—and created the enduring standard for how it should sound. But the Stones never strayed far from their roots in Chicago, Detroit, and the American South. Their more experimental tracks and albums sounded instantly contrived and dated, whereas their increasingly personal variations on Chess Records blues, hard country music, Motown, Stax, and countless black performers from James Brown to Tina Turner were often riveting. The Stones affirmed the primacy of the electric guitar as Keith Richards succeeded Chuck Berry as rock's primary riff-meister; Richards and Mick Jagger wrote classic melodies and pithy, unsentimental, and frequently just plain cruel lyrics that were the equal of their 1960s rivals Bob Dylan and the Beatles; and the group's rhythm section, anchored by the peerless Charlie Watts, made it all swing like nobody's business. Only problem is, the Stones kept the money machine in motion long after their artistic drive waned. Like their blues heroes, the Stones entered their 50s still singing about their overworked mojos and cranking out competent product that bespoke professionalism rather than inspiration.

what to buy: *Aftermath* 𝄞𝄞𝄞𝄞 (Abkco, 1966, prod. Andrew Loog Oldham) marked the entry of these erstwhile blues traditionalists into the album-rock pantheon alongside Dylan and the Beatles, with its canny use of sitar, marimba, and dulcimer (all performed by Brian Jones) to augment Jagger's multifaceted star turn as a vocalist on "Paint It Black," "Lady Jane," and "Under My Thumb." The weakest cuts on *Beggars Banquet* 𝄞𝄞𝄞𝄞 (Abkco, 1968, prod. Jimmy Miller) are its best known: "Street Fighting Man" offers a rare political commentary that is musically stirring but lyrically ambivalent; and "Sympathy for the Devil" finds Jagger pandering to the group's bad-boy image. Otherwise, the disc is a tour de force of acoustic-tinged savagery and slumming sexuality, particularly the gleefully flippant "Stray Cat Blues." *Let It Bleed* 𝄞𝄞𝄞𝄞𝄞 (Abkco, 1969, prod. Jimmy Miller) slams the door on the 1960s with such harrowing anthems as "Gimme Shelter" and "You Can't Always Get What You Want." *Exile on Main Street* 𝄞𝄞𝄞𝄞𝄞 (Virgin, 1972, prod. Jimmy Miller) got some bum reviews when first issued for its muddy sound and decadent atmospherics. It's now rightly hailed as a masterpiece, and from the passionate yearning of the gospel-tinged "Let It Loose" to the demon fury of "Rip This Joint," it remains a towering survey of the Stones as they reinvent their influences.

what to buy next: *Big Hits/High Tide and Green Grass* 𝄞𝄞𝄞𝄞 (Abkco, 1966, prod. Andrew Loog Oldham) is an impeccable, 12-cut summary of the Stones' pre-*Aftermath* singles; of the hits collections, it's surpassed only by the pricy but worth-it box set *The Singles Collection* 𝄞𝄞𝄞𝄞 (Abkco, 1989, prod. various), which documents the band's first and best decade of music-making. *Sticky Fingers* 𝄞𝄞𝄞𝄞 (Virgin, 1971, prod. Jimmy Miller) has the most famous cover art of any Stones album (Andy Warhol's zippered crotch shot) and—"Brown Sugar" excepted—among the most darkly weary music. But amid the druggy drama, the luminous beauty of "Sway" and "Moonlight Mile" is redemptive. *Some Girls* 𝄞𝄞𝄞𝄞 (Virgin, 1978, prod. the Glimmer Twins, a.k.a. Mick Jagger and Keith Richards) is the last gasp of greatness, with Richards's "Before They Make Me Run" serving as what should have been a fitting epitaph: "See my tail lights fading/Not a dry eye in the house." Those who insist on owning something from the latter-day, Steel Wheelchairs-era Stones should head straight for *Stripped* 𝄞𝄞𝄞 (Virgin, 1995, prod. Don Was, the Glimmer Twins), the first live album by the group that isn't superfluous, with its revelatory

Mick Jagger of the Rolling Stones (© Ken Settle)

"unplugged" treatment of several classic tracks compensating for a tepid cover of Dylan's "Like a Rolling Stone."

what to avoid: Before *Stripped*, the Stones released five live albums, all of them stiffs. None offer tracks that improve upon the studio originals, including *Got Live if You Want It* 🎜 (Abkco, 1966, prod. Andrew Loog Oldham); the overrated *Get Yer Ya's Out* 🎜🎜 (Abkco, 1970, prod. Glyn Johns, the Rolling Stones), *Love You Live* 🎜 (Rolling Stones, 1977, prod. the Glimmer Twins), *Still Life* 🎜 (Rolling Stones, 1982, prod. the Glimmer Twins), and *Flashpoint* 🎜 (Rolling Stones, 1991, prod. Chris Kimsey, the Glimmer Twins).

the rest:

The Rolling Stones: England's Newest Hit Makers 🎜🎜🎜🎜 (Abkco, 1964)
12 X 5 🎜🎜🎜🎜 (Abkco, 1964)
The Rolling Stones, Now! 🎜🎜🎜🎜 (Abkco, 1965)
Out of Our Heads 🎜🎜🎜 (Abkco, 1965)
December's Children 🎜🎜🎜🎜 (Abkco, 1965)
Between the Buttons 🎜🎜🎜🎜 (Abkco, 1967)
Flowers 🎜🎜🎜 (Abkco, 1967)
Their Satanic Majesties Request 🎜🎜 (Abkco, 1967)
Through the Past Darkly (Big Hits, Vol. 2) 🎜🎜🎜🎜 (Abkco, 1968)
Hot Rocks 1964–71 🎜🎜🎜🎜 (Abkco, 1972)
More Hot Rocks: Big Hits and Fazed Cookies 🎜🎜🎜 (Abkco, 1973)
Goats Head Soup 🎜🎜 (Rolling Stones/Virgin, 1973)
It's Only Rock 'N' Roll 🎜🎜🎜 (Rolling Stones/Virgin, 1974)
Made in the Shade 🎜🎜🎜 (Rolling Stones/Virgin, 1975)
Black and Blue 🎜🎜🎜 (Rolling Stones/Virgin, 1976)
Emotional Rescue 🎜🎜 (Rolling Stones/Virgin, 1980)
Sucking in the Seventies 🎜🎜🎜 (Rolling Stones, 1981)
Tattoo You 🎜🎜🎜 (Rolling Stones/Virgin, 1981)
Undercover 🎜🎜 (Rolling Stones, 1983)
Rewind (1971–84) 🎜🎜🎜 (Rolling Stones, 1984)
Dirty Work 🎜🎜🎜 (Rolling Stones, 1986)
Steel Wheels 🎜🎜🎜 (Rolling Stones, 1989)
Voodoo Lounge 🎜🎜🎜 (Virgin, 1994)
Bridges to Babylon 🎜🎜🎜 (Virgin, 1997)

worth searching for: *Jump Back: The Best of the Rolling Stones* (Virgin, 1993, prod. various) is a sparkling sounding U.K. compilation spanning 1971–93, with exceptional liner notes.

influences:

◀◀ Willie Dixon, Muddy Waters, Chuck Berry, Buddy Holly, Sam Cooke, James Brown, Jackie Wilson, Ike & Tina Turner, the Beatles, Bob Dylan

▶▶ New York Dolls, Aerosmith, Guns N' Roses, Black Crowes, Tom Petty

Greg Kot

The Ronettes /Ronnie Spector

Formed as The Darling Sisters (later Ronnie & the Relatives), 1959, in New York, NY.

Veronica (Bennett) Spector (born August 10, 1943, in New York, NY), vocals; Estelle Bennett (born July 22, 1944, in New York, NY), vocals; Nedra Talley (born January 27, 1946, in New York, NY), vocals.

As the lead singer of the Ronettes, Ronnie Bennett's precocious vibrato brought an aura of teen vulnerability and eroticism to the 1960s girl group sound. As a solo artist, she made some affecting sides with limited commercial success. Bennett, her sister Estelle, and cousin Nedra Taylor formed their first group, the Darling Sisters (later Ronnie & the Relatives), in 1959. By the time Stu Phillips of Colpix Records signed them in 1961, they had perfected their stage show and look (Spanish Harlem "tough girl chic"), but musically, they weren't quite ready. Records such as "I Want a Boy" and "What's So Sweet about Sweet Sixteen" were cute tunes by some nice kids, but that was all. Their second release ("Silhouettes"), billed the group as the Ronettes, but despite the name change, their early singles flopped. The Ronettes' first recordings for Phil Spector's Philles label in 1963 were the fast, danceable tunes that went over well in their live gigs at the Peppermint Lounge and in Murray the K's Fox Revues, but Spector was looking for something with more heart. Giving full-vent to Bennett's Frankie Lymon-influenced tremolo, creating the perfect blend of virgin and vixen, "Be My Baby" was one of Spector's finest productions and the group's lone Top 10 record. Follow-up singles such as "Baby I Love You" and "(The Best Part Of) Breaking Up" were rife with hungry sexuality but made less impact.

Spector's growing infatuation with Bennett began to yield negative results in 1964. He recorded Bennett solo on the wonderful "So Young," then quickly pulled it from release. Sure hits such as "Chapel of Love" were shelved in favor of less likely material, and some recordings made by the Ronettes inexplicably appeared on LPs by the Crystals. Spector's quirky genius reasserted itself briefly for the Top 20 hit "Walking in the Rain," which won a Grammy Award for its use of sound effects. Ronnie was not allowed to tour with the Beatles in 1965 (her cousin Elaine substituted), as an increasingly jealous and possessive Spector manipulated her into virtual seclusion. The effect of this missed promotional opportunity became apparent as subsequent singles charted in low positions. The Ronettes broke up in 1966, and Spector and Bennett married shortly after. Ronnie Spector was allowed to record unsuccessful singles produced by her husband for A&M and the Beatles' Apple label. After enduring several years of emotional abuse and bizarre behavior, Ronnie divorced Spector in 1974. Attempting a comeback, she recorded two poor singles for Buddah Records with new Ronettes, Chip Fields and Denise Edwards. She stayed active working oldies concerts, but solo singles on the Tom Cat label did little for her new career. Subsequent recordings featuring Bruce Springsteen's E Street Band for Epic/Cleveland International and a single written for her by Billy Joel, "Say Goodbye to Hollywood," garnered more publicity than sales. Ronnie was semi-retired in 1986 when rocker Eddie Money called her to do a cameo vocal on his single "Take Me Home Tonight." The record was a Top 5 pop hit and led to her best solo LP, 1987's *Unfinished Business*. These days Ronnie Spector is happily remarried, quietly raising a family in Connecticut, and when she chooses to work, she is still one of pop music's sexiest and most expressive vocalists.

what to buy: Some of Phil Spector's greatest recordings—meaning some of the greatest records ever made—were written for, and spectacularly sung by, Ronnie Spector, and they're all included on *The Best of the Ronettes* 𝄞𝄞𝄞𝄞 (Abkco, 1992, prod. Phil Spector). You'll instantly recognize the hits, but if you're not already familiar with the equally stunning misses (such as "Do I Love You" and "You Came, You Saw, You Conquered"), then by all means put this book down *immediately* and head for the nearest record store!

what to buy next: The Ronettes' versions of "Frosty the Snowman," "Sleigh Ride," and "I Saw Mommy Kissing Santa Claus" off Phil Spector's *A Christmas Gift for You* 𝄞𝄞𝄞𝄞 (Philles, 1963/Abkco, 1990, prod. Phil Spector) have become Yuletide standards. The non-Spector recordings are best represented by *The Colpix and Buddah Years* 𝄞𝄞𝄞 (Sequel, 1994, prod. various) and *Dangerous, 1976–1987* 𝄞𝄞𝄞 (Raven, 1996, prod. various), both fine overviews which demonstrate, to varying degrees, how a voice as potent as Spector's can overcome even the most vacuous of material (the stock, sub-Brill schmaltz of much of the Colpix sides) and accompaniment (the bombastic E Street Band only tends to get in the way of a performer as nuanced as Spector).

worth searching for: In a well-meaning if misguided attempt to "update" Spector's sound, *Siren* 𝄞𝄞𝄞 (Polish, 1980, prod. Genya Raven) does contain one deliciously sublime moment: a version of the Ramones' "Here Today, Gone Tomorrow," which demonstrates that while Deborah Harry and Chrissie Hynde may have had the money and push behind them at the time, Spector still had the Real Thing—and *then* some.

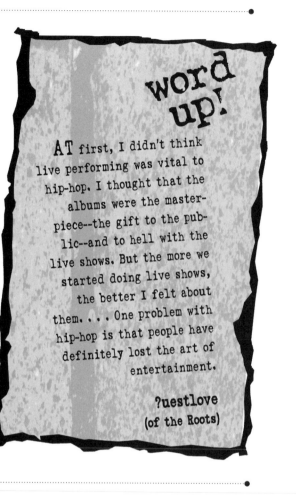

word up!

AT first, I didn't think live performing was vital to hip-hop. I thought that the albums were the masterpiece--the gift to the public--and to hell with the live shows. But the more we started doing live shows, the better I felt about them. . . . One problem with hip-hop is that people have definitely lost the art of entertainment.

?uestlove
(of the Roots)

influences:
◀◀ Frankie Lymon, the Chantels, Little Anthony & the Imperials
▶▶ Joey Ramone, the Bangles, SWV (Sisters with Voices)

Ken Burke and Gary Pig Gold

The Roots

Formed 1987, in Philadelphia, PA.

Black Thought, vocals; Malik B., vocals; Leonard Hubbard, bass; B.R.O.theR. ?uestion/?uestlove, drums; Rahzel the Godfather of Noyze, vocals, percussion; Kamal, keyboards (1995–present).

Gang Starr's DJ Premiere and A Tribe Called Quest's Ali Shaheed gave hip-hop its first notable jazz infusion via their crafty, swinging samples, and Guru's guest-driven Jazzmatazz project followed by introducing the notion of using actual jazz musicians (instead of samples) behind the MC. It was only a matter of time, then, before a group would emerge playing live, jazz-inspired hip-hop without the help of any hired guns. Though Branford Marsalis's Buckshot LeFonque made a fair attempt, the group was far more bop than hip-hop and didn't really register with the rap nation. The Roots leaned just as far the other way, and for that very reason (along with their chops and vision, of course), they were embraced by those rap fans who had been waiting for somebody to stop talking all that jazz and, instead, just play it. By recording their breakthrough *Do You Want More?!!!??!* without the use of samples or even electronic drum machines, the Roots also didn't promise something on wax that they wouldn't be able to deliver live. In fact, their sweaty, relentless performances and impressive musicality earned them a reputation as one of the best, most dynamic live hip-hop acts of the post-Run-D.M.C. era.

what to buy: *Do You Want More?!!!??!* ✶✶✶✶ (DGC, 1995, prod. B.R.O.theR. ?uestion, Black Thought, Rahzel, others) has been hailed by some as one of the more progressive recordings in 1990s rap. But that's not quite right. Although the album is certainly different in its approach (a self-contained hip-hop *band* playing without samples?!), the Roots actually look back for inspiration, employing everything from old-soul Fender Rhodes licks and jazz-funk basslines to old-school vocal interplay on such standouts as "Mellow My Man" and "Proceed." Beatboxer extraordinaire Rahzel takes you way back, too, with his vocal percussion work on the "Show'-y ? vs. Rahzel," although it's actually ?uestion himself who proves to be the star of the lyrically positive album with his taut beats and vast vocabulary.

what to buy next: The newly renamed ?uestlove apparently lost his thesaurus before recording the Roots's followup, *Illadelph Halflife* ✶✶✶ (DGC, 1996, prod. ?uestlove, others), as the album features a narrower range of beats and fills. Samples enter the mix, too, as do guest MCs (Bahamadia, Common, Q-Tip), but the most notable new addition here is the dark tone of the lyrics, which are already bracing for the new millennium. For all the talk about the group's fusing of jazz and hip-hop, the most stunning element of either Roots album actually comes on this record's "Concerto of the Desperado," with Amel Larrieux suddenly in your *aria.*

worth searching for: The Roots call their self-released 1993 debut *Organix* a demo, but the recording is more than just a rough introduction. Although available as a bootleg on the Internet, the album may be reissued in 1998.

influences:

◀◀ Stetsasonic, D.J. Jazzy Jeff & the Fresh Prince, Schoolly D, Sha-Key, Gang Starr/Jazzmatazz, A Tribe Called Quest

▶▶ Erykah Badu, Boogie Monsters, Bahamadia

Josh Freedom du Lac

Rose Royce

Formed as Total Concept Unlimited, 1973, in Los Angeles, CA.

Gwen "Rose" Dickey, vocals (1976–77, 1978–80); Kenji Brown, guitar (1973–80); Kenny Copeland, trumpet; Freddie Dunn, trumpet; Michael Moore, saxophone; Terral Santiel, percussion; Victor Nix, keyboards (1973–77); Lequeint "Duke" Job, bass; Henry Gamer, drums; Rose Norwalt, vocals (1977); Ricci Benson (1980–87); Michael Nash, keyboards (1977–present); Walter McKinney, guitar (1980–present); Lisa Taylor, vocals (1987–present).

Rose Royce spent the first few years of its career as a backing band, supporting Edwin Starr (as Total Concept Unlimited), Yvonne Fair (as Magic Wand), the Temptations, and the Undisputed Truth. The group followed producer Norman Whitfield from Motown to his own Whitfield Records imprint, added singer Gwen Dickey, changed its name and landed in a fine situation, recording music for the disco-oriented soundtrack to the hit film *Car Wash.* Launched by the movie's theme songs—as well as "Put Your Money Where Your Mouth Is" and "In Full Bloom"—Rose Royce parlayed its fine start into a number of hits in both the U.S. and the U.K. Suffering assorted membership changes, it parted ways with Whitfield in 1980, following Dickey's second departure from the band. The group never quite equaled the impact of *Car Wash,* but it maintains a strong overseas following and still tours.

what to buy: *Car Wash* ✶✶✶✶ (MCA, 1976, prod. Norman Whitfield, others) is arguably as valid a reflection of the mid-1970s disco movement as *Saturday Night Fever*—perhaps more so because of this album's grittier urban sensibility. Among its highlights are collaborations between Rose Royce and the Pointer Sisters.

what to buy next: *In Full Bloom* ✶✶✶✶ (Whitfield, 1977/O' Skool, 1996, prod. Norman Whitfield) is a fine follow-up, with ace material such as "Do Your Dance," "It Makes You Feel Like Dancing," and "Wishing on a Star." There's a sense, albeit a brief one, that Rose Royce could become a real force.

what to avoid: *The Best of Rose Royce from "Car Wash"* ✶ (MCA, 1988/MCA Special Products, 1993) is a 10-track redundancy that offers nothing over the original soundtrack album.

the rest:
Greatest Hits ♫♫♫♪ (Warner Bros., 1976)
Perfect Lover ♫♫♪ (Atlantic, 1989)

worth searching for: Rose Royce's guest appearance on "It's Not Over" from hip-hop master Dr. Dre's *The First Knockout* (Triple X, 1996) is worth a listen.

influences:

◀◀ Sly & the Family Stone, Edwin Starr, the Temptations, the Funk Brothers

▶▶ The Trammps, Dr. Dre, Mother's Finest, Lakeside

Gary Graff

Diana Ross

Born March 26, 1944, in Detroit, MI.

Smokey Robinson was the king of Motown, Ross was the label's queen. As the focal point of the Supremes, her delicate features, doe-eyed expressions and clear—if sometimes thin—vocals became symbols for the company's desired image of sophistication and glamour. Motown lore is filled with trash talk about Ross: ego, ambition, *espirit de Me.* And when you read her self-celebratory autobiography, *Secrets of a Sparrow,* or look at the photo of magazine covers she's graced in the booklet for *The Ultimate Collection,* it does seem that modesty is not among Ross's virtues. But she must be given her due as a distinctive talent, with a drive that established her star not only in music but also in movies (*Lady Sings the Blues, Mahogany*). She left Motown to record for RCA in 1981, but eight years later she was back "home," and whatever else is said about her, it's certain that no one would be talking unless she was a star.

what to buy: With only six of its 20 songs overlapping with Supremes anthologies, *The Ultimate Collection* ♫♫♫♫ (Motown, 1994, prod. various) is a good way to sample Ross's solo career, from the epic schmaltz of "Ain't No Mountain High Enough" to heartfelt ode to Marvin Gaye, "Missing You." *Diana* ♫♫♫♫ (Motown, 1980, prod. Nile Rodgers) was a smart move forward, bringing in Chic's Nile Rodgers and Bernard Edwards to modernize Ross's sound and launch two of her biggest solo hits, "Upside Down" and "I'm Coming Out."

what to buy next: *Diana & Marvin* ♫♫♫ (Motown, 1973, prod. various) is a pleasant summit from two of Motown's brightest lights that was reportedly driven by some real sparks (of anger) in the studio.

what to avoid: The box set *Forever Diana* ♫♫ (Motown, 1993, prod. various) is a padded vanity project that was initially with-

drawn from sale due to its poor sound quality (which was corrected upon reissue).

the rest:
Lady Sings the Blues ♫♫♫ (Motown, 1972)
Touch Me in the Morning ♫♫♪ (Motown, 1973)
Ain't No Mountain High Enough ♫♫♫♪ (Motown 1979/1989)
The Boss ♫♫♫ (Motown, 1979)
Anthology ♫♫♫♫ (Motown, 1986)
Diana's Duets ♫♫♫ (Motown)
Diana Ross ♫♫♫♪ (Motown, 1989)
Live at Caesar's Palace ♫♫♪ (Motown, 1990)
All the Great Hits ♫♫♫♪ (Motown, 1991)
An Evening with Diana Ross ♫♫ (Motown, 1991)
The Force Behind the Power ♫♫ (Motown, 1991)
Diana Ross's Greatest Hits ♫♫♫♫ (Motown, 1991)
Stolen Moments: The Lady Sings Jazz & Blues ♫♫ (Motown, 1993)
Extended—The Remixes ♫♫♪ (Motown, 1994)
Take Me Higher ♫♫♫ (Motown, 1995)
Greatest Hits: The RCA Years ♫♫♫♪ (RCA, 1997)

worth searching for: Diana, Placido, and Jose? That's Domingo and Carreras to you non-opera buffs, and they make for a classy kind of Supremes on *Christmas in Vienna* ♫♫♪ (Sony Classical, 1993).

influences:

◀◀ Billie Holiday, Ella Fitzgerald, Smokey Robinson

▶▶ Donna Summer, Cher, Dionne Warwick, Brandy

see also: *The Supremes*

Gary Graff

Rottin Razkals

Formed 1992, in East Orange, NJ.

Diesel, vocals; Fam, vocals; Chap, vocals.

Truly a family affair, the Razkals were the second project from Naughty by Nature's Illtown Records venture and featured Jeff "Diesel" Ray, the brother of Naughty co-frontman Anthony "Treach" Criss. Developed as a vehicle for Ray, the Razkals came together with the addition of Fam, who had rapped on the 1993 hit single, "Hey, Mr. D.J." by Zhane—Illtown's first act. Once together, the Razkals honed their act opening on tour for Naughty and debuted on wax on "Knock 'Em Out Da Box" from Naughty's 1993 album *19NaughtyIII.*

what's available: The Razkals' debut, *Rottin' Ta Da Core* ♫♫♫ (Illtown/Motown, 1995, prod. Naughty by Nature, others), es-

tablishes the trio as a bona-fide group, with bone-shaking jams such as "Oh, Yeah" and "A-Yo."

influences:
◀◀ Naughty by Nature

Eric Deggans

Royal Crescent Mob

Formed 1985, in Columbus, OH. Disbanded 1994.

David Ellison, lead vocals, harmonica; B, guitar, vocals; Harold Chichester, bass, vocals; Billy Schwers, drums (1985); Carlton Smith, drums (1986–94).

This band garnered critical acclaim for combining dirty rock guitar and a funky backbeat. David Ellison was fond of pointing out that he mowed the lawn of the Ohio Players' Leroy (Sugar) Bonner while growing up and absorbed both funk and punk. The band was put together from the pieces of two groups competing in a local battle of the bands, so they could better use the contest prize: studio time. After two small releases, the band was signed by Sire records. But its producers at Sire, Richard Gottehrer and Eric Calvi, were not well suited to funk and whitewashed the proceedings. Despite critical appreciation, record sales were disappointing, and Sire did not keep the group. Royal Crescent Mob, always hot live, continued gigging and put out a 1992 concert recording, *Destruction 13*, on its own Mobco imprint. The band then retreated to its hometown, playing within driving range on weekends, and managed to put out a final album before Chichester left to spend more time with his family, which ultimately ended the band's run. Chichester later showed up in Howlin' Maggie, playing in a related but inferior style.

what to buy: *Omerta* 𝄽𝄽𝄽𝄽 (Moving Target, 1987, prod. Jonathon Myner, Royal Crescent Mob, Montie Temple) is by far the band's best work, with "Get on the Bus" and covers of "Fire" and "The Big Payback." Funky, hard-driving, showing no mercy, it's the must-own album. Fortunately, it was reissued on CD just before the band's demise.

what to avoid: *Midnight Rose's* 𝄽𝄽 (Sire, 1991, prod. Eric Calvi) has a few funky tracks, but largely sounds like Calvi was aiming for too heavy and dense of a sound.

the rest:
Spin the World 𝄽𝄽𝄽 (Sire, 1989)

Diana Ross (© Jack Vartoogian)

worth searching for: Some of the band's funky but hard to find collections include *Good Lucky Killer* 𝄽𝄽𝄽 (Enemy, 1993, prod. Royal Crescent Mob, Montie Temple), *Something New, Old and Borrowed* 𝄽𝄽𝄽 (Moving Target, 1988), and the live *13 Destruction* 𝄽𝄽𝄽𝄽 (Mobco, 1992, prod. Royal Crescent Mob, Montie Temple).

solo outings:
Howling Maggie:
Honeysuckle Strange 𝄽𝄽 (Columbia, 1996)

influences:
◀◀ Ohio Players, James Brown, the Stooges, the Dead Kennedys
▶▶ Infectious Grooves, Mind Funk

Steve Holtje

Royal Flush

Born Ramel Govantes, in Queens, NY.

Introduced to the world by fellow Flushing rapper Mic Geronimo on *The Natural*, Royal Flush is part of the new wave of Queens MCs that includes Nas, Mobb Deep, and, of course, Geronimo. As with Geronimo, Flush's player-obsessed lyrical concerns are conspiciously similar to Nas and Mobb Deep's. Like the burough's prodigal son, Nas, though, Flush is an exceptional lyricist who makes his verses sound like street poetry, and not just pretentious bravado. Signed to Geronimo's label after his guest turn on *The Natural*, Flush dropped a trio of well-received singles of his own, then vanished for more than six months as sample-clearance and other problems delayed his full-length debut.

what's available: *Ghetto Millionaire* 𝄽𝄽𝄽𝄽 (Blunt/TVT, 1997, prod. Buckwild, Da Beatminerz, L.E.S., EZ Elpee) embodies both what's wrong and right with Royal Flush. What's wrong are the same generic Big Willie themes found in dozens of records that were released following the success of Notorious B.I.G.'s *Ready to Die* and Mobb Deep's *The Infamous*. You can only get so much mileage out of high-stakes fantasies about "iced down medallions" and jetting off in Lears, and at least a fourth of the album sounds like run-of-the-mill New York gangsterism. The inclusion of a handful of obligatory R&B crossover tracks doesn't help, either. What's right, though, are the production touches and Flush's knack for churning out exceptional lyrics. Over a sound that's noticeably jazzier and, ultimately, more interesting than the gloom-and-doom soundtracks Mobb Deep and its minions are known for, Flush shows signs of brilliance on tracks such as the instantly classic Queens anthem, "Worldwide," and the domestic violence vignette, "Family Problems."

While it's hard not to reach for the fast forward button at times, there are still enough strong moments on *Ghetto Millionaire* to make it worthwhile.

worth searching for: Flush's third single, "Rotten Apple" (Blunt/TVT, 1996), was released as a promo, but never saw the light of day commercially (either as a single or album cut) because of sample-clearance problems. It's not as good as Flush's first two singles, "Movin On Ya Weak Production" and "Worldwide," but "Rotten Apple" still would have been one of the better songs on *Ghetto Millionaire*.

influences:

◀◀ Nas, Mobb Deep, Mic Geronimo

▶▶ Capone-N-Noreaga

Oliver "O-Dub" Wang

David Ruffin

See: The Temptations

Jimmy Ruffin

Born May 7, 1939, in Colinsville, MS.

Jimmy Ruffin has had the not-so-unique misfortune of being a fine singer with a brother whose talent fairly eclipsed his own. It was both Jimmy and brother David Ruffin who were asked to join the Temptations. While David accepted and passed into R&B history with an extraordinary string of searingly sung hits throughout the 1960s, Jimmy declined, preferring to sing backup. Also traveling on his own throughout Motown's subsidary labels, Ruffin's own career was middling, although he did put one right down the middle with "What Becomes of the Brokenhearted?" in 1966. A strong tune straight out of the Motown machinery, it got the lesser known brother a Top 10 hit and set the tone for a number of singles, less successful ones, over the next handful of years. Since his last hit in 1980, "Hold on to My Love," he has spent his time on endless tours. Although he did pop up briefly on record with Paul Weller in 1984, he has apparently been unable to corral an album's worth of material on his own.

what's available: Both Jimmy and David's solo hits are included on *Motown Superstar Series, Vol. 8* 𝄞𝄞 (Motown, prod. various), a somewhat skimpy package that again, throws Ruffin in the looming shadow of his brother.

Chaka Khan (© Jack Vartoogian)

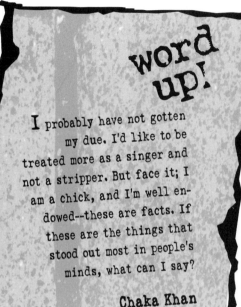

word up!

I probably have not gotten my due. I'd like to be treated more as a singer and not a stripper. But face it; I am a chick, and I'm well endowed--these are facts. If these are the things that stood out most in people's minds, what can I say?

Chaka Khan

influences:

◀◀ David Ruffin, the Temptations, Enchantment

Allan Orski

Rufus /Chaka Khan

Rufus formed 1970, in Chicago, IL. Disbanded 1983. Chaka Khan born Yvette Marie Stevens, in Great Lakes, IL, March 23, 1953.

Chaka Khan, vocals; Kevin Murphy, keyboards; Ron Stockert, guitar (1970–74); Tony Maiden, guitar (1974–83); Al Ciner, guitar (1970–74); Dennis Belfield, bass (1970–74); Bobby Watson, bass (1974–83); Dennis Belfield, keyboards (1970–73); Nate Morgan, keyboards (1973–77); David "Hawk" Wolinski, keyboards (1977–83); Andre Fisher, drums (1970–78), Richard "Moon" Calhoun, drums (1978–79); John "J.R." Robinson, drums (1979–83).

Dedicated to a career as a singer by her teens, a young Chaka Khan (a stage name derived from an African shaman, a brief marriage, or her nickname among friends in the 1960s-era Black Panther Party, depending on who you believe) kicked around Chicago-area clubs, eventually hooking up with a Top

40 band called Ask Rufus. Before long, Khan's spellbinding vocals convinced the group to head West and audition for ABC Records in Los Angeles. By 1973, the group had released its first record, though it wasn't until the band's second album—featuring the smash "Tell Me Something Good," written by Stevie Wonder specifically for Khan—that Rufus joined the R&B elite. Featuring a whipcrack, funky backing band of studio whiz players and Khan's incendiary voice, Rufus ruled the R&B charts for years, with the singer eventually getting top billing, then striking out on her own during the late 1970s. Khan kept recording with the band until 1983, eventually leaving the group for good (it broke up shortly afterwards) to concentrate on her own solo releases—often mesmerizing collections of soulful dance-pop and contemporary jazz selections, pieced together by the industry's most talented producers. But R&B's turn toward youthful, hip-hop influenced divas pulled the commercial rug out from under the Grammy-winning singer (she's got seven, total), relegating Khan's efforts to occasional appearances on other artists' albums and film soundtracks. Her latest gig, appearing at comic Sinbad's *Summer Soul Jam* aired on the HBO cable channel in 1995, only underscores her fall to the nostalgia circuit.

what to buy: In a catalog that spans some 15 albums, the high points are many. As a band, Rufus connected with R&B history on *Rags to Rufus* ♪♪♪♪ (ABC, 1974/MCA, 1990, prod. Rufus, Bob Monaco), the album with "Tell Me Somthing Good" and the Ray Parker Jr.-penned classic workout "You Got the Love." On her own, Khan scored with *Chaka Khan* ♪♪♪♪ (Warner Bros., 1982, prod. Arif Mardin), a collection of high-quality, well-produced tunes topped with astounding vocals, including the ballad "Got to Be There" and jazzy excursion "Be Bop Medley."

what to buy next: *Rufus Featuring Chaka Khan* ♪♪♪♪ (ABC, 1975/MCA, 1990, prod. Rufus) boasts ear candy such as the simmering "Sweet Thing" and boisterous "Dance with Me." Khan's *I Feel for You* ♪♪♪♪ (Warner Bros., 1984, prod. Arif Mardin) adds a heavy synthesizer and DJ touch, from the hit title track to a stratospheric remake of Gary Wright's "My Love Is Alive."

what to avoid: As good as Rufus and Chaka Khan were at crafting hit singles, consistent albums were never their strong suit. Together, their worst effort still in print is probably *Stompin' at the Savoy* **woof!** (Warner Bros., 1983, prod. Russ Titleman), an uninspiring collection of live performaces and studio cuts redeemed only by the inventive, last-gasp hit "Ain't Nobody."

the rest:
Rufus Featuring Chaka Khan:

Rufus ♪♪♪ (ABC, 1973)
Rufusized ♪♪♪ (ABC, 1974/MCA, 1990)
Ask Rufus ♪♪♪ (ABC, 1977/MCA, 1992)
Street Player ♪♪ (ABC, 1978)
Numbers ♪♪ (ABC, 1979)
Masterjam ♪♪♪ (MCA, 1979)
The Very Best of Rufus Featuring Chaka Khan ♪♪♪♪ (MCA, 1997)

Chaka Khan:

Chaka ♪♪♪ (Warner Bros., 1979)
Naughty ♪♪♪ (Warner Bros., 1980)
What 'Cha Gonna Do for Me? ♪♪♪♪ (Warner Bros., 1981)
Destiny ♪♪♪ (Warner Bros., 1986)
C.K. ♪♪♪ (Warner Bros., 1988)
Life Is a Dance (The Remix Project) ♪♪ (Warner Bros., 1989)
The Woman I Am ♪♪♪ (Warner Bros., 1992)
Epiphany: The Best of Chaka Khan ♪♪♪ (Reprise, 1996)

worth searching for: Contributing a stirring version of "My Funny Valentine" to the soundtrack for *Waiting to Exhale* ♪♪♪♪ (Arista, 1996, prod. various), Khan proves once again she knows her way around a jazz tune quite well, indeed.

influences:

◀◀ Betty Carter, Aretha Franklin, Gladys Knight

▶▶ Mary J. Blige, Faith Evans, Monica, Cheryl Lynne, Vesta Williams

Eric Deggans

Run-D.M.C.

Formed 1981, in Hollis, Queens, NY.

Run (born Joseph Simmons), vocals; D.M.C. (born Darryl McDaniels), vocals; Jam Master Jay (born Jason Mizell), DJ.

No group was more responsible for taking hip-hop into the pop-culture mainstream than Run-D.M.C. The trio broke through with a canny mixture of streetwise image (a casual jock-inspired look and attitude known as "b-boy"); clever, conversational wordplay; and, most of all, stripped-down beats that drew as much on hard rock as funk. On 1984's self-titled debut album, Run-D.M.C. established its signature sound; nothing in rap sounded quiet so hard and minimalist as "Sucker M.C.'s" and "It's Like That," reprised from the trio's groundbreaking 1983 single. The debut also introduced the wailing, P-Funk-like guitar of Eddie Martinez, who returned on the title track of the 1985 album, *King of Rock*—a boast the group would make good on the next year, when Aerosmith's Steven Tyler and Joe Perry collaborated with the rappers on a remake of Aerosmith's cock-rock standard "Walk This Way."

The track launched Aerosmith's comeback and, as the cornerstone of the multimillion-selling *Raising Hell* album, established Run-D.M.C. as an arena act. Unfortunately, the group's attempt to expand its success with a 1988 movie and album of the same name, *Tougher Than Leather*, bombed, and the increasing political militancy and verbal explicitness of a new breed of hip-hop groups eventually made Run-D.M.C. sound quaint and dated. But live, as occasional club and arena dates have demonstrated through the mid-'90s, the still-intact threesome remains a powerhouse.

what to buy: *Raising Hell* 𝄞𝄞𝄞𝄞 (Profile, 1986, prod. Russell Simmons, Rick Rubin) has its thin moments, but the initial burst of "Peter Piper," "It's Tricky," "My Adidas," and "Walk This Way" is as powerful an opening sequence as any rap or rock record of the 1980s could hope for. While *Raising Hell* is as much a cultural milestone as a musical one, the aural pleasures are packed wall to wall on the thumping *Together Forever: Greatest Hits 1983–1991* 𝄞𝄞𝄞𝄞 (Profile, 1991, prod. various).

what to buy next: The debut, *Run-D.M.C.* 𝄞𝄞𝄞𝄞 (Profile, 1984, prod. Russell Simmons, Larry Smith), is another milestone: the first true hip-hop album, though it may sound a tad too stripped down and insular to rap nonbelievers. With its minimal but meaty rhythms and strident vocal cadences, even the tracks without electric guitar still rock.

what to avoid: *Back From Hell* 𝄞𝄞 (Profile, 1990, prod. Run-D.M.C., Jam Master Jay) is a transparent attempt to keep up with foul-mouthed gangsta rappers; for the first time the group is chasing trends rather than starting them.

the rest:
King of Rock 𝄞𝄞𝄞 (Profile, 1985)
Tougher Than Leather 𝄞𝄞 (Profile, 1988)
Down with the King 𝄞𝄞𝄞 (Profile, 1993)

worth searching for: The debut 12-inch single, "It's Like That"/"Sucker M.C.'s" 𝄞𝄞𝄞𝄞 (Profile, 1983, prod. Russell Simmons, Larry Smith) is a hip-hop classic, with an extended mix of "It's Like That" and instrumental versions of both tracks perfect for your own karaoke party.

influences:
◀◀ Grandmaster Flash, Parliament-Funkadelic, James Brown, Afrika Bambaataa, Kool DJ Herc, Queen, Aerosmith, Kurtis Blow

▶▶ Public Enemy, N.W.A., the Beastie Boys, Rage Against the Machine, Boogie Down Productions

Greg Kot

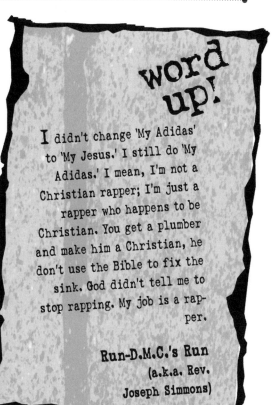

word up!

I didn't change 'My Adidas' to 'My Jesus.' I still do 'My Adidas.' I mean, I'm not a Christian rapper; I'm just a rapper who happens to be Christian. You get a plumber and make him a Christian, he don't use the Bible to fix the sink. God didn't tell me to stop rapping. My job is a rapper.

Run-D.M.C.'s Run (a.k.a. Rev. Joseph Simmons)

Otis Rush

Born April 29, 1934, in Philadelphia, MS.

Otis Rush is arguably the greatest living bluesman, with only John Lee Hooker and B.B. King to rival him as a guitar and vocal stylist. Hooker and King have had long, continuously productive recording careers, however, whereas Rush's discography is shockingly thin (and erratic) for a blues legend in his mid-60s. From 1956–58, his string of truly great singles for Cobra, a Chicago blues label, revealed an amazingly expressive, intense electric guitarist and powerful singer. Playing the instrument lefthanded and upside down (as did Jimi Hendrix), with a distinctive picking style, Rush sounded—and still sounds—utterly unique. Those sides—"I Can't Quit You Baby," "All Your Love (I Miss Loving)," and others—not only formed the basis of the "West Side" style of Chicago blues (with the contemporaneous work of Magic Sam and Buddy Guy), but also inspired several generations of guitarists to play Fender Stratocasters and cover his tunes (Led Zeppelin and Eric Clapton played Rush songs, and Stevie Ray Vaughan named his band Double Trouble after a Cobra title). His slow minor blues started a much-imitated trend, and his band was the first to use electric bass.

Growing up in the country in Mississippi, Rush sang in church choirs and played guitar casually; mostly, though, he learned from his two older brothers and from records (lacking access to a live scene). When he moved to Chicago in 1948 at age 14, he started listening to more blues records, mostly the Delta performers popular in Chicago's largely transplanted black community. Within a few years he was playing covers of classic Delta blues in small clubs, but the influences of more guitar-solo-oriented performers—the epitome of whom was B.B. King—began to influence his thinking; he also took lessons from a local jazz session guitarist, Reggie Boyd, and learned from Kenny Burrell and George Benson records. The West Side style, so-called because its practitioners played in clubs in the western part of Chicago, was built of these materials, and it was from those clubs that Cobra owner Eli Toscano drew his talent. But Toscano was a gambler, and after he lost all his money (which included money owed to his artists), Cobra went out of business and Toscano died mysteriously (if unsurprisingly, considering whom he owed). Subsequently, circumstances were less kind to Rush himself than to his legacy. He joined his Cobra producer, Willie Dixon (who had written much of Rush's material), at Chess for two years, but had only one single released ("So Many Roads, So Many Trains"); moving to Duke for five years, he again put out only one single (1962's "Homework"). Rush's fortunes changed somewhat after he recorded five songs for Vanguard's *Chicago/The Blues/Today!* series in 1966—this helped expose him to the burgeoning white audience for the blues. But when Rush finally got to record some albums, the results were disastrous. His first album, recorded for a subsidiary of Atlantic Records, was a totally botched production by two white Chicago blues musicians (the outstanding Paul Butterfield guitarist Mike Bloomfield and Electric Flag vocalist/keyboardist Nick Gravenites). His second album had no such production problems, but for some reason (perhaps poor sales of other blues titles on the label) Capitol refused to release *Right Place, Wrong Time* after having put a lot of money into it, granting its title a hideous irony. Rush was finally able to buy back the tapes five years later and release it on an indie label. At one point he was

semi-retired, playing occasional gigs to pay the rent but mostly, he says, shooting pool. He fortunately found a sympathetic label, Delmark (in conjuction with the Japanese label Trio), for a few albums, while also recording for European labels. In yet another bizarre development, when Alligator reissued the 1977 Sonet album *Troubles, Troubles*, retitling it *Lost in the Blues*, Lucky Peterson was brought in to overdub organ and piano, much to Rush's disdain. Some of his guitar solos were even edited out. Rush's suspicion of record companies, however justified, has clearly interfered with his productivity; he even blew off a session that Rooster Blues had set up, with many top sidemen hired, because he didn't like his amplifier. Perhaps as a result, most of his albums since then have been live recordings, but finally, more than two decades after *Right Place, Wrong Time*, he received another major-label studio production of equal care and love thanks to John Porter, and this time it came out right away. It also marked his return to using the solid-body Strat after a long period of favoring a bright red hollowbody Gibson Epiphone. But whatever momentum he might have gathered from the Mercury album was lost to the nebulous career malady "personal problems," though now he's been signed to the new House of Blues label and may once again revive his career. Though Rush has often been an erratic performer, at his peak he remains capable of vocals packing stunning emotional intensity and highly individual guitar solos of shocking impact and originality.

what to buy: Rush's Cobra material is required for every blues and R&B lover's collection. At the moment there are two main options. *1956–1958 Cobra Recordings* ♫♫♫♫ (Paula, 1991, prod. various) has all the Cobra material—16 songs and four alternate takes. "I Can't Quit You Baby," "Groaning the Blues," "Double Trouble," and "All Your Love (I Miss Loving)" have to be heard to be believed; that some of the Willie Dixon-penned songs are trivial doesn't matter a bit once Rush unleashes his guitar fury on them. *The Cobra Records Story: Chicago Rock and Blues 1957–1958* ♫♫♫♫ (Capricorn, 1993, prod. various) is a two-CD set with not only all the Rush tracks but also a healthy sampling of Cobra's other singles, including everyone from Sunnyland Slim, Magic Sam, and Buddy Guy to Harold Burrage, Betty Everett, and Ike Turner's Kings of Rhythm (Turner also plays, magnificently, with Rush on "Double Trouble"). The enclosed booklet (which includes Rush's memories of the period) is well-done, and those interested in Chicago blues can have not only the crucial Rush sides but also a fine cross-section of the milieu in which he was operating. *Right Place, Wrong Time* ♫♫♫♫ (Bullfrog/Hightone, 1976, prod. Nick

Gravenites, Otis Rush) has plenty of intense slow blues tracks, always Rush's most reliably awe-inspiring material, and he sounds good on the soul and uptempo numbers, too, which are so often his downfall. Production-wise, the guitar and vocals are recorded and mixed well, and Rush sings and plays as though his life depends on it.

what to buy next: *So Many Roads* 🎵🎵🎵🎵 (Delmark, 1978, prod. Steve Tomashefsky) is his best live recording and offers an unbeatable combination of classic songs in a stretched-out format allowing maximum expression of his guitar prowess. *Ain't Enough Comin' In* 🎵🎵🎵🎵 (This Way Up/Mercury, 1994, prod. John Porter) has the best sound of any Rush album. The production is elaborate without being busy or distracting from Rush's generally excellent performance, and rock fans will note that Billy Payne of Little Feat and Ian McLagan of the Rolling Stones add spicy piano and organ. The album lacks only the manic edge that Rush sometimes summons, but he's hardly coasting.

what to avoid: Don't be tempted by a personnel list that includes Duane Allman (strictly rhythm guitar) and Jerry Jemmott (bass): *Mourning in the Morning* 🎵🎵 (Cotillion/Atlantic, 1969, prod. Mike Bloomfield, Nick Gravenites) is a production nightmare, with Rush's vocals (poorly recorded) and guitar buried under overdubbed horns, female backing vocals, and lots of other bad ideas, including tacky electric piano.

the rest:
Cold Day in Hell 🎵🎵🎵 (Delmark, 1975)
Screamin' and Cryin' 🎵🎵🎵🎵 (Disques Black and Blue, 1975, France/Evidence, 1992, U.S.)
Blues Interaction: Live in Japan 1986 🎵🎵
Tops 🎵🎵🎵🎵 (Blind Pig, 1988)
Lost in the Blues 🎵🎵🎵🎵 (Alligator, 1991)
Live in Europe 🎵🎵🎵🎵 (Evidence, 1993)

worth searching for: Rush has five tracks on *Chicago/The Blues/Today! Vol. 2* 🎵🎵🎵 (Vanguard, 1966, prod. Sam Charters), with James Cotton and Homesick James filling out the other two-thirds of the album.

influences:
 John Lee Hooker, Muddy Waters, T-Bone Walker, B.B. King, Kenny Burrell

▶▶ Bobby "Blue" Bland, Eric Clapton, the Rolling Stones, Jimi Hendrix, Led Zeppelin, Duane Allman, Mike Bloomfield, Lurrie Bell, Stevie Ray Vaughan

Steve Holtje

Patrice Rushen

Born September 30, 1954, in Los Angeles, CA.

If you needed to explain Patrice Rushen to the uninitiated, it might be best to use Quincy Jones as a good point of reference. Growing up in Los Angeles blanketed by music, she was quickly recognized as a child prodigy on the piano, and serious training on the instrument began at age three. She continued to play during her elementary and high school education, and a performance in her high school's All-Star Jazz Band at the Monterey Jazz Festival in 1972 lead to a recording contract with Fantasy Records' Prestige division. She issued three highly acclaimed, though, now, sadly out-of-print, albums at Prestige. Always growing, developing, and experimenting, Rushen parted ways with Prestige as she was looking to express herself in more than a strictly instrumental jazz vein. Her need for creative freedom was satisfied at Elektra Records, a label that in 1978 was not known for its forays into black music. Elektra's gamble in its laissez faire approach paid off: Rushen scored 12 R&B hit singles—half of those in the Top 10—and six hit albums during her seven-year association with the imprint. In 1986 she moved to Arista Records, where she continued to strike gold, but the relationship was truncated in 1987 over creative differences. In a way, it was time for her to move on: now fluent in directing her own musical course, she—like Q—needed a new challenge. That challenge manifested itself in film and television theme scoring, producing other artists (notably Sheena Easton), and musical direction (she helmed Janet Jackson's "janet" tour, the Emmy Awards in 1991 and 1992, the 1993 People's Choice Awards, and she's been the Musical Director for the NAACP Image Awards since 1989). Despite all of these accomplishments—many of them firsts for a black woman—Rushen is not one to rest on her laurels, and in 1994 she started from square one, issuing her first album in eight years and serving notice that she intends to remain a powerful force in music for years to come.

what to buy: The two records that are mandatory are *Haven't You Heard: The Best of Patrice Rushen* 🎵🎵🎵🎵 (Rhino, 1996, prod. Charles Mims Jr., Patrice Rushen, Reggie Andrews) and *Straight from the Heart* 🎵🎵🎵🎵 (Elektra, 1982/Rhino Five-Star Soul, 1996, prod. Charles Mims Jr., Patrice Rushen). *Haven't You Heard* collects 14 tracks—many of them in their unedited album length—from the zenith of her career, 1978–86. The collection is full of the smooth and mellow yet bright and effervescent jazz/R&B/pop/funk fusion that was not only ruling the airwaves at home, but was also the blueprint for many pop/soul outfits that were forming abroad. Equally impressive is *Straight from the Heart*, her fourth album for Elektra. The album is a powerhouse, featuring "Forget Me Nots," "Breakout!," "I Was Tired of Being Alone," and the rare groove instrumental "Number One." To flesh out the reissue, Rhino included extended 12" and 7" edits of "Forget Me Nots," "Breakout!," and "Number One." But this album would be just as potent and would remain a must-have were only the original track tracks featured.

what to buy next: On *Signature* ♪♪♪ (Discovery, 1997, prod. Patrice Rushen) she returns to her roots—instrumental jazz—and she's found, or rediscovered, a comfortable idiom where she can let herself flow. Though the album has the feel of some many other modern urban-contemporary jazz albums, this has a soul that many of its siblings in the style don't have, and a soul that only Patrice Rushen can offer. For those expecting *Signature* to pick up where "Number One" left off, however, it's bound to disappoint. Yet for those who have long curled their nose at modern fusion, *Signature* is bound to surprise with its cool, controlled, and sophisticated swing and soul.

what to avoid: *Anything But Ordinary* ♪♪ (Sin-Drome, 1994, prod. Patrice Rushen) is a tentative return to the spotlight. Rushen couldn't choose a path for this record, and though there are hints of the magic of her Elektra years, it's missing the seamless mix and that vital spark that made her Elektra recordings unique.

influences:

◀◀ Valerie Simpson, Gloria Jones, Syreeta

▶▶ Mary J. Blige, Heavy D., Janet Jackson, Sheena Easton, Paul Weller, Tracie

Dana G. Smart

Brenda Russell

Born Brenda Gordon, in Brooklyn, NY.

A contemplative songwriter, arranger, and session musician who made the most of her shot at solo recording success, Brenda Russell knocked the pop and R&B worlds on their collective ear in 1988 with one of the most hauntingly beautiful ballads to hit the singles lists before or since, "Piano in the Dark." The key track off her most honored album to date, *Get Here*, "Piano" became a Top 5 hit on both the R&B and pop charts, earning her three Grammy nominations including Song of the Year and Best Pop Female Vocalist. Launching her career in her native New York after being raised in Toronto from the age of 12, she later returned to Toronto to join the cast of the musical *Hair* and married Canadian songwriter Brian Russell. The couple co-hosted the Canadian TV series *Music Machine*,

then moved to Los Angeles in 1973, where they were discovered by Elton John and signed to his Rocket Records label. Recording under the name Brian & Brenda, the duo couldn't make beautiful music together; they divorced in 1978. She signed with A&M the next year as a solo artist, cutting two albums for the label (including her well-received debut, *Brenda Russell*) before jumping to Warner Bros. to record the LP *Two Eyes*. Moving to Sweden in 1984 for an extended period, she eventually returned to the States and A&M to contribute lead vocals for label boss Herb Alpert's project *Wild Romance* before *Get Here* propelled her talents out of the dark. By 1993 she was signed to EMI Records and released the album *Soul Talkin'*. While not as distinctive a performer as contemporaries like Angela Winbush or Patrice Rushen, as a writer-producer Russell's songs have been covered by an impressive array of performers throughout her career, including Barbra Streisand, Diana Ross, Luther Vandross ("If Only for One Night"), Rufus, and Earth, Wind & Fire. Should she be inspired enough to create another "Piano in the Dark," however, it's a safe bet she'll keep it for herself.

what to buy: There is much to commend on *Get Here* ♪♪♪♪ (A&M, 1988, prod. Stanley Clarke, Brenda Russell, others) beyond "Piano in the Dark," although that track alone would make the LP a worthy addition to any CD collection. It's her first album on which Russell plays no instruments, and what she loses in hands-on touch and artistry is more than balanced by her concentration on vocal expression. The focus here is on ballads, particularly the emotional, often-covered title song and the savory "Le Restaurant," featuring sax embellishments by David Sanborn.

what to buy next: Russell's music is so tasteful and consistent without becoming uninteresting that there's little difference in quality between her first album and her last. However, her debut LP, *Brenda Russell* ♪♪♪♪ (Horizon, 1979, prod. Andre Fischer) is a treasure, a gentle pop confection full of spare piano arrangements and quietly desperate vocals. It's the kind of work that sneaks up on you, returning to your melodic memory long after you've played it. Highlights include the ballad "Think It Over," her original version of "If Only for One Night," and her first Top 40 solo hit, "So Good, So Right,"

the rest:
Love Life ♪♪♪ (A&M, 1981)
Two Eyes ♪♪♪ (Warner Bros., 1983)
Kiss Me with the Wind ♪♪♪♪ (A&M, 1991)
Greatest Hits ♪♪♪♪ (A&M, 1992)
Soul Talkin' ♪♪♪♪ (A&M, 1993)

influences:

◄◄ Barbra Streisand, Donna Summer, Bette Midler, Elton John, Roberta Flack, Luther Vandross, Carol Bayer Sager, Patrice Rushen, Dusty Springfield

▶▶ Oleta Adams, Chante Moore, Mona Lisa, Donna Lewis

Jim McFarlin

S

Saafir
/The WhoRidas

Rappers are always trying to create new styles of delivery (at least the good ones are), some coming with fluid verses, others experimenting with on-beat/off-beat cadences. After getting his start on Digital Underground's *Body Hat Syndrome* and Casual's *Fear Itself*, though, Saafir became recognizable for having no real style at all, bulling his way through beats with no technical logic whatsoever. His sardonic sense of humor makes him one of the funniest MCs around and an easy point-person for his West Oakland crew, the Hobo Junction, which includes the group the WhoRidas (King Sann, Mr. Taylor, and Big Nouz), plus IQ, Arrogant, 3rd Rail, K/Top, J-Groove, Hollywood, Poke Martian, Sleuth Pro, and Jay-Z (not to be confused with the Brooklyn artist of the same name). In one of the most successful PR ploys in 1990s hip-hop, Saafir challenged his one-time friend Casual (and, by nature, Casual's entire Hieroglyphics crew) to a rhyme battle in late 1994. The ensuing Hieroglyphics-versus-Hobo Junction battle (played out on the radio and elsewhere) resonated with hip-hop heads worldwide and became a part of hip-hop lore. Informal surveys gave Saafir and Hobo Junction the win—but only barely.

what's available: Saafir has one of those rigid, slightly abrasive rhyming styles that you either love or hate. Those who appreciate change and experimentation will also appreciate the rapper's debut, *Boxcar Sessions* 𝄢𝄢𝄢𝄢 (Qwest/Warner Bros., 1994, prod. Jay-Z, J-Groove). The album is noisy and cacophonous in spots, but Saafir's rhymes are truly a spectacle to behold. "Battle Drill," as its name suggests, is a deft pairing of the rapper's warrior-like savvy with a rapid-fire drum beat, and "Can You Feel Me?" is a rare daydream-like tune. Saafir's Hobo Junction crewmates, the WhoRidas, recite playa rhymes with skill usually found in lyrically focused underground crews. The group's

debut, *Whoridin* 𝄢𝄢𝄢𝄢 (Southpaw/Delicious Vinyl, 1997, prod. the WhoRidas), is a pretty narcotic affair, featuring drop-top ridin' anthems like "Taxin" and "Shot Callin' and Big Ballin'."

worth searching for: Some of Saafir's best verses have come on cameos, including the B.U.M.S.' "Rain" (Priority, 1995) and the wild *Street Fighter Soundtrack* (VRS, 1994) entry, "Come Widdit," featuring Ahmad and Ras Kass.

influences:

◄◄ Digital Underground, Hieroglyphics, Organized Konfusion, Kool G Rap

▶▶ Ras Kass, Ahmad

Jazzbo

Sade

Born Helen Folsade Adu, January 19, 1959, in Lagos, Nigeria.

Reared as the daughter of a Nigerian teacher and English nurse, Sade moved to London with her mother at age four when her parents split. A design student at St. Martin's College in London, the singer made a minor name for herself as a clothes designer during the 1980s before turning heads in London fronting the jazz-funk band Pride. Joined by keyboardist Andrew Hale, bassist Paul Denman, and guitarist/saxophonist Stuart Matthewman, Sade organized her own self-named band in 1984, eventually forging a mix of cool-school jazz and smoldering funk that brought the group to worldwide attention. Though critics have often focused on Sade herself—a coffee-colored beauty with a fashion model's face and jazzy, delicate vocal chops—the publicity-shy singer has always insisted others accept Sade as a band. And while some have found the group's laid back instrumental mix a bit boring, their signature sound has garnered a wide and loyal fan base. The group's first record spent 81 weeks on the *Billboard* sales charts—earning a Best New Artist Grammy award—and collectively, their four original music albums have sold more than 27 million copies. While the singer welcomed a new daughter, Ila, in 1996, her bandmates crafted an album of ambient soul grooves without her under the name Sweetback (and Matthewman worked with hot newcomer Maxwell). Early in 1997, Sade's only activity was in court—she faced disorderly conduct charges related to some traffic infractions in Jamaica—with no firm plans for a new album.

what to buy: Following a four-year layoff, Sade added 1990s-style reggae touches for her best effort yet, *Love Deluxe* 𝄢𝄢𝄢𝄢 (Epic, 1992, prod. Sade, Mike Pela), a heady mix of tunes fu-

eled by the burning, sensual grooves "No Ordinary Love" and "Cherish the Day."

what to buy next: It wasn't until her second album, *Promise* 𝄞𝄞𝄞𝄞 (CBS/Portrait, 1986, prod. Sade, Ben Rogan, Mike Pela, Robin Miller), that Sade began to live up to the promise in her own jazz/pop/soul sound. Veering from the percolating hit "The Sweetest Taboo" to the jazzy minor-chord lament "Mr. Wrong" and the semi-funky, lounge-tinged workout "Never As Good As the First Time," the singer's detached cool mixes with her crack backing band to bring some truly inspired moments.

what to avoid: Though her debut album, *Diamond Life* 𝄞𝄞𝄞 (CBS/Portrait, 1985, prod. Robin Miller) made a splash by introducing the world to her jazz-influenced, ice-queen persona, the songs here are a little too restrained, with the hit single "Smooth Operator" as the only exception. Elsewhere, funky stuff such as "Cherry Pie" feels stilted, while "Your Love Is King" winds on like an overbearing lounge singer that doesn't know when to call it a night.

the rest:
Stronger Than Pride 𝄞𝄞𝄞𝄞 (CBS/Portrait, 1988)
The Best of Sade 𝄞𝄞𝄞𝄞 (Epic, 1994)

worth searching for: You'd never guess from their cool-school records that Sade is a smoking live band, but the 90-minute concert video *Sade Live* (Sony, 1993), which captures one of the band's more inspired 1993 performances, should change that idea in a hurry.

influences:
◀◀ Nina Simone, Billie Holiday, Marvin Gaye

▶▶ Des'ree, Basia

Eric Deggans

Salt-N-Pepa
Formed as Super Nature, 1985, in Queens, NY.

Salt (Cheryl James), vocals; Pepa (Sandy Denton), vocals; Latoya Hanson, DJ (1985–86); Spinderella (Dee Dee Roper), DJ (1987–present).

Before they adopted their current moniker, Cheryl James and Sandy Denton scored a minor hit with "The Show Stoppa"—a distaff dis to Doug E. Fresh and Slick Rick's "The Show"—under the name Super Nature in late 1985. One year later, as the

Sade (© Ken Settle)

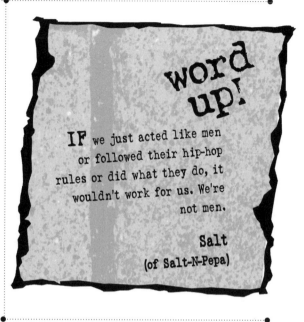

rechristened Salt-N-Pepa, the Queens-based rappers released their first full-length album. *Hot, Cool & Vicious* ignited dance floors with the heavy-breathing crossover smash "Push It," and commandeered a place for themselves on hip-hop's front lines. What's remarkable about Salt-N-Pepa, though, is not that they managed a hit-filled debut ("Push It," "Tramp," "My Mic Sounds Nice," and "Chick on the Side" all notched the R&B charts), nor even that they were the first female rap act to meet with substantial commercial success, but that they have parlayed that success into an artistically exceptional, decade-long-plus career.

Dee Dee "Spinderella" Roper joined the fold on 1988's *A Salt with a Deadly Pepa*, replacing former DJ Latoya Hanson (who, confusingly, was credited as "Spinderella" on *Hot, Cool & Vicious*). Propelled by Roper's sophisticated turntable textures and producer Hurby "Luv Bug" Azor's ever-improving studio craft, Salt-N-Pepa transformed from saucy, streetwise tomboys with a Run-D.M.C. fixation, to smooth-singing, body-sculpted temptresses, over the course of just a few albums. The culmination of that transformation was 1993's *Very Necessary*, a quintuple-platinum coup whose biggest hit, "Whatta Man" (a rewrite of Linda Lyndell's "What a Man"), paired the trio with R&B's reigning funky divas, En Vogue. Since the release of *Very Necessary*, Salt-N-Pepa have kept a relatively low profile, every now

Salt-N-Pepa (© Ken Settle)

and then contributing to various multi-artist projects, including soundtracks for *Space Jam* (a cover of Diana Ross's "Upside Down") and *Bulletproof* ("Champagne"), as well as the all-female charity album *Ain't Nuthin' but a She Thing* (the title track).

what to buy: Situated midway between the crushing breakbeats of their early albums and the svelte grooves of their recent work, Salt-N-Pepa's third joint, *Blacks' Magic* ♫♫♫ (Next Plateau/London, 1990), is a masterstroke. A celebration of African American accomplishment and feminist empowerment that doesn't forget to kick out the party jams, *Blacks' Magic* opens with the funky juggernaut "Expression" and includes the mirror-ball romp "Let's Talk about Sex." *Very Necessary* ♫♫♫ (Next Plateau/London, 1993) explores the ladies' newfound sexual candor—not to mention sexuality—to stunning effect. If this blockbuster extinguished any hopes of Salt-N-Pepa returning to their B-girl roots, it nonetheless demonstrated that they could engage mainstream R&B with panache and conviction.

what to avoid: *A Blitz of Salt-N-Pepa Hits* ♫♫ (Next Plateau/London, 1990) is a greatest-hits remix collection for completists only.

the rest:
Hot, Cool & Vicious ♫♫♫ (Next Plateau/London, 1986)
A Salt with a Deadly Pepa ♫♫♫ (Next Plateau/London, 1988)
Brand New N/A (Red Ant/London, 1997)

worth searching for: The six-song remix EP *None of Your Business* ♫♫♫ (Next Plateau/London, 1994) features the kind of imaginative remixes so conspicuously absent on *A Blitz of Hits*, including DJ Muggs's blistering hard-rock version of the title track.

influences:

◀◀ Run-D.M.C., Dana Dane, Grandmaster Flash, George Clinton, the Supremes, Doug E. Fresh

▶▶ Roxanne Shante, MC Lyte, Kid 'N Play, TLC, En Vogue, Mary J. Blige, Antoinette, Bahamadia

Greg Siegel

Sam & Dave

Formed in 1961. Disbanded in 1970.

Sam Moore (born October 12, 1935, in Miami, FL), vocals; Dave Prater (born May 9, 1937, in Ocilla, GA, and died April 11, 1988, in Atlanta, GA), vocals.

Soul men indeed, Sam Moore and Dave Prater could trade vocals with both ease and urgency that seemed almost instinctive. Using the call-and-response technique that harkened back to both their beginnings as gospel singers, Prater and Moore slipped around each other's vocal lines like cracking bullwhips. Their Stax/Volt recordings, largely written and produced by the team of Isaac Hayes and David Porter, rank with the finest works in the field, records that have been covered by a disparate group of artists such as Elvis Costello, Fabulous Thunderbirds, Tom Jones, and Carl Wilson of the Beach Boys. The duo first paired in 1961 and recorded several unsuccessful singles for the Roulette label before producer Jerry Wexler of Atlantic Records signed them and put the duo in the bosom of Memphis soul, where Hayes and Porter supervised a string of hit singles beginning with the timeless "Hold On I'm Coming," one of the definitive records of 1960s soul and a title allegedly inspired by repeated calls for songwriter Hayes to return to a session from the bathroom. After Stax folded its tent, the duo continued to record for Atlantic under a procession of different producers—notably Wexler and Tom Dowd, and Miami's Brad Shapiro and Dave Crawford—although without much success. Personal conflicts led to a split in 1970. They rejoined a number of times briefly, but nothing they ever did again on their own or as a team matched the incendiary force of their Stax/Volt recordings. Prater died in a 1988 car crash, after the Blues Brothers hit version of their "Soul Man" reignited interest in their work. Moore continues to ply his trade, notably singing harmonies on the 1992 Bruce Springsteen album *Human Touch*, a 1994 duet with Conway Twitty on the country and soul collaboration *Rhythm Country and Blues*, and a terrific live performance with John Fogerty at the Concert for the Rock and Roll Hall of Fame in 1995.

what to buy: The double-disc retrospective, *Sweat 'N' Soul: Anthology 1965–1971* ♪♪♪♪ (Rhino, 1993, prod. various) combines all the duo's famed highspots with rewarding gems plucked from the dusty corners of their estimable body of work.

what to buy next: All the individual original Stax albums boast non-single tracks steeped in that greasy fatback sound of Memphis soul, but *Soul Men* ♪♪♪♪ (Stax, 1967, prod. Isaac Hayes, David Porter) holds a slight edge with cuts such as "Broke Down Piece of Man" (later covered by Southside Johnny & the Asbury Jukes), "May I Baby," and their delicious take on the Everly Brothers' "Let It Be Me."

what to avoid: Moore remade the duo's signature tune as the title track for the soundtrack to the 1987 movie *Soul Man*, with—of all people—Lou Reed. The intended irony falls somewhat flat.

the rest:
Hold On I'm Coming ♪♪♪ (Stax, 1966)
Double Dynamite ♪♪♪ (Stax, 1966)
I Thank You ♪♪♪ (Stax, 1968)

worth searching for: *The Stax/Volt Revue Volume One—Live in London* ♪♪♪♪ (Stax, 1967, prod. Jim Stewart) contains a spellbinding live version of their drop-dead soul ballad "When Something Is Wrong with My Baby" alongside another pair of Sam & Dave performances, not to mention cuts by Otis Redding, Booker T. and the MG's, Eddie Floyd, and others.

influences:
◀◀ Sam Cooke, Jackie Wilson, Sims Twins
▶▶ Righteous Brothers, Blues Brothers

Joel Selvin

Sam the Sham & the Pharaohs

Formed 1963, in Dallas, TX. Disbanded 1966.

Sam the Sham (born Domingo Samudio), lead vocals, organ; David Martin, bass; Ray Stinnet, guitar; Jerry Patterson, drums; Butch Gibson, saxophone (1965–66).

With a crazed yelp of "Uno, dos, one-two-tres *quatro!*," Sam the Sham burst into the spotlight seemingly out of nowhere with the classic "Wooly Bully," the second-best selling single of 1965, and the sight of his band, festooned in garish mock-Egyptian garb, was a refreshing if somewhat bizarre distraction from the Merseybeat and Motown-infested mid-1960s. Unfairly categorized even then as a mere novelty act despite solid, groundbreaking musicianship, Sam the Sham, with roots deep-set in Southern-fried R&B, can rightfully lay claim today to being one of the principle architects of the entire Tex-Mex genre. After a four-year Navy stint and time spent at Arlington State College studying classical music by day (and club-hopping by night), Samudio formed his first group of Pharaohs during the early 1960s, performing sets full of songs by John Lee Hooker, Jimmy Reed, and Elmo James to the denizens of Dallas juke joints. Quickly tiring of the five-dollar-per-man-per-night regimen,

Samudio disbanded this outfit soon afterwards, but not before acquiring the moniker "Sam the Sham" due to his penchant for enthusiastically MC-ing the act (a.k.a. "shamming") as opposed to simply planting himself dourly behind his organ on stage. A subsequent stint as a carnival barker led to the formation of his next band with old school pal David Martin, who told his partner all they really needed to escape the drudgery of the Southwest bar circuit was "one gold record." The first step towards this goal was the release of "Haunted House" in May of 1964, which fared pretty well on local radio despite stiff competition from a rival version by rockabilly legend Gene Simmons. This brought them to the attention of Sun Records alumnus Stan Kesler, who arranged to release a version of a song (about Sam's cat!) that the band had ad-libbed on stage. Licensed to MGM Records in 1965, "Wooly Bully" went on to sell 3.5 million copies, and the Pharaohs toured the world in their trademark turbans, as well as making frequent television appearances and even walk-ons in a couple of quickie MGM movie musicals. The Pharaohs disbanded the following year however, leaving Sam to cut his second-biggest hit, "Little Red Riding Hood," in New York with studio musicians. This arrangement, complete with a chorus of back-up singer/dancers ("the Shamettes"), grew into the full-scale Sam the Sham Revue, which cut an additional album for MGM in 1967 before Sam went totally solo with the wonderful *Sam, Hard and Heavy* album in 1970, cut with Duane Allman and the Dixie Flyers for Atlantic Records. This record won Sam his first and only Grammy Award—for its *liner notes!*—but it wasn't until more than a decade later that he resurfaced on disc, alongside Ry Cooder, composing music for *The Border* soundtrack. Today, offering his services strictly in the name of the lord, Sam can be found preaching on Memphis street corners and performing for the inmates of Tennessee jails when not readying and recording new songs at home on his acoustic guitar ("You've heard of Unplugged?," Sam asks. "This is *Disconnected!*") He was recently honored with the prestigious Desi Award in recognition of his achievements as a Mexican American, and at the gala presentation ceremonies leapt on stage to perform a blistering "Wooly Bully" accompanied by, appropriately enough, one of his many heirs-apparent, the Texas Tornados.

what to buy: The stupendous *Pharaohization: The Best of Sam the Sham & the Pharaohs* 🎜🎜🎜 (Rhino, 1985, prod. various) demonstrates that this band had far more to offer than the mere novelties of it two biggest hits. Left to its own devices, its rockabilly-fused pure Louisiana R&B was practically without precedent during the mid-1960s and greatly influenced many artists to come.

what to buy next: With every single one of their spectacular MGM albums sorrowfully out of print, and until some visionary soul decides to issue Sam's newest recordings, we can all more than make due with the fine, fun *Turban Renewal: A Tribute to Sam the Sham & the Pharaohs* 🎜🎜🎜 (Norton, 1994, comp. Billy Miller and Mark Natale), in which 26 acts (28 on the double-vinyl edition) pay homage-in-party to one of Tex-Mex's founding fathers.

influences:

◀◀ Otis Rush, Screamin' Jay Hawkins, Booker T. & the MG's

▶▶ Sir Douglas Quintet, Joe "King" Carrasco, Texas Tornados

Gary Pig Gold

David Sanborn

Born July 30, 1945, in Tampa, FL.

One of the most lyrical and expressive saxophone players in the pop, R&B, and jazz realms, David Sanborn's alto work is never less than far above average; he's often imitated but never quite duplicated. And it's true what they say about his style—it takes hearing a mere note or two to know it's Sanborn's distinctive work. He's also a player who puts his whole body into it, thrusting notes out from his once-delicate, polio-ridden lungs with surprising power (it was polio that led him to the sax as a form of physical therapy). Equally adept at gentle love ballads and searing funk, multiple Grammy-winner Sanborn's talent also has made him one of the most successful jazz crossover artists. Though considered a jazz cat, he's known more for his R&B-flavored music than his jazz influences, and he actually started out playing R&B with Albert King and Little Milton. He hit the Chicago area—and its R&B clubs—during the early 1960s as a college student before moving to Los Angeles in 1967. There Sanborn hooked up with the Paul Butterfield Blues Band, whom he would accompany to Woodstock. That was just the first of his rock forays; he would later play with David Bowie (the distinctive riffing on "Young Americans" is his), Paul Simon, Bruce Springsteen, Stevie Wonder, Steely Dan, the Rolling Stones, Roger Waters, B.B. King, and others. Called the white Junior Walker because of his natural R&B ability, Sanborn has no trouble flipping from soul to pop to blues to jazz and back. His jazzier collaborations have been with the Brecker brothers, Michael Franks, Gil Evans, and Al Jarreau, and he's seen regularly sitting in with Paul Shaffer and his band on *The Late Show with David Letterman.* For two years, Sanborn also hosted his own television show, the syndicated *Night Music,* with an esoteric array of artists appearing in interview and performance formats. It died from lack of sponsorship. He also had a syndicated radio show for a while during the early 1990s.

what to buy: On *Voyeur* 𝄞𝄞𝄞𝄞 (Warner Bros., 1981, prod. Michael Colina, Ray Bardani), Sanborn surrounded himself with impeccable players, including Hamish Stuart of the Average White Band, Tom Scott, Valerie Simpson, Patti Austin, Marcus Miller, and others. Together they created a blend of funk and soul that's smooth and quite seductive. "Wake Me When It's Over," with its doubling effects, is terrific. Also, pick up *Backstreet* 𝄞𝄞𝄞𝄞 (Warner Bros., 1983, prod. Marcus Miller, Ray Bardani, Michael Colina), which explores even more of his soulful, sensuous side without abandoning interludes of muscular funk. There's also some Vocoder experimentation on here, perhaps suggesting influences by such fusion artists as Herbie Hancock, who released "Rockit" the same year.

what to buy next: *Upfront* 𝄞𝄞𝄞 (Elektra, 1992, prod. Marcus Miller), features more of Sanborn's fluid artistry. *Straight to the Heart* 𝄞𝄞𝄞 (Warner Bros., 1984, prod. Marcus Miller) has a killer version of the R&B standard "Love and Happiness" with lead vocals by Hamish Stuart.

what to avoid: *Pearls* 𝄞𝄞𝄞 (Elektra 1995, prod. Tommy LiPuma, Johnny Mandel) is not your usual Sanborn output; one for the jazz fans, it's filled with standards such as "Smoke Gets in Your Eyes" and unexpected versions of "Try a Little Tenderness," "This Masquerade," and "Nobody Does It Better" (with Oleta Adams on vocals). It's not unpleasant at all, but it contains less funk than fans might be seeking.

the rest:
Taking Off 𝄞𝄞𝄞 (Warner Bros., 1975)
Sanborn 𝄞𝄞𝄞 (Warner Bros., 1976)
Heart to Heart 𝄞𝄞𝄞 (Warner Bros., 1978)
Hideaway 𝄞𝄞𝄞 (Warner Bros., 1979)
As We Speak 𝄞𝄞𝄞 (Warner Bros., 1982)
Double Vision 𝄞𝄞𝄞 (Warner Bros., 1984)
Change of Heart 𝄞𝄞𝄞 (Warner Bros., 1987)
CloseUp 𝄞𝄞𝄞 (Reprise, 1988)
Hearsay 𝄞𝄞𝄞 (Elektra, 1994)
Best of David Sanborn 𝄞𝄞𝄞𝄞 (Reprise, 1994)
Love Songs 𝄞𝄞𝄞 (Warner Bros., 1995)
Songs from the Night Before 𝄞𝄞𝄞 (Elektra, 1996)

worth searching for: *Another Hand* 𝄞𝄞𝄞𝄞 (Elektra, 1991, prod. Hal Willner) is another step into more straight jazz, with fine results. Among its surprises are contributions by members of NRBQ, Syd Straw, and other notables.

influences:

◀◀ Gil Evans, the Breckers, Hank Crawford, Charlie Parker, Jackie McLean, King Curtis, Junior Walker

▶▶ Kenny G, Kenny Blake, Dave Koz

Lynne Margolis

Deion Sanders

Born August 9, 1967, in Fort Meyers, FL.

"This album is for real. . . . This ain't no joke." So said superstar *athlete* Deion "Prime Time" Sanders about his first—and, thankfully, only—album, *Prime Time*. Sorry, but we beg to differ.

what to avoid: Despite help from the likes of Too $hort and Ant Banks, Sanders stinks it up big time on *Prime Time* **woof!** (Bust It, 1994, prod. various), delivering cliched lyrics in a voice that only a record-company-running friend (i.e. Hammer) could love. Heck, the song titles alone are enough to make you run the other way: "2 B Me," "House of Prime," "Time For Prime," "Prime Time Keeps on Ticking," "Y U NV ME?" and so on. Hardly an all-pro effort.

influences:

◀◀ Hammer, Ant Banks, Too $hort, Snoop Doggy Dogg, Notorious B.I.G.

Josh Freedom du Lac

Boz Scaggs

Born William Royce Scaggs, June 8, 1944, in OH.

Before he started making hits during the 1970s as a sophisticated, soulful crooner, Boz Scaggs was a cohort of Steve Miller, whom he met at St. Mark's Preparatory School in Dallas during in the late 1950s. Both attended the University of Wisconsin, then separated when Scaggs moved to England during the mid-1960s. Returning to San Francisco in 1967, Scaggs hooked up with the Steve Miller Band for two albums of psychedelic blues before the singer-guitarist decided to go solo. His debut, *Boz Scaggs*, was co-produced by *Rolling Stone* magazine publisher Jann Wenner and features one of Duane Allman's seminal solos on "Loan Me a Dime." Gradually eschewing rockers for ballads, Scaggs began working with the cream of L.A.'s studio crop and fashioned a slick, Teflon soul sound that hit its peak with *Silk Degrees*, a five-million seller that made him one of pop's hottest commodities during the mid-1970s. During the past 16 years, however, he's spent more time nurturing his Bay Area club, Slim's, than making music; he's only released three albums, returning to the bluesy R&B tenor of his early solo recordings. He was also planning a box set for late 1997.

what to buy: *Silk Degrees* 𝄞𝄞𝄞𝄞 (Columbia, 1976, prod. Joe Wissert) shines with the laid-back cool elegance of "Lowdown" and the chugging "Lido Shuffle." The Muscle Shoals house band provides hot backing on the rootsy debut *Boz Scaggs* 𝄞𝄞𝄞𝄞 (Atlantic, 1969/1988, prod. Boz Scaggs, Jann Wenner, Marlin Greene), and Allman's slide guitar on "Loan Me a Dime" is a seminal moment in rock history.

what to buy next: *Some Change* 𝄞𝄞𝄞 (Virgin, 1994, prod. Boz Scaggs, Ricky Fataar) is a sincere comeback that has a down-home comfort. Scaggs sounds assured and inspired, and Booker T. Jones on the organ doesn't hurt, either.

what to avoid: *Other Roads* 𝄞𝄞 (Columbia, 1988, prod. Bill Schnee, Stewart Levine), which came after an eight-year hiatus, is so anti-climatic it makes you wonder if he shouldn't stick to running his restaurant.

the rest:
Slow Dancer 𝄞𝄞𝄞 (Columbia, 1974)
Down—Two Then Left 𝄞𝄞𝄞 (Columbia, 1977)
Hits! 𝄞𝄞𝄞 (Columbia, 1980)
Come on Home 𝄞𝄞𝄞 (Virgin, 1997)
My Time: A Boz Scaggs Anthology 𝄞𝄞𝄞𝄞 (Legacy, 1997)

worth searching for: The out-of-print *My Time* 𝄞𝄞𝄞𝄞 (Columbia, 1972) features the last of Scaggs's rockers, "Full-Lock Power Slide" and "Dinah Flo"—pretty charged-up stuff, considering what the next 20 years would hold.

influences:
◀◀ Lightnin' Hopkins, Lou Rawls, Dan Penn, Steve Miller Band, Motown

▶▶ Phil Collins, Huey Lewis & the News, Michael Bolton, Tony Rich

Allan Orski

Schoolly D

Born Jesse B. Weaver, June 22, 1966, in Philadelphia, PA.

More than a decade after he released an untitled album on his own record label, Schoolly D's impact on hip-hop is not lost. Generally regarded as the first-ever gangsta rapper, Schoolly D was a master lyricist who ushered in a new era in hip-hop: hardcore. The consummate street poet, he had a terse delivery and trademark sinister drawl that, along with his DJ Code Money's crashing drum breaks, resonated the hardened attitude of life in gangs, on the streets, and in the projects. Schoolly claims he was once a member of the Park Side Killas gang in North Philadelphia, and that was reflected in the violent energy he conjured up in his songs. He rapped about murders and drugs, Gucci and Filas—even his gun-packing mother. He came to rap's party, and nothing was ever the same. But amidst the rumors of Schoolly D's "dusted" persona existed a twisted irony: Many who came into contact with the rapper insisted he was just a nice, ordinary guy. Some even doubted his association with the Park Side Killas gang he immortalized in the song "PSK." Had Schoolly D calculated his attitude and concocted this thuggish, violent imagery and the almost-mythological street life to make a name for himself and sell records? Truly ahead of his time.

what to buy: Almost to spite the growing tide of Afrocentricity that was emerging in hip-hop at the end of the 1980s—especially since his hardened persona was in such stark contrast to it—Schoolly D released *Am I Black Enough for You?* 𝄞𝄞𝄞𝄞 (Jive/Zomba, 1989, prod. Schoolly D, DJ Code Money), an album of black power anthems in which his gangsta persona still rings true. Songs such as "Gangsta Boogie" and "Black Power" combine Schoolly's rhymes, attitude, and underlying sense of self-preservation with an undeniable booming bass that's hard to resist.

the rest:
The Adventures of Schoolly D 𝄞𝄞𝄞 (Rykodisk, 1987)
How a Blackman Feels 𝄞 (Capitol, 1991)
Welcome to America 𝄞𝄞 (Columbia/Ruffhouse, 1994)
Reservoir Dog 𝄞𝄞𝄞 (Contract/PSK, 1995)

worth searching for: Many of Schoolly's best records are out of print, including his seminal untitled debut (Schoolly D, 1986), which contains "Put Your Filas On," "Gucci Time," and, of course, "PSK." *Saturday Night!—The Album* (Jive/RCA, 1987) and *Smoke Some Kill* (Jive/RCA, 1988) are also considered classics and are certainly worth scavenging for.

influences:
◀◀ Afrika Bambaataa, Grandmixer D. St

▶▶ N.W.A., Cypress Hill, Scarface, Kool G Rap, Boogie Down Productions, Beastie Boys

Jazzbo

Dred Scott

Producer/rapper Scott emerged in the early 1990s from the San Fernando Valley, hooking up with Tragedy the Intelligent Hoodlum who led him to a record deal.

what's available: *Breaking Combs* ✍✍✍ (Tuff Break, 1993, prod. Dred Scott) presents the kind of upbeat, positive rap that seems so unfortunately out-of-fashion now. Dred Scott is a rapper in touch with the continuity of black life, but his record was released during the rise of G-funk. On such infectious tracks as "Back in the Day," "Check the Vibe," or "Can't Hold It Back," Scott instead opts for a clean, horn-laden, flute-inflected, jazz-and-breakbeat sound more akin to East Coasters Pete Rock or 1990s-era Marley Marl. And, lyrically, he refuses to indulge in new jack gangsta posturing, instead either celebrating the joys a decade in hip-hop has brought him or examining male-female relationships in a sharp way. Unfortunately, this likely made him impossible to market during the summer months of the gangsta lean and the Death Row ride. If you want well-crafted songs and thoughtful rhyming, though, you can't do much better.

influences:

◄◄ A Tribe Called Quest, Marley Marl, Brand Nubian, Pete Rock & C.L. Smooth

Jeff "DJ Zen" Chang

Gil Scott-Heron

Born April 1, 1949, in Chicago, IL.

Along with the Last Poets and Watts Prophets, Gil Scott-Heron is one of the founding fathers of hip-hop. Starting as an angry, somewhat one-dimensional and unsympathetic poet, he broadened his outlook and empathy to become an astute and articulate observer of sociopolitical issues, always retaining enough of his anger with injustice to give his work an edge. Early on he incorporated music into his art, and eventually became an effective singer in a mildly jazzy R&B context. Scott-Heron debuted with an album of poems accompanied by percussion, 15 short tracks that packed a big wallop and, as much as they were of their time, remain relevant (which says as much about the United States as it does about the poet). On his next record he added more music to his sound (he plays keyboards as well as singing) but continued to rap. Whether or not listeners shared the sentiments of such hard-hitting tracks as "Whitey on the Moon" (which criticized spending money on the space program while there was poverty in the inner-city) or the famous "The Revolution Will Not Be Televised" (the mature Scott-Heron would not be guilty of the cheap shot at "hairy-armed women's liberationists"), it was clear he had a way with words and a distaste for politicians' bullshit and hypocrisy regardless of color. After three albums on Flying Dutchman

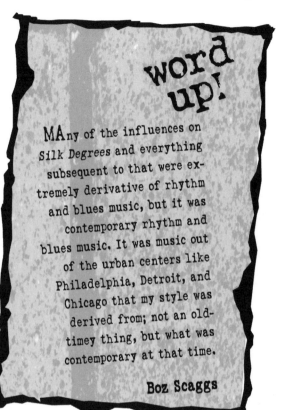

MAny of the influences on *Silk Degrees* and everything subsequent to that were extremely derivative of rhythm and blues music, but it was contemporary rhythm and blues music. It was music out of the urban centers like Philadelphia, Detroit, and Chicago that my style was derived from; not an old-timey thing, but what was contemporary at that time.

Boz Scaggs

(owned by John Coltrane producer Bob Thiele), he made one classic album on Strata-East and then became the first artist signed by Arista. All the while he was adding more and more music to his records, and his Arista albums were typically pop-oriented R&B and funk, abetted by his long collaboration with flutist/keyboardist Brian Jackson (who sometimes took the lead vocals and often shared billing on the albums). They even made an anti-drinking ditty, "The Bottle," appealing enough that it was a dance hit in 1974. His 10-year Arista period overlapped considerably with the Reagan Era, inspiring two of his best political songs, "'B' Movie" and "Re-Ron," and found Scott-Heron taking an increasingly universal outlook as reflected in the classic "(What's the Word) Johannesburg," which he performed as one of *Saturday Night Live*'s first musical guests. But his #30-charting 1975 Arista debut was his only album to reach the Top 50, and urban hits such as the anti-drug "Angel Dust" never broke out into the mainstream, though his popularity was broad-based enough that he was more than a cult artist. The early 1990s surprisingly found Scott-Heron combating substance abuse—apparently a winning battle, as he made a comeback with an album for TVT. Not surprisingly, the artist is still receiving props from the more thoughtful present-day rappers for his influence and example.

what to buy: *The Revolution Will Not Be Televised* ♫♫♫♫ (RCA, 1988, prod. Bob Thiele) is audacious and revolutionary (in several senses of the word). This newer version (an LP compilation with the same title had less material) adds bits from his first two albums on Flying Dutchman to the entire *Pieces of a Man* ♫♫♫♫ (Flying Dutchman, 1973, prod. Bob Thiele).

what to buy next: *The Best of Gil Scott-Heron* ♫♫♫♫ (Arista, 1984, prod. various) is the only Arista album still in print, a scandalous situation made even worse by the fact that this collection still skimpily consists of the same nine tracks as when it came out on LP. It has the best-known Arista tracks ("Winter in America," "The Bottle," "Johannesburg," "Angel Dust," "'B' Movie," "Re-Ron," etc.) and is the only option for those not willing to search used LP bins.

what to avoid: It's not hard to avoid *1980* ♫ (Arista, 1980, prod. Gil Scott-Heron, Brian Jackson, Malcolm Cecil), since it's out of print, but the combination of overly disco-ized production and weak material and ideas (the result of putting out albums at a furious pace) make this Scott-Heron's limpest album. After the thoughtful, articulate anti-nuke plant "We Almost Lost Detroit" on *Bridges*, "Shut 'Um Down" was mere sloganeering, showing as much imagination as the album title.

the rest:
Pieces of a Man ♫♫♫◊ (Flying Dutchman, 1971/1995)
Small Talk at 125th and Lenox ♫♫♫◊ (Flying Dutchman, 1972/1995)
Free Will ♫♫♫◊ (Flying Dutchman, 1972/1995)
Spirits ♫♫♫ (TVT, 1994)

worth searching for: *From South Africa to South Carolina* ♫♫♫♫ (Arista, 1975, prod. Gil Scott-Heron, Brian Jackson, the Midnight Band) is not only one of the greatest political albums of the 1970s, it's also got some of the best grooves—funky but often infused with elliptical African rhythm patterns. While connecting the racism in "Johannesburg" and "South Carolina (Barnwell)," the album also showcases a gentle, personalized optimism on "Beginnings (First Minute of a New Day)" and "A Lovely Day." The only flaw is Jackson's strained, out-of-tune singing on some tracks.

influences:
◀◀ Langston Hughes, Amiri Baraka, Last Poets

▶▶ Sekou Sundiata, Public Enemy, KRS-One, Spearhead, Dana Bryant

Steve Holtje

Seal

Born Sealhenry Samuel, February 19, 1963, in Paddington, England.

Seal strikes an imposing figure—six-foot-plus, shaved head, odd facial scars, swathed in black leather. His music is only slightly less imposing, mixing Seal's sweet voice, Trevor Horn's impeccable production and polyrhythmic dance rhythms, and soaring melodies for something close to pop perfection. Like Peter Gabriel, he's titled each of his two albums *Seal*.

what to buy: The infectious single "Crazy" was the calling card for the first *Seal* ♫♫♫♫ (ZTT/Sire/Warner Bros., 1991, prod. Trevor Horn), a wholly splendid effort in which every song carries weight and significance.

the rest:
Seal ♫♫♫ (ZTT/Sire/Warner Bros., 1994, prod. Trevor Horn)

worth searching for: *The Acoustic Session* ♫♫♫ (ZTT/Sire/Warner Bros., 1991, prod. Dick Meanie) is a promotional CD that features wonderfully stripped-down reinterpretations of songs from his debut.

influences:
◀◀ Peter Gabriel, Joni Mitchell, Trevor Horn, George Michael, Jimi Hendrix

▶▶ Maxwell, D'Angelo, Duncan Sheik

Aidin Vaziri

Marvin Sease

Born 1947, in Blackville, SC.

Give Marvin Sease credit for living up to his credo—he never gave up. Raised in the cotton fields of South Carolina, he suffered frequent whippings by his sharecropper father for singing as he worked. Sease also sang in church and gradually developed a dream of singing professionally, starting in gospel in Charleston, South Carolina, New Jersey, and Brooklyn, then moving back down south to sing the blues. He moved back to New York during the early 1980s and began singing in bars and clubs, finally recording an album called *Ghetto Man* for his own Early Records label. He peddled his wares store to store, convincing retailers to play it on their in-house systems so that customers could hear it. Sease's tireless self promotion—including posters plastered around New York—attracted the attention of PolyGram Records, which signed him to a contract in 1987. Sease's music, however, is Barry White done bad; it's lover man stuff, but there's nothing particularly subtle or romantic about songs such as "Candy Licker," "I Ate You for My Breakfast," and the infidelity celebration "Motel Lover." Sease—married with nine children—delivers these salacious come-ons with such sincerity that it's almost comical, and while he claims there's humor intended in his lyrics it sounds like he decided that *after* he recorded them. Sease developed a cult following but no real fan base, and though he hasn't recorded in several years he still tours and hopes to one day record a gospel album.

what's available: *The Best of Marvin Sease* 🎵🎵 (Mercury Chronicles, 1997, prod. Marvin Sease) collects songs from his four PolyGram albums, reasonably smooth soul melodies that collapse when his lyrics are added. Sease's work ethic is laudable—he wrote, arranged, and produced these 14 songs—but there's something unsavory and, worse, truly disinteresting about this stuff.

influences:

◀◀ Smokey Robinson, Aretha Franklin, Sam Cooke, Marvin Gaye, Barry White

▶▶ R. Kelly

Gary Graff

Shabba Ranks

Born Rexton Rawlston Fernando Gordon on January 17, 1966, in St. Ann's Parish, Jamaica.

The ranking sex symbol of Jamaican dancehall swing and self-proclaimed "Mr. Loverman," Shabba Ranks—the first reggae artist ever to win a Grammy Award—exploded on the international music scene with a series of crossover hits in the early 1990s, powered by his ragged, booming vocals. Developing his uniquely raunchy rap-and-reggae style for a decade before becoming an overnight sensation, Ranks sang and recorded in small Jamaican clubs and studios under the name "Co-Pilot," enjoying considerable success regionally and in the Caribbean sections of major cities like New York and London. Choosing "Shabba" after two local gangsters with the same name died, Ranks developed a musical variation all his own, combining the sounds of reggae, dancehall, and hip-hop with blatantly sexual lyrics in a style called "slackness." During the peak of his stardom from 1989 to 1991, he released 50 singles, made a now-

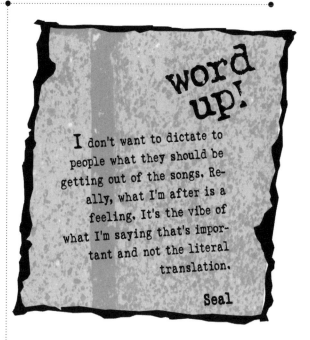

word up!

I don't want to dictate to people what they should be getting out of the songs. Really, what I'm after is a feeling. It's the vibe of what I'm saying that's important and not the literal translation.

Seal

legendary helicopter-drop entrance at Reggae Sunsplash 1989, won his first of two Grammys for the 1991 LP *As Raw as Ever*, and signed a major three-album deal with Epic/Sony. Immodestly releasing a greatest-hits album the following year, Shabba's meteoric rise was blunted by an accusation of rape (for the fourth time in his life) by a woman who appeared in his "Trailer Loada Girls" video; he compounded the controversy around him in an interview on British television in which he said gays "deserve to be crucified," making him a target of GLAAD protesters. Nonetheless, Ranks claimed a string of crossover U.S. hits, including the Top 10 R&B tunes "Housecall (Your Body Can't Lie to Me)," "Mr. Loverman," "Slow and Sexy," and the #1 remake of Sly & the Family Stone's "It's a Family Affair" off the *Addams Family Values* movie soundtrack. He continues to be an extremely popular attraction outside the U.S., particularly in Japan and Europe.

what to buy: Though he released not one but two "greatest hits" packages called *Rough & Ready* in the early 1990s, the subsequent 1995 double-disc set *Caan Dun: The Best of Shabba* 🎵🎵🎵🎵 (VP, 1995, compilation prod. David Sanguinetti, Derrick Moo-Young), graced with the gift of perspective, stands as a much more fulfilling overview of a dynamically unique performer. The Caribbean hits that spurred his emergence, like "Live Blanket" and "Wicked in Bed," are prominent here, as are the majority of his international victories, led by "Mr. Loverman" and "Best Baby Father." A fine introduction to Shabba in all his guttural, gritty glory.

what to buy next: His second Grammy-winning LP, *X-tra Naked* ♫♫♫ (Epic, 1992, prod. Wycliffe Johnson), finds the singer maximizing the style which propelled him to fame while giving the people what he believes they want: All his creativity is concentrated below the waist. Featuring his hit "Slow and Sexy" duet with Johnny Gill, and contributions from rappers Queen Latifah and Chubb Rock, the Shabba beats are fresh, challenging, nasty, and definitely not for the pure of spirit.

what to avoid: A rehashing of Shabba's best tunes repackaged without enhancement, *Shabba Ranks/J.C. Lodge* ♫♫ (Pow Wow, prod. various) adds nothing significant to his body of recordings, appearing to be more of a device to place Lodge within the fringe of his spotlight.

the rest:
Rappin' with the Ladies ♫♫♫ (VP, 1988)
Just Reality ♫♫♫ (VP, 1990)
Best Baby Father ♫♫ (VP, 1990)
Golden Touch ♫♫♫ (VP, 1990)
As Raw as Ever ♫♫♫♫ (Epic, 1991)
Mr. Maximum ♫♫♫ (Pow Wow, 1992)
Rough & Ready, Vol. 1 ♫♫♫♫ (Epic, 1992)
Rough & Ready, Vol. 2 ♫♫♫ (Epic, 1993)
No Competition ♫♫♫ (Critique, 1993)
A Mi Shabba ♫♫♫♫ (Epic, 1995)

worth searching for: A brilliant roster of reggae and jazz talents—including Sly & Robbie, Bootsy Collins, Herbie Hancock, Bernie Worrell, and Fred Wesley and Maceo Parker in the horn section—surround fellow guest artist Shabba in the future-pop album from Material, *The Third Power* ♫♫♫♫ (Axiom, 1991). Ranks isn't the whole show here, but he steals it when he appears.

influences:
◀◀ Yellowman, Josey Wales, General Echo, King Jammy, Brigadier Jerry

▶▶ Maxi Priest, Buju Banton

Andre McGarrity

Sha-Key

Sha-Key is a poet-cum-MC who began to make noise in the early 1990s as part of the same vibrant East Coast poetry movement that spawned the careers of Dana Bryant and Reg E.

Gaines. Sha-Key's crews, the Vibe Khameleons and the Boom Poetic Movement—which included everyone from J-Live to Rahzelle the Godfather of Noise—infused their work with a hip-hop sensibility, so the transition from poems to raps was seamless. Meanwhile, Sha-Key's work with the Prodigy on-line service during the pre-World Wide Web days and also with the monthly electronic hip-hop newsletter *Guillotine* made her one of the first members of the rap nation to exploit Cyberspace as a communication medium.

what's available: Though droning and terse at times, there are moments on Sha-Key's only album, *A Head Nadda's Journey to Adidi Skizm* ♫♫♫ (Imago, 1994, prod. Earl Blaize), that should satisfy those fiending for pure lyricism, a la Freestyle Fellowship or Hieroglyphics. Rahzelle, whose notoriety has skyrocketed since his work as noisemaker for the Roots, is featured on several songs, including "Children of the Corn."

influences:
◀◀ Freestyle Fellowship, Heiroglyphics, Reg E. Gaines, Last Poets, Maya Angelou

▶▶ The Roots, Dana Bryant, Priest and Beans

Jazzbo

Tupac Shakur
See: 2Pac

Shalamar
Formed 1977, in Los Angeles, CA. Disbanded 1990.

Jody Watley, vocals (1977–83); Jeffrey Daniels, vocals (1977–83); Gary Mumford, vocals (1977), Gerald Brown, vocals (1977); Howard Hewett, vocals (1978–86); Delisa Davis, vocals (1984–90); Micki Free, guitar, vocals (1984–90); Sidney Justin, vocals (1987–90).

When Shalamar's first single, "Uptown Festival," was released in 1977, the group had no actual members except for the entity's creators, British producer Simon Soussan and Dick Griffey, a booking agent for the TV dance show *Soul Train*. The success of the Motown medley tune prompted them to form a touring group, starting with Jody Watley and Jeffrey Daniels, a popular pair of dance partners from *Soul Train*. Gerald Brown soon replaced third member Gary Mumford and was in turn replaced on the second album by Howard Hewett. Starting with "Take That to the Bank," this carefully constructed, model early 1980s pop-soul group scored several major hits, from peppy post-disco dance grooves to sensitive ballads, most produced by Leon Sylvers. The last album with the three central members was a big European hit. Amid rumors of persistent in-fighting,

Daniels and Watley left in 1983. Hewett replaced them in 1984 with Delisa Davis and Micki Free, who both contributed more to the group's collective good looks than they did its musical direction. No matter; by then, the magic was lost, and the sound had been tweaked decidedly towards rock, an idea hinted at by Daniels years before. Hewett left for a solo career in 1986 and was replaced by Sidney Justin. Watley's star rose as a solo artist, but the more talented Hewett enjoyed only moderate success. Daniels recently worked on radio in Japan.

what to buy: *Three for Love* ♫♫♫ (Capitol/Solar, 1981/The Right Stuff, 1997, prod. Leon Sylvers III) finds Shalamar in its glory period, producing hit singles and creating enduring ballads.

what to buy next: Rather than wading painfully through the dated album cuts in the early life of the group, pick up *Greatest Hits* ♫♫♫♫ (Solar, 1982, prod. various).

what to avoid: By the time the group made *Wake Up* ♫ (Solar, 1990, prod. various), Shalamar had none of its original members and no collective personality to speak of.

the rest:
Uptown Festival ♫♫ (Soul Train/Solar, 1977/The Right Stuff, 1997)
Big Fun ♫♫♫ (Solar, 1979)
Friends ♫♫♫ (Solar, 1982)
Look ♫♫♫ (Solar, 1983)
Heartbreak ♫♫♫ (Solar, 1984)
Circumstantial Evidence ♫♫ (Solar/Epic, 1987)

worth searching for: Several of the group's works are out of print, including *Go for It* ♫♫♫ (Solar, 1981, prod. Leon Sylvers III) and *Disco Gardens* ♫♫ (RCA/Solar, 1978, prod. Dick Griffey).

influences:

◀◀ Hues Corporation, the Sylvers, Peaches & Herb

▶▶ Atlantic Starr, Midnight Starr, Starpoint

see also: *Howard Hewett, Jody Watley*

Franklin Paul

Sham & the Professor

Formed in New York, NY.

Having found favor with Todd Terry, one of New York's favorite remixers, along with Kenny "Dope" Gonzales, Sham & the Professor emerged in the early 1990s, releasing four singles on Freeze Records before finally unleashing the 1994 album, *Split Personalities*. With the blessing of Terry's presence, Sham & the Professor had a string of club hits, beginning with "Who's at the Door" in 1993 and continuing through a fierce Kenny Dope remix of "So-Low-Ist" later that same year. Though the in-

fluences were clearly New York, the duo's singles found favor on both coasts, mostly relying on grooving production by Terry and decent, though not exceptional, lyrical performances by Sham & the Professor. After their 1994 debut album fared poorly, Sham & the Professor fell largely silent. In retrospect, though, their recordings foreshadowed the coming prominence of New York party rhymers and producers like Frankie Cutlass.

what's available: Sham & the Professor's only album, *Split Personalities* ♫♫♫ (Freeze, 1994, prod. Todd Terry, Sam Sever, Kenny Dope, Sham & the Professor, others), wasn't able to capitalize on the popularity of the group's singles. While the lyrics work OK on the singles "So-Low-Ist" and "Who's At the Door," their pair's gift of lip only takes the two so far, and the poorer production on the album reveal the weaknesses in the overall effort. Their politics are admirable, though, especially in their call for police accountability on "Justice for All." And they also show a keen sense of humor with the skit "Grammy Smokeout," in which Sham pokes fun at some mainstream hip-hop favorites, including Snow, Marky Mark, and Me Phi Me. What's worth listening to is Side B of the album, which features three of the album's best tracks—and, not coincidentally, three of the singles, including "The Light's Gone Out."

worth searching for: "Who's at the Door" (Freeze, 1993) is an underground club classic, filled with a chunky bass line and infectious hook. It offers little by way of content—after all, the song's about the "buddha man"—but for the head-nodding crowd, it gets the nod of approval. "The Light's Gone Out" 12-inch (Freeze, 1994) contains a remix and an unreleased track that are both worth checking out. Diehards might also scan for the group's first single, "Coney Island" (Freeze, 1992), which sounded as dated then as it does now. Neither the single nor its B-side made the group's only album.

influences:

◀◀ Nine, Todd Terry, Kenny Dope

▶▶ Frankie Cutlass

Oliver "O-Dub" Wang

Shanice

Born Shanice Wilson on May 14, 1973, in Pittsburgh, PA.

Shanice Wilson was a seasoned performer long before she got a record contract at the ripe old age of 11. She sang in musicals, starred in a Kentucky Fried Chicken commercial alongside Ella Fitzgerald, and performed on *Star Search*. A&M Records executive John McClain signed the adolescent Shanice and they released her first album in 1987. Shanice scored with "(Baby Tell Me) Can You Dance" and "No 1/2 Steppin," but waited a long three years to follow up the debut. She reappeared in 1990 with a new name (just "Shanice"), a new label (Motown), and a higher echelon of producers, including Narada Michael Walden. He gave her the huge hit "I Love Your Smile," but again she had a hard time sustaining momentum, possibly because, despite her capable voice, her sound was still candy-coated. She tried to shed that image on her last album, titled "21 Ways to Grow," but few people noticed.

what to buy: Shanice, like all of Walden's pupils, can do wonders with a big ballad. *Inner Child* 🎜🎜🎜 (Motown, 1991, prod Narada Michael Walden) gives her several juicy opportunities, like "Silent Prayer" and "I'm Crying." But beware of the dance cuts.

the rest:
21 Ways to Grow 🎜🎜🎝 (Motown, 1994)

worth searching for: *Discovery* 🎜🎜🎝 (A&M, 1987, prod. Bryan Loren) may have produced two uptempo hits, but it was Shanice's chilling delivery of the ballad "Just a Game" that showed she truly was talented. "If I Never Knew You," her 1995 duet with Jon Secada for the soundtrack to *Pocahontas*, does the same.

influences:
◀◀ Stacey Lattisaw, New Edition, Johnny Gill

▶▶ Monica, Aaliyah

Franklin Paul

Roxanne Shante

Born Lolita Shante Gooden, March 8, 1970, in Long Island City, NY.

Walking down the street near New York's Queensbridge housing projects in 1985, 14-year-old runaway Lolita Gooden heard three men complaining about how the rap group U.T.F.O. had stood them up, canceling a show they'd promoted—even though the trio had helped break the group's single, "Roxanne, Roxanne," on New York's WHBI-FM. With characteristic guts, Gooden offered to cut an answer record to U.T.F.O.'s "Roxanne," a song that criticizes a woman as "stuck up, devious, and sinister" because she resists them. After demonstrating her freestyle prowess, the men—including soon-to-be-legendary producer Marley Marl—cut "Roxanne's Revenge" in Marl's family room, creating a groundbreaking single that simultaneously established Marl's reputation, dissed U.T.F.O., and spawned at least 102 more answer-record knock-

offs. The single was a hit before it was even pressed on a record, thanks to heavy underground airplay of the reel-to-reel master. Christened Roxanne Shante, Gooden immediately earned a reputation as a tough-talking female MC who refused to take any crap from her macho male counterparts. U.T.F.O. eventually forced Marl and Shante to re-cut "Revenge" to eliminate a sample of the first "Roxanne" single, but Shante's career was already off and running. Though she released a host of singles—including one with funkmaster Rick James—it would be four more years before Shante released her first album, a profanity-laced demonstration of her considerable skills. But her focus on touring and erratic work schedule (her second album came three years after the first) allowed the fast-paced world of rap to leave her behind, with only occasional appearance on old-school radio jams to mark her passing.

what to buy: The biggest problem in unearthing the best work of early rappers is that so much of their initial success came from hit singles never found on subsequent albums. Fortunately, Shante got a greatest hits record on the market a few years ago—*Roxanne Shante's Greatest Hits* 🎜🎜🎜 (Cold Chillin', 1995, prod. Marley Marl, others)—that collects many of her best singles on one disc. From the brazen, in-your-face attitude of "Roxanne's Revenge," on which she tells the members of U.T.F.O. they "don't really know how to operate," to "Have a Nice Day" and "Go On, Girl" (lyrics courtesy of Big Daddy Kane), this collection offers a good overview of why Roxanne is still considered one of the hardest female MCs from back in the day.

what to avoid: Shante's second record, *The Bitch Is Back* **woof!** (Cold Chillin', 1992, prod. Marley Marl, Kool G Rap, Large Professor, Grandmaster Flash), is a curiously toned-down version of the R-rated raps that made her such a hit in the first place. Shows what a little easy living and overproduction can do for you.

the rest:
Bad Sister 🎜🎜🎝 (Cold Chillin', 1989)
Def Mix #1 🎜🎜 (Cold Chillin', 1989)
Roxanne 🎜🎜🎝 (Columbia)

worth searching for: Shante and Rick James teamed up on the memorable #1 R&B hit, "Loosey's Rap" (Reprise, 1988).

influences:
◀◀ Betty Thomas, Millie Jackson, Marlena Shaw, Marley Marl

▶▶ The Real Roxanne, Yo Yo, Lil' Kim, Foxy Brown, Biz Markie

Eric Deggans

Shinehead (© Jack Vartoogian)

Sheila E.

Born Sheila Escovedo, December 17, 1957, in Oakland, CA.

A featured performer in father Pete Escovedo's renowned Latin-jazz band Azteca before she was old enough to drive, Sheila E. had a growing career as a percussionist/backing vocalist for stars such as Lionel Richie, Diana Ross, and George Duke before Prince "discovered" her in 1983. Amazingly, the funk pioneer—who also tapped her to play on albums by Apollonia 6 and the Time—had to talk Sheila E. into singing the duet "Erotic City" (she felt more comfortable in the background than in the limelight then). He also produced her solo debut the same year, building an album so grounded in his own sounds that Escovedo sounded like a guest star on her own record. Still, that album and her sophomore record both went gold, selling more than 500,000 copies each. But when she took control of her own sonic destiny in 1987, there wasn't much to replace his vision. A short stint as drummer for Prince's backing band during the late 1980s did little to establish her solo career, and when she finally released a solo album worthy of her talents in 1991,

persistent health problems kept her from promoting it to anyone who would care. She formed a jazz band called E-Train with fellow Prince alumnus Eric Leeds on sax in 1994, and also recorded and performed with a number of acts, including Gloria Estefan, Placido Domingo, Najee, and Carlene Carter.

what to buy: As a showcase for her full range of talent—songwriting, producing, playing, and singing—*Sex Cymbal* ♫♫♫♫ (Warner Bros., 1991, prod. Sheila E., Peter Michael Escovedo) stands as Sheila E.'s most arresting and underrated effort. Featuring thickly layered funk of "Loverboy," the title track's danceable pop, the slick ballad "Heaven," and various percussion jams, this record is her most complete individual statement as a solo artist.

what to buy next: Her solo debut *The Glamorous Life* ♫♫♫ (Warner Bros., 1984, prod. Sheila E., the Starr Company (a.k.a. Prince)) created the Prince-derived, bodacious babe-behind-the-timbales persona fans knew best, buoyed by the sax-laden dance groove of the title track.

what to avoid: Though it boasts a standout track in the ballad "Hold Me," the rest of *Sheila E.* **woof!** (Paisley Park, 1987, prod. Sheila E., David Z.) is lifeless, directionless filler.

the rest:

Romance 1600 ♪♪♪ (Paisley Park, 1985)

worth searching for: For evidence of her prowess behind a drum kit, check *16* ♪♪♪ (Warner Bros., 1996, prod. Prince), the powerhouse debut album by the jazz-fusion band Madhouse—created by Prince and also featuring backing players Levi Seacer Jr. and Eric Leeds.

influences:

◀◀ Prince, Santana, Tito Puente, Azteca

▶▶ Crystal Taliefero, Me'Shell Ndegeocello

Eric Deggans

Shep & the Limelites
See: The Heartbeats

Shinehead
Born Edmund Carl Aiken, April 10, 1962, in London, England.

Raised in both the center of reggae (Jamaica) and the birthplace of rap (the Bronx), it's no wonder Shinehead became one of the first artists to fuse the two genres. Less evident, though, is why he began remaking old pop, rock, and soul songs, although it's hard to quibble with most of the results. Still, hearing Boston's rock hit "More Than a Feeling" in a reggafied hip-hop context is a bit jarring.

what to buy: On his expertly produced major-label debut, *Unity* ♪♪♪♪ (Elektra, 1988, prod. Claude Evans, Jam Master Jay, Davy D.), the even-keeled toaster-of-the-town gets a little help from the Beatles, using "Come Together" as the foundation for the self-explanatory title track. Even better, though, is "Chain Gang (Rap)," a warm, funky, and funny update of the Sam Cooke song. And Shinehead gets topical, too, serving up a sort of dancehall "White Lines" for the hubba era with "Gimme No Crack."

the rest:

The Real Rock ♪♪♪ (Elektra, 1990)
Sidewalk University ♪♪ (Elektra, 1992)
Troddin' ♪♪ (Elektra, 1994)

influences:

◀◀ Don Baron, Asher D & Daddy Freddy

▶▶ Snow

Josh Freedom du Lac

The Shirelles
Formed 1957, in Passaic, NJ.

Shirley Owens (1957–75); Addie "Micki" Harris (died June 10, 1982); Doris Coley (1957–68, 1975–present); Beverly Lee.

One of the first and defining practitioners of the Girl Group sound, and one of the few who actually had a hand in writing their own material, the Shirelles were rarely out of the Top 10 between 1960 and 1963, and their songs and style had a major impact on the way pop and R&B sounded during the early 1960s. Originally formed as the Poquellos in high school, the quartet sang semi-professionally at dances and parties where one of their own compositions, "I Met Him on a Sunday," came to the attention of a fellow classmate named Mary Jane Greenberg, whose mother Florence ran a small record company out of her living room. Changing their name to the Shirelles, Florence released the song on her Tiara label, and it was so successful locally that Decca Records picked it up for national release during the summer of 1958. Shortly thereafter, Greenberg, now officially managing the group, formed a new label with writer/producer Luther Dixon called Scepter. They released a Shirelles version of the Five Royales' "Dedicated to the One I Love" but, lacking national distribution, the record stalled at #83 in mid-1959. A year later, however, the Owens/Dixon song "Tonight's the Night" became a Top 40 R&B and pop success, and the hits continued through 1961 with "Will You Still Love Me Tomorrow" (the first-ever Girl Group chart-topper), "Mama Said," and even a reissue of "Dedicated," which this time soared to #3. In 1962, both the Burt Bacharach-Hal David-composed "Baby It's You" and "Soldier Boy," the latter written in a matter of minutes by Greenberg and Dixon as mere album filler, continued the group's remarkable string of hits. But following Dixon's departure from Scepter in 1963, the group placed only one final release in the Top 20.

By now, however, their impact internationally was already being acknowledged (for example, the Beatles recorded *two* Shirelles songs on their first album), but competition at home increased dramatically as producers such as Phil Spector and Berry Gordy Jr. began flooding the charts with artists and records fashioned on the Shirelles' sound. A three-year legal dispute with Greenberg prevented the band from recording new material until 1967 (though Scepter continued to release old masters—with little success—during the interim) and the group, now reduced to a trio with the temporary departure of Coley, spent the majority of their time touring the rock 'n' roll revival circuit while recordings for Mercury, Bell, and RCA failed to chart. Following one such appearance in 1982, Harris died of heart failure, and it was not until a decade later that the group, after a prolonged court case, was awarded $1 million in royalties owed them and former Scepter label-mates Gene Pitney and B.J. Thomas. In 1994, the three surviving original Shirelles reunited for the first time in 19 years to perform at the Rhythm and Blues Foundation's Pioneer Awards show, and they were subsequently inducted into the Rock and Roll Hall of Fame in recognition not only of their ground-breaking initial successes, but for their decades spent on the road continuing to bring the sound they helped fashion to new generations of eager students and listeners the world over.

what to buy: Despite a dizzying array of greatest hits albums available, *Anthology, 1959–1964* ᴊᴊᴊᴊ (Rhino, 1986) contains all of the Shirelles' greatest recordings, many tastefully remixed into digital stereo for the first time from the original multi-track tapes.

what to buy next: With access to some of the greatest songwriters of the time (i.e. Goffin and King) and the winning combination of Owens' lead vocals and Dixon's arrangements and production, *Shirelles Sing to Trumpets and Strings* ᴊᴊᴊ (Scepter, 1961/Sundazed 1994, prod. Luther Dixon), *Baby It's You* ᴊᴊᴊᴊ (Scepter, 1962/Sundazed, 1993, prod. Luther Dixon), and *Foolish Little Girl* ᴊᴊᴊ (Scepter, 1963/Sundazed, 1994, prod. Luther Dixon) are surprisingly free of the clutter which padded most albums during the early 1960s.

what to avoid: The promisingly titled *Shirelles and King Curtis Give a Twist Party* ᴊᴊᴊ (Scepter, 1962/Sundazed, 1993, prod. Luther Dixon) contains only one real "duet" between the group and their sax player.

worth searching for: *The Shirelles* ᴊᴊᴊ (RCA Victor, 1972) is a more-than-competent return to form for the group, no doubt bolstered by the presence of strong material from Bill Withers, Marvin Gaye, and even the Bee Gees.

influences:

◀◀ The Chantels, the Five Royales

▶▶ The Crystals, Martha & the Vandellas, the Shangri-La's, Bananarama, Spice Girls

Gary Pig Gold

Showbiz & A.G.

Formed early 1990s, in Bronx, NY.

Andre the Giant/A.G., vocals; Showbiz/Show, DJ.

Showbiz & A.G. have come to define what *real* hip-hop is in the wake of gangsta permeation and G-funk excess. Hailing from the Patterson projects in the Boogie Down Bronx, the two met while working on Lord Finesse's debut. Showbiz's funkdafied, party-groove style is similar to that of his Diggin' in the Crates brethren Lord Finesse, Diamond D, and Buckwild, and his production talents have been featured on records by everyone from Finesse and Organized Konfusion to O.C. and KRS-One.

what to buy: *Can I Get a Soul Clap?* ᴊᴊᴊᴊ EP (London/Payday, 1992, prod. Showbiz, Diamond D) is one of the most auspicious debuts the hip-hop world has ever heard. A.G.'s no-frills lyricism is a perfect match for Show's horn-laced bass ditties, and the influential tracks "Soul Clap" and "Party Groove" are potent, uncut, street-level basement jams that universally rocked the hip-hop world. Both songs (plus others from the EP) are included on the full-length *Runaway Slave* ᴊᴊᴊᴊ (London/Payday, 1992, prod. Showbiz, Diamond D).

the rest:

Goodfellas: The Medicine ᴊᴊᴊ (Payday, 1995)

influences:

◀◀ Lord Finesse, Grandmaster Flash & the Furious Five, Nice & Smooth, Beatnuts

▶▶ O.C., Jeru, Fat Joe, Big L, Black Moon, Black Sheep

Jazzbo

The Showmen

Formed early 1960s, in Norfolk, VA. Disbanded 1967.

Norman Johnson; Leslie Fenton; Milton Wells; Dorsey Knight; Gene Knight; Danny Woods.

The Showmen had minimal impact on the charts of their time, but the group produced two songs of lasting impact: the rock 'n' roll anthem "It Will Stand" and "39-21-46," a minor 1967 hit that has become a standard on the Carolina beach-music scene. The group's lead singer, Norman Johnson, would add a General to his name and lead the Chairmen of the Board from 1969 to 1974, along with former Showmen member Danny Woods, Eddie Curtis from Lee Andrew's Hearts, and Harrison Kennedy from the Stone Soul Children. He also wrote such hits as "Patches" for Clarence Carter, "Wants Ads" for the Honey Cone, and Freda Payne's "Bring the Boys Home."

what's available: *It Will Stand* ᴊᴊᴊ (Collectables, 1994)—the Showmen came out of the doo-wop tradition, but with Johnson's raspy, pleading vocals up front, their records sometimes bore the stamp of gospel shouts. Minimally produced, with piano and horns way up in the mix, these aren't great records, but Johnson's singing style gives them a sense of urgency. This collection includes "39-21-46" (listed incorrectly as "39-21-40 Shape," though that's what Johnson actually sings in the song), two versions of "It Will Stand," and four other previously unissued recordings.

influences:

◀◀ The Four Tops, the Isley Brothers

▶▶ The Honey Cone, Freda Payne

see also: *The Chairmen of the Board*

Brian Mansfield

Shyheim

Born Shyheim Franklin, 1980, in Staten Island, NY.

Just past his 14th birthday when his first record dropped, young Shyheim burst out of the projects in Staten Island with a tough gangsta pose few MCs 10 years his senior could muster. Affiliated with the Wu-Tang Clan, a Staten Island group long obsessed with movies, Shyheim eventually revealed talents as an actor, turning a role as a street kid in rap trio TLC's video for "Waterfalls" into parts in Fred Williamson's *Original Gangstas* and Whitney Houston's mega-starring vehicle, *The Preacher's Wife*.

what to buy: High-pitch-voiced Shyheim pulled no punches on his first record, *a.k.a. the Rugged Child* ⚡⚡⚡ (Virgin, 1994, prod. RNS, Prince Rakeem), cutting up the competition with jeep-ready jams such as "On and On" and "Here Come the Hits."

what to avoid: Between-album success in Hollywood and a maturing voice (now a smooth-around-the-edges baritone) couldn't help Shyheim avoid the sophomore jinx with *The Lost Generation* ⚡⚡ (Virgin, 1996, prod. RNS, L.E.S., RZA, others), a disc as confused as its title might suggest. The Wu-Tang generation, however, should note that Wu headmaster RZA checks in on "Young Godz."

influences:

◀◀ Wu-Tang Clan, Mobb Deep, Da Youngsta's

▶▶ Pop the Brown Hornet

Eric Deggans

Silk

Formed early 1990s, in Atlanta, GA.

Timothy Cameron, vocals; Jimmy Gates, vocals; Gary "Big G" Glenn, vocals; Gary "Lil' G" Jenkins, vocals; Jonathan Rasboro, vocals.

The talented five-man vocal group, which was discovered in 1991 by Keith Sweat after he heard them perform at a local barbecue, was one of the first to capitalize on the swell of interest in R&B "guy" groups after Boyz II Men exploded onto the scene. Jimmy Gates and Jonathan Rasboro started Silk, but Sweat fired the first fifth band member and replaced him with Nashville native Gary Jenkins, who become the lead singer. Though they hit the big time with the single "Freak Me," the tune's sexually aggressive lyrics may have distracted the group's audience from their high level of talent. Fearful of remaining in Sweat's shadow, they severed creative ties with him for their second album, which explored a style of soul that was more grownup than that of their peers. But the well crafted work was lost in the crowd of harmonic groups emerging at the time.

what to buy: Their sophomore effort, *Silk* ⚡⚡⚡⚡ (Elektra, 1995, prod. various), is mature, racy, and exciting, with the group confidently tackling dreamy ballads as well as uptempo jams. No less than three of the members eagerly tackle complex lead vocals, putting them in the same talent plateau as Boyz II Men, minus the bubblegum.

the rest:

Lose Control ⚡⚡⚡ (Elektra, 1992)

influences:

◀◀ Boyz II Men, the O'Jays , New Edition

Franklin Paul

Joe Simon

Born September 2, 1943, in Simmesport, LA.

A little bit country and a little bit R&B, Joe Simon blended the two forms to create his own unique delivery that was soulful and down-home, but in a manner entirely different from the gritty soul styles being created in Memphis and Muscle Shoals. Simon moved from Louisiana to California during the late 1950s, performing first with a gospel group called the Goldentones, then going secular after Vee-Jay Records picked up his 1962 single, "My Adorable One." His country-R&B approach was unique, and by the late 1960s Simon was landing hits such as "Nine Pound Steel," "(You Keep Me) Hangin' On," and "The Chokin' Kind," which hit #1 on the R&B charts and was a Top 20 pop hit as well. During the early 1970s he worked with Kenny Gamble and Leon Huff in Philadelphia, then went to Nashville for his *Simon Country* album, which preceded his turn at disco. Simon recorded into the mid-1980s, but he's seldom heard from anymore, devoting most of his time to the church.

what to buy: *The Chokin' Kind: Golden Classics* ⚡⚡⚡⚡ (Collectables, 1993, prod. various) is Simon at his best, 14 songs that showcase his crucial 1960s output. *The Best of Joe Simon* 🎵🎵🎵 (Columbia Special Products, 1993, prod. various) is drawn from his later recordings for Spring Records, including his work with Gamble and Huff.

the rest:
Lookin' Back—The Best of Joe Simon 🎵🎵🎵 (Ripete, 1996)
Music in My Bones N/A (Rhino, 1997)

worth searching for: The import *Mood, Heart & Soul/Today* 🎵🎵🎵 (Polydor, 1974/Spring, 1976/Southbound, 1991) is a two-fer import that combines two of his adequate but unremarkable outings. Any copy of *Simon Country* 🎵🎵🎵 (Spring, 1974) is well worth hearing.

influences:
◀◀ Jerry Butler, Joe Tex, Big Joe Turner, Elvis Presley, Sam Cooke, Ray Charles

▶▶ Tyrone Davis, John Mellencamp

Gary Graff

Simply Red

Formed 1982, in Manchester, England.

Mick Hucknall, vocals; Sylvan Richardson, guitar (1985–89); Fritz McIntyre, keyboards; Tony Bowers, bass; Chris Joyce, drums; Tim Kellett, horns, keyboards; Aziz Ibrahim, guitar (1989–91); Ian Kirkham, sax (1989).

With its polished commercial soul sound and R&B riffs, Simply Red was a fresh-sounding new force when it landed in the U.S. during the 1980s. Lead singer and band leader Hucknall, who sang in punk bands during the late 1970s and early 1980s, was the key to this success, singing in a plaintive high tenor that evokes yearning and loss and has just enough texture to make it interesting. It continues to provide a good counter to the band's slick and slightly tame arrangements, which have worked for the occasional hit—"Holding Back the Years" in 1985 and its cover of Harold Melvin and the Blue Notes' "If You Don't Know Me by Now" four years later.

what to buy: *Picture Book* 🎵🎵🎵 (Elektra, 1985, prod. Stewart Levine), the band's debut, was a revelation that showcased Richardson's classical background and Hucknall's tremendously emotional singing. The result is Stax/Volt meets Philly soul and two of the year's best singles in "Holding Back the Years" and the group's rendition of "Money$ Too Tight to Mention." *Greatest Hits* 🎵🎵🎵 (EastWest America, 1996, prod. various) isn't quite as cohesive, but it has all the songs you should own.

what to buy next: After some middling releases in-between, *Stars* 🎵🎵🎵 (EastWest, 1991) is Simply Red's strongest album since its debut.

what to avoid: Coming after such a stellar debut, *Men & Women* 🎵🎵 (Elektra, 1987, prod. Alex Sadkin) is a significant sophomore slump—even though Hucknall had Motown great Lamont Dozier as a collaborator.

the rest:
A New Flame 🎵🎵🎵 (Elektra, 1989)
Life 🎵🎵🎵 (EastWest, 1995)

influences:
◀◀ Bobby Purify, Smokey Robinson, the Dells, Harold Melvin & the Blue Notes

▶▶ Lisa Stansfield, Rick Astley, the Commitments

Patrick McCarty

Sir Mix-a-Lot

Born Anthony Ray, August 12, 1963, in Seattle, WA.

Melding a salacious sense of humor with a serious mack daddy vibe, Sir Mix-a-Lot rode a fine line between old-school party records and the traditional rap game, lucking into a taste of pop success that would make him king of Seattle's often-ignored rap scene. Boasting a stage name that came from his days DJ'ing at dances in Seattle's Central District projects, Mix-a-Lot burst onto the national stage in 1985 with "Square Dance Rap." Fueled by a cover of Black Sabbath's "Iron Man" (recorded by Seattle thrash band Metal Church) and the memorable hit "Posse on Broadway," Mix-a-Lot's first album sold over 1 million copies and was followed by a Public Enemy-influenced sophomore album that went gold. Mix-a-Lot remained an artist better known for his music than his image, until the arrival of 1992's *Mack Daddy* and its tribute to women with large behinds, "Baby Got Back." Turned into a monster hit by constant MTV play, "Baby Got Back" became the second-largest selling single of the year, notching 2.5 million in sales even as critics accused the rapper of everything from misogyny to racism. The criticisms didn't stop Mix-a-Lot from accepting a Grammy for Best Rap Performance. A year later, he released an album that lacked *Mack Daddy*'s commercial potential and, by 1995, the rapper had accepted a starring role in the ill-fated UPN-TV show *The Watcher*. He eventually released another record that sank without a trace.

what to buy: It's not often that an artist's strongest creative work is also his best-selling stuff, but Mix-a-Lot's *Mack Daddy* 🎵🎵🎵

(Rhyme Cartel/Def American, 1992, prod. Sir Mix-a-Lot, Nate Fox, Strange) presents the best balance between the rapper's swaggering player persona and clownish side while also presenting the monster hit "Baby Got Back." But there's more here than tribute to oversize bottoms; check out the humor in "Swap Meet Louie" (while ignoring the politically incorrect jabs at Korean merchants) and the groove of "One Time's Got No Case."

what to buy next: Although the rapper hadn't yet refined his mix of hard-edged rhymes and bad-boy humor, *Swass* ♬♬♬ (Nastymix, 1987, prod. Sir Mix-a-Lot) is still a worthy find. The debut contains "Square Dance Rap" (perhaps the first hip-hop hoedown in history), as well as another honky-tonk slammer, "Buttermilk Biscuits (Keep on Square Dancin')." But it's actually "Posse on Broadway" that best represents the signature Mix-a-Lot sound. *Seminar* ♬♬♬ (Nastymix, 1989, prod. Sir Mix-a-Lot) features a hilarious commentary on the hip-hop nation's dependence on pagers ("Beepers"), as well as an ode to the ever-popular oversized ride ("My Hooptie").

the rest:
Chief Boot Knocka ♬♬♭ (Rhyme Cartel/American, 1994)
Return of the Bumpasaurus ♬♬♭ (Rhyme Cartel/American, 1996)

worth searching for: Mix-a-Lot brings the noise with another Seattle rock band, Mudhoney, on the powerhouse tune ""Freak Mama" from the soundtrack for the film *Judgment Night*. There's no place for grunge, though, on *Seattle. . .The Dark Side* ♬♬♭ (Rhyme Cartel/American, 1994, prod. various), a sampler that showcases some of Seattle's unsigned rap and R&B talent and also includes a Mix-a-Lot track that's unavailable elsewhere.

influences:
◄◄ 2 Live Crew, Slick Rick, Blowfly, Dolomite, Too $hort
►► Ant Banks, Geto Boys, Kid Sensation

Eric Deggans and Spence D.

Sister Sledge
Formed 1970, in Philadelphia, PA.

Joni Sledge, vocals; Kathie Sledge, vocals; Kim Sledge, vocals; Debra Sledge, vocals.

Much to the delight of their parents, who were both entertainers, and their grandmother, opera singer Viola Williams, the

Mick Hucknall of Simply Red (© Jack Vartoogian)

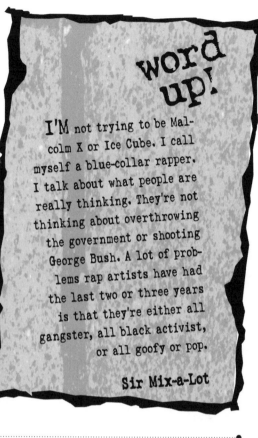

word up!

I'M not trying to be Malcolm X or Ice Cube. I call myself a blue-collar rapper. I talk about what people are really thinking. They're not thinking about overthrowing the government or shooting George Bush. A lot of problems rap artists have had the last two or three years is that they're either all gangster, all black activist, or all goofy or pop.

Sir Mix-a-Lot

Sledge sisters began singing together when they were children. The quartet often entertained friends and family at parties and in church under the name Mrs. Williams' Grandchildren. They were only teens when they recorded as Sister Sledge for the Philadelphia-based Money Back label in 1971. Their debut, appropriately titled *Time Will Tell*, was produced by Marty Bryant, who produced the Stylistics. After *Time Will Tell*, Sister Sledge sang back-up vocals for Kenneth Gamble and Leon Huff's productions, then signed with Atlantic in 1973. The records they made during the next five years weren't successful, but in 1979 they broke onto the charts, peaking at #3, with the gold *We Are Family* on the Cotillion label. The hit singles "He's the Greatest Dancer" and the album's title track both went to #1 on *Billboard* R&B charts; the latter became an anthem for the Pittsburgh Pirates during the 1979 World Series and for gay rights demonstrators who marched in Washington, D.C., that same year. Sister Sledge made *Love Somebody Today* in 1980 and began producing their own records in 1981, beginning with *All American Girls*. They entered the charts again in 1982 with a cover of Mary Wells's 1964 hit "My Guy." But after disco's decline during the 1980s, the group's popularity in the U.S. slipped considerably. But they had one major hit single in the U.K., "Frankie," in 1985. Kathy Sledge made a solo record in 1992, while avant-garde British punks the Fall made a predictably twisted cover version of Sister Sledge's "Lost in Music" in 1993.

what to buy: *The Best of Sister Sledge (1973–85)* 🎵🎵🎵🎵 (Rhino, 1992, prod. various) includes the hits and some remixes.

what to buy next: *We Are Family* 🎵🎵🎵🎵 (Cotillion, 1979/Rhino, 1995, prod. Bernard Edwards, Nile Rodgers) shows Sister Sledge at its peak, thanks to the Chic production team, which also played on the album and wrote the songs. There's also a guest appearance by Luther Vandross.

the rest:
Love Somebody Today 🎵🎵🎵 (Cotillion, 1980/Rhino)
All American Girls 🎵🎵🎵✧ (Cotillion, 1981/Rhino, 1995)

influences:
◀◀ Aretha Franklin, the Supremes, Martha & the Vandellas, the Shangri-La's, the Ronnettes
▶▶ TLC, SWV, the Braxtons, Spice Girls

Norene Cashen

Sister Souljah
Born Lisa Williamson.

This untalented rapper's claim to infamy came in 1992, when Bill Clinton was seeking to defeat George Bush for the presidency. Trying to distance himself from liberal power-broker Jesse Jackson—without alienating Jackson's widespread and loyal African American following—Clinton ripped on one of the speakers at Jackson's Rainbow Coalition conference. That speaker, Sister Souljah, had made a previous comment about killing white people to make up for years of black slavery and oppression. Souljah, an unofficial member of Public Enemy for exactly one album, had been a nobody before Clinton's speech; she became a trivia question afterwards. The strident, forceful speaker had actually been exaggerating—in fine rap style—to make her point about racism in the U.S. Unfortunately, she was a God-awful rapper and, despite an autobiography a few years after the election, faded quickly from public view.

what to avoid: It's unclear why any record company would have released Souljah's solo album, *360 Degrees of Power* **woof!** (Epic, 1992, prod. Street Element), which is nothing more than an endless stream of bland rhetoric above uninteresting beats and no funk at all. How Souljah earned the attention of Chuck D., and guest rapper Ice Cube, is beyond most hip-hop fans.

influences:
◀◀ Ice Cube, Public Enemy
▶▶ Nonchalant

Steve Knopper

Skee-Lo
Born Antoine Roundtree in Los Angeles, CA.

Self-parody isn't well-known territory for most Los Angeles rappers. But, then, this former regular of South Central's Good Life cafe shuns convention in more ways than one. Who else but Skee-Lo would dress the part of Forrest Gump in a video for his chart-topping single "I Wish"? Who else could earn a Grammy nomination while being such an outsider and upstart in the hip-hop establishment? A careful observer of Crenshaw Boulevard culture, Skee-Lo offers an anti-flossin' message with lyrics that shine a spotlight on the materialism that surrounds, tempts, and threatens to undo him and those he knows. Luckily, Skee-Lo's a stronger soul, reconciling his life as an endearing loser and fighting in his own small way against the tyranny of bullies and the cool crowd. Call it reality rap for the underdog.

what's available: *I Wish* 🎵🎵🎵✧ (Scotti Brothers, 1995, prod. various) debuted this comical and conversational storyteller to a national audience. A timely diversion from typically hardcore L.A. themes, Skee-Lo's radio hits "Top of the Stairs" and "I Wish" narrate a scrappy and humorous struggle into stardom—and the dramatically different life before. On the latter cut, Skee-Lo puts it best, lamenting: "Dag y'all! I never understood, black, why the jocks get the fly girls/And me, I get the hood rats."

influences:
◀◀ Ahmad, Pharcyde, Fresh Prince

Corey Takahashi

Skyy
See: Brass Construction

Slave
/Steve Arrington

Formed 1975, in Dayton, OH.

Steve Arrington, drums, vocals (1979–82); Steve Washington, trumpet (1975–79); Mark "The Hansolor" Adams, bass; Floyd Miller, vocals, horns; Danny Webster, vocals, guitar; Mike Williamson, vocals; Mark "Drac" Hicks, keyboards; Rodger Parker, drums.

Slave was one of the premier funk/disco bands to come out of the Midwest during the 1970s, only to be out-funked by Parliament-Funkadelic and the crossover king, Earth, Wind & Fire. Slave's 1977 debut went gold, thanks to the hit single "Slide," and also represents the outfit's commercial peak. Washington left the group to form Aurra in 1979, and Steve Arrington became Slave's lead singer on *Stone Jam*, keeping the group's profile high with hits such as "Watching You." Arrington left for a solo career of his own in 1982, carving out a niche for himself with Atlantic Records. He also worked with George Johnson of the Brothers Johnson during the early 1980s. Slave survived the loss of Arrington and other member changes, moving on to Atlantic for one record, then to Ichiban with modest success.

what to buy: *Stellar Fungk: the Best of Slave* 𝄞𝄞𝄞𝄞 (Rhino, 1994, prod. various) features Steve Arrington and Slave at their very best.

what to buy next: *Stone Jam* 𝄞𝄞𝄞𝄢 (Cotillion, 1980/Atlantic, 1996) includes Atlantic and Atco remasters of the original album plus three extra tracks: "Feel My Love," "Sizzlin' Hot," and "Watching You."

the rest:
Masters of the Fungk 𝄞𝄞𝄢 (Ichiban, 1996)

worth searching for: Arrington's solo albums are out of print. *Steve Arrington's Hall of Fame: I* 𝄞𝄞𝄞𝄞 (Atlantic, 1983) is his best known, most successful, and most interesting.

influences:
◀◀ George Clinton, Parliament-Funkadelic, Earth, Wind & Fire, Sly & the Family Stone, Kool & the Gang

▶▶ The Brothers Johnson, Prince

Norene Cashen

Percy Sledge

Born November 25, 1940, in Leighton, AL.

The diminutive former boxer with the huge voice will forever be remembered for his 1966 hit "When a Man Loves a Woman," a majestic ballad that still moves the soul, regardless of how many weddings you've heard it at. While Sledge never pretended to possess the up-tempo, bone-rattling excitement of more celebrated peers such as Otis Redding or Sam & Dave, he was virtually unchallenged when it came to ballads, heartbreakers in particular. Sledge hit the mark, and the charts, many times during the late 1960s with weepers marked by his warm, expressive vocal delivery.

what to buy: With 22 tracks, *It Tears Me Up: The Best of Percy Sledge* 𝄞𝄞𝄞𝄞 (Rhino, 1992, prod. Quin Ivy, Marlin Greene) offers the most comprehensive collection on the market, covering all his great tear-jerkers from 1966–71, including his carefully executed renditions of "The Dark End of the Street," "Love Me Tender," and "Try a Little Tenderness." Sledge, his timbre undiminished, returned after a 21-year absence with *Blue Night* 𝄞𝄞𝄞𝄞 (Pointblank, 1994, prod. Saul Davis, Barry Goldberg), which features top-notch material and help from old hands such as Steve Cropper, Bobby Womack, and former Rolling Stone Mick Taylor. Rising to the level of his surroundings, his performance is emotionally centered and nothing less than inspiring.

the rest:
The Best of Percy Sledge 𝄞𝄞𝄞 (Atlantic, 1969/1989)
The Ultimate Collection: When a Man Loves a Woman 𝄞𝄞𝄞 (Atlantic, 1987)
Greatest Hits: When a Man Loves a Woman 𝄞𝄞𝄢 (Hollywood/Rounder)
Best of 𝄞𝄞 (Curb, 1996)

influences:
◀◀ Sam Cooke, Dan Penn, Bobby Womack, the Chi-Lites

▶▶ Luther Vandross, Peabo Bryson

Allan Orski

Sleeping Bag/Fresh Records

Club-friendly New York indie label Sleeping Bag/Fresh didn't live to see hip-hop's big payday during the mid-1990s. Thus, much of its entertaining and innovative music has gone unsung. The label's debut in 1985 came at a transitional point in hip-hop, but luckily, the company had a versatile and prolific artist in the hugely talented Mantronix (a.k.a. Curtis Kahleel). Kahleel would go on to produce classic sides by Just Ice and T La Rock for the label, as well as Latin flavored dance hits by Nocera and Joyce Sims; the most important tracks—including Just Ice's "Cold Gettin' Dumb" and T La Rock's "Breakdown"—are included on *The Rap Pack* 𝄞𝄞𝄞𝄞 (Fresh, 1987, prod. various). But 1988 would be the label's biggest year, with significant releases in Just Ice's *Kool and Deadly* and Cash Money and Marvelous' *Where's the Party At?* The breakout success of EPMD's *Strictly Business* was an encouraging sign, too. *The Rap Pack II* ✍✍✍✍ (Fresh, 1988, prod. various) documents this amazing period, with added butters from Mantronix for good measure. Despite promising debuts from Stezo and Nice & Smooth and the release of EPMD's *Unfinished Business* the following year, though, the label soon closed its doors. If only it had made it to the 1990s, Sleeping Bag/Fresh would have received its share of critical accolades for a catalog that included some of hip-hop's most important artists.

Jeff "DJ Zen" Chang

Slick Rick

Born Ricky Walters, January 14, 1965, in London, England.

Slick Rick's place in the history of hip-hop was well established even before he had recorded any of his three solo albums. His songs with Doug E. Fresh, "La Di Da Di" and "The Show," were the type of irresistible throwdowns that made people fall in love with hip-hop and the art of the rhyme. Slick Rick was a master of narratives, and his storytelling abilities are legendary. His sleepy-voiced delivery and penchant for imitating characters in the middle of a rhyme or introducing musical quotes from such groups as the Beatles made him easily recognizable to any rap fan. His uniqueness was enhanced by the patch he wore around his eye, the $60,000 worth of gold jewelry around his neck, and the old-world gangster image he projected. Born in London and raised in the Bronx from the age of 12, Slick Rick became almost as infamous for his troubles outside of music. While driving with his pregnant girlfriend in July of 1990, Rick chased down and shot at Mark Plummer, his cousin and hired bodyguard. Rick missed, injuring a bystander in the ankle instead. Plummer had allegedly been extorting money from Rick and threatening his family. In fact, weeks earlier, Rick had been shot and injured himself in a club in the Bronx, so he viewed his actions as self-defense. But in June the following year, Rick was convicted of attempted murder in the second degree (a felony) and sentenced to 3 to 10 years in prison. (Plummer was eventually shot and killed.) After serving the minimum time in prison, the parole board pulled Rick from his work-release program and threatened to deport him back to the U.K., citing an unapologetic attitude on Rick's part. In early 1996, though, Rick was released. Ironically, one of Rick's best-known songs is 1988's "Children's Story," which details an incident that's eerily similar to the real-life one that would take place in 1990.

what to buy: Slick Rick's first album, *The Great Adventures of Slick Rick* ✍✍✍✍ (Def Jam/CBS, 1988, prod. Ricky Walters, Hank Shocklee, Eric Sadler, others) made Rick one of rap's first commercial stars. It also helped shore up his place as one of hip-hop's greatest storytellers, with "Treat Her Like a Prostitute," "Children's Story," and "The Moment I Feared" among the album's classic narratives.

the rest:
The Ruler's Back ✍✍✍ (Def Jam/Columbia, 1991)
Behind Bars ✍✍ (Def Jam, 1994)

influences:
◄◄ Spoonie Gee, Treacherous Three, Doug E. Fresh
►► Dana Dane, Special Ed, Snoop Doggy Dogg

Jazzbo

Sly & the Family Stone

Formed 1967, in San Francisco, CA.

Sly Stone (born Sylvester Stewart), keyboards, guitar, vocals; Freddie Stone, guitar, vocals; Larry Graham, bass, vocals (1967–72); Rosie Stone, keyboards, vocals; Greg Errico, drums (1967–72); Jerry Martini, saxophone; Cynthia Robinson, trumpet.

Sly Stone dragged black music into the modern era. He bridged the worlds of traditional R&B and the new 1960s rock sound with a dazzling amalgam of rock, soul, and gospel, and music was never the same again. By the time Sly and his Family Stone burst onto the radio with the 1968 hit, "Dance to the Music," the bandleader had already amassed an extraordinary background in music. His recording career dates back to a childhood 78 rpm gospel record he made with his family, the Stewart Family Four, and he notched a regional doo-wop hit before he was out of high school in Vallejo, California. As a disc jockey, he was the fastest talking, jivingest spieler on two Bay Area soul stations. As a house producer for San Francisco-based Autumn Records, he supervised hit records by Bobby Freeman ("C'mon and Swim"), the Beau Brummels ("Laugh Laugh"), and an assortment of lesser knowns like the Great Society, which featured a young, pre-Airplane Grace Slick. But with the Family Stone—the rich, throbbing thump-and-pluck bass of Larry Graham, colorful contrapuntal vocal harmonies, and sassy, brassy, downright uppity sloganeering songs—Sly led his band to the mountain of Woodstock and beyond before succumbing to massive drug abuse and titanic flights of ego. One of the most talented musicians to ever tackle the soul scene, Stone himself was reduced to a cocaine ravaged wraith, a fugitive from justice for several years during the late 1980s and into the 1990s. But his vast influence becomes only more pervasive as the years pass.

what to buy: The band's fourth album, *Stand!* 𝄢𝄢𝄢𝄢 (Epic, 1969, prod. Sly Stone) remains Stone's towering achievement, an album by turns militant ("Don't Call Me Nigger, Whitey"), paranoid ("Somebody's Watching You"), and inspirational ("Everyday People," "You Can Make It If You Try").

what to buy next: Although the band's record label has done an abysmal job of introducing the full body of work to the digital domain, the unheralded first three albums—*A Whole New Thing* 𝄢𝄢𝄢 (Epic, 1967, prod. Sly Stone), *Life* 𝄢𝄢𝄢 (Epic 1968), and *Dance to the Music* 𝄢𝄢𝄢 (Epic, 1968, prod. Sly Stone)— have been made available with previously unreleased bonus tracks. His epic, angry, and sarcastic masterpiece, *There's a Riot Goin' On* 𝄢𝄢𝄢𝄢 (Epic, 1971, prod. Sylvester Stewart), is a bitter, snarling diatribe that presaged his downfall.

the rest:
Greatest Hits 𝄢𝄢𝄢𝄢 (Epic 1970)
Anthology 𝄢𝄢𝄢𝄢 (Epic, 1981)

worth searching for: A collection of largely unreleased Autumn Records solo recordings and productions, *Precious Stone: In the Studio with Sly Stone 1963–1965* 𝄢𝄢𝄢 (Ace, 1994, prod. Sly Stone) was released in England, where his 1972 album, *Fresh* 𝄢𝄢𝄢𝄢 (Edsel, 1987, prod. Sly Stone), is also available. In used record stores, it is still possible to find the Billy Preston album, *The Wildest Organ in Town* 𝄢𝄢 (Capitol, 1966, prod. Steve Douglas), with Sly playing piano and the original version of what later became the Sly & the Family Stone standard, "I Want to Take You Higher."

influences:
◀◀ Otis Redding, Lenny Bruce, Swan Silvertones

▶▶ Temptations, Stevie Wonder, Miles Davis, Funkadelic, Prince, Red Hot Chili Peppers

Joel Selvin

Smif-N-Wessun /Da Cocoa Brovaz

Formed in Brooklyn, NY.

Tek, vocals; Steele, vocals.

The Bucktown duo was the second group to emerge from the Black Moon camp (collectively known as the Boot Camp Clik), and like their predecessors, Tek and Steele are solid practitioners of the laid-back, moody, hardcore style, serving slow and rugged rhymes over minimal, low-end grooves. As a result of pressure applied by the gun company of the same (albeit differently spelled) name, the two rappers have rechristened themselves Da Cocoa Brovaz—a name they'd used amongst themselves since their inception, anyway.

what to buy: The duo's debut, *Dah Shinin'* 𝄢𝄢𝄢𝄢 (Nervous/Wreck Records, 1995, prod. Da Beatminerz), is a masterwork of mellow madness, with Da Beatminerz taking the minimalistic rhythm foundation first explored by Black Moon to another level. Rumbling bass and tight snare workouts are the norm, and Da Beatminerz have dug up some seriously dusted grooves. The result is a brilliant balance of ghetto dub machinations and rugged funk that's hard around the edges but smooth in the middle. "Wrektime" is filled with nice scratch inserts, blurting horn cuts, and a loping bassline that shuffles endlessly underneath the duo's chocolate-y flow. The ominous "Wontime" rides a thundering bass and tight backbeat. "Sound Bwoy Bureill" is a sneaky, twisted rude-bwoy ragga blitz. And "Let's Git It On" features a thick bass lick and haunting tones. The album also contains Smif-N-Wessun's underground hit, "Bucktown," which, with its echoing horn loops, taut drum snaps, and compelling lyrical cadence, is a modern-day classic.

influences:
◀◀ Black Moon, EPMD, Gang Starr, Eric B. & Rakim

▶▶ Boot Camp Clik, Finsta & Bundy, Heltah Skeltah, O.G.C., Shades of Brooklyn

Spence D.

Bessie Smith

Born April 15, 1894, in Chattanooga, TN. Died September 26, 1937, in Clarksdale, MS.

After being unmarked for 30 years, Bessie Smith's grave now reads, "The Greatest Blues Singer in the World Will Never Stop Singing." That's due in part to Janis Joplin. And it's true. Though Smith has been dead well over 50 years, her legacy lives on in nearly every blues singer and song. Smith was the unparalleled blues artist of her time, and she well deserved the title "Empress of the Blues" not only for her vocal mastery, dancing, and acting, but for the tragedy that haunted her life from the very beginning: Her parents and two of her six brothers and sisters died before she was nine. By the age of 16, she hooked up with a vaudeville show and met her mentor and friend, Gertrude "Ma" Rainey, who may have had the greatest influence on introducing Smith to jazz and blues. Smith traveled the country performing at the turn of the century, eventually settling in New York in 1923 after marrying her second husband, Jack Gee. That same year, she recorded her greatest record ever: "Gulf Coast Blues," with Alberta Hunter's "Downhearted Blues" on the flipside. It sold 780,000 copies in six months and suddenly, Bessie Smith was a superstar. She began touring the country in a custom-designed railway car with a show called "Harlem Frolics," then another, "Mississippi Days." Her temper and carousing were legendary; she was known to drink excessively, carry on affairs with men and women, and nearly beat her husband's mistress to death. In his biography *Bessie,* Chris Albertson relates that Smith once singlehandedly chased off a horde of Ku Klux Klansmen before a show in North Carolina. During a career cut tragically short, she recorded 160 songs—all before the stock market crash completely eliminated Columbia Records' "race" records division—and performed with many of the greats of her time, like Louis Armstrong, Coleman Hawkins, James P. Johnson, and Charlie Green. Though she struggled with her career during the Great Depression, there was talk of a new recording contract, a Carnegie Hall show with John Hammond, and a movie, when an auto accident abruptly ended her life in 1937. Edward Albee's play *The Death of Bessie Smith* perpetuated the popular myth that Smith was denied treatment at a whites-only hospital and died by the time she could be taken to a facility that admitted blacks. That story may be just hyperbole. But Smith's injuries were grievous, and neither an arm amputation (after having it severed in the crash) nor a blood transfusion could save her. Nearly 10,000 people visited her casket prior to the most lavish and impressive funeral accorded any African American of her era. During her performing days, Bessie Smith had no competition, and because of that, her immense talent lives on in all those she has influenced. As her grave marker attests, she's singing still.

what to buy: Sony released the complete recordings of Bessie Smith, but five volumes over nine discs is a little daunting. For the blues traveler wanting just a sample of the ultimate female artist, *Bessie Smith—The Collection* ♪♪♪♪ (Sony, 1989, prod. John Hammond, Frank Walker) serves up 16 of her greatest tracks for a modest price. Not only is this disc the best introduction available to Smith's catalog, but it also features some of the most legendary blues and jazz musicians of the 1920s and 1930s, such as Benny Goodman, Coleman Hawkins, Charlie Dixon, Billy Taylor, and Buck Washington.

what to buy next: Should you decide you love blues in general and Bessie Smith in particular, take the plunge and drop the bucks—about double the cost of a single CD— for *The Complete Recordings, Vol.1* ♪♪♪♪ (Sony, 1991). This set collects all

of Smith's album tracks that were rereleased in the 1970s. A stunning collection, the first volume features Bessie's best-known number, "Tain't Nobody's Bizness If I Do," with which she was tearing up blues joints 20 years before Billie Holiday, and gives a more complete aural portrait of Bessie than *Collection. The Complete Recordings, Vol.2* ♪♪♪♪ (Sony, 1991) is a hot mix of middle-career Bessie, especially her collaborations with Louis Armstrong. Smith belts her vocals so powerfully that she overcomes the pitfalls of the grainy, primitive recording technology of the era. This collection spotlights nine songs with Armstrong, including "St. Louis Blues" and "I Ain't Goin' to Play Second Fiddle."

the rest:
Empty Bed Blues ♪♪♪♪ (ASV/Living Era, 1971)
1925–33 ♪♪♪♪ (Nimbus, 1987)
Sings the Jazz ♪♪♪♪♪ (EPM/Jazz Archives, 1991)
The Complete Recordings, vol.3 ♪♪♪♪♪ (Sony, 1992)
The Complete Recordings, vol.4 ♪♪♪♪♪ (Sony, 1993)
Bessie's Blues ♪♪♪♪ (Hallmark, 1993)
The Complete Recordings, vol.5 ♪♪♪♪ (Sony, 1994)
1923 ♪♪♪♪ (Jazz Chronological Classics, 1994)
1923–24 ♪♪♪♪ (Jazz Chronological Classics, 1994)
1923–25 ♪♪♪♪ (Jazz Chronological Classics, 1994)
1923–27 ♪♪♪♪ (Jazz Chronological Classics, 1994)
1923–28 ♪♪♪♪ (Jazz Chronological Classics, 1994)
1923–29 ♪♪♪♪ (Jazz Chronological Classics, 1994)
1923–33 ♪♪♪♪ (Jazz Chronological Classics, 1994)
Mama's Got the Blues ♪♪♪♪♪ (Topaz Jazz, 1994)
Blue Spirit Blues ♪♪♪♪ (Drive)
Sings the Blues ♪♪♪♪♪ (Sony, 1996)

worth searching for: Named for the title bestowed upon Bessie as unchallenged queen of the blues world for 20 years, *Empress of the Blues* ♪♪♪♪ (Collector's Edition/Charly, 1971/1992) is a worthy disc now available on CD that offers sublime recordings of Smith's choicest works.

influences:

◀◀ Blind Lemon Jefferson, Alberta Hunter, Ma Rainey

▶▶ Billie Holiday, Ida Cox, Dinah Washington, Janis Joplin, Aretha Franklin, Ethel Waters, Carmen McRae, Sarah Vaughan, Koko Taylor

Chris Tower

Huey "Piano" Smith

Born October 10, 1924, in New Orleans, LA.

Huey "Piano" Smith's best records were group-sung nonsense songs that sounded as if they were recorded at a New Orleans rent party. Smith's first hit, the oft-covered "Rockin' Pneumonia and the Boogie Woogie Flu" in 1957, showcases all the best elements of his sound: a loping second-line rhythm, half-chanted vocals, good-humored funny lyrics, and a superb rolling piano. Before Smith began his solo career, he played in Lloyd Price's and Earl King's road bands, and worked on recording sessions for such notables as Smiley Lewis and Little Richard (who can only play in one key). In 1955, Smith played piano on one of Ace Records' first hits, Earl King's "Those Lonely Lonely Nights." Various incarnations of Smith's band, the Clowns, featured some of the best musicians (Lee Allen, Alvin Tyler, Robert Parker, Mac Rebennack/Dr. John) in the New Orleans area. Smith supplemented his erratic singing with a series of vocalists (the great Bobby Marchan, Bobby Roosevelt, Gerry Hall, Eugene Francis, Junior Gordon, and Roland Cook, among others), and they gave his records a sense of good-humored variety. After "Rockin' Pneumonia" in 1957, Smith and the Clowns hit the pop Top 10 in 1958 with the two-sided smash "Don't You Just Know It" b/w "High Blood Pressure." Their follow-up, "Don't You Know Yockomo," was every bit as entertaining and danceable, but a lesser hit. (Perhaps it was too funny.) Smith wrote inventive lyrics, but he continually reprised his musical arrangements from his big hits. On LP, this method is a bit tedious, but in the days of the 45 rpm single, this repetition just seemed like a periodic continuation of the last recorded party. When he wasn't touring, Smith and his band did session work behind Jimmy Clanton and Frankie Ford (whose hits "Sea Cruise" and "Roberta" were actually Huey Smith tracks with Smith's vocals erased). During the late 1960s, Smith tried to retool his sound for the soul generation, and he recorded for a variety of labels under the names Shindig Smith & the Soul Shakers, the Pitter Pats, and the Hueys. Smith's last chart entry was "Coo Coo Over You" for the Cotillion label in 1968. During the 1970s, Smith became a Jehovah's Witness, and he seldom plays music anymore. Don't you just know it?

what to buy: *Rock 'n' Roll Revival* 🎵🎵🎵🎵 (Ace, 1991, prod. Johnny Vincent) has all the big hits ("Rockin' Pneumonia," "High Blood Pressure," "Don't You Just Know It") and others, plus two previously unreleased tracks. Frankie Ford and Bobby Marchan guest.

what to buy next: *Good Ole Rock 'n' Roll* 🎵🎵🎵🎵 (Ace, 1991, prod. Johnny Vincent) contains 16 non-hit tracks, showcasing some fine New Orleans-style party music including "Educated Fool," "Won't You Turn Me On," and "At the Mardi Gras."

what to avoid: *Huey "Piano" Smith & Friends* 🎵🎵 (Charly, 1987, prod. various) features several 1960s soul-style remakes of

Smith's hits from the 1950s for Joe Banashak's Cotillion label. The original recordings are still the best.

the rest:
Pitta Pattin' 🎵🎵🎵 (Charly, 1988)
Snag-A-Tooth Jeannie 🎵🎵🎵 (Night Train, 1996)

worth searching for: *Serious Clownin'—The Best of Huey Piano Smith* 🎵🎵🎵🎵 (Rhino, 1989, prod. Johnny Vincent) is a 14-track compilation of quality. It's out of print, but some stores still have it on their stock lists if you prefer vinyl.

influences:
◀◀ Earl King, Professor Longhair
▶▶ Frankie Ford, Bobby Marchan, Dr. John

Ken Burke

Smoothe Da Hustler

Smoothe Da Hustler represents the rough-n-tumble Brownsville area of Brooklyn and, like his contemporaries M.O.P., uses a ruff, rugged, and extremely raw rhyme style that reflects the toughness of the hard-rock neighborhood.

what's available: Smoothe's gruff, gravely growl dominates *Once Upon a Time in America* 🎵🎵🎵 (Profile, 1996, prod. various), spiking the smoothed-out soul- and funk-tinged tracks with hard-hitting lyrics of fury. Rapping about survival of the fittest on the mean streets of Brooklyn, Smoothe attacks a musical foundation that ranges from the dark, psych-out funk of "Dollar Bill" and the bare-boned hardcore crunch of "Broken Language" to the melodious, laid-back, (Stevie) Wonderful groove of "Only Human."

influences:
◀◀ M.O.P., Nine
▶▶ Trigger Tha Gambler

Spence D.

Snoop Doggy Dogg
Born Calvin Broadus, October 20, 1972, in Long Beach, CA.

"What's my name?" So asked Snoop Doggy Dogg on "Who Am I (What's My Name)?" the first single from his first album, *Doggystyle*. Of course, all of America already knew the answer to the rhetorical question long before they'd even heard the soon-to-be-gold single. Indeed, Snoop had earned the biggest buzz for a new artist in rap history by stealing the vocal show on

snoop doggy dogg

mentor Dr. Dre's smash album, *The Chronic*, and, also, by running into trouble with the law by getting arrested in connection with the murder of an alleged Los Angeles gang member, who was shot by Snoop's bodyguard. The murder indictment, coupled with lyrics on Dre's album that touched on themes of gang violence, immediately made the tall, lanky, charismatic kid from Long Beach with the disarming sing-song drawl the poster boy for the troubled-rap-artist movement. As such, well before the release of *Doggystyle*, Snoop had already appeared on the covers of *Rolling Stone, Vibe,* and even *Newsweek*. It came as no surprise, then, when Snoop's controversial debut entered the charts at #1, selling nearly a million copies alone in its first week of release. Recorded for Death Row Records, the dominant gangsta-rap label from *The Chronic* on, the album is the fastest-selling debut in pop history. Snoop, though, was eventually pushed out of the spotlight some by his embattled, ever-controversial friend 2Pac, who perpetually made headlines for all the wrong reasons on his way to becoming the best-selling artist not just on Death Row, but in gangsta rap, period. But when 2Pac and his rival East Coast counterpart, the Notorious B.I.G., were murdered within about six months of each other, Snoop regained his status as the living leader of the troubled gangsta pack, even if his sophomore album, *Tha Doggfather*, both suffered without the helping hand of Dre and presented a kinder, gentler Snoop, who was apparently affected by fatherhood and an acquittal on the murder charges.

what to buy: On *Doggystyle* ♫♫♫♫ (Death Row/Interscope, 1993, prod. Dr. Dre), Snoop presents himself as rap's most loveable gangsta, inviting you into his world with a warm, un-threatening delivery that's nothing short of mesmerizing and offering occasionally riotous (albeit largely offensive) lyrics over the masterfully funky production work of Dr. Dre. Although Snoop raps early and often about the harsher side of hood life (the eerily prescient "Murder Was the Case," "Serial Killa," "Pump Pump"), he also enjoys throwing a good Dogg-house party, taking you on a retro tour of his "Doggy Dogg World" on a song that reintroduced the soul-singing Dramatics to the world, or just rapping about pot and his favorite beverage, "Gin and Juice," on a smash hit that popularized the drink just as the Beastie Boys' "Brass Monkey" had done to that obscure concoction several years earlier. For good offensive measure, Snoop and the then-unheard of Dogg Pound attempt to both shack and offend as many women as possible with their nasty, X-rated posse cut, "Ain't No Fun (If the Homies Can't Have None)."

what to avoid: Although lyrically unfocused and thematically unclear (a cover of Biz Markie's "Vapors"?!?!), *Tha Doggfather* ♫♫ (Death Row/Interscope, 1996, prod. DJ Pooh, Dat Nigga Daz, others) disappoints most with its wholly average production. It's obvious the Dr. (Dre, that is) was out during the recording of this record. Thankfully, Snoop and Dre are expected to reunite for a 1998 album with the working title *Break Up to Make Up*.

the rest:

Dogggumentary N/A (Death Row/Interscope EP, 1997)

worth searching for: Dr. Dre's masterful *Chronic* album may be the recording that turned most of America on to Snoop's mysterious persona and compelling sing-song drawl, but the rapper actually first made noise in the hip-hop world with another Dre duet, "Deep Cover" (Solar, 1992).

influences:

◀◀ Dr. Dre, Rakim, Biz Markie, Slick Rick, MC Eiht

▶▶ Tha Dogg Pound, Illegal, Warren G

Josh Freedom du Lac

Snow

Born Darrin O'Brien, October 30, 1969, in North York, Toronto, ON, Canada.

Can a white man toast the dancehall? Sure. Can he be credible? Depends on who you ask—and when you ask it. Much like the white rap group 3rd Bass, the white dancehall rapper Snow garnered much attention for his music . . . before people figured out he wasn't actually black. The lyrically indecipherable but catchy-as-all-hell "Informer" had butts shaking from coast to coast, for sure, but when the song's video began appearing on MTV, suddenly, people weren't so sure they liked this skinny, snow-white Canadian kid anymore. No Vanilla Ice he, though—Snow actually had talent.

what to buy: Mixing jazz samples and hip-hop with Jamaican dub and reggae rhythms and inflections, Snow sets himself apart from his contemporaries with his diversity on *12 Inches of Snow* ♫♫♫♪ (EastWest America, 1993, prod. M.C. Shan, others). The debut includes the essential hit, "Informer," which still doesn't sound dated. That's no small feat.

what to buy next: Two years and one big skin-color-controversy later, Snow issued *Murder Love* ♫♫♫ (EastWest American, 1995, prod. M.C. Shan, Junior Reid, Hurby "Luv Bug" Azor, others), an

Snoop Doggy Dogg (© Ken Settle)

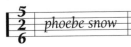

album highlighted by a duet with reggae's Junior Reid and Nin-jaman ("Si Wi Dem Nuh Know We"). About that credibility: The album was recorded at the Mixing Lab in Jamaica.

the rest:
Justuss 𝄞𝄞𝄞 (EastWest American, 1997)

influences:
◀◀ Shinehead, Don Baron

                                        Christina Fuoco

Phoebe Snow

Born July 17, 1952, in New York, NY.

The purity of Phoebe Snow's instrument has always been dis-arming. A rich contralto with versatility of nearly limitless pro-portions, she has never been properly established as the major talent she is. The problem has always been where and how to house her fluid chops. Similarly, poor production, nasty label relations, and her own decision (albeit admirable) to provide home-care for her autistic daughter have seriously hampered her commercial viability. From her jazzy-folk beginnings in the 1970s all the way up to her solid return in 1989, Snow has been an undeniable talent, in search of worthy surroundings. She is currently without a record deal.

what to buy: *Phoebe Snow* 𝄞𝄞𝄞𝄞 (Shelter–A&M, 1974/Right Stuff, 1995, prod. Dino Airali) is an auspicious coffeehouse folk debut which reveals an emotional assuredness underneath her considerable vocal range. It contains her biggest hit, "Poetry Man," as well as the gutsy "Harpo's Blues" and an interesting cover of Sam Cooke's "Good Times."

what to buy next: Snow's emotional urgency on the title track alone makes *Something Real* 𝄞𝄞𝄞 (Elektra, 1989, prod. Rob Fraboni, Ricky Fataar) cost-effective. Overall, the album's tone is surprisingly relaxed, given that this was her first recording in eight years. Elektra apparently expected desperation and dropped her quick.

what to avoid: Snow is clearly not a singles-churning hit ma-chine, making brief best of's such as *The Best of Phoebe Snow* 𝄞𝄞𝄞 (Columbia, 1981, prod. Phil Ramone) a bit short-sighted and unrevealing.

the rest:
Second Childhood 𝄞𝄞𝄞 (Columbia, 1976/1988)
It Looks Like Snow 𝄞𝄞𝄞 (Columbia, 1976/1989)
Never Letting Go 𝄞𝄞𝄞 (Columbia, 1977/1990)

worth searching for: *Against the Grain* 𝄞𝄞𝄞 (Columbia, 1978) is a bit slick, but has a good version of Paul McCartney's "Every

Night." On *Rock Away* 𝄞𝄞𝄞 (Mirage/Atlantic, 1981), Snow tries her hand at rock, covering everything from Rod Stewart's "Gasoline Alley" to Bob Dylan's "I Believe in You."

influences:
◀◀ Sarah Vaughan, Bob Dylan, Paul Simon, Joan Baez, Judy Collins, Joni Mitchell

▶▶ Dionne Farris, Tracy Chapman

                                        Allan Orski

Solar Records

In 1977, disco ruled R&B's roost, and bands had a significant place alongside singers for the first time since doo-wop's golden age of the late 1950s. Enter Solar—the Sound of Los Angeles Records. Established by industry vet Dick Griffey, Solar was big on groove but also valued acts (including an unusually high number of ensembles) that could write well and present them-selves well on stage. Griffey assembled a formidable lineup— the Whispers, Midnight Star, Lakeside, Shalamar, Klymaxx, the Deele—that became an Old School source for myriad hip-hop-pers during the late 1980s and 1990s. At the time of its 20th an-niversary, Solar was embarking on an ambitious celebration, re-releasing many of its original albums along with a box set of the label's hits and anthologies from several of its acts.

                                        Gary Graff

Solo

Formed 1994, in New York, NY.

Darnell Chavis, vocals; Eunique Mack, vocals; Daniele Stokes, vocals; Robert Anderson, acoustic bass.

The label New Classic Soul may be the creation of some record company employee, but it really does sum up the vibe of Solo—a thoroughly current sound with clearly traced lines to doo-wop and soul music roots. The group was formed in stages: first Eunique Mack and Darnell Chavis hitchhiked from Hollywood to New York, where they met Daniele Stokes. Then the trio performed on street corners and in the Manhattan sub-ways, adding bassist Robert Anderson. By coincidence, produc-ers Jimmy "Jam" Harris III and Terry Lewis heard them doo-wop-ping on different street corners in the same day and eventually signed them. The group distinguishes itself by bringing to its music the same energy and dynamic, harmonic voices they used to turn heads on the city streets. Further, led by Mack's husky tenor (which is strikingly similar to that of Sam Cooke), the group sounds just as comfortable singing a hip-hop tune as they do remaking the Drifters' "Under the Boardwalk."

what's available: These guys know they sound like the O'Jays, the Temptations, and other classic artists, and that's what makes *Solo* ✍✍✍ (Perspective/A&M, 1995, prod. various) so great—they dare walk on sacred ground, and they do it with reverence and impressive quality. Is this what the mighty Temptations would sound like in the 1990s? Quite possibly.

influences:

◀◀ Sam Cooke, Otis Redding, the Temptations, the O'Jays

Franklin Paul

Son of Bazerk

Back at the beginning of the decade, when video shows like *Pump It Up!* ruled the airwaves, Son of Bazerk somehow made sense. Combining the funk of a '50s doo-wop group with the sonic-boom production talents of the Bomb Squad (the crew responsible for the noisy, layered sound of Public Enemy's records), Son of Bazerk and his friends, No Self Control and the Band, weren't so much a hip-hop group as they were a raucous attempt at recreating the James Brown style for modern times. In fact, it wasn't only samples they borrowed from the Godfather, but also his catch-phrases, the look of his old bands, and even one of his old album covers. As hip-hop evolved out of its James Brown and Parliament-Funkadelic stage, though, so did it outgrow the quirky, but dated, sound of Son of Bazerk.

what's available: The group's only album, *Son of Bazerk Featuring No Self Control and the Band* ✍✍ (MCA, 1991, prod. the Bomb Squad), has all the elements of its time: James Brown's style, the Public Enemy sound (they shared producers, plus DJ Terminator X), and the whimsy of artists like Chubb Rock and the Beastie Boys. Ultimately, though, songs like "Change the Style" and "What Could Be Better Bitch" had as much lasting power as the Afros. Right: *Who?*

influences:

◀◀ James Brown, Public Enemy, Digital Underground

▶▶ Afros

Jazzbo

The S.O.S. Band

Formed 1977, in Atlanta, GA.

Mary Davis, lead vocals, keyboards (1977–86, 1995–present); Jason "T.C." Bryant, keyboards; Billy R. Ellis, saxophone (1977–89); James Earl Jones III, drums (1977–82); Willie "Sonny" Killebrew, saxophone, flute (1977–86); John Simpson, bass (1977–89, 1991–present); Bruno Speight, guitar; Abdul Ra'oof, trumpet, vocals (1981–present); Fredi Grace, backing vocals (1981–90); Jerome "J.T." Thomas, drums (1982–89); Marcus Williams, drums (1989–present); Penny Ford, lead vocals, (1987–89); Chandra Currelly, lead vocals (1989–95); Kurt Williams, bass (1989–91).

Credited with inspiring artists ranging from Janet Jackson to Maxwell, the S.O.S. Band remains one of the most underrated and underappreciated R&B acts around. Originally christened the Sounds of Santa Monica while performing in Atlanta-area clubs, the band's name was changed by Tabu Records head Clarence Avant once he signed them to his label (S.O.S. stands for Sounds of Success). It made a quick mark with the R&B hit "Take Your Time (Do It Right), Part 1," which first offered the band's sprawling trademark sound—funky synthesized bass line, percolating percussion, and Davis' powerful, soul-drenched vocals. Though their next few albums failed to catch fire, by 1982 they had teamed with Time members Jimmy Jam and Terry Lewis (the two were fired from the band by Prince when they missed a tour date while producing S.O.S.' fourth album). Helped by Jam and Lewis, the band's 1983 single "Just Be Good to Me" reestablished the group's hold on the R&B and pop charts—a grip solidified by the 1984 single "Just the Way You Like It" and 1986's "The Finest." But the rise in rap and hip-hop sounds—combined with Jam and Lewis' commitment to the Janet Jackson whirlwind—led to tough times for the band by the mid-1980s. Davis decided to go solo in 1987, and the band floundered as it searched for a replacement. Penny Ford held down the job for a few years before leaving to join Snap, and Chandra Currelly took over. Interest in the band—always better known for its songs than its image, even among R&B fans—waned in America, forcing S.O.S. to work more in Europe and Japan. By 1995, Davis had reunited with S.O.S., but, lacking a stateside record deal, it's tough to gauge whether anyone cared.

what to buy: Expert at creating shimmering, post-disco R&B singles, the S.O.S. Band had trouble stretching that quality into a consistent album. That's why a new fan might be best served by the greatest hits collection *The Best of the S.O.S. Band* ✍✍✍ (Tabu, 1995, prod. various), which strings together classic singles such as "Just Be Good to Me" and "Just the Way You Like It" without any of the horrible filler.

what to buy next: If you insist on buying another S.O.S. record, *Sands of Time* ✍✍✍ (Tabu, 1986, prod. James "Jimmy

Jam" Harris III, Terry Lewis) is the record in which Jam and Lewis finally nailed the production formula they would eventually put to work for everyone from Cherelle and Alexander O'Neal to the Human League. From shimmering singles such as "The Finest" to sultry ballads such as "Borrowed Love," the production is glossy and Davis' vocals shine like they never have before. *Just the Way You Like It* ♪♪♪ (Tabu, 1984, prod. James "Jimmy Jam" Harris III, Terry Lewis) offers less production mastery but stronger songs, including the breezy "Weekend Girl," "No One's Gonna Love You," and the grooving title track.

what to avoid: One listen to the pedestrian grooves and predictable melodies clogging the group's sophomore record *Too woof!* (Tabu, 1981, prod. Sigidi Abdallah) and it's obvious how much Jam and Lewis brought to the group's sound a few years later—and easy to see why the charts pretty much ignored this one.

the rest:
The S.O.S. Band ♪♪♥ (Tabu, 1980)
On the Rise ♪♪♪ (Tabu, 1983)
Diamonds in the Raw ♪♪ (Tabu, 1987)
The Way You Like It ♪♪♪ (CBS Special Products, 1988)
One of Many Nights ♪♪ (A&M, 1991)

worth searching for: The S.O.S. Band contributes backing for former Temptations lead singer Eddie Kendrick on his solo record *I Got My Eyes on You* (Ms Dixie, 1983), which offers some exciting soul cuts powered by a legendary voice.

influences:
◀◀ Earth, Wind & Fire, Con Funk Shun, Fatback, Frankie Beverly & Maze

▶▶ Maxwell, Cherelle, Lisa Keith, En Vogue

Eric Deggans

Soul Stirrers

Formed 1926, in Trinity, TX. Disbanded early 1970s.

Robert H. Harris, lead vocals (1937–50); Sam Cooke, lead vocals (1950–57); Jesse J. Farley, bass; S.R. Crain, first tenor; R.B. Robinson, baritone; Paul Foster, second tenor (1949–63); T.L. Brewster; Julian Cheeks; Johnnie Taylor; Willie Rogers; Martin Jacox; Richard Miles; Jimmy Outler.

As one of the longest standing and certainly most successful gospel vocal groups in history, the Soul Stirrers will most likely be remembered as the vehicle that gave Sam Cooke his thrust into the world's spotlight. However, it was an unequaled force long before Cooke joined ranks. The Stirrers were akin to all their peers, beginning as a traditional quartet. But the addition of a fifth member, Harris in 1937, changed the gospel format forever. Harris further pushed the Stirrers to the top of the national circuit during the mid-1940s by splitting from the jubilee tradition into modern gospel while simultaneously introducing a second lead voice to the mix, an unprecedented move. By the time of his departure in 1950, his powerful voice and phrasing, both sweet and coarse, was to be a telling influence on the young Cooke, whose initial style bore more than a passing resemblance to Harris. With Cooke, life became as wild and frenzied as church singing gets, for the Stirrers not only had national admiration but also thousands of fawning young ladies eager to clutch the hem of the handsome singer's garment. Besides pre-dating the Beatles hysteria, the 19-year-old was shedding his Harris influence like dry skin, emitting a nuanced tenor the likes of which no congregation had ever heard. Sensing the steeple could scarcely contain his potential, he slowly pulled the Stirrers towards the secular world. The group's unwillingness to crossover resulted in his departure from the group and into pop history in 1956. A flurry of lead men—including Johnnie Taylor, Willie Rogers, Martin Jacox, and Richard Miles—were able to carry the group onward. With Taylor, the Stirrers were one of the first acts signed to Cooke's fledgling SAR label (designed specifically for gospel). Perhaps because of the precarious balance between secular and gospel material, the Stirrers stopped recording during the early 1970s.

what to buy: For those who doubt that Cooke's gospel singing was any less exciting than his pop breakthroughs, *Sam Cooke with the Soul Stirrers* ♪♪♪♪ (Specialty, 1991) presents a compelling argument. One only needs to hear him forming his trademark yodel and precise rhythmic phrasing in front of a suitably spartan accompaniment to realize that, if anything, the reverse is true. *Legends of Gospel Series: Shine on Me* ♪♪♪♪ (Specialty, 1992) features the mighty Harris in all his sweeping glory as the group's pre-Cooke rise to national prominence took hold. This was the first time in gospel a lead sang in front of a four-part harmony.

what to buy next: *Heaven Is My Home* ♪♪♪♪ (Specialty, 1993) compiles the best of the post-Cooke years with the able Johnny Taylor at the helm. There's plenty of alternate takes here to satisfy the insatiable gospel completist in all of us.

what to avoid: Of the various compilations available, *Heritage Vol. 1* ♪♪ (Jewel, 1996) and *Heritage Vol. 2* ♪♪ (Jewel, 1996) are both too skimpy to be bothered with.

the rest:

Jesus Gave Me Water ♪♪♪ (Specialty, 1992)

When the Saints Go Marching In ♪♪♪ (MCA, 1993)

The Last Mile of the Way ♪♪♪ (Specialty, 1994)

Strength, Power and Love ♪♪ (Jewel, 1996)

influences:

◀◀ The Pilgrim Travellers, the Highway QCs

▶▶ Sam Cooke, Johnny Taylor, Sounds of Blackness, the Four Tops, the Temptations, the O'Jays

Allan Orski

The Soul Survivors

Formed 1966, in New York, NY. Disbanded 1970. Re-united 1974.

Kenneth Jeremiah, vocals; Richard Ingui, vocals; Charles Ingui, vocals; Paul Venturini, organ; Edward Leonetti, guitar; Joey Forigone, drums.

The Soul Survivors had only one hit, but it was a big one. In 1967, "Expressway to Your Heart" reached the Top 5 on both the pop and R&B charts. Unfortunately, the lone in-print album, *When the Whistle Blows Anything Goes* ♪ (Collectables, 1993), points to the weaknesses of the group; the Soul Survivors couldn't write and, except for the one hit, made poor song selections. Better to find "Expressway" on a good oldies collection.

Patrick McCarty

Soul II Soul

Formed 1982, in London, England.

Jazzie B (born Beresford Romeo), producer, vocals; Nellee Hooper, producer, arranger (1985–91).

Soul II Soul started out as a traveling sound-system, modeled after the mobile dub crews of the Caribbean. After years of supplying DJs and equipment to warehouse parties around England on a freelance basis, the collective started organizing its own events. Things took off for the group after Nellee Hooper, a member of Bristol's Massive Attack, joined the fold in 1985. After securing a residency at the Africa Centre in Covent Garden, the group started making its own demos, which attracted the attention of Virgin. Releasing a pair of singles ("Fairplay," "Feel Free") with modest success in 1988, Soul II Soul struck paydirt with "Keep On Movin'," a song that featured the band's trademark sound in full—lush strings, soaring vocals, and an inescapable rhythm. The group's debut album *Club Classics Vol I* went platinum shortly thereafter, and Hooper and Jazzie B became coveted producers, scoring their biggest success arranging Sinead O'Connor's "Nothing Compares 2 U" in 1990. Soul II Soul became one of the most influential dance acts on Britain's early 1990s scene. The band released its second album, *Vol II: 1990—A New Decade*, to much critical and commercial acclaim, but started to disintegrate shortly thereafter. Hooper, arguably the most talented member of the collective, returned to his Massive Attack duties, while Jazzie B pressed forth with a pair of dismal follow-up albums (*Volume III: Just Right* and *Volume V: Believe*). The group was abruptly dropped by Virgin in 1995, closing the chapter on one of England's most important musical movements of the decade.

what to buy: Caron Wheeler's astral vocals and the Jazzie B/Hooper production team make *Club Classics Vol I* ♪♪♪♪ (Virgin, 1989, prod. Soul II Soul) an indispensable document of the innovation coming out of England at the beginning of the decade. Mixing dub and R&B influences with contributions from Wheeler and the Reggae Philharmonic Orchestra, this album justifiably made Soul II Soul an international sensation at the time of its release, launching hit singles with "Keep On Movin'" and "Back to Life (However Do You Want Me)."

what to buy next: While not as startlingly brilliant as its predecessor, *Vol II: 1990—A New Decade* ♪♪♪ (Virgin, 1990, prod. Soul II Soul) further helped establish Soul II Soul's distinctive sound. Although it lacks Wheeler's voice, the album features some of Soul II Soul's most innovative work, particularly the symphonic "Get a Life" and "A Dream's a Dream."

what to avoid: When Hooper left Soul II Soul after its second album, the group lost its spark. *Volume III: Just Right* ♪ (Virgin, 1992, prod. Jazzie B) and *Volume V: Believe* ♪ (Virgin, 1995, prod. Jazzie B) are tiresome listens, fruitlessly rehashing the textures of the first two albums without gelling into anything beyond ear candy.

worth searching for: Released only in the U.K., *Vol IV: The Classic Singles* ♪♪♪ (Virgin U.K., 1993) compiles all the band's best material on one convenient disc and tacks on some remixes as bonus tracks. It's a good way to avoid the filler on the second and third albums.

influences:

◀◀ Augustus Pablo, Sade, James Brown, De La Soul

▶▶ Portishead, Sinead O'Connor, Massive Attack, Madonna, Tricky

Aidin Vaziri

Sounds of Blackness

Formed 1971, in Minneapolis, MN.

The massive vocal-instrumental ensemble Sounds of Black-

Sounds of Blackness (© Jack Vartoogian)

ness defies limitation in both sound and scope. An imposing assemblage of 30 voices and 10 musicians, the troupe has been a vibrant foundation of the burgeoning Minneapolis black music scene for more than a quarter-century, working with and alongside such talents as the Artist Formerly Known as Prince, Sheila E., Alexander O' Neal, and Jimmy Jam and Terry Lewis. Led by eclectic ex-bodybuilder Gary Hines, the group's conductor and driving spirit, Sounds of Blackness emerged from Macalester College in St. Paul, Minnesota, growing out of the heightened African American consciousness and black arts programs that swept across college campuses in the early 1970s. Though the troupe doesn't label itself as a gospel act, its heady blend of blues, jazz, R&B, funk, and rap is rooted in the black gospel choral tradition, resulting in an exhilarating, all-encompassing sound that has enamored them to a wide cross-section of music lovers. After struggling for years as a local Twin Cities attraction playing churches, halls, and Urban League meetings, Sounds of Blackness received its big break when Janet Jackson's pro-

ducers, Jam and Lewis, took her to one of their concerts. The production duo was considering signing the group, but Jackson's unbridled excitement over what she had seen became the deciding factor. Sounds of Blackness became the first act to release product on Jam & Lewis' Perspective label, with the award-winning studio team producing the majority of songs on their first three albums. The impressive results so far have included a string of crossover pop hits, two Grammys, an NAACP Image Award, and a spot as opening act on R&B superstar Luther Vandross' highly successful "Power of Love" tour.

what to buy: The title, *The Evolution of Gospel* ♪♪♪♪ (Perspective, 1991, prod. Gary Hines, Jimmy Jam, Terry Lewis), perfectly describes the awesome musical task this concept LP tackles—and achieves. Encompassing everything from timeless Negro Spirituals to the urban contemporary rhythms of today, the Grammy-winning project yielded the hit crossover singles "Optimistic," "Pressure, Pt.1," and "Testify," while playing a major role in defining the future sound and course that contemporary gospel music would take.

what to buy next: *Africa to America (The Journey of the Drum)* ✍✍✍ (Perspective, 1994, prod. Gary Hines, Jimmy Jam, Terry Lewis) takes on the same ambitious assignment as *Evolution of Gospel*—attempting to tell a sprawling historical saga through modern urban music on a single LP—and does so while opting for a decidedly harder, street-savvy direction.

the rest:

The Night Before Christmas: A Musical Fantasy ✍✍ (Perspective, 1992)
Time for Healing ✍✍✍ (Perspective, 1997)

influences:

◀◀ Quincy Jones, Curtis Mayfield, BeBe & CeCe Winans, Marvin Gaye, Stevie Wonder, Hampton Hawes, the Jacksons, Jimmy Jam & Terry Lewis

▶▶ Donald Lawrence, Kirk Franklin & the Family, Hezekiah Walker, Christopher Gray

Tim A. Smith

Southside Johnny & the Asbury Jukes

Formed 1974, in Asbury Park, NJ.

Southside Johnny (born John Lyon, December 4, 1948, Neptune, NJ), vocals, harmonica; Billy Rush, guitar (1974–85); Kevin Kavanaugh, keyboards; Al Berger, bass (1974–80); Kenny Pentifallo, drums (1974–77); Carlo Novi, tenor sax (1974–77); Eddie Manion, baritone sax (1974–82); Tony Palligrosi, trumpet (1974–78); Ricky Gazda, trumpet (1974–82); Richie "La Bamba" Rosenberg, trombone (1974–82); Steve Becker, drums (1977–91); Bob Muckin, trumpet (1978–80); Joey Stann, baritone sax, tenor sax (1980–1982, 1986–1991); Rusty Cloud, keyboards (1983–present); Mark Pender, trumpet (1983–86); Al Torrente, trumpet (1983–85); Bobby Ferrel, trombone (1983–86); Frank Elmo, saxophone (1983–86, 1991); George L. Ruiz, bass (1986); Bobby Bandiera (1986–present); Barry Danielian, trumpet; Dan Levine, trombone; Jerry Vivino Jr., tenor sax; David Hayes.

Southside Johnny & the Asbury Jukes came out of the same Asbury Park, New Jersey, scene that produced Bruce Springsteen, and at roughly the same time. In fact, the group's leader, Southside Johnny Lyon, and Springsteen occasionally played in the same bands during the early 1970s. But where Springsteen leaned toward rock and Phil Spector records, Lyon preferred urban blues and horn-band R&B, leading him to form the Jukes.

Lyon is an excellent, gravel-voiced white-soul singer, but the Springsteen connection has been a double-edged sword. Springsteen has written much of the Jukes' best-known material ("Hearts of Stone," "The Fever"), which has gained the group fans while creating a shadow from it has been unable to emerge. And when the group has abandoned the Springsteen connection (as on 1979's *The Jukes*, when guitarist Billy Rush became the primary songwriter), it has faltered. But Lyon and the Jukes have remained great performers in the New Jersey R&B/rock vein, if more limited in appeal than their more famous colleague. (Southside also sang the theme song for the CBS television sitcom *Dave's World*.)

what to buy: *Havin' a Party with Southside Johnny* ✍✍✍✍ (Epic, 1979/1990, prod. Miami Steve) is a solid, if a bit skimpy, hits collection with an added live recording of Sam Cooke's "Havin' a Party." It's a great white-soul, horn-band album that features tunes by Springsteen and cameos by Ronnie Spector and Lee Dorsey.

what to buy next: *Better Days* ✍✍✍ (Impact, 1991, prod. Little Steven) finds Southside Johnny making his peace with his place in New Jersey music—and with Springsteen's shadow—reuniting with the Miami Horns for one of his toughest, most exciting albums. Little Steven (earlier known as Miami Steve) returned to the production board, and Springsteen and Jon Bon Jovi contributed guest vocals. *All I Want Is Everything: The Best of Southside Johnny & the Asbury Jukes 1979–1991* ✍✍✍✍ (Rhino, 1993, prod. various) captures the best of the group's recordings immediately after the Epic years. *Live/Reach Up and Touch the Sky* ✍✍✍✍ (Mercury, 1981/1990, prod. John Lyon, Stephan Galfas) shows the band in its natural element.

what to avoid: *Trash It Up* ✍✍ (Mirage, 1983, prod. Nile Rodgers) totally removes Southside from his Jersey bar roots and places him in some parallel MTV-spawned R&B universe. Instead of sounding passionate, he sounds merely lascivious.

the rest:

I Don't Want to Go Home ✍✍✍ (Epic, 1976/1987)
This Time It's for Real ✍✍✍ (Epic, 1977/Legacy, 1990)
Hearts of Stone ✍✍✍✍ (Epic, 1978/1990)
The Jukes ✍✍ (Mercury, 1979/Off Beat, 1995)
Love Is a Sacrifice ✍✍✍ (Mercury, 1980)
The Best of Southside Johnny and the Asbury Jukes ✍✍✍✍ (Epic/Legacy, 1992)
Jukes Live at the Bottom Line ✍✍✍✍ (Tristar Music Imports, 1996)

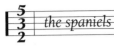

worth searching for: *At Least We Got Shoes* 🐾🐾🐾 (Atlantic, 1986, prod. John Lyon, John Rollo) contains a marvelous rave-up of the Dusty Springfield chestnut "I Only Want to Be with You."

solo outings:
Southside Johnny:
Slow Dance 🐾🐾🐾 (Cypress, 1988/A&M, 1993)

influences:
◄◄ Bruce Springsteen, the Coasters, the Drifters, Gary U.S. Bonds, James Brown, Wilson Pickett

►► Jack Mack & the Heart Attack, Iron City Houserockers

see also: *Little Steven*

Brian Mansfield

The Spaniels
Formed 1952, as the Hudsonaires. Renamed the Spaniels in 1953.

James "Pookie" Hudson, lead vocals; Ernest Warren, first tenor; James "Dimples" Cochran, first tenor; Willis C. Jackson, second tenor; Donald Porter, second tenor; Opal Courtney Jr., baritone vocals; Calvin Carter, baritone vocals; Carl Rainge, baritone vocals; Bill Carey, baritone vocals; Gerald Gregory, bass vocals; Andy McGruder, bass vocals; Ricky Burden, bass vocals; Lester Williams, bass vocals; Pete Simmons, guitar, bass vocals; Charles Douglas, first tenor; Alvin Wheeler, second tenor; Alvin Lloyd, baritone vocals.

The Spaniels were one of the most versatile doo-wop groups of the 1950s. Their vocal harmonies masterfully embraced soulful cheek-to-cheek balladry, Chicago-style jump blues, and inspired, comic rock 'n' roll. Before turning pro, the group was known as the Hudsonaires (named after leader James Hudson). They changed their name to the Spaniels in part as a zany response to a heckler who shouted "Y'all sound like a pack of dogs!" and as a way to distinguish themselves from the famous groups with bird names. In 1953, the Spaniels were the very first act signed to Vee-Jay Records. That year Vee-Jay leased the Spaniels' first record, "Baby It's You," to the Chance subsidiary, and it became a solid R&B hit. Their first release on Vee-Jay was the 1954 classic "Goodnight, Sweetheart, Goodnight." Written by Hudson and producer Calvin Carter, "Goodnight Sweetheart" is one of the most enduring doo-wop ballads of all time. Its resurrection as something of a lullaby (as done in the hit film *Three Men and a Baby*) seems strange in light of the lyrics which tell of a frustrated late night tryst. "Painted Pictures" wasn't nearly as big a hit, but it kept them on the charts until the U.S. Army

drafted some members and internal squabbles estranged others. A new line-up of the Spaniels, featuring Hudson, began hitting the R&B charts again in 1957 with "Everyone's Laughing," "I Know," "False Love," and their absolute finest performance as a group, the beautiful "(You Gave Me) Peace of Mind." After several break-ups and make-ups, the Spaniels left Vee-Jay in 1960. Various incarnations of the group (usually fronted by Hudson) recorded for labels such as Neptune, Jamie, Double-L, North American, Calla, and Buddah, though only one single made any noise on the charts, 1970's "Fairy Tales." Many of the Spaniels have disappeared into obscurity, but through the continual anthologizing of "Goodnight, Sweetheart, Goodnight" and others, their fame as a group lives on.

what to buy: *The Spaniels* 🐾🐾🐾🐾 (Dipper, 1997, prod. Calvin Carter), *Goodnight Sweetheart, Goodnight* 🐾🐾🐾🐾 (Vee-Jay, 1993, prod. Calvin Carter), and *Golden Hits* 🐾🐾🐾🐾 (Jukebox Treasures, 1994) are all compilations featuring the big hits "Goodnight Sweetheart, Goodnight," "Baby It's You," "Everyone's Laughing," and several showy covers of standards such as "Stormy Weather," "A Rockin' Good Way," and some previously unreleased songs.

what to buy next: *Heart & Soul Vol. 2* 🐾🐾🐾 (Vee-Jay, 1993) contains 25 tracks of lesser known material such as the amazing "Great Googly Moo," "Baby Sweets," and "Automobiles," plus 10 previously unreleased songs and alternates.

what to avoid: *The Spaniels 40th Anniversary 1953–1993* 🐾🐾 (Collectables, 1995, prod. Jim Meyers) is more misleading than bad, as it features remixes and re-recordings of the group's big hits. It's a pleasant outing, but if you're looking for the original Vee-Jay sounds, this doesn't have them.

the rest:
Play It Cool 🐾🐾🐾 (Charly, 1990)
Accapella Collection 🐾🐾🐾 (Jukebox Treasures, 1993)

worth searching for: *Recorded Live* 🐾🐾🐾 (New Rose, 1993) is a nine-song 1985 live show from Andover, Maryland, with a splashy opening medley and crowd pleasing renditions of their big hits.

influences:
◄◄ The Orioles, the Ravens, the Flamingos
►► The Gladiolas, the Neville Brothers

Ken Burke

Special Ed

Born Edward Archer.

Special Ed has always been considered one of the freshest, most gifted rappers in hip-hop—a pure MC who occupies the same realm as folks like Kool G Rap, Rakim, and KRS-One. Ever since he was a confident and somewhat arrogant 17-year old proclaiming he was the "Youngest in Charge," Special Ed has been mesmerizing listeners with his captivating voice and bugged-out lyricism. While out of the spotlight for a couple of years, Special Ed kept busy playing ornate side-men on *The Cosby Show* and in the movie *Juice* before reentering hip-hop's consciousness with an acclaimed showing as part of the Crooklyn Dodgers (with Masta Ace and Buckshot) for Spike Lee's *Crooklyn* soundtrack.

what to buy: Ed's natural skills as a wordsmith piqued the interest of his record label, but it was his sheer, unabashed enthusiasm and confidence that sealed the deal. Crafted when he was only 17, his first album, *Youngest in Charge* ♨♨♨♨ (Profile, 1987, prod. Howie Tee), captures the sound that marks the beginning of hip-hop's strongest era and, with the help of his DJ, Akshun, and longtime producer, "Hit Man" Howie Tee, is responsible for introducting several classics in the hip-hop pantheon, including "I Got It Made," "Taxing," "I'm the Magnificent," and the title track.

what to buy next: The follow-up, *Legal* ♨♨♨ (Profile, 1990, prod. Howie Tee) is Ed's way of proclaiming to the world (and to the ladies) that he's come of age. The title track and such cuts as "Come On Let's Move" reveal that, though his skills haven't diminished, perhaps the sound listeners want to hear has.

the rest:

Revelations ♨♨♨ (Profile, 1995)

worth searching for: Though Special Ed ended his nearly 10-year relationship with Profile after *Revelations* proved nothing special, a former A&R man at the company gave the rapper another shot with his fledgling label, Sure Shot. At last glance, the vinyl-only single "Think Twice" was creating a buzz on college radio and mix shows.

influences:

◀◀ Steady B, Ultramagnetic MC's, Rakim, Slick Rick

▶▶ Gang Starr, MC Lyte, Del Tha Funkee Homosapien

Jazzbo

Phil Spector

Born December 24, 1940, in the Bronx, NY.

The trademark mulched sound of Spector's glorious productions—borrowed equally from Frank Guida and Leiber and Stoller—didn't survive the transfer into the digital domain with all their majesty intact. But his landmark work, probably best heard on the original 45s, commands an incomparable position in the realm of rock's history. His story is well known and, in fact, reads like fiction—the high school senior who wrote a #1 record (the Teddy Bears' "To Know Him Is to Love Him") from his father's epitaph and "retired" at age 25 to live the life of a reclusive Beverly Hills millionaire, only to return to the studio to re-mix the tapes from the Beatles' arduous *Let It Be* sessions. Spector was rock's ultimate *auteur,* a visionary—and a notorious eccentric, to be kind—who imprinted his artistic signature so thoroughly on the records he made during the early 1960s for his own Philles Records that they are universally known as Phil Spector records and not by the name of the titular artists—who, by the way, included Gene Pitney, the Crystals, the Ronettes, Darlene Love, and the Righteous Brothers' "You've Lost That Lovin' Feelin'." Most recently, he produced sessions for Canadian chanteuse Celine Dione that she chose not to use, so Spector keeps threatening to put out *his* version of the album. Virtually every musician who stepped into a recording studio in his wake owes Spector a debt.

what's available: Spector personally oversaw the production of the four-disc boxed set *Back to Mono (1958–1969)* ♨♨♨♨ (Abkco, 1991, prod. Phil Spector), so he has nobody else to blame for the indifferent, cloudy digital transfers of his masterpieces. In addition to his brilliant 1963 Christmas album, included on its own disc, the set spans his entire career—from "To Know Him Is to Love Him" to Tina Turner's "River Deep—Mountain High" and a selection of rare and unissued latter-era studio experiments.

worth searching for: Spector so carefully rewrites his own history, he breezes through his wilderness years hitting just a few successful highpoints. But a Japanese import, *Twist and Shout* ♨♨♨ (WEA, 1989, prod. Phil Spector), collects 12 early productions he did for Atlantic Records that capture the artist in transition. They aren't uniformly great records, but the original singles are so hard to find, this set offers an unparalleled glimpse of the young Spector.

influences:

◀◀ Gary U.S. Bonds, the Drifters, Frankie Lymon & the Teenagers

▶▶ The Beach Boys, the Beatles, the Ramones, U2, Steve Lilly-white, Don Was, James "Jimmy Jam" Harris III & Terry Lewis, Kenneth "Babyface" Edmonds

Joel Selvin and Gary Graff

Ronnie Spector

See: The Ronettes

The Spice Girls

Formed 1994, in London, England.

Geri "Ginger Spice" Halliwell, vocals; Victoria "Posh Spice" Adams, vocals; Melanie "Sporty Spice" Chisolm, vocals; Melanie "Scary Spice" Brown, vocals; Emma Lee "Baby Spice" Bunton.

So tell us what you want, what you really really want. If it's radio-ready pop pap of the most disposable variety, wrapped in a pretty package and run up the flagpole with the most calculating of marketing schemes, the Spice Girls may just be the group for you. The Spice Girls scored the highest-charting British debut single ever with "Wannabe" in 1996. But that accomplishment was only a modest warning of the media tempest that followed them afterwards. The story goes that the five young women were brought together by a greedy producer (or a would-be team of svengalis—such are the vagaries of marketing, you know), but upon meeting one another broke out on their own, eschewing the virtues of "Girl Power!" and crafting their catchy but dispos-able debut album *Spice*. In reality, the whole thing was contrived, from the image to the sloganeering to the music. But that didn't stop the group from scoring several international hits with adult-contempo synth songs like "Say You'll Be There" and "2 Become 1." Crass, maybe, but on the other hand, don't hate them be-cause they're (sort of) beautiful. Sometimes, as in the tradition of the Monkees, New Edition, Wham!, and countless other manu-factured bands, the Spice Girls rise above their very real limita-tions and create some of the most enticing ear and eye candy in recent pop music history. And if we forget them tomorrow, what harm will have been done?

what's available: The hype accompanying the Spice Girls' megaselling worldwide smash *Spice* ♫♫♫ (Virgin, 1996, prod. Stannard & Rowe, Absolute) has been so enduring and so fevered, that the experience of sitting down and actually listen-ing to the thing, as opposed to merely having an opinion about it, seems almost irrelevant. But no; *Spice*, it turns out, is actu-ally an enjoyable pop trifle, full of hooky choruses, danceable grooves, and yes, tolerable singing. The girl-power anthem

"Wannabe" is an obvious winner, and the follow-up, "Say You'll Be There" charms with a surprising touch, a Stevie Wonder-like harmonica in the instrumental break. *Spiceworld* N/A (Virgin, 1997), the group's second album, was released in late 1997.

influences:

◀◀ Madonna, Wham!, Margaret Thatcher

Daniel Durchholz and Aidin Vaziri

Spice 1

Born in Bryson, TX.

East Oakland's Spice 1 did for gangsta rap what Too $hort did for the pimp/playa/mack style of rap. Starting in 1988 with an appearance on a Too $hort-organized Dangerous Crew compi-lation, and continuing with the indie release of the 1991 EP, *Let It Be Known*, Spice 1 literally transformed the face of gangsta rap, not only removing its focus from the streets of L.A., but also redefining its storytelling methods. The Texas-born rapper was raised in Hayward and neighboring Oakland, and every-thing he raps about is rooted in the cold, hard reality of the streets. His violent lyrics bring to light the darkside of the East Bay Area—the no-man's land between Oakland and Hayward, where D Boys slang dope and jealous fools pack gats, waiting to steal a sucker's ride, jewels, or cash. In Spice 1's world, you either roll strapped or wind up dead. In the rapumentary, *Rhyme and Reason,* Spice is even shown talking lovingly about his mother—and insisting that his gun-toting crew provide pro-tection for her at a show. As the one-time outlaw declared in a minor 1992 hit of the same name: "Welcome to the Ghetto."

what to buy: Like Too $hort, Spice developed a distinct style and stuck to it, making fine-tune adjustments (and minor additions) all the while. The best of his albums is his third, *187 He Wrote* ♫♫♫ (Jive, 1993, prod. Ant Banks, Too $hort, MC Eiht, EA-Ski, oth-ers), on which he mixes reggae slang (first explored on his previ-ous album) and a stutter-stop style with chilling pistol-grip im-agery. Although Compton's Most Wanted's MC Eiht teams up with Spice on "The Murda Show," the album's key track is "Trigga Gots No Heart," a streetwise rumination on the old addage "guns don't kill people, people do." *1990-Sick* ♫♫♫ (Jive, 1996, prod. Ant Banks, others) covers familiar teritory, both lyrically and musi-cally, with even previous guests (MC Eiht, E-40) coming back for more. There is a surprise, though: "Sucka Ass Niggas," in which Spice gives Run-D.M.C.'s old-school classic "Sucka MC's" the 187 treatment, making for a curbside classic of his own.

what to buy next: The debut EP, *Let It Be Known* ♫♫♫ (Triad, 1991, prod. Ant Banks, others), is packed with slanky Ant Banks funk, but it's Spice who stars here, with his lickety-split delivery and hard-edged imagery. The key track is "187 Proof," a ghetto fairy tale in which all the characters are named after popular alcoholic drinks from around the hood. *Spice 1* ♬♬♬ (Jive, 1992, prod. Ant Banks, Spice 1, others) reprises and reworks some of the EP tracks and includes a host of new material, not to mention a new style; proving that he's not a one-trick pony, Spice debuts his weirdly infectious stop-stutter delivery on "Money Gone." *Amerikkka's Nightmare* ♬♬♬ (Jive, 1994, Ant Banks, others) is packed with raw ghetto reality that stings with its intensity. On "Jealous Got Me Strapped," for instance, Spice and 2Pac examine how a simple emotion can lead to death. It's a killer.

the rest:
The Black Bossalini (a.k.a. Dr. Bomb From Da Bay) N/A (Jive, 1997)

influences:
◀◀ Too $hort, Ant Banks
▶▶ E-40, EA-Ski

Spence D.

The Spinners
Formed 1957, in Detroit, MI.

Bobbie Smith, tenor vocals; Pervis Jackson, bass vocals; Henry Fambrough, baritone vocals; Billy Henderson, tenor-baritone vocals; George Dixon, tenor vocals (1957–62); Edgar Edwards, tenor vocals (1962–66); G.C. Cameron, tenor vocals (1967–72); Phillipe Wynne (died July 13, 1984), tenor vocals (1972–77); John Edwards, tenor vocals (1977–present).

The Spinners' easy soul is so eminently likable and immediate it's easy to take the group for granted. The singers spent most of the 1960s spinning their wheels at Motown, but the group hit gold with a move to Atlantic and the patronage of producer Thom Bell in 1972. Bell crafted breathtakingly smooth songs which the Spinners nailed in performance, culminating in 17 charted singles and five gold albums—figures that rivaled the group's chief counterparts of Philly soul, the O'Jays. Flanked by sweet harmonies and deceptively simple strings and brass, newcomer Wynne—gruff yet sensitive, versatile yet controlled—was one of the best soul singers of the 1970s. Wynne left for a solo career in 1977 and died of a heart attack onstage seven years later. Although Edwards is a strong frontman, Bell was only able to channel the new blood into one more hit in 1979. But the Spinners clearly have enough material to fill the shows the group continues to play on the oldies circuit.

what to buy: The hit parade began with *Spinners* ♬♬♬♬ (Rhino, 1973/1995, prod. Thom Bell) with the buoyant likes of "I'll be Around," "One of a Kind (Love Affair)," "Ghetto Child," and "Could It Be I'm Falling in Love." *Pick of the Litter* ♬♬♬♬♬ (Rhino, 1975/1995, prod. Thom Bell) is the most fully conceptualized Spinners album, containing the group's best song, "Games People Play."

what to buy next: *One of a Kind Love Affair: The Anthology* ♬♬♬♬♬ (Rhino, 1991, prod. various) brilliantly seams the group's best work together on a two-disc, 30-track whopper. In addition to the obvious, it also includes the pre-Wynne hit "It's a Shame" (featuring the long-forgotten G.C. Cameron's shining moment) as well as later disco pop-offs such as "The Rubberband Man." On *Mighty Love* ♬♬♬♬ (Rhino, 1975/1995, prod. Thom Bell), Wynne stakes his claim as the decade's most exciting soul man, particularly with his blissful, extemporaneous vocal on the title track.

what to avoid: The 13-track *Best of the Spinners* ♬♬ (Rebound Records, 1994, prod. Howard Smiley) hardly realizes the scope of the group's work and is skimpy in comparison to *One of a Kind Love Affair*.

the rest:
Best of the Spinners ♬♬ (Rhino, 1978/1986)
Dancin' and Lovin' ♬♬♬ (Rhino, 1979/1992)
Best of the Spinners ♬♬♥ (Motown, 1988)
Down to Business ♬♬♥ (Volt, 1989)
New and Improved ♬♬♬ (Rhino, 1995)

worth searching for: The out-of-print *Spinners Live* ♬♬♬ (Atlantic, 1975) showed the group could do it onstage, too.

influences:
◀◀ Smokey Robinson & the Miracles, the Temptations, the Drifters, the O'Jays, Major Lance
▶▶ The Trammps, Frankie Beverly & Maze, the Dazz Band

Allan Orski

Lisa Stansfield
Born April 11, 1966, in Rochdale, England.

Lisa Stansfield had all the makings of another teen diva, coming up through the talent contest and TV show ranks. But her tastes ran not towards pop but to soul, which isn't surprising considering that she hung around R&B-loving Manchester quite a bit. She started out in a group called Blue Zone with former schoolmates Andy Morris and Ian Devaney; the group—or, rather, Stansfield's—break came when the British production team Coldcut recorded its "People Hold On," which became a Top 20 hit. Arista Records signed Stansfield, and Morris and Devaney stayed on as her producers, songwriters, and backing musicians. Her career has been sporadic; she never really capitalized after a big beginning with *Affection*, and a five-year break during the mid-1990s left her in an unenviable comeback position when she re-emerged during 1997.

what to buy: Her debut, *Affection* ♫♫♫♫ (Arista, 1989, prod. Ian Devaney, Andy Morris) was a deserving smash—lush, sultry, and buoyant all at the same time. The songs—including the hits "All Around the World" and "You Can't Deny It"—are deft pop confections, and Stansfield's performance is absolutely outstanding. *Lisa Stansfield* ♫♫♫ (Arista, 1997) marked a welcome return to form, with lush production and improved songwriting.

the rest:
Real Love ♫♫♫ (Arista, 1991)
So Natural ♫♫ (Arista, 1993)

influences:
◀◀ Barry White, Annie Lennox, Tracy Thorn (Everything but the Girl)

▶▶ Ambershower, Maxwell, D'Angelo, Spice Girls

Gary Graff

The Staple Singers

Formed 1953, in Chicago, IL.

Roebuck "Pops" Staples, vocals, guitar; Mavis Staples, vocals; Cleo Staples, vocals; Pervis Staples, vocals (1953–71); Yvonne Staples, vocals (1966–present).

The Staple Singers began as a gospel group founded by parents Pops and Oceola Staples, who migrated to Chicago from Mississippi during the early 1940s. Enlisting their two older daughters and one son, they began performing in church and, during the 1950s, started recording for the Vee-Jay label. Youngest daughter Yvonne joined during the 1960s, and the Staples became one of the country's most beloved Southern-style gospel ensembles. The family edged into non-religious pop as the 1960s rolled on, then turned into a mainstream soul act upon signing to the legendary Stax label. Their churchy testifying worked perfectly against the backdrop of the funky soul that Stax provided—scoring hits such as "Respect Yourself" and "I'll Take You There"—though many in the gospel world never forgave the group for giving in to the temptations of secular music. What these purists failed to recognize is that the

Staples' spiritual message was a powerfully uplifting force on black radio. While the Staples' hits continue to be sampled by hip-hop artists, Pops and Mavis (who collaborated with Prince during the late 1980s) continue to pursue solo interests.

what to buy: *The Best of the Staple Singers* ♫♫♫♫ (Stax, 1986, prod. Al Bell) features most of their most familiar tracks in a good-vibes marathon.

what to buy next: *Uncloudy Day/Will the Circle Be Unbroken* ♫♫♫♫ (Vee-Jay, 1957/1992), an early recording of joyous and resonant spiritual music.

what to avoid: The cassette collection *Greatest Hits* ♫♫♫ (RSP, 1992, prod. various) has plenty of good songs but is skimpy. If you need something for the car, tape *The Best of*.

the rest:
Freedom Highway ♫♫♫ (Epic, 1965/Legacy, 1991)
Soul Folk in Action ♫♫♫ (Stax, 1968/1991)
We'll Get Over ♫♫♫ (Stax, 1968/1995)
Staple Swingers ♫♫♫ (Stax, 1971/1994)
Be Altitude: Respect Yourself ♫♫♫♫ (Stax, 1972)
Be What You Are ♫♫♫ (Stax, 1973/1990)
City in the Sky ♫♫♫ (Stax, 1974/1996)
Great Day ♫♫♫♫ (Milestone, 1975/1990)
Turning Point ♫♫♫ (Private I, 1984/Legacy, 1995)

worth searching for: *Let's Do It Again* ♫♫♫♫ (Curtom, 1975, prod. Curtis Mayfield) is worth owning just for its gorgeously sexy title track. The group's gospel side is faithfully anthologized on the out-of-print *Chronicle* ♫♫♫♫ (Fantasy, 1985, prod. various).

solo outings:
Mavis Staples:
Mavis Staples ♫♫♫ (Stax, 1969)
Only for the Lonely ♫♫♫ (Stax, 1976)
A Piece of the Action ♫♫♫ (Curtom, 1976)
Oh, What a Feeling ♫♫♫ (Warner Bros., 1979)
Time Waits for No One ♫♫♫ (Paisley Park, 1989)
The Voice ♫♫♫ (Paisley Park, 1993)

Pops Staples:
Peace to the Neighborhood ♫♫♫ (Pointblank/Charisma, 1992)

influences:
◀◀ Charley Patton, Howlin' Wolf, Ray Charles, Mahalia Jackson, the Impressions, Aretha Franklin, Sam Cooke

▶▶ Salt-N-Pepa, Madonna, Prince, Talking Heads, Spearhead, Arrested Development, Me'Shell Ndegeocello

Simon Glickman and Gary Graff

Edwin Starr

Born January 21, 1942, in Nashville, TN.

Edwin Starr never really achieved a consistent string of R&B hits (or albums for that matter), but when you cut a single as cataclysmic as "War," such observations seem like nitpicking. Starr proves he can shout with the best of 'em on this 1970 protest anthem, a heaving ground-shaker and easily the most visceral thing ever to come out of Motown. Prior to that, he charted with "25 Miles," which was nearly as good. Most of Starr's material doesn't pack the same wallop as "War," which means that at worst he's merely energetic.

what to buy: *Motown Legends: War—Twenty Five Miles* 𝄢𝄢𝄢 (ESX Entertainment, 1994) has the edge for containing material from his long-deleted first album in addition to "War" and "25 Miles."

the rest:

Motown Superstars Series, Vol. 3 𝄢𝄢𝄢 (Motown, 1980)
The Very Best of the Motor City Recordings 𝄢𝄢𝄢 (Hot, 1996)

influences:

◀◀ The Temptations, the O'Jays, the Isley Brothers, James Brown, Wilson Pickett

▶▶ Ted Hawkins, Bruce Springsteen

Allan Orski

Candi Staton
/Candi Staton-Sussewell

Born Canzata Maria Staton, May 13, 1940, in Hanceville, AL.

Gospel songbird, blues princess, or disco diva, Candi Staton has forged a multi-decade career that defies categorization—or easy explanation. The Alabama church-bred "Sweetheart of Soul" has recorded sparkling, hit-potential music in every genre she's attempted: Her bittersweet 1976 anthem "Young Hearts Run Free," for example, is one of the few surviving classics of the disco era, and experienced a resurgence of popularity in 1996 on the soundtrack to the modern film remake of *Romeo & Juliet*. Yet Staton never seemed to attain a level of success equal to her talent, either because of record label mishandling or her own early self-destructive tendencies. A member of the Jewel Gospel Trio in her teens, she left the group when she came of age to marry singer Lou Rawls, but the plans fell through. Shortly after, her brother dared her to compete on amateur night in a Birmingham nightclub, and her winning rendition of Aretha Franklin's "Do Right Woman" landed her a

booking to open for blues giant Clarence Carter—whom she eventually did marry. Her secular career jump-started, Staton recorded her first million-selling single, the blues-based "I'd Rather Be an Old Man's Sweetheart (Than a Young One's Fool)" in 1969, followed by a string of Southern soul hits like "I'm Just a Prisoner (of Your Good Lovin')," "As Long as He Takes Care of Home," and her first major pop success, an R&B version of Tammy Wynette's "Stand By Your Man." The mid-1970s saw her segue smoothly into disco with the #1 "Young Hearts Run Free" and the subsequent dance dazzlers "Victim," "When You Wake Up Tomorrow," and "Chance." Staton conquered a personal battle with alcoholism and became a born-again Christian in 1982; she has since recorded nine gospel LPs (including two Grammy winners) while establishing the Atlanta-based Beracah Ministries with her fourth husband, former Ashford & Simpson and Diana Ross drummer John Sussewell. Since 1996 Staton has hosted her own weekly variety show, *Say Yes*, on the Trinity Broadcasting Network.

what to buy: In keeping with her up-and-down career fortunes, the best collection of Staton's work, *Young Hearts Run Free: The Best of Candi Staton* 𝄢𝄢𝄢𝄢 (WEA/Warner Bros., 1995, comp. prod. Gregg Geller) doesn't contain all of her best recordings. It omits her first big hit, "I'd Rather Be an Old Man's Sweetheart," the disco tracks "Chance" and "Honest I Do," and her most successful single you've probably never heard—"You Got the Love," her 1991 dance smash that hit #1 on British pop charts and sold nearly 2½ million copies worldwide. Despite its string of questionable choices, what is included is a representative (if not comprehensive) review of Staton's discography.

what to buy next: Her 1997 gospel release *Cover Me* 𝄢𝄢𝄢 (PGD/A&M/CGI, 1997, prod. Marcus Williams) is indicative of where Staton's sound has progressed and how her musical influences have coalesced. It includes spiritually reworked cover versions of "Bridge over Troubled Water" and "Hold On, I'm Coming," with down-home testifyin' numbers like "He Set My Spirit Free," and a new rendition of her 1987 Grammy-nominated gospel song, "The First Face I Want to See."

the rest:

Nightlites 𝄢𝄢 (Sequel, 1993)
It's Time! 𝄢𝄢𝄢 (Intersound, 1995)

worth searching for: Staton's albums for the defunct Fame label, particularly *I'm Just a Prisoner* 𝄢𝄢𝄢𝄢 (Fame, 1969) are out of print, as are her early gospel LPs like *Make Me an Instrument* 𝄢𝄢𝄢𝄢 (Beracah, 1985) and *Love Lifted Me* 𝄢𝄢𝄢𝄢 (Beracah, 1988), but are worth the effort to hunt down.

influences:

◀◀ The Soul Stirrers, Jewel Gospel Trio, the Staple Singers, Aretha Franklin, Mighty Clouds of Joy, Clarence Carter, Bobby Womack, Patti LaBelle

▶▶ Luther Vandross, Gloria Gaynor, Jennifer Holliday, Vickie Winans

Jim McFarlin

Stax-Volt

Motown called itself the Sound of Young America. But many R&B fans during the 1960s considered Memphis-based Stax-Volt Records to be the sound of black America. Where Motown was smooth and urbane, Stax was gritty and rural. Motown was polished; Stax was passionate. These are, of course, easy generalities, but it can't be argued that what was produced in Memphis was a soul music of another breed than what was being made in Detroit—not better, but certainly different.

Stax began during the late 1950s as Satellite Records and was started by Jim Stewart, a songwriter and country musician whose day job was in banking, and his sister, Estelle Axton. Chips Moman, a producer, songwriter, and guitarist, was also an integral part of the operation. Satellites first success was Carla and Rufus Thomas' "'Cause I Love You"; he paid one Nashville disc jockey a percentage of the royalties to play the song, and Carla's father Rufus, who was a DJ, lobbied his colleagues to play it as well. The song sold 15,000 copies locally, attracting Atlantic Records' Jerry Wexler, who licensed the song from Stewart and began a lengthy association between the labels.

Satellite became Stax—a combination of Stewart and Axton's surnames—in 1960 and became a powerhouse operation, with a hall of fame–caliber roster of artists that included Otis Redding, Sam & Dave, Eddie Floyd, Albert King, and the Staple Singers. Isaac Hayes, destined to be a star himself, wrote hits with David Porter. The house band—Booker T. & the MG's—were good enough to have their own hits, too, such as the seminal "Green Onions." Stax was a major American power through 1968, weathering even Redding's death in a plane crash in 1967.

In 1968, Stewart ditched his Atlantic connection and entered into an agreement with Gulf & Western, which began Stax's demise—though there would be a steady stream of hits into the early 1970s. But by the time Stax closed its doors in 1976, the label was a shadow of its former self, though the memories are of a great, groundbreaking label that was responsible for releasing some of the most memorable pop music the world has ever heard.

what to buy: It's hard to call a nine-volume box set an essential purchase, but that's just the case with *The Complete Stax/Volt Singles, Volume 1: 1959–1968* 𝄞𝄞𝄞𝄞 (The Atlantic Group, 1991, prod. various). It's a staggering collection, with nary a loser amongst its 240-plus songs. More than just a box set, it's an aural documentary. Stax produced two more massive box sets covering its later years, but fans who want to dabble in the post-Atlantic years might first want to consider the single-disc set *Top of the Stax: Twenty Greatest Hits* 𝄞𝄞𝄞𝄞 (Stax/Fantasy, 1988, prod. various).

what to buy next: Though not as awesomely consistent as the first volume, the next two Stax sets—the nine-volume *The Complete Stax/Volt Singles, Volume 2: 1968–1971* 𝄞𝄞𝄞 (Stax/Fantasy, 1993, prod. various) and the 10-volume *The Complete Stax/Volt Singles, Volume 3: 1972–1975* 𝄞𝄞𝄞 (Stax/Fantasy, 1994, prod. various)—are worthwhile, with plenty of memorable hits and lots of obscure gems that languished out of print for years.

worth searching for: *Stax Greatest Hits* 𝄞𝄞𝄞𝄞 (Stax/Fantasy, 1986, prod. various) is a top-notch single collection from Japan that will be of interest to anyone looking for a good taste of the label's post-1968 period.

Gary Graff

Stereo MC's

Formed late 1980s, in East London.

Rob B. (born Rob Bich), vocals; the Head (born Nick Hallam), DJ; Owen If (born Owen Rossiter), drums.

While many groups have attempted to bridge the gap between funk, hip-hop, and dance music, few have done it as well as the Stereo MC's. Maintaining a musical vibe that was simultaneously upbeat and down-n-dirty soulful, the group perfected the synthesis of hip-hop beats and milky acid-jazz infused dance grooves. While the popular Manchester sound of the time melded slinky dance grooves and rock 'n' roll, the Stereo MC's cast their eye not on rock, but on the traditional trappings of American hip-hop. Rapper Rob B., DJ-remixer the Head, and drummer Owen If may have lacked the hardcore posturing of their New York rap contemporaries, but they more than made up for it with sheer sonic verve. Indeed, whatever you thought of their Euro-Anglo accents (and Rob B. does deserve credit for staunchly refusing to emulate his East Coast counterparts by copping a fake inner-city drawl), you simply couldn't front on their impeccable production. Giving a nod to the New York old school, the group featured not only a real DJ, but also an actual drummer both on their studio recordings and in their live sets (a practice was later adopted by the likes of the Digable Planets, the Roots, and Snoop Doggy Dogg). Yet despite their links to the old school and, more significantly, the endorsement of both the Beatnuts and the Jungle Brothers' Afrika Baby Bam, the Stereo MC's failed to connect with the American hip-hop community, which has traditionally ignored European artists. The crew subsequently turned its attention to production under the moniker Ultimatum and remixed songs for the likes of U2, the Jungle Brothers, PM Dawn, and the Disposable Heroes of Hiphoprisy.

what to buy: *Supernatural* 🎵🎵🎵 (4th and B'way/Island, 1990, prod. Afrika Baby Bambaataa, the Beatnuts, Stereo MC's) came in two flavors: the original, 16-track album and a reduced, 12-track "American Mix." The 16-track version is far superior, containing the Afrika Baby Bam-and-Beatnuts-produced "Watcha Gonna Do?" and Baby Bam's nearly eight-minute funk jam, "Smokin' with the Motherman." The Stereo MC's shake things up, too, with "Two Horse Town" (which grabs the now-popular cowboy/outlaw thematic by the reigns), "Goin' Back to the Wild" (which offers a verbal link between Baby Bam and Rob B.), and "Lost in Music" (a shuffling, jazzy rump-shaker supreme). But true star here is the upbeat, dancy "Elevate My Mind," whose electro-charged bpms match perfectly with Rob B.'s slinky, decidedly British flow. The "American Mix" album is most notable for its Groove Holmes-styled remix of "Lost in Music."

what to buy next: *Connected* 🎵🎵🎵 (Gee St./Island, 1992, prod. Stereo MC's) is not a hip-hop album in the pure sense. As if in frustration over the lack of support it received from stateside hip-hop heads, the Stereo MC's shift to a more dance-oriented approach here. Yet, where many dance groups might pump out soulless music tailored for the masses, the Stereo MC's infuse theirs with plenty of earthy soul and even a touch of down-in-the-gutter funk. This time out, the trio is joined by the sultry singers Cath Coffey, Andrea Groves, and Verona Davis, who provide sensuous backing vocals.

worth searching for: The five-song EP *Stereo MC's* 🎵🎵🎵 (4th and B'Way/Island, 1989, prod. Stereo MC's) is the group's most hip-hop-oriented release, featuring the Run-D.M.C.-meets-Van McCoy turntablized funk of "What Is Soul," the rapid-fire lyrical assault of "Bring It On," and the old-school beat snatching of "Neighborhood."

influences:

◀◀ Massive Attack, Hijack, PM Dawn

▶▶ O.M.C.

Spence D.

Stetsasonic
/Daddy-O
/Prince Paul
/Gravediggaz

Formed 1981, in Brooklyn, NY.

Daddy-O (born Glenn Bolton), vocals; Delite (born Martin Wright), vocals; Fruitkwan (born Bobby Simmons), vocals, drums; Wise (born Leonard Roman), beatbox; DBC (born Marvin Nemley), keyboards, turntables, drums; Prince Paul (born Paul Houston), turntables, samplers.

If to some hip-hop represented the promise of postmodern method, the ultimate egalitarian fusion of all sounds and genres, then it needed someone to make the commercial leap. So it was up to such innovators as Stetsasonic, billed as the "original hip-hop band," to become the musical recombinant that could demonstrate the range of forms available to the next generation of sampler-dependent producers and post-hip-hop instrumentalists. It's no surprise that it would be Stet that would summarize hip-hop's musical strategy in the manifesto entitled "Talking All That Jazz." Main Stet alum Prince Paul would go on to apply his lessons directly with "sons" De La Soul, setting the stage for hip-hop's sonic and artistic entropy.

what to buy: When Stet decided to throw out coherence and flow with its interests, the group came up with the endlessly enjoyable *In Full Gear* 🎵🎵🎵🎵 (Tommy Boy, 1988, prod. Stetsasonic), a map for many of the vectors hip-hop and pop music generally would take in the next decade. There's a look back to the Last Poets and the Watts Prophets on Daddy-O's "Freedom or Death." The revisionist Sly & the Family Stone on "It's in My Song" points to Rage Against the Machine. There's a concession to the James Brown sampling craze on "DBC Let the Music Play," a venture into dancehall on "The Odad," and a reverent take on "Miami Bass." And "Talking All That Jazz" anticipates both Us3 and Gang Starr, while Prince Paul's "Music for the Stetfully Insane" prefigures MoWax and the instrumental hip-hop craze.

what to buy next: A crew merging live drumming with drum machines, turntables, old-school-influenced MCs, and a human beatbox could go in many directions, and the debut, *On Fire* 𝄞𝄞𝄞 (Tommy Boy, 1986, prod. Stetsasonic), finds the band feeling out its possibilities at a transitional period in hip-hop. Much of the album sounds like A&R by the numbers—a metal-rap fusion track here, a Def Jam-styled track there, a Roxanne-type track and a bunch of park-jam rhymes over drum machines. The exuberance of the rhyme trio energizes the basic 808 thump of "4 Ever My Beat" and "My Rhyme." "Go Stetsa 1" is the real gem, with Nawthar Muhammed's powerful drum rolls and memorable verses from the entire crew. *Blood, Sweat & No Tears* 𝄞𝄞𝄞 (Tommy Boy, 1991, prod. Stetsasonic) doesn't reach nearly as far as its predecesor, *In Full Gear*, but maintains a steady, relaxing groove. Daddy-O and Deite keep their rhymes positive and direct while Prince Paul's off-kilter humor provides the counterpoint.

the rest:
Daddy-O:
You Can Be a Daddy But Never Be Daddy-O 𝄞𝄞 (Island, 1993)

The Gravediggaz:
6 Feet Deep 𝄞𝄞𝄞 (Gee Street, 1994)
The Pick, the Sickle, and the Shovel N/A (Gee Street, 1997)
Six Feet Deep N/A (Gee Street, 1997)

Prince Paul:
Psychoanalysis 𝄞𝄞𝄞 (WordSound, 1996)

influences:
◄◄ Run-D.M.C., Public Enemy

►► De La Soul, MoWax, Dr. Octagon, the Roots, Wu-Tang Clan

Jeff "DJ Zen" Chang

Rod Stewart

Born January 10, 1945, in London, England.

Former frontman for the Jeff Beck Group and Faces, Rod Stewart has been written off so many times that critics could use him as a tax deduction. Granted, consistency has never been his forte: even *Foolish Behaviour*, *Tonight I'm Yours*, and *A Night on the Town*—his best, hardest-rocking albums since his early 1970s heyday with the Faces—were uneven, reneging on the promise of his classic 1972 album title, *Never a Dull Moment*. But "Maggie May," "You Wear It Well," and "Stay with Me" still sound great on radio, and even in middle age, that soulful howl can wring emotion from the sappiest of love songs. Credit Stewart's longevity to a thrilling live show (save for his yawn-inducing 1996 tour that inexplicably found him performing his hits in chronological order) and an impeccable

taste in cover songs that over the years has included Eddie Cochran's "Cut Across Shorty," Bobby Womack's "It's All Over Now," Jimi Hendrix's "Angel," Cat Stevens' "The First Cut Is the Deepest," Tom Waits' "Downtown Train," and the Blue Nile's "Downtown Lights."

what to buy: *Every Picture Tells a Story* 𝄞𝄞𝄞𝄞 (Mercury, 1971, prod. Rod Stewart) and *Never a Dull Moment* 𝄞𝄞𝄞𝄞 (Mercury, 1972, prod. Rod Stewart) make up one of the most overwhelming one-two punches in rock history. Acoustic guitars, mandolins, organs, and drums collide with Stewart's potent, scruffy, pipes. Gloriously reckless but never sloppy.

what to buy next: *The Rod Stewart Album* 𝄞𝄞𝄞 (Mercury, 1969, prod. Lou Reizner) offers a formative glimpse at his songwriting ("An Old Raincoat Won't Ever Let You Down") and interpretive prowess (the Rolling Stones' "Street Fighting Man," Michael D'Abo's "Handbags and Gladrags"). *A Night on the Town* 𝄞𝄞𝄞 (Warner Bros., 1976, prod. Tom Dowd) plays to his strengths as a balladeer ("Tonight's the Night," "The First Cut Is the Deepest") and barroom rocker ("The Balltrap," "The Wild Side of Life"). *Absolutely Live* 𝄞𝄞𝄞 (Warner Bros., 1982, prod. Rod Stewart) is a sweat-soaked document of one of his strongest post-Faces tours, with roof-raising versions of "Hot Legs," Chuck Berry's "Sweet Little Rock 'n' Roller," and a smoking medley of "Little Queenie" and "She Won't Dance with Me."

what to avoid: *Body Wishes* **woof!** (Warner Bros, 1983, prod. Rod Stewart, Tom Dowd), is a wimpy, synthesizer-drowned album notable only for its utter lack of artistic relevance. The hit was "Baby Jane," if that tells you anything.

the rest:
Gasoline Alley 𝄞𝄞𝄞 (Mercury, 1970)
Sing It Again Rod 𝄞𝄞𝄞 (Mercury, 1972)
Smiler 𝄞𝄞 (Mercury, 1974)
Atlantic Crossing 𝄞𝄞𝄞 (Warner Bros., 1975)
Footloose and Fancy Free 𝄞𝄞 (Warner Bros., 1977)
Blondes Have More Fun 𝄞𝄞 (Warner Bros., 1978)
Greatest Hits 𝄞𝄞 (Warner Bros., 1979)
Foolish Behaviour 𝄞𝄞𝄞 (Warner Bros., 1980)
Tonight I'm Yours 𝄞𝄞𝄞 (Warner Bros., 1981)
Camouflage 𝄞𝄞 (Warner Bros., 1984)
Rod Stewart 𝄞𝄞 (Warner Bros., 1986)
Out of Order 𝄞 (Warner Bros., 1988)

Rod Stewart (© Ken Settle)

Storyteller: The Complete Anthology 1964–1990 🐾🐾🐾🐾 (Warner Bros., 1989)

Downtown Train: Selections from Storyteller 🐾🐾 (Warner Bros., 1990)

Vagabond Heart 🐾🐾 (Warner Bros., 1991)

The Mercury Anthology 🐾🐾🐾🐾 (Polydor, 1992)

Unplugged . . . and Seated 🐾🐾🐾 (Warner Bros., 1993)

Vintage 🐾🐾🐾🐾 (Mercury, 1993)

The Best of Rod Stewart featuring Reason to Believe 🐾🐾🐾 (Rebound, 1994)

A Spanner in the Works 🐾🐾🐾 (Warner Bros., 1995)

Face of the Sixties 🐾🐾🐾 (Griffin, 1995)

If We Fall in Love Tonight 🐾🐾🐾 (Warner Bros., 1996)

worth searching for: The European import *Lead Vocalist* 🐾🐾🐾 (Warner Bros., 1993, prod. various) mixes hits with five tracks from an aborted Trevor Horn-produced album, including covers of Stevie Nicks' "Stand Back" and the Rolling Stones' "Ruby Tuesday."

influences:

◀◀ Sam Cooke, Otis Redding

▶▶ Dan Baird, Black Crowes, Bash & Pop

David Okamoto

Stories

Formed 1971, in New York, NY. Disbanded 1975.

Michael Brown (born Michael Lookofsky), keyboards (1971–73); Ian Lloyd (born Ian Buoncocglio), vocals, bass; Steve Love, guitar, vocals; Bryan Madey, drums, vocals (1971–75); Kenny Aaronson, bass (1971–75); Ken Bichel, keyboards (1971–75); Rick Ranno, drums (1974–75).

After the dissolution of the Left Banke and his stint as songwriter for the group Montage, keyboardist/songwriter Brown co-founded Stories. Lead singer Lloyd's raspy, Rod Stewart-like vocals don't complement Brown's melodic compositions quite as well as Steve Martin's in the Banke, but Stories still managed to produce two enjoyable albums and become something of a journeyman band that opened for anyone who would take them on the road. Lloyd also became an in-demand background singer.

what's available: The second LP, *About Us* 🐾🐾🐾🐾 (Kama Sutra, 1973/Original Buddah Classics, 1996), put Stories over the top with its #1 cover of Hot Chocolate's "Brother Louie," which was actually released as a single and appended to the album when it hit big, which was after Brown left the group.

worth searching for: *Stories* 🐾🐾🐾 (Kama Sutra, 1972) is out of print, but worth searching for thanks to the unlikely Top 40 hit

"I'm Coming Home" as well as strong tracks such as "Hello People," "Step Back," and "Take Cover."

influences:

◀◀ Rod Stewart, Sam Cooke, the Chambers Brothers, the Isley Brothers

▶▶ Foreigner, Rick James, Dan Reed Network

Mike Greenfield

Style Council

Formed 1983, in London, England. Disbanded 1989.

Paul Weller, guitar, bass, keyboards, vocals; Mick Talbot, keyboards, vocals; Dee C. Lee, vocals (1986–89).

If the Jam's punk-rock roots were too confining for Paul Weller's expanding musical interests, the Style Council gave him an open door to unrestricted excess. Backed by an army of jazz and funk session musicians, Weller and keyboardist Mick Talbot (formerly of the Merton Parkas and Dexy's Midnight Runners) fused R&B, soul, funk, and jazz, straining it all through European elitism and Weller's growing leftist political ideologies. While the music was highly polished and sophisticated, it could be wildly pretentious and slick as well, produced at times with layered synth brass and drum machines. Nevertheless, the Style Council demonstrated what could be done with a palette of divergent styles, setting a trend that was echoed in the work of other former punk artists, including the Clash's Mick Jones (in Big Audio Dynamite) and Bow Wow Wow's Matthew Ashman (in Chiefs of Relief). By 1988, the Style Council was tripping over its own self-importance, and, as slipping album sales indicated, no one really cared anymore. Weller wisely abandoned the project, married vocalist Dee C. Lee, and, following a lengthy sabbatical, launched a successful solo career.

what to buy: *Our Favourite Shop* 🐾🐾🐾🐾 (Polydor, 1985, prod. Peter Wilson, Paul Weller) is more consistent than anything that preceded it and more optimistic than anything that would follow it. (Weller admits he lost interest in the band after this release.) For once the group's varied styles worked together in a surprisingly coherent mix of funk ("The Lodgers"), soul ("Shout to the Top"), and classic instrumentation ("A Stone's Throw Away"). (Note: This album was also released as *Internationalists* 🐾🐾🐾🐾 (Geffen, 1985), with a different cover, alternate mixes, and a slightly revised track list. It is currently not available on CD.)

what to buy next: As greatest hits offerings go, *The Style Council Collection* 🐾🐾🐾🐾 (Polydor, 1996, prod. Peter Wilson, Paul

Weller) is just about perfect, emphasizing the band's early hits ("Speak Like a Child," "Long Hot Summer," "My Ever Changing Moods") and tossing in several excellent non-LP tracks ("It Just Came to Pieces in My Hands," "Ghosts of Dachau") for good measure. Oddly, some of the Style Council's best work appeared not on albums but on singles and EPs. *Here's Some That Got Away* 🎵🎵🎵 (Pony Canyon, 1994, prod. Peter Wilson, Paul Weller) serves them up on one fine disc. Among the treats are the lovely and wistful "The Piccadilly Trail" and Talbot's rousing instrumental "Party Chambers."

what to avoid: Weller's disgust with everything (including the Style Council) comes across loud and clear on *Confessions of a Pop Group* 🎵 (Polydor, 1988, prod. Peter Wilson, Paul Weller). Opening with a toilet flush, the album wearily concludes with a 10-minute orchestral suite, complete with doo-wop chorus.

the rest:
Cafe Bleu 🎵🎵🎵 (Polydor, 1984)
My Ever Changing Moods 🎵🎵🎵 (Geffen, 1984)
Live! The Style Council, Home & Abroad 🎵🎵 (Polydor, 1986)
The Singular Adventures of the Style Council (Greatest Hits Vol. 1) 🎵🎵🎵 (Polydor, 1989)

worth searching for: The seven-song CD *Introducing the Style Council* 🎵🎵🎵🎵 (Polydor, 1983, prod. Peter Wilson, Paul Weller) brims with enthusiasm and breezy soul. Standouts include the group's debut single, "Speak Like a Child," the moody hit "Long Hot Summer," and an excellent alternate version of "The Paris Match."

influences:
◀◀ Curtis Mayfield, Marvin Gaye, Steely Dan, Modern Jazz Quartet, Dexter Gordon

▶▶ Big Audio Dynamite, Chiefs of Relief, Everything But the Girl, Communards, Us3, Guru

Christopher Scapelliti

The Stylistics

Formed 1968, in Philadelphia, PA.

Russell Thompkins Jr., vocals; James Smith, vocals (1968–80); Airrion Love, vocals; James Dunn, vocals (1968–80); Herbie Murrell, vocals.

Formed from the remnants of two rival vocal groups, the Monarchs and the Percussions, the Stylistics were the personal domain of famed Philadelphia producer Thom Bell. With lyricist Linda Creed, Bell gave the Stylistics lush, romantic fare such as "You Make Me Feel Brand New," "I'm Stone in Love with You," "You Are Everything," and "Betcha By Golly, Wow" (recently covered by the Artist Formerly Known as Prince)—a batch of material tailor made for the group's exquisite five-part harmonies. You can't argue with the success; during the early 1970s, the Stylistics had 12 consecutive Top 10 singles. The bottom didn't quite fall out when the group split with Bell to work with Van McCoy, but the Stylistics' commercial success gradually slowed, though the group's material remained popular in the U.K. Now it exists as a trio, playing oldies bills and still sounding sweet, if not as full as they once did.

what to buy: *The Best of the Stylistics* 🎵🎵🎵🎵 (Amherst, 1975, prod. Thom Bell) has just 10 songs, but they're all revelatory gems and will doubtlessly lead you to *The Best of the Stylistics, Vol. 2* 🎵🎵🎵🎵 (Amherst, 1976/1985).

what to buy next: *Love Talk* 🎵🎵🎵 (Amherst, 1991, prod. various) is a strong latter-day studio album on which the band recasts some of its old hits and delivers some strong new numbers produced by Burt Bacharach and Carole Bayer Sager, among others. *The Stylistics* 🎵🎵🎵🎵 (Avco Embassy, 1971/Amherset, 1995, prod. Thom Bell) and *Round 2* (Amherst, 1972/1992, prod. Thom Bell) have their share of filler but also hold many of those tremendous early hits.

what to avoid: *All Time Classics* 🎵🎵 (Delmark, 1976) is just another R&B act—albeit a talented one—indulging itself in pop standards.

the rest:
Greatest Love Hits 🎵🎵🎵 (Amherst, 1985)
Stylistics Christmas 🎵🎵🎵 (Amherst, 1992)
Love Is Back in Style 🎵🎵 (Bellmark, 1996)

worth searching for: *Heavy* 🎵🎵🎵 (Avco Embassy, 1974, prod. Van McCoy) begins the group's post-Bell period on an ambitious note that's worth hearing.

influences:
◀◀ Al Green, the Temptations, the Impressions

▶▶ The Spinners, Honey Cone, Main Ingredient, DeBarge

Gary Graff

Sugar Hill Records

Hard to believe, but once upon a time hip-hop was all about fun: "Throw your hands in the air and wave 'em like you just don't care," or variations thereof, among them Super-Wolf imploring the faithful to "Get up and party/And don't ask why/I just want everybody/To shake your gluteus maximi." The carefree contributions of Super-Wolf and a host of better-known acts, including the seminal Grandmaster Flash & the Furious Five and the Sugarhill Gang, are preserved on *The Sugar Hill Records Story* 🎵🎵🎵🎵 (Rhino, 1997, prod. various), an essential five-CD slice of urban history. Rap was still pretty much a street art, practiced by DJs and MCs at rent parties and barbecues in the South Bronx, when husband-and-wife music-industry veterans Joe and Sylvia Robinson started pressing up a 12-inch single called "Rapper's Delight" by the Sugarhill Gang in 1979. The track, which turned the bass line from Chic's disco hit "Good Times" into an epic breakbeat that just wouldn't quit and then topped it with a series of joyously silly rhymes, ushered in the commercial hip-hop era. Appropriately, it kicks off this comprehensive collection of 12-inch singles, which includes plenty of fluff, a handful of classics, and a bunch more variations on "Good Times" and whatever other groove proved trendy at the time. Grandmaster Flash & the Furious Five's "The Message" and "White Lines (Don't Do It)" demonstrated this music had a conscience too, on par with Marvin Gaye's "What's Going On" and Stevie Wonder's "Livin' for the City," and wasn't to be just a fad. But mostly, *The Sugar Hill Records Story* is the soundtrack for a party that started in the ghetto and wound up rocking both suburbia and Wall Street.

Greg Kot

The Sugarhill Gang

Formed 1979, in NJ or NY.

Master Gee (born Guy O'Brien), vocals; Wonder Mike (born Michael Wright), vocals; Big Bank Hank (born Henry Jackson), vocals.

To this date, the origins of the Sugarhill Gang remain vague. The story goes that Sugar Hill Records founder Sylvia Robinson sent out her son, Joey Robinson Jr., to put the group together for her new label after hearing some rappers at her birthday party at New York's Harlem World. An impromptu audition with Big Bank Hank inside a parked car attracted the attention of Wonder Mike and Master Gee, and the trio was born on the spot. Lifting the bassline and rhythm from Chic's "Good Times," the Sugarhill Gang's first single, "Rapper's Delight," became the first internationally recognized hip-hop hit, charting in the American Top 40 shortly after its release. No rap track had ever even cracked the Top 100 before, and, certainly, none had sold as much: According to Sugar Hill Records, the single sold more than 2 million U.S. copies. The Sugarhill Gang's success rankled other members of New York's budding hip-hop community, who were disturbed that the first rap group through the mainstream door hadn't paid its dues, and was mediocre, anyway. Plus, the group had roots in New Jersey, which drove the New

York purists crazy. It wasn't long, though, before the Sugarhill Gang lost its King-of-the-Hill status; although the group released a string of 12-inch singles ("8th Wonder," "Apache"), none fully recreated the success of the debut, which ironically and appropriately clocks in at just under 15 minutes.

what's available: *Rapper's Delight: The Best of the Sugarhill Gang* 🎵🎵🎵 (Rhino, 1996, prod. various) compiles the group's variable work, from the pathbreaking title track up to 1985's "Work, Work, the Body."

influences:

◀◀ King Tim III, Treacherous Three, Kurtis Blow, DJ Hollywood, Kool Herc, Grandmaster Flash & the Furious Five, Grandmaster Caz & the Cold Crush Brothers

▶▶ Hip-hop and everything after

Aidin Vizari

Donna Summer

Born Donna Gaines, December 31, 1948, in Boston, MA.

Disco had a queen, and it was Summer. Nurtured in church choirs and in theater troupes, Summer—in cahoots with producers Giorgio Moroder and Pete Bellote—delivered a breathless, orgasmic performance on "Love to Love You Baby" that stirred loins on dance floors around the world in 1975 and eventually scaled the pop charts. That was the start of something big, as Summer reeled off a five-year string of club and radio hits ("I Feel Love," "Last Dance," an epic rendition of Jimmy Webb's dynamically twisted "MacArthur Park"). But Summer and her producers were savvy enough to follow the trends; as disco ebbed at the end of the 1970s, she moved subtly into dance-rock on albums such as *Bad Girls* and *The Wanderer* and continued to broaden her reach and embrace her born-again faith (she won a Grammy for Best Inspirational Vocal in 1984)—even though the hits slowed and eventually stopped during the 1980s. Summer hasn't necessarily given up, but when you see her perform these days it's little more than a trip down a polyester memory lane.

what to buy: The compact, 18-song *Endless Summer: Donna Summer's Greatest Hits* 🎵🎵🎵🎵 (Mercury/Casablanca, 1984, prod. various) is a nonstop treat of pleasures—guilty in some cases, but well worth having in the collection.

what to buy next: *Bad Girls* 🎵🎵🎵🎵 (Mercury/Casablanca, 1979, prod. Giorgio Moroder, Pete Bellote) added rock to Summer's dance-oriented palette via the title track and the wonderful

"Hot Stuff." *The Wanderer* 🎜🎜🎜 (Geffen, 1980/Casablanca-Mercury, 1994, prod. Giorgio Moroder, Pete Belotte) branches out even further, with contributions from Jeff Beck and Billy Idol. *The Donna Summer Anthology* 🎜🎜🎜 (Casablanca/Chronicles, 1993, prod. various) offers a broader sampling than *Endless Summer*.

what to avoid: *Another Place and Time* 🎜 (Atlantic, 1989, prod. Mike Stock, Matt Aitken, Waterman) is bland and soulless, diluting Summer's powerful presence in the antiseptic arrangements that are the British production trio's stock in trade.

the rest:

Love to Love You Baby 🎜🎜🎜 (Mercury/Casablanca, 1975/1992)
A Love Trilogy 🎜🎜 (Mercury/Casablanca, 1976/1992)
The Four Seasons of Love 🎜🎜 (Mercury/Casablanca, 1976/1991)
I Remember Yesterday 🎜🎜 (Mercury/Casablanca, 1977/1991)
Once Upon a Time 🎜🎜 (Mercury/Casablanca, 1977/1991)
Live and More 🎜🎜 (Mercury/Casablanca, 1978/1990)
On the Radio: Greatest Hits 🎜🎜🎜 (Mercury/Casablanca, 1979)
Walk Away: Collector's Edition 🎜🎜🎜 (Mercury/Casablanca, 1982)
Donna Summer 🎜🎜🎜 (Geffen, 1982/Mercury-Casablanca, 1994)
She Works Hard for the Money 🎜🎜🎜 (Mercury, 1983)
Cats Without Claws 🎜🎜 (Geffen/Mercury, 1984)
All Systems Go 🎜🎜 (Mercury/Casablanca, 1987)
Dance Collection 🎜🎜🎜 (Mercury/Casablanca, 1987)
Mistaken Identity 🎜🎜 (Atlantic, 1991)
Christmas Spirit 🎜🎜🎜 (Mercury, 1994)

worth searching for: Summer has made lots of guest appearances, ranging from the ridiculous—Kiss' *Gene Simmons* 🎜🎜 (Mercury, 1978)—to her sublime vocals on Brooklyn Dreams' *The Music, Harmony and Rhythm* 🎜🎜🎜 (Mercury/Casablanca, 1996).

influences:

◀◀ Mahalia Jackson, Aretha Franklin, Nico, Kraftwerk, Gloria Gaynor

▶▶ Irene Cara, Grace Jones, Madonna, Paula Abdul, Taylor Dayne

Gary Graff

The Supremes

Formed as the Primettes, 1959, in Detroit, MI.

Diana (Diane) Ross, vocals (1959–69); Florence Ballard, vocals (1959–1967); Mary Wilson, vocals; Betty McGlown, vocals (1959–60); Barbara Martin, vocals (1960–63); Cindy Birdsong, vocals (1967–71, 1974–76); Jean Terrell, vocals (1970–74); Lynda Laurence, vocals

(1972–74); Scherrie Payne, vocals (1974–77); Susaye Greene, vocals (1976–77).

The Supremes were as much about sugary pop confection and image as about R&B; they were Berry Gordy Jr.'s ticket to the Copacabana and other mainstream trappings he craved, which (along with his romance with Diana Ross) helps explain why they were the most successful of Motown's female vocal groups. It's hard to overstate the magic of Holland-Dozier-Holland's hits and, to a slightly lesser extent, Ross' dynamic and striking lead vocals. Balancing choreographed stage glamour with alternatingly cool and flirty coyness, the Supremes' sweet vocals epitomized the everyone-welcome crossover nature of the Motown sound. Along with the Beatles, the Supremes defined Top 40 pop during the 1960s. But after Ross' departure for a career as a solo artist and movie star, the Supremes were placed on Motown's back burner; the gradual departure of Holland-Dozier-Holland's songs and the label's decreased support left the group floundering until it folded in 1977, though Wilson continues to tour using the Supremes moniker.

what to buy: *Anthology* 🎜🎜🎜🎜 (Motown, 1970, prod. various) contains every single Motown hit the group recorded—an awesome display of timeless music making that's still amazing to behold.

what to buy next: *Greatest Hits and Rare Classics* 🎜🎜🎜🎜 (Motown, 1991, prod. various) is an informative supplement to *Anthology* for those interested in the post-Ross years.

what to avoid: *The Best of the Supremes & the Four Tops* 🎜🎜 (Motown, 1991, prod. various) is a skimpy compilation that sells both groups short.

the rest:

Merry Christmas 🎜🎜🎜 (Motown, 1965)
The Supremes Sing Country, Western & Pop 🎜🎜 (Motown, 1965/1994)
I Hear a Symphony 🎜🎜🎜 (Motown, 1966)
Supremes A-Go-Go 🎜🎜🎜🎜 (Motown, 1966/1989)
Reflections 🎜🎜🎜 (Motown, 1968/1991)
Great Songs & Performances That Inspired Motown 25 🎜🎜🎜 (Motown, 1983/1991)
Greatest Hits, Vol. I 🎜🎜🎜 (Motown, 1986)
Greatest Hits, Vol. II 🎜🎜🎜 (Motown)
Greatest Hits, Vol. III 🎜🎜🎜 (Motown, 1991)
Motown Superstar Series, Vol. 1 🎜🎜🎜🎜 (Motown)
Live at London's Talk of the Town 🎜🎜🎜 (Motown)
Captured Live On Stage 🎜🎜🎜 (Motown)
Every Great #1 Hit 🎜🎜🎜🎜 (Motown)
Motown Legends: Stoned Love 🎜🎜 (ESX Entertainment, 1995)
The Ultimate Collection 🎜🎜🎜🎜 (Motown, 1997)

worth searching for: Look for *Where Did Our Love Go* ♫♫♫ (Motown, 1964), the trio's sophomore effort and one of Ross' great pre-vanity showcases.

influences:

◄◄ The Shangri-las, the Chiffons

►► The J. Geils Band, TLC, SWV, the Braxtons, Luther Vandross, Brandy

see also: *Diana Ross*

Allan Orski

Al B. Sure!

Born Al Brown in 1969, Boston, MA.

Al Brown was Sure! of himself and his potential for pop-soul stardom long before bursting onto the national recording scene in the late 1980s. The Boston native, raised in Mount Vernon, New York, gave up a football scholarship to the University of Iowa to pursue a music career—and made the gamble pay off handsomely. The New Jack balladeer scored his first hit single at age 19 with the smooth and sensual "Nite and Day" from his platinum debut LP *In Effect Mode*, then reinforced his heartthrob appeal and vocal range with his bouncy followup single "Off on Your Own (Girl)." But Sure! (yes, the exclamation point is an affectation, but correct) shrewdly positioned himself as a New Jack Swinger for the sensitive-male 1980s. Rather than rhapsodize about animal magnetism and female undergarments, his songs like "If I'm Not Your Lover" chides women about relationships based purely on sex: "I'm just a man who comes around at night/And to leave you girl/Baby that ain't right." As his prominence in the industry escalated—enough to merit a romantic duet with Queen Motown herself, Diana Ross, on his sophomore LP *Private Times . . . and the Whole 9!*—Sure! has branched out into other areas of the business, writing songs and producing such acts as Jodeci, Johnny Gill, and Tevin Campbell while taking time to provide guest vocals on albums by Chubb Rock, David Bowie, Big Daddy Kane, and Barry White. His last solo release, the EP *Right Now*, is available only by special order.

what to buy: The first Sure! LP, *In Effect Mode* ♫♫♫ (Warner Bros./Uptown, 1988, prod. Kyle West, Teddy Riley, Al B. Sure!), remains his finest total effort, establishing the artist as a sexy, sincere individualist with the emotional balladry of "Nite and Day," "If I'm Not Your Lover," and a credible cover of Roberta Flack's timeless "Killing Me Softly."

what to buy next: Sticking with his tradition of including at least one cover on each album, *Private Times . . . and the Whole*

9! ♫♫♫ (Warner Bros./Uptown, 1990, prod. various) is notable for its soaring, funkified version of the Eagles' "Hotel California." However, Sure!'s masterful songweaving continues on this album with the sultry "Touch You," "Shades of Grey," and the Diana Ross duet "No Matter What You Do." "Missunderstanding," with its machine-gun drum effects and New Jack attitude, is the original highlight of the LP. Perhaps his album titles don't make immediate sense, but his music does.

the rest:
Sexy Versus ♫♫ (Warner Bros., 1992)
Right Now ♫♫♥ (Warner Bros., 1992)

influences:

◄◄ Barry White, Sam Cooke, Motown artists

►► R. Kelly, Johnny Gill, Tevin Campbell, Boyz II Men

Christina Fuoco

Surface

Formed mid-1980s, in NJ.

Bernard Jackson, vocals, guitar, bass, synthesizer; David "Pic" Conley, synthesizer, flute, percussion, drum programming; David Townsend, guitar, keyboards, vocals.

Surface arrived with a musical pedigree: David Townsend is the son of producer/songwriter Ed Townsend, while David Conley served time with Mandrill. The trio specializes in quiet, smooth jams—not quite Barry White-style bedroom music but certainly romantic and pleasantly sophisticated. They've had a smattering of commercial success, including the #1 hit "First Time" and Top 20 titles "Happy," "Never Gonna Let You Down," and "Shower Me with Your Love."

what to buy: *The Best of Surface: A Nice Time for Lovin'* ♫♫♫ (Columbia, 1991) has all the hits and even a holiday song, "Christmas Time Is Here," but at 10 songs it's a bit skimpy and wrongly excludes "Hold On to Love," a collaboration with a then-fledgling Regina Belle from the *2nd Wave* album.

what to buy next: Acquire *2nd Wave* ♫♫♫ (Columbia, 1988) to get the must-have "Hold On to Love."

the rest:
Surface ♫♫♫ (Columbia, 1987)
3 Deep ♫♫♫ (Columbia, 1990)
Surface 10 ♫♫♥ (Hypnotic, 1996)

Keith Sweat (© Ken Settle)

influences:

◀◀ Barry White, John Klemmer, the Stylistics, the Crusaders

▶▶ Portrait, Joe

Gary Graff

Keith Sweat

Born 1963, in New York, NY.

Harlem-born soul singer/songwriter Keith Sweat knows how to do one thing—sing slow, bass-heavy, somewhat cornball ballads with infectious hooks, a formula he's used to sell nearly 10 million albums. The former Wall Street brokerage assistant, whose voice recalls that of 1970s singer Steve Arrington, scored his first big hit in 1987 with "I Want Her," a dance tune produced by Teddy Riley. The groundbreaking single ushered in the genre New Jack Swing, a hybrid of traditional soul melodies with hip-hop's harder edge. Though critics often malign his "I'm pleading for your love" style, Sweat has consistently made R&B and crossover hits by communicating masculine, adult emotions inside a comfort zone neither supersensitive nor super-macho.

what to buy: His seminal work, *Make It Last Forever* 𝄞𝄞𝄞𝄞 (Elektra, 1988, prod. Keith Sweat, Teddy Riley), introduced us to Sweat's offbeat voice and delivered lasting, trend-setting songs such as "Something Just Ain't Right," and "Don't Stop Your Love." Because of Sweat's generally unchanging style, it sounds as current today as it did when it was released.

what to buy next: *Keith Sweat* 𝄞𝄞𝄞𝄞 (Elektra, 1996, prod. Keith Sweat), finds Sweat upholding his tradition nearly a decade after his debut, and includes a cover of one of Arrington's biggest hits, "Just a Touch."

what to avoid: *Get Up On It* 𝄞𝄞 (Elektra, 1994, prod. Keith Sweat) finds the formula intact but getting a little less interesting with repetition.

the rest:

I'll Give All My Love to You 𝄞𝄞𝄞 (Elektra, 1990)

Keep It Comin' 𝄞𝄞𝄞 (Elektra, 1991)

(With Gerald Levert and Johnny Gill) *Levert. Sweat. Gill.* N/A (EastWest America, 1997)

influences:

◀◀ Steve Arrington, Teddy Pendergrass, Ronald Isley

▶▶ Joe, Gerald Levert, Jeff Redd

Franklin Paul

Switch

Formed 1975, in Mansfield, OH.

Phillip Ingram, vocals (1975–80); Bobby DeBarge (died 1985), keyboards (1975–early 1980s); Tommy DeBarge, bass (1975–early 1980s); Greg Williams, horns; Eddie Fluellen, horns; Jody Sims, drums; Renard Gallo, percussion, vocals (early 1980s–?); Gonzales Ozen, percussion, vocals (early 1980s–?); Attala Zane, keyboards (early 1980s–?).

Despite a few Top 10 R&B singles during the late 1970s—"I Call Your Name," "There'll Never Be," "Love Over and Over Again"—Switch is something of a footnote in R&B history. A discovery of Jermaine Jackson's for Motown, it made the most news after two key members—Bobby and Tommy DeBarge—turned Jackson on to their younger siblings back in Grand Rapids, Michigan, and eventually left themselves for the more lucrative fortunes of the family act, effectively scuttling Switch's ambitions.

what's available: *The Best of Switch* 𝄞𝄞𝄞𝄞 (Motown, 1991, prod. various) shows that Switch deserves a little more respect than it receives. The songwriting is strong, and there are several tracks that are as enjoyable as the hits. For now, this remains Switch's only title in print.

influences:

◀◀ The Jacksons, the Sylvers, the Emotions

▶▶ DeBarge, New Edition

Gary Graff

SWV

Formed 1989, in New York, NY.

Cheryl "Coko" Gamble, vocals; Leanne "Lelee" Lyons, vocals; Tamara "Taj" Johnson, vocals.

New York City-bred Cheryl Gamble, Leanne Lyons, and Tamara Johnson started as a hip-hopping, TLC-like outfit called Female Edition, in reverence to their idols, New Edition. The three high school friends soon became SWV—Sisters with Voices—and had a huge commercial success with their debut album. Though the album went double platinum and scored several hit singles, the trio appeared to be a textbook "girl group"—one standout voice (Coko), two silent members in the background, all under the guidance of a male writer and producer (Brian Alexander Morgan). SWV's second complete album dispelled that notion as each member carved out vocal niches, wrote songs, and brought in a bevy of producers to give it variety. Throw in a grown-up look in their videos and the group had managed a rare feat—transforming from kids to adults right in plain site. They also managed to keep themselves grounded in the hip-hop community with several well-chosen guest appearances, including the remix to "Anything," a collaboration with Wu-Tang Clan that appeared on the soundtrack to the film *Above the Rim,* and Teddy Riley's popular remix of their "Right Here/Human Nature," that featured samples of Michael Jackson's hit, "Human Nature."

what to buy: SWV was aiming to distinguish their separate voices on *New Beginning* 🎵🎵🎵 (RCA, 1996, prod. various) and instead managed to create a mature, gelled, and singularly defining sound, as evidenced on "Use Your Heart" and "That's What I'm Here For."

what to buy next: *It's About Time* 🎵🎵🎵 (RCA, 1992, prod. Brian A. Morgan) sounds almost childish in theme and execution by comparison, but tender love songs such as "Weak" and "You're Always on My Mind" are still pleasant.

the rest:
The Remixes EP 🎵🎵🎵 (RCA, 1994)
Release Some Tension 🎵🎵🎵🎵 (RCA, 1997)

worth searching for: Nowhere can the trio's grownup sexuality be seen better than on "Can We," their entry to the movie soundtrack *Booty Call* 🎵🎵🎵 (Jive, 1997, prod. various).

influences:
◀◀ New Edition, the Jackson 5
▶▶ Xscape, 702, Brownstone

Franklin Paul

The Sylvers

Formed 1972, in Memphis, TN. Disbanded 1985.

Leon Frank Sylvers III; Olympia-Ann Sylvers; Charmaine Sylvers; James Sylvers; Foster Sylvers; Edmund Sylvers; Ricky Sylvers; Angela Sylvers; Pat Sylvers.

Along with Tavares and the Jackson 5, the nine siblings in the Sylvers were among the most popular family-based acts of the dance-oriented 1970s. The four oldest children—Leon, Olympia-Ann, Charmaine, and James—had performed for years as the Little Angels before the Sylvers' first records, made for Pride Records in the early 1970s. Brothers Foster, Edmund, and Ricky joined the act for the first recordings. By the time the group hit its peak with songs such as "Boogie Fever" and "Hot Line," sisters Angela and Pat had also joined. The Sylvers had their biggest successes working with writer/producer Freddie Perrin, who had also worked with Tavares and the J5, but their records

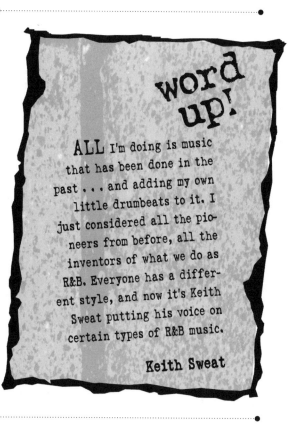

identified them so strongly with disco that as that trend faded, so did the band. The Sylvers released their last record as a group for Geffen in 1984, though Foster has recorded solo and Leon went on to some success as a producer.

what to buy: *Boogie Fever: The Best of the Sylvers* 🎵🎵🎵 (Razor & Tie, 1995, prod. various) contains all 16 of the Sylvers' charting hits (including solo singles by Foster and Edmund), from the Jackson 5-influenced "Stay Away from Me" to the synthesizer-fattened "In One Love and Out the Other." The best records, though, remain the group's crossover disco smashes—"Boogie Fever," "Hot Line," and "High School Dance."

what to avoid: *Greatest Hits* 🎵🎵 (Curb, 1994, prod. various) is an inferior compilation that duplicates a lot of the material from *Boogie Fever.*

influences:
◀◀ Jackson 5
▶▶ Tavares, New Edition

Brian Mansfield

Sylvester

Born Sylvester James, Sept 1944, in Los Angeles, CA. Died 1988.

Sylvester James is recognized as one of the pioneers of disco music. One of the first openly gay artists in the music industry, he mixed funk, R&B, and gospel into his music. He came along when the disco genre began to flourish and produced some of the era's finest material. His stage shows presented him in full transvestite regalia and earned him a huge gay following nationwide. Before his solo career, he performed with a cross-dressing vocal group, the Cockettes. His background vocalists included Jeanie Tracy and the Two Tons O'Fun (Martha Wash, Izora Rhodes). After making an indelible mark on the industry, Sylvester died from AIDS-related complications in 1988.

what to buy: *Greatest Hits* 𝒜𝒜𝒜𝒜 (Fantasy, 1988, prod. various) contains all of the classics, including "You Make Me Feel Mighty Real," "Stars," and "Disco Heat." A terrific introduction to his music and an excellent representation of his body of work.

what to buy next: *Greatest Hits: Non-Stop Dance Party* 𝒜𝒜𝒜𝒜 (Fantasy, 1983, prod. various) presents many of the same songs in special dance remixes—perhaps the definitive way to experience Sylvester's music.

what to avoid: During the mid-1980s, Sylvester reached a crossroads. R&B was becoming stale and formulaic, and his new label, Megatone, was unsure of how to market him. So avoid the wannabe commercial stylings of *Call Me* 𝒜 (Megatone, 1984), *M-1015* 𝒜 (Megatone, 1984), and *Mutual Attraction* 𝒜𝒜 (Megatone, 1987).

the rest:
Step II 𝒜𝒜𝒜 (Fantasy, 1978)
Living Proof 𝒜𝒜𝒜 (Fantasy, 1979)
Mighty Real 𝒜𝒜𝒜 (Fantasy, 1980)

influences:
◀◀ Little Richard, B.B. King, Mahalia Jackson, James Brown, Sly Stone

▶▶ Rick James, Jermaine Stewart, Boy George, Grace Jones, Duran Duran, Michael Jackson, RuPaul, Frankie Knuckles, Ten City

Damon Percy

Syreeta

Born Rita Wright, 1946, in Pittsburgh, PA.

Imagine being married to Stevie Wonder—and trying to have a musical career of your own. Such was the dilemma faced by Syreeta Wright, a onetime choir singer at Mather Academy in South Carolina who became a secretary and background vocalist at Motown during the mid-1960s. She started recording on her own in 1968, with Holland-Dozier-Holland producing and Ashford & Simpson writing songs for her. But when Syreeta began to write her own material, Wonder took an interest, which eventually became more than musical. The two were only married for a couple of years, but they've remained friends and professional collaborators throughout both of their careers—right up to Syreeta's 1983 album *Spell*. Syreeta never had great commercial success on her own, but she's certainly a strong footnote in Motown's history.

what's available: All that remains in print is *Stevie Wonder Presents Syreeta* 𝒜𝒜𝒜 (Motown, 1974/1994, prod. Stevie Wonder), on which Wonder and Syreeta wrote all the material. Ultimately, he should have written more, and for as talented as he was, maybe letting Syreeta be part of Motown's well-oiled production machine wouldn't have been such a bad idea.

worth searching for: Syreeta worked with another famous keyboard player on *Billy Preston & Syreeta* 𝒜𝒜𝒜 (Motown, 1991) to somewhat better results, as Preston takes the kind of control Wonder probably should have.

influences:
◀◀ Stevie Wonder, Marvin Gaye, Martha Reeves, Carla Thomas
▶▶ Jean Carne, Irene Cara

Gary Graff

Tag Team

Formed 1983, in Denver, CO.

DC the Brain Supreme (born Cecil Glenn), vocals; Steve Roll'n (born Steve Gibson), vocals.

"One-hit wonder, that's what they say/Well all y'all can kiss my A." So declared Tag Team on "Here It Is! Bam," the bass music duo's failed attempt at a second hit. Of course, even without another hit under their belt, DC the Brain Supreme and Steve Roll'n can still get away with telling people to kiss off; their song "Whoomp! (There It Is)" stands as one of the best-selling singles in pop history, with over 4 million U.S. music consumers served. The smash hit also wound up making a major contribution to the

American lexicon, as the *New York Times* called "Whoomp! There It Is"—and 95 South's variation on the theme, "Whoot, There It Is"—the hottest new phrase in the country in 1993. While Jacksonville, Florida's, 95 South released "Whoot!" a month before Tag Team's "Whoomp!" hit the market, DC the Brain Supreme claimed that he had been leading the cry "Whoomp, there it is" as a club DJ since 1990 to rev up the dance floor. "Whoomp" was his own variation of Arsenio Hall's trademark bark, and DC decided to use it with Steve Roll'n, his rap partner of 10 years. Eventually, he began spinning a rough cut of "Whoomp!" at an Atlanta nightclub, which members of 95 South heard and decided to make into a song of their own. With the two songs on the market simultaneously in 1993, it's quite possible that "Whoomp!" lost out on its chance to become the top-selling single in history because of the confusion about which song was which. Still, DC and Steve Roll'n harbored no ill will toward 95 South, even appearing on the *The Arsenio Hall Show* with their rivals for a combined "Whoot"/"Whoomp!" performance.

what's available: Only the group's mediocre sophomore effort, *Audio Entertainment* ♪♪ (Life, 1995), is still in print.

worth searching for: The single "Whoomp! (There It Is)" (Life, 1993) is all the Tag Team you'll need. Although the vocals are spotty and the refrain is downright silly, the exuberant, bass-driven song is still a load of fun and, certainly, a bass-music classic. Call it the "Louie, Louie" of southern hip-hop. Proving that they don't take themselves too seriously, Tag Team reprise their hit with "MC Mouse" on the out-of-print collection *Mickey Unrapped* (Disney, 1994).

influences:

◀◀ Magic Mike, 2 Live Crew

▶▶ 95 South, Freak Nasty, 69 Boyz, A-Town Players, 12 Gauge

Josh Freedom du Lac

Taj Mahal

See: Mahal, Taj

Take 6

Formed 1980, in Huntsville, AL.

Mark Kibble, first tenor; Claude V. McKnight III, first tenor; David Thomas, second tenor; Cedric Dent, baritone vocals; Alvin Chea, bass vocals; Mervyn Warren, second tenor (1980–90); Joey Kibble, second tenor (1990–present).

The incomparably tight vocal harmonies of Take 6 have had a significant impact on the musical directions of contemporary R&B, jazz, and pop, while renewing interest in and expanding the dimensions of *a capella* singing. Though still a gospel group at its core, the sextet has seemingly taken up permanent residence as Best Jazz Vocal Group in *Down Beat* magazine's Readers and Critics Polls, appeared on numerous movie soundtracks, and recorded with such diverse artists as k.d. lang, Ella Fitzgerald, Don Henley (on "The End of the Innocence"), Quincy Jones, and Branford Marsalis. Formed in the acoustically favorable men's rooms of Alabama's tiny Oakwood College, Take 6 evolved from its original identity of The Gentlemen's Estate Quartet to the Sounds of Distinction to Alliance, changing the last name after discovering it was already in use by another group. Each member an accomplished musician in his own right (baritone Dent is completing his Ph.D. in Music Theory), Take 6 provided what little instrumental accompaniment they required on their early albums with their voices alone. Although they have been criticized by gospel purists for their unique bond to both the mainstream and Christian music communities, the sextet has always remained true to their gospel roots.

what to buy: The eponymous album that introduced their unparalleled artistry to the world, *Take 6* ♪♪♪♪ (Reprise, 1988, prod. Mark Kibble, Claude V. McKnight III, Mervyn Warren) mixed innovative reworkings of classic spirituals and dynamic original tunes—all sung completely *a capella*—and provided a gust of fresh air to an industry that was, and in many ways still is, starving for new creative juices. *Join the Band* ♪♪♪♪ (Reprise, 1994, prod. various) was a landmark LP for the sextet, incorporating instruments into their music (as performed by the likes of Herbie Hancock and Gerald Albright), recording cover versions of secular hits ("Biggest Part of Me"), and inviting guest vocalists such as Ray Charles and Queen Latifah. The overt attempt to curry mainstream favor was met with a Grammy Award and a gold-record plaque, proving the experiment a rousing success.

what to buy next: *So Much 2 Say* ♪♪♪♪ (Reprise, 1990, prod. Take 6) was the last album to feature original second tenor Mervyn Warren, who left to pursue a career as a producer. The disc produced a hit single, "I L-O-V-E U," and established the fact that Take 6 would have staying power beyond the curiosity of a novelty vocal group.

the rest:
He Is Christmas ♪♪♪ (Reprise, 1991)
Brothers ♪♪♪ (Reprise, 1996)

worth searching for: The Quincy Jones album *Back on the Block* (Qwest, 1989) is a must-have recording for a Take 6 fan, showcasing the group on numerous tracks including an "*a cap-*

pella party" with Bobby McFerrin and the hauntingly beautiful Brazilian wedding song, "Setembro." So flawless are the group's voices that Take 6 sounds have been sampled and cut up for studio producers. Kurzweil is offering a "Take 6 Sample Library" featuring vocal sustains, accents, percussion, and rhythm loops, for a mere $399.

influences:

⏮ Fairfield Four, Persuasions, Isley Brothers, Andrae Crouch

⏭ Boyz II Men, Coming of Age, DC Talk

Tim A. Smith

Al Tariq

See: Beatnuts

A Taste of Honey

Formed 1972, in Los Angeles, CA.

Hazel Payne, vocals, guitar; Janice Marie Johnson, vocals, bass; Perry L. Kibble, keyboards, vocals; Donald R. Johnson, drums, vocals.

R&B was always ahead of the trend curve in popular music, and the mixed-gender makeup of this band presaged that development in rock and pop by nearly two decades. Thanks to the disco smash "Boogie Oogie Oogie," its eponymous debut album sold more than a million copies in 1978, and the quartet won the Grammy Award for Best New Artist for that year. Alas, the award's curse snared our heroes, who quietly faded away despite Johnson's and Payne's best efforts to make a go of it.

what's available: *Beauty and the Boogie* 🎵🎵 (EMI, 1997, prod. various) shows why A Taste of Honey's career was short-lived. There are a few modestly successful grooves, but even "Boogie Oogie Oogie"—included in its hit single and extended remix versions here—couldn't be considered top-shelf disco.

influences:

⏮ Brass Construction, the Whispers, Donna Summer, Barry White

Gary Graff

Tavares

Formed 1959, in New Bedford, MA.

Ralph Tavares; Arthur "Pooch" Tavares; Feliciano "Butch" Tavares; Perry Lee "Tiny" Tavares; Antone "Chubby" Tavares.

There may, in fact, be hell to pay when the litany of disco performers are summoned on judgment day, but Tavares will most likely skate by unscathed. Such immunity stems from the fact that the five brothers were weaned on Cape Verde (where the family history originates) folk songs and doo wop. That and a healthy dose of R&B led the group to make a danceable music that crossed disco lines without completely severing the roots from which it grew. By 1974, Tavares had gone past its New England club circuit with ballads such as their cover of Hall and Oates' "She's Gone," which led them to a former Motown producer who gelled the brother's harmonies into dance floor success (10 singles in the latter half of the 1970s). The group's popularity peaked with its single "More Than a Woman" from the hyper-selling *Saturday Night Fever* soundtrack in 1978. It proved to be a questionable feat, however, since it forever saddled the group with the disco tag, soon to be the kiss of death. Tavares has since relied on its live drawing power rather than its record selling potency, which seems to have irrevocably waned. Ralph left the group in 1983, opting to spend time with his family.

what's available: The only album left in print is the recent compilation, *It Only Takes a Minute: A Lifetime with Tavares* 🎵🎵🎵 (EMI, 1997). Although it's by no means complete (it omits "She's Gone" and "More Than a Woman") it does contain the bulk of the group's better known material such as "It Only Takes a Minute," "Heaven Must Be Missing an Angel," and "Remember What I Told You to Forget."

influences:

⏮ The Jackson Five, Marvin Gaye, the Temptations

⏭ Boyz II Men, New Edition, Hall and Oates

Allan Orski

Johnnie Taylor

Born May 5, 1938, in Crawfordsville, AK.

One of the last great "testifyin'" soul singers of his era, Taylor undoubtedly developed his tortured, electrifying blues-growl style in church. He started with a Chicago-based gospel group called the Highway QCs in the mid-1950s, even though he was raised closer to the pure Memphis R&B sound. Taylor was also a member of the Five Echoes gospel quintet until turning to commercial soul in the late 1960s, as Sam Cooke's hand-picked choice to replace him in the Soul Stirrers. He left the group for a brief fling as a preacher; then he truly got funky. By his early 30s, Taylor had gone solo and released his signature hit, "Who's Makin' Love (To Your Old Lady/While You Was Out Makin' Love)," in 1968, which peaked at #5 nationally. The album of the same name is still available, and remains a flawless example of late 1960s soul shoutin'. Proclaimed the "Philosopher of Soul" by the Stax PR machine and specializing in lyrical tales of cheatin' lovers, Taylor had a five-year wait before his next chart success, "Cheaper to Keep Her," a Top 20 hit in 1973 (and surely one of the last publicly endorsed statements of political incorrectness). But the late 1970s saw Taylor go the way of many of his stone soul brothers—disco—a move which ironically produced his only #1 single, "Disco Lady." Mixing a slow Memphis-inspired groove with a sensuous disco rhythm, "Disco Lady" hit the top spot on April 3, 1976, and remained there four weeks overall. Taylor's last chart hit, the optimistically titled "Disco 9000," came in 1977. Most recently, Taylor has been recording for the Malaco label.

what to buy: The Taylor trademark *Who's Makin' Love* ♪♪♪ (Stax, 1990, prod. Don Davis, Al Jackson Jr.)—featuring the Memphis Horns, Booker T. and the MG's, and Isaac Hayes on guitar!—is obviously a good place to start, but the J.T. experience is perhaps best realized through the hard-to-find *Chronicle: 20 Greatest Hits* ♪♪♪♪ (Stax, 1977, prod. Don Davis). The title may be a slight overstatement, but most of Taylor's pop and R&B victories are definitely on board.

what to buy next: Many of Taylor's earliest Stax R&B recordings from 1971–73, including "Cheaper to Keep Her" and "We're Getting Careless with Our Love," are now available on *Taylored in Silk* ♪♪♪♪ (Stax, 1995, prod. various).

what to avoid: *Super Hits* ♪ (Stax, 1989, prod. various) is a true misnomer: a rehashed greatest-hits package, poorly produced.

the rest:
Raw Blues ♪♪♪ (Stax, 1987)
Ugly Man ♪♪ (Ichiban, 1989)
I Know It's Wrong, But I Just Can't Do Right ♪♪ (Malaco, 1991)
The Johnnie Taylor Philosophy Continues ♪♪♪♪ (Stax, 1991)
Little Bluebird ♪♪♪ (Stax, 1991)
Wanted: One Soul Singer ♪♪♪ (Rhino, 1991)
Greatest Hits, Vol. 1 ♪♪♪ (RSP, 1992)
Real Love ♪♪♪ (Malaco, 1994)
Stop Half-Loving These Women ♪♪♪ (Paula, 1996)
Good Love! ♪♪♪ (Malaco, 1996)
One Step Beyond ♪♪ (Stax, 1996)
Rated X-Traordinaire: The Best of Johnnie Taylor ♪♪♪♪ (Legacy, 1996)
In Control ♪♪ (Malaco)

worth searching for: Try to find the cassette-only reissue of *Eargasm* (Columbia, 1989), one of the few discs Taylor did not wax for Stax.

influences:
◀◀ Sam Cooke, the Soul Stirrers, James Brown

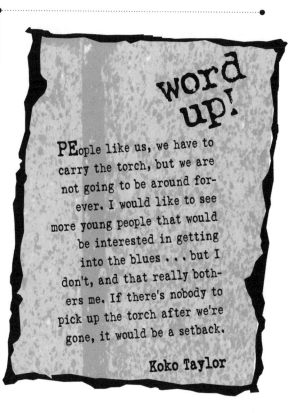

> PEople like us, we have to carry the torch, but we are not going to be around forever. I would like to see more young people that would be interested in getting into the blues . . . but I don't, and that really bothers me. If there's nobody to pick up the torch after we're gone, it would be a setback.
>
> **Koko Taylor**

▶▶ Wilson Pickett, Otis Redding, Al Green, Bobby Womack, Teddy Pendergrass, Latimore, Dennis Edwards, Rod Stewart

Bob Paxman

Koko Taylor

Born Cora Walton, September 28, 1935, in Memphis, TN.

Koko Taylor—best known for her growling belt of a voice, heavy nightclub touring even as she approaches 60, and facial features so distinctive and charismatic she earned a cameo in the David Lynch movie *Wild at Heart*—began her singing career after she moved to Chicago in 1953. It was just soon enough; by the early 1960s, just before Chicago's famed Chess Records lost momentum to rock 'n' roll, she hooked up with songwriter-producer Willie Dixon and squeezed out the terrific blues anthem "Wang Dang Doodle." Though that 1965 hit, a stomping, funky description of an all-night house party, continues to be the Queen of the Blues' main show-stopper, Taylor has put out

Koko Taylor (© Ken Settle)

nine straightforward blues albums since then. She has been one of the most reliable and consistent performers on the blues circuit; while some blues heroes and heroines, like Taylor's immediate predecessor Etta James, have experimented with different sounds to reach a broader audience, Taylor has held firm to her strengths. You can count on her traveling through your town, with a band of hot instrumentalists playing no-frills 12-bar electric blues songs, before the year is out.

what to buy: Because Taylor has such a visual presence, her ferocious onstage energy rarely comes across on record; her Alligator debut, *I Got What It Takes* ♫♫♫ (Alligator, 1975, prod. Koko Taylor, Joe Young, Bruce Iglauer) showcases her hunger to make an impact, with hot guitarist Mighty Joe Young, great songs by Willie Dixon and Otis Spann, and a pure-blues cover of the R&B classic "Mama, He Treats Your Daughter Mean." Like Lonnie Brooks, Luther Allison, and, heck, the Ramones, she basically put out the same album every few years after that; *Force of Nature* ♫♫♫ (Alligator, 1993, prod. Criss Johnson,

Koko Taylor, Bruce Iglauer) gets a boost from guest guitarist Buddy Guy and explosive readings of "Born Under a Bad Sign" and "Hound Dog," and is her best recent album.

what to buy next: Especially on the fast stuff, *The Earthshaker* ♫♫♫ (Alligator, 1978, prod. Bruce Iglauer), shows Taylor using her big voice to great effect. The pre-Alligator album you want, with frequently funny collaborations from creative partner Willie Dixon, is *Koko Taylor* ♫♫♫ (Chess, 1972, prod. Willie Dixon). *Queen of the Blues* ♫♫♫ (Alligator, 1985, prod. Koko Taylor, Bruce Iglauer, Criss Johnson) features guest guitarists Albert Collins, Son Seals, and Lonnie Brooks.

what to avoid: Taylor's one-dimensional blues approach sometimes lodges her in a rut, which is the case on *From the Heart of a Woman* ♫♫ (Alligator, 1981, prod. Bruce Iglauer) and *Jump for Joy* ♫♫ (Alligator, 1990, prod. Bruce Iglauer).

the rest:
Basic Soul ♫♫ (Chess, 1972)

Live from Chicago—An Audience with the Queen ♫♫♫ (Alligator, 1987)

What It Takes ♫♫♫ (Chess/MCA, 1991)

worth searching for: Her first album, *Koko Taylor* ♫♫♫ (USA, 1963, prod. Big Bill Hill) doesn't use Taylor's still-maturing voice to great effect, but it's a nice historical document of her early career. Because Taylor has her record company's consummate sound—straight-ahead blues with big vocals and lots of guitar solos—devotees will want to try *The Alligator Records 20th Anniversary Collection* ♫♫♫ (Alligator, 1991, prod. various) and the *Alligator Records 25th Anniversary Collection* ♫♫♫ (Alligator, 1996, prod. various).

influences:

◀◀ Muddy Waters, Bessie Smith, Etta James, Willie Dixon, B.B. King, Big Mama Thornton, Buddy Guy

▶▶ Katie Webster, Son Seals, Big Time Sarah, PJ Harvey, Janis Joplin, Melissa Etheridge

Steve Knopper

The Temptations

Formed 1961, in Detroit, MI.

Otis Williams (born Otis Miles), vocals; Eddie Kendricks (died October 5, 1992), vocals (1961–72); Paul Williams (died August 17, 1973), vocals (1971–72); Melvin Franklin (born David English; died February 23, 1995), vocals (1971–95); Elbridge Bryant, vocals (1961–63); David Ruffin (died June 1, 1991), vocals (1963–68); Dennis Edwards, vocals (1968–77, 1979–83, 1986–87); Ricky Owens, vocals (1972); Damon Harris, vocals (1972–75); Richard Street, vocals (1972–93); Glenn Leonard, vocals (1975–83); Louis Price, vocals (1977–79); Ron Tyson, vocals (1983–present); Ali Ollie Woodson, vocals (1983–86, 1987–present); Theo Peoples, vocals (1993–present); Ray Davis, vocals (1995–present).

With respect to the Four Tops—who deserve much credit for their longevity and wonderful body of work—the Temptations are *it* when it comes to Motown male vocal groups. The visceral power of the Tempts' five voices combined with its high-stepping stage show (a cross between the Tops' smooth 'n' natural and the Contours' chaos) super-charged the vocal group model to another level; when you hear "Get Ready," it's not just a song—it's a command. The Tempts' history is both blessed and cursed. It's been blessed with some otherwordly lead singers (Paul Williams, Ruffin, Kendricks, Edwards) and some of Motown's top producers and writers (Smokey Robinson, Norman Whitfield). The group has had some luck, too; Robinson and Ronnie White could have kept "My Girl" for their own group,

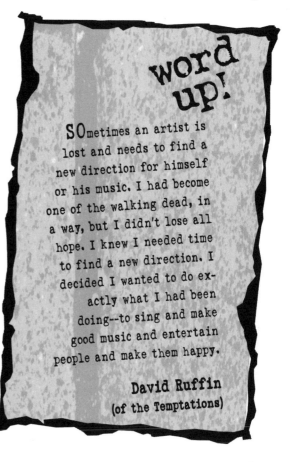

word up!

SOmetimes an artist is lost and needs to find a new direction for himself or his music. I had become one of the walking dead, in a way, but I didn't lose all hope. I knew I needed time to find a new direction. I decided I wanted to do exactly what I had been doing--to sing and make good music and entertain people and make them happy.

David Ruffin (of the Temptations)

the Miracles. But the Tempts' dominance came with a price; four members are dead from tragic circumstances (suicide, drug OD, lung cancer, a brain seizure). Otis Williams, the band's biographer, is the sole founding member left, but he's been carrying the torch through decades of internal squabbling and ego battles. The Temptations of today surely aren't on a par with the classic lineup of the 1960s, but the incredible battery of songs—"The Way You Do the Things You Do," "Girl (Why You Wanna Make Me Blue)," "Ain't Too Proud to Beg," "I Wish It Would Rain," "Cloud Nine," "Just My Imagination (Running Away With Me)"—usually will out.

what to buy: *The Temptations Anthology* ♫♫♫♫♫ (Motown, 1995, prod. various) packs 46 hits onto two CDs, with not a bad note to be found.

what to buy next: A more total—and worthwhile—immersion can be made with *Emperors of Soul* 𝄪𝄪𝄪𝄪 (Motown, 1995, prod. various), a regally titled box set that, at five discs, needs to be considered before purchase. *One by One* 𝄪𝄪𝄪𝄪 (Motown, 1995, prod. various) offers a well chosen collection of solo recordings by Kendricks, Ruffin, Edwards, and Paul Williams. *The Temptations Sing Smokey* 𝄪𝄪𝄪𝄪 (Motown, 1965/1989, prod. Smokey Robinson) is a nicely conceived collaboration between the Tempts and one of the group's chief patrons.

what to avoid: After all that great music, it's hard to swallow *For Lovers Only* 𝄪𝄪 (Motown, 1995, prod. Richard Perry) and its lush covers of "Some Enchanted Evening," "Night and Day," and "You Send Me."

the rest:
Meet the Temptations 𝄪𝄪𝄪 (Motown, 1964/1992)
The Temptin' Temptations 𝄪𝄪𝄪 (Motown, 1965/1990)
Gettin' Ready 𝄪𝄪𝄪 (Motown, 1966/1989)
Greatest Hits, Vol. 1 𝄪𝄪𝄪𝄪 (Motown, 1966)
In a Mellow Mood 𝄪𝄪𝄪 (Motown, 1967/1969)
I Wish It Would Rain 𝄪𝄪𝄪 (Motown, 1968)
Cloud Nine 𝄪𝄪𝄪 (Motown, 1969)
Psychedelic Shack 𝄪𝄪𝄪 (Motown, 1970/1989)
Puzzle People 𝄪𝄪𝄪𝄪 (Motown, 1970/1989)
Christmas Card 𝄪𝄪𝄪 (Motown, 1970/1989)
Give Love at Christmas 𝄪𝄪 (Motown)
Greatest Hits, Vol. II 𝄪𝄪𝄪𝄪 (Motown, 1970)
Sky's the Limit 𝄪𝄪𝄪 (Motown, 1971/1990)
All Directions 𝄪𝄪𝄪 (Motown, 1972)
Masterpiece 𝄪𝄪𝄪𝄪 (Motown, 1973/1989)
A Song for You 𝄪𝄪𝄪 (Motown, 1975)
All the Million Sellers 𝄪𝄪𝄪𝄪 (Motown, 1981)
Reunion 𝄪𝄪𝄪 (Motown, 1982)
Great Songs & Performances That Inspired Motown 25 𝄪𝄪𝄪 (Motown, 1983)
Truly for You 𝄪𝄪 (Motown, 1984/1989)
To Be Continued 𝄪𝄪𝄪 (Motown, 1986)
Special 𝄪𝄪 (Motown, 1989)
Milestone 𝄪𝄪𝄪 (Motown, 1991)
Hum Along and Dance: More of the Best (1963–1974) 𝄪𝄪𝄪𝄪 (Rhino, 1993)
Motown Legends: My Girl—(I Know) I'm Losing You 𝄪𝄪𝄪 (ESX, 1994)
Motown Legends: Just My Imagination—Beauty Is Only Skin Deep 𝄪𝄪𝄪 (ESX, 1994)
The Ultimate Collection 𝄪𝄪𝄪𝄪 (Motown, 1997)

worth searching for: You may not be able to see 'em, but the Tempts' voices on *Temptations Live!* 𝄪𝄪𝄪𝄪 (Motown, 1967) convey enough of the show's excitement to compensate.

solo outings:
Eddie Kendricks:
People Hold On 𝄪𝄪𝄪 (Motown, 1972/1991)

At His Best 𝄪𝄪𝄪 (Motown, 1990)

David Ruffin:
At His Best 𝄪𝄪𝄪 (Motown, 1991)

Jimmy & David Ruffin:
Motown Superstar Series Volume 8 𝄪𝄪𝄪 (Motown)

influences:
◄◄ The Soul Stirrers, the Falcons, the Drifters
►► The Jackson 5, the Commodores, the Ohio Players, Maze

Gary Graff

Joe Tex

Born Joe Arrington Jr., August 8, 1933, in Rogers, TX. Died August 13, 1982, in Navasota, TX.

Joe Tex was a typical struggling singer on Texas' vast 1950s R&B circuit, relatively unheralded until he stepped into a King recording studio in 1955. He cut several regional hits but still couldn't crack that break-out hit. A brief stint with New Orleans' Ace label didn't shake the trees, but it did get him noticed by Nashville country producer Buddy Killen. In 1965, Killen cut Tex's breakthrough smash "Hold What You've Got" on his Dial imprint. "Hold What You've Got," a churchy ballad pleading for steadfast love that was powered by the vocalist's unique jackleg country preacher rap/singing style, was archetypical Joe Tex. Between 1966–72, Tex steadily rammed the show stage as well as the R&B charts, scoring with the tracks such as "A Sweet Woman Like You," "S.Y.S.L.J.F.M. (The Letter Song)," "Show Me," the phenomenal "Skinny Legs and All," the swamp jive of "I Gotcha," and "Ain't Gonna Bump No More (With No Big Fat Woman)," his discsofied last hurrah. The hits faded for Tex as the 1970s wore on, but his legendary live shows (capped by his acrobatic microphone stand manipulations) still drew crowds. In his later years, Tex became a member of the Nation of Islam, changed his name to Joe X, and performed sporadically until his death in 1982.

what to buy: *The Very Best of Joe Tex* 𝄪𝄪𝄪 (Rhino, 1996, prod. Buddy Killen, Joe Tex) has all of Tex's hits, some of his hip B-sides, and a couple of filler tunes. A excellent compilation with informative, though brief, liner notes that puts Tex in the historical relevance he deserves.

what to avoid: *Greatest Hits* **woof!** (Columbia Special Products, 1993) is, at 28-minutes, damn near actionable.

the rest:
I Believe I'm Gonna Make It: The Best of Joe Tex 𝄪𝄪𝄪 (Rhino, 1988/1993)

The Best of Joe Tex ◊◊◊◊ (King, 1993)
His Best ◊◊◊ (K-Tel, 1997)
Greatest Hits ◊◊◊◊ (I.T.C. Masters, 1997)

worth searching for: Two generous import collections, *You're Right, Joe Tex* ◊◊◊◊ (Kent U.K., 1995) and *Skinny Legs and All* ◊◊◊◊ (Kent U.K., 1995), show off his vintage years with 22 and 24 tracks, respectively.

influences:

◀◀ James Brown, Little Willie John, Esquerita

▶▶ Percy Sledge, James Carter, Clarence Carter, Lou Rawls

Tom Terrell and Gary Graff

Tha Dogg Pound

See: Dogg Pound, Tha

Them

Formed 1963, in Belfast, Northern Ireland. Disbanded 1966.

Van Morrison, vocals; Billy Harrison, guitar; Alan Henderson, bass; Ronnie Millings, drums.

Them was a bruising R&B unit, featuring the gruff vocals of a young Morrison. Its brief recording career (three years) spawned few singles, but Morrison's fierce passion and the raw power of the hits left a more significant impression in the U.S. than many of the other British Invasion acts with whom they were grouped. The classic "Gloria" remains their defining moment—just three chords and feral growls, but its mark can be felt not only in its stomping performance but also in the innumerable cover versions that have surfaced since then (not counting every garage and bar band that peels through the song at a moment's notice).

what's available: The group's catalog is woefully underrepresented; *Them Featuring Van Morrison* ◊◊◊◊ (Deram, 1965, prod. various) is the only compilation currently available, and while it's by no means complete, it does contain its best-known work, including "Gloria" and the crashing "Mystic Eyes," as well as the searing "Baby, Please Don't Go" (on which Jimmy Page reportedly supplied the fiery solo).

influences:

◀◀ John Lee Hooker, Fats Domino, Muddy Waters

▶▶ U2, Graham Parker, Thin Lizzy

see also: *Van Morrison*

Allan Orski

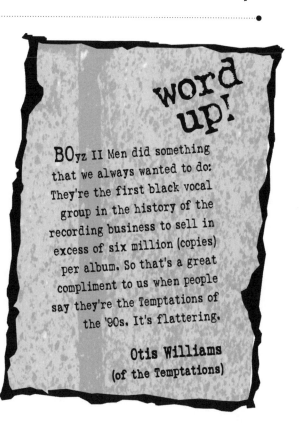

word up!

BOyz II Men did something that we always wanted to do: They're the first black vocal group in the history of the recording business to sell in excess of six million (copies) per album. So that's a great compliment to us when people say they're the Temptations of the '90s. It's flattering.

Otis Williams
(of the Temptations)

3rd Bass

Formed 1988, in New York, NY. Disbanded 1992.

MC Serch (born Michael Berrin), vocals; Prime Minister Pete Nice (born Peter Nash), vocals; Daddy Rich (born Richard Lawson), DJ; Sam Sever, DJ (1988–91).

While 3rd Bass wasn't the first white rap group, it was the first to complicate the race issue in hip-hop. Because of their deep Brooklyn and Queens-accented voices and undeniably funky deliveries, MC Serch and Prime Minister Pete Nice didn't sound the way white rappers were *supposed* to sound, especially since the only previous model was established by the raucous Beastie Boys. But 3rd Bass wasn't gimmicky. The group didn't use its whiteness as a selling point. Instead, 3rd Bass just made incredibly good hip-hop music with friends from KMD to Prince Paul, music that spoke for itself. Rightly conscious of rap's predominantly black roots, hip-hop fans didn't quite know how to react when told that the slamming "Gas Face" song they were rockin' to was made by a couple of white guys. 3rd Bass forced hip-hop to deal with the makeup of its own culture, whose partisans were beginning to include an increasing number of whites, Latinos, and Asians. The group's preeminence also caused people to ponder the roles of other white rappers, such as the Beastie Boys, Vanilla Ice, and, later, the pro-Irish House of Pain. Interestingly, 3rd Bass never had a camaraderie with any of these groups, lambasting the Beasties in the press, or making a song dedicated to smacking Vanilla Ice ("Pop Goes the Weasel"). Rumor was that the Beasties were so fed up with 3rd Bass that they wanted to put a photo of a naked MC Serch on the cover of one of their *Paul's Boutique*-era singles.

3rd Bass' dynamic was intriguing from the beginning. Pete Nice and Serch were actually separate rappers in the Russell Simmons-controlled RUSH management labyrinth. Thinking the two would survive as a unit rather than separate entities, Simmons introduced the two to the idea of forming a group, along with DJ Sam Sever, who later left 3rd Bass to form Downtown Science with another critically acclaimed white MC, Bosco Money. Sever was later replaced with floating member Richie "Daddy" Rich, who was black. Although pairing people with no previous history together is actually commonplace in hip-hop (see Gang Starr and Group Home), the lack of a true bond ultimately wore on 3rd Bass, coming to a head during a tour to promote *Derelicts of the Dialect*. The dissolution of the group left both Serch and Pete Nice to pursue solo careers and other business opportunities. Pete Nice (whom Daddy Rich sided with) formed the HoppoH management company with Bobitto Garcia, a New York radio personality and overall hip-hop icon, and worked with the likes of KMD and Kurious. Serch had a somewhat even more successful run with Serchlite Management, working with Nas and OC. He also spent time as an executive with now-defunct Wild Pitch Records.

what to buy: The music of 3rd Bass was nothing short of extraordinary. Their debut, *The Cactus Album* 🎜🎜🎜🎜 (Def Jam/Columbia, 1989, prod. Prince Paul, Sam Sever, Hank Shocklee, others) combines the layered funk of Hank Shocklee's Bomb Squad (Public Enemy) with the quirky influence of Prince Paul, who had just finished crafting a similarly styled album for De La Soul. Add to that Serch and Pete Nice's complimentary, unapologetic lyrical flows and you have such upbeat classics as "The Gas Face," "Triple Stage Darkness," and "Steppin' to the A.M."

what to buy next: Shit happens, and by the time 3rd Bass recorded its second album, *Derelicts of Dialect* 🎜🎜🎜🎜 (Def Jam/Columbia, 1991, prod. Prince Paul, Sam Sever, 3rd Bass),

M.C. Hammer and Vanilla Ice had happened, becoming major commercial-rap success stories. Feeling some sort of responsibility to address the situation, 3rd Bass recorded its most commercial-sounding hit, "Pop Goes the Weasel," a forgettable song with a humorous video in which an Ice-like figure is mocked throughout. Still, such cuts as the dark and dusty title track or the silky-smooth "Herbalz in Your Mouth" are gems worth discovering. Midway through the recording of this album, Sam Sever left to form Downtown Science, and Daddy Rich—primarily the group's tour DJ—stepped in as the group's beat creator.

the rest:
Cactus Album Revisited 🎜🎜🎜 (Def Jam/Columbia, 1990)

worth searching for: After 3rd Bass broke up, both Serch and Pete Nice floundered as solo artists. Serch fared better with *Return of the Product* 🎜🎜🎜 (Chaos/Sony, 1992, prod. T.Ray, Wolf, others) which is mostly ordinary, though the live sound of "Here It Comes" is refreshing.

influences:
◄◄ KMD, Stetsasonic, De La Soul
►► Downtown Science, Kurious, Nas

Jazzbo

Third World
Formed 1973, in Kingston, Jamaica.

Stephen "Cat" Coore, guitar; Michael "Ibo" Cooper, keyboards; William "Bunny Rugs" Clark, vocals (1977–present); Milton "Prilly" Hamilton, vocals (1973–77); William "Willie" Stewart, drums (1977–present); Cornel Marshall, drums (1973–77); Richard Daley, bass; Irvin "Carrot" Jarrett, percussion (1973–89).

When classical cellist/guitarist Cat Coore (son of Jamaica's Minister of Finance) and keyboardist Ibo Cooper formed Third World in response to the dearth of live reggae music in 1973, they had no idea that they would still be on the set 24 years later. Barnstorming the island with their cohorts (Daley, Marshall, and Hamilton), Third World soon became the buzz of Jamaica with their original tunes and covers of American R&B hits. Aided by a loan of £4000, they traveled to London with one thing in mind—securing a contract with Island Records, the home of Bob Marley & The Wailers. Within weeks, they signed and opened for Marley at his legendary Lyceum concert preserved on Marley's *Live* LP. In late 1976, Island released Third World's ground-breaking, self-titled debut. Not the roots or militant styles of reggae that carried the swing at that time, Third World was an audacious, decidedly pop-rock version of the form, more Santana, Kool & the Gang, and Beatles than Abyssinians or Burning Spear. Unfortunately, the album also revealed the band's weakness—inconsistency. The next year, Third World replaced Hamilton and Marshall with Clark and Stewart, and created their masterwork, *96 Degrees in the Shade*. A killah mix of anthemic originals ("Jah Glory," "Rhythm of Life," the title tune) and an inspired, almost definitive version of Bunny Wailer's "Dreamland," this is a triumph of reggae genre expansion. *96 Degrees in the Shade* was not well-received, but its followup, *Journey to Addis*, was. Propelled by the radio/club smash "Now That We Found Love," the album crossed Third World into the pop mainstream. Now a truly global reggae band, Third World slipped into a long-term strategy of diminishing returns: they would reduce their touring to select venues and would make records with one or two blockbusters and cool but underachieving filler tracks. The hits—"Try Jah Love," "Sense of Purpose," "Lagos Jump"—followed (albeit sporadically), yet by the mid-1980s they were relegated to nostalgia act status. They continue with their salad days membership intact, but today they seem sadly past their time.

what to buy: *96 Degrees in the Shade* 𝄫𝄫𝄫𝄫 (Mango, 1977/1996, prod. Third World) is ground zero for reggae-pop. Sure, Bob Marley is the King, but this album is fighting for a corner of his throne. Essential.

what to buy next: *Reggae Ambassadors: 20th Anniversary* 𝄫𝄫𝄫 (Island Chronicles, 1993, prod. various) is not the definitive Third World anthology. Although it contains a few songs from the band's Columbia and later Mercury tenures, this is basically a by-the-numbers Third World hits package. There's just not enough from crucial out-of-print Island tracks (from *Prisoner in the Streets*, *Third World*, and *Arise in Harmony*) or the Columbia stuff. Hopefully, someday justice will be done.

what to avoid: During the 1990s, the group put together its own label to release its albums, but *Live It Up* 𝄫𝄫 (Third World, 1995) leaves you wondering if they'd be able to get a label interested, anyway.

the rest:
Reggae Greats 𝄫𝄫𝄫 (Mango)
Rock the World 𝄫𝄫𝄫 (Columbia, 1981/1989)
You've Got the Power 𝄫𝄫𝄫 (Columbia, 1982)
Sense of Purpose 𝄫𝄫𝄫 (Columbia, 1985)
Hold On to Love 𝄫𝄫 (Columbia, 1987)
All the Way Strong 𝄫𝄫 (Columbia, 1989)
Serious Business 𝄫𝄫𝄫 (Mercury, 1989)
Committed 𝄫𝄫𝄫 (Mercury, 1992)
The Best of Third World 𝄫𝄫𝄫 (Legacy, 1993)

worth searching for: *Aiye Keta* 𝄫𝄫𝄫 (Edsel U.K., 1973/1997) an interesting though intermittently successful collaboration with Steve Winwood.

influences:

◀◀ Bob Marley, Santana, Paragons

▶▶ Foundation, Steel Pulse, UB40, 311

Tom Terrell and Gary Graff

Carla Thomas

Born December 21, 1942, in Memphis, TN.

The mighty Stax/Volt label got its start from an 18-year-old college girl on summer vacation. Not that Carla Thomas was just any co-ed; her father, Rufus Thomas, a ground floor soul man, had been grooming her since childhood through his own career and their duet, "'Cause I Love You." The young woman's first single, "Gee Whiz (Look at His Eyes)" in 1961 for the fledgling Satellite label (soon to be renamed Stax/Volt), was not only the first Memphis soul song to gain a national audience, it paved the road for Stax's inception. Thomas subsequently remained an integral part of the Stax line-up throughout the label's life span, which ended in 1976. During those years, she nailed a string of hits stamped with her tart innocence and liberated sass, which reached their apex with two historic pairings with Otis Redding, "Tramp" and "Knock on Wood." The fact that she is not regarded as highly as her more celebrated labelmates has long been a point of contention in the Stax/Volt community. True, Thomas delivers a steady dependability, albeit with a lack of urgency that allowed the eruptive powers of Redding and Sam and Dave to cast an obstructive shadow. The fact that she retired from recording soon after Stax folded, opting for the club circuit, assured her place in the label's history but also closed the door on future endeavors that may have helped elevate her standing.

what to buy: *Gee Whiz: The Best of Carla Thomas* 𝄫𝄫𝄫 (Rhino, 1994, comp. Steve Greenberg) compiles nearly everything to get a full picture of Thomas as her early shyness develops into womanly allure during the 22 tracks. Bursting forth on "Tramp," she goes head to head with Redding and hurls everything she's got in a frolicking dis session. Rounding out Thomas' career is *Hidden Gems* 𝄫𝄫𝄫 (Stax/Fantasy, 1992, comp. Jim Stewart), showing there was more water in the well than just her charting singles. Made up of obscure album tracks, B-sides, and unreleased material, it's another study of

Carla Thomas (© Jack Vartoogian)

Thomas' natural ability to get inside a song. Neither compilation includes the heaving "Knock on Wood," unfortunately.

the rest:
Memphis Queen 🎵🎵🎵♪ (Stax, 1968)
Comfort Me 🎵🎵🎵 (Rhino, 1991)
Carla 🎵🎵🎵 (Rhino, 1991)
Sugar 🎵🎵🎵♪ (Stax, 1995)

worth searching for: There are many solid moments to be found on many of Thomas' out-of-print records, such as *King & Queen* 🎵🎵🎵🎵 (Stax, 1967), an album of duets with Otis Redding, or *Love Means* 🎵🎵🎵 (Stax, 1966), a studio album from Stax's glory years.

influences:
◄◄ Mary Wells, the Shangri-La's, Rufus Thomas, Doris Troy
►► Diana Ross, Martha and the Vandellas

Allan Orski

Irma Thomas

Born February, 18, 1941, in Ponchatoula, LA.

The title "Queen of Soul" is usually reserved for one woman only, with a Detroit address. But down in New Orleans, another female singer has been elevated to the throne. While Irma Thomas hasn't enjoyed the commercial success of Aretha Franklin or some of her other more famous peers, her vocal ability stands on its own among the pantheon of top soul divas. Married at 14 and a mother soon after, Thomas also started her music career at an early age. Discovered by noted bandleader Tommy Ridgley while waiting tables at a New Orleans nightclub, Thomas was invited on stage to sing a few numbers. She did so well that Ridgley decided to include her as a regular feature of his act. Ridgley was also instrumental in helping Thomas to secure her first recording contract, cutting sides for Joe Ruffino's Ron Records. She scored a hit right out of the box with the now-classic "(You Can Have My Husband but Please) Don't Mess with My Man." After a year with Ron she moved to

Minit Records, hitting again with Jesse Hill's "Ooh Poo Pah Doo," destined to become a Basin Street standard. It was during her stay with Minit that Thomas formed a relationship with legendary record producer and New Orleans music icon Allen Toussaint, who was going about the task of updating the traditional New Orleans sound for modern consumption. Almost every successful R&B artist in the Big Easy passed through his able hands during the 1960s and early 1970s. The Minit years were to produce some of Thomas' most significant work, including the 1963 track "Ruler of My Heart." Although the song was a commercial flop for her, Otis Redding thought enough of it to cut a slightly reworked version, renaming it "Pain in My Heart." The Redding treatment crossed over and peaked at #61 on the pop charts. After Toussaint left to join the service, Thomas switched labels again, moving this time to Imperial, a small brand under the umbrella of Liberty Records. It was here that she recorded what was to become her most famous song, "Time Is on My Side," which was covered shortly after its release by the Rolling Stones and became the British band's first Top 10 hit. By the late 1960s, after doing a stint on the Chess label and several unreleased sides at Muscle Shoals, Thomas relocated to California and recorded for several companies while also working a series of day jobs. In 1974 she returned to New Orleans, which was by then in the midst of a musical renaissance, finally giving credit and respect to the unsung heroes of its R&B past. Though she hasn't graced the charts in almost 20 years, her records now on the Rounder label are of standout quality. Thomas continues to play selected dates worldwide and also packs the house regularly at her own club, The Lion's Den, in New Orleans.

what to buy: The greatest-hits set *Sweet Soul Queen of New Orleans: The Irma Thomas Collection* 𝄢𝄢𝄢𝄢🕭 (Razor & Tie, 1996) covers most of Irma's best work on both the Minit and Imperial labels. While most of this material failed to chart, it has rightfully come to the attention of listeners through reissues. The disc finds the singer interpreting songs by Randy Newman (one of his first tunes ever recorded, "While the City Sleeps"), Burt Bacharach and Hal David, Jerry Ragovoy and Van McCoy. Highlights include the hit "I Wish Someone Would Care" and, of course, "Time Is on My Side." The all-gospel record *Walk Around Heaven: New Orleans Gospel Soul* 𝄢𝄢𝄢𝄢🕭 (Rounder, 1994, prod. Scott Billington, Irma Thomas) sounds as if it came straight out of the gospel tent at the New Orleans Jazz and Heritage Festival. Like that other noted Queen of Soul, Thomas shows here that she'll never turn her back on her church roots. An excellent backup unit, led by organist Sammy Berfect and New Orleans

drum great Herman Ernst, expand the dimensions of faith with full choir accompaniment on this very satisfying work.

what to buy next: Irma's first recording for Rounder Records, *The New Rules* 𝄢𝄢𝄢 (Rounder, 1986, prod. Scott Billington, Irma Thomas) was also her first release in several years. Rounder gave her more artistic control than ever before, and she's been with the label ever since. *The Way I Feel* 𝄢𝄢𝄢 (Rounder, 1988, prod. Scott Billington, Irma Thomas) shows the evolution of her sound during the late 1980s while combining elements of her past work through songs by Allen Toussaint and Jerry Ragavoy. Also included are her takes on the signature Motown hit "Dancing in the Street" and the Ronettes' "Baby I Love You," with backing from her own band, the Professionals. *The Story of My Life* 𝄢𝄢𝄢 (Rounder, 1977, prod. Scott Billington, Irma Thomas) features a gutsy rendition of "Dr. Feelgood" and songs by Dan Penn and Toussaint. New Orleans all-stars David Torkanosky on keyboards and George Porter on bass help propel Thomas' soulful vocals.

what to avoid: *Soul Queen of New Orleans* 𝄢 (Mardi Gras, 1996) and the British import *Time Is on My Side Plus* 𝄢 (Kent, 1996), ragged compilation LPs of inferior production quality.

the rest:
Ruler of Hearts 𝄢𝄢 (Charly, 1989)
Something Good: The Muscle Shoals Chess Sessions 𝄢𝄢𝄢𝄢 (MCA Chess, 1990)
Simply the Best: Live! 𝄢𝄢𝄢𝄢🕭 (Rounder, 1991)
Safe With Me/Live at the Kingfish 𝄢𝄢𝄢𝄢 (RCS, 1991)
True Believer 𝄢𝄢𝄢𝄢 (Rounder, 1992)
Turn My World Around 𝄢𝄢𝄢 (Shanachie, 1993)

worth searching for: A vinyl copy of *In Between Tears* (Capricorn, 1973), the most significant and listenable product of her California years, produced by the "Swamp Dogg," Jerry Williams.

influences:
◄◄ New Orleans gospel, Annie Laurie, Percy Mayfield
►► The Rolling Stones, Tracy Nelson, Charmaine Neville

Matt Lee

Rufus Thomas

Born March 26, 1917, in Casey, MS.

The son of a Mississippi sharecropper, Rufus Thomas may be known as the clown prince of soul, the man who brought the phrase "Funky Chicken" into America's consciousness during the 1970s. But a deeper look into the singer's history reveals a performer who not only bridged the gap between two distinct eras of American entertainment but also helped lay the foundation for what became the Memphis Sound. After his family relocated to Memphis during the 1930s, Thomas broke into showbiz as part of a tap-dance duo in the Rabbit Foot Minstrel Show, later incorporating blues singing into his act. After the demise of traveling shows in the South, Thomas moved back to Memphis and began appearing at local talent contests. It was at this time that one his former high school teachers got him a gig broadcasting on legendary Memphis radio station WDIA. The first station in America to employ black talent as broadcasters, WDIA's 50,000-watt signal became a beacon of listening for blacks throughout the South, also giving rise to the career of blues giant B.B. King. Thomas, the popular afternoon personality, soon parlayed his celebrity into a recording contract with another soon-to-be-legendary operation, Sam Phillips' Sun Records. In 1953, Thomas scored Sun's first hit with "Bearcat," a song Phillips wrote in response to Big Mama Thornton's smash "Hound Dog." But after Phillips discovered Elvis Presley, all other acts on Sun—especially black ones—were given low priority or discarded altogether. This turned into a blessing for Thomas, who subsequently signed with the fledgling Stax label, where he would become a major force for years to come. After minor hits on the Meteor label, Thomas teamed with his teenage daughter Carla to record "'Cause I Love You"; released on Stax, it became one of the company's first hits. Rufus scored his first Top 10 hit at the age of 46 with "Walkin' the Dog," a follow-up to his lesser-known "The Dog." These songs were written to accompany a hot dance craze and often included references to animals. Known for his outlandish costumes and comic stage patter, Thomas continued to entertain crowds worldwide—he is to Italians what Jerry Lewis is to the French—even during commercial lulls. People still recall Thomas' appearance at the 1972 Wattstax concert in California leading thousands to dance his "Funky Chicken" *en masse* while stealing the show from many of the most popular artists of the day. Television commercials and print ads continue to keep Thomas in the public eye; at 80, the self-proclaimed "world's oldest teenager" is still going strong, hosting a radio show on WDIA to this day.

what to buy: *The Best of Rufus Thomas: Do the Funky Somethin'* 𝄞𝄞𝄞𝄞 (Rhino, 1996) represents the best overview of Thomas' work. Included in the collection are the early hits "Bearcat" and "'Cause I Love You," in addition to such novelty songs as "Do the Funky Chicken," "Do the Funky Penguin," "Can Your Monkey Do the Dog?," "Somebody Stole My Dog," and, of course, "Walkin' the Dog." The original Stax/Atlantic release that started it all for Thomas, *Walkin' the Dog* 𝄞𝄞𝄞𝄞

(Stax/Atlantic Remasters, 1963, prod. Jim Stewart) also features excellent covers, such as the New Orleans classic "Ooh-Poo-Pah-Doo" and Wilson Pickett's "Land of 1,000 Dances."

what to buy next: *Rufus Thomas Live* 𝄞𝄞𝄞 (Stax, 1994, prod. Al Bell) showcases the artist in two different settings, with two different backup bands. Both groups were later to become successful in their own right: the first half of the LP features LTD (with Jeffrey Osborne on drums, before he became a lead singer); the second half, recorded at the Wattstax event, finds Thomas supported by the band which would later become hitmakers as Con Funk Shun. Both units would back Thomas often at L.A. area appearances. *Did You Hear Me* 𝄞𝄞𝄞 (Stax, 1972, prod. Tom Nixon, Al Bell) is Rufus in his post-*Walkin' the Dog* period, backed by such Memphis standouts as the Bar-Kays, the Memphis Horns, and Thomas' son, Marvell, on keyboards. Included are the dance tracks "The Breakdown Parts 1 & 2" and "The Funky Penguin Parts 1 & 2."

the rest:
Chronicle: Rufus and Carla Thomas 𝄞𝄞𝄞 (Stax, 1974)

influences:

◄◄ Bill "Bojangles" Robinson, Pigmeat Markham

►► Elvis Presley, B.B. King, Otis Redding, Al Green, Ernie K. Doe, D.J. Jazzy Jeff & the Fresh Prince

Matt Lee

Tony Thompson
See: Hi-Five

Big Mama Thornton
Born Willie Mae Thornton, December 11, 1926, in Montgomery, AL. Died July 25, 1984, in Los Angeles, CA.

Nothing against Elvis Presley, but Willie Mae Thornton's original version of "Hound Dog" communicates much more power and emotion than the King's million-selling rock classic. Her 1953 #1 R&B hit (written by Jerry Leiber and Mike Stoller) is filled with playful howling noises and a certain bottom-line funk that Presley, despite his controversial hip-shaking, smoothed out. It's too bad Thornton's great career has been, because of that song, relegated to a rock footnote; her explosive singing bridged the gap between Bessie Smith's no-nonsense proto-feminism and later soul and rock heroes such as Etta James, Aretha Franklin, Janis Joplin, and even Alanis Morissette. Thornton, whose mother sang in church, joined a traveling revue in 1941 before moving to Houston and becoming a solo singer (and drummer and harpist). There she hooked up with Johnny Otis, the great R&B bandleader, and Peacock Records' Don Robey; the connections led to some phenomenal, hard-hitting R&B songs, including "Ball and Chain," "Yes Baby," "The Fish," "They Call Me Big Mama," and, of course, "Hound Dog." Like many other blues originals who were pushed aside for rock 'n' roll, her career slipped in the 1960s. The blues revival gave her some touring clout in Europe, and she continued to record and play international festivals.

what to buy: *Hound Dog: The Peacock Recordings* ♪♪♪ (MCA, 1992, prod. various) includes all of Thornton's most famous material; the most welcome revelation is how wonderful Otis' jump and swing bands sound underneath the singer's booming voice.

what to buy next: Thornton's career as an album artist began in the 1960s, and it has excellent moments, but it's not nearly as consistent as her old singles. Still, *Jail* ♪♪♪ (Vanguard, 1975) contains fun new versions of "Ball and Chain," Willie Dixon's "Little Red Rooster," and "Hound Dog."

the rest:
In Europe ♪♪♪ (Arhoolie, 1966)
Chicago Blues ♪♪♪ (Arhoolie, 1967)
Ball and Chain ♪♪♪ (Arhoolie, 1968)
Stronger Than Dirt ♪♪ (Mercury, 1969)
She's Back ♪♪ (Backbeat, 1971)
Sassy Mama ♪♪♪ (Vanguard, 1975)
Mama's Pride ♪♪♪ (Vanguard, 1978)

worth searching for: Thornton's best-known song drops into *Blues Masters, Vol. 5: Jump Blues Classics* ♪♪♪♪ (Rhino, 1992, prod. various), landing comfortably among Wynonie Harris' "Good Rockin' Tonight" and Big Jay McNeely's "Deacon's Hop." She even blows away the disc's closer, Ruth Brown.

influences:
◀◀ Memphis Minnie, Ma Rainey, Bessie Smith, Billie Holiday, Johnny Otis

▶▶ Janis Joplin, Etta James, Aretha Franklin, Elvis Presley, Koko Taylor

Steve Knopper

Three Times Dope

Formed in Philadelphia, PA.

EST, vocals; Chuck Nice, programming; DJ Woody Wood (born Duer-wood Beale), DJ.

Unlike their serious-minded and competition-obsessed brothers and sisters in the Big Apple, Philadelphia's Three Times

Dope—like cross-town contemporaries Cash Money and Marvelous and D.J. Jazzy Jeff & the Fresh Prince—were concerned with keeping records spinning, rhymes flowing, crowds moving. No gangsta pretensions and paranoid fantasies here. And in that respect, they were years ahead of their time, paving the way for the pop crossover success of like-minded groups Naughty by Nature and the Pharcyde in the 1990s.

what's available: *Original Stylin'* ♪♪♪ (Arista, 1989, prod. Lawrence Goodman, Chuck Nice) is a sunny LP, with just enough bass, just enough scratching, just enough attitude to show they're not suckers—but perhaps not enough to inspire fear or awe. There's a lot to like about the gold-digger riffs ("Funky Dividends") and chest-thumping boasts ("Improvin Da Groovin," "Greatest Man Alive"). Of course, there's also the Philly crew LP standby (the DJ showcase cut), wherein Woody Wood takes care of business on "Who Is This?" *Live from Acknicklous Land* ♪♪♪ (Arista, 1990, prod. Chuck Nice) is slightly better, as Chuck Nice's production takes it up a couple notches. Flavorful samples, steady flows, and scratch-infested choruses abound in such tracks as "Mr. Sandman," the comical "10 Lili Sucka Emceez," and the hype title track.

influences:
◀◀ D.J. Jazzy Jeff & the Fresh Prince, Steady B, Tat Money

▶▶ Kwame, Larry Lar

Jeff "DJ Zen" Chang

Tim Dog

This Bronx-bred bomber has links to the Ultramagnetic MC's and is generally considered to be a peripheral member of that pioneering rap group. Of course, although Tim Dog first appeared on the Ultra cut "Chorus Line," it wasn't until 1991 that he really rocked the house, telling the world how he felt about the westside connection.

what to buy: *Penicillin on Wax* ♪♪♪ (Ruffhouse/Columbia, 1991, prod. various) is worth the price of admission if only for the shear audacity of the hit single "Fuck Compton." Coming at the height of Compton success (N.W.A., Ice Cube, DJ Quik, Compton's Most Wanted), the East Coast anthem was rally cry for those who were tired of gangsta rap's domination of the hip-hop world. Tim Dog's rugged-n-ruff delivery, coupled with thick, chunky slabs of funk (courtesy of Ultra's Moe Luv, TR Luv, and Ced Gee), hits you like a mutant flu virus, working its way into your system and eventually knocking you flat on your ass. The lyrics are a mixture of over-the-top bravado and L.A. bash-ing, although, just to be fair, Tim Dog also hammers wack-ass dancers-turned-rappers (a la M.C. Hammer), fake-ass Afrocentric rappers, and just about everyone else. Boasting, bragging, dissin', and baggin', Tim Dog takes you back to the early days of the dozens with his songs ("Step to Me," "Bronx Nigga," "You Ain't Shit," "Fuck Compton"). Sure, his bark is ultraloud, and at times it's hard to discern if it's worse than his bite—but, then, that's half the fun of this album.

what to buy next: *Do or Die* ♪♪♪ (Ruffhouse, 1993, prod. various) contains a noteworthy cameo by Bronx heavyweight KRS-One (on the Ultra-produced "I Get Wrecked") and some nice and smooth layouts on "Skip to My Loot" that come courtesy of Smooth B. Aside from that, though, Tim Dog's energy lags, and the beats don't carry the powerful impact of the debut's. On the underground indie release, *Ultra* ♪♪♪ (Our Time, 1997, prod. various), Tim is reunited with Ultramagnetic frontman Kool Keith. While the rhymes are on point, there's a sameness to the beats.

worth searching for: Tim Dog's first appearance on wax came on "Chorus Line," the B-side to the Ultramagnetic MC's 12-inch "Traveling at the Speed of Thought." Tim Dog joined Ultra again in 1991 for "Chorus Line Pt. 2," the flip side to the single "Make It Happen." You can also catch some rare live Tim Dog on "Tim Dog Live on Capitol Radio" off the Ultramagnetic MC's *New York—What Is Funky* (Tuff City, 1996), a compilation of unreleased studio recordings and outtakes.

influences:
◀◀ Ultramagnetic MC's

Spence D.

The Time

Formed 1981, in Minneapolis, MN. Disbanded in 1984. Re-formed in 1990 and in 1995.

Morris Day, vocals; Jesse Johnson, guitars, vocals; Jellybean Johnson, drums; Terry Lewis, bass (1981–83, 1990); James "Jimmy Jam" Harris III, keyboards (1981–83, 1990); Monte Moir, keyboards (1981–83, 1990, 1995); Gerry Hubbard, bass (1983–84); Paul "St. Paul" Peterson, keyboards, vocals (1983–84); Mark Cardenas, keyboards (1983–84).

Originally formed as a convenient home for Prince songs too conventionally funky for the diminutive funk master's own records, the Time grew into the ultimate R&B party band—also becoming the most successful spin-off from the Minneapolis-based wunderkind's stable of mid-1980s acts. Though its 1981 debut album features a band on the cover, it was actually recorded entirely by Prince and Day. Eventually, Minneapolis' hottest funk band was

recruited to back Day, and the Time was born. By its second album—also bearing the heavy sonic stamp of its producer, Jaime Starr, a.k.a. Prince—the band's roles had solidified, offering forward-looking funk jams knit together by electric synthesizer licks and Day's own class-clowning, party animal image. Unfortunately, efforts by Harris and Lewis to produce other artists got them forced out of the group (they went on to produce hits for Janet Jackson, the Human League, and many others), followed shortly by Moir. The remaining band, showcased in Prince's breakthrough *Purple Rain* movie, had nonetheless lost its magic. Regrouping in 1990 after a six-year hiatus—for another Prince film, *Graffiti Bridge*—the classic lineup found modern production techniques couldn't make up for a lack of passion. The latest incarnation has yet to produce an album.

what to buy: Every so often, a band manages to bring its creative best at a time when the world is perfectly poised to hear it. For the Time, *What Time Is It?* ♪♪♪♪ (Warner Bros., 1982, prod. Jamie Starr) is that record. Tracks such as "777-9311" and "Wild and Loose" meld incendiary funk, playing with the band's image as slick-suited, perfectly coifed party dogs, while the ballad "Gigolos Get Lonely Too" show they can work a slowjam to death as well.

what to avoid: Besides the mostly forgettable solo stuff cranked out by the individual members, *Ice Cream Castle* **woof!** (Warner Bros., 1984, prod. Prince, Morris Day) is a popified rehash of the band's vibe, built around the two songs featured in the *Purple Rain* movie—"Jungle Love" and "The Bird." Though this album won the band lots of new fans, those who'd been around from the early days knew it was the beginning of the end.

the rest:
The Time ♪♪♪ (Warner Bros., 1981)
Pandemonium ♪♪♪ (Reprise, 1990)

worth searching for: A slick promotional piece for *Pandemonium* that includes a digital clock in the packaging (the Time—get it?). A fun way to own an otherwise mediocre album.

solo outings:
Morris Day:
Color of Success ♪♪ (Warner Bros., 1985)
Daydreaming ♪♪ (Warner Bros., 1987)

Jesse Johnson:
Jesse Johnson's Revue ♪♪♪ (A&M, 1985)
Shockadelica ♪♪♪ (A&M, 1986)
Every Shade of Love ♪♪♪ (A&M, 1988)

influences:
◀◀ James Brown, Prince, Parliament/Funkedelic, Ohio Players

▶▶ Chuckii Booker, Tony! Toni! Tone!, the Wooten Brothers

see also: *Jimmy Jam & Terry Lewis*

Eric Deggans

TLC
Formed 1991, Atlanta, GA.

T-Boz (Tionne Watkins), vocals; Left Eye (Lisa Lopes), vocals; Chilli (Rozonda Thomas), vocals.

More a marketable synthesis of package and production than a bona fide creative unit, Atlanta-based hip-hoppers TLC are one of the most successful female groups of all time. Assembled and managed by R&B songstress Pebbles, TLC hit it big from the get-go, selling more than four million copies of their debut, *Ooooooohhh...On the TLC Tip*. The follow-up, *CrazySexyCool*, was even more successful (10 million copies sold), if not as artistically accomplished as its predecessor.

what to buy: *Ooooooohhh...On the TLC Tip* 𝄢𝄢𝄢 (LaFace, 1992, prod. various). On jams such as "Ain't 2 Proud 2 Beg," "What About Your Friends," and "Hat 2 Da Back" (a spirited defense of TLC's cartoonish, baggy-shorts-and-baseball-cap image), producer Dallas Austin undergirds Left Eye's hip-shooting with gripping grooves that are slick but never soft. But on their chart-topping ballad "Baby-Baby-Baby"—written and produced by LaFace Records founders L.A. Reid and Babyface with Daryl Simmons—TLC turn down the lights and turn on their grown-up charms, demanding "conversation with *their* sex" and teasing, "Baby, long as you know I could have any man I want/Baby, that's actual and factual."

the rest:
CrazySexyCool 𝄢𝄢𝄢 (LaFace, 1994)

influences:
◀◀ Salt-N-Pepa, En Vogue, Pebbles, L.A. Reid and Babyface
▶▶ Toni Braxton, Mary J. Blige

Greg Siegel

Tommy Boy

Manhattan club impresario Tom Silverman saw the future, and its name was hip-hop. And so his self-named label latched onto hip-hop, using three breakdancing silhouettes (along with DJ-friendly BPM listings) on its imprint and landing the genre's godfather as the cornerstone of its roster. Indeed, in 1982, just as hip-hop was beginning to gain an international audience,

the label released Afrika Bambaataa and the Soul Sonic Force's "Planet Rock"—a single with an impact on pop music unequaled since the Sex Pistols' "Anarchy in the UK" and that no song would have again until Nirvana's "Smells Like Teen Spirit." Other early Tommy Boy hits included G.L.O.B.E. and Whiz Kid's "Play That Beat (Mr. D.J.)," Planet Patrol's "Play at Your Own Risk," and Keith LeBlanc's "Malcolm X," all of which are included on *Tommy Boy's Greatest Beats* 𝄢𝄢𝄢𝄢 (Tommy Boy, 1985, prod. various), an essential document of the electro sound. During this period, the label also became almost as legendary for what it didn't release; reportedly a response to one of Tommy Boy's megamix contests, the influential turntablist classic "The History of Hip-Hop, Parts 1, 2, and 3" by Double Dee and Steinski, for instance, was issued only as a promotional vinyl single for DJs. Through the early 1990s, the label peaked as hip-hop did, releasing smashes by Stetsasonic, De La Soul, Digital Underground, House of Pain, Naughty by Nature, and Paris, and signing a distribution deal with Warner Bros. After building a reputation through its first decade as a label committed to setting the stylistic edge via hip-hop, Tommy Boy reevaluated its position, and in the next decade, the phenomenally successful Coolio would come to symbolize the label's new attitude: world-wise, media-friendly, and entirely cross-marketable.

Jeff "DJ Zen" Chang

Tone-Loc
Born Anthony Terrell Smith, March 3, 1966, in Los Angeles, CA.

Even if it weren't for the fact that he was the first African American rapper to summit *Billboard*'s pop album chart, Tone-Loc would still be remembered for his one-of-a-kind baritone croak, and for "Wild Thing," the crossover smash that thrust those sandpaper-rough pipes into the spotlight in late 1988. As is often the case when a new artist strikes it big with a novelty-ish single, the double-platinum "Wild Thing"—a humorous sexcapade built on a bare-bones beat and snatches of Van Halen's "Jamie's Cryin'"—would prove first a blessing, and then a curse: Loc would never fully escape its stifling shadow.

what to buy: Besides "Wild Thing," Loc's debut album, *Loc-ed After Dark* 𝄢𝄢𝄢 (Delicious Vinyl, 1989, prod. the Dust Brothers, others) made a stir with another (structurally similar) Young M.C.-penned hit, "Funky Cold Medina," a paean to the aphrodisiacal potency of its namesake. Add to these his epic ode to herb, "Cheeba Cheeba" (a slow-burn funk flavor-ite featuring some stunningly soulful wailing by guest vocalist N-Dea), and

Loc's image as the West Coast's easygoing, fun-lovin' rhymester was all but chiseled in stone. Sure, *Loc-ed After Dark* contains its share of filler—the pointless instrumental "Loc'in on the Shaw," the toke-along friends-fest "The Homies"—but it's still one helluva good time. (Incidentally, it's also a great place to hear three early examples of the Dust Brothers' symphonic use of sampled technology.)

what to avoid: The party didn't last for long. By the time Loc released his sophomore effort, *Cool Hand Loc* ♫♫ (Delicious Vinyl, 1991, prod. the Dust Brothers, others), the hip-hop landscape had become a veritable battleground, in which black nationalists, original gangstas, New Jack swingers, old-school MCs, whitebread phonies, dance DJs, acid-jazzers, and crossover teddy bears (like Loc) all scuffled for artistic legitimacy and commercial hegemony. In this context, *Cool Hand Loc* is a fascinating case study in identity crisis. Thematically, the songs run the gamut from gun-toting shit talkin' ("Funky Westside" and "Pimp Without a Caddy") to muddle-headed pot-smoking ("Mean Green"); from harmless perversion ("Freaky Behavior") to acute castration anxiety ("Fatal Attraction"); from claims of superhuman virility ("I Adore You") to soft-spoken pledges of everlasting love ("All Through the Night" and "Why"). Musically, the album is nearly as schizophrenic, zigzagging between unctuous slow-jam soul (check out Loc's Barry White-isms in "Why"), snazzy urban-contemporary, and hard-edged rap. On the album's penultimate track, Tone-Loc—a onetime superstar now in desperate pursuit of some street cred—surveys the exploding rap scene, reflects on his uncertain place in it, and concludes: "Hip-Hop It Is Kinda Different." Sometimes the only language left is truism.

influences:

◄◄ Young M.C., Dust Brothers, LL Cool J

►► Young M.C., Candyman

Greg Siegel

Tony D

Born Tony Dofat, in Trenton, NJ.

A producer who worked with a variety of acts, including close friends Poor Righteous Teachers, Tony D embodies the period in hip-hop between 1989 and 1991, when fast, rugged, funk-driven hip-hop beats dominated the landscape.

Raphael Saddiq of Tony! Toni! Tone! (© Ken Settle)

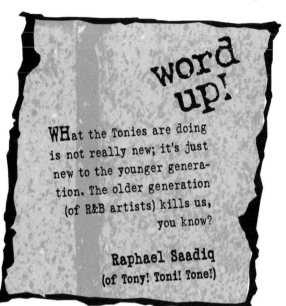

> **WH**at the Tonies are doing is not really new; it's just new to the younger generation. The older generation (of R&B artists) kills us, you know?
>
> **Raphael Saadiq**
> **(of Tony! Toni! Tone!)**

what's available: One of the first artists to both produce and rap, Tony D released only one album, *Droppin' Funky Verses* ♫♫ (4th and B'Way/Island, 1991, prod. Tony D)—a recording that demonstrates why Tony has always been known more as a beat creator than a lyricist. Yet the title track and "Harvey Wallbangar" still managed to rock some parties.

influences:

◄◄ Stetsasonic, Superlover Cee, Casanova Rud

►► Diamond D

Jazzbo

Tony! Toni! Tone!

Formed 1986, in Oakland, CA.

Raphael Saddiq (ne Wiggins), bass, guitar, keyboards, vocals; D'wayne Wiggins, guitar, vocals; Timothy Christian Riley, keyboards, drums.

It seemed appropriate that Tony! Toni! Tone! titled its fourth album *House of Music*; the title reflects the trio's upbringing in Oakland, California. Brothers Raphael and D'wayne Wiggins (Raphael changed his surname to Saddiq to express his Muslim faith) and cousin Timothy Christian Riley were exposed to a melting pot of popular music while growing up, from Al Green,

musicHound r & b

5
6 *too $hort*
8

the Temptations, and Marvin Gaye, to Joni Mitchell, Miles Davis, the Doobie Brothers, and lots of disco. They've filtered it all into their music, creating some of the most strikingly melodic work in contemporary R&B. Rather than rely on tape loops, drum machines, and sampled sounds, the trio loyally adheres to the idea of actually playing music, an old school philosophy that it blends with decidedly modern sonic ideas—one foot in the past, the other in the future, as it were. That's given Tony! Toni! Tone! a remarkable cache, though the group has curiously never been able to develop a live reputation, particularly because it hasn't felt able to afford the large band it requires to put its songs over onstage; the last time it did, for an opening stint on Janet Jackson's 1993–94 world tour, it wound up leaving early because of alleged mistreatment. Saddiq, meanwhile, has become an in-demand collaborator, working with, among others, rockers such as John Mellencamp and the Bee Gees.

what to buy: *Sons of Soul* 𝄞𝄞𝄞𝄞 (Wing, 1993, prod. Tony! Toni! Tone!) is a masterpiece, proof that classic soul music conventions can still be delivered without sounding dated. But make no mistake; the Tonys emphasis is on "real" songs, and the results—"What Goes Around Comes Around," "Slow Wine," "Pillow (Lay Your Head on Mine)"—are sumptuous.

what to buy next: *House of Music* 𝄞𝄞𝄞 (Mercury, 1996, prod. Tony! Toni! Tone!) is nearly as good, from the Al Green knockoff "Thinking of You" to the funky "Let's Get Down," which features a guest appearance by rapper DJ Quik.

the rest:
Who? 𝄞𝄞𝄞 (Wing, 1988)
The Revival 𝄞𝄞𝄞𝄾 (Wing, 1990)
Greatest Hits 𝄞𝄞𝄞𝄾 (Mercury, 1997)

worth searching for: Saddiq's intriguing contributions to a couple of veteran rock 'n' roll acts' albums, John Mellencamp's *Mr. Happy Go Lucky* (Mercury, 1996) and the Bee Gees' *Still Waters* (Polydor, 1997), are worth seeking out.

influences:
◄◄ Al Green, Earth, Wind & Fire, the Time, Brass Construction, the Commodores, Kool & the Gang

Gary Graff

Too $hort

Born Todd Anthony Shaw, April 28, 1966, in Los Angeles, CA.

Way back in 1983, Shaw was transformed into the freak-nasty supreme MC, Too $hort. As legend has it, Oakland transplant $hort and his partner, Freddy B., were slangin' tapes like kilos,

selling them out of the trunks of cars and on the back seats of city buses; the pair sold thousands of recordings, and $hort eventually signed a sweet deal with Jive. In the years since, Too $hort has created a platinum rap empire based largely on one word: "bitch," which he drags out to "biiiiiiiiiiiiiiiiiiitch!" He's also become the most influential hip-hop artist in the San Francisco Bay Area, not only for his lyrics and sound, but for his initial do-it-your-damn-self ethic, too. In 1996, $hort announced his "retirement" and even conducted press conferences at which he declared that *Gettin' It* (Jive, 1996) would be his 10th and final album. But there was a loophole: although $hort has so far kept his promise, he's still surfaced on a slew of *other* people's records, most notably Ant Banks' *Big Thangs*, on which $hort and Ice Cube team up for the title track.

what to buy: *Short Dog's in the House* 𝄞𝄞𝄞𝄞 (Jive, 1990, prod. Too $hort, DJ Pooh, Sir Jinx) is historical in that it was the first rap LP to come in two entirely different versions: a "dirty" Parental Advisory version and a clean, radio-playable version. Amusingly, Ice Cube and $hort team up for the "bitch"-and-"fuck"-filled "Ain't Nothin' But a Word to Me," which, on the "clean" version, is nothing more than bleeps running over a fat bassline; it's one of the best (recorded) illustrations ever of how censorship can inhibit artistic expression. The album itself is also $hort's best ever. Too $hort handles much of the production on the album, but Sir Jinx and DJ Pooh are on board, too, adding a shot of West Coast gangsta boogie. The album isn't exactly stereotypical gangsta fare, though, as $hort steps to the positivity pulpit on "It's Your Life" to warn about the dangers of slangin' dope. The album also features $hort's heady reworking of Donny Hathaway's "The Ghetto," his first crossover hit.

what to buy next: By the time $hort released his Jive debut, *Born to Mack* 𝄞𝄞𝄞 (Jive, 1986, prod. Too $hort), he was already a legend throughout the streets of Oakland and the Bay Area at large. This is the album, though, that gave the rest of the world its first taste of $hort's graphic raps and definitive West Coast funk sound, and essentially put East Oakland on the rap map in the process. Some seminal $hort material is on this album, including the 10-minute opus, "Freaky Tales," which is the undisputed blueprint for all freaky-deaky sexcapade rhymes to come. In addition, "Dope Fiend Beat," with its rumble-quake bass, became pimped by every wannabe rapper from Vallejo to Hayward. $hort's self-produced tracks are entirely sample free and heavy on the keyboards and programmed 808 beats, with some mild scratching thrown in for effect. The cover of the platinum follow-up, *Life Is...Too $hort*

♫♫♫♫ (Jive, 1988, prod. Too $hort, Al Eaton), features a tombstone on which the following epitaph is carved: "John Sucker M.C. Doe—Born: On Stage—Died: On Wax—Rest in Peace." The message seems to be directed at the East Coast, which had failed to grasp $hort's mack attitude and anti-sampling funk. Once again, $hort mans the boards, but the father of the Oaktown sound, Al Eaton, is here, too, playing guitar and co-producing three tracks. "Oakland" and "City of Dope" are declarations of civic pride, $hort-style, but it's "Don't Fight the Feeling" that's the album's most notable track—a nasty posse cut which unites Oakland and San Francisco and introduces Rappin' 4-Tay to the world.

the rest:

$horty the Pimp ♫♫♫ (Jive, 1992)
Get in Where You Fit In ♫♫♫ (Jive 1993)
Cocktails ♫♫♫ (Jive, 1995)
Gettin' It (Album Number Ten) ♫♫♫ (Jive, 1996).

worth searching for: The rare 75 Girls releases *Don't Stop Rappin'*, *Players*, and *Raw, Uncut and X-Rated* provide an early glimpse of the soon-to-be icon. Such tracks as "She's a Bitch" and "Invasion of the Flat Bootied Bitches" contain the word that $hort would turn into his trademark cat call: "Biiiiiiiiiiiiiiiiiiiitch!" Showing true marketing savvy, $hort voluntarily put his own warning labels on the tapes (they say "Explicit Lyrics" and "Dirty Rapps Inside"), which only helped to sell more copies. The tapes are all long out of print; in 1993, though, In-A-Minute Records released *Too $hort: Greatest Hits Volume 1—The Player Years, 1983–1988*, a double set that includes many of $hort's early street hits. While not exactly a full-fledged Too $hort endeavor, the Dangerous Crew compilation, *Don't Try This at Home* ♫♫♫ (Jive, 1995, prod. various), still features the $hort one on several tracks.

influences:

◀◀ Iceberg Slim, *The Mack,* Blowfly

▶▶ Rappin' 4-Tay, Spice 1, Pooh-Man, Dru Down, E-40, and just about any other rapper to emerge from the Bay Area

Spence D.

Peter Tosh

Born October 9, 1944, in Westmoreland, Jamaica; died September 11, 1987, Barbican, St. Andrew, Jamaica.

Of the three original Wailers—along with Bunny Livingstone and Bob Marley—Peter Tosh was certainly the most limited vocally, his gruff baritone being no match for Livingstone's mystical warmth nor Marley's sage-like delivery. But as the reggae supergroup became Marley's show, the street-wise tenacity in Tosh erupted. A swaggering bravado, which would provide back-up to no man, took over, and the solo work he had dabbled with in the Wailers became a full-time endeavor. And perhaps not so surprisingly, his career brimmed with a rebellion and staunch Rastafarian ideology that neither Marley nor Livingstone (commonly known as Bunny Wailer by the 1970s) approached with their respective romantic noodlings and murky spirituals. The same man who announced "I'm the Toughest" in the 1960s, charged into the 1970s championing marijuana, simultaneously butting heads with the police (who nearly beat him to death in 1978) and releasing earthbound reggae albums that were as gritty as they were non-compromising. Though his work waned during the 1980s, he remained a strident mouthpiece against Jamaican government, which some feel led to his murder in 1987. To this day, accusations fly that the three pistol waving men who killed the singer were carrying out a political execution. Two others were fatally shot and four more wounded in the course of the robbery (as it was officially reported) of Tosh's home.

what to buy: Tosh's first two efforts, *Legalize It* ♫♫♫♫ (Columbia, 1976, prod. Peter Tosh) and *Equal Rights* ♫♫♫♫ (Columbia, 1977, prod. Peter Tosh) both stand as defiant cornerstones, not merely in reggae terms but also in Tosh's refusal to be eclipsed by Marley's stardom. "Legalize It" hoists ganga up the topical flagpole while "Equal Rights" blisters in both political and personal warnings, as in the sharp "Stepping Razor."

what to buy next: A decidedly more mainstream album, replete with a Motown-like duet, *Wanted Dread and Alive* ♫♫♫ (EMI, 1981, prod. Peter Tosh) makes up for Tosh's Marvin Gaye flip-out with the captivating "Reggae Mylitis"; this ode to reggae "disease" is an unexpected playful peak, while the more typically defiant title track and "Cold Blood" stand among his best work.

what to avoid: Since it's out of print, *Mystic Man* ♫♫♫ (Rolling Stones, 1979) is easy to avoid. It suffers mostly from uneven material and an abundance of murk.

the rest:

Bush Doctor ♫♫♫ (Rolling Stones, 1978)
The Toughest ♫♫♫ (Capitol, 1988)
Dread Don't Die ♫♫ (EMI, 1995)
Honorary Citizen ♫♫♫♫ (Legacy, 1997)

influences:

◀◀ The Wailers, Bob Marley, Bunny Wailer, Desmond Dekker

Allan Orski

Allen Toussaint

Born January 14, 1938, in New Orleans, LA.

Through the course of his five-decade career, outside influences never interfered with the basic integrity of Allen Toussaint's brilliant, evocative productions and songwriting. Deeply rooted in the traditional jazz and parade rhythms of his native New Orleans, Toussaint has always evolved and grew based on his own artistic premises. He rarely leaves New Orleans, which is why artists as distinguished as the Band and Paul McCartney have traveled to him to have Toussaint help them make records. His productions have ranged from 1970s hits with Dr. John and Labelle to minor masterpieces by a galaxy of home grown New Orleans R&B stars such as Irma Thomas, Ernie K-Doe, Lee Dorsey, Chris Kenner, the Meters, and virtually anyone who mattered after Fats Domino on that city's rich and colorful scene.

But Toussaint's own recordings have been quizzical affairs, undermined by his own insecurities in himself as a vocalist, although artists like Bonnie Raitt, Esther Phillips, Boz Scaggs, and others have recorded songs off his solo albums. But his solid sense of craftsmanship, his own slightly florid but mellifluous piano playing, always informed all his own records with a scrupulous sense of purpose and powerful musicality.

what to buy: His lack of commercial success as a recording artist has left his infrequent solo outings largely out of print and difficult to find, so most people will have to make do with *The Allen Toussaint Collection* ✍✍✍ (Reprise, 1991), a selection drawn from solo albums recorded from 1970–78.

what to buy next: *Connected* ✍✍✍ (NYNO, 1996, prod. Allen Toussaint) shows that Toussaint hasn't lost his elegant touch after all these years.

what to avoid: His instrumental debut credited to Tousan, *The Wild Sound of New Orleans* ✍✍ (RCA, 1957), which has been released on European CDs, may have yielded the hit "Java" for Al Hirt, but is largely an uninteresting—if jaunty—exercise in Longhairish pianistics.

worth searching for: His album *Southern Nights* ✍✍✍✍ (Reprise, 1975, prod. Allen Toussaint, Marshall Sehorn) is a marvel, his vocals bathed in shimmering vocals effects, the supple majesty of the production lighting each of the intricately wrought compositions. His first two solo albums, *From a Whisper to a Scream* ✍✍✍ (Scepter, 1970, prod. Allen Toussaint, C. Greene) and *Life, Love and Happiness* ✍✍✍ (Reprise, 1972, prod. Allen Toussaint), have been released on CD in Europe.

influences:

◀◀ Professor Longhair, Fats Domino

▶▶ Neville Brothers, Boz Scaggs

Joel Selvin

Tower of Power

Formed 1968, in Oakland, CA.

Rufus Miller, vocals (1969–70); Rick Stevens, vocals (1970–72); Lenny Williams, vocals (1973–75); Hubert Tubbs, vocals (1975–76); Edward McGee, vocals (1976); Michael Jeffries, vocals (1977–79); Ellis Hall, vocals, keyboards, guitar (1987–present); Tom Bowes, vocals (1991–94); Brent Carter, vocals (1995–present); Emilio Castillo, alto sax, tenor sax, vocals; Greg Adams, trumpet, flugelhorn, vocals (1968–93); Lenny Pickett, reeds, vocals (1973–79); Steve Kupka, baritone sax, oboe, English horn, vocals; Skip Mesquite, tenor sax, flute, vocals (1968–72); Richard Elliot, alto sax, tenor sax, lyricon (1987); David Mann, sax (1994–present); David Padron, trumpet (1968–70); Mic Gillette, brass, vocals (1970–79); Lee Thornburg, brass, vocals (1987–93); Barry Danielian, trumpet, flugelhorn (1995–present); Bill Churchill, trumpet, flugelhorn, trombone (1995–present); Jay Spell, keyboards (1972); Chester Thompson, keyboards, vocals (1973–79); Nick Milo, keyboards (1991–present); Willie Fulton, guitar, vocals (1968–72, 1987); Bruce Conte, guitar, vocals (1973–78); Danny Hoefer, guitar (1979); Carmen Grillo, guitar, vocals (1991–present); Francis Rocco Prestia, bass (1968–76, 1991–present); Victor Conte, bass (1978); Vito San Filippo, bass, vocals (1979); Dave Garibaldi, drums, vibes, vocals (1968–76, 1979); Brent Byars, percussion (1972–74); David Bartlett, drums (1975); Ronnie Beck, drums, vocals (1976–78); Mick Mestek, drums (1987); Russ McKinnon, drums, piano (1991–93); Herman Matthews, drums (1995–present).

When Lenny Williams was its florid lead vocalist, Tower of Power was in the first rank of funk, artistically and commercially. Even without him, its funky rhythm section and tight, jazzy horns are always worth hearing. Throughout the group's many personnel changes, most of the horn section has been constant; however, its best-known member, Lenny Pickett, went to New York, joined the *Saturday Night Live* band, and worked with avant-garde musicians, though as a guest he took five solos on 1993's *T.O.P.*, the pinnacle of the group's comeback. TOP's horn sound was especially distinctive thanks to Steve Kupka's use of baritone sax for a fat low end, and the arrangements at their best emphasized intricately interlocking parts. The horn section found itself an in-demand brand-name entity, spicing up countless sessions by bands across the rock and R&B spectrums—including Huey Lewis & the News, Michael Bolton, Poison, Public Image Ltd.,

Victoria Williams, Phish, Link Wray, Santana, Elton John, Luther Vandross, Sammy Hagar, Spyro Gyra, Bobby Caldwell, Ray Charles, Joe Louis Walker, John Hiatt, and the Rolling Stones. During the dark decade of the 1980s, in fact, the group practically disbanded while the horns worked more away from the band than with it. The challenge for TOP has always been to retain its trademark sound yet stay up-to-date, a challenge that has been met with varying degrees of success during the past two decades. Throughout all the ups and downs, however, TOP has been a thrilling live band with a huge repertoire of classic funk to sustain it.

what to buy: *Urban Renewal* 🎵🎵🎵🎵 (Warner Bros., 1975, prod. Emilio Castillo, TOP) has the amazingly tight rhythm section interplay among Thompson, Conte, Prestia, and Bartlett that makes "Maybe It'll Rub Off," "Give Me the Proof," "Only So Much Oil in the Ground," and "It's Not the Crime" so funky they hurt. Williams' fervid singing is front and center on the ballads "I Won't Leave Unless You Want Me To" and "Willing to Learn."

what to buy next: *Tower of Power* 🎵🎵🎵🎵 (Warner Bros., 1973) contains "What Is Hip?" and the ultra-funky "Soul Vaccination." *Back to Oakland* 🎵🎵🎵🎵 (Warner Bros., 1974) offers "Don't Change Horses (In the Middle of a Stream)." Both albums feature Williams on vocals.

what to avoid: *Ain't Nothin' Stoppin' Us Now* 🎵 (Columbia, 1976, prod. Emilio Castillo, TOP) has dated production along with the annoying vibrato and thin voice of McGee, who oozes insincerity. *Power* 🎵 (Cypress/A&M, 1987, prod. Emilio Castillo, Ellis Hall) fails not only because Ellis Hall is a forced, unsoulful singer, but also because there's too much unidiomatic synthesizer and formulaic arranging.

the rest:
East Bay Grease 🎵🎵🎵 (San Francisco/Atlantic, 1971)
Bump City 🎵🎵🎵 (Warner Bros., 1972)
In the Slot 🎵🎵🎵 (Warner Bros., 1975)
Live in Living Color 🎵🎵🎵🎵 (Warner Bros., 1976)
We Came to Play! 🎵🎵🎵 (Columbia, 1978)
Back on the Streets 🎵🎵🎵🎵 (Columbia, 1979)
Direct 🎵🎵🎵 (Sheffield Lab, 1981)
Monster on a Leash 🎵🎵🎵 (Epic, 1991)
T.O.P. 🎵🎵🎵🎵 (Epic, 1993)
Souled Out 🎵🎵 (Epic, 1995)
Rhythm & Business 🎵🎵🎵🎵 (Epic, 1997)

worth searching for: Many of the TOP horn section's guest appearances on other artists' albums are for only a tune or two, and they've been exceedingly indiscriminate in whom they lend their talents to. But the horns were an integral part of Little

Feat's transition into a funkier sound on *Time Loves a Hero* (Warner Brothers, 1977, prod. Ted Templeman) and many tracks on the subsequent live double album *Waiting for Columbus* (Warner Brothers, 1978, prod. Lowell George)

influences:

◀◀ Stan Kenton, James Brown, Sam & Dave, Otis Redding, Sly & the Family Stone

▶▶ Cameo, Uptown Horns, Incognito, Weapon of Choice

Steve Holtje

The Trammps

Formed 1972, in Philadelphia, PA.

John Hart, lead vocal; Jimmy Ellis, lead vocal; Harold Wade, first tenor; Stanley Wade, second tenor; Robert Upchurch, lead vocal, baritone; Earl Young, bass.

Cult favorites of the early disco underground, the Trammps were an exciting and innovative vocal group whose exuberant dance records helped ignite the disco explosion of the 1970s. Building respectfully on the models of the past, the Trammps added a Philadelphia dance beat to 1950s doo-wop to create some of the strongest vocal-group records of the 1970s. The key elements of the Trammps' unique sound were the hard-edged soul shouting of lead singer Jimmy Ellis and the deep, pumping bass singing of Earl Young, who doubled as the drummer for TSOP (The Sound of Philadelphia), the extraordinary rhythm section behind the great Gamble & Huff-produced Philadelphia sound of the 1970s. The Trammps are best remembered for their biggest hit, "Disco Inferno," which appeared in the soundtrack for the film *Saturday Night Fever.* But their more obscure material—remakes of "Zing Went the Strings of My Heart," "Ninety-Nine and a Half," "Shout," and "Sixty Minute Man," as well as fetching early disco songs such as "Trusting Heart" and "Where Do We Go from Here"—are a better representation of this highly underrated group's skills.

what to buy: *This Is Where the Happy People Go: The Best of the Trammps* 🎵🎵🎵🎵 (Rhino, 1994, prod. Ronald Baker, Norman Harris, Earl Young) has just about everything you need. *Trammps* 🎵🎵🎵🎵 (Golden Fleece, 1975/Philadelphia International, 1977, prod. Ronald Baker, Norman Harris, Earl Young) was their first released LP (some earlier 45s were later collected as *The Legendary Zing Album;* see below), and represents their freshest work, including early disco classics such as "Love Epidemic," "Where Do We Go from Here," and "Trusting Heart."

what to buy next: *The Legendary Zing Album, Featuring the Fabulous Trammps* ♫♫♫ (Buddah, 1975/Kent U.K., 1995, prod. Ronald Baker, Norman Harris, Earl Young) is a collection of their first singles; this set includes "Sixty Minute Man," which isn't on the Rhino set, and "Hold Back the Night," later covered by Graham Parker, among others. Also released as *Golden Classics* (Collectables, 1992).

the rest:
Where the Happy People Go ♫♫♫ (Atlantic, 1976)
Disco Inferno ♫♫♫ (Atlantic, 1977)
The Trammps III ♫♫♫ (Atlantic, 1977)
Best of the Trammps ♫♫♫ (Atlantic, 1978)
The Whole World's Dancing ♫♫♫ (Atlantic, 1979)

influences:
◄◄ Billy Ward & the Dominoes, the Drifters, the Dells, the Five Royales, the Isley Brothers, the Coasters, Wilson Pickett

►► Boyz II Men, the Bee Gees, Harold Melvin & the Blue Notes, the O'Jays

Bill Pollak

Ralph Tresvant
See: New Edition

A Tribe Called Quest
Formed 1988, in Queens, NY.

Q-Tip (born Jonathan Davis), vocals; Phife (born Malik Taylor), vocals; Jarobi, vocals (1988–91); Ali Shaheed Muhammad, DJ.

Celebrated for its easy funkiness and positive vibe, A Tribe Called Quest has set trends for nearly a decade. Along with DJ Premier, Ali Shaheed Muhammad is most responsible for moving hip-hop production away from Afrika Bambaataa's breakbeat canon and towards 1960s and 1970s jazz fusion. Q-Tip's ability to naturalize rhythm rhyming as part of the total musical flow makes him one of the best rappers ever to grace a mic. And Phife's earthy humor grounds the group and prevents Tribe from becoming highbrow.

what to buy: The group's first three records are all highly recommended. *People's Instinctive Travels and the Paths of Rhythm* ♫♫♫ (Jive, 1990, prod. A Tribe Called Quest) is set up as a personal journey into a realized Afrocentric aesthetic,

Q-Tip of A Tribe Called Quest (© Ken Settle)

word up!

HIp-hop is about rhymes and beats and having fun. It's skills and all that. But we also dig in a little bit deeper and just kick it from a spiritual level. Life is not supposed to be about being careless. It's supposed to be about having compassion and caring for the next human being. So when you're doing hip-hop--or entertainment in general--you need to be more responsible because you have power.

Ali Shaheed Muhammad (of A Tribe Called Quest)

moving from birth through discovery and loss—and, finally, to comfort and pride. While the unseen hand of the Jungle Brothers is there, Q-Tip dominates the record. Yet the humor leavens the morality plays. *The Low End Theory* ♫♫♫ (Jive, 1991, prod. A Tribe Called Quest) has been praised for creating the so-called hip-hop-jazz sound, but that minimizes the album's considerable achievement. *The Low End Theory* not only presents the group at the height of its confidence and creative powers, it also attempts to place hip-hop within the black cultural continuum as a whole. On "Excursions," Q-Tip and Ali map the path from be-bop to the Last Poets and then into the 1990s. On the very next track, "Buggin Out," the trio applies its low end theory (we're talking low end in the sense of class, ass, and bass) and Phife emerges as a rhyme animal. On "Jazz," Phife epitomizes the group's—and all of hip-hop's—great leap forward when he declares: "The low end theory's here, so it's time to wreck shop!" An absolute classic. *Midnight Marauders* 🎵🎵🎵🎵 (Jive, 1993, prod. A Tribe Called Quest) has a different, if no less ambitious, goal: it seeks to redefine black pop on singles like "Oh My God," "Award Tour," and "Electric Relaxation." Ali's sound is expansive, subtle and hook-filled, and Q-Tip and Phife have never been more direct in approach.

what to buy next: After the first three Tribe records, *Beats, Rhymes and Life* 🎵🎵🎵 (Jive, 1996, prod. A Tribe Called Quest) sounds like a big letdown, as if the group has discovered limits it can't overcome. Q-Tip admits as much on "Keep It Moving," saying: "Hip-hop/A way of life/It doesn't tell you how to raise a child or treat a wife." "1nce Again" even sounds like a step backward, reprising *The Low End Theory*'s "Check the Rhime" and "Verses from the Abstract" in a refinement of a formula that's strictly for the radio.

worth searching for: *Revised Quest for the Seasoned Traveller* 🎵🎵🎵 (Jive UK, 1992, prod. various) is an interesting import, featuring mostly uptempo British remixes from the first two albums.

influences:

◄◄ Jungle Brothers, Biz Markie, Public Enemy, De La Soul, K-Rob

►► Main Source, Hieroglyphics, Dream Warriors, Brand Nubian, Da Bush Babees, Us3

Jeff "DJ Zen" Chang

Trouble Funk

Formed in Washington, DC.

Robert "Dyke" Reed, lead vocals, guitar, keyboards; Tony Fisher, vocals, keyboards, bass guitar; James Avery, keyboards, vocals; Taylor Reed, trumpet, vocals; Timothy "T-Bone" David, percussion, vocals; Mack Carey, drums, percussion; Emmett Nixon, drums; Alonzo Robinson, drums, percussion; Dean Harris, horns; David Rudd, horns; Chester Davis, guitar.

Briefly in the mid-1980s, it seemed as if Washington, D.C.'s homegrown funk variant—that cowbell ringing, call-and-response family jam known as go-go—might be ready for the world. Island Records honcho Chris Blackwell decided it would be the biggest thing since reggae, and he set up singles, compilations, and tours and even bankrolled a studio movie starring Art Garfunkel to foist the genre on an unsuspecting public.

At the center of the marketing plan was the mighty, mighty Trouble Funk, a forward-thinking, sweat-inducing 11-piece outfit already legendary among the first generation of B-boys and B-girls in Philadelphia and New York. But when the 1990s came, the hype was over. Spike Lee had beaten arch-enemy Blackwell to history's door with E.U.'s "Da Butt" in his flick *School Daze*. Trouble Funk was an oft-sampled footnote (see LL Cool J's "Rock the Bells," Brand Nubian's "Drop the Bomb"). And go-go's shake-shakey beats had been assimilated into both hip-hop (see Doug E. Fresh's "The Show," Slick Rick's "Children's Story") and New Jack swing (see Teddy Riley and Guy). So go-go returned to D.C., where ghetto youth, black collegiates, and the next wave of all-night bands and MCs (Backyard, Junkyard, Rare Essence, DJ Kool) kept the backsides burning. Lest anyone forget, though, Trouble Funk was once the only answer when the question was: Where's the party at?

what to buy: In the late 1970s, Trouble Funk backed go-go godfather Chuck Brown (see "Ashley's Roachclip," the oft-sampled drum loop that appears on Eric B. & Rakim's "Paid in Full" and LL Cool J's "Jack the Ripper"). But it wasn't long before they emerged as the genre's hottest act. With a dual-drummer/triple-percussionist attack, they had a rhythmic density and power akin to the Meters multiplied by three. Onstage, in two-hour nonstop sets, Robert Reed led the crowd in continuous call-and-response, while co-writers Tony Fisher and James Avery threw in the spacey keyboard hooks that signaled the turns in the limelight for Taylor Reed's effusive horn section and T-Bone's roaring breakdowns. Constant touring and sides for local indie label T.T.E.D. (otherwise known as D.E.T.T.) brought the explosive beats to hip-hop heads in the Northeast, and in 1982, Trouble Funk released the classic *Drop the Bomb* album on Sugar Hill Records. D.E.T.T. later released the double LP *In Times of Trouble*. While both albums have been deleted, go-go fanatic Rick Rubin did the world a huge favor by commissioning collections of early Trouble work for his reissue label, Infinite Zero. If you ignore Henry Rollins' embarrassing whiteboy-in-a-black-club liner notes that are short on history and long on voyeurism, you can enjoy a small treasure trove of extremely rare recordings. *Early Singles* 🎵🎵🎵🎵 (Infinite Zero/American, 1997) includes the club monster "Trouble Funk Express," the regional hit "Super Grit," and the irrepressible "So Early in the Morning." Better yet, check *Live* 🎵🎵🎵🎵 (Infinite Zero/American, 1996). Originally available only as a bootleg, the record captures the go-go sound entirely within context, broken up only by the original LP's requisite fade-outs. The energy, crowd participation, endless shout-outs, the go-go community in a deep sweat—exactly as it was always meant to be heard. It's a necessity for completists and a seminar for new jacks, one of the best live go-go recordings ever.

what to buy next: Blackwell moved in just as the band was cutting some of its best sides, including "Say What" and "Let's Get Small." These cuts, and an update of "Drop the Bomb," were compiled onto the excellent primer *Go-Go Crankin'* ♫♫♫♫ (Island, 1985). "Good to Go" and "Still Smokin" showed up on the soundtrack to the aborted movie project *Good to Go* ♫♫♫ (Island, 1986). But these tracks never made it onto a Trouble Funk full-length. Instead, Island released the live sides from *In Times of Trouble* on *Saturday Night Live from Washington D.C.* ♫♫♫ (Island, 1985). Of course, the performance is incredible, and much of it shows up on hip-hop records to this day; but the record was meant merely to be a cost-effective EP, so it's short on what you need.

what to avoid: When go-go didn't become the new hip-hop, the band underwent a crisis of faith and released the squeaky-clean *Trouble over Here* ♫♫ (Island, 1987, prod. Rob Fraboni, Maxx Kidd). Not worth the trouble.

worth searching for: Worth the trouble, though, is *Drop the Bomb* ♫♫♫♫ (Sugar Hill, 1982, prod. Reo Edwards), which includes "Hey Fellas," "Drop the Bomb," and the classic "Pump Me Up." The studio sides of *In Times of Trouble* ♫♫♫♫ (D.E.T.T., 1983, prod. Robert Reed, Tony Fisher, James Avery) feature "Say What" and "Spin Time," while the aforementioned live sides bring the house down. Many live bootleg cassettes of the band are in circulation, a practice that continues today with the new generation of go-go bombers. Finally, for the hard-core, collaborations with Kurtis Blow and 2 Live Crew ("The Bomb Has Dropped") are also worth mentioning.

influences:

◄◄ Chuck Brown and the Soul Searchers

►► Hot Cold Sweat, Junkyard Band, Rare Essence, Backyard, Little Benny and the Masters

Jeff "DJ Zen" Chang

Tuff Crew

Hailing from Philadelphia and New Jersey, the talented Tuff Crew seemed to register below the radar of most hip-hop historians. Despite credentials as proteges of Ultramagnetic MC's, the group's catalog remains a largely forgotten crate of gems, demonstrating a grasp of styles from L.A.- and Miami-styled bass to Bomb Squad-styled blasts. And with DJ Too Tuff, the

Crew created three turntablist tracks that were to be powerfully influential on the next generation of DJs. If they had emerged in the late 1990s, they might have been celebrated as indie-label overachievers; but during the late 1980s, their distribution situation was more a liability than a badge of honor. Hip-hop heads are advised to catch up on the story through Warlock's reissues.

what to buy: *Back to Wreck Shop* ♫♫♫ (Soo Def/Warlock, 1989, prod. LA Kid, Tuff Crew) is the Crew's pinnacle. Stylistic eclecticism—from bass to JB breaks—becomes coherent through the Crew's focused rhythmic blasts. "What You Don't Know," "Nut," and "Show 'Em Hell" find the rhymers at their most aggressive. Too Tuff's wrist-flipping blitz on "Behold the Detonator" and "Soul Food" make them early turntablist classics.

what to buy next: *Phanjam* ♫♫ (Soo Def, 1987, prod. Tuff Crew, Ced Gee, Kool Keith) is an uneven debut. Generally, Ced's production work on "Kick the Ball" and "B-Boy Document" echoes the spare, hard work he did for *Criminal Minded.* Otherwise, the Crew's broad tastes prove distracting. "So Ridiculous" nods toward the Boys (Fat and Beastie), while "Art of Love" tries for the "I Need Love" market. The best track—the gripping "Techno-Tuff"—most explicitly demonstrates the Tuff Crew's electro fetish. *Danger Zone* ♫♫♫ (Soo Def/Warlock, 1988, prod. L.A. Kid, Too Tuff, Tone Love) is much more consistent in tempo and feel. The herky-jerky "Feel So Good" reveals the Crew's debts to Ultramagnetics, while, in comparison to Ultra's "Travellin' at the Speed of Thought," "My Part of Town" leaps beyond. None of the rhymers has the charisma of Ced Gee or the brilliance of Kool Keith, but DJ Too Tuff emerges as the hero. His pacing and production light up "It's Mad" and "Detonator," and in the first of his seminal DJ-only sides, Too Tuff creates enough tension and release to fill a big-screen thriller in "Deuce, Ace, Housin'." But he's gone on *Still Dangerous* ♫♫♫ (Warlock, 1991, prod. L.A. Kid), and the album is largely L.A. Kid's show. More consistently uptempo, the content moves decidedly in the direction of streetwise attitude *a la* Kool G Rap or the Geto Boys.

influences:

◄◄ Ultramagnetic MC's

Jeff "DJ Zen" Chang

Big Joe Turner

Born Joe Vernon Turner, May 18, 1911, in Kansas City, MO. Died November 24, 1985, in Los Angeles, CA.

When Atlantic Records signed Big Joe Turner in 1952, he was the first top artist to be associated with the fledgling R&B company. The Atlantic partners knew Turner well from the minor boogie-woogie craze the barrel-chested vocalist stirred in New York during the early 1940s with pianist Pete Johnson. In fact, Turner was probably deemed past his commercial prime at the time, although he went on to make his greatest records with Atlantic during the 1950s. Turner was the last bastion of the Kansas City school of blues shouting, a relaxed, easy moaning style, swung with a voice that sounded like it came from the bottom of a well. He was an unlikely teenage rock 'n' roll star, but after Bill Haley transformed Turner's "Shake, Rattle and Roll" into a rock evergreen—recorded subsequently by everyone from Elvis Presley to Huey Lewis and the News—Turner himself followed Haley into the Top 40 with "Corrine Corrina" in 1956. At the same time, Atlantic showed good taste by reteaming Turner and pianist Johnson for an album, *The Boss of the Blues*, now recognized as a classic.

what to buy: It took a three-disc retrospective to encompass the breadth of Turner's almost 50 years of recording. *Big, Bad & Blue: The Big Joe Turner Anthology* ♫♫♫ (Rhino, 1994, prod. various) runs from his 1939 sessions with pianist Johnson through a 1983 date with jump band revivalists Roomful of Blues.

what to buy next: While he was touring on package rock 'n' roll tours with the teen heartthrobs of the day, Turner took time to recreate the classic Kansas City jazz sound of his youth on *The Boss of the Blues* ♫♫♫♫ (Atlantic, 1956, prod. Nesuhi Ertegun, Jerry Wexler), an utterly magnificent chapter in American music.

what to avoid: Turner recorded extensively during the 1980s, often with indifferent results, and was not at his best in the informal, jazz-like settings he received on *Stormy Monday* ♫♫ (Pablo, 1976).

the rest:
Big Joe Rides Again ♫♫♫ (Atlantic, 1959)
Rhythm and Blues Years ♫♫♫ (Atlantic, 1988)
I've Been to Kansas City ♫♫♫ (Decca, 1990)
Tell Me Pretty Baby ♫♫♫♫ (Arhoolie, 1992)
Every Day in the Week ♫♫♫ (Decca, 1993)
Jumpin' with Joe: The Complete Aladdin & Imperial Recordings ♫♫♫ (EMI, 1993)

worth searching for: The rollicking backdrop provided by relative youngsters Roomful of Blues made *Blues Train* ♫♫♫♫ (Muse, 1983, prod. Doc Pomus, Bob Porter) one of the most satisfying Turner outings since he left Atlantic 20 years earlier.

influences:

◀◀ Jimmy Rushing

▶▶ James Brown, Chuck Berry, Little Richard, Mick Jagger, Otis Redding, Sam and Dave, Bruce Springsteen

Joel Selvin

Ike & Tina Turner
/Tina Turner
/Ike Turner

Tina Turner (born Annie Mae Bullock, November 26, 1938, in Brownsville, TN); Ike Turner (born Izear Luster Turner, November 5, 1931, in Clarksdale, MS).

The saga of Tina Turner's escape from an abusive relationship with husband Ike has often obscured the duo's status as seminal R&B and rock 'n' roll pioneers. Ike first came to prominence as leader of the Kings of Rhythm, a group that recorded "Rocket 88"—widely cited as the first rock 'n' roll tune because of its fuzz guitar sound, the result of a broken amp—in 1951 at Sun Studios. Taking the Kings of Rhythm on the club circuit, Ike met Tina at a St. Louis club and eventually she convinced him to let her sing with the band. In 1956, she became a sometimes member of the group and married Ike two years later. When a singer failed to show for a session in 1960, Tina sang lead vocals on the band's first hit, "A Fool in Love." Ike decided to focus the show on Tina, hiring a trio of backing singers and creating the Ike and Tina Turner Revue. Hitting big with soulfully rocking covers of tunes such as Creedence Clearwater Revival's "Proud Mary" and the Beatles' "Come Together," the Revue particularly enthralled British artists such as the Rolling Stones, who invited them on tour, and producer Phil Spector, who produced Tina's first solo hit, "River Deep, Mountain High." But the beatings Tina received from Ike and his escalating drug use—Ike has said his bills were $35,000 to $75,000 monthly—eventually prompted her to leave him in 1976. Though Tina's comeback was rocky at first—she wound up singing covers in Las Vegas lounges for a time—her friendship with members of British synth-popsters Heaven 17 convinced them to produce her next solo hit, a cover of Al Green's "Let's Stay Together." The single led to an album deal of similar material, balancing her soulful, unrestrained vocals with well-produced pop/rock tracks. With the support of rockers such as Elton John, the Stones, and Bryan Adams, Tina became a superstar pop vocalist, while Ike's continuing drug problems led to a short prison stay, further damaging his already diminishing prospects.

what to buy: For an accurate take on the arc of this amazing duo's career, the greatest hits collection *Proud Mary: The Best of Ike and Tina Turner* ♫♫♫♫ (EMI, 1991, prod. various) pulls together seminal cuts such as "A Fool in Love" and Tina's contribution to the film version of the Who's *Tommy,* "The Acid Queen." Fortified by impressive liner notes, this collection is a must for any fan seeking a full history. On her own, Tina's greatest success on record remains her solo debut, *Private Dancer* ♪♪♪♪ (Capitol, 1984, prod. Rupert Hine, Britten Sample, Wilton Felder, Ndugu Chancler, Martin Ware, Carter and Walsh), which bounds effortlessly from the midtempo hit "What's Love Got to Do with It?" to the synthesizer-laden soul of "I Can't Stand the Rain."

what to buy next: As Ike and Tina's most successful album together, *Workin' Together* ♪♪♪♪ (Liberty, 1970) contains their breakthrough hit "Proud Mary" along with tasty nuggets of the group's R&B/early rock sound, including a masterful cover of "Ooh Poo Pah Doo." *Bold Soul Sister: The Best of the Blue Thumb Recordings* ♪♪♪♪ (Hip-O, 1997, prod. various) is another ace collection of early material. Tina's next-best solo work isn't even a "real" album; the soundtrack to her autobiographical film *What's Love Got to Do with It* ♪♪♪♪ (Virgin/EMI, 1993, prod. Chris Lord-Alge, Roger Davies, Tina Turner, Bryan Adams, Robert "Mutt" Lange, Rupert Hine, Terry Britten) finds the singer re-creating classic Ike and Tina cuts with a better band and better production. Though some later hits are here, updated versions of tunes such as "A Fool in Love," "Nutbush City Limits," and "Rock Me Baby" are the real reason to get this one.

what to avoid: Marrying Tina's earthy, powerful vocals with producer Phil Spector's wall of sound proved a deadly, misguided combination, sinking half the material on *River Deep, Mountain High* ♪♪ (Philles, 1966/A&M, 1969, prod. Phil Spector, Ike Turner). It's no wonder that, when the record failed to do well in the U.S., Spector went into a three-year seclusion. On her own, Tina loses more of her distinctive soul flair and rock energy with every record, sublimating those distinctive qualities in favor of a generic pop appeal. Small wonder that her last two solo albums, *Foreign Affair* **woof!** (Capitol, 1989, prod. Tina Turner, Dan Hartman) and *Wildest Dreams* ♪ (Virgin, 1997, prod. various) are the worst—just a bunch of generic pop tunes linked solely by Tina's vocals.

the rest:
Ike and Tina Turner:
The Soul of Ike and Tina Turner ♪♪♪♪ (Sue, 1960/Collectables, 1994)
Dance with Ike and Tina Turner ♪♪♪♪ (Sue, 1962/Collectables, 1996)
It's Gonna Work Out Fine ♪♪♪ (Sue, 1963/Collectables)
The Great Rhythm & Blues Sessions ♪♪♪♪ (Tomato, 1968/1991)
Come Together ♪♪♪ (Liberty, 1970/Laserlight, 1995)
Live at Carnegie Hall/What You Hear Is What You Get ♪♪♪♪ (United Artists, 1971/EMI, 1996)
Nutbush City Limits ♪♪♪♪ (United Artists, 1973/Laserlight, 1995)

> *I was born singing, so to speak. I remember mother standing me on a stool and I was singing for the ladies in the shop where she worked. I always like to think I can make really good music that can fit in some kind of way with today's music.*
>
> **Tina Turner**

Greatest Hits, Vol. 1 ♪♪♪ (Saja, 1989)
Greatest Hits, Vol. 2 ♪♪♪ (Saja, 1989)
Greatest Hits, Vol. 3 ♪♪♪ (Saja, 1989)
The Collection ♪♪♪ (Castle, 1990)
Greatest Hits ♪♪ (Curb, 1990)
The Best of Ike and Tina Turner ♪♪♪ (CEMA Special Products, 1992)
Too Hot to Hold ♪♪ (Charly, 1992)
Sexy, Seductive, Provocative ♪♪♪♪ (Paula, 1993)
Shake, Rattle and Roll ♪♪♪ (Laserlight, 1994)
Rockin' and Rollin' ♪♪ (Laserlight, 1995)
Livin' for the City ♪♪ (Laserlight, 1995)
Keep on Pushing ♪♪♪ (Laserlight, 1995)
Ike and Tina Turner ♪♪♪ (King, 1996)
Back in the Day ♪♪♪ (32 Records, 1997)
Golden Classics ♪♪♪ (Collectables)

Tina Turner:
Break Every Rule ♪♪♪ (Capitol, 1986)
Tina Live in Europe ♪♪ (Capitol, 1988)
Simply the Best ♪♪♪ (Capitol, 1991)
Collected Recordings: '60s to '90s ♪♪♪ (Capitol, 1994)

Ike Turner:

1958–1959 ♪♪♪ (Paula, 1993)
I Like Ike! The Best of Ike Turner ♪♪♪♪ (Rhino, 1994)

worth searching for: *I, Tina,* Turner's autobiography, is spell-binding as it recounts her abusive relationship with Ike, her subsequent escape, and career rehabilitation. She narrates the audiotape version herself.

influences:

◀◀ Bessie Smith, Big Mama Thornton

▶▶ Nona Hendryx, Chaka Khan, Eurythmics

Eric Deggans and Gary Graff

The Twinz

Formed 1992, in Long Beach, CA.

Trip Locc (Dion Williams), vocals; Wayniac (DeWayne Williams), vocals.

Brothers of the same mind, the Long Beach two throw lyrics back and forth like a game of verbal football. One starts a sentence, the other wraps it up, all in a seamless symbiotic flow of quick wit and boasting. Unlike most hip-hop duos, though, neither MC seems to dominate the mic. What else to expect from fraternal rapping twins? Although dwarfed by other giants of the Long Beach scene, these MCs maintain consistently solid rhymes blessed with the production of neighborhood guru Warren G. Classic G-funk meets traditional family values.

what's available: *Conversation* ♪♪♪♪ (Def Jam, 1995, prod. Warren G, others) is the debut from these underrated Long Beach rappers that would rather recreate adolescent nostalgia than depict the violent undercurrents of their native LBC. Graced with the able hands of Warren G on production, their LP rides to a G-funk melody but contains a more immediate lyrical punch than Warren's slow-flowing efforts. Songs like "Round & Round" and "Eastside LB" capture the crew's accessible mid-tempo energy, while "First Round Draft Pick" offers an example of them in pseudo-gangsta capacity.

influences:

◀◀ Warren G, Snoop Doggy Dogg, Dove Shack

▶▶ L.B.C. Crew

Corey Takahashi

Tina Turner (© Ken Settle)

2 Live Crew

Formed 1985, in Miami, FL. Disbanded 1991. Re-formed 1994.

Luke Skyywalker (born Luther Campbell), vocals; Fresh Kid Ice (born Christopher Wong-Won), vocals; Brother Marquis (born Mark Ross), vocals (1985–91); Mr. Mixx (born David Hobbs), DJ (1985–91); Verb (born Larry Dotson), vocals (1994–present).

Obsessively vulgar and unrelenting in its search for the best party, 2 Live Crew is a cadre of rappers more likely to be remembered for the legal battles it won than any music it might have made. Known mostly among Florida-area fans of Miami bass-style deep backbeats, the Crew developed a shtick taken from ribald, old-time black comics such as Blowfly and Dolomite, presenting an image as bad-ass party boys who always get the girls. The group burst onto the national stage in 1989 with "Me So Horny," an explicit single built around a sample of a Vietnamese hooker's come-on line from the film *Full Metal Jacket.* Some Florida authorities didn't get the joke, however, arresting two retailers for selling the record, *As Nasty As They Wanna Be,* and arresting the band for performing songs from the album at a club in Hollywood, Florida. The resultant legal battle went all the way to the U.S. Court of Appeals, garnering the group support from such unlikely artists as Bruce Springsteen and Sinead O'Connor—and eventually concluding in 2 Live Crew's favor. Capitalizing on the newfound notoriety, Campbell got the Crew a distribution deal with Atlantic Records, refitting Springsteen's most popular anthem into a cut called "Banned in the U.S.A." Still, it wasn't long before the group was in court again—this time, over a parody of Roy Orbison's classic "Pretty Woman" that appeared on the so-called clean version of the *Nasty* album, *As Clean As They Wanna Be.* Sued by Orbison's publisher, Acuff-Rose music, 2 Live Crew again found itself defending artists' rights to parody a song—this time before the Supreme Court. Again, the group won. But demands for the Crew's music had rarely matched demands for its presence in courtrooms, so 2 Live Crew disbanded in 1991. Campbell found brief success with a singing trio called H-Town on his Luke Records in 1993 (a suit by *Star Wars* creator George Lucas forced Campbell to drop the Skyywalker name), and he had convened another version of 2 Live Crew by 1994. But the excesses of gangsta rappers such as Dr. Dre and Snoop Doggy Dogg made the 2 Live concept look both tame and amateurish by comparison, so the new Live Crew's effort was largely ignored.

what to buy: Chock full of the booming synth bass, scratching effects, sound samples, and sex raps that made the group a household name, *Greatest Hits* ♪♪ (Luke, 1992, prod. various) gives most people all the 2 Live Crew they ever need (or probably could stand) to hear. Of course, the classic "Me So Horny" is here, along with the Crew's unofficial anthem, "We Want Some Pussy," and 2 Live standards such as "Throw The D" and "Move Somethin'."

what to buy next: As the album that made Tipper Gore's hair stand on end and sent Florida officials into hyperdrive, *As Nasty As They Wanna Be* &? (Luke Skyywalker, 1989, prod. 2 Live Crew) is a collector's item of sorts, officially declared obscene by then-Florida Governor Robert Martinez. Musically, the record offers a passable introduction to the group's depraved image through songs such as "Put Her in the Buck" and "Dirty Nursery Rhymes." A clean version of the record, *As Clean As They Wanna Be* &?, is notable only for its inclusion of the group's other lawsuit-generating single, "Oh, Pretty Woman."

what to avoid: Though some critics might suggest avoiding the group's entire catalog, 2 Live Crew's debut album, *2 Live Crew Is What We Are* **woof!** (Luke Skyywalker, 1986, prod. David Hobbs) is particularly awful—mostly because Campbell was not yet a full member of the group and hadn't yet brought what little style and wit the Crew presents on subsequent releases.

the rest:
Move Somethin' &&? (Luke Skyywalker, 1987)
Live in Concert &? (Effect, 1990)
Banned in the U.S.A. & (Luke, 1990)
Sports Weekend (As Nasty As They Wanna Be, Part II) &&? (Luke, 1991)
Back at Your Ass for the Nine-4 &? (Luke, 1994)
The Original 2 Live Crew & (Luke, 1995)
Shake a Lil' Somethin &? (Luke, 1996)
Goes to the Movies N/A (Lil' Joe, 1997)

solo outings:
Luke, a.k.a. Luther Campbell:
I Got Shit on My Mind & (Luke, 1992)
In the Nude & (Luke, 1993)
Freak for Life & (Luke, 1994)
Greatest Hits & (Luke, 1996)

influences:
◄◄ Egyptian Lover, Uncle Jamm's Army

►► Sir Mix-a-Lot, Afro-Rican, H.W.A., N2Deep, Miami Bass

Eric Deggans

2Pac/Thug Life/Makaveli

Born Tupac Amaru Shakur, June 16, 1971, in New York, NY. Died September 13, 1996.

The message that was tattooed across Tupac Shakur's abdomen offers an incomplete lesson. "Thug Life," it read.

"Equals Thug Death" is the part that was missing. A rapper and actor whose life was so intertwined with his art that misguided souls are still poring over his albums for signs that his violent death was faked, Shakur's legacy is hard to pin down. His work in films such as *Juice* and *Poetic Justice* prove him a talent that had arrived, yet his rap skills were still not fully formed. His rep owed at least as much to his run-ins with the law (he was arrested a number of times and finally convicted of sexual assault, for which he served time) and to his Freddy-like ability to rise from the nearly dead (he survived being shot four times in a New York mugging the night before his conviction) as it owed to beats and, especially, rhymes, which were often double tracked to hide his vocal shortcomings. Still, the part of Shakur that can be found in the grooves of his records reveals a canny rapper blessed with charisma, if not flow, expressing often articulate rage over racial injustice and nonsensical braggadocio in the face of the East Coast/West Coast rift. We'll never know where it all would have taken him, unless those nuts on the Internet are right, and under the guise of his final pseudonym, Makaveli, Shakur will rise from the shadows and turn the rap game on its ear once and for all. Although the Tupac-isn't-dead rumors have been bolstered by the rapper's guest turns on albums by Scarface, Lady of Rage, Bone Thugs-N-Harmony, and Ant Banks nearly 10 months after his (supposed) death, don't hold your breath.

what to buy: If ever an album title summed up an artist's worldview, *Me Against the World* &&&& (Out da Gutta/Interscope/Atlantic, 1995, prod. various) is it. Paranoid, perhaps, but that didn't mean the world wasn't out to get him. On such tracks as "If I Die 2Nite," "Death Around the Corner," and the title cut, Pac coolly comments on his impending demise as if he's ordering dinner (perhaps a last meal?). Elsewhere, "Dear Mama" pays tribute to the hood's positive female role models, and "Can U Get Away" offers support to women in abusive relationships. Pac is perhaps the most contradictory figure in rap history, boasting his gangsta connections on the one hand, decrying violence on the other; slapping "bitches" down one minute, offering them solace the next. That he can keep all this up in the air at once is what makes *Me Against the World* so fascinating.

what to buy next: Overlong and a mishmash of styles, *All Eyez on Me* &&&? (Death Row/Interscope, 1995, prod. Dr. Dre, others) is still a worthwhile ride that provides a glimpse of a side of 2Pac seldom seen since his days as a Digital Underground roadie-turned-associate ("Same Song"). Rather than the fatalistic jams that dominate his own previous albums, *All Eyez* is almost a party album—perhaps to celebrate his release from prison or his signing on to the Death Row family. Whatever the reason, the double set *rocks.* "California Love," bolstered by the masterful production of Dr. Dre, is Pac's most memorable single ever, and there are a wealth of notable cameos by Snoop, Nate Dogg, K-Ci and Jo-Jo, George Clinton, and others.

what to avoid: 2Pac's debut, *2Pacalypse Now* 🎵🎵 (Interscope, 1991, prod. various), offers boilerplate portraiture of inner-city strife, casual violence, and overconfidence the too-friendly grooves can't back up.

the rest:

Strictly 4 My Niggaz 🎵🎵🎵 (TNT/Interscope/Atlantic, 1993)

(As Thug Life)*Thug Life (Volume 1)* 🎵🎵🎵 (Out da Gutta/Interscope/Atlantic, 1994)

(As Makaveli)*The Don Killuminati: The 7 Day Theory* 🎵🎵🎵 (Death Row/Interscope, 1996)

influences:

◀◀ Digital Underground, Ice-T, Geronimo Pratt

▶▶ Notorious B.I.G.

Daniel Durchholz

The Tymes

Formed as the Latineers, 1959, in Philadelphia, PA.

George Hilliard, tenor (1959–early 1970s); Donald Banks, bass; George Williams, lead (1959–70s); Albert Berry, tenor (1959–70s, 1990–present); Norman Burnett, baritone; Charles Nixon, tenor (early 1970s); Dave James (1990s).

The hits have been sporadic, but the Tymes have been together in some form for four decades. The first success came with "So Much in Love" in 1963; the single was a #4 R&B hit, but it topped the pop chart. The follow-ups "Wonderful! Wonderful!" and "Somewhere" also performed well. The group hooked up with Leon Huff and his Winchester label during the mid-1960s, before the producer's glory days, but returned with the hit "People" in 1968 on Columbia. "You Little Trustmaker" made the Top 40 R&B and pop charts in 1974, and "Ms. Grace," written by John and Johanna Hall, reached #1 in the U.K. though it was only a minor single in the U.S. It has since become one of the group's best-known records as a beach-music classic favored in the Carolinas. The group still tours, though "It's Cool" was its last charting hit—#3 in 1976.

what's available: *Great Soul Hits* N/A (Koch, 1997) was slated for late 1997 release, much to the delight of fans of the Tymes.

worth searching for: "Ms. Grace" is available on a number of compilations, including the four-disc set *Beach Music Anthol-*

ogy 🎵🎵🎵 (Ripete, 1992, prod. various), and other individual Tymes recordings can be found here and there. Collectors are directed to the group's first album, *So Much in Love* 🎵🎵🎵 (Pathways, 1963), and *Trustmaker* 🎵🎵🎵 (RCA, 1974), which contains "You Little Trustmaker" and "Ms. Grace."

influences:

◀◀ Johnny Mathis, the Embers

▶▶ Archie Bell & the Drells, Harold Melvin & the Blue Notes

Brian Mansfield

UB40

Formed 1978, in Birmingham, England.

Ali Campbell, lead vocals, rhythm guitar; Robin Campbell, lead guitar, vocals; Earl Falconer, bass; Mickey Virtue, keyboards; Brian Travers, saxophone; Jim Brown, drums; Norman Hassan, percussion; "Yomi" Babayemi, percussion (1979–80); Terence "Astro" Wilson, toaster, vocals.

Named after the United Kingdom's unemployment benefit form and possessing an uncanny knack for creating hits out of grizzled cover tunes by stirring in reggae flavoring, UB40 is a non-Jamaican reggae band conceived in England while its core members stood in line "on the dole," and has maintained the working-class grit and multicultural gusto of its origins. Singer Ali Campbell (with his brother, Rob, sons of famed Scottish folk singer Ian Campbell) bought the group's first instruments with money from a barroom-brawl settlement, even though most of the members didn't know how to play them; within a year, at Chrissie Hynde's invitation, they were opening for the Pretenders on their U.K. tour. Fusing British soul, funk, and a dash of Euro-pop with its ska-reggae underpinnings, UB40 signed in 1979 with the small indie label Graduate, despite heated interest from major companies, because Graduate promised them total creative control—but no advance money, which kept the band poor but proud at the beginning of its recording career.

They scored a Top 5 U.K. hit with "Food for Thought" off their first album, *Sign Off,* but their dream deal with Graduate crumbled quickly when the label cut the anti-apartheid song "Burden of Shame" from the South African release of the LP. They left Graduate shortly afterward and formed their own label under the auspices of Virgin Records, spinning a string of highly successful albums in the U.K. (and their first #1 single with a cover of Sonny & Cher's "I Got You, Babe," with Hynde providing the female lead) but didn't make a major splash in the States until 1988. That year, the group performed their copy of Neil Diamond's "Red, Red Wine"—which had topped the British charts five years earlier off their *Labour of Love* album—at a Nelson Mandela tribute concert, prompting a Phoenix radio station to dredge up the single and begin playing it. In short order, it became a #1 U.S. hit. Seeing no reason to fix something that wasn't broken, UB40 released *Labour of Love II* in 1990, another album filled with reggae treatments of classic songs that went platinum. Believing in the power of recycling, they released *Labour of Love, Vol. I and II* in 1994 and *The Best of UB40 Vol. 2* in 1995. It's hard to tell whether having such phenomenal success retreading old hits is a good thing or a disservice to the group's ability, but there can be no denying that UB40's musical formula is infectious and extraordinarily profitable. They are, in fact, the only artists in history to copy an Elvis Presley song and beat the King at his own game: Their cover of "Can't Help Falling in Love" from the movie *Sliver* went to #1 in 1993; Presley's never charted higher than #2.

what to buy: Considering the wealth of their archives, the compilation albums *The Best of UB40, Vol. 1* ✧✧✧ (Virgin, 1995, prod. various) and *The Best of UB40, Vol. 2* ✧✧✧ (Virgin, 1995, prod. various) are more than enough to provide all the smoothly sanitized UB40 reggae any beginner could want. The LPs include the second-time-around classics "Don't Let It Pass You By/Don't Slow Down," "Red, Red Wine," and "I Got You, Babe" (on Vol. 1), and "Breakfast in Bed," "The Way You Do the Things You Do," and "Here I Am (Come and Take Me)" (on Vol. 2). Of particular interest on the second disc is "One in Ten," UB40's blistering—and original—political commentary on Britain's unemployment rate.

what to buy next: It hit #1 in Britain in 1983 and remained on the charts there for 18 months, but *Labour of Love* ✧✧✧ (A&M, 1983/1997, prod. UB40) didn't break UB40 in America until 1988. It is a classic work, featuring the hits "Please Don't Make Me Cry" and "Many Rivers to Cross" in addition to the first recording of "Red, Red Wine."

what to avoid: Just what you'd expect from a decades-old Russian import, *UB40 CCCP: Live in Moscow* ✧✧ (A&M, 1987, prod. UB40) is a poorly produced, uninspiring concert obligation.

the rest:
Signing Off ✧✧✧ (Virgin, 1980/1994)

Present Arms ✧✧✧ (Virgin, 1981/1992)
Live ✧✧✧ (Virgin, 1983/1994)
Geffery Morgan (Loves White Girls) ✧✧✧ (A&M, 1984/1997)
Baggariddim ✧✧✧✧ (Virgin, 1985/1997)
Little Baggariddim ✧✧ (A&M, 1985/1989)
Rat in the Kitchen ✧✧✧ (A&M, 1986/1997)
UB40 ✧✧✧✧ (Virgin, 1988/1997)
Labour of Love II ✧✧✧✧ (Virgin, 1989)
Promises and Lies ✧✧✧ (Virgin, 1993)
Guns in the Ghetto ✧✧✧ (Virgin, 1997)

solo outings:
Ali Campbell:
Big Love ✧✧✧ (Kuff/Virgin, 1995)

influences:

◀◀ Bob Marley, the Pretenders, Jimmy Cliff, Tony Tribe, the Specials, Al Green

▶▶ Fine Young Cannibals, Us3, Sublime, No Doubt

Andre McGarrity

James Blood Ulmer

Born February 2, 1942, in St. Matthews, SC.

Free-funk jazzman Blood Ulmer has one of the most distinctive guitar sounds in music today; his sharp, staccato attack alternates flurries of notes with raw chord tones and distortions. Starting out in 1959, Ulmer was a journeyman when a mid-1970s meeting with Ornette Coleman converted him to the harmolodic school of free jazz and subsequent pairings with such players as Arthur Blythe, Ronald Shannon Jackson, and David Murray. Ulmer adds his rough vocal skills to the more blues and rock-oriented records, though these generally don't stand up as strongly as his harmolodic forays—which lately have been made under the name Music Revelation Ensemble.

what to buy: A series of duets with lead hornmen lifts the Music Revelation Ensemble's *In the Name of . . .* ✧✧✧✧ (DIW, 1994, prod. James Blood Ulmer, Kazanori Sugiyama) with its odd stretched-out melodies and Ulmer's slash-and-run chording. Ulmer steps into the rock arena with *Blues Preacher* ✧✧✧✧ (DIW, 1994, prod. James Blood Ulmer) and, aside from his unengaging vocal style, pulls it off with elan. "Cheering" is a slow groove on which he shows off some Hendrix chops.

James Blood Ulmer (© Jack Vartoogian)

what to buy next: *Revealing* ♪♪♪ (In + Out, 1990, prod. James Blood Ulmer) is a compilation of earlier tapes, but it cooks in a jazzy vein as Ulmer's splashes around the musical water with saxophonist George Adams.

what to avoid: *The Blues Allnight* ♪♪ (In + Out, 1995, prod. James Blood Ulmer, Frank Kleinschmidt) aims high and misses the mark as far as the blues is concerned. Again, Ulmer's voice grates on the nerves.

the rest:
America—Do You Remember the Love? ♪♪♪ (Blue Note, 1987)
Electric Jazz ♪♪♪ (DIW, 1990)
Blues in the East ♪♪♪ (Axiom, 1994)

worth searching for: When Ulmer heads outside, he's at his best, and *Music Revelation Ensemble* ♪♪♪ (DIW, 1988, prod. James Blood Ulmer) finds him grinding, cutting, and exploring beyond the horizon.

influences:
◀◀ Jimi Hendrix, Ornette Coleman

▶▶ Jon Butcher, Helmet, Jon Spencer Blues Explosion

Lawrence Gabriel

Ultramagnetic MC's

Formed mid-1980s, in the Bronx, NY.

Kool Keith/Rhythm X (born Keith Thornton), vocals; Ced Gee (Cedric Miller), vocals, producer; TR Luv (Trevor Randolph), vocals, producer; Moe Luv (Maurice Smith), DJ.

Just as Rakim was talking 'bout being "serious as cancer," the Ultramagnetic MC's were going off the rails on the crazy train. Their mission? Make it safe to rhyme *un*self-consciously about intergalactic adventures, pornographic encounters, heat misers, and even defiled and exiled rabbits over blasting breakbeats. By the time they were through, sometime Creedmore Hospital resident Kool Keith had been installed as the patron rhyme-saint of the freestyle underground. But the Ultramagnetics were also built on the mighty musical strengths of TR Luv, DJ Moe Luv, and, especially, rhymer/producer Ced Gee, the unsung musical force behind Boogie Down Productions' *Criminal Minded* and Eric B. & Rakim's *Paid in Full*. As proteges of influential producer/engineer Paul "Paul C." McKasty, the Ultramagnetics quickly distinguished themselves from the late 1980s pack with their collective ability—in the tradition of a Sun Ra, Lee "Scratch" Perry, or Can—to make eccentricity sound vitally hardcore. By the time 1996's *New York—What Is Funky* was released, the Ultramagnetics as we knew them were dormant.

what to buy: With a series of classic sides—including "Give the Drummer Some," "Ego Trippin'," "Funky," "Ease Back," and "Chorus Line, Pt. 1" (which introduces a growling Tim Dog)—the Ultramagnetic MC's made their mark. *Critical Beatdown* ♪♪♪♪ (Next Plateau, 1988, prod. Ced Gee, Ultramagnetic MC's, Paul C.) collects all but the latter. The dusty-sounding record is one of hip-hop's greatest achievements, full of elusively shifty polyrhythms, bizarre lyrical concerns, and relentlessly raw energy.

what to buy next: *Funk Your Head Up* ♪♪♪ (Mercury, 1992, prod. Ultramagnetic MC's, Dr. Jam, Charlie Beats) is diffuse in comparison, although Keith's turns on "MC Champion," "Bust the Facts," "Make It Happen," and "Poppa Large" make the record worth getting. On *The Four Horsemen* ♪♪♪♪ (Wild Pitch, 1993, prod. Ultramagnetic MC's, Godfather Don), the group polished its sound and focused more expertly on thematics. The result is a movement from strength to strength—from Keith's battle flows on "One Two One Two" to his comedic riffs on "Two Brothers with Checks" to the streetside docudramas of "Raise It Up" and "Time to Catch a Body," and, finally, the poignant Negro baseball league tribute "Saga of Dandy, The Devil and Day." Worth getting.

the rest:
The Basement Tapes ♪♪♪ (Tuff City, 1994)
New York—What Is Funky ♪♪♪ (Tuff City, 1996)
B-Sides Companion N/A (Next Plateau/Roadrunner, 1997)

influences:
◀◀ Afrika Bambaataa, Red Alert, Public Enemy, Paul C.

▶▶ Boogie Down Productions, Eric B. & Rakim, Tuff Crew, Organized Konfusion, Chino XL, Freestyle Fellowship, Ras Kass, Prodigy

see also: *Kool Keith*

Jeff "DJ Zen" Chang

The UMCs

Formed in Staten Island, NY.

Kool Kim (born K. Sharpton), vocals; Hass G (born C. Evans), vocals.

Before there was the Wu-Tang Clan, spreading love about its home borough of Staten Island, the UMCs had already put Staten on the hip-hop map, rhyming about "blue cheese," Side Show Bob (from *The Simpsons*), and Never-Never Land. The Peter Pan reference seems to be an apt summarization of the duo's attitude, circa 1991; the early singles and first album were filled with youthful exuberance and "happy" rhymes that weren't just fluff, making for an entertaining soundtrack filled with jazz- and soul-influenced production that was aesthetically closer to the Native Tongues than it was to the moody perspectives of their Wu-Tang boroughmates. However, by the release of their next album four years later, the UMCs had changed their happy-go-lucky ways and decided to get down and dirty. The title of one of their B-sides reveals it all: "Ill Demonic Clique." The change didn't bode well for the UMCs continued success, as their sophomore album was a disappointment. With their former label, Wild Pitch, but a memory, the UMCs have gone the indie route, with Kool Kim testing the waters with a solo single on Broken Records.

what's available: While the title probably incurred some backlash from those who believe hip-hop = hardcore, the UMCs first album, *Fruits of Nature* ♫♫♫ (Wild Pitch, 1991, prod. Hass G and RNS), is an unsung classic that captures some of the creativity that the new school phase of hip-hop embodied from the late 1980s to early 1990s. "Fun" is an operative word here, especially on the likes of "Blue Cheese" (the first single) and "It's Gonna Last"—tracks that, while filled with braggadocio, go for witty jabs rather than gun-filled manifestos. "Morals" gets a little more serious in content, as Hass and Kim drop cautionary tales, but RNS' soulful production is really the lesson that is remembered. Listening to the perky, swinging beats on "Fruits of Nature," it's hard to believe that RNS was the mentor to Shaolin's other famous producer, the Wu-Tang Clan's RZA, who now specializes in dark and haunting melodies. RNS' shuffling beats, bright hi-hats, and bouncy basslines are a world away and a big reason why this album caught the attention of listeners on both coasts.

worth searching for: "Blue Cheese" was better known, but "One to Grow On" b/w "Swing It to the Area" (Wild Pitch, 1991) unquestionably represents the height of the UMCs abilities. While "One to Grow On" itself was a fine track, what with its fast, jazzy groove and well-utilized scratching, the real gem of the single is the remix of "Swing It to the Area." The original album version (named "Island Nation Anthem" on the 12-inch) switches tempos two-thirds in and becomes a short, jamming rhyme session between Kim and Hass. On the remix, "Side Show Bob Recreation," the UMCs extend the end segment into a full-length track that's years ahead of the current freestyle craze. Also, though the weakest of their three singles, the promo-only "Never Never Land" b/w "Hey Here We Go" (Wild Pitch, 1992) contains an exclusive remix of "Never Never Land," making it a choice find for UMC completists.

influences:
◀◀ Native Tongues

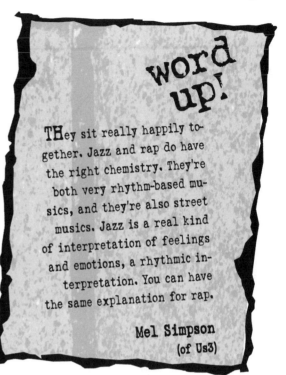

word up!

THey sit really happily together. Jazz and rap do have the right chemistry. They're both very rhythm-based musics, and they're also street musics. Jazz is a real kind of interpretation of feelings and emotions, a rhythmic interpretation. You can have the same explanation for rap.

Mel Simpson
(of Us3)

▶▶ Wu-Tang Clan, Shyheim, the Nonce

Oliver "O-Dub" Wang

The Undisputed Truth

Formed 1970, in Detroit, MI. Disbanded early 1980s.

Joe Harris, vocals; Billie Rae Calvin, vocals (1970–73); Brenda Evans, vocals (1970–73); Tyrone Berkeley, vocals (1973–early 80s); Tyrone Douglas, vocals (1973–76); Calvin Stevens, vocals (1973–early 80s); Virginia McDonald, vocals (1973–76); Taka Boom, vocals (1976–early 80s).

The Undisputed Truth was the brainchild of producer Norman Whitfield who, flush with success from working with the Temptations, sought to make a new group with backup singers Billie Rae Calvin and Brenda Evans. Whitfield brought in Joe Harris, a former baseball player who had been in the band Stone Soul Children. The group hit off the bat; the foreboding, slightly paranoid "Smiling Faces Sometimes" was a #3 smash in 1971, but it would also represent the group's commercial zenith. It soldiered on for nearly a decade, using Rose Royce as its touring band, and weathering a number of personnel changes—and a label switch to Warner Bros. during the mid-1970s—before it quit shortly after the turn of the decade.

what's available: *Motown Milestones* 𝄢𝄢𝄢𝄢 (Motown, 1995, prod. various) is your one and only choice at the moment. It has "Smiling Faces Sometimes" as well as other tracks—including the original version of the Temptations' hit "Papa Was a Rollin' Stone"—that prove the group was more than a one-hit wonder.

influences:

◄◄ The Temptations, the Four Tops, Edwin Starr, Marvin Gaye, the O'Jays

►► Lakeside, DeBarge, the Family

see also: *Rose Royce*

Gary Graff

Us3

Formed 1992, in London, England.

Mel Simpson; Geoff Wilkinson.

The duo of club deejay Wilkinson and studio arranger Simpson came up with a novel twist on early 1990s acid-jazz: British jazz cats and guest rappers playing live over bop samples from the classic Blue Note jazz catalog. The pair actually landed with Blue Note in a roundabout way. After Wilkinson and Simpson used an uncleared sample of Grant Green's "Sookie Sookie" on their London club hit "The Band Played the Boogie," Capitol Records, the guardian of all things Blue Note (including "Sookie Sookie"), brought not a lawsuit, but rather an offer to sift through the massive Blue Note catalog. The result was Us3's 1993 debut, *Hand on the Torch*, which went on to become the top-selling album in Blue Note's history.

what to buy: The formula was good for one album, *Hand on the Torch* 𝄢𝄢𝄢 (Blue Note/Capitol, 1993, prod. Mel Simpson, Geoff Wilkinson). Well, actually, it was good for one single: "Cantaloop (Flip Fantasia)," a brilliant recasting of Herbie Hancock's "Cantaloupe Island" as a cool club groove that is destined to be on Rhino (if not K-Tel) compilations someday. The rest of *Hand on the Torch* isn't as inspired, but still goes down easily, coasting on samples from Art Blakey, Donald Byrd, and Thelonious Monk.

what to avoid: Us3's heart seems to be in the right place on the follow-up, *Broadway & 52nd* 𝄢𝄢 (Blue Note/Capitol, 1997, prod. Geoff Wilkinson, Jim Hawkins), with a title that references the address of New York's fabled Birdland nightclub and some

serious content from guest rappers KCB and Shabaam Sahdeeq. But Simpson is gone, and so is much of the chemistry that made the debut so enjoyable. *Broadway & 52nd* just never quite makes it out of second gear.

influences:

◄◄ Gang Starr, Jazzmatazz, Digable Planets, A Tribe Called Quest, Lucas

David Menconi

U.T.F.O.

Formed 1983, in Brooklyn, NY. Disbanded in 1991.

Doctor Ice, vocals; The Kangol Kid, vocals; The Educated Rapper (a.k.a. EMD), vocals; Mix-Master Ice (1986–91), vocals, scratching.

Cyrano de Bergerac would have thought he was being asked to make a comeback in the winter of 1984. You couldn't go near any radio in America—hell, anywhere on the planet, for that matter—without hearing somebody saying *something* about a beauty named Roxanne. In one of the more memorable examples of mass insanity in record industry history, a novelty rap single called "Roxanne, Roxanne," about a gorgeous newcomer who moves into a New York neighborhood and busts the chops of its street corner Romeos, exploded into an international #1 hit, inspired over 100 "answer" recordings, and launched a wave of careers among female rap artists. The credit (or blame) for this mania belongs to U.T.F.O. (a weird acronym for Untouchable Force), an East Flatbush trio that won a breakdance contest as the Keystone Dancers, went on a European tour with Whodini, then cut a record that dominated radio and dance floors for months while dramatically expanding the audience for rap. Backed by the beats and production of Full Force, U.T.F.O.'s tale of empowering female aloofness and men being rejected by an unattainable goddess (again) seemed to strike universal chords; at the peak of their popularity, the group appeared on the *Donahue* TV show and received an invitation from Dustin Hoffman to perform at his daughter's birthday party. But then a 14-year-old rapper named Lolita Shante Gooden, angered over what she felt was the song's unflattering portrayal of women, changed her performing name to Roxanne Shante and cut a single with producer Marley Marl called "Roxanne's Revenge," copying U.T.F.O.'s background music exactly and sparking a brief dispute between record labels. This prompted U.T.F.O. to briefly add a female rapper and counter Shante's response record with a response of their own, "The Real Roxanne." Before the madness had subsided, countless "Roxanne" singles had surfaced from all corners, including "Roxanne's Mother," "Roxanne's Doctor," "Roxanne's Psychiatrist"—even "Roxanne's a Man"—and rappers Shante, the Real Roxanne, and Roxanne, among others, had established their careers. U.T.F.O. released a second LP, *Skeeter Pleaser*, in 1985 and three subsequent albums thereafter, but never again came anywhere near the success of "Roxanne." The group broke up in 1991, reuniting in 1995 for a one-shot "pioneers of rap" concert in New York City and the chance to rhapsodize over Roxanne one more time.

what to buy: *The Best of U.T.F.O.* 🎵🎵🎵 (Select, 1996, prod. various) isn't the only music from the group still in print, but given the fleeting, faddish nature of their success, it's the only one worth having. And even its value is primarily as 1980s cultural memorabilia—or if you know someone named Roxanne.

what to avoid: The 1991 LP *Bag It & Bone It* **woof!** (Jive, 1991, prod. Full Force) was U.T.F.O.'s last-gasp attempt to salvage their act, but the LP's tired rhymes and weak beats only reconfirmed why they needed to retire. When you're a novelty group, long-term music trends can really pass you by.

solo outings:
Doctor Ice:
Rely on Self 🎵🎵 (Select, 1994)

influences:
◀◀ Sugarhill Gang, Grandmaster Flash & the Furious Five, Whodini, Kurtis Blow, Full Force

▶▶ Roxanne Shante, Real Roxanne, Roxanne, the Time, D.J. Jazzy Jeff & the Fresh Prince

Andre McGarrity

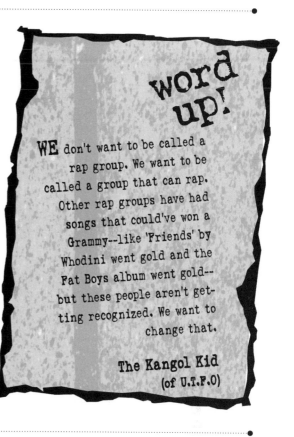

word up!

WE don't want to be called a rap group. We want to be called a group that can rap. Other rap groups have had songs that could've won a Grammy--like 'Friends' by Whodini went gold and the Fat Boys album went gold-- but these people aren't getting recognized. We want to change that.

The Kangol Kid
(of U.T.F.O)

V

Frankie Valli
/The Four Seasons

Formed as the Four Lovers, 1956, in Newark, NJ. Disbanded 1974. Reformed 1980.

Frankie Valli, vocals; Tommy Devito, guitar (1956–70); Nick Devito, guitar (1956–60); Hank Majewski, bass (1956–60); Bob Gaudio, keyboards (1960–74); Nick Massi, bass (1960–65); others.

Spanning 40 years and more than 100 million record sales, the Four Seasons are the longest surviving and most successful doo-wop group ever. The main focus has always been Valli and his soaring three-octave tenor, which shifts with frightening ease. Hopping constantly over the years from frontman to solo performer, Valli has nearly always struck commercial gold, whether it be with the street-corner harmonies of "Sherry" or the unbearable disco dreck of "Grease." The Four Seasons has re-formed countless times (usually for the worse), but by 1976 it was still capable of something as engaging as "December 1963 (Oh What a Night)," which hit #1 and has re-charted with an inhuman regularity ever since—most recently as part of the soundtrack for *Forrest Gump*.

what to buy: Since the band's catalog is a virtually endless stream of repackaged collections of their greatest hits, only the most noteworthy are listed. Pinning down what to buy is maddening, as every album has a gem such as "Big Girls Don't Cry" along with something unbearable like "Grease." *25th Anniversary* 🎵🎵🎵 (Rhino, 1987, prod. various), a three-disc set, is by far the most comprehensive document of the band's output (in-

cluding Valli's solo excursions) and contains virtually everything you do and don't want to hear. *Anthology* 🎵🎵🎵 (Rhino, 1988, prod. Bill Inglot) is a more streamlined 26-track single disc that doesn't wallow too long in the disco years.

what to buy next: *Greatest Hits Vol. 1* 🎵🎵🎵 (Rhino, 1991, prod. Bob Crewe) compacts most of the early hits like "Walk Like a Man" and "Sherry." *Greatest Hits Vol. 2* 🎵🎵🎵 (Rhino, 1991, prod. various) focuses more on the later material. If you must own "Swearin' to God" and "Who Loves You," this is probably the most painless of the later era compilations on the market.

what to avoid: We could dance to the originals just fine, thank you, so steer clear of *Dance Album* 🎵 (Curb, 1993).

the rest:
Working My Way Back to You and More 🎵🎵🎵🎵 (Rhino, 1966)
Christmas Album 🎵🎵 (Rhino, 1967)
Rarities Vol. 1 🎵🎵🎵 (Rhino, 1990)
Rarities Vol. 2 🎵🎵🎵 (Rhino, 1990)

influences:
◀◀ The Drifters, the Platters, the Penguins
▶▶ The Beach Boys, the Beatles, Billy Joel

Allan Orski

Luther Vandross

Born April 20, 1951, in New York, NY.

Now known as an R&B balladeer who's found some success on the pop charts, Luther Vandross started out as a session singer during the 1970s, working for the U.S. Army, Carly Simon, Barbra Streisand, and David Bowie—even helping co-write (with Bowie and John Lennon) the art-rocker's 1975 hit "Fame." After singing on hits by R&B groups such as Chic and Change, Vandross scored his own record deal, releasing an album that surrounded his silky smooth tenor with up-to-date R&B sounds and evocative ballads. Eventually teaming up with jazz artists such as Nat Adderly Jr. and former Miles Davis bassist Marcus Miller, Vandross crafted a signature sound that favored mid- to slow-tempo numbers with plenty of keyboard textures and room for his impressive vocal chops. Though he remained an R&B star through the 1980s, it took the commercial-sounding hit "Here and Now" to put him on the pop charts, where he's found intermittent success. Like fellow R&B/pop powerhouse Anita Baker, Vandross's sonic formula has narrowed to a strait-

jacket in recent years, resulting in albums that often sound identical to previous work, with a few changed lyrics.

what to buy: As a distillation of all the qualities that have made Vandross a star, no single album does it like *The Night I Fell In Love* 🎵🎵🎵 (Epic, 1985, prod. Luther Vandross, Marcus Miller), combining textured, atmospheric soul cuts like the title track with an evocative take on Stevie Wonder's "Creepin'" and the uppity "'Til My Baby Comes Home." For a better collection of Vandross's work, you'd have to go to a greatest-hits collection, *The Best of Luther Vandross . . . The Best of Love* 🎵🎵🎵🎵 (Epic, 1989, prod. Luther Vandross, Marcus Miller, Jacques Fred Petrus). Though no double-album could fit all the hits the singer had to this point, it's still the best way to sample his best—from the early party hit "Bad Boys" to the majestic "Stop to Love."

what to buy next: Though it sounds a little dated more than 15 years later, Vandross's debut album, *Never Too Much* 🎵🎵🎵 (Epic, 1981, prod. Luther Vandross), bears the early signs of his trademark material—from the soaring title track to the legendary R&B lament "A House Is Not a Home."

what to avoid: Vandross's later records have been stifled by the very formula that made his early efforts such a success. Nowhere is this syndrome more apparent than on *Songs* **woof!** (Sony, 1994, prod. Walter Afanasieff), Vandross's collection of cover tunes that slaps his distinctive vocalese on songs such as Lionel Richie's "Hello," Heatwave's "Always and Forever," and a duet with Mariah Carey on "Endless Love." It's a move that only shows how moribund and predictable Vandross's original material has become lately, making you wonder when he'll get around to crafting some new classics of his own.

the rest:
Forever for Always for Love 🎵🎵🎵 (Epic, 1982)
Busy Body 🎵🎵🎵 (Epic, 1983)
Give Me the Reason 🎵🎵🎵🎵 (Epic, 1986)
Any Love 🎵🎵🎵🎵 (Epic, 1988)
Power of Love 🎵🎵🎵 (Epic, 1991)
Never Let Me Go 🎵🎵🎵 (Epic, 1993)
This Is Christmas 🎵🎵🎵 (Epic, 1995)
Your Secret Love 🎵🎵🎵 (Epic, 1996)
One Night with You: The Best of Love, Vol. 2 🎵🎵🎵🎵 (Epic, 1997)

worth searching for: Vandross lent superior lead vocals to the singles "Searchin'" and "Glow of Love" from the album *Glow of Love* 🎵🎵🎵🎵 (Warner Bros., 1980, prod. Jacques Fred Petrus) by the R&B band Change.

influences:
◀◀ Sam Cooke, Lionel Richie, Marvin Gaye, Dionne Warwick

Luther Vandross (© Ken Settle)

▶▶ Johnny Gill, Freddie Jackson, Alexander O'Neal

Eric Deggans

Vanilla Ice

Born Robert Van Winkle, October 31, 1968, in Miami Lakes, FL.

Rap's all-time favorite punch line, Vanilla Ice is also the most hated figure in hip-hop history. A scrawny, skinny white kid with some decent dance moves, a goofy Evel Knievel look, a phony story about growing up in the 'hood, and very little lyrical ability, Ice somehow became an instant video-age icon with his lightweight song, "Ice Ice Baby," which blatantly ripped off David Bowie and Queen's "Under Pressure" much in the same way Hammer's "U Can't Touch This" stole from Rick James. (In fact, Ice is probably the one artist whose music would be chosen *after* Hammer's by any hip-hop purist in a game of desert-island discs.) Hip-hop's Pat Boone parlayed his two-hit success ("Play That Funky Music" was the other) into a stint as an actor, starring in the laughable *Cool As Ice,* in which he actually says: "Yo, Kat, drop that zero and get with this hero." Instead of allowing us to laugh with him, though, Ice made us laugh at him by demanding respect he simply didn't deserve.

After Ice's entertainment career froze, he began concentrating on water sports, an arena in which he actually became competitive. But Ice couldn't resist making at least one ill-fated comeback attempt, and so he resurfaced in 1994 with penitentiary braids and bad songs about good dope. *Spin* magazine probably summed it up best: "Oh God—he's back!"

what to avoid: *To the Extreme* ♪ (SBK, 1990, prod. Vanilla Ice) features "Ice Ice Baby," but so what? The soundtrack to *Cool As Ice* **woof!** (SBK, 1991, prod. Vanilla Ice) and the horrid live album *Extremely Live* **woof!** (SBK, 1991, prod. Vanilla Ice) are both out of print—and rightly so. *Mind Blowin'* ♪ (SBK, 1994, prod. Vanilla Ice) isn't really.

influences:
◀◀ New Kids on the Block, M.C. Hammer
▶▶ Marky Wahlberg

Josh Freedom du Lac

Sarah Vaughan

Born March 27, 1924, in Newark, NJ. Died April 3, 1990.

Sarah Vaughan earned the nickname "Sassy" for her feistiness, but as a vocal performer she was nothing short of divine. Ella Fitzgerald once called Vaughan "the greatest singing talent in the world today." And Frank Sinatra thought her one of the finest vocalists in the history of pop music. She was considered bop's greatest diva, the queen of jazz vocals, who wielded her voice like a brass horn. She could improvise, quickly change a song's mood, and embellish it with rhythms and melodies that made any music to which she contributed unique and inspired. The daughter of a carpenter father and laundress mother, Vaughan began her singing career in church choir, notably Mt. Zion Baptist Church, and by the age of 12 was the church's organist. In 1942, her professional singing career was launched when she won a Harlem talent contest and then began touring with Earl Hines' band. Vaughan made her recording debut when Billy Eckstine left Hines' band and formed his own in 1944. She went solo in 1945 and worked as a solo artist for the rest of her long and amazing career. She continued to collaborate with Eckstine, though one of her breakthrough songs was the jazz tune "Lover Man," which she recorded with Dizzy Gillespie and Charlie Parker in 1945. She married trumpeter George Treadwell in 1947 but divorced him years later.

Though her roots were in jazz, she recorded many albums at the beginning of her career simply backed by an orchestra. When Vaughan hopped to Mercury in 1954, she began working in jazz again and collaborated with some of the greats of her time, including Count Basie, Clifford Brown, and Cannonball Adderley; she made some of best music during this period, especially her big hit "Broken-Hearted Melody." By the 1950s, she was an international star, touring the world and drawing huge crowds for her concerts in the United States. She moved from company to company in the 1960s, continuing to record great music with an emphasis on jazz. She took a break from recording for five years and returned in 1971, though many of her ventures during the 1970s were disappointing, her Duke Ellington songbook project with Count Basie and Oscar Peterson was a career standout. Vaughan's health declined during the 1980s, forcing her to cut back on her performances. In 1989, she won a Grammy for her Lifetime Achievement in music. That same year, she was diagnosed with cancer and died in 1990. Not just the music world, but the entire world mourned the loss of one of the greatest vocal talents of all time. To list the number of performers whom she inspired would be an impossible task. Since her death, her albums have been reissued by the dozens, though many Vaughan fans are still not satisfied and wait for more of the great diva's work to be reissued and collected.

what to buy: Though you can get *In the Land of Hi-Fi* ♪♪♪♪♪ (Verve/Emarcy, 1955) if you buy the massive (and pricey) *The*

Complete Sarah Vaughan on Mercury, Vol. 1, the individual album is a good place to start. One of Vaughan's best efforts, this album offers up some solid jazz with an Ernie Wilkins orchestra that features a young Cannonball Adderley. Besides, any album with "Hi-Fi" in the title is usually high quality. *Sarah Sings Soulfully* ♬♬♬ (EMD/Capitol, 1963/1993) was Vaughan's final Roulette session before returning to Mercury, and features some of the best vocals of her career on such songs as "A Taste of Honey," "What Kind of Fool Am I," "'Round Midnight," and "Moanin'." This disc will demonstrate how she earned the nickname "Sassy." If you need collections, check out *1960s Vol. 4* ♬♬♬♬ (PGD/Verve, 1963, prod. various) and *Columbia Years 1949–1953* ♬♬♬ (Deuce/Sony, 1949, prod. various), which feature a wider selection of some of Sassy's best work.

what to buy next: If you get the *1960s Vol. 4*, you get a lot of the material on *Sassy Swings the Tivoli* ♬♬♬♬ (Verve, 1963/1987, prod. Quincy Jones), but this individual release shows how Sassy does the songs live with great accompaniment on "I Cried For You," "Misty," and "Tenderly." Likewise, if you're looking for hip Sassy that busts loose and hits the stratosphere in that best-of-career way, then *With Clifford Brown* ♬♬♬♬ (Verve/Emarcy, 1954) is a choice pick. Vaughan didn't record as much with Brown as she should have, but the light that burns half as long burns twice as bright, and this one's blinding. *Crazy and Mixed Up* ♬♬♬♬ (Fantasy, 1982/Pablo, 1987, prod. Sarah Vaughan) is Sassy in total control and at her best. This is not a reissue; in 1982, Vaughan had been singing and recording for almost 50 years. As a golden anniversary, this one can't be beat.

what to avoid: Picking Vaughan releases to avoid is like a chocolate lover making value judgments on which chocolate is best. If you love chocolate, you're not willing to avoid any of it. Still, with Vaughan, she has some weak collections, including *Rodgers & Hart Songbook* ♬♬ (Verve, 1954) and the unfortunate *Send in the Clowns* ♬♭ (Sony, 1981, prod. Norman Granz). The songbook does not feature Vaughan at her best; Rodgers & Hart is not the kind of music that made her famous. And "Send in the Clowns" is considered cruel and unusual torture in some countries.

the rest:
It's You or No One ♬♬♬ (Pair, 1946/1992)
Duke Ellington Songbook #1 ♬♬♬ (Fantasy, 1953)
Swingin' Easy ♬♬♬ (Verve, 1954)
Great Jazz Years 54–56, Vol. 1 ♬♬♬ (PGD/Verve, 1954)
Gershwin Songbook #1 ♬♬♬ (Verve, 1955)
At Mister Kelly's ♬♬♬ (PGD/Verve, 1957)
Great Show on Stage 54–56 ♬♬♬ (PGD/Verve, 1957)

Live: Compact Jazz ♬♬♬ (PGD/Verve, 1957)
Misty ♬♬♬ (PGD/Verve, 1958/1964)
Gershwin Songbook #2 ♬♬♬ (Verve, 1958)
Golden Hits ♬♬♬ (Verve, 1958)
Roulette Years ♬♬♬ (EMD/Capitol, 1960)
After Hours ♬♬♬ (EMD/Capitol, 1961)
Best Of ♬♬♬ (Fantasy, 1961)
1963 Live Guard Sessions ♬♬♬ (Jazz Band, 1963)
Sassy Swings Again ♬♬♬ (Verve, 1967)

word up!

PEople often say to me, 'Oh, you're singing about love again,' and the tone is, 'Why don't you talk about politics or other things in your lyrics? Why aren't you Bob Dylan?' Well, I'm not. Those are things I choose to read about. I choose to sing about that part of a person's life which affects his emotional standing. Other people are called upon to write about politics and other issues. For me, I didn't want to do that. I'm a soul man; I want to sing about what goes on in the heart, in the soul . . . in everyone's lives.

Luther Vandross

Jazz Fest Masters ♫♫♫♪ (WEA, 1969/1992)
I Love Brazil! ♫♫♫ (Fantasy, 1977)
Copacabana ♫♫♫ (Fantasy, 1979)
Duke Ellington Songbook #2 ♫♫♫♪ (Fantasy, 1979)
Gershwin Live! ♫♫♫♪ (Sony, 1982)
Mystery of Man ♫♫♪ (Kokopelli, 1984)
The Complete Sarah Vaughan on Mercury, Vol. 1 ♫♫♫♪ (Mercury, 1986)
The Complete Sarah Vaughan on Mercury, Vol. 2 ♫♫♫♪ (Mercury, 1986)
The Complete Sarah Vaughan on Mercury, Vol. 3 ♫♫♫♪ (Mercury, 1986)
The Complete Sarah Vaughan on Mercury, Vol. 4 ♫♫♫♪ (Mercury, 1986)
Compact Jazz ♫♫♪ (Verve, 1987/Emarcy, 1990)
Song of the Beatles ♫♫♫♪ (WEA/Atlantic, 1990)
Essential-Great Songs ♫♫♫♪ (PGD/PolyGram, 1992)
Jazz 'Round Midnight ♫♫♫♪ (PGD/Verve, 1992)
Sassy Sings & Swings ♫♫♫♪ (Capitol, 1992)
16 Most Requested Songs ♫♫♫♪ (Sony, 1993)
Benny Carter Sessions ♫♫♫♪ (EMD, 1994)
Essence of Sarah Vaughan ♫♫♪ (Sony, 1994)
Vol. 18–Verve Jazz Masters ♫♫♫♪ (Verve, 1994)
Vol. 42–Verve Jazz Masters ♫♫♫♪ (Verve, 1995)
Memories ♫♫♫♪ (Black Label)
Sings Broadway ♫♫♫♪ (PGD/Verve, 1995)
Sings Great American Songs, Vol. 2, '56–'57 ♫♫♫♪ (Verve)
This Is Jazz #20 ♫♫♪ (Sony, 1996)
You're Mine You ♫♫♫♪ (Member's Edition, 1997)

worth searching for: When Fantasy reissued *How Long Has This Been Going On* ♫♫♫♪ (Fantasy, 1978/Pablo, 1987), Vaughan fans wept, and if you can track this one down, you won't be sorry. This disc collects 10 best of Vaughan selections that will not disappoint the newcomer and veteran Vaughan lover alike. Likewise, if you need a good Vaughan fix, *No Count Sarah* ♫♫♫♪ (PGD/Verve, 1958) offers her collaboration with the Count Basie Orchestra, which is ultimate Vaughanism. If you don't want to by the Mercury set that includes this disc, find it individually and enjoy one of the best Vaughan recordings of all time.

influences:

◀◀ Billie Holiday, Bessie Smith, Ella Fitzgerald

▶▶ Carmen McRae, Shirley Horn, Lena Horne, Maxine Sullivan, Diana Ross, Whitney Houston, Gladys Knight, Bette Midler, Barbra Streisand

Chris Tower

The Village People

Formed 1977, in New York, NY.

Felipe Rose (the Indian); Alexander Briley (the G.I.); Glenn Hughes (the Leatherman); David Hodo (the Construction Worker) (1977–82, 1987–present); Randy Jones (the Cowboy) (1977–80); Victor Willis (the Cop) (1977–79); Ray Simpson (1979–82, 1987–present); Miles Jaye (1982–85); Jeff Olsen (1980–present).

One of the shrewdest, most cleverly manufactured groups ever, the Village People began life as a sly mockery of New York's gay subculture and ended up—for two years anyway—becoming one of the most successful groups on the planet, their very exclusive sense of musical and visual humor helping initiate countless millions of unsuspecting listeners into the exotic world of hardcore dance music. Wandering the streets of Greenwich Village late one night in 1976, French record producer Jacques Morali encountered a dancer named Felipe Rose, dressed in full Native American regalia, en route to his job at the notorious Anvil Club. Intrigued, he followed Rose inside where he was joined at the bar by another dancer, this one resplendent in an outrageous Wild West outfit. This incongruous image—a cowboy and an Indian drinking and dancing together at four in the morning—led Morali to form a group that, in parodying stereotypes of American masculinity, would put a face to what was already being called a faceless genre: disco. He then concocted four songs celebrating four centers of the American gay underground ("San Francisco (You've Got Me)," "Fire Island," "In Hollywood (Everybody Is a Star)," and "Village People"), recorded them with Broadway vocalist Victor Willis, and sold the album to Neil Bogart's hot new Casablanca label.

American Bandstand called soon afterwards, requesting the "band" (which had already entered the U.K. charts with "San Francisco") to perform on national television. Running an ad in the trade papers which began with the words "Macho Types Wanted: Must Have Mustache," Morali quickly cast the remaining four "characters" for the group, and their very first live appearance together, in February of 1977 at Brooklyn's 2001 Odyssey club (where much of *Saturday Night Fever* had just been filmed), was an overwhelming success. The next songs Morali wrote for his creations—"Macho Man," "YMCA," and "In the Navy"—were all huge international hits, and the Village People as a result became the first disco act to mount and sell out a worldwide stadium tour. However, while preparing to shoot their movie *Can't Stop the Music* in 1979, Willis left to embark on an ultimately unsuccessful solo career. His replacement was Ray Simpson, brother of singer/composer Valerie Simpson, and himself a veteran of much session work as a back-up vocalist, but the group and its movie both soon afterwards fell victim to the gigantic anti-disco backlash then sweeping the U.S. A 1981 album for RCA, *Renaissance*, was a feeble attempt to cash in on the burgeoning New Romantic movement from Britain, and Hodo and Simpson duly left the group, the latter being briefly replaced by Miles Jaye, who also enjoyed a successful post-People career under the auspices of Teddy Pendergrass.

The band all but disappeared for next several years (though each of its remaining members, thanks to Morali's exceedingly generous contract with them, were very well off financially). Inspired by the Monkees' 20th anniversary reunion tours, the Village People began performing again in 1987, ironically only now beginning to pay their dues on the bar circuit. But in the decade since, they've doggedly worked their way back up—maybe not to the prominence of their salad days, but to a lucrative career entertaining at business conventions, sporting events, and nostalgia fests. Disco now being cool (or at least "camp") again, their story, along with that of the late Morali, is currently under development at Columbia Pictures, and not a week goes by that doesn't find the Village People playing to increasingly large and enthusiastic crowds of insurance agents, baseball fans, and even families at Disney World, all of whom innocently stand on their seats, arms in the air, spelling out the letters "YMCA" as each show comes to a boisterous end.

what to buy: It's sometimes hard to believe that the songs contained on *The Best of the Village People* 🎵🎵🎵 (Casablanca/Mercury, 1994, prod. Jacques Morali, Henri Belolo) sold more than 40 million records between 1977–80, but if you let your guard down (and let your legs do the thinking), it's not very hard at all to be swept up in the good, semi-clean fun these 14 tracks (including several sizzling 12-inch dance mixes) represent.

what to buy next: All of the group's original Morali-produced Casablanca LPs were reissued on CD by Mercury in 1996, so if the *Best Of* doesn't satisfy, try also *Cruisin'* 🎵🎵🎵 (Casablanca, 1978/Mercury, 1996, prod. Jacques Morali) and *Macho Man* 🎵🎵🎵 (Casablanca, 1978/Mercury, 1996, prod. Jacques Morali). The oh-so-accurately-titled *Live and Sleazy* 🎵🎵🎵 (Casablanca, 1979/Rebound, 1994, prod. Jacques Morali) also makes for an interesting evening's entertainment—while we wait for Columbia's bio-pic, that is.

what to avoid: *Can't Stop the Music* 🎵🎵 (Casablanca, 1980/Mercury, 1996)—but, oh, sometimes we'd like to.

the rest:
Village People 🎵🎵🎵 (Casablanca, 1977/Mercury, 1996)
Go West 🎵🎵🎵 (Casablanca, 1979/Mercury, 1996)

solo outings:
Miles Jaye:
Miles 🎵🎵🎵 (Island, 1987)

word up!

HAmmer doesn't just borrow stuff; he takes it all. He uses the name of the song and everything and calls it his song. Hammer's a good friend of mine. I knew him before he ever got started, so I don't want to cut him down and say anything bad. But that's not the way I want to do things.

Vanilla Ice

Irresistible 🎵🎵🎵 (Island, 1989)
Strong 🎵🎵 (Island, 1991)

influences:

⏪ Bette Midler, Disco Tex and the Sex-O-Lettes, *The Boys in the Band*

⏩ Culture Club, David Lee Roth, Pet Shop Boys

Gary Pig Gold

Vinx

Born Vincent De'Jon Parrette, in Kansas City, MO.

For all of Vinx's achievements—including scoring the second-best triple jump in the world to qualify for the 1980 Moscow Olympics (the ones the United States boycotted)—it's amazing he's not more renowned as a multi-dimensional performer, athlete, or visual artist. A singer and percussionist who started his career playing with Taj Mahal in 1978, Vinx continued to pursue

his Olympic goals, moving to Los Angeles in 1984. Sidelined by an injury at the trials, however, he turned his attention to music. His first recording session, with saxophonist Ernie Watts (*Musician*), earned a Grammy in 1986. The following year, crooner Tom Jones recorded the Vinx tune "Touch My Heart." In 1988, Vinx turned up on TV in memorable commercials for Levis 501 jeans and Sprite, and toured with Rickie Lee Jones, Toni Childs, Teena Marie, and others. Just as his own career was taking off, Vinx experienced a brutal loss: his father was murdered during a mugging while visiting family in Detroit. Despite losing his biggest musical influence, Vinx continued performing and touring, heading to Europe with his drum band, the Barkin' Feet, and appearing on Herbie Hancock's Showtime *Coast to Coast* show with Bonnie Raitt, Bruce Hornsby, B.B. King, Lou Reed, and Woody Harrelson.

After he joined Sting on *The Soul Cages* album, Sting and I.R.S. Records head Miles Copeland (brother of ex-Police drummer Stewart) signed Vinx to Sting's own I.R.S. imprint, Pangea. His debut release was 1991's *Rooms in My Fatha's House*, with Taj Mahal, Herbie Hancock, Sting, Sheryl Crow, Branford Marsalis, and other guests. A baritone compared vocally to Al Jarreau, Bobby McFerrin, Donny Hathaway, and Nat "King" Cole, Vinx proved a commanding (and funny) stage act as the opener and percussionist/backing vocalist for Sting's *Soul Cages* tour. His song "While the City Sleeps" became the soundtrack to the opening dance segment of the Fox TV show *In Living Color*. In 1992, Vinx headed to Santa Fe, where he sold his first painting and released his next CD, *I Love My Job* with a jazz/soul approach and guests such as Patrice Rushen, Zap Mama, and Hiroshima's Don Kuromoto. Another Vinx composition, "There I Go Again," was heard on TV's *Northern Exposure* and became the subject of so many inquiries it wound up on a compilation of the show's most requested songs. During 1993, Vinx released his third album, *Storyteller*, with Stevie Wonder and Cassandra Wilson, and moved to Boston. The following year, he turned out a pilot for Oprah Winfrey's Harpo Productions and played and co-emceed at Woodstock '94. He also hit the road with the Spin Doctors, Cracker, and the Gin Blossoms.

In 1995, he served as a U.S. State Department cultural attache on a four-month tour of Africa, then toured with Me'Shell Ndegeocello. His fourth CD, *Lips Stretched Out*, was released in 1996 on his own Internet label H.O.E. (Heroes of Expression) Records. He also had a gallery show, wrote a children's book,

Vinx (© Ken Settle)

> **word up!**
>
> AS a kid I played pots and pans . . . and sang, learning how to develop my own style from an early age. That was very important in my family. Unless you sounded like yourself, you didn't exist. When we put a record on, if we couldn't tell who it was in two notes, you were not respected by my family.
>
> **Vinx**

and made a belated appearance at the Olympics—this time as a performer at the Summer Olympics in Atlanta. In 1997, he took his own band, Jungle Funk (with Will Calhoun and Doug Wimbish of Living Colour and Bernie Worrell of Parliament/Funkadelic) on a tour of Europe. Not a bit afraid to genre-jump, his eclectic abilities allow him to cross over in a broad range of categories, from funk and R&B to jazz, soul, blues, world beat, reggae, salsa, urban, and pop. Vinx is likely to turn up exactly where he might be least expected—as he did at the 1997 NFL playoff game between the New England Patriots and the Pittsburgh Steelers, where he sang the "Star Spangled Banner."

what to buy: *Rooms in My Fatha's House* 🎵🎵🎵🎵 (Pangea/I.R.S., 1991, prod. Sting, John Eden, Greg Poree, Vinx) is an inviting place—subtle, passionate, witty, never overdone, and filled with charisma. Among the friends hanging out are Taj Mahal, Herbie Hancock, Sheryl Crow, and Branford Marsalis.

what to buy next: *The Storyteller* 🎵🎵🎵 (Pangea/I.R.S., 1993, prod. Greg Poree, Vinx) features a huge list of contributors, including Harvey Mason (drums), Cassandra Wilson (vocals), and Stevie Wonder (piano). It's sometimes categorized as rock, but is full of eclectic fusions and other non-categorizable, uniquely Vinx sounds. *I Love My Job* ♫♫♫ (Pangea/I.R.S., 1992, prod. Greg Poree, Vinx) is equally offbeat, soulful, and clever.

the rest:
Lips Stretched Out ♫♫♫ (H.O.E., 1996)

worth searching for: Cassandra Wilson's *Blue Light Til Dawn* (Blue Note, 1993), on which Vinx delivers percussion and vocals, and Sting's *The Soul Cages* (A&M, 1991), on which he plays percussion.

influences:
◀◀ Sting, Herbie Hancock, Stevie Wonder, Gerald Albright, Bobby McFerrin, Prince, Al Jarreau, Nat "King" Cole, Leslie Jackson Parrette Sr.

▶▶ Cassandra Wilson, Bobby McFerrin

Lynne Margolis

Volume 10

Born Dino Hawkins.

Hailing from the once-prolific L.A. underground, Volume 10 is a terror on the microphone. His rugged ferocity and stop-and-go freestyle prowess—a common trait amongst his Heavyweights crew brethren (Freestyle Fellowship, Abstract Rude, etc.)—was honed during his many appearances at the Good Life Cafe, a weekly straight-edge rhyming session in South Central that has come to be an icon for the city. A father of two, Volume 10 debuted on the seven-minute, free-spirited posse cut "Heavyweights" from the Freestyle Fellowship's *Inner City Griots* album.

what's available: Though supremely talented, Volume 10 had a hard time establishing a single direction in which to move forward. With the rapper caught between being an underground lyricist and a funk-latent street G, his only album to date, *Hip-Hoppera* ♫♫♫ (Immortal/RCA, 1994, prod. Fat Jack, Baka Boyz, DJ Homicide, others) suffers a bit from inconsistency. Still, the songs on which it all seemed to work ("Where's the Sniper," "Tricks 'N' Hoes," the surprisingly optimistic "Sunbeams") are worth the album in its entirety, simply because Volume 10 possessed a style that has yet to be rivaled.

worth searching for: The single "Pistol Grip Pump" (later changed to just "Pump" because of its supposedly violent title), features a jazz remix that provides a much better context

for Volume 10's lyricism than its original funk version (Immortal/RCA, 1994).

influences:
◀◀ Freestyle Fellowship
▶▶ Bone Thugs-N-Harmony, WhoRidas

Jazzbo

Narada Michael Walden

Born April 23, 1952, in Kalamazoo, MI.

It can be said that Narada Michael Walden has had two careers, one as a musician and the other as a prominent producer of other pop and R&B artists. An accomplished drummer, he lent his jazz-fusion style to recordings by Jeff Beck, John McLaughlin, Robert Fripp, Herbie Hancock, Santana, Chick Corea, and others during the early 1970s. Walden made his first R&B solo record, *Garden of Love Light*, for Atlantic in 1975. It was produced by Tom Dowd and featured Jeff Beck, Santana, and singer Cissy Houston. *Awakening*, released in 1979, charted along with the dance single "I Don't Want Nobody (Else to Dance With)," and was the beginning of a string of hit albums in the early 1980s. Around that same time Walden produced his first hit single, Stacy Lattisaw's disco-driven "Jump to the Beat." He also produced Sister Sledge's album *All American Girls* in 1981, and later records for George Benson and Don Cherry. Walden was in demand in the studio by the middle of the decade, putting his signature on Aretha Franklin's "Freeway of Love," Jermaine Stewart's "We Don't Have to Take Our Clothes Off," and Whitney Houston's "I Wanna Dance with Somebody" and "How Will I Know." He continued making his own records during the 1990s but has maintained a more fruitful production career, working with Mariah Carey, Angela Bofill, and Shanice Wilson. Walden was named Top Singles Producer by *Billboard* magazine in 1987.

what's available: *Ecstasy's Dance: The Best of Narada Michael Walden* ♫♫♫♫ (Rhino, 1996, prod. Narada Michael Walden) offers up the best of Walden's self-produced solo recordings, most of which were on Atlantic and weren't terribly essential individually.

worth searching for: The guest-filled *Awakening* ✍✍✍ (Atlantic, 1977, prod. Narada Michael Walden) is the best of Walden's mixed bag of albums available only on vinyl.

influences:

◀◀ Jeff Beck, Chick Corea, John McLaughlin, Herbie Hancock

▶▶ Tevin Campbell, the Brecker Brothers, Eric Benet

Norene Cashen

Junior Walker & the All-Stars

Formed 1964, in Detroit, MI.

Original members: Junior Walker (born Oscar G. Mixon, a.k.a. Autry DeWalt III, June 14, 1931, in Blytheville, AK; died December 23, 1995, in Battle Creek, MI), tenor sax, vocals; Vic Thomas, keyboards; Willie Woods, guitar; James Graves, drums.

Mixing southern fatback funk with gritty vocals and hard-blowing tenor sax straight from the roadhouse, Arkansas-born Junior Walker became an unlikely mid-1960s star at Motown. His wasn't the assembly-line "Sound of Young America" that Berry Gordy had envisioned; in the beginning, Junior & the All Stars' groove was rawer and raunchier than anything else on the label (their single, "Shoot Your Shot," was banned from the airwaves during the Detroit riots in the summer of 1967). The group had immediate success with a series of classic singles—"Shotgun" and "Road Runner" among them—which established Walker, along with King Curtis and New Orleans' Lee Allen, as one of the legends of rock 'n' roll sax. Though he never again reached the frenetic heights of those early singles, Walker enjoyed a successful career with Motown well into the 1970s, recording more mainstream fare such as "What Does It Take" and "These Eyes." He continued to play and tour until his death in 1995.

what to buy: One of the most influential R&B albums of the 1960s is *Shotgun* ✍✍✍✍ (Motown, 1965, prod. Berry Gordy, Lawrence Horn). The first side alone includes "Road Runner," "Shotgun," "Shake and Fingerpop," "Shoot Your Shot," and the much-covered, moody instrumental "Cleo's Mood." Aside from James Brown's band, this was the tightest, most raucous funk outfit around during the mid-1960s. For a complete career overview, *Nothing but Soul: The Singles (1962–1983)* ✍✍✍✍ (Motown, 1994, prod. various) contains all the essential early singles, as well as more polished later hits like "What Does It Take," "Do You See My Love," "These Eyes," and "Way Back Home."

what to buy next: For a taste of Walker's late 1960s live shows, check out *Junior Walker & the All-Stars—Live!* ✍✍✍ (Motown, 1969).

what to avoid: The numerous and needlessly duplicated "best-of" sets Motown has churned out over the years; there are currently six Junior Walker "greatest hits" collections on CD. Stick with *Nothing but Soul*.

the rest:

Road Runner ✍✍✍ (Motown, 1966)
Gotta Hold on to This Feeling ✍✍✍ (Motown, 1967)
Home Cookin' ✍✍✍ (Motown, 1968)
The Ultimate Collection ✍✍✍✍ (Motown, 1997)

worth searching for: An original vinyl pressing of the *Shotgun* album—a strong argument for the sonic superiority of the LP vs. the CD.

influences:

◀◀ Illinois Jacquet, Louis Jordan, Coleman Hawkins, Ray Charles

▶▶ Maceo Parker, Morphine, Prince, David Sanborn

Doug Pippin

T-Bone Walker

Born Aaron Thibeaux Walker, May 28, 1910, in Linden, TX. Died March 16, 1975, in Los Angeles, CA.

The undisputed cornerstone of the modern electric blues guitar movement, T-Bone Walker single-handedly revolutionized the blues. With elegant fluidity and a unique gritty sophistication, Walker triumphed throughout the 1940s and 1950s as the pathfinder of the modern electric guitar movement; every blues guitarist after him bears his influence. He was the original link between the rural blues of singers like Blind Lemon Jefferson and the contemporary blues of the electric combos he pioneered. First to record electric blues, Walker was a commanding guitarist, excellent vocalist, and author of numerous blues classics. His fascination with electrified guitar led him to experiment with amplification, an interest that had to do with his crossing paths earlier with another electrified guitar proponent, Charlie Christian. Smitten by wanderlust and a love of the entertainment world while still in grade school, Walker ran off with a medicine show. His insatiable thirst for learning instrumental and performing skills led him to a week's membership in the Cab Calloway Band. After he took a solo gig in Houston, playing banjo and doing splits and dance moves, Walker was a hit, and by the early 1930s had logged numerous miles on the road and was already beginning to fall victim to health and drinking problems. Walker found a new audience in the European tour circuit in the 1960s, when a new generation discovered the magic of his anthem, "Stormy Monday," through its considerable exposure by the Allman Brothers Band. Despite declining health and a car accident, Walker mounted a domestic comeback of sorts in the early 1970s. Health and financial setbacks got the best of him, and he never fully recovered after being sidelined by a stroke in 1974. Walker's overwhelming contributions virtually define what the blues is today.

what to buy: The vast and rich Walker discography is complete enough to satisfy the most avid collector or casual listener. Must-haves for collectors include *The Complete Capitol/Black and White Recordings* ♪♪♪♪ (Capitol, 1995, prod. Pete Welding), 75 tracks on three CDs that chronicle the 1940s phase, with extensive notes and many alternate takes. Another collector's dream set is the specially priced, two-disc *The Complete Imperial Recordings* ♪♪♪♪ (EMI, 1991), which covers his prolific early 1950s stint with Imperial. Among the 52 selections are the stellar instrumental "Strollin' with Bones." For those who are not ready to invest as heavily, try the single-disc *T-Bone Blues* ♪♪♪♪ (Atlantic Jazz, 1989, prod. Bob Porter), a solid collection of some better known Walker compositions, including the classic "Stormy Monday."

what to buy next: Originally recorded in the late 1960s for the Black and Blue label, *I Want a Little Girl* ♪♪♪♪ (Delmark, 1973, prod. Robert Koester) is another winner. Backed by a polished and empathetic band, T-Bone radiates all that he is legendary for—from uptempo jazz/blues grooves to smoldering slow blues. Originally recorded in France in 1969, *Good Feelin'* ♪♪♪ (Verve, 1993) is rather uneven instrumentally, with the French backup band not quite meshing as well as others have with T-Bone. Oddly, this effort won Walker a Grammy, belatedly, toward the end of his life.

what to avoid: Unless you just want another version of "Stormy Monday," steer clear of *Rare T-Bone Walker* ♪♪ (Offbeat, 1996).

the rest:
Rare and Well Done ♪♪♪♪ (Magnum)
Inventor of the Electric Blues Guitar ♪♪♪ (Blues Collection, 1991)
T-Bone Shuffle: Charly Masterworks, Vol. 14 ♪♪♪♪ (Charly, 1992)
Good Feelin' ♪♪♪ (Verve, 1994)
Stormy Monday ♪♪♪ (Laserlight, 1996)
Legendary T-Bone Walker ♪♪♪ (Brunswick, 1996)
(With Eddie Vinson) *Blues Collective* ♪♪♪ (Laserlight, 1997)

worth searching for: Another compelling six-disc collection, *The Complete Recordings of T-Bone Walker, 1940–1952* ♪♪♪♪ (Mosaic, 1990) again demonstrates Walker's remarkable impact on the music world.

influences:
◀◀ Blind Lemon Jefferson, Charlie Christian

▶▶ Freddie King, B.B. King, Albert Collins, Eric Clapton, Robert Cray, Stevie Ray Vaughan

Tali Madden

War
Formed 1969, in Long Beach, CA.

Lonnie Jordan, vocals, keyboards, bass; Howard Scott, vocals, guitar; Charles Miller, woodwinds (1969–79); B.B. Dickerson, vocals, bass (1969–78); Harold Brown, drums, percussion (1969–83, 1993–present); Papa Dee Allen (died August 30, 1988, in Vallejo, CA), vocals, keyboards (1969–88); Lee Oskar, harmonica (1969–92); Pete Rosen (died in 1969), bass (1969); Luther Rabb, bass (1978–84); Ricky Green, bass (1984–89); Pat Rizzo, reeds (1979–86); Ron Hammon, percussion (1979–present); Alice Tweed Smyth, vocals (1978–82); Tetsuya "Tex" Nakamura, harmonica (1993–present); Rae Valentine (born Harold Rae Brown Jr.), programming (1993–present); Kerry Campbell, saxophone (1993–present); Sal Rodriguez, drums, vocals (1993–present); Charles Green, reeds (1993–present).

Some of the best groove music ever laid down was done by War during the 1970s. With its Latin percussion and Angelino concerns, War was the southwest's flagship entry into the funk fray. And it represented it well with memorable jams such as "Low Rider," "Cisco Kid," "The World Is a Ghetto," and more. War initially formed as a backup group for pro-footballer Deacon Jones and got the attention of U.K. rocker Eric Burdon, who was also looking for a backup group. Adding the Danish-born Oskar, whose harmonica brought a trademark sound to the band, Burdon and War had a smash hit with "Spill the Wine." After two years and two albums, during which the group jammed with Jimi Hendrix the night before he died, the band bid Burdon adieu and went on to even greater accomplishments on its own. Despite numerous personnel changes and flagging sales—particularly during the 1980s—War kept touring until the hip-hop community began embracing its old records. The group then set up an innovative lend-lease kind of arrangement, ensuring that a) it was compensated for the use of its music, and b) that it would be able to cash in on the newfound exposure.

what to buy: *All Day Music* ♪♪♪♪ (United Artists, 1971/Avenue, 1994, prod. Jerry Goldstein, Chris Huston, War) is an awesome coming of age album, with "Slippin' into Darkness" leading the way. *Anthology, 1970–1994* ♪♪♪♪ (Avenue, 1994, prod. various) touches all the essential moments and includes a version of "Don't Let No One Get You Down" that was recorded with hip-hop's Hispanic MC's.

what to buy next: *The World Is a Ghetto* 🎧🎧🎧🎧 (United Artists, 1972/Avenue, 1992, prod. Jerry Goldstein, Lonnie Jordan, Howard Scott) has "The Cisco Kid" and the pointed, poignant title track as cornerstones for another superlative album. *Rap Declares War* 🎧🎧🎧🎧 (Avenue, 1992, prod. various) is a fascinating look—through the vantage point of one group's music—at how hip-hop cleverly appropriates and blends older sounds into its mix.

what to avoid: *The Best of War . . . and More* 🎧 (Priority, 1987/Avenue, 1991, prod. various), a skimpy, poorly chosen (no "The World Is a Ghetto"?) collection that deserves instant deletion from the catalog.

the rest:
(With Eric Burdon) *Eric Burdon Declares War* 🎧🎧🎧 (MCA, 1970/Avenue, 1992)
(With Eric Burdon) *The Black-Man's Burdon* 🎧🎧 (MCA, 1970/Avenue, 1992)
War 🎧🎧🎧 (United Artists, 1971/Avenue, 1992)
Deliver the Word 🎧🎧🎧🎧 (United Artists, 1973/Avenue, 1992)
War Live 🎧🎧🎧🎧 (United Artists, 1974/Avenue, 1992)
Why Can't We Be Friends? 🎧🎧🎧🎧 (United Artists, 1975/Avenue, 1992)
(With Eric Burdon) *Love Is All Around (Early Recordings)* 🎧🎧 (ABC, 1976/Avenue, 1992)
Greatest Hits 🎧🎧🎧🎧 (United Artists, 1976/Avenue, 1995)
Platinum Jazz 🎧🎧🎧 (Blue Note, 1977/Avenue Jazz, 1993)
Galaxy 🎧🎧🎧 (MCA, 1977/Avenue, 1993)
Outlaw 🎧🎧 (RCA, 1982/Avenue, 1995)
Peace Sign 🎧🎧🎧 (Avenue, 1994)
(With Eric Burdon) *Best of Eric Burdon and War* 🎧🎧🎧🎧 (Avenue, 1995)
The Best of War . . . and More, Vol. 2 🎧🎧 (Avenue, 1996)
Coleccion Latina 🎧🎧🎧🎧 (Avenue/Rhino, 1997)

worth searching for: The late 1970s couplet *The Music Band* 🎧🎧🎧🎧 (MCA, 1979, prod. Jerry Goldstein, Lonnie Jordan, Howard Scott) and *The Music Band 2* 🎧🎧🎧 (MCA, 1979, prod. Jerry Goldstein, Lonnie Jordan, Howard Scott) gave War a bit of a revival in the midst of its commercial doldrums.

influences:
◄◄ Sly & the Family Stone, Los Bravos
►► Groove Collective, Los Lobos

Lawrence Gabriel and Gary Graff

Dionne Warwick

Born December 12, 1940, in East Orange, NJ.

Dionne Warwick's gospel beginnings, if nothing else, prepared her for belting out the intricate pop songs that have marked her solo career. When budding songwriter Burt Bacharach spotted Warwick singing backup on the Drifter's "Mexican Divorce" session in 1961, he immediately seized the opportunity to align himself—along with his Brill Building partner, lyricist Hal David—with the relatively unknown singer. It was a shrewd move indeed, for their association garnered a virtual non-stop run of hits (all but one bearing Bacharach/David songwriting credits) and an armful of Grammys for Warwick. The whole of the Warwick/Bacharach/David union (1962–75) was significantly out of kilter with the pop mainstream in Bacharach's shifting time signatures, complex arrangements, and maddeningly melodic sensability. Warwick herself brought a crystallized ringing vitality that could be tool-like in its precision and also capable of a near operatic sweeping intensity. When Bacharach and David split unexpectedly in 1974, Warwick basically floundered for the remainder of the decade. She did bounce back, commercially speaking, with a slew of pallid duets in the 1980s, earning her fifth Grammy alongside Elton John, Gladys Knight, and Stevie Wonder with the saccharine do-gooder "That's What Friends Are For" in 1985. In a flatline epilogue, Warwick now blandly hawks the Psychic Friends Network in gurgling late night infomercials, apparently under a spell.

what to buy: A walloping 24 singles comprise *The Dionne Warwick Collection: Her All-Time Greatest Hits* 🎧🎧🎧🎧 (Rhino, 1989, compilation prod. Bill Inglot), and you'll be hard pressed to find a clunker in the bunch. The best tracks—"Walk on By," "Always Something There to Remind Me," "Do You Know the Way to San Jose?" and "Trains and Boats and Planes"—unfold like lessons in melody. And when Warwick pines for unrequited love, she mesmerizes.

what to buy next: *Hidden Gems* 🎧🎧🎧🎧 (Rhino, 1992) is a more subdued but solid collection of B-sides and overlooked album tracks, some of which are as sprightly and challenging ("I Smiled Yesterday") or as lilting ("Wishin' and Hopin'") as her more celebrated work.

what to avoid: Hooking up with niece Whitney Houston ups the bland quotient on *Friends Can Be Lovers* 🎧🎧 (Arista, 1993, prod. Burt Bacharach). Lisa Stansfield, Luther Vandross, and Darlene Love jump aboard as well. Even Bacharach can't save it.

the rest:
The Sensitive Sound of Dionne Warwick 🎧🎧🎧🎧 (Scepter, 1965/MSI, 1997)
Here Where There Is Love 🎧🎧🎧 (Scepter, 1967/MSI, 1997)
Valley of the Dolls 🎧🎧🎧 (Scepter, 1968/MSI, 1997)
The Windows of the World 🎧🎧🎧🎧 (Scepter, 1968/MSI, 1997)
Soulful 🎧🎧 (Scepter, 1969/MSI, 1997)
Friends 🎧🎧 (Arista, 1985)

was (not was)

At Her Very Best 🐾🐾🐾 (Pair, 1989)
Greatest Hits: 1979–1990 🐾🐾🐾 (Arista, 1989)
Sings Cole Porter 🐾🐾🐾 (Arista, 1990)
Aquarela Do Brasil 🐾🐾🐾 (Arista, 1994)
Love Songs 🐾🐾🐾 (Warner Special Products, 1994)
From the Vaults 🐾🐾🐾 (Ichiban, 1995)
Her Greatest Hits 🐾🐾 (Special Music Company, 1996)
Her Classic Songs 🐾🐾🐾 (Curb, 1997)

worth searching for: "Then Came You," her hit 1974 duet with the Spinners, best found on that group's *One of a Kind Love Affair: The Anthology* (Rhino, 1991, prod. various).

influences:

⏪ Dusty Springfield, Aretha Franklin, Dee Dee Warwick, Herb Alpert, Englebert Humperdinck

⏩ Whitney Houston, Luther Vandross, Gladys Knight, Elton John

Allan Orski

Was (Not Was)

Formed 1980, in Detroit, MI. Disbanded 1993.

Don Fagenson (a.k.a. Don Was), bass, etc.; David Weiss (a.k.a. David Was), reeds, etc.; Sweet Pea Atkinson, vocals; Sir Harry Bowens, vocals; Donald Ray Mitchell, vocals; others.

Utterly unclassifiable, Was (Not Was) is a combination studio project and rock/R&B/funk collective whose offbeat lyricism—mostly from Weiss—nods to beat culture, Frank Zappa, and Captain Beefheart. The Was brothers' anything goes sensibility brought together a wildly eclectic group of guests for its albums, including Ozzy Osbourne, Frank Sinatra Jr., Iggy Pop, Mel Torme, Leonard Cohen, Mitch Ryder, Marshall Crenshaw, and members of the Knack, the MC5, Parliament-Funkadelic, and Wild Cherry. A Top 10 hit with "Walk the Dinosaur" in 1989 took the group on the road, but Fagenson's Grammy-winning production work—his credits include the Rolling Stones, Bonnie Raitt, Bob Dylan, the B-52's, Willie Nelson, Ringo Starr, and the Highwaymen—put the group on ice, while Was went on to his own production career, as well as commercial work. By the early 1990s Was (Not Was) was on an extended hiatus—though there was reunion talk during 1997.

what to buy: *What Up, Dog?* 🐾🐾🐾🐾 (Chrysalis, 1988, prod. Don Was, David Was) is Was (Not Was)'s shining moment. The guest list was interesting—Sinatra Jr. and a co-writing credit to Elvis Costello—but this is the album where a true band identity surfaced, thanks to the singers and to an ace group of Detroit players. The songwriting is solid, particularly on "Spy in the House of Love" and "Boy's Gone Crazy," and Weiss' psycho tone-poem "Dad, I'm in Jail" is tremendous comedy.

what to buy next: Either of *Dog's* predecessors—*Was (Not Was)* 🐾🐾🐾 (Ze/Island, 1981, prod. Don Was, David Was) and *Born to Laugh at Tornadoes* 🐾🐾🐾🐾 (Ze/Geffen, 1983, prod. Don Was, David Was)—are worthwhile. The latter is guest-drenched; check out Osbourne rapping on "Shake Your Head." The first album is a bit funkier and more subversive, with dance club hits such as "Out Come the Freaks" and "Tell Me That I'm Dreaming."

what to avoid: *Are You Okay?* 🐾🐾🐾 (Chrysalis, 1990, prod. Don Was, David Was) isn't awful, but it's more convoluted than the group's other offerings—particularly a rapified version of the Temptations' "Papa Was a Rolling Stone"—and is therefore the last one to acquire.

worth searching for: *Hello, Dad . . . I'm in Jail* 🐾🐾🐾🐾 (Fontana, 1992, prod. Don Was, David Was) is a British best-of that captures the essential tracks and includes the updated "Shake Your Head," featuring Osbourne and actress Kim Basinger.

influences:

⏪ 1960s classic rock, Motown, Stax, Parliament-Funkadelic, Duke Ellington, Charlie Parker, John Coltrane, various world musics

⏩ None; Was (Not Was) is an unusually unique venture whose influence was more in spirit—any modern rock band with a touch of funk—than directly in music.

Gary Graff

Dinah Washington

Born Ruth Lee Jones, August 29, 1924, in Tuscaloosa, AL. Died December 14, 1963, in Chicago, IL.

You probably don't know this but, unquestionably, Dinah Washington is one of the greatest, most versatile voices in the entire canon of American song. A consummate master of jazz, blues, R&B, and pop, Washington spent most of her career imprisoned in the ghetto divadom constructed for the likes of Ella Fitzgerald, Billie Holiday, and Sarah Vaughan (she didn't escape until 1959's "What a Diff'rence a Day Makes"). Washington's ascent to that point was long and arduous, yet fruitful. She started as a piano prodigy in her mother's church at the age of 10. In 1939, a 15-year-old Ruth won an amateur contest at Chicago's famous Regal Theater, singing "I Can't Face the Music." From that point on, the sinful call of the sec-

ular world was ringing in her ears. The gospel circuit beckoned, but by the early 1940s, Dinah Washington (as she was
now called) quit that and plunged into the jazz underworld.
After a brief stint with trumpeter Henry Red Allen, Washington
hooked up with Lionel Hampton's big band. Her work with
him earned a contract with Keynote Records, and her first single, 1943's "Evil Gal Blues," heralded the promise of a new
voice to jukeboxes throughout African-America. By the 1950s,
Washington became a quiet people's favorite, triumphing
with excellent and pedestrian material alike. More prolific
than most (she would cut almost 500 sides for the Emarcy,
Keynote, Mercury, and Wing labels between 1943 and 1961),
when she finally hit her stride she was unbeatable. Her
crossover successes ("Unforgettable," "This Bitter Earth,"
and "Baby, You've Got What It Takes"), plus 1960 duets with
Brook Benton on "A Rockin' Good Way to Mess Around" and
"Fall in Love," made her the toast of pop and the darling of *Jet*
magazine. Washington would leave Mercury in 1961 for a
more lucrative deal with Roulette Records, but she never had
the same impact again. She died from an accidental overdose
of diet pills in 1963. Since her prominence as the musical leit-
motif of Clint Eastwood's film *The Bridges of Madison County*,
Washington's legacy has undergone a renaissance. For an
artist of her caliber, it's long-overdue.

what to buy: *First Issue: The Dinah Washington Story* 🎵🎵🎵🎵🎵
(Verve, 1993, prod. various) is the definitive collection. Buy it.
Her classic *What a Diff'rence a Day Makes* 🎵🎵🎵🎵🎵 (Mercury,
1959/1987) is also available in a nicely polished Mobile Fidelity
audiophile issue released in 1997.

what to buy next: *Mellow Mama* 🎵🎵🎵🎵 (Delmark, 1945/1993,
prod. Robert Koester, Steve Wagner) and *Dinah Jams* 🎵🎵🎵🎵🎵
(PSM, 1954/Verve, 1997) are tremendous early works that
set the tone for her future magic. *The Bessie Smith Songbook* 🎵🎵🎵🎵 (Emarcy, 1957/1986) is one of the finest interpretive efforts of our time. *The Best of Dinah Washington: The
Roulette Years* 🎵🎵🎵🎵🎵 (Roulette, 1993) is a fine chronicling of
her later work.

what to avoid: *Golden Classics* 🎵🎵 (Collectables, 1990) is a
hodgepodge affair that doesn't serve Washington's memory
well, though she sounds fine throughout.

the rest:
For Those In Love 🎵🎵🎵🎵 (Emarcy, 1955/1992)
In the Land of Hi-Fi 🎵🎵🎵🎵 (Emarcy, 1956/1987)
Dinah 🎵🎵🎵 (Emarcy, 1956/1991)
The Fats Waller Songbook 🎵🎵🎵🎵 (Emarcy, 1957/1987)

word up!

THe essence of it is, we're
trying to make a few seemingly disparate elements
collide. . . . Sometimes huge
success takes you off track.
I don't want that to happen
to me. I feel like we're on a
creative roll now, and I
don't want something to happen to mess that up. As long
as we can get to the next
record and keep the band together, I'm happy.

Don Was
(of Was (Not Was))

Unforgettable 🎵🎵🎵 (Mercury, 1959/1991)
(With Brook Benton) *The Two of Us* 🎵🎵🎵🎵 (Verve, 1960/1995)
Dinah '63 🎵🎵 (Roulette, 1963/1990)
Compact Jazz 🎵🎵🎵🎵 (Verve, 1987)
Compact Jazz: Dinah Washington Sings the Blues 🎵🎵🎵🎵 (Verve,
1987/1990)
The Complete Dinah Washington on Mercury, Vol. 1–7 🎵🎵🎵🎵 (Mercury,
1989)
In Love 🎵🎵🎵 (Roulette, 1991)
The Essential Dinah Washington: The Great Songs 🎵🎵🎵🎵 (Verve, 1992)
Jazz 'Round Midnight 🎵🎵🎵 (Verve, 1993)
Verve Jazz Masters #19 🎵🎵🎵🎵 (Verve, 1994)
Sings Standards 🎵🎵🎵🎵 (Verve, 1994)
Blue Gardenia: Songs of Love 🎵🎵🎵🎵 (Emarcy, 1995)
Jazz Profile 🎵🎵🎵🎵 (Blue Note, 1997)
Back to the Blues 🎵🎵🎵🎵 (Blue Note, 1997)

worth searching for: The 1992 video *The Swingin' Years: Vintage Jazz Classics*, which features performances by Washington, Stan Kenton, Louis Jordan, and others on a 1960 telecast hosted by Ronald Reagan.

influences:

◄◄ Maxine Sullivan, Sarah Vaughan, Mildred Bailey

►► Patti LaBelle, Patti Austin, Aretha Franklin, Erykah Badu

Tom Terrell and Gary Graff

Grover Washington Jr.

Born December 12, 1943, in Buffalo, NY.

After starting his career as a blues and R&B sideman in Philadelphia, saxophonist Grover Washington Jr. found himself on Creed Taylor's Kudu label, where he created several fine jazz fusion LPs during the 1970s, among them the hit *Mister Magic* and its follow-up, *Feels So Good* (not to be confused with Chuck Mangione's album of the same name). Next to *Mister Magic,* however, Washington's biggest commercial success came with an Elektra product, *Winelight*, which spawned the notable single "Just the Two of Us" (with vocals by Bill Withers). While none of his work qualifies as the definitive yardstick by which to measure the jazz-fusion genre, *Mister Magic*, a sexy sax exploration that helped bring fusion to the non-hardcore-jazz masses, comes close. On it, Washington melds jazz and funk perfectly into a tasty rhythmic, melodic blend—smooth as silk and full of soul. Washington has label-hopped over the years, from the now-defunct Kudu to Elektra, Motown, and, currently, Columbia; fortunately, his Kudu output was reissued during the 1980s by Motown. He also might be credited with (or accused of) paving the way for the even more blatant commercialism of fellow saxophonist Kenny G.; Washington's work has always been carefully crafted for maximum mass appeal—a trait his often too self-important pure jazz counterparts regard with icy disdain.

what to buy: On *Mister Magic* &&&& (Kudu, 1975/Motown, 1995, prod. Creed Taylor), the combination of Washington's saxes and the efforts of sidemen Eric Gale, Ralph MacDonald, and Harvey Mason, with Bob James' impeccable arrangements, is intoxicating. *Inner City Blues* &&&&& (Kudu, 1972/Motown, 1995, prod. Creed Taylor) set the tone for what was to follow. It also features Gale, James, Ron Carter, Airto Moreira, and Thad Jones—versatile players who would move in and out of Washington's professional circle often over the years.

what to buy next: *Winelight* &&&& (Elektra, 1980, prod. Grover Washington Jr., Ralph MacDonald), Washington's well-crafted double-Grammy winner, is fine mood music, as the name implies.

what to avoid: Good as it is, pop and R&B lovers won't find what they're looking for on *Then and Now* &&&& (Columbia, 1988, prod. Grover Washington Jr.), a more straight-ahead jazz outing with standards such as "Stella by Starlight" and "In a Sentimental Mood."

the rest:
Feels So Good &&&& (Kudu, 1975)
A Secret Place &&& (Kudu, 1977)
Live at the Bijou &&&& (Kudu, 1977/Motown, 1978)
Paradise &&& (Elektra, 1979)
Reed Seed &&&& (Motown, 1979)
Skylarkin' &&& (Motown, 1980)
Baddest &&& (Motown, 1981)
Come Morning &&& (Elektra, 1981)
Inside Moves &&& (Elektra, 1984)
The Best Is Yet to Come &&& (Elektra, 1987)
Strawberry Moon &&& (Columbia, 1987)
Time Out of Mind &&& (Columbia, 1989)
Next Exit &&& (Columbia, 1992)
All My Tomorrows &&& (Columbia, 1994)
Soulful Strut &&& (Columbia, 1996)

worth searching for: *Grover Washington Jr. Anthology* &&&&& (Motown, 1981), a two-CD set that features three Marvin Gaye tunes, "Mister Magic," and other choice cuts from Washington's 1970s output. Also, *All the King's Horses* &&&& (Kudu, 1972, prod. Creed Taylor), which includes covers of "Where Is the Love," the title tune, and "Lean on Me," as well as terrific supporting players. Also worth hearing is *Fire Into Music* &&&&& (CTI/Kudu, 1975, prod. various), a compilation of labelmates that also includes performances by Deodato, George Benson, Freddie Hubbard, Stanley Turrentine, Hubert Laws, and others, at a time when all the most successful pop/jazz players were recording for Creed Taylor.

influences:

◄◄ Chet Baker, Sonny Rollins, Dexter Gordon, Coleman Hawkins, Gerry Mulligan, Joe Henderson

►► Kenny G., Kenny Blake, David Sanborn

Lynne Margolis

Keith Washington (© Ken Settle)

Keith Washington

Born in Detroit, MI.

With a smooth voice, a cool loverman persona, and a face made for TV, Washington rose to the top of the soul crooner pile during the early 1990s after scoring big with his first single, "Kissing You." The former *Star Search* contestant and backup singer for Miki Howard parlayed his quick success into a small part on the ABC soap opera *General Hospital* and found other acting jobs. But he failed to sustain that momentum in his music career. His second album, for which he co-wrote most of the songs, proved that perhaps he was simply better at creating a romantic mood than singing a stirring song.

what to buy: *Make Time for Love* ♫♫♫ (Qwest, 1991, prod. Terry Coffey), his debut, contains some cooly melodic tunes, led by his big hit, "Kissing You," which was nominated for a Grammy Award.

the rest:
You Make It Easy ♫♫♫ (Qwest, 1993)

worth searching for: Washington blends well with Chante Moore on the duet "Candlelight and You," from her album *Precious* (MCA, 1992, prod. various).

influences:
◄◄ Luther Vandross, Babyface, James Ingram
►► Christopher Williams

Franklin Paul

Crystal Waters

Born 1964, in Philadelphia, PA.

Crystal Waters' "la da dee, la da dah" chorus, from her 1991 summer dance hit "Gypsy Woman (She's Homeless)," was intensely catchy, and it made this unknown Washington, D.C., singer-songwriter—the daughter of jazz musician Jr. Waters and niece of singer Ethel Waters—a star. Waters has at least as much dance-hall savvy as Paula Abdul, and she's a better lyric writer, but she still hasn't been able to click for more than a hit or two per album. "100% Pure Love," an overproduced but catchy song from her second album, hit #11 on the pop singles charts, but it was "I Believe I Love You," buried between mostly overproduced dance music on that same album, that truly showcased her talent. The song is a Stax-Motown-style soul classic, with perfect sound effects, a funky groove, and a Janet Jackson-style delivery.

what to buy: The sophomore album *Storyteller* ♫♫♫ (Mercury, 1994, prod. Basement Boys) is full of much stronger songwriting, with the wonderful "I Believe I Love You," but its electrodance-funk production wears thin too fast.

what to buy next: *Crystal Waters* ♫♫♫ (Mercury, 1997, prod. Jimmy Jam, Terry Lewis) is more gimmicky, playing up Waters' apparent interest in basketball (it includes her *NBA at 50* soundtrack song, "Say . . . If You Feel Alright," and a collaboration with hoops nutcase Dennis Rodman); the dance grooves, especially on "Love I Found," are strong as usual.

the rest:
Surprise ♫♫♫ (Mercury, 1991)

influences:
◄◄ Diana Ross, Donna Summer, Janet Jackson, Roberta Flack, Madonna
►► En Vogue, TLC, Fugees, Brandy

Steve Knopper

Muddy Waters

Born McKinley Morganfield, April 4, 1915, in Rolling Fork, MS. Died April 30, 1983, in Chicago, IL.

"The blues had a baby," Muddy Waters sang in 1977, "and they named it rock and roll." It was *his* baby. Inspired by Robert Johnson, Son House, and the other talented local bluesmen, the young McKinley Morganfield picked up an acoustic guitar and immediately established himself as a peer. Even as a young man, his voice was deep and charismatic; his untrained guitar tones on "Honey Bee" and "Rollin' Stone"—the latter inspired both the band and the Bob Dylan hit—sounded so new and out of the ordinary that they inspired such torch-carriers as Charlie Parker, Chuck Berry, Elvis Presley, and Keith Richards. At a time when pop music was still defined by George and Ira Gershwin, such "black music" was considered dirty and uncouth, and Waters' gravelly voice and forthright lyrics did little to combat this perception. He didn't earn his legend until the 1950s, when he moved to Chicago and picked up an electric guitar. Recording for Chicago's Chess Records, the label at the right place at the right time, Waters developed a sharp, piercing blues sound that influenced generations of blues and rock players and launched the careers of harpist James Cotton and pianist Otis Spann, who both played in Waters' band. He reeled off countless classics—"Hoochie Coochie Man," "You Shook Me," "Got My Mojo Workin'," "Mannish Boy"—many written by Chess session bassist Willie Dixon. His career sagged slightly, and ironically, after Elvis Presley merged Waters' electric blues with Kentucky bluegrass music, but it picked up again when the Rolling

Stones began dropping his name in America. Waters performed with his proteges several times, including once at Chicago's still-thriving Checkerboard Lounge, and was a prominent figure in the 1960s blues revival. During the 1970s, he hooked up with guitar hero Johnny Winter and, playing his distinctive electric tones off Winter's spastic solos, found renewed creative power. He died in 1983 as perhaps the world's best-known and most influential bluesman. Others still base their entire career on the fact that they once played with him. And many thriving blues clubs, including Antone's in Austin, Texas, market themselves with huge pictures and T-shirts of Muddy Waters.

what to buy: It's tough to navigate Waters' 20-plus albums, many of which were released simply to promote a single or two, so the best starting point is the comprehensive career retrospective *The Chess Box* 𝄚𝄚𝄚𝄚 (Chess-MCA, 1989, prod. various), which has simply everything, plus critic Robert Palmer's must-read liner notes dissecting Waters' unique musical style. Two other worthwhile collections are *The Best of Muddy Waters* 𝄚𝄚𝄚𝄚 (Chess, 1958/Chess-MCA, 1987, prod. various) and *His Best: 1947–1955* 𝄚𝄚𝄚𝄚 (Chess-MCA, 1997, prod. various). Both contain "I Can't Be Satisfied" and other important studio tracks from 1948–54.

what to buy next: To build a good Waters collection, it's advisable to sample a key album from every phase of his career. *Down on Stovall's Plantation* 𝄚𝄚𝄚𝄚 (Testament, 1966, prod. Alan Lomax) is a collection of folklorist Alan Lomax's acoustic 1941 field recordings; the scholar was trying to find Robert Johnson in the Delta, but failed and was referred to the similar-sounding Waters instead. The 1950s sides are best collected on *Trouble No More: Singles, 1955–1959)* 𝄚𝄚𝄚𝄚 (Chess-MCA, 1989, prod. various). Waters' 1960s material is less spontaneous, though *The Real Folk Blues* 𝄚𝄚𝄚𝄚 (Chess, 1966/MCA, 1987, prod. Marshall Chess) contains "40 Days & 40 Nights" and "Mannish Boy," which influenced the Stones, Led Zeppelin, Bo Diddley, and every living bluesman. The better-known version of "Mannish Boy," at least the one rock radio stations still play from time to time, is off *Muddy "Mississippi" Waters Live* 𝄚𝄚𝄚𝄚 (Blue Sky, 1979, prod. Johnny Winter), a fiery collection with Winter's electric guitar smashing dangerously into Waters' confident, perfectly timed chiming notes and friendly vocal growl.

what to avoid: Even Waters put out some lemons, most notably *The Muddy Waters Woodstock Album* 𝄚 (Chess, 1975, prod. Henry Glover), which gives the legendary upstate New York town a bad name.

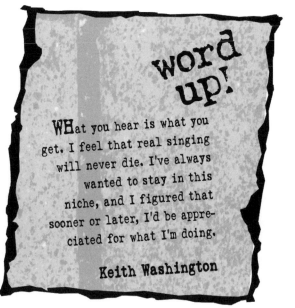

word up!

WHat you hear is what you get. I feel that real singing will never die. I've always wanted to stay in this niche, and I figured that sooner or later, I'd be appreciated for what I'm doing.

Keith Washington

best of the rest:

At Newport 𝄚𝄚𝄚𝄚 (Chess, 1960/Chess-MCA, 1986)
Sings Big Bill Broonzy 𝄚𝄚𝄚𝄚 (Chess, 1960)
Folk Singer 𝄚𝄚𝄚𝄚 (Chess, 1964)
More Real Folk Blues 𝄚𝄚𝄚𝄚 (Chess, 1967/Chess-MCA, 1988)
Fathers and Sons 𝄚𝄚𝄚 (Chess, 1969)
The London Muddy Waters Sessions 𝄚𝄚𝄚 (Chess, 1972/Chess-MCA, 1989)
Hard Again 𝄚𝄚𝄚 (Blue Sky, 1977)
I'm Ready 𝄚𝄚𝄚 (Blue Sky, 1978)
Rolling Stone 𝄚𝄚𝄚 (Chess, 1982/Chess-MCA, 1984)
Rare and Unissued 𝄚𝄚𝄚 (Chess, 1982/Chess-MCA, 1991)
His Best: 1956–64 𝄚𝄚𝄚𝄚 (Chess-MCA, 1997)

worth searching for: The two-albums-on-one-CD combination of *Folk Singer/Sings Bill Broonzy* 𝄚𝄚𝄚𝄚 (Chess-MCA, 1987), two of Waters' finest albums from the early 1960s.

influences:

◀◀ Robert Johnson, Son House, Charley Patton

▶▶ Buddy Guy, Jimi Hendrix, Bob Dylan, the Rolling Stones, Led Zeppelin, PJ Harvey, Johnny Winter, Elvin Bishop, Paul Butterfield Blues Band, Allman Brothers Band, Eric Clapton

Steve Knopper

Jody Watley

Born January 30, 1959, in Chicago, IL.

Jody Watley had—and still has, though her commercial prime is past—a number of advantages over her 1980s R&B diva competition. Being a bit older than most of them, and coming out of the group Shalamar, she came up when singing involved understanding melody and how to build to a climax, rather than starting frenetic and mangling producer-penned drivel with wild melismas to make up for poor writing. Her material was better-written for similar reasons, plus her producer was often Andre Cymone (ex-Prince & the Revolution), who secretly married her. And her trademark long hair was her own, and don't think Watley didn't flaunt it proudly (except for an image change that lasted only one album). It was a quirk in the Grammy Award rules that allowed Watley to win Best New Artist in 1987 for her debut, for she was a show-biz veteran (she was, however, new as a solo act). Living in Los Angeles, she and friend Jeffrey Daniels were dancers on *Soul Train* when they were recruited for Shalamar, which had started in 1977 as a studio group but had to tour behind its immediate hits. The group had a string of high-charting singles, but Watley felt stuck behind lead singer Howard Hewett, not getting the opportunities she was starting to deserve. She left in 1984 and moved to England for a while, doing session work and modeling. She returned to L.A. and hooked up with Cymone, and her dance-pop debut spawned three Top 10 hits: "Looking for a New Love," "Don't You Want Me," and "Some Kind of Lover." With dark, minor-key moods and a high-tech sheen clearly descended from the Prince/Jimmy Jam & Terry Lewis school, her music was forward-thinking but still fit into mid-1980s urban radio formats. She was perceived as a less ingenuous Janet Jackson—or, if you will, a less bitchy Karyn White—but with better vocal technique and a smoother, purer voice. Watley and Cymone pursued changing dance-pop trends with equal success on her follow-up, *Larger Than Life*, which again yielded a trio of Top 10 hits and paired her with hip-hoppers Eric B. & Rakim on "Friends." Their third album followed the same formula with diminished returns, both commercially and artistically, and Watley moved towards ballads on her next release, which revived her artistically but was chart death. After breaking up with both her husband and her label, she continues to pursue her muse with enjoyable results if not big sales numbers, her lyrics becoming more intimate and personal. As always, despite modern accoutrements of production, her songs look back to a golden age of R&B writing with solid structures and pacing.

what to buy: Much more than a few hits and a bunch of filler, *Larger Than Life* ♪♪♪♪ (MCA, 1989, prod. Andre Cymone) sustains a high level of quality throughout and fills in the outlines of Watley's persona more completely.

what to buy next: *Jody Watley* ♪♪♪♪ (MCA, 1987, prod. Andre Cymone, David Z., Bernard Edwards, Patrick Leonard) is just barely more tentative than the follow-up, and is also quite consistent.

what to avoid: Only suitable for late-on-the-uptake DJs and completist fans, *You Wanna Dance with Me?* ♪♪ (MCA, 1990, prod. Andre Cymone, others) recycles Watley's hits in dance remixes and doesn't even really function as a greatest hits album, unless clubs are where the listener learned to like the songs. Even then, it only covers her first two albums. If you only want the hits, go for the real *Greatest Hits*.

the rest:
Affairs of the Heart ♪♪♪ (MCA, 1991)
Intimacy ♪♪♪ (MCA, 1993)
Affection ♪♪♪ (Avitone/Bellmark, 1995)
Greatest Hits ♪♪♪♪ (MCA, 1996)

worth searching for: Watley covers "After You, Who" on the Cole Porter tribute/AIDS benefit *Red Hot + Blue* ♪♪♪♪ (Chrysalis, 1990, prod. various).

influences:
◀◀ Shalamar, Prince, S.O.S. Band, the Time, Vanity 6
▶▶ Mary J. Blige

see also: *Shalamar*

Steve Holtje

WC and the MAAD Circle

Formed in 1991.

Although his profile has been elevated somewhat recently with the success of the Westside Connection, rapper WC is still one of L.A.'s most underrated MCs. In 1988, WC and the noted turntablist DJ Aladdin turned heads when they caught wreck on Ice-T's compilation album *Rhyme Syndicate Comin' Through*. Calling themselves Low Profile, the two were subsequently signed to Priority Records and released an album in 1989. But by 1990, they had disbanded, with Aladdin moving on to work with Ice-T. However, WC reemerged in 1991 as the leader of a new crew called the MAAD Circle (Minority Alliance Against Discrimination), which has released two albums to date and is credited with launching the career of mega-star Coolio. Still the leader of MAAD Circle, WC also claims membership in the Westside Connection, an ad hoc supergroup he formed with Ice Cube and Mack 10.

what to buy: On WC and the MAAD Circle's debut, *Ain't A Damn Thang Changed* ♫♫♫♫ (Priority, 1991, prod. Crazy Toones, Sir Jinx, WC, others), the group busts straight outta L.A. with some heavy-ended, underground, hardcore funk that deserves to be heard. WC's own appeal lies in his rhyme flow, which is smooth and clear. Lyrically, he and his crew wax poetic about everything from poverty and unemployment to police brutality and plain-old life in the streets. "Fuck My Daddy" is pointed social commentary that examines the absent-father syndrome plaguing many inner-city families. "Dress Code" takes on the rats who judge you by the clothes you wear. "Behind Closed Doors" examines the wonderful world of AmeriKKKan demonocracy. This record is deep, both lyrically and musically (with beats supplied by WC's DJ-brother, Crazy Toones). A minor classic, it also gave the world its first taste of Coolio.

what to buy next: *Curb Servin'* ♫♫♫ (Payday/London, 1995, prod. Ice Cube, Crazy Toones, others) is a tasty slice of Los Angeles funk that's rough, rugged, and sticky. Although some of the beats can sound dangerously familiar, WC's verbal tenacity raises the album above standard L.A. gangsta fare. On "Kill a Habit," WC even finds himself wrestling with past addictions. To be sure, there are some choice *sounding* cuts, too: The hand waving shuffle of "West Up!" (featuring Ice Cube and Mack 10) and the infectiously slinky funk of "The One" are juicy delights, making for an album that both bumps the trunk and stimulates the mind.

worth searching for: Prior to drawing up the MAAD Circle, WC rocked the mic in Low Profile with DJ Aladdin. The duo's only album, *We're in This Together* ♫♫♫♫ (Priority, 1989, prod. various), contains 11 tracks, each one a well-crafted, funky-ass slammer. From Aladdin's quick-wristed scratchmatic embellishment on the opening "Funky Song" and his brilliant turntable terrorism on "Aladdin on a Rampage," to WC's you-gotta-earn-the-right-to-flip-on-the-mic words in "PayYa Dues," the album is flawless, making it an undisputed classic (not to mention a highly prized out-of-print hip-hop collectible).

influences:

◄◄ N.W.A., Ice-T, KDAY Mixmasters

►► Coolio, Mack 10, Westside Connection, Tha Alkaholiks

see also: *Ice Cube, Coolio*

Spence D.

Junior Wells

Born Amos Blackmore, December 9, 1934, in Memphis, TN.

Blues lore has it that a 12-year-old Junior Wells worked for a week to buy a harmonica he had seen at a pawnshop. Upon being told that it cost $2.00, he threw down his weeks' wages of $1.50 and ran out with the harp. When a judge asked why he had done this, Junior replied that he just had to have it. The judge asked him to play it, and upon hearing the precocious kid, gave the complainant 50 cents and dismissed the case. It's probably an apocryphal tale, but some things are true even if they never happened. Wells is one of a handful of people, along with Little Walter, the two Sonny Boy Williamsons, and James Cotton, who wrote the book on Mississippi Delta/Chicago-style harmonica playing. Wells replaced Walter in Muddy Waters' seminal band in 1952. He began making solo recordings the following year while AWOL from the army. In 1966, Wells began a lengthy partnership with Buddy Guy which resulted in some of the guitarist's finest recorded work.

what to buy: Years of playing South Side blues clubs, often backed by Guy, honed Wells' chops as he developed an expansive, new, hardened style, adding heavy dollops of urban menace and James Brown-style proto-funk to his traditional Chicago blues. The result, *Hoodoo Man Blues* ♫♫♫♫ (Delmark, 1965, prod. Robert Koester), is not only Wells' finest moment, but a modern blues masterpiece that leaps out of the gate with "Snatch It Back and Hold It," a burst of funky R&B fun, and never looks back, with Wells and Guy constantly prodding each other to new heights. *It's My Life, Baby!* ♫♫♫♫ (Vanguard, 1966, prod. Samuel Charters) is almost as strong. Of his co-headlining albums with Guy, *Drinkin TNT 'N' Smokin' Dynamite* ♫♫♫♫ (Blind Pig, 1974/1988, prod. Bill Wyman) is by far the best, documenting a fiery 1974 live performance with a band including pianist Pinetop Perkins and Rolling Stones bassist Wyman.

what to buy next: *On Tap* ♫♫♫♫ (Delmark, 1966/1991, prod. Robert Koester) is a laid-back treat, capturing the feel of a typical Wells South Side performance. The mostly acoustic *Come on in This House* ♫♫♫♫ (Telarc, 1996, prod. John Snyder), on which Wells is joined by young guitarists, including Corey Harris, Sonny Landreth, and John Mooney, is a remarkable achievement: a top-notch album cut years after Wells was written off as a creative force.

what to avoid: On *Coming at You* ♫♫♫ (Vanguard, 1969/1989), Wells and Guy are weighed down by a superfluous horn section. Wells' first album in years was the lifeless *Better off with the Blues* ♫♫ (Telarc, 1993).

the rest:

Blues Hit Big Town ♫♫♫♪ (Delmark, 1954/1967)

Southside Blues Jam ♫♫♫♪ (Delmark, 1970)

(With Buddy Guy) *Play the Blues* ♫♫♫ (Atco, 1972/1992)

(With Buddy Guy) *Live In Montreux* ♫♫♫ (Evidence, 1977/1991)

Pleading the Blues ♫♫♫ (Evidence, 1979/1993)

(With Buddy Guy) *Alone & Acoustic* ♫♫ (Alligator, 1981/1991)

(With Carey Bell, James Cotton, and Billy Branch) *Harp Attack* ♫♫♫♫ (Alligator, 1990)

1957–63: Messin' with the Kid ♫♫♫♪ (Paula, 1991)

Everybody's Gettin' Some ♫♫♫ (Telarc, 1995)

influences:

◀◀ Sonny Boy Williamson II, James Cotton, Little Walter, Big Walter Horton

▶▶ Carey Bell, Billy Branch, Sugar Blue, John Popper

Alan Paul

Mary Wells

Born May 13, 1943, in Detroit, MI. Died July 26, 1992, in Los Angeles, CA.

Motown's first bona fide star, Mary Wells is remembered, perhaps unfairly, for her 1964 smash "My Guy." The song, one of many collaborations with Smokey Robinson, became her biggest seller and overshadowed everything else she did. Wells didn't have much luck after her bitter split with Motown, but she continued to record and perform until her death from throat cancer.

what to buy: *Looking Back: 1961–1964* ♫♫♫♫ (Motown, 1993, prod. various) is a two-disc set that offers the best representation of the singer's most famous period; all her hits came from the Motown years. "The One Who Really Loves You," "You Beat Me to the Punch," and "My Guy" are all here, in addition to interviews with friends and associates.

what to buy next: *Never, Never Leave Me/The 20th Century Sides* ♫♫♫ (Ichiban, 1996, prod. various) reveals that Wells had more to say after "My Guy." Compiling material from sessions immediately after her Motown split, this has no big hits but plenty of decent, lightweight soul. Wells' chirpy innocence had begun to subside a bit by this point, leading to more versatile interpretations.

what to avoid: The too-puny *Greatest Hits* ♫♫ (Motown, 1964/1989, prod. various).

Junior Wells (© Linda Vartoogian)

the rest:

My Guy ♫♫♫ (Motown, 1964/1989)

Motown Legends: You Beat Me to the Punch-My Guy ♫♫♫♪ (ESX, 1994)

Ain't It the Truth ♫♫♫ (Varese Vintage, 1994)

Dear Lover: The Atco Sessions ♫♫♫ (Ichiban, 1995)

influences:

◀◀ Della Reese, Judy Garland, Smokey Robinson

▶▶ The Supremes, Diana Ross, Martha & the Vandellas

Allan Orski

Fred Wesley

Famed for his time with both James Brown (starting in 1968) and Parliament-Funkadelic and its various offshoots, trombonist Fred Wesley has consistently been the most jazz-oriented of the many horn players (including saxophonists Maceo Parker and Pee Wee Ellis) in those and similar contexts—but then, Wesley also played in the Count Basie big band. Since Wesley was often the James Brown band's musical director (Brown said he preferred Wesley's arranging to Ellis', and that Wesley had a better sense of rhythm), it was logical that he would be the leader of the JBs when they recorded as a separate act. Later, in the period when P-Funk mastermind/ringleader George Clinton was recording his sprawling organization under as many names as possible (and for as many different labels), the horn section of Wesley, Parker, and trumpeters Rick Gardner and Richard "Kush" Griffith was christened the Horny Horns, with Wesley the leader. In the years since all those bands' heydays, Wesley has worked off and on with Brown and Clinton, and more frequently with Parker and Ellis as the JB Horns, also appearing on Parker's albums (and Parker on Wesley's). Since 1990, Wesley's albums have focused on jazz, with his funk impulses being mostly channeled into his non-leader work. As a jazz trombonist he favors an extremely rich and darkly mellifluous tone, which sets him apart from most current peers, though he requires distinctive contexts to make it into a compelling sonic package.

what to buy: *New Friends* ♫♫♫♫ (Antilles/Island, 1990, prod. Steve Meyner, Fred Wesley) is a tour-de-force that puts Wesley solidly in the jazz tradition, but connects it with R&B at the same time through a series of inspired covers: Duke Ellington's "Rockin' in Rhythm," Clyde McPhatter & the Drifters' lascivious "Honey Love," Thelonious Monk's "Bright Mississippi" and "Blue Monk," the Dells' "Love We Had Stays on My Mind" (with a great vocal on Wesley's version by Carmen Lundy), Quincy Jones' "Plenty, Plenty Soul," Dizzy Gillespie's "Birks Works," and Elmo Hope's "Eyes So Beautiful." Equally impressive is Wesley's remake of his Horny Horns tune "Peace Fugue," rewritten for four trombones, while his jazzy "For the Elders" allows everyone to stretch out. "D-Cup and Up" is the only outright funk number, but it's as deeply grooving as anything he's ever done. The other players are young, respected jazz musicians who know how to get down, making this album a varied joy from start to finish.

what to buy next: The first two albums billed as by Fred Wesley and the Horny Horns, *A Blow for Me, a Toot for You* ♫♫♫ (Atlantic, 1977, prod. George Clinton, William "Bootsy" Collins) and *Say Blow By Blow Backwards* ♫♫♫ (Atlantic, 1979/AEM, 1994, prod. George Clinton, William "Bootsy" Collins, Fred Wesley), sometimes sound like they were thrown together without much care, with flubbed notes and half-assed vocals, and a number of tunes recycled from P-Funk albums. But for all that there are still great moments, and whatever happens, it's funky. And surprisingly, the two new remixes per CD work well. *The Final Blow* ♫♫♫♫ (AEM, 1994, prod. George Clinton) seems to be from the same period as those two albums, but is tighter, more musically interesting and inventive, and doesn't suffer from the lackadaisical mass vocals of the other efforts; five of the seven tracks are instrumentals (with only minimal lead vocals on the other two) and "Bells" might be the best thing they ever did.

what to avoid: The JB Horns' *Pee Wee, Fred & Maceo* ♫ (Gramavision, 1990, prod. Jim Payne) is pedestrian hackwork, by-the-numbers funk that's not very funky and all blurs together. *To Someone* ♫♫ (Hi Note/Rough Trade, 1990) is Wesley's most hardcore jazz album, but that's not what's wrong with it. His tone is a bit blowzy, which after a while becomes irritating on a quartet date where he's the only horn; even worse, bassist Ken Walker's lines are turgid and unimaginative.

the rest:
(With the JBs) *Damn Right I Am Somebody* ♫♫♫ (People/Polydor, 1974)
(With the New JBs) *Breakin' Bread* ♫♫♫ (People/Polydor, 1974)
Comme Ci Comme Ca ♫♫♫ (Antilles/Island, 1991)
Swing and Be Funky ♫♫♫ (Minor Music, 1992)

worth searching for: Fred Wesley and the JBs' *Doing It to Death* ♫♫♫ (People/Polydor, 1973, prod. James Brown) features the #1 R&B title hit. If the rest feels a bit like filler, it's damn funky filler, and one wonders why this LP (and for that matter the other JBs stuff) has been out of print for so long (though the 10-minute title track is available on various James Brown anthologies). The four-group collection *Jim Payne's New York Funk! Vol. 1* ♫♫♫ (Gramavision, 1993, prod.

Jim Payne) includes three tracks by a Wesley-led quintet, including Kenny Garrett (alto sax), recorded specifically for this anthology. The import-only *Amalgamation* ♫♫♫ (Minor Music, 1994, prod. Stephan Meyner, Fred Wesley) is so funky that even a cover of Wham's "Careless Whisper" grooves, though the highlight is the tightly percolating "Herbal Turkey Breast."

influences:
◀◀ James Brown, Parliament-Funkadelic, J.J. Johnson
▶▶ Tower of Power, Brand New Heavies, Heavy Metal Horns

Steve Holtje

Kim Weston

Born Agatha Natalie Weston, in Detroit, MI.

Too often a footnote in Motown's rich history, Kim Weston made her name as Marvin Gaye's second duet partner, following Mary Wells. With Gaye, the church-trained Weston—who married Motown exec Mickey Stevenson—scored a series of hits, including "It Takes Two" in 1967. Weston actually preceded Motown to the West Coast, moving to Los Angeles in 1967 to record for MGM, then Stax and Stevenon's Banyan Tree label. She still performs on occasion and spends much of her time doing charitable and community work in Detroit.

what to buy: *Greatest Hits and Rare Classics* ♫♫♫♫ (Motown, 1991, prod. William Stephenson) features 20 tracks, including three duets with Gaye.

the rest:
Very Best Of ♫♫♫ (Hot, 1996)

worth searching for: Weston's quintessential work with Gaye is available on a number of his collections, including *Marvin Gaye & His Girls* ♫♫♫♫ (Motown, 1969/1990) and *The Master, 1961–1984* ♫♫♫♫♫ (Motown, 1995).

influences:
◀◀ Mahalia Jackson, Dinah Washington, Aretha Franklin, Mary Wells
▶▶ A Taste of Honey, Stephanie Mills, Diana Ross, Ann Peebles

Gary Graff

Westside Connection

See: Ice Cube

The Whispers

Formed 1964, in Los Angeles, CA.

Gordy Harmon, vocals (1964–73); Walter Scott, vocals; Wallace Scott, vocals; Marcus Hutson, vocals; Nicholas Caldwell, vocals; Leaveil Degree, vocals (1973–present).

Because of slow-burn hits such as "Seems Like I Gotta Do Wrong," "A Mother for My Children," "Lady," and "Living Together (In Sin)," the Whispers are often categorized as R&B "love men." But the fact of the matter is the vocal group has been just as successful with its more uptempo grooves—or have you forgotten "And the Beat Goes On," "In the Raw," "One for the Money (Part 1)," and "Rock Steady"? Like the finest of their contemporaries—the Temptations, the O'Jays, the Spinners, the Chi-Lites—the Whispers are a facile group that offers a varied and versatile package. Formed on the street corners of Watts, the quintet was recording by 1964 and was on the charts five years later with "The Time Will Come." Label hopping from Dore, to Soul Clock, to Janus, to Soul Train, to Solar—and even weathering a membership change when Gordy Harmon left and was replaced by Leaveil Degree—the Whispers enjoyed a steady stream of hits into the early 1990s. The group's 1987 smash, "Rock Steady," was the first hit by a then-new production team—Antonio "L.A." Reid and Kenneth "Babyface" Edmonds—who went on to become one of the most successful and influential production teams in pop history. With an enviable catalog of hits—47 charted singles at last count—the Whispers continue to be in-demand as a live act, not having to rely on current hits to bring crowds to their shows.

what to buy: *Greatest Hits* 🎵🎵🎵🎵 (The Right Stuff, 1997, prod. various) does an outstanding job of collecting the cream of the Whispers' hits and displaying the wide stylistic range the group has explored over the years. *The Whispers* 🎵🎵🎵🎵 (Solar, 1980/Sequel, 1996, prod. various) contains "And the Beat Goes On" and "Lady," and is easily the best of their individual titles.

what to buy next: *Toast to the Ladies* 🎵🎵🎵 (Capitol/EMI, 1995, prod. various) isn't quite as gentle as the title makes it sound— at least not with a number called "Pissed Off (Baby Come Back)." *Greatest Slow Jams, Vol. 1* 🎵🎵🎵🎵 (The Right Stuff, 1993/1996, prod. Tom Cartwright) is the kind of collection you want to keep on hand for candlelight dinners. *Just Gets Better With Time* 🎵🎵🎵 (Solar, 1987/The Right Stuff, 1996, prod. various) has "Rock Steady" and a number of other nicely crafted and well-produced songs that showed the Whispers were still a viable entity.

what to avoid: *Christmas Moments* 🎵 (Capitol/EMI, 1994), a yawner of a seasonal offering and not nearly as interesting as the group's 1985 release *Happy Holidays to You*.

the rest:

Open Up Your Love 🎵🎵🎵 (Soul Train, 1977/The Right Stuff, 1996)
Headlights 🎵🎵🎵 (Solar, 1978/The Right Stuff, 1997)
Imagination 🎵🎵🎵 (Solar, 1981/Sequel, 1996)
Love Is Where You Find It 🎵🎵🎵 (Solar, 1982/The Right Stuff, 1996)
Happy Holidays to You 🎵🎵🎵 (Solar, 1985/The Right Stuff, 1996)
Vintage 🎵🎵 (Solar/Epic, 1989)
Somebody Loves You 🎵🎵 (Quicksilver, 1991)

worth searching for: *30th Anniversary Anthology* 🎵🎵🎵🎵 (Sequel, 1994, prod. various) is a British import that offers a more in-depth look at the Whispers' legacy.

influences:

◀◀ The Impressions, the Drifters, the Platters

▶▶ Harold Melvin & the Bluenotes, the Jackson 5, the Commodores, New Edition, Boyz II Men

Gary Graff

Barry White

Born September 12, 1944, in Galveston, TX.

If Barry White received a royalty for every time someone imitated his rumbling baritone, he'd never have to worry about selling another record. White is pop music's penultimate Love Man, wrapping his murmured come-hither lyrics in lush, silky arrangements filled with the strings and sweet harmonizing background vocals of his 40-piece Love Unlimited Orchestra. Where does such a big sound come from? Texas, of course. But White was raised in Los Angeles, where he played piano on Jesse Belvin's hit "Goodnight My Love" when White was just 11. By 1960 he was fronting vocal groups such as the Upfronts, the Atlantics, and the Majestics. He wound up working as a talent scout for the Mustang/Bronco label in Hollywood, where he was mentored in the music business by company executive Larry Nunes. So by the time he began recording in earnest during the early 1970s, White had his vocal chops and plenty of business acumen—all the better to put together the Love Unlimited package. He hit quickly; during 1973–74, White reportedly sold more than $16 million worth of records, scoring with his own hits ("Can't Get Enough of Your Love, Babe," "Never, Never Gonna Give You Up," "It's Ecstasy When You Lay Down Next to Me"), as well as with recordings by the Love Unlimited backup singers and the Love Unlimited Orchestra. All machines need retooling, however, and White rode his influential pillow

talk formula a bit too long, tapping out by the late 1970s. But he resurged in 1989, with a guest appearance on Quincy Jones' single "Secret Garden" that led to a new recording contract and renewed popularity. The best thing about White is that, despite his sincerity, he's smart enough to laugh at himself, whether it's participating in David Letterman's shenanigans or letting MTV's "Beavis and Butthead" have their way with him (oh, you know what we mean). It's likely that more babies have been conceived to Barry White music than any other performer, and there are far worse legacies to have as an artist.

what to buy: One knock on White's albums is that his formula became so ingrained they tend to be interchangeable. That's why *All Time Greatest Hits* 𝄞𝄞𝄞𝄞 (Mercury, 1994, compilation prod. Harry Weinger) is the best first stop. Not only does it have all the hits, as well as excellent liner notes by R&B biographer David Ritz, but it gives the impression that there was greater variety to White's 1970s output than there really was. However, *The Icon Is Love* 𝄞𝄞𝄞 (A&M, 1994, prod. various) is a strong comeback, as White lets other producers—notably Chuckii Booker and Jimmy Jam & Terry Lewis—take hold of his sound to infuse some modernism without losing the classic elements of his sound.

what to buy next: If you want a representative look at White's peak period, try *Can't Get Enough* 𝄞𝄞𝄞 (20th Century, 1974/Mercury, 1996, prod. Barry White), which hit #1 on the *Billboard* charts and includes hits such as "Can't Get Enough of Your Love, Babe" and "You're the First, My Last, My Everything."

what to avoid: The three-disc boxed set *Just for You* 𝄞𝄞 (Casablanca, 1992, prod. various) is simply too much, illustrating the sameness of much of White's music rather than celebrating his career.

the rest:
I've Got So Much to Give 𝄞𝄞𝄞 (20th Century, 1973/Polydor, 1994)
Stone Gon' 𝄞𝄞𝄞 (20th Century, 1973/Polydor, 1994)
Just Another Way to Say I Love You 𝄞𝄞𝄞 (20th Century, 1975/Mercury, 1996)
Greatest Hits, Vol. 1 𝄞𝄞𝄞 (Casablanca, 1975)
Let the Music Play 𝄞𝄞𝄞 (20th Century, 1976/Mercury, 1996)
Barry White Sings for Someone You Love 𝄞𝄞𝄞 (20th Century, 1977/Mercury, 1996)
Man 𝄞𝄞 (20th Century, 1978/Mercury, 1996)
I Love the Songs I Sing 𝄞𝄞 (20th Century, 1979/Mercury, 1996)
Sheet Music 𝄞𝄞 (Priority, 1980/1992)

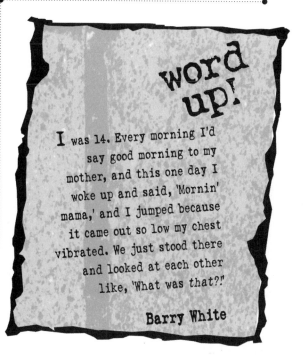

word up!

I was 14. Every morning I'd say good morning to my mother, and this one day I woke up and said, 'Mornin' mama,' and I jumped because it came out so low my chest vibrated. We just stood there and looked at each other like, 'What was that?'

Barry White

(With Glodean James) *Barry & Glodean* 𝄞𝄞𝄞 (Priority, 1981)
Let 'Em Dance 𝄞𝄞 (Priority, 1981)
Greatest Hits, Vol. 2 𝄞𝄞𝄞 (Casablanca, 1981)
Change 𝄞𝄞 (Priority, 1982)
Dedicated 𝄞𝄞 (Priority, 1983)
The Man Is Back! 𝄞𝄞 (A&M, 1989)
(With Love Unlimited Orchestra) *Back to Back: Their Greatest Hits* 𝄞𝄞𝄞 (Rebound, 1996)
Boss Soul: The Genius of Barry White N/A (Del-Fi, 1997)

worth searching for: White has made many guest appearances on other artists' albums during his career. One of the most unexpected was on pop singer Edie Brickell's solo debut, *Picture Perfect Morning* 𝄞𝄞𝄞 (Geffen, 1994, prod. Paul Simon, Roy Halee), on which the Love Man lends his sexy tones to the song "Good Times."

influences:

◄◄ Al Green, Marvin Gaye, Isaac Hayes

►► Michael Jackson, Prince, Al B. Sure!, Lisa Stansfield, El DeBarge, Maxwell, LL Cool J

see also: *Love Unlimited Orchestra*

Gary Graff

Barry White (© Ken Settle)

Karyn White

Born October 14, 1965, in Los Angeles, CA.

On her way to R&B-feminist "Superwoman" status, singer Karyn White worked after high school as a change counter in the L.A. bus terminal and a retail clerk. At the same time she was taking paltry gigs as a recording session vocalist. Her determination and self-assurance, along with touring with R&B artist O'Bryan and providing the lead vocal on jazzman Jeff Lorber's "Facts of Life," propelled her lifelong ambition to become an "overnight" sensation. The Lorber gig led to her signing with Warner Bros. Records and a 1988 debut album that exploded to #1 on the R&B charts, selling over 2 million copies on the strength of three Top 10 singles: "The Way You Love Me," "Love Saw It," and the definitive anthem "Superwoman," an empowering pro-woman ballad so compelling that at least three soul divas (Patti LaBelle, Gladys Knight, and Dionne Warwick) have covered the song. Almost as a male counterattack, photographers began to focus on the former beauty pageant winner's physical attributes rather than her impressive singing or heartfelt insights on the woman's view of romantic relationships. Spending increasing amounts of time in Minneapolis at the Flyte Time studios of Jimmy Jam and Terry Lewis, who produced her 1991 followup LP *Ritual of Love*, White's view of romance soon focused on Lewis; they eventually wed and had a daughter, Ashley. The real-life "Superwoman" demands of marriage and motherhood have kept White largely out of the R&B spotlight in recent years, but with her undeniable skills and easy access to one of pop music's hottest production teams, she should never be absent from the top of the charts for long.

what to buy: White's pop-R&B premiere, *Karyn White* ♫♫♫♫ (Warner Bros., 1988, prod. L.A. Reid, Babyface, others), still stands as one of the most remarkable solo female introductions in recent memory; a high-concept, multifaceted showcase for a powerful vocal talent, guided by dazzling but understated production and a storehouse of odds-on hits.

what to buy next: Still searching for love and championing the right of women to stand on equal romantic footing with men, *Ritual of Love* ♫♫♫ (Warner Bros., 1991, prod. various) was a consistent and commendable encore to her self-titled debut. White takes part in her own production here and assumes a firmer hand in her musical interpretations, belting out "Romantic" with every ounce of lung capacity and getting in the face of unfaithful lovers everywhere with "Walkin' the Dog."

the rest:
Make Him Do Right ♫♫♫ (Warner Bros., 1994)

worth searching for: She's a mother now, so she should be singing lullabies. And White's tender, pristine version of the rock 'n' roll standard "Dream" becomes standout music for cradle rocking on the Disney Records all-star compilation *Rock-A-Bye-Baby* ♫♫♫ (Disney, 1996), a collection of rock classics transformed into kiddie night-night tunes.

influences:

◀◀ Gladys Knight, Patti LaBelle, Whitney Houston, Janet Jackson, Babyface, Jody Watley, Vanessa Williams, Madonna

▶▶ Taylor Dayne, Tamia, Toni Braxton

Andy Ernst and Andre McGarrity

Wild Cherry

Formed 1970s, in Steubenville, OH.

Bob Parissi, lead vocals, guitar; Bryan Bassett, guitar; Mark Auset, keyboards; Allen Wentz, bass; Ron Beitle, drums.

In a classic case of bar-band-makes-good—at least, temporarily—Wild Cherry became wildly popular in its native Steubenville and the northern Ohio areas of Canton and Akron, then enjoyed a brief moment in the national spotlight with its lone hit, "Play That Funky Music." The song sparked controversy in the mid-1970s, as it was often mistitled, "Play That Funky Music, White Boy"; the "white boy" was certainly an integral part of the lyric, but was never included (or even parenthesized) in the song's title. Nonetheless, propelled by one of the more memorable guitar hooks of the past 20 years, "Play That Funky Music" roared to #1 in September of 1976 and stayed there for three weeks. That was, however, the first and final hurrah for the group. None of Wild Cherry's follow-up singles, through 1977, even sniffed the Top 40. Evidently Parissi, who wrote and produced for the band, was a one-shot talent who never got his groove back. Astonishingly, the band's only album, *Wild Cherry* ♫♫ (Epic, 1990, prod. Bob Parissi), is still in print, and "Play That Funky Music" is still heard widely in club mixes and hip-hop samples. Depending upon your view of the song, that's either a miracle or a mockery.

influences:

◀◀ Average White Band, the Jaggerz, KC & the Sunshine Band, Hall & Oates

▶▶ Dexy's Midnight Runners, Huey Lewis & the News

Bob Paxman

Deniece Williams

Born Deniece Chandler, June 3, 1951, in Gary, IN.

Deniece Williams began her career in 1971 working as a backup singer for Stevie Wonder. In 1975 she went solo and signed with Columbia Records, debuting with *This Is Niecy* in 1976. The album—which was produced by Earth, Wind & Fire's Maurice White—entered the pop charts quickly, as did its singles, "Free" and "That's What Friends Are For." But Williams couldn't maintain the momentum, and her next album, *Songbird*, went unnoticed. She made *That's What Friends Are For* with Johnny Mathis the following year, then began recording for White's ARC label, where she debuted with *When Love Comes Calling* in 1979. Two albums later she was back with Columbia, where she made it big in 1984 with "Let's Hear It for the Boy," a #1 *Billboard* hit included on the soundtrack for the movie *Footloose*. This was the last of her hit pop recordings, but Williams' return to her gospel roots during the mid-1980s brought her back to a position of acclaim, especially with *So Glad I Know*, which won two Grammy Awards.

what to buy: *Gonna Take a Miracle: The Best of Deniece Williams* 𝄢𝄢𝄢𝄢 (Legacy, 1996, prod. various) features the singer's finer pop moments, including collaborations with Johnny Mathis, Lee Oskar, George Duke, Ray Parker Jr., Richard Elliot, Philip Bailey, and Victor Feldman.

what to buy next: *So Glad I Know* 𝄢𝄢𝄢𝄢 (Sparrow, 1986, prod. Brad Westering) is part of Williams' triumphant return to her gospel roots. It features guest artists Sandi Patti and Paul Jackson Jr.

what to avoid: *My Melody* 𝄢𝄢𝄢 (Columbia, 1981), evidence of her commercial and artistic decline in the pop world.

the rest:
This Is Niecy 𝄢𝄢𝄢𝄢 (Columbia, 1976)
From the Beginning 𝄢𝄢𝄢𝄢 (Sparrow, 1986)
Let's Hear It for the Boy 𝄢𝄢𝄢 (Columbia, 1989)
As Good as It Gets 𝄢𝄢𝄢𝄢 (Columbia, 1991)
Deniece Williams: Greatest Gospel Hits 𝄢𝄢𝄢𝄢 (Sparrow, 1994)
Love Solves It All 𝄢𝄢𝄢 (P.A.R., 1996)

worth searching for: Williams sang with Stevie Wonder's Wonderlove on *Talking Book* (Motown, 1972) and *Songs in the Key of Life* (Motown, 1976).

influences:

◀◀ Tammi Terrell, Stevie Wonder, Dionne Warwick

▶▶ Whitney Houston, Stephanie Mills, Anita Baker, Brandy

Norene Cashen

Larry Williams

Born Lawrence E. Williams, May 10, 1935, in New Orleans, LA. Died January 7, 1980.

Though a version of his 1950s classic "Bad Boy" is currently the theme to the TV sitcom *Men Behaving Badly*, Larry Williams is nearly forgotten today, even though he is a deserving and influential artist of hall of fame caliber. Williams was Lloyd Price's chauffeur, valet, and road pianist during the mid-1950s. When Price left Specialty to form his own label, Williams was hired to take his place. After his first hit (a version of Price's "Just Because"), Williams was encouraged to imitate the departing Little Richard, but he didn't need to be anybody's copycat. He was a talented songwriter with an ear for teenage slang and idioms on the order of Chuck Berry, as well as an underrated musician who brought fresh musical hooks to his songs. Most of his best work at Specialty featured many of the same musicians who played on sessions for Little Richard, Lloyd Price, and Fats Domino, but they showcased twangy guitar accents and fills, brassier horn sections, and Williams' own pounding piano and neat whistling ability. Williams wrote the Top 5 hit "Short Fat Fanny" as a comedic counterpoint to Little Richard's run of hits, and its many references to other top songs of the day made it a favorite among kids and DJs alike. When producer Art Rupe suggested he write a song about a skinny girl, Williams came up with "Bony Moronie," a solid Top 15 hit and an enduring rock and soul standard. Williams' fourth release was one of the greatest two-sided singles in early rock history—"Dizzy Miss Lizzy" b/w "Slow Down"—yet it was a only a minor hit. Real rock 'n' roll was giving way to the forces of teen pop by this time, and Williams' career suffered as a result. After some hard times (Specialty dropped him after he was arrested on narcotics charges in 1959), Williams' fortunes reversed themselves when the Beatles recorded dazzling versions of "Slow Down," "Dizzy Miss Lizzy," and "Bad Boy." Hired as a staff producer at Okeh Records, he teamed with Johnny "Guitar" Watson and began forging a new career in soul music that featured the hits "Mercy, Mercy, Mercy" and "Nobody." Williams produced several sessions for the comebacking Little Richard (including his live *Greatest Hits* LP) and tried to update his former labelmate's sound with slick horn arrangements and guitars, but Richard was an unconvincing soul singer. Despite positive reviews and a potent live show, Williams' recording career petered out in the late 1960s. He financed his lavish lifestyle by trafficking in drugs and prostitution. Williams cut one final (rather dreadful) LP for Fantasy in 1979. The following year, Williams was found in his mansion, dead from a self-inflicted bullet wound or a professional hit (depending on whom you talk to). It was a sad, grisly end for someone whose music reflected so much joy, humor, and spirit.

what to buy: *Bad Boy* 🎵🎵🎵🎵 (Specialty, 1990, prod. Art Rupe, Bumps Blackwell) has 23 tracks—all the big rock 'n' roll hits, all the best B-sides and LP cuts, and six previously unreleased tracks and alternate takes. *Best of Larry Williams* 🎵🎵🎵🎵 (Ace, 1991, prod. Art Rupe, Bumps Blackwell) is a nearly identical set of hits and LP cuts. *Here's Larry Williams* 🎵🎵🎵🎵 (Specialty, 1991, prod. Art Rupe, Bumps Blackwell) is a 12-track reissue of Williams' 1959 LP and features "Dizzy Miss Lizzy," "You Bug Me," "Bony Moronie," and "Short Fat Fanny." It's a fine starter set.

what to buy next: *Larry Williams Show* 🎵🎵🎵 (Decca, 1965/Edsel, 1992, prod. Larry Williams) is an entertaining example of how Williams was transforming from a rocker to a soul artist.

what to avoid: *That's Larry Williams* **woof!** (Fantasy, 1979, prod. various) features several soul/funk remakes of his original hits. For masochistic completists only.

the rest:
Hocus Pocus 🎵🎵🎵 (Specialty, 1986)
Unreleased Larry Williams 🎵🎵🎵 (Specialty, 1986)

worth searching for: *Two for the Price of One* 🎵🎵🎵 (Collector's Series, 1995, prod. various) contains Williams' last chart records, "Nobody" and "Mercy, Mercy, Mercy." Williams and Johnny "Guitar" Watson's work with the psychedelic band Kaleidoscope is innovative, though it may be a stretch for fans of his more straightforward 1950s sides.

influences:
◀◀ Lloyd Price, Little Richard
▶▶ The Beatles, Johnny "Guitar" Watson

Ken Burke

Maurice Williams & the Zodiacs

Formed 1960, in New York, NY.

Maurice Williams (born April 26, 1938, in Lancaster, NC), lead vocals; Wiley Bennett, vocals; Albert Hill, vocals; Henry Gaston, vocals; Charles Thomas, vocals; Little Willie Morrow, vocals.

Maurice Williams has written hundreds of songs during his long career in vocal-group soul, including one, "Little Darlin'," that didn't become a huge 1950s hit until it was covered by a white group of the era, the White Diamonds. But it was with his quartet the Zodiacs that Williams achieved musical immortality with the 1960 doo-wop confection "Stay," laced with its piercing falsetto melody and shifting pseudo-Latin rhythms. The song actually did better on the pop charts than it did on the R&B charts, crossing over to become a #1 national smash, and it still stands as one of the hallmark tunes of early rock 'n' roll. "Stay" has been covered by countless acts since the 1960s and seems to have a life of its own, experiencing revivals in popularity every few years, most recently as a key part of the *Dirty Dancing* movie soundtrack. It was a vindicating achievement for Williams, who formed his first quartet, the Charms, while still in his teens. He had to change group names (and members) repeatedly, from the Charms (fearing confusion with the Charms of Otis Williams and their hit "Hearts of Stone") to the Royal Charms, the Gladiolas, the Excellos, and, finally, the Zodiacs. On the heels of "Stay," Williams and the Zodiacs toured constantly with artists like James Brown, and released a series of follow-up singles, including "Come Along," "I Remember," "Running Around," and "Come and Get It." But they all paled in comparison to "Stay." For some groups, one timeless classic is enough: after a failed attempt as a solo act, Williams re-formed the Zodiacs and has been one of the top attractions on the eastern seaboard oldies/beach music circuit into the 1990s.

what to buy: Though it seems like one "greatest hits" collection would be overstating the case where Williams and the Zodiacs are concerned, there are actually two such releases available by the group, and there isn't much to distinguish one from the other. Identically titled, *The Best of Maurice Williams & the Zodiacs* 🎵🎵🎵 (Collectables, 1994, prod. various) and *The Best of Maurice Williams & the Zodiacs* 🎵🎵🎵 (Relic, 1991, prod. various) both have "Stay" as their centerpiece. Take your pick.

the rest:
Anthology 🎵🎵🎵 (Ripete, 1996)
Live at Myrtle Beach '65 🎵🎵🎵 (Night Train, 1996)

worth searching for: The Gladiolas' rendition of both "Little Darlin'" and "Stay" are featured on the superb box set *The Doo Wop Box: 101 Vocal Group Gems from the Golden Age of Rock 'n' Roll* 🎵🎵🎵🎵🎵 (Rhino, 1994, prod. Bob Hyde, Walter DeVenne). It's the very best of Williams, set in context alongside dozens of his contemporaries.

influences:
◀◀ The Charms, Frankie Lymon & the Teenagers, Clyde McPhatter & the Drifters, the Platters
▶▶ Frankie Valli & the Four Seasons, Sha Na Na, Otis Day & the Knights

Jim McFarlin

Vanessa Williams

Born March 18, 1963, in Buffalo, NY.

For those who still believe the adage that there are no second acts in American lives, take a quick look at the ride Vanessa Williams has been on. Triumphant as the first black Miss America, Williams was stripped of her crown after nude photos of her surfaced, a blow that would have flattened most would-be showbiz careers. Not Williams'. After a few TV and film appearances, she landed a recording contract, emerging a wiser and more empowered woman. If her early recorded work is perfunctory, it's interesting to note just how much she's grown over the course of five albums, moving from the standard-issue dance music of *The Right Stuff* to signature ballads such as "Save the Best for Last" and "The Sweetest Days." Williams' talent continues to grow in other ways as well. She's won accolades for her work in the Broadway smash *Kiss of the Spider Woman* and in films such as the otherwise forgettable *Eraser* and *Harley Davidson and the Marlboro Man.* She may still have her detractors, but it's hard to deny success this hard won.

what to buy: It wasn't her biggest hit, but Williams' third album, *The Sweetest Days* ✓✓✓✓ (Wing/Mercury, 1995, prod. various), is her most fully realized work, shaking off her ambitions of being a dance-floor diva in favor of a classier, multifaceted approach that shows off her vocal talents across a wide range of material, including jazz- and latin-tinged styles ("Ellamental" and "Constantly," respectively). Especially fine are two Babyface numbers, "Betcha Never" and "You Can't Run," which show off Williams' heretofore unexplored lower register.

what to buy next: Williams' sophomore set, *The Comfort Zone* ✓✓✓✓ (Wing/Mercury, 1991, prod. various), proved to be her defining moment, spawning the #1 hit ballad "Save the Best for Last."

the rest:
The Right Stuff ✓✓✓ (Wing/PolyGram, 1988)
Star Bright ✓✓✓ (Mercury, 1996)
Next ✓✓✓✓ (Mercury, 1997)

worth searching for: Two of Williams' biggest hits weren't even on her own albums. "Love Is," a duet with Brian McKnight, can be found on *Beverly Hills 90210: The Soundtrack* ✓✓✓ (Giant, 1992), while "Colors of the Wind" is on the mostly instrumental soundtrack for *Pocahontas* ✓✓✓ (Disney, 1995).

influences:
◀◀ Patti Austin, Janet Jackson, Whitney Houston

▶▶ Brandy, Chante Moore

Daniel Durchholz

Chuck Willis

Born Harold Willis, January 31, 1928, in Atlanta, GA. Died April 10, 1958, in Atlanta, GA.

Chuck Willis was dubbed the King of the Stroll during the 1950s, but this Turban-wearing cat provided more than just background music for a dance craze. In fact, he was one of R&B's finest singer/songwriters. Willis was discovered by popular disc jockey Zenas "Daddy" Sears and steered to Columbia Records in 1951. After one release, his contract was shuttled to their Okeh subsidiary, where his bittersweet vocal style and prolific pen scored major R&B hits such as "My Story," "Don't Deceive Me," "I Feel So Bad," "You're Still My Baby," and a cover of Fats Domino's "Going to the River." Willis' luck on the charts ran out in 1954, and Okeh let his contract expire. Atlantic Records signed him in 1956 and began to accentuate Willis' poignant vocals with lush choruses, xylophones, and a generally slicker sound. "It's Too Late" was his major comeback hit, and it glowed with soulful self-pity. A bigger smash was his reworking of the old folk ballad "C.C. Rider" (it stood for County Circuit Rider, though Willis and others after him sang the phrase as if it were someone's name). With its slow shuffling beat and rolling xylophone, it became the perfect accompaniment for teens doing the Stroll, which turned it into a major pop hit. In 1958, Willis required emergency abdominal surgery for bleeding ulcers; his death by peritonitis intensified the impact of the remarkable "What Am I Living For" b/w "Hang Up My Rock 'n' Roll Shoes," and both were major hits as well as spooky deathbed statements. Two posthumous singles, "My Life" and "Keep-a-Drivin'," were also hits before the year was out. Willis' best known songs lived on in cover versions by Ruth Brown, Elvis Presley, LaVern Baker, Jerry Lee Lewis, Conway Twitty, Roy Orbison, Mitch Ryder, Derek & the Dominoes, and many others.

what to buy: *Stroll On: The Chuck Willis Collection* ✓✓✓✓✓ (Razor & Tie, 1994, compilation prod. Dave Booth) features Willis' great run at Atlantic Records. All the big hits are here, as well as 20 other tracks. It's one of the finest reissues of all-time. *Let's Jump Tonight! The Best of Chuck Willis, 1952–1956* ✓✓✓✓ (Legacy, 1994, compilation prod. Bob Irwin) is a 26-track compilation of Willis' years at Columbia/Okeh and features "Don't Deceive Me," "My Story," "Goin' to the River,'" and "I Feel So Bad," plus two previously unreleased tracks.

the rest:
My Story ✓✓✓✓ (Collector's Series, 1993)
influences:
◀◀ Ivory Joe Hunter, Johnny Ace

▶▶ Sammy Turner, Ruth Brown, Elvis Presley

Ken Burke

Al Wilson

Born June 19, 1939, in Meridian, MS.

Blessed with crystal-clear phrasing and a vibrant, pleading voice, Mississippi-born singer and drummer Al Wilson racked up a string of Top 10 singles with distinctive novelty themes from the late 1960s through the early 1970s. After relocating from the Deep South to the West Coast in the late 1950s, Wilson sang with a group called the Rollers from 1960 to 1962 and was a member of Johnny Harris and the Statesmen in the mid-1960s. He then signed with Soul City Records as a solo performer and began his run on the R&B and pop charts in 1968 with "The Snake," a parable of good vs. evil set to a saucy horn arrangement. Wilson achieved his biggest success in 1973 with the million-selling single "Show and Tell," a romantic takeoff on the childhood school activity. Though his lyrics were a bit offbeat, his voice was rooted in classic southern soul emotion and supported by glossy instrumentation. Wilson had other respectable hits before getting to #3 on the R&B lists one more time in 1976, with "I've Got a Feeling (We'll Be Seeing Each Other Again)" on the Playboy label.

what's available: The only Al Wilson album still in print, *Show and Tell* ∅∅∅ (Rocky Road, 1973, prod. various), is fortunately also his best. Although hard to find, it's full of the type of slick, Vegas style glitz-on-grits that defined a soul music period in the early 1970s, with Wilson's voice adding an oily coat of sophistication.

influences:

◀◀ Joe Tex, Rufus Thomas, Ben E. King, Johnnie Taylor, Johnny Mathis, Johnny Nash

▶▶ Gerald Alston, Jim Croce, Bill Withers, Maxwell

Jim McFarlin

Jackie Wilson

Born June 9, 1934, in Detroit, MI. Died January 21, 1984.

Reputedly the most exciting, acrobatic live performer of his time, Jackie Wilson could sizzle when he sang. His darting, arching shrieks sound like exposed nerves. His greatest recording, "(Your Love Keeps Lifting Me) Higher and Higher," could well be the best single ever made. But Wilson's body of work is riddled with material far less sublime. Under the dubious influence of a manipulative manager and insensitive record label, this great vocal talent was wasted on projects as odious as an entire album of Al Jolson songs. His longings for conventional show business respectability may have mirrored the mores of his generation of black entertainers, but it meant that Wilson would leave behind a recorded legacy more frustrating for what might have been than what he actually accomplished. A onetime professional boxer, he apprenticed as lead tenor with Billy Ward and the Dominoes, replacing the estimable Clyde McPhatter in the lineup. His earliest rock 'n' roll records, which were also the first hits for fledgling songwriter and future Motown chief Berry Gordy Jr., throbbed with his incessant pleading vocals. But after parting ways with Gordy, Wilson fell under the unenlightened artist and repertoire direction of Brunswick Records, the same people that gave you Buddy Holly with strings. His singles had stopped making the charts at all when "Higher and Higher," a record Wilson cut with moonlighting Motown sidemen behind him, blasted off in 1965, setting the stage for what could have been one of the more extraordinary comebacks in soul history. His decision the following year to leave his longtime, mob-affiliated manager—who also owned Brunswick Records—may have helped sabotage that possibility. The 1969 murder of his 16-year-old son, Jackie Wilson Jr., turned Wilson into a further tragic figure. But the story gets downright Dickensian after his on-stage collapse from an apparent heart attack in 1975 at the Latin Casino in Cherry Hill, New Jersey. Shipped out of the emergency room in a coma, possibly the product of improper medical care, Wilson lay speechless and motionless in a hospital bed while a long-forgotten ex-wife and attorneys began fighting over his inert body. When it became apparent there was no money anyway, Wilson wound up a ward of the state, alone, abandoned, and comatose for eight years before he finally died.

what to buy: The highpoints of 15 years of recording can all be found on *The Jackie Wilson Story* ∅∅∅∅ (Epic, 1983, prod. various), a 24-song collection that qualifies as one of the backbones of modern soul music.

what to buy next: The three-disc boxed set *Mr. Excitement* ∅∅∅∅ (Rhino, 1992) covers the Jackie Wilson legacy in considerable detail that mixes key his singles with album tracks, including collaborations with Count Basie and the Chi-Lites.

what to avoid: *Merry Christmas from Jackie Wilson* ∅ (Brunswick, 1963/Rhino, 1991, prod. Nat Tarnapol) is not only a lame Jackie Wilson album, recorded at the nadir of his career, but it's not a very good Christmas album, either.

the rest:
Live at the Copa ∅∅ (Brunswick, 1962/Rhino, 1995)
The Very Best of Jackie Wilson ∅∅∅∅ (Rhino, 1994)
Higher and Higher ∅∅∅ (Rhino, 1995)

worth searching for: An X-rated version of the duet with LaVern Baker, "Think Twice," has been only infrequently bootlegged.

influences:

◄◄ Clyde McPhatter, Little Willie John, Roy Hamilton

►► Elvis Presley, Marv Johnson, Michael Jackson, Chuckii Booker

Joel Selvin

Nancy Wilson

Born February 20, 1937, in Chillicothe, OH.

By the mid-1960s, Nancy Wilson's distinctive sound had transitioned from jazz to pop and R&B, although she would continue to shift gears between styles throughout her career. Like many singers, Wilson developed at an early age, singing in choirs and dance bands as a teenager in Columbus, Ohio. In 1956 she joined Rusty Bryant's Carolyn Club Band and made her first recordings for Dot Records. Her next collaboration was with Cannonball Adderley in 1959. Still hooked on straight jazz, Wilson recorded her first hit with Adderley, "Save Your Love for Me," in 1962. From there she picked up a more pop-oriented style and a new momentum, putting 33 albums on the charts between 1962 and 1977. Some of the hit songs from that period include "Peace of Mind," "Don't Come Running Back to Me," "Face It Girl, It's Over," and "Now I'm a Woman." Wilson's "How Glad I Am" won a Grammy for Best R&B Song in 1964. In 1983 she won a song festival award in Tokyo and recorded five albums for Japanese labels over the next few years. During that time she also made one pop record in the U.S., *The Two of Us*, with Ramsey Lewis. Wilson let the stops out on her pop sensibilities when she made *With My Lover Beside Me* with Barry Manilow, who performed on and produced the album. The lyrics were based on the poetry of Johnny Mercer, who died in 1983. Her latest album, *If I Had My Way*, proves that, regardless of style, this singer is still going strong.

what to buy: *Ballads, Blues, and Big Bands: The Best of Nancy Wilson* ♪♪♪♪ (Capitol, 1996, prod. various) is a three-disc set of Wilson's recordings between 1959 and 1969. It includes performances with Cannonball Adderley and the George Shearing Quintet.

what to buy next: *Nancy Wilson: The Jazz and Blues Sessions* ♪♪♪♪ (Blue Note, 1996, prod. various) features work with Cannonball Adderley, Hank Jones, George Shearing, and Ben Webster. *Nancy Wilson/Cannonball Adderley* ♪♪♪♪ (Capitol, 1961/1993) features Adderley on sax and the hit "Save Your Love For Me."

what to avoid: *With My Lover Beside Me* ♪♪ (Columbia, 1991, prod. Barry Manilow), a fallow piece of pop pap that's more about Manilow than Wilson.

the rest:

(With George Shearing) *The Swingin's Mutual* ♪♪♪♪ (Capitol, 1961/1992)
Yesterday's Love Songs, Today's Blues ♪♪♪ (Blue Note, 1963/1991)
Welcome to My Love ♪♪ (Blue Note, 1967/1994)
Lush Life ♪♪♪ (Capitol 1967/1995)
But Beautiful ♪♪♪♪ (Capitol, 1969/1990)
Keep You Satisfied ♪♪♪ (Columbia, 1986/1989)
Forbidden Lover ♪♪♪♪ (Columbia, 1987)
Nancy Now! ♪♪♪ (Columbia, 1988)
Lady with a Song ♪♪♪♪ (Columbia, 1990)
I Wish You Love ♪♪♪ (CEMA Special Products, 1992/1994)
Love, Nancy ♪♪♪ (Columbia, 1994)
Spotlight on Nancy Wilson ♪♪♪ (Capitol, 1995)
If I Had My Way ♪♪♪♪ (Columbia, 1997)

worth searching for: *The Two of Us* ♪♪♪♪ (Columbia, 1984), her enjoyable collaboration with Ramsey Lewis that marked her last appearance on *Billboard*'s pop album chart.

influences:

◄◄ Little Jimmy Scott, Nat King Cole, Billy Eckstine, Louis Jordan, LaVern Baker, Dinah Washington, Ruth Brown

►► Daryl Coley, Patti LaBelle, Anita Baker, Phyllis Hyman

Norene Cashen

The Winans

Formed 1970s, in Detroit, MI.

Carvin Winans, vocals; Marvin Winans, vocals; Ronald Winans, vocals; Michael Winans, vocals.

Through talent and a series of well-chosen secular guest apperances, these four brothers have become gospel's preeminent crossover act, the spearhead of an immensely talented family of 10 children, all of whom—plus the parents—have recorded at one point or another. The Winans grew up singing in church but were also schooled by Motown, which can be heard in the quartet's mix of chorale and ensemble approaches to its work. Performing first as the Testimonial Signers, the quartet changed it name in 1982, signed its first recording contract, and released three warmly received albums before Quincy Jones signed the group to his Qwest label. While there, the Winans contributed background vocals to Michael Jackson's 1987 smash "Man in the Mirror" and also recorded with Anita Baker, Stevie Wonder, Ladysmith Black Mambazo, and many others.

what to buy: *Return* ♪♪♪♪ (Qwest, 1990, prod. Michael Powell) is the Winans' finest secular moment, a smooth R&B album with stellar guests (Stevie Wonder, Teddy Riley) and some of

the group's best material, including "It's Time," "Gonna Be Alright," and "Together We Stand." *Tomorrow & More* 🎵🎵🎵 (Light, 1984, prod. Bill Maxwell) is the quartet's shining gospel moment. The updated CD adds six bonus tracks.

what to buy next: *Decisions* 🎵🎵🎵 (Qwest, 1987, prod. the Winans), is bolstered by guest appearances from Baker, Michael McDonald, and younger brother CeCe Winans. *Let My People Go* 🎵🎵🎵 (Qwest, 1985, prod. Carvin Winans) shows a jazzier side of the Winans' artistry, with a guest appearance by Vanessa Bell Armstrong.

what to avoid: *All Out* 🎵🎵 (Qwest, 1993, prod. various) isn't terrible, but it's flawed by a sameness and a somewhat dated R&B approach.

the rest:
Introducing the Winans 🎵🎵🎵 (Light, 1981)
Tomorrow and More 🎵🎵🎵 (A&M/CGI, 1984)
Long Time Comin' 🎵🎵🎵 (Light, 1985/CGI, 1993)
Heart & Soul 🎵🎵🎵 (Qwest/Warner Bros., 1995)

worth searching for: The video *Return* 🎵🎵🎵 (Warner Bros., 1990), which gives a sense of the Winans' skill as performers, with some of the material from their best album.

solo outings:
Ronald Winans:
Presents Family and Friends IV 🎵🎵🎵 (Selah, 1996)

influences:
◀◀ Andrae Crouch, Aretha Franklin, the Temptations, the Four Tops, the Soul Stirrers

▶▶ BeBe & CeCe Winans, Commissioned, the Clark Sisters, Anita Baker

Gary Graff

Angie & Debbie Winans

Formed 1986, in Detroit, MI.

Angie Winans (born March 4, in Detroit, MI), soprano vocals; Debbie Winans (born September 3, in Detroit, MI), alto vocals.

The youngest members of the proclaimed "First Family of Gospel Music," sisters Angie and Debbie Winans traveled along much the same musical course as their older siblings. In fact, after BeBe and CeCe Winans left the PTL Singers to forge their own career in 1986, Angie and Debbie traveled the exact same

path, singing backup vocals for their Grammy-winning brother and sister for nearly a decade. Yet upon branching out to create their own identity as a recording duo, the ladies have managed to deliver a brand of slickly-produced, message-filled urban contemporary gospel music which pays tribute to, but doesn't copy, the Winans family style. Among the performing highlights for Angie and Debbie thus far was a national tour with Whitney Houston, serving as the R&B/pop diva's opening act. Their second album, 1997's *Bold*, was released on their own Against the Flow label and produced by Cedric Caldwell, Angie's husband.

what's available: The sisters' first LP, *Angie & Debbie* 🎵🎵🎵 (Capitol/Frontline, 1993, prod. various), stands as proof that these young ladies drank deeply from the Winans talent gene pool. The songs "Light of Love" and "What a Place" made the gospel charts, but this deserving release never really got into the mainstream, due primarily to record label problems. *Bold* 🎵🎵🎵 (Against the Flow, 1997, prod. Cedric Caldwell) contains more of Angie and Debbie's urban gospel vocals.

influences:
◀◀ The entire Winans family, Whitney Houston, Tramaine Hawkins, Vanessa Bell Armstrong, Cissy Houston, Yolanda Adams, Commissioned

Tim A. Smith

BeBe & CeCe Winans

Formed 1982, in Detroit, MI.

BeBe (Benjamin) Winans, vocals; Priscilla (CeCe) Winans, vocals.

The professional relationship BeBe and CeCe Winans have enjoyed came about more so because of chronological order than anything else. While the pair were in high school, four of their brothers—Marvin, Carvin, Ronald, and Michael—went on to form the ground-breaking gospel group the Winans. Initially a part of a family team known as the Winans Part II, BeBe and CeCe began singing together with the PTL Singers in 1982, making frequent nationwide TV appearances as well as recording a gospelized version of "Up Where We Belong" (with the PTL Singers), from the movie *An Officer and a Gentleman*. Inevitably the duo came to the attention of music industry executives, and in 1987 was signed by Sparrow Records. During their 10 years together, the siblings have churned out hit after hit. The success of crossover hits like "Addictive Love," "I'll Take You There," and "It's O.K." clearly shows the duo has been embraced by core gospel fans as well as mainstream music connoisseurs. In addition, BeBe and CeCe have lent their songwriting and singing tal-

Nancy Wilson (© Jack Vartoogian)

ents to such noteworthy mainstream artists as Whitney Houston, M.C. Hammer, Phil Perry, Mavis Staples, Gerald Albright, Chante Moore, Melba Moore, and Gladys Knight.

what to buy: *Greatest Hits* ♪♪♪♪ (Sparrow, 1996, prod. various) is a music collector's delight. If you missed picking up any of BeBe and CeCe's previous albums, never fear; all of the hits are here. An added treat is the addition of two bonus tracks, "Feels Like Heaven (with You)" and a new version of the song that got them going, "Up Where We Belong."

what to buy next: *Different Lifestyles* ♪♪♪ (Sparrow, 1991, prod. various) and *Heaven* ♪♪♪ (Sparrow 1988, prod. Keith Thomas) are both recommended, showing the duo's mainstream appeal. Luther Vandross and Whitney Houston make guest vocal appearances, respectively.

the rest:
First Christmas ♪♪♪ (Sparrow, 1993)
Relationships ♪♪ (Sparrow, 1994)

worth searching for: The true talent that excited both mainstream and gospel industry types and fans comes through on *BeBe & CeCe Winans* ♪♪♪ (Sparrow, 1987), the duo's debut album.

solo outings:
BeBe Winans:
BeBe Winans ♪♪ (Atlantic, 1997)

influences:
◀◀ The Hawkins Family, Andrae Crouch, the Winans

▶▶ Whitney Houston, Jars of Clay

Tim A. Smith

Vickie Winans

Born Vickie Bowman, in Detroit, MI.

Although the former Vickie Bowman became part of America's "First Family of Gospel Music" by marriage (to Rev. Marvin Winans, leader of the superstar brother act the Winans), she has enhanced the family heritage gloriously while establishing herself as a major musical talent of diva proportions on her own. A soloist since the age of eight, Vickie originally met Marvin through her church singing, and her subsequent support of his career allowed her the avenue to take her vocal abilities to the next level. She was initially a member of the group the Winans Part II, with BeBe and CeCe Winans, Daniel Winans, and Marvie Wright. When BeBe and CeCe left to launch their career as a duo, the group eventually dissolved, but Vickie was encouraged by a close friend to continue her career as a solo artist. Since that time, the three-time Grammy nominee (1985, 1989, and 1992) has not only become one of gospel music's most charismatic female performers, with her blend of traditional and contemporary sounds, but also serves as host of *Singsation,* a nationally-syndicated gospel television show. Noted for her opulent gowns and glamorous demeanor, Vickie has additionally appeared as a stage actress in such plays as *Don't Get God Started* and *Perilous Times,* and has been national spokesperson for the Quaker Oats Company and its "Voices of Tomorrow" gospel singing competition since 1992. Her oldest son, Mario "Skeeter" Winans, has been signed as a solo artist by Motown Records.

what to buy: Take your choice: either *Be Encouraged* ♪♪♪ (Light, 1987, prod. Marvin Winans, Vickie Winans)—Vickie's first Grammy-nominated work, which contains her signature song "We Shall Behold Him"—or its followup, *Total Victory* ♪♪♪ (Light, 1989, prod. Marvin Winans, Vickie Winans), are marvelous additions to any musical collection, regardless of one's favorite genre. Vickie's is simply a voice that demands to be heard and admired.

what to buy next: After a more than three-year hiatus from recording, Vickie resurfaced with an intensely personal live LP, *Vickie Winans Live in Detroit* ♪♪♪♪ (GCI, 1997, prod. Vickie Winans, Steven Ford), recorded at the Motor City's majestic Straight Gate Church. Blending such timeless hymns as "Great Is Thy Faithfulness" and "No Cross, No Crown," with uptempo selections like her remake of Candi Staton's "The Blood Rushes," the album is a jubilant celebration of faith. Fellow singers Inez Andrews, Kim Stratton, Yolanda Adams, and Albertina Walker were on hand to lend moral support to Winans' effort, which was ultimately a bittersweet triumph: it was her last concert attended by her father, Aaron Bowman, who died just months later.

the rest:
Best of All ♪♪♪ (CGI, 1991)
Vickie Winans ♪♪♪ (Intersound, 1994)

worth searching for: Vickie Winans as urban dance queen? *The Lady* ♪♪♪ (MCA, 1991) is actually a superior album, but was flatly rejected by gospel purists, ignored by the radio community, and underpromoted by the record company because it veered so unexpectedly from her fans' spiritual expectations. Highlighted by a remixed version of the track "Don't Throw Your Life Away," featuring New Jack Swingster R. Kelly, *The Lady* is a great example of how not to make a good LP successful.

influences:

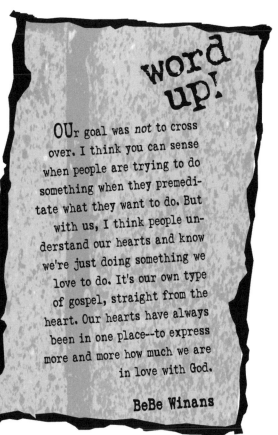 Clara Ward, the Clark Sisters, Rev. James Cleveland, Shirley Caesar, the Winans, BeBe & CeCe Winans, Albertina Walker, Anita Baker

▶▶ Rev. Daryl Coley, Iona Locke, Kirk Franklin, DeLeon Richards, Mario Winans, Vanessa Bell Armstrong

Tim A. Smith

Angela Winbush

Born in St. Louis, MO.

Someday, years from now, Angela Winbush will be showered with accolades that so far have eluded this accomplished writer, producer, arranger, and performer. Winbush, a former schoolteacher, began her career during the late 1970s, singing background for the likes of Eddie Money, Jean Carne, and Stevie Wonder. But even as a student at Howard University, she had been writing songs, including "I Have Learned to Respect the Power of Love," which became a hit for Stephanie Mills. In Los Angeles in 1977, she formed a songwriting team with Rene Moore, but they were eventually signed as a singing duo in 1980. Rene & Angela recorded almost a dozen R&B hits before a messy split in 1985, when both embarked on solo endeavors. Winbush, a four-octave soprano, recorded three albums during the next nine years, scoring moderate success. Her legacy may well rest in the songs she's written and produced for others, such as Mills, Lalah Hathaway, and the Isley Brothers. Much of her most recent work has been created in tandem with her husband, Ronald Isley of the Isley Brothers.

what to buy: *Angela Winbush* ✍✍✍ (Elektra, 1994, prod. Angela Winbush) draws upon all of Winbush's emotional and musical experiences, and enlists the help of Isley, Chuckii Booker, and George Duke to help her through the rough spots.

the rest:
Sharp ✍✍✍ (Mercury, 1985)

worth searching for: *It's the Real Thing* ✍✍✍ (Mercury, 1989, prod. Angela Winbush) is remarkable mainly for Winbush's version of her tune "I've Learned to Respect the Power of Love."

influences:

◀◀ Aretha Franklin

▶▶ Dionne Farris, Billy Lawrence

see also: *Rene & Angela*

Frank Paul

---

word up!

OUr goal was not to cross over. I think you can sense when people are trying to do something when they premeditate what they want to do. But with us, I think people understand our hearts and know we're just doing something we love to do. It's our own type of gospel, straight from the heart. Our hearts have always been in one place--to express more and more how much we are in love with God.

BeBe Winans

Edgar Winter

Born December 28, 1946, in Beaumont, TX.

Winter may have composed "Frankenstein," that monster of hard rock redundancy, but fans should rejoice that he first formed White Trash. The band was meaner looking than a half-dozen Jerry Lee Lewises and twice as rocking, with a decidedly R&B bent. Winter, who is guitar great Johnny Winter's younger brother, is a multi-instrumentalist; his sax and keyboard work are complex, and his technique sways between subtle and ferocious. His vocals could peel a banana or soothe a fevered baby. His take of "Tobacco Road," from his debut album *Entrance*, is nearly unhinged and completely unforgettable. But for all of his talents, Winter's recordings since the 1970s have been sporadic in both volume and quality.

what to buy: *Edgar Winter's White Trash* 🎵🎵🎵🎵 (Epic, 1971/1989, prod. Rick Derringer) covers hard rock, soul, funk, and blues—often at a blistering pace. The impassioned "Save the Planet" and melodic "Where Would I Be" accompany a salvo of rocking R&B in "I've Got News for You" and "Give It Everything You Got."

what to buy next: *The Edgar Winter Collection* 🎵🎵🎵 (Rhino, 1989, prod. various) samples from Winter's 1970s catalog and highlights his most familiar work. "Frankenstein" is part of Winter's hard rocking *They Only Come Out at Night* 🎵🎵🎵 (Epic, 1972, prod. Rick Derringer), which also spawned the play-it-'til-it-melts "Free Ride."

what to avoid: *The Real Deal* 🎵🎵 (Intersound, 1996) isn't. Flawless playing can't overcome this sterile recording, which is as clinical as a jingle house.

the rest:
Entrance 🎵🎵🎵 (Epic, 1970/1992)
(With Johnny Winter) *Together: Live* 🎵🎵🎵 (Blue Sky, 1970/Epic, 1992)
Roadwork 🎵🎵🎵🎵 (Epic, 1972/1989)
Shock Treatment 🎵🎵🎵 (Epic, 1974/Legacy, 1990)
I'm Not a Kid Anymore 🎵🎵 (Thunderbolt, 1994)
Come Back Baby 🎵🎵🎵 (Collectables, 1996)

worth searching for: On Johnny Winter's *Hey, Where's Your Brother?* 🎵🎵🎵🎵 (Point Blank, 1992), Edgar provides keyboard, sax, and vocal support on his big brother's strongest gig of the 1990s.

influences:

◀◀ Johnny Winter, Blood, Sweat & Tears, the Blues Project, Sly & the Family Stone, Them

▶▶ Stevie Wonder, Rare Earth, Was (Not Was)

Patrick McCarty

Bill Withers

Born July 4, 1938, in Slab Fork, WV.

Although he's hardly a household name, Withers has nonetheless lingered on the threshold with a handful of memorable and oft-covered singles he's written and recorded. In 1970, his recently recorded demos attracted the attention of Booker T. Jones, leading to his first record deal. With other members of Booker T. & the MG's on hand to record his debut, the music had a spare and quietly brooding quality which steered the single "Ain't No Sunshine." By 1972, Withers had developed a low-key, bluesy approach with feel-good vibes, culminating in the #1 crossover hit "Lean on Me." Although "Lean on Me" represents his commercial peak, a string of singles followed through

the 1970s. In 1980, he resurfaced on Grover Washington Jr.'s *Winelight* album with another smash, "Just the Two of Us," which he co-wrote and sang. Since then he records and performs only on occasion.

what to buy: The most thorough compilation available, *Lean on Me: The Best of Bill Withers* 🎵🎵🎵🎵 (Columbia/Legacy, 1994, compilation prod. John Snyder) presents Withers as a songwriter, which is the most flattering light to present him in. As such, he's responsible for a handful of tracks that straddle R&B and pop with relative ease. As a performer, his understated vocal delivery becomes merely underwhelming when stretched out over an hour.

the rest:
Still Bill 🎵🎵🎵 (Sussex/Columbia, 1972)
Greatest Hits 🎵🎵🎵 (Columbia, 1989)
Live at Carnegie Hall N/A (Legacy, 1997)

influences:

◀◀ Smokey Robinson, Sam Cooke, Booker T. & the MG's

▶▶ Paul McCartney, Thelma Houston, the Winans, Michael Jackson, Grover Washington Jr., Club Nouveau

Allan Orski

Peter Wolf

Born Peter Blankfield, March 6, 1946, in the Bronx, NY.

The J. Geils Band's white-boy R&B ran toward the music's roots, but singer Peter Wolf, a supporter of Boston's R&B scene since his days as a DJ at WBCN, looked toward more modern sounds after leaving the group in 1983, even hooking up with early rap hero Michael Jonzun. He had some initial success with his solo outings—more, certainly, than the Wolf-less J. Geils Band—and placed three singles ("Lights Out," "I Need You Tonight," and "Come As You Are") in the Top 40. Subsequent releases have not been received as well, however, and have become more infrequent.

what to buy: Wolf had been writing songs with R&B singer Don Covay ("Lights Out") and Jonzun when he was squeezed out of J. Geils. Those songs emerged on *Lights Out* 🎵🎵🎵 (EMI, 1984, prod. Michael Jonzun, Peter Wolf), whose playful approach to the music proved an excellent foil for Wolf's white-funk jive.

Peter Wolf (© Ken Settle)

what to buy next: On *Come As You Are* ♫♫♫ (EMI, 1987, prod. Peter Wolf, Eric "E.T." Thorngren) Wolf continued to work with hot hip-hop producers—this time with Thorngren, who had come to fame remixing Grandmaster Flash's records. Wolf and Thorngren turn up the guitars while retaining the grooves, but beyond the title track and a couple other cuts, they can't maintain the party atmosphere in which Wolf has cut his best records.

what to avoid: Written and co-produced with two Nashville songwriters, *Up to No Good* ♫♫ (MCA, 1990, prod. Peter Wolf, Robert White Johnson, Taylor Rhodes) doesn't have the spark of his work with R&B musicians.

the rest:
Long Line ♫♫♫ (Reprise, 1996)

worth searching for: The 12-inch dance mixes of "Lights Out" and "Come As You Are" are among the best rock remixes of the mid-1980s.

influences:

◀◀ The J. Geils Band, Bobby Womack, the Rolling Stones, Blondie, Jackie Wilson, doo wop

▶▶ Robert Palmer, Mick Jagger

see also: *J. Geils Band*

Brian Mansfield

Womack & Womack

Formed early 1980s.

Cecil Womack (born in 1947, in Cleveland, OH), guitars, vocals; Linda Womack (born in 1952), keyboards, vocals.

The husband-and-wife duo of Womack & Womack bring a deep family tradition to their soulful music. Cecil started performing as a teenager with the Womack Brothers gospel group, which evolved into the influential R&B band the Valentinos and, in turn, launched brother Bobby Womack's solo career. And Linda is the daughter of Sam Cooke. Before partnering as performers, they wrote songs individually for artists such as Aretha Franklin and Teddy Pendergrass. In 1983 they produced their first album as a duo, *Love Wars*. Interestingly, for a couple who appear to be the picture of domestic bliss on their album covers, Womack & Womack's lyrics often explore the tenuous realms of infidelity, betrayal, and lost love. Though displaying a skilled sense of contemporary songwriting, the feeling and flavor of soul music's roots are crucial elements in all their work. This is mature, seasoned stuff—which probably explains their lack of airplay and resultant journeys from one record label to another.

what to buy: *Love Wars* ♫♫♫♫ (Elektra, 1983, prod. Stewart Levine) remains their best, with a solid studio band adding muscle to classic soul grooves and well-crafted tunes.

what to buy next: On *Conscience* ♫♫♫♫ (Island, 1988, prod. Chris Blackwell, the Gypsy Wave Power Co.), a multi-layered southern soul guitar mix gives a mellower feel to some of Womack & Womack's best material, including "Good Man Monologue," later covered (in spirit, at least) by Bonnie Raitt and Delbert McClinton.

the rest:
Radio M.U.S.I.C. Man ♫♫♫ (Elektra, 1985)
Family Spirit ♫♫♫ (RCA, 1991)
Transformation to the House of Zekkariyas ♫♫ (Warner Bros., 1993)

worth searching for: Any of the Valentinos recordings, some of which can be found on *Sam Cooke's SAR Story* (Abkco, 1994, prod. Sam Cooke).

influences:

◀◀ Bobby Womack, Sam Cooke, the Impressions, the Staple Singers

▶▶ Arrested Development, Me Phi Me, Fugees

Doug Pippin

Bobby Womack

Born March 4, 1944, in Cleveland, OH.

Helping to fill the bill after Sam Cooke's death in 1964, Bobby Womack—who was Cooke's guitar player—embarked on a solo career. He wrote or co-wrote some key rock 'n' roll songs, played guitar on a lot of crucial sessions, and had rumblings of R&B success, with a gritty soul voice and an advanced sense of soul writing and arrangement. When he and his brothers were signed to Cooke's label as the Womack Brothers, he changed their name to the Valentinos, and they tasted their first success with "Looking for a Love" and "It's All Over Now," which later became key hits for the J. Geils Band and the Rolling Stones, respectively. Lapses in his career were said to be caused by drug abuse; pronounced comebacks accompanied several clean-ups. After he helped out on more than a couple of Stones albums, the band repaid him when Ron Wood issued Womack's 1994 comeback on his own label and enlisted superstar rock friends to help out. Womack sees himself as a soul survivor in a field decimated over the decades. He's certainly been able to maintain a major-label career as his peers struggled, although the big fame has so far eluded him.

what to buy: The numbers of Womack titles currently in print are conspicuously spotty, with early 1970s recordings much more readily available than mid- to late 1980s successes. There's never been a loss in Womack compilations, though. *Only Survivor: The MCA Years* ♪♪♪ (MCA, 1996, prod. various) stands out because it collects such otherwise unavailable songs as "I Wish He Didn't Trust Me So Much" and the stirring "I'll Still Be Looking Up to You (No Matter How High I Get)." *The Soul of Bobby Womack: Stop on By* ♪♪♪ (EMI, 1996, compilation prod. Leo Sacks) gathers 15 solid favorites from the early and mid-1970s.

what to buy next: *The Poet* ♪♪♪ (Beverly Glen Music, 1981/Razor & Tie, 1993, prod. Bobby Womack), the first of two strong *Poet* albums that mounted a comeback of sizzling R&B tracks, such as "If You Think You're Lonely Now." *Midnight Mover: The Bobby Womack Collection* ♪♪♪ (EMI, 1993, prod. various) covers a lot of ground: the first nine years of his solo recording career, which included over 11 albums for Minit, Liberty, and United Artists, from 1967 to 1975.

what to avoid: Although it boasts grittier production and a wonderful remake of the Temptations' "I Wish It Would Rain," Womack's last album for United Artists, *Safety Zone* ♪♪ (United Artists, 1972/The Right Stuff, 1994, prod. David Rubinson), ended with a dismal eight-minute disco stab, "I Feel a Groove Coming On."

the rest:
Communication ♪♪♪ (United Artists, 1971/The Right Stuff, 1994)
Understanding ♪♪♪ (United Artists, 1972/The Right Stuff, 1994)
Facts of Life ♪♪♪ (United Artists, 1973/The Right Stuff, 1994)
Looking for a Love Again ♪♪♪ (United Artists, 1974/ The Right Stuff, 1994)
The Poet II ♪♪♪ (Beverly Glen Music, 1984)
Lookin' for a Love: The Best of Bobby Womack, 1968–1975 ♪♪♪ (Razor & Tie, 1993)
Resurrection ♪♪♪ (Slide/Continuum, 1994)
The Soul of Bobby Womack: Stop on By ♪♪♪ (EMI, 1996)

worth searching for: *Someday We'll All Be Free* ♪♪♪ (Beverly Glen Music, 1985, prod. Bobby Womack, Patrick Moten) may be the best of the many out-of-print Womack titles. This could have been *The Poet III*, since it was his next album in that series on that small label and boasted workouts such as "I Wish I Had Someone to Go Home To" and the Donny Hathaway-penned title song.

influences:
◄◄ Sam Cooke, Wilson Pickett, Friendly Womack

word up!

THere's always expectations. If you listen to every single opinion and every single thing people say to you, you'll go crazy. One person says, 'Stevie, I like your corn rows,' and the next one will say, 'Stevie, I like your afro.' I don't really trip on other people's expectations. I trip on my own expectations first; ultimately, I have to answer to myself. And I'm my own worst critic.

Stevie Wonder

▶▶ Womack & Womack, Tony Rich Project, Babyface

Roger Catlin

Stevie Wonder

Born Steveland Morris, May 13, 1950, in Saginaw, MI.

Out of all the stars that came out of the Motown stable, Stevie Wonder's has shined the brightest and the longest. Already a star as Little Stevie Wonder in 1971, the maturing musician fought Motown president Berry Gordy for artistic control of his music—and won. Wonder went on to become the 800-pound gorilla of pop during the 1970s, with a distinctive sound that borrowed freely from funk, rock, classical, jazz, country, and even reggae. His immense genius absorbed it all into a pre-

cisely layered and melodic music that had no peer. From "Fingertips Part 2," his first hit at the age of 13, to "I Just Called to Say I Love You" and beyond, Wonder's oeuvre encompasses a treasure trove of ageless songs—"My Cherie Amour," "You Are the Sunshine of My Life," "Superstition," "Golden Lady." Paul Simon put it all in perspective when accepting a Grammy for 1975's *Still Crazy After All These Years*: he thanked Wonder for not putting out a record that year. Wonder was instrumental in the campaign to get Martin Luther King Jr.'s birthday declared a national holiday and has been active in exposing African and Caribbean musicians to American audiences. Though not in the spotlight as much as before, Wonder is still a top pop star with the ability to put his finger on the pulse of the people and compose a tune that goes right to the heart of the matter.

what to buy: Wonder seemed an absolute pop music genius during the 1970s, and *Innervisions* ♪♪♪♪♪ (Motown, 1973, prod. Stevie Wonder) is the pinnacle of that sensibility. Nearly every song—"Too High," "Golden Lady," "Don't You Worry 'Bout a Thing," "All in Love Is Fair"—is a classic. But it was the gritty "Living for the City" that really set folks on their ears. *Talking Book* ♪♪♪♪♪ (Motown, 1972, prod. Stevie Wonder) was almost as good; "Superstition" and "You Are the Sunshine of My Life" gave an inkling of what was to come.

what to buy next: A lot of folks thought Wonder had gone off the deep end when the double album *Songs in the Key of Life* ♪♪♪♪♪ (Motown, 1976, prod. Stevie Wonder) came out, with its blend of funk and jazz influences, but it yielded hits such as "Sir Duke" and "Isn't She Lovely" to turn minds around. *Where I'm Coming From* ♪♪♪♪ (Motown, 1972, prod. Stevie Wonder) is the first album that Wonder had complete creative control over and the only one of his adult years that he gave significant songwriting space to someone else—then-wife Syreeta Wright. The album gave us "If You Really Love Me" and "Never Dreamed You'd Leave Me in Summer." *Song Review: A Greatest Hits Collection* ♪♪♪♪♪ (Motown, 1997, prod. various) can't tell the whole story, even with two discs, but it's a solid gathering of most of his best-known material.

what to avoid: *Journey Through the Secret Life of Plants* ♪♪♪ (Motown, 1979, prod. Stevie Wonder) has well-crafted instrumentals that lean toward the New Age vibe, but was outside the pop mainstream. It's a testament to Wonder's clout that Gordy even allowed this to be released.

Stevie Wonder (© Ken Settle)

the rest:
The Jazz Soul of Little Stevie Wonder ♪♪♪ (Motown, 1963)
With a Song in My Heart ♪♪♪ (Motown, 1966)
Down to Earth ♪♪♪ (Motown, 1967)
I Was Made to Love Her ♪♪♪ (Motown, 1967)
Someday at Christmas (Motown, 1967) ♪♪♪
For Once in My Life ♪♪♪♪ (Motown, 1968)
Greatest Hits, Vol. 1 ♪♪♪♪♪ (Motown, 1968)
My Cherie Amour ♪♪♪ (Motown, 1969)
Signed, Sealed and Delivered ♪♪♪♪ (Motown, 1970)
Greatest Hits, Vol. 2 ♪♪♪♪ (Motown, 1972)
Music of My Mind ♪♪♪♪♪ (Motown, 1972)
Fulfillingness' First Finale ♪♪♪♪ (Motown, 1974)
Hotter Than July ♪♪♪♪ (Motown, 1980)
Original Musiquarium I ♪♪♪♪ (Motown, 1982)
The Woman in Red ♪♪♪ (Motown, 1984)
In Square Circle ♪♪♪ (Motown, 1985)
Characters ♪♪♪ (Motown, 1987)
Jungle Fever ♪♪♪ (Motown, 1991)
Motown Legends: I Was Made to Love Her—Uptight ♪♪♪♪ (ESX Entertainment, 1994)
Conversation Peace ♪♪♪♪ (Motown, 1995)
Natural Wonder ♪♪♪ (Motown, 1995)

worth searching for: The import *Essential Stevie Wonder* ♪♪♪♪♪ is the only comprehensive collection of Wonder's 1963–71 work, a period no single domestic release covers completely.

influences:
◄◄ Ray Charles, Duke Ellington, Smokey Robinson, Marvin Gaye, Frankie Lymon, Miles Davis

►► Lionel Richie, Lenny Kravitz, Luther Vandross, Howard Jones, Michael Jackson

Lawrence Gabriel

Wreckx-N-Effect /Wrecks-N-Effect

Formed c. 1987, in Harlem, NY.

Markell Riley, DJ; Keith KC, lead vocals (left group in 1988); Aquil Davidson, vocals; Brandon Mitchell (died 1990), vocals.

Wreckx-N-Effect reached the peak of its popularity in 1992 with the runaway hit "Rump Shaker." With Teddy Riley (DJ Markell's brother) lending his production expertise to the track, "Shaker" bounced Wreckx into multiplatinum status. Formed around 1987 by Riley family neighbor Aquil Davidson, the quartet soon signed with Atlantic Records and released its first album, simply titled *Wrecks-N-Effect*. The album is notable for the memorable, genre-defining track "New Jack Swing." The following year, the group moved to Motown Records and dropped its second eponymous LP—this time spelled *Wreckx-N-Effect*. Despite the absence of lead rapper Keith KC—or perhaps because of it—the second release featured a more polished sound. Unfortunately, the group went from a trio to a duo in 1990 when Brandon Mitchell was shot dead. Markell and Davidson continued as Wreckx-N-Effect on MCA Records and released the double-platinum *Hard or Smooth*; with "Rump Shaker" as its foundation hit single, *Hard or Smooth* was the album that defined the group's 15 rump-shaking minutes of fame.

what to buy: *Hard or Smooth* ♫♫ (MCA, 1992, prod. Teddy Riley, others) is the best of the Wreckx, which isn't saying a whole lot. But the monster jam "Rump Shaker" (which rides a sample of N2Deep's hit, "Back to the Hotel") and a few other agreeable tracks make the album an adequate outing.

the rest:
Wrecks-N-Effect ♫♫ (Atlantic, 1988)
Wreckx-N-Effect ♫♫♫ (Motown, 1990)
Rap's New Generation ♫♪ (MCA, 1996)

influences:
◀◀ Whodini, Run-D.M.C., 2 Live Crew, Guy, N2Deep
▶▶ Jodeci, BLACKstreet

Andre McGarrity

Betty Wright

Born December 21, 1953, in Miami, FL.

Mother Wit was way ahead of Alanis Morissette and the rest of the female angst crowd. Her "Clean Up Woman," a Top 10 hit in 1971 (when she was only 18), was just one of a series of songs she infused with her strong, no-nonsense attitude about the opposite sex. Wright's strong-woman philosophy remains a hallmark of her work today, though she tours more than she records these days. Wright started singing as a child in the family's gospel group, Echoes of Joy. She made the switch to R&B as a pre-teen when she was discovered by writer-producers Willie Clarke and Clarence Reid. They released her first single, "Paralyzed," cut when Wright was 12, on their Deep City label. Its regional success led to a deal with Henry Stone's Alston label and Wright's first national hit, "Girls Can't Do What the Guys Do," recorded at the ripe age of 14. "Clean Up Woman," about a woman who has to clean up her man's messes, followed four years later and helped put the Miami sound on the map. Alston was part of the T.K. Records group, with a roster of local talent that made significant inroads with R&B and, soon after, disco fans. Among its biggest success stories was KC &

the Sunshine Band, who's front man, Howard Casey, once worked as Wright's secretary. Wright continued to make the R&B charts during the 1970s with hits such as "Tonight's the Night," "Shoorah! Shoorah!," and "Baby Sitter." When T.K. folded, she moved to Epic for a couple of albums, one featuring a duet with Stevie Wonder and the other produced by Marlon Jackson. Her recorded output has been sporadic since. Wright formed her own Ms. B Productions to release her occasional album and single, remains a strong live performer—Tina Turner's got nothing on this sister—and in recent years has teamed up with kindred spirit Millie Jackson.

what to buy: Most of her studio albums are long out of print. Fortunately, Wright's singles and concert staples were rounded up into the 20-song collection *The Best of Betty Wright* ♫♫♫ (Rhino, 1992, compilation prod. David Booth), the perfect assemblage of her sassy, sexy, strong persona that covers the length of her recording career.

what to buy next: *Betty Wright: Live* ♫♫♪ (Alston, 1978/Rhino, 1991, prod. Howard Albert, Ron Albert) includes her famous "Clean Up Woman" medley that works as a song suite about love, heartbreak, and ultimate happiness. It quotes from "Me and Mrs. Jones," "Midnight at the Oasis," and "You Are My Sunshine."

what to avoid: An ill-advised collection of covers and a less-than-stellar remake of "Clean Up Woman" mar *The Best of Betty Wright* ♫♫ (Black Tiger, 1995, prod. various).

the rest:
Passion & Compassion ♫♫♫ (Ms.B/Vision, 1964/1990)
Mother Wit ♫♫♪ (Ms.B/Vision, 1988)
4U2NJoy ♫♫♪ (Ms. B/Vision, 1989)

influences:
◀◀ Aretha Franklin
▶▶ Millie Jackson, Tina Turner, Denise LaSalle

Doug Pullen

Charles Wright & the Watts 103rd Street Rhythm Band

Formed 1963, in Los Angeles, CA. Disbanded 1973.

Charles Wright (born 1940, in Clarksdale, MS), guitar, vocals, keyboards; James Gadson, drums; Melvin Dunlap, bass; Al McKay, guitar; Ray Jackson, trombone; Gabe Flemings, piano, trumpet; Big John Rayford, saxophones; Bill Cannon, saxophones.

The LA/West Coast music scene in the late 1960s was in constant flux. Even though James Brown had invented the funk years before, many R&B groups were absorbing rock and other influences that were sure to take soul music in different directions. Charles Wright and his band were signed to Warner Bros. in 1969 and became the first R&B act to attain major chart success for the label. Moving from his native Mississippi in his early teens, Wright looked up L.A. singing sensation Jessie Belvin's number in the phone book. Belvin—at the time the godfather of southern California soul vocalists—liked Wright's guitar playing and began using him on various sessions. By the early 1960s, Wright had started his band, originally called the Soul Runners, and became an attraction on the South Central and Hollywood club scenes. It was during this period that the famous L.A. disc jockey "The Magnificent Montague" took a Wright composition called "Spreadin' Honey" and made it his theme song. After Bill Cosby gave the band a boost by using them on an album and at his gigs, Wright secured a deal with Warners. While waiting for his finished record to be released, Wright assembled a different group to tour, eventually replacing his original lineup with these members, whom he thought best fit his loose-jointed, free-flowing brand of funk. Their improvised jams often turned into fully realized songs. The band's biggest and most distinctive hit, "Express Yourself," featured Wright singing an almost stream-of-consciousness lyric over a prickly instrumental groove. (The tune was used recently as the TV commercial soundtrack for a national burger chain, encouraging customers to express themselves by having burgers their way!) The Watts 103rd Street Rhythm Band also cracked the Top 20 with "Do Your Thing," "Till You Get Enough," and the ballad "Love Land," but when their last group single, "High As Apple Pie," failed to chart, many of the band's members began backing singer-songwriter Bill Withers. Guitarist Al McKay and drummer James Gadson eventually joined Earth, Wind & Fire. Wright continued to record, though never again recapturing the innovative, exhilarating vibe of his group at its peak.

what to buy: The 16-song compilation *Express Yourself: The Best of Charles Wright and the Watts 103rd Street Band* ♫♫♫♫ (Warner Archives, 1994, compilation prod. Gregg Geller, Charles Wright) showcases the raw exuberance of a band that often sounded as if it was making up the music as it went along. "Express Yourself," which hit #12 on the pop charts in 1970, remains a heavily-sampled track for rap and hip-hop acts to this day. The collection also includes the early radio attention-grabber "Spreadin' Honey" and the previously unreleased Wright creations "Keep Saying," "Tell Me What You Want Me to Do," and "Sweet Lorene."

what to buy next: The reissue *In the Jungle, Babe/Express Yourself* ♫♫♫ (Ol' Skool, 1997, prod. Charles Wright) combines two albums originally released in 1969 and 1970, respectively. While many of the tunes are the same as those found on the 1994 "greatest hits" package—particularly the wonderful Wright original "Love Land," on which the 103rd soars behind what may be Wright's strongest vocal track ever—this grouping also includes covers of the Sly Stone classic "Everyday People," Wilson Pickett's "I'm a Midnight Mover," and Edwin Starr's "25 Miles."

influences:

◀◀ James Brown, Otis Redding, Bill Cosby, Booker T. & the MG's, Sly & the Family Stone

▶▶ Earth, Wind & Fire, War, N.W.A., Brand New Heavies

Matt Lee

O.V. Wright

Born Overton Vertis Wright, October 9, 1939, in Leno, TN. Died November 16, 1980, in Mobile, AL.

Let's not mince words: O.V. Wright was the greatest deep-soul singer ever. By the time he cut his first secular recording—1964's "That's How Strong My Love Is"—Wright was already a well-known and successful gospel singer, having sung and recorded with gospel groups such as the Spirit of Memphis Quartet and the Sunset Travelers. Wright is by no means the only artist to abandon the sanctuary of the church in search of the rewards and temptations of the secular world. The pop recordings of Sam Cooke, Al Green, Aretha Franklin, and Johnnie Taylor all make overt or oblique reference to the trauma of this self-imposed exile. But in the work of no other artist, with the possible exception of Green, does this exile play so central a role. Wright's recordings are unmistakably the work of a spiritually troubled man. As if to underscore the gravity of his choice, Wright's secular recordings, more than those of any of his peers, cleave faithfully to the style, structure, and, most importantly, the feeling and fervor of the deepest and most heartfelt gospel music. The presence of this theme in all of his strongest performances—"You're Gonna Make Me Cry," "Eight Men, Four Women," "Everybody Knows (The River Song)," "Born All Over," "Heartaches, Heartaches," "Memory Blues"—give them a timeless universality that places them on a par with the hymns of Mahalia Jackson, the blues of Robert Johnson, or the country music of Hank Williams.

There were two distinct periods in Wright's 15-year secular career, delineated by the demise of his first record label, Back

Beat, which had been owned and operated by the don of Houston R&B, Don Robey. Midway in his career, Wright migrated to Hi Records, where his longtime producer Willie Mitchell was the principal talent director. Few artists in any medium exhibit so huge a gap between artistic quality and commercial success as O.V. Wright. Wright's two most successful records, "You're Gonna Make Me Cry" and "Eight Men, Four Women," came early on in his career at Back Beat, and neither recording received any airplay outside the circumscribed world of 1960s R&B radio. In fact, R&B radio in the late 1960s, the heyday of southern gospel-inflected soul music, is the only radio format during the years spanned by Wright's career in which it is possible to imagine Wright's chilling statements from the spiritual void finding a home. Wright is an artist whose reputation is destined to grow with the historical perspective afforded by time. Willie Mitchell's production values and house musicians (the Hi Rhythm Section, among others) were essential elements in the brilliance of Wright's recordings. Mitchell had achieved great commercial and artistic success helping Al Green craft a new kind of Memphis soul music in the 1970s. Undoubtedly motivated by the desire to help Wright achieve more of the success and recognition that he so deserved, Mitchell attempted to adapt this softer, more melodic sound to Wright's recordings during Wright's later period at Hi Records. That this sound was not entirely suited to Wright's unique gifts provides one explanation for the relative superiority of the Back Beat recordings. Another factor is that, by all accounts, the O.V. Wright who recorded for Hi was deteriorating from a drug habit that ultimately claimed his life. A comparison of the photographs from the Back Beat albums and the later Hi albums provides stark evidence of his physical deterioration. He died in an ambulance, en route to the hospital, at the age of 41, consumed by the music that haunted him and the life that went with it.

what's available: *The Soul of O. V. Wright* ♪♪♪♪ (MCA, 1992, prod. Willie Mitchell) is the only Wright CD readily available these days. It's not enough, not by a long shot, but for now, it's the best there is, and it includes most of the essential recordings. With track time so precious on a single CD that purports to represent the best of these stirring performances, however, it's hard to comprehend the inclusion of "Monkey Dog," a throwaway that is of interest only as Mitchell & Co.'s take on the Bo Diddley beat.

worth searching for: A couple of imports that help round out the story: *The 45's* ♪♪♪♪ (Hi U.K., 1994, prod. Willie Mitchell), which is just what the title says; and *The Wright Stuff/Live in Memphis*

♪♪♪♪ (Hi U.K., 1994, prod. Willie Mitchell), which puts together well-regarded albums from 1977 and 1979, respectively.

influences:

◀◀ Rev. R.H. Harris/the Soul Stirrers, Sam Cooke, Rev. Morgan Babb/Radio Four, Rev. Claude Jeter/Swan Silvertones, Johnnie Taylor, Willie Mae Ford Smith, Johnny Ace, Bobby "Blue" Bland, Al Green, Joe Hinton

▶▶ Otis Clay, Robert Cray

Bill Pollak

Wu-Tang Clan

Formed 1992, in Staten Island, NY.

Prince Rakeem/The RZA (born Robert Diggs), vocals, producer; Method Man (Clifford Smith), vocals; U-God (Lamont Hawkins), vocals; Inspektah Deck (Jason Hunter), vocals; Chef Raekwon (Corey Woods), vocals; Ghost Face Killa (Dennis Coles), vocals; Ol' Dirty Bastard (Russell Jones), vocals; Genius/GZA (Gary Grice), vocals; Masta Killa (Elgin Turner), vocals.

They began as nine MCs who were either unknowns or major-label cast-offs, but together as the Wu-Tang Clan, RZA, Method Man, U-God, Inspektah Deck, Raekwon, Ghost Face Killa, ODB, Genius, and Masta Killa have transformed into the most dominant crew in hip-hop. Though the numbers may not match rap's biggest sellers (with each Wu-related album selling between 500,000 and 2 million copies), the Clan has established a franchise that will surely pay dividends for many years to come. There are only officially nine in the immediate crew, but the Wu-Tang Clan apparently consists of more than 200 members, all from the fifth—and sometimes "forgotten"—borough of Staten Island. The unifying principle of the Wu is based on an Asiatic philosophy and mythology developed by the Buddhist monks of the Shao Lin Monastery in ancient times; the Wu-Tang was regarded as one of the deadliest combat techniques that was more mental than physical. Shrouding yourself in an Asiatic discipline may be interpreted as a marketing gimmick. But is it? The Wu gambinos frequently quote text from the likes of Sun Tzu's *Art of War,* the I Ching, and the Koran; chess has become the crew's favorite pastime; and headmaster RZA—who not only organized the Clan but also drew up its guiding principles and has produced almost all of the group's influential beats—can fully explain to you the philosophy at any time.

Flash back to 1992, and RZA doesn't yet have the hip-hop nation as his captive audience. But he's plotting. Both RZA and his cousin, Genius, had already had somewhat sour experiences in the record industry during their solo careers, and others in the Clan had been turned down by record companies. Before the Clan would surface, RZA first wanted to make sure everyone in the group was on the same page. A business plan was crafted, and after pooling together what little resources they had, Wu-Tang dropped 500 vinyl copies of a single—"Protect Ya Neck" b/w "After the Laughter Comes Tears"—on its own Wu-Tang Records. The single served as a demo tape for the labels, with the added effect of showing off the group's potential popularity; college radio jocks had taken to the single and were beginning to bump it across the country. Sure enough, the plan worked. Within two years, Wu-Tang Clan had signed on with a major label (Loud) and landed a distribution deal for Wu-Tang Records, RZA had signed two different production-company deals, six of the group's members had inked solo artist deals, and a clothing line (Wu-Wear) had become a hit. As such, the Wu-Tang Clan has become admired not only for its musical prowess, but for its business acumen as well.

what to buy: Not everybody had been sold on the Wu-Tang Clan with its debut single, re-released as "Protect Ya Neck" b/w "Method Man." When the group's full-length debut came out, though, everything changed. *Enter the Wu-Tang (36 Chambers)* 🎜🎜🎜🎜 (Loud/RCA, 1993, prod. RZA) is one of those landmark records, a truly original creation that changed people's perception of music. It's a gritty, grimy record that goes against all conventions—and indeed, that's its charm. Songs such as "C.R.E.A.M. (Cash Rules Everything Around Me)" and "Can It Be All So Simple" became street anthems, while the other cuts highlighted the crew's many different personalities. After the first record, a steady stream of solo records were issued, keeping the Wu-Tang on the forefront of the hip-hop nation's minds from 1993 on—for better or for worse. After Method Man and Ol' Dirty Bastard issued their albums (both acquired tastes), Raekwon dropped *Only Built for Cuban Linx . . .* 🎜🎜🎜🎜🎜 (Loud/RCA, 1995, prod. RZA, 4th Disciple), a recording that truly surprised. Arguably even better than the first Wu album, it's tight, concise, and highly cinematic, with "Incarcerated Scarfaces," "Rainy Dayz," and other sonically—if not visually—stunning tunes. And who knew that Raekwon and his partner, Ghost Face Killa, were the two best lyricists in the crew?

what to buy next: Genius/GZA's first (pre-Wu) album, *Words from the Genius* 🎜🎜🎜 (Cold Chillin', 1991/1994, prod. Genius, Prince Rakeem, Easy Mo Bee, others), is a great recording, but the rapper lost his initial label deal when sales didn't live up to

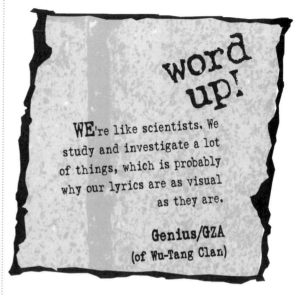

word up!

WE're like scientists. We study and investigate a lot of things, which is probably why our lyrics are as visual as they are.

Genius/GZA
(of Wu-Tang Clan)

expectations. Still, the title track and "Phony As You Want to Be" established the Genius as a gifted MC—one who has always lurked in the Wu shadows. Cold Chillin' reissued the album to capitalize on Wu-mania, replacing "Come Do Me" with "Pass the Bone," which features Prince Rakeem/The RZA. Genius maintains his understated, smooth, and compelling style—albeit in a darker fashion—on his post-Wuxplosion solo record, *Liquid Swords* 🎜🎜🎜🎜 (Geffen, 1995, prod. RZA). Though a little more chaotic-sounding than Raekwon's, Genius' lyrical flow is rivaled by few. Ghost Face Killa, meanwhile, may have played a secondary role on Raekwon's record, but it's the other way around on his own solo debut, *Ironman* 🎜🎜🎜🎜 (Epic, 1996, prod. RZA, True Masta). Wucomer Cappadonna (born Darryl Hill), first introduced on Raekwon's album, also plays a significant role here. Though you'd think people might be getting a little Wu-zy after hearing five Wu-related albums in just over three years, hearing Ghost Face go off on "Wildflower," and Ghost Face, Raekwon, and Cappadonna exchange verses on "Camay" and "Daytona 500," is simply intoxicating.

what to avoid: In the summer of 1997, the Wu-Tang Clan regrouped for a sophomore album that was one of the most highly anticipated hip-hop records ever. But *Wu-Tang Forever* 🎜🎜 (Loud/RCA, 1997, prod. RZA, others) is a dramatic disappointment. RZA's production on some songs ("Reunited" with its flipping violins, the haunting "The City") proves that he's got an ear for music. But part of what made Wu-Tang Clan so good initially was its grittiness, and that's abandoned on this slick, seemingly made-for-profit record. The album's size (two hours of music spread out over two discs) is excessive. This easily could have been a tight, single album.

solo outings:
Method Man:
Tical 𝄢𝄢𝄢 (Def Jam, 1994)

Ol' Dirty Bastard:
Return to the 36 Chambers 𝄢𝄢 (Elektra, 1995)

GP-Wu:
The Grain N/A (MCA, 1997)

worth searching for: In 1991, RZA released the single "Ooh! I Love You Rakeem" (with "Deadly Venoms" and "Sexcapades") on Tommy Boy. If you can find the single, you'll also find some of the first Wu-Tang remixes.

influences:
◀◀ Prince Paul, Kool G Rap, Public Enemy, Cypress Hill
▶▶ GP-Wu, Killarmy, Shyheim, Capone-N-Noreaga, AZ, King Just

see also: *Stetsasonic*

Jazzbo

X-Clan

Formed in Brooklyn, NY.

Professor X (born Lumumba Carson), vocals; Brother J (Jason Hunter), vocals; Grand Architect Paradise; Rhythm Provider Sugar Shaft.

The revolution may not be televised, but it could well happen over the airwaves. And who knows? MTV and BET just might follow suit after all. Following the literally revolutionary success of Public Enemy, X-Clan arrived in the middle of rap's Afrocentric period and quickly established itself as one of the most uncompromisingly pro-black groups, decorating its album cover with African symbolism and rapping thoughtfully about the red, the black, and the green at the crossroads. A massive spoonful of funk made the biting, occasionally pedantic lyrical medicine go down, although X-Clan lost its standing as the pro-black movement lost its steam, and rumors swirled about the band's seemingly hypocritial actions, including out-of-race dating.

what to buy: On the funky, sample-driven sophomore album *Xodus: The New Testament* 𝄢𝄢𝄢𝄢 (Polydor, 1992, prod. Jason Hunter, others), Brother J and Professor X prove themselves to be two of rap's most authoritative, commanding voices, both with their socially conscious, racially aware lyrical concerns and, of course, their booming, forceful deliveries.

the rest:
To the East, Blackwards 𝄢𝄢𝄢 (4th & Broadway, 1990)

solo outings:
Professor X:
Puss 'N Boots (The Struggle Continues . . .) 𝄢𝄢 (Polydor, 1993)

Dark Sun Riders Featuring Brother J:
Seeds of Evolution 𝄢𝄢𝄢 (Island, 1996)

influences:
◀◀ Public Enemy, Brand Nubian, Boogie Down Productions, Jungle Brothers
▶▶ Lin Que (Isis), Queen Mother Rage, Dark Sun Riders

Josh Freedom du Lac

Yagg Fu Front

Formed 1989, in Raleigh, NC.

D'Ranged & Damaged (born Brad Thompson); Spin 4th (born Torin McBynum); Jingle Bell (born Tyrone Burres).

To call Yagg Fu Front positive is to ascribe a seriousness to them that they just don't have. Take the teenage concerns of Fresh Prince, fast-forward a few years to college, and you'll have Yagg Fu Front (which stands for "You Are Gonna Get Fucked Up If You Front").

what's available: There's an appealingly collegiate feel to the group's debut, *Action Packed Adventure* 𝄢𝄢𝄢𝄢 (Mercury, 1994, prod. Yagg Fu Front), which addresses such weighty topics as the dangers of credit card ownership. The album is great fun—equal parts radio play, "Urban Home Companion," and imaginary soundtrack—with jazz-inflected grooves as playful as the light-hearted subject matter. Of particular note is "Black Liquid," in which a bummer day at school becomes an attack of the 50-foot undergrad after the protagonist drinks a mysterious liquid in chemistry lab. "Stay in school, please," it concludes, "or you'll have nuts like these runnin' the country." We could do a lot worse.

influences:

⏪ De La Soul, Digable Planets

David Menconi

Yarbrough & Peoples

Formed late 1970s, in Dallas, TX.

Cavin Yarbrough, vocals, keyboards, percussion; Alisa Peoples, vocals, keyboards, percussion.

A one-hit wonder—O.K., two hits, but that's stretching it—of the post-disco era, this duo played pleasant, lively records of middling consequence during the early and mid-1980s. That's not to say there's no talent here: the childhood friends wowed congregants at their church, and Cavin Yarbrough toured with Leon Russell for a time. Upon his return, they began cutting demo tapes and got one to Charlie Wilson of the Gap Band, who engineered their singing to Total Experience Records. They were a hit out of the box; "Don't Stop the Music" was #1 on the R&B charts for five weeks during early 1981. They didn't return to the top until three years later with "Don't Waste Your Time," but after the 1986 album *Guilty*, the couple—who married in 1987—stepped out of the spotlight. They haven't been heard from since, but they don't rule out future recordings, either.

what's available: *The Best of Yarbrough & Peoples* ⚂⚀ (Mercury Chronicles, 1997, prod. various) is all that's in print. It's a worthwhile but inessential collection; "Don't Stop the Music" is a good dance tune, but you're better off finding it on a various artists compilation. And there's little on this collection that will make you feel like the duo didn't get its due.

influences:

⏪ Andrae Crouch, Marvin Gaye & Tammi Terrell, Marilyn McCoo & Billy Davis Jr., the Gap Band

⏩ Lisa Stansfield, Deee-Lite

Gary Graff

Yo Yo

Born Yolanda Whitaker, August 4, 1971, in Los Angeles, CA.

Though she's had her ups and downs, Yo Yo is one of the most positive black women ever to rock a microphone. Ironically, the South Central product first received the opportunity to flex her lyrical skills on "It's a Man's World," a song from veteran West Coast rapper Ice Cube's seminal 1990 LP *AmeriKKKa's Most Wanted*. The following year, Yo Yo made her solo debut with *Make Way for the Motherlode*, an album consisting almost entirely of demos she'd made while working with producer-mentor Cube. But the single "You Can't Play with My YoYo" (*also featuring Ice Cube*) was a hit, and Yo Yo's future in the rap game was assured. During the height of her success, she founded the Intelligent Black Women's Coalition, an organization designed to help empower young black women in the areas of self-esteem and career planning. As much an activist as an artist, Yo Yo also testified at the Congressional hearings on gangsta rap and presently volunteers at women's shelters when not writing her advice column for *Vibe* magazine. She also hosts a Los Angeles radio show and has even dabbled in acting (*Boyz N the Hood, Panther, New York Undercover, Martin*). Somehow, Yo Yo also found time to rock the cradle, becoming a mother in 1994.

what to buy: Yo Yo's first solo effort, *Make Way for the Motherlode* ⚂⚂⚂ (EastWest America, 1991, prod. Ice Cube, Sir Jinx), remains her most powerful album to date—a brazen and aggressive statement of attitude and feminist fury that comes across on every track through top-rate production.

what to buy next: Rebounding from the lackluster sales and critical accusations of turning soft and light on her sophomore album, *Black Pearl*, Yo Yo's third release, *You Better Ask Somebody* ⚂⚂⚂ (EastWest America, 1993, prod. Ice Cube, others), is a solid return to form, displaying a fully realized rapper and woman—feisty, funky, and extremely focused—supported by such guests as funnyman Martin Lawrence and the acid-jazz-dropping Brand New Heavies.

the rest:

Black Pearl ⚂⚂ (EastWest America, 1992)
Total Control ⚂⚂ (EastWest America, 1996)

influences:

⏪ Teena Marie, Queen Latifah, Ice Cube, MC Lyte, Salt-N-Pepa

⏩ Lady of Rage, Patra, Champ MC, Adina Howard, Brandy

Andre McGarrity

Young Black Teenagers

Formed in NY.

Firstborn, vocals; Kamron, vocals; A.T.A., vocals; DJ Skribble, DJ.

This group caused quite a stir when it emerged on longtime Public Enemy associate Bill Stephney's Soul Records label in 1990 because, well, none of the Young Black Teenagers were actually black. The group insisted that the moniker was a sociopolitical statement and that black was a state of mind. Many scoffed at this rhetoric, but few could deny that the group's three MCs were competent rhymers. Ultimately, though, despite a solid debut, the group became a minor footnote in hip-hop history: Following the group's eponymous debut and resultant hubbub, leader Kamron appeared in *House Party 2* and a second album was released. Then the group disappeared.

what to buy: Metaphysical ruminations regarding what it means to be black aside, *Young Black Teenagers* (Soul Records, 1991, prod. the Bomb Squad) is filled with some tasty tracks, thanks in large part to the beat manipulations of the Bomb Squad. "Daddy Called Me Niga Cause I Liked to Rhyme" is a pointed twist on the "Parents Just Don't Understand" theme, with much more punch. "To My Donna" is a timely shot at Madonna, who had sampled Public Enemy without credit or permission—just as sample-clearance was becoming a white-hot topic.

what to avoid: The dreaded sophomore jinx sets in on *Dead Enz Kidz Doin' Lifetime Bidz* (Soul Records, 1992, prod. Keith Shocklee, Grandmaster Flash, Terminator X, Gary G-Wiz). Although "Tap the Bottle" became a minor hit, the album's lackluster production and ho-hum songs suggest that the Teenagers have hit a creative dead end. The group does, however, deserve minor credit for trying to rework Rush's classic "Tom Sawyer" break in "Time to Make the Dough Nutz."

influences:

◀◀ 3rd Bass, Public Enemy

Spence D.

Young-Holt Unlimited

Formed 1965, in Chicago, IL.

Eldee Young, bass; Isaac "Red" Holt, percussion; Hysear Don Walker, piano.

In 1965, bassist Eldee Young and drummer Isaac "Red" Holt, two-thirds of the phenomenally successful Ramsey Lewis Trio, did the unthinkable: they left the group at the height of its success, in the wake of hits such as "The 'In' Crowd" and "Hang On Sloopy." They formed their own jazz-soul collective, the Young-Holt Trio (with the addition of pianist Hysear Don Walker), at Chicago's Brunswick Records. The group hit out of the box; its debut, the bouncingly funky "Wack Wack," was a Top 20 R&B single at the end of 1966. They released four more singles in their hip jazz-soul style, changing their name along the way to Young-Holt Unlimited. But the records had a cool reception, none making a dent on the R&B or pop charts. The tide turned in the autumn of 1968 with the release of "Soulful Strut," a mellow, magic-carpet-ride of a song with an infectious horn line, a funky rhythm, and a sweet, lyrical piano lead. An instrumental version of Barbara Acklin's "Am I the Same Girl" (issued prior to Acklin's vocal), "Strut" would be Young-Holt's biggest hit and one of the songs, along with Jackie Wilson's "(Your Love Keeps Lifting Me) Higher and Higher," that would be at the top in the Brunswick canon. Though their future looked hopeful, the group would return to the R&B chart only once more, and disappointingly, with "Just a Melody." With the flip of the decade, Young-Holt moved to Atlantic's Cotillion subsidiary, though the move failed to produce any chart hits.

what's available: The best of their Brunswick output is collected on *The Best of Young-Holt Unlimited* (Brunswick, 1995, prod. various). The set features the hits "Soulful Strut" and "Wack Wack," along with lesser known but equally striking tracks, such as their ain't-nothin'-but-a-party-y'all take on Johnnie Taylor's "Who's Makin' Love," the sly "Baby Your Light Is Out," and the fantastic live medley "The 'In' Crowd/Wade In the Water/Ain't There Something Money Can't Buy." The omission of "Just a Melody," YHU's only other charting single, is a shame, as is the exclusion of other great Young-Holt tracks that would easily have fit on the disc. Nevertheless, *The Best of Young-Holt Unlimited* shows how gifted Eldee Young and "Red" Holt are on these 12 coolly sophisticated tracks.

influences:

◀◀ Ramsey Lewis, Ahmad Jamal

▶▶ Vince Montana, Paul Weller, the Dust Brothers

Dana G. Smart

Young Lay

Born Lathan Williams, in Vallejo, CA.

Young Lay first started rapping in junior high, but it was while he was serving time at a ranch for juvenile lawbreakers that he really honed his rap skills. Eventually, fellow Vallejo rapper Mac Mall hooked Young Lay up with producer Khayree, who in turn introduced Lay to another NorCal rapper, Ray Luv. The four collaborated on "All About My Fetti," a gold single off the *New Jersey Drive* soundtrack, and Lay landed an album deal. Prior to the completion of his solo debut, though, he was shot in the head and spent several weeks in a coma. Miraculously, he recovered and was able to complete his album.

what's available: *Black 'N Dangerous* 𝄞𝄞𝄞 (Young Black Brotha/Atlantic, 1996, prod. Khayree, others) is a perfect example of the NorCal rap sound. Vallejo producer and multi-instrumentalist Khayree instills Lay's debut with slinky guitar, slithery keyboards, and just-plain-funky ambiance. Lay laces the groove with a competent flow, dishing out low-n-slow playa slang and even some quick-tongued verse.

influences:
◀◀ E-40, Mac Dre, Mac Mall, Ray Luv

Spence D.

Young M.C.

Born Marvin Young, May 10, 1967, in London, England.

Back in 1957, Chuck Berry's "School Days" celebrated the freedom of the three o'clock bell and the pleasures of the local juke joint. It drove parents nuts. In 1989, Young M.C.'s "Principal's Office"—a good-humored ditty about getting busted for passing notes in class—gave parents a reason to rejoice. At a time when hip-hop was being blamed for every societal evil under the sun, Young, who was raised in a middle-class neighborhood in Queens and educated at the University of Southern California, must've seemed like a godsend.

what to buy: Released on a start-up label owned by fellow Trojans Matt Dike and Michael Ross, Young's debut, *Stone Cold Rhymin'* 𝄞𝄞𝄞𝄞 (Delicious Vinyl, 1989) was one of the first rap albums to enjoy across-the-board appeal, reaching #9 on *Billboard*'s pop album chart in September of 1989. Rippling with clever turns of phrase and lightning-strike syntax, old-school flows like "I Come Off," "Non Stop," and "Roll with the Punches" leave little doubt as to Young's keen wit and mastery of mic calisthenics. Indeed, you can almost take him at his word when, in "Got More Rhymes," he quips: "I got more rhymes than the other guys do/They're just a monkey, I'm the whole damn zoo/I got more rhymes than water seen by a sailor/More than husbands of Elizabeth Taylor." Young's knack for phat grooves ain't too shabby either. Powered by a tangled bass vamp (courtesy of the Red Hot Chili Peppers' Flea) and Crystal Blake's delicious coo-cooing, "Bust a Move" is as good as it gets in the realm of Top 40 rap; save for the puritanical closing track—the Quincy Jones Jr.-produced "Just Say No"—so is the rest of *Stone Cold Rhymin'*.

the rest:
Return of the 1 Hit Wonder 𝄞𝄞 (Overall, 1997)

worth searching for: *Brainstorm* 𝄞𝄞𝄞 (Capitol, 1991) and *What's the Flavor?* 𝄞𝄞𝄞 (Capitol, 1993)—the two albums that

immediately followed *Stone Cold Rhymin'*—are both out of print. The former saw Young M.C. striving for social consciousness, while the latter added jazz stylings and edgier beats to the mix. If you can't get enough Young M.C., you might want to check the used CD bins.

influences:
◀◀ D.J. Jazzy Jeff & the Fresh Prince, Tone-Loc
▶▶ Skee-Lo, Ahmad

Greg Siegel

The Young Rascals /The Rascals

Formed 1965, in New York, NY. Disbanded 1972.

Felix Cavaliere, vocals, keyboards; Dino Danelli, drums; Eddie Brigati, vocals (1965–71); Gene Cornish, guitar (1965–71); Buzzy Feiten, guitar (1970–71); Robert Popwell, bass (1971–72); Ann Sutton, vocals (1971–72).

With three-part vocal harmonies rooted in R&B and floating atop an ocean of sound from Felix Cavaliere's Hammond B-3 organ, the Young Rascals were one of the original "blue-eyed soul" bands, bringing the energy and excitement of R&B to the masses by covering Wilson Pickett, Sir Mack Rice, and other soul stirrers. Wearing Little Lord Fauntleroy outfits at nightclub gigs across Long Island, Manhattan, and New Jersey, the Young Rascals offered an American alternative to the British invaders. The band's uptempo cover of the Olympics' "Good Lovin'," its first #1 single, erupts with such rhythmic fury that it endures as one of the greatest dance-rock numbers ever recorded. The band tried a softer touch with the syrupy "Groovin'," another chart-topper that, unfortunately, marked a shift away from raw R&B to polished pop. In 1967, the Rascals dropped the "Young" from its name and the knickers from their stage show, seeking a maturity and awareness appropriate to the times. It was a good fit for a while, as heard in "See," "Ray of Hope," and "People Got to Be Free," the group's last #1 hit. The Rascals experimented with lengthy jazz episodes—working with guests such as David Sanborn, Ron Carter, Hubert Laws, and Alice Coltrane—before fading from the charts and dissolving in 1972. There have been periodic, short-term reunions since, and the group was inducted into the Rock and Roll Hall of Fame in 1997, where it spent much of its time backstage singing doo wop numbers with fellow inductees George Clinton and the Parliaments.

what to buy: *Time Piece: The Rascals' Greatest Hits* 𝄞𝄞𝄞𝄞𝄞 (Atlantic, 1968, prod. the Rascals) crystallizes the band's most exuberant years into one tidy package of essentials ("Good Lovin'," "Mustang Sally," "I Ain't Gonna Eat Out My Heart Anymore," "You Better Run," and "Groovin'"). The two-disc, 44-song set *The Rascals Anthology, 1965–1972* ♫♫♫♫ (Rhino, 1992, prod. various) is also a superb overview from Young Rascals to the old, the good, the not-so-good, and the awful ("Real Thing," "Brother Tree").

what to buy next: The group's debut album, *The Young Rascals* ♫♫♫♫ (Atlantic, 1966/Warner Special Products, 1988, prod. the Young Rascals, Tom Dowd, Arif Mardin), can't be beat for sheer energy and exuberance, even though the group only wrote one of its tunes.

what to avoid: After Brigati and Cornish left, the Rascals lost their R&B heart and replaced it with an artificial jazz pump. Pull the plug on the lifeless *Peaceful World* **woof!** (Atlantic, 1971, prod. Felix Cavaliere) and *The Island of Real* **woof!** (Atlantic, 1972, prod. Felix Cavaliere).

the rest:
Collections ♫♫♫ (Atlantic, 1966/Warner Special Products, 1988)
Groovin' ♫♫♫ (Atlantic, 1967)
Once Upon a Dream ♫♫ (Atlantic, 1968/Rhino, 1993)
Freedom Suite ♫♫♫ (Atlantic, 1969/Rhino, 1993)
See ♫♫ (Atlantic, 1969)
Search and Nearness ♫ (Atlantic, 1971)
The Ultimate Rascals ♫♫♫♫ (Warner Special Products, 1986)
Groovin' ♫♫♫♫ (Warner Special Products, 1988)
The Very Best of the Rascals ♫♫♫♫♫ (Rhino, 1993)
Good Lovin' ♫♫♫♫ (Rhino, 1993)

solo outings:
Felix Cavaliere:
Felix Cavaliere ♫♫♫ (Bearsville, 1974)
Destiny ♫♫ (Bearsville, 1975)
Treasure ♫♫♫ (Epic, 1976)
Castles in the Air ♫♫ (Epic, 1980)
Dreams in Motion ♫♫ (Karambolage, 1994)

Eddie Brigati:
Brigati ♫♫ (Elektra, 1976)

influences:
◀◀ Ray Charles, Booker T. Jones, Stax-Volt, Motown

▶▶ Hall & Oates, Huey Lewis & the News, Robert Palmer, Gin Blossoms

David Yonke

Paul Young
Born January 17, 1956, in Luton, Bedfordshire, England.

The son of an auto plant worker who logged some time in the factory himself, Paul Young developed a simultaneous affection for New Wave rock and 1960s soul into a singular solo voice during the 1980s. Starting as a semi-pro bassist with Kat Koland and the Kool Kats, he gained early notice as lead vocalist for the British soul/horn band the Q-Tips. Young was signed to a solo deal by Columbia Records in 1981, eventually dropping a record that expertly blended the New Wave and dance sounds of the day with old-time soul vocal gymnastics, presenting covers of both Marvin Gaye's "Wherever I Lay My Hat (That's My Home)" and Joy Division's "Love Will Tear Us Apart." His next efforts further refined that signature sound, blunting the force of his soul sources with increasing amounts of pop flavor. Though a passable songwriter himself, most of Young's big hits were covers of other artists' material, from Gaye to Daryl Hall and John Oates. Unfortunately, the proportion of slickness to soul in his records kept tilting toward pop blandness until U.S. listeners—who had never fully embraced him anyway—stopped caring.

what to buy: Young's debut record, *No Parlez* ♫♫♫♫ (Columbia, 1983, prod. Laurie Latham), is both his most eclectic and impressive recorded effort, bridging the gap between arty New Wave and funky soul sounds in a vibrant new way. From the dreamy cover of Marvin Gaye's obscure ballad "Wherever I Lay My Hat (That's My Home)" to the drum machine and sequencer-fed dance excursion, "Sex," and atmospheric lead-off single "Come Back and Stay," this record offers an inspired mix of styles unified by Young's own impassioned blue-eyed soul vocal licks.

what to buy next: His second album, *The Secret of Association* ♫♫♫♫ (Columbia, 1985, prod. Laurie Latham), is the only other Young record that doesn't completely sacrifice passion for precision, as the singer allows a little funky heat to build on cuts like the fretless bass-fueled dance workouts "I'm Gonna Tear Your Playhouse Down," "Bite the Hand That Feeds," and "Hot Fun." But the only hit here, a pop-ified cover of Hall and Oates' "Every Time You Go Away," hints of the mistakes to come.

what to avoid: The rest of Young's catalog, basically. For his next two records, the singer seemed to turn his back on the very soul influences that made him a success in the first place, with *Between Two Fires* **woof!** (Columbia, 1986, prod. Paul Young, Hugh Padgham) drowning in its own pop slickness (and a preponderance of Young-penned tunes) and *Other Voices*

Paul Young (© Ken Settle)

6/4/0 *zapp*

woof! (Columbia, 1990, prod. Nile Rodgers, Peter Wolf) rocking out a collection of forgettable songs.

the rest:
From Time to Time: The Singles Collection ✇✇✇ (Columbia, 1991)
The Crossing ✇✇✇ (Columbia, 1993)
Reflections ✇✇✇ (Columbia, 1994)
Paul Young ✇✇✇ (Columbia, 1997)

worth searching for: A rare recording of a pre-stardom Young performing with the Q-Tips in concert, *Live at Last* ✇✇✇ (Stoic Records/Rewind Records) is available only as an import and offers early versions of the singer's take on Smokey Robinson's "Tracks of My Tears" and his own strongest original tune, "Broken Man."

influences:
◀◀ Rod Stewart, Paul Rodgers, Robert Palmer, Marvin Gaye
▶▶ Go West

Eric Deggans

Zapp
/Zapp & Roger
Formed late 1970s, in Dayton, OH.

Roger Troutman, lead vocals, talkbox, various instruments; Lester Troutman, drums, percussion; Larry Troutman, congas, percussion; Zapp (Tony) Troutman, bass; Carl Cowen, horns.

A longtime friendship with Bootsy Collins and too much free time to play around with an electronic voice-altering device led to the creation of Zapp—a quirky minor satellite act in George Clinton's vast P-Funk universe—by Ohio's Troutman brothers in the late 1970s. Zapp founder and do-everything mastermind Roger Troutman released an early LP under the band name Roger and the Human Body. That album went nowhere. Then Troutman held old pal Bootsy to a promise to help him if Collins ever became successful. Troutman landed a gig with Funkadelic (playing on the *Electric Spanking of War Babies* album), which led to Collins and Troutman co-producing the 1980 debut LP for Zapp (the nickname of one of Troutman's brothers). Their music, distinguished by smooth funk rhythms and Troutman singing through a processor that gave his voice a

reedy, robotic sound, became a change-of-pace favorite of club DJs with songs like "More Bounce to the Ounce" and the #1 R&B hits "Dance Floor" and the remake of "I Heard It Through the Grapevine." Troutman eventually spun off as a separate but equal entity, releasing solo albums as Roger in addition to working with Zapp. The group frequently opened for P-Funk in concert and continues to perform live. Roger served as a guest artist on 1990s albums by Tupac Shakur, Johnny Gill, and Curtis Mayfield.

what to buy: Zapp and Roger have two "greatest hits" collections in print, but Troutman's eccentric vocal style can wear thin quickly. Of the two, *All the Greatest Hits* ✇✇✇ (Reprise, 1993, prod. Roger Troutman) offers a 17-song dose of choice moments from both Zapp the group and Roger the soloist, which should be more than enough to suffice. A remix of "(In the) Midnight Hour—Live '93" is a highlight, along with all the tracks Zapp fans would expect: "More Bounce to the Ounce," "I Heard It Through the Grapevine," "Dance Floor," "Do It Roger," and "Computer Love."

what to buy next: *Zapp* ✇✇✇ (Warner Bros., 1980, prod. Bootsy Collins, Roger Troutman) is noteworthy for the production inspiration of Collins (absent on all subsequent albums), the energetic performance given to what was then a fresh concept, and a couple of songs too odd to ever appear in a "best of" compilation, but intriguing nonetheless: "Be Alright," an absurdly drippy ballad, and the electric blues jump "Coming Home," the first evidence of Troutman's affection for the blues.

what to avoid: The only Roger solo album still in print, *Unlimited!* ✇ (Reprise, 1987, prod. Roger Troutman) suggests that his creativity as well as his gimmickry were wearing thin.

the rest:
Zapp II ✇✇✇ (Warner Bros., 1989)
The New Zapp IV U ✇✇✇ (Warner Bros., 1989)
Zapp V ✇✇ (Reprise, 1989)
The Compilation: Greatest Hits II ✇✇✇ (Reprise, 1996)

worth searching for: The earliest Roger solo LPs, particularly his first, *The Many Facets of Roger* ✇✇✇ (Warner Bros., 1981), which confirmed him as one of the most peculiar and distinctive mainstream funk artists in history. It's available as a Japanese import.

influences:
◀◀ George Clinton, James Brown, Bootsy Collins, Marvin Gaye, Buddy Guy, Wilson Pickett
▶▶ Chess, Prince, Cybotron

Jim McFarlin

Zhane

Formed 1990, in Philadelphia, PA.

Renee Neufville, vocals; Jean Norris, vocals.

This harmonizing duo met while attending Temple University and started singing together when both broke up with boyfriends within the same 24-hour period. Given a hip-hop edge by Kay Gee of the rap group Naughty by Nature, they formulated a smooth, sing-along style dance groove. Neither their voices nor their songwriting talents are extraordinary, but a certain earnestness and around-the-way-girl familiarity permeates Zhane's tunes, setting them apart from their overproduced peers. A jazz vibe only hinted at on their debut album is explored more deeply on the follow-up—a sign of growth to some, but a departure of sorts for those seeking another album of party jams.

what to buy: O.K., so *Pronounced Jah-Nay* ✧✧✧✧ (Motown, 1994, prod. various) isn't exactly polished. But try to avoid doing a little dance when infectious party cuts like "Hey Mr. D.J." begin to thump.

what to buy next: *Saturday Night* ✧✧✧✧ (Motown, 1997, prod. various) successfully walks the line between moody, almost-jazz grooves and party time, though the latter has a "been there" feeling to it.

worth searching for: "Shame," a cut on the soundtrack to the 1994 film *A Low Down Dirty Shame,* confidently updates the Evelyn "Champagne" King classic.

influences:
◀◀ Evelyn "Champagne" King, Maze featuring Frankie Beverly

Franklin Paul

Zimbabwe Legit

Akiro Ndlovu; Dumisani Ndlovu.

The hook with this duo was that the two members were natives of Zimbabwe who rapped in their native tongue. What Zimbabwe Legit turned out to be, though, was an exercise in whimsy by their label, Hollywood BASIC.

what's available: Their only release, *Zimbabwe Legit* ✧ (Hollywood BASIC, 1992, prod. DJ Shadow, Mista Lawnge, Phase 5, others), is a tough call. The EP's lead song, "Doin' Damage In My Native Language," is completely forgettable, as are the different vocal and instrumental mixes from such producers as Black Sheep's Mista Lawnge. But the EP is completely worth the money—and might even have collector-type value, too—because of "Shadow's Legitimate Mix," a seven-minute opus that marks the official recording debut of DJ Shadow. The instrumental cut, based on Idris Muhammad's version of Grover Washington Jr.'s "Loran's Dance," was actually supposed to have vocals, but BASIC head Dave Funkenklein was so enamored by Shadow's version that he left it as is. A year later, Mo Wax head James Lavelle heard the song and was inspired to track Shadow down and sign him.

influences:
◀◀ Fab 5 Freddy, Last Poets
▶▶ DJ Shadow

Jazzbo

musicHound

Resources and
Other Information

Books, Magazines, and Newspapers

Web Pages

Music Festivals

Radio Stations

Record Labels

Five-Bone Albums

Compilation Albums

Can't get enough R&B? Here are some books, magazines, and newspapers you can check out for further information. Happy reading!

Books

BIOGRAPHIES

As Nasty As They Wanna Be : The Uncensored Story of Luther Campbell of the 2 Live Crew
Luther Campbell and John R. Miller (Barricade Books, 1992)

Bessie
Chris Albertson (Stein & Day, 1985)

Bessie Smith (Out Lines)
Jackie Kay (Absolute Press, 1997)

Between Each Line of Pain and Glory: My Life Story
Gladys Knight (Hyperion, 1997)

Brother Ray: Ray Charles' Own Story
Ray Charles, with David Ritz (Da Capo Press, 1992)

Dancing in the Street: Confessions of a Motown Diva
Martha Reeves and Mark Bego (Hyperion, 1994)

Divided Soul: The Life of Marvin Gaye
David Ritz (Da Capo Press, 1991)

Don't Block the Blessings: Revelations of a Lifetime
Patti LaBelle (Putnam, 1996)

Elvis
Albert Goldman (McGraw-Hill, 1981)

Elvis
Dave Marsh (Times Books, 1982)

Elvis and Me
Priscilla Beaulieu Presley and Sandra Harmon (G.P. Putnam's Sons, 1985)

Goodnight Sweetheart, Goodnight: The Story of the Spaniels
Richard G. Carter (August Press, 1994)

I Make My Own Rules
LL Cool J (St. Martin's, 1997)

I Will Survive
Gloria Gaynor (St. Martin's, 1997)

Jackie Wilson: Lonely Teardrops
Tony Douglas (Omnibus Press, 1997)

James Brown: The Godfather of Soul
James Brown, with Bruce Tucker (Thunder's Mouth Press, 1997)

Jimi Hendrix: The Final Days
Tony Brown (Omnibus Press, 1997)

Let the Good Times Roll: The Story of Louis Jordan and His Music (Michigan American Music Series)
John Chilton (University of Michigan Press, 1997)

Living in America: The Soul Saga of James Brown
Cynthia Rose (Serpents Tail, 1991)

Miss Rhythm: The Autobiography of Ruth Brown, Rhythm and Blues Legend
Ruth Brown and Andrew Yule (FINE, 1996)

Prince: Inside the Purple Reign
Jon Bream (Collier Books, 1984)

Rap: Portraits and Lyrics of a Generation of Black Rockers
Bill Adler (St. Martin's, 1991)

Save the Last Dance for Me: The Musical Legacy of the Drifters, 1953–1993 (Rock & Roll Remembrances, No. 11)
Tony Allan and Faye Treadwell (Popular Culture Ink, 1994)

The Spice Girls
Anna Louise Golden (Ballantine Books, 1997)

Stars of Soul and Rhythm & Blues: Top Recording Artists and Showstopping Performers, from Memphis and Motown to Now
Lee Hildebrand (Watson Guptill, 1994)

The Temptations
Ted Cox (Chelsea House, 1997)

Tupac Shakur
Editors of *Vibe* magazine, ed. (Crown, 1997)

You Send Me: The Life and Times of Sam Cooke
Daniel Wolff, S.R. Crain, Clifton White, and G. David Tenenbaum (Quill, 1996)

GENERAL INTEREST

A 2 Z : The Book of Rap & Hip-Hop Slang
Lois Slavsky, I.E. Mozeson, and Dani Reyes Mozeson (Boulevard, 1995)

A wop bop a loo bop, A lop bam boom: The Golden Age of Rock
Nik Cohn (Da Capo Press, 1996)

All Music Guide to Rock
Michael Erlewine, Vladimir Bogdanov, and Chris Woodstra, ed. (Miller Freeman, 1995)

Beale Black & Blue: Life and Music on Black America's Main Street
Margaret McKee and Fred Chisenhall (Louisiana State University Press, 1993)

Big Al Pavlow's The R&B Book: A Disc-History of Rhythm & Blues
Big Al Pavlow (Music House, 1983)

The Billboard Book of Number One Rhythm & Blues Hits
Adam White and Fred Bronson (Billboard Publications, 1993)

Black and White Blues
Marc Norberg and B. Martin Pederson (Graphis Press, 1996)

Black Music
Leroi Jones (William Morrow, 1968)

Black Noise: Rap Music and Black Culture in Contemporary America
Tricia Rose (Wesleyan University Press, 1994)

The Blackwell Guide to Soul Recordings
Robert Pruter, ed. (Blackwell, 1993)

Blue Rhythms: Six Lives in Rhythm and Blues (Music in American Life)
Chip Deffaa (University of Illinois Press, 1996)

Blues People: Negro Music in White America
Imamu Amiri Baraka (William Morrow & Co., 1983)

Bring the Noise: A Guide to Rap Music and Hip-Hop Culture
Havelock Nelson and Michael A. Gonzales (Harmony Books, 1991)

Bronzeville: A History of Chicago Rhythm & Blues
Oscar A. Jackson (Heno, 1995)

Buppies, B-Boys, Baps & Bohos: Notes on Post-Soul Black Culture
Nelson George (HarperCollins, 1992)

Chicago Soul
Robert Pruter (University of Illinois Press, 1992)

Christgau's Record Guide: The '80s
Robert Christgau (Da Capo Press, 1994)

The Death of Rhythm & Blues
Nelson George (Obelisk, 1991)

The Early Years of Rhythm & Blues: Focus on Houston
Alan B. Govenar (Rice University Press, 1990)

Encyclopedia of Pop, Rock, and Soul
Irwin Stambler (St. Martin's, 1989)

Encyclopedia of Rock Stars
Dafydd Rees and Luke Crampton (Dorling Kindersley, 1996)

Fight the Power: Rap, Race, and Reality
Chuck D. and Yusuf Jah (Delacorte Press, 1997)

Find That Tune: An Index to Rock, Folk-Rock, Disco, and Soul in Collections, Vol. 2
Sue Sharma, with William Gargan, ed. (Neal Schuman Pub., 1988)

Funk: The Music, the People, and the Rhythm of the One
Rickey Vincent (St. Martin's Griffin, 1996)

Girl Groups: The Story of a Sound
Alan Betrock (Delilah, 1982)

Give the Drummers Some! The Great Drummers of R&B, Funk, and Soul
Jim Payne, with Harry Weinger, ed. (Warner Bros., 1997)

Goin' Back to Memphis: A Century of Blues, Rock 'n' Roll, and Glorious Soul
James Dickerson (Simon & Schuster, 1996)

Group Harmony: Behind the Rhythm and the Blues
Todd R. Baptista (TRB Enterprises, 1996)

Heart & Soul: A Celebration of Black Music Style in America, 1930–1975
Bob Merlis and Davin Seay (Stewart Tabori & Chang, 1997)

The Heart of Rock and Roll
Dave Marsh (Penguin, 1989)

Hip-Hop: The Illustrated History of Breakdancing, Rap Music, and Graffiti
Steve Hager (St. Martin's, 1984)

I Hear You Knockin': The Sound of New Orleans Rhythm and Blues
Jeff Hannusch (Swallow, 1985)

Joel Whitburn's Top R&B Singles, 1942–1995
Joel Whitburn (Record Research, 1996)

Making Tracks: Atlantic Records and the Growth of a Multi-Billion Dollar Industry
Charlie Gillet (Souvenir, 1974)

Nowhere to Run
Gerri Hirshey (Da Capo Press, 1995)

Poetic License: In Poem and Song
Curtis Mayfield (Dove Books, 1996)

Rap Attack: African Jive to New York Hip-Hop
David Toop (South End Press, 1984)

Rap Attack 2: African Rap to Global Hip-Hop
David Toop (Serpent's Tail, 1991)

Rap Whoz Who: The World of Rap Music
Steven Stancell (Schirmer Books, 1996)

Rhythm and Blues in New Orleans
John Broyen (Pelican, 1983)

The Rhythm and Blues Story
Gene Busnar (J. Messner, 1985)

Rhythm and the Blues
Jerry Wexler, with David Ritz (Random House, 1993)

Rhythm Oil
Stanley Booth (Pantheon, 1991)

Rock Albums of the '70s: A Critical Guide
Robert Christgau (Da Capo Press, 1990)

Rolling Stone Album Guide
Anthony DeCurtis and James Henke, ed., with Holly George-Warren (Random House, 1992)

The Roots & Rhythm Guide to Rock
Frank Scott and Al Ennis (A Cappella Books, 1993)

Say It Loud: The Story of Rap Music
K. Maurice Jones (Millbrook Press, 1994)

Signifying Rappers: Rap and Race in the Urban Present
Mark Costello and Davis Foster Wallace (Echo Press, 1990)

The Soul Book
Ian Hoare, Clive Anderson, Tony Cummings, and Simon Frith (Methuen, 1975)

Soul Music A–Z
Hugh Gregory (Da Capo Press, 1995)

Soul Music: The Birth of a Sound in Black America
Michael Haralambos (Da Capo Press, 1985)

Soulsville, USA: The Story of Stax Records
Robert Bowman (Macmillan, 1997)

The Sound of Philadelphia
Tony Cummings (Methuen, 1975)

Swamp Pop: Cajun and Creole Rhythm and Blues (American Made Music Series)
Shane K. Bernard (University Press of Mississippi, 1996)

Sweet Soul Music: Rhythm and Blues and the Southern Dream of Freedom
Peter Guralnick (HarperCollins, 1986)

They All Sang on the Corner: A Second Look at New York City's Rhythm and Blues Vocal Groups
Philip Groia (Phillie Dee Enterprises, 1983)

A Touch of Classic Soul: Soul Singers of the Early 1970s
Marc E. Taylor (Aloiv Publications, 1996)

The Ultimate Soul Music Trivia Book: 501 Questions and Answers about Motown, Rhythm & Blues, and More
Bobby Bennett and Sarah Smith (Citadel Press, 1997)

Up From the Cradle of Jazz: New Orleans Music Since World War II
Jason Berry (Da Capo Press, 1986)

Upside Your Head! Rhythm and Blues on Central Avenue
Johnny Otis (Wesleyan University Press, 1995)

Where Did Our Love Go? The Rise and Fall of the Motown Sound
Nelson George (St. Martin's, 1987)

Will You Still Love Me Tomorrow? Girl Groups from the '50s On
Charlotte Greig (Virago, 1989)

Magazines and Newspapers

Billboard
1515 Broadway
New York, NY 10036
(212) 764-7300

Blues & Rhythm
1 Cliffe Ln.
Thornton, Bradford, BD13 3DX, U.K.
44 (0) 1234 826158

CMJ New Music Monthly
11 Middleneck Rd.
Suite 400
Great Neck, NY 11021
(516) 466-6000

Down Beat
102 N. Haven Rd.
Elmhurst, IL 60126
(800) 535-7496

Goldmine
700 E. State St.
Jola, WI 54990
(715) 445-4612

ICE
PO Box 3043
Santa Monica, CA 90408
(800) 647-4ICE

Musician
1515 Broadway
New York, NY 10036
(212) 536-5208

Rap Pages
8484 Wilshire Blvd.
Beverly Hills, CA 90211
(213) 651-5400

Rap Sheet
6733 S. Sepulveda
Suite 106
Los Angeles, CA 90045
(310) 670-7200

Rolling Stone
1290 Avenue of the Americas
2nd Floor
New York, NY 10104
(212) 484-1616

The Source
215 Park Ave. South
11th Floor
New York, NY 10003
(212) 253-8700

URB
1680 N. Vine St.
Suite 1012
Los Angeles, CA 90028

VIBE
205 Lexington Ave.
3rd Floor
New York, NY 10016
(212) 522-7092

R&B is everywhere, even out in cyber-space. Point your Web browser to these pages for more information on your favorite artists or R&B in general.

Artists

Aaliyah
http://members.aol.com/TommyChill
/Aaliyah-Main.html
http://www.geocities.com/SunsetStrip/
Club/4654/

Gregory Abbott
http://www.aimcmc.com/abbott.html

Paula Abdul
http://www2.southwind.net/~ksims/
abdul/Abdul.html
http://www.virginrecords.com/artists/
VR.cgi?ARTIST_NAME=Paula_
Abdul

Ace of Base
http://www.aristarec.com/aob/
http://www.dacc.cc.il.us/~mulberry/
music/aceofbase/
http://home.earthlink.net/~hanner/

Oleta Adams
http://www.decca.com/polygram/
mercury/artists/adams_oleta/
oleta.html

Akinyele
http://www.sonicnet.com/sonicore/
chat/bios/bioakinyele.html

Gerald Albright
http://www.cnotes.com/cnotes.artists/
albright.html

Arthur Alexander
http://www.fame2.com/fame/alexande.
htm

Louis Armstrong
http://www.trb.ayuda.com/~dnote/
louisa.html
http://192.108.254.18/~rfrederi/
wlouis01.htm

Arrested Development
http://www.eden.com/magical/45/
arrested_development.html

Art of Noise
http://rtt.colorado.edu/~baur/aon/
aon.html

Ashford & Simpson
http://www.ashfordandsimpson.com/

Patti Austin
http://www.mca.com/grp/grp/artists/
austin.rel.html

Average White Band
http://www.paulin.demon.co.uk/AWB
WEB/CONTENT/main.htm

Roy Ayers
http://www.soros.org.mk/mk/skopje/
jazz/en/roy.htm
http://www.music.sony.com/Music/
ArtistInfo/RoyAyers.html

Babyface
http://members.aol.com/icefm/baby
face.htm

Erykah Badu
http://www.kedar.com/kedar20.htm
http://www.wsu.edu:8080/~dstrolis/
badu1.html

Anita Baker
http://www.prism.gatech.edu/~kd26/
menu/a-frame.html

LaVern Baker
http://rockhall.com/induct/bakelave.
html

Hank Ballard & the Midnighters
http://rockhall.com/induct/ballhank.
html
http://www.onlinetalent.com/Ballard
_homepage.html

Afrika Bambaataa
http://www.sonicnet.com/sonicore/
chat/bios/bioafrika.html

The Bar-Kays
http://www.rsimusic.com/bar-kays.
htm
http://www.abc.se/~m8877/
TheBarKays.html

Fontella Bass
http://members.gnn.com/concerted/
bass.htm
http://pilot.msu.edu/user/andrycoc/
fontella.html

Shirley Bassey
http://www.geocities.com/Broadway/
Stage/3331/

Beastie Boys/DJ Hurricane/Money Mark
http://www.musick.com/BeastieBoys/
Press/Newspaper/
http://www.buzznet.com/03/beats/
4080/hurra/index.html
http://www.cmd.uu.se/AcidJazz/
Backup/1996-Apr/0401.html

http://www.sonicnet.com/sonicore/
chat/bios/biomoneymark.html

The Beatnuts
http://www.streetsound.com/inter
views/intbeatnuts66.html

Beck
http://www.rain.org/~truck/beck/
http://pages.infinit.net/zmehari/

Regina Belle
http://www.music.sony.com/Music/
ArtistInfo/ReginaBelle/reachin.htm

Chuck Berry
http://www.surfin.com/TheBlueFlame
Cafe/Chuck_Berry.html
http://shell.ihug.co.nz/~mauricef/
frames9.htm

Big Chief
http://www.biddeford.com/~gighag/

Big Daddy Kane
http://www.mca.com/mca_records/
library/bios/bio.bigdaddy.html

Biz Markie
http://hamp.hampshire.edu/~edgF91/
BIZ.html

Black Moon
http://www.streetsound.com/inter
views/intblkmn71.html

Blackbyrds
http://www.fantasyjazz.com/black
byrds.html

Blahzay Blahzay
http://www.decca.com/polygram/
mercury/artists/blah-zay/blah-zay.
html

Bobby "Blue" Bland
http://malaco.com/blues/bbb/index.
html

Mary J. Blige
http://stallion.jsums.edu/~awil0997/
mary.htm

Bloods & Crips
http://www.lowyzucker.com/new/
bloods.html

Blues Brothers
http://www.cs.monash.edu.au/~
pringle/bluesbros/section2.html
http://www.math.unl.edu/~augustyn/
Sounds/BluesBrothers.shtml

Gary U.S. Bonds
http://www.crl.com/www/users/ts/
tsimon/bonds.htm

Bone Thugs-N-Harmony/Flesh-N-Bone
http://members.aol.com/bonez357/
index.htm
http://www.sonicnet.com/sonicore/
chat/bios/biofleshnbone.html

Boogie Down Productions/KRS-One
http://www.uvm.edu/~jdjohnso/
teacher.html

Boogie Monsters
http://www.krib.com/links/hiphop.
html

James Booker
http://www.gis.net/~gottlieb/booker
_essay.html

Booker T. & the MG's
http://www.music.sony.com/Music/
ArtistInfo/BookerTAndTheMGs_
ThatsTheWayItShouldBe.html
http://www.rockhall.com//induct/
bookert.html

Jean-Paul Bourelly
http://www.w2.com/trippin.html

David Bowie/Tin Machine
http://www.davidbowie.com/2.0/
http://www.algonet.se/~bassman/
BOWIE.html

Boyz II Men
http://www.geocities.com/Hollywood/
Lot/2302/
http://www.cyber-dyne.com/~Jenh/

Brand New Heavies
http://www.dvinyl.com/bnh/html/
bnh.html
http://www.webpro.se/bnh/

Brand Nubian/Grand Puba/Masters of Ceremony/Sadat X
http://www.loud.com/sadat/sadat.
html

Brandy
http://www.usvi.net/cobex/people/
matthew/html/brandy.htm
http://www-und.ida.liu.se/~andwa984/
musik/brandy.html

Toni Braxton
http://www.lafacerecords.com/
braxton.html
http://www.geocities.com/Sunset
Strip/8614/tonibraxton.html

James Brown
http://www.onlinetalent.com/
MRBrown_homepage.html

Shirley Brown
http://malaco.com/blues/shirleyb/

Peabo Bryson
http://www.music.sony.com/Music/
ArtistInfo/PeaboBryson.html

Buckshot Lafonque
http://www.netcetera.nl/marsalis.
html

B.U.M.S.
http://www.gointeract.com/instinct/
bums.html

Solomon Burke
http://www.moosenet.com/burke.
html

C+C Music Factory
http://www.music.sony.com/Music/
ArtistInfo/C%2bCMusicFactory_
AnythingGoes.html

Cadillacs
http://bmi.com/repertoire/awards/
cadlacs.html

Shirley Caesar
http://www.gospelroots.com/
mainmenu/shirleycaesar.html

Cameo
http://stud-www.uni-marburg.de/~
Cagalj/

Tevin Campbell
http://www.wbr.com/tevin/

Camp Lo
http://www.hippatodahoppa.com/ro/

Mariah Carey
http://www.music.sony.com/Music/
ArtistInfo/MariahCarey/
http://www.geocities.com/Sunset
Strip/8218/

Cella Dwellas
http://www.sonicnet.com/sonicore/
chat/bios/biocella.html

Gene Chandler
http://www.crl.com/www/users/ts/
tsimon/chandler.htm

Ray Charles
http://www.raycharles.com/
http://www.mrshowbiz.com/starbios/
raycharles/index.html

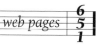

http://www.surfin.com/TheBlueFlame
Cafe/Ray_Charles.html
http://www.fantasyjazz.com/charles.
html

Chubby Checker
http://scriptorium.lib.duke.edu/sgo/
texts/checker.html
http://www.ozemail.com.au/~facerg/
sound.htm

Neneh Cherry
http://www.sheenaweb.com/neneh/

Chic
http://www.slip.net/~spage/chic/

Lou Christie
http://www.crl.com/www/users/ts/
tsimon/christie.htm

Otis Clay
http://centerstage.net/chicago/music/
whoswho/OtisClay.html

Jimmy Cliff
http://www.onf.ca/FMT/E/musi/Cliff_
Jimmy.html

George Clinton
http://www.music.sony.com/Music/
CDEXTRA/george.html

The Coasters
http://t-e-i.com/coasters.html

Natalie Cole
http://www.atlcom.net/~tac1/natalie.
html

Bootsy Collins
http://www.netcetera.nl/collins.html

Color Me Badd
http://www.revolution-online.com/
CMB/bio.html

The Commodores
http://t-e-i.com/commodores.html

Sam Cooke
http://www.eyeneer.com/Labels/
Abcko/night.beat.html

Coolio
http://home1.swipnet.se/~w-10840/

The Counts
http://www.acerecords.co.uk/gotrt/
aug96/counts01.html

The Coup
http://www.tc.umn.edu/nlhome/
g368/nola0010/

Randy Crawford
http://www.blackworld.com/proffs/
artistes/crawford.htm

Robert Cray
http://www.vivanet.com/~catbauer/
bio/bobcray1.html

Crucial Conflict
http://members.aol.com/raplord/
index.html

The Crystals
http://www.crl.com/www/users/ts/
tsimon/crystals.htm

Culture Club/Boy George
http://www-personal.umich.edu/%7
Egeena/boygeorge.html

Cypress Hill
http://www.music.sony.com/Music/
ArtistInfo/CypressHill/index.html
http://reality.sgi.com/employees/
sprout_corp/vibrations/cypress/

Da Brat
http://www.music.sony.com/Music/
ArtistInfo/DaBrat/Bio2.html

D'Angelo
http://www.seanet.com/~dean206/
dangelo.htm

Terence Trent D'Arby
http://comspan.com/BIGSTAR/
WHITENITES/TTD.html

Bobby Darin
http://www.bxscience.edu/alum/
darin.html

Das Efx
http://www.sonicnet.com/sonicore/
chat/bios/biodasefx2.html

Sammy Davis Jr.
http://www.schoolroom.com/videos/
v12092.htm
http://www.io.org/~wad/sambio.
html
http://www.skypoint.com/members/
happyjac/samdisc.html

Tyrone Davis
http://www.jazzcentralstation.com/
jcs/station/jazzdest/festivals/
deltablu/artists/davis.html

Taylor Dayne
http://pouncer.simplenet.com/taylor/

De La Soul
http://people.clarkson.edu/~currieat/
dela/faq.html

http://pathfinder.com/altculture/
aentries/d/dexlaxso.html

Deee-Lite
http://www.pathfinder.com/altculture
/aentries/d/deeexlite.html
http://gene.wins.uva.nl/~stkok/
deeelite.html

Def Jef
http://www.island.co.uk/cat/cat_d/
defjef.html

Defunkt
http://www.rykodisc.com/3/catalog/
album/41.html
http://www.fred.net/jbowie/classic.
html

**Del Tha Funk Homosapien/Souls of
Mischief/Casual/Extra Prolific**
http://www.hieroglyphics.com/stinke/
artists/souls/
http://www.rcavictor.com/rca/diehard/
extra-p.html

The Delfonics
http://www.onlinetalent.com/
Delfonics_homepage.html

Delinquent Habits
http://www.peeps.com/dhabits/bio.
html

Dexy's Midnight Runners
http://ubl.com/artists/003264.html

Manu Dibango
http://www.ina.fr/music/Artistes/
manu_dibango/index.en.html

Bo Diddley
http://www.codeblue-records.com/
diddley.html

Dion & the Belmonts
http://www.wintermute.co.uk/users/
gwatson/

Dirty Dozen Brass Band
http://www.rounder.com/rounder/
catalog/byartist/d/dirty_dozen_
brass_band/

Digital Underground/Raw Fusion
http://www.peeps.com/critique/
c_du_index.html
http://www.schmooze.net/pwcasual/
zines/exclaim/9610/nf/reviews/
nxt/03.htm

DJ Kool
http://www.euronet.nl/users/schalk/
lyrics/lyricsdjkoolletmeclearyourt
hroat.html
http://american.recordings.com/
cgi-bin/imagemap/kool?218,148

DJ Krush
http://www.fly.co.uk/krush1.htm

DJ Quik
http://www.geocities.com/Hollywood/
1561/quik.html

DJ Shadow
http://www.spy.net/~hoover/shadow.
html

Dr. Dre
http://www.aswellas.se/drdre/sounds.
html

Dr. John
http://www.netcetera.nl/john-dr.html
http://www.drjohn.com/

Tha Dogg Pound
http://www.hotwired.com/music/95/
51/dogg.html

Fats Domino
http://www.crl.com/www/users/ts/
tsimon/domino.htm
http://www.glue.umd.edu/~lukey/
fats/fats.htm

Lee Dorsey
http://www.crl.com/www/users/ts/
tsimon/dorsey.htm

The Dove Shack
http://www.umr.edu/~rabrooks/
index.html

The Drifters
http://www.srv.net/~roxtar/drifters.
html

Dru Down
http://www.buzznet.com/04/beats/
4080/drudown/index.html

George Duke
http://www.wins.uva.nl/~heederik/
zappa/faq/whatever/GeorgeDuke.
html

Earth, Wind & Fire
http://home.sn.no/~gege/ewf/

Sheena Easton
http://www.sheenaweb.com/

Eazy-E
http://www.pathfinder.com/altculture/
aentries/e/eazyxe.html
http://users.deltanet.com/users/rick/
eazy.html

Duke Ellington
http://www.ilinks.net/~holmesr/duke.
htm
http://duke.fuse.net/

En Vogue
http://www.angelfire.com/fl/envogue/
index.html
http://www.elektra.com/randb_club/
en_vogue/en_vogue_press.html

EPMD/Erick Sermon/PMD
http://www.sonicnet.com/sonicore/
chat/bios/biosermon.html

Eric B. & Rakim
http://www.shu.edu/~martelfr/
contents/music/ericb.html

Gloria Estefan & Miami Sound Machine
http://www.globalxs.nl/home/p/
porky/discogra.htm

Eurythmics
http://www.ubl.com/artists/005462.
html

Everything but the Girl
http://www.terabit.net/icho/ebtg1.htm

Fat Joe
http://www.sonicnet.com/sonicore/
chat/bios/biofatjoe.html
http://www.yale.edu/ydn/paper/10.2
7.95al/10.27.95storyno.ACal.html

Rachelle Ferrell
http://www.bluenote.com/ferrell.html

Fine Young Cannibals
http://www.dsv.su.se/~mats-bjo/
fyc/fychome.html

Fishbone
http://www.risingsun.com/fishbone/

Ella Fitzgerald
http://www.enviromedia.com/ella/

Five Satins
http://lemur.stanford.edu/albumd
base/Doo-wop/16.html

Roberta Flack
http://pathfinder.com/@@nq014HJon
QEAQNyi/people/rock/wherenow/
flack.html

The Flamingos
http://www.bmi.com/flamingo.html

The Four Tops
http://home.dti.net/warr/fourtops.
html

Aretha Franklin
http://web3.starwave.com/starbios/
arethafranklin/b.html
http://www.wallofsound.com/artists/
arethafranklin/index.html

Kirk Franklin & the Family
http://www.ccmcom.com/ccmmag/
96aug/0896kirk_cover.html

Freestyle Fellowship/Aceyalone/Project Blowed
http://imusic.com/cgi-bin/bbs/bbs.
cgi?x=freestylefellowship

Fugees
http://www.music.sony.com/Music/
ArtistInfo/Fugees/
http://www.geocities.com/South
Beach/2903/fugees.htm

Funkmaster Flex
http://www.loud.com/flex/flex.html

G. Love & Special Sauce
http://www.music.sony.com/Music/
ArtistInfo/GLoveAndSpecialSauce.
html

Warren G
http://www.defjam.com/artists/
warren/warren.html

Gang Starr/Jazzmatazz/Guru
http://www.netcetera.nl/guru.html

Marvin Gaye
http://www.motown.com/motown/
artists/Marvin_Gaye/gaye_M.html
http://www.sedgsoftware.com/sedg.
htm

Gloria Gaynor
http://www.soon.org.uk/page32.htm
http://pathfinder.com/@@nq014HJon
QEAQNyi/people/rock/wherenow/
gaynor.html

J. Geils Band
http://www.dancefloor.com/ROCK/
JGB.html

Geto Boys/Scarface/Facemob/Bushwick Bill/Willie Dee/Big Mike
http://www.pathfinder.com/altculture/
aentries/g/getoxboys.html

http://emusic.com/browse/8694613/
181870/all1

The Goats
http://www.music.sony.com/Music/
ArtistInfo/TheGoats.html

The Goodie Mob
http://www.creativeloafing.com/new
sstand/atlo21096/V_HEAT.HTM
http://www.uvm.edu/~jdjohnso/
good.html

Berry Gordy
http://www.polygram.com/motown/
60_Main.html
http://www.rockinwoman.com/
oldies5.html

Grandmaster Flash & the Furious Five
http://www.wbls.com/dj_folder/dj_
show.gmf.html

Dobie Gray
http://songs.com/noma/noma/dobie/
dobiegray.html

Al Green
http://www.memphisguide.com/
Music/AlGreen.html
http://www.mca.com/mca_records/
library/bios/bio.algreen.html

Groove Theory
http://www.music.sony.com/Music/
ArtistInfo/GrooveTheory_Groove
Theory.html

Group Home
http://www.sonicnet.com/sonicore/
chat/bios/biogrphome.html

Buddy Guy
http://www.surfin.com/TheBlueFlame
Cafe/Buddy_Guy.html
http://www.math.clemson.edu/~mc
mike/music.html

Bill Haley & the Comets
http://www.odyssee.net/~epronovo/
haley/haley.htm
http://www.101strings.com/bhaley.
html

Daryl Hall & John Oates
http://www.cs.uit.no/Music/View/
hall+%2526+oates/daryl+hall+%
2526+john+oates/230/
http://www9.pair.com/iwc/hall_oates/

Herbie Hancock
http://www.jazzcentralstation.com/
jcs/station/featured/hhancock/
index.html

http://spider.media.philips.com/poly
gram/mercury/artists/hancock_
herbie/hancock_herbie.html

Ben Harper
http://www.rosebudus.com/harper/
index.html

Lalah Hathaway
http://www.enews.com/data/
magazines/alphabetic/all/vibe/
Archive/060194.11
http://www.mbmgroup.com/music/
htmlband/lelahtml.html

Richie Havens
http://www.pathfinder.com/@@d
RvrcgYAKuXZACG3/Life/rocknroll/
classic/havens.html

Screamin' Jay Hawkins
http://www.crl.com/www/users/ts/
tsimon/jhawkins.htm

Isaac Hayes
http://www.memphisguide.com/
Music/IHayes.html

The Heartbeats
http://www.classique-productions.
com/pages/PAGE7D.HTM

Heavy D. & the Boyz
http://www.mca.com/mca_records/
library/bios/bio.heavyd.html

Heltah Skeltah
http://fbox.vt.edu:10021/M/mshabazz/
Artists.html

Jimi Hendrix
http://www.jimi-hendrix.com/
http://www.inconnect.com/~hendrix/
http://www.geocities.com/Sunset
Strip/Stage/4863/
http://www.lionsgate.com/music/
hendrix/

Howard Hewett
http://www.blackworld.com/proffs/
artistes/hhewett.htm

Z. Z. Hill
http://malaco.com/blues/zzhill/

Holland, Dozier & Holland
http://rockhall.com/induct/hdh.html
http://www.sioux.demon.co.uk/hdh.
htm

Billie Holiday
http://users.bart.nl/~ecduzit/billy/
index.html

Brenda Holloway
http://www.rtd.com/~harvey/
holloway.html

John Lee Hooker
http://www.vivanet.com/~catbauer/
bio/johnlee.html
http://www.abel.co.uk/~milne/jl
hooker/netindex.html

Son House
http://www.en.utexas.edu/~sbowen/
314spring/tom/index.html

House of Pain
http://www.geocities.com/South
Beach/Sands/8501/
http://noether.math.uwaterloo.ca/
~jmclachl/hopinfo.html

Cissy Houston
http://hobmusic.com/cissy2.html
http://www.peeps.com/cissy/

Thelma Houston
http://pathfinder.com/@@nqo14HJon
QEAQNyi/people/rock/wherenow/
thelma.html

Whitney Houston
http://fanasylum.com/whitney/

Howlin' Wolf
http://hob.com/essential/howl.html
http://www.rockhall.com/induct/wolf
howl.html

Phyllis Hyman
http://www.peeps.com/hyman/index.
html

Ice Cube
http://www.pathfinder.com/altculture/
aentries/i/icexcube.html

Ice-T
http://www.pathfinder.com/altculture/
aentries/i/icextx.html

Ill Al Scratch
http://www.phantom.com/~street/
intlg.htm

Immature
http://www.mca.com/mca_records/
library/bios/bio.immature.html

The Impressions
http://rockhall.com/induct/impressi.
html

Incognito
http://arla.rsn.hk-r.se/incognito/

Intelligent Hoodlum
http://www.streetsound.com/interviews
/intintellhoodlum68.html

The Intruders
http://www.best.com/~mjq/intruders.
htm

Isley Brothers
http://www2.uic.edu/~wcloyd1/Isley.
html
http://www.geocities.com/Sunset
Strip/Alley/1973/

Jackson 5/Jacksons/Jermaine Jackson
http://www.srv.net/~roxtar/jackson5.
html
http://www.pathfinder.com/@@s868l
wYAvuWD8oPk/Life/rocknroll/
classic/jacksons.html
http://www.galactica.it/101/black/
ajjcksn3.html

Freddie Jackson
http://www.pyramid-ent.com/
fjackson.htm

Janet Jackson
http://ubl.com/artists/001060.html

Michael Jackson
http://msn.yahoo.com/Entertainment
/Music/Artists/Jackson__Michael/
http://www.tshirtnow.com/tshirtnow/
mjlp.html

Millie Jackson
http://www.acerecords.co.uk/labels/
southbound/cdsewd_100.html

Jimmy Jam & Terry Lewis
http://www.galactica.it/101/black/
ajjmtlw.html

Elmore James
http://www.deltablues.com/elmo.htm

Etta James
http://hob.com/bn/97/01/20/profile2.
html

Rick James
http://www.galactica.it/101/black/
arjms.html
http://home.dti.net/warr/rjames.html

Jamiroquai
http://www.jamiroquai.co.uk/

Al Jarreau
http://fringe.lib.ecu.edu/JoynerLib/
LibraryDepts/MusicLib/Bibs/Jazz
Art/jarreau.html

Blind Lemon Jefferson
http://www.eyeneer.com/America/
Genre/Blues/Profiles/lemon.html

Garland Jeffreys
http://ubl.com/artists/012655.html

Jeru the Damaja
http://ubl.com/artists/003068.html

Jodeci
http://www.euronet.nl/users/schalk/
jodeci/jodeci.html

Johnnie Johnson
http://www.metroactive.com/papers/
metro/05.16.96/blues2-9620.
html

Marv Johnson
http://www.typearts.com/Originals/
Volume5.html#johnson

Robert Johnson
http://www-ts.cs.oberlin.edu/wt94/
RobertJohnson.html

Grace Jones
http://www.tvguide.com/movies/
mopic/wideangl/features/honor3.
htm
http://pathfinder.com/@@Dvni3d
GrJgAAQIRO/people/gallery/exley/
grace.html

Quincy Jones
http://www.duke.edu/~jcf3/

Albert King
http://www.geocities.com/Bourbon
Street/Delta/1225/bdn8.html

B.B. King
http://www.worldblues.com/bbking/
default.asp
http://bbking.mca.com/
http://www.teleport.com/~boydroid/
blues/bbking.htm
http://Prairie.Lakes.com/~jkerekes/

Freddie King
http://www.mazeppa.com/fking.html
http://home1.gte.net/deltakit/
freddieking.htm

King Curtis
http://www.crl.com/www/users/ts/
tsimon/curtis.htm

King Tee
http://www.mca.com/mca_records/
library/bios/bio.kingtee.html
http://www.aftermath.com/kingt.html

Gladys Knight & the Pips
http://rockhall.com/induct/knigglad.
html
http://www.mca.com/mca_records/
library/bios/bio.knight.html

Lenny Kravitz
http://www.virginrecords.com/kravitz
/home.html
http://www.geocities.com/Sunset
Strip/Stage/5948/

Kris Kross
http://www.music.sony.com/Music/
ArtistInfo/KrisKross/html/
kkhmpge.html

Kurious
http://www.music.sony.com/Music/
ArtistInfo/Kurious.html

Kwest
http://american.recordings.com/
American_Artists/Kwest_tha_
Madd_Lad/kwest_home.html

Patti LaBelle
http://www.pattilabelle.com/map.
html
http://www.geocities.com/Sunset
Strip/Palms/4524/

Lady of Rage
http://www.geocities.com/Hollywood
/1561/rage.html

Denise LaSalle
http://malaco.com/blues/dls/index.
html

Last Poets
http://www.trilliumproductions.com/
tlphp.htm

Kenny Lattimore
http://www.music.sony.com/Music/
ArtistInfo/KennyLattimore/

Leadbelly
http://www.surfin.com/TheBlueFlame
Cafe/Leadbelly.html
http://www.island.net/~blues/huddy.
html

Leaders of the New School/Busta Rhymes
http://www.elektra.com/hiphop_club/
busta/busta.html

Gerald & Eddie Levert
http://www.elektra.com/randb_club/
levert/levert.html

Jerry Lee Lewis
http://www.elektra.com/country_
club/jerrylee/jerry.html
http://members.tripod.com/~Jerry9/
Fire.htm

Ramsey Lewis
http://www.afgsoft.com/ramsey/
default.htm

Little Anthony & the Imperials
http://www.onlinetalent.com/Anthony
_homepage.html

Little Richard
http://www.sjoki.uta.fi/~latvis/artists
/peach.html

Living Colour
http://www.willamette.edu/~cwick/
lc/

LL Cool J
http://www.geocities.com/Hollywood/
Hills/1569/allworld.html
http://llcoolj.starplanet.com/
http://www.defjam.com/artists/
llcoolj/llcoolj.html

Lordz of Brooklyn
http://american.recordings.com/
Ventrue/Artists/Lordz_Of_Brooklyn/
index.html

Luniz
http://www.virginrecords.com/artists/
NT.cgi?ARTIST_NAME=Luniz

Madonna
http://www.wbr.com/madonna/
http://www.madonnafanclub.com/
http://www.geocities.com/SoHo/Loft
s/3425/MadonnaLand.html
http://www.madonnaweb.com/

Massive Attack
http://www.virginrecords.com/artists/
VR.cgi?ARTIST_NAME=Massive_
Attack

Curtis Mayfield
http://www.hh.se/stud/d96join/cm/
curtis.html

MC Lyte
http://www.elektra.com/randb_club/
mclyte/mclyte.html
http://www.geocities.com/Sunset
Strip/3937/mclyte.html

MC 900 FT. Jesus
http://american.recordings.com/
American_Artists/MC_900FT_
Jesus/mc_home.html

Mobb Deep
http://www.loud.com/mobb/mobb.
html
http://www.geocities.com/Hollywood/
7488/MobbDeep.html

Nas
http://www.music.sony.com/Music/
ArtistInfo/Nas/
http://www.shu.edu/~martelfr/
contents/music/nas.html

Naughty By Nature
http://www.naughtybynature.com/
http://flavorunit.com/naughty.htm

Me'Shell Ndegeocello
http://www.wbr.com/maverick/
meshell/

New Edition
http://www.mcarecords.com/amp15/f.
newedition.html
http://www.hare.net.au/~ken12/

Notorious B.I.G.
http://www.wallofsound.com/artists/
thenotoriousbig/index.html
http://members.aol.com/subseven/
biggie.html

N.W.A.
http://pathfinder.com:80/altculture/
aentries/n/n.w.a.html

Shaquille O'Neal
http://www.interscoperecords.com/
shaq1.html

Onyx
http://www.defjam.com/artists/onyx/
onyx.html

OutKast
http://www.geocities.com/SunsetStrip/
Palms/3190/
http://www.geocities.com/SunsetStrip/
2457/OutKast.htm

Paris
http://www.scarface.com/

Pebbles
http://member.aol.com/pebbspage/
index.html

Pharcyde
http://www.hlindustries.com/
pharcyde/

P.M. Dawn
http://www.polygram.com/polygram/
island/artists/pm_dawn/

Prince
http://love4oneanother.com
http://www.nuvo.net/hammer/prince.
html
http://www710.univ-lyon1.fr/
~burzlaff/uptown.html
http://student.uq.edu.au/~s339290/
prince.htm
http://www.mcs.net/~nation/home/
cpn.htm

Public Enemy
http://www.defjam.com/artists/pe/
enemy.html
http://louis.ecs.soton.ac.uk/~rvn95r/
public_e/pe.html

Ray J
http://pathfinder.com/people/970623/
features/norwood.html

Otis Redding
http://ernie.bgsu.edu/~adavoli/otis.
html
http://ourworld.compuserve.com/
homepages/Luke_THE_GR8/

The Roots
http://www.geffen.com/roots/

Diana Ross
http://dianaross.com/welcome.htm#
Welcome!
http://www.ccn.cs.dal.ca/~ag249/
ross.html
http://utopia.knoware.nl/users/ross/
ross1.htm

Run DMC
http://www.users.interport.net/
~tjbeat/code/rdmain.html

Sade
http://www.epix.net/~akwarner/sade/

Salt-n-Pepa
http://www.execpc.com/~mwildt/snp.
html

Snoop Doggy Dogg
http://www.wallofsound.com/artists/
snoopdoggydogg/index.html
http://www.geocities.com/Colosseum/
Field/8927/snoop.html

Spice Girls
http://www.virginrecords.com/spice_
girls/spice.html
http://www.geocities.com/Sunset
Strip/Stage/1032/index.html

TLC
http://www.geocities.com/Sunset Strip/Palms/2154/tlc.html

Tony! Toni! Tone!
http://www.mercuryrecords.com/ mercury/artists/toni_tony_tone/ ttt_homepage.html

A Tribe Called Quest
http://www.algonet.se/~top/tribe.htm

Tina Turner
http://www.digiwing.com/tina/
http://www.toptown.com/centralpark/ tina/

2Pac
http://members.aol.com/BondsRules/ homepage.html

Vanilla Ice
http://www.manifest.com/~dopey/ LTC/ice.html

Jody Watley
http://members.aol.com/ffunzo/diva. htm

The Whispers
http://members.aol.com/ecmaj7/ Whispers.html

Vanessa Williams
http://www.mercuryrecords.com/ mercury/artists/williams_vanessa/ williams_v.html
http://www.geocities.com/Hollywood/ 9696/

Stevie Wonder
http://www.polygram.com/polygram/ motown/artists/wonder_stevie/S tevie.html
http://www.xmission.com/ ~matthewc/wonder/stevie.html
http://student- www.uchicago.edu/users/ jrgenzen/stevie.html

Wu-Tang Clan
http://www.loud.com/wu/wu.html
http://www.geocities.com/Sunset Strip/Towers/9022/
http://www.geocities.com/NapaValley/ 4035/wu.html

Other R&B and Music- Related Sites

Another Phat R&B Page
http://james.simplenet.com/

Azzam's Hip-Hop Site
http://www.total.net:8080/~affan/ HIPHOP.html

Best of Rap and R&B on the Web
http://www.lookup.com/Homepages/ 82075/music.html

Billboard Magazine
http://www.billboard.com/

Blues and Soul Magazine
http://www.bluesandsoul.co.uk/

Blues and Soul Music Primer
http://dialspace.dial.pipex.com/town/ square/e035/

BMG Music Service
http://www.bmgmusicservice.com/

Club H
http://www.highrise.nl/club/

Columbia House Music Club
http://www.columbiahouse.com

CyberSoul
http://coconet-j.com/cybersoul/ e-soul.htm

Da Hip-Hop Dimension
http://www.geocities.com/CollegePark/ 2757/MUSIC.htm

Davey D's Hip-Hop Corner
http://www.daveyd.com/hindex.html

D.J. Danny Boy's Hip-Hop Forum
http://udel.edu/~raekwon/index2. html

Drive-By
http://home.sol.no/gerardo/drive-in. html

88 Hip-Hop
http://www.88hiphop.com/

4080 Hip-Hop Online
http://www.buzznet.com/4080/index. html

Funky Soul Web
http://www.slamp.com/

Hip-Hop Alternative
http://www.geocities.com/Sunset Strip/Alley/2201/

Hip-Hop Reviews
http://www.ai.mit.edu/~isbell/HFh/ reviews/000-toc.html

Hip-HopSite.Com
http://www.hiphopsite.com/Home. html

ICE Magazine
http://www.icemagazine.com/

iMusic Newsagent
http://www.imusic.interserv.com/ newsagent/

Internet Soul Archive
http://www.echonyc.com/~spingo/ Soul/

Koolout
http://pseudo.com/netcast/shows/ koolout/

Li'l Flava's Hip-Hop Nation
http://www.geocities.com/Sunset Strip/3428/index1.html

Loop Hole
http://source.syr.edu/Loophole/

Mr. Hyde's Hip-Hop Sector
http://www.netspace.org/~sureel/ warning.html

MTV
http://www.mtv.com

Multimedia Hip-Hop on the Web
http://members.aol.com/e2thag/hip hop/index.html

The Music Page
http://www.ugrad.cs.jhu.edu/~tavon/ secular.html

Nobby's Soul on 45 RPM
http://www.pluto.dti.ne.jp/~nobbyy/

Old Soul Music Page
http://ourworld.compuserve.com/ homepages/glyn_valleyradio/

On Point Magazine
http://www.mindspring.com/ ~onpoint/index2.html

R&B Page
http://www.rbpage.com/

The Rap Game
http://wci2.wcinet.net/~cajun/

The Rap Lyrics Page
http://www.geocities.com/Broadway/ 2682/RAP.HTM

Rap.Org
http://www.rap.org/

Rolling Stone Magazine
http://www.rollingstone.com

Ro's Phat Hip-Hop Page
http://www.geocities.com/Hollywood/ 7488/

Soul Dogg
http://web.kyoto-inet.or.jp/people/
dad6fnp/

Soul of the Net
http://www.cet.ac.il/personnel/yonin/

Support Online Hip-Hop
http://www.sohh.com/

The Totally Unofficial Rap Dictionary
http://www.sci.kun.nl/thalia/rapdict/

24 Seven Hip-Hop
http://www.geocities.com/Sunset
Strip/Alley/4604/

UK Soul Page
http://www.amdragon.com/matt/
uksoul.htm

Ultimate Rap Audio Files
http://www.geocities.com/Silicon
Valley/2387/index.html

Ultimate Soul and Dance Directory
http://www.spods.dcs.kcl.ac.uk/
~richii/soulandance.html

unfURLed
http://www.unfurled.com/

URB Magazine
http://www.urb.com/urb/

USA TODAY (Music Page)
http://www.usatoday.com/life/enter/
music/lem99.htm

VH1
http://www.vh1.com/

VIBE Magazine
http://www.vibe.com/

Wall of Sound
http://www.wallofsound.com/

Westside
http://westside.simplenet.com/

Worldwide Unda-Ground Hip-Hop Site
http://www.illcrew.com/

If you want to see some R&B music performed live, we suggest you check out some of these North American music festivals. (For more information on these and other music festivals, consult Visible Ink Press' Music Festivals from Bach to Blues.)

UNITED STATES

Alabama

Birmingham
Birmingham Jam
Columbus Day weekend, Friday–Sunday
(205) 323-0569
WWW: http://www.bhm.tis.net/bhmjam/

Arizona

Flagstaff
Arizona Jazz, Rhythm & Blues Festival
A weekend in late June or early July
(800) 520-1646
(520) 744-9675

California

Indian Wells
New Year's Jazz at Indian Wells

December 29, 30 and 31
(310) 799-6055

Long Beach
Southern California Cajun & Zydeco Festival
First weekend in June
(310) 427-3713
(310) 595-5944
(818) 794-0070
(415) 386-8677

Los Angeles
Watts Towers Jazz Festival
Last Sunday in September
(213) 847-4646

San Rafael
Bay Area Cajun & Zydeco Festival
First weekend in October
(415) 472-3500
(415) 386-4553
(415) 386-8677

South Lake Tahoe
Rhythm and Brews Beer Tasting Festival
Third Saturday in July
(916) 541-4975
(800) 553-1022

Georgia

Atlanta
Freak Nik
A weekend in April
(404) 521-6600

Kentucky

Ashland
Summer Motion
July 4 and the nearest weekend
(800) 765-7464

Somerset
Master Musicians Festival
First week after Labor Day
(606) 678-2225

Louisiana

Lafayette
Festival International de Louisiane
Last week in April, Tuesday–Sunday
(318) 232-8086
WWW:http://www.usl.edu/Regional/Festival/

Monroe
Louisiana Folklife Festival
Second full weekend in September, Saturday and Sunday
(318) 329-2375

New Orleans
Cutting Edge Music Business Conference
Thursday–Sunday preceding Labor Day
(504) 827-5700
E-mail: 74777.754 @compuserve.com

French Quarter Festival

Second full weekend in April, Friday–Sunday
(504)566-5011

New Orleans Jazz and Heritage Festival
Last weekend in April (Friday–Sunday) and first weekend in May (Thursday–Sunday)
(504) 522-4786

Super Sunday
Sunday closest to March 19
(504) 568-1239

Maryland

Mount Airy
Bayou Razz-Jazz Wine Festival
Third weekend in August, Saturday and Sunday
(800) 514-8735
(301) 831-5889

Michigan

Kalamazoo
Kalamazoo Blues Festival
A weekend in mid-July, Thursday–Sunday
(616) 381-6514

Mississippi

Canton
Elmore James Hickory Street Festival
First Saturday in September
(601) 859-5703

Jackson
Farish Street Heritage Festival
Fourth weekend in September, Friday and Saturday
(601) 960-2383
(601) 960-1891

Missouri

Kansas City
18th & Vine Heritage Jazz Festival
Last weekend in August, Saturday and Sunday
(816) 474-1080
E-mail: vinejazz@worldmall.com

St. Louis
St. Louis Blues Heritage Festival
Labor Day weekend, Saturday and Sunday
(314) 241-2583
(800) 325-7962
(314) 534-1111

Nevada

Sparks
Fiesta Nevada Celebration
First weekend in May
(702) 353-2291

Ohio

Columbus
Big Bear Rhythm & Food Festival
Memorial Day weekend, Friday–Sunday
(419) 243-8024

Toledo
Toledo Rock, Rhythm and Blues Festival
Memorial Day weekend, Friday–Sunday
(419) 243-8024

Oklahoma

Rentiesville
Dusk 'Til Dawn Blues Festival
Labor Day weekend, Friday–Sunday
(918) 473-2411

Oregon

Portland
North by Northwest
A weekend in September or October
(512) 467-7979
E-mail: 72662.2465@compuserve.com

Pennsylvania

Philadelphia
USAir Jambalaya Jam
Memorial Day weekend, Saturday–Monday
(215) 636-1666

Yo! Philadelphia Festival
Labor Day weekend, Sunday and Monday
(215) 636-1666

Rhode Island

Escoheag
Big Easy Bash
Last weekend in June
(401) 351-6312
(800) 738-9808

Newport
Newport Rhythm and Blues Festival
Last weekend in July, (Saturday and Sunday)
(401) 847-3700

South Carolina

Charleston
Lowcountry Cajun Festival
Third or fourth Saturday in April
(803) 762-2172

Tennessee

Memphis
Beale Street Music Festival
First weekend in May
(901) 525-4611

Memphis Music & Heritage Festival
Second weekend in July
(901) 525-3945

Texas

Austin
Antone's Anniversary Party
Ten days usually ending July 15
(512) 474-5314

South by Southwest
Third week in March, Wednesday–Sunday
72662.2465@compuserve.com
WWW: http://monsterbit.com/sxsw.html

Port Arthur
Gulf Coast Jam
Last weekend in July or first weekend in August

Janis Joplin's Birthday Bash
Second Saturday in January
(409) 722-3699

Virginia

Norfolk
Bayou Boogaloo and Cajun Food Festival
A weekend in mid-June, Friday–Sunday
(804) 441-2345

Portland
Umoja Festival
Third weekend in September
(800) 767-8782
(804) 393-8481
E-mail: portsva@aol.com

Wolf Trap Farm/Vienna
Louisiana Swamp Romp
Sunday of the first weekend in June
(703)218-6500

(703) 255-1860
WWW: http://www.wolf.trap.org/

Wolf Trap's Jazz and Blues Festival
A weekend in late June, Thursday–Sunday
(703) 218-6500
(703) 255-1860
WWW: http://www.wolf.trap.org/

West Virginia

Clifftop
Doo-Wop Saturday Night
Third Saturday in July
(304) 558-0220
(304) 438-6429

Wisconsin

Milwaukee
Summerfest
Eleven days beginning the last Thursday in June
(800) 273-3378
(414) 273-3378

CANADA

Nova Scotia

Halifax
Halifax Pop Explosion
Second week in October, Wednesday–Sunday
865-1715
535-2586

Ontario

Toronto
North by Northeast
Third weekend in June, Thursday–Saturday
(416) 469-0986
(512) 467-7979
E-mail: 72662.2465@compuserve.com

The following U.S. radio stations serve up some fine R&B. (Warning: radio formats often change like the weather, so if you're looking for SWV and end up with ELO, don't blame us!)

Alabama

Birmingham
WATV (900 AM)
WBHJ (95.7 FM)
WBHK (98.7 FM)
WENN (107.7 FM)
WJLD (1400 AM)
WTUG (92.9 FM)

Dothan
WJJN (92.1 FM)
WZHT (105.7 FM)

Huntsville
WEUP (92.1 FM)

Mobile
WBLX (92.9 FM)
WDLT (98.3 FM)
WYOK (104.9 FM)

Montgomery
WMCZ (97.1 FM)
WXVI (1600 AM)
WZHT (105.7 FM)

Tuscaloosa
WBHJ (95.7 FM)

WNPT (102.9 FM)
WQLW (104.3 FM)
WTUG (92.9 FM)
WWPG (1280 AM)

Arizona

Phoenix
KISO (1230 AM)
KMJK (106.9 FM)

Arkansas

Little Rock
KIPR (92.3 FM)
KYFX (99.5 FM)

California

Fresno
KQEQ (1220 AM)

Los Angeles
KACE (103.9 FM)
KJLH (102.3 FM)
KKBT (92.3 FM)
KPWR (105.9 FM)

Montgomery/Salinas/Santa Cruz
KLYZ (99.1 FM)

Riverside/San Bernardino
KMEN (90.3 FM)

San Diego
XHTZ (90.3 FM)

San Francisco
KBLX (102.9 FM)
KDIA (1310 AM)
KMEL (106.1 FM)
KSOL (98.9 FM)

San Jose
KBLX (102.9 FM)
KMEL (106.1 FM)
KYLZ (99.1 FM)

Colorado

Denver/Boulder
KDKO (1510 AM)

Connecticut

Hartford/New Britain/Middletown
WKND (1480 AM)

New Haven
WNHC (1340 AM)
WYBC (94.3 FM)

District of Columbia

Washington
WHUR (96.3 FM)
WKYS (93.9 FM)
WMMJ (102.3 FM)
WPGC (1580 AM)
WPGC (95.5 FM)

Florida

Daytona Beach
WJHM (101.9 FM)
WPUL (1590 AM)

Gainesville/Ocala
WNFQ (100.5 FM)
WTMG (101.3 FM)
WWLO (1430 AM)

Jacksonville
WJBT (92.7 FM)
WOBS (1530 AM)
WSOL (101.5 FM)
WXQL (105.7 FM)

Lakeland/Winterhaven
WHNR (1360 AM)
WWAB (1330 AM)

Melbourne/Titusville/Cocoa
WXXU (1300 AM)

Miami/Fort Lauderdale/Hollywood
WEDR (99.1 FM)
WHQT (105.1 FM)
WYFX (1040 AM)

Orlando
WJHM (101.9 FM)

Pensacola
WBLX (92.9 FM)
WRNE (980 AM)

Tallahassee
WHBT (1410 AM)
WHBX (96.1 FM)

WHGH (840 AM)
WWSD (1230 AM)

Tampa/St. Petersburg/Clearwater
WRBQ (1380 AM)
WRXB (1590 AM)
WTMP (1150 AM)

West Palm Beach/Boca Raton
WEDR (99.1 FM)
WHQT (105.1 FM)
WYFX (1040 AM)

Georgia

Albany
WJIZ (96.3 FM)
WQVE (105.5 FM)

Atlanta
WALR (1340 AM)
WALR (104.7 FM)
WHTA (97.5 FM)
WVEE (103.3 FM)

Augusta
WAEG (92.3 FM)
WAEJ (100.9 FM)
WAKB (96.9 FM)
WFXA (103.1 FM)
WKIM (1230 AM)

Columbus
WAGH (98.3 FM)
WFXE (104.9 FM)
WKZJ (95.7 FM)
WOKS (1340 AM)

Macon
WIBB (97.9 FM)
WPGA (100.9 FM)
WRBG (101.7 FM)

Savannah
WEAS (93.1 FM)
WHBZ (99.7 FM)
WLVH (101.1 FM)
WSGF (103.9 FM)
WSKX (92.3 FM)

Illinois

Champaign
WBCP (1580 AM)

Chicago
WEJM (950 AM)
WEJM (106.3 FM)

WGCI (1390 AM)
WGCI (107.5 FM)
WVAZ 9102.7 FM)

Peoria
WBGE (92.3 FM)

Fort Wayne
WJFX (107.9 FM)

Indianapolis
WGGR (106.7 FM)
WGLD (93.9 FM)
WTLC (105.7 FM)

South Bend
WSMK (99.1 FM)
WUBU (106.3 FM)

Iowa

Quad Cities (Davenport/Rock Island/Moline)
KFQC (1580 AM)

Kentucky

Lexington/Fayette
WTKT (1580 AM)

Louisville
WGZB (96.5 FM)
WMJM (101.3 FM)

Louisiana

Alexandria
KBCE (102.3 FM)

Baton Rouge
KBRH (1260 AM)
KCLF (1500 AM)
KQLX (106.5 FM)

Lafayette
KFXZ (106.3 FM)
KJCB (770 AM)
KNEK (104.7 FM)
KRRQ (99.5 FM)
KVOL (1330 AM)
KVOL (105.9 FM)

Lake Charles
KXZZ (1580 AM)
KZWA (105.3 FM)

Monroe
KRVV (100.1 FM)
KTRY (94.3 FM)

KYEA (98.3 FM)

New Orleans
KMEZ (102.9 FM)
WQUE (93.3 FM)
WYLD (98.5 FM)

Shreveport
KDKS (103.7 FM)
KMJJ (99.7 FM)

Maryland

Baltimore
WERQ (92.3 FM)
WWIN (95.9 FM)
WXYV (102.7 FM)

Salisbury/Ocean City
WRKE (101.7 FM)

Massachusetts

Boston
WILD (1090 AM)
WJMN (94.5 FM)

Michigan

Detroit
WCHB (105.9 FM)
WDRQ (93.1 FM)
WGPR (107.5 FM)
WJLB (97.9 FM)
WMXD (92.3 FM)
WQBH (1400 AM)

Flint
WDZZ (92.7 FM)
WOWE (98.9 FM)
WTLZ (107.1 FM)

Grand Rapids
WKWM (1140 AM)

Kalamazoo
WNWN (1560 AM)

Lansing/East Lansing
WQHH (96.5 FM)
WXLA (1180 AM)

Saginaw/Bay City/Midland
WOWE (98.9 FM)
WTLZ (107.1 FM)

Minnesota

Minneapolis/St. Paul
KSGS (950 AM)

Mississippi

Biloxi/Gulfport/Pascagoula
WBSL (1190 AM)
WJZD (94.5 FM)

Jackson
WJMI (99.7 FM)
WKXI (1400 AM)
WKXI (107.5 FM)
WONG (1150 AM)

Laurel/Hattiesburg
WJMG (92.1 FM)
WJXX (102.5 FM)

Meridian
KSLY (104.9 FM)
WALT (910 AM)
WNBN (1290 AM)
WZKS (104.1 FM)

Tupelo
WESE (92.5 FM)

Missouri

Kansas City
KPRS (103.3 FM)

St. Louis
KATZ (100.3 FM)
KMJM (107.7 FM)
KXOK (97.1 FM)
WESL (1490 AM)

Nebraska

Omaha/Council Bluffs
KBBX (1420 AM)

New Jersey

Atlantic City/Cape May
WBNJ (105.5 FM)
WTTH (96.1 FM)

New York

Buffalo/Niagara Falls
WBLK (93.7 FM)
WUFO (1080 AM)

WWWS (1400 AM)

New York
WBLS (107.5 FM)
WQHT (97.1 FM)
WRKS (98.7 FM)

Rochester
WDKX (103.9 FM)

Syracuse
WRDS (102.1 FM)

North Carolina

Charlotte/Gastonia/Rock Hill
WBAV (1600 AM)
WBAV (101.9 FM)
WPEG (97.9 FM)

Fayetteville
WLRD (107.7 FM)
WZFX (99.1 FM)

Greensboro/Winston Salem/High Point
WAAA (980 AM)
WJMH (102.1 FM)
WQMG (97.1 FM)

Greenville/New Bern/Jacksonville
WCOO (1380 AM)
WELS (102.9 FM)
WIKS (101.9 FM)

Raleigh/Durham
WDUR (1490 AM)
WFXC (107.1 FM)
WFXK (104.3 FM)
WLLE (570 AM)
WQOK (97.5 FM)

Wilmington
WMNX (97.3 FM)

Ohio

Akron
WTOU (1350 AM)

Cinncinnati
WCIN (1480 AM)
WIZF (100.9 FM)

Cleveland
WJMO (1490 AM)
WJTB (1040 AM)
WZAK (93.1 FM)

Columbus
WCKX (106.3 FM)
WJZA (107.5 FM)
WSMZ (103.1 FM)
WVKO (1580 AM)

Dayton
WDAO (1210 AM)
WRNB (96.9 FM)
WROU (92.1 FM)

Toledo
WIMX (95.7 FM)
WLQR (1470 AM)

Youngstown/Warren
WRBP (101.9 FM)

Oklahoma

Oklahoma City
KVSP (1140 AM)

Tulsa
KJMM (105.3 FM)

Oregon

Portland
KBMS (1480 AM)

Pennsylvania

Harrisburg/Lebanon/Carlisle
WTCY (1400 AM)

Philadelphia
WDAS (105.3 FM)
WUSL (98.9 FM)

Pittsburgh
WAMO (860 AM)
WAMO (106.7 FM)
WXVX (1510 AM)

South Carolina

Charleston
WMGL (101.7 FM)
WPAL (730 AM)
WPAL (100.9 FM)
WWBZ (98.9 FM)
WWWZ (93.3 FM)

Columbia
WLXC (98.5 FM)
WOIC (1230 AM)
WWDM (101.3 FM)

Florence
WCMG (94.3 FM)
WYNN (106.3 FM)

Greenville/Spartanburg
WASC (1530 AM)
WBAV (101.9 FM)
WJMZ (107.3 FM)

Myrtle Beach
WCKN (1270 AM)
WDAI (98.5 FM)

Tennessee

Chattanooga
WJTT (94.3 FM)
WMPZ (93.7 FM)
WNOO (1260 AM)

Jackson
WFKX (95.7 FM)
WKBJ (1600 AM)

Knoxville
WKGN (1340 AM)
WNOX (99.1 FM)

Memphis
KJMS (101.1 FM)
WDIA (1070 AM)
WHRK (97.1 FM)
WJCE (680 AM)

Nashville
WJCE (101.1 FM)
WMDB (880 AM)
WQQK (92.1 FM)
WVOL (1470 AM)

Texas

Austin
KJCE (1370 AM)

Beaumont/Port Arthur
KZWA (105.3 FM)

Bryan/College Station
KHRN (94.3 FM)

Dallas/Fort Worth
KKDA (730 AM)
KKDA (104.5 FM)
KRBV (100.3 FM)

Houston/Galveston
KBXX (97.9 FM)
KMJQ (102.1 FM)

Kileen/Temple
KIIZ (92.3 FM)

San Antonio
KSJL (96.1 FM)

Texarkana
KTOY (104.7 FM)
KXAR (101.7 FM)
KZRB (103.5 FM)

Tyler/Longview
KZEY (690 AM)

Virginia

Charlottesville
WCHV (1260 AM)

Norfolk/Virginia Beach/Newport News
WCKO (1110 AM)
WMYK (92.1 FM)
WOWI (102.9 FM)
WSVY (107.7 FM)

Richmond
WCDX (92.1 FM)
WCLM (1450 AM)
WPLZ (99.3 FM)
WSOJ (100.3 FM)

Roanoke/Lynchburg
WJJS (106.1 FM)
WTOY (1480 AM)

Washington

Seattle/Tacoma
KBLV (1540 AM)
KRIZ (1420 AM)
KZIZ (1560 AM)

West Virginia

Wheeling
WDIG (950 AM)

Wisconsin

Milwaukee/Racine
WKKV (100.7 FM)
WMCS (1290 AM)
WNOV (860 AM)

The following record labels are just some of the labels that have substantial R&B catalogs. You may want to contact them if you have questions regarding specific releases.

A & M Records
1416 N. La Brea Ave.
Hollywood, CA 90028
(213) 469-2411
Fax: (213) 856-2600

Alligator Records
PO Box 60234
Chicago, IL 60660
(312) 973-7736
Fax: (312) 973-2088

Almo Sounds
360 N. La Cienega Blvd.
Los Angeles, CA 90048
(310) 289-3080
Fax: (310) 289-8662

American Recordings
3500 W. Olive Ave., Ste. 1550
Burbank, CA 91505-4628
(818) 973-4545
Fax: (818) 973-4571

Arista Records
6 W. 57th St.
New York, NY 10019
(212) 489-7400
Fax: (212) 830-2238

Atlantic & Associated Labels
75 Rockefeller Plz.
New York, NY 10019
(212) 275-2995
Fax: (212) 275-3985

Bellmark Records/Life Records
7060 Hollywood Blvd., 10th Floor
Hollywood, CA 90028
(213) 464-8492
Fax: (213) 464-0785

Big Beat Records
14 E. 60th St., 8th Floor
New York, NY 10022
(212) 508-5400
Fax: (212) 527-0950

Black Top
PO Box 56691
New Orleans, LA 70156
(504) 895-7239
Fax: (504) 891-1510
E-Mail: blacktnola@aol.com

Blue Note/Metro Blue Records
1290 Avenue of the Americas, 35th Floor
New York, NY 10104
(212) 492-5300
Fax: (212) 492-5458

Blue Thumb Records
555 W. 57th St.
New York, NY 10019
(212) 424-1000
Fax: (212) 424-1007

Blunt Records
23 E. Fourth St.
New York, NY 10003
(212) 979-6410
Fax: (212) 979-6489

Capitol-EMI
1750 N. Vine St.
Hollywood, CA 90028
(213) 462-6252
Fax: (213) 467-6550

Capricorn Records
2205 State St.
Nashville, TN 37203
(615) 320-8470
Fax: (615) 320-8479

Columbia Records
550 Madison Ave.
New York, NY 10022-3211
(212) 833-8000
Fax: (212) 833-7731

The Curb Group
47 Music Sq. E.
Nashville, TN 37203
(615) 321-5080
Fax: (615) 327-3003

Death Row Records
9171 Wilshire Blvd., Ste. 302
Beverly Hills, CA 90210
(310) 786-8459
Fax: (310) 786-8467

Decca Records
60 Music Sq. E.
Nashville, TN 37203
(615) 244-8944
Fax: (615) 880-7475

Def Jam Music Group
160 Varick St.
New York, NY 10013
(212) 229-5200
Fax: (212) 675-3588

EastWest
75 Rockefeller Plz.
New York, NY 10019
(212) 275-2500
Fax: (212) 974-9314

Elektra Entertainment
75 Rockefeller Plz.
New York, NY 10019-6907
(212) 275-4000
Fax: (212) 974-9314

Epic Records
550 Madison Ave.
New York, NY 10022-3211
(212) 833-8000
Fax: (212) 833-5134

57 & Shotput Records
3155 Roswell Rd., Ste. 330
Atlanta, GA 30305
(404) 237-5757
Fax: (404) 237-5739

Fox Music
PO Box 900
Beverly Hills, CA 90213-0900
(310) 369-3349
Fax: (310) 369-1516

GRP Records
555 W. 57th St.
New York, NY 10019
(212) 424-1000
Fax: (212) 424-1007

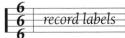

6
6 *record labels*
6

Geffen/DGC
9130 Sunset Blvd.
Los Angeles, CA 90069-6197
(310) 278-9010
Fax: (310) 273-9389

Giant Records
1514 South St.
Nashville, TN 37212
(615) 256-3110
Fax: (615) 742-1560

Hollywood Records
500 S. Buena Vista St.
Burbank, CA 91521
(818) 560-5670
Fax: (818) 841-5140

Ichiban Records
PO Box 724677
Atlanta, GA 31139-1677
(770) 419-1414
Fax: (770) 419-1230

Impulse!
555 W. 57th St.
New York, NY 10019
(212) 424-1000
Fax: (212) 424-1007

Interscope Records
10900 Wilshire Blvd.
Los Angeles, CA 90024
(310) 208-6547
Fax: (310) 208-7343

Intersound/Branson Entertainment
PO Box 1724
Roswell, GA 30077
(770) 664-9262
Fax: (770) 664-7316
E-mail:
  intersound@intersound
  music.com

Island Records
825 Eighth Ave., 24th Floor
New York, NY 10019
(212) 333-8000
Fax: (212) 603-3965

JVC/Vertex
3800 Barham Blvd., Ste. 305
Los Angeles, CA 90068
(213) 878-0101
Fax: (213) 878-0202

Jive/Silvertone
137-139 W. 25th St., 11th Floor

New York, NY 10001
(212) 727-0016
Fax: (212) 645-3783

LaFace Records
3350 Peachtree Rd., Ste. 1500
Atlanta, GA 30326
(404) 848-8050
Fax: (404) 848-8051

Lava Records
75 Rockefeller Plz.
New York, NY 10019
(212) 265-3440
Fax: (212) 265-7706

London Records
825 Eighth Ave., 23rd Floor
New York, NY 10019
(212) 333-3999
Fax: (212) 333-8030

Loose Cannon Records
825 Eighth Ave., 23rd Floor
New York, NY 10019
(212) 603-7692
Fax: (212) 333-1460

Loud Records
8360 Melrose Ave., 2nd Floor
Los Angeles, CA 90069
(213) 653-0891
Fax: (213) 653-6250

MCA Records
70 Universal City Plz.
Universal City, CA 91608
(818) 777-4000
Fax: (818) 733-1407

MCG/Curb
3907 W. Alameda Ave., Ste. 101
Burbank, CA 91505
(818) 843-1616
Fax: (818) 843-5429

Magnatone Records
1516 16th Ave. S.
Nashville, TN 37212
(615) 383-3600
Fax: (615) 383-0020

Maverick
8000 Beverly Blvd.
Los Angeles, CA 90048
(213) 852-1177
Fax: (213) 852-1505

Mercury Records
World Wide Plz., 825 Eighth Ave.
New York, NY 10019
(212) 333-8000
Fax: (212) 333-1093

Metropolitan Recording Corp.
900 Passaic Ave.
East Newark, NJ 07029
(201) 483-8080
Fax: (201) 483-0031

Motown Records
825 Eighth Ave., 28th Floor
New York, NY 10019
(212) 294-9516
Fax: (212) 946-2615

NooTrybe Records
338 N. Foothill Rd.
Beverly Hills, CA 90210
(310) 288-1444
Fax: (310) 288-2470

Pandisc Records
6157 NW 167th St., Ste. F-9
Miami, FL 33015
(305) 557-1914
Fax: (305) 557-9262

Priority Records
6430 Sunset Blvd., 9th Floor
Hollywood, CA 90028
(213) 467-0151
Fax: (213) 856-0150

Private Music
8750 Wilshire Blvd.
Beverly Hills, CA 90211
(310) 358-4500
Fax: (310) 358-4520

Profile
740 Broadway, 7th Floor
New York, NY 10003
(212) 529-2600
Fax: (212) 420-8216

Qwest Records
3800 Barham Blvd., Ste. 503
Los Angeles, CA 90068
(213) 874-7770
Fax: (213) 874-5049

RCA Records
1540 Broadway
New York, NY 10036
(212) 930-4000
Fax: (212) 930-4468

Razor & Tie Records
214 Sullivan St., #4A
New York, NY 10012
(212) 473-9173
Fax: (212) 473-9174
E-mail: razrntie@ad.com

Relativity Records
79 Fifth Ave., 16th Floor
New York, NY 10003
(212) 337-5300

Reprise Records
3300 Warner Blvd.
Burbank, CA 91505-4694
(818) 846-9090
(818) 953-3223
Fax: (818) 953-3211

Restless Records
1616 Vista Del Mar Ave.
Hollywood, CA 90028
(213) 957-4357
(800) 573-7853
Fax: (213) 957-4355

Rhino Records
10635 Santa Monica Blvd.
Los Angeles, CA 90025-4900
(310) 474-4778
Fax: (310) 441-6575

The Right Stuff
1750 N. Vine St.
Hollywood, CA 90028
(213) 960-4634
Fax: (213) 960-4666

Rounder Records
One Camp St.
Cambridge, MA 02140
(617) 354-0700
Fax: (617) 491-1970

Ruthless Records
21860 Burbank Blvd., Ste. 100
Woodland Hills, CA 91367
(818) 710-0060
Fax: (818) 710-1009

Rykodisc
27 Congress St.
Salem, MA 01970
(508) 744-7678
Fax: (508) 741-4506

Scotti Brothers Records
808 Wilshire Blvd.
Santa Monica, CA 90401
(310) 656-1100
Fax: (310) 656-7430

Sire
75 Rockefeller Plz., 21st Floor
New York, NY 10019
(212) 275-4000
Fax: (212) 581-6416

Solar Records
1635 N. Cahuenga Blvd.
Los Angeles, CA 90028
(213) 461-0390
Fax: (213) 461-9032

Sony 550 Music
550 Madison Ave.
New York, NY 1022
(212) 833-8000
Fax: (212) 833-7120

TVT Records
23 E. Fourth St.
New York, NY 10003
(212) 979-6410

Fax: (212) 979-6489
E-Mail: general@tvtrecords.com

Tag Recordings
14 E. 60th St., 8th Fl.
New York, NY 10022
(212) 508-5450
Fax: (212) 593-7663

Thump Records
PO Box 445
Walnut, CA 91788-0445
(909) 595-2144
Fax: (909) 598-7028
E-mail: thump4cds@aol.com

Tommy Boy Music
902 Broadway, 13th Floor
New York, NY 10010
(212) 388-8300
Fax: (212) 388-8400

Universal Records
1325 Ave. of the Americas, 5th Floor
New York, NY 10019
(212) 373-0600
Fax: (212) 489-8195

Uptown Records
1755 Broadway, 8th Floor
New York, NY 10019
(212) 841-8114
Fax: (212) 841-8142

Verve Records
825 Eighth Ave., 26th Floor
New York, NY 10019
(212) 333-8000
Fax: (212) 333-8194

Virgin
338 N. Foothill Rd.
Beverly Hills, CA 90210

(310) 278-1181
Fax: (310) 278-6231

Warner Bros. Records
3300 Warner Blvd.
Burbank, CA 91510
(818) 846-9090
(818) 953-3223
Fax: (818) 846-8474

Wax Trax
23 E. Fourth St.
New York, NY 10003
(212) 979-6410
Fax: (212) 979-6489

The Work Group
2100 Colorado Ave.
Santa Monica, CA 90404
(310) 449-2666
Fax: (310) 449-2095

The following albums by individual artists or groups achieved the highest rating possible—5 bones—from our discriminating MusicHound R&B *writers. You can't miss with any of these recordings.*

Arthur Alexander
The Ultimate Arthur Alexander (Razor & Tie, 1993)

Joan Armatrading
Greatest Hits (A&M, 1996)
Joan Armatrading (A&M, 1976)

Louis Armstrong
The Complete Studio Recordings of Louis Armstrong and the All Stars (Mosaic, 1993)
Ella Fitzgerald and Louis Armstrong (Verve, 1957)
Hot Fives and Hot Sevens—Vol. 2 (CBS, 1926/Columbia, 1988)
Louis Armstrong and Earl Hines (CBS, 1927/Columbia Jazz Masterpieces, 1989)
Portrait of the Artist as a Young Man, 1923–1934 (Columbia/Legacy, 1994)

Arrested Development
3 Months, 5 Months & 2 Days in the Life of . . . (Chrysalis/EMI, 1992)

Hank Ballard
Sexy Ways: The Best of Hank Ballard and the Midnighters (Rhino, 1993)

Dave Bartholomew
The Spirit Of New Orleans: The Genius of Dave Bartholomew (EMI, 1992)

Beck
Odelay (DGC, 1996)

Chuck Berry
The Chess Box (Chess/MCA, 1988)
Chuck Berry Is On Top (Chess, 1959)
The Great Twenty-Eight (Chess, 1982)

Bobby "Blue" Bland
I Pity the Fool/The Duke Recordings Vol. 1 (MCA, 1992)
Turn On Your Love Light (MCA, 1994)
Two Steps from the Blues (MCA, 1961/1989)

Boogie Down Productions
Criminal Minded (B Boy, 1987)

James Booker
New Orleans Piano Wizard: Live! (Rounder, 1981)
Spiders on the Keys (Rounder, 1993)

Booker T. & the MG's
Hip Hug-Her (Stax, 1967/Rhino, 1992)

Earl Bostic
25 Years of Rhythm and Blues Hits (King, 1960)

David Bowie
Aladdin Sane (RCA, 1973)
Hunky Dory (RCA, 1971)
The Rise and Fall of Ziggy Stardust and the Spiders from Mars (RCA, 1972)
The Singles 1969–1993 (Ryko, 1993)

Young Americans (RCA, 1975)

The Brand New Heavies
The Brand New Heavies (Delicious Vinyl, 1991)

Brand Nubian
One for All (Elektra, 1990)

James Brown
Live at the Apollo (King, 1963/Polydor, 1990)
Live at the Apollo, Vol. 2 (Rhino, 1985)
Solid Gold: 30 Golden Hits (Polydor, 1986)
Star Time (Polydor, 1991)

Roy Brown
Good Rocking Tonight: The Best of Roy Brown (Rhino, 1994)

Ruth Brown
Miss Rhythm: Greatest Hits and More (Atlantic, 1989)
Rockin' In Rhythm—The Best of Ruth Brown (Rhino, 1996)

Peabo Bryson
Live and More (Atlantic, 1980)
Reaching for the Sky (Capitol, 1978)

Solomon Burke
The Best of Solomon Burke (Atlantic, 1989)
Rock 'N Soul (Atlantic, 1961)

Jerry Butler
Best of Jerry Butler (Rhino, 1987)

Cab Calloway
Are You Hep to the Jive? (Legacy, 1994)

Ray Charles
Anthology (Rhino, 1988)

The Best of Ray Charles: The Atlantic Years (Rhino, 1994)
The Birth of Soul: The Complete Atlantic Rhythm & Blues Recordings, 1952–1959 (Rhino, 1991)
Genius & Soul: The 50th Anniversary Collection (Rhino, 1997)
Modern Sounds in Country and Western Music (ABC, 1963)

Chef Raekwon (of Wu-Tang Clan)
Only Built For Cuban Linx . . . (Loud/RCA, 1995)

Dee Clark
Raindrops (Vee-Jay, 1993)

Otis Clay
Live in Japan (JVC Japan, 1981)

Jimmy Cliff
The Harder They Come (Island, 1972)

George Clinton/Parliament-Funkadelic
Funkadelic's Greatest Hits (Westbound, 1975)
Mothership Connection (Casablanca, 1975)
One Nation Under a Groove (Warner Bros., 1987/Priority, 1993)

Nat King Cole
Anatomy of a Jam Session (Black Lion, 1945)
The Complete After Midnight Sessions (Capitol/EMI, 1996)
The Complete Capitol Recordings of the Nat King Cole Trio (Capitol/EMI, 1991)
The Greatest Hits (Capitol/EMI, 1994)
Jazz Encounters (Blue Note, 1992)
Lush Life (EMI/Capitol, 1993)
Nat King Cole (Capitol/EMI, 1992)
The Very Thought of You (Capitol/EMI, 1991)

Natalie Cole
Inseparable (Capitol, 1975)

Sam Cooke
The Man and His Music (RCA Victor, 1986)
Night Beat (RCA, 1963/Abkco, 1995)
One Night Stand: Live At the Harlem Square Club, 1963 (RCA Victor, 1985)
Sam Cooke with the Soul Stirrers (Specialty, 1991)

Hank Crawford
Heart and Soul: The Hank Crawford Anthology (Rhino, 1994)

Andrae Crouch
Mercy (Qwest, 1994)

The Crusaders
The Crusaders: Way Back Home (GRP-Blue Thumb, 1996)

Cypress Hill
Cypress Hill (Ruffhouse/Columbia, 1991)

Terence Trent D'Arby
Introducing the Hardline According to Terence Trent D'Arby (Columbia, 1987)

Tyrone Davis
Greatest Hits (Rhino, 1992)

De La Soul
3 Feet High and Rising (Tommy Boy, 1989)

Defunkt
Thermonuclear Sweat (Hannibal, 1982)

DJ Red Alert
Let's Make It Happen (Next Plateau, 1990)

Fats Domino
Antoine "Fats" Domino (Tomato, 1992)
Fats Domino: The Fat Man, 25 Classics (EMI, 1996)
My Blue Heaven (EMI, 1990)
Out of New Orleans (Bear Family, 1993)
They Call Me the Fat Man (EMI, 1991)

The Dominoes
Sixty Minute Men: The Best of Billy Ward & the Dominoes (Rhino, 1993)

The Drifters
1959–1965: All-Time Greatest Hits and More (Atlantic, 1988)

George Duke
Don't Let Go (Legacy, 1990)
Muir Woods Suite (Warner Bros., 1996)

Dyke & the Blazers
So Sharp! (Kent/Ace U.K., 1991)

Earth, Wind & Fire
Spirit (Columbia, 1976)

Duke Ellington
All Star Road Band Vol. 2 (Signature, 1957/CBS Special Products, 1990)
Anatomy of a Murder (Anadisq, 1959)
The Best of Duke Ellington (Blue Note, 1995)
Black, Brown, & Beige—Mastersound Series (Columbia, 1994)
Blues in Orbit—1960 (Columbia, 1988)

The Cornell University Concert—December 1948 (Musicmasters, 1995)
Duke Ellington & His Famous Orchestra: Fargo, North Dakota, Nov. 7, 1940 (VJC)
Duke Ellington & His Orchestra Live at Newport—1958 (Columbia/Legacy, 1994)
Duke Ellington: The Blanton-Webster Band, 1939–1942 (Bluebird, 1986)
Duke Ellington: Greatest Hits (RCA, 1996)
Duke Ellington Meets Coleman Hawkins (MCA, 1986)
Duke Ellington, 1924–1930—Box Set (Classics 6, 1995)
Duke Ellington, Vol.2: Swing 1930–1938 (ABC Music, 1994)
Duke Ellington's My People (Red Baron, 1992)
Duke's Big Four (Pablo, 1973/1988)
Ellington at Basin Street East: The Complete Concert of 14 January 1964 (Music & Arts, 1996)
Ellington at Newport (Columbia, 1956/1987)
Ellington Indigos: Sept–Oct. 1957 (Columbia, 1989)
Ellingtonia (Fat Boy, 1996)
The Great London Concerts—1964 (MusicMasters, 1993)
The Great Paris Concert (Atlantic, 1963/1989)
In a Mellotone—1940–1944 (RCA, 1995)
Live at the Blue Note (Roulette Jazz, 1994)
Lullaby of Birdland (Intermedia)
Money Jungle—1962 (Blue Note, 1986)
Mood Indigo (EPM Musique, 1994)
New Orleans Suite–1970 (Atlantic)
Original Hits, Vol. 1: 1927–31 (King Jazz, 1993)
Original Hits, Vol. 2: 1931–38 (King Jazz, 1993)
The Pianist 1966, 1970 (Fantasy, 1992)
The Piano Album (Capitol, 1989)
The Private Collection, Vol. 5: "The Suites" 1968 (Saja, 1989)
Satin Doll, 1958–1959 (Jazz Time, 1995)
70th Birthday Concert—Nov. 1969 (Blue Note, 1995)
Side by Side (Verve, 1986)
Sophisticated Lady: Masters of the Big Bands (Bluebird, 1986)
Uptown Downbeat w/his Orchestra: Cotton Club, Jungle Band 1927–1940 (Empire/Avid, 1995)
Uptown—Early 1950s (Columbia, 1987)

Vol. 4: The Mooche, 1928 (EPM Musique, 1996)

Vol. 9: Mood Indigo—1930 (EPM Musique, 1996)

Eric B. & Rakim
Paid In Full (4th & Broadway/Island, 1987)

Ella Fitzgerald
The Best Is Yet to Come (Pablo, 1996)
The Best of Ella Fitzgerald & Louis Armstrong on Verve (Verve, 1997)
The Cole Porter Songbook (Verve, 1956)
The Complete Duke Ellington Songbook (Verve, 1956)
The Complete Ella Fitzgerald & Louis Armstrong on Verve (Verve, 1997)
The Complete Ella Fitzgerald Song Books (Verve, 1993)
Ella Fitzgerald & Duke Ellington: The Stockholm Concert Feb. 7, 1966 (Pablo, 1989)
Ella Fitzgerald/Count Basie/Joe Pass: Digital III at Montreux (Pablo)
Ella: The Legendary Decca Recordings (Decca Jazz, 1995)
First Lady of Song (Verve, 1993)
Love Songs: Best of the Verve Songbooks (Verve, 1996)
Mack the Knife: The Complete Ella in Berlin Concert (Verve, 1993)
75th Birthday Celebration (Decca, 1993)
Sings the Rodgers & Hart Songbook (Verve, 1997)
These Are the Blues (Verve, 1986)

The "5" Royales
Monkey Hips and Rice: The "5" Royales Anthology (Rhino, 1994)

Roberta Flack
Softly with These Songs: The Best of Roberta Flack (WEA/Atlantic, 1993)

The Four Tops
Anthology (Motown, 1989)
Greatest Hits (Motown, 1967/1987)

Aretha Franklin
Amazing Grace (Atlantic, 1972)
I Never Loved a Man (the Way I Loved You) (Atlantic, 1967)
Lady Soul (Atlantic, 1968)
The Queen of Soul (Rhino/Atlantic, 1992)
30 Greatest Hits (Atlantic, 1985)

Freestyle Fellowship
Inner City Griots (Island, 1993)
To Whom It May Concern (Sun, 1991)

Gap Band
Best of Gap Band (Mercury Funk Essentials, 1994)
Gap Gold/Best of Gap Band (Mercury, 1985)

Marvin Gaye
Anthology (Motown, 1995)
The Master, 1961–1984 (Motown, 1995)
What's Going On (Motown, 1971)

J. Geils Band
Houseparty: The J. Geils Band Anthology (Atlantic & Atco Remasters/Rhino, 1993)

Al Green
Anthology (The Right Stuff, 1997)
Call Me (Hi, 1973/The Right Stuff, 1994)
Greatest Hits (Hi, 1975/The Right Stuff, 1995)

Daryl Hall
Sacred Songs (RCA, 1980)

Daryl Hall & John Oates
Greatest Hits (Razor & Tie/BMG Direct Marketing, 1997)

Herbie Hancock
Empyrean Isles (Blue Note, 1964/1985)
Maiden Voyage (Blue Note, 1965)

Wynonie Harris
Bloodshot Eyes—The Best of Wynonie Harris (Rhino, 1994)

Isaac Hayes
Hot Buttered Soul (Enterprise, 1969/Stax, 1987)

Jimi Hendrix
Are You Experienced? (Reprise, 1967/Experience Hendrix/MCA 1997)
Axis: Bold As Love (Reprise, 1967/Experience Hendrix/MCA, 1997)
Electric Ladyland (Reprise, 1968/Experience Hendrix/MCA 1997)
The Essential Jimi Hendrix (Reprise, 1978)

Billie Holiday
The Complete Decca Recordings (GRP, 1991)

Holland, Dozier & Holland
The Composers Series: Holland-Dozier-Holland (Motown)

John Lee Hooker
Chill Out (Point Blank, 1995)

**
The Ultimate Collection, 1948–1990 (Rhino, 1991)

Howlin' Wolf
The Chess Box (Chess, 1991)

Ivory Joe Hunter
Since I Met You Baby: The Best of Ivory Joe Hunter (Razor & Tie, 1994)

Ice Cube
AmeriKKKa's Most Wanted (Priority, 1990)

The Impressions
The Anthology, 1961–1977: Curtis Mayfield and the Impressions (MCA, 1992)
Keep On Pushing/People Get Ready (ABC-Paramount, 1964/ABC-Paramount, 1965/Kent, 1996)

Jackson 5
The Ultimate Collection (Motown, 1995)

Elmore James
The Sky Is Crying: The History of Elmore James (Rhino, 1993)

Jamiroquai
The Return of the Space Cowboy (Columbia, 1994)

Al Jarreau
We Got By (Warner Bros., 1975)

Blind Lemon Jefferson
Blind Lemon Jefferson (Milestone, 1992)
Blind Lemon Jefferson: Complete Works, 1926–1929 (Document, 1991)

Robert Johnson
King of the Delta Blues Singers (Columbia, 1961)
Robert Johnson: The Complete Recordings (Columbia, 1990)

Syl Johnson
Back For a Taste of Your Love/Diamond in the Rough (Hi 1973/1995)
Best of the Hi Records Years (Capitol/The Right Stuff, 1995)
Music to My Ears (Hi, 1991)

Janis Joplin (with Big Brother & the Holding Company)
Cheap Thrills (Columbia, 1968)

Louis Jordan
The Best of Louis Jordan (MCA, 1975)

Jungle Brothers
My Jimmy Weighs a Ton (Warner Bros., 1993)

Just Ice
Kool and Deadly (Justiclzms) (Fresh, 1987)

Albert King
Born under a Bad Sign (Atlantic, 1967)

B.B. King
The Best of B.B. King, Vol. One (Flair/Virgin, 1991)
Live at the Regal (MCA, 1971)

Earl Klugh
Solo Guitar (WEA/Warner Bros., 1989)

Kool & the Gang
The Best of Kool and the Gang, 1969–1976 (Mercury/Chronicles, 1993)

Last Poets
Be Bop or Be Dead (Axiom, 1993)
The Blue Guerrilla (Collectibles, 1990)
Hustler's Convention (Celluloid, 1984)
Last Poets (Celluloid, 1984)

Little Richard
The Georgia Peach (Specialty, 1991)
Little Richard's Greatest Hits (Epic, 1988)

Little Willie John
Fever: The Best of Little Willie John (Rhino, 1993)

LL Cool J
Mama Said Knock You Out (Def Jam/Columbia, 1990)

Darlene Love
The Best of Darlene Love (Abkco, 1992)

Cheryl Lynn
The Best of Cheryl Lynn: Got to Be Real (Legacy Records, 1996)

Taj Mahal
Mo' Roots (Columbia, 1974)

Main Source
Breaking Atoms (Wild Pitch, 1991)

The Manhattans
Dedicated to You (Carnival, 1966)
Dedicated to You/For You and Yours (Kent/UK, 1993)
Dedicated to You: Golden Carnival Classics, Pt. 1 (Collectables, 1991)
Follow Your Heart (Solid Smoke, 1981)
For You and Yours: Golden Carnival Classics, Pt. 2 (Collectables, 1991)
I Wanna Be Your Everything (DJM, 1976)

Bob Marley & the Wailers
Burnin' (Island, 1973)

Legend (Tuff Gong/Island, 1984)
Natty Dread (Island, 1974)

Martha & the Vandellas
Motown Milestones (Motown, 1995)

Massive Attack
Blue Lines (Wild Bunch/EMI, 1991)

Johnny Mathis
Johnny's Greatest Hits (Columbia, 1958/1988)

Curtis Mayfield
People Get Ready (Rhino, 1996)
Superfly (Curtom, 1972/Rhino, 1997)

Maze
Anthology (The Right Stuff, 1996)

Harold Melvin & the Blue Notes
Collector's Item (Sony, 1976)

Amos Milburn
The Best of Amos Milburn—Down the Road Apiece (EMI, 1993)

The Mills Brothers
The Mills Brothers: The Anthology (1931–1968) (MCA, 1995)

Van Morrison
Astral Weeks (Warner Bros., 1968)
Moondance (Warner Bros., 1970)

Maria Muldaur
Maria Muldaur (Reprise, 1973/Warner Archives, 1993)

Laura Nyro
The First Songs (Columbia, 1973)
New York Tendaberry (Columbia, 1969)

The O'Jays
Back Stabbers (Philadelphia International, 1972/Legacy, 1996)
Love Train: The Best of the O'Jays (Epic/Legacy, 1994)

Osibisa
Woyaya (MCA, 1971/AIM, 1993)

The Persuasions
Man, Oh Man: The Power of the Persuasions (EMI, 1997)

The Platters
Four Platters and One Lovely Dish (Bear Family, 1994)
The Magic Touch—An Anthology (Mercury, 1991)

The Very Best of the Platters (Mercury, 1991)

The Pointer Sisters
Fire: The Very Best of the Pointer Sisters, 1973–1986 (RCA, 1996)

Prince
Dirty Mind (Warner Bros., 1980)
1999 (Warner Bros., 1982)
Sign O' the Times (Paisley Park/Warner Bros., 1987)
The White Album (Neutral Zone, 1989)

Professor Longhair
Mardi Gras in New Orleans (Nighthawk, 1981)
Rock 'n' Roll Gumbo (Barclay, 1974/Dancing Cat, 1985)

Ma Rainey
Ma Rainey (Fantasy/Milestone, 1975)
Ma Rainey's Black Bottom (Yazoo, 1975)

Otis Redding
Live In Europe (Stax, 1967)
Otis Blue (Stax, 1965)
The Very Best of Otis Redding (Rhino, 1992)

Jimmy Reed
Speak the Lyrics to Me Mama Reed (Vee-Jay, 1993)

Smokey Robinson & the Miracles
Anthology: The Best of Smokey Robinson & the Miracles (Motown, 1995)

The Rolling Stones
Aftermath (Abkco, 1966)
Big Hits/High Tide and Green Grass (Abkco, 1966)
Exile on Main Street (Virgin, 1972)
Let It Bleed (Abkco, 1969)
The Singles Collection (Abkco, 1989)

Diana Ross
The Ultimate Collection (Motown, 1994)

Run-D.M.C.
Together Forever: Greatest Hits, 1983–1991 (Profile, 1991)

Otis Rush
1956–1958 Cobra Recordings (Paula, 1991)
Right Place, Wrong Time (Bullfrog/Hightone, 1976)

Sly & the Family Stone
Stand! (Epic, 1969)

FIVE-BONE ALBUMS

Bessie Smith
Bessie Smith—The Collection (Sony, 1989)
The Complete Recordings, Vol.1 (Sony, 1991)
The Complete Recordings, Vol.3 (Sony, 1992)
Mama's Got the Blues (Topaz Jazz, 1994)
Sings the Blues (Sony, 1996)
Sings the Jazz (EPM/Jazz Archives, 1991)

Huey "Piano" Smith
Rock 'n' Roll Revival (Ace, 1991)
Serious Clownin'—The Best of Huey Piano Smith (Rhino, 1989)

Soul Stirrers
Sam Cooke with the Soul Stirrers (Specialty, 1991)

Soul II Soul
Club Classics Vol I (Virgin, 1989)

The Spinners
One of a Kind Love Affair: The Anthology (Rhino, 1991)
Pick of the Litter (Rhino, 1975/1995)
Spinners (Rhino, 1973/1995)

Rod Stewart
Every Picture Tells a Story (Mercury, 1971)

Sylvester
Greatest Hits (Fantasy, 1988)
Greatest Hits: Non-Stop Dance Party (Fantasy, 1983)

Take 6
Take 6 (Reprise, 1988)

The Temptations
The Temptations Anthology (Motown, 1995)

Third World
96 Degrees in the Shade (Mango, 1977/1996)

The Time
What Time Is It? (Warner Bros., 1982)

Tony! Toni! Tone!
Sons of Soul (Wing, 1993)

Too $hort
Short Dog's in the House (Jive, 1990)

Tower of Power
Urban Renewal (Warner Bros., 1975)

The Trammps
Trammps (Golden Fleece, 1975/Philadelphia International, 1977)

A Tribe Called Quest
The Low End Theory (Jive, 1991)

Trouble Funk
Live (Infinite Zero/American, 1996)

Big Joe Turner
The Boss of the Blues (Atlantic, 1956)

Ultramagnetic MC's
Critical Beatdown (Next Plateau, 1988)

Sarah Vaughan
Crazy and Mixed Up (Fantasy, 1982/Pablo, 1987)
How Long Has This Been Going On (Fantasy, 1978/Pablo, 1987)
In the Land of Hi-Fi (Verve/Emarcy, 1955)
1960s Vol. 4 (PGD/Verve, 1963)
No Count Sarah (PGD/Verve, 1958)
Sarah Sings Soulfully (EMD/Capitol, 1963/1993)
Sassy Swings the Tivoli (Verve, 1963/1987)
With Clifford Brown (Verve/Emarcy, 1954)

T-Bone Walker
The Complete Capitol/Black and White Recordings (Capitol, 1995)
The Complete Imperial Recordings (EMI, 1991)
The Complete Recordings of T-Bone Walker, 1940–1952 (Mosaic, 1990)
I Want A Little Girl (Delmark, 1973)

Dinah Washington
First Issue: The Dinah Washington Story (Verve, 1993)
What a Diff'rence a Day Makes (Mercury, 1959/1987)

Grover Washington Jr.
Grover Washington Jr. Anthology (Motown, 1981)
Inner City Blues (Kudu, 1972/Motown, 1995)
Mister Magic (Kudu, 1975/Motown, 1995)

Muddy Waters
The Best of Muddy Waters (Chess, 1958/Chess-MCA, 1987)
The Chess Box (Chess-MCA, 1989)
Down on Stovall's Plantation (Testament, 1966)
His Best: 1947–1955 (Chess-MCA, 1997)
The Real Folk Blues (Chess, 1966/MCA, 1987)
Trouble No More: Singles, 1955–1959 (Chess-MCA, 1989)

WC (with Low Profile)
We're In This Together (Priority, 1989)

Junior Wells
Hoodoo Man Blues (Delmark, 1965)

Fred Wesley
New Friends (Antilles/Island, 1990)

The Whispers
Greatest Hits (The Right Stuff, 1997)

Barry White
All Time Greatest Hits (Mercury, 1994)

Chuck Willis
Stroll On: The Chuck Willis Collection (Razor & Tie, 1994)

Jackie Wilson
The Jackie Wilson Story (Epic, 1983)

BeBe & CeCe Winans
Greatest Hits (Sparrow, 1996)

Stevie Wonder
Essential Stevie Wonder (Import)
Innervisions (Motown, 1973)
Songs in the Key of Life (Motown, 1976)
Talking Book (Motown, 1972)

O.V. Wright
The Soul of O. V. Wright (MCA, 1992)

Wu-Tang Clan
Enter the Wu-Tang (36 Chambers) (Loud/RCA, 1993)

The Young Rascals
Time Piece: The Rascals' Greatest Hits (Atlantic, 1968)

If you're looking for some R&B music by a variety of performers, these compilation albums would be a good place to start.

Decades

Didn't It Blow Your Mind! Soul Hits of the '70s: Vol. 1 ♪♪♪♪ (Rhino, 1991)

Didn't It Blow Your Mind! Soul Hits of the '70s: Vol. 2 ♪♪♪♪ (Rhino, 1991)

Didn't It Blow Your Mind! Soul Hits of the '70s: Vol. 3 ♪♪♪♪ (Rhino, 1991)

Didn't It Blow Your Mind! Soul Hits of the '70s: Vol. 4 ♪♪♪ (Rhino, 1991)

Didn't It Blow Your Mind! Soul Hits of the '70s: Vol. 5 ♪♪ (Rhino, 1991)

Didn't It Blow Your Mind! Soul Hits of the '70s: Vol. 6 ♪♪♪♪ (Rhino, 1991)

Didn't It Blow Your Mind! Soul Hits of the '70s: Vol. 7 ♪♪♪ (Rhino, 1991)

Didn't It Blow Your Mind! Soul Hits of the '70s: Vol. 8 ♪♪♪♪ (Rhino, 1991)

Didn't It Blow Your Mind! Soul Hits of the '70s: Vol. 9 ♪♪♪♪ (Rhino, 1991)

Didn't It Blow Your Mind! Soul Hits of the '70s: Vol. 10 ♪♪♪ (Rhino, 1991)

Didn't It Blow Your Mind! Soul Hits of the '70s: Vol. 11 ♪♪ (Rhino, 1991)

Didn't It Blow Your Mind! Soul Hits of the '70s: Vol. 12 ♪♪♪ (Rhino, 1991)

Didn't It Blow Your Mind! Soul Hits of the '70s: Vol. 13 ♪♪ (Rhino, 1991)

Didn't It Blow Your Mind! Soul Hits of the '70s: Vol. 14 ♪♪ (Rhino, 1991)

Didn't It Blow Your Mind! Soul Hits of the '70s: Vol. 15 ♪♪♪♪ (Rhino, 1991)

Didn't It Blow Your Mind! Soul Hits of the '70s: Vol. 16 ♪♪♪ (Rhino, 1991)

Didn't It Blow Your Mind! Soul Hits of the '70s: Vol. 17 ♪♪♪♪ (Rhino, 1991)

Didn't It Blow Your Mind! Soul Hits of the '70s: Vol. 18 ♪♪ (Rhino, 1991)

Didn't It Blow Your Mind! Soul Hits of the '70s: Vol. 19 ♪♪ (Rhino, 1991)

Groove Me ('70s Soul) ♪♪♪ (Dominion)

#1 Soul Hits from the '60s (and some that should have been), Vol. 1: Tell It Like It Is ♪♪♪♪ (Relativity, 1997)

#1 Soul Hits from the '60s (and some that should have been), Vol. 2: Tighten Up ♪♪♪♪ (Relativity, 1997)

#1 Soul Hits from the '60s (and some that should have been), Vol. 3: Papa's Got a Brand New Bag ♪♪♪♪ (Relavity, 1997)

'70s Soul Revue ♪♪♪♪ (Warner Bros., 1997)

16 #1 Hits from the Early '60's ♪♪♪♪ (Motown)

16 #1 Hits from the Late '60's ♪♪♪♪ (Motown)

Soul Brothers and Sisters of the '60s ♪♪ (K-Tel, 1997)

Soul Brothers and Sisters of the '70s ♪♪♪ (K-Tel, 1997)

Soul Classics: Best of the '70s ♪♪ (Rebound, 1997)

Soul Classics: Best of the '80s ♪♪♪ (Rebound, 1997)

Soul Shots: A Collection of Sixties Soul Classics ♪♪♪♪♪ (Rhino, 1988)

Soul Shots: A Collection of Sixties Soul Classics, Vol. 2 ♪♪♪♪♪ (Rhino, 1988)

Soul Shots: A Collection of Sixties Soul Classics, Vol. 3 ♪♪♪♪ (Rhino, 1988)

Soul Shots: A Collection of Sixties Soul Classics, Vol. 4 — Urban Blues ♪♪♪♪♪ (Rhino, 1988)

12 #1 Hits from the '70s ♪♪ (Motown, 1980)

Video Soul: Best Soul of the '80s, Vol. 1 ♪♪♪ (Rhino, 1995)

Video Soul: Best Soul of the '80s, Vol. 2 ♪♪♪ (Rhino, 1995)

Disco (Bumpin')

Billboard Dance Hits: 1976 ♪♪♪♪ (Rhino, 1992)

Billboard Dance Hits: 1977 ♪♪♪ (Rhino, 1992)

Billboard Dance Hits: 1978 ♪♪♪ (Rhino, 1992)

Billboard Dance Hits: 1979 ♪♪ (Rhino, 1992)

Billboard Dance Hits: 1980 ♪♪♪ (Rhino, 1992)

Classic Club Mix: R&B Grooves ♪♪♪ (Cold Front, 1997)

Club Epic, Vol. 1 ♪♪♪♪ (Epic, 1994)

Club Epic, Vol. 2 ♪♪♪ (Epic, 1994)

Club Epic, Vol. 3 ♪♪♪ (Epic, 1994)

Club Epic, Vol. 4 ♪♪♪♪ (Epic, 1995)

Disco Fever ♪♪ (K-Tel, 1994)

Disco Fever: Rock the Planet ♪♪♪ (Warner Special Products, 1995)

Disco 54 ♪♪♪♪ (Hip-O, 1997)

Disco Queens: The '70s ♪♪♪♪ (Rhino, 1997)

Disco Queens: The '80s ♪♪♪♪ (Rhino, 1997)

The Disco Years, Vol. 1: Turn the Beat Around (1974–1978) 𝄞𝄞𝄞𝄞 (Rhino, 1992)

The Disco Years, Vol. 2: On the Beat (1978–1982) 𝄞𝄞𝄞𝄞 (Rhino, 1992)

The Disco Years, Vol. 3: Boogie Fever 𝄞𝄞𝄞 (Rhino, 1992)

The Disco Years, Vol. 4: Lost in Music 𝄞𝄞𝄞𝄞 (Rhino, 1992)

The Disco Years, Vol. 5: Must Be the Music 𝄞𝄞𝄞 (Rhino, 1992)

Discomania 𝄞𝄞 (K-Tel, 1997)

DJ Disco Mix 𝄞𝄞𝄞𝄞 (Beast, 1996)

Hot Nights—Disco Light 𝄞𝄞 (K-Tel, 1996)

Mighty Real 𝄞𝄞𝄞𝄞 (EMI, 1995)

Non-Stop Disco, Vol. 1 𝄞𝄞𝄞𝄞 (Chronicles, 1997)

Non-Stop Disco, Vol. 2 𝄞𝄞𝄞𝄞 (Chronicles, 1997)

Old School Boogie 𝄞𝄞𝄞𝄞 (Thump, 1996)

Pure Disco 𝄞𝄞𝄞𝄞 (Polydor, 1996)

Doo Wop

The Best of Doo Wop Ballads 𝄞𝄞𝄞𝄞𝄞 (Rhino, 1989)

The Best of Doo Wop Uptempo 𝄞𝄞𝄞𝄞𝄞 (Rhino, 1989)

The Doo Wop Box 𝄞𝄞𝄞𝄞𝄞 (Rhino, 1993)

The Doo Wop Box II 𝄞𝄞𝄞𝄞 (Rhino, 1996)

Funk

All Platinum Funk 𝄞𝄞𝄞 (Charly, 1995)

Back in the Day Jamz 𝄞𝄞𝄞 (Critique/PolyGram, 1997)

Classic Funk, Vol. 1 𝄞𝄞𝄞 (MVP/PolyGram, 1996)

Classic Funk, Vol. 2 𝄞𝄞𝄞 (MVP/PolyGram, 1996)

Classic Jazz Funk 𝄞𝄞𝄞𝄞 (MVP/EMI, 1996)

Cosmic Funk 𝄞𝄞𝄞𝄞 (Chronicles, 1997)

Funk Nation 𝄞𝄞𝄞 (Cold Front, 1996)

Funkalogy, Vol. I: Got to Give it Up 𝄞𝄞𝄞𝄞 (Motown, 1995)

Funkalogy, Vol. II: Behind the Groove 𝄞𝄞𝄞 (Motown, 1996)

In Yo' Face: The History of Funk, Vols. 1–5 𝄞𝄞𝄞𝄞 (Rhino, 1993)

Old School Funk 𝄞𝄞𝄞𝄞 (Thump, 1996)

Old School Mixx 𝄞𝄞𝄞𝄞 (Thump, 1997)

Rare Grooves: Straight Funk 𝄞𝄞𝄞 (Priority, 1997)

Standing on the Verge: The Roots of Funk 𝄞𝄞𝄞𝄞 (Shanachie)

Stax Funx 𝄞𝄞𝄞 (Ace, 1997)

Street Jams: Electric Funk, Vol. 1 𝄞𝄞𝄞𝄞 (Rhino, 1992)

Street Jams: Electric Funk, Vol. 2 𝄞𝄞𝄞 (Rhino, 1992)

Street Jams: Electric Funk, Vol. 3 𝄞𝄞𝄞𝄞 (Rhino, 1992)

Street Jams: Electric Funk, Vol. 4 𝄞𝄞𝄞 (Rhino, 1992)

Street Jams: Electric Funk, Vol. 1–4 𝄞𝄞𝄞𝄞𝄞 (Rhino, 1996)

Vintage Funk, Vol. 1 𝄞𝄞𝄞 (MVP/PolyGram, 1997)

Vintage Funk, Vol. 2 𝄞𝄞𝄞 (MVP/PolyGram, 1997)

Up for the Down Stroke: Uncut Funk, Vol. 1 𝄞𝄞𝄞 (Polydor, 1992)

Hip-Hop/Rap

America Is Dying Slowly 𝄞𝄞𝄞𝄞 (EastWest, 1996)

. . . And Then There Was Bass 𝄞𝄞𝄞 (LaFace/Arista, 1997)

Answer LP: Rap vs. Rap 𝄞𝄞𝄞 (Priority, 1990)

Assassin Hitworks 𝄞𝄞𝄞 (Arrogant/Bonafyed, 1996)

Bass Hits from Da Bottom, Vol. II 𝄞𝄞𝄞 (Lil' Joe, 1997)

Bass Mix U.S.A. 𝄞𝄞𝄞 (Cold Front, 1997)

Bay Area Playaz 𝄞𝄞𝄞 (Anonymous, 1995)

B-Ball's Best Kept Secret 𝄞𝄞 (Immortal/Epic, 1994)

Beats & Rhymes: Hip-Hop of the '90s, Vol. 1 𝄞𝄞𝄞𝄞 (Rhino, 1997)

Beats & Rhymes: Hip-Hop of the '90s, Vol. 2 𝄞𝄞𝄞 (Rhino, 1997)

Beats & Rhymes: Hip-Hop of the '90s, Vol. 3 𝄞𝄞𝄞 (Rhino, 1997)

Best of Bass 1 𝄞𝄞 (Priority, 1994)

Best of Bass 2 𝄞𝄞 (Priority, 1994)

Best of Bass 3 𝄞𝄞 (Priority, 1994)

The Best of Black Market Records: Hounds of Tha Underground 𝄞𝄞𝄞 (Black Market, 1997)

Best of the Box: Rap 𝄞𝄞𝄞 (K-Tel, 1992)

Best of the Wake-Up Show, Vol. 1 𝄞𝄞𝄞𝄞 (All City, 1996)

Best of the Wake-Up Show, Vol. 2 𝄞𝄞𝄞 (All City, 1996)

Best of the Wake-Up Show, Vol. 3 𝄞𝄞𝄞𝄞 (All City, 1996)

Big Phat Ones of Hip-Hop: Volume 1 𝄞𝄞𝄞 (BOXTunes, 1995)

Blunt Special Blends 𝄞𝄞𝄞 (Blunt, 1996)

Bomb Hip-Hop Compilation 𝄞𝄞𝄞 (PGA, 1995)

The Bomb Hip-Hop, Vol. 1 𝄞𝄞𝄞𝄞 (Backstage, 1996)

Booty and the Beat: Bass Jams, Vol. 1 𝄞𝄞 (Priority, 1996)

Booty Bass Mix, Vol. 1 𝄞𝄞 (Priority, 1997)

Booty Mix '96 𝄞𝄞 (Intersound, 1996)

Bounce '96 𝄞𝄞𝄞 (Rip-It, 1996)

Bust a Rap 𝄞𝄞𝄞𝄞 (Priority, 1993)

Cell Block Compilation 𝄞𝄞𝄞 (Cell Block, 1996)

Classic Club Mix: R&B Grooves 𝄞𝄞𝄞 (Cold Front, 1997)

Classic Hip-Hop Mastercuts, Vol. 1 𝄞𝄞𝄞𝄞 (Beechwood, 1995)

Classic Hip-Hop Mastercuts, Vol. 2 𝄞𝄞𝄞𝄞 (Beechwood, 1996)

Compton's Greatest Rap, Vol. 1 𝄞𝄞𝄞𝄞 (Priority, 1993)

Compton's Greatest Rap, Vol. 2 𝄞𝄞𝄞𝄞 (Priority, 1993)

Da Shit 𝄞𝄞𝄞𝄞 (Ummm, 1995)

Da Underground Sound, Vol. 1: East Side 𝄞𝄞𝄞𝄞 (Priority, 1996)

Da Undaground Sound, Vol. 2: West Side 𝄞𝄞𝄞 (Priority, 1996)

Da Undaground Sound, Vol. 3: Hip-Hop East Meets West 𝄞𝄞𝄞 (Priority, 1997)

Death Row's Greatest Hits 𝄞𝄞𝄞𝄞𝄞 (Death Row/Interscope, 1996)

Deep Concentration 𝄞𝄞𝄞𝄞𝄞 (OM, 1997)

Def Jam Classics, Vol. 1 𝄞𝄞𝄞𝄞 (Def Jam, 1989)

Def Jam Classics, Vol. 2 𝄞𝄞𝄞𝄞 (Def Jam, 1995)

Def Jam Greatest Hits 𝄞𝄞𝄞 (Def Jam, 1997)

Def Jam Greatest Hits Hardcore 𝄞𝄞𝄞𝄞 (Def Jam, 1997)

Def Jam Music Group 10th Anniversary Box Set 𝄞𝄞𝄞𝄞𝄞 (Def Jam, 1995)

Diggin' the Crates (for the Beats, Y'all) 𝄞𝄞𝄞𝄞 (Perfect Beat, 1986/Profile, 1994)

Down South Hustlers: Bouncin' and Swingin' 𝄞𝄞𝄞 (No Limit, 1995)

D-Shot Presents Boss Ballin' 𝄞𝄞𝄞 (Shot, 1995)

Eargasms (Crucial Poetics), Vol. 1 𝄞𝄞𝄞𝄞 (Manic, 1997)

East vs. West 𝄞𝄞𝄞 (K-Tel, 1991)

Explicit Rap 𝄞𝄞𝄞𝄞 (Priority, 1991)

First Generation of Rap: The Old School, Vol. 1 𝄞𝄞𝄞𝄞 (Collectables, 1994)

First Generation of Rap: The Old School, Vol. 2 𝄞𝄞𝄞𝄞 (Collectables, 1994)

First Generation of Rap: The Old School, Vol. 3 𝄞𝄞𝄞𝄞 (Collectables, 1994)

First Generation of Rap: The Old School, Vol. 4 𝄞𝄞𝄞 (Collectables, 1994)

1st Ladies of Rap 𝄞𝄞𝄞𝄞 (K-Tel, 1992)

Flippin' the Script: Rap Meets Poetry 🦴🦴🦴🦴 (Mouth Almighty/Mercury, 1996)

4080 Compilation Album, Vol. 1: Mobbin' Thru the Bay 🦴🦴🦴 (Swerve, 1996)

14 Fathoms Deep 🦴🦴🦴 (Loosegroove, 1996)

Funkin' It Up 🦴🦴🦴 (K-Tel, 1994)

Gangsta Nation: Rap's Hardest Songs 🦴🦴🦴 (Ruthless/Relativity, 1996)

Ghetto Rap 🦴🦴🦴 (Priority, 1993)

Ghetto Style DJ's Bass, Vol. 1 🦴🦴🦴🦴 (Lil' Joe, 1996)

Gimme Some Skins: Rap's Dirtiest Songs 🦴🦴🦴 (Ruthless/Relativity, 1996)

Groove Active 🦴🦴🦴🦴 (OM, 1995)

Hard Rap 🦴🦴 (Priority, 1990)

The Hill That's Real 🦴🦴🦴 (4th & B'way, 1992)

Hip-Hop Back in the Day 🦴🦴🦴🦴 (Priority, 1995)

Hip-Hop Classics, Vol. 1 🦴🦴🦴🦴 (Priority, 1996)

Hip-Hop Classics, Vol. 2 🦴🦴🦴🦴🦴 (Priority, 1996)

Hip-Hop Classics, Vol. 3 🦴🦴🦴🦴 (Priority, 1997)

Hip-Hop Greats: Classic Raps 🦴🦴🦴🦴 (Rhino, 1990)

Hip-Hop Mix 🦴🦴 (Max Music & Entertainment, 1996)

Hip-Hop's Most Wanted 🦴🦴🦴 (Priority, 1996)

Hip-Hop's Most Wanted 2 🦴🦴🦴🦴 (Priority, 1997)

Hip Ol' Skool 🦴🦴🦴🦴 (Hip-O/MCA, 1997)

History of Miami Bass 🦴🦴🦴🦴 (K-Tel, 1997)

History of Rap, Vol. 1 🦴🦴🦴🦴 (Cold Front, 1996)

History of Rap, Vol. 2 🦴🦴🦴 (Cold Front, 1996)

History of Rap, Vol. 3 🦴🦴🦴🦴 (Cold Front, 1996)

The Hit List 🦴🦴🦴 (Intersound, 1997)

Hurby's Machine: The House That Rap Built 🦴🦴🦴🦴 (Next Plateau, 1988)

In tha Beginning ... There Was Rap 🦴🦴🦴 (Priority, 1997)

International Blunt Funk 🦴🦴🦴 (In-a-Minute/Handlebar, 1997)

Jointz from Back In Da Day 🦴🦴🦴 (Quality/Warlock, 1994)

Jointz from Back In Da Day, Vol. 2 🦴🦴🦴 (Quality/Warlock, 1994)

The Juice Crew Story 🦴🦴🦴🦴 (Cold Chillin', 1995)

Kool Rap 🦴🦴🦴 (Priority, 1989)

Kurtis Blow Presents: The History of Rap, Vol. 1 🦴🦴🦴🦴🦴 (Rhino, 1997)

Kurtis Blow Presents: The History of Rap, Vol. 2 🦴🦴🦴🦴🦴 (Rhino, 1997)

Kurtis Blow Presents: The History of Rap, Vol. 3 🦴🦴🦴🦴 (Rhino, 1997)

Latin Hip-Hop Flava 🦴🦴🦴 (Priority, 1996)

Latin Lingo 🦴🦴🦴 (Rhino/Skankless, 1995)

Latin Lingo: Hip-Hop from La Raza, Vol. 2 🦴🦴🦴 (Skankless/Rhino, 1997)

The Lawhouse Experience, Vol. 1 🦴🦴🦴 (Street Life, 1997)

Legal Dope 🦴🦴 (Priority, 1995)

Loud '95 Nudder Budders (EP) 🦴🦴🦴 (Loud/RCA, 1994)

Major Flavas: Rap Classics 🦴🦴🦴 (Rebound, 1996)

Master P Presents: West Coast Bad Boyz, Vol. I 🦴🦴🦴 (No Limit, 1994/Priority, 1997)

Master P Presents: West Coast Bad Boyz, Vol. II 🦴🦴🦴 (No Limit/Priority, 1997)

Maximum Rap 🦴🦴🦴🦴 (Elektra, 1997)

Miami Bass: Heat Mix, Vol. 2 🦴🦴 (Cold Front, 1997)

Mobbin' Thru the Bay 🦴🦴🦴 (Swerve, 1996)

Nervous Hip-Hop 🦴🦴🦴 (Nervous, 1995)

The Next Chapter 🦴🦴 (Immortal/Epic, 1995)

NFL Jams 🦴🦴 (Castle, 1996)

Ol' Skool Butta, Vol. 1 🦴🦴🦴🦴 (Right Stuff, 1996)

Ol' Skool Butta, Vol. 2 🦴🦴🦴🦴 (Right Stuff, 1996)

Old School Rap, Vol. 1 🦴🦴🦴 (Thump, 1994)

Old School Rap, Vol. 2 🦴🦴🦴🦴 (Thump, 1995)

Old School Rap, Vol. 3 🦴🦴🦴 (Thump, 1996)

Old School Rarities: The Funky Drum Jams 🦴🦴🦴🦴 (Ol' Skool Flava, 1995)

One-Hit Compilation: Take Your Hit & Pass It 🦴🦴 (Rob No-Kneez, 1997)

One Million Strong 🦴🦴🦴🦴 (Mergela, 1995)

Pass the Mic: The Posse Album 🦴🦴🦴🦴 (Priority, 1996)

Phat Blunts: Rap Unda Tha Influence 🦴🦴🦴🦴 (Priority, 1996)

Phat Rap Flava '95 🦴🦴🦴 (Cold Front, 1995)

Pimps, Players & Poets 🦴🦴🦴 (Cold Front, 1995)

Planet Rap: A Sample of the World 🦴🦴🦴🦴 (Tommy Boy, 1993)

Pump Ya Fist: Hip-Hop Inspired by the Black Panthers 🦴🦴🦴🦴 (Avatar, 1995)

The Pusha' Man 🦴🦴 (The Road Productions, 1996)

Queens of Rap 🦴🦴🦴🦴 (Priority, 1989)

Raiders of the Lost Art ... 🦴🦴🦴🦴 (Street Life, 1994)

Rap Archives, Vol. 1 🦴🦴🦴🦴 (Sounds of Urban London, 1996)

Rap Beat from the Street 🦴🦴🦴🦴 (K-Tel, 1992)

Rap Declares War 🦴🦴🦴🦴 (Avenue/Rhino, 1992)

Rap G Style 🦴🦴🦴🦴 (Priority, 1995)

Rap: Ghetto Trax 🦴🦴🦴 (K-Tel, 1993)

Rap: Hall of Fame 🦴🦴🦴🦴 (K-Tel, 1992)

Rap Hitz 🦴🦴🦴 (Priority, 1993)

Rap Jams 🦴🦴🦴 (Priority, 1992)

Rap Miami Style 🦴🦴🦴 (Pandisc, 1990)

Rap: Most Vaulable Players 🦴🦴🦴🦴 (K-Tel, 1992)

Rap: On the Lighter Tip 🦴🦴🦴 (K-Tel, 1992)

Rap: Straight Outta the Ghetto 🦴🦴🦴🦴 (K-Tel, 1992)

Rap: 10 Years of Gold (1985–1994) 🦴🦴🦴 (K-Tel, 1995)

Rap: Today's Greatest Hits 🦴🦴🦴🦴 (K-Tel, 1993)

Rap Wit'Cha 🦴🦴🦴 (K-Tel, 1990)

Rap Wit'Cha 2 🦴🦴🦴 (K-Tel, 1990)

Rapmasters: From Tha Priority Vaults, Vol. 1 🦴🦴🦴 (Priority, 1996)

Rapmasters: From Tha Priority Vaults, Vol. 2 🦴🦴🦴 (Priority, 1996)

Rapmasters: From Tha Priority Vaults, Vol. 3 🦴🦴🦴🦴 (Priority, 1996)

Rapmasters: From Tha Priority Vaults, Vol. 4 🦴🦴🦴 (Priority, 1996)

Rapmasters: From Tha Priority Vaults, Vol. 5 🦴🦴🦴 (Priority, 1997)

Rapmasters: From Tha Priority Vaults, Vol. 6 🦴🦴🦴 (Priority, 1997)

Rapmasters: From Tha Priority Vaults, Vol. 7 🦴🦴 (Priority, 1997)

Rapmasters: From Tha Priority Vaults, Vol. 8 🦴🦴🦴 (Priority, 1997)

Rap's Biggest Hits 🦴🦴🦴🦴 (K-Tel, 1990)

Rap's Greatest Disses 🦴🦴🦴🦴 (Priority, 1993)

Rap's Greatest Hits, Vol. 1 🦴🦴🦴🦴 (Priority, 1997)

Rap's Greatest Hits, Vol. 2 🦴🦴🦴🦴 (Priority, 1997)

Rap's Greatest Hits, Vol. 3 🦴🦴🦴🦴 (Priority, 1997)

Rap's Greatest Stories 🦴🦴🦴🦴 (Priority, 1993)

Rare Grooves, Vol. 1: The Originals 🦴🦴🦴 (Priority, 1996)

The Rebirth of Cool, Vol. 3 🦴🦴🦴🦴 (4th & Broadway, 1995

Relativity Urban Assault 🦴🦴🦴🦴 (Relativity, 1996)

Return of the DJ (Bomb Hip-Hop, 1996)

Roll Wit Tha Flava (Epic, 1993)

Saucy, Vol. 1 (Ichiban, 1997)

Seattle . . . The Dark Side (Rhyme Cartel, 1993)

Select Old School Hip-Hop (Select, 1995)

Show Me the Money: Hip-Hop Pays (Priority, 1997)

Sick Wid' It Records Compilation: The Hogg In Me (Sick Wid' It/Jive, 1995)

Slammin' Ol' Skool Trax (Scotti Brothers, 1996)

So So Def Bass All-Stars (So So Def, 1996)

So So Def Bass All-Stars, Vol. II (So So Def, 1997)

Southwest Riders (Sick Wid' It/Jive, 1997)

Spittin' Lingo (Scotti Brothers, 1995)

Spread Yo' Hustle (Swerve, 1997)

State of Emergency: Society In Crisis, Vol. 1 (Motown, 1994)

Stop the Gunfight: Untold Stories (Intersound, 1997)

Straight from Da Streets (Priority, 1994)

Straight from the Hood (Profile, 1991)

Str8 Up Loco (Moola, 1995)

Street Jams: Back to the Old Skool, Vol. 1 (Rhino, 1992)

Street Jams: Back to the Old Skool, Vol. 2 (Rhino, 1992)

Street Jams: Back to the Old Skool, Vol. 3 (Rhino, 1992)

Street Jams: Hip-Hop from the Top, Vol. 1 (Rhino, 1992)

Street Jams: Hip-Hop from the Top, Vol. 2 (Rhino, 1992)

Street Jams: Hip-Hop from the Top, Vol. 3 (Rhino, 1994)

Street Jams: Hip-Hop from the Top, Vol. 4 (Rhino, 1994)

Street Soldiers (Priority, 1992)

Street Stories (Rhythm Street, 1996)

Suave House (Suave, 1997)

Subterranean Hitz, Vol. 1 (WordSound, 1997)

The Sugar Hill Records Story (Rhino, 1997)

10th Anniversary: Rap-A-Lot Records (Rap-A-Lot, 1996)

This Is Bass (Hot Productions, 1989)

Time to Taste Bass (Chaos, 1994)

True School: Lyrical Lessons from the Rap Legends, Vol. 1 (Cold Front, 1996)

True School: Lyrical Lessons from the Rap Legends, Vol. 2 (Cold Front, 1996)

True School: Lyrical Lessons from the Rap Legends, Vol. 3 (Cold Front, 1996)

Ultimate Hip-Hop Party 1998 (Arista, 1997)

Urban Beats, Vol. 1 (Next Plateau, 1996)

Uptown MTV Unplugged (MCA, 1993)

Uptown's Block Party, Vol. 1 (Universal, 1996)

Uptown's Block Party, Vol. 2 (Universal, 1996)

West Coast Rap, Vol. 1: The First Dynasty (Rhino, 1992)

West Coast Rap, Vol. 2: The First Dynasty (Rhino, 1992)

West Coast Rap, Vol. 3: The First Dynasty (Rhino, 1992)

West Coast Rap: The Renegades (Rhino, 1992)

What's Up? Rap Hits of the '90s (Rhino, 1995)

Yo! MTV Raps (Def Jam, 1997)

Young Southern Playaz, Vol. 1 (Priority, 1996)

History/General R&B Collections

The ABC's of Soul (Hip-O, 1996)

All Black Enough For You? (Legacy, 1995)

Beg, Scream & Shout! The Big Ol' Box of '60s Soul (Rhino, 1997)

Billboard Hot R&B Hits: 1980 (Rhino, 1996)

Billboard Hot R&B Hits: 1981 (Rhino, 1996)

Billboard Hot R&B Hits: 1982 (Rhino, 1996)

Billboard Hot R&B Hits: 1983 (Rhino, 1996)

Billboard Hot R&B Hits: 1984 (Rhino, 1996)

Billboard Hot R&B Hits: 1985 (Rhino, 1996)

Billboard Hot R&B Hits: 1986 (Rhino, 1996)

Billboard Hot R&B Hits: 1987 (Rhino, 1996)

Billboard Hot R&B Hits: 1988 (Rhino, 1996)

Billboard Hot R&B Hits: 1989 (Rhino, 1996)

Brown Eyed Soul: The Sound of East L.A., Vol. 1 (Rhino, 1997)

Brown Eyed Soul: The Sound of East L.A., Vol. 2 (Rhino, 1997)

Brown Eyed Soul: The Sound of East L.A., Vol. 3 (Rhino, 1997)

Classic Soul (MVP/PolyGram, 1997)

Deep Soul, Vol. 2 (Priority, 1996)

East Coast Family, Vol. 1 (Motown)

Golden Age of Black Music (Atlantic, 1989)

High on the Hog: The Sweet Sounds of Muscle Shoals (Overture, 1996)

Inner City Blues: The Music of Marvin Gaye (Motown, 1995)

Legacy Rhythm & Soul Revue (Legacy, 1995)

Lionel Richie: The Composer Series (Motown)

New Jack Hits (Rhino, 1996)

Old School, Vol. 1 (Thump, 1994)

Old School, Vol. 2 (Thump, 1994)

Old School, Vol. 3 (Thump, 1994)

Old School, Vol. 4 (Thump, 1994)

Old School, Vol. 5 (Thump, 1994)

On the Real Side (Sequel, 1991)

Only Soul 1985–1989 (Warner Special Products, 1996)

Phat Trax: The Best of the Old School, Vol. 1 (Rhino, 1994)

Phat Trax: The Best of the Old School, Vol. 2 (Rhino, 1994)

Phat Trax: The Best of the Old School, Vol. 3 (Rhino, 1994)

Phat Trax: The Best of the Old School, Vol. 4 (Rhino, 1994)

Phat Trax: The Best of the Old School, Vol. 5 (Rhino, 1994)

Phat Trax: The Best of the Old School, Vol. 6 (Rhino, 1994)

Phat Trax: The Best of the Old School, Vol. 7 (Rhino, 1994)

Pimps, Players & Private Eyes (Sire/Warner Bros., 1991)

Pure Soul (Polygram, 1997)

Soul Motion (OM, 1996)

Soul Soldiers (Ace, 1988)

Soulful Grooves: R&B Instrumental Classics, Vol. 1 (Hip-O, 1996)

Sweet Soul Music: Voices from the Shadows (Sire, 1992)

Urban Fire (Hip-O, 1997)

Vintage Soul, Vol. 1 (MVP, 1997)

Vintage Soul Classics 🎵🎵 (Boomerang, 1997)

Holidays

Christmas Cheer from Motown 🎵🎵🎵 (Motown)

Christmas Rap 🎵🎵🎵 (Priority, 1987)

Handel's Messiah: A Soulful Celebration 🎵🎵🎵 (Reprise, 1992)

A LaFace Family Christmas 🎵🎵🎵🎵 (LaFace, 1994)

A Motown Christmas 🎵🎵🎵🎵 (Motown)

A Motown Christmas Carol 🎵🎵🎵 (Motown)

Soul Christmas 🎵🎵🎵🎵 (Atlantic & Atco Remasters, 1991)

Ladies

Atlantic Sisters of Soul 🎵🎵🎵🎵 (Rhino, 1992)

Cheatin' from a Woman's Point of View, Vol. 1 🎵🎵🎵 (Ichiban, 1995)

Dance Floor Divas: The '70s 🎵🎵🎵🎵 (Rhino, 1996)

Disco Queens: The '70s 🎵🎵🎵🎵 (Rhino, 1997)

Disco Queens: The '80s 🎵🎵🎵🎵 (Rhino, 1997)

Divas of Dance, Vol. 1 🎵🎵🎵🎵 (DCC, 1996)

Divas of Dance, Vol. 2 🎵🎵🎵🎵 (DCC, 1996)

Divas of Dance, Vol. 3 🎵🎵🎵 (DCC, 1996)

Divas of Dance, Vol. 4 🎵🎵🎵 (DCC, 1996)

Divas of Dance, Vol. 5 🎵🎵🎵 (DCC, 1996)

Funkalogy, Vol. III: Dance Divas 🎵🎵🎵 (Motown, 1996)

Motown's Leading Ladies 🎵🎵🎵 (Motown, 1995)

R&B Heroines: Goldner's Golden Girls 🎵🎵🎵 (Sequel, 1997)

Soulful Ladies of the '80s 🎵🎵🎵 (Hip-O, 1996)

The Stax Soul Sisters 🎵🎵 (Fantasy, 1988)

New Orleans

The Best of New Orleans Rhythm & Blues, Vol. 1 🎵🎵🎵🎵 (Rhino, 1988)

The Best of New Orleans Rhythm & Blues, Vol. 2 🎵🎵🎵🎵 (Rhino, 1988)

Highlights from Crescent City Soul: Sound of New Orleans, 1947–1974 🎵🎵🎵🎵 (EMI, 1996)

Record Label Collections

A Decade of Hits: Philly International's Greatest 🎵🎵🎵 (CBS, 1984)

A Postcard from Philly 🎵🎵🎵 (Legacy, 1997)

The Brunswick Years, Vol. I 🎵🎵🎵🎵 (Brunswick, 1995)

Chess Soul: A Decade of Chicago's Finest 🎵🎵🎵🎵 (Chess/MCA, 1997)

The Cobra Records Story 🎵🎵🎵🎵 (Capricorn/Warner Bros., 1993)

The Complete Stax/Volt Singles, Vol. 1: 1959–1968 🎵🎵🎵🎵🎵 (The Atlantic Group, 1991)

The Complete Stax/Volt Singles, Vol. 2: 1968–1971 🎵🎵🎵🎵 (Stax/Fantasy, 1993)

The Complete Stax/Volt Singles, Vol. 3: 1972–1975 🎵🎵🎵 (Stax/Fantasy, 1994)

Cruizin' to Motown 🎵🎵 (Thump, 1995)

Every Great Motown Song: The First 25 Years, Vol I: The '60s 🎵🎵 (Motown, 1986)

Every Great Motown Song: The First 25 Years, Vol II: The '70s 🎵🎵 (Motown, 1986)

The Fire/Fury Records Story 🎵🎵🎵🎵 (Capricorn/Warner Bros., 1993)

Hi Times/Hi Records: The R&B Years 🎵🎵🎵🎵🎵 (Hi/The Right Stuff, 1995)

Hitsville U.S.A.: The Motown Singles Collection, 1959–1971 🎵🎵🎵🎵🎵 (Motown, 1992)

Hitsville U.S.A., Vol. 2: The Motown Singles Collection, 1972–1992 🎵🎵🎵🎵 (Motown, 1993)

Hush Productions: The Music Makers, Vol. 1 🎵🎵🎵 (EMI, 1996)

The Memories, the Music, the Magic of Motown: A Tribute to Berry Gordy 🎵🎵🎵 (Motown, N/A)

Motown Blues Evolution 🎵🎵 (Motown)

Motown Classic Hits, Vol. I 🎵🎵🎵 (Motown, 1995)

Motown Classic Hits, Vol. II 🎵🎵🎵 (Motown, 1995)

Motown Classic Hits, Vol. III 🎵🎵🎵 (Motown, 1995)

Motown Classic Hits, Vol. IV 🎵🎵🎵 (Motown, 1995)

Motown Classic Hits, Vol. V 🎵🎵 (Motown, 1995)

Motown Comes Home 🎵🎵🎵 (Motown)

Motown Love Songs 🎵🎵🎵 (PolyGram, 1994)

Motown Meets the Beatles 🎵🎵 (Motown)

Motown Year by Year: The Sound of Young America—1964 🎵🎵🎵 (Motown, 1995)

Motown Year by Year: The Sound of Young America—1966 🎵🎵🎵 (Motown, 1995)

Motown Year by Year: The Sound of Young America—1968 🎵🎵🎵 (Motown, 1995)

Motown Year by Year: The Sound of Young America—1969 🎵🎵🎵🎵 (Motown, 1995)

Motown Year by Year: The Sound of Young America—1970 🎵🎵🎵🎵 (Motown, 1995)

Motown Year by Year: The Sound of Young America—1973 🎵🎵🎵 (Motown, 1995)

Motown Year by Year: The Sound of Young America—1975 🎵🎵🎵 (Motown, 1995)

Motown Year by Year: The Sound of Young America—1976 🎵🎵 (Motown, 1995)

Motown Year by Year: The Sound of Young America—1980 🎵🎵🎵 (Motown, 1995)

Motown Year by Year: The Sound of Young America—1982 🎵🎵🎵 (Motown, 1995)

Motown Year by Year: The Sound of Young America—1985 🎵🎵🎵🎵 (Motown, 1995)

Motown Year by Year: The Sound of Young America—1987 🎵🎵🎵 (Motown, 1995)

Philadelphia Classics 🎵🎵🎵 (CBS, 1977)

The Philly Sound: Kenny Gamble, Leon Huff & the Story of Brotherly Love (1966–1976) 🎵🎵🎵🎵 (Epic/Legacy, 1997)

RCA Victor Blues & Rhythm Revue 🎵🎵🎵🎵 (RCA, 1988)

The Red Bird Story 🎵🎵🎵🎵 (Charly, 1991)

The Scepter Records Story 🎵🎵🎵🎵 (Capricorn/Warner Bros., 1992)

16 #1 Hits from the Early '60s 🎵🎵🎵 (Motown, 1982)

Stax/Volt Revue, Vol 2: Live in Paris (Atlantic, 1966)

Sweet Soul Music: The Stax Groups 🎵🎵🎵 (Fantasy, 1988)

3000 Volts of Stax 🎵🎵 (Ace, 1994)

Top of the Stax: 20 Greatest Hits 🎵🎵🎵🎵 (Fantasy, 1988)

Top of the Stax: Vol. II 🎵🎵🎵🎵 (Fantasy, 1991)

The Westbound Sound of Detroit: Sensational Motor City Groups, 1969–75 🎵🎵🎵🎵 (Westbound/Ace, 1995)

Slow Jams (Humpin')

Baddest Love Jams, Vol. 1: A Quiet Storm 🎵🎵🎵🎵 (Motown, 1995)

Baddest Love Jams, Vol 2: Fire Desire 🎵🎵🎵 (Motown, 1995)

Baddest Love Jams, Vol. 3: After the Dance 🎵🎵🎵 (Motown, 1996)

Between the Sheets, Vol. 1 🎵🎵 (Epic, 1995)

Between the Sheets, Vol. 2 🎵🎵 (Epic, 1995)

Between the Sheets, Vol. 3 🦴🦴 (Epic, 1995)

Between the Sheets, Vol. 4 🦴🦴 (Epic, 1995)

Classic Mellow, Vol. 1 🦴🦴🦴🦴 (MVP, 1997)

Classic Mellow, Vol. 2 🦴🦴🦴 (MVP, 1997)

Classic Mellow, Vol. 3 🦴🦴🦴 (MVP, 1997)

18 Soulful Ballads 🦴🦴🦴 (Warner Special Products, 1996)

Endless Love: Motown's Greatest Love Songs 🦴🦴 (Motown, 1995)

From Philly with Love 🦴🦴🦴 (Legacy, 1995)

The Glory of Love: '50s 🦴🦴🦴🦴 (Hip-O, 1997)

The Glory of Love: '60s 🦴🦴🦴🦴 (Hip-O, 1997)

The Glory of Love: '70s 🦴🦴🦴🦴 (Hip-O, 1997)

The Glory of Love: '80s 🦴🦴🦴 (Hip-O, 1997)

The Glory of Love: Sweet and Soulful Love Songs 🦴🦴🦴 (Hip-O, 1997)

Love Jams, Vol. 1 🦴🦴🦴🦴 (Warner Bros., 1996)

Love Jams, Vol. 2 🦴🦴🦴 (Warner Bros., 1996)

Love's Train: The Best of Funk Essentials Ballads 🦴🦴🦴🦴 (Mercury, 1995)

Maximum Slow Jams 🦴🦴🦴🦴 (Elektra, 1997)

Motown Love Songs 🦴🦴🦴 (Motown, 1996)

Old School Love Songs, Vol. 1 🦴🦴🦴 (Thump, 1995)

Old School Love Songs, Vol. 2 🦴🦴 (Thump, 1995)

Old School Love Songs, Vol. 3 🦴🦴🦴 (Thump, 1995)

Old School Love Songs, Vol. 4 🦴🦴 (Thump, 1997)

The Power of Love: Best of the Soul Essentials Ballads 🦴🦴🦴🦴 (Polydor, 1996)

Quiet Storms, Vol. 1 🦴🦴🦴🦴 (MCA, 1996)

Quiet Storms, Vol. 2 🦴🦴🦴 (MCA, 1995)

Risque Rhythm: Nasty 50's R&B 🦴🦴🦴🦴 (Rhino, 1991)

Sex & Soul, Vols. 1–3 🦴🦴🦴 (EMI, 1996)

Slow Grind 🦴🦴🦴 (Priority, 1996)

Slow Groove Love Jams of the '70s 🦴 (K-Tel, 1995)

Slow Jams, Vols. 1–7 🦴🦴🦴 (The Right Stuff, 1995)

Slow Jams of the '60s, Vols. 1–2 🦴🦴🦴 (The Right Stuff, 1994)

Slow Jams of the '70s, Vols. 1–5 🦴🦴🦴🦴 (The Right Stuff, 1993)

Slow Jams of the '80s, Vols. 1–4 🦴🦴🦴 (The Right Stuff, 1997)

Smooth Grooves: A Sensual Collection, Vol. 1 🦴🦴🦴🦴 (Rhino, 1995)

Smooth Grooves: A Sensual Collection, Vol. 2 🦴🦴🦴🦴 (Rhino, 1995)

Smooth Grooves: A Sensual Collection, Vol. 3 🦴🦴🦴 (Rhino, 1995)

Smooth Grooves: A Sensual Collection, Vol. 4 🦴🦴🦴 (Rhino, 1995)

Smooth Grooves: A Sensual Collection, Vol. 5 🦴🦴🦴 (Rhino, 1995)

Smooth Grooves: A Sensual Collection, Vol. 6 🦴🦴🦴🦴 (Rhino, 1996)

Smooth Grooves: A Sensual Collection, Vol. 7 🦴🦴🦴 (Rhino, 1996)

Smooth Grooves: A Sensual Collection, Vol. 8 🦴🦴🦴🦴 (Rhino, 1996)

Smooth Grooves: A Sensual Collection, Vol. 9 🦴🦴🦴 (Rhino, 1996)

Smooth Grooves: The '60s, Vol. 1 🦴🦴🦴 (Rhino, 1997)

Smooth Grooves: The '60s, Vol. 2 🦴🦴🦴 (Rhino, 1997)

Smooth Grooves: The '60s, Vol. 3 🦴🦴🦴 (Rhino, 1997)

Smooth Love Jams of the '90s, Vol. 1 🦴 (Beast, 1996)

Smooth Luv: The Luv Collection 🦴🦴🦴 (EMI, 1996)

Soul Serenade: Intimate R&B 🦴🦴🦴 (Rhino, 1997)

Strip Jointz 🦴🦴🦴 (Robbins, 1996)

Soundtracks

A Low Down Dirty Shame 🦴🦴🦴 (Jive, 1994)

Above the Rim 🦴🦴🦴🦴 (Death Row/Interscope, 1994)

Addams Family Values 🦴🦴🦴🦴 (Atlas, 1993)

Bad Boys 🦴🦴🦴 🦴🦴🦴 (Work, 1995)

Beverly Hills Cop III 🦴🦴🦴 (MCA, 1994)

Blankman 🦴🦴🦴 (Epic Soundtrax, 1994)

Boomerang 🦴🦴🦴🦴 (LaFace/Arista, 1992)

Booty Call 🦴🦴🦴 (Jive, 1997)

Boyz 'N the Hood 🦴🦴🦴🦴 (Qwest/Warner Bros., 1991)

Breakin' 🦴🦴🦴🦴 (Polydor, 1984)

Breakin' 2: Electric Boogaloo 🦴🦴 (Polydor, 1985)

Bulletproof 🦴🦴🦴🦴 (MCA Soundtracks, 1996)

Car Wash 🦴🦴🦴🦴 (MCA, 1976/1996)

CB4 🦴🦴🦴🦴 (MCA, 1992)

Cleopatra Jones 🦴🦴🦴🦴 (Warner Bros., 1973)

Clockers 🦴🦴🦴 (40 Acres and a Mule/MCA Soundtracks, 1995)

Colors 🦴🦴🦴🦴🦴 (Warner Bros., 1988)

Coming to America 🦴🦴 (Atco, 1988)

The Commitments 🦴🦴🦴 (MCA, 1991)

The Commitments, Vol. 2 🦴🦴🦴 (MCA, 1992)

Corrina, Corrina 🦴🦴🦴 (RCA, 1994)

Crooklyn: A Spike Lee Joint! Vol. 1 🦴🦴🦴🦴 (40 Acres and a Mule/MCA Soundtracks, 1994)

D.C. Cab 🦴 (MCA, 1984)

Dangerous Ground 🦴🦴🦴 (Jive, 1997)

Dangerous Minds 🦴🦴🦴 (MCA Soundtracks, 1995)

Dead Presidents 🦴🦴🦴🦴 (Underworld, 1995)

Deep Cover 🦴🦴🦴🦴 (Solar, 1992/The Right Stuff, 1996)

Disorderlies 🦴🦴 (Polydor, 1987)

Do the Right Thing 🦴🦴🦴🦴 (Motown, 1989)

Don't Be a Menace to South Central While Drinking Your Juice in the Hood 🦴🦴🦴 (Island, 1996)

Eddie 🦴🦴🦴 (Island/Hollywood, 1996)

The Five Heartbeats 🦴🦴🦴🦴 (Virgin, 1991)

Fresh 🦴🦴🦴🦴🦴 (Loud/RCA, 1994)

Friday 🦴🦴🦴🦴 (Priority, 1995)

Get on the Bus 🦴🦴🦴🦴 (40 Acres and a Mule/Interscope, 1996)

Girl 6 🦴🦴🦴🦴 (Warner Bros., 1996)

Girls Town 🦴🦴🦴🦴 (Mercury, 1996)

The Golden Child 🦴🦴 (Capitol, 1987)

Good Burger 🦴🦴🦴 (Capitol, 1997)

Gravesend 🦴🦴🦴 (Island, 1997)

Great White Hype 🦴🦴🦴🦴 (Hudlin Bros./Epic Soundtrax, 1996)

Gridlock'd 🦴🦴🦴🦴 (Death Row/Interscope, 1997)

Gunmen 🦴🦴🦴 (MCA, 1993)

High School High 🦴🦴🦴🦴 (Big Beat, 1996)

Higher Learning 🦴🦴🦴🦴 (550/Epic Soundtrax, 1994)

Hoodlum 🦴🦴🦴 (Loud/Interscope, 1997)

Hoop Dreams 🦴🦴🦴 (MCA, 1994)

House Party 🦴🦴🦴🦴 (Motown, 1990)

House Party 2 🦴🦴🦴 (MCA, 1991)

House Party 3 🦴🦴🦴 (Select/Street, 1994)

How to Be a Player 🦴🦴🦴 (Def Jam, 1997)

I Like It Like That 🦴🦴🦴 (Columbia, 1994)

I'm Bout It 🦴🦴🦴 (No Limit/Priority, 1997)

Into the Night 🦴🦴🦴🦴 (MCA, 1985)

Jason's Lyric 🦴🦴🦴🦴 (Mercury, 1994)

Judgment Night 🦴🦴🦴🦴🦴 (Immortal/Epic, 1993)

Juice 🦴🦴🦴🦴 (MCA, 1992)

Krush Groove 🦴🦴🦴🦴 (Warner Bros., 1985)

The Last Dragon 🦴🦴 (Motown, 1985)

Lean on Me 🦴🦴🦴🦴 (Warner Bros., 1989)

Less than Zero 🦴🦴🦴🦴 (Def Jam, 1987)

Livin' Large! 🦴🦴🦴🦴 (Def Jam, 1991)

A Low Down Dirty Shame 𝄞𝄞 (Hollywood/Jive, 1994)

Made in America 𝄞𝄞𝄞 (Elektra, 1993)

Malcolm X 𝄞𝄞𝄞 (Qwest/Reprise, 1992)

Marked for Death 𝄞𝄞𝄞 (Delicious Vinyl, 1990)

The Mask 𝄞𝄞𝄞 (Chaos, 1994)

Men in Black 𝄞𝄞𝄞𝄞 (Columbia/Sony Soundtrax, 1997)

Menace II Society 𝄞𝄞𝄞𝄞 (Jive, 1993)

Mo' Money 𝄞𝄞𝄞𝄞 (Perspective, 1992)

Money Talks 𝄞𝄞𝄞 (Arista, 1997)

Money Train 𝄞𝄞𝄞 (550/Epic Soundtrax, 1995)

Murder Was the Case 𝄞𝄞𝄞𝄞 (Death Row/Interscope, 1994)

New Jack City 𝄞𝄞𝄞𝄞 (Giant/Reprise, 1991)

New Jersey Drive, Vol. 1 𝄞𝄞𝄞𝄞 (Tommy Boy, 1995)

New Jersey Drive, Vol. 2 (EP) 𝄞𝄞𝄞 (Tommy Boy, 1995)

New York Undercover 𝄞𝄞𝄞𝄞 (Uptown/MCA, 1995)

Nothing to Lose 𝄞𝄞𝄞𝄞 (Tommy Boy, 1997)

The Nutty Professor 𝄞𝄞𝄞𝄞 (Def Jam, 1996)

Old School Friday: More Music from Friday 𝄞𝄞𝄞 (Priority, 1995)

Original Gangstas 𝄞𝄞𝄞 (Noo Trybe, 1996)

Panther 𝄞𝄞𝄞𝄞 (Mercury, 1995)

Phat Beach 𝄞𝄞𝄞 (TVT, 1996)

Poetic Justice 𝄞𝄞𝄞𝄞𝄞 (Epic, 1993)

Posse 𝄞𝄞𝄞 (A&M, 1993)

Rhyme & Reason 𝄞𝄞𝄞𝄞 (Priority, 1997)

RIOT 𝄞𝄞𝄞 (Rhino Movie Music, 1997)

Running Scared 𝄞𝄞𝄞 (MCA, 1986)

Saturday Night Fever 𝄞𝄞𝄞𝄞𝄞 (RSO, 1977)

School Daze 𝄞𝄞𝄞𝄞 (EMI-Manhattan, 1988)

Set It Off 𝄞𝄞𝄞𝄞 (EastWest, 1996)

The Show 𝄞𝄞𝄞𝄞 (Def Jam, 1995)

Sister Act 𝄞𝄞 (Hollywood, 1992)

Sister Act 2: Back in the Habit 𝄞 (Hollywood, 1993)

The 6th Man 𝄞𝄞𝄞 (Hollywood, 1997)

Soul In the Hole 𝄞𝄞𝄞𝄞 (Loud/RCA, 1997)

Soul Man 𝄞𝄞𝄞𝄞 (A&M, 1986)

Soul Food 𝄞𝄞𝄞𝄞 (Arista, 1997)

South Central 𝄞𝄞𝄞𝄞 (Hollywood BASIC, 1992)

Space Jam 𝄞𝄞𝄞𝄞 (Warner Sunset/Atlantic, 1996)

Sprung 𝄞𝄞𝄞 (Qwest/Warner Bros., 1997)

Steel 𝄞𝄞𝄞 (Qwest/Warner Bros., 1997)

Streetfighters 𝄞𝄞𝄞𝄞 (VRS, 1994)

Strictly Business 𝄞𝄞𝄞𝄞 (MCA, 1991)

The Substitute 𝄞𝄞 (Priority, 1996)

Sugar Hill 𝄞𝄞𝄞 (Fox, 1994)

Sunset Park 𝄞𝄞𝄞 (Flavor Unit/EastWest, 1996)

Supercop 𝄞𝄞 (Interscope, 1996)

Tales from the Hood 𝄞𝄞𝄞𝄞 (40 Acres and a Mule/MCA Soundtracks, 1995)

Tap 𝄞𝄞𝄞 (Epic, 1989)

Teenage Mutant Ninja Turtles 𝄞𝄞𝄞 (SBK, 1990)

Teenage Mutant Ninja Turtles II: The Secret of the Ooze 𝄞 (SBK, 1991)

Thank God It's Friday 𝄞𝄞𝄞𝄞 (Casablanca, 1978)

A Thin Line Between Love & Hate 𝄞𝄞𝄞 (Jac-Mac/Warner Bros., 1996)

To Wong Foo, Thanks for Everything! Julie Newmar 𝄞𝄞𝄞𝄞 (MCA, 1995)

Trespass 𝄞𝄞𝄞𝄞 (Sire, 1992)

Waiting to Exhale 𝄞𝄞𝄞𝄞 (Arista, 1995)

When We Were Kings 𝄞𝄞𝄞𝄞 (DAS/Mercury, 1997)

White Men Can't Jump 𝄞𝄞𝄞 (EMI, 1992)

Who's the Man? 𝄞𝄞𝄞 (Uptown/MCA, 1993)

Wild Style 𝄞𝄞𝄞𝄞𝄞 (Rhino Movie Music, 1997)

The Wiz 𝄞𝄞𝄞𝄞 (MCA, 1978/1997)

musicHound

Indexes

Band Member Index

Producer Index

Roots Index

Category Index

Can't remember what band a certain musician or vocalist is in? Wondering if a person has been in more than one band? The Band Member Index will guide you to the appropriate entry (or entries).

Aaronson, Kenny *See* Stories

Abrams, Bryan *See* Color Me Badd

Aceyalone *See* Freestyle Fellowship

Adam, George *See* Fatback Band/Fatback

Adams, Billy *See* Dexy's Midnight Runners/Kevin Rowland & Dexy's Midnight Runners

Adams, Clifford *See* Kool & the Gang

Adams, Mark "The Hansolor" *See* Slave/Steve Arrington

Adams, Victoria "Posh Spice" *See* The Spice Girls

ADMoney *See* Lordz of Brooklyn

Afloat, Yusef *See* The Nonce

Ajile *See* Arrested Development/Speech/Dionne Farris

Albin, Peter *See* Janis Joplin/Big Brother & the Holding Company

Alexander, Fred Jr. *See* Lakeside

Alexander, James *See* The Bar-Kays

Allen, Jeff *See* Mint Condition

Allen, Papa Dee *See* War

Allen, Rick *See* The Box Tops

Allison, Verne *See* The Dells

Almo, Michael *See* Kid Creole & the Coconuts/Dr. Buzzard's Original Savannah Band

Alston, Barbara *See* The Crystals

Alston, Gerald *See* The Manhattans

Amao, Loughty Lasisi *See* Osibisa

Amarfio, Sol *See* Osibisa

Anderson, Al *See* Bob Marley & the Wailers

Anderson, Alfa *See* Chic

Anderson, Katherine *See* The Marvelettes

Anderson, Keith *See* Dirty Dozen Brass Band

Anderson, Robert *See* Solo

Anderson, Stan *See* The Chi-Lites

Andre the Giant/A.G. *See* Showbiz & A.G.

Andrew, Sam *See* Janis Joplin/Big Brother & the Holding Company

Andrews, Mark "Sisqo" *See* Dru Hill

Andrews, Revert *See* Dirty Dozen Brass Band

Andy, Horace *See* Massive Attack/Protection

Anthony, Larry "Jazz" *See* Dru Hill

Archer, Clifford *See* Atlantic Starr

Arrington, Steve *See* Slave/Steve Arrington

Ashford, Nickolas *See* Ashford & Simpson

Ashford, Rosalind *See* Martha & the Vandellas

A.T.A. *See* Young Black Teenagers

Atkinson, Sweet Pea *See* Was (Not Was)

Avery, James *See* Trouble Funk

Axton, Packy *See* The Mar-Keys

B *See* Royal Crescent Mob

Babayemi, "Yomi" *See* UB40

Baby Gerry *See* Full Force

Baby-D *See* J.J. Fad

Bailey, James "J.R." *See* The Cadillacs

Bailey, John "Buddy" *See* The Clovers

Bailey, Philip *See* Earth, Wind & Fire/Maurice White

Baker, Ronnie *See* MFSB

Ball, Roger *See* Average White Band

Ballard, Florence *See* The Supremes

Ballin, Christopher *See* Incognito

Bambaataa, Afrika Baby *See* Jungle Brothers

Bandiera, Bobby *See* Southside Johnny & the Asbury Jukes

Banks, David *See* Enchantment

Banks, Donald *See* The Tymes

Banks, Patryce "Chocolate" *See* Graham Central Station/Larry Graham

Banks, Ron *See* The Dramatics

Baptiste, David Russell *See* The Meters

Barbarella, Tommy *See* New Power Generation

Barker, Francine *See* Peaches & Herb

Barker, Gary *See* The Catalinas

Barker, Johnny *See* The Catalinas

Brewster, Ray *See* The Cadillacs

Brewster, T.L. *See* Soul Stirrers

Brice, Sheila "Mother" *See* Kirk Franklin & the Family

Bricker, Gene *See* The Marcels

Bridges, Gil *See* Rare Earth

Brigati, Eddie *See* The Young Rascals/The Rascals

Bright, Jeryl *See* Cameo

Bright, Ronnie *See* The Cadillacs; The Coasters

Briley, Alexander *See* The Village People

Brooks, Arthur *See* The Impressions

Brooks, Charles "Buddy" *See* The Cadillacs

Brooks, Dolores "La La" *See* The Crystals

Brooks, John *See* One Way/Alicia Myers

Brooks, Richard *See* The Impressions

Brother J *See* X-Clan

Brother Marquis *See* 2 Live Crew

B.R.O.theR. ?uestion/?uestlove *See* The Roots

Brown, Bill *See* The Dominoes

Brown, Billy *See* Ray, Goodman & Brown/The Moments

Brown, Bobby *See* New Edition

Brown, Charlie *See* Leaders of the New School/Busta Rhymes

Brown, Douglas *See* The El Dorados

Brown, Errol *See* Hot Chocolate

Brown, George "Funky George" *See* Kool & the Gang

Brown, Harold *See* War

Brown, Jim *See* UB40

Brown, Jimmy *See* Brick

Brown, Johnny *See* The Cadillacs

Brown, Kenji *See* Rose Royce

Brown, Lawrence *See* Harold Melvin & the Blue Notes

Brown, Melanie "Scary Spice" *See* The Spice Girls

Brown, Michael *See* Roachford

Brown, Michael *See* Stories

Brown, Ray *See* Jimmy Castor/The Jimmy Castor Bunch

Brown, Samuel *See* The Intruders

Brown, Steven *See* The Cadillacs; The Charts

Brown, Tommy *See* Hues Corporation

Bruce, Paul *See* Roachford

Bryant, Elbridge *See* The Temptations

Bryant, Jason "T.C." *See* The S.O.S. Band

Bryant, Sharon *See* Atlantic Starr

Bryant, William *See* Maze

Buchanan, Wallis *See* Jamiroquai

Buckshot *See* Black Moon/Boot Camp Clik

Buford, Ross *See* The Charts

Bunny D. *See* L'Trimm

Bunton, Emma Lee "Baby Spice" *See* The Spice Girls

Burden, Ricky *See* The Spaniels

Burnett, Norman *See* The Tymes

Bushwick Bill *See* Geto Boys

Busta Rhymes *See* Leaders of the New School/Busta Rhymes

Butler, Floyd *See* Friends of Distinction

Butler, Huey "Billy" *See* Archie Bell & the Drells

Butler, Jerry *See* The Impressions

Butterfly *See* Digable Planets

Byers, Marilyn *See* The Crystals

Byrd, Donald *See* The Blackbyrds

Caesar, Suave Sonny *See* Onyx

Cain, Randy *See* The Delfonics

Calderon, Mark *See* Color Me Badd

Caldwell, Nicholas *See* The Whispers

Caldwell, Ronnie *See* The Bar-Kays

Calhoun, Michael *See* The Dazz Band

Calhoun, William *See* Living Colour

Calloway, Reggie *See* Midnight Star

Calloway, Vincent *See* Midnight Star

Calvin, Billie Rae *See* The Undisputed Truth

Cameron, G.C. *See* The Spinners

Cameron, Timothy *See* Silk

Campbell, Ali *See* UB40

Campbell, Kerry *See* War

Campbell, Luther *See* 2 Live Crew

Campbell, Robin *See* UB40

Campbell, Thomas *See* Cameo

Capitol Q *See* Dream Warriors

Capone *See* Capone-N-Noreaga

Cardenas, Mark *See* The Time

Carey, Bill *See* The Spaniels

Carey, Mack *See* Trouble Funk

Carnegie, Lorenzo *See* L.T.D./Jeffrey Osborne

Carroll, Earl "Speedo" *See* The Cadillacs; The Coasters

Carroll, Porter *See* Atlantic Starr

Carter, Calvin *See* The Spaniels

Carter, John *See* The El Dorados

Carter, Johnny *See* The Dells

Carter, Melvin *See* Con Funk Shun

Carter, Nick *See* Backstreet Boys

Carter, Obadiah *See* The "5" Royales

Carter, Roy *See* Heatwave

Casey, Harry Wayne *See* KC & the Sunshine Band

Cash, Fred *See* The Impressions

Castor, Jimmy *See* Jimmy Castor/The Jimmy Castor Bunch

Cauley, Ben *See* The Bar-Kays

Cavaliere, Felix *See* The Young Rascals/The Rascals

Cave, Claude "Coffee" *See* Mandrill

Ced Gee *See* Ultramagnetic MC's

Cee-Lo *See* Goodie Mob

Cenad, Ben "Cozmo D" *See* Newcleus

Cenad, Yvette *See* Newcleus

Cenas, Bundie *See* Mandrill

Chambers, George *See* The Chambers Brothers

Chambers, Joe *See* The Chambers Brothers

Chambers, Karl *See* MFSB

Chambers, Lester *See* The Chambers Brothers

Chambers, Roland *See* MFSB

Chambers, Willie *See* The Chambers Brothers

Chap *See* Rottin Razkals

Charles, Martin *See* Jimmy Castor/The Jimmy Castor Bunch

David, Timothy "T-Bone" *See* Trouble Funk

Davidson, Aquil *See* Wreckx-N-Effect/Wrecks-N-Effect

Davis, Billy Jr. *See* The Fifth Dimension

Davis, Carrie "Mousey" Young *See* Kirk Franklin & the Family

Davis, Chester *See* Trouble Funk

Davis, Delisa *See* Shalamar

Davis, Gregory *See* Dirty Dozen Brass Band

Davis, Henry *See* L.T.D./Jeffrey Osborne

Davis, Huey *See* The Contours

Davis, Kirk *See* The Cadillacs

Davis, Jimmie *See* L.T.D./Jeffrey Osborne

Davis, Mary *See* The S.O.S. Band

Davis, Ray *See* The Temptations

Davis, Theresa *See* The Emotions

Davis, William "Bill" *See* The Crows

Davis, Willie *See* The Cadets

Dawn, Sandra *See* The Platters

Dawson, Tarik *See* Da Youngsta's/Illy Funkstas

Day, Morris *See* The Time

Daye, Corey *See* Kid Creole & the Coconuts/Dr. Buzzard's Original Savannah Band

DBC *See* Stetsasonic/Daddy-O/Prince Paul/Gravediggaz

DC the Brain Supreme *See* Tag Team

DeBarge, El *See* DeBarge/El DeBarge

DeBarge, Bobby *See* Switch

DeBarge, Bunny *See* DeBarge/El DeBarge

DeBarge, Eldra *See* DeBarge/El DeBarge

DeBarge, James *See* DeBarge/El DeBarge

DeBarge, Mark *See* DeBarge/El DeBarge

DeBarge, Randy *See* DeBarge/El DeBarge

DeBarge, Tommy *See* Switch

Deff Jeff *See* Almighty RSO

DeGrate, Dalvin "Mr. Dalvin" *See* Jodeci

DeGrate, Donald "DeVante Swing" *See* Jodeci

Degree, Leaveil *See* Friends of Distinction; The Whispers

Delite *See* Stetsasonic/Daddy-O/Prince Paul/Gravediggaz

Delmar, Marco *See* Basehead

Demery, Fred *See* Fatback Band/Fatback

Demps, Larry *See* The Dramatics

DeMudd, Pierre *See* The Dazz Band

Dent, Cedric *See* Take 6

Derrick X/Sadat X *See* Brand Nubian

Deuce Deuce *See* D.R.S. (Dirty Rotten Scoundrels)

Devito, Nick *See* Frankie Valli/The Four Seasons

Devito, Tommy *See* Frankie Valli/The Four Seasons

DeVoe, Ronnie *See* New Edition

DeWald, Bob *See* Basehead

Dickerson, B.B. *See* War

Dickey, Gwen "Rose" *See* Rose Royce

Dickson, Damon *See* New Power Generation

Diesel *See* Rottin Razkals

Dinco D *See* Leaders of the New School/Busta Rhymes

Dino Botz *See* Lordz of Brooklyn

Dixon, George *See* The Spinners

Dixon, Reather *See* The Bobbettes

DJ Alamo *See* Brand Nubian

DJ Apollo *See* Buckshot Lefonque

DJ Fuze *See* Digital Underground

DJ Hurricane *See* Beastie Boys/DJ Hurricane/Money Mark

D.J. Jazzy Jeff *See* D.J. Jazzy Jeff & the Fresh Prince/Will Smith

DJ Lethal *See* House of Pain

DJ Minutemix *See* PM Dawn

DJ Muggs *See* Cypress Hill

DJ On-e *See* Deee-lite

D.J. Polo *See* Kool G Rap and D.J. Polo

DJ Premier *See* Buckshot Lefonque; Gang Starr

DJ Skribble *See* Young Black Teenagers

DJ Towa Tei *See* Deee-lite

DJ Woody Wood *See* Three Times Dope

DJ Zero *See* MC 900 FT Jesus

D.M.C. *See* Run-D.M.C.

Dobbins, Georgia *See* The Marvelettes

Dr. Dre *See* N.W.A.

Doctor Dre *See* Doctor Dre and Ed Lover

Doctor Ice *See* U.T.F.O.

Dr. Octagon *See* Kool Keith/Dr. Octagon

Dogg, Ray *See* Almighty RSO

Doitall *See* Lords of the Underground

Doodlebug/Knowledge *See* Digable Planets

Dorough, Howie *See* Backstreet Boys

Dorsey, Eric *See* The Dayton Family

Dorsey, Ira *See* The Dayton Family

Dortch, Darwin *See* The Ohio Players

Douglas, Charles *See* The Spaniels

Douglas, Tyrone *See* The Undisputed Truth

Doulphin, Edward *See* The Channels

Dow, Gary *See* Cameo

Dowd, Christopher Gordon *See* Fishbone

Downie, Tyrone *See* Bob Marley & the Wailers

Draffen, Willis *See* Bloodstone

Drake, LaVerne *See* The Cadillacs

D'Ranged & Damaged *See* Yagg Fu Front

Dre *See* OutKast

Dres *See* Black Sheep

Drummond, Jon "J.D." *See* Kirk Franklin & the Family

D-Shot *See* E-40 and the Click

DTTX *See* Lighter Shade of Brown (LSOB)

Dudley, Anne *See* The Art of Noise

Dudley, Curtis *See* One Way/Alicia Myers

Duhe, Robin *See* Maze

Duke, Calvin *See* Heatwave

Duke, George *See* George Duke/The Clarke/Duke Project

Duncan, Cleveland *See* The Penguins

Duncan, Malcolm *See* Average White Band

Dunn, Donald "Duck" *See* Booker T. & the MG's; The Mar-Keys

Dunn, Freddie *See* Rose Royce

Dunn, James *See* The Stylistics

Funches, Johnny *See* The Dells

Fuqua, Charlie *See* The Ink Spots

Fuqua, Harvey *See* The Moonglows/Harvey Fuqua

G. Love *See* G. Love & Special Sauce

Gadson, James *See* Booker T. & the MG's

Gail, Irving Lee *See* The Cadillacs

Gaines, Rosie *See* New Power Generation

Gaines, Tony *See* The Cleftones

Gaining, Cub *See* The Cadillacs

Gale, Gretchen *See* The Crystals

Gallo, Renard *See* Switch

Gamble, Cheryl "Coko" *See* SWV

Gamer, Henry *See* Rose Royce

Gant, Kenneth *See* Midnight Star

Ganxsta Ridd *See* Boo-Yaa T.R.I.B.E.

Garcia, Mayte *See* New Power Generation

Gardner, Bruce "Cool Aid" *See* Basehead

Gardner, Carl *See* The Coasters

Garrett, Seidah *See* The Brand New Heavies

Gaston, Henry *See* Wild Cherry

Gates, Jimmy *See* Silk

Gathers, Helen *See* The Bobbettes

Gatling, Timmy *See* Guy

Gaudio, Bob *See* Frankie Valli/The Four Seasons

Gazda, Ricky *See* Southside Johnny & the Asbury Jukes

Geils, J. (Jerome) *See* J. Geils Band/Bluestime

General Jeff *See* Rodney O & Joe Cooley

Genius/GZA *See* Wu-Tang Clan

Gentry, Melvin *See* Midnight Star

George, Langston *See* Gladys Knight & the Pips

George, Paul Anthony *See* Full Force

Getz, David *See* Janis Joplin/Big Brother & the Holding Company

Ghost Face Killa *See* Wu-Tang Clan

Gibb, Barry *See* The Bee Gees

Gibb, Maurice *See* The Bee Gees

Gibb, Robin *See* The Bee Gees

Gibbs, Charles *See* Archie Bell & the Drells

Gibson, Butch *See* Sam the Sham & the Pharaohs

Gibson, Douglas *See* Jimmy Castor/The Jimmy Castor Bunch

Gibson, Hillard *See* Jimmy Castor/The Jimmy Castor Bunch

Gift, Roland *See* Fine Young Cannibals

Gill, Johnny *See* New Edition

Gipp *See* Goodie Mob

Gittens, Ronnie *See* The Catalinas

Gizmo *See* Audio Two/Milk

Glaser, Gabrielle *See* Luscious Jackson

Glasper, Robert *See* The El Dorados

Glenn, Gary "Big G" *See* Silk

Glover, Corey *See* Living Colour

Glynn, Stephanie "Chicken" *See* Kirk Franklin & the Family

Godfather Rock "Te" *See* Boo-Yaa T.R.I.B.E.

Gondwe, Hawi *See* Roachford

Gooden, Sam *See* The Impressions

Gooding, Cuba *See* The Main Ingredient

Goodman, Al *See* Ray, Goodman & Brown/The Moments

Goodman, Qu'ran *See* Da Youngsta's/Illy Funkstas

Goodman, Taji *See* Da Youngsta's/Illy Funkstas

Gordon, Billy *See* The Contours

Gordon, Florence LaRue *See* The Fifth Dimension

Gordon, Marc *See* Levert

Goring, Sonia *See* The Chantels

Gorrie, Alan *See* Average White Band

GP-Wu *See* Wu-Tang Clan

Grace, Fredi *See* The S.O.S. Band

Graham, Johnny *See* Earth, Wind & Fire/Maurice White

Graham, Larry *See* Graham Central Station/Larry Graham; Sly & the Family Stone

Grand Architect Paradise *See* X-Clan

Grand Puba Maxwell *See* Brand Nubian

Grandmaster Flash *See* Grandmaster Flash & the Furious Five/Melle Mel & the Furious Five

Grandy, Keisha *See* Kirk Franklin & the Family

Granolio, Paolo *See* Change

Graveravin' *See* Flatlinerz

Graves, Cliff *See* The Dominoes

Graves, James *See* Junior Walker & the All-Stars

Graves, Pete *See* The Moonglows/Harvey Fuqua

Gravitte, O.C. *See* The Catalinas

Gray, James *See* Disposable Heroes of Hiphoprisy/Spearhead

Green, Charles *See* War

Green, Eddie *See* MFSB

Green, Greg *See* One Way/Alicia Myers

Green, James "Woody" *See* Dru Hill

Green, Ricky *See* War

Greenberg, Larry *See* Brass Construction/Skyy

Greenberg, Steve *See* Lipps, Inc.

Greene, Bobby *See* Enchantment

Greene, Linda *See* Peaches & Herb

Greene, Susaye *See* The Supremes

Greenwood, Clarence "Citizen Cope" *See* Basehead

Gregory, Gerald *See* The Spaniels

Grier, Joe *See* The Charts

Griffin, Mark *See* MC 900 FT Jesus

Griffin, William *See* Smokey Robinson & the Miracles

Griffiths, Marcia *See* Bob Marley & the Wailers

Grimes, Jeffrey *See* Jimmy Castor/The Jimmy Castor Bunch

Grudge, Mickey *See* Brass Construction/Skyy

Guest, Eleanor *See* Gladys Knight & the Pips

Guest, William *See* Gladys Knight & the Pips

Guiterriez, Juan *See* The Diablos

Gunter, Cornell/Cornelius *See* The Coasters

Gurley, James *See* Janis Joplin/Big Brother & the Holding Company

Guru *See* Gang Starr

Ill *See* Ill Al Skratch

Imani *See* Incognito

Indo *See* D.R.S. (Dirty Rotten Scoundrels)

Ingram, Phillip *See* Switch

Ingram, Ripley *See* The Five Keys

Ingui, Charles *See* The Soul Survivors

Ingui, Richard *See* The Soul Survivors

Inspektah Deck *See* Wu-Tang Clan

Irby, Treston *See* Hi-Five

Irons, Eddie *See* Brick

Irons, Jack *See* Red Hot Chili Peppers

Isles, Bill *See* The O'Jays

Isley, Ernie *See* Isley Brothers

Isley, Marvin *See* Isley Brothers

Isley, O'Kelly *See* Isley Brothers

Isley, Ronald *See* Isley Brothers

Isley, Rudolph *See* Isley Brothers

Israel, Yackov Ben *See* Earth, Wind & Fire/Maurice White

Ives *See* Delinquent Habits

Ivey, Michael *See* Basehead

Jackson, Al Jr. *See* Booker T. & the MG's

Jackson, Anthony *See* MFSB

Jackson, Bernard *See* Surface

Jackson, Glenmore *See* The Charts

Jackson, Jackie *See* Jackson 5/The Jacksons

Jackson, Janet *See* Jackson 5/The Jacksons

Jackson, Jermaine *See* Jackson 5/The Jacksons

Jackson, Jerome *See* The Main Ingredient

Jackson, Kurt *See* Portrait

Jackson, LaToya *See* Jackson 5/The Jacksons

Jackson, Marlon *See* Jackson 5/The Jacksons

Jackson, Maureen *See* Jackson 5/The Jacksons

Jackson, Michael *See* Jackson 5/The Jacksons

Jackson, Pervis *See* The Spinners

Jackson, Randy *See* Jackson 5/The Jacksons

Jackson, Tito *See* Jackson 5/The Jacksons

Jackson, Wayne *See* The Mar-Keys

Jackson, Willis C. *See* The Spaniels

Jacobs, Perk *See* The Blackbyrds

Jacox, Martin *See* Soul Stirrers

Jagger, Mick *See* The Rolling Stones

Jail Bait *See* D.R.S. (Dirty Rotten Scoundrels)

Jam Master Jay *See* Run-D.M.C.

Jamal *See* Illegal/Jamal

James, Charlie *See* The Cleftones

James, Dave *See* The Tymes

James, David *See* Disposable Heroes of Hiphoprisy/Spearhead

James, Glodean *See* Love Unlimited Orchestra/Love Unlimited

James, Kenny *See* Rare Earth

James, Linda *See* Love Unlimited Orchestra/Love Unlimited

Jamison, Le Le *See* Disposable Heroes of Hiphoprisy/Spearhead

Jarobi *See* A Tribe Called Quest

Jarrett, Irvin "Carrot" *See* Third World

Jasper, Chris *See* Isley Brothers

Jaye, Miles *See* The Village People

Jazzie B *See* Soul II Soul

J-Dee *See* Da Lench Mob

Jean, Nel Wyclef *See* Fugees

Jeczalik, J.J. *See* The Art of Noise

Jeffries, Otto *See* The "5" Royales

Jenkins, Gary "Lil' G" *See* Silk

Jenkins, Tomi *See* Cameo

Jensen, Harry *See* Jimmy Castor/The Jimmy Castor Bunch

Jeremiah, Kenneth *See* The Soul Survivors

Jingle Bell *See* Yagg Fu Front

Job, Lequeint "Duke" *See* Rose Royce

Johnny Z *See* N2Deep

Johns, Eric *See* Heatwave

Johnson, Alan *See* The Marcels

Johnson, Billy *See* The Moonglows/Harvey Fuqua

Johnson, Billy "Shoes" *See* Maze

Johnson, Clarence *See* The Chi-Lites

Johnson, Cynthia *See* Lipps, Inc.

Johnson, Danny *See* The Chi-Lites

Johnson, Donald R. *See* A Taste of Honey

Johnson, Dwight *See* Harold Melvin & the Blue Notes

Johnson, Emanuel "EJ" *See* Enchantment

Johnson, Fred *See* The Marcels

Johnson, George "Lightnin' Licks" *See* The Brothers Johnson

Johnson, Gregory *See* Cameo

Johnson, Hubert *See* The Contours

Johnson, Janice Marie *See* A Taste of Honey

Johnson, Jeannette *See* Kirk Franklin & the Family

Johnson, Jellybean *See* The Time

Johnson, Jesse *See* The Time

Johnson, Kirk *See* New Power Generation

Johnson, Louis "Thunder Thumbs" *See* The Brothers Johnson

Johnson, Norman *See* Chairmen of the Board; The Showmen

Johnson, Phillip *See* Portrait

Johnson, Ralph *See* Earth, Wind & Fire/Maurice White; The Impressions

Johnson, Robert *See* KC & the Sunshine Band

Johnson, Stephen *See* The Blackbyrds

Johnson, Tamara "Taj" *See* SWV

Johnson, Terry *See* The Mar-Keys

Johnson, Wesley *See* The Blackbyrds

Jones, Benny *See* Dirty Dozen Brass Band

Jones, Booker T. *See* Booker T. & the MG's

Jones, Brian *See* The Rolling Stones

Jones, Creadel *See* The Chi-Lites

Jones, Dorothy *See* The Cookies

Jones, Efrem *See* Dirty Dozen Brass Band

Jones, James Earl III *See* The S.O.S. Band

Jones, Jamie *See* All-4-One

Jones, Jerome "Romeo" *See* Immature

Jones, Jewel *See* The El Dorados

Jones, Kendall Rey *See* Fishbone

Jones, Marshall "Rock" *See* The Ohio Players

Jones, Maxine *See* En Vogue

Jones, Mitchell *See* Commissioned

Jones, Orville "Hoppy" *See* The Ink Spots

Jones, Phalon *See* The Bar-Kays

Jones, Randy *See* The Penguins

Jones, Randy *See* The Village People

Jones, Robert "Kuumba" *See* The Ohio Players

Jones, Will "Dub" *See* The Cadets; The Coasters

Jones, William *See* Heatwave

Jordan, Lonnie *See* War

Joseph, Charles *See* Dirty Dozen Brass Band

Joseph, Kirk *See* Dirty Dozen Brass Band

Joseph, Quinton *See* MFSB

Josephsberg, Mark *See* Kid Creole & the Coconuts/Dr. Buzzard's Original Savannah Band

Joyce, Chris *See* Simply Red

J-Ro *See* Tha Alkaholiks

J-Sublimi *See* Freestyle Fellowship

JuJu *See* Beatnuts

Junior, Marvin *See* The Dells

Justman, Seth *See* J. Geils Band/Bluestime

Kae, Fudgie *See* Mandrill

Kamal *See* The Roots

Kamron *See* Young Black Teenagers

Kangol Kid, The *See* U.T.F.O.

Kashif *See* B.T. Express

Katona, Gabriel *See* Rare Earth

Katz, Simon *See* Jamiroquai

Kavanaugh, Kevin *See* Southside Johnny & the Asbury Jukes

Kaves *See* Lordz of Brooklyn

Kay Gee *See* Naughty By Nature

Kay, Jason *See* Jamiroquai

K-Cut *See* Main Source/Large Professor

K-Def *See* Real Live

Keck, Mike *See* Mother's Finest

Keenan, Brian *See* The Chambers Brothers

Keith KC *See* Wreckx-N-Effect/Wrecks-N-Effect

Kellett, Tim *See* Simply Red

Kelley, H. Ann *See* Hues Corporation

Kelly, Betty *See* Martha & the Vandellas

Kelly, Kenneth *See* The Manhattans

Kelly, Tonya *See* Jade

Kemo *See* Delinquent Habits

Kendo *See* Hyenas in the Desert

Kendrick, Kevin *See* Cameo

Kendricks, Eddie *See* The Temptations

Kennedy, Delious *See* All-4-One

Kennedy, Harrison *See* Chairmen of the Board

Kennedy, Hershall "Happiness" *See* Graham Central Station/Larry Graham

Kennedy, Joyce *See* Mother's Finest

Kennibrew, Dee Dee *See* The Crystals

Kenny, Bill *See* The Ink Spots

Kenny, Herb *See* The Ink Spots

Kessee, Kelton "Little Drummer Boy" *See* Immature

Keys, Jimmy *See* The Chords

Khalil *See* Force M.D.'s

Khan, Chaka *See* Rufus/Chaka Khan

Khudjo *See* Goodie Mob

Kibble, Joey *See* Take 6

Kibble, Mark *See* Take 6

Kibble, Perry L. *See* A Taste of Honey

Kibby, Walter Adam *See* Fishbone

Kid *See* Kid 'n Play

Kidd Creole *See* Grandmaster Flash & the Furious Five/Melle Mel & the Furious Five

Kiedis, Anthony *See* Red Hot Chili Peppers

Kilkenny, Giorgio *See* Dexy's Midnight Runners/Kevin Rowland & Dexy's Midnight Runners

Killebrew, Willie "Sonny" *See* The S.O.S. Band

Killgo, Keith *See* The Blackbyrds

Kilo *See* Crucial Conflict

Kincaid, Jan *See* The Brand New Heavies

Kinchen, Ricky *See* Mint Condition

King Ad-Rock (a.k.a. Adam Horovitz) *See* Beastie Boys/DJ Hurricane/Money Mark

King, Ben E. *See* The Drifters

King, Ian *See* Hot Chocolate

King, Jay *See* Club Nouveau

King, Jimmy *See* The Bar-Kays

King, Johnny *See* Fatback Band/Fatback

King Lou *See* Dream Warriors

King, William *See* Jimmy Castor/The Jimmy Castor Bunch; The Commodores/Lionel Richie

Kirby, Lady Miss Kier *See* Deee-lite

Kirkham, Ian *See* Simply Red

Kirkland, Eric *See* Portrait

Klein, Danny *See* J. Geils Band/Bluestime

Klepto *See* Junior M.A.F.I.A./Lil' Kim

KM.G the Illustrator *See* Above the Law

Knauss, Richard *See* The Marcels

Knight, Brenda *See* Gladys Knight & the Pips

Knight, Dorsey *See* The Showmen

Knight, Gene *See* The Showmen

Knight, Gladys *See* Gladys Knight & the Pips

Knight, Jon *See* New Kids on the Block

Knight, Jordan *See* New Kids on the Block

Knight, Merald "Bubba" *See* Gladys Knight & the Pips

Knox, Richard *See* Dirty Dozen Brass Band

Knumskull *See* Luniz

Kobra *See* Boo-Yaa T.R.I.B.E.

Kool Ass Fash/Al Tariq *See* Beatnuts

Kool G Rap *See* Kool G Rap and D.J. Polo

Kool Keith/Rhythm X *See* Ultramagnetic MC's

Kool Kim *See* The UMCs

Kool Rock-ski *See* Fat Boys

Krayzie Bone *See* Bone Thugs-N-Harmony

Krazy Drayz *See* Das EFX/Bobby Sichran

KRS-One *See* Boogie Down Productions/KRS-One

Kurupt *See* Tha Dogg Pound

Kwesi *See* Arrested Development/Speech/Dionne Farris

La Rock, Scott *See* Boogie Down Productions/KRS-One

L.A. Sno *See* Duice

LaCroix, Jerry *See* Rare Earth

Lady Anna *See* J.J. Fad

Marley, Rita *See* Bob Marley & the Wailers

Marley, Robert Nesta *See* Bob Marley & the Wailers

Marley, Stephen *See* Ziggy Marley & the Melody Makers

Marsalis, Branford *See* Buckshot Lefonque

Marshall, Cornel *See* Third World

Marshall, Jenell *See* Dirty Dozen Brass Band

Marshall, Joi *See* Jade

Martin, Barbara *See* The Supremes

Martin, Cedric *See* Con Funk Shun

Martin, David *See* Sam the Sham & the Pharaohs

Martin, Kenny *See* Defunkt

Martin, Luci *See* Chic

Martin, Sennie "Skip" *See* The Dazz Band

Martinez, Cliff *See* Red Hot Chili Peppers

Martinez, Paul *See* Jimmy Castor/The Jimmy Castor Bunch

Martinez, Roland *See* The Cadillacs

Martini, Jerry *See* Sly & the Family Stone

Marvin, Julian "Junior" *See* Bob Marley & the Wailers

Massey, Bobby *See* The O'Jays

Massi, Nick *See* Frankie Valli/The Four Seasons

Masta Killa *See* Wu-Tang Clan

Master Gee *See* The Sugarhill Gang

Maulkie *See* Da Lench Mob

Maunick, Jean-Paul "Bluey" *See* Incognito

Maurice, Brian *See* Dexy's Midnight Runners/Kevin Rowland & Dexy's Midnight Runners

Mayes, Lenny *See* The Dramatics

Mayfield, Curtis *See* The Impressions

Mazik *See* Blood of Abraham

MC Breed *See* MC Breed & the DFC

MC J.B. *See* J.J. Fad

M.C. Ren *See* N.W.A.

MC Serch *See* 3rd Bass

MCA *See* Beastie Boys/DJ Hurricane/Money Mark

McArthur, Keith *See* Disposable Heroes of Hiphoprisy/Spearhead

McBride, Roger *See* Rare Earth

McCain, Tiemeyer *See* Lakeside

McCall, Louis *See* Con Funk Shun

McCary, Michael *See* Boyz II Men

McClain, Marlon *See* The Dazz Band

McClain, William "Buzzy" *See* The Cleftones

McClary, Thomas *See* The Commodores/Lionel Richie

McConnell, Tommy *See* Brass Construction/Skyy

McCoo, Marilyn *See* The Fifth Dimension

McCord, Kevin *See* One Way/Alicia Myers

McCormick, Charles *See* Bloodstone

McCrae, Saunders *See* Fatback Band/Fatback

McCraw, Lloyd *See* The Cadets

McCrea, Ethel "Earl-Jean" *See* The Cookies

McDonald, Virginia *See* The Undisputed Truth

McDonald, Yolanda "Yo" *See* Kirk Franklin & the Family

McFadden, Gene *See* McFadden & Whitehead

McGhee, John *See* L.T.D./Jeffrey Osborne

McGill, Mike *See* The Dells

McGlown, Betty *See* The Supremes

McGowan, Johnny "Jayski" *See* Quad City DJ's

McGruder, Andy *See* The Spaniels

McIntosh, Robbie *See* Average White Band

McIntyre, Fritz *See* Simply Red

McIntyre, Joe *See* New Kids on the Block

McIntyre, Onnie *See* Average White Band

McKay, Al *See* Earth, Wind & Fire/Maurice White

McKee, Julius *See* Dirty Dozen Brass Band

McKeehan, Toby *See* DC Talk

McKenzie, Derrick *See* Jamiroquai

McKinney, Niles *See* The Dazz Band

McKinney, Walter *See* Rose Royce

McKnight, Claude V. III *See* Take 6

McLean, A.J. *See* Backstreet Boys

McLemore, LaMonte *See* The Fifth Dimension

McNeil, David *See* The Dominoes

McPhatter, Clyde *See* The Dominoes; The Drifters

McPherson, Donald *See* The Main Ingredient

McQuater, Matthew *See* The Clovers

McRae, Floyd "Buddy" *See* The Chords

Meadows, Jonathan "Corky" *See* One Way/Alicia Myers

Medley, Bill *See* Righteous Brothers

Melle Mel *See* Grandmaster Flash & the Furious Five/Melle Mel & the Furious Five

Melvin, Harold J. *See* Harold Melvin & the Blue Notes

Merchant, Jimmy *See* Frankie Lymon & the Teenagers

Mercury *See* Force M.D.'s

Merle, Milton *See* The Dominoes

Mesa, Omar *See* Mandrill

Method Man *See* Wu-Tang Clan

Meyer, Bob *See* The Catalinas

Michael, George *See* George Michael/Wham!

Michael, Prakazrel *See* Fugees

Mickens, Robert "Spike" *See* Kool & the Gang

Middlebrooks, Ralph "Pee Wee" *See* The Ohio Players

Middleton, Mark *See* BLACKstreet

Mikah Nine/Microphone Mike *See* Freestyle Fellowship

Mike D *See* Beastie Boys/DJ Hurricane/Money Mark

Mike G *See* Jungle Brothers

Mikey D *See* Main Source/Large Professor

Miles, Richard *See* Soul Stirrers

Milk *See* Audio Two/Milk

Miller, A.J. "Onion" *See* L.T.D./Jeffrey Osborne

Miller, Charles *See* War

Miller, Floyd *See* Slave/Steve Arrington

Milligan, Delores Dunning *See* Brass Construction/Skyy

Millings, Ronnie *See* Them

Mills, Aaron *See* Cameo

Mills, Donald *See* The Mills Brothers

Mills, Harry *See* The Mills Brothers

Mills, Herbert *See* The Mills Brothers

Mills, John Jr. *See* The Mills Brothers

Mills, John H. Sr. *See* The Mills Brothers

Mills, John H. II *See* The Mills Brothers

Mills, Ken *See* Jimmy Castor/The Jimmy Castor Bunch

Ming, Leslie *See* B.T. Express

Minus, Rene *See* The Chantels

Mista Lawnge *See* Black Sheep

Mr. Cheeks *See* Lost Boyz

Mr. Funky *See* Lords of the Underground

Mr. Hayes *See* New Power Generation

Mr. Man *See* Da Bush Babees

Mr. Mixx *See* 2 Live Crew

Mitchell, Brandon *See* Wreckx-N-Effect/Wrecks-N-Effect

Mitchell, Donald Ray *See* Was (Not Was)

Mix-Master Ice *See* U.T.F.O.

MJG *See* Eightball & MJG

Moc *See* Fu-Schnickens

Modeliste, Zig *See* The Meters

Moir, Monte *See* The Time

Mondo *See* Boogiemonsters

Monette, Ray *See* Rare Earth

Money B *See* Digital Underground

Money Mark *See* Beastie Boys/DJ Hurricane/Money Mark

Monsta "O" *See* Boo-Yaa T.R.I.B.E.

Montana, Vince *See* MFSB

Moore, Angelo Christopher *See* Fishbone

Moore, Garry *See* Mother's Finest

Moore, Jimmy *See* The "5" Royales

Moore, Johnny *See* The Drifters

Moore, Larry *See* MFSB

Moore, Michael *See* Rose Royce

Moore, Pauline *See* The Chantels

Moore, Rene *See* Rene and Angela

Moore, Sam *See* Sam & Dave

Moore, Stephen *See* Cameo

Moore, Warren "Pete" *See* Smokey Robinson & the Miracles

Morgan, Nate *See* Rufus/Chaka Khan

Morris, Billy *See* The Channels

Morris, Nathan *See* Boyz II Men

Morris, Wanya *See* Boyz II Men

Morrison, Van *See* Them

Morrison, Walter "Junie" *See* The Ohio Players

Morrow, Little Willie *See* Wild Cherry

Morvan, Fabrice *See* Milli Vanilli

Mosely, Alex "Spandor" *See* Lisa Lisa & Cult Jam

Moses, Pirkle Lee *See* The El Dorados

Moss, Jon *See* Culture Club/Boy George

Mowatt, Judy *See* Bob Marley & the Wailers

Muckin, Bob *See* Southside Johnny & the Asbury Jukes

Muhammad, Ali Shaheed *See* A Tribe Called Quest

Mulkerin, John *See* Defunkt

Muller, Randy *See* Brass Construction/Skyy

Mumford, Eugene *See* The Dominoes

Mumford, Gary *See* Shalamar

Mundy, Ronald *See* The Marcels

Murdock, Glenn *See* Mother's Finest

Murphy, Kevin *See* Rufus/Chaka Khan

Murray, Barbara *See* The Chantels

Murrell, Herbie *See* The Stylistics

Mushroom *See* Massive Attack/Protection

Myers, Alicia *See* One Way/Alicia Myers

Myers, Edward *See* The Dazz Band

Myntric *See* Boogiemonsters

Nadirah *See* Arrested Development/Speech/Dionne Farris

Nakamura, Tetsuya "Tex" *See* War

Nash, Michael *See* Rose Royce

Navarro, Dave *See* Red Hot Chili Peppers

Ndlovu, Akiro *See* Zimbabwe Legit

Ndlovu, Dumisani *See* Zimbabwe Legit

Neal, Russell *See* Hi-Five

Negroni, Joe *See* Frankie Lymon & the Teenagers

Nelson, Nate *See* The Platters

Nelson, Shara *See* Massive Attack/Protection

Neufville, Renee *See* Zhane

Nevarez, Alfred *See* All-4-One

Never *See* Crucial Conflict

Neville, Aaron *See* The Neville Brothers

Neville, Art *See* The Meters; The Neville Brothers

Neville, Charles *See* The Neville Brothers

Neville, Cyril *See* The Meters; The Neville Brothers

Nice, Chuck *See* Three Times Dope

Nice, Gregg *See* Nice & Smooth

Nice, Prime Minister Pete *See* 3rd Bass

Nicholas, James Dean "J.D." *See* The Commodores/Lionel Richie; Heatwave

Nickens, Richard *See* The El Dorados

Nilija *See* Last Poets

Nino Brown *See* Junior M.A.F.I.A./Lil' Kim

Nix, Don *See* The Mar-Keys

Nix, Victor *See* Rose Royce

Nixon, Charles *See* The Tymes

Nixon, Emmett *See* Trouble Funk

Nocentelli, Leo *See* The Meters

Noreaga *See* Capone-N-Noreaga

Norfleet, Michael *See* The Dazz Band

Norman, Jimmy *See* The Coasters

Norris, Jean *See* Zhane

Norton, Daniel "Sonny" *See* The Crows

Norwalt, Rose *See* Rose Royce

Novi, Carlo *See* Southside Johnny & the Asbury Jukes

Nunn, Bobby *See* The Coasters

Nuriddin, Jalal/Alfia Pudim/Lightnin' Rod *See* Last Poets

Oates, John *See* Daryl Hall & John Oates

Oatie Kato *See* Goats

O'Brien, Matt *See* Big Chief

O'Dell, Homer *See* Mint Condition

ODM *See* Lighter Shade of Brown (LSOB)

O.G. Style *See* Delinquent Habits

Oje, Baba *See* Arrested Development/Speech/Dionne Farris

Ol' Dirty Bastard *See* Wu-Tang Clan

Santiago, Herman *See* Frankie Lymon & the Teenagers

Santiago, Neftali *See* Mandrill

Santiel, Robert *See* L.T.D./Jeffrey Osborne

Santiel, Terral *See* Rose Royce

Sapp, Marvin *See* Commissioned

Satchell, Clarence "Satch" *See* The Ohio Players

Saulsberry, Michael Angelo *See* Portrait

Saunders, Nick *See* The Cleftones

Saunders, Orville *See* The Blackbyrds

Scarface *See* Geto Boys

Schellenbach, Kate *See* Beastie Boys/DJ Hurricane/Money Mark; Luscious Jackson

Schoefield, Willie *See* The Falcons

Schott, Peter *See* Kid Creole & the Coconuts/Dr. Buzzard's Original Savannah Band

Schwers, Billy *See* Royal Crescent Mob

Scorpio/Mr. Ness *See* Grandmaster Flash & the Furious Five/Melle Mel & the Furious Five

Scott, David *See* The Chi-Lites

Scott, Howard *See* War

Scott, Sherry *See* Earth, Wind & Fire/Maurice White

Scott, Wallace *See* The Whispers

Scott, Walter *See* The Whispers

Scotty Edge *See* Lordz of Brooklyn

Seacer, Levi Jr. *See* New Power Generation

Seavers, Vernon *See* The Heartbeats/Shep & the Limelites

Seay, Jerry *See* Mother's Finest

Self-Jupiter *See* Freestyle Fellowship

Sen Dog *See* Cypress Hill

Sermon, Erick *See* EPMD

Sever, Sam *See* 3rd Bass; Downtown Science

Sevilla, Mickey *See* Kid Creole & the Coconuts/Dr. Buzzard's Original Savannah Band

Shaggy 2 Dope *See* Insane Clown Posse

Shaheed, Fatima *See* J.J. Fad

Sheard, Karen Clark *See* The Clark Sisters

Shelby, Thomas *See* Lakeside

Shelter, Tom *See* The Falcons

Shelton, Earl *See* Fatback Band/Fatback

Shelton, Seb *See* Dexy's Midnight Runners/Kevin Rowland & Dexy's Midnight Runners

Sheppard, James "Shep" *See* The Heartbeats/Shep & the Limelites

Sherman, Jack *See* Red Hot Chili Peppers

Shock G *See* Digital Underground

Shockley, Stephan *See* Lakeside

Shorty *See* Da Lench Mob

Showbiz/Show *See* Showbiz & A.G.

Shy Shy *See* Full Force

Sichran, Bobby *See* Das EFX/Bobby Sichran

Sierra, Anibal "Butch" *See* Brass Construction/Skyy

Simmons, Bill *See* Midnight Star

Simmons, Luther Jr. *See* The Main Ingredient

Simmons, Pete *See* The Spaniels

Simpson, Chris "Sweetie" *See* Kirk Franklin & the Family

Simpson, John *See* The S.O.S. Band

Simpson, Mel *See* Us3

Simpson, Ray *See* The Village People

Simpson, Valerie *See* Ashford & Simpson

Sims, Jody *See* Switch

Sincere Allah *See* Brand Nubian

Singleton, Charlie *See* Cameo

Sir Scratch *See* Main Source/Large Professor

Skillings, Muzz *See* Living Colour

Skoob *See* Das EFX/Bobby Sichran

Skratch, Al *See* Ill Al Skratch

Sledge, Debra *See* Sister Sledge

Sledge, Joni *See* Sister Sledge

Sledge, Kathie *See* Sister Sledge

Sledge, Kim *See* Sister Sledge

Slim Kid 3 *See* Pharcyde

Slovak, Hillel *See* Red Hot Chili Peppers

Smith, Annette *See* The Chantels

Smith, Arlene *See* The Chantels

Smith, Bobbie *See* The Spinners

Smith, Carlton *See* Royal Crescent Mob

Smith, Chad *See* Red Hot Chili Peppers

Smith, Charles *See* Kool & the Gang

Smith, Dickie *See* The Five Keys

Smith, Earl *See* Bob Marley & the Wailers

Smith, George "Smitty" *See* The Manhattans

Smith, James *See* The Stylistics

Smith, Jerome *See* KC & the Sunshine Band

Smith, Jerry Lee "Smoochie" *See* The Mar-Keys

Smith, Kenneth *See* Bloodstone

Smith, Kevin *See* DC Talk

Smith, Parrish *See* EPMD

Smith, Ron *See* Maze

Smith, Ronnie *See* KC & the Sunshine Band

Smith, Sidney *See* The Catalinas

Smith, Toby *See* Jamiroquai

Smith, Will (a.k.a. The Fresh Prince) *See* D.J. Jazzy Jeff & the Fresh Prince/Will Smith

Smooth Bee *See* Nice & Smooth

Smyth, Alice Tweed *See* War

Sondoobie *See* Funkdoobiest

Sonny T. *See* New Power Generation

Southside Johnny *See* Southside Johnny & the Asbury Jukes

Spann, Patricia *See* The Cleftones

Sparks, Willie "Wild" *See* Graham Central Station/Larry Graham

Spartacus R. *See* Osibisa

Speare, Paul *See* Dexy's Midnight Runners/Kevin Rowland & Dexy's Midnight Runners

Special One *See* Conscious Daughters

Spector, Ronnie (Veronica Bennett Spector) *See* The Ronettes/Ronnie Spector

Speech *See* Arrested Development/Speech/Dionne Farris

Speight, Bruno *See* The S.O.S. Band

Spencer, Bobby *See* The Cadillacs

Spencer, Caddy *See* The Cadillacs

Spigg Nice *See* Lost Boyz

Spin 4th *See* Yagg Fu Front

Spinderella *See* Salt-N-Pepa

Spratelly, William *See* Harold Melvin & the Blue Notes

Stallings, Jack *See* The Catalinas

Stann, Joey *See* Southside Johnny & the Asbury Jukes

Stanton, Terry *See* The Dazz Band

Staples, Cleo *See* The Staple Singers

Staples, Mavis *See* The Staple Singers

Staples, Pervis *See* The Staple Singers

Staples, Roebuck "Pops" *See* The Staple Singers

Staples, Yvonne *See* The Staple Singers

Starang Wondah *See* O.G.C. (Originoo Gun Clappaz)

Staton-Sussewell, Candi *See* Candi Staton/Candi Staton-Sussewell

Steele *See* Smif-N-Wessun/Da Cocoa Brovaz

Steele, David *See* Fine Young Cannibals

Steinberg, Lewis *See* Booker T. & the MG's

Stevens, Calvin *See* The Undisputed Truth

Stevens, Cliff *See* One Way/Alicia Myers

Stevie D. *See* Force M.D.'s

Stewart, Dave *See* Eurythmics

Stewart, Reggie *See* The Dazz Band

Stewart, William "Willie" *See* Third World

Stickyfingaz *See* Onyx

Stinnet, Ray *See* Sam the Sham & the Pharaohs

Stockert, Ron *See* Rufus/Chaka Khan

Stockman, Shawn *See* Boyz II Men

Stokes, Daniele *See* Solo

Stokes, Otis *See* Lakeside

Stone, Rosie *See* Sly & the Family Stone

Stone, Sly *See* Sly & the Family Stone

Stone, Freddie *See* Sly & the Family Stone

Strain, Sammy *See* The O'Jays

Street, Richard *See* The Temptations

Strong, Nolan *See* The Diablos

Strozier, Gordon *See* Ready for the World

Stuart, Hamish *See* Average White Band

Stubbs, Joe *See* The Falcons

Stubbs, Levi *See* The Four Tops

Sub Commander Ras I Zulu *See* Disposable Heroes of Hiphoprisy/Spearhead

Subroc *See* KMD

Sudderth, William *See* Atlantic Starr

Suede, Geechi *See* Camp Lo

Suga T *See* E-40 and the Click

Summers, Eddie *See* Bloodstone

Sun, Ahaguna G. *See* Maze

Super DJ Dmitry *See* Deee-lite

Sutton, Ann *See* The Young Rascals/The Rascals

Swayzack *See* Goats

Sylvers, Angela *See* The Sylvers

Sylvers, Charmaine *See* The Sylvers

Sylvers, Edmund *See* The Sylvers

Sylvers, Foster *See* The Sylvers

Sylvers, James *See* The Sylvers

Sylvers, Leon Frank III *See* The Sylvers

Sylvers, Olympia-Ann *See* The Sylvers

Sylvers, Pat *See* The Sylvers

Sylvers, Ricky *See* The Sylvers

Sylvester, Tony *See* The Main Ingredient

Tait, Michael *See* DC Talk

Talbot, Mick *See* Style Council

Talley, Gary *See* The Box Tops

Talley, Nedra *See* The Ronettes/Ronnie Spector

Tame One *See* Artifacts

Tanner, Aisha *See* Atlantic Starr

Tanner, Johnny *See* The "5" Royales

Taree, Aerle *See* Arrested Development/Speech/Dionne Farris

Tash *See* Tha Alkaholiks

Tate, Bruce *See* The Penguins

Tatum, Robby *See* The Heartbeats/Shep & the Limelites

Tavares, Antone "Chubby" *See* Tavares

Tavares, Arthur "Pooch" *See* Tavares

Tavares, Feliciano "Butch" *See* Tavares

Tavares, Perry Lee "Tiny" *See* Tavares

Tavares, Ralph *See* Tavares

Taylor, Chris *See* Roachford

Taylor, Derrick *See* Roachford

Taylor, James "J.T." *See* Kool & the Gang

Taylor, Johnnie *See* Soul Stirrers

Taylor, Lisa *See* Rose Royce

Taylor, Mick *See* The Rolling Stones

Taylor, Richard *See* The Manhattans

Taylor, Ted *See* The Cadets

Taylor, Zola *See* The Platters

T-Bone *See* Da Lench Mob

T-Boz *See* TLC

T.C.D. *See* Force M.D.'s

T-Double *See* MC Breed & the DFC

Tek *See* Smif-N-Wessun/Da Cocoa Brovaz

Temperton, Rod *See* Heatwave

Tempest *See* Flatlinerz

Terminator X *See* Public Enemy

Terrell, Elbertina "Twinkie" Clark *See* The Clark Sisters

Terrell, Jean *See* The Supremes

Terry, Phil *See* The Intruders

Thaler, Les *See* The Dazz Band

Thomas, Alex *See* Earth, Wind & Fire/Maurice White

Thomas, Charles *See* Wild Cherry

Thomas, Danny *See* Con Funk Shun

Thomas, David *See* Take 6

Thomas, Dennis "D.T." *See* Kool & the Gang

Thomas, Gerry *See* Jimmy Castor/The Jimmy Castor Bunch

Thomas, Jerome "J.T." *See* The S.O.S. Band

Thomas, Joe "Jobie" *See* Enchantment

Thomas, Mary *See* The Crystals

Thomas, Vic *See* Junior Walker & the All-Stars

Thomas, Wayne *See* Maze

Thome, Rob *See* The Catalinas

Thompkins, Russell Jr. *See* The Stylistics

Thompson, Marshall *See* The Chi-Lites

Thompson, Rick *See* B.T. Express

Thompson, Tony *See* Chic; Hi-Five

Thorn, Tracey *See* Everything but the Girl

Thorne, Rufus *See* Harold Melvin & the Blue Notes

Thornton, Kevin *See* Color Me Badd

The Producer Index compiles the albums in Music-Hound R&B that have a producer noted for them. (These are usually recommended discs, but we like to credit the producer for albums in the "What to Avoid" section, too, so a few of these could be downright dogs!) Under each producer's name is the name of the entry (or entries) in which the album can be found, followed by the album title. If an album is produced by more than one individual/group, the album name will be listed separately under the names of each of the individuals/ groups who had a hand in producing it.

Gregory Abbott
Gregory Abbott, *Shake You Down*

Sigidi Abdallah
The S.O.S. Band, *Too*

Above the Law
Above the Law, *Time Will Reveal*

Herb Abramson
Ruth Brown, *Rockin' In Rhythm—The Best of Ruth Brown*

Absolute
The Spice Girls, *Spice*

Aceyalone
Freestyle Fellowship, *All Balls Don't Bounce*

George Acogny
Manu Dibango, *Wakafrika*

Bryan Adams
Ike & Tina Turner/Tina Turner/Ike Turner, *What's Love Got to Do with It*

Joe Adams
Ray Charles, *Anthology*
Ray Charles, *Modern Sounds in Country and Western Music*

Terry Adams
Johnnie Johnson, *Johnnie B. Bad*

Nat Adderly Jr.
New Edition, *Johnny Gill*

ADK
One Way/Alicia Myers, *Who's Foolin' Who*

ADMoney
Lordz of Brooklyn, *All In the Family*

Walter Afanasieff
All-4-One, *Hunchback of Notre Dame Soundtrack*
Mariah Carey, *Mariah Carey*
Mariah Carey, *Merry Christmas*
Mariah Carey, *MTV Unplugged*
New Kids on the Block, *Face the Music*
Luther Vandross, *Songs*

Afro Rican
Afro Rican, *Give It All You Got 95*

Ahmad
Ahmad, *Ahmad*

Dino Airali
Phoebe Snow, *Phoebe Snow*

Matt Aitken
Donna Summer, *Another Place and Time*

Howard Albert
Betty Wright, *Betty Wright: Live*

Ron Albert
Betty Wright, *Betty Wright: Live*

Gerald Albright
Gerald Albright, *Live at Birdland West*

James Alexander
The Bar-Kays, *48 Hours*

Tha Alkaholiks
King Tee, *Tha Triflin Album*

Reggie Andrews
Patrice Rushen, *Haven't You Heard: The Best of Patrice Rushen*

Apache
Apache, *Apache*

Arcadia
Grace Jones, *So Red the Rose*

Joan Armatrading
Joan Armatrading, *Hearts and Flowers*

Art of Noise
The Art of Noise, *The Ambient Collection*
The Art of Noise, *The Best of the Art of Noise*
The Art of Noise, *Daft*
The Art of Noise, *The Drum and Bass Collection*
The Art of Noise, *The FON Mixes*
The Art of Noise, *In Visible Silence*
The Art of Noise, *Who's Afraid Of? (The Art of Noise!)*

Artifacts
Artifacts, *Between a Rock and a Hard Place*

Ashford & Simpson
Ashford & Simpson, *Been Found*
Ashford & Simpson, *Capitol Gold—The Best of Ashford & Simpson*

Beck
Beck, *One Foot in the Grave*

The Bee Gees
The Bee Gees, *Cucumber Castle*
The Bee Gees, *Spirits Having Flown*

Michael Beinhorn
Red Hot Chili Peppers, *Mother's Milk*
Red Hot Chili Peppers, *The Uplift Mofo Party Plan*

Al Bell
Eddie Floyd, *Baby Lay Your Head Down*
Isaac Hayes, *Hot Buttered Soul*
The Staple Singers, *The Best of the Staple Singers*
Rufus Thomas, *Did You Hear Me*
Rufus Thomas, *Rufus Thomas Live*

Ricky Bell
New Edition, *Poison*

Thom Bell
James Ingram, *Never Felt So Good*
The Spinners, *Mighty Love*
The Spinners, *Pick of the Litter*
The Spinners, *Spinners*
The Stylistics, *The Best of the Stylistics*
The Stylistics, *Round 2*
The Stylistics, *The Stylistics*

William Bell
William Bell, *Bedtime Stories*
William Bell, *On a Roll*
William Bell, *Vol. 1—Greatest Hits*
William Bell, *Vol. 2—Greatest Hits*

Pete Bellote
Donna Summer, *Bad Girls*

Henri Belolo
The Village People, *The Best of the Village People*

Pete Belotte
Donna Summer, *The Wanderer*

LaMont Bench
The Edwin Hawkins Singers, *Oh Happy Day*

Vassal Benford
Oleta Adams, *Moving On*
Jade, *Jade to the Max*

H.B. Bennett
Otis Clay, *The Soul Collection*

George Benson
George Benson, *Big Boss Band*

Howard Benson
Ice-T, *Violent Demise: The Last Days*

Chuck Berry
Chuck Berry, *Golden Hits*

Andre Betts
Living Colour, *Stain*
Me'Shell Ndegeocello, *Plantation Lullabies*

Frankie Beverly
Maze, *Golden Time of Day*
Maze, *Live in Los Angeles*
Maze, *Live in New Orleans*
Maze, *Maze Featuring Frankie Beverly*
Maze, *Silky Soul*
Maze, *We Are One*

Chris Biando
Chuck Brown & the Soul Searchers, *The Other Side*

William Bickelhaupt
Major Lance, *Now Arriving*

Big Chief
Big Chief, *Face*
Big Chief, *Mack Avenue Skullgame*
Big Chief, *Platinum Jive*

Big Daddy Kane
Big Daddy Kane, *It's a Big Daddy Thing*

Joe Bihari
Richard Berry, *Get Out of the Car*

Scott Billington
Johnny Adams, *Good Morning Heartache*
Johnny Adams, *Johnny Adams Sings Doc Pomus: The Real Me*

Johnny Adams, *One Foot in the Blues*
Johnny Adams, *Walking on a Tightrope: The Songs of Percy Mayfield*
James Booker, *Classified*
James Booker, *Resurrection of the Bayou Maharajah*
James Booker, *Spiders on the Keys*
Dirty Dozen Brass Band, *Jelly*
Dirty Dozen Brass Band, *Voodoo*
Irma Thomas, *The New Rules*
Irma Thomas, *The Story of My Life*
Irma Thomas, *Walk Around Heaven: New Orleans Gospel Soul*
Irma Thomas, *The Way I Feel*

Martin Bisi
Bill Laswell/Material, *Memory Serves*

Michael Bivins
New Edition, *Poison*

Biz Markie
Biz Markie, *All Samples Cleared*
Biz Markie, *The Biz Never Sleeps*
Biz Markie, *I Need A Haircut*
Grand Daddy I.U., *Smooth Assassin*
Illegal/Jamal, *The Untold Truth*
Kid Capri, *Kid Capri: The Tape*

Black Sheep
Chi-Ali, *The Fabulous Chi-Ali*

Black Thought
The Roots, *Do You Want More?!!!??!*

Larry Blackmon
Cameo, *She's Strange*
Cameo, *Word Up*
New Edition, *King of Stage*

Bumps Blackwell
Jesse Belvin, *The Blues Balladeer*
Little Richard, *The Georgia Peach*
Little Richard, *Shag On Down By the Union Hall*

Little Richard, *The Specialty Sessions*
Larry Williams, *Bad Boy*
Larry Williams, *Best Of Larry Williams*
Larry Williams, *Here's Larry Williams*

Chris Blackwell
Bob Marley & the Wailers, *Babylon by Bus*
Bob Marley & the Wailers, *Burnin'*
Womack & Womack, *Conscience*

Earl Blaize
Sha-Key, *A Head Nadda's Journey to Adidi Skizm*

Allen Blazek
J. Geils Band/Bluestime, *Blow Your Face Out*
J. Geils Band/Bluestime, *Hotline*

Adam Block
Charles Brown, *Driftin' Blues: The Best of Charles Brown*

Bloodstone
Bloodstone, *The Ultimate Collection*

Mike Bloomfield
Otis Rush, *Mourning in the Morning*

Kurtis Blow
Kurtis Blow, *The Best of Kurtis Blow*

Richard Bock
The Crusaders, *Lighthouse 68*

Angela Bofill
Angela Bofill, *Too Tough*

The Bomb Squad
Paula Abdul, *Shut Up and Dance (The Dance Mixes)*
Ice Cube, *AmeriKKKa's Most Wanted*
Public Enemy, *Muse Sick-N-Hour Mess Age*
Son of Bazerk, *Son of Bazerk Featuring No Self Control and the Band*
Young Black Teenagers, *Young Black Teenagers*

Christopher Bond
Maria Muldaur, *Southern Winds*

Bone
Bone Thugs-N-Harmony, *Faces of Death*

Boogiemen
Del Tha Funkee Homosapien/Souls of Mischief/Casual/Extra Prolific, *I Wish My Brother George Was Here*

Boogiemonsters
Boogiemonsters, *God Sound*
Boogiemonsters, *Riders of the Storm: The Underwater Album*

Booker T. & the MG's
Booker T. & the MG's, *Melting Pot*

Chuckii Booker
Chuckii Booker, *Niice 'n' Wiild*

David Booth
Chuck Willis, *Stroll On: The Chuck Willis Collection*
Betty Wright, *The Best of Betty Wright*

Boots
The Coup, *The Coup: The EP*
The Coup, *Genocide & Juice*
The Coup, *Kill My Landlord*

Boo-Yaa T.R.I.B.E.
Boo-Yaa T.R.I.B.E., *New Funky Nation*
Boo-Yaa T.R.I.B.E., *Rumours of a Dead Man*

Sam Bostic
E-40 and the Click, *The Mailman*

Carl E. Bourelly
New Edition, *Poison*

Jean-Paul Bourelly
Jean-Paul Bourelly, *Fade to Cacophony*
Jean-Paul Bourelly, *Jungle Cowboy*
Jean-Paul Bourelly, *Saints & Sinners*
Jean-Paul Bourelly, *Sonya*
Jean-Paul Bourelly, *Trippin'*

Byron Bowie
Defunkt, *Defunkt*

David Bowie
David Bowie, *Aladdin Sane*
David Bowie, *Heroes*
David Bowie, *Never Let Me Down*
David Bowie, *The Rise and Fall of Ziggy Stardust and the Spiders from Mars*
David Bowie, *Station To Station*

Joe Bowie
Defunkt, *Thermonuclear Sweat*

Joe Boyd
James Booker, *Junco Partner*
Defunkt, *Thermonuclear Sweat*
Maria Muldaur, *Maria Muldaur*
Maria Muldaur, *Pottery Pie*
Maria Muldaur, *Waitress in a Donut Shop*

The Brand New Heavies
The Brand New Heavies, *The Brand New Heavies*
The Brand New Heavies, *Brother Sister*
The Brand New Heavies, *Heavy Rhyme Experience: Vol. 1*
The Brand New Heavies, *Shelter*
Masta Ace, *Heavy Rhyme Experience Volume 1*

Brand Nubian
Brand Nubian, *In God We Trust*
Brand Nubian, *One for All*

Wayne Brathwaite
Will Downing, *A Dream Fulfilled*

Michael H. Brauer
Roachford, *Roachford*

Toni Braxton
Toni Braxton, *Secrets*

Stephen Bray
Madonna, *True Blue*

Terry Britten
Ike & Tina Turner/Tina Turner/Ike Turner, *What's Love Got to Do with It*

Broadway
King Tee, *IV Life*

Bruce Bromberg
Robert Cray, *Bad Influence*
Robert Cray, *Strong Persuader*
Ted Hawkins, *Happy Hour*

Chuck Brooks
J. Blackfoot, *City Slicker*

Michael Brooks
Commissioned, *Commissioned Complete*
Billie Holiday, *Lady in Satin*
Billie Holiday, *The Quintessential Billie Holiday*

B.R.O.theR. ?uestion
The Roots, *Do You Want More?!!!??!*

Bobby Brown
New Edition, *Don't Be Cruel*

Ezo Brown
Poor Righteous Teachers, *The New World Order*

James Brown
Afrika Bambaataa, *Unity*
James Brown, *Live at the Apollo*
James Brown, *Soul Pride: The Instrumentals 1960-1969*
Fred Wesley, *Doing It to Death*

Morrie Brown
Evelyn "Champagne" King, *Get Loose*

Ollie E. Brown
The Fifth Dimension, *In the House*

Sherman M. Brown
Commissioned, *Irreplaceable Love*

Shirley Brown
Shirley Brown, *Diva of Soul*
Shirley Brown, *If This Is Goodbye*

Peabo Bryson
Peabo Bryson, *Reaching for the Sky*

Mickey Buckins
Johnny Nash, *The Reggae Collection*

Buckshot
Heltah Skeltah, *Nocturnal*
O.G.C. (Originoo Gun Clappaz), *Da Storm*

Buckwild
Big L, *Lifestylez Ov Da Poor & Dangerous*
Brand Nubian, *Everything Is Everything*
Brand Nubian, *Wild Cowboys*
Kool G Rap and D.J. Polo, *4,5,6*
Madd Skillz, *From Where???*
Mic Geronimo, *The Natural*
Notorious B.I.G., *Life After Death*
O.C., *Word Life*
Organized Konfusion, *The Equinox*
Organized Konfusion, *Stress: The Extinction Agenda*
Royal Flush, *Ghetto Millionaire*

James Bullard
Al Green, *One in a Million*

Selassie Burke
Solomon Burke, *Live at the House of Blues*

Henry Bush
Albert King, *I'll Play the Blues for You*

Bushwick Bill
Geto Boys, *We Can't Be Stopped*

Busta Rhymes
Leaders of the New School/Busta Rhymes, *The Coming*
Keith Murray, *The Most Beautifulest Thing in This World*

Buster & Shavoni
Kirk Franklin & the Family, *Whatcha Lookin' 4?*

Chris Cuben-Tatum
Me Phi me, *One*

Culture Freedom
Poor Righteous Teachers, *The New World Order*

Jill Cunniff
Luscious Jackson, *Natural Ingredient*

Ian Curnow
Rick Astley, *Whenever You Need Somebody*

Michael Cuscuna
Nat King Cole, *Jazz Encounters*
Buddy Guy, *Buddy Guy & Junior Wells Play the Blues*

Frankie Cutlass
Frankie Cutlass, *Politics & Bullshit*
Doug E. Fresh, *Play*

Cutmaster Cool V
Grand Daddy I.U., *Smooth Assassin*

Andre Cymone
Jody Watley, *Jody Watley*
Jody Watley, *Larger Than Life*
Jody Watley, *You Wanna Dance with Me?*

Davy D.
Shinehead, *Unity*

Tony D
Kwest Tha Madd Lad, *This Is My First Album*
Tony D, *Droppin' Funky Verses*

Da Baka Boyz
The B.U.M.S., *Lyfe and Tyme*
Kwest Tha Madd Lad, *This Is My First Album*
Volume 10, *Hip-Hoppera*

Da Beatminerz
Artifacts, *That's Them*
Bahamadia, *Kollage*
Black Moon/Boot Camp Clik, *Diggin' In Dah Vaults*
Black Moon/Boot Camp Clik, *Enta Da Stage*
Doug E. Fresh, *Play*
Heltah Skeltah, *Nocturnal*
Mic Geronimo, *The Natural*
O.C., *Jewelz*
Royal Flush, *Ghetto Millionaire*

Smif-N-Wessun/Da Cocoa Brovaz, *Dah Shinin'*

Daddy-O
Junior M.A.F.I.A./Lil' Kim, *Conspiracy*
Queen Latifah, *All Hail the Queen*

Miki Dallon
J.J. Jackson, *The Great J.J. Jackson*

D'Angelo
D'Angelo, *Brown Sugar*

Terence Trent D'Arby
Terence Trent D'Arby, *Introducing the Hardline According to Terence Trent D'Arby*
Terence Trent D'Arby, *Neither Fish Nor Flesh*
Terence Trent D'Arby, *Symphony Or Damn*
Terence Trent D'Arby, *Vibrator*
Des'ree, *Symphony or Damn*

August Darnell
Kid Creole & the Coconuts/Dr. Buzzard's Original Savannah Band, *In Praise of Older Women and Other Crimes*
Kid Creole & the Coconuts/Dr. Buzzard's Original Savannah Band, *Off the Coast of Me*
Kid Creole & the Coconuts/Dr. Buzzard's Original Savannah Band, *Wise Guy*

Das EFX
Das EFX/Bobby Sichran, *Dead Serious*

Dat Nigga Daz
Lady of Rage, *Necessary Roughness*
Snoop Doggy Dogg, *Tha Doggfather*

Terry Date
Fishbone, *Give a Monkey a Brain and He'll Swear He's the Center of the Universe*

Roger Davies
Joe Cocker, *Have a Little Faith*

Ike & Tina Turner/Tina Turner/Ike Turner, *What's Love Got to Do with It*

Carl Davis
Walter Jackson, *It's All Over*
Walter Jackson, *Send in the Clowns*
Walter Jackson, *Welcome Home*
Major Lance, *Everybody Loves a Good Time!*

Don Davis
The Dramatics, *Drama V*
The Dramatics, *Dramatically Yours*
Johnnie Taylor, *Chronicle: 20 Greatest Hits*
Johnnie Taylor, *Who's Makin' Love*

Quint Davis
Dirty Dozen Brass Band, *My Feet Can't Fail Me Now*

Saul Davis
Percy Sledge, *Blue Night*

Morris Day
The Time, *Ice Cream Castle*

Daz
Tha Dogg Pound, *Dogg Food*

De La Soul
De La Soul, *3 Feet High and Rising*
De La Soul, *Stakes Is High*

El DeBarge
DeBarge/El DeBarge, *In a Special Way*

Bert deCoteaux
Z.Z. Hill, *Love Is So Good When You're Stealing It*

Deee-Lite
Deee-lite, *Dancefloor Oddities & Sampladelic Relics—Deee Remixes*
Deee-lite, *Infinity Within*
Deee-lite, *World Clique*

Def Jef
Def Jef, *Just A Poet with Soul*
Def Jef, *Soul Food*
Shaquille O'Neal, *Shaq Diesel*

Eddie del Barrio
Dianne Reeves, *Art + Survival*

Donald DeGrate
Jodeci, *Diary of a Mad Band*
Jodeci, *Forever My Lady*

Del Tha Funkee Homosapien
Del Tha Funkee Homosapien/Souls of Mischief/Casual/Extra Prolific, *I Wish My Brother George Was Here*
Del Tha Funkee Homosapien/Souls of Mischief/Casual/Extra Prolific, *No Need for Alarm*
New Kingdom, *Heavy Load*

Cerwin "C-Dawg" Depper
Public Enemy, *Apocalypse '91 . . . The Enemy Strikes Black*

Rick Derringer
Edgar Winter, *Edgar Winter's White Trash*
Edgar Winter, *They Only Come Out at Night*

Des'ree
Des'ree, *I Ain't Movin'*

Ian Devaney
Lisa Stansfield, *Affection*

Walter DeVenne
The Channels, *The Doo-Wop Box: 101 Vocal Group Gems from the Golden Age of Rock 'n' Roll*
The Charms, *The Doo-Wop Box: 101 Vocal Group Gems from the Golden Age of Rock 'n' Roll*
The Charts, *The Doo Wop Box: 101 Vocal Group Gems from the Golden Age of Rock 'n' Roll*
The El Dorados, *The Doo Wop Box II: 101 More Vocal Group Gems from the Golden Age of Rock 'n' Roll*
The Five Keys, *The Doo Wop Box II*
The Five Keys, *The Doo Wop Box: 101 Vocal Group*

*Gems from the Golden
Age of Rock 'n Roll*
The Moonglows/Harvey
Fuqua, *On Stage*
Maurice Williams & the Zodi-
acs, *The Doo-Wop Box:
101 Vocal Group Gems
from the Golden Age of
Rock 'n' Roll*

Ronnie DeVoe
New Edition, *Poison*

Mohandas Dewese
Kool Moe Dee, *How Ya Like
Me Now*
Kool Moe Dee, *Knowledge Is
King*

D-Flo
Digital Underground, *Body
Hat Syndrome*

Diamond D
Tha Alkaholiks, *Coast II Coast*
Apache, *Apache*
Brand Nubian, *In God We
Trust*
Brand Nubian, *Wild Cowboys*
Cypress Hill, *Unreleased & Re-
vamped*
Diamond D, *Passion, Hatred
and Infidelity*
Diamond D, *Stunts, Blunts
and Hip-Hop*
Ed O.G. and Da Bulldogs, *Rox-
bury 02119*
Fat Joe Da Gangsta, *Jealous
One's Envy*
Fu-Schnickens, *Nervous
Breakdown*
Fugees, *The Score*
Illegal/Jamal, *The Untold
Truth*
Lord Finesse, *Funky Techni-
cian*
Lord Finesse, *Return of the
Funky Man*
Showbiz & A.G., *Runaway
Slave*

Denny Diante
Angela Bofill, *Teaser*

Manu Dibango
Manu Dibango, *Live 91*

J. Dibbs
Joe, *All That I Am*

Joe, *Everything*

Jim Dickinson
G. Love & Special Sauce,
Coast to Coast Motel

Nathan DiGesare
Commissioned, *Irreplaceable
Love*

Digital Underground
Digital Underground, *Body
Hat Syndrome*
Digital Underground, *Future
Rhythm*
Digital Underground, *Sex
Packets*
Digital Underground, *Sons of
the P*
Digital Underground, *This Is
an EP Release*

Moses C. Dillard Jr.
Al Green, *White Christmas*

The Dirty Dozen
Dirty Dozen Brass Band, *ears
to the wall*

Divine Styler
Divine Styler, *Spiral Walls
Containing Autumns of
Light*
Divine Styler, *Word Power*

Luther Dixon
The Shirelles, *Baby It's You*
The Shirelles, *Foolish Little
Girl*
The Shirelles, *Shirelles and
King Curtis Give a Twist
Party*
The Shirelles, *Shirelles Sing to
Trumpets and Strings*

Willie Dixon
Charles Brown, *Southern
Blues 1957–1963*
Koko Taylor, *Koko Taylor*

DJ Battlecat
Dana Dane, *Rollin' with Dana
Dane*
Domino, *Domino*

DJ Clark Kent
Junior M.A.F.I.A./Lil' Kim, *Conspiracy*

DJ Code Money
Schoolly D, *Am I Black
Enough for You?*

DJ Darryl
Richie Rich, *Seasoned Veteran*

DJ Daryl
Richie Rich, *Half Thang*

DJ Evil D
O.G.C. (Originoo Gun Clappaz), *Da Storm*

DJ Fuze
Dru Down, *Can You Feel Me*

DJ Gill
All-4-One, *All-4-One*

DJ Homicide
Chino XL, *Here To Save You All*
Volume 10, *Hip-Hoppera*

DJ Honda
DJ Honda, *DJ Honda*

DJ Irv
Mic Geronimo, *The Natural*

DJ Kool
DJ Kool, *Let Me Clear My
Throat*

DJ Krush
DJ Krush, *DJ Krush*
DJ Krush, *Meiso*

DJ Lethal
House of Pain, *House of Pain*

DJ Mark the 45 King
Chill Rob G, *Ride the Rhythm*
Def Jef, *Soul Food*
Diamond D, *Stunts, Blunts
and Hip-Hop*
DJ Kool, *Let Me Clear My
Throat*
Doctor Dre and Ed Lover, *Back
up off Me*
King Sun, *XL*
Queen Latifah, *All Hail the
Queen*

DJ Mista Cee
Masta Ace, *Take a Look
Around*

DJ Muggs
Boogie Down
Productions/KRS-One, *I
Got Next*

Cypress Hill, *Black Sunday*
Cypress Hill, *Cypress Hill*
Cypress Hill, *Cypress Hill III—
Temples of Boom*
Funkdoobiest, *Brothas Doo-
bie*
Funkdoobiest, *Which Doobie
U B?*
House of Pain, *House of Pain*

D.J. Polo
Kool G Rap and D.J. Polo,
Road to the Riches
Kool G Rap and D.J. Polo,
Wanted Dead or Alive

DJ Pooh
Color Me Badd, *Time and
Chance*
Tha Dogg Pound, *Dogg
Food*
Kam, *Neva Again*
King Tee, *Act a Fool*
King Tee, *At Your Own Risk*
King Tee, *IV Life*
King Tee, *Tha Triflin Album*
Snoop Doggy Dogg, *Tha Dog-
gfather*
Too $hort, *Short Dog's in the
House*

DJ Premier
Bahamadia, *Kollage*
Buckshot Lefonque, *Buckshot
LeFonque*
Fat Joe Da Gangsta, *Jealous
One's Envy*
Gang Starr, *Daily Operation*
Gang Starr, *Hard to Earn*
Gang Starr, *No More Mr. Nice
Guy*
Group Home, *Livin' Proof*
Jay-Z, *Reasonable Doubt*
Jeru the Damaja, *The Sun
Rises in the East*
Jeru the Damaja, *The Wrath of
the Math*
Lady of Rage, *Necessary
Roughness*
Lord Finesse, *Funky Techni-
cian*
Nas, *Illmatic*
Notorious B.I.G., *Life After
Death*
Notorious B.I.G., *Ready to Die*
O.C., *Jewelz*

DJ Quik
Bo$$, *Born Gangstaz*
DJ Quik, *Quik Is the Name*
DJ Quik, *Safe & Sound*
DJ Quik, *Way 2 Fonky*
Kam, *Made in America*

DJ Shadow
DJ Shadow, *Entroducing . . .*
DJ Shadow, *Latyrx*
Zimbabwe Legit, *Zimbabwe Legit*

DJ Slip
MC Eiht/Compton's Most Wanted, *Death Threatz*
MC Eiht/Compton's Most Wanted, *We Come Strapped*

DJ Uneek
Bone Thugs-N-Harmony, *Creepin On Ah Come Up*
Bone Thugs-N-Harmony, *E. 1999 Eternal*

DJ Yella
Dr. Dre, *Concrete Roots*
Eazy-E, *Eternal E*

D-Maq
Anotha Level, *On Anotha Level*

Brian "the Wino" Dobbs
Coolio, *Gangsta's Paradise*

D.O.C.
The D.O.C., *Helter Skelter*

Dr. Dre
2Pac/Thug Life/Makaveli, *All Eyez on Me*
The D.O.C., *No One Can Do It Better*
Dr. Dre, *The Chronic*
Dr. Dre, *Concrete Roots*
Dr. Dre, *First Round Knockout*
Eazy-E, *Eternal E*
J.J. Fad, *Supersonic*
N.W.A., *Straight Outta Compton*
Nas, *It Was Written*
Snoop Doggy Dogg, *Doggystyle*

Dr. Freeze
Color Me Badd, *C.M.B.*
New Edition, *Poison*

Dr. Jam
Lifers Group, *Lifers Group*
Lifers Group, *Living Proof*
Ultramagnetic MC's, *Funk Your Head Up*

C.S. Dodd
Bob Marley & the Wailers, *The Birth of a Legend*

Larry Dodson
The Bar-Kays, *48 Hours*

Tha Dogg Pound
M.C. Hammer, *The Funky Headhunter*

Fats Domino
Fats Domino, *Christmas Is a Special Day*

Domino
Del Tha Funkee Homosapien/Souls of Mischief/Casual/Extra Prolific, *Fear Itself*
Del Tha Funkee Homosapien/Souls of Mischief/Casual/Extra Prolific, *Like It Should Be*
Del Tha Funkee Homosapien/Souls of Mischief/Casual/Extra Prolific, *'93 Til Infinity*
Del Tha Funkee Homosapien/Souls of Mischief/Casual/Extra Prolific, *No Man's Land*
Del Tha Funkee Homosapien/Souls of Mischief/Casual/Extra Prolific, *No Need for Alarm*
Domino, *Physical Funk*

Joel Dorn
Roberta Flack, *First Take*
Billie Holiday, *The Complete Commodore Recordings*
King Curtis, *King Curtis & Champion Jack Dupree: Blues at Montreux*

Double X
Double XX Posse, *Put Ya Boots On*

Alan Douglas
Jimi Hendrix, *Voodoo Soup*
Albert King, *Red House*

Steve Douglas
Sly & the Family Stone, *The Wildest Organ in Town*

Tom Dowd
Buddy Guy, *Buddy Guy & Junior Wells Play the Blues*
Wilson Pickett, *The Sound of Wilson Pickett*
Rod Stewart, *Body Wishes*
Rod Stewart, *A Night on the Town*
The Young Rascals/The Rascals, *The Young Rascals*

Tyrone Downie
Ziggy Marley & the Melody Makers, *Hey World*
Ziggy Marley & the Melody Makers, *Play the Game Right*

Will Downing
Will Downing, *A Dream Fulfilled*
Will Downing, *Love's the Place to Be*
Will Downing, *Moods*

Downtown Science
Downtown Science, *Downtown Science*

O'landa Draper
Jennifer Holliday, *On & On*

Dream Warriors
Dream Warriors, *And Now the Legacy Begins*
Dream Warriors, *Subliminal Simulation*

Dres
Fu-Schnickens, *F.U. Don't Take It Personal*

Frank Driggs
Robert Johnson, *King of the Delta Blues Singers*
Robert Johnson, *Robert Johnson: The Complete Recordings*

Skip Drinkwater
Taj Mahal, *Like Never Before*

DTTX
Lighter Shade of Brown (LSOB), *Hip-hop Locos*

Anne Dudley
The Art of Noise, *Below The Waste*
The Art of Noise, *In No Sense? Nonsense!*

George Duke
Philip Bailey, *Continuation*
Anita Baker, *Rhythm of Love*
George Duke/The Clarke/Duke Project, *The Clarke/Duke Project*
George Duke/The Clarke/Duke Project, *Muir Woods Suite*
Rachelle Ferrell, *Rachelle Ferrell*
Dianne Reeves, *Dianne Reeves*

Jermaine Dupri
Da Brat, *Funkdafied*
Da Bush Babees, *Ambushed*
Junior M.A.F.I.A./Lil' Kim, *Hard Core*
Kris Kross, *Totally Krossed Out*
MC Lyte, *Bad as I Wanna B*
Richie Rich, *Seasoned Veteran*

The Dust Brothers
Beastie Boys/DJ Hurricane/Money Mark, *Paul's Boutique*
Beck, *Odelay*
Boo-Yaa T.R.I.B.E., *New Funky Nation*
Def Jef, *Just A Poet with Soul*
Tone-Loc, *Cool Hand Loc*
Tone-Loc, *Loc-ed After Dark*

Arthur Dyer
Kirk Franklin & the Family, *Kirk Franklin & the Family*

EA-Ski
Luniz, *Operation Stackola*
Spice 1, *187 He Wrote*

Earth, Wind & Fire
Earth, Wind & Fire/Maurice White, *Open Our Eyes*

Earthquake Brothers
Freestyle Fellowship, *Inner City Griots*

Barry J. Eastmond
Anita Baker, *Rhythm of Love*

Louis Jordan, *The Best of
Louis Jordan*
Louis Jordan, *Just Say Moe!
Mo' of the Best of Louis
Jordan*

Pete Gage
Joan Armatrading, *Back To the
Night*

Rosie Gaines
Rosie Gaines, *Arrival*
Rosie Gaines, *Caring*

Stephan Galfas
Southside Johnny & the Asbury Jukes, *Live/Reach Up
and Touch the Sky*

Peter Gallway
Laura Nyro, *Time and Love:
The Music of Laura Nyro*

Albhy Galuten
The Bee Gees, *Spirits Having
Flown*

Kenneth Gamble
Jerry Butler, *Iceman—Mercury
Years Anthology*
Harold Melvin & the Blue
Notes, *Collector's Item*
Harold Melvin & the Blue
Notes, *Greatest Hits*
Harold Melvin & the Blue
Notes, *If You Don't Know
Me By Now—Best of*
Laura Nyro, *Gonna Take a Mir-
acle*
The O'Jays, *Back Stabbers*
The O'Jays, *Give the People
What They Want*
The O'Jays, *Love Train: The
Best of the O'Jays*
Teddy Pendergrass, *Teddy
Live! Coast to Coast*
Wilson Pickett, *Wilson Pickett
in Philadelphia*
Lou Rawls, *Lou Rawls Live*

David Gamson
Me'Shell Ndegeocello, *Peace
Beyond Passion*
Me'Shell Ndegeocello, *Planta-
tion Lullabies*

Val Garay
Joan Armatrading, *The Key*

Joey Gardner
K7, *Swing Batta Swing*

Janos Gat
Defunkt, *Defunkt*

Timmy Gatling
New Edition, *Poison*

Bob Gaudio
Clifford Curry, *The Ultimate
Collection*
Marvin Gaye, *Dream of a Life-
time*

Marvin Gaye
Marvin Gaye, *Let's Get It On*
Marvin Gaye, *Midnight Love*
Marvin Gaye, *What's Going On*

J. Geils Band
J. Geils Band/Bluestime, *Blow
Your Face Out*
J. Geils Band/Bluestime, *Mon-
key Island*

Gregg Geller
Candi Staton/Candi Staton-
Sussewell, *Young Hearts
Run Free: The Best of
Candi Staton*
Charles Wright & the Watts
103rd Street Rhythm
Band, *Express Yourself:
The Best of Charles
Wright and the Watts
103rd Street Band*

Genius
Wu-Tang Clan, *Words from the
Genius*

David Getz
Janis Joplin/Big Brother & the
Holding Company,
Cheaper Thrills

Lee Gillette
Nat King Cole, *The Christmas
Song*
Nat King Cole, *Nat King Cole*

Verna Gillis
Bill Laswell/Material, *Live
from Soundscape*

Gabby Glaser
Luscious Jackson, *Natural Ingredient*

Pete Glenister
Alison Moyet/Yaz/Yazoo,
Hoodoo

Henry Glover
Roy Brown, *Greatest Hits*
Roy Brown, *Mighty Mighty
Man*
Little Willie John, *Fever: The
Best of Little Willie John*
Little Willie John, *Mister Little
Willie John*
Little Willie John, *Sure Things*
Muddy Waters, *The Muddy
Waters Woodstock Album*

Godfather Don
Ultramagnetic MC's, *The Four
Horsemen*

Gerry Goffin
The Cookies, *Complete Cookies*

Barry Goldberg
Percy Sledge, *Blue Night*

Stephan Goldman
Randy Crawford, *Raw Silk*

Jerry Goldstein
War, *All Day Music*
War, *The Music Band*
War, *The Music Band 2*
War, *The World Is a Ghetto*

G-One
DJ Quik, *Safe & Sound*

Lawrence Goodman
Three Times Dope, *Original
Stylin'*

Marc Gordon
Levert, *Just Coolin'*

Berry Gordy
Junior Walker & the All-Stars,
Shotgun

Michael Gore
Irene Cara, *Fame*

Steve Gottlieb
LaVern Baker, *The Sullivan
Years—The Rhythm &
Blues Revue*

Larry Graham
Graham Central Station/Larry
Graham, *Graham Central
Station*
Graham Central Station/Larry
Graham, *One in a Million
You*

Leo Graham
The Manhattans, *Sweet Talk*

Grand Puba Maxwell
Brand Nubian, *One for All*
Brand Nubian, *Reel to Reel*

Grandmaster Flash
Roxanne Shante, *The Bitch Is
Back*
Young Black Teenagers, *Dead
Enz Kidz Doin' Lifetime
Bidz*

Norman Granz
Louis Armstrong, *Ella Fitzger-
ald and Louis Armstrong*
Duke Ellington, *Compact Jazz:
And Friends*
Ella Fitzgerald, *The Cole
Porter Songbook*
Ella Fitzgerald, *The Complete
Duke Ellington Songbook*
Ella Fitzgerald, *The Complete
Ella Fitzgerald Song
Books*
Ella Fitzgerald, *Wishes You a
Swinging Christmas*
Sarah Vaughan, *Send in the
Clowns*

Nick Gravenites
Otis Rush, *Mourning in the
Morning*
Otis Rush, *Right Place, Wrong
Time*

Eric "IQ" Gray
Poor Righteous Teachers, *Holy
Intellect*

Jimmy Gray
E.U. (Experience Unlimited),
Free Yourself

Jay Graydon
Al Jarreau, *Jarreau*

Al Green
Al Green, *Anthology*
Al Green, *Call Me*
Al Green, *Greatest Hits*

Al Green, *One in a Million*

Jerry Greenberg
Average White Band, *Benny and Us*
Average White Band, *Pickin' Up the Pieces: The Best of the Average White Band, 1974–80*

Steve Greenberg
Lipps, Inc., *Funkyworld: The Best of Lipps, Inc.*

C. Greene
Allen Toussaint, *From a Whisper to a Scream*

Marlin Greene
Boz Scaggs, *Boz Scaggs*
Percy Sledge, *It Tears Me Up: The Best of Percy Sledge*

Peter Grendysa
Ruth Brown, *Rockin' In Rhythm—The Best of Ruth Brown*

Dick Griffey
Shalamar, *Disco Gardens*

Gene Griffin
New Edition, *Don't Be Cruel*

Mark Griffin
MC 900 FT Jesus, *Hell with the Lid Off*
MC 900 FT Jesus, *One Step Ahead of the Spider*
MC 900 FT Jesus, *Too Bad*
MC 900 FT Jesus, *Welcome to My Dream*

Onaje Allan Gumbs
Will Downing, *A Dream Fulfilled*
Will Downing, *Moods*

Guru
Gang Starr, *Daily Operation*
Gang Starr, *Guru's Jazzmatazz: Vol. I*
Gang Starr, *Hard to Earn*
Gang Starr, *No More Mr. Nice Guy*

Buddy Guy
Buddy Guy, *Live! The Real Deal*

The Gypsy Wave Power Co.
Womack & Womack, *Conscience*

Lew Hahn
Culture Club/Boy George, *From Luxury to Heartache*

Roy Halee
Johnny Nash, *The Reggae Collection*
Laura Nyro, *New York Tendaberry*

Daryl Hall
Daryl Hall & John Oates, *Private Eyes*
Daryl Hall & John Oates, *Three Hearts in the Happy Ending Machine*
Daryl Hall & John Oates, *Voices*

Dave Hall
Joe, *All That I Am*
Joe, *Everything*

Ellis Hall
Tower of Power, *Power*

Rick Hall
Clarence Carter, *Sixty Minutes with Clarence Carter*
Clarence Carter, *Snatching it Back: The Best of Clarence Carter*

Fred Hammond
Commissioned, *Commissioned Complete*

John Hammond
Billie Holiday, *The Quintessential Billie Holiday*
Bessie Smith, *Bessie Smith—The Collection*

Herbie Hancock
Herbie Hancock, *Head Hunters*
Herbie Hancock, *Monster*
Herbie Hancock, *The Other Side of Round Midnight*
Herbie Hancock, *Round Midnight*
Herbie Hancock, *Sound-System*

Bernie Hanighen
Billie Holiday, *The Quintessential Billie Holiday*

Jomo Hankerson
Aaliyah, *One in a Million*

Jeff Hannusch
Johnny Adams, *I Won't Cry: From the Vaults of Ric & Ron Records*

Kevin "K-Def" Hansford
Lords of the Underground, *Here Come the Lords*
Lords of the Underground, *Keepers of the Funk*

Phil Harding
Rick Astley, *Whenever You Need Somebody*

Ben Harper
Ben Harper, *Fight for Your Mind*
Ben Harper, *Welcome to the Cruel World*

James "Jimmy Jam" Harris III
Change, *Change of Heart*
Cherrelle, *Affair*
Cherrelle, *Fragile*
Cherrelle, *High Priority*
Color Me Badd, *Time and Chance*
Janet Jackson, *Control*
Janet Jackson, *Rhythm Nation 1814*
Ann Nesby, *I'm Here for You*
New Edition, *Heart Break*
New Edition, *Johnny Gill*
Alexander O'Neal, *All True Man*
Alexander O'Neal, *Hearsay*
The S.O.S. Band, *Just the Way You Like It*
The S.O.S. Band, *Sands of Time*
Sounds of Blackness, *Africa to America (The Journey of the Drum)*
Sounds of Blackness, *The Evolution of Gospel*
Crystal Waters, *Crystal Waters*

Norman Harris
The Trammps, *The Legendary Zing Album, Featuring the Fabulous Trammps*
The Trammps, *This Is Where the Happy People Go: The Best of the Trammps*
The Trammps, *Trammps*

Pete Q. Harris
D.J. Jazzy Jeff & the Fresh Prince/Will Smith, *He's the D.J., I'm the Rapper*

Jerry Harrison
Fine Young Cannibals, *The Raw and the Cooked*

Dan Hartman
Ike & Tina Turner/Tina Turner/Ike Turner, *Foreign Affair*

Donny Hathaway
Donny Hathaway, *Everything Is Everything*

Michael Haughton
Aaliyah, *One in a Million*

Richie Havens
Richie Havens, *Richie Havens Sings the Beatles and Bob Dylan*

Havoc
Almighty RSO, *Doomsday: Forever RSO*
Foxy Brown, *Ill Na Na*
Mobb Deep, *Hell On Earth*
Nas, *It Was Written*
Notorious B.I.G., *Life After Death*

Jim Hawkins
Us3, *Broadway & 52nd*

Isaac Hayes
The Bar-Kays, *Black Moses*
The Emotions, *Chronicle: Greatest Hits*
Isaac Hayes, *Double Feature*
Isaac Hayes, *The Isaac Hayes Movement*
Isaac Hayes, *Shaft*
Sam & Dave, *Soul Men*

Heavy D.
Heavy D. & the Boyz, *Nuttin' But Love*

Jimmy Henchmen
Groove Theory, *Groove Theory*

Ashley Ingram
Des'ree, *I Ain't Movin'*

At'c Inoue
Bootsy Collins, *Keepin' Dah Funk Alive 4 1995*

Jimmy Iovine
Eurythmics, *Greatest Hits*
Mother's Finest, *Live*
Alison Moyet/Yaz/Yazoo, *Raindancing*

Bob Irwin
Janis Joplin/Big Brother & the Holding Company, *18 Essential Songs*
Chuck Willis, *Let's Jump Tonight! The Best of Chuck Willis, 1952–1956*

Afrika Islam
Divine Styler, *Word Power*
Ice-T, *Iceberg/Freedom of Speech . . . Just Watch What You Say*

Isley Brothers
Isley Brothers, *3 + 3*
Isley Brothers, *The Heat Is On*
Isley Brothers, *In the Beginning . . .*

Michael Ivey
Basehead, *Play with Toys*

Quin Ivy
Percy Sledge, *It Tears Me Up: The Best of Percy Sledge*

Al Jackson Jr.
Shirley Brown, *Woman to Woman*
Eddie Floyd, *Baby Lay Your Head Down*
Albert King, *Born under a Bad Sign*
Otis Redding, *Good to Me*
Johnnie Taylor, *Who's Makin' Love*

Brian Jackson
Gil Scott-Heron, *1980*
Gil Scott-Heron, *From South Africa to South Carolina*

Chuck Jackson
Natalie Cole, *The Natalie Cole Collection*
Michael Henderson, *Slingshot*

Janet Jackson
Janet Jackson, *Control*
Janet Jackson, *Rhythm Nation 1814*

Michael Jackson
Michael Jackson, *Off the Wall*
Michael Jackson, *Thriller*

Millie Jackson
Millie Jackson, *Rock 'n' Soul*

The Jacksons
Jackson 5/The Jacksons, *Destiny*
Jackson 5/The Jacksons, *Triumph*
Michael Jackson, *Triumph*
Michael Jackson, *Victory*

Daniel Jacoubovitch
Johnnie Johnson, *Rockin' Eighty-Eights*

Mick Jagger
The Rolling Stones, *Some Girls*

Jam Master Jay
Bo$$, *Born Gangstaz*
Onyx, *Bacdafucup*
Run-D.M.C., *Back From Hell*
Shinehead, *Unity*

Fred James
Clifford Curry, *The Provider*

Palmer James
Al Green, *Anthology*

Rick James
Rick James, *Bustin' Out of L7*
Rick James, *Come Get It*
Rick James, *The Flag*
Rick James, *Street Songs*
Rick James, *Throwin' Down*
Teena Marie, *Greatest Hits*

Jay-Z
Saafir/The WhoRidas, *Boxcar Sessions*

Jazzie B
Soul II Soul, *Volume III: Just Right*
Soul II Soul, *Volume V: Believe*

Jazzy Jeff
D.J. Jazzy Jeff & the Fresh Prince/Will Smith, *Code Red*
D.J. Jazzy Jeff & the Fresh Prince/Will Smith, *Rock the House*

The JBL
Public Enemy, *Apocalypse '91 . . . The Enemy Strikes Black*

J.J. Jeczalik
The Art of Noise, *Below The Waste*
The Art of Noise, *In No Sense? Nonsense!*

Garland Jeffreys
Garland Jeffreys, *Escape Artist*

Arthur Jenkins
Johnny Nash, *The Reggae Collection*

J-Groove
Saafir/The WhoRidas, *Boxcar Sessions*

Joe
Joe, *All That I Am*
Joe, *Everything*

Glyn Johns
Joan Armatrading, *Joan Armatrading*
The Rolling Stones, *Get Yer Ya's-Ya's Out*

Criss Johnson
Koko Taylor, *Force of Nature*
Koko Taylor, *Queen of the Blues*

Jellybean Johnson
Janet Jackson, *Rhythm Nation 1814*
Whitney Houston, *Whitney*

Jesse Johnson
Paula Abdul, *Forever Your Girl*
Janet Jackson, *Dream Street*

Robert White Johnson
Peter Wolf, *Up to No Good*

Syl Johnson
Syl Johnson, *Brings Out the Blues in Me*

Syl Johnson, *Ms. Fine Brown Frame*
Syl Johnson, *This Time Together by Father and Daughter*

Wycliffe Johnson
Shabba Ranks, *X-tra Naked*

Joker/Buddha
Ace of Base, *The Bridge*
Ace of Base, *The Sign*

Allen Jones
The Bar-Kays, *Money Talks*
Isaac Hayes, *Hot Buttered Soul*
Albert King, *I'll Play the Blues for You*

Booker T. Jones
Booker T. & the MG's, *The Way It Should Be*

Gordon Jones
New Edition, *Don't Be Cruel*

Grace Jones
Grace Jones, *Inside Story*

James Earl Jones Jr.
Heavy D. & the Boyz, *Nuttin' But Love*

Kipper Jones
Brandy, *Brandy*

Quincy Jones
Arrested Development/ Speech/Dionne Farris, *Malcolm X Soundtrack*
Patti Austin, *Every Home Should Have One*
George Benson, *Give Me the Night*
The Brothers Johnson, *Blam*
The Brothers Johnson, *Greatest Hits*
The Brothers Johnson, *Light Up the Night*
The Brothers Johnson, *Look Out for #1*
The Brothers Johnson, *Mellow Madness*
The Brothers Johnson, *Right on Time*
James Ingram, *It's Your Night*
Michael Jackson, *Off the Wall*
Michael Jackson, *Thriller*

The Village People, *Macho Man*

Brian A. Morgan
SWV, *It's About Time*

Tom Morgan
Amos Milburn, *Johnny Otis Presents . . .*
Johnny Otis, *The Capitol Years*
Johnny Otis, *Johnny Otis Presents . . .*

Paul Morley
The Art of Noise, *Who's Afraid Of? (The Art of Noise!)*

Giorgio Moroder
Donna Summer, *Bad Girls*
Donna Summer, *The Wanderer*

Andy Morris
Lisa Stansfield, *Affection*

Van Morrison
Van Morrison, *Hymns to the Silence*
Van Morrison, *Inarticulate Speech of the Heart*
Van Morrison, *Irish Heartbeat*
Van Morrison, *Moondance*
Van Morrison, *A Night in San Francisco*
Van Morrison, *St. Dominic's Preview*
Van Morrison, *Too Long in Exile*
Van Morrison, *Van Morrison His Band and the Street Choir*

Mike Mosely
Celly Cel, *Killa Kali*
E-40 and the Click, *Down and Dirty*
E-40 and the Click, *Game Related*
E-40 and the Click, *In a Major Way*
E-40 and the Click, *The Mailman*
Mac Mall, *Untouchable*

Mickie Most
Hot Chocolate, *Everyone's a Winner*

Patrick Moten
Bobby Womack, *Someday We'll All Be Free*

Tom Moulton
Grace Jones, *Muse*

Robert Mugge
Al Green, *Anthology*

Muggs
Cypress Hill, *The Soul Assassins*
Cypress Hill, *Unreleased & Revamped*

Ali Shaheed Muhammad
Da Bush Babees, *Ambushed*
D'Angelo, *Brown Sugar*
Shaquille O'Neal, *Shaq Diesel*

Maria Muldaur
Johnny Adams, *Fanning the Flames*
Maria Muldaur, *Fanning the Flames*
Maria Muldaur, *Jazzabelle*

Randy Muller
B.T. Express, *Do It ('Til You're Satisfied)*
Brass Construction/Skyy, *Get Up to Get Down: Brass Construction's Funky Feeling*

Nick Mundy
Color Me Badd, *C.M.B.*

Shirley Murdock
Shirley Murdock, *Let There Be Love!*

Mark Murray
Color Me Badd, *Time and Chance*

Jonathon Myner
Royal Crescent Mob, *Omerta*

Hitoshi Namekata
Rachelle Ferrell, *First Instrument*

George Nash Jr.
Eric Benet, *True to Myself*

Johnny Nash
Johnny Nash, *I Can See Clearly Now*
Johnny Nash, *The Reggae Collection*

David Nathan
Arthur Conley, *Sweet Soul Music: The Best of Arthur Conley*

Pete Nathan
Syl Johnson, *Back In the Game*

Opal Louis Nations
Otis Clay, *Ring Them Golden Bells: The Best of the Gospel Songbirds*

Naughty By Nature
Eazy-E, *Eternal E*
Naughty By Nature, *19NaughtyIII*
Naughty By Nature, *Naughty By Nature*
Naughty By Nature, *Poverty's Paradise*
Rottin Razkals, *Rottin' Ta Da Core*

Andy Nehra
Kid Rock, *Fire It Up*

Mike Nehra
Kid Rock, *Fire It Up*

Bryan "Chuck" New
D.J. Jazzy Jeff & the Fresh Prince/Will Smith, *He's the D.J., I'm the Rapper*

Chuck Nice
Three Times Dope, *Live from Acknicklous Land*
Three Times Dope, *Original Stylin'*

Pete Nice
Kurious, *A Constipated Monkey*
3rd Bass, *Dust to Dust*

David Nichtern
Maria Muldaur, *Open Your Eyes*
Maria Muldaur, *Sweet and Slow*

Joe "The Butcher" Nicolo
Boo-Yaa T.R.I.B.E., *New Funky Nation*
Disposable Heroes of Hiphoprisy/Spearhead, *Home*
Goats, *Tricks of the Shade*

Phil Nicolo
Big Chief, *Platinum Jive*

Tom Nixon
Rufus Thomas, *Did You Hear Me*

Reggie Noble
Redman, *Dare Iz a Darkside*
Redman, *Muddy Waters*

The Nonce
The Nonce, *World Ultimate*

Gill Norton
Roachford, *Permanent Shade of Blue*

Notorious B.I.G.
Junior M.A.F.I.A./Lil' Kim, *Conspiracy*
Junior M.A.F.I.A./Lil' Kim, *Hard Core*

NPG
New Power Generation, *Exodus*
New Power Generation, *Gold Niggaz*
New Power Generation, *Good Life*

Jack Nuber
Bob Marley & the Wailers, *Babylon by Bus*

Laura Nyro
Laura Nyro, *Eli & the 13th Confession*
Laura Nyro, *Mother's Spiritual*
Laura Nyro, *New York Tendaberry*

John Oates
Daryl Hall & John Oates, *Private Eyes*
Daryl Hall & John Oates, *Voices*

Tim O'Brien
All-4-One, *All-4-One*
All-4-One, *And the Music Speaks*
The Chambers Brothers, *The Chambers Brothers' Greatest Hits*

The Ohio Players
The Ohio Players, *Honey*

Slick Rick, *The Great Adventures of Slick Rick*

Keith Shocklee
New Edition, *Poison*
Public Enemy, *Fear of a Black Planet*
Young Black Teenagers, *Dead Enz Kidz Doin' Lifetime Bidz*

Sig Shore
Earth, Wind & Fire/Maurice White, *That's the Way of the World*

Showbiz and A.G.
Black Sheep, *Non-Fiction*

Showbiz
Big L, *Lifestylez Ov Da Poor & Dangerous*
Boogie Down Productions/KRS-One, *I Got Next*
Diamond D, *Stunts, Blunts and Hip-Hop*
Lord Finesse, *Funky Technician*
Lord Finesse, *Return of the Funky Man*
Nice & Smooth, *Jewel of the Nile*
Organized Konfusion, *The Equinox*
Showbiz & A.G., *Runaway Slave*

Dick Shurman
Otis Clay, *When a Guitar Plays the Blues*
Robert Cray, *Showdown!*

Louil Silas Jr.
New Edition, *Don't Be Cruel*
New Edition, *Greatest Hits, Vol. 1*

Tom Silverman
James Brown, *Unity*

Daryl Simmons
Tevin Campbell, *I'm Ready*
New Edition, *Johnny Gill*

Lonnie Simmons
Gap Band, *Ain't Nothing But a Party*
Gap Band, *Gap Band VI*

Russell Simmons
Run-D.M.C., *Raising Hell*
Run-D.M.C., *Run-D.M.C.*

John Simon
Janis Joplin/Big Brother & the Holding Company, *Cheap Thrills*

Mel Simpson
Us3, *Hand on the Torch*

Sir Jinx
Ice Cube, *Death Certificate*
Ice Cube, *Lethal Injection*
Kool G Rap and D.J. Polo, *Live and Let Live*
Too $hort, *Short Dog's in the House*
WC and the MAAD Circle, *Ain't A Damn Thang Changed*
Yo Yo, *Make Way for the Motherlode*

Sir Mix-a-Lot
Sir Mix-a-Lot, *Mack Daddy*
Sir Mix-a-Lot, *Seminar*
Sir Mix-a-Lot, *Swass*

Gary Skardina
Anita Baker, *Rapture*

Brett Ski
MC Breed & the DFC, *Funkafied*

Slip
MC Eiht/Compton's Most Wanted, *It's a Compton Thang*
MC Eiht/Compton's Most Wanted, *Music to Driveby*
MC Eiht/Compton's Most Wanted, *Straight Checkn 'Em*

Gerard Smerek
Anita Baker, *Rhythm of Love*

Howard Smiley
The Spinners, *Best of the Spinners*

Bubba Smith
Shirley Caesar, *He Will Come: Live*

Douglas Smith
Millie Jackson, *Rock 'n' Soul*

Larry Smith
Run-D.M.C., *Run-D.M.C.*

Scott V. Smith
Andrae Crouch, *Mercy*

Steve Smith
Robert Palmer, *Sneakin' Sally through the Alley*

Lester Snells
J. Blackfoot, *Love-A-Holic*
J. Blackfoot, *Room Service*

John Snyder
Johnny Adams, *Fanning the Flames*
George Benson, *I Like Jazz: The Essence of George Benson*
Charles Brown, *Honey Dripper*
Charles Brown, *These Blues*
Louis Jordan, *Rock 'n' Roll Call*
Maria Muldaur, *Fanning the Flames*
Junior Wells, *Come on in This House*
Bill Withers, *Lean on Me: The Best of Bill Withers*

Somthin' for the People
Brandy, *Brandy*

Soul II Soul
Soul II Soul, *Club Classics Vol I*
Soul II Soul, *Vol II: 1990—A New Decade*

Souls of Mischief
Del Tha Funkee Homosapien/Souls of Mischief/Casual/Extra Prolific, *'93 Til Infinity*
Del Tha Funkee Homosapien/Souls of Mischief/Casual/Extra Prolific, *No Man's Land*

Special Ed
Junior M.A.F.I.A./Lil' Kim, *Conspiracy*

Phil Spector
The Crystals, *The Best of the Crystals*
Darlene Love, *The Best of Darlene Love*
Darlene Love, *A Christmas Gift for You*

The Ronettes/Ronnie Spector, *The Best of the Ronettes*
The Ronettes/Ronnie Spector, *A Christmas Gift for You*
Phil Spector, *Back to Mono (1958–1969)*
Phil Spector, *Twist and Shout*
Ike & Tina Turner/Tina Turner/Ike Turner, *River Deep, Mountain High*

Speech
Arrested Development/Speech/Dionne Farris, *3 Months, 5 Months & 2 Days in the Life of . . .*
Arrested Development/Speech/Dionne Farris, *Speech*
Arrested Development/Speech/Dionne Farris, *Unplugged*

Alvin Speights
Arrested Development/Speech/Dionne Farris, *Unplugged*

Spice 1
Spice 1, *Spice 1*

David Spinozza
Garland Jeffreys, *Matador and More*

Spoon
Coolio, *Gangsta's Paradise*

Spring Heel Jack
Everything but the Girl, *Walking Wounded*

Bruce Springsteen
Gary U.S. Bonds, *The Best of Gary U.S. Bonds*

Spur of the Moment
Stacy Lattisaw, *Spuraddict*

Stannard & Rowe
The Spice Girls, *Spice*

The Starr Company (a.k.a. Prince)
Sheila E., *The Glamorous Life*
The Time, *What Time Is It?*

Maurice Starr
New Kids on the Block, *Hangin' Tough*

Ed Stasium
Living Colour, *Biscuits*
Living Colour, *Time's Up*

Wolf Stephenson
Bobby "Blue" Bland, *Sad Street*
Shirley Brown, *Z.Zelebration: A Tribute to the Late Great Z.Z. Hill*
Denise LaSalle, *Hittin' Where It Hurts*
Denise LaSalle, *Lady in the Street*
Denise LaSalle, *Love Me Right*

William Stephenson
Kim Weston, *Greatest Hits and Rare Classics*

Bill Stepheny
Public Enemy, *Yo! Bum Rush the Show*

Charles Stepney
Earth, Wind & Fire/Maurice White, *Spirit*
Ramsey Lewis, *Maiden Voyage (and More)*
Ramsey Lewis, *Sun Goddess*

Stereo MC's
Stereo MC's, *Connected*
Stereo MC's, *Stereo MC's*
Stereo MC's, *Supernatural*

Stetsasonic
Stetsasonic/Daddy-O/Prince Paul/Gravediggaz, *Blood, Sweat & No Tears*
Stetsasonic/Daddy-O/Prince Paul/Gravediggaz, *In Full Gear*
Stetsasonic/Daddy-O/Prince Paul/Gravediggaz, *On Fire*

Monte Steward
Howard Hewett, *It's Time*

Art Stewart
Teena Marie, *Greatest Hits*

Dave Stewart
Eurythmics, *1984*
Eurythmics, *Be Yourself Tonight*
Eurythmics, *Greatest Hits*
Eurythmics, *Sweet Dreams (Are Made of This)*

David A. Stewart
Daryl Hall & John Oates, *Three Hearts in the Happy Ending Machine*

Jim Stewart
Booker T. & the MG's, *Hip Hug-Her*
Booker T. & the MG's, *The Stax/Volt Revue: Volume 2—Live In Paris*
Booker T. & the MG's, *The Stax/Volt Revue: Volume One—Live In London*
Shirley Brown, *If This Is Goodbye*
Shirley Brown, *Woman to Woman*
Otis Redding, *Live In Europe*
Otis Redding, *Otis Blue*
Sam & Dave, *The Stax/Volt Revue Volume One—Live in London*
Rufus Thomas, *Walkin' the Dog*

Rod Stewart
Rod Stewart, *Absolutely Live*
Rod Stewart, *Body Wishes*
Rod Stewart, *Every Picture Tells a Story*
Rod Stewart, *Never a Dull Moment*

Sylvester Stewart
Sly & the Family Stone, *There's a Riot Goin' On*

Winston Stewart
Shirley Brown, *If This Is Goodbye*

Stickyfingaz
Onyx, *All We Got Iz Us*

Robert Stigwood
The Bee Gees, *Cucumber Castle*

Stimulated Dummies
KMD, *Mr. Hood*

Sting
Vinx, *Rooms in My Fatha's House*

Mike Stock
Donna Summer, *Another Place and Time*

Chris Stokes
Immature, *We Got It*

Michael Stokes
Enchantment, *If You're Ready: The Best of Enchantment*

Mike Stoller
The Drifters, *The Very Best of the Drifters*
Ruth Brown, *Rockin' In Rhythm—The Best of Ruth Brown*

Sly Stone
Sly & the Family Stone, *Dance to the Music*
Sly & the Family Stone, *Fresh*
Sly & the Family Stone, *Precious Stone: In the Studio with Sly Stone 1963–1965*
Sly & the Family Stone, *Stand!*
Sly & the Family Stone, *A Whole New Thing*

Strange
Sir Mix-a-Lot, *Mack Daddy*

Street Element
Sister Souljah, *360 Degrees of Power*

Stretch Armstrong
Junior M.A.F.I.A./Lil' Kim, *Hard Core*

Studio Ton(e) Capone
Celly Cel, *Killa Kali*
E-40 and the Click, *Down and Dirty*
E-40 and the Click, *Game Related*
E-40 and the Click, *Hall of Game*
E-40 and the Click, *In a Major Way*
E-40 and the Click, *The Mailman*
Mac Mall, *Untouchable*

Kazunori Sugiyama
Jean-Paul Bourelly, *Fade to Cacophony*
Jean-Paul Bourelly, *Saints & Sinners*
James Blood Ulmer, *In the Name of . . .*

Dwayne Sumal
Boogie Down Productions/KRS-One, *Live, Hardcore & Worldwide*

Super DJ Dmitry
Deee-lite, *Dewdrops in the Garden*

Al B. Sure!
Al B. Sure!, *In Effect Mode*
Jodeci, *Forever My Lady*

Al Sutton
Big Chief, *Face*
Big Chief, *Mack Avenue Skullgame*

Keith Sweat
Keith Sweat, *Get Up On It*
Keith Sweat, *Keith Sweat*
Keith Sweat, *Make It Last Forever*

Leon Sylvers III
Shalamar, *Go for It*
Shalamar, *Three for Love*

Bill Szymczyk
B.B. King, *Completely Well*
J. Geils Band/Bluestime, *Blow Your Face Out*
J. Geils Band/Bluestime, *Hotline*

Kaname Tajima
Al Green, *Anthology*

Take 6
Take 6, *So Much 2 Say*

Nat Tarnapol
Jackie Wilson, *Merry Christmas from Jackie Wilson*

Donald Tavie
Norman Connors, *Easy Living*

Creed Taylor
George Benson, *The Best of George Benson*
George Benson, *George Benson in Concert: Carnegie Hall*
George Benson, *White Rabbit*
Grover Washington Jr., *All the King's Horses*
Grover Washington Jr., *Inner City Blues*

Grover Washington Jr., *Mister Magic*

Gary Taylor
The Manhattans, *Sweet Talk*

Koko Taylor
Koko Taylor, *Force of Nature*
Koko Taylor, *I Got What It Takes*
Koko Taylor, *Queen of the Blues*

Skip Taylor
John Lee Hooker, *Hooker 'N' Heat*

Troy Taylor
Boyz II Men, *Cooleyhighharmoney*

T-Bone
Da Lench Mob, *Guerillas In Tha Mist*

Tears For Fears
Oleta Adams, *The Seeds of Love*

Howie Tee
Special Ed, *Legal*
Special Ed, *Youngest in Charge*

John Telfer
Johnny Adams, *Lost in the Stars: The Music of Kurt Weill*

Rod Temperton
Patti Austin, *Every Home Should Have One*
Mica Paris, *Whisper a Prayer*

Montie Temple
Royal Crescent Mob, *13 Destruction*
Royal Crescent Mob, *Good Lucky Killer*
Royal Crescent Mob, *Omerta*

Ted Templeman
Van Morrison, *St. Dominic's Preview*

Terminator X
Young Black Teenagers, *Dead Enz Kidz Doin' Lifetime Bidz*

Todd Terry
Doug E. Fresh, *Play*
Sham & the Professor, *Split Personalities*

Joe Tex
Joe Tex, *The Very Best of Joe Tex*

Bob Thiele
Louis Armstrong, *What a Wonderful World*
Gil Scott-Heron, *Pieces of a Man*
Gil Scott-Heron, *The Revolution Will Not Be Televised*

3rd Bass
3rd Bass, *Cactus Album Revisited*
3rd Bass, *Derelicts of Dialect*

Third World
Third World, *96 Degrees in the Shade*

Damon Thomas
Brandy, *Brandy*

Irma Thomas
Irma Thomas, *The New Rules*
Irma Thomas, *The Story of My Life*
Irma Thomas, *Walk Around Heaven: New Orleans Gospel Soul*
Irma Thomas, *The Way I Feel*

Keith Thomas
BeBe & CeCe Winans, *Heaven*

Marvell Thomas
Isaac Hayes, *Hot Buttered Soul*

Tracey Thorn
Everything but the Girl, *Acoustic*
Everything but the Girl, *Amplified Heart*
Everything but the Girl, *Language of Life*

Eric "E.T." Thorngren
Peter Wolf, *Come As You Are*

Thrill Da Playa
Quad City DJ's, *Get on Up and Dance*

Russ Titleman
George Benson, *20/20*
The Cookies, *Complete Cookies*
Graham Central Station/Larry Graham, *Graham Central Station*
Rufus/Chaka Khan, *Stompin' at the Savoy*

Andres Titus
Black Sheep, *Non-Fiction*
Black Sheep, *A Wolf In Sheep's Clothing*

Jon Tiven
Don Covay, *Back to the Streets: Celebrating the Music of Don Covay*

Steve Tomashefsky
Otis Rush, *So Many Roads*

Tone Love
Tuff Crew, *Danger Zone*

Tony D
King Sun, *Righteous but Ruthless*
Poor Righteous Teachers, *Holy Intellect*
Poor Righteous Teachers, *Pure Poverty*
Queen Latifah, *Black Reign*
Tony D, *Droppin' Funky Verses*

Tony! Toni! Tone!
Tony! Toni! Tone!, *House of Music*
Tony! Toni! Tone!, *Sons of Soul*

Too $hort
Kid Rock, *Grits Sandwiches for Breakfast*
Spice 1, *187 He Wrote*
Too $hort, *Born to Mack*
Too $hort, *Life Is...Too $hort*
Too $hort, *Short Dog's in the House*

Too Tuff
Tuff Crew, *Danger Zone*

TOP
Tower of Power, *Ain't Nothin' Stoppin' Us Now*
Tower of Power, *Urban Renewal*

Peter Tosh
Peter Tosh, *Equal Rights*
Peter Tosh, *Legalize It*
Peter Tosh, *Wanted Dread and Alive*

Allen Toussaint
Lee Dorsey, *Can You Hear Me*
Lee Dorsey, *Lee Dorsey*
Lee Dorsey, *Night People*
Dr. John, *In the Right Place*
The Meters, *Looka Py-Py*
The Meters, *Rejuvenation*
The Neville Brothers, *The Wild Tchoupitoulas*
Allen Toussaint, *Connected*
Allen Toussaint, *From a Whisper to a Scream*
Allen Toussaint, *Life, Love and Happiness*
Allen Toussaint, *Southern Nights*

Ed Townsend
The Impressions, *Lasting Impressions*

TrackMasters
Foxy Brown, *Ill Na Na*
Nas, *It Was Written*

A Tribe Called Quest
Apache, *Apache*
Fu-Schnickens, *F.U. Don't Take It Personal*
A Tribe Called Quest, *Beats, Rhymes and Life*
A Tribe Called Quest, *The Low End Theory*
A Tribe Called Quest, *Midnight Marauders*
A Tribe Called Quest, *People's Instinctive Travels and the Paths of Rhythm*

Didier Tricard
Buddy Guy, *Alone and Acoustic*
Buddy Guy, *Stone Crazy*

Roger Troutman
Eric Benet, *True to Myself*
Shirley Murdock, *Let There Be Love!*
Shirley Murdock, *Roger & Zapp, The Compilation: Greatest Hits II and More*
Zapp/Zapp & Roger, *All the Greatest Hits*

Hal Willner
Johnny Adams, *Lost in the Stars: The Music of Kurt Weill*
David Sanborn, *Another Hand*

Bryce P. Wilson
Groove Theory, *Groove Theory*

Charlie Wilson
Gap Band, *Ain't Nothing But a Party*

Peter Wilson
Style Council, *Confessions of a Pop Group*
Style Council, *Here's Some That Got Away*
Style Council, *Introducing the Style Council*
Style Council, *Our Favourite Shop*
Style Council, *The Style Council Collection*

The Winans
The Winans, *Decisions*

BeBe Winans
The Clark Sisters, *Miracle*

Carvin Winans
The Winans, *Let My People Go*

Marvin Winans
Vickie Winans, *Be Encouraged*
Vickie Winans, *Total Victory*

Vickie Winans
Vickie Winans, *Be Encouraged*
Vickie Winans, *Total Victory*
Vickie Winans, *Vickie Winans Live in Detroit*

Angela Winbush
Angela Winbush, *Angela Winbush*

Angela Winbush, *It's the Real Thing*

George Winston
Professor Longhair, *Rock 'n' Roll Gumbo*

Johnny Winter
Muddy Waters, *Muddy "Mississippi" Waters Live*

Stefan Winter
Jean-Paul Bourelly, *Jungle Cowboy*

Joe Wissert
Earth, Wind & Fire/Maurice White, *Head to the Sky*
Earth, Wind & Fire/Maurice White, *Last Days and Time*
Boz Scaggs, *Silk Degrees*

Peter Wolf
Chuckii Booker, *Indian Summer*
Peter Wolf, *Come As You Are*
Peter Wolf, *Lights Out*
Peter Wolf, *Up to No Good*
Paul Young, *Other Voices*

Elliot Wolff
Paula Abdul, *Forever Your Girl*
Paula Abdul, *Shut Up and Dance (The Dance Mixes)*

Tom "T-Bone" Wolk
Daryl Hall & John Oates, *Three Hearts in the Happy Ending Machine*

Bobby Womack
Bobby Womack, *The Poet*
Bobby Womack, *Someday We'll All Be Free*

Stevie Wonder
Whitney Houston, *I'm Your Baby Tonight*

Minnie Riperton, *Perfect Angel*
Syreeta, *Stevie Wonder Presents Syreeta*
Stevie Wonder, *Innervisions*
Stevie Wonder, *Journey Through the Secret Life of Plants*
Stevie Wonder, *Songs in the Key of Life*
Stevie Wonder, *Talking Book*
Stevie Wonder, *Where I'm Coming From*

Danny Wood
Marky Mark, *You Gotta Believe*

John Wood
James Booker, *Junco Partner*

Betty Wright
Millie Jackson, *Rock 'n' Soul*

Charles Wright
Charles Wright & the Watts 103rd Street Rhythm Band, *Express Yourself: The Best of Charles Wright and the Watts 103rd Street Band*
Charles Wright & the Watts 103rd Street Rhythm Band, *In the Jungle, Babe/Express Yourself*

Bill Wyman
Junior Wells, *Drinkin TNT 'N' Smokin' Dynamite*

Yagg Fu Front
Yagg Fu Front, *Action Packed Adventure*

Yaz
Alison Moyet/Yaz/Yazoo, *Upstairs at Eric's*

Douglas Yeager
Richie Havens, *Richie Havens Sings the Beatles and Bob Dylan*

Yella
Bone Thugs-N-Harmony, *Creepin On Ah Come Up*
Eazy-E, *It's On (Dr. Dre) 187Um Killa*
N.W.A., *Straight Outta Compton*

Young Disciples
Masta Ace, *Road to Freedom*

Earl Young
The Trammps, *The Legendary Zing Album, Featuring the Fabulous Trammps*
The Trammps, *This Is Where the Happy People Go: The Best of the Trammps*
The Trammps, *Trammps*

Harry Young
Arthur Conley, *Sweet Soul Music: The Best of Arthur Conley*

Joe Young
Koko Taylor, *I Got What It Takes*

Paul Young
Paul Young, *Between Two Fires*

David Z.
Jody Watley, *Jody Watley*

Erik Zobler
Rachelle Ferrell, *Rachelle Ferrell*

Which artists or groups have had the most influence on the acts included in MusicHound R&B? *The Roots Index will help you find out. Under each artist or group's name—not necessarily an R&B act— are listed the acts found in* MusicHound R&B *that were influenced by that artist or group. By the way, James Brown is the influence champ: he appears in the* ◀◀ *section of a whopping 58 artists or groups.*

A-Town Players
Quad City DJ's

ABBA
Ace of Base

Above the Law
Dove Shack
Warren G

Johnny Ace
Bobby "Blue" Bland
Chuck Willis
O.V. Wright

Roy Acuff
Bobby Hebb

Yolanda Adams
Angie & Debbie Winans

Cannonball Adderley
Booker T. & the MG's
George Duke
The Mar-Keys

Aerosmith
Run-D.M.C.

Afro Rican
Duice

Ahmad
Ras Kass
Skee-Lo

Doris Akers
Andrae Crouch

Gerald Albright
Portrait
Vinx

Rance Allen
John P. Kee

All-4-One
Backstreet Boys

Mose Allison
Van Morrison

Herb Alpert
Dionne Warwick

Herb Alpert & the Tijuana Brass
Gloria Estefan

Albert Ammons
Professor Longhair

Ivie Anderson
Minnie Riperton

Inez Andrews
Linda Jones

Lee Andrews & the Hearts
Chairmen of the Board

The Andrews Sisters
The Pointer Sisters

Horace Andy
Massive Attack

Maya Angelou
Sha-Key

The Animals
The Chambers Brothers

Anthrax
Public Enemy

Joan Armatrading
Des'ree

Jo Armstead
Barbara Acklin

Louis Armstrong
Dave Bartholomew
Nat King Cole
Billie Holiday
Louis Jordan

Vanessa Bell Armstrong
Angie & Debbie Winans

Billy Boy Arnold
Syl Johnson

Eddy Arnold
Arthur Alexander

Arrested Development
Basehead
Fugees
Me Phi Me

Steve Arrington
Keith Sweat

Art of Origin
Flatlinerz
Naughty by Nature

Asher D & Daddy Freddy
Shinehead

Ashford & Simpson
Peaches & Herb
Rene & Angela

Chet Atkins
Earl Klugh

Atlantic Starr
O'Bryan

Brian Auger
Average White Band

Patti Austin
Regina Belle
Jennifer Holliday
Vanessa Williams

Gene Autry
Hank Ballard

Average White Band
The Brand New Heavies

Roy Ayers
The Blackbyrds
The Brand New Heavies
Incognito
Jamiroquai

AZ
Foxy Brown

Azteca
Sheila E.

Rev. Morgan Babb/Radio Four
O.V. Wright

Babyface
Tevin Campbell
Tony Rich Project
Keith Washington
Karyn White

Burt Bacharach
Isaac Hayes

Burt Bacharach & Hal David
Ashford & Simpson
Holland, Dozier & Holland

Bad Brains
Beastie Boys
Living Colour

Joan Baez
Laura Nyro
Phoebe Snow

Mildred Bailey
Dinah Washington

Pearl Bailey
Freda Payne

Anita Baker
Oleta Adams
Will Downing
Rachelle Ferrell
Lalah Hathaway
Shirley Murdock
Mica Paris
Vickie Winans

Chet Baker
Beck
Grover Washington Jr.

Josephine Baker
Shirley Bassey

LaVern Baker
The Bobbettes
Denise LaSalle

Little Eva
Esther Phillips
Nancy Wilson

Hank Ballard
Etta James

Hank Ballard & the Midnighters
James Brown
Wilson Pickett

Afrika Bambaataa
Afro Rican
DJ Red Alert
DJ Shadow
Jungle Brothers
K7
Newcleus
Run-D.M.C.
Schoolly D
Ultramagnetic MC's

Ant Banks
Dru Down
Deion Sanders
Spice 1

The Bar-Kays
E.U. (Experience Unlimited)
The Ohio Players

Amiri Baraka
Gil Scott-Heron

Don Baron
Shinehead
Snow

Dave Bartholemew
Lee Dorsey

Rob Base and DJ EZ-Rock
Coolio
Nice & Smooth

Count Basie
Ray Charles
Hank Crawford
Johnnie Johnson
Johnny Otis

Joe Bataan
Mandrill

Bay City Rollers
New Kids on the Block

The Beach Boys
The Bee Gees

The Beastie Boys
Cypress Hill
Goats
House of Pain
Insane Clown Posse
Kid Rock
Lordz of Brooklyn
Luscious Jackson
MC 900 FT Jesus

The Beatles
The Bee Gees
The Box Tops
Joe Cocker
Richie Havens
Jimi Hendrix
Hot Chocolate
PM Dawn
Prince
The Rolling Stones

The Beatnuts
Chi-Ali
Luniz

Sidney Bechet
Duke Ellington

Beck
DC Talk

Jeff Beck
Narada Michael Walden

Harry Belafonte
Shirley Bassey
Richard Berry

Thom Bell
Ray, Goodman & Brown

Regina Belle
Lalah Hathaway

Jesse Belvin
Richard Berry
The Penguins

Tony Bennett
Robert Palmer

George Benson
Incognito
Kashif
Earl Klugh

Brook Benton
Isaac Hayes
Johnny Mathis
Teddy Pendergrass

Chuck Berry
Richard Berry
Jimi Hendrix
Jessie Hill
The Rolling Stones

Bessie Smith
Sarah Vaughan

Frankie Beverly & Maze
One Way
The S.O.S. Band
Zhane

Big Daddy Kane
Biz Markie
Craig G
Def Jef
Grand Daddy I.U.
King Sun
Masta Ace

Big Maceo
Professor Longhair

Big Maybelle
Esther Phillips

Biz Markie
Beastie Boys
Craig G
Craig Mack
DJ Kool
Doug E. Fresh
Grand Daddy I.U.
Kwest Tha Madd Lad
Main Source
Pharcyde
Snoop Doggy Dogg
A Tribe Called Quest

Black Flag
House of Pain
Ice-T

Black Moon
Blahzay Blahzay
Cella Dwellas
Heltah Skeltah
O.G.C. (Originoo Gun Clappaz)
Smif-N-Wessun

Black Sheep
Chi-Ali

The Blackbyrds
Jamiroquai

Robert Blair and the Fantastic Violinaires
Solomon Burke

Art Blakey
The Crusaders

Bobby "Blue" Bland
Johnny Ace
Johnny Adams
Tyrone Davis
Latimore
Little Milton
The Platters
O.V. Wright

Mary J. Blige
Brandy

The Blind Boys
Gerald Alston

Blondie
Peter Wolf

Blood, Sweat & Tears
The Commodores
The Dazz Band
Edgar Winter

Michael Bloomfield
Buddy Miles

Kurtis Blow
Big Daddy Kane
D.J. Jazzy Jeff & the Fresh
   Prince
Fat Boys
Full Force
Kool Moe Dee
LL Cool J
Public Enemy
Run-D.M.C.
The Sugarhill Gang
U.T.F.O.

Blowfly
Sir Mix-a-Lot
Too $hort

The Blues Project
The Blues Brothers
Edgar Winter

Buddy Bolden
Louis Armstrong

The Bomb Squad
Cypress Hill

Gary U.S. Bonds
Little Steven
Southside Johnny & the As-
   bury Jukes
Phil Spector

Bone Thugs-N-Harmony
Crucial Conflict

Boogie Down Productions
Arrested Development
Rob Base & D.J. E-Z Rock
Chubb Rock
The Coup
Fat Joe Da Gangsta
Just Ice
N.W.A.
Public Enemy
X-Clan

James Booker
Dr. John

Booker T. & the MG's
The Bar-Kays
The Meters
Sam the Sham & the
   Pharaohs
Bill Withers
Charles Wright & the Watts
   103rd Street Rhythm Band

Bo$$
Conscious Daughters
Da Brat

Earl Bostic
Gerald Albright
King Curtis

Connee Boswell
Ella Fitzgerald

Bow Wow Wow
Culture Club

David Bowie
Culture Club

Boy George/Culture Club
Rick Astley

Boyz II Men
Dru Hill
Jade
Portrait
Silk

Brand New Heavies
Buckshot Lefonque

Brand Nubian
Dred Scott
KMD
X-Clan

Brandy
Ray J

Brass Construction
A Taste of Honey
Tony! Toni! Tone!

Toni Braxton
Chante Moore

The Breckers
David Sanborn

Brick
Eddie Murphy

Brigadier Jerry
Shabba Ranks

Big Bill Broonzy
Long John Baldry

The Brothers Johnson
O'Bryan

Bobby Brown
Backstreet Boys
Ray J

Charles Brown
Ray Charles
Sam Cooke
Amos Milburn

**Chuck Brown & the Soul
Searchers**
E.U. (Experience Unlimited)
Trouble Funk

Clarence "Gatemouth" Brown
B.B. King

Clifford Brown
Lucas

H. Rapp Brown
Last Poets

James Brown
Average White Band
Afrika Bambaataa
The Bar-Kays
Big Chief
The Blues Brothers
Chuckii Booker
Brass Construction
Chuck Brown & the Soul
   Searchers
B.T. Express
Cameo
The Chambers Brothers
Chic

George Clinton
Joe Cocker
Bootsy Collins
The Commodores
Con Funk Shun
The Counts
Defunkt
Dyke & the Blazers
Earth, Wind & Fire
Fishbone
J. Geils Band
Geto Boys
Herbie Hancock
Roy Head
Hot Chocolate
Incognito
Isley Brothers
Michael Jackson
Jackson 5
Rick James
Syl Johnson
M.C. Hammer
The Meters
Buddy Miles
Van Morrison
One Way
Robert Palmer
Prince
Public Enemy
Queen Latifah
The Rolling Stones
Royal Crescent Mob
Run-D.M.C.
Son of Bazerk
Soul II Soul
Southside Johnny & the As-
   bury Jukes
Edwin Starr
Sylvester
Johnnie Taylor
Joe Tex
The Time
Tower of Power
Fred Wesley
Charles Wright & the Watts
   103rd Street Rhythm Band
Zapp

James Brown/the JBs
Brick

Maxine Brown
Gloria Gaynor

Roy Brown
James Brown
Little Richard

musicHound **i n d e x e s**

andrae crouch 7
4
1

Chubb Rock
Akinyele

Chuck Chillout
Funkmaster Flex

Eric Clapton
Robert Cray
G. Love & Special Sauce

Dr. Mattie Moss Clark
Vanessa Bell Armstrong
The Clark Sisters

The Clark Sisters
Vickie Winans

Stanley Clarke
Norman Connors
Marcus Miller

Otis Clay
Tyrone Davis

Clarence Clemons
Gerald Albright

Rev. James Cleveland
Vanessa Bell Armstrong
The Edwin Hawkins Singers
John P. Kee
Vickie Winans

Jimmy Cliff
UB40

George Clinton
Bootsy Collins
Del Tha Funkee Homosapien
Geto Boys
Ice Cube
MC Breed & the DFC
Buddy Miles
Me'Shell Ndegeocello
Salt-N-Pepa
Slave
Zapp

The Clovers
Arthur Alexander
The Dells
The Penguins

The Coasters
The Chords
Ernie K-Doe
Southside Johnny & the As-
    bury Jukes
The Trammps

Arnett Cobb
King Curtis

Leonard Cohen
Laura Nyro

Coke La-Rock
Kurtis Blow

Cold Crush Brothers
Jungle Brothers
Leaders of the New School
M.C. Shan

Nat King Cole
Jesse Belvin
Brook Benton
Charles Brown
Ray Charles
Natalie Cole
Will Downing
Marvin Gaye
Isaac Hayes
Walter Jackson
Al Jarreau
Marv Johnson
Ramsey Lewis
Johnny Mathis
Brian McKnight
Lou Rawls
Vinx
Nancy Wilson

Ornette Coleman
James Blood Ulmer

Albert Collins
Robert Cray

Bootsy Collins
Gap Band
Me'Shell Ndegeocello
Zapp

Judy Collins
Laura Nyro
Phoebe Snow

John Coltrane
Norman Connors
Herbie Hancock
Janis Joplin
Bill Laswell
Maceo Parker
Was (Not Was)

Commissioned
Angie & Debbie Winans

The Commodores
Atlantic Starr

Commissioned
Tony! Toni! Tone!

**Compton's Most Wanted
featuring MC Eiht**
Eightball & MJG

Con Funk Shun
The S.O.S. Band

Norman Connors
Michael Henderson

Conscious Daughters
Da Brat
Passion

Contortions
Defunkt

Sam Cooke
Gerald Alston
Rick Astley
William Bell
Bobby "Blue" Bland
Maxine Brown
Peabo Bryson
Dee Clark
Arthur Conley
Eddie Floyd
Aretha Franklin
Dobie Gray
Al Green
Richie Havens
Ted Hawkins
Z.Z. Hill
The Intruders
Isley Brothers
Chuck Jackson
Garland Jeffreys
Ernie K-Doe
Ben E. King
Gladys Knight & the Pips
Major Lance
The Manhattans
Johnny Mathis
Maxwell
Maze
Van Morrison
Johnny Nash
Billy Ocean
The O'Jays
Ann Peebles
Teddy Pendergrass
Bobby and James Purify
Lou Rawls
Otis Redding
Smokey Robinson & the Mira-
    cles

The Rolling Stones
Sam & Dave
Marvin Sease
Joe Simon
Percy Sledge
Solo
The Staple Singers
Rod Stewart
Stories
Al B. Sure!
Johnnie Taylor
Luther Vandross
Bill Withers
Womack & Womack
Bobby Womack
O.V. Wright

Cookie Crew
L'Trimm

Coolio
Ray J

Alice Cooper
Insane Clown Posse

Chick Corea
George Duke
Narada Michael Walden

The Corvettes
Ray, Goodman & Brown

Bill Cosby
Charles Wright & the Watts
    103rd Street Rhythm Band

James Cotton
Junior Wells

The Coup
The B.U.M.S.

Craig G
Ed O.G. and Da Bulldogs

Hank Crawford
David Sanborn

Charlie Creath
Earl Bostic

Bing Crosby
Roy Brown
The Mills Brothers

Andrae Crouch
Kirk Franklin & the Family
The Edwin Hawkins Singers
The Neville Brothers
Take 6

Muddy Waters

Paul C
Main Source
Ultramagnetic MC's

Les Paul
Earl Klugh

Pavement
Beck

Peaches & Herb
Rene and Angela
Shalamar

Pebbles
TLC

Ann Peebles
Mary J. Blige
Jean Carne
Jean Knight
Melba Moore

Barron Peeler
Chante Moore

Teddy Pendergrass
Colonel Abrams
Jodeci
Joe
Montell Jordan
Maxwell
Stephanie Mills
Keith Sweat

The Penguins
Boyz II Men
The Catalinas
The Cleftones
Frankie Valli

Dan Penn
Boz Scaggs
Percy Sledge

Roy "Boogie Boy" Perkins
Lloyd Price

Persuasions
Take 6

Oscar Peterson
Herbie Hancock
Ramsey Lewis

Pharcyde
Ahmad
Anotha Level
Boogiemonsters
Skee-Lo

Esther Phillips
LaVern Baker
Shuggie Otis

Sam Phillips
Berry Gordy Jr.

Wilson Pickett
Average White Band
J. Blackfoot
The Box Tops
The Chambers Brothers
The Counts
Tyrone Davis
Dyke & the Blazers
Ted Hawkins
Isaac Hayes
Garland Jeffreys
Buddy Miles
Robert Palmer
Southside Johnny & the As-
bury Jukes
Edwin Starr
The Trammps
Bobby Womack
Zapp

The Pilgrim Travellers
Soul Stirrers

Fats Pinchon
Dave Bartholomew

Pink Floyd
David Bowie
Rare Earth

The Pips
The Braxtons

Planet Patrol
Force M.D.'s

The Platters
The Channels
The Contours
The Fifth Dimension
Gladys Knight & the Pips
Frankie Valli
The Whispers
Maurice Williams & the Zodi-
acs

PM Dawn
DC Talk
Me Phi Me
Stereo MC's

Poor Righteous Teachers
Brand Nubian

Gang Starr
Goodie Mob

Bud Powell
Johnnie Johnson

Powerule
Kurious

Geronimo Pratt
2Pac/Thug Life/Makaveli

The Premiers
Frankie Lymon & the
Teenagers

Elvis Presley
The Coasters
Tyrone Davis
Fine Young Cannibals
Joe Simon

Billy Preston
Michael Henderson

The Pretenders
Grace Jones
UB40

Leontyne Price
Friends of Distinction

Lloyd Price
Larry Williams

Charley Pride
Little Milton

Prince
Babyface
Chuckii Booker
Tevin Campbell
D'Angelo
Terence Trent D'Arby
Sheena Easton
Guy
Janet Jackson
Jodeci
Lenny Kravitz
Teena Marie
M.C. Hammer
Mint Condition
Me'Shell Ndegeocello
New Power Generation
O'Bryan
PM Dawn
Ray J
Ready for the World
Sheila E.
The Time
Vinx

Jody Watley

Prince Paul
Automator
Downtown Science
Wu-Tang Clan

The Prisonaires
The Persuasions

Procol Harum
Rare Earth

Professor Longhair
Dr. John
Fats Domino
Jessie Hill
The Meters
The Neville Brothers
Huey "Piano" Smith
Allen Toussaint

Arthur Prysock
Brook Benton
Chuck Brown & the Soul
Searchers
Walter Jackson

Public Enemy
Arrested Development
Beck
Brand Nubian
Chill Rob G
Chubb Rock
The Coup
Cypress Hill
Digital Underground
Disposable Heroes of Hipho-
prisy
Geto Boys
Hyenas in the Desert
Ice Cube
Paris
Queen Latifah
Sister Souljah
Son of Bazerk
Stetsasonic
A Tribe Called Quest
Ultramagnetic MC's
Wu-Tang Clan
X-Clan
Young Black Teenagers

Tito Puente
Gloria Estefan
Sheila E.

Puff Daddy
Tracey Lee

Bobby Purify
Simply Red

Flora Purim
Dianne Reeves

Queen
Culture Club
Run-D.M.C.

Queen Latifah
Bo$$
Lady of Rage
Monie Love
Naughty by Nature
Nonchalant
Pete Rock & C.L. Smooth
Yo Yo

? and the Mysterians
Garland Jeffreys

Raekwon
AZ
Nas

Raelettes
Darlene Love

Ma Rainey
Mahalia Jackson
Bessie Smith
Big Mama Thornton

Rakim
Capone-N-Noreaga
Common
King Tee
Mobb Deep
Nas
N.W.A.
Shaquille O'Neal
Paris
Snoop Doggy Dogg
Special Ed

Rammellzee & K-Rob
Cypress Hill

Rappin' 4-Tay
Celly Cel
Herm
JT the Bigga Figga
Luniz
Mac Mall
Passion

Rare Earth
Bloodstone
Ray Parker Jr.

Rare Essence
DJ Kool

The Ravens
The Charms
The Dominoes
The Drifters
The Moonglows
The Spaniels

Lou Rawls
Eddie Floyd
Billy Paul
Boz Scaggs

Red Alert
Jungle Brothers
Ultramagnetic MC's

Red Hot Chili Peppers
MC 900 FT Jesus

Otis Redding
J. Blackfoot
The Box Tops
Clarence Carter
The Chambers Brothers
Arthur Conley
Eddie Floyd
Dobie Gray
Al Green
Ted Hawkins
Z.Z. Hill
The Intruders
McFadden & Whitehead
Alexander O'Neal
Sly & the Family Stone
Solo
Rod Stewart
Tower of Power
Charles Wright & the Watts
    103rd Street Rhythm Band

Redman
Craig Mack
Keith Murray

Jimmy Reed
Arthur Alexander
Syl Johnson
Albert King

Della Reese
Martha & the Vandellas
Mary Wells

Martha Reeves
Melba Moore
Freda Payne
Syreeta

Django Reinhardt
B.B. King

Kid Rena
Louis Armstrong

Rene & Angela
Atlantic Starr

Ricky Ricardo
Kid Creole & the Coconuts

Buddy Rich
Buddy Miles

Lionel Richie
James Ingram
Billy Ocean
Luther Vandross

Richie Rich
Dru Down
Luniz

Nelson Riddle
MFSB

The Righteous Brothers
Roy Head

Minnie Riperton
Angela Bofill
Mariah Carey
Phyllis Hyman
Margie Joseph
Chante Moore

Ritz Brothers
De La Soul

Johnny Rivers
The Fifth Dimension
Willie Hutch

Bill "Bojangles" Robinson
Sammy Davis Jr.
Rufus Thomas

Smokey Robinson
Ashford & Simpson
Peabo Bryson
D'Angelo
Fine Young Cannibals
Holland, Dozier & Holland
Willie Hutch
Jackson 5
Kashif
The Marvelettes
Diana Ross
Marvin Sease
Simply Red

Mary Wells
Bill Withers
Stevie Wonder

**Smokey Robinson & the
Miracles**
Enchantment
The Spinners

Betty Roche
Minnie Riperton

Pete Rock & C.L. Smooth
Common
Dred Scott
Ill Al Skratch

Rodgers and Hart
Holland, Dozier & Holland

Paul Rodgers
Paul Young

Rodney O and Joe Cooley
DJ Quik

Roger/Zapp
EPMD

Rogers and Hammerstein
Holland, Dozier & Holland

The Rolling Stones
Terence Trent D'Arby
J. Geils Band
Prince
Peter Wolf

Sonny Rollins
George Duke
Grover Washington Jr.

The Ronnettes
Love Unlimited Orchestra
Sister Sledge

Roots
Boogiemonsters

Rosie & the Originals
The Crystals

Diana Ross
Natalie Cole
Whitney Houston
Janet Jackson
Michael Jackson
Madonna
Chante Moore
Pebbles
Crystal Waters

Diana Ross & the Supremes
Sheena Easton
Gloria Gaynor

Roswell Rudd
Defunkt

David Ruffin
Colonel Abrams
Jimmy Ruffin

Rufus
Mother's Finest

Run-D.M.C.
Audio Two
Rob Base & D.J. E-Z Rock
Boogie Down Productions
Da Youngsta's
EPMD
Ice-T
Ill Al Skratch
LL Cool J
Lords of the Underground
MC Lyte
Nice & Smooth
Salt-N-Pepa
Stetsasonic
Wreckx-N-Effect

Rush
Fishbone

Otis Rush
Buddy Guy
Freddie King
Sam the Sham & the
    Pharaohs

Patrice Rushen
Gerald Albright
Brenda Russell

Jimmy Rushing
Hank Ballard
Wynonie Harris
Big Joe Turner

Brenda Russell
Anita Baker

Leon Russell
Gap Band

RZA
Mobb Deep

Saafir
The B.U.M.S.
Ras Kass

Sade
Groove Theory
Incognito
Chante Moore
Soul II Soul

Carol Bayer Sager
Brenda Russell

Salt-N-Pepa
Bahamadia
Mary J. Blige
J.J. Fad
Kid 'n Play
L'Trimm
MC Lyte
Monie Love
TLC
Yo Yo

Sam & Dave
Arthur Conley
Daryl Hall & John Oates
McFadden & Whitehead
Roachford
Tower of Power

Santana
Mandrill
Mellow Man Ace
Sheila E.
Third World

Carlos Santana
Prince

Johnny Sayles
Tyrone Davis

Boz Scaggs
The Pointer Sisters

Scarface
Goodie Mob
Lifers Group

Schoolly D
Beastie Boys
Boogie Down Productions
Geto Boys
Kool G Rap and D.J. Polo
Mobb Deep
Nas
The Roots

Little Jimmy Scott
Nancy Wilson

Tom Scott
Gerald Albright

Gil Scott-Heron
Disposable Heroes of Hipho-
    prisy
Geto Boys
Public Enemy

Seal
Eric Benet
DC Talk

Erick Sermon
Shaquille O'Neal

7A3
Coolio
Cypress Hill
Gerardo
Mellow Man Ace

The Sex Pistols
Neneh Cherry
Red Hot Chili Peppers

Shabba Ranks
Mad Lion

Sha-Key
The Roots

Shalamar
Midnight Star
Jody Watley

Sham & the Professor
Frankie Cutlass

The Shangri-La's
Sister Sledge
The Supremes
Carla Thomas
Love Unlimited Orchestra

Del Shannon
Lou Christie

Roxanne Shante
Biz Markie
J.J. Fad
MC Lyte

Sha-Rock
Bahamadia

Sonny Sharrock
Bill Laswell

Marlena Shaw
Roxanne Shante

George Shearing
Herbie Hancock

Shinehead
Snow

The Shirelles
The Chiffons
The Cookies
The Crystals
The Marvelettes

Showbiz and A.G.
Big L
Black Moon
Black Sheep

Horace Silver
Kool & the Gang

Paul Simon
Phoebe Snow

Nina Simone
Oleta Adams
Shirley Bassey
Donny Hathaway
Robert Palmer
Sade

Valerie Simpson
Patrice Rushen

Sims Twins
Sam & Dave

Frank Sinatra
Brook Benton
Bobby Darin
Marvin Gaye
Johnny Mathis
Lou Rawls

Sir Mix-a-Lot
Ant Banks
Candyman

Sister Sledge
Van McCoy

69 Boyz
Quad City DJ's

Skatalites
Bob Marley & the Wailers

Slayer
Ice-T

Percy Sledge
The Box Tops
Isaac Hayes
Luther Ingram

Rod Stewart
Stories
Paul Young

Sting
Vinx

Sly Stone
E.U. (Experience Unlimited)
Fishbone
Graham Central Station
Sylvester

Stone Soul Children
Chairmen of the Board

The Stooges
Big Chief
Royal Crescent Mob

Barbra Streisand
Irene Cara
Sheena Easton
Brenda Russell

Levi Stubbs (the Four Tops)
Colonel Abrams
Garland Jeffreys

Stuff
Change

The Stylistics
Surface

Sugarhill Gang
Fat Boys
Newcleus
Puff Daddy
U.T.F.O.

Maxine Sullivan
Ella Fitzgerald
Roberta Flack
Dinah Washington

Donna Summer
Paula Abdul
The Brand New Heavies
Irene Cara
Taylor Dayne
Deee-lite
Gloria Estefan
KC & the Sunshine Band
Evelyn "Champagne" King
Mica Paris
Brenda Russell
A Taste of Honey
Crystal Waters

Sun Ra
George Clinton

Super Cat
Mad Lion

Superlover Cee
Tony D

The Supremes
The Braxtons
En Vogue
Love Unlimited Orchestra
Van McCoy
The Pointer Sisters
Salt-N-Pepa
Sister Sledge

Swan Silvertones
The Impressions
Wilson Pickett
Sly & the Family Stone

Keith Sweat
R. Kelly

SWV
The Braxtons

The Sylvers
DeBarge
Shalamar
Switch

Sylvester
Chic

Syreeta
Patrice Rushen

Tag Team
Quad City DJ's

Take 6
Brian McKnight

Tangerine Dream
The Art of Noise

Tat Money
Three Times Dope

Art Tatum
Charles Brown

Tavares
The Chi-Lites

Eddie Taylor
Freddie King
Jimmy Reed

Johnnie Taylor
Luther Ingram
Latimore
The Manhattans
Billy Paul
Al Wilson
O.V. Wright

The Temptations
BLACKstreet
Bloodstone
Boyz II Men
The Commodores
The Dramatics
Fine Young Cannibals
Guy
Daryl Hall & John Oates
Hot Chocolate
Jackson 5
KC & the Sunshine Band
Lakeside
The Persuasions
Rare Earth
Roachford
Rose Royce
Jimmy Ruffin
Solo
The Spinners
Edwin Starr
The Stylistics
Tavares
The Undisputed Truth
The Winans

Tammi Terrell
Wild Cherry

Clark Terry
Quincy Jones

Sonny Terry and Brownie McGhee
Van Morrison

Todd Terry
Sham & the Professor

Joe Tex
Joe Simon
Al Wilson

Sister Rosetta Tharpe
Dr. Mattie Moss Clark
Syl Johnson

Margaret Thatcher
The Spice Girls

Them
Edgar Winter

3rd Bass
Blood of Abraham
Chubb Rock
Downtown Science
KMD
Kurious
Young Black Teenagers

Betty Thomas
Roxanne Shante

Carla Thomas
Jean Knight
The Mar-Keys
Syreeta

Irma Thomas
Maxine Brown
Margie Joseph

Rufus Thomas
D.J. Jazzy Jeff & the Fresh
    Prince
Isaac Hayes
The Mar-Keys
Carla Thomas
Al Wilson

Tracy Thorn (Everything but the Girl)
Lisa Stansfield

Big Mama Thornton
Etta James
Koko Taylor
Ike & Tina Turner

Gerhart Thrasher
Clyde McPhatter

The Three Degrees
Hues Corporation

Three Times Dope
Candyman

The Time
Babyface
Club Nouveau
Mint Condition
New Power Generation
Ready for the World
Tony! Toni! Tone!
Jody Watley

Timex Social Club
Club Nouveau

C.A. Tindley
Shirley Caesar

Shuggie Otis
Otis Rush

Fats Waller
Duke Ellington
Ivory Joe Hunter

Anita Ward
Evelyn "Champagne" King

Billy Ward
Clyde McPhatter

Billy Ward & the Dominoes
Arthur Alexander
The Mills Brothers
The Trammps

Celia Ward
Aretha Franklin

Clara Ward
Fontella Bass
Shirley Brown
Dr. Mattie Moss Clark
Vickie Winans

Guy Warren
Osibisa

Dee Dee Warwick
Dionne Warwick

Dionne Warwick
Babyface
Angela Bofill
The Fifth Dimension
Whitney Houston
Walter Jackson
Kashif
Evelyn "Champagne" King
Luther Vandross
Wild Cherry

Dinah Washington
Patti Austin
Fontella Bass
Shirley Bassey
Maxine Brown
Ruth Brown
Jean Carne
The Chantels
Randy Crawford
Gladys Knight & the Pips
Denise LaSalle
Mica Paris
Billy Paul
Esther Phillips
Della Reese
Kim Weston

Nancy Wilson

Grover Washington
Gerald Albright

Keith Washington
Brian McKnight

Tuts Washington
James Booker
Dr. John

Muddy Waters
Long John Baldry
Chuck Berry
Jean-Paul Bourelly
Bo Diddley
Buddy Guy
Richie Havens
Screamin' Jay Hawkins
Elmore James
Syl Johnson
Percy Mayfield
Van Morrison
The Rolling Stones
Otis Rush
Koko Taylor
Them

Jody Watley
Karyn White

Johnny "Guitar" Watson
Robert Cray

Watts 103rd Street Rhythm Band
B.T. Express

Watts Prophets
Freestyle Fellowship
N.W.A.

WC
Mack 10

WC and the MAAD Circle
Tha Alkaholiks
Coolio
Da Lench Mob

Weather Girls
L'Trimm

Weather Report
Incognito

Wee Papa Girl Rappers
L'Trimm

Junior Wells
Buddy Guy

Syl Johnson

Mary Wells
Barbara Acklin
Gladys Knight & the Pips
Cheryl Lynn
Carla Thomas
Kim Weston

Rudy West
Marvin Gaye

Kim Weston
Freda Payne

Wham!
The Spice Girls

The Whispers
A Taste of Honey

Barry White
Big Daddy Kane
Freddie Jackson
Latimore
Maxwell
Teddy Pendergrass
Marvin Sease
Lisa Stansfield
Al B. Sure!
Surface
A Taste of Honey

Thomas A. Whitfield
Andrae Crouch
The Edwin Hawkins Singers

The Who
David Bowie

Whodini
LL Cool J
U.T.F.O.
Wreckx-N-Effect

Williams Brothers
Harold Melvin & the Blue Notes

Deniece Williams
Chante Moore

Hank Williams
Arthur Alexander
Chuck Berry

Joe Williams
Jerry Butler
Walter Jackson
Lou Rawls

Marion Williams
Shirley Brown

Maurice Williams
Philip Bailey

Maurice Williams & the Zodiacs
The Catalinas

Mentor Williams
Dobie Gray

Paul Williams
Dobie Gray

Vanessa Williams
Karyn White

Sonny Boy Williamson I
The Blues Brothers
Howlin' Wolf
Elmore James
Van Morrison

Sonny Boy Williamson II
Junior Wells

Bob Wills
Bill Haley

Charlie Wilson
L.V.

Delroy Wilson
Desmond Dekker

Jackie Wilson
Dee Clark
The Contours
Enchantment
J. Geils Band
Willie Hutch
Jackson 5
Michael Jackson
Marv Johnson
Linda Jones
Gladys Knight & the Pips
Van Morrison
The O'Jays
Teddy Pendergrass
Smokey Robinson & the Miracles
The Rolling Stones
Sam & Dave
Peter Wolf

Nancy Wilson
Regina Belle
Friends of Distinction
Phyllis Hyman

The Category Index represents an array of categories put together to suggest some of the many groupings under which R&B music and R&B acts can be classified. The Hound welcomes your additions to the existing categories in this index and also invites you to send in your own funny, sarcastic, prolific, poignant, or exciting ideas for brand new categories.

Acronyms
A.G. (Andre the Giant)
A.O.K. (All Out Kings)
AWB (Average White Band)
BB&Q Band (Brooklyn, Bronx & Queens)
Bone (Brewed Out Niggas Everyday/Brothers On Normal Elimination) Thugs-N-Harmony
B.T. (Brooklyn Trucking) Express
B.U.M.S. (Brothas Unda Madness)
B.W.P. (Bytches With Problems)
CMW (Compton's Most Wanted)
D.R.S. (Dirty Rotten Scoundrels)

EPMD (Erick and Parrish Makin' Dollars)
Gap (Greenwood, Archer, and Pine) Band
H.W.A. (Hoez With Attitude)
Big Daddy Kane (King Asiatic Nobody's Equal)
B.B. (Blues Boy) King
KRS-One (Knowledge Reigns Supreme Over Nearly Everyone)
LL Cool J (Ladies Love Cool James)
LSOB (Lighter Shade of Brown)
L.T.D. (Love, Togetherness, and Devotion)
MFSB (Mother, Father, Sister, Brother)
N.W.A. (Niggaz With Attitude)
O.G.C. (Originoo Gun Clappers)
PM (Prince B, DJ Minute Mix) Dawn
S.O.S. (Sounds of Success) Band
TLC (T-Boz, Left Eye, Chilli)
YBT (Young Black Teenagers)
WC and the MAAD (Minority Alliance Against Discrimination) Circle

Afro-Centric
Brothers Johnson
Bootsy Collins
The Commodores
The Jackson 5
Kid 'n Play

Sly Stone

Bass-O-Matics
Stanley Clarke
Bootsy Collins
Donald "Duck" Dunn
Bernard Edwards
Melvin Franklin
Larry Graham
Isaac Hayes
James Jamerson
Louis Johnson
Marcus Miller
Jaco Pastorius
Don Was
Barry White
Verdine White

Black Pride
Black Moon
Black Sheep
The Blackbyrds
J. Blackfoot
Larry Blackmon
BLACKstreet
Sounds of Blackness
Young Black Teenagers

Blue-Eyed Soul
David Bowie
Boy George/Culture Club
Alex Chilton
Dion DiMucci
Daryl Hall & John Oates
Roy Head
Mick Hucknall (Simply Red)
Everything but the Girl
Annie Lennox/Eurythmics
Teena Marie

George Michael/Wham
Robert Palmer
The Righteous Brothers/Bill Medley
Johnny Rivers
Mitch Ryder
Boz Scaggs
Dusty Springfield
Lisa Stansfield
Rod Stewart
Steve Winwood
Peter Wolf
Paul Young

Book 'Em, Dan-O!
Above the Law
Arrested Development
Capone-N-Noreaga
Criminal Element Orchestra (Arthur Baker)
Delinquent Habits
Naughty By Nature
Public Enemy
Rottin Razkals

Braves
Apache
Big Chief
Boo-Ya Tribe
Mic Geronimo
Redman

Building Supplies
Brass Constructon
Brick
Otis Clay
M.C. Hammer
Level 42

Geography 101
The Chi-Lites
The Dayton Family
DC Talk
The Detroit Emeralds
The Manhattans
95 South
The Ohio Players
Paris
The Watts 103rd St. Band

Hi Society
Bobby "Blue" Bland
Quinton Claunch
Otis Clay
Al Green
Syl Johnson
Willie Mitchell
Ann Peebles
Tommy Tucker
O.V. Wright

Jocks
Muhammad Ali (the original
    rapper)
Shaquille O'Neal
Deion Sanders

Just Chillin'
Chill Rob G
Cold Crush Brothers
Cool C
DJ Chuck Chillout
Joe Cooley
Coolio
Fresh Kid Ice
Ice Cube
Ice-T
Just Ice
Kid Frost
Kool & the Gang
Kool Ass Fashion
Kool DJ Herc
Kool DJ Red Alert
Kool G Rap
Kool Keith
Kool Kim
Kool Moe Dee
L.A. Sno
Snow
Vanilla Ice

Kid Stuff
Kid Capri
Kid Creole & the Coconuts
Kid Frost
Kid 'n Play
Kid Rock

New Kids on the Block

Large and in Charge
B-Fats
Big Bank Hank
Big Boi
Big Daddy Kane
Big D.S.
Big Joe Turner
Big L
Big Lady K
Big Mama Thornton
Big Maybelle
Big Mike
Big Money Odis (a.k.a. Gold
    Money)
Big Noyd
Chubb Rock
Chubby Checker
Chubby Chubb (Cosmic Force)
Chunky A
Da Big Kahuna
Fat Boys
Fat Joe
Fat Larry's Band
Fatback Band
Fatlip
Fats Domino
Heavy D.
JT the Bigga Figga
Large Professor
Mo B. Dick
Notorious B.I.G.
Overweight Pooch
Pudgee, Tha Phat Bastard
Top Dog

Last Night a DJ Saved My Life
DJ Aladdin
DJ Alamo
DJ Cash Money
DJ Chuck Chillout
DJ Clark Kent
DJ Daryl
DJ E-Z Rock
DJ Fuze
DJ Hollywood
DJ Homicide
DJ Honda
DJ Hurricane
DJ Jazzy Jeff
DJ Kool
DJ Krush
DJ Lethal
DJ Minutemix
DJ Muggs
DJ Polo
DJ Pooh

DJ Premier
DJ Quest
DJ Quik
DJ Ralph M
DJ Red Alert
DJ Shadow
DJ Skribble
DJ Slip
DJ Smurf
DJ Taz
DJ Too Tuff
DJ U-Neek
DJ Woody Wood
DJ Yella
Kool DJ Herc
Pete DJ Jones
Quad City DJ's
Unknown DJ

Medicine Men
Dr. Dre
Dr. Funkenstein (George Clin-
    ton)
Doctor Ice (U.T.F.O.)
Dr. Jeckyll & Mr. Hyde
Dr. John
Doc Magic Hands (a.k.a. Mar-
    ley Marl)
Dr. Octagon
Doc Pomus
Dr. Rock and Dr. Shock (Force
    M.D.'s)
Dr. Who (Masters of Cere-
    mony)

Military
The Cadets
Colonel Abrams
The Commodores
Dream Warriors
General Johnson
Major Harris
Major Lance
Massive Attack

Minneapolis
Andre Cymone
Morris Day
Cat Glover
Jimmy Jam & Terry Lewis
Jellybean Johnson
Monte Moir
The New Power Generation
Alexander O'Neal
Prince
The Revolution
Sheila E.
The Time

Vanity 6
Wendy & Lisa

Motown
Ashford & Simpson
J.J. Barnes
H.B. Barnum
Benny "Papa Zita" Benjamin
Boyz II Men
Johnny Bristol
Jean Carne
The Commodores
Contours
DeBarge/El DeBarge
Detroit Spinners
Lamont Dozier
Dennis Edwards
The Elgins
The Four Tops
Harvey Fuqua
Marvin Gaye
Johnny Gill
Cuba Gooding
Holland, Dozier & Holland
Brenda Holloway
Willie Hutch
The Isley Brothers
Chuck Jackson
The Jackson 5
Jermaine Jackson
Michael Jackson
James Jamerson
Rick James
Mabel John
Marv Johnson
Eddie Kendricks
Maurice King
Gladys Knight & the Pips
Stacy Lattisaw
Betty LaVette
Shorty Long
Martha & the
    Vandellas/Martha Reeves
The Marvelettes
The Mary Jane Girls
Amos Milburn
Stephanie Mills
The Originals
Parliament/George Clinton
Wilson Pickett
Bonnie Pointer
Billy Preston
Rose Royce
Diana Ross
David Ruffin
Jimmy Ruffin

Smokey Robinson & the Miracles
Edwin Starr
Barrett Strong
The Supremes
Richard Tee
The Temptations
Tammi Terrell
The Undisputed Truth
The Velvelettes
Junior Walker & the All-Stars
Leon Ware
Mary Wells
Kim Weston
Grover Washington Jr.
Mary Wilson
Syreeta Wright
Stevie Wonder

Muscle Shoals
Arthur Alexander
LaVern Baker
Barry Beckett
Bobby "Blue" Bland
Ruth Brown
Shirley Brown
Solomon Burke
Clarence Carter
Ray Charles
Otis Clay
Joe Cocker
Don Covay
Aretha Franklin
Marlin Greene
Rick Hall
Roger Hawkins
Z.Z. Hill
Eddie Hinton
David Hood
Millie Jackson
Etta James
Jimmy Johnson
King Curtis
Laura Lee
Mighty Sam
Dorothy Moore
Dan Penn
Wilson Pickett
James & Bobby Purify
Norbert Putnam
The Rolling Stones
Roscoe Shelton
Joe Simon
Paul Simon
Percy Sledge
The Staple Singers
Joe South

Dusty Springfield
Candi Staton
The Tams
Johnnie Taylor
Ted Taylor
Irma Thomas
Bobby Womack

N'awlins
Johnny Adams
Harold Battiste
Roy Brown
Jean Carne
Dixie Cups
Dr. John
Fats Domino
Lee Dorsey
Barbara George
Betty Harris
Thurston Harris
Jessie Hill
The House Rockers
Etta James
Margie Joseph
Ernie K-Doe
King Floyd
Jean Knight
Smiley Lewis
Little Richard
Barbara Lynn
Tami Lynn
Professor Longhair
Bobby Marchan/The Clowns
The Meters
The Neville Brothers/Aaron
  Neville
Robert Parker
Lloyd Price
Wardell Quezergue
Shirley & Lee
Huey "Piano" Smith
Soul Machine
Irma Thomas
Allen Toussaint
Larry Williams

New Jacks
BLACKstreet
Boyz II Men
Bobby Brown
El DeBarge
Guy
Aaron Hall
Jodeci
R. Kelly
Teddy Riley
Keith Sweat

New Jills
Aaliyah
Erykah Badu
Mary J. Blige
Brandy
Missy Misdemeanor Elliot
Faith
Angie Martinez
Monica
Salt-N-Pepa
702
SWV
TLC
Xcape

Numerology
All-4-One
Audio Two
Awesome 2
Boyz II Men
Chapter 8
Cold 187um
Disco Three
E-40
Eightball & MJG
11/5
Fantastic Five
Fantasy 3
The Fifth Dimension
5ft. Excellerator
The Five Keys
The Five Royales
The Five Satins
The Five Stairsteps
Force One Network
40 Thevz
415
The Four Seasons
The Four Tops
Funky Four +1
G-One
Grandmaster Flash & the Furious Five
Hi-Five
The Jackson 5
KRS-One
K7
Mack 10
Mark V's
Mark the 45 King
MC Eiht
MC 900 Ft. Jesus
Mikah Nine
Nine
95 South
98 Degrees
N2Deep

Oaktown 3-5-7
112
187 Fac
Paulie Two Times
Proper Dos
Rappin 4-Tay
2nd II None
7A3
702
Shaggy 2 Dope
69 Boyz
Slim Kid 3
Soul II Soul
Special One
Spice 1
Tame One
3rd Bass
3T
3-2
Three Times Dope
Three Times Krazy
Treacherous Three
12 Gague
Twilight 22
2 in a Room
2 Live Crew
2Pac
2-Scoop
UB40
Us3
Vanity 6
Vicious 4
Volume 10

Old 'Uns/Young 'Uns
Babe-Face Kaos
Baby Gerry
Baby-D
Babyface
Afrika Baby Bambaataa
Big Daddy Kane
Da Bush Babees
Da Youngsta's
Daddy Mack
Daddy-O
Good Girls
Junior
Junior M.A.F.I.A.
Kid Capri
Kid Creole
Kid Frost
Kid Rock
Ol' Dirty Bastard
Father MC
Godfather Rock
Grand Daddy I.U.
Mack Daddy

Puff Daddy
Slim Kid
Young Lay
Young M.C.

One-Name Bandits
Aaliyah
Babyface
Beck
Brandy
D'Angelo
Faith
Ginuwine
Des'ree
Joe
Madonna
Maxwell
Monica
Mtume
Nas
Prince
Rakim
Sade

Otis, M'Man!
Otis Clay
Johnny Otis
Shuggie Otis
Otis Redding
Otis Rush

Play that Funky Music
Steve Arrington
Average White Band
The Bar-Kays
Brass Construction
Brick
Brothers Johnson
Chuck Brown & the Soul
    Searchers
James Brown
B.T. Express
Cameo
Jimmy Castor Bunch
George Clinton
Bootsy Collins/Bootsy's Rub-
    ber Band
The Dazz Band
Earth, Wind & Fire
The Gap Band
Larry Graham/Graham Central
    Station
Al Green
Isaac Hayes
The Isley Brothers
Rick James
The JBs
Kool & the Gang

Curtis Mayfield
The Ohio Players
Maceo Parker
Parliament-Funkadelic
Rare Earth
Red Hot Chili Peppers
Rufus featuring Chaka Khan
Slave
Sly & the Family Stone
The Staple Singers
Joe Tex
Rufus Thomas
Tower of Power
Ike & Tina Turner
War
Was (Not Was)
Johnny "Guitar" Watson
Wild Cherry
Charles Wright & the Watts
    103rd St. Rhythm Band
Zapp

**Rappers Who Use Their Real
Names**
Tracey Lee
Keith Murray
Erick Sermon and Parrish
    Smith

Royalty
King Sunny Ade
Count Basie
Nat "King" Cole
The Counts
Disco King Mario
George Duke
Duke Ellington
Albert King
B.B. King
Ben E. King
Evelyn "Champagne" King
Freddie King
Gladys Knight
Robert Knight
The Five Crowns
The Five Royales
King Curtis
King Floyd
Kings of Rhythm
King Tee
Lord Finesse
Lords of the Underground
Lordz of Brooklyn
Prince
Queen Latifah
Royal Crescent Mob
Royal Flush
Sir Mix-a-Lot

Short Stuff
Buckshot Shorty
Lil' Dap
Lil' Kim
Lil' 1/2 Dead
Little Anthony & the Imperials
LIttle Eva
Little Milton
Little Richard
Little Steven
Little Willie John
MC Lyte
Slim Kid 3
Too $hort

Single-Letters Bar
A+
A-Town Players
Chunky A
B-Fine
B-Legit
B Real
B-Rock
Brucie B
Eric B.
Heather B.
Jazzie B (Soul II Soul)
Money B
Rob B.
Sammy B
Steady B
C-Bo
C-Knight
Cool C
Paul C
Asher D
Baby-D
Bunny D.
Chuck D.
Creo-D
Diamond D
Dinco D
Grandmixer D.St
Heavy D
MC Shy D
Mike D
Mikey D
Nikki D
Schoolly D
Stevie D.
Tony D
Willie D
D-Loc
D-Maq
D-Nice
D-Shot
D-Wyze

E-40
E-Roc
E-Swift
E-Vocalist
D.J. E-Z Rock
Eazy-E
Chill Rob G
Craig G
Hass G
Mike G
Shock G
Warren G
G. Love
G-One
Kool G Rap
H-Town
Brother J
Chopmaster J
Double J
LL Cool J
Ray J
Violent J
J-Dee
J-Groove
J-Live
J-Ro
J-Sublimi
Big Lady K
Ernie K-Doe
K-Ci
K-Cut
K-Dee
K-Rob
K7
K-Solo
Positive K
Big L
DJ Ralph M
Daddy-O
Monsta "O"
Rodney O
Johnny P
Master P
Percee P
Capitol Q
Q-Tip (A Tribe Called Quest)
R. Kelly
Booker T. (& the MG's)
Ice-T
Suga-T
3T
T-Bone
T-Boz
T-Double
T-La Rock
T-Lowe
T-Mo

musicHound **n o t e s**

FREE MUSIC from **Mercury Records**

1. **THE GREAT PRETENDER**

   THE PLATTERS

   One of the early crossover R&B hits, "The Great Pretender" is classic romantic R&B, soaring with lovelorn angst. The Platters were inducted into the Rock and Roll Hall of Fame in 1990.

2. **SMOOTH OPERATOR**

   SARAH VAUGHAN

   Down Beat magazine once deemed the singer "the greatest vocal artist of the century." Better known for her lengthy body of jazz vocals, Vaughan reigned as a pop diva from 1953 to 1959, releasing songs like "C'est la Vie," "Mr. Wonderful," "The Banana Boat Song," and "Smooth Operator."

3. **OUT OF SIGHT**

   JAMES BROWN

   The Godfather of Soul released this gem on Smash Records (a subsidiary of Mercury) in 1964. It charted within the Top 25 and helped establish the dance-funk genre. Brown was inducted into the Rock and Roll Hall of Fame in 1986.

4. **ONLY THE STRONG SURVIVE**

   JERRY BUTLER

   A former member of the Impressions (1991 Rock and Roll Hall of Fame inductees), the Ice Man had a major crossover soul hit with this tune, which helped establish the Philly sound of writers/producers Kenny Gamble and Leon Huff.

5. **FIRE**

   THE OHIO PLAYERS

   Released in late 1974 and certified gold just two weeks later, this classic funk song hit #1 on the *Billboard* charts in February of 1975. It was one of a steady stream of hits for the band from Dayton, Ohio.

6. **MAMA USED TO SAY**

   JUNIOR

   A massive urban radio/club hit in the early 1980s, this track helped blaze the trail for a new generation of British soul stars in the United States and was Junior's biggest success.

7. **FLASHLIGHT**

   PARLIAMENT

   Often referred to as the "Stairway to Heaven" of old-school funk, this is George Clinton and his P-Funk crew at their finest. Parliament-Funkadelic were inducted into the Rock and Roll Hall of Fame in 1997.